Reference Books for Young Readers

The Bowker Buying Guide Series

Reference Books for Young Readers

Authoritative Evaluations of Encyclopedias, Atlases, and Dictionaries

Marion Sader
Editor

Brent Allison

Shirley A. Fitzgibbons

Rebecca L. Thomas
Consultants

R. R. Bowker Company
New York & London

Published by R. R. Bowker Company, a division of
  Reed Publishing (USA) Inc.
Copyright © 1988 by Reed Publishing USA
All rights reserved
Printed and bound in the United States of America

Library of Congress Cataloging-in-Publication Data

Reference books for young readers.

  (The Bowker Buying Guide Series)
  Bibliography: p. 589
  Includes index.
  1. Children's reference books—Bibliography.
2. Libraries, Children's—Book lists.   3. Libraries,
Young people's—Book lists.   I. Sader, Marion.
II. Series.
Z1037.1.R43   1988   [PN1009.A1]   011'.02   87-38234
ISBN 0-8352-2366-3

**Editorial Development and Production
by Visual Education Corporation,
Princeton, NJ**

Contents

Preface

Reference Books for Young Readers, the first volume in the Bowker Buying Guide Series, is the result of R. R. Bowker's long association with school, public, and academic librarians. For people making reference purchase decisions or answering patron queries, this series offers the advantage of having all the relevant information in one place at one time, and having it there in an orderly and accessible form.

A wide range of publications exists to help librarians make collection development and selection decisions. While these are certainly useful tools, in general, works are evaluated individually and with minimal comparison to similar titles; consistent criteria may be applied less rigorously from work to work; and the idiosyncrasies and preconceptions of individual reviewers often tend to reduce objectivity. Faced with shrinking budgets and a preponderance of reference books from which to choose, many librarians find themselves overwhelmed.

Bowker offers its new Buying Guide Series as a solution to that dilemma. Each guide has been designed to meet the specific needs of librarians. This guide, *Reference Books for Young Readers*, is designed primarily for those librarians who serve children and young adults—from preschool and kindergarten through elementary, middle school, and high school—in a reference capacity. It presents approximately 200 extensive, descriptive evaluations of encyclopedias (online as well as printed versions), world atlases, dictionaries and word books, and large-print reference works that are generally considered to be appropriate for age levels from preschool through high school.

The list of general encyclopedias, dictionaries, and atlases included is comprehensive within the following limits. First, we include those general reference works which have been published in the United States. Second, the editions reviewed were those in print and readily available for purchase on August 1, 1987, by school and public libraries and their patrons—educators, parents, and young readers. Only in-print titles, which in most cases can be obtained from the usual retail and distribution outlets, meet this requirement. (Librarians who wish to purchase out-of-print works or works not readily available may wish to consult back issues of journals listed in the bibliography [Appendix A] that begins on page 589.)

We have made every effort to identify all appropriate *general* reference works for young readers, and have given publishers every opportunity to submit information on and copies of their general reference books for inclusion in this guide. Publishers were also consulted for facts about forthcoming editions and new titles; in a few cases (noted in the individual reviews) publishers kindly supplied advance copies for review before publication. Several publishers were able to supply advance proofs of standard reference works that have recently undergone major revision but that were not yet generally available by August 1, 1987, our closing date for inclusion. In such cases, these editions have been listed and reviewed. On the other hand, some titles available on August 1, 1987, may have gone out of print shortly thereafter, and new ones may have been introduced, as publishers' lists are constantly changing. Similarly, while the prices given in the "Facts at a Glance" boxes were accurate as of our closing date, they are always subject to change without notice.

The text of *Reference Books for Young Readers* is divided into five main parts, with two appendixes and an index. We recommend that you first read the introductory, "Using This Book," which serves as a road map to the main features of the guide and describes the structure of this volume.

A few special features are worth noting here. Because many librarians and consumers will not have the opportunity to see all the reference books from which they may choose, we have included a generous selection of facsimiles of actual book pages from encyclopedias and of selected entries from dictionaries. These facsimiles include keyed labels (call-outs) to the major features of a book's page design or typical entry. Six pages of generic maps illustrate "What to Look for in Atlases." Another special feature is the glossary of terms at the end of each "What to Look for . . ." chapter. Each glossary explains potentially unfamiliar or specialist terms that may appear in the individual reviews in that chapter.

Ultimately, *Reference Books for Young Readers* is designed to serve two audiences: the professional librarian and the general public. Librarians can use this guide as a collection development and selection aid, and to provide reference service assistance to members of the public. Library patrons, including parents, teachers, and those students mature enough to select their own reference books, may want to consult the guide to identify the works best suited to their particular needs and to compare different works before making a major purchase. *Reference Books for Young Readers*, then, is designed to be useful on both sides of the reference desk.

Given its comprehensive overview of general reference titles, this guide will also be useful for students in professional library training, or as a refresher for practicing librarians. It provides the reader with an in-depth look at the problems of creating reference works and keeping them current, an understanding of the complexities and specialized terminology of each of the three major categories, and a guide to assessing each one's value and use.

A word or two about authority. The R. R. Bowker Company has been publishing authoritative books and other professional reference materials for librarians for over 115 years. Among its well-known reference tools are *Books in Print*, *Children's Books in Print*, *Best Books for Children*, and *The Reader's Adviser*. Bowker's commitment to libraries and to librarians is unquestioned, as is demonstrated once again in the professional expertise that is the foundation of the Bowker Buying Guide Series. All of the reviews were created by professional librarians and subject matter specialists, listed on pages ix–x along with their current affiliations. They have given generously of their time, effort, and experience to assist with the preparation of this Buying Guide. Three librarian-consultants functioned as arbiters in the matters of which works to include and what criteria to use for each category of work; they read and re-read all of the reviewers' evaluations and gave painstaking advice; they offered additional comparisons among the works, and generally ensured that *Reference Books for Young Readers* is a truly professional, useful, and unbiased book.

In addition to the consultants, a number of contributors and reviewers (librarians, educators, and subject specialists) wrote and revised the profiles and essays. The careful process of preparing these expert evaluations ensures that each review represents a balanced, thoroughly considered judgment. Special thanks are due to John F. Drexel and Ann M. Harvey for their editorial guidance during this project, and to Anita Black for overseeing production.

Reference Books for Young Readers presents the most extensive, methodical reviews of all three categories of general reference books that have yet been compiled into one comprehensive volume. These reviews are considerably more descriptive and comparative than those of any journal can be. We hope that they prove useful to librarians, to educators, and to parents engaged in the difficult task of selecting the best and the most useful works of reference for young readers of all ages.

Marion Sader
Executive Editor
Professional and Reference Books
R. R. Bowker Company
January 1988

Reviewers, Contributors, and Consultants

Consultants

Brent Allison
Head, Map Library
Humanities/Social Sciences Libraries
University of Minnesota, Twin Cities
Minneapolis, MN

Shirley A. Fitzgibbons
Associate Professor
School of Library and Information
Sciences
Indiana University
Bloomington, IN

Rebecca L. Thomas
Librarian
Boulevard Elementary School
Shaker Heights, OH
and
Visiting Assistant Professor
School of Library Science
Kent State University
Kent, OH

Subject Consultants

Gerald Friedman
Assistant Professor
Department of Economics
University of Massachusetts
Amherst, MA

Robert George
Assistant Professor
Public Law and Jurisprudence
Department of Politics
Princeton University
Princeton, NJ

Clinton W. Hatchett
Astronomical Writer/Producer
American Museum—
Hayden Planetarium
New York, NY

John R. Michener
Principle Investigator
Electron Beam Testing
Siemens RTL
Princeton, NJ

Lynn Nadel
Professor of Cognitive
Science
Department of Psychology
University of Arizona
Tucson, AZ

Reviewers and Contributors

Carole A. Barham
Head Librarian
Columbia High School Library
Maplewood, NJ

Sandra J. Barnard
Editorial Consultant
Chicago, IL

W. F. Bolton
Professor of English
Rutgers University

Jeanne Hardendorff Burr
Children's Librarian
Jaffrey Public Library
Jaffrey, NH

April Carlucci
Map Reference Specialist
New York Public Library
New York, NY

Ester Connelly
ESL Consultant
Consultant, Time to Read
Trenton, NJ

James A. Coombs
Map Librarian
Southwest Missouri State University
Springfield, MO

Astrid S. Dadourian
   Editorial Consultant
Berkeley Heights, NJ

Priscilla L. Drach
   Children's Services Manager
Cuyahoga County Public Library
Cleveland, OH

Michael Dulka
   Map Librarian
Dag Hammarskjold Library
United Nations
New York, NY

Keith P. Fleeman
   Community Librarian
Little Falls Library
Bethesda, MD

Louise G. Fradkin
   Retired, Head Reference Librarian
Trenton State College
Trenton, NJ

Cindy George
   Educational Consultant
Princeton, NJ

Sally G. Gillmore
   Head Librarian
Mayfield High School
Mayfield, OH
      and
   Adjunct Assistant Professor
Kent State University
School of Library Science
Kent, OH

Helen M. Gothberg
   Library Consultant
      and
   Associate Professor
Graduate Library School
The University of Arizona
Tucson, AZ

Jeannette Handler
   Children's Librarian II
Rockville Regional Library
Rockville, MD

William Hoffman
   Director
Fort Myers–Lee County Public Library
Fort Myers, FL

Susan Dye Lee
   History Instructor
North Park College
Chicago, IL

Lauren E. Lepow
   Editorial Consultant
Princeton, NJ

Gloria R. Mosesson
GRM Associates, Inc.
New York, NY

Princeton Research Forum
   Editorial Associates
Princeton, NJ

Ann M. Rogers
   Library Media Specialist
Evergreen Junior High School
Evergreen, CO

Chris Sokol
   Monograph Cataloger
Holland Library
Washington State University
Pullman, WA

Tyler W. Wasson
   Editorial Consultant
New York, NY

Teri Wilbur
Office of Instructional Technology
University of Delaware
Newark, DE

Using This Book

Reference Books for Young Readers is divided into five main parts: Part I, Introduction; Part II, Encyclopedias; Part III, Atlases; Part IV, Dictionaries and Word Books; and Part V, Large-Print Reference Books. In Part I you will find four chapters that provide background information. Chapter 1, "The History of General Reference Books," reviews the history of general reference books, including landmarks in the development of works for young readers, and describes current trends. Chapter 2, "Choosing General Reference Books," details the differences between adult and juvenile reference materials and the criteria one may wish to consider, in general. Chapter 3, "Librarians Rate General Reference Books for Young Readers," may be useful to librarians at either end of the selection process. It begins by describing a national survey undertaken at the beginning of preparation for this new guide in which public and school librarians were asked to evaluate and rate encyclopedias, dictionaries, and atlases, and to answer questions about their libraries' reference services for young readers. The general results of this survey are presented and analyzed, with representative comments from the respondents quoted. For each question, responses are broken down according to library type—that is, by public library, elementary school, middle school, and high school library. An overall summary of the total responses to each question is also given. The results of this survey can be used either as an initial guide to those titles potential purchasers of reference books may wish to consider or, alternatively, the survey results can be consulted after readers have drawn their own preliminary conclusions.

Chapter 4 is comprised of comparative charts that display key information on encyclopedias, dictionaries, and atlases reviewed in this volume. These "at-a-glance" charts serve as a detailed table of contents; they provide ready reference to each work's quantitative data; and they enable the reader to make direct comparisons of factual data among similar works. For each title included, such information as reading level, number of volumes, pages, articles, words, illustrations, index pages, cross-references, price, and publisher are listed. By helping the pro-

spective purchaser identify, at the outset, those particular reference titles that might be of interest, these charts should simplify the selection process.

Parts II, III, IV, and V contain detailed evaluations of encyclopedias, atlases, dictionaries and word books, and large-print reference books, respectively. Depending upon your current needs, you may wish to move from Part I directly to whichever of the subsequent parts addresses the kind of reference book you require. For ease of accessibility as well as comparison, each part follows the same structure and includes similar features. The first chapter in each of Parts II, III, and IV is entitled "What to Look for in [type of reference book]." These chapters detail the criteria used in this guide to judge the particular reference works. It should be noted that these are not newly minted criteria; rather, they are the tried and true specifications that librarians and educators have used for many years when assessing reference books. For example, in "What to Look for in Encyclopedias," the following characteristics are defined and discussed: *scope* (breadth and depth of coverage); *authority* (reputation, contributors' qualifications, and general reliability); *currency*; *accuracy*; *clarity*; *objectivity*; *accessibility* (arrangement, cross-referencing, and indexing); *special features* (such as illustrations, maps, and bibliographies); and *format* (a brief physical description of the encyclopedia). Each work is thus examined in light of each of the appropriate criteria. Note, too, that at the end of each of the "What to Look for . . ." chapters you will find a glossary of terms used in that chapter.

The individual reviews begin with a box of summary data called "Facts at a Glance." These fact boxes are a finding aid to help readers identify works of particular interest to them before reading the entire evaluation. The summary information includes such items as the work's full title, publisher, editor; initial copyright date or the edition reviewed; quantitative data such as the number of volumes, entries or maps, pages, illustrations (and the number in color); trim size and binding; price; intended readership; and where the reference work is sold.

Each review within a category follows a standard outline. Specific numbered subheadings vary among the categories, but will generally cover such criteria as *scope*, *authority*, *clarity*, *objectivity*, and *accessibility*, in addition to criteria that are specific to each type of work, such as *quality and currency of entries* in dictionaries and *scale and projections* in atlases. Each review concludes with a summary, in which the book is evaluated in light of its overall quality and potential use to readers. When appropriate, the *summary* section may also compare this particular work with similar works.

One of the special features of this guide is the inclusion of facsimile pages. These facsimiles are reproductions of typical pages or entries from many of the encyclopedias and dictionaries reviewed, along with keyed annotations that identify particular features—especially those cited in the evaluations. These will be of special value to people who use the guide to comparison shop prior to purchasing reference books, and for those who cannot personally examine each work. These illustrations provide an invaluable gauge to a particular work's appropriateness for a specific reader. For example, an authoritative encyclopedia packed with entries may sound like a good idea—until you see what a representative page looks like filled with small type and minimal white space. Both can be very important factors in reference works for younger readers who generally benefit from clear type, crisp illustrations, and an open page design. Readers of this guide should note that facsimiles of encyclopedias are reduced to fit on our pages; a note below the facsimile indicates the amount of this reduction. Dictionary facsimiles are reproduced actual size. Facsimiles are not included for atlases and word books because they could not give the reader an accurate impression of those works' contents. However, "What to Look for in Atlases" includes six pages of generic maps that illustrate various elements found in atlases. These maps are accompanied by text that describes how atlases are designed.

Facsimile pages have been selected to illustrate representative samples of the design and editorial features of various titles. Wherever these pages have been reduced in size, the percentage of reduction is indicated. The reproduction process necessarily results in some loss of image quality, especially when converting a color page to black and white. The facsimiles therefore do not represent the clarity of the original works.

Finally, *Reference Books for Young Readers* concludes with two appendixes and an index. Appendix B provides an alphabetical list of publishers and distributors along with their addresses. This list includes all of the publishers and distributors cited in the individual reviews. Information is current as of August 1, 1987. Appendix A is a bibliography that includes titles of related reference works and professional journals that may be of particular interest to the reference librarian. Finally, the index includes all titles reviewed, as well as other titles mentioned in the evaluations. The index is amply cross-referenced.

In using this guide, you may find it helpful to start with a checklist of those criteria that are most important to you, in order of consideration. For example, if you are shopping for a dictionary, does the need for currency take precedence over the pronunciation guide? Are simplified definitions more important than number of entries? Are the special features such as separate biographical and geographical listings or a list of abbreviations less important than usage examples? And what role does price play given your budget? With this checklist in hand, you can create your own comparative chart of the several books you have chosen for careful consideration and consult it to help you toward your final selection.

Reference Books for Young Readers

PART ONE

Introduction

Chapter 1
The History
of General
Reference Books

Introduction

Reference Books for Young Readers considers three types of general reference works: encyclopedias, dictionaries and other books relating to words and the use of words, and atlases.

Encyclopedias categorize knowledge, giving a survey of what is currently known about a myriad of specific topics. They present an orderly assembly of the facts essential to an understanding of each topic. Modern encyclopedias are designed to serve as a point of reference from which the reader can proceed to other sources that contain more specific and detailed information. The term used for these works is derived from the expression the classical Greeks used to describe a "rounded out" education or "circle of learning"—*enkyklios paideia*.

If encyclopedias can be characterized as telling about *things*, then dictionaries can be described as telling about *words*. Dictionaries and their close counterparts, such as thesauruses and etymologies, deal with words as words. They describe the derivation, pronunciation, and definitions of words, and the relationships words have to each other. The English name for these books is a translation of a medieval Latin word, *dictionarium*, which in turn was derived from the classical Latin *dictio*, "word" or

"speech," *dicere*, "to say, to speak," and *arium*, a connecting thing or place.

Atlases describe the surface of the world and its features, both natural and artificial. The maps in atlases are abstract representations of the earth. In addition to words, atlases use special symbols to depict special features of the earth. The term *atlas* came to be used after early mapmakers illustrated the covers of their map collections with pictures of the titan Atlas. In Greek mythology, Atlas was made to carry the heavens on his shoulders for eternity after the gods of Olympus defeated the titans for control of the universe. The modern world atlas has a burden too—the accurate, up-to-date representation of the world, its political boundaries, cities, and salient features.

The history of all these reference books is closely tied to the development of the written word. The written word is a form of memory that enables a literate person to arrange and store not only his or her own knowledge but also that possessed by others. This capacity allows human knowledge to accumulate and be transmitted from one generation to another. It also enables individuals to learn with relative ease about places they have never visited and about subjects of which they have no prior knowledge or experience.

The compiling of reference works is a response to the same human impulses that created systems of writing. Only by defining and agreeing to an arbitrary collection of signs to represent spoken language could a permanent record of information be accumulated and passed on to the official in the next village, to the scholar in the next country, or to the leaders in the next generation.

The earliest reference systems were mnemonic aids—pictures and symbols used to prompt the recollection of information. Contemporary examples of such aids include the rosaries still used by the Buddhist, Catholic, Hindu, and Muslim faithful to prompt the ordered repetition of a prayer sequence. The notched Maori genealogy sticks of New Zealand and the knotted strands of the Inca quipu were also memory aids. They made possible the recording of history and other information.

Like the memory aids, Sumerian cuneiform, Egyptian hieroglyphics, and other early writing systems allowed ancient peoples to measure time, to record genealogies and transactions, and to represent various aspects of myth, religion, and ritual. These systems, however, could only record the concrete; the abstract, unseen, and unknowable aspects of religion could not be recorded unless they were first reduced to concrete terms.

The urge to record the most abstract thoughts that language can express led to the development of the alphabet. The first true alphabet, which emerged around 1000 B.C. in the Phoenician city of Byblos, had a liberating effect on the recording of knowledge. By separating language into sounds, the alphabet made it possible to use a finite number of symbols to represent an infinite number of words. More flexible and economical than hieroglyphics, pictograms, or ideograms, this alphabet could be used to record the most abstract statements. As a result, subsequent generations were able to refine the abstract concepts they inherited in light of new as well as accumulated information.

Moreover, the alphabet allowed writers and readers to switch from one language to another with greater ease than did the earlier systems of writing. And, though its creators could not have foreseen it, the alphabet would be the perfect partner for the advanced printing techniques that would culminate in movable type and the eventual mass distribution of books.

Encyclopedias

The Beginning of Classification in Ancient Greece and Rome

Improved writing systems resulted in a vastly expanded accumulation of knowledge. The need arose to classify information in order to manage or absorb it easily. In classical Greece, philosophers such as Socrates and Plato taught that the good life required thought and that thought, in turn, required an encompassing knowledge of all things. Books that could capture all known information in easily absorbed form seemed to be a solution, and the reference work was born.

The Greek approach to encyclopedic writing was to record the spoken word. In a sense, Plato became the first encyclopedist when he set down the only known record of Socrates's discourses. Plato's status as the first encyclopedist is further bolstered by his

development of taxonomy, the rules or laws of ordering information. In the fourth century B.C. there were two systems of classification. Plato used both in efforts to codify and explain the universe. The first of these systems was by category, in which sets and members of sets were established. Categorization established a finite set of "containers" and sorted any information in such a way that it could be appropriately "contained." The second method of classification was by hierarchy. Under a hierarchical system, knowledge was ranked as superordinate and subordinate. In his teaching, Plato was to synthesize both systems, radically altering the way human beings looked at life and the universe.

Just as the alphabet freed writers from the restraints of hieroglyphics, so Plato liberated taxonomy to deal with ideas. Plato believed that objects in the world are imperfect reflections, or representations, of perfect ideas, ideas that exist in a nonmaterial world. Therefore, he reasoned, just as objects can be sorted into containers, so ideas can be sorted into categories. Plato also noted the order that results from the stratification of government and society and from ranking soldiers in an army. Ideas and intellectual disciplines, he concluded, could also be arranged in terms of "higher" and "lower."

Plato's ideas of taxonomy and his ordering of the universe were recorded by his nephew and disciple, Speusippus. Although no complete plan or outline for Speusippus's writings has survived, the existing fragments indicate that he was attempting a sort of encyclopedic reference work. By recording Plato's words, he sought to preserve the accumulation of the then-known arts and sciences within the orderly framework Plato had constructed for the universe.

Plato's actual "encyclopedia," however, was a living one. In order to gather and classify all knowledge into a single entity, he founded the Academy in Athens in 338 B.C. Here "perfect" ideas were both categorized and ranked hierarchically in the creation of a curriculum in which students could learn politics, aesthetics, philosophy, interpersonal relations, and benefit from a broad *paideia*, the training, disciplining, and education of the young.

Plato's best known disciple at the Academy, Aristotle, concentrated on and classified only the knowable as he moved away from Plato's idealism toward what is now called realism. Aristotle's emphasis on facts and observation were central to the curriculum of the Academy's rival school, the Lyceum, which he established in 335 B.C. Both the categories and the hierarchy classifications taught in the Lyceum survived in the ideals of Greek education that were spread through the far-flung military conquests of

Aristotle's student, Alexander of Macedon (Alexander the Great). This "all around" or general education, called *enkyklios paideia*, remains the standard for a liberal arts education even today. Aristotle's surviving lecture notes are encyclopedic in the sense that they show how the Lyceum sought to present and preserve a comprehensive background for learning.

The seven categories of the *enkyklios paideia* developed in the Hellenistic era were divided into three lower categories (grammar, rhetoric, and logic/dialectic) and four higher categories (arithmetic, geometry, astronomy, and music/harmony). Not only did the seven disciplines of the *enkyklios paideia* become the seven "liberal arts," but they also became the basis for the first written encyclopedias, which appeared in Hellenized Rome.

Unlike the Greeks, Roman writers did not seek to preserve the spoken word but rather to collect existing knowledge and present it in a readable form. This practice was in keeping with the value the Romans placed on acquiring the knowledge necessary for the execution of practical tasks. The first known Roman effort to summarize all usable knowledge was a series of letters from Marcus Porcius Cato (Cato the Censor) to his son. The collection, known as the *Praecepta ad filium* (Advice to His Son, ca. 183 B.C.), survives only in fragments, but it is known that in this encyclopedic work, Cato sought to provide an education for his reader as well as references that could be used in solving practical problems. The *Praecepta* included all the subjects Cato considered essential for the Roman citizen: agriculture, rhetoric, medicine, law, and the art of war.

A more direct link to the *enkyklios paideia* was established by another Roman writer, Marcus Terentius Varro. His *Disciplinae* (The Disciplines, ca. 30 B.C.) consisted of nine volumes, one devoted to each of the seven liberal arts, and one each to medicine and architecture. This work also exists only in fragments.

The earliest *enkyklios paideia* to survive in its entirety was compiled by Pliny the Elder (ca. A.D. 23–79). His *Historia Naturalis* (Natural History or General Knowledge, A.D. 77) is by far the most influential of all the Roman encyclopedias and served as a major source for other encyclopedias for the next fifteen centuries. Although the term encyclopedia, which first appears in medieval Latin, was never used to describe reference works in the ancient world, Pliny's *Historia Naturalis* is often cited as the first true encyclopedia.

Pliny's encyclopedia is an immense work. He collected all the information about the natural world he could locate from the writings of 473 Greek and Roman authors. The 37 books that comprise the work divided "all known" knowledge into 2,500 chapters and included such diverse categories as the physical composition of the universe, geography and ethnography, anthropology and human physiology, zoology, minerals and their uses, and painting and sculpture. The content of this last category remains a primary reference work on ancient Roman art.

The Middle Ages

After the fall of the Roman Empire in the fifth century A.D., trade and communications throughout Europe waned, cities declined, law and order disintegrated, and educational institutions were disbanded. As Europe was fragmented into numerous small kingdoms, the middle class shrank and life for the masses was reduced to subsistence level. The single unifying force in Europe during the Middle Ages (fifth to fifteenth centuries) was the Christian Church. The Church not only provided some social services for the sick and indigent, but also fostered learning in the monasteries where many of the classical texts were preserved.

The early Church fathers, in establishing the monastic tradition of scholarship, sought to preserve the learning of the classical pagan world while reconciling it with Christian beliefs and doctrine. During this period, encyclopedias were compiled so that existing knowledge could be interpreted and codified in accordance with orthodox theology. Despite their theocentric purpose, these works fulfilled the traditional goal of the *enkyklios paideia* by preserving all known knowledge throughout an era that was largely inimical to it.

In 551, the Roman statesman and writer Cassiodorus withdrew to a monastery and began work on an encyclopedia that was to establish the tone for Christian encyclopedias in the Middle Ages. His *Institutiones divinarum et saecularium litterum* (Institutes of Divine and Secular Literature) set an example for presenting encyclopedia entries in order of their perceived importance. Cassiodorus drew clear distinctions between sacred and profane teachings and ranked them hierarchically in his encyclopedia, with Scripture and Church topics considered first and in detail. Such topics as arithmetic and geometry appeared last and were given only minor attention.

Between 600 and 630, Isidore of Seville (Archbishop and Saint) compiled an encyclopedia for the education of the newly converted population of Spain. The *Etymologiae* or *Origenes* (Etymologies or Beginnings) was an ambitious collection of 20 books in which Isidore attempted to give the definition and etymology of every term relating to an academic discipline. The books were arranged topically and at the beginning of each major division, Isidore offered a brief historical summary of the subject to be examined. This vast compilation included not only the classical *enkyklios paideia* subjects, but also theology, Church history, languages, nations, cities, animals, and gardening. Following the example of Cassiodorus, Isidore organized his encyclopedia in an ordered fashion.

Because Isidore considered the liberal arts and secular learning to be the true basis of a Christian education, he dealt first with such subjects as liberal arts and medicine, then with the Bible and Church teachings, and finally with such practical topics as agriculture, warfare, shipping, and furniture. Isidore's work was treated with great respect and was reprinted as late as the sixteenth century.

During the next five centuries, European encyclopedias were generally undistinguished and were designed to be read by a learned few. Because they were intended as tools for professional scholars, content was organized to reflect a train of thought, not for ease in usage.

There were, however, three minor but notable departures. At the beginning of the twelfth century, a reference work called the *Suidas* or *Suda* first used alphabetical order, and its practical information ensured its popularity for several centuries. At the end of the twelfth century, the Abbess of Herrad compiled what is probably the first encyclopedia to be written by a woman. Her work was intended to educate and edify the nuns of her abbey. The idea of an encyclopedia for readers other than male clerics was taken a step further by Bartholomaeus Angelicus, who designed *De proprietibus rerum* (1220–40) for the lay reader. This encyclopedia, based on Pliny and Isidore's works, remained the most popular European encyclopedia for the next three hundred years.

The most outstanding encyclopedia of the Middle Ages was the authoritative work of Vincent of Beauvais, who compiled it at the request of Louis IX of France (ca. 1244). Vincent, a Dominican monk, gathered all the knowledge of the Middle Ages into three comprehensive works: the *Speculum naturale* (Mirror of Nature), the *Speculum doctrinale* (Mirror of Doctrine), and the *Speculum historiale* (Mirror of History). Together with a fourth book, the *Speculum morale* (Mirror of Morals), an anonymous work added after Vincent's death, this encyclopedia is known as the *Speculum maius* (Greater Mirror).

Vincent's portion of the *Speculum maius* consists of 80 books and is divided into 9,785 chapters. Almost equal space is allotted to each of the three

sections. In the *Speculum naturale*, Vincent drew not only on Latin writings, but also on Greek, Arabic, and Hebrew sources to summarize all natural history known to Western thought in the thirteenth century: it covered God and the Creation as part of natural history. The *Speculum doctrinale* discussed practical matters and the scholastic knowledge of the period. Intended as a practical handbook for the student or public official, it included the classical *enkyklios paideia*, with chapters ranging from grammar to the art of poetry, from war to mythology. In the *Speculum historiale*, Vincent summarized the first two "Mirrors," recounted the history of the world from Creation to the Crusade of St. Louis (1254), and predicted the extinction of the human race and the end of the world (2376).

The *Speculum maius* was translated into several languages and was reprinted in its entirety until the end of the nineteenth century. Its value is unequaled as the repository of fragmentary documents of classical antiquity and as a detailed and contemporary history of the early thirteenth century. In 1485, it was printed in an English translation by William Caxton as *The Myrror of the Worlde*, the first encyclopedia to be produced with movable type.

The fourth part of the *Speculum maius* was based principally on the work of St. Thomas Aquinas. Responding to the need for standardized training of the clerical ranks, as well as the continuing need to reconcile sacred dogma and secular thought, Aquinas and his fellow scholastics attempted to categorize all the knowledge into rigid, unchanging containers. Because dogma could not brook criticism or questioning, the work of the scholastics took on some of the mystique and authority of the Scriptures.

The awe in which recorded knowledge was held during the Middle Ages and the unquestioning attitude toward knowledge approved by the scholastics can still be found in the attitudes of some users of modern reference works. There is a tendency to accept what is written in encyclopedias and dictionaries as the absolute truth, and to regard an encyclopedia as the repository of all possible information on a subject. However, as indicated earlier, encyclopedias in the Middle Ages were intended to be read from beginning to end, like textbooks, and not to be consulted for specific information, as are modern encyclopedias. Encyclopedists usually created their work for scholars and the clergy, not for the general public. Indeed, few people could read.

There were, however, two encyclopedists of the Middle Ages who did write for the public: one was the previously mentioned Bartholomeus Anglicus and the other was Dante Alighieri's teacher, Brunetto Latini. Latini wrote the first vernacular encyclopedia in French, which at that time was the common language of the cultured and mercantile classes in Italy. Latini called his work *Li livres dou tresor* (Treasure Books, ca. 1266), and though it was much more concise than Vincent's *Speculum maius*, it followed the same classification system.

Islamic Reference Works in the Middle Ages

Clerics in European monasteries were not the only scholars who were preserving classical learning during the Middle Ages. Medieval Islamic scholars were also collecting and analyzing classical writing as they created encyclopedic reference works that served as repositories of knowledge and attempted to reconcile the philosophies of the ancient classical world with their own religious teachings.

Early Arabic encyclopedic works include the *Catalogue of Sciences* by al-Farabi of Baghdad (ca. 870–950), a work that was translated into Latin and read widely in Europe during the Middle Ages. Al-Farabi was aware of the *enkyklios paideia* and divided his work into eight similar categories: logic (including rhetoric and poetry), mathematics (including optics, astronomy, weights and measures, and mechanics), physics (including botany, meteorology, psychology, and zoology), politics, law, and theology. Al-Farabi's work still exists in manuscript form in the Escorial in Spain.

Like the Roman and Christian encyclopedists, Arabic writers compiled highly structured works, classifying their information into the categories of the scholastic disciplines. The Arabic writers also showed a preference for arranging their work hierarchically.

The pattern for many later works was set by the first true Arabic encyclopedia, the *Kitab'Uyun al-Akhbar* (The Best of Traditions), written by Ibn Qutayba (828–89). Whereas Cassiodorus gave pride of place to the Scriptures and Isidore of Seville honored the liberal arts, Ibn Qutayba reflected the needs of his cultural milieu by beginning with power, war, and nobility and ending with food and women, with asceticism and prayers coming in between.

About a century later, another Arabic encyclopedia, written by the Persian statesman-scholar al-Khwarizmi, drew a clear line between the sacred and the profane. He divided the *Mafatih al-Ulum* (Key to the Sciences, ca. 975–77) into two major categories, distinguishing between the indigenous Islamic sciences (Koranic jurisprudence, theological philosophy, Arabic grammar, secretarial duties, history, poetry, and prosody) and the "foreign" sciences. Although they were not identical to the seven disciplines of the *enkyklios paideia*, the "foreign" sciences he included reflected the Greek ideas that were being synthesized by the Islamic world—philosophy, logic, medicine, arithmetic, geometry, astronomy, music, and mechanics.

The Age of Reason

With the invention of movable printing type (ca. 1450), books could be mass produced and sold relatively cheaply. As more and more people learned to read and write, the Church found it increasingly difficult to monopolize the written word. Exposure to old ideas and the ability to communicate new ones, together with the changes brought about by geographic and scientific discoveries, ushered in the age of reason and scientific inquiry.

The English philosopher Francis Bacon (1561–1626) proposed that the new age needed a new kind of reference work, one that took a scientific approach to learning. Bacon regarded the encyclopedia not as a compendium of all knowledge, but as a systematic categorization of knowledge that included only information that could be observed or empirically confirmed. The work that he planned, the *Instaturatio magna* (Great Renewal), would reflect his rational attempts to find the basic forms of nature. The 130 sections of the work were to be divided into three major categories: external nature, man, and man's actions on nature. Bacon did not complete his outline and his encyclopedia was never written, but his ideas exerted a revolutionizing effect both on encyclopedia making and on the categorization of knowledge.

After Bacon, European encyclopedias evolved from repositories of all information available at the time— whether true or not—into collections of verified knowledge. One of the first such works was Johann Heinrich Alsted's *Encyclopedia septem tomis distincta* (Encyclopedia Arranged in Seven Volumes, 1630). Like previous encyclopedias, Alstead's work was arranged topically but included a 119-page index for enhanced accessibility. It was one of the last encyclopedias to be written topically and in Latin. Thereafter encyclopedias were arranged alphabetically and written in the vernacular. This was a reflection not only of a realization that the body of knowledge had so expanded that alphabetization was the only sensible way to organize the material, but also of the decreasing importance of Latin to a broader base of readership.

Forerunners of the Modern Encyclopedia

Public preference for vernacular, alphabetical encyclopedias was shown by the immediate success of Louis Moreri's *Grand Dictionaire Historique* (1674). Moreri's work, which emphasized geographical and biographical material, is acknowledged to be the inspiration for encyclopedias that were soon published in England, Germany, the Netherlands, and Switzerland.

A further step toward the format of today's encyclopedias was taken in 1704 with the publishing of the German *Konversations-Lexicon* (Dictionary of Conversation), which established a pattern for later works by presenting a collection of short, cross-referenced articles by different writers. Prior to this work, encyclopedias were written wholly by their compilers.

Despite its Latin title, the *Lexicon technicum* (1704), compiled by John Harris, was the first modern encyclopedia written in English. This alphabetically arranged work contained clear, practical articles written by specialists, with bibliographies for its more important articles. The *Lexicon technicum* was subtitled the *Universal Dictionary of Arts and Sciences*.

The same subtitle was incorporated in 1728 in another outstanding English encyclopedia, Ephraim Chambers's two-volume *Cyclopaedia*. Although Chambers's *Cyclopaedia* was designed to be a comprehensive reference work that would also show the relationships among the various areas of knowledge, it included no geographical, historical, or biographical information. Its content is characterized by scholarly articles from a number of contributors and by systematic cross-referencing. Its design and layout resemble those of present-day encyclopedias. Two other distinguishing features of the *Cyclopaedia* were its 21 large plates of illustrations and an elaborate preface depicting the divisions and subdivisions of knowledge in schematic form.

Possibly the most important aspect of Chambers's *Cyclopaedia* is the work that it inspired in France. Originally, a Paris publisher named André Breton planned to publish the French *Encyclopédie* as a translation and modest expansion of Chambers's work. The project was given to the philosopher Denis Diderot and the mathematician Jean d'Alembert to complete. In their hands the *Encyclopédie* (1751–65) grew into a gargantuan 28-volume work. Abandoning the idea that an encyclopedia should include entries on all subjects, they endeavored to produce writing of the highest standard in articles that championed rationalism, the scientific method, and republican ideals. The initial subscription to this polemical work was 2,000 and the number of subscribers grew as papal and governmental censorship added to its popularity. The *Encyclopédie* is commonly regarded as having played a significant role in helping to ignite the French Revolution (1789).

The next major landmark in encyclopedia making was the *Encyclopaedia Britannica*, conceived by two

Edinburgh Scots, Andrew Bell and Colin Macfarquhar, and edited by William Smellie. The first edition (1768–71) was published in three volumes, weighed 12 pounds, and contained 2,659 pages with some 160 copperplate engravings. The *Britannica* favored a monographic approach, highlighting long, comprehensive articles, although it also included some shorter entries. It was an extremely popular work despite its sometimes startling inaccuracies, like a description of California as a country in the West Indies. A second edition, edited by William Tytler and published between 1777 and 1784, greatly improved the *Britannica*'s accuracy and extended its scope. The 29-volume eleventh edition of the *Britannica* (1910–11) was sponsored by Cambridge University. Because of its rich leisurely prose, it is considered by many to be the finest encyclopedia ever published. The eleventh edition doubled the number of entries without greatly expanding its size by splitting up the lengthy, comprehensive treatises of former editions into shorter, more comprehensible articles.

Pirated editions of the *Encyclopaedia Britannica* were printed in the United States as early as 1798; it was not until the fourteenth edition (1929) that the *Britannica* was officially published in New York as well as in London. In 1941, the *Britannica* was taken over by a corporation with strong ties to the University of Chicago, and its publishing headquarters were moved to Chicago, where they are located today.

Both the French *Encyclopédie* and the British *Encyclopaedia Britannica* contained extended learned discussions as well as some short articles. The next major encyclopedia to appear challenged that format. The *Brockhaus Konversations-Lexicon* began in 1796 as a German encyclopedia for women and then was taken over by Friedrich Arnold Brockhaus, who brought out his first edition between 1796 and 1811. Its brief, unsigned articles were written in a popular style. The *Brockhaus* did not claim to be an encyclopedia of universal knowledge; instead, it concentrated on subjects of interest to Germans. As the first national encyclopedia, the *Brockhaus* served as a model for later American, British, and European works. This model of a national encyclopedia is still followed by some publishers and has heirs in such works as the 65-volume *Bolshaya sovetskaya entsiklopedya* (Great Soviet Encyclopedia, 1926–47).

The first American encyclopedia was the *Encyclopedia Americana*, published between 1829 and 1833 in Philadelphia. Its editor was a German immigrant, Francis Lieber, who based his work on the seventh edition of the *Brockhaus*. The *Americana* has gone through many revisions and editions since the first 13-volume set was published; it is still in print.

An English translation of the *Brockhaus* provided the format for the *Chambers's Encyclopedia*, which had no relationship to Ephraim Chambers's *Cyclopedia* of 1728. The new work was the creation of Robert and William Chambers and was published in Edinburgh between 1859 and 1868. The 10-volume set was issued simultaneously in Philadelphia by J. B. Lippincott & Company.

The subtitle of the Chambers's work, *A Dictionary of Universal Knowledge for the People*, indicates that by the middle of the nineteenth century the encyclopedia as a reference book had assumed virtually its present form. In their preface to the first edition, the Chambers brothers wrote: "The several topics are not handled with a view to the technical instruction of those who have to make a special study of particular branches of knowledge or art. The information may be characterized as *non-professional*, embracing those points of the several subjects which every intelligent man or woman may have occasion to speak or think about. At the same time," they went on, "every effort is made that the statements, so far as they go, shall be precise and scientifically accurate." These are essentially the same criteria as those of today's encyclopedia makers.

Young Readers' Encyclopedias

"Suppose a boy of ten were to spend fifteen minutes a day in reading these pages . . . he would at thirteen know more about the earth and the life on it than the wisest man knew a few generations ago." (Preface to the *Book of Knowledge*, 1910.) Encyclopedias for children emerged long after adult encyclopedias had evolved into their modern form. It is therefore interesting to observe that the first children's encyclopedias reverted to the basic form of *enkyklios paideia* embraced by Pliny and the early encyclopedists. Moreover, they reflected the new ideas of childhood education that developed in seventeenth-century Europe and America.

Just before the start of the eighteenth century, a professor at Altdorf University in Germany published the first known encyclopedia for young readers. Johann Christoph Wagenseil's *Pera librorum juvenilium* (1695) was a collection of essays and stories, literally a set of books intended to serve as a young reader's complete library at a time when almost no books were printed for children. Characteristically, this first youth encyclopedia mirrored the role played by encyclopedias in adult education. Wagenseil was essentially a storyteller, and his most lasting contri-

bution to literature was the telling of folk stories that were retold by later German writers. His *Von der Meister-Singer Holdseligen Kunst* (The Master Singer's Gracious Art, 1697), for example, found new life when E. T. A. Hoffman told the tale of *Der Kampf der Sänger* (The Struggle of the Singer, 1818). Wagenseil's model of encyclopedist as storyteller was clearly in keeping with John Locke's revolutionary educational concepts, which governed progressive education in the eighteenth and nineteenth centuries. Locke, in *Some Thoughts Concerning Education* (1693), argued that children should be encouraged to acquire the pleasant habit of reading rather than to store up facts.

The next large-scale encyclopedias for children did not appear until the twentieth century. However, the progression of children's literature throughout the eighteenth and nineteenth centuries established a tradition of interesting, entertaining encyclopedic reading.

The Englishman John Newbery, the first bookseller and publisher to see the potential market for children's books, initially issued children's stories in the tradition of the popular chapbooks. Newbery (for whom the American Library Association's annual award for the most distinguished American children's book is named) recognized the value of printing intriguing stories for instruction, and introduced one of the first reference books for children, *Circle of Sciences* (1745). Some of Newbery's adult authors, including Oliver Goldsmith, contributed to the work.

By the end of the eighteenth century, progressive educators were beginning to come under the influence of the ideas of Jean-Jacques Rousseau. According to Rousseau, children learned best by observing nature, and by doing things themselves under the guidance of wise and friendly adults. That education should, above all, be interesting was emphasized by Rousseau in *Emile* (1762), the chronicle of a boy whose learning was based on his interests.

Despite a characteristic tendency to moralize, children's literary classics of the nineteenth century maintained the tradition of instruction through entertaining reading. Many of these works presented factual information and moral precepts wrapped in engrossing tales. Fantasy (*King of the Golden River* by John Ruskin, 1840) and adventure (Johan Rudolf Weiss's *Swiss Family Robinson*, 1812–13) led the way. Real places were described in Mark Twain's novels *Tom Sawyer* (1876) and *Huck Finn* (1884), and in Johanna Spyri's *Heidi* (1880). Real social issues were examined in such classics as *Black Beauty* (1877, Anna Sewell).

The growing acceptance and popularity of story collections moved children's literature toward the format of the modern encyclopedia. Like encyclopedias, these collections grouped stories by topic and summarized information in an easily accessible format. Charles and Mary Lamb's *Tales from Shakespeare* (1808) experimented with the rewriting of adult literature for children, while Jakob and Wilhelm Grimm (1812–22) and Hans Christian Andersen (1835–72) codified children's tales. Nathaniel Hawthorne's *A Wonder Book*, published in 1852, retold Greek myths in children's language. Robert Louis Stevenson's *A Child's Garden of Verses* (1885) went one step further in telling of the world not only in terms that a child could understand but also from a child's point of view. In his *Jungle Book* collections (1874, 1895), Rudyard Kipling also wrote from a child's perspective and in *Just So Stories* (1902) went so far as to present scientific "reasons" born of children's fantasies.

Another early form of encyclopedic reading for the young can be found in children's magazines. These periodicals mixed essays and fairy tales, moral lessons and natural science articles in the tradition of a general and liberal education. Early examples were the *Leipziger Wochenblatt für Kinder* (Leipzig Children's Weekly, 1798) and the *Gaceta de los Niños* (Children's Magazine), first published in Spain in 1798.

The most influential early magazine for children in the United States was *St. Nicholas*. Its first editions (1873) were edited by Mary Mapes Dodge, best known as the author of *Hans Brinker, or The Silver Skates* (1865). *St. Nicholas* emphasized articles on science and history as well as stories. The first Canadian children's magazine, *The Snow Drop* (1847), was also encyclopedic, but featured moralistic tales. The Spanish tradition of magazines for children was carried on in the Americas by José Martí, Cuba's liberator, who began publishing *La Edad de Oro* (The Golden Age) in 1889.

That children's literature, as a genre, now had official sanction was evident in 1900 when the American Library Association first included a children's section. As the twentieth century opened, then, the stage was set for the coalescence of children's literature into a formal encyclopedia. In 1908, the *Children's Encyclopedia* was published in England and two years later the Grolier Society issued an American version, *The Book of Knowledge*, subtitled "The Children's Encyclopedia That Leads to Love of Learning."

In keeping with Locke and Rousseau's ideals of education, these early encyclopedias provided general information in short, interesting segments. Stories, poetry collections, games, and hobby instructions were interspersed among topically arranged articles that described natural phenomena and historical events. Rousseau's theories were reflected in departments as varied as "The Fine Arts" (where "The child becomes familiar with the best, and learns unconsciously to recognize true beauty") and "Things to Make and Things to Do" (where "The child, while amusing himself, learns to use his hands, to carry out an idea").

The popularity of the *Children's Encyclopedia* and *The Book of Knowledge* encouraged other publishers to produce youth and school versions of encyclopedias. Like adult encyclopedias, their articles were cross-indexed and arranged alphabetically. *The World Book* (now titled THE WORLD BOOK ENCYCLOPEDIA), written specifically for children of elementary and junior high school age, appeared in 1918. In 1925, *The World Book* adopted a policy of continuous revision and the publication of yearly supplements intended to update each edition.

In 1922, *Compton's Pictured Encyclopedia* took youth encyclopedias a step further, from tools for a general education to ones geared for formal education. *Compton's* was designed for use in junior and senior high schools for student research and included a "Fact-Index" in each volume. It is published today as COMPTON'S ENCYCLOPEDIA. *Britannica Junior* (later *Britannica Junior Encyclopaedia* and now out of print), written for elementary school children, was first published in 1934, also with a policy of continuous revisions.

Finally, in the 1960s, Grolier Inc. brought youth encyclopedias full cycle, publishing its heavily illustrated *Encyclopedia International* (1963, now out of print) for older secondary school students and education-minded adults, and a completely new work for younger readers, the NEW BOOK OF KNOWLEDGE (1966), a 20-volume reference work with topics arranged alphabetically.

The modern children's encyclopedias reviewed in *Reference Books for Young Readers* are heirs to this legacy of children's literature and educational thought. In our reviews and evaluations we have measured them by the standards to which enlightened educators have always held children's books—standards that include sensitivity to the learning and interest cycles of young people and the role assigned to reading by the current prevailing philosophies of education.

An examination of youth encyclopedias as children's literature reveals the roots of the modern encyclopedia in early children's storybooks and story collections. The youth encyclopedia's debt to these origins may have been partially repaid when its name was given to a hero of modern children's books, a boy named Encyclopedia Brown. Donald J. Sobol's character admits that though his head is so full of facts that his friends call him a walking encyclopedia, his success as a detective comes from his ability to use facts to interpret what he observes. Professional encyclopedists would applaud.

Encyclopedias Today

The goals of today's encyclopedia are fairly standard. Encyclopedias are intended for use by the majority of the people in a society and as such are marketed not only to scholarly and academic institutions and libraries but also to homes. In this sense, encyclopedias have become democratized. General encyclopedias are no longer created by learned experts who present scholarly treatises exploring every facet of a topic. Rather, they are created by teams of specialists brought together for the specific task of synthesizing the ever-expanding body of accessible knowledge in their fields.

Modern encyclopedia makers have similar standards as well as similar goals, markets, and ways of creating their works. In general, publishers have elected to avoid polemical articles in favor of ones that codify knowledge in an impartial way. When sensitive and controversial topics are included, reputable publishers go to great lengths to make them objective. Among other standards held by reputable encyclopedia makers today are the inclusion of such items as selected bibliographies, illustrations, cross-references, and separate indexes. The articles themselves are generally short and written in a simple, straightforward style; the trend toward short articles can be seen by comparing entries in the NEW ENCYCLOPAEDIA BRITANNICA's Micropaedia and Macropaedia.

In each of its evolutionary forms, encyclopedists have tried to satisfy the needs of their age. When the Greeks placed a premium on the ability to think, encyclopedias recorded the thought process; when the Romans learned to prize practicality, Cato and Pliny recorded and summarized useful knowledge. When the religious and political temper of the Middle Ages demanded the rationalization of science within an orthodox framework, the encyclopedists complied; and when political questioning became popular, Diderot's inflammatory work found a receptive audience.

Encyclopedias also have varied purposes. Initially, they were meant to instruct, to lead the reader through the *enkyklios paideia*. Their second goal emerged as the impulse to preserve for future generations the accumulation of all that was known to the current generation of scholars. For most of their history, encyclopedias have been meant to instruct or preserve.

In the scientific era, the reading population became less passive and demanded more of the encyclopedia. The knowledge of the ages was now safely preserved, they felt, and their own intellects could instruct them if they were given the proper resources. The reader now demanded a usable and reliable source of data to use as the basis for self-instruction and further research. Again, the encyclopedists complied. How well the publishers of today's encyclopedias are responding to the needs of the reader is the focus of the reviews in chapter 6 of this book.

Even now, encyclopedia publishers are attempting to anticipate the needs of future users through the application of computer and telecommunications technology. The use of data processing and electronic text storage has facilitated the revision and updating of encyclopedic works, and several publishers now offer access to their titles through on-line delivery services or on laser-read compact discs. In the future, vast data banks may be available to subscribers, together with pictures, charts, recordings of music and speeches, and other features that have, until recently, been inconceivable.

Dictionaries

Roots of the English Dictionary

Although the word *dictionarius* cannot be found in classical Latin, it appears as early as A.D. 1225 in medieval Latin as a term for lists of Latin words that every educated person should know. As time passed, the *dictionarius* was joined by the glossary, a list of annotations (glosses) giving vernacular equivalents for selected Latin words in a specific book. A gloss is intended to define difficult words in context and thus help the reader through a passage. Glosses and glossaries are still used in modern textbooks. In Shakespeare anthologies, for example, the modern equivalents of archaic terms are provided as glosses. In foreign-language texts and readers, glosses as well as glossaries give English synonyms for foreign words that are necessary to the passage but have not been introduced to the as-yet limited vocabulary of the reader.

The earliest known English-Latin dictionary was intended as a glossary for children and clerics. Written in manuscript, perhaps as early as 1440, the *Promptorium* was literally a "storehouse" of words to be used in completing translations. The *Promptorium* appeared in print in 1499, a result of the introduction of movable-type printing to England by William Caxton in 1476. Caxton's interest in glossaries had already been evidenced by his printing of an untitled English-French glossary in 1480.

The first important Latin-English dictionary to be created in England was a collection of glossaries arranged conceptually by topic, not by a single alphabetical listing. Published in 1500, it was called the *Hortus Vocabularium* (Garden of Words).

In 1538, Sir Thomas Elyot's Latin-English glossary was published as the *Dictionary* and, in the absence of copyright laws, was absorbed by Thomas Cooper in his *Thesaurus* (1565), demonstrating a pattern of "borrowing" that has characterized dictionary-making throughout its history. (Cooper's work, incidentally, did not spring effortlessly into print, despite the borrowing. Cooper's wife, irritated at his neglect of her during long nights of compiling dictionary entries, burned half of his completed manuscript.)

Richard Huloet's *Abecedarium Anglo-Latinum* (1552) brought the bilingual glossary a few steps closer to the form of the modern dictionary by including not only English and Latin equivalents but also their French equivalents and brief definitions of the English words. Another English-Latin work of the period, *A Shorte Dictionarie for Young Begynners* (1553), added the dimension of a dictionary as a tool for learning, not just for translation. Its author, John Withal, introduced his work as a teaching manual for Latin classes.

While the interlingual dictionary increased in scope and standard, the English-language dictionary was beginning to take shape. In 1582, for example, Richard Mulcaster published a list of 8,000 English words, without definitions. It was called the *Elementarie*, and with its publication Mulcaster defended English as an important language in its own right, one that deserved its own dictionary. Mulcaster further expressed the wish that someone "wold gather all the words which we use in our English tung." This was attempted in 1596 by Edmund Coote, who, in his *Englishe Scholemister* (*English School-Master*), included a lexicon of 1,400 English words and definitions, as well as comments on grammar, prayers, and the catechism.

Robert Cawdrey's *A Table Alphabeticall* (1604), based on the *English School-Master*, is generally considered to be the first true dictionary in English. In addition to supplying definitions for 3,000 words, Cawdrey's dictionary included rudimentary etymologies, using symbols to designate which English words were derived from Greek or French. Cawdrey, however, bowed to the tradition of the glossary by including some entries he referred to as "hard usuall wordes borrowed from the Hebrew, Greeke, Latine, or French. &c . . . gathered for . . . Ladies, Gentlewomen, or any and other unskillful persons."

The next true dictionary, *An English Expositor* by John Bullokar, was registered in 1610 and printed in 1616. It contained twice as many words as Cawdrey's dictionary, but actually was less "English" than the *Table* because many of its "hard words" were merely pseudo-Anglicizations of Latin words. To increase the usefulness of his work, Bullokar sometimes identified the field in which a word was generally used and included archaisms, which he tagged as "only used of some ancient writers and now growne out of use." His own work remained in print through fourteen editions, the last appearing in 1731.

In 1623, Henry Cockeram borrowed heavily from Bullokar in creating *The English Dictionarie: or, An Interpreter of Hard English Words*, including many ersatz terms coined from Latin. To borrow one of Cockeram's words, the "prodigity" of his listings made this dictionary what the preface claimed it to be: the most complete dictionary of any yet published.

An important step in dictionary making was taken by Thomas Blount in *Glossographia: or A Dictionary Interpreting all such Hard Words . . . as are now used in our refined English Tongue* (1656). In this ambitious work, Blount listed, and often cited sources for, words that he had encountered and found difficult in his own reading. The *Glossographia* included scientific and technical terms as well as words that had recently entered the English language, and it also attempted to trace the etymologies of all entries.

As has been noted, lexicographers of this period borrowed quite heavily, usually without acknowledgment, from previous works. The first open conflict over this practice arose when Edward Phillips, a nephew of the English poet John Milton, published *The New World of English Words* in 1658. Blount bitterly attacked the work as a plagiarism of his 1656 dictionary. Although Phillips's work was clearly imitative of Blount's, often repeating Blount's errors, it did introduce one new idea. By claiming, albeit without proof, that specialists had helped write his dictionary, Phillips introduced into lexicography the practice of enlisting experts to support the authority of a dictionary.

An English Dictionary (1676) by Elisha Cole, the most comprehensive dictionary to appear up to this time, featured 25,000 entries, including archaic terms from Chaucer's time and, for the first time in any dictionary, dialectal terms and cant (the secret slang used by thieves and beggars). Nevertheless, like its predecessors, Cole's *Dictionary* mainly included "hard words," not a general vocabulary as dictionaries do today.

The Eighteenth Century

With the eighteenth century came the work of John Kersey, who is regarded by historian Allen Walker Read as the first professional lexicographer. As the editor of *A New English Dictionary* (1702), Kersey moved away from the "hard words" tradition of English dictionaries toward the concept of a general dictionary by using common as well as difficult or esoteric words. It was a consciously English work that avoided Latin, archaic, or overspecialized words. Although the definitions for its 28,000 entries were often brief to the point of being inadequate, it was so popular that it remained in print for 70 years.

In his next work, a 1706 revision of Edward Phillips's *New World of English Words*, Kersey made another departure by listing multiple meanings for words. In a language as polysemous as English, this advance did much to improve the value of dictionary definitions. Kersey also included an impressive list of technical and scientific terms and doubled the size of Phillips's dictionary to 38,000 words.

It then only remained for a schoolmaster, Nathan Bailey, to solidify the modern concept of a dictionary as a collection of all recognized words in use at a given time. His 1721 edition of *An Universal Etymological English Dictionary* listed "four-letter" words as well as dialectic, archaic, and literary terms. Bailey, a professional lexicographer and the master of a boarding school, incorporated not only etymologies but also earlier forms of words. Bailey's dictionary was reprinted throughout the eighteenth century and supplementary volumes were issued to add to the 40,000 entries in the first edition. Later editions added syllabication and syllable stress marks.

Bailey further developed the practice of lexicography in his *Dictionarium Britannicum*, an encyclopedic work published in 1730. Its 48,000 words excluded mere oddities of the language, and, like many present-day dictionaries, it listed geographical and biographical entries separately. Bailey's collaborators included such specialists as a botanist and a mathematician. This comprehensive work served as the base for one of the most notable and influential dictionaries in English, Samuel Johnson's *A Dictionary of the English Language*.

Dr. Johnson's Dictionary

In the first half of the eighteenth century, a number of notable writers began to express concern with what they felt was a decay in the English language. Jonathan Swift and Daniel Defoe, for example, proposed establishing authoritative standards that would keep English "pure" by halting changes in the language. Thomas Addison proposed that this might be done, if not by an Academy, as in France, then with a dictionary that would include literary quotations to illustrate the standard use of the entries. Alexander Pope also proposed such a dictionary.

This challenge was taken up by Samuel Johnson, a critic and poet who had no experience as a lexicographer. In 1747, Johnson presented his *Plan of a Dictionary of the English Language* to a potential patron, Lord Chesterfield. In his *Plan*, Johnson seems to agree with Swift and Defoe that the English language was in need of preservation. "The chief intent of [the *Dictionary*] is to preserve the purity and ascertain the meaning of our English idiom," he wrote. He went on to state that his goal was to create "a dictionary by which the pronunciation of our language may be fixed . . . [and] by which its purity may be preserved."

In an effort to include "the whole of the English language," Johnson made liberal use of Nathan Bailey's word stock and added to it words gleaned from his own scholarly reading. Contrary to popular belief, Johnson's word stock of 40,000 entries was not the largest of its day. What made Johnson's dictionary a masterpiece and a landmark in dictionary making was the inclusion of 118,000 amplifying quotations that recorded the usage of words by some of the most illustrious writers of the sixteenth and seventeenth centuries.

When Johnson's *Dictionary of the English Language* appeared in 1755, it incorporated all of the features of its immediate predecessors—multiple definitions, etymologies, quotations, stress marks— but used them with new authority. Its reputation as the finest dictionary in the English language remained secure for more than a century both in Great Britain and the United States.

Happily, although Johnson had set out to standardize the English language, he found that the living language refused to calcify and continued to grow. To accommodate this change, Johnson supervised three revisions of his work during his lifetime, with the fourth edition (1773) receiving particular attention. After his death in 1784, the *Dictionary* was revised by Henry John Todd, and with the 1818 and 1827 editions it became known as the *Todd-Johnson*.

Pronouncing Dictionaries

Following the publication of Johnson's master work, most dictionary makers concentrated on creating pronouncing dictionaries. Their intention was to satisfy the same fixative urge that lay behind Johnson's

Dictionary. In particular, the pronouncing dictionaries of the late eighteenth century were meant to oppose the tide of alternative pronunciations presented by Irish, Scottish, and American English.

The first of these pronouncing dictionaries, the *Linguae Britannica* was produced in 1757 by James Buchanan. William Johnson's *Pronouncing and Spelling Dictionary* followed in 1764. Both works sought to remedy the "manglings" and innovations of "illiterate Court fops, half-witted poets and University boys" that Jonathan Swift had excoriated in his diatribes against the sullying of "pure English." These two works introduced the practice of providing the actual pronunciation of a word in addition to stress marks, and they experimented with the use of diacritical marking systems.

The Irish actor and elocution teacher Thomas Sheridan employed both conventions and added phonetic respellings in his 1780 work, *A General Dictionary of the English Language.* Sheridan particularly hoped that his dictionary would correct the "mistakes" made by "well-educated natives of Ireland."

Although he had advocated language preservation, Samuel Johnson came to modify his views. He recognized that a living language is in constant transition and that no clear choice could be made from among several acceptable pronunciations. In his *Life of Johnson* (1791), James Boswell recorded Johnson's reaction to Sheridan's pronouncing dictionary. When he embarked on his own work, Johnson recalled, "Lord Chesterfield told me that the word *great* should be pronounced so as to rhyme to *state*; and Sir William Younge sent me word that it should be pronounced so as to rhyme to *seat*, and that none but an Irishman would pronounce it *grait*." Johnson cautioned that if "two men of the highest rank" disagreed, a lexicographer would be out of place in claiming only one pronunciation.

Nevertheless, Sheridan's work gained wide use and, with a later work by another actor, John Walker (1791), was considered authoritative, especially in the United States, where the spirit of revolution and a growing pride in American usage had not dimmed the zeal to speak English "properly." Sheridan, incidentally, went on to a lucrative career giving lectures in Ireland on proper English pronunciation.

Noah Webster and the American Dictionary

At the time of the American Revolution, the use of dictionaries was well established in American schools. In his *Ideas of the English School* (1751), Benjamin Franklin had recommended that "Each boy should

have an English dictionary to help him over difficulties." A New York schoolmaster went Franklin one better by stipulating that every student should have Johnson's *Dictionary.*

Despite his admiration for the English dictionary, Franklin had no use for the chaos that characterized English spelling at that time. In 1768, he published a paper calling for spelling reform and described a special typeface he had cut for a new alphabet. Franklin's plan was not carried out, but it did inspire a system of American spelling and a dictionary to rival Johnson's—both by Noah Webster.

Noah Webster's first work was the 1783 "blue-backed" *American Speller*, designed for elementary schools. Over 8 million copies of the *Speller* were sold in Webster's lifetime. At a royalty of one cent per copy, the success of the *Speller* gave Webster the financial freedom to devote his life to promoting the spelling, pronunciation, and grammar of American English at a time when it was rapidly acquiring its own distinctive characteristics.

By 1789, Webster had proposed many Americanized spellings. They included dropping the *u* from *-our* words (*colour/color, honour/honor*); changing *-re* endings to *-er* (*fibre/fiber, theatre/theater, centre/center*); subsituting *c* for *k* or *ck* (*kerb/curb, musick/music*); and simplifying vowel sounds (*plough/plow, tyre/tire*). These spelling changes might have occurred naturally, but the patriotic Webster felt that decisive action was necessary to encourage a separate American culture. "Our honor," he wrote in *Dissertations on the English Language* in 1789, the year when the first American president was inaugurated and the constitution came close to final ratification, "requires us to have a system of our own language, as well as government." Webster's first dictionary for schools, the *Compendious Dictionary for the English Language* (1806), satisfied his honor by using American spellings and by including more than 5,000 words that were native to America (such as *canoe*) among its 37,000 entries. To conform to etymology and rules of analogy, however, Webster refrained from such extremes as the substitution of *tuf* for *tough* and *bred* for *bread*, which Franklin had suggested.

For the next two decades, Webster continued to study language usage, and in 1828, at the age of 70, he saw the publication of his master work, *An American Dictionary of the English Language.* In this work, he showed greater conservatism than in his earlier years, noting that "The body of the language is the same as in England, and it is desireable [*sic*] to perpetuate that sameness."

In 1830, an important rival to Webster's *Dictionary* was brought out by a man who did not have

Webster's reputation as a reformer and innovator. Joseph Emerson Worcester was a quiet traditionalist but a competent lexicographer, who had worked previously on Webster's *Dictionary*. His *Comprehensive Pronouncing and Explanatory Dictionary of the English Language* and his later (1846) *A Universal and Critical Dictionary of the English Language* were in many ways more authoritative, accurate, and lexicographically correct than Webster's dictionaries. Webster promptly accused Worcester of plagiarism. Thus, what became known as the "war of the dictionaries" began.

Although some learned partisans of Webster and Worcester argued over lexicographical matters, the "war of the dictionaries" was primarily a marketing competition with sales of dictionaries for classroom use as the prize. After Webster's death in 1843, his son-in-law sold Webster's interests to the publishing firm of G. & C. Merriam in Springfield, Massachusetts. Aggressive Merriam sales agents decided the outcome of the "war" by convincing state legislatures to adopt Webster's book and place it, by decree, in all schoolhouses.

Worcester quietly fought back by introducing *A Dictionary of the English Language* (1860), the first dictionary to include illustrations and synonyms, features that were included in most subsequent dictionaries. In 1864, the G. & C. Merriam Company countered with an "unabridged" Webster's that included authoritative etymologies by a noted German scholar, Karl Augustus Friedrich Mahn. After the Webster-Mahn publication, Worcester's publishers gave up their unequal struggle, recognizing that the new Merriam product had adopted the virtues of Worcester's work and excised the faults of Webster's, and stopped publishing Worcester's books. The Webster-Mahn *Dictionary of the English Language* became the basis for a long and successful line of dictionaries, which are now called the Merriam-Webster dictionaries.

The Oxford English Dictionary

While the Americans debated the merits of their rival dictionaries, a group of scholars in Great Britain were preparing for a truly monumental dictionary-making project. Now that scientific principles of lexicography had been established, the Philological Society in Great Britain began to call for a full-scale historical dictionary. To that end, the society established an "Unregistered Words Committee." In 1857, encouraged by the Dean of Westminster, Richard Chevinex Trench, the society set about to create a dictionary of "all the words that have formed the English vocabulary from earliest records on" and "all

relevant facts concerning their form, sense, history, pronunciation and etymology." The new work was to be called *A New English Dictionary on Historical Principles*.

Beginning in 1858, volunteer readers began to compile quotation slips and subeditors began to work in 1862 under the direction of the editor Fredrick James Furnivall, who for a while had a co-editor, Herbert Coleridge, grandson of the poet Samuel Taylor Coleridge. In 1879, the task of editing the new dictionary was given to a Scot, James Augustus Henry Murray. Although Murray was later joined by three other editors, he was referred to as the first (chief) editor. For the next half century Murray shepherded the new dictionary into print. The first copy went to the printer in 1882 and the last portion in 1928.

The final work exceeded 15,500 pages, with three columns of type on each page, and included 1,827,306 of the nearly 6 million quotations that were submitted to the editors. The size of the work, however monumental, was secondary to the skill and authority of the lexicographers in presenting the full scope of the English language. The authority of the dictionary is such that it has not been revised; instead, supplements have been issued since 1928. The complete work was reprinted in 1933 as a 12-volume set under a new title, *The Oxford English Dictionary*. In the preface, the editors paid tribute to their lexicographical progenitors and expressed pride in their own work by stating *The Oxford English Dictionary* was the "oak" that had grown from "Cawdrey's acorn," *A Table Alphabeticall*.

Dictionaries in the Modern Era

After the *Oxford English Dictionary*, dictionary makers in England and America concentrated their efforts less on inclusiveness than on the creation of dictionaries designed for particular markets. One example of this trend was the start of publication in the 1940s of college dictionaries for burgeoning numbers of college students. So-called collegiate dictionaries had been published as early as 1898 (Merriam-Webster's), but they were seen as handy abridgments of larger works, not as important works in their own rights.

The first college dictionary was the *American College Dictionary*, edited by Clarence Barnhart and published by Random House. It quickly became a favorite not only with scholars but also with the general public. Encouraged by its success, the publisher issued *The Random House Dictionary*, *College Edition* (later called THE RANDOM HOUSE COLLEGE

DICTIONARY), which contained more entries (155,000) than any previous collegiate dictionary and set a standard for the inclusion of scientific and technical terms in an encyclopedic way. The guiding principle of this Random House dictionary and its successors was to help the student find the meaning of terms encountered in a lecture or textbook.

Publishers have continued to design dictionaries for specific markets, and the variety of dictionaries available today is remarkable. Modern dictionaries range from big, unabridged versions to small pocket versions. Some are designed specifically for children and are published in carefully graded series. Others are written for non-native speakers of English and may also be published as a series of graded versions with varying degrees of sophistication.

Whatever their intended market, dictionaries have maintained their traditional role of presenting a working vocabulary in a practical manner. In the reviews that follow, our reviewers measure the dictionaries and similar word books by Samuel Johnson's practical standard. "It is not enough," he wrote, "that a dictionary delights the critic, unless at the same time it instructs the learner; as it is to little purpose that an engine amuses the philosopher by the subtilty [*sic*] of its mechanism, if it requires so much knowledge in its application as to be no advantage to the common workman."

Along with the criteria given in this Buying Guide for examining dictionaries, the person selecting a dictionary might do well to consider how the dictionary was made. Traditionally, there have been two ways of making a dictionary: by borrowing a word list from another source and constructing revised definitions or adding features such as pronunciation guides; and by collecting citations and constructing a whole new word list. The *Oxford English Dictionary* represented the apotheosis of the latter method. Presently, the market for dictionaries is extensive; however, the market for any specific type of dictionary cannot now support a colossal effort such as the five-decade process that created the *Oxford English Dictionary*. Some dictionary makers have therefore reverted to borrowing word lists, sometimes buying another publisher's word list and sometimes appropriating an old, out-of-print list. These dictionary makers usually are publishers whose major project line is not dictionaries. Using a previously published word list, however, is not always a sign of shoddy workmanship. Many dictionary makers, such as Merriam-Webster, have used teams of lexicographers, trained definers, consultants, and experts in specific fields to create new,

authoritative works with borrowed, carefully edited lists.

As computers become increasingly sophisticated, they may be able to provide a way for dictionary makers to combine both traditional methods of constructing dictionaries in an economical way. Citations as well as word lists can be kept on data bases and if editors, consultants, and other experts could be placed on-line with the data base, new dictionaries could be produced without putting together prohibitively expensive in-house staffs.

The computer revolution has opened another possibility for dictionary makers: the creation of dictionaries that are accessed directly by the user. Two types of user-accessed computerized dictionaries are presently being explored.

With the first type, the user keyboards the desired term and the computer displays it. Phonetic searches are being developed that would help the user find a word that he or she cannot spell. Other avenues of computer research are developing methods of presenting a definition and preferred usage even if a variant of the term is keyboarded.

The second type of computerized dictionary being considered is usually linked to a specific piece of text stored in the computer. As the user reads the text on the screen and comes upon an unknown term, he or she can ask for the dictionary entry, read it, and then continue to move further along in the text.

In attempting to define what a dictionary is, some have defined it by comparison with an encyclopedia. A dictionary, they say, explains words, while an encyclopedia explains things. But while encyclopedias are dictionaries in that they give the meanings of words, dictionaries are not considered encyclopedias. Computerized dictionaries could forever blur these distinctions, however, if an item in the text could be looked up not only as a dictionary entry, but also as an encyclopedia entry.

Future dictionary makers will certainly have access not only to new methods of creating dictionaries but also to new methods of presenting their work to users. As descendants of Samuel Johnson they will have to seek ways to delight not only the critic but to satisfy the needs of the learner. To do this they will have to find a way to approximate the most practical of all uses of the print dictionary throughout history—the serendipitous learning that occurs when users get sidetracked while looking up a word.

As reviewers we look for delight in the dictionaries we review; at the same time we also seek the match between the needs of intended user and the "subtilty [*sic*] of the mechanism."

Atlases

The modern atlas is a systematic collection of maps, usually but not always uniform in size and format. An atlas may contain maps of many kinds: political, topographic, transportation, meteorological, or climatic. They may also represent such themes as land use, population density, or the distribution of languages and religions.

It is not known when mankind first attempted to represent the surface of the earth symbolically. Among the very earliest recorded maps are Assyrian clay tablets dating from around 3800 B.C. that list properties and describe civil boundaries for administrative purposes such as tax collections. Ramses II commissioned a map of the Nile empire in 1225 B.C., also for taxation purposes, while the earliest surviving papyrus map (1320 B.C.) is one of a Nubian gold mine. Even nonliterate early peoples used utilitarian maps. For example, the cave dwellers in prehistoric southern Europe drew cave wall sketches showing hunting spots. It is also known that the Polynesian navigators constructed maps from the latticed spines of palm branches to show wind and sea currents as references for finding islands, which were represented by sea shells.

The first known atlas was made by Ptolemy (A.D. 90–168), a Greek in Hellenic Alexandria. Ptolemy's work, called *Geographike hyphegesis* (Guide to Geography) was published in eight volumes in A.D. 160. It contained 27 maps, which treated the earth as a sphere, and listed 8,000 place names. In the eighth volume, Ptolemy offered instructions on mapmaking and discussed the mathematical principles of geography. His work represented an important step toward a scientific approach to geography and cartography. Ptolemy's concept of maps and map collections was surprisingly close to the modern encyclopedic ideal. Maps, he said, were "a representation in picture of the whole known world, together with the phenomena contained therein."

The growing influence of the Roman world partially eclipsed Ptolemy's ideas of mathematical geography because the Romans sought practical maps for warfare and administration. The dislocations and decline of learning in the Western world during the first centuries of the Christian era also obscured Ptolemaic ideas of geography. Fortunately, Ptolemy's *Geography* was preserved by the Nestorians, a Christian sect that fled to Persia to escape persecution by the Orthodox Byzantines. There, in the centers of

Islamic culture and learning, the science of geography was cultivated by Arab scholars who translated the *Geography* and added to it their own discoveries. Their pioneering use of the compass, for example, enabled Islamic scholars to measure part of the meridian and thus add to the concept of the 360-degree circle, Ptolemy's concept of a spherical earth. Islamic cartographic principles, as well as copies of Ptolemy's *Geography*, were introduced into Europe through the Moors and by refugees who fled to Italy after the fall of Byzantium in the late fourteenth century. In Florence, Ptolemy's *Geography* was translated into Latin in 1400. In 1477, it was printed in Bologna, the first atlas as well as the first classical Greek work to be printed with movable type. The Bologna *Geography* was also the first to use copper-engraved maps instead of woodcuts.

Throughout the fifteenth and sixteenth centuries, cartographers followed Ptolemy's ideal of a map collection as an index of contemporary geographic information. As late as 1570, a Roman mapmaker, Lafreri, described his collection of maps as being "arranged in Ptolemy's order." Lafreri, incidentally, was the first cartographer to illustrate a collection of maps with the symbolic figure of Atlas supporting the world.

The first modern general atlas was published in 1570 in Antwerp by Abraham Ortelius. Ortelius was a successful cartographer who had already published a world map in eight sheets in 1565 as well as two-sheet maps of Egypt in 1565 and Asia in 1567. When Ortelius decided to expand his scope by publishing a collection of maps, he noted that all previous collections included maps of varying sizes and format and often included contradictory depictions of the same country created by different authors. In the work he edited and published, Ortelius standardized the format of all the maps included and used only one cartographer for each country. Ortelius's work was titled the *Teatrum Orbis Terrarum* (Theater of the World).

Even before the publication of the *Teatrum* in 1570, a colleague of Ortelius, Gerardus Mercator, had outlined a plan for a systematic and comprehensive collection of maps of uniform size and format. Mercator, who was Flemish, did not live to complete the collection, but he managed to publish two of its three sections before his death in 1594. His son, Rumold, carried out the project, and Mercator's atlas was published posthumously in 1595 as the *Atlas sive Cosmographicae meditationes de fabrica mundi et fabricati figura* (Atlas, or Cosmographical meditations upon the creation of the universe, and the universe as created). It is the first recorded use of the word "atlas" for a collection of maps.

Gerardus Mercator also gave his name to the Mercator Projection, the depiction of the earth from a globe to a flat surface, first published by him in 1568. Its great value, in spite of attendant distortions, lies in its use in navigation. In fact, the Mercator Projection has been more generally used than any other projection for navigators' maps of the world.

Although atlases were expensive and available only to a limited number of people, they became common during the sixteenth and seventeenth centuries, the great age of maritime exploration and discovery. The initiative in atlas making was retained by the Dutch, whose efforts reached a zenith in 1662 with the publication of Willem Janszoon Blaeu's 11-volume *Atlas Major*. During this period, Dutch mapmakers also brought out a number of small, or pocket, atlases based on the works of Ortelius, Mercator, and others.

During the eighteenth century, advances in astronomy, mathematics, and meteorology led to the development of increasingly accurate maps. As surveying and triangulation techniques grew more sophisticated, mapmakers abandoned the tradition of decorative, often highly fanciful cartography that had characterized earlier works and concentrated instead on precise instrumental observations. At the same time, the rise of maritime commerce and the nation-state encouraged many European governments to commission meticulous topographical surveys of their territories. The first such national survey was the French *Carte Geometrique de la France*, published in 1794 in 182 sheets and rendered at a scale of 1:86,400. During the nineteenth century, this highly detailed work was followed by similar efforts in England, Spain, Austria, Germany, and many other nations, including Japan.

In addition, the discovery of lithography in 1796 by Alois Senefelder made the duplication of maps less expensive and easier. This broadened the availability of atlases in the nineteenth century. The late 1800s also saw the first indexed world atlases, published by such firms as Adolf Stieler and Richard Andree. The increase in an atlas's utility through the addition of an index cannot be overstated. There was also a sharp rise in the publication of "school atlases" during this period. Further developments in the nineteenth century were the emergence of international cooperation on standards of measurement, the adoption of a prime meridian, and a proposal for an International Map of the World, all sheets of which would be drawn on a scale of 1:1,000,000 (1 cm = 10 km).

Mapmaking has advanced rapidly in the twentieth century. Techniques of aerial photography that started during World War I developed into major cartographic tools during World War II, permitting efficient mapping of vast areas with unparalleled accuracy. Also during World War II, many of the blank spaces on world maps were filled by military maps, especially aeronautical charts. Since then, developments in photographic emulsions, lenses, and the science of photogrammetry (taking measurements from photographs) have advanced to such a degree that overlapping strips of film shot from specialized aircraft can be used to create maps showing virtually any feature on the face of the earth. Political and military alliances have also contributed to mapmaking during the twentieth century. The members of the North Atlantic Treaty Organization (NATO), for example, agreed upon the use of standard map symbols, scales, and formats, and the United Nations has standardized map features while offering technical advice and a clearinghouse service for international cartographic information.

Still further advances have been made possible by techniques of remote sensing coupled with orbiting satellites. Landsat and other satellites equipped with electromagnetic sensing devices have produced countless images of the earth's surface, revealing not only geographic features but also environmental pollution, crop diseases, and the location of mineral deposits. Although these images are not actual maps, they provide new and highly accurate data for the creation of many types of maps.

The word *map* comes from the Latin word for *napkin*, and it conjures up images of Roman diners sketching out maps on a napkin to give directions to some faraway city in the empire or to sketch a battlefield. The image is apt. In choosing whether or not to pocket the napkin drawing for future reference, the diners are assessing the long-term utility of the map. The same process—determining utility—is the overriding factor in choosing an atlas. The reviews in this guide have been written to assist you in that process.

A Note on Out-of-Print Titles

As anyone involved in acquisitions will be aware, general reference books tend to have longer life spans than do the majority of trade books. Yet reference books do not remain in print indefinitely. Many of the encyclopedias and atlases reviewed in this Buying Guide are revised annually, and upon issuing a revised edition the publisher usually declares the previous edition out of print. Dictionaries are revised less frequently, but the process by which a new edition supersedes an older one is similar.

However, many reference titles that go out of print are not replaced with updated editions. This has become increasingly the case in the 1980s, as publishing mergers and acquisitions have meant that publishing decisions are dictated more and more by economics, and less by the merits of the individual book. It also means that individual works have a shorter life span in print than they might have had 10 or 20 years ago. In many cases this has also made it difficult for librarians to acquire the books they need or would like for their collections.

A number of standard reference books that have recently gone out of print, however—especially those that established strong reputations during their heyday—may still be of interest to some librarians and library patrons. These works, in a sense, form part of the continuum of the history of reference books, and may have practical as well as historical value. What they lack in currency, they sometimes more than make up for in authority, and they can remain important research tools long after having been removed from the publisher's list.

Encyclopedias

Many librarians, students, and general readers will be familiar with certain well-known encyclopedias that have recently gone out of print. Some of these volumes may still be found in remainder outlets, or may even show up in tag sales and used book sales.

Encyclopedias go out of print for a number of reasons, which may or may not have to do with the quality of the encyclopedia itself. Very often, the reason is financial. The length of time it takes to recoup editorial and production costs may make it risky and prohibitively expensive for publishers to undertake an extensive revision.

Unlike multivolume encyclopedias, most single-volume encyclopedias are not designed for regular revision. Thus, after a period of time, although they may maintain their authority, clarity, and accessibility, they are no longer able to compete with newer works in their coverage of recent events or new discoveries. The cost of revising such works often runs into the millions of dollars.

Among the most prominent single-volume titles removed from publishers' lists in recent years are the *New Columbia Encyclopedia*, the *Random House Encyclopedia*, *Pears Cyclopaedia*, and *Junior Pears Encyclopaedia*.

The *New Columbia Encyclopedia* (a revision of the *Columbia Encyclopedia*) was withdrawn from the

market in the mid-1980s. *Columbia* and *New Columbia* were highly respected reference works, and many users continue to find them authoritative and reliable, especially in their coverage of historical topics. For single-volume encyclopedias, they were remarkably comprehensive and included much information that remains valid. (For further information about these titles, see the review of the CONCISE COLUMBIA ENCYCLOPEDIA beginning on page 112.)

The Random House Encyclopedia, introduced in 1977 and last revised in 1983, is another notable single-volume general reference work that is no longer in print. The *RHE* was best known for its profuse illustrations and informal, informative writing style; it was also heavily criticized for its complex organization and difficult accessibility.

Pears Cyclopaedia, published regularly in the U.K. since 1897, was recently withdrawn from sale in the United States. Heavily British in its orientation, this work in many respects bore more resemblance to an almanac than to an encyclopedia. Its companion volume, *Junior Pears Encyclopaedia*, has also been withdrawn. This book, which first appeared in 1961, contained encyclopedia-style entries but made no effort to be comprehensive. Like *Pears Cyclopaedia* it belonged largely to the domain of the almanac, and was also British in flavor.

Three multivolume encyclopedias that until recently were available in the United States may also be familiar to readers of this Buying Guide. Like the two Pears titles, these works are of British origin. They are the 15-volume *Chambers's Encyclopaedia*, last revised in 1979; the 20-volume *New Caxton Encyclopaedia*, last revised in 1979; and the 12-volume *Everyman's Encyclopaedia*, the print version of which was last revised in 1978. (For a review of the current online version of EVERYMAN'S, see page 127.)

Basically, there are three reasons for the withdrawal of these encyclopedias from the American market. First, because of their British orientation, they were perceived to be of value to only a small portion of American library patrons, and to virtually no school students. Second, unlike American multivolume encyclopedias, these works were not revised annually. Thus, in the 1980s, these works have increasingly suffered from lack of currency, especially when compared to their American competitors. And third, budget cutbacks in United States libraries mean that many institutions no longer have the luxury of choosing a third or fourth encyclopedia for their general reference collection. Few American libraries, if any, will choose a British encyclopedia as their first or second general reference encyclopedia, no matter how prestigious or authoritative. In short, these titles have been unable to compete against a strong field of encyclopedias created by the major reference publishers in the United States.

Nevertheless, these works do have considerable merit, and in general terms hold their own against the large American encyclopedias. *Chambers's*, whose origins have already been discussed in this chapter, was noted for its scholarly content, while the more "popular" *New Caxton*, first published under this title in 1966, was especially renowned for its illustrations (including reproductions of important works of art) and was lauded by such British critics as Auberon Waugh and Nicholas Tucker. *Everyman's* was a solid (if unexciting), well-established set.

Britannica Inc. has announced that it will issue *Children's Britannica*, a new 20-volume encyclopedia for youngsters in grades 3 through 8, in April 1988. This set will presumably fill the void left when the popular *Britannica Junior Encyclopaedia* was withdrawn from the market in 1984.

While this Buying Guide could not secure any specific information from the publishers of these works regarding future revision and re-publication, it is possible that some of these encyclopedias may be revised in the future and once again placed "in print."

Atlases

In the atlas genre, the profusion of titles may cause particular confusion. In preparing this Buying Guide, the editors discovered that some titles believed to be in print had been, or were about to be, deleted from publishers' lists. Currently several dozen atlases suitable for young readers and high school students are in print, but there can be no guarantee that all of these will remain in print for any length of time under their present titles. As with dictionaries, atlas titles do go out of print but are frequently repackaged and marketed by another publisher.

It is important to keep in mind that because cartography is a complex, exacting, and expensive craft, few general reference publishers produce their own maps. Rather, they purchase or commission maps from one of the major cartographic firms, which also usually publish atlases under their own imprint. In the United States, Hammond Incorporated and Rand McNally & Company are the two largest and best-known cartographic houses. In addition to producing their own atlases, they also provide maps for ency-

clopedias, textbooks, and other educational books. (On the other hand, the National Geographic Society, which maintains a distinguished cartographic operation, produces maps exclusively for its own publications.) In Great Britain, John Bartholomew & Son, Ltd. and George Philip & Son, Ltd., are two highly reputable cartographers whose maps have been packaged by American publishers. Together, these four cartographers provide maps for the majority of atlases sold in the United States and Canada. A few atlases reviewed in this Buying Guide use cartography supplied by German and Scandinavian mapmakers.

In the same way that these atlas makers have stood for excellence over the years, reputable dictionary and encyclopedia publishers will continue to revise and update their standard works with the same care as always. Names like Encyclopaedia Britannica and World Book, Merriam-Webster and Houghton Mifflin, stand for reliability, continuity, and high quality in the field of reference books for young readers.

Dictionaries

In general, the standard dictionaries on which schools and libraries rely for young readers do not go out of print but rather are revised and repackaged. Rather than removing an established, successful hardbound children's dictionary from their list, reputable publishers will make a conscientious effort to revise and improve it. If a good dictionary does go out of print, chances are that it will later reappear in a revised form under a different title. Occasionally, the same dictionary will be issued simultaneously by several publishers in several formats. For example, the MACMILLAN DICTIONARY FOR CHILDREN is also published in two other editions: the BEGINNING DICTIONARY and the CHILDCRAFT DICTIONARY.

Paperback dictionaries are another story. These tend to be reformatted and reprinted, but the amount of revision is often minimal. In general, paperbacks are not revised as extensively as hardcover editions; frequently, they are much less up-to-date than their hardcover counterparts despite the reputation of the dictionary's title. In other words, in paperback dictionaries, the title alone is not a guarantee of quality. Nor does the fact that a paperback dictionary is in print mean that it is contemporary.

Chapter 2
Choosing
General
Reference Books

Introduction

To help readers make a judicious choice of general reference works for their collections, *Reference Books for Young Readers* reviews current atlases, dictionaries, and encyclopedias and discusses how to make the most effective use of the reviews, including, in each "What to Look for" section, an examination of appropriate criteria for evaluating such works. This chapter offers suggestions to help school librarians, public librarians, and teachers clarify their collection development goals. It is also addressed to parents who are considering the purchase of general reference books for their children.

Although the purchase of any book merits careful thought, the acquisition of general reference titles involves special considerations. Many such works, particularly encyclopedias and large atlases, are far more expensive than the average volume and, in view of their cost, must be suitable for extended use. At the same time, the need for current information demands a systematic program of replacement. General reference works must also serve a broad range of readers whose ages, reading levels, and reference needs may differ widely. The prospective purchaser may feel perplexed, if not discouraged, when he or she considers that no reference work is capable of satisfying a universal readership; *general* is a relative term.

Nevertheless, reference books can be evaluated according to certain criteria and in light of your particular circumstances: your budget, the size of your collection, the needs of your library patrons. First, however, it is essential to understand both the nature and inherent limitations of each type of general reference work.

Encyclopedias

The sale of encyclopedias and materials to supplement them generates over $500 million in revenues each year. Encyclopedias are found in approximately one out of every four homes in the United States, and the average public library may have anywhere from four to twelve different sets on its shelves.

The high cost of a multivolume encyclopedia is a major consideration. These works represent a large investment to the publisher—especially when they are revised frequently—and hence to the purchaser. Revision is essential if a work is to be current, although there is a limit to its value if much information about current or recent events can be located in other, less expensive sources such as yearbooks, almanacs, and other annuals. Some publishers revise their titles only sporadically, but a responsible publisher makes a long-term commitment to keeping its works as current as possible through a regular cycle of continuous revision in which a certain portion of the content (usually around 10 percent) is replaced or updated each year. The changes may range from minor updating of existing articles to entirely new entries about recent events or personalities. Every several years the publisher may also undertake a major revision that results in substantial rewriting and the publication of a new edition. If you are thinking about replacing an old set with a revised one, ask for detailed information about the amount and type of changes to help you decide whether they in fact warrant the cost of replacement.

Multivolume encyclopedias treat their subjects in far greater depth than do one- or two-volume sets. Smaller sets are extremely useful for ready reference information, such as a capsule biography or the geographical features of a country. Despite the need to squeeze a large amount of information into a small space, most abridged encyclopedias are illustrated with photographs, maps, or charts.

In addition to an encyclopedia's depth of coverage, two other factors to be considered in its purchase are currency and accuracy. These criteria are discussed at length in the section, "What to Look for in Encyclopedias," but, in general, encyclopedia publishers update their works in different ways. Continuous or annual revision means that a certain portion of the set (usually around 10 percent) is replaced with new material or brought up to date with more current information. Every few years, the publisher may also undertake a substantial revision that involves the rewriting, addition, or removal of hundreds or even thousands of articles. In such cases, the publisher should provide prospective purchasers with detailed information so that they can make an informed decision as to whether or not to replace an earlier edition they may have in their collections.

Buyers expect encyclopedias to be substantially accurate, but no encyclopedia is absolutely error-free. Many critics feel that encyclopedias err more often by omitting important information than through mistakes in the information they do include, particularly in regard to complex or controversial subjects.

A meticulously compiled index is especially important in an encyclopedia, not only because it contains so much information, but also because information on a given topic may appear in several articles. If a subject is covered in an encyclopedia, there should be logical references to it in one or more places in the index. Moreover, a useful index should not require a great deal of prior knowledge about the subject on the part of the reader. Students, for instance, should not have to know the name of the Sherman Anti-Trust Act in order to locate information about restraint of trade, trusts, or anti-trust laws. Cross-references to these topics, or others, such as monopolies, should lead them to a complete picture of the subject in relevant articles or portions of articles.

Multivolume and small-volume encyclopedias are available for both adults and children. Adult encyclopedias assume that a reader's skills will be at the high school level or above. Children's encyclopedias, in which entries are often arranged topically rather than alphabetically, and which may include stories and activities in addition to more standard encyclopedic entries, are usually (but not always) written at upper elementary school reading levels. Encyclopedias considered appropriate for "young adults" usually have a reading level in the junior high school range. Note, however, that reading levels within an encyclopedia may vary considerably, according to the complexity of the subjects.

Most children's encyclopedias are prepared with the assistance of reading specialists, who make certain that the reading levels are appropriate for the intended grade range. They are also often written in a so-called *pyramid* style, in which the article first presents basic concepts or facts about the subject in simple language and form, and then progresses to more complex information and concepts. This pyramid structure enables young readers of varying ages and abilities to use the same encyclopedia.

The principal differences between adult and children's encyclopedias lie in their reading levels, in the nature and extent of their illustrations, and in the complexity of subject matter discussed. To some extent, the content of children's and young adult encyclopedias is dictated by "current curricula." A less-important difference is that encyclopedias for children usually define difficult or technical words used in the text, whereas adult ones assume either knowledge on the reader's part or the ability of the reader to locate it in another source.

Some publishers are inaccurate in their claims about the readability levels of their works. They may indicate levels, for instance, for use in one grade or a span of grades that prove to be either too high or too low for the grade or grades suggested for its use. Some ways in which you can spot this are: Check to see if difficult vocabulary words are defined; test the readability level against standardized measurements; and examine the text for the use of the pyramid style. An excellent final check involves using children who are at the levels of the intended audience, and having them read sample articles and sections. Checking comprehension and getting their verbal responses will help you to determine if the publisher's claims about readability are accurate, for children will report if something is too easy, as well as if it is too hard. This is an especially good test for encyclopedias that have adults as their primary audience, but that are also recommended by their publishers as being suitable for children.

When selecting a children's encyclopedia, a distinction must be made between those published for older students and sets for younger students. The sets for older students are designed for ages 9 through 18, and they generally require junior high reading ability. These encyclopedias, which include the WORLD BOOK ENCYCLOPEDIA, COMPTON'S ENCYCLOPEDIA, and the MERIT STUDENTS ENCYCLOPEDIA, most closely resemble adult sets in the depth and comprehensiveness with which they cover their subjects, and they are most useful to upper-grade students in completing many school-assigned research projects.

Encyclopedias for young students are written for children ages 7 through 14 and require reading skills at third-grade level and above. Children's encyclopedias are not, obviously, as comprehensive as either adult ones or those for junior high and high school students. Their goal is to be interesting and to deal with their subject matter at a level appropriate for the intended age span. As previously mentioned, they are sometimes arranged topically rather than alphabetically and therefore must be well-indexed and easy to use.

Some encyclopedias, written for ages 4 through 10, are not conventional reference works, but are collections of stories, fairy tales, things to do, rhymes, riddles, or suggested activities. As chapter 1 points out, this format has enjoyed a long tradition of acceptance, especially in the United States. COMPTON'S PRECYCLOPEDIA and CHILDCRAFT are examples of this genre. Sets of this type can be entertaining and instructive. Although they can encourage children to read and browse for information, they are not designed primarily as reference tools.

Children's encyclopedias are most attractive to their readers when they are richly illustrated. Their usefulness is enhanced when they are structured so that entries on specific topics can be found quickly. However, alert purchasers should also be aware of how many articles and subjects are covered in the set; that is, is the range limited or broad, repetitious or comprehensive. Since students are usually instructed to use encyclopedias to gain an overview of a subject, a set that includes bibliographies or study guides listing other sources of information offers something extra. This is a particularly useful feature in the many encyclopedias that have been designed to conform to basic elementary school curricula. Some encyclopedias can be purchased as part of a "package" consisting of dictionaries, yearbooks, maps, and other add-ons that may enhance their overall value for certain readers.

Dictionaries

When the distinguished librarian Lawrence Clark Powell was asked what book he would choose to take with him to a desert island, his selection was *Webster's Unabridged Dictionary*. "What a glorious prospect," he declared, "to be alone on an island with the opportunity to sit back against a banana tree, and read all the way from aardvark to zymurgy." Since unabridged dictionaries contain more than 250,000 entries, a shipwrecked Powell would have ensured himself of reading material for a very long time.

Dictionaries are broadly classified, according to the number of entries they contain, as unabridged, semi-unabridged, abridged, and paperback or pocket-sized. The largest unabridged dictionary in existence is the 13-volume *Oxford English Dictionary* (*OED*), which to date has been augmented with four supplements and costs about $1,600. A two-volume photographically reduced *OED* (accompanied by a magnifying glass) is available as a book-club membership premium for under $40. A semi-unabridged dictionary contains 130,000 to 250,000 entries; an abridged dictionary ranges from 55,000 entries for a concise or desk edition to 130,000 or more for a college dictionary, and a paperback dictionary may have about 55,000 entries. Very small pocket-size (or vest pocket size) dictionaries may contain less than half that number of entries.

An abridged dictionary omits thousands of obscure, uncommon, archaic, and technical words—and often vulgar or taboo words—as well as certain other features of larger works. The number of meanings for each entry is reduced, synonyms and antonyms are eliminated, or alternate spellings and pronunciations are left out. When considering a dictionary, keep in mind that the number of entries is only one of many factors. It offers a rough guide to a work's scope, but is no measure of its quality or currency. In fact, the number of entries can vary widely between two dictionaries that, based on publishers' claims, appear to be nearly the same size. This is true because some publishers count every form and variant of a word as a separate entry, whereas others count only the main entry for each word. Thus, one dictionary that claims to define a certain number of words may actually have far fewer than another, for which its publisher has taken credit for only main entry words.

Dictionaries are produced by staffs of editors and specialists who decide how pronunciations are shown, how technical words are defined, which new words have entered the standard lexicon, what new meanings have been attached to old words, and other matters. Most new dictionary entries come from files of citations, continuously updated collection of words with illustrative examples of use that staffs cull from current books, periodicals, newspapers, and other sources. *Lexicographers* (dictionary makers) continually debate whether a dictionary should provide authoritative guidance to correct English or describe current usage, but most try to strike a balance somewhere between those two extremes. Most dictionaries provide standard words and meanings, but will also include colloquial or slang words, and usage commonly employed in books, magazines, and newspapers.

Some dictionaries have more components than others, but a standard entry in an abridged dictionary provides the spelling, pronunciation, syllabication, parts of speech, basic definitions, plurals, and inflected forms of each word. In more comprehensive dictionaries, the main entries may also include derivative words (words obtained by adding prefixes and suffixes), the etymology or history of the word, synonyms and antonyms, and usage labels. Usage labels indicate whether or not a word is current in a particular science or field of knowledge, such as geology or music, or if the word is archaic, nonstandard, poetic, regional, or slang. Dictionaries may also provide several examples or quotations showing how the word is used in standard written English. They also serve a variety of purposes other than simply spelling or defining words. They may contain tables of weights and measures, proofreading marks, biographical entries, geographical entries, a table of alphabets, lists of colleges and universities, maps, and other useful facts. This kind of information is called "encyclopedic information."

Generally, only librarians, scholars, teachers, and writers need unabridged dictionaries. The average adult recognizes only about 20,000 words and customarily uses far fewer than this number in both writing and speech, so an abridged dictionary will be adequate for most households. College students may require a semi-unabridged or abridged dictionary, depending on their fields of study, but younger students will probably find that an abridged dictionary or a school or children's dictionary suits their needs and language skills. A school or children's dictionary is written to high school, middle school, or elementary school reading levels and the entries are selected on the basis of the frequency of their appearance in the textbooks and literature commonly used in the classroom. Etymologies are usually omitted or simplified and definitions emphasize standard usage.

A separate category of books that are also called dictionaries are those created for preschoolers and beginning readers. These take almost as many forms as their authors and illustrators choose but have several characteristics in common: they are highly illustrated in full color; include a very limited and selective range of vocabulary (usually not more than 1,000 or 1,200 words, and frequently as few as a couple of hundred); depend heavily on illustrative sentences and humor for their definitions; have no complexities like word variants, syllabication, pronunciation, or etymologies; and often use the illustrations to get the meanings of words across to the reader. Many require the participation of an adult, which makes them almost picture books. "Dictionaries" at this age level are quickly outgrown, and, if used in the library or classroom, are often correlated with curriculum materials. Thus, when the student moves to a higher grade level or increased reading ability, the picture dictionary has no further educational value.

Picture dictionaries can provide young children with important early experience in "looking up" words. However, special care must be used in their purchase; there is a wide variation in quality among them. Attractive illustrations alone do not make a good picture dictionary. It is also important to consider such details as the correlation between art and text, the suitability of the concepts and words included, and the accurate presentation of words.

A good-quality children's dictionary must be constructed of durable materials, since it must withstand extensive use that is often not gentle. In addition, good organization and pleasing graphics, such as large type and well-drawn or photographed illustrations, are particularly important elements in children's dictionaries if they are to appeal to young and inexperienced users.

Atlases

Atlases are collections of maps of a specified area— a region, a nation, the lands or oceans of the world, the solar system, or the universe, and so on. This Buying Guide evaluates only world atlases. In a world atlas, the maps can be *political*, showing the boundaries of nations, territories, cities or towns; *physical*, showing natural features, such as shorelines, elevations, and climate; or *thematic*, showing populations, economic features, or other specialized data. Atlas maps often delineate a great many details, such as lakes, rivers, highways, railroad lines, and airports. The maps are usually arranged to show a large area, a continent, for example, and then smaller segments of the same area, such as each nation on the continent. When purchasing an atlas, examine the scales used to draw each map. Readability is an important and desirable feature in maps. Scales may vary from 1:24,000 for regional maps to 1:10,000,000 for continental and world maps. The larger the scale, that is, the smaller the ratio, the more details that can be included. However, larger-scale maps also require larger pages or more pages on which to print them. Although atlases frequently include photographs, drawings, charts, and text as well as maps, it is the quality and quantity of the maps that count in selecting an atlas for purchase.

A family may require a world atlas as part of an encyclopedia set or as a companion to a world globe. A library may need several world atlases, and, depending on the population range it serves, may select various types of atlases (that is, political, physical, and thematic). Obviously, if a library serves a school population below the junior high level, it may not need the more sophisticated thematic atlases, but it will need one or more that is tied into the social-studies curriculum. High school libraries will require atlases that are sufficiently correlated to the subjects that are taught in the school. For instance, the library of an academic high school has much more need of a variety of thematic atlases than would that of a commercial or vocational high school. Public library needs in this area will vary according to the size of the population and the type of community served. A farming or rural community would have quite different requirements from that of a large urban area with a more diverse population.

Although there are dozens of world atlases on the market, most of the maps they include are produced by a relatively small number of cartographic firms. In the United States, Rand McNally and Hammond are the leading mapmakers. The premier cartographers in England are John Bartholomew & Son, Ltd., and George Philip & Son, Ltd. Bartholomew's maps are the basis for the highly esteemed *Times Atlas of the World*, for example, and Rand McNally's maps are used in GOODE'S WORLD ATLAS, an atlas that is found in many school libraries.

If you are choosing an atlas from among a selection offered by a single publisher, you should be aware that the differences are primarily in format and price; publishers generally use the same basic maps in all their atlases. However, while the maps may be virtually the same, the selection, order of presentation, and number included in a particular atlas may vary widely. Therefore, such details as the overall size of the book, the quality of the paper, printing, and binding, the additional text, statistical tables, index, and special features should all be weighed in the final purchase decision.

Reference Books in School and Public Libraries

If you are selecting general reference books for a public library, you will have to meet the needs of a very broad range of younger readers, their parents, and their teachers (and the type of community that the library serves will also be a factor in this range). They may include students at all age and grade levels from preschool through community college and university. One way to accomplish this is to choose a range of atlases, dictionaries, and encyclopedias that complement and supplement each other.

Because general reference books are used for so many different purposes, libraries need to keep their reference collections up-to-date. However, currency may not be as critical as some reviewers suggest. Most information in a general reference book remains accurate for many years; only a small percentage of its contents becomes outdated each year. Knowledgeable reference librarians suggest that a useful rule of thumb is to replace encyclopedias every five years. However, this is an arbitrary cutoff time, and it is not necessarily a valid guide for collection development. A variety of other factors may influence the time spans for making such changes.

For example, if an encyclopedia is strong on historical data and general background information that does not change rapidly with time, it may be worthwhile to retain the set for even seven or eight years if the library also has other encyclopedias that have been updated annually or is in a position to acquire a new set that is current. The two (the old and the new) can then supplement each other. In any event, you will have to determine what policy is feasible in your library. The other important factor in all this, of course, is the financial one, as you must weigh the need for replacements against possible budgetary limitations. Your choice may ultimately be influenced by the costs of competing sets.

In many libraries, the process of weeding out old, inaccurate materials from the reference collections is informal and unsystematic. Some libraries maintain standing orders with publishers for the purchase of new editions as they become available. In such cases, the old editions may either be discarded or placed in open circulation.

A typical small public library might have three or four multivolume adult sets and one or two small-volume sets. It might also have at least one or two young adult or children's multivolume encyclopedias. The library would probably also have one or more unabridged dictionaries, in addition to a selection of abridged or college dictionaries. (An interesting side note to choosing dictionaries concerns the "Webster's" designation that so many bear. Although the original Webster Company was sold to G. & C. Merriam, which continues to use "Webster" in the names of its dictionaries, in actual fact, the Webster name is out of copyright and in the public domain—and has been for years. Thus, anyone is free to use it in a dictionary title, and the name carries such weight that many do so just to give credibility and authenticity to their books, with no actual basis for any connection with the original Webster.)

Even a small library is likely to have several atlases. In addition to a world atlas, it is desirable to have a historical atlas as well as any thematic one that fits in with the broad general interests of the specific community the library serves.

Most school libraries probably need more than one adult multivolume encyclopedia. This is especially the case if the school is a large one whose population includes many advanced level students in the high-school grades. In addition, many schools would need at least two or three sets of young adult and children's encyclopedias. Again, the number will depend on the size and the age range of the school population, the demands made by the curriculum, and teachers' policies on students' use of encyclopedias for research. The library should also have several school versions of dictionaries and atlases in addition to, or in place of, standard editions of these reference works. In selecting reference books, many school librarians consider the advice of teachers, curriculum requirements, and their own professional judgment and research.

Unlike most public libraries, many school libraries may need several sets or copies of particular reference books on hand to satisfy the needs of a large number of users (that is, students) who may all need timely access to these works in order to complete their class assignments. The library has to balance this demand with the fact that, for long intervals, these extra volumes may go unused.

Home Use

Most family reference-book needs can be met with one or two dictionaries, a thesaurus, a world atlas, and a general encyclopedia. These may be supplemented with a *Bartlett's Familiar Quotations* and an almanac, as well as any other special-interest works that are appropriate for that specific family.

Age ranges in a family may vary widely. This range, as well as any variation in the interests of the family members, must be considered carefully, especially in the acquisition of encyclopedias. Thus, it may be that a young adult set, written in pyramid style, is a wise choice to serve the needs of most or all of the children in a family.

Dictionaries fall into a different purchase category. They are far less expensive than are encyclopedias, so it may be worthwhile for each child to have his or her own dictionary, appropriate to the child's age level.

Aside from the dictionary, which is a reference tool that may be in constant use in either home or library, it is possible that a family might not need to purchase either an atlas or the more expensive encyclopedia set that they may have thought was necessary. It is important to evaluate how much use a set like this might get. If the children in a family are going to be assigned only a handful of projects among them, parents should consider encouraging them to use the local public library, as well as their school library, if convenient. (In addition, many public libraries will have circulating volumes.) This would save the family the cost of the sets and at the same time offer them the advantage of the updated reference materials that are available in the library's collection. Again, this is something that the individual family will have to consider in terms of convenience, the quality of the public library, and personal needs.

An important factor, but one easily overlooked, is the size of the reference books a family may plan to purchase. Will they fit on already-existing shelves? Can they be stored in a convenient location? How much space will they take up? Will they be too heavy or bulky for the family's children to handle?

Binding, paper, typography, and layout are all components of book format. Proposed purchases should be examined with these details in mind, particularly the bindings, which are vulnerable to strain and breaking. Books considered for purchase should be examined carefully, and if there is a possibility that they will not lie flat or will be susceptible to breakage, this should be weighed into the purchase decision.

The size of the type should also be examined, as young children cannot accommodate their reading skills to small type. Of course, the content itself is of paramount importance. At the same time, however, the contents will be of little value if the writing level is too advanced for the reader—or if, by the same token, it is below the child's reading ability.

Finally, of course, price will be a significant factor. Options such as deluxe bindings, yearbooks, accompanying atlases or globes, and other supplementary materials and research services, can add considerably—as much as several hundred dollars in some cases—to the cost of a multivolume encyclopedia. For instance, yearbooks usually do not add considerably to the basic value of an encyclopedia, as they have only a year's worth of updating in them, and at the end of two or three years, their use may become cumbersome. Likewise, the family may already have the atlases, dictionaries, or other extras that appear to be part of the basic encyclopedia purchase. So it is worthwhile to ascertain what the cost of the encyclopedia itself is, if it can be purchased separately, and then to decide how many of the extras, if any at all, the family would like to acquire at the same time. This guide will show the general price range of encyclopedias, and a buyer can match them against prices quoted by a salesman. Shipping and sales tax costs are always additional, so this should be kept in mind.

The purpose of price comparison is to determine the lowest price for the best reference book in a given category. Even in comparing the cost of two abridged dictionaries, for example, you will sometimes note sharp differences. Often, these are based on production quality, but in many cases the price differential is caused by the additional, nondictionary material in the book, often advertised on the jacket as "special features." It then becomes a question of deciding if these extra features are worth the higher price.

Many publishers today are turning out dictionaries at apparently bargain prices, and the temptation is to acquire one or more of these very inexpensive volumes. Often, however, the bargain price is possible only because the dictionary is a reprint of one that has become obsolete and has simply been reformatted and packaged to make it look new. As this Buying Guide reminds readers, keeping reference books up-to-date requires intensive editorial and writing effort, with concomitant costs. So anything that seems to be too great a bargain—whether dictionary, atlas, or encyclopedia—should be checked for copyright dates as well as a random sampling of entries to determine just how old its content really is.

There are, however, other ways to reduce the cost of acquiring reference books. Bookstore specials are one way, although this may sometimes mean that the purchaser will have to settle for the title that is on sale, rather than buying the book that would otherwise be his or her first choice. Second-hand books may also be purchased for a fraction of their original cost, and watching classified ads, garage sales, and so on will often lead to true bargains. Although scientific and technological information, as well as the latest in current history and political matters may become outdated quickly, a considerable portion of all reference works remains valid for a fairly long time, so if the proposed purchase is not absolutely ancient, and the volumes are in good physical shape, their purchase is worth consideration. Used encyclopedias that are only a year or two old may be as much as 15 to 20 percent less expensive than new sets. Some retail outlets specialize in selling sets that are fairly new—just not absolutely new—and these advertise nationally. Likewise, from time to time, some of the major book clubs offer dictionaries, atlases, and even one-volume encyclopedias—as well as thesauruses, books of quotations, and other reference materials—as premiums or at greatly reduced prices. It is worth watching the advertisements for such offers and deciding if the reduced cost, plus the book club obligation that is entailed, is warranted.

How to Select General Reference Books

The first step in choosing general reference books is identifying need. In library terms, this means having a sense of your patrons' requirements. In order to determine how often to add to your dictionary, encyclopedia, and atlas collections, you might ask the following questions:

- How often do you get requests for materials that are not in your library?
- How much of your collection is in constant use? Is there a long "waiting list" of requests for reference books that are being used?
- How many of your reference volumes seem never to be used, and actually to be gathering dust on the shelves?

- How many complaints do you get about obsolete books? Do you check the copyright dates in your collection periodically?
- What does your inspection tell you about the physical condition of your collection? Are the books in good condition, or do they show moderate or heavy signs of use, with concomitant damage to pages, binding, and so on?
- Do you have a formal plan, whether by standing order with publishers or some built-in system in your library, for the replacement of worn or obsolete materials with fresh, current volumes?

The need-identification stage is perhaps the most difficult to complete. However, once you have done so, this Buying Guide will be most helpful to you because of the variety of information it contains to assist you in making a choice of purchases. For instance, the comparative charts give comparisons of price, reading levels, numbers of volumes, illustrations, maps, publishers, and indexes, and are starting points for you to decide on the works you would like to consider in greater detail. The "What to Look for" sections describe in detail the criteria used by the Buying Guide reviewers, and are just as applicable to librarian or individual use as they are to the reviewers. Each review is prefaced by a "Facts-at-a-Glance" box that summarizes background data provided by the publisher about the material being evaluated.

Assume, for example, that you are shopping for an unabridged dictionary. Consult the comparative chart for this category of book and select several titles that seem to meet your requirements. Then read the "What to Look for in a Dictionary" chapter and the reviews of the titles you've chosen in the product-evaluations section. Once you have read the evaluations, consider the strengths and weaknesses of each work in terms of your specific needs. For instance, it may not be important to you if the dictionary is well illustrated, but you may be concerned with its currency. Thus, the book you finally select should be noted as one that has been updated recently and contains current terms, even if the comments indicate that its graphics are not as good as those of another dictionary.

In this connection, it is worthwhile for you to start with a checklist of those criteria that are most important to you, in order of consideration. For example, does currency come before graphics? Is size of type more important than number of entries? Are the extras at the back less important than usage examples? With this in hand, you can use the evalua-

tions to create your own comparative chart of the several books you've chosen for careful consideration, and consult this to help you toward your final selection.

This Buying Guide also has an extensive bibliography that you can consult for other sources of information on choosing and purchasing reference books of all types. The average public library will have one or more of these books in its reference collection. Many of the evaluation sections in this guide cite critical comments from other publications, and you can find an extensive list of other review media in the bibliography.

No matter how many reviews you read, there is no substitute for comparing actual copies of reference books you are considering for purchase. You can comparison shop for many dictionaries and atlases in bookstores, where you can leaf through the volumes, examine the indexes, read samples of the text, and look at the maps, illustrations, and extra features they offer. Read the prefaces and other introductory materials and look for a statement of purpose, a description of special features, and information about the latest revision. One way to check currency of a dictionary is to have a list of some of the newest words in technology and science, or colloquial or idiomatic expressions that have become common enough to have entered the language, and to check on whether or not they are in the dictionaries you are considering. Likewise, you can compare maps of identical areas in atlases to see how they are handled, and in the case of countries whose names have been changed, and so on, you can check on whether or not the maps show the revisions.

Bookstores also carry small-volume encyclopedias, so you can do some comparison shopping of these in the same way. Again, follow the same procedure of comparing the identical subject's handling in each of the works you are considering, and decide which has covered it best. At the same time, you can be judging accessibility (which encyclopedia was easiest to use in terms of locating the new material sought), and currency by selecting "new" topics, such as arms control or abortion and seeing whether or not they are included, as well as comparing the way they are handled.

Multivolume encyclopedias are not as easy to compare because, for the most part, they are not a bookstore item. Rather, most multivolume sets are sold directly by salespeople who visit the home and/or library and make direct presentations. Remember, the promotional material presented by the sales rep will, of course, describe the sets as advantageously as possible. These are advertising materials that may or may not be strictly accurate.

One way it may be possible for you to examine a set without pressure and to think carefully about its value for your purposes is to ask the sales rep if he or she can leave a set with you on a trial basis, for at least a week. This will afford you an opportunity to examine the set, and to arrive at some conclusions based on the criteria outlined in the reviews in this Buying Guide. It will also give you time to make notes about these, which will later allow you to make comparisons with other sets. Always insist that the sales rep leave the entire set. One volume alone, out of context, does not give you a chance to check a full range of articles and index entries, nor does it afford you the opportunity to note how cross-references are handled from one volume to another. Other possibilities for comparing encyclopedias include visiting other school and public libraries, and examining sets on display at library convention exhibits.

Some companies, including Grolier, World Book, and Encyclopaedia Britannica, have what they call "satisfaction guaranteed" policies. Under these, following the purchase there is an examination period (usually 15 or 30 days) during which you may, if not satisfied, cancel your order and receive a full refund. The grace periods and stipulations are specific to various publishers, and since these can change from time to time, this Buying Guide does not spell them out. Return privileges, of course, carry with them the obligation that the merchandise must be in good, clean, resalable condition.

This is a major purchase that requires a careful decision that should not be rushed, so be certain that the work you are considering satisfies the needs of the intended users before you agree to the purchase or waive your return privileges under an examination-period option.

Encyclopedia Publishers

As already noted, encyclopedias are costly to write and produce, so that there are very few new publishers entering this market. In fact, the number of encyclopedia publishers has been consolidated in recent years, and there are now four firms that dominate this market in the United States. These four, whose sales account for more than four-fifths of all encyclopedias sold, are Encyclopaedia Britannica, Inc., World Book, Inc., Grolier, Inc., and Macmillan Educational Company, Inc. Each produces high-priced multivolume sets. Encyclopaedia Britannica, Inc., not only produces its namesake set, but also COMPTON'S ENCYCLOPEDIA and COMPTON'S PRECYCLOPEDIA. Grolier publishes the ENCYCLOPEDIA AMERICANA, the NEW BOOK OF KNOWLEDGE, and the ACADEMIC AMERICAN ENCYCLOPEDIA. In the early 1980s, the

Arete Publishing Company, the creators of the ACADEMIC AMERICAN, did try to penetrate this "closed" market and, during its first two years of existence, sold some 3,000 sets of its 21-volume work, primarily to libraries and institutions. However, it could not penetrate the lucrative home market, possibly because it tried to sell its sets in bookstores only, rather than door to door. When its efforts failed, Arete (a subsidiary of Verenigde Nederlandse Uitgeversbedrijven [VNU], a Dutch publishing conglomerate) licensed Grolier to publish the encyclopedia in both print and database format in the United States. A few years later, Grolier purchased the encyclopedia outright, and therefore uses its database.

World Book enjoys the largest in-home sales share and the highest sales in both dollars and units sold of these four companies. Encyclopaedia Britannica is a distant second. After the NEW ENCYCLOPAEDIA BRITANNICA was introduced in 1975, sales increased for a time, but they have since leveled off again. Grolier is in third place, and Macmillan has the least volume and unit sales of the top four. The only other American encyclopedia publishers of note are Funk & Wagnalls, which publishes FUNK & WAGNALLS NEW ENCYCLOPEDIA and the Standard Educational Corporation, which produces the NEW STANDARD ENCYCLOPEDIA.

FUNK & WAGNALLS NEW ENCYCLOPEDIA is the best-selling set in the supermarket field. The pattern of supermarket sales usually varies considerably from that of the door-to-door market. As a general rule, the first volume is offered at a greatly reduced price, and subsequent volumes are offered at full price. A complete set purchased in this manner is usually substantially less costly than a comparable set purchased through a distributor. For instance, a complete set of 27 volumes of the FUNK & WAGNALLS NEW ENCYCLOPEDIA, which includes 13,000 pages and 25,000 entries, costs $140. By comparison, the 21-volume ACADEMIC AMERICAN, priced at $850 for individuals, includes over 28,000 entries in 9,750 pages. The 22-volume WORLD BOOK costs $599 for individuals and has 18,000 entries in its 14,000 pages. A complete list of all the publishers and distributors of all the encyclopedias evaluated in this Buying Guide is in Appendix B.

Encyclopedia Sales Tactics

A substantial percentage of the cost of an encyclopedia set covers the commission that the sales representative earns for persuading you to purchase it. It is to be expected, therefore, that a fair number of "aggressive" selling techniques are employed in such contacts. These range from price offerings linked to timely "bargains" to statistics on the improvement in the family's cultural life and educational standings of its children. There was a time when the tactics also included fraudulent claims and promises, including returns and refund privileges that did not exist. However, consumer protection legislation has curbed such sales practices so that it is relatively rare for the average consumer today to be confronted with them—and even more important, should someone fall into such a trap inadvertently, it is far easier to extricate one's self than in the past. This Buying Guide will not, therefore, spend time discussing these deceptive practices but will rather focus on the types of questions and "resistance" that you may want to offer an overly persistent salesperson.

The first step in the selling process is the contact. Salespersons must find a way to meet you and to persuade you to set aside some time to speak with them in your home.

The follow-up varies considerably from simply knocking on the door unannounced and requesting an opportunity to present the set to calling to make a formal appointment to talk with the prospective purchaser. Some people find it difficult to say "no" in such situations and, whether interested or not, will permit the salesperson to enter, or will make an appointment, whereas others can be quite negative about such sales meetings and refuse either entry or an appointment. It is often not easy to say "no" to them at the outset. The meeting is, of course, just the beginning of the sales campaign.

That campaign usually focuses on two aspects of encyclopedia acquisition—the need for every home to have such a general reference work, and the need of the family's children to have it in order to attain high achievement in their school work. This chapter has already discussed some of the questions that you should ask about the contents of the encyclopedia being offered, the costs, the return privileges, the examination options, and so on. The important aspects, therefore, of such home sales offers are to ask those questions; to be firm in your resolve about what you can and cannot manage financially; to give yourself time to consider your decision; and most of all, to resist the ultimate sales pitch—that you will have demonstrated poor parental judgment and a lack of interest in your children's future by not having made the purchase on the spot!

The situation is different in the case of sales to schools and libraries. Even if salespeople call on acquisition personnel there, the pressure is different, partly because the purchase must fit into a budget, and partly because professional personnel are trained to evaluate encyclopedias. In many cases, salesper-

sons do not call on institutions, since orders are handled directly by the publishers' marketing departments.

Consumers should be aware that as part of the various restrictions placed on door-to-door encyclopedia publishers and sales personnel, there are several procedures that all must follow. These include clear identification of the salesperson as someone who is selling a set (and, of course, the name of the set and the publisher) and notifying prospective customers that someone will call on them.

Consumer-Protection Laws

The Federal Trade Commission is one of the oldest regulatory bodies in the United States. Among its various responsibilities is that of regulating commercial advertising which, since 1972, has included the requirement that manufacturers substantiate all advertising claims. It also has the responsibility of enforcing consumer-protection laws. Such laws cover purchases, loans, credit approvals, and debt collection. It is worthwhile to discuss briefly the consumer-protection laws that most closely affect encyclopedia sales (and other door-to-door purchases).

The Truth-in-Lending Law

This is a 1958 statute that requires the seller to inform the buyer of all credit charges involved in the sale, including the total dollar amount of any loan, the finance charges, and the annual percentage rate of interest on the loan. The annual percentage rate is considered the true cost of borrowing money, in contrast to a simple interest rate, which does not reflect total loan costs, or finance charges. All contracts for installment payments—a method by which encyclopedias are frequently purchased—must include this information.

The Cooling-Off Period

This 1974 Federal Trade Commission regulation mandates that all purchases from door-to-door salespersons are subject to cancellation within a cooling-off period of three business days after signing the contract. This is enforceable even if there is a signed contract and the merchandise has been delivered. This provision is protection for the consumer who is not strong enough to resist a forceful sales approach, but who seriously reconsiders when he or she has time and is not under pressure. As additional protection in such circumstances, not only must the salesperson tell the customer this verbally, but a statement to this effect must appear in at least ten-point type on the sales contract next to the space reserved for the purchaser's signature. A notice-of-cancellation form for the buyer's use if the option to cancel is to be exercised must be attached to the sales agreement.

The seller also has some protection in such cases. The decision to cancel must be communicated in writing within that three-day period, either with the notice-of-cancellation form attached to the contract or by letter. In either case, the notice must be post-marked within the three-day period. Certified or Return Receipt Requested mail is recommended.

The seller is additionally protected by your obligation to return the merchandise in substantially the same condition as that in which you received it; that is, it must be salable so that the seller can offer it to another prospective purchaser. At the same time, the seller must return to you any papers that you signed, refund any payments you made, return any product you might have traded in as part of the purchase, and pick up the unwanted merchandise within 20 days of receiving your notice of cancellation. Alternatively, if it is mutually acceptable, you can return the merchandise by mail or other common carrier, at the seller's expense.

As a matter of consumer interest, you should be aware that this cooling-off-period rule applies to all sales other than those made at the seller's normal place of business. This would include, among others, sales at a product party, whether in a home or a public place like a hotel or restaurant. It does not apply to sales made in a store, or by phone, or by mail order, and the purchase price must be no less than $25.

The Negative-Option Plan

This applies primarily to mail-order sales of books, records, collectibles, and similar products. The buyer is permitted to inform the seller each month (or whatever the sales intervals are) whether or not he or she wishes to purchase the next offering, about which the purchaser is supposed to be informed well in advance—at least 10 days—of its proposed mailing date. The offering usually comes with a complete description and a form to be used in indicating whether or not it should be sent. The form also indicates the price as well as shipping and handling charges, if any. If you do not return the form or otherwise instruct the seller not to ship the offering to you, it will come automatically at the specified time. If you have returned the form and you still receive the selection, you have the option of returning it. Negative-option plans usually permit the subscriber to cancel after a

specified period and/or number of purchases after the first one.

The Federal Trade Commission has considerably strengthened consumer rights in negative-option plans. The seller's notices and promotional materials must clearly spell out how the selection can be declined, how buyers can resign from the plan after they have fulfilled its minimum requirements, the costs of shipping and handling charges, how unwanted selections can be returned, and the schedule of notices and announcements on an annual basis.

This regulation applies to encyclopedia purchases, as some publishers use negative-option plans for the yearbooks and educational supplements that accompany the sets.

The Equal Credit Opportunity Act

This act was passed by Congress in 1975 and requires lenders and granters of credit to apply the same standards for granting or denying credit to women as to men. It also grants married women the right to credit in their own names and prohibits lenders from denying women credit if their marital status has changed through death, divorce, or separation. A woman who can prove that she has been unfairly denied credit can use this law to collect up to $10,000 in punitive damages from the vendor who discriminated against her. This is relevant to encyclopedia sales because so many of them are sold on the installment plan, which involves receiving credits or loans.

The Fair Credit Billing Act

This 1975 statute offers consumers protection in instances of disputes over billing practices. Creditors must acknowledge consumer complaints within 30 days and process them within 90 days. The creditor is required to investigate the complaint and either issue a corrected invoice or justify his original charges. During this 90-day period, consumers have the right to withhold payment of the disputed amount, and creditors may not pursue its payment. And, while the dispute is still pending, they may not bring suit or issue an adverse credit report on the consumer.

The Fair Debt Collection Practices Act

This is a 1977 statute whose purpose is to protect consumers against unfair debt-collection practices of creditors and collection agencies. It mandates that creditors may not contact the debtor at work or contact his employer, may not use foul or obscene language, may not threaten or harass debtors, may not telephone debtors before 8 a.m. or after 9 p.m., and may not reveal in any way to third parties that they are trying to collect a debt. If the debtor has an attorney, creditors may deal only with the attorney, and if they bring a lawsuit against the debtor, it must be where he or she lives, not in a distant jurisdiction.

These laws were not specifically designed to protect purchasers of encyclopedias and other types of books because their applicability is extensive and covers all types of merchandise. However, since abusive practices could occur in any sales situation, prospective purchasers of encyclopedias should be aware of their rights.

World Book, Encyclopaedia Britannica, and Grolier all belong to the Direct Selling Association, and subscribe to its code of ethics. Among other things, this code requires sales representatives of the Association's 100 member firms to identify themselves as such at the beginning of a sales call and to give clear and accurate information about the company's products, prices, services, and credit terms. Encyclopaedia Britannica and Grolier also have order-verification systems. Nonsales employees contact a buyer after a sale to make sure that he or she understands all the terms of the sale. Both also have customer-service telephone numbers through which the firm can be contacted with complaints, and an effort is then made to resolve them.

Avoiding Unscrupulous Sellers

Although there is far less abuse today than there was in the past, buyers may still occasionally meet an overly aggressive salesperson or a dishonest distributor selling encyclopedias. Here are a few suggestions for avoiding trouble:

- Never admit an encyclopedia salesperson who does not present proper identification.
- Examine the terms of all offers before agreeing to a purchase. Offers that seem too good to be true usually are. Promotional and advertising claims tend to exaggerate—after all, they're selling—so don't be misled by them. Compare the claims to the facts as presented by objective reviews, such as the ones in this Buying Guide and in the other reviews and guides listed in the bibliography.
- Before you sign a sales contract, read it carefully, and be sure you understand all its terms, including price, extra fees, finance charges, payment schedules, and any other details of the financial obligation you are assuming. If you are unsure of any item, ask the sales rep for an explanation. Do some

arithmetic and make sure that you can afford the monthly payments and the total cost.
- Set a limit to the amount of time you will spend with the salesperson. Any presentation should be completed in less than an hour. If you find that it is going on too long, you may also find yourself being worn down by a persistent salesperson. Likewise, sales calls should not start too late in the evening, when you may be tired and less able to resist sales pressure.
- Make sure you understand all the terms of the firm's "satisfaction guaranteed" period. A firm that does not have one, and that refuses to leave a demonstration set for at least a week, is a firm to avoid.
- Do not sign a blank sales contract, even if the salesperson assures you that he or she will fill in all the blanks according to your understanding at a later time. Do not even sign one with only some of the blanks empty. You cannot be sure about what will be filled in later. Be sure you receive a duplicate copy of the agreement as soon as you sign it; it should be identical to the salesperson's copy and should correctly spell out all the terms and conditions of the purchase, including a description of the merchandise. Make sure that it includes provisions for the three-day cooling-off period, and that a notice of cancellation is attached to it.
- Negative-option plans frequently include the distribution of one or more expensive add-ons every year. If you know that you will not want these at the time you make the original purchase, be sure to have the salesperson cross out and initial the applicable contract terms about this. Conversely, you may have the option to select the negative-option plan at the time you make the contract, by signing or filling in an applicable box. This will entitle you to receive yearbooks and other extras, as specified. If, however, you decide to cancel your participation in this plan at a later date, you may do so by writing to the company. Again, certified mail, with a return receipt requested, protects you from a company's claim that it never received your cancellation notification.
- Oral promises are not binding unless they are translated to written form, so make sure that the contract includes any such promises made by the salesperson. If the merchandise comes

with a guarantee, be sure to get it in writing when you sign the agreement.

- A delivery obligation, within a reasonable time or a specified time as set forth in the contract, is part of the seller's obligation. The risk of loss or damage from common-carrier shipment is the purchaser's unless the seller also signs a shipping or destination contract, preferably as part of the sales agreement. Both of these put the burden of damage or loss on the seller until the set reaches you and you have signed for its receipt.

- If you believe that you have been victimized in any of the ways described in this Buying Guide—or in any other ways—report this to the Federal Trade Commission, to your local consumer protection agency, and to your local Better Business Bureau. This helps prevent a recurrence of the practice, and may even help you to get recourse for the problem. You may also want to contact Consumer's Union, as they frequently cover such practices in their publications, and may thus alert other consumers to potential problems.

Chapter 3 Librarians Rate General Reference Books for Young Readers

A buying guide, in the best sense, has the following characteristics: it is systematic, it evaluates all works of the same type and class, it applies clearly defined criteria in making evaluations, and it compares works of the same type and class when appropriate. In other words, this new title in the Bowker Buying Guide series is more than a guide to the most popular reference books for young readers. The methodology of the reviews insures that each work is fairly and objectively considered. In fact, this carefully prepared guide will help potential buyers to separate the facts from opinions on general reference volumes for the intended readers.

In the review chapters that follow, *Reference Books for Young Readers* provides the kind of balanced, systematic analysis that librarians, educators, and other readers need to select general reference books. The evaluations, prepared in conjunction with a board of professional librarians, measure encyclopedias, atlases, and dictionaries against a prescribed set of criteria appropriate to the category of work and to the age, skill level, and potential needs of young readers. These criteria are more fully described in the "What to Look for" chapters—chapters 5, 7, and 9. Care has been taken to separate the promotional claims of the publisher as well as the reputation of the individual reference works from reality. However, it is important to describe and organize opinion, particularly the opinions of those experts who select and use these atlases, encyclopedias, and dictionaries on a daily basis. Such information can be especially useful to librarians if it comes from their peers—other professional librarians in a wide range of settings, serving similar populations and selecting general reference materials for young readers.

At the beginning of preparation for *Reference Books for Young Readers*, a survey was conducted by a professional market research group in which librarians across the country were asked to evaluate and rate a sample of encyclopedias, atlases, and dictionaries, the majority of them profiled in this Buying

Guide.[1] The survey was mailed to a statistically valid random selection of librarians in the United States. Recipients of the survey were 120 elementary school librarians, 100 secondary school librarians, and 30 public librarians serving children and young adults.

Using a carefully compiled list of general reference works in the three major review categories (encyclopedias, dictionaries, atlases), a 14-question survey was developed for use by the librarian respondents. The questionnaire focused on encyclopedias, atlases, and dictionaries, and prompted the respondents to consider which works in each of three categories were most useful for each population: *elementary students, middle school students,* and *high school students.* In general, librarians receiving the survey were asked to rank order these choices. Other questions were designed to discover which works were actually in the libraries' collections, which works students consulted most frequently, and which ones teachers were most likely to recommend for student use. Finally, several questions addressed special needs, selected computerized reference works, recommendation policies, and criteria the librarians used when making purchasing decisions.

The results from this specially prepared survey were analyzed and are reported here. Part **I. Multivolume Encyclopedias,** consists of four questions and their results; part **II. Desk Encyclopedias,** one question with results; part **III. Dictionaries,** two questions with results; part **IV. Atlases,** two questions with results; part **V. General Reference Information,** five questions with results. Note that some questions are multipart, and that the results for such questions frequently include a breakdown of data by public, elementary school, middle school, and high school libraries with excerpted comments as appropriate. Part **VI. Conclusions,** provides just that, along with references in support of the survey.

---

[1]Questionnaires were mailed in late November 1986 to 250 libraries, which closely parallel the proportion of school and public libraries in the U.S. Returns were received from 69 libraries as follows:

Public librarians (children's/YA)	= 17 (25%)
Elementary school librarians	= 25 (36%)
Middle school librarians	= 15 (22%)
High school librarians	= 12 (17%)

Questionnaires were mailed to librarians in 47 states and returns were received from librarians in 30 states. Libraries were randomly selected by an independent agency, MARKET DATA RETRIEVAL of Shelton, Connecticut.

I. Multivolume Encyclopedias

Multivolume general encyclopedias are those reference works in three or more volumes that serve as the backbone of a library's reference collection. These sets usually represent a substantial portion of the librarian's budget. The average school reference collection has at least four sets, including duplicates and older circulating editions. Given the importance—and the cost—of multivolume encyclopedias, four of the survey's fourteen questions were devoted to this primary category of reference work.

Across all four questions and all four types of libraries, WORLD BOOK garnered the highest percentage of "first choice" ratings. Not only did 99% of the responding librarians have one or more sets of WORLD BOOK in their collections, but they also tended to recommend it first to all age groups. One might wonder which came first, WORLD BOOK or the recommendations, but it should be remembered that these same libraries do have other encyclopedias in their reference collections. Nonetheless, WORLD BOOK is clearly seen by librarians as the preeminent encyclopedia for collections serving young readers.

Second choice encyclopedias vary depending upon the type of library, the audience served, and the content area emphasized. The prospective purchaser will want to take all of these factors into account when considering the results of the survey. A public or school library necessarily serves a wide range of patrons with varying needs, while a home reference collection must suit the needs of a particular student or family. As always, the reference needs of the user should be considered first rather than any more general criteria.

Below are the four questions on multivolume encyclopedias posed by the survey with the results, divided into five segments: **All Libraries, Public Libraries, Elementary School Libraries, Middle School Libraries,** and **High School Libraries.** Within each, responses appear in rank order with the percentage of respondents selecting them. Where available, typical comments are excerpted and presented under the label *Selected Comment(s)*. After each question, a *Summary* section provides a capsule review of how the librarians responded to the question.

1. Which of the following general multivolume encyclopedias are included in your library's reference collection?

_____ ACADEMIC AMERICAN
_____ CHILDCRAFT

_____ COLLIER'S ENCYCLOPEDIA
_____ COMPTON'S ENCYCLOPEDIA
_____ COMPTON'S PRECYCLOPEDIA
_____ ENCYCLOPEDIA AMERICANA
_____ FUNK & WAGNALLS NEW ENCYCLOPEDIA
_____ MERIT STUDENTS ENCYCLOPEDIA
_____ NEW BOOK OF KNOWLEDGE
_____ NEW ENCYCLOPAEDIA BRITANNICA
_____ NEW STANDARD ENCYCLOPEDIA
_____ TELL ME WHY
_____ WORLD BOOK ENCYCLOPEDIA
_____ YOUNG CHILDREN'S ENCYCLOPEDIA
_____ OTHER

All Libraries

The responses from all types of libraries showed the following encyclopedias in the library collections:[2]

99% WORLD BOOK ENCYCLOPEDIA
78% NEW BOOK OF KNOWLEDGE
71% COMPTON'S ENCYCLOPEDIA
59% MERIT STUDENTS ENCYCLOPEDIA
58% ACADEMIC AMERICAN
51% COLLIER'S ENCYCLOPEDIA
46% CHILDCRAFT
46% NEW ENCYCLOPAEDIA BRITANNICA
41% ENCYCLOPEDIA AMERICANA
20% ENCYCLOPEDIA INTERNATIONAL
19% COMPTON'S PRECYCLOPEDIA
13% BRITANNICA JUNIOR ENCYCLOPEDIA
 6% YOUNG CHILDREN'S ENCYCLOPEDIA
 3% NEW STANDARD ENCYCLOPEDIA
 3% TELL ME WHY
 1% FUNK & WAGNALLS NEW ENCYCLOPEDIA

Public Libraries

The returns from the children's and young adult librarians in public libraries reflected similar trends to the group at large, but with fewer titles in higher percentages:

100% WORLD BOOK ENCYCLOPEDIA
 88% NEW BOOK OF KNOWLEDGE
 76% MERIT STUDENTS ENCYCLOPEDIA
 71% ACADEMIC AMERICAN
 70% NEW ENCYCLOPAEDIA BRITANNICA
 59% COMPTON'S ENCYCLOPEDIA
 59% COLLIER'S ENCYCLOPEDIA
 47% CHILDCRAFT
 35% ENCYCLOPEDIA AMERICANA
 1% COMPTON'S PRECYCLOPEDIA
 1% ENCYCLOPEDIA INTERNATIONAL

---

[2]Based upon the 69 responses to the survey.

1% TELL ME WHY
1% BRITANNICA JUNIOR
1% YOUNG STUDENT'S ENCYCLOPEDIA
1% CATHOLIC ENCYCLOPEDIA
1% CHILDREN'S FIRST ENCYCLOPEDIA
1% "OLD" BRITANNICA

Selected comment: "[We have] far more sets of WORLD BOOK than any other."

Elementary Libraries

The elementary library returns showed again that WORLD BOOK ENCYCLOPEDIA was owned by all, and secondly, from comments, it appears also to be both the most recently purchased and the most duplicated set. The returns are:

100% WORLD BOOK ENCYCLOPEDIA
 88% NEW BOOK OF KNOWLEDGE
 80% COMPTON'S ENCYCLOPEDIA
 72% CHILDCRAFT
 48% MERIT STUDENTS ENCYCLOPEDIA
 40% COMPTON'S ENCYCLOPEDIA
 24% ACADEMIC AMERICAN
 16% YOUNG CHILDREN'S ENCYCLOPEDIA
 16% BRITANNICA JUNIOR
 16% ENCYCLOPEDIA AMERICANA
 12% NEW ENCYCLOPAEDIA BRITANNICA
 8% ENCYCLOPEDIA INTERNATIONAL
 4% NEW STANDARD ENCYCLOPEDIA
 4% TELL ME WHY

Selected comments: "CHILDCRAFT circulates and is no longer a complete set"; "[We have] four sets of WORLD BOOK."

Middle School Libraries

Middle school responses varied little from the elementary schools in the three sets most often owned:

100% WORLD BOOK ENCYCLOPEDIA
 87% COMPTON'S ENCYCLOPEDIA
 80% NEW BOOK OF KNOWLEDGE
 67% ACADEMIC AMERICAN
 60% COLLIER'S ENCYCLOPEDIA
 60% MERIT STUDENTS ENCYCLOPEDIA
 53% NEW ENCYCLOPAEDIA BRITANNICA
 53% ENCYCLOPEDIA AMERICANA
 33% CHILDCRAFT
 33% ENCYCLOPEDIA INTERNATIONAL
 20% BRITANNICA JUNIOR
 6% NEW STANDARD ENCYCLOPEDIA
 6% LEXICON UNIVERSAL ENCYCLOPEDIA

High School Libraries

The high school responses showed that although WORLD BOOK was not in all respondents' collections, there were few encyclopedia sets in a collection when WORLD BOOK was not included. Out of the eight sets most frequently found in high school library reference collections, four are adult encyclopedias.

92%   WORLD BOOK ENCYCLOPEDIA
83%   ACADEMIC AMERICAN
75%   NEW ENCYCLOPAEDIA BRITANNICA
75%   ENCYCLOPEDIA AMERICANA
58%   COLLIER'S ENCYCLOPEDIA
58%   COMPTON'S ENCYCLOPEDIA
58%   MERIT STUDENTS ENCYCLOPEDIA
58%   NEW BOOK OF KNOWLEDGE
42%   ENCYCLOPEDIA INTERNATIONAL
8%   COMPTON'S PRECYCLOPEDIA
8%   CHILDCRAFT

Selected comment: "We are in need of a general encyclopedia to replace *Britannica Junior* which is no longer being published. With its demise, we don't have an encyclopedia for the lower elementary reading level."

Summary: It may be useful to note that the average number of encyclopedia titles owned by the respondents at this level was 6.1 sets. The range in *public libraries* was from two sets to eleven sets; in *elementary libraries* the range was from four to eight sets; in *middle school libraries* the range was from four to ten sets; in *high school libraries* the range was from two to nine sets. Within these averages, WORLD BOOK is clearly the primary encyclopedia. However, note that NEW BOOK OF KNOWLEDGE is a popular second or third encyclopedia in public, elementary, and middle school libraries, with COMPTON'S and (to a lesser degree) the MERIT STUDENTS ENCYCLOPEDIA as other popular choices. But for high school libraries, ACADEMIC AMERICAN AMERICANA, and NEW BRITANNICA are the secondary choices—all sets usually considered "Adult."

2. Which general encyclopedia do you recommend that patrons consult first when they are looking for information about the following subjects:

____   HISTORY
____   CURRENT EVENTS
____   BIOGRAPHICAL MATERIAL
____   GEOGRAPHY
____   SCIENCE AND MEDICINE
____   SOCIAL STUDIES
____   NATURE/NATURAL HISTORY

All Libraries

Overall responses from all types of libraries showed WORLD BOOK as the most frequently recommended encyclopedia. Respondents did not always answer each part of this question. Results, therefore, are based on the number of answers in each category.

Public Libraries

The results are:

History:
48%   WORLD BOOK
24%   NEW BRITANNICA
14%   AMERICANA
5%   MERIT STUDENTS
5%   COLLIER'S

Current Events:
67%   WORLD BOOK
25%   ACADEMIC AMERICAN
8%   WORLD BOOK YEAR BOOK

Biographical Material:
53%   WORLD BOOK
20%   ACADEMIC AMERICAN
7%   NEW BRITANNICA
7%   AMERICANA
7%   MERIT STUDENTS
7%   WORLD BOOK YEAR BOOK

Geography:
67%   WORLD BOOK
17%   AMERICANA
8%   NEW BOOK OF KNOWLEDGE
8%   ACADEMIC AMERICAN

Science and Medicine:
60%   WORLD BOOK
30%   NEW BRITANNICA
10%   COLLIER'S

Social Studies:
83%   WORLD BOOK
8%   COLLIER'S
8%   ACADEMIC AMERICAN

Nature/Natural History:
70%   WORLD BOOK
20%   ACADEMIC AMERICAN
10%   MERIT STUDENTS

Selected comments: "I don't make much of a discrimination by subject areas with children"; "I don't use general encyclopedias for any of these. I use special sources, such as biographical encyclopedias or science encyclopedia."

Elementary School Libraries

The results are:

History:
- 85%   WORLD BOOK
- 5%   NEW BOOK OF KNOWLEDGE
- 5%   ACADEMIC AMERICAN
- 5%   MERIT STUDENTS

Current Events:
- 94%   WORLD BOOK
- 6%   NEW BOOK OF KNOWLEDGE

Biographical Material:
- 88%   WORLD BOOK
- 6%   COLLIER'S
- 6%   NEW BOOK OF KNOWLEDGE

Geography:
- 100%   WORLD BOOK

Science and Medicine:
- 73%   WORLD BOOK
- 13%   NEW BOOK OF KNOWLEDGE
- 6%   ACADEMIC AMERICAN
- 6%   COLLIER'S

Social Studies:
- 100%   WORLD BOOK

Nature/Natural History:
- 80%   WORLD BOOK
- 20%   NEW BOOK OF KNOWLEDGE

Selected comments: "[We do] not use general [encyclopedias]; use biographical dictionary or wildlife dictionary"; "For current events use Newsbank."

Middle School Libraries

The results are:

History:
- 39%   WORLD BOOK
- 28%   AMERICANA
- 11%   COLLIER'S
- 11%   MERIT STUDENTS
- 5%   ACADEMIC AMERICAN
- 5%   NEW BRITANNICA

Current Events:
- 64%   WORLD BOOK
- 18%   ACADEMIC AMERICAN
- 9%   COLLIER'S
- 9%   NEW BOOK OF KNOWLEDGE

Biographical Material:
- 42%   WORLD BOOK
- 33%   AMERICANA

- 8%   COLLIER'S
- 8%   ACADEMIC AMERICAN
- 8%   NEW BRITANNICA

Geography:
- 63%   WORLD BOOK
- 13%   COLLIER'S
- 13%   AMERICANA
- 6%   INTERNATIONAL
- 6%   MERIT STUDENTS

Science and Medicine:
- 46%   WORLD BOOK
- 15%   COMPTON'S
- 15%   NEW BRITANNICA
- 8%   COLLIER'S
- 8%   INTERNATIONAL
- 8%   AMERICANA

Social Studies:
- 47%   WORLD BOOK
- 18%   COLLIER'S
- 18%   INTERNATIONAL
- 18%   AMERICANA

Nature/Natural History:
- 64%   WORLD BOOK
- 14%   NEW BRITANNICA
- 7%   COLLIER'S
- 7%   AMERICANA
- 7%   ACADEMIC AMERICAN

Selected comments: "WORLD BOOK—the students favor it so I usually recommend it unless the student is low"; "Current events: I prefer to send them to newspapers and periodicals"; "Depends on the reading level—I recommend the student look at two or three and choose!"

High School Libraries

The results are:

History:
- 50%   WORLD BOOK
- 25%   NEW BRITANNICA
- 25%   AMERICANA

Current Events:
- 40%   WORLD BOOK
- 20%   AMERICANA
- 20%   NEW BRITANNICA
- 20%   MERIT STUDENTS

Biographical Material:
- 60%   WORLD BOOK
- 20%   AMERICANA
- 20%   NEW BRITANNICA

Geography:
    86% WORLD BOOK
    14% NEW BRITANNICA

Science and Medicine:
    50% WORLD BOOK
    33% NEW BRITANNICA
    17% COLLIER'S

Social Studies:
    63% WORLD BOOK
    25% ACADEMIC AMERICAN
    12% NEW BRITANNICA

Nature/Natural History:
    50% WORLD BOOK
    33% NEW BRITANNICA
    17% COLLIER'S

Selected comments: "WORLD BOOK for elementary and low reading level Senior High; AMERICANA or NEW BRITANNICA for other Senior High"; "Current events: Whatever is our latest"; "Current events: *Reader's Guide*"; "Biographical material: None— *Biography Index, Current Biography*, etc." (One respondent listed special reference books for each answer rather than any general encyclopedias.)

Summary: While many respondents did name an encyclopedia—usually WORLD BOOK—written comments indicated that a number of librarians were more comfortable with other, topical or subject sources for these special areas.

3. Which multivolume encyclopedia do patrons consult most frequently?
    elementary: _____
    middle school: _____
    high school: _____

The public librarians generally answered for all three levels of students, while the school librarians answered mainly for their own level. However, librarians were not asked which grade levels were in their schools. In a few cases, the schools may actually cover slightly more or slightly fewer grades than "elementary," "middle," or "high school" generally implies; for example, one librarian specified: "We are grades 5–6 only."

Public Libraries

The results are:

Elementary:
    84% WORLD BOOK
    11% MERIT STUDENTS
     5% NEW BOOK OF KNOWLEDGE

Middle school:
    84% WORLD BOOK
    11% ACADEMIC AMERICAN
     5% MERIT STUDENTS

High school:
    47% WORLD BOOK
    26% ACADEMIC AMERICAN
    11% AMERICANA
     5% COLLIER'S
     5% MERIT STUDENTS
     5% NEW BRITANNICA

Elementary Libraries

The results showed:

Elementary level:
    92% WORLD BOOK
     4% COMPTON'S
     4% NEW BOOK OF KNOWLEDGE

Middle school level: Eight respondents listed WORLD BOOK but did not indicate what grades were included in their school.

Middle School Libraries

The middle school librarians also responded strongly for WORLD BOOK (82%). MERIT STUDENTS, AMERICANA, and ACADEMIC AMERICAN each received 4% as the encyclopedias most frequently consulted.

High School Libraries

The high school librarians had more diverse perceptions as to which encyclopedias the students preferred:

    64% WORLD BOOK
    21% AMERICANA
     7% NEW BRITANNICA
     7% ACADEMIC AMERICAN

Summary: In question 3 the survey sought to discover what gap, if any, existed between encyclopedias the library had versus encyclopedias patrons actually preferred. The gap as reported here is not great. While percentages vary, the rank order tends to remain the same for each group, with WORLD BOOK clearly in the number one position.

4. Which multivolume encyclopedia do you generally find most useful for:
    elementary students: _____
    middle school students: _____
    high school students: _____

Public Libraries

The public librarians again responded to all three levels of student users. Their responses are:

Elementary students:
- 79% WORLD BOOK
- 11% NEW BOOK OF KNOWLEDGE
- 5% CHILDCRAFT
- 5% BRITANNICA JUNIOR

Middle school students:
- 72% WORLD BOOK
- 11% ACADEMIC AMERICAN
- 6% NEW BOOK OF KNOWLEDGE
- 6% AMERICANA
- 6% MERIT STUDENTS

High school students:
- 37% WORLD BOOK
- 26% ACADEMIC AMERICAN
- 17% AMERICANA
- 17% NEW BRITANNICA
- 5% COLLIER'S

Elementary Libraries

The elementary school librarians responded for their own level, and several responded for the other levels (the numbers at the other levels are not significant to this report). The encyclopedias that respondents use most to help students are:

- 88% WORLD BOOK
- 4% NEW BOOK OF KNOWLEDGE
- 4% CHILDCRAFT
- 4% COLLIER'S

Middle School Libraries

The middle school librarians responded to which encyclopedia was most useful for use with students as follows:

- 72% WORLD BOOK
- 11% MERIT STUDENTS
- 5% COLLIER'S
- 5% ACADEMIC AMERICAN
- 5% AMERICANA

High School Libraries

Among high school librarians, WORLD BOOK was considered most helpful by 60%, followed by AMERICANA with 30% and ACADEMIC AMERICAN with 10%.

Summary: Similar to question 3, question 4 was included to define any gap that might exist between which encyclopedias were available, which encyclopedias patrons seemed to prefer, and which ones the librarians found most useful for the target population. Once again, the percentages vary but the rank order remains the same with WORLD BOOK the first choice on everybody's list.

II. Desk Encyclopedias

In one or two volumes of reasonable dimensions and weight, desk encyclopedias attempt to offer a reader the comprehensive breadth vis-à-vis topics covered in the multivolume encyclopedia. Generally breadth and brevity cannot both be achieved within one or two volumes. The more successful, or at least long-lived, examples provide somewhat less comprehensiveness in exchange for longer entries where needed. In the main, desk encyclopedias are designed for the home or the classroom as adjuncts to the material available in a public or school library's reference collection; still, many libraries do place one or more desk encyclopedias within the reference area.

Question 5 from the survey attempts to discover which desk encyclopedias *patrons* seem to find most useful. The survey did not require that respondents indicate which titles their libraries had, nor which they, as librarians, found most useful. Responses are in rank order preceded by the associated percentages. Not all respondents answered this question; thus, the percentages do not always total 100.

5. Which of the following desk encyclopedias (i.e., single- or two-volume) do patrons consult most frequently?

    ____ CONCISE COLUMBIA ENCYCLOPEDIA
    ____ LINCOLN LIBRARY OF ESSENTIAL
    INFORMATION
    ____ NEW COLUMBIA ENCYCLOPEDIA
    ____ RANDOM HOUSE ENCYCLOPEDIA
    ____ THE VOLUME LIBRARY

Public Libraries

The public librarians' responses are:

- 41% LINCOLN LIBRARY
- 18% NEW COLUMBIA
- 12% CONCISE COLUMBIA
- 6% RANDOM HOUSE
- 41% None

Elementary Libraries

The elementary librarians' responses are:

- 24% RANDOM HOUSE
- 20% LINCOLN LIBRARY

4%   CONCISE COLUMBIA
4%   NEW COLUMBIA
64%   None

Middle School Libraries

The middle school librarians' responses are:

53%   LINCOLN LIBRARY
27%   NEW COLUMBIA
13%   RANDOM HOUSE
33%   None

High School Libraries

The high school librarians' responses are:

33%   LINCOLN LIBRARY
8%   NEW COLUMBIA
8%   RANDOM HOUSE
58%   None

Selected comment: "Have but do not use much."

Summary: Since the question does not reveal how many libraries own each of these sets, we cannot presume anything other than which ones are perceived by the librarians to be most often consulted. A total of 51% of the respondents indicated that the listed desk encyclopedias were never consulted, or that they did not own them. The percentages often add up to more than 100% because some respondents listed more than one encyclopedia.

III. Dictionaries

English language dictionaries abound, even within the "general" category. This is no less the case when separating out those general dictionaries designed primarily *for* young readers, or accessible to them. The sheer diversity of reading levels among young readers accounts, in part, for the great number of dictionaries made available. In addition, there are dictionaries intended specifically for school use, often in conjunction with a reading or language arts textbook series, and there are dictionaries meant for home use by a wider range of children. The number of available works can overwhelm both librarians and consumers. This fact, along with similarities among titles and apparent provenances, accounts for a good part of the confusion surrounding the question of "best dictionaries." As librarians know, it is not enough to cite "Webster's" or the "American Heritage" when each of those names may actually refer to a number of various reference works. Note that the survey list includes general dictionaries only; thesauruses and other special purpose dictionaries or word books were not included in the survey, al-

though many such titles appropriate for young readers are reviewed in this Buying Guide.

In this section of the survey librarians were asked two basic questions concerning dictionaries. In the first, a list was provided, to be rank ordered. In the second, librarians simply wrote in their choices for each user level. For each question, responses were tabulated by type of library with rank orderings within that type.

6.   Which of the following children's/young adult dictionaries are included in your library reference collection?

_____ AMERICAN HERITAGE CHILDREN'S DICTIONARY
_____ AMERICAN HERITAGE FIRST DICTIONARY
_____ AMERICAN HERITAGE STUDENT'S DICTIONARY
_____ HBJ SCHOOL DICTIONARY
_____ MACMILLAN DICTIONARY
_____ MACMILLAN FIRST DICTIONARY
_____ MACMILLAN DICTIONARY FOR CHILDREN
_____ MACMILLAN DICTIONARY FOR STUDENTS
_____ MACMILLAN SCHOOL DICTIONARY
_____ WEBSTER'S ELEMENTARY DICTIONARY
_____ WEBSTER'S II RIVERSIDE CHILDREN'S DICTIONARY
_____ WEBSTER'S NEW WORLD DICTIONARY FOR YOUNG READERS
_____ WEBSTER'S INTERMEDIATE DICTIONARY
_____ WEBSTER'S NEW WORLD DICTIONARY (STUDENT EDITION)
_____ WEBSTER'S HIGH SCHOOL DICTIONARY
_____ RANDOM HOUSE SCHOOL DICTIONARY
_____ SCOTT, FORESMAN BEGINNING DICTIONARY
_____ SCOTT, FORESMAN INTERMEDIATE DICTIONARY
_____ SCOTT, FORESMAN ADVANCED DICTIONARY

Since there are many children's and young adult dictionaries on the list, the responses are listed only for the top five or six in each category of library. A number of respondents listed other dictionaries that their libraries owned, but these were often adult level works and, therefore, less relevant to this question.

Public Libraries

The public library responses are:

47%   MACMILLAN DICTIONARY FOR CHILDREN

29% WEBSTER'S NEW WORLD (STUDENT EDITION)
29% WORLD BOOK DICTIONARY
6% HBJ SCHOOL DICTIONARY
6% WEBSTER'S ELEMENTARY DICTIONARY
6% WEBSTER'S INTERMEDIATE DICTIONARY

Elementary Libraries

The elementary library responses are:

40% WEBSTER'S ELEMENTARY DICTIONARY
28% AMERICAN HERITAGE STUDENT'S DICTIONARY
28% WEBSTER'S NEW WORLD (STUDENT EDITION)
16% WEBSTER'S INTERMEDIATE DICTIONARY
16% RANDOM HOUSE SCHOOL DICTIONARY
16% SCOTT, FORESMAN INTERMEDIATE DICTIONARY

Middle School Libraries

The middle school library responses are:

33% AMERICAN HERITAGE STUDENT'S DICTIONARY
33% MACMILLAN DICTIONARY
33% WEBSTER'S ELEMENTARY DICTIONARY
33% WEBSTER'S INTERMEDIATE DICTIONARY
33% WEBSTER'S NEW WORLD (STUDENT EDITION)
33% RANDOM HOUSE SCHOOL DICTIONARY

High School Libraries

The high school library responses are:

42% RANDOM HOUSE SCHOOL DICTIONARY
33% AMERICAN HERITAGE STUDENT DICTIONARY
33% None from the list

Summary: Clearly no *one* dictionary is suitable for all young readers at all grade levels. To a great extent, dictionaries fall into groups for specific reading levels; one would not expect to find, for example, the MACMILLAN DICTIONARY FOR CHILDREN prominent in high school or even middle school libraries. Still, the librarians' responses give some indication as to which dictionaries they have and find useful for each audience.

7. Which dictionaries do you find most useful for:
    elementary students: _____
    middle school students: _____
    high school students: _____

Many responses to this question did not specify particular dictionary titles, but rather dictionary publishers (for example, Merriam-Webster or Macmillan). Also, since the librarians were not asked to restrict their responses to only those dictionaries on the list in question 6, a number of respondents listed the names of other dictionaries, some of which are usually considered adult level. Still other librarians chose not to answer this question at all; hence, percentages do not always add up to 100.

Public Libraries

The public library responses are:

Elementary students:
29% MACMILLAN DICTIONARY FOR CHILDREN
18% WORLD BOOK DICTIONARY
12% WEBSTER'S BEGINNING DICTIONARY
6% WEBSTER'S INTERMEDIATE
6% SCOTT, FORESMAN INTERMEDIATE
6% MACMILLAN SCHOOL DICTIONARY
6% RANDOM HOUSE SCHOOL DICTIONARY

Middle school students:
29% WEBSTER'S NEW COLLEGIATE
18% WORLD BOOK
12% WEBSTER'S ELEMENTARY DICTIONARY
12% MACMILLAN DICTIONARY FOR STUDENTS
6% AMERICAN HERITAGE DICTIONARY
6% WEBSTER'S INTERMEDIATE
6% WEBSTER'S NEW WORLD

High school students:
53% WEBSTER'S NEW COLLEGIATE
12% AMERICAN HERITAGE
12% WEBSTER'S THIRD UNABRIDGED
6% WORLD BOOK DICTIONARY

Elementary School Libraries

The elementary school librarians' responses are:

24% WEBSTER'S ELEMENTARY
16% MACMILLAN
12% AMERICAN HERITAGE STUDENT
12% WEBSTER'S INTERMEDIATE
8% SCOTT, FORESMAN BEGINNING
8% WORLD BOOK
4% RANDOM HOUSE

Selected comment: "We have none appropriate at this level."

Middle School Libraries

Responses from the middle schools are:

33% Webster's Collegiate
20% Webster's New World
20% Webster's Intermediate
20% American Heritage
 7% Scott, Foresman Intermediate
 7% World Book
 7% Random House School
 7% Webster's Third Unabridged

Selected comment: "Our middle school students do not want to use intermediate dictionaries—they want 'grown-up' dictionaries."

High School Libraries

High school responses are:

42% Webster's Collegiate
17% American Heritage
 8% Webster's New World
 8% World Book
 8% Webster's Third Unabridged

Selected comment: "All—depending on student ability" (this respondent had listed dictionaries owned by the library).

Summary: Librarians seem to consider Webster's [New] Collegiate to be the most useful dictionary for middle school and older students. There appears to be little consensus on the utility of other titles, and given the incompleteness of many title citations or publisher references by the respondents, few conclusions can be drawn.

IV. Atlases

Despite the plethora of atlases published, many libraries are forced to rely on a very few titles for a wide range of students and student needs. Library reference budgets are often limited; therefore, it may be difficult to justify purchasing a variety of atlases—political, historical, "picture," and the like—for a variety of levels of young users. As a result, most juvenile reference collections, in school and in public libraries, rely on one or two good general atlases for each major category of user (elementary, middle, and high school students). These are of course supplemented by the map portions of encyclopedias and topical reference works.

The survey asked the librarians two questions about atlases, the first to discover which atlases were actually in their reference collections, and the second to determine which works the librarians found most useful for each level of student. Note that while many atlases are less specific to grade levels than many dictionaries, more segmentation occurs here than among encyclopedias. As a result, one company may publish four or more juvenile atlases—which can lead to confusion in title references for librarians and for consumers.

8. Which of the following world atlases are included in your library's reference collection?

_____ Ambassador World Atlas
_____ Britannica Atlas
_____ Children's First Atlas
_____ Citation World Atlas
_____ Colorprint Scholastic World Atlas
_____ Colorprint World Atlas
_____ Comparative World Atlas
_____ Gage Atlas of the World
_____ Goode's World Atlas
_____ The Great World Atlas
_____ Hammond Headline World Atlas
_____ Hammond Large Type World Atlas
_____ Hammond World Atlas: Gemini Edition
_____ Intermediate World Atlas
_____ International World Atlas
_____ Macmillan School Atlas
_____ Maps on File
_____ National Geographic Atlas of the World
_____ New Penguin World Atlas
_____ Prentice-Hall Modern Home Atlas
_____ Rand McNally Children's Atlas of the World
_____ Rand McNally Classroom Atlas
_____ Rand McNally Student's World Atlas
_____ Scott, Foresman World Atlas
_____ Signet-Hammond World Atlas
_____ Viking Children's World Atlas
_____ Viking Student World Atlas
_____ Wonderful World of Maps
_____ World Atlas for Students
_____ Other

Because of the lengthy listing of atlases, the results reported are confined to the top ten or so atlases in each category.

All Libraries

The overall results are:

69% Goode's World Atlas

66% NATIONAL GEOGRAPHIC ATLAS OF THE WORLD
42% AMBASSADOR WORLD ATLAS
36% CITATION WORLD ATLAS
33% BRITANNICA ATLAS
25% HAMMOND WORLD ATLAS: GEMINI EDITION
23% MAPS ON FILE
20% RAND MCNALLY STUDENT'S WORLD ATLAS
19% WORLD BOOK ATLAS
17% INTERNATIONAL WORLD ATLAS
14% RAND MCNALLY CHILDREN'S ATLAS OF THE WORLD
13% HAMMOND MEDALLION ATLAS
11% HAMMOND LARGE TYPE WORLD ATLAS

Public Libraries

Public library responses are:

59% GOODE'S WORLD ATLAS
53% AMBASSADOR WORLD ATLAS
47% NATIONAL GEOGRAPHIC ATLAS
35% MAPS ON FILE
24% BRITANNICA ATLAS
24% HAMMOND WORLD ATLAS: GEMINI EDITION
18% CITATION WORLD ATLAS
18% RAND MCNALLY STUDENT'S WORLD ATLAS
18% CHILDREN'S WORLD ATLAS

Selected comments: "MAPS ON FILE—do not like these maps"; "Atlases circulate."

Elementary Libraries

Elementary school library responses are:

52% NATIONAL GEOGRAPHIC ATLAS OF THE WORLD
44% GOODE'S WORLD ATLAS
36% CITATION WORLD ATLAS
28% AMBASSADOR WORLD ATLAS
28% RAND MCNALLY CHILDREN'S ATLAS OF THE WORLD
24% WORLD BOOK ATLAS
24% BRITANNICA ATLAS
20% MAPS ON FILE
12% HAMMOND MEDALLION
12% INTERNATIONAL WORLD ATLAS

Middle School Libraries

Middle school library responses are:

87% GOODE'S WORLD ATLAS

60% NATIONAL GEOGRAPHIC ATLAS OF THE WORLD
53% AMBASSADOR WORLD ATLAS
40% RAND MCNALLY STUDENT'S WORLD ATLAS
33% BRITANNICA ATLAS
33% CITATION WORLD ATLAS
27% HAMMOND WORLD ATLAS: GEMINI EDITION
20% HAMMOND MEDALLION WORLD ATLAS
20% WORLD BOOK WORLD ATLAS
20% HAMMOND HEADLINE WORLD ATLAS

High School Libraries

The high school library responses are:

75% GOODE'S WORLD ATLAS
58% NATIONAL GEOGRAPHIC ATLAS OF THE WORLD
42% BRITANNICA ATLAS
42% HAMMOND WORLD ATLAS: GEMINI EDITION
25% AMBASSADOR WORLD ATLAS
25% CITATION WORLD ATLAS
25% COMPARATIVE WORLD ATLAS
25% MAPS ON FILE
25% RAND MCNALLY STUDENT'S WORLD ATLAS
25% HAMMOND MEDALLION

Summary: GOODE'S WORLD ATLAS is always the most prevalent choice for young reader reference collections. The next most popular atlases are the NATIONAL GEOGRAPHIC ATLAS OF THE WORLD and the AMBASSADOR WORLD ATLAS. A basic collection, then, should contain at least these three, according to the librarians surveyed.

9. Which world atlas do you generally find most useful for:
elementary students: _____
middle school students: _____
high school students: _____

All Libraries

The complete set of responses found the most useful atlases to be:

Elementary students:

1. NATIONAL GEOGRAPHIC PICTURE ATLAS
2. WORLD BOOK ATLAS/OR/HAMMOND AMBASSADOR

Middle school students:

1. GOODE'S ATLAS

2. National Geographic Atlas of the World

High school students:

Goode's Atlas

Summary: These results suffer somewhat from requiring the respondents to "write in" their choices. Moreover, neither the *World Book Atlas* nor the *National Geographic Picture Atlas* were in print when this survey was taken. Nonetheless, it is clear that the three most prevalent atlases are also considered the three most useful: Goode's World Atlas, National Geographic Atlas of the World, and the Ambassador World Atlas.

V. General Reference Information

This portion of the survey was designed for those questions and trends not tracked elsewhere in the survey. The first question represents an effort to discover which general reference works, if any, teachers required their students to use. The second two questions address special user needs (for example, large-print materials and computerized general reference materials, both of which are costly to acquire and rarely as up-to-date as traditional print versions). And lastly, the survey posed two questions to the librarians as consumers and consumer advisors.

10. Are there any particular titles teachers regularly require their students to use for assignments?
    encyclopedia: _____
    dictionary: _____
    atlas: _____

Most of the respondents wrote "none" across the entire question or left it blank. However, 17% of the *public* and *elementary school* librarians indicated that World Book Encyclopedia is assigned. A few *elementary* librarians mentioned some dictionaries by publisher rather than title: for example, Random House, Webster's, and Macmillan. No mention was made of teacher assignments for atlases at this level.

A slightly larger percentage (19%) of *middle school* and *high school* librarians listed World Book as being assigned by teachers. *High school* librarians also mentioned New Britannica and Academic American. Webster's Dictionary (without more specific identification) was mentioned by several *middle* and *high school* librarians as being assigned. Atlases assigned for use in 13% of the *middle schools* were: National Geographic and Goode's.

Selected comments: "Some say 'No World Book'"; "often say they may not use a multivolume encyclopedia"; "World Book is frequently *suggested* by teachers"; "frequently teachers ask that an encyclopedia not be used for an assignment."

Summary: World Book Encyclopedia continues to be the encyclopedia of choice among teachers as well as librarians and students. However, note the all-too-familiar request that students *not* use an encyclopedia for an assignment. Dictionary preferences seem more vague, with librarians repeating that teachers recommend works by publisher rather than by specific title. With respect to atlases, once again Goode's World Atlas and the National Geographic Atlas of the World seem popular, although the respondents did not offer much information about these.

11. Does your collection include any general reference works for patrons with special needs (e.g., braille, large-print, or foreign-language editions)?
    Yes 30%   No 70%
    How often do patrons request such reference works?
    never 40%   sometimes 16%
    rarely 30%   frequently 6%

Of the public librarians, only 24% indicated that they have reference works for special patrons and noted that these are in the area of large-print books. Similarly, just 20% of the elementary school librarians reported having reference materials for special patrons; some have large-print items and some have items in foreign languages depending upon the school population. The percentage of middle schools with special materials was higher (40%).

Selected comments: "Braille [materials]—kept on loan for one student . . . not here permanently"; "We order tapes and braille books from [the] state library for two blind students but do not have them in our collection."

Only 8% of the high school librarians indicated any special items, and no mention was made of what kind they were.

Summary: Reference materials to meet special needs do not appear to play a major role in permanent juvenile reference collections, either in school or public library collections for younger readers. One would expect braille or large-print reference works to appear in only those collections with a sizable population needing or requesting them. For all others, loaned materials appear to suffice.

12. Does your library use any encyclopedic data-bases or other on-line or CD-ROM encyclopedias?
Yes _4%_   No _96%_
If Yes, please specify: _____
_____

The positive responses came from several public libraries and from one middle school library.
Selected comments: "In adult reference"; "ACA-DEMIC AMERICAN through CompuServ."
Summary: While computerized reference works make headlines and are widely advertised, most juvenile collections do not have them, probably mainly for budgetary reasons, but presumably also because access is complex, time consuming, and expensive, and because the products provide neither the necessary currency nor the illustrations that young readers require.

13. Which criteria are most important to you in deciding whether to purchase a particular reference work? Write 1 for most important, 2 for 2nd most important, and so forth.

_____ PRICE
_____ CURRENCY
_____ EASE OF USE (QUALITY OF LAYOUT, INDEXES, CROSS-REFERENCES)
_____ READING LEVEL
_____ COMPREHENSIVENESS
_____ FAVORABLE REVIEWS IN PROFESSIONAL JOURNALS
_____ OTHER: _____

All Libraries

The librarians responding to the survey indicated that the most important criteria in purchase of a particular reference work are:

1. ease of use and comprehensiveness
2. currency
3. reading level
4. price
5. favorable reviews

Criteria that were also mentioned are patron demand and graphic quality.
Summary: While budgets may be slim, note that librarians rank price as one of the less important criteria in selecting reference works for young readers.

14. Do patrons ever ask you to recommend specific dictionaries, encyclopedias, or atlases they should purchase for themselves or their children?

never _13%_   sometimes _57%_
rarely _19%_   frequently _10%_
Do you ever make specific recommendations?
Yes _53%_   No _47%_
If No, how do you generally respond to such requests? _____
_____

Selected comments: "Give them [a] guide to encyclopedias"; "Show them what we own and refer to *Encyclopedia Buying Guide* or other guides (usual request is for encyclopedia[s])"; "We refer patrons to use current reviews and then to examine the reference work if we own it"; "I have never been approached for recommendations"; "Usually we try to refer them to *Encyclopedia Buying Guide* and *Dictionary Buying Guide* for comparisons and evaluations. We also use evaluations published in *Booklist*"; "Depending upon the age of children in question and purpose of purchase I will often recommend WORLD BOOK or CHILDCRAFT"; "Tell them to think about: (1) who will use them (age level); (2) seek up-to-date source—look for new articles; (3) can supplements be acquired/traded in old for new"; "School district has a policy prohibiting such"; "WORLD BOOK for general use by students; I don't recommend dictionaries—just let them look; atlas—GOODE's."
Summary: Note that librarians are fairly evenly split on how to handle patron requests for recommendations. Of those who do recommend specific titles, WORLD BOOK was the most often cited encyclopedia, and GOODE's the most often cited atlas. Of the librarians who offer advice (but do not provide title recommendations), the preferred strategy involves: (1) reading reviews (whether in professional journals or buying guides); (2) actually perusing the reference works; and (3) considering the consumer's individual and family needs in light of (1) and (2). This is a thumbnail sketch of the strategy recommended by the American Library Association and also by this Buying Guide. Consumers should note that many school districts and libraries have an explicit policy prohibiting librarians from advocating one reference book over another. Most librarians can advise and guide consumers in the selection process, but few are permitted to recommend by specific title.

VI. Conclusions

At the beginning of this chapter it was suggested that the role of expert opinions and qualitative ratings in a buying guide are ancillary to more quantitative, controlled evaluations of the works in question. Some librarians will concur with this opinion; others may not. In either case, this chapter and the survey it describes allow each librarian and consumer to make up his or her own mind, to decide whether to consider the foregoing ratings or not when making a purchasing or selection decision. Fact—in the form of the careful evaluations presented in the following chapters of *Reference Books for Young Readers*—has been separated from opinion—actually, the opinions of the sixty-nine librarians who responded to this specially prepared survey. The reader of this Buying Guide can combine the opinions expressed in the survey with the evaluations to whatever degree seems most useful in the selection of general reference titles for young readers.

Many conclusions can be drawn from this survey, and many more questions are suggested by the results. One of the more obvious conclusions is that the librarians surveyed and their patrons prefer WORLD BOOK ENCYCLOPEDIA whether for an elementary school library or a high school library. However, it may be equally important to note that high school librarians and students indicate that they frequently use other, adult encyclopedias as well. Depending upon an individual school and its needs, or an individual family, a less well-known title may be the most appropriate. Knowing which books are best sellers or the most frequently consulted is useful, and reassuring, but it is only one of many considerations in purchasing a reference work.

For example, librarians at all levels indicated there was little use made of desk encyclopedias in their libraries. For the consumer, however, a desk encyclopedia may be an appropriate purchase. Desk encyclopedias are convenient and generally less costly than multivolume encyclopedias. For a family with a limited budget and ready access to a good public library, a desk encyclopedia may even be the best choice—certainly better than no encyclopedia at all provided one understands its limitations. For the classroom or home reference shelf, a current desk encyclopedia may often be preferred to a seriously out-of-date multivolume set relied upon blindly for any and all reference questions.

Dictionaries are one area where librarians are not at all in agreement about the best or most useful titles to own. The list of available choices is, of course, almost overwhelming, and the differences among several titles from a given publisher can be confusing. This is apparent in questions where the librarian was asked to write in dictionary titles, and frequently the answer was only a publisher's name. In addition, high school librarians indicate that adult, and not juvenile, dictionaries are preferred by those students; in fact, all levels indicated the need for some adult dictionaries to be available.

What *can* be concluded is that choosing a dictionary requires more effort and consideration than one might expect. Consumers and librarians need to clarify their needs first, and then look carefully at those dictionaries that seem generally appropriate. Relying upon a publisher's name is not a sufficient guide, as one publisher may offer five or more similarly titled works. The consumer will need to learn a little about the features of dictionaries and how each answers his or her needs before making a decision.

The number of atlases available is also large but not quite so confusing. Two atlases showed up at all levels as being the most often owned and consulted: GOODE'S WORLD ATLAS and NATIONAL GEOGRAPHIC ATLAS. In the question dealing with the most useful atlases in the library, many librarians also cited historical atlases, which indicates that students' geographical questions frequently concern history rather than current political or geographical boundaries and features. While it may be desirable to have a wide variety of atlases at every student level, at the very least a juvenile reference collection needs a good, up-to-date general atlas as well as a historical atlas suited to each student level it serves.

A final note is needed here on copyright dates: Respondents were not required to comment on the currency of their reference holdings. The several who did list copyright dates included atlases that were more than ten years old (and, therefore, clearly obsolete), encyclopedias which were well over the generally recommended five-year relevancy date, and some dictionaries that were as much as twenty years old. Some of the results reported on the relative usefulness of specific reference items, as well as patron preference for these items, must be considered in light of the fact that use and preference is often affected by the currency of the material in a general reference work. An encyclopedia that makes no mention of the space shuttle, a dictionary that does not include the word *program* in its computer-related sense, and an atlas that does not reflect recent political and territorial changes in Africa, should not be counted among the possible mainstays of any reference collection for young readers.

Chapter 4
Comparative
Charts

The following comparative charts provide basic factual information about every reference book or set evaluated in *Reference Books for Young Readers*. Organized for quick and easy reference, the charts break down titles according to the broad age and grade levels for which the books are intended.

There are three **Encyclopedia Comparative Charts**. The first of these includes all titles appropriate for *Preschool and Elementary School Children*. The second lists titles in the *Multivolume Secondary School* category. The third contains information about *Small-Volume Secondary School* encyclopedias.

There are two **Atlas Comparative Charts**. The first presents information about those atlases generally considered appropriate for use at the elementary, middle school, or high school level; it is headed *Elementary School through High School*. The second chart lists atlases that are only appropriate for *High School* students. In most cases, these are atlases designed primarily for adult or general readers but nonetheless sold to high school libraries or commonly used by high school students. The distinction is not always cut-and-dried; in determining in which chart to place a particular atlas, we have relied upon publishers' descriptions, the survey results, our consultants' advice, and inspection of the atlases.

The three **Dictionary Comparative Charts** divide the dictionaries included in the reviews into *Preschool through Elementary School*, *Middle School and Junior High School*, and *High School* categories. A fourth chart is devoted to all **Thesauruses and Word Books**.

The information given in the charts has been compiled from fact information request forms sent to the publishers of the respective titles, and in many cases from additional direct contact with the publishers. We have made every effort to ensure that this information is complete and up-to-date. When publishers were unable to provide us with precise figures about their books, we have relied upon their estimates or upon the careful estimates of our reviewers. We have also, in cases where publishers reported the intended readership in terms of age or school type, converted those figures into grade levels to allow for easy direct comparison among different books.

Encyclopedia Comparative Chart

Title	Publisher	Edition Reviewed (© Date)	Grade Level	Number of Volumes	Number of Entries
Preschool and Elementary School					
Childcraft, The How and Why Library	World Book, Inc.	1985	Ages 4 to 12 (Preschool–Elementary)	15	3,000
Compton's Precyclopedia	Encyclopaedia Britannica, Inc.	1985	Ages 4 to 8	16	642
Tell Me Why: Answers to Hundreds of Questions Children Ask	Grosset & Dunlap	1986	Ages 7 to 12	4	900
Webster's Beginning Book of Facts	Merriam-Webster, Inc.	1978	Ages 4 to 8	1	88
The Young Children's Encyclopedia	Encyclopaedia Britannica, Inc.	1985	Ages 4 to 8	16	642
Multivolume Secondary					
Academic American Encyclopedia	Grolier, Inc.	1987	Grade 6 and up	21	28,600
Collier's Encyclopedia	Macmillan Educational Company	1986	Grade 9 and up	24	25,000
Compton's Encyclopedia	Encyclopaedia Britannica, Inc.	1987	Grades 2 to 12	26	4,300
The Encyclopedia Americana	Grolier, Inc.	1987	Grade 6 and up	30	52,000
Funk & Wagnalls New Encyclopedia	Funk & Wagnalls, Inc.	1986	Grade 5 and up	29	25,000

Number of Pages	Number of Words	Number of Contributors	Number of Illustrations	Number of Maps	Number of Index Entries	Price Individual/ School-Library
5,000	750,000	25 for Vol. 15— Guide for Parents; Staff Written, largely	4,500	0	20,000	$199/$170
2,944	361,740	Not available	3,423	18	2,700	$249/$239
832	360,000	Not available	400 b/w	0	2,600	$9.95/—
2,560	339,000	Not available	400	Not available	0	$9.95/—
384	Not available	48	2,675 color 48 b/w	17	0	$149.50/—
9,744	9,040,000	2,300	12,500 color 4,150 b/w	1,080	200,000	$850/$650
19,750	21,000,000	4,600	1,750 color 15,600 b/w	1,600	400,000	$1,099.50/$744
9,500	7,000,000	500	15,000 color 7,500 b/w	2,000	60,000	$699/$525
26,965	30,800,000	6,460	3,184 color 19,468 b/w	1,279	353,000	$1,200/$869
13,024	9,000,000	1,033	3,332 color 5,849 b/w	317	130,000	$139.81

Encyclopedia Comparative Chart

Title	Publisher	Edition Reviewed (© Date)	Grade Level	Number of Volumes	Number of Entries
Multivolume Secondary (cont.)					
Merit Students Encyclopedia	Macmillan Educational Company	1986	Grades 3 to 12	20	21,000
The New Book of Knowledge	Grolier, Inc.	1987	Grades 2 to 8	21	9,002
New Encyclopaedia Britannica	Encyclopaedia Britannica, Inc.	1986	Grade 9 and up	32	61,680
New Standard Encyclopedia	Standard Educational Corporation	1986	Grades 7 to 12	17	30,960
World Book Encyclopedia	World Book, Inc.	1987	Grade 6 and up	22	18,300
Small-Volume Secondary					
The Concise Columbia Encyclopedia	Columbia University Press	1983	Grade 9 and up	1	15,000
The Lincoln Library of Essential Information	The Frontier Press Company	1985	Grade 9 and up	2	26,000
The New American Desk Encyclopedia	New American Library	1985	Grade 7 and up	1	13,000
The Volume Library	The Southwestern Company	1986	Grade 9 and up	2	unspecified

Number of Pages	Number of Words	Number of Contributors	Number of Illustrations	Number of Maps	Number of Index Entries	Price Individual/ School-Library
12,300	9,000,000	2,300	5,000 color 15,000 b/w	1,570	140,000	$1,099.50/$525
10,540	6,800,000	1,506	20,300 color 2,200 b/w	1,062	10,540	$800/$529.50
32,000	44,000,000	4,000	8,164 color 16,000 b/w 16,000 b/w	1,000	399,000	$1,249/$999
10,100	6,400,000	700	2,300 color 9,700 b/w	642	0	$649.50/$422.50
14,000	10,000,000	3,000	14,500 color 14,500 b/w	2,300	150,000	$599/$499
943	1,000,000	33	117 b/w	73	0	$25.95 cloth, $14.95 paper/ —
2,323	3,500,000	125	145 color 800 b/w	139	26,000	$139.95/—
1,305	1,000,000	31	35 color 225 b/w	225	0	$6.95/—
2,519	2,500,000	200	unspecified; several thousand, both color and b/w	over 200	22,000 (estimated)	$145.00/—

Atlas Comparative Chart

Title	Publisher	Copyright Date	Grade Level (Intended Readership)	Number of Maps	Number of Pages	Number of Index Entries	Price
Elementary School through High School							
Colorprint Scholastic World Atlas	American Map Corporation	None given	Grade 3 and up	36	46	2,400 +	$2.95
Colorprint Student's Atlas of the World	American Map Corporation	1963	Grade 3 and up	14	22	2,300 +	$2.25
Colorprint World Atlas	American Map Corporation	1959	Grade 3 and up	14	14	0	$1.50
The Gage Atlas of the World	Gage Educational Publishing Ltd.	1985	Grades 7 to 12	170	192	10,500	$13.95 (Canadian price)
Comparative World Atlas	Hammond, Inc.	1985	Grades 8 to 12	84	60	6,500	$3.75
Hammond Headline World Atlas	Hammond, Inc.	1986	Grade 9 and up	59	48	unspecified	$2.95
Intermediate World Atlas	Hammond, Inc.	1984	Grades 7 and 8	80	80	958	$3.95
International World Atlas	Hammond, Inc.	1986	Grade 7 and up	265	200	unspecified	$14.95
Hammond World Atlas: Gemini Edition	Hammond, Inc.	1986	Grade 7 and up	262	200	unspecified	$9.95
The Macmillan School Atlas	Macmillan Publishing Company, Inc.	1982	Grades 4 to 8	105	128	2,200	$8.75 (Canadian price)
Rand McNally Children's Atlas of the World	Rand McNally, Inc.	1985	Grades K to 6	34	96	500	$11.95

Atlas Comparative Chart

Title	Publisher	Copyright Date	Grade Level (Intended Readership)	Number of Maps	Number of Pages	Number of Index Entries	Price
Elementary School through High School							
Rand McNally Classroom Atlas, 8th Edition	Rand McNally, Inc.	1986	Lower Elementary to High School	82	96	2,000	$3.95
Rand McNally Quick Reference World Atlas	Rand McNally, Inc.	1986	General	49	64	4,000	$3.95
Rand McNally Student's World Atlas	Rand McNally, Inc.	1982	Lower Elementary to High School	60	96	500	$3.75
Simon & Schuster Young Readers' Atlas	Simon & Schuster, Inc.	1983	Grades 4 to 9	46	187	1,160	$6.95
Student's World Atlas	Sharon Publications, Inc.	1984	Grades 2 to 9	55	48	286	$3.95
Viking Children's World Atlas	Viking-Penguin Inc.	1981	Grades K to 6	20	48	0	$8.95
Viking Student World Atlas	Viking-Penguin Inc.	1986	Grades K to 6	31	64	1,800	$9.95
Wonderful World of Maps	Hammond, Inc.	1986	Grades 3 and 4	48	64	164	$8.95
World Atlas for Students	Hammond, Inc.	1985	Grades 8 to 12	83	128	300	$3.45
Ambassador World Atlas	Hammond, Inc.	1986	Grade 9 and up	415	500	148,000	$29.95
Britannica Atlas	Encyclopaedia Britannica, Inc.	1986	Grade 9 and up	301	568	160,000	$79.50

Atlas Comparative Chart

Title	Publisher	Copyright Date	Grade Level (Intended Readership)	Number of Maps	Number of Pages	Number of Index Entries	Price
Elementary School through High School							
Citation World Atlas	Hammond, Inc.	1986	Grade 9 and up	400	364	25,000	$24.95
Concise Earthbook	Graphic Learning International Publishing Corporation	1987	Grade 9 and up	70	215	20,000	$12.95
Diplomat World Atlas	Hammond, Inc.	1986	Grade 9 and up	302	272	5,000	$24.95
Earthbook	Graphic Learning International Publishing Corporation	1987	Grade 9 and up	185	327	46,000	$65.50
The Great World Atlas	American Map Corporation	1986	Grade 6 and up	158	352	100,000	$39.95
Hammond Large Type World Atlas	Hammond, Inc.	1986	Grade 4 and up	52	144	3,100	$24.95
Hammond New Horizon World Atlas	Hammond, Inc.	1984	Grade 9 and up	302	272	5,000	$13.95
Maps on File	Facts on File, Inc.	1986	Grade 9 and up	400	varies	1,400	$145.00
National Geographic Atlas of the World, 5th edition	National Geographic Society	1981	Grade 3 and up	138	386	155,000	$44.95
New Penguin World Atlas	Viking-Penguin Inc.	1979	Grade 9 and up	44	96	17,000	$9.95

Atlas Comparative Chart

Title	Publisher	Copyright Date	Grade Level (Intended Readership)	Number of Maps	Number of Pages	Number of Index Entries	Price
Elementary School through High School							
Prentice-Hall New World Atlas	Prentice-Hall Inc.	1984	Grade 9 to adult	128 pp of maps	284	45,000	$16.95
Prentice-Hall Pocket Atlas of the World	Prentice-Hall Inc.	1983	Grade 6 to adult	26 pp of maps	100	11,000	$3.95
Rand McNally Family World Atlas	Rand McNally, Inc.	1986	Grade 9 to adult	216	256	30,000	$14.95
Rand McNally Goode's World Atlas	Rand McNally, Inc.	1986	Grade 9 to adult	396	384	36,000	$22.95
Rand McNally Images of the World	Rand McNally, Inc.	1983	Grade 9 to adult	151	160	0	$24.95
The Random House Concise World Atlas	Random House Inc.	1984	Grade 9 to adult	120	208	20,000	$7.95
The Random House Mini World Atlas	Random House Inc.	1985	Grade 9 to adult	120	208	20,000	$4.95
Scott, Foresman World Atlas	Scott, Foresman and Company	1982	Grade 7 to 12	139	128	7,500	$5.80
VNR Pocket Altas	Van Nostrand Reinhold	1983	Grade 9 to adult	80	233	13,500	$8.95
Whole Earth Atlas	Hammond, Inc.	1986	Grade 9 to adult	302	256	unspecified	$8.95

Dictionary Comparative Chart

Title	Publisher	Edition Reviewed	Intended Readership	Binding	Price
Preschool through Elementary School					
The American Heritage First Dictionary	Houghton Mifflin Company	1986	Kindergarten to Grade 3	Cloth	$10.95
The American Heritage Picture Dictionary	Houghton Mifflin Company	1986	Kindergarten to Grade 1	Cloth	$7.95
Beginning Dictionary	Macmillan Publishers, Inc.	1987	Grades 3 to 5	Cloth	$22.00
The Cat in the Hat Beginner Book Dictionary	Random House Inc.	1964	Preschool to Kindergarten	Cloth	$7.95
The Doubleday Children's Picture Dictionary	Doubleday & Company, Inc.	1986	Grades 1 to 3	Cloth	$11.95
English Picture Dictionary	National Textbook Company	1986	Kindergarten to Grade 3	Cloth	$7.95
The First Thousand Words: A Picture Word Book	EDC Publishing	1979	Preschool to Grade 6	Cloth	$10.95
Macmillan Dictionary for Children	Macmillan Publishers, Inc.	1982	Grades 2 to 6	Cloth	$13.95
Macmillan First Dictionary	Macmillan Publishing Company, Inc.	1987	Grades 1 to 2	Cloth	$16.77
The Macmillan Picture Wordbook	Macmillan Publishing Company, Inc.	1982	Ages 2 to 5	Cloth	$7.95
Macmillan Very First Dictionary! A Magic World of Words	Macmillan Publishing Company, Inc.	1983	Preschool to Grade 2	Cloth	$10.95
My First Picture Dictionary	Random House Inc.	1978	Preschool to Kindergarten	Paper	$1.95
My First Picture Dictionary	Scott, Foresman and Company	1987	Grade 1	Cloth	$5.99
My Pictionary	Scott, Foresman and Company	1987	Kindergarten to Grade 1	Cloth	$9.12
My Picture Dictionary	Silver Burdett and Ginn, Inc.	1985	Kindergarten to Grade 1	Cloth	$5.35
My Second Picture Dictionary	Scott, Foresman and Company	1987	Grade 2	Cloth	$13.54
My Second Picture Dictionary	Silver Burdett and Ginn, Inc.	1985	Grades 1 to 2	Cloth	$10.25

Trim Size	Number of Volumes	Number of Pages	Number of Entries	Number of Illustrations
7⅞″ × 10¹³⁄₁₆″	1	360	1,700	600
8½″ × 11″	1	144	900	649
8″ × 10″	1	816	30,000	1,200
8¼″ × 11¼″	1	133	1,350	760
9″ × 11″	1	199	1,500	256
7¾″ × 10½″	1	82	1,200	82
9″ × 12″	1	63	1,000+	1,000+
8″ × 10″	1	784	30,000	1,200
8½″ × 11″	1	264	1,500	500
8½″ × 11″	1	80	46	80
8½″ × 11″	1	264	1,500	500
8″ × 8″	1	31	500	250+
7½″ × 9¼″	1	192	914	770
7½″ × 9³⁄₁₆″	1	96	548	476
6½″ × 9″	1	48	582	277
7½″ × 9³⁄₁₆″	1	384	4,099	1,178
7″ × 9″	1	220	135	790

Dictionary Comparative Chart

Title	Publisher	Edition Reviewed	Intended Readership	Binding	Price
Preschool through Elementary School					
The New Color-Picture Dictionary for Children	Delair Publishing Company	1977	Kindergarten to Grade 2	Paper over boards	$14.95
Open Sesame Picture Dictionary	Oxford University Press	1982	Grades 2 to 6	Paper	$4.95
Scott, Foresman Beginning Dictionary	Scott, Foresman and Company	1988	Grades 3 to 5	Cloth	$16.49
The Sesame Street Dictionary	Random House Inc.	1980	Preschool to Kindergarten	Cloth	$12.95
Middle School and Junior High School					
The American Heritage Children's Dictionary	Houghton Mifflin Company	1986	Grades 3 to 6	Cloth	$13.95
The American Heritage Student's Dictionary	Houghton Mifflin Company	1972	Grades 7 to 10	Cloth	$11.95
Childcraft Dictionary	World Book, Inc.	1982	Grades 3 to 6	Cloth	$25.00
The Christian Student Dictionary	Bob Jones University Press	1982	Grades 2 to 5	Cloth	$16.90
The Grosset Webster Dictionary	Grosset & Dunlap, Inc.	1985	Grades 8 to 12	Paper	$6.95
The HBJ School Dictionary	Harcourt Brace Jovanovich, Inc.	1985	Grades 4 to 9	Cloth	$17.97
Holt School Dictionary of American English	Holt, Rinehart and Winston	1981	Grades 3 to 7	Cloth	$22.64
Macmillan Dictionary	Macmillan Publishers, Inc.	1987	Grades 8 to 12	Cloth	$22.68
Macmillan Dictionary for Students	Macmillan Publishers, Inc.	1984	Grades 6 to 8	Cloth	$16.95
Macmillan School Dictionary	Macmillan Publishers, Inc.	1987	Grades 5 to 7	Cloth	$22.12
New Scholastic Dictionary of American English	Scholastic Inc.	1981	Grades 9 to 12	Paper	$6.95
Oxford Children's Dictionary	Oxford University Press	1985	Grades 3 to 7	Cloth	$11.95

Trim Size	Number of Volumes	Number of Pages	Number of Entries	Number of Illustrations
8″ × 10⅞″	1	256	1,500	800
8½″ × 11″	1	83	550+	68
8″ × 10″	1	832	28,000	1,275
8½″ × 11″	1	253	1,300+	1,250
7½″ × 9⅞″	1	864	36,000	1,500
7½″ × 10″	1	992	70,000	2,000
7¼″ × 9¾″	1	800	30,000	1,000
8″ × 10″	1	864	13,000	1,400
7″ × 9¼″	1	648	75,000	1,000
8″ × 10″	1	1,100	65,000	2,075
7½″ × 9³⁄₁₆″	1	1,056	40,000	1,482
8″ × 10″	1	1,232	90,000	1,800
8″ × 10″	1	1,216	90,000	1,800
8″ × 10″	1	1,168	65,000	1,500
5¼″ × 7⅝″	1	1,024	40,000	1,450
5″ × 7¾″	1	322	12,000	215

Dictionary Comparative Chart

Title	Publisher	Edition Reviewed	Intended Readership	Binding	Price
Middle School and Junior High School					
The Random House School Dictionary	Random House, Inc.	1984	Grades 9 to 12	Cloth	$15.99
Scott, Foresman Advanced Dictionary	Scott, Foresman and Company	1983	Grades 7 to 12	Cloth	$16.94
Scott, Foresman Intermediate Dictionary	Scott, Foresman and Company	1983	Grades 5 to 8	Cloth	$16.69
Simon & Schuster's Illustrated Young Reader's Dictionary	Simon & Schuster, Inc.	1981	Grades 5 to 9	Paper	$5.95
Student's Webster Dictionary of the English Language	Sharon Publications, Inc.	1983	Grades 9 to 12	Paper	$2.95
Webster's Elementary Dictionary	Merriam-Webster, Inc.	1986	Grades 6 to 8	Cloth	$10.95
Webster's Intermediate Dictionary	Merriam-Webster, Inc.	1986	Grades 7 to 9	Cloth	$9.95
Webster's New World Dictionary for Young Readers	Simon & Schuster, Inc.	1983	Grades 6 to 9	Cloth	$14.95
Webster's New World Dictionary: Student Edition	Simon & Schuster, Inc.	1981	Grades 7 to 12	Cloth	$15.95
Webster's Scholastic Dictionary	Airmont Publishing Company	1985	Grades 6 to 12	Paper	$2.95
Webster's School Dictionary	Merriam-Webster, Inc.	1986	Grades 9 to 12	Cloth	$11.95
Webster's II Riverside Children's Dictionary	Houghton Mifflin Company	1984	Grades 3 to 6	Cloth	$8.95

Trim Size	Number of Volumes	Number of Pages	Number of Entries	Number of Illustrations
6⁹⁄₁₆″ × 9⅝″	1	908	24,500	1,160
7⅝″ × 9³⁄₁₆″	1	1,312	100,000	1,500
8″ × 10″	1	1,104	68,700	1,637
4¾″ × 7⅜″	1	240	7,700	175
8″ × 11″	1	48	15,000	0
8″ × 10 ″	1	600	32,000	600
7¼″ × 9½″	1	943	65,000	1,000
8″ × 10″	1	880	50,000	1,000
7⁷⁄₁₆″ × 9⅝″	1	1,130	108,000	1,500
7¼″ × 4½″	1	416	30,000	47
8″ × 10″	1	1,184	85,000	953
7⅞″ × 9⅞″	1	800	40,000	1,200

Dictionary Comparative Chart

Title	Publisher	Edition Reviewed	Intended Readership	Binding	Price
High School					
The American Heritage Desk Dictionary	Houghton Mifflin Company	1981	Grade 9 and up	Cloth	$10.95
The American Heritage Dictionary	Dell Publishing Company	1983	Grade 7 and up	Paper	$4.95
The American Heritage Dictionary: Second College Edition	Houghton Mifflin Company	1976	Grade 9 and up	Cloth	$18.95
The Concise American Heritage Dictionary	Houghton Mifflin Company	1980	Grade 7 and up	Cloth	$7.95
The Doubleday Dictionary for Home, School, and Office	Doubleday Publishing Company	1975	Grade 7 and up	Cloth	$11.95
Everyday American English Dictionary	National Textbook Company	1984	Grade 4 and up	Cloth	$7.95
Fearon New School Dictionary	David S. Lake Publishers	1987	Grade 7 and up	Cloth	$12.75
The Little Oxford Dictionary of Current English	Oxford University Press	1986	Grade 9 and up	Paper	$9.95
The Little Webster	Langenscheidt Publishers, Inc.	1987	Grade 7 and up	Paper	$2.00
Longman Dictionary of American English: A Dictionary for Learners of English	Longman, Inc.	1983	Grade 8 and up	Cloth	$10.95
The Merriam-Webster Dictionary	Pocket Books	1974	Grade 7 and up	Paper	$3.95
New American Webster Handy College Dictionary	New American Library	1981	Grade 6 and up	Paper	$2.95
The New Century Vest-Pocket Webster Dictionary	New Century Publishers	1975	Grade 7 and up	Paper	$2.95

Trim Size	Number of Volumes	Number of Pages	Number of Entries	Number of Illustrations
6¾″ × 9⁹⁄₁₆″	1	1,152	100,000	1,000
4¼″ × 6³⁄₁₄″	1	880	60,000	400
6¾″ × 9⁹⁄₁₆″	1	1,600	200,000	3,000
6⅛″ × 9³⁄₁₄″	1	820	55,000	300
5¾″ × 8½″	1	906	85,000	970
5¼″ × 7½″	1	400	5,500	1
4¼″ × 7″	1	1,280	70,000	0
4″ × 6″	1	720	25,000	0
1½″ × 2″	1	640	7,000+	0
5½″ × 9¾″	1	792	60,000	300
4⅛″ × 6¾″	1	848	57,000	0
4¼″ × 7″	1	640	115,000	0
3″ × 5½″	1	304	12,000	243

Dictionary Comparative Chart

Title	Publisher	Edition Reviewed	Intended Readership	Binding	Price
High School					
Oxford Student's Dictionary of American English	Oxford University Press	1983	Grade 8 and up	Cloth	$15.95
The Random House American Dictionary: New Revised Edition	Random House, Inc.	1984	Grade 7 and up	Paper	$2.95
The Random House College Dictionary: Revised Edition	Random House, Inc.	1984	Grade 9 and up	Cloth	$14.95
The Random House Dictionary	Ballantine Books	1980	Grade 8 and up	Paper	$3.50
The Random House Dictionary: Concise Edition	Random House, Inc.	1983	Grade 9 and up	Cloth	$5.95
The Scribner-Bantam English Dictionary	Bantam Books	1985	Grade 9 and up	Paper	$3.95
The Thorndike Barnhart Handy Pocket Dictionary	Bantam Books	1985	Grade 6 and up	Paper	$3.50
Webster Comprehensive Dictionary: Encyclopedic Edition	J.G. Ferguson Publishing Company	1984	Grade 7 and up	Cloth	$49.95
Webster Comprehensive Dictionary: International Edition	J.G. Ferguson Publishing Company	1984	Grade 7 and up	Cloth	$39.95
Webster Illustrated Contemporary Dictionary	J.G. Ferguson Publishing Company	1984	Grade 7 and up	Cloth	$17.95
Webster's Concise Family Dictionary	Merriam-Webster, Inc.	1975	Grade 6 and up	Cloth	$8.95
Webster's Dictionary for Everyday Use	Barnes & Noble, Inc.	1985	Grade 7 and up	Paper	$4.95

Trim Size	Number of Volumes	Number of Pages	Number of Entries	Number of Illustrations
5½″ × 9¾″	1	710	19,000	135
2⅞″ × 5⅜″	1	315	30,000	0
6⁹⁄₁₆″ × 9⅝″	1	1,600	170,000	1,700
4¼″ × 6⅞″	1	1,055	70,000	0
4⅛″ × 7″	1	1,070	74,000	0
6½″ × 9½″	1	1,120	80,000	0
4¼″ × 7″	1	450	36,000	0
8½″ × 11¾″	2	1,702	175,000	2,043
8½″ × 11¾″	2	1,536	175,000	2,000
7⅛″ × 10¼″	1	1,122	85,000	970
6″ × 9¼″	1	848	57,000	0
5¼″ × 7¾″	1	446	50,000	0

Dictionary Comparative Chart

Title	Publisher	Edition Reviewed	Intended Readership	Binding	Price
High School					
Webster's New Compact Dictionary for School and Office	Thomas Nelson Publishers	1986	Grade 9 and up	Paper	$2.95
Webster's New World Compact Dictionary of American English	Prentice Hall Press	1981	Grade 7 and up	Paper	$4.95
Webster's New World Compact School & Office Dictionary	Prentice Hall Press	1982	Grade 9 and up	Paper	$5.95
Webster's New World Dictionary: Second College Edition	Prentice Hall Press	1986	Grade 9 and up	Cloth	$16.95
Webster's New World [Handy] Pocket Dictionary	Prentice Hall Press	1977	Grade 9 and up	Paper	$2.95
Webster's New World Vest Pocket Dictionary	Simon & Schuster, Inc.	1977	Grade 9 and up	Paper	$1.95
Webster's Ninth New Collegiate Dictionary	Merriam-Webster, Inc.	1986	Grade 10 and up	Cloth	$16.95
Webster's Super New School and Office Dictionary	Fawcett Crest	1975	Grade 8 and up	Paper	$3.50
Webster's II New Riverside Dictionary	Berkeley Publishing Group	1984	Grade 8 and up	Paper	$3.95
Webster's II New Riverside Pocket Dictionary	Houghton Mifflin Company	1978	Grade 9 and up	Paper	$2.95
Webster's Vest Pocket Dictionary	Merriam-Webster, Inc.	1981	Grade 10 and up	Paper	$2.25
The World Book Dictionary	World Book, Inc.	1987	Grade 6 and up	Cloth	$75.00

Trim Size	Number of Volumes	Number of Pages	Number of Entries	Number of Illustrations
3½″ × 5¼″	1	504	30,000	0
3″ × 4½″	1	630	38,000	0
5″ × 8¼″	1	540	56,000	0
7⅜″ × 9″	1	1,692	160,000	1,300
3″ × 5½″	1	316	22,000	0
3″ × 5¼″	1	188	15,000	0
7″ × 9½″	1	1,568	156,000	573
4⅛″ × 6⅞″	1	888	63,000	0
4¼″ × 7″	1	824	55,000	200
3½″ × 5½″	1	256	35,000	200
3¼″ × 5⅜″	1	384	38,000	0
8⅜″ × 10⅞″	2	2,554	225,000	3,000

Thesaurus and Word Books Comparative Chart

Title	Publisher	Intended Readership	Edition Reviewed
Allen's Synonyms and Antonyms	Barnes & Noble	Grade 9 and up	1972
The Basic Book of Synonyms and Antonyms	New American Library	Grade 6 and up	1978
The Clear and Simple Thesaurus Dictionary	Putnam Publishing Group	Grades 2 to 7	1971
Concise Dictionary of Correct English	Littlefield, Adams & Company	Grade 8 and up	1979
Dictionary of Problem Words and Expressions	Washington Square Press	Grade 8 and up	1975
A Dictionary of Synonyms and Antonyms	Warner Books	Grade 6 and up	1961
The Doubleday Children's Thesaurus	Doubleday Publishing Company	Grades 3 to 8	1987
Funk & Wagnalls Standard Handbook of Synonyms, Antonyms, and Prepositions	Harper & Row, Publishers, Inc.	Grade 8 and up	1947
In Other Words, A Beginning Thesaurus	Scott, Foresman and Company	Grades 3 to 4	1987
In Other Words, A Junior Thesaurus	Scott, Foresman and Company	Grades 5 to 8	1987
Joan Hansen Word Books (11 volumes)	Lerner Publications	Preschool to Grade 3	1972, 1973, 1976, 1979
The Merriam-Webster Pocket Dictionary of Synonyms	Pocket Books, Inc.	Grade 9 and up	1972
Nelson's New Compact Roget's Thesaurus	Thomas Nelson Publishers	Grade 6 and up	1978

Binding	Price	Trim Size	Number of Pages	Number of Entries
Paper	$4.95	5½″ × 8″	427	12,000
Paper	$3.95	4¼″ × 7″	413	4,000
Paper	$7.95	6¼″ × 9¼″	319	6,500
Paper	$1.50	5½″ × 8⁷⁄₁₆″	166	940
Paper	$4.95	4⅛″ × 6¾″	369	1,500+
Paper	$2.95	4¼″ × 7″	384	3,000+
Paper	$10.95	7⅜″ × 10¼″	198	6,000+
Cloth	$13.95	8½″ × 11″	515	726
Cloth	$9.96	7½″ × 9¼″	240	100
Cloth	$12.67	7½″ × 9¼″	447	2,636
Laminated paper over boards	$4.95 each	7¼″ × 7¼″	32 per volume	27
Paper	$3.95	4⅛″ × 6¾″	441	unspecified
Paper	$2.45	3½″ × 5¼″	314	1,000

Thesaurus and Word Books Comparative Chart

Title	Publisher	Intended Readership	Edition Reviewed
The New American Roget's College Thesaurus in Dictionary Form	New American Library	Grade 10 and up	1985
The Penguin Pocket Thesaurus	Viking-Penguin Inc.	Grade 10 and up	1985
The Penguin Roget's Thesaurus of English Words and Phrases	Viking-Penguin Inc.	Grade 7 and up	1985
The Random House Basic Dictionary of Synonyms and Antonyms	Ballantine Books	Grade 7 and up	1960
The Random House Thesaurus: A Dictionary of Synonyms and Antonyms	Random House, Inc.	Grade 6 and up	1960
The Random House Thesaurus: College Edition	Random House, Inc.	Grade 9 and up	1984
The Right Word II: A Concise Thesaurus	Houghton Mifflin Company	Grade 8 and up	1983
Roget's International Thesaurus: Fourth Edition	Harper & Row Publishers, Inc.	Grade 9 and up	1984
Roget's Pocket Thesaurus	Pocket Books	Grade 9 and up	1946
Roget's II: The New Thesaurus	Houghton Mifflin Company	Grade 8 and up	1980
The Scholastic Dictionary of Synonyms, Antonyms, Homonyms	Scholastic, Inc.	Grades 3 to 8	1965
The Simon & Schuster Young Readers' Thesaurus	Wanderer Books, Simon & Schuster, Inc.	Grades 5 to 9	1984
Webster's New World Thesaurus	Warner Books	Grade 6 and up	1974
Webster's School Thesaurus	Merriam-Webster, Inc.	Grade 9 and up	1978

Binding	Price	Trim Size	Number of Pages	Number of Entries
Paper	$3.95	5¼″ × 8″	649	20,000 +
Paper	$3.50	4⅜″ × 7¹⁄₁₆″	514	814
Paper	$7.50	5″ × 7¾″	776	990
Paper	$1.50	4¼″ × 6⅞″	137	4,000
Paper	$2.95	2⅞″ × 5⅜″	261	4,500
Cloth	$14.95	6⁹⁄₁₆″ × 9⅝″	812	11,000
Laminated paper over boards	$3.95	4″ × 5½″	288	unspecified
Cloth	$12.45	8½″ × 11″	1,318	256,000
Paper	$3.95	4¼″ × 6¹¹⁄₁₆″	479	1,000
Cloth	$11.95	6¾″ × 9⁹⁄₁₆″	1,088	250,000
Paper	$1.95	4³⁄₁₆″ × 6¾″	224	12,000
Paper	$5.95	4¾″ × 7⅜″	192	6,100
Paper	$3.50	4¼″ × 6⅞″	530	17,500
Cloth	$9.95	8″ × 10″	512	43,000 +

PART TWO

Encyclopedias

Chapter 5
What to Look for in Encyclopedias

Encyclopedias have many similarities, but no two are exactly the same. A set that may be ideal for one user may be of little value for another simply because the two user's needs differ greatly. Therefore, the first question a prospective purchaser needs to ask is: Why do I need an encyclopedia? Why will I be using it, and what sort of help do I expect to get from it? If an adult is purchasing an encyclopedia for a child, he or she will have to consider the child's needs. These and other broad considerations are discussed in chapter 2, "Choosing General Reference Books." Once those questions have been answered, the individual will be in a position to judge whether a particular encyclopedia is suitable for his or her purposes.

Encyclopedias may be assessed according to a number of criteria. The importance of each criterion may differ from reader to reader, depending upon his or her needs. For the reader's convenience, each encyclopedia review in this Buying Guide is divided into the following sections: *Introduction*, *Scope*, *Authority*, *Currency*, *Accuracy*, *Clarity*, *Objectivity*, *Accessibility*, *Special Features*, *Format*, *Other Opinions*, and *Summary*. "What to Look for in Encyclopedias" explains the considerations and clarifies the criteria that are the bases for each evaluation; it also gives the reader a sound basis for making a personal evaluation of these works. It describes some of the things a prospective purchaser should look for—and should look out for—when shopping for an encyclopedia.

"Facts at a Glance". Each review is preceded by a "Facts at a Glance" box that provides statistical information about the encyclopedia: the publisher and editors; price; reader suitability; number of volumes, pages, illustrations, and so forth. This information enables the prospective purchaser to determine immediately if the encyclopedia would be of interest and might meet the intended user's particular requirements. In every case, the "Facts at a Glance" information has been provided to the Buying Guide by the publisher. Publishers often present such material in their promotional literature as well.

Introduction. Each review begins with a statement about the intended purpose of the encyclopedia under discussion. In many cases, the publisher has provided an overview of the set and explained some of its basic principles. Naturally, each publisher can be expected to present its products in the best possible light. In some instances, publishers' claims about their encyclopedias are made for advertising purposes and may tend toward hyperbole. Whenever possible, we have quoted pertinent statements by the publisher, since part of the function of the review is to examine whether the publisher's claims are accurate, and to determine whether they stand up to scrutiny.

Scope. Why is scope an important consideration? It gives the reader an idea of what is in the encyclopedia, as well as what is not. For example, a user with a frequent need for information about science would not be well served by an encyclopedia whose content was weighted heavily toward humanities subjects.

The scope section begins by reporting some basic statistics about the encyclopedia, such as the number of words it contains, the average length of a typical article, and the general maximum and minimum lengths of articles. Scope also tells the reader what sort of subjects are covered, and tries to give an accurate assessment of the depth of coverage of various subject-matter areas. Scope also looks at the percentage of overall coverage accorded to major subject areas (e.g., humanities, sciences, history, biography, how-to). It also examines the extent of coverage of non-American content. It points out any serious omissions and identifies areas in which the encyclopedia's coverage is particularly strong.

Authority. Most people take it for granted that an encyclopedia will be a trustworthy source of information, and that the authors of encyclopedia articles are well qualified to write about their chosen subjects. The very titles of some well-known sets have become bywords for authority. But is there any guarantee that the word of the encyclopedia contributor is more authoritative than that of the average person in the street?

An encyclopedia is the result of a massive collaborative effort involving hundreds (and often thousands) of scholars, scientists, writers, editors, and other specialists and generalists. The excellence of any encyclopedia depends largely upon the qualifications and experience of the individuals who write, edit, and organize it. In the context of these evaluations, *authority* refers to the reputation of the publishing firm and the qualifications of the work's editors and contributors. An encyclopedia of questionable authority is unlikely to be a source of sound and comprehensive information. An encyclopedia whose contributors are known to be well versed in their fields is more likely to provide such information.

The section begins with a brief history of the particular encyclopedia under consideration. Most encyclopedias now on the market had their genesis early in this century; one (the NEW ENCYCLOPAEDIA BRITANNICA) is heir to a tradition older than the United States, while others (for example, the ACADEMIC AMERICAN ENCYCLOPEDIA) are of relatively recent origin. In any event, the pedigree and reputation of earlier editions of a given work are often reflected in the current edition. Times do change, however, and with them, standards; an illustrious history is not necessarily a warranty that quality has been maintained. Thus, the review tries briefly to recapitulate the fortunes and misfortunes of publishers and their encyclopedias, and to determine whether today's set resembles yesterday's in name only or is its true successor.

This portion of the review also examines the credentials of the contributors. It asks who they are, and whether or not their contributions are likely to be genuinely authoritative. Here, name recognition of contributors and consultants is important, but should not be considered as the only factor in assessing an encyclopedia's authority. Often, an encyclopedia's unsung staff writers and editors may be as knowledgeable in particular subjects as well-known academics. And these professional writers are frequently able to convey the essence of the subject in a clearer, more direct manner—one more appropriate to the encyclopedia user's needs.

Many academics and other well-known figures are very active in writing or otherwise contributing substantially to encyclopedias. However, the prospective buyer should be alert to the occasional instance when an encyclopedia retains well-known authorities simply for the prestige associated with their names. Often, such so-called contributors have had little actual input to the work. Signed or initialed articles offer the reader some assurance that the cited authority has, theoretically at least, read the article before publication and has verified its accuracy or made suggestions for revision.

The reader should also note whether or not the encyclopedia relies heavily upon corporations, professional organizations, or government agencies for information. Such practices may raise doubts about the encyclopedia's objectivity.

Occasionally, encyclopedia credits will identify certain contributors as "deceased," or the user may happen to know that a famous individual has been dead for some time. In either case, it is clear that the individual had little or no input in the latest edition. (This could also indicate that the article has not been revised recently.) A high proportion of deceased contributors should lead the user to question the authority of the current edition of the encyclopedia.

Currency. An encyclopedia cannot provide the same sort of "contemporary" or "newsworthy" information as newspapers, magazines, and specialized journals. Nor is that its primary function. However, it should reflect conditions based on the information available at the time its entries were being revised (such as the general economic and political situation in a particular nation, the status of research into a deadly disease, the death of a world leader). However, currency is a marginal consideration when the general reader is looking for information about such subjects as medieval society or the American Civil War, in which facts have been well established and are not likely to change from one edition to another.

Many publishers revise and reissue their encyclopedias annually. The extent of revision varies from publisher to publisher, and it may take several forms. And some subjects require more revision than others.

For instance, knowledge changes rapidly in the sciences and technology, so an encyclopedia that is current at the time it is published may become obsolete in a few years. What is believed to be true in

1986 may have been proven so (or proven false) in 1987. By its very nature, there can never be an entirely up-to-date encyclopedia, although online or "electronic" encyclopedias may be able to come close to this.

In examining encyclopedias for currency, readers are advised to pay particular attention to three volatile areas in which this is a major consideration: 1) science, health, and technology; 2) contemporary biography (especially for political figures, creative artists, and entertainers); and 3) politics and international affairs.

By the same token, encyclopedias must be careful not to make sweeping predictions about the future, such as, "By the year 2000, there will probably be colonies on the moon," or "new farming methods are expected to solve the food shortage in Africa in the next few years." Although such forecasts might seem reasonable when the encyclopedia is published, they could prove embarrassingly off the mark a few years later.

While taking note of any obvious instances of currency or datedness, our reviewers paid particular attention to a number of set entries. These subjects include, but are not limited to, **AIDS**, **Woody Allen**, **Ronald Reagan**, **South Africa**, **Soviet Union**, **space exploration**, **sports medicine**, **videocassette**, **terrorism**, and the role of **women** in contemporary American society. We believe that these entries, because of their volatility and the high degree of contemporary interest in each, serve as appropriate benchmarks in assessing overall currency. Whenever possible, the reviews also note the number of entirely new articles in the present edition, as well as the number of articles substantially revised from the previous edition. Examples of new and revised entries are given. When appropriate, the reviewers also commented on the currency of an encyclopedia's illustrations, maps, and statistics.

Accuracy. As educational tools and self-styled repositories of human knowledge, encyclopedias have a large responsibility to present accurate information. A generally inaccurate encyclopedia has no value other than as a curiosity. Unfortunately, a printed falsehood often acquires the authority of truth, especially when it appears in a reference work. Many readers take it for granted that everything they read in an encyclopedia must be true—otherwise, why would it be in the encyclopedia? However, this is not always the case.

Most errors are the result of the writer's or editor's uncritical acceptance of a piece of information that, on the surface, seems perfectly plausible. The publisher employs researchers, editors, and subject specialists (i.e., consultants) to help ensure that the published work is accurate. However, in the course of assembling an encyclopedia, certain errors and inconsistencies inevitably find their way into print. In an accurate encyclopedia, these errors and inconsistencies are for the most part so slight as to be insignificant.

Apart from errors, other factors may contribute to an encyclopedia's inaccuracy. These include oversimplification, generalization, and imprecise writing. A set's currency also may have a direct bearing on its accuracy.

To assess the accuracy of each encyclopedia reviewed, the Buying Guide has drawn on the expertise of a number of scholars and scientists. Each of these individuals read several entries in his or her field of knowledge, and commented on their accuracy. The same subjects were read from each encyclopedia being reviewed, thereby allowing for direct comparative evaluation. The subjects reviewed for accuracy include **Henry the Navigator, bill of rights, brain, money, Saturn, transistors**, and several others. These articles, falling within a wide spectrum of subjects, allowed our reviewers to assess an encyclopedia's overall accuracy in its coverage of history, geography, biography, natural history and life sciences, physical sciences, and other significant areas. Additionally, in the course of examining each encyclopedia, our general reviewers made spot-checks and noted any glaring instances of inaccuracy that they happened upon. Captions were also spot-checked for accuracy, as were statistics such as population figures.

Clarity. Accurate information is of little value if it is presented at a level beyond the reader's comprehension, or if it is poorly organized, or if it is presented unclearly. Clarity refers to an encyclopedia's readability, as well as to the overall quality of its writing.

In considering clarity, the prospective purchaser may ask a number of questions of an encyclopedia. Are articles geared to an appropriate reading level? Is the writing style suited to the audience that the encyclopedia purports to serve? Is there a clear and consistent internal structure to articles (e.g., "*pyramid*" style—beginning with basic, simple facts and progressing to more complex material)?

In addition to these considerations, the evaluations also describe the general writing style (is it dull, lively, journalistic, scholarly?), and discuss the major benefits and drawbacks of the particular type of writing. Again, the suitability of the style to the subject and to the intended reader is a prime consideration.

To allow the Buying Guide reader an opportunity to compare writing style and clarity from encyclopedia to encyclopedia, each review includes an extended quotation from the beginning of one article. **Lighthouse** was chosen as a representative selection for several reasons. This subject is of general interest, yet it presents enough technical aspects to reveal the writer's and editor's ability to convey information clearly. It is a straightforward and uncontroversial topic; therefore, the article's focus would be on present facts in a clear and readable manner, rather than on engaging in speculation. Furthermore, it is a subject that would be of potential interest to readers of different ages and of varying reading abilities.

Objectivity. Individuals consult an encyclopedia in order to learn facts, from which they may draw their own conclusions, not to be persuaded to believe in one cause or another. An encyclopedia article is not the same type of writing as a newspaper editorial. An encyclopedia serves its purpose only if it presents accurate information without bias.

One of the responsibilities of encyclopedia editors is to filter out the contributors' biases, whether they are deliberate or unconscious. Moreover, good editors attempt to ensure that controversial subjects receive dispassionate and evenhanded coverage, with all sides of an issue presented in a manner that does not give undue weight to any particular viewpoint or interpretation. Among other things, the objective article should note when controversy exists, and explain its nature. It should also make clear distinctions among fact, theory, supposition, belief, and doctrine, and cite evidence to support any controversial claim.

The prospective purchaser may test an encyclopedia's objectivity by asking several questions. How does it deal with controversial or potentially controversial issues? Does it ever take a particular stance on such issues? Is a political viewpoint evident? Does it ignore controversy altogether?

In examining each encyclopedia's objectivity, our reviewers evaluated a number of specific entries chosen for their high potential for controversy. These subjects include **abortion**, **homosexuality**, **evolution** and **scientific creationism**, **South Africa**, and **Andrew Jackson**. Of course, these are not the only subjects that could be used to test objectivity, but they are representative of the kinds of subjects likely to provoke debate. When appropriate, the reviews also note instances of exceptional objectivity or bias in other subjects.

For example, an encyclopedia article could treat the subject of **abortion** strictly in physiological or medical terms, ignoring the moral, ethical, and political dilemmas surrounding it. Such a presentation, however, would not give a fair and full overview of abortion as it relates to contemporary society. At the other extreme, the article could take a frankly or subtly biased stance, starting from the belief that abortion ought to be universally permitted or that it ought to be prohibited. The nearly ideal and "objective" article would describe the medical procedure and circumstances in which it might be carried out, explain why it is controversial, outline the arguments both pro and con, and explain why people hold opposing opinions on the issue. It would also describe important relevant legislation and court rulings, and their effect on individuals and society.

The purchaser might also want to examine the encyclopedias for evidence of political bias. Among questions he or she might ask, are: How does the encyclopedia treat Communist or other totalitarian/authoritarian/"non-democratic" governments and value systems? Is the United States always used as a central point of reference? What is the encyclopedia's attitude toward private enterprise? Does it tend to favor capitalism over socialism, or vice versa? In dealing with specific political figures and movements, is there a predominantly "liberal" or "conservative" tone or subtext?

The reader may want to consider whether or not the encyclopedia gives well-rounded portraits of historical figures who have been traditionally venerated as heroes but who have later been discovered to have flaws that may challenge or contradict their images. For an indication of this, our reviewers examined all entries for **Andrew Jackson**, a figure who is sometimes portrayed as an unblemished hero but who, in spite of his accomplishments, approved of the institution of slavery, owned slaves, disregarded the rights of the Cherokees, and defied the Supreme Court.

Encyclopedias may reflect other types of bias as well. The reader can ask if contributors ever express personal opinions. If so, how does this affect the overall objectivity of a particular article? And finally, are the encyclopedia's illustrations generally objective?

Accessibility. Most encyclopedias contain thousands of pages, tens of thousands of entries, and several million words. With all this material, how can the user locate particular information quickly? How easy is it for the user to locate *all* the information he or she requires?

Fortunately, encyclopedias provide a number of tools for locating information. For starters, an encyclopedia's preface generally contains information about the set's finding aids. Many sets contain an introduction on "How to Use This Encyclopedia," or a similar title. The most important of these tools is the index. The index helps users who may not know which subject headings to consult. Many indexes also refer the user to related articles that contain information about the subject. For example, in addition to the article on **Marie Curie**, she may also be discussed in the article on **physics**. For a variety of reasons, some encyclopedias, notably the single-volume NEW AMERICAN DESK ENCYCLOPEDIA and NEW COLUMBIA ENCYCLOPEDIA and the multivolume NEW STANDARD ENCYCLOPEDIA, dispense with indexes altogether, relying instead on cross-references to supply the desired accessibility. Such substitutes may work to varying degrees, but a comprehensive index is still the rule rather than the exception.

Cross-references within articles are also important finding aids—at times, they can be more immediately valuable than the index itself. For example, an article on **jazz** may contain cross-references to entries on specific jazz musicians. Had the first article not contained these cross-references, the reader might never have found out about other articles that may contain highly pertinent additional information.

An encyclopedia's layout and design can also hinder or enhance accessibility. Therefore, the reviews tell whether entries are alphabetized letter-by-letter or word-by-word, and describe any anomalies in alphabetization. Running heads of entry words and page numbers are also described. Moreover, the reviews discuss the use of subheads within articles, and alert the reader to any serious inconsistencies in the structure of similar articles.

Special Features. Although its articles are the heart of any encyclopedia, most encyclopedias attempt to enhance their usefulness with a number of special features. The significance of these features may vary according to the user's needs and interests. For example, a reader interested in art history may be greatly concerned with the quality of the encyclopedia's art reproductions. The student of history may want to know about the quality of a set's maps, and whether it includes historical maps.

The special features most commonly found in encyclopedias include illustrations (photographs, art reproductions, drawings, and diagrams); maps; and charts, graphs, and tables. The reader may want answers to several questions before he or she can determine whether or not the special features will have

an important bearing on what he or she gets out of the set. Are the illustrations clear—that is, in the most literal sense, are they good illustrations? Do they clearly represent what they are intended to represent? Are reproductions of adequate quality? And are the illustrations appropriate to the text they are intended to supplement?

Similarly, are the maps of good quality and will they be helpful to the reader? (The basic criteria that apply to the maps in the Atlas section of this Buying Guide—see pages 216–21—apply to the maps in encyclopedias.) Does the encyclopedia make good use of charts, graphs, and tables?

The reviews note any other important special features and assess their usefulness. These may include bibliographies, phonetic pronunciations for foreign words, and so on.

Format. Often, some fundamental aspect quite unrelated to the intellectual quality of the encyclopedia may be a determining factor in deciding whether to purchase a particular encyclopedia. For example, an individual who lives in a cluttered studio apartment might not have the space necessary to accommodate a 32-volume set, even though on all other counts that encyclopedia might be appropriate for this particular reader. The person who orders an encyclopedia without any idea of its size and appearance may be in for a surprise when the set arrives and he or she finds out that each book weighs twelve pounds and is bound in a dayglow-pink paper cover. This example is of course a deliberate exaggeration, but it illustrates a point that many consumers overlook.

Other Opinions. To balance the assessments of our own reviewers, the Buying Guide includes excerpts from reviews that have appeared in review journals, reference book guides, and other pertinent media. Among the sources we have drawn from are such publications as *Library Journal*, *School Library Journal*, and *American Reference Books Annual*. These excerpts are cited without comment, so that the reader is offered an unbiased account and may draw his or her own conclusions.

Summary. Each review concludes with a brief summary of the main points. The reviewer assesses the set's overall strengths and weaknesses, and also notes for whom and for what purposes the particular encyclopedia would be most useful. The summary also includes direct overall comparisons with other encyclopedias evaluated in the Buying Guide. Here and elsewhere in the review, cross-references refer the reader to reviews of these other titles.

Finally, the review concludes with information about how to order the set. The review notes when the set is available in different bindings or when special discounts are offered.

Glossary

In the event that users of this guide are unfamiliar with the terms employed in these reviews, the following glossary is provided:

authenticate. To establish as being genuine, accurate, and authentic any article or information contained in an encyclopedia.

authenticator. A qualified authority responsible for critically examining an article and ensuring its reliability and authenticity.

completely revised edition. Any edition of a previous work which has been critically reviewed, authenticated, revised, brought up-to-date, re-edited, and re-set.

consultant. An expert or specialist who provides professional advice, reviews an original entry on a specific topic, and makes recommendations to the **editor.** See also **contributor**; **editor**; **authenticator**.

continuous revision. The practice of most encyclopedia publishers in which major and minor changes are made in the content of a publication for succeeding printings. Generally, about 10 percent of a work's contents are revised each year.

contributor. A person (whether a consultant, freelance specialist or staff writer) who provides written information for inclusion in a text. See also **consultant**; **editor**; **authenticator**.

cross-reference. A finding aid (a word or phrase, often in italics or boldface type) that directs the reader to another related entry or article for additional information. **An external or main entry cross-reference** is found as a separate entry in the main alphabetical sequence; it indicates that information on the topic named in the **entry** term is found under another title. An **internal cross-reference** is found within or at the end of an article **distribution**. The system by which general reference works are sold. Marketing or merchandising either by mail order, direct sales, retailers, jobbers, or directly from the publisher.

distributor. A person or organization that markets or delivers an encyclopedia for a publisher. See also **vendor**.

edition. The entire number of copies of a work printed at one time and having the same (unaltered) content. Note the difference between an annually revised "printing" of a work, which may include only minor additions and changes, in contrast to a **completely revised edition**, or a **revised edition**.

editor. The person with responsibility for the contents and organization of a written work.

entry. A self-contained article, listed under a subject heading (also called the entry word[s] or title) and dealing with that subject.

entry-specific. Refers to an entry that focuses on a single, narrow subject or on a single aspect of a broader subject (such as one historical figure rather than a historical period). Usually concise rather than discursive, entry-specific articles concentrate on the main facts related to the subject. Also called **specific entry**.

external or main entry cross-reference. See **cross-reference**.

general entry. An entry that is broadly focused or deals with a large subject (such as an entire historical period rather than a single historical figure). Often lengthy and discursive, general-entry articles may include interpretations of the subject in addition to specific facts.

internal cross-reference. See **cross-reference**.

major revision. For reference books, an edition which is changed beyond the regularly scheduled programs between printings (See **continuous revision**). A major revision requires re-editing, resetting of type, new illustrations, and more extensive inclusion of new material. The resulting work may be referred to as a **new edition**, as opposed to a **completely revised edition** of a work.

minor revision. The slight changes in the content of a reference work usually accomplished in regularly scheduled programs between printings (See **continuous revision**). These can include correction of typographical errors, facts, figures, or updates of events.

multivolume. As used in this Buying Guide, any encyclopedia in which information is presented in four or more separate books or volumes.

new (e.g., "new encyclopedia") An encyclopedia never before offered to the public and freshly composed from original material based on available data but not specifically on any previous publication. Also, an encyclopedia which has been so completely rewritten, redesigned and re-typeset as to be unrecognizably related to any previous work. See also **new edition.**

new edition. A work that has been overhauled, beyond the extent of a **minor revision,** but not so extensively as to be described as **completely revised edition,** nor a **major revision.** A new edition would contain new material considerably beyond the standard annual **continuous revision** program. These would include, for example, significant reworking of specific subject areas or categories of information (maps, statistics, etc.) from a previous edition.

online encyclopedia. electronic database that can be accessed with a personal computer.

ready reference. A phrase describing a reference work that provides concise, easily accessible, factual information.

revise. To change or edit material in order to improve it. If material in an encyclopedia has been checked and reviewed, and actual changes are made, it has been "revised"; if the material has been checked and no changes are necessary, it has been "authenticated." See **authenticate.**

revised edition. A work that has been changed in some way from an earlier edition. These alterations can range from minor corrections in typography, and updating certain facts and figures, to a **completely revised edition** that entails extensive new research and rewriting. See also **major revision; continuous revision; minor revision.**

small volume. As used in this Buying Guide, any encyclopedia in which information is presented in four or fewer separate books or volumes.

specific entry. See **entry.**

up-to-date. The timeliness or degree of currency of an encyclopedia. Generally, a minimum of 10 percent of the material contained within an encyclopedia should undergo a thorough revision or review in order to be considered current. This is often accomplished through the annual **continuous revision** process.

vendor. The service or organization that carries **online encyclopedia**s and other electronic databases and communications via computer for subscribers.

Chapter 6
Evaluations of
Encyclopedias

Academic American

Facts at a Glance

Full Title: **Academic American Encyclopedia.**
Publisher: Grolier Incorporated, Sherman Turnpike, Danbury, CT 06816.
Editors: Bernard S. Cayne, Editorial Director; K. Anne Ranson, Editor-in-Chief.

Copyright: 1987.
Number of Volumes: 21.
Number of Contributors: 2,300.
Number of Entries: 28,600.
Number of Pages: 9,744.
Number of Words: 9,040,000.
Number of Maps: 1,080.
Number of Cross-references: 67,000.
Number of Indexes: 1.
Number of Index Entries: 200,000.
Number of Illustrations: 12,500 color; 4,150 black-and-white.
Trim Size: 8″ × 10″.

Intended Readership: upper elementary grades through adult.
Price: $850 plus shipping and handling for individuals; $650 plus shipping and handling school/library discount.
Sold directly by the publisher and door-to-door. ISBN 0-7172-2016-8.
Revised annually.

I. Introduction

The *Academic American Encyclopedia* is a 21-volume work designed to "[meet] the reference needs of students in upper elementary grades, junior high school, high school, or college and of the inquisitive adult." To fulfill this aim, the publishers attempt to "[make] available to nonspecialist readers definitive information on the broadest possible range of subjects."

Moreover, according to the publisher, *Academic American* was designed to meet four criteria: 1) to

Academic American

cient, a hydraulic rather than a cable-and-drum mechanism is used. The cab is supported on top of a steel piston enclosed in a cylinder that is sunk into the ground to a depth equal to the rise of the elevator. To raise the car, a pump forces oil into the cylinder, moving the piston upward. When the car descends, valves control the release of oil from the cylinder. Shaft, car guides, and controls are similar to those in cable elevator installations. HARRY S. NACHMAN

Bibliography: Strakosch, G. R., *Vertical Transportation: Elevators and Escalators* (1967).

11th Amendment

The 11th Amendment to the CONSTITUTION OF THE UNITED STATES, proposed in 1794 and ratified 339 days later, became effective in January 1798. It limits federal court jurisdiction by providing that the citizens of one state cannot bring suit in federal court against the government of another state except by its consent, nor can the subjects of any foreign country. This limitation was extended later by the Supreme Court to include suits against a state by its own citizens or by a foreign state. This amendment, provoked by the Supreme Court's decision in *Chisholm v. Georgia* (1793), reversed the part of Article III, Section 2 of the Constitution, which extended federal jurisdiction to such actions.

The amendment, however, places this constraint only upon the power to bring "any suit in law or equity, commenced or prosecuted"; it is not a constraint upon the power of federal judicial review; that is, it does not restrict the rights of individuals to appeal a decision from the highest court of any state to the U.S. Supreme Court in cases involving federal laws or constitutional issues. Moreover, officers of a state may not use the amendment for protection against suits on grounds of individual performance.

elf: see FAIRY.

Elgar, Sir Edward [el'-gahr]

Sir Edward Elgar is widely regarded as the first internationally prominent English composer since the 17th century. Admired for their brilliant orchestration, Elgar's works include symphonies, concertos, overtures, marches, and oratorios. In 1904, Elgar was knighted by King Edward VII; as master of the king's music, he was made a baronet in 1931.

Sir Edward Elgar, b. near Worcester, June 2, 1857, d. Feb. 23, 1934, is generally considered England's greatest native-born composer since Henry PURCELL. He received his early musical training from his father, a music seller, violinist, and organist of St. George's Roman Catholic church in Worcester. In 1879 he had a few violin lessons in London, but as a composer Elgar was self-taught. He succeeded (1885) his father as church organist in Worcester and pursued a minor, local career—teaching, conducting, and composing. In 1889 he married his student and admirer, Caroline Alice Roberts, whose love and encouragement transformed him; their marriage of three decades coincided with the most creative period of Elgar's life.

Elgar's compositions, especially his oratorios and other choral music and his orchestral works, won him growing success and prestige. He was knighted in 1904, appointed master of the king's music in 1924, and made a baronet in 1931. Identified with the Edwardian era and the British Empire, he became, despite his Roman Catholicism, a symbol of English national pride. In 1920, however, he was devastated by his wife's death, and his later years were lonely and unproductive.

Most popularly remembered for the first of his five *Pomp and Circumstance Marches*, Elgar wrote magnificent orchestral scores in the late romantic tradition: concertos for violin (1910) and cello (1919), two symphonies (in A-flat, 1908; in E-flat, 1911), the buoyant *Cockaigne* (In London Town) overture (1901), the celebrated *Enigma Variations* (1899), and the symphonic study *Falstaff* (1913); as well as chamber music, piano pieces, songs, church music, and incidental music for the stage. His music for string orchestra includes a lovely serenade in E minor (1892) and the spirited *Introduction and Allegro* (1905). His oratorio *The Dream of Gerontius* (1900), based on a poem by Cardinal Newman, is considered by many to be Elgar's masterpiece. An authoritative conductor of his own music, Elgar was the first major composer to record his works systematically for the phonograph.

JOHN W. BARKER

Bibliography: Hurd, Michael, *Elgar* (1969); Kennedy, Michael, *Portrait of Elgar* (1968); McVeagh, Diana M., *Edward Elgar* (1955); Moore, Jerrold N., *Elgar* (1972); Parrott, Ian, *Elgar* (1971; repr. 1977).

Elgin, Thomas Bruce, 7th Earl of [el'-gin]

The 7th earl of Elgin, b. July 20, 1766, d. Nov. 14, 1841, was the British diplomat who negotiated the removal to England of important classical Greek sculptures from the ACROPOLIS in Athens. The sculptures, known as the ELGIN MARBLES, were secured by Lord Elgin while he served in Constantinople as ambassador to Turkey (1799–1803). In 1816 the British Museum purchased the marbles, which include sizable portions of the frieze, pediments, and metopes of the Parthenon and a caryatid from the Erechtheum. Lord Elgin also served as a diplomat in Brussels and Berlin.

Elgin, James Bruce, 8th Earl of

James Bruce, 8th earl of Elgin, b. July 20, 1811, was a notable British colonial administrator. Son of the 7th earl, he was educated at Eton and Oxford and succeeded to the earldom in 1841. After serving (1842–46) as governor of Jamaica, he became governor-general of Canada (1847–54), where he oversaw the granting and implementation of responsible government. Sent (1857) as a special envoy to China after armed British intervention in Canton, he negotiated (1858) the Treaty of Tientsin (1858; see TIENTSIN, TREATIES OF); and when the Chinese refused to honor it, he returned with an Anglo-French force in 1860, captured Peking, and burned the imperial summer palace. Appointed viceroy of India in 1861, Elgin died there on Nov. 20, 1863. PETER J. KING

Bibliography: Morison, J. L., *The Eighth Earl of Elgin* (1928).

Elgin Marbles [el'-gin]

The Elgin Marbles are an important group of ancient Greek sculptures collected in Athens between 1801 and 1803 and taken to England by Thomas Bruce, 7th earl of ELGIN. They comprise works from the ACROPOLIS, including a frieze by PHIDIAS and a caryatid. The sculptures were purchased by the British government in 1816 and are now exhibited in the British Museum.

Elgon, Mount [el'-gahn]

Mount Elgon is a large extinct volcano on the Kenya-Uganda border. At its base the mountain is about 80 km (50 mi) in diameter. Its crater is about 8 km (5 mi) across and nearly 610 m (2,000 ft) deep. The crater contains several peaks, the highest reaching 4,321 m (14,178 ft). Its lower slopes are densely populated and planted with coffee and grains.

Page shown at 67% of actual size.

1 Main entry: Academic American contains 28,600 entries, arranged alphabetically word-by-word. A rule separates the entry title from the article itself.

2 Cross-reference entry

3 Illustration: Academic American includes 16,650 illustrations, of which seventy-five percent are in color.

4 Caption: Captions in Academic American often add to the information presented in the main text.

5 Guide words

6 Page number

7 Bibliography: More than forty percent of Academic American's articles include a bibliography.

8 Cross-references: Academic American contains 67,000 cross-references.

9 Contributor's credit: Academic American has 2,300 contributors. Seventy-five percent of all articles are signed.

10 Pronunciation: Foreign or other difficult entry words are followed by phonetic pronunciation.

provide quick access to definitive factual information; 2) to provide a readily intelligible general overview of a subject that does not compel the reader to grasp intricate subtleties or wade through a drawn out historical analysis; 3) to give students a starting point for further research by isolating key concepts, outlining the structure of a subject, and directing the reader to more specialized primary and secondary goals; and 4), to help readers visualize or recognize people, places, objects, and processes by means of maps, photographs, and drawings.

II. Scope

The *Academic American Encyclopedia* contains 28,600 articles, the majority of which are of the specific entry type. More than half of the content is presented in articles that are less than 500 words long.

As an indication of how space is apportioned among different subjects, **Charlemagne** receives about one and one-sixth pages, while **Konstantin Chernenko** is covered in approximately one-fourth of a page. **Ray Charles** is treated in 11 lines, as is **Ty Cobb** (although his entry is accompanied by a photograph). The U. S. **Civil War** is discussed in 19 pages; the entry for **Christianity** is about two pages long; and **China** is the subject of a ten-page article (including a two-page map). Readers should note, however, that the **history of China** is treated as a separate article (nearly seven and one-half pages long). Indeed, because the *AAE* is an entry-specific work, individual aspects of a broad topic are generally covered under separate entries. At the same time, however, there is often a good deal of overlap among different articles. For example, both **space exploration** and **space shuttle** present information about the shuttle, the *Challenger* disaster, and its effects on the American space program.

The publisher has provided the following breakdown of total space allocated to different subject areas: humanities and the arts, 36 percent; science and technology, 35 percent; social science, 14 percent; geography, 13 percent; sports and contemporary life, 2 percent. Thirty-five percent of all entries are biographical, although the percentage of actual pages is much smaller.

The *AAE* was originally compiled in the United States under the aegis of a Dutch publisher, and its content was written primarily for North American readers. Moreover, as the Preface notes, "the list of entries (and their lengths) reflects the curriculum of American schools and universities." The publisher also remarks, however, that articles on general topics "grant appropriate recognition to the diversity of practice throughout the world." As an indication of

the attention given to non-American subjects, a section chosen at random (Volume 7, pages 102–135) includes the following entries: **Elat** (Israeli town), **Elba**, **Elbe River**, **Mount Elbrus**, **Elburz Mountains**, **Elche** (Spanish city), **Eleanor of Aquitaine**, **Eleatic School**, **Electra** (mythology), **Electra** (play), **Elegy Written in a Country Churchyard**, **Eleusinian Mysteries, Eleusis.** Note that these amount to only 13 entries out of 91 in this page span. The majority of other entries in this segment are devoted to scientific, technical, or natural subjects which have no particular national orientation. Indeed, this is the pattern for the entire *AAE*. In general, entries for foreign places and people tend to be brief.

III. Authority

The *Academic American Encyclopedia* is the newest encyclopedia on the market; in fact, it is the only encyclopedia now in print to have been created since the advent of COLLIER'S ENCYCLOPEDIA and the MERIT STUDENTS ENCYCLOPEDIA in the 1950s.

The set was originally published in Princeton, New Jersey by the Arete Publishing Company, Inc., an American subsidiary of the Dutch publishing conglomerate VNU. The encyclopedia was Arete's first production. *AAE* has the distinction of being the first set to make use of computer technology in planning, editing, and revising an encyclopedia. This allows the publisher to revise the set quickly and at less expense. Most other encyclopedia publishers have since followed Arete's lead.

As noted, the *AAE* was designed specifically for the American market, and is not based on any previous encyclopedia, foreign or domestic. The encyclopedia's editorial staff was American, and the contributors were drawn mainly from American universities. Upon publication, the first edition met with general acclaim for accuracy, currency, and objectivity.

In 1982, the set was acquired by the well-known Connecticut-based publisher, Grolier, Inc., who also publishes the ENCYCLOPEDIA AMERICANA and the NEW BOOK OF KNOWLEDGE. As its title implies, the *AAE* is the product of extensive scholarship. Some 2,300 contributors, many of whom are internationally known authorities in their fields, were drawn mainly from American universities. In addition, the list of entries was prepared by a board of 25 distinguished scholars and other prominent authorities. The editorial staff works under the direction of Bernard S. Cayne, Grolier's Editorial Director, and K. Anne Ranson, the Editor-in-Chief, who served as a Supervisory Editor of the first edition. All in all, the credentials of the contributors appear impeccable; the authority of the *AAE* appears to be of the highest quality.

IV. Currency

As a fairly new encyclopedia, the *AAE* has an automatic advantage over older encyclopedias in terms of currency. The *AAE* is revised annually. The 1987 edition features a revision rate of about 11 percent of the total text pages, plus the entire index. More than 130 new articles were added; 55 were replaced; and another 170 received major revision. According to the publisher, "less extensive but nonetheless significant" revisions were made in 1,270 other articles.

As a result of this process, the *AAE* is extremely up-to-date. Most entries on volatile topics include important developments through the end of 1986. For example, the article on **AIDS** includes information about the antiviral drug AZT, which was approved for the treatment of AIDS patients late in 1986. The article also notes that "the first U.S. hospital devoted solely to AIDS treatment and research opened in Houston, Tex., in 1986."

The **South Africa** entry mentions the new constitution of 1984, as well as the abolition of the pass laws and the declaration of a state of emergency in 1986. The article ends with the general comment: "An international campaign to impose economic sanctions against South Africa and encourage foreign-owned businesses to halt investment there gained momentum."

The entry on **Ronald Reagan** was virtually up-to-the-minute at the time the 1987 edition of *AAE* was published. The article mentions his approval (October 1986) of the tax reform measure, the Iceland summit meeting with Mikhail Gorbachev (also October 1986), and the Democrats' capture of the Senate in the November elections. The article concludes with the statement that "shortly after [the election], Reagan and his aides were embroiled in controversy over revelations of secret arms sales to Iran, some of the profits of which were diverted to the Nicaraguan 'contras.' " **Nicaragua** includes the 1984 election of Daniel Ortega Saavedra and the Reagan administration's support of the contras. The article ends by saying that "Efforts by four Latin American nations . . . to mediate a regional peace settlement made little progress, and no end to the civil conflict or resolution of U. S.-Nicaraguan differences was in sight."

The *AAE*'s coverage of **terrorism** is fairly up-to-date, but concentrates on the legal definition and political implications of terrorism rather than on the history of terrorism. Relatively few specific terrorist incidents are mentioned; the 1985 *Achille Lauro* highjacking is the most recent of these.

A four-page article on **women in society** reflects contemporary trends and attitudes.

The article **Space Shuttle** contains three paragraphs that discuss the January 1986 Challenger explosion, the inquiry into the disaster, and the possible consequences for the United States space program. Additionally, the *AAE* contains biographical entries for each of the seven crew members killed in the explosion. Other new biographical entries in the 1987 edition include **Corazon Aquino, Jerry Falwell, Lee Iacocca, Jack Kemp, Neil Kinnock, Daniel Ortega Saavedra,** and **Manuel Puig.**

The *AAE* also includes up-to-date entries dealing with many aspects of contemporary technology. Among these are an extensive (five-page) article on **video,** plus a number of related topics including **music video, video art, video camera, video display terminal, video game, video recording, video technology, videodisc, videotape,** and **videotex.** There are also entries on the **compact disc** and **digital technology,** as well as for such computer-related subjects as **personal computer, computer-aided design** and **computer-aided manufacturing, computer crime, computer graphics,** the **computer industry, computer languages, computer memory, computer modeling, computer networking, computer software,** and **computers and privacy.**

For the 1987 edition of *AAE*, such articles as **common cold, computer, depression, history of Europe,** and **Halley's Comet** were entirely rewritten (or replaced by new articles on these subjects) in order to reflect more recent knowledge or revised views. A new article on the Vietnam War "reflects the changed perspective that the passage of time has allowed," in the words of the publisher.

Entirely new subject entries include **Chernobyl, computers in education, childhood diseases, literary modernism, privatization, Progressive Era,** and **Vietnam Veterans Memorial.**

In addition to its up-to-date text, the *AAE* also features an exceptionally up-to-date illustration program. Among new photographs included in the 1987 edition are those of Corazon Aquino, P. W. Botha, the Supreme Court (with new justice Antonin Scalia), the *Challenger* explosion, and Halley's Comet. Moreover, the *AAE*'s photographs, apart from those of specifically historical interest, are not dated in any manner. Like its text, the illustrations in *AAE* are as up-to-date as those in any general multivolume encyclopedia currently on the market.

V. Accuracy

More so than any of its competitors, the *Academic American* is geared to the presentation of fact; there is very little speculative or discursive material. The publisher asserts that in order to ensure the encyclopedia's accuracy, "a large team of research editors—all specialists in their field—verified every fact, inference, and conclusion against primary and other authoritative sources in several of the world's largest libraries . . . ."

Academic American is the only encyclopedia reviewed in this Buying Guide that does not succumb to the popular and erroneous claim that **Henry the Navigator** established a school of navigation at Sagres, nor does it depict him as a beneficent patron of Portugese explorers. Rather, it acknowledges that "his explorations were motivated as much by hatred of the Muslims and hunger for gold as they were by the desire for geographical knowledge."

Our subject specialists also remarked on the high degree of accuracy in most of the articles they examined. **Bill of Rights** includes useful summaries of the first ten amendments, although it does not mention the important concept of "incorporation." The well written entry on **money**, contributed by a prominent economist, is concise and touches on most aspects of the subject that one would expect in an adult presentation, but will not be suitable for younger readers. Similarly, the article on the **brain** is accurate but will also be difficult for young readers to understand. The entry does not deal with **cognitive psychology**, **memory**, **perception**, or **problem solving**, but each of these is the subject of a separate article. The entry on **Saturn** is concise and detailed, and is careful to note that in astronomy, measurements are not absolute but relative. **Transistors** has an excellent description of how transistors work. There are cross-references to related entries on **semiconductors**, **electron tubes**, **integrated circuits**, and **microelectronics**.

VI. Clarity

Although the publisher claims that the set is geared to school curricula, there has been no evident attempt to write the text to a controlled reading level. A number of critics have claimed that *Academic American*'s text is too advanced for the average user, whether student or adult. (See *Other Opinions.*) Sentences tend to be long, syntax is often unnecessarily complex, and difficult or unusual terms are not always explained in context. These problems are particularly evident in articles on scientific or technical subjects.

A few examples will illustrate. The first sentence in the article **solar system** reads: "The solar system is the group of celestial bodies, including the Earth, orbiting around and gravitationally bound by the star known as the SUN, one of at least a hundred billion stars in our galaxy." In the following sentence, the planets are described as "the Sun's retinue." The first sentence in **electron** reads: "The electron is often described as a particle of ELECTRICITY, a definition that reflects its role as a piece of matter and suggests its relationship to electrical phenomena."

Entries on highly technical subjects also make extensive use of acronyms, formulae, and jargon. Although these are usually explained, they are nonetheless often presented at a level that requires a college-level mastery of the subject. Mathematical and chemical formulae are strewn profusely through such articles. Again, they require the reader to have a fundamental grasp of the discipline and of the terminology used in that discipline, and will be of limited use to the average reference book user. For example, the third paragraph of the article on the **electron** quoted above reads as follows:

> Modern measurements have determined the mass of the electron to be 9.1083×10^{-28} grams, about $1/1836$ of the mass of the proton. The charge is 4.80×10^{-10} electrostatic units, or 1.60×10^{-19} coulombs. Even more useful to scientists is the ratio of charge to mass, e/m, since this term appears in many calculations. Its value is 1.759×10^{11} coulombs/kg.

While this information may indeed be important to an understanding of the electron, it is presented in a way that is beyond the grasp of the average reader who has little or no previous knowledge of the subject.

The following extract from **lighthouse** illustrates the style of a typical (and less technical) entry in the *AAE*:

> **lighthouse** A lighthouse is a structure designed to provide ships with a navigational point of reference by day and by night, and often to indicate dangerous rocks or shoals as well. Used since ancient times, lighthouses have evolved from beacon fires burning on hilltops to modern masonry or steel-frame towers that are capable of resisting the severest storms and are equipped with optical and sound signalling systems.
>
> **HISTORY**
>
> Although the Phoenicians and Egyptians are thought to have built lighthouses, there are no records of their accomplishments.
>
> **Construction.** The first lighthouse for which a detailed account remains was the great Pharos of Alexandria, considered one of the SEVEN WONDERS OF THE WORLD. A stone structure about 107 m (350 ft) high with a wood fire at the top, the Pharos, built c.280 BC, took its name from the island on which it was built. After withstanding

winds and waves for many centuries, it was toppled by an earthquake in the 14th century. The Romans built lighthouses along the European coastline, sometimes fortifying them for military use. Roman lighthouses still stand inside the walls of Dover Castle (England) and at Coruña, Spain....

VII. Objectivity

The editors of the *Academic American Encyclopedia* acknowledge that "scholars may differ among themselves even on questions that do not involve social policy." One of the functions of the encyclopedia, therefore, is "to reflect those differences and to consider alternative theories or interpretation as well as opposing points of view . . . ." On the whole, the encyclopedia achieves this aim.

Occasionally, however, *Academic American*'s bias toward scientific and technical subjects affects not only the extent of its coverage of such subjects, but also the tone and point of view inherent in this coverage. For example, in its treatment of the evolution-creationism debate, *Academic American* cannot be considered strictly objective. The extensive entry on **evolution** contends that "Exactly how evolution occurs is still a matter of debate, but that it occurs is a scientific fact . . . . It is plausible that all organisms can be traced back to the origin of life from inanimate matter." Similarly, the article on **prehistoric humans** declares that "the human species . . . is related, in descending order of closeness, to apes, monkeys, tarsiers, and lemurs." A much shorter entry on **creationism** notes fundamentalists' objections to evolution and their efforts to mandate the teaching of creationism in public schools. The article distinguishes between religious and scientific grounds for creationism, and notes that " 'creation science' papers . . . have also been reviewed by established scientific journals and rejected for lack of scientific coherency and documentation."

The *AAE*'s discussion of **abortion** is generally objective. The article is broken down into four subsections, which treat "Medical Aspects," "Legal Aspects," "Impact of Legalization," and "Ethical Aspects." This last section briefly recapitulates contemporary arguments both for and against abortion.

The discussion of the history of the **Bill of Rights** takes a somewhat dismissive and sectarian tone in discussing the Federalist argument against the necessity for such a bill.

The two-and-one-quarter page article on **Andrew Jackson** is evenhanded, neither ignoring nor sensationalizing the controversy that surrounded his political career. He is fairly described as "a man of strong convictions, iron will, and fiery temperament." The main facts relating to his presidency are presented in a straightforward and objective manner.

VIII. Accessibility

The *Academic American* is generally well designed and contains a number of basic finding aids that should make it readily accessible to the average intended user. The Preface, located at the front of Volume 1, describes the set's organization and the different elements involved. However, unlike most other general multivolume encyclopedias reviewed in this Buying Guide, it does not give specific instructions on how to use the set.

Entries are arranged alphabetically, word by word. Names beginning with *Mc* are treated as though they begin with *Mac*; the same rule applies to the use of the abbreviation *St.* for *Saint*.

Page numbers are located at the top of each page, flush with the outside margin. Guide words indented from the page numbers indicate the first entry on the left-hand page and the last entry on the right-hand page.

Article headings are printed in 10-point boldface type. A rule separates the heading from the article text.

The main key to the *AAE*'s accessibility is its index, which contains more than 200,000 entries and occupies all of Volume 21. A "Guide to the Use of This Encyclopedia" at the front of the index describes the index's features and explains how to use it. As an indication of the scope and style of individual entries, the reader searching for information about Marie Curie will find the following index entry:

CURIE, MARIE AND PIERRE 4:328

illus.; **5:**391–392 *bibliog.*,

illus.; **15:**286 *illus.*

polonium **15:**417

radioactivity **16:**60–61 *illus.*

radium **16:**68

The set's accessibility is further enhanced by some 67,000 cross-references. These are of three types: cross-reference entries; cross-references within article text, which are printed in small capital letters; and "See also" references that occur at the ends of articles. Both the index and the cross-references are well designed, and serve to tie together separate articles on related subjects—particularly crucial in a specific-entry encyclopedia.

IX. Special Features

Of its several special features, the *AAE* has been most highly praised for the excellence of its illustrations. Fully three-quarters of its more than 16,000 illustrations are in color. Among its competitors, only WORLD BOOK, with 29,000 illustrations, can boast a more extensive illustration program.

Altogether, the *AAE*'s photographs, maps, and commissioned artwork occupy one-third of the set's available editorial space. The editors' use of illustrations reflects great care and creativity. The publisher claims that "many of the major articles are so profusely illustrated and extensively captioned that the reader will acquire a basic comprehension of the subject as well as considerable factual information by studying the illustrations and captions alone." While this statement may be dismissed as advertising hyperbole, it is not totally without merit. Very few of the illustrations can be characterized as dull; most are stimulating and will lead to a greater understanding of the subject they illustrate. The publisher's claim that "each [illustration] was carefully selected to explain, support, or expand ideas in the text" is borne out by an examination of the set.

Photographs of individuals have been carefully selected. The publisher notes that "whenever possible the traditional postage-stamp-size 'mug shot' was avoided, and photos that reveal more of the subject's personality were selected." This claim too is generally true.

In addition to excellent photographs, the *AAE* also makes extensive use of commissioned drawings and diagrams. The full-color drawings that accompany many of the entries on specific mammals and birds are particularly outstanding. Readers will also find the full-color illustrations of various aircraft quite useful. Anatomical and technical drawings throughout the encyclopedia are similarly distinguished.

Photographs and drawings alike are supported by captions that not only identify the illustration they accompany, but also often provide information not found in the main text. Moreover, the captions often reinforce the text. For example, the caption accompanying the photograph of a sailplane for the article **glider** reads: "The long, thin wings of a glider, or sailplane, enable the craft to remain aloft by soaring on rising air currents. Gliders, the first heavier-than-air vehicles to achieve sustained flight, are flown today both for recreation and as a competitive sport." Captions that accompany technical drawings and cross-section diagrams frequently identify and explain various numbered elements in the illustration.

The *Academic American* contains over 1,000 maps covering all the continents and countries of the world, all U. S. states and Canadian provinces, and nearly 50 of the world's major cities. In addition, there are hundreds of historical and thematic maps. In their clarity, currency, and accuracy of detail, the maps in the *AAE* (created by the cartographers of Rand McNally, R. R. Donnelley Cartographic, Lothar Roth and Associates, and the Arete/Grolier staff) are second to none.

Standardized "fact boxes" accompany entries on individual nations, states, Canadian provinces, and U. S. presidents, presenting important statistical and general information on the subject. These features are well designed and up-to-date. Tables, graphs, and lists accompany other entries where pertinent, providing the reader with an accessible source of basic information.

Foreign or difficult entry words are immediately followed by a phonetic pronunciation. The *AAE* uses a pronunciation system similar to that used by *Time* magazine. For example, the pronunciation for **Agamemnon** is given as *ag-uh-mem'-nahn*; the pronunciation for **Gibraltar** is given as *juh-brawl'-tur*.

Selected bibliographies accompany about 40 percent of all entries. According to the editors, the bibliographies are intended "to furnish a well-chosen list of standard and recently published works to which readers may turn for further information or additional development of particular points of view. Leading textbooks, paperbacks, and recordings are included, as well as occasional periodical references." However, the editors note that "we have not attempted, especially in science, to furnish the most definitive work in the field if, in our opinion, that work would be well beyond the comprehension of the intended reader. . . . [E]very effort has been made to refer to books currently in print." In general, the bibliographies are up-to-date and diverse. However, as they are not annotated, the reader cannot tell which titles might be most appropriate to his or her needs. Moreover, unlike COLLIER'S and WORLD BOOK, the bibliographies do not distinguish between books that are appropriate for students and those that are more suited to adult readers, an omission that may limit their usefulness.

X. Format

The 21-volume *Academic American Encyclopedia* comes in one print format and in several electronic formats. (For information on the electronic formats, see pages 88–91.) Like the NEW STANDARD ENCYCLOPEDIA and WORLD BOOK, among others, volumes in the *AAE* are arranged by letter. That is (with the exception of entries beginning with A, C, and S, which are spread over two volumes each), entries for each letter are contained within a single volume. Some volumes contain all the entries for two, three, or four letters.

The typeface is also worthy of comment. Apart from FUNK & WAGNALLS NEW ENCYCLOPEDIA, the *AAE* is the only encyclopedia to use sans serif typeface, which has a lighter, more functional look than the traditional typefaces used by other encyclopedias. Some readers, however, find this typeface more difficult to read. The relatively small 8 on 9 point type size may also discourage younger readers. The *AAE* is the only encyclopedia to use a "ragged," rather than a justified, right-hand margin.

Each volume is bound in a durable blue and red McCain Sewn, Lexotone binding that should stand up well to frequent use. The paper quality is good. The encyclopedia's title and the volume number and letter are stamped in gold lettering on the spine and front of each volume. The entire set takes up slightly more than two feet of horizontal shelf space.

XI. Other Opinions

ARBA 81 (Janet H. Littlefield): "[*Academic American*] features higher coverage of the sciences than other general encyclopedias. . . . Orientation of the encyclopedia is international, stressing coverage of Asia, Africa, and South America, as well as North America and Europe. Coverage of geography, especially, is less than in other encyclopedias, necessitating the elimination of many smaller American cities from consideration."

College and Research Libraries, January 1982 (Wendy Pradt Lougee): "*Academic American Encyclopedia* . . . appears to have a competitive edge in terms of currency, contemporary biography, and graphics. It is well researched, well written, and a strikingly attractive set. In comparison to similar multivolume encyclopedias, *AAE* is noticeably more compact. . . . Its short entry format . . . makes it particularly appropriate for library 'ready reference' collections. . . . The text has a reasonable level of technical and scholarly sophistication, but maintains accessibility as well. . . . It is neither elementary nor overwhelming. . . . Clearly the articles can best serve as aids in definition and as starting places for further investigation. Although *AAE*'s brevity may fail to capture adequately the nuances that only length can bring to a subject, its format does provide quick and easy access to concise information. One must rely,

however, on the index and textual cross-references to maintain the integrity of the overall coverage of a topic."

Wilson Library Journal, February 1982 (James Rettig): "*Academic American*'s strengths are its currency, its accessibility, and its graphics. . . . No other English-language, general encyclopedia has graphics comparable to [*AAE*'s]. . . . For ready-reference and fact-finding purposes, *Academic American* is the best of the general encyclopedias. However, as a source for broad industry information or as an overview on any but the narrowest subjects, others—notably BRITANNICA, AMERICANA, and COLLIER'S—are superior even if not as current. . . . High school, public, and academic libraries should have this [set] to complement other encyclopedias."

Library Journal, May 15, 1982: "The *AAE* is a superior, short-article encyclopedia. The *AAE*'s strengths are its objective treatment of controversial subjects, its coverage of science, and its articles on contemporary people and events. The *AAE*'s more than 16,000 photographs, maps, diagrams, and drawings, plus its general layout, make it the most visually pleasing general encyclopedia on the market. . . . Librarians will find it useful for ready reference questions."

ARBA 84 (G. Edward Evans): "None of the other encyclopedias packs as much information into as little space as does *AAE*. . . . Brevity does have a price, however, and a student certainly would have to consult other encyclopedias to get a full sense of interrelationships within an area. Users may decide it is better to start with longer articles, such as those in AMERICANA, WORLD BOOK, or COLLIER'S, than to begin with *AAE* and then move on to those other encyclopedias before getting to primary sources. . . . Overall, *AAE* is a sound purchase for high school and undergraduate libraries for use as a ready-reference tool. It cannot be thought of as a replacement for WORLD BOOK, AMERICANA, or COLLIER'S . . . but rather as a supplement to these works. It is a good buy for the money, but it does need to be used with caution."

Booklist (*Reference Books Bulletin*), November 15, 1986: "Because of its recent creation . . ., and since it is supported by Grolier's aggressive revision program, *AAE* is one of the most up-to-date encyclopedias in the world. . . . It is hard to find an area where *AAE* is not up-to-date. . . . Because *AAE* is such a new encyclopedia, it is not burdened with a legacy of dated photographs. . . . *Academic American Encyclopedia* remains one of the best English-language encyclopedias for junior high, high school, college, and adult use. If Grolier continues its program of updating the accurate, excellently illustrated contents, this encyclopedia will be one of the premier works of its kind for many years to come.''

XII. Summary

The newest multivolume encyclopedia on the market, and the first to use computer technology in storing and collating information and in typesetting, the *Academic American* garners top honors as an up-to-date source of basic factual information. It covers many topics of contemporary interest not included in other encyclopedias, and with noteworthy accuracy. In short, the *AAE* is an outstanding ready-reference encyclopedia, especially in its coverage of science, technology, and contemporary biography.

Nevertheless, because its articles are limited in depth, the *AAE* cannot be recommended as a first choice for most families with school-age children. Many users will find that the science entries are written at too advanced a level to be helpful to the average layperson, student or adult. However, school and public libraries will find it an excellent source of ready-reference answers to specific questions from patrons. It is highly factual, accurate, current, and objective, and its outstanding illustrations and maps are a decided plus.

Academic American is not a direct competitor to any other encyclopedia now on the market. Its entries are briefer and less discursive than those in COLLIER'S, ENCYCLOPEDIA AMERICANA, and NEW BRITANNICA. At the same time, its reading level is more difficult than that of WORLD BOOK, although it is visually similar. The prospective purchaser's decision may depend upon whether a good "support" encyclopedia is needed to supplement a main encyclopedia. The *AAE*'s excellent coverage of science and technology topics and its currency may be deciding factors. The *AAE* costs $850 to individuals and $650 to institutions—a reasonable price at current market rates.

Individuals wishing to purchase the *Academic American Encyclopedia* may contact the publisher, Grolier Incorporated, at Sherman Turnpike, Danbury, CT 06816, or telephone (800) 243-7256. Schools and libraries should address their orders to Grolier Educational Corporation at the same address or phone number.

For information about the online and CD-ROM versions of the *AAE*, consult the reviews that follow.

Academic American Encyclopedia (online)

Facts at a Glance

Full Title: **Academic American Encyclopedia** (online version).
Publisher: Grolier Incorporated, Sherman Turnpike, Danbury, CT 06816. Produced by Grolier Electronic Publishing, Inc., 95 Madison Avenue, New York, NY 10016.
Editors: Bernard S. Cayne, Editorial Director; K. Anne Ranson, Editor-in-Chief.
Online Vendors: Bibliographic Retrieval Services; CompuServe; Dialog; Dow Jones News/Retrieval; IHS Online; InfoMaster; QuantumLink; Startext; The Source; VU/TEXT. See list of Publishers and Distributors for addresses and phone numbers.
Copyright: 1987.

Number of Entries: over 28,600.
Number of Words: over 9,000,000.
Number of Cross-references: over 67,000.
No index in online version.

Intended Users: upper elementary grades through adult.
Price: Each online service has its own pricing structure. In general, the *AAE* is offered either on a subscription basis or at an hourly royalty rate.
Revised quarterly.

I. Introduction

The online version of the *Academic American Encyclopedia* contains the same text as recent editions of the print version, so the two are closely similar in their contents and approach. (For fuller information, see the review that begins on page 80.) But the online version does not include any of the finding devices, notably the index, of the print version. Nor does it include any of the print edition's many illustrations.

II. Accessibility

The online version of the *Academic American Encyclopedia* is carried by several vendors of online database services, including Bibliographic Retrieval Services, Inc., CompuServe, Inc., Dialog Information Services, Inc., Dow Jones News/Retrieval, and VU/TEXT Information Services, Inc. It is also available through services that package access to the vendors, such as InfoMaster (a feature of Western Union's EasyLink), which was used to conduct this review. The user cannot access the *AAE* directly, and without direct access the user's experience of the encyclopedia will depend somewhat on the interface provided by the particular vendor. Some are probably a bit swifter or more flexible than others. For example, BRS, Dialog, VU/TEXT, Data Star, and The Source all provide full-text searching. The Source also allows users to search by article headings alone. The other services that carry *AAE* online permit searching by partial or full article headings only. This is the case with InfoMaster.

Accessing information in the *AAE* usually entails the following steps:

I

1. Boot system
2. Load communications program
3. Dial vendor or service
4. Connect, give user ID
(5. Select vendor if a service is used)

II

1. Select database
2. Select topic
3. Conduct database search
4. Display text
5. Respond to prompt for next action

With InfoMaster, the final choice takes the user all the way back to II.1, reasonably supposing that the next search may require a different database. The time required between a "hit" (a match between the search string and an entry in the database) and the text display depends on the length of the entry: the lengthier entries take considerably longer. Even for a short entry such as **Ty Cobb**, however, section II takes about two minutes. Section I takes about three minutes, so from cold boot to display of the entry can take at least five minutes, by which time the user is as grouchy as dour old baseball Titan Cobb—and with far fewer hits to show for it. However, the reader should note that other online/videotex networks may allow a more expeditious search than is possible with InfoMaster.

III. Locating Information

The index that occupies all of Volume 21 of the print *AAE* and is crucially important to an entry-specific encyclopedia such as this one, is not available in the online version. Rather, with services that do not allow full-text searching, the user locates information on a given topic by searching for the entry title, in effect attempting to reconstruct the table of contents *verbatim* by guesswork. A search for **Meniere's Dis-**ease was unsuccessful when it tried "Meniere" as the search word, and again when it used the Boolean string "ears AND disease." The correct entry titles are **Meniere's Disease** and **Ear Disease**; the latter includes a cross-reference to the former (but not vice versa).

The entire text of the *AAE* resides in the database, so in theory it should be possible to carry out a thorough and efficient electronic search by using logical operators. In actuality, this is possible only with those vendors that offer full-text searching. Otherwise, online searches do not explore the text of the entries, just the entry titles; and they provide a hit only on an absolute match. If the search does not provide a hit, the user must expend at least two minutes retracing the way through a succession of menus back to the desired topic.

IV. Cost

All the while the meter is ticking. As an example, InfoMaster charges 15¢ per minute for connection through a local network node (35¢ for a WATS connection), plus an $8 per topic search fee (waived if no hits are made). That can be a high price for the seven-line entry on **Meniere's Disease** which, like many of the shorter entries, includes no bibliography. Other services have comparable rates. Under an FCC proposal, connection fees would increase by $4 or $5 per hour. Even at current rates, a hundred average searches of the online *AAE* will pay for the print version. Grolier reports that the *AAE* online is presently offered "either on a subscription basis or at an hourly royalty rate."

V. Currency

In theory, an online database can readily be updated; that is why the *Oxford English Dictionary* is going online, and why many library catalogues are following suit. Print, whether encyclopedia volume or catalog card, resists change. Electronic databases, by contrast, merge and purge effortlessly.

The publisher claims that "the online edition . . . is updated four times each year and includes information that is not found in the print edition." While this is undoubtedly the case, as of mid-June 1987 the electronic version of the *AAE* actually appeared far *less* up-to-date than the 1987 print version in many areas. For example, it did not mention the following items new in the 1987 print version: the antiviral drug AZT for AIDS; Manuel Puig; the nuclear disaster at Chernobyl; privatization; or President Reagan's approval of the tax reform measure, or his Iceland summit meeting with Mikhail Gorbachev (both October 1986), or indeed anything later than his cancer surgery in July 1985. On the other hand, the online version did mention that "the first U.S. hospital devoted solely to AIDS treatment and research opened in Houston, Texas, in 1986," and it included the entry on **Corazon Aquino** that is new to the 1987 print edition. On the whole, the online version appears to be a blend of the 1987 and earlier print editions.

The advantage of the print edition over the electronic version can be reversed, and perhaps it shortly will. The editors have used advanced computer technology in preparing the print version, so its up-to-date information must exist on electronic media somewhere; the job of transferring it to the online databases should not be too difficult. But the theoretical advantage of electronic information storage and retrieval is not *automatically* realized in practice, as the *AAE* amply showed at the time of this review.

VI. Accuracy, Objectivity, and Clarity

In terms of accuracy and objectivity, the online *AAE* bears a close resemblance to its justly admired print namesake. But in the matter of clarity the electronic version is at a considerable disadvantage, because it includes no illustrations; Grolier acknowledges that "current technology precludes the delivery of high-quality graphics." The print version contains some 16,650 pictures, three-quarters in color and many with useful captions. These illustrations occupy one-third of the set's available space, enabling the reader to, in the publisher's words, "acquire a basic comprehension of the subject as well as considerable factual information by studying the illustrations and captions alone." The publisher's further claim that "each [illustration] was carefully selected to explain, support, or expand ideas in the text" only shows how devastating the loss really is, for the online version gives no evidence that the entries were rewritten to compensate for the absence of the illustrations.

Digitizing scanners should enable the publisher to incorporate the graphics into the online database, where modern high-speed modems along with EGA or VGA boards and monitors will enable the user to retrieve and display them. Such developments would help put the online *AAE* in an advanced technical position comparable to that occupied by the print version.

VII. Summary

The print *AAE* has been chiefly praised as a ready-reference tool, especially for its index, its graphics, and its inclusion of the latest information. In comparison, the online edition must be judged a crippled version at best. The user in search of ready reference

must leap numerous electronic hurdles before even arriving at the database; electronic search methods could, but do not, make up for the loss of the print version's 200,000-entry index; computed at 1,000 words per picture, the nonillustrated online version is some 16,650,000 words' worth less informative than the print edition; and the electronic information is often older than the print.

That said, however, it should be noted that of the three online encyclopedias currently available to library and home subscribers (the other two are EVERYMAN'S ENCYCLOPAEDIA and the KUSSMAUL ENCYCLOPEDIA), the *AAE* is the only one backed by the resources of a major American reference publisher (Grolier). It is likely that the company and its electronic publishing division will continue to update the database and improve accessibility.

Individuals and institutions interested in acquiring the *AAE* online may contact any of the vendors listed in "Facts at a Glance" at the head of this review; addresses and phone numbers are listed in the Publishers and Distributors appendix beginning on page 595. Since services and charges vary from vendor to vendor, consumers are advised to examine the total package offered by vendors before subscribing.

Academic American (CD-ROM)

Facts at a Glance

Full Title: **Academic American Encyclopedia** (CD-ROM version).

Alternate Title: The Electronic Encyclopedia.

Publisher: Grolier Incorporated, Sherman Turnpike, Danbury, CT 06816.

Editors: Bernard S. Cayne, Editorial Director; K. Anne Ranson, Editor-in-Chief.

Copyright: 1987.

Number of Volumes: 1 Compact Disc.
Number of Contributors: 2,300.
Number of Entries: 28,600.
Number of Words: 9,040,000.
Number of Cross-references: 67,000.
Number of Indexes: 1.
Number of Index Entries: 200,000.

Intended Readership: upper elementary grades through adult.
Price: $299.
Sold directly by the publisher.
Revised annually.

The CD-ROM version of the *Academic American Encyclopedia*—popularly known as *The Electronic Encyclopedia*—was introduced by Grolier, Inc., in January, 1986. It contains the same text as the 20-volume print edition on one compact disc less than 4 3/4″ in diameter. However, it lacks the illustrations that are a major strength of the print edition.

The library survey conducted for Bowker's *Reference Books for Young Readers* indicates that only 6 percent of the libraries surveyed as yet use online or, in some cases, CD-ROM encyclopedias. Overall, very few libraries possess the technology necessary to use these electronic information systems. The feeling among most librarians seems to be that a CD-ROM encyclopedia does not match the print version in accessibility. Today, most students have some training in the use of computers from an early age, but once the novelty of the computer has worn off, most express a preference for a book version of a large reference work. Books have the advantage of being portable: the student can sit down at a desk with a book and take notes, whereas in order to use *The Electronic Encyclopedia* the student must be present at the computer. Furthermore, as W. F. Bolton, professor of English at Rutgers University and an expert on electronic reference sources, has noted, electronic encyclopedias do not easily allow the serendipitous experiences that are inherent in the use of encyclopedias in book format.

The Electronic Encyclopedia does possess two advantages over the print edition. Most obviously, with its entire contents contained on one small disc, it takes up much less space than does a multivolume print encyclopedia—in fact, it quite literally takes up next to no space at all. And its price ($299) is considerably less expensive than the school and library discount price of $650 for the print version. In comparison with the *Academic American* online, it is fairly accessible, and bypasses many of the problems that make online reference works difficult to use. The user need not go through all the steps of dialing a vendor and selecting the reference information from a menu of different services, as is the case with all online encyclopedias. And there are no online charges. This can represent considerable savings over the long run.

However, the hardware needed to drive and read the CD-ROM version is still prohibitively expensive for most institutions. Unless this equipment is already in place, or unless the institution is already planning to install it to accommodate a wide range of CD-ROM software, the initial investment required will simply be beyond the average school or public library's resources. The most advanced research libraries in the country are only now beginning to test or use this technology. In short, the idea of the CD-ROM encyclopedia is tremendously exciting, but its practicability for the typical library's general reference services will remain in doubt for some time.

According to the publisher, the CD-ROM *Academic American* is accompanied by "the Knowledge Retrieval System, a powerful, full-text search and retrieval program that allows the user to search for any word or combination of words in seconds." The system's full retrieval program incorporates Boolean logic and is screen-prompted. Grolier notes further that "search results can be printed out or saved to disk in one of three types of word processing files."

More than one half of the CD memory is occupied by an extensive index. *School Library Journal* (June-July 1987) reports that this index "allows users to locate a listing of every entry containing a reference to a particular subject. A further refinement allows a user to narrow any topic by employing two search terms to get a display of entries mentioning, for example, both religion and China. Obviously, this capability saves a great deal of time." It also gives the CD-ROM version a distinct advantage over the online version, which does not have this capability, where accessibility is concerned.

For complete information about the contents of *The Electronic Encyclopedia*, see the review of the print edition of the ACADEMIC AMERICAN ENCYCLOPEDIA that begins on page 80.

The Electronic Encyclopedia can be ordered directly from the publisher, Grolier Incorporated, Sherman Turnpike, Danbury, CT 06816, telephone (800) 243-7256. Grolier can also arrange a demonstration of the system.

Childcraft, The How and Why Library

Facts at a Glance

Full Title: **Childcraft, The How and Why Library.**
Publisher: World Book, Inc.
Editors: William H. Nault, Robert O. Zeleny,
   Dominic Miccoles, and Harry R. Snowden.
Copyright: 1985.

Number of Volumes: 15.
Number of Entries: 3,000.
Number of Words: 750,000.
Number of Pages: 5,000.
Number of Indexes: 18.
Number of Index Entries: 20,000.
Number of Illustrations: 4,500.

Intended Readership: preschool through
    elementary grades.
Trim Size: 7¼″ × 9¾″.

Price: $199 plus 14.50 shipping and handling; $159
    when purchased with *World Book*; $170 to
    schools and libraries.
Sold directly by the publisher.
ISBN 0-7166-0187-7.
Revised periodically.

I. Introduction

Childcraft, the How and Why Library is a 15-volume
resource set designed for young children. According
to the publisher, "While the set is especially appropriate for early childhood education, *Childcraft* also
appeals to the older child who needs high-interest,
easy-to-read material." As the title suggests, *The How
and Why Library* is intended to provide answers to
the questions young children ask. The set is intended
for preschool through elementary school. Reading
levels range from fourth through sixth grades according to the Fry Readability Scale, although the
profuse illustrations do make the set appropriate for
younger children.

II. Authority

Childcraft is published by World Book, Inc., a firm
respected for such reference works as the WORLD
BOOK ENCYCLOPEDIA and WORLD BOOK DICTION-
ARY. The work originated in 1934 as a seven-volume
set largely about, rather than for, children. Since its
first edition, it has undergone substantial revision.
When World Book acquired the six-volume *How and
Why Library* in 1964 both the title and the scope of
the set were altered. Over the years it has been translated into French, Spanish, Swedish, Hebrew, Japanese, and several other languages.

William H. Nault, an experienced authority on
children's books who also serves as publisher, heads
a four-member editorial advisory board. Robert O.
Zeleny, Editor-in-Chief of WORLD BOOK, serves in
the same capacity for *Childcraft*. The library consultants' committee consists of six public and school
library professionals, while the publisher also maintains a small staff of editors, artists, and researchers.
Volumes 4 through 14 were published chiefly by
members of this staff and are unsigned. Volumes 1
through 3 contain the signed work of many well-
known writers of children's literature, including such
Newbery Award winners and Caldecott medalists as
Beverly Cleary, Scott O'Dell, Robert McCloskey,

and Ezra Jack Keats. In addition, many of the illustrations are the work of Caldecott Award-winning
artists.

Volume 15, the Guide for Parents, was prepared
with assistance from more than 25 physicians, psy-
chiatrists, dentists, and educators who are acknowledged in the volume's frontmatter.

III. Scope

Childcraft contains some 3,000 entries of varying
length. Most articles in Volumes 4 through 14 take
up approximately two pages, including illustrations,
and contain an average of 250 words. Unlike the
other sets for young children evaluated in this Buying
Guide, many of the illustrations in this set are captioned.

Each volume covers a broad subject area. Volumes 1 through 3 are collections of children's literature, both traditional and contemporary, by noted
authors, illustrators, and poets such as Laura Ingalls
Wilder, Kenneth Grahame, A. A. Milne, Maurice
Sendak, Arnold Lobel, John Ciardi, and Sara Teas-
dale. The rhymes, fables, and tales in Volume 1 are
intended to be read aloud to preschoolers; primary
grade children may be able to read the stories and
poems in Volumes 2 and 3 by themselves.

Volumes 4 through 7 are devoted to science and
technology and are titled, respectively, World and
Space, About Animals, The Green Kingdom, and
How Things Work.

The next three volumes cover social studies topics.
Volume 8, About Us, containing articles about families, religions, rules and laws, housing, and foods,
explains how diverse cultures share similar needs and
interests. Volume 9, Holidays and Birthdays, organized by month, explains more than 100 holidays.
The first section of the volume discusses holidays,
birthdays, anniversaries, calendar systems, and how
the days of the week were named. Each succeeding
section opens with a monthly calendar noting the
birthdays of famous musicians, writers, political figures, inventors, and others. The May calendar, for
example, includes the birthdays of Golda Meir, Hor-
ace Mann, Nellie Bly, Robert Browning, and Gabriel
Fahrenheit, among others. The calendar is followed
by an informative article telling how the month was
named, as well as articles about holidays celebrated
world-wide during that month.

The publisher accurately describes Volume 10,
Places to Know, as "a travel book for children." The
volume contains more than 150 entries about historic
places, marketplaces, seats of government, museums, architectural and archaeological wonders.

Volumes 11 (Make and Do) and 12 (Look and Learn) cover creative activities and the arts. Make and Do provides instructions for projects using paper, paint, papier mâché, clay, and wood. The woodworking section describes the tools and skills needed for woodworking, and offers simple instructions for making a toy tugboat and barge, wind chimes, stilts, an African thumb piano, a scooter, and a stool. The book is organized by medium (e.g., clay, wood, paper) or theme (e.g., gifts, nature crafts, puppets). For example "Gifts to Give" tells how to make gift items such as key rings, note boards, and stuffed animals, and concludes with an article on making imaginative gift wraps. Another section contains instructions for making several types of puppets and a puppet stage, and for presenting a play. Group games, card games, pencil and paper games, guessing games, and magic tricks are also described. The volume ends with a 15-page manual for planning a party.

In Volume 12, Look and Learn, children explore how people communicate through colors, gestures, facial expressions, and signs and symbols. This chapter includes a delightful section on cartoonists' symbols, such as the light bulb for an idea, or the cloud over a character's head for unspoken thoughts.

Mathemagic, Volume 13, uses puzzles, humor, number lore, and projects to present topics such as geometry, measurement, probability and the origin of numbers, and discusses the people who work with numbers, such as engineers, physicists, accountants, astronomers, and statisticians. Volume 13 also has two bibliographies: one for 5- through 8-year-olds and another for children in the 9- to 12-year-old group.

Volume 14, About Me, deals sensitively with birth; family, physical, and intellectual growth; and individuality—all topics of great interest to the intended reader.

The final volume, Guide for Parents, provides expert advice to help parents and teachers understand children's problems and concerns. The first of its four sections deals with human growth and development from birth to early adolescence. The second considers special topics such as adoption, divorce, handicaps, and drugs, and includes a list of child welfare organizations in the United States and Canada. The third section, a medical guide, offers practical, authoritative suggestions on caring for a sick child. Its 142 pages discuss childhood illnesses and physical abnormalities, as well as treatments for common childhood diseases and injuries. The final section, a guide and index to *Childcraft*, describes the set's organization and suggests ways of using *Childcraft* with different age groups, from toddler through sixth graders. One part of this section, Curriculum En-

richment Guides, correlates *Childcraft* with the subjects commonly taught in the elementary grades—language arts, mathematics, science, social studies, health, and creative arts. Arranged alphabetically by topic rather than by title of the articles, these guides furnish the volume and page numbers where related articles can be found. The rest of Volume 15 is a General Index (for a complete description see *Accessibility*).

The contents of most volumes are organized in sections. For example, How Things Work is divided into sections on electricity, machines, matter, sound, temperature, and other topics. Each section contains several entries. The section on temperature, titled "Hot and Cold," includes articles about heat produced by friction and the relative heat of objects; an experiment to observe the different speeds at which molecules move; an article explaining how a thermometer works; instructions for making a solid thermometer; articles on heat conduction, ice, and steam; four pages of magic tricks using heat; an article on hot air balloons; an experiment to weigh air; an article on removing heat (refrigeration); a Paiute Indian legend about fire; an article explaining how a picnic cooler works; and an experiment to test heat-saving materials.

Explanatory articles are followed by instructions for a project or experiment. For example, after learning how a thermometer works, the reader learns how to make one. To maintain interest, the factual content of this section is interspersed with several entertaining pages of magic tricks that use scientific principles, and a story about fire.

IV. Currency

According to the publisher, approximately 30 percent of the content is revised in each new edition of *Childcraft*. Over the years, several volumes have been dropped, others added, and some completely revised. Because most of the material is general in nature, currency is not as important a factor in this set as it is in works for older children. Nevertheless, *Childcraft* is noticeably up-to-date. Certain contemporary issues, such as environmental pollution, are treated directly and seriously. In Volume 3, About Animals, this problem is discussed in a concise paragraph:

Animals need clean air and water. Many animals cannot breathe air that has lots of smoke and soot in it. Fish and other animals can't live in lakes and rivers that have lots of garbage and waste materials in them. When oil covers the waters of the ocean, many sea animals and birds are killed. And insect sprays kill other animals besides insects.

Many stories and poems in *Childcraft* reflect the increasing participation of girls in games once played exclusively by boys. For example, in the section of poems about sports in Volume 3, "The Sidewalk Racer" by Lillian Morrison is about skateboarding and "The New Kid" by Mike Makley concerns a baseball player who, it turns out, is a girl.

Childcraft's artwork is often more up-to-date than its photographs, some of which show the short hemlines and bouffant hairdos of the 1960s and 1970s. Many of the set's color photographs, however, are of recent vintage.

V. Accuracy

Frequent revision has enhanced not only the currency but also the accuracy of *Childcraft*'s articles. For example, according to the 1986 edition, the "Dimetredon [a prehistoric reptile] is a puzzle to scientists. It had a big fin like a sail on its back. No one knows what this was for." In the 1987 edition this description has been revised to incorporate new findings:

> Dimetredon had a big fin like a sail on its back. Scientists think the fin helped a Dimetredon warm up or cool off. After a cool night, a stiff, cold Dimetredon might lie with its fin facing the sun, and the fin would get quickly warm. The warmth would spread into Dimetredon's body. But a Dimetredon that was too hot could lie with the thin edge of the fin facing the sun. Then the fin would cool off.

A spot-check by our reviewers of dates in biographical entries, phonetic pronunciations of difficult or unfamiliar words, and other factual material confirmed the overall accuracy of the set.

The following excerpt from Volume 7, How Things Work, is a good example of a concept accurately and plainly stated:

> Noise is hard to stop. Like other sounds, it travels through air and through solid things—even walls. And it bounces off floors, ceilings, or any smooth, hard surface. This makes noisy places even noisier! But some materials actually 'soak up' noise. They absorb sound waves and keep them from traveling. These materials are called insulators (IHN suh LAY tuhrz) because they are sound stoppers.
>
> Inside a building, rugs and curtains soak up sound. The soft threads and tiny air spaces in the material help trap the vibrations.

VI. Accessibility

As noted earlier, *Childcraft* is arranged by topic, each volume dealing with a broad subject. Individual volumes are indexed and Volume 15, Guide for Parents, provides a 112-page general index to the entire set as well as a two-page guide to its use.

Volumes 1, 2, and 3 contain four indexes each: author, title, and subject indexes, plus a first-line index to poetry. The latter is especially useful for young children who may remember how a favorite poem begins but cannot recall the title. The author index lists the author's name in boldface followed by the selections and page numbers, as in this example:

Milne, A. A.
  Furry Bear, 164
  Hoppity, 189

The title index cites titles in boldface followed by the author's name in parentheses and the page numbers, as in the following:

Millions of Cats
  (Wanda Gág), 238

The first-line index alphabetically lists the first lines of all poems in the book, followed by the pages where they can be found. The subject index is useful when trying to locate poems and stories about a particular subject. Subject headings are in boldface, followed by an alphabetical list of related entries and page number citations. For example:

City
  City, 290
  City Lights, 290
  Rosa-Too-Little (story), 287
  Snowy Morning, 291

The indexes for Volumes 4 through 14 are prefaced by detailed yet simple instructions on how to use them. This feature should help young readers learn about indexes and prepare them to use the more complex indexes they will encounter later in advanced reference books.

The General Index in Volume 15 is a comprehensive key to the information in all 15 volumes. However, it does not include the titles of poems in the first three volumes, which are more than adequately indexed in those volumes.

Because different aspects of a subject may be covered in more than one volume, the General Index is an important tool for locating specific information. Boldface entries indicate either general or specific topics. General entries, and some specific, are subdivided to help readers find the exact information they are looking for. As a further aid, identifying labels are often provided in parentheses. A typical specific entry looks like this:

Cortes, Hernando (explorer)
Conquering the Aztecs, **10**/285,
with pictures; **12**/192–193,
with pictures

A typical general listing looks like this:

communication
drum messages, **8**/210–211, with picture
gestures, **8**/200–201, with pictures
history of, **8**/199, with picture
language, **8**/202, with pictures
letter writing, pictures, **8**/214–217
newspapers, **8**/208–209, with pictures
picture signs, **8**/205, with pictures
telephone, pictures, **8**/211
television, **8**/213, with pictures
writing, **8**/206, with pictures
see also **radio**

The "see also" reference at the end of the citation further enhances the set's accessibility.

Because some illustrations extend to the page margin, some pages are unnumbered, which may confuse young readers. This is also the case in YOUNG CHILDREN'S ENCYCLOPEDIA and COMPTON'S PRECYCLOPEDIA.

VII. Clarity

Childcraft is written at an elementary level; its essential points are conveyed with clarity. In their promotional material the publishers suggest that *Childcraft* will often be read aloud to children. Vocabulary throughout the set is appropriate for most elementary school children. Difficult words are usually defined and a phonetic pronunciation supplied, as in this passage: "Then, about three hundred years ago, a man named Christian Huygens invented a clock with a pendulum (PEN juh luhm). A pendulum is a long swinging weight that moves back and forth. With a pendulum, which swings at a steady, even pace, clocks could be made to keep time more accurately."

Sentences and paragraphs are usually short enough for beginning readers to understand the concepts presented, as in the following excerpt:

What makes the light bulb give off light?

If you hold your hand above a light bulb, you'll find a clue. The bulb is hot! When the light is on, electricity runs through a tiny wire inside the bulb. This makes the wire get hot. And when the wire gets hot enough, something begins to happen.

Like everything else, the wire is made of atoms. And in the atoms are electrons. As the wires in the light bulb get hot, the electrons soak up energy. And when they are loaded with energy, they throw it off. The bundles of energy thrown off by the electrons are light.

The bundles of energy have a special name. They are called photons (FOH tahnz). Photo is a word part that means 'light,' and on at the end means 'a bit.' So photons are 'bits of light.'

Another example of clarity is shown by the following instructions for making a Catch-can:

Catch-can is a skill game you can play by yourself. Ask a grown-up to use a hammer and nail to punch a hole in the bottom of a small vegetable or soup can. Thread about 12 inches (30 cm) of string through the hole. Tie a heavy button to each end of the string. Let the string hang down outside the can. Hold the can in your hand. Now swing the string and try to catch it in the can.

The accompanying illustration shows not only the Catch-can itself, but also how the game is played.

Colorful, well-designed layouts and instructive illustrations enhance the entire set. As one reviewer noted in *ARBA 80*, "one should not overlook the effective use of white space, yielding uncluttered pages that direct the eye to visuals or the text," an observation that also applies to the current edition.

Childcraft's clarity becomes particularly evident when the set is compared with its closest competitors, COMPTON'S PRECYCLOPEDIA and YOUNG CHILDREN'S ENCYCLOPEDIA. The following excerpt about Susan B. Anthony is from *Childcraft*:

Susan Anthony was born February 15, 1820. At that time, women had few rights under the law. In most states women could not own property or vote. When Susan Anthony grew up, she worked for equal rights for women—especially the right to vote.

Susan Anthony did not live to see her dream come true. She died in 1906, fourteen years before women won the right to vote.

Compare this with the following passage found in both COMPTON'S PRECYCLOPEDIA and YOUNG

CHILDREN'S ENCYCLOPEDIA, which begins by describing Anthony's attempt to vote in the 1872 presidential election:

> About a dozen women were talking to the voting judges, men who were in charge of making sure that the voting was fair. One of the women was Susan B. Anthony. Even though she was having a very important argument with the men around her, she spoke calmly. Susan B. Anthony and 12 of her friends had come to vote for the next president. . . The voting judge explained that women were simply not allowed to vote. It had always been that way in America. . . Susan B. Anthony worked hard so that women could have all the same rights as men. She gave speeches all around America. She wrote stories for a newspaper. . . These campaigns by Susan B. Anthony made people—both men and women—think more about being fair to women. But it was nearly 50 years before a new law was passed giving all women the right to vote.

In two concise paragraphs, *Childcraft* tells when Anthony lived, what she did, and when. The second selection, with its vague, rambling style, provides little factual information and gives no context for the event.

VIII. Objectivity

Because *Childcraft* does not purport to be a general encyclopedia, the criteria of objectivity that apply to a true encyclopedia are less important here. Nonetheless, reviews of earlier editions criticized the set for its "pervasive middle-class orientation" (Kister, *Best Encyclopedias*, 1986). Our reviewers found, however, that the editors have taken steps to rectify this bias. Members of minority groups appear frequently in the illustrations, and most articles avoid sexual stereotyping.

Childcraft's balance and sensitivity are most readily apparent in two volumes that deal with children and their concerns: Volume 8, About Us, and Volume 14, About Me. The former is about life in different parts of the world and in different cultures. The first entry, "Who Are We?", discusses differences and similarities among people and emphasizes the positive aspects of human diversity:

> . . . Some of us have warm, tan skins like sunlight on sand. Some of us have deep brown skins, like rich chocolate. Some of us have rosy pink skins, the color of the sky at dawn. And some of us have skins that are touched with the red glint of copper or the tawny gleam of gold. We come in many colors, and all the colors are beautiful. . . . We have many different ways of life. We have

> many different beliefs and customs. We like different kinds of foods. We build our houses in different ways. But we're very much alike in many important ways. We must all have food. We all want to be comfortable and happy. We all need love and friendship. . . .

The entry on religion, "We Believe," presents factual, straightforward information about the world's major religions and religious practices. There are individual stories about Hinduism, Judaism, Christianity (Roman Catholicism, Eastern Orthodoxy, and Protestant denominations), Buddhism, Islam, Shinto, and animism. The feature "Where Did We Come From?" tells nine stories (based on various religious traditions, myths, and science) about the creation of the world and the first people. These features illustrate the diversity of the human experience simply, effectively, and without bias. Throughout the volume, photographs give the reader positive impressions of life in various parts of the world.

Similarly, the text of Volume 14, About Me, is sensitive to the differing circumstances of contemporary families. The section "Me and My Family" tells that some children live with their natural parents, others with the parents who adopted them, and some with a natural parent and a step-parent. Others, it says, may live with a single parent. The text emphasizes the positive aspects of both traditional and nontraditional family life. Some of the older photographs in this volume do reflect a white middle-class norm. The great majority of photos, however, are contemporary and show children and adults of diverse backgrounds in a wide variety of non-stereotypic settings. The larger message of the volume is that it is acceptable for a child to be "different" from others, that "there's nobody exactly like me."

IX. Special Features

Childcraft contains several special features. The medical guide, curriculum guides, and general index are all contained in the Guide for Parents, itself a special feature. (See also *Scope* and *Accessibility*.)

Six of the volumes (4, 5, 7, 8, 13, and 14) contain **New Words** lists. The list in the Green Kingdom begins with these instructions: "Here are some of the words you've met in this book. They may be new to you. Many of them are words you'll meet again in other books—so they're good words to know. Some of them are flower names that may be hard for you to pronounce. Next to each word you are shown how to say it correctly: acid (AS ihd). Put the emphasis on the part of the word shown in capital letters. Under each word, the meaning is given in a complete sentence."

Following the text in Volumes 7 and 13 are two lists of **Books to Read,** one for ages 5-8 and the other for ages 9-12. These bibliographies enable children to investigate further their interest in physical science and mathematics.

Two special features of the literature volumes are worth noting. Several stories are followed by paragraphs referring readers to additional stories by the same author. Others are followed by descriptive paragraphs suggesting similar stories that the child might enjoy.

Several stories are preceded by biographical notes on the authors.

Each year, the publisher offers a supplementary volume, *The Childcraft Annual.* Instead of updating the set, the *Annual* gathers articles and stories on a particular topic of interest to children. The 1986 *Annual*, for example, is titled "Mysteries and Fantasies."

X. Other Opinions

ARBA 80 (Lillian Biermann Wehmeyer): "*Childcraft* is best seen as a motivator, designed to evoke a sense of wonder, rather than as an information source. Still, because it is generally readable and accurate, the set is a good starting place for primary-grade readers. . . [the set] enables children to see classifications and relationships, yet avoids the common failing of 'too much, too soon.' "

Reference Books for Children, 1981 (Carolyn Sue Peterson, Ann D. Fenton): "While *Childcraft* is not an encyclopedia, it contains such a wealth of material to teachers, parents, and children that it should definitely be considered as a basic reference source. Its information and appeal easily justify the expense of a circulating set or sets plus one for reference."

Kenneth Kister, *Best Encyclopedias*, Oryx, 1986: "[*Childcraft*'s illustrations are] first-rate, and the writing style is captivating."

XI. Summary

Childcraft is a 15-volume collection of factual articles, literature, and activities designed to motivate young children and some older ones who need high-interest, easy-to-read material. The writing is clear, concise, and appropriate for young readers without being too simple or coy. When adults read to children, adults are apt to find the selections appealing and interesting.

Extensive indexing makes the content of *Childcraft* readily accessible, and frequent revisions keep the set current and pertinent to the interests of its

intended readers. The set's sturdy binding, high-quality paper, and washable covers will withstand heavy use.

Although *Childcraft* lacks some of the encyclopedic features of YOUNG CHILDREN'S ENCYCLOPEDIA and COMPTON'S PRECYCLOPEDIA, its abundant factual information and creative activities make the set one that children can use for a significantly longer time. Priced at about $200, between YOUNG CHILDREN'S ENCYCLOPEDIA at $149 and COMPTON'S PRECYCLOPEDIA at $249, *Childcraft* is a good buy. The set is highly recommended for school, library, and home use.

Collier's Encyclopedia

Facts at a Glance

Full Title: **Collier's Encyclopedia**.
Publisher: Macmillan Educational Company, 866 Third Avenue, New York, NY 10022.
Editors: William D. Halsey, Editorial Director; Emanuel Friedman, Editor-in-Chief.
Copyright: 1986.

Number of Volumes: 24.
Number of Contributors: 4,600.
Number of Entries: 25,000.
Number of Pages: 19,750.
Number of Words: 21,000,000.
Number of Maps: 1,600.
Number of Cross-references: 13,000.
Number of Indexes: 1.
Number of Illustrations: 1,750 color; 15,600 black-and-white.
Trim Size: 8¼″ × 10⅝″.

Intended Readership: high school through adult.
Price: $1,099.50 to individuals; $744 plus $20 shipping to schools and libraries ($709 plus shipping for two or more sets).
Sold door-to-door, directly to libraries and schools, and by direct mail.
Revised annually.

I. Introduction

Collier's Encyclopedia is a 24-volume general reference work described by its editors as "a scholarly, systematic, continuously revised summary of the knowledge that is most significant to mankind." Its articles cover "the curricula of colleges and secondary schools, as well as the upper grades." However, while the material is intended to be within the grasp

Collier's Encyclopedia

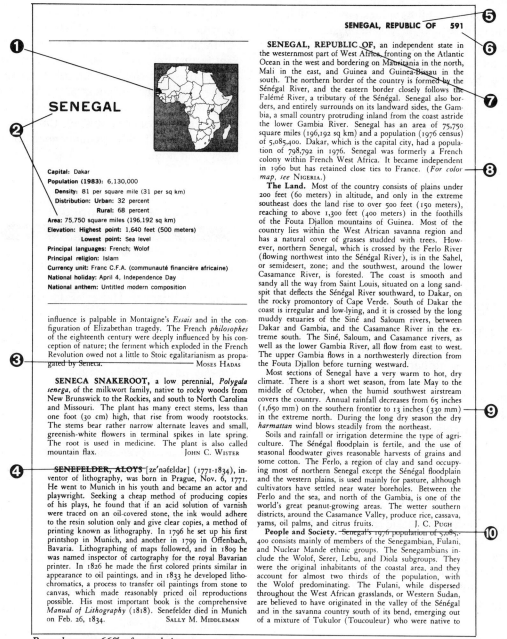

❶ SENEGAL

❷

Capital: Dakar
Population (1983): 6,130,000
Density: 81 per square mile (31 per sq km)
Distribution: Urban: 32 percent
Rural: 68 percent
Area: 75,750 square miles (196,192 sq km)
Elevation: Highest point: 1,640 feet (500 meters)
Lowest point: Sea level
Principal languages: French; Wolof
Principal religion: Islam
Currency unit: Franc C.F.A. (communauté financière africaine)
National holiday: April 4, Independence Day
National anthem: Untitled modern composition

influence is palpable in Montaigne's *Essais* and in the configuration of Elizabethan tragedy. The French *philosophes*
of the eighteenth century were deeply influenced by his conception of nature; the ferment which exploded in the French
Revolution owed not a little to Stoic egalitarianism as propa-
❸ gated by Seneca. ——————————— Moses Hadas

SENECA SNAKEROOT, a low perennial, *Polygala
senega*, of the milkwort family, native to rocky woods from
New Brunswick to the Rockies, and south to North Carolina
and Missouri. The plant has many erect stems, less than
one foot (30 cm) high, that rise from woody rootstocks.
The stems bear rather narrow alternate leaves and small,
greenish-white flowers in terminal spikes in late spring.
The root is used in medicine. The plant is also called
mountain flax. John C. Wister

❹ **SENEFELDER, ALOYS** [ze'nəfeldər] (1771-1834), inventor of lithography, was born in Prague, Nov. 6, 1771.
He went to Munich in his youth and became an actor and
playwright. Seeking a cheap method of producing copies
of his plays, he found that if an acid solution of varnish
were traced on an oil-covered stone, the ink would adhere
to the resin solution only and give clear copies, a method of
printing known as lithography. In 1796 he set up his first
printshop in Munich, and another in 1799 in Offenbach,
Bavaria. Lithographing of maps followed, and in 1809 he
was named inspector of cartography for the royal Bavarian
printer. In 1826 he made the first colored prints similar in
appearance to oil paintings, and in 1833 he developed litho-
chromatics, a process to transfer oil paintings from stone to
canvas, which made reasonably priced oil reproductions
possible. His most important book is the comprehensive
Manual of Lithography (1818). Senefelder died in Munich
on Feb. 26, 1834. Sally M. Middleman

❺ SENEGAL, REPUBLIC OF   591 **❻**

SENEGAL, REPUBLIC OF, an independent state in **❻**
the westernmost part of West Africa, fronting on the Atlantic
Ocean in the west and bordering on Mauritania in the north,
Mali in the east, and Guinea and Guinea-Bissau in the
south. The northern border of the country is formed by the
Sénégal River, and the eastern border closely follows the **❼**
Falémé River, a tributary of the Sénégal. Senegal also borders, and entirely surrounds on its landward sides, the Gambia, a small country protruding inland from the coast astride
the lower Gambia River. Senegal has an area of 75,750
square miles (196,192 sq km) and a population (1976 census)
of 5,085,400. Dakar, which is the capital city, had a population of 798,792 in 1976. Senegal was formerly a French
colony within French West Africa. It became independent
in 1960 but has retained close ties to France. (*For color* **❽**
map, see Nigeria.)
The Land. Most of the country consists of plains under
200 feet (60 meters) in altitude, and only in the extreme
southeast does the land rise to over 500 feet (150 meters),
reaching to above 1,300 feet (400 meters) in the foothills
of the Fouta Djallon mountains of Guinea. Most of the
country lies within the West African savanna region and
has a natural cover of grasses studded with trees. However, northern Senegal, which is crossed by the Ferlo River
(flowing northwest into the Sénégal River), is in the Sahel,
or semidesert, zone; and the southwest, around the lower
Casamance River, is forested. The coast is smooth and
sandy all the way from Saint Louis, situated on a long sand-
spit that deflects the Sénégal River southward, to Dakar, on
the rocky promontory of Cape Verde. South of Dakar the
coast is irregular and low-lying, and it is crossed by the long
muddy estuaries of the Siné and Saloum rivers, between
Dakar and Gambia, and the Casamance River in the extreme south. The Siné, Saloum, and Casamance rivers, as
well as the lower Gambia River, all flow from east to west.
The upper Gambia flows in a northwesterly direction from
the Fouta Djallon before turning westward.
Most sections of Senegal have a very warm to hot, dry
climate. There is a short wet season, from late May to the
middle of October, when the humid southwest airstream
covers the country. Annual rainfall decreases from 65 inches
(1,650 mm) on the southern frontier to 13 inches (330 mm) **❾**
in the extreme north. During the long dry season the dry
harmattan wind blows steadily from the northeast.
Soils and rainfall or irrigation determine the type of agriculture. The Sénégal floodplain is fertile, and the use of
seasonal floodwater gives reasonable harvests of grains and
some cotton. The Ferlo, a region of clay and sand occupying most of northern Senegal except the Sénégal floodplain
and the western plains, is used mainly for pasture, although
cultivators have settled near water boreholes. Between the
Ferlo and the sea, and north of the Gambia, is one of the
world's great peanut-growing areas. The wetter southern
districts, around the Casamance Valley, produce rice, cassava,
yams, oil palms, and citrus fruits. J. C. Pugh
People and Society. Senegal's 1976 population of 5,085,- **❿**
400 consists mainly of members of the Senegambian, Fulani,
and Nuclear Mande ethnic groups. The Senegambians include the Wolof, Serer, Lebu, and Diola subgroups. They
were the original inhabitants of the coastal area, and they
account for almost two thirds of the population, with
the Wolof predominating. The Fulani, while dispersed
throughout the West African grasslands, or Western Sudan,
are believed to have originated in the valley of the Sénégal
and in the savanna country south of its bend, emerging out
of a mixture of Tukulor (Toucouleur) who were native to

Page shown at 66% of actual size.

❶ Location map: Collier's contains 1,600 maps in all.

❷ Nation and state entries include a "fact box" showing the place's location and presenting basic statistics about geography, population, and economy.

❸ Contributor's credit: Collier's has more than 4,600 contributors. Virtually all articles are signed.

❹ Pronunciation: Foreign or other difficult entry words are followed by phonetic pronunciation.

❺ Guide Words

❻ Page number

❼ Main entry: Collier's Encyclopedia contains 25,000 entries, arranged alphabetically, letter-by-letter. Entry words are printed in bold-face capitals.

❽ Cross-reference: Collier's contains 13,000 cross-references. Titles of cross-referenced entries are printed large and small caps.

❾ Metric approximation are given for customary measures.

❿ Article subhead

of readers in "the upper grades," the editors state that "an attempt is made to prepare the reader by references to preliminary reading in more elementary related articles." This suggests that portions of the text may be somewhat advanced for many secondary students.

Today, *Collier's* is regarded as one of the "big three" scholarly encyclopedias on the market—the other two being the ENCYCLOPEDIA AMERICANA and NEW ENCYCLOPAEDIA BRITANNICA. As such, it is directly competitive with these two sets.

II. Scope

Collier's Encyclopedia contains 25,000 articles and a total of 21 million words, making it just in terms of size the smallest of the "big three." Articles average 840 words, or approximately one-and-one-quarter pages in the encyclopedia's two-column page format. Actual article lengths vary from short entries such as the five-line **Acheron** to the 75-page overview of the **United States of America**.

As an indication of how space is apportioned among different subjects, **Charlemagne** receives two-and-one-half pages, **Konstantin Chernenko** gets approximately one-half page, **Grover Cleveland** is accorded two pages, and **Ty Cobb** is given about one-quarter of a page. The article on **China** is 63 and one-half pages, the **U.S. Civil War** is covered in 38 pages, and 8 pages are devoted to **Christianity**.

The articles in *Collier's* cover all of the major academic disciplines as well as practical information of general interest. Geographical, biographical, and historical subjects are treated thoroughly and consistently. In addition, conceptual topics such as **Apostasy** and **A priori** are covered, as are practical subjects such as **Safety**, which *New Britannica* totally omits.

Collier's coverage of international subjects, both in the geographical entries and elsewhere, is similarly broad. Articles on major countries include color maps and other illustrations. International political, historical and cultural figures of importance are discussed either in individual articles or within longer articles accessible through the index.

As an indication of the attention *Collier's* gives to foreign subjects, the entries from **Bartolome Mitre** to **Mohammed**, inclusive, include the following: **Mitre** (Argentine statesman), **Mitsubishi** (Japanese conglomerate), **Francois Mitterand** (French president), **Miyazaki** (Japanese city), **Moab** (ancient Near Eastern kingdom), **Mobutu Sese Seko** (Zairean president), **Modena** and **Modica** (Italian cities), **Amadeo Modigliani** (Italian artist), **Mödling** (Austrian city),

Jorgen Moe (19th century Norwegian writer), **Mogadishu** (Somalian capital), **Mogilev** (Soviet city), and **Mohammed**. This represents 15 entries out of a total 33 in this span.

North America is also particularly well covered, with illustrated articles on each of the 50 states and Canadian provinces. Since these regions feature prominently in school curricula, the articles devoted to them should be most helpful to students.

Popular subjects of current interest are added to the encyclopedia with each revision. Thus, the 1986 edition includes new entries on **Fred Astaire**, **Larry Bird**, and **Stephen Sondheim**. The same edition also introduced new entries on **Rajiv Gandhi**, **Edward Koch**, and **Desmond Tutu**, among others, thus keeping abreast of world affairs.

Collier's Encyclopedia includes a considerable number of longer survey articles which discuss aspects of a general topic that might be treated only as shorter separate entries in other encyclopedias. For example, the article on **American Literature** spans 30 pages and includes sections on Herman Melville, Walt Whitman, Henry James, and others. The survey article format is extremely useful for the reader who requires an overview of American literature and it provides a convenient alternative to consulting numerous cross-references as a means of studying a broad subject. But since only certain subjects are treated in this manner the reader is not always so accommodated, and the broad entry format does not facilitate locating specific information. (See also *Accessibility*.)

III. Authority

Collier's Encyclopedia is published by the Macmillan Educational Company (MEC), a division of the Macmillan Publishing Company. Well known in the reference field and one of the four leading publishers of general encyclopedias in the United States, MEC also publishes the *Merit Students Encyclopedia*, reviewed on page 147 of this Buying Guide. Conceived early in the postwar period, *Collier's* first appeared in 1950 and was favorably received. Since that time the encyclopedia has established a strong reputation as an authoritative reference work, particularly in the library and school market.

Editorial Director William D. Halsey and Editor-in-Chief Emanuel Friedman oversee the editing of both *Collier's* and *Merit*. They are assisted on *Collier's* by a staff of 24 house editors. In addition, the front matter lists three advisory boards (Library, Curriculum, and International), giving the credentials and affiliations of each member. The publisher reports that the members of these boards "contributed to the development" of the encyclopedia. The front matter also includes a list of senior editors and advisors, classified under the broad subject categories of Biological Sciences, Physical Sciences, Humanities, Regional Studies, and Social Sciences.

Collier's boasts an impressive roster of contributors—some 4,600 in all—drawn mainly from North American and British universities. Among its many notable contributors are agricultural researcher and Nobel laureate Norman Borlaug; child psychologist Bruno Bettelheim; novelist Kingsley Amis; sociologist Lewis Mumford; linguist Mario Pei; economist and Nobel laureate Milton Friedman; historians Barbara Tuchman, Asa Briggs, and A. L. Rowse; and British political figure Shirley Williams. A number of *Collier's* outstanding contributors, such as legal scholar Felix Frankfurter, anthropologist Margaret Mead, theologian Reinhold Niebuhr, art critic Herbert Read, and aviation engineer Igor Sikorsky, have been deceased for some time; however, this in no way diminishes the authority of their original contributions. (The list of contributors identifies deceased contributors as such.) Lesser known figures who have contributed to this encyclopedia appear to be respected authorities in their fields as well. Like both Encyclopedia Americana and New Encyclopaedia Britannica, *Collier's* list of contributors gives its contributors' academic degrees, professional affiliations, and titles of selected relevant books they have authored.

Most of the articles in *Collier's* are signed; in the cases of extended articles in which different sections were written by separate contributors, each section is signed. Some of the signatures are preceded by "Reviewed by," indicating that the contributor reviewed a prepared article; others are signed with more than one name, indicating joint authorship.

On the whole, the editors have taken meticulous care to ensure the authority of each entry, and to faithfully document this authority. The result is an encyclopedia whose authority rivals, and frequently excels, that of Encyclopedia Americana and New Britannica.

IV. Currency

The editors and publisher of *Collier's Encyclopedia* maintain a laudable policy of annual revision. According to the editors, the last five revisions have averaged about 2,000 revised pages each; this represents an annual revision of about 10 percent, which is standard for the industry. As a result, the 1986 edition is up-to-date to the time of publication in

most important factual areas. Ongoing lists such as heads of state and recipients of awards are current to the mid-1980s.

The article on the **Republic of South Africa** reports recent activity there, with information such as "In July 1985 the government proclaimed a state of emergency in large parts of South Africa. Military repression intensified." The article on **Nicaragua** reports events of 1984, explaining that "Intensified U.S. support enabled the counter-revolutionaries to increase their attacks . . ." and mentions the Sandinistas' 1984 presidential victory. The article on **Acquired Immune Deficiency Syndrome (AIDS)** reflects understanding of the disease current at the time the article was written, and mentions attempts by researchers in the United States and elsewhere to develop a vaccine.

Inevitably, some portions of the text are not quite up-to-date. For example, the entries on the **Republic of Ireland** and **Northern Ireland** fail to mention the 1985 agreement between Great Britain and the Republic granting the Republic a voice in the government of Northern Ireland. The article on **Margaret Thatcher** fails to mention in 1983 re-election victory, which was a significant event marking widespread support for the Conservative Party at that time. **Papacy** refers to Pope John Paul II only in passing and does not mention the fact that his selection as the first pope from an Eastern bloc country signaled a major development in the history of the Catholic Church. In Volume 10 (page 396) the caption of a photograph of Jean-Paul Sartre and Simone de Beauvoir is written in the present tense although Sartre died in 1980. However, since the encyclopedia is continuously revised, those sections that are less current at present would presumably receive attention in a future revision.

The choice of topics for articles also reflects the editorial goal of maintaining an up-to-date picture of events. New articles on **Mikhail Gorbachev** (general secretary of the Communist Party of the Soviet Union from March 1985), **Ted Hughes** (appointed poet laureate in Great Britain in 1984), and **Shimon Peres** (prime minister in Israel's coalition government in 1984) show the effort to incorporate new figures in the arts and international affairs. The articles on **Nuclear Fission**, **Elementary Particles**, and **Desalinization** have been completely rewritten for the 1986 edition, presenting new developments in science and technology. However, our reviewers noted some curious omissions. For example, the article **sound recording and reproduction** does not mention digital technology, which was introduced on a wide scale in the early 1980s and is now central to the recording industry. Moreover, the article discusses quadrophonic recording technology as though this was still in vogue; in fact, virtually all record companies had abandoned this process by 1980. The encyclopedia does not contain entries for digital recording or the compact disc.

The statistics reported in the articles, like most other factual material, are generally up-to-date. *Collier's* population figure for the U.S.S.R. dates from 1983—a reasonably up-to-date statistic for a 1986 encyclopedia. The entry's tables for the civilian labor force, industrial production, mineral production, principal exports and imports, and the consolidated state budget, all date from 1978. However, given the difficulty of obtaining current economic statistics from the Soviet Union, these tables are not unreasonably outmoded. Population figures for **Africa** and **Afghanistan** date from 1985 and 1983, respectively. However, the figure for **Bhopal** State dates from 1961; the population figure for the city of Bhopal is more recent (1981). The entry does not mention the 1984 industrial disaster at the Union Carbide plant there. The articles on **Advertising**, **Divorce**, the **Electrical Industry**, and **Frozen Foods** all include tables in which the figures date from 1975, but these are exceptions and most of the tables are reliably up-to-date.

The vast size of *Collier's Encyclopedia*, set against the pace of changing events in the world, makes the task of updating such a work most challenging. On balance, *Collier's* editors have succeeded in producing a work that is reasonably current, and they have demonstrated their commitment to keeping it up to the same standard in subsequent editions. Students should be able to turn to this encyclopedia for recent information in most fields with confidence.

V. Accuracy

The articles in *Collier's Encyclopedia* are consistently accurate in reporting information. The careful preparation, editorial review, and frequent revision are evident throughout and generate a high standard of reliability. For example, the long article on **Printing** provides a thorough explanation of the typesetting, printing, and binding processes, in sufficient detail to serve as a helpful review for the professional, and with attention to the latest technology and computerization of the industry.

The article on **Ronald Wilson Reagan** covers Reagan's early life and acting career, the major events of his early political career, and details of his presidency through late 1985. The level of detail provided is appropriate, with the most detailed discussion devoted to the years since 1980.

With only one exception, our content reviewers report that the articles they have examined are highly accurate and useful. *Collier's* entry on the **brain** is fairly complete and straightforward, taking into account such important aspects of the subject as the specialized functions of the right and left brain, theories of memory and learning, and neurotransmitters (although the coverage of this last item is not as current as it could be). The article on the **Bill of Rights** is thorough and good. Taking the historical approach, the entry covers the English Bill of Rights, the Virginia Declaration, and the first ten amendments to the U.S. Constitution, illuminating the relationships among the three. Our astronomy consultant reports that, of all encyclopedia articles on **Saturn**, *Collier's* is clearly the best. The article provides a good balance between hard factual information and reasonable speculative information, and should remain accurate and reliable for some time. The encyclopedia's coverage of **transistors** is similarly excellent. The entry provides a good description of different types of transistors, their behavior, and their applications. There are helpful and appropriate cross-references to related entries. However, our consultant also notes that some of the discussion in transistors is likely to be too advanced for many readers.

Collier's entry on **money** is less reliable than its coverage of the subjects just discussed. It is significantly narrower in scope than the article in NEW BRITANNICA, and difficult even for an economist to understand. It contains some serious errors and biases that, on the whole, render it of little value to the general reader. However, such examples are the rare exception rather than the rule. In general, *Collier's* accuracy is second to none, and this encyclopedia maintains a high standard of excellence.

VI. Clarity

Collier's Encyclopedia is intended for secondary school students and adults. While the discussion of complex and technical subjects may be difficult for junior high school readers to follow, they are certainly suitable for high school students and adults. The Preface announces that the articles "have been constructed according to carefully designed patterns. Typically, such a pattern provides for immediate definition, for simple explanation, and for presentation of the basic facts early in the article." A random review confirms that long articles are indeed often introduced in this fashion. The structure of the articles aids the reader by presenting material in a logical sequence and highlighting specific aspects. This is especially valuable in the survey articles. For example, the article on **Chess** begins as described above, with a succinct definition and some general information. This is followed by sections introduced with bold headings on "Rules of Chess," "Notation," "Chess Theory," "A Classical Game," and so on. Whether the reader is looking for an overview of the subject or a specific piece of information, this format should pose little difficulty.

The writing style is generally clear and scholarly but may vary considerably from article to article. Compare this passage from the article on **Archaeology**: "Now this may all seem simple and unexciting; but an archaeologist is an outsider to the men and cultures with which he chooses to deal" with a sentence from the article **Chord**: "This distinction between several tones heard simultaneously but independently and those perceived as a homogeneous union is the distinction between contrapuntal ("horizontal") and harmonic ("vertical") texture in music." The two *Collier's* articles dealing with evolution (**evolution of man** and **organic evolution**) are both highly technical and may be beyond the grasp of the typical reader. Each assumes that the reader possesses a fairly thorough familiarity with genetics, anthropology, and paleontology.

For the most part, though not always and not consistently, technical terms are defined in context. Individuals are occasionally mentioned by surname only, without identification or an explanation of their relationship to the subject at hand. For example, the article on **T. S. Eliot** includes this statement: "Through Russell he met Clive Bell, who introduced him to members of the so-called Bloomsbury Group." This is the first and only mention of (Bertrand) Russell, who may be unfamiliar to the reader and should perhaps be identified more fully. Minor stylistic inconsistencies also occur; for example in Volume 8 (pages 284 and 285) the captions to the two photographs of the Indonesian capital use different spellings of the city's name, Jakarta and Djakarta. However, such lapses are few, and with the exception of the occasional article, the overall style of this encyclopedia is lucid and easy to follow.

The following extract from **lighthouse** illustrates the style of a typical entry in *Collier's Encyclopedia*:

LIGHTHOUSE, a structure located in or adjacent to navigable waters, designed to serve as a visual guide by day and to support a light or lights for display at night to warn mariners of dangers and to assist them in determining their safe course. Identification by day is through physical description and at night by characteristic light occultations, flashes, colors, and so forth.

Because of the development of additional navigational safeguards over the first half of the twentieth century, lighthouse structures now often house other important signaling equipment. These include sound fog signals, operating during obscured weather, and radio beacons. The latter, because of their great effective range (200 miles or more), are often operated on published clear-weather schedules as well as during periods of local fog, smoke, or snow. Lighthouses may also, because of their well-publicized and accurately charted locations and because of operating economies, serve advantageously as sites for radar beacons to guide ships locally or as transmitting stations for other electronic signals, such as loran, for guidance of vessels far at sea. Developed during World War II, loran has a signaling range of 1,500 miles. . . .

VII. Objectivity

Like its major competitors, Encyclopedia Americana and New Encyclopaedia Britannica, *Collier's* is in the main an objective, well-balanced encyclopedia. The Preface states that "to insure objectivity, articles involving key issues are submitted to authorities representing all major points of view." Thus, in areas where controversy exists, it is usually mentioned.

For example, the entry on **abortion** summarizes the main arguments held by those who favor the legalization of abortion and those who oppose it. The article notes that the subject continues to raise controversy, and mentions further legislation and court rulings affecting abortion in the United States during the 1970s and 1980s. The article also deals with other problematic aspects of the subject. For example, it points out that "to what extent, if any, access to legal abortion has led to a deterioration of contraceptive practice is a matter of contention. A section on "Complications and Aftereffects" deals with *psychological reactions*—an area not addressed in the abortion entries of any other encyclopedia.

Collier's articles on **organic evolution** and **evolution of man** mention pre-Darwinian views on these subjects, but allude only briefly to contemporary challenges to evolutionary theory. Neither creationism nor scientific creationism are mentioned by name, and this encyclopedia does not contain an entry under either heading. This is a rare instance in which *Collier's* does not address an alternative viewpoint on a major issue.

Collier's coverage of controversial historical figures is well balanced. For example, the entry on **Henry Kissinger** describes Kissinger's successes in negotiations with the Soviet Union, the People's Republic of China, North Vietnam, Israel, and Egypt, but also notes that his "tenure was flawed by much controversy" in matters concerning Cambodia, Chile, and Angola.

The entry on **Andrew Jackson** gives a full and rounded account of his personality and his career. Early in the article we read that "the gay, headstrong youth often seemed more interested in horse racing, cockfighting, gambling, and girls than in study or his career." Later, he is described as "trigger-touchy concerning slights to his 'honor' or to [his wife's] sacred name"; the article also reports that he killed one opponent in a duel, and that he "owned 20 slaves." Jackson's many involvements in political controversy during his presidency are also noted, but his positive achievements are emphasized. A *summation* section states that "most historians rate Jackson not only as a 'great' president but as a 'strong' one. . . . His strength lay in the firmness and decisiveness of his conduct of the office, particularly in instances of conflict with Congress, and in his resistance in the name of 'equal protection and equal benefits' to domination of government by special interests."

VIII. Accessibility

Collier's Encyclopedia is well organized and most specific information can be easily located. Entries are arranged alphabetically in a letter-by-letter system. Names beginning with *Mc* are alphabetized as though they began with *Mac*; names beginning with *St.* are likewise alphabetized as though *Saint* were spelled out. Entry headings are in bold capital letters, with several levels of subheads in bold or italic type depending on the complexity of the article. Subheads in historical articles are in chronological order; those in articles on authors often identify individual works; still other subheads help to distinguish various aspects of the topic under discussion.

Several special features to the system of organization serve as aids to the reader. Glossaries of technical terms appear at the end of many articles, such as **Archaeology** and **Archery**. The articles on states include lists of prominent state citizens with brief descriptions of their contributions. Some longer articles, such as **Astronomy** and **Automobile**, are accompanied by boxes containing a brief explanation of how the article is organized. These aids are useful since the survey article format incorporates a great deal of information in each article.

Subjects are listed under their most familiar names. Thus, authors appear under their pseudonyms with cross-references under their real names sometimes, but not always, supplied. The use of familiar names leads to some inconsistencies; for example, the

brothers of the French emperor Napoleon I are all discussed in Volume 4 under their surname Bonaparte, whereas the article on the emperor appears under Napoleon I in Volume 17. But decisions such as this are necessary and have been made logically in most cases.

There are some 13,000 cross-references (fewer than one per page), appearing at the ends of articles or sections of articles, as suggestions for further reading, or following an entry title where the entry itself appears elsewhere. In a sense, the broad entry format makes some cross-references unnecessary by bringing related material together.

Articles on related subjects frequently overlap and information on a similar theme may thus appear in different volumes. For this reason, and because much information appears under a single title in survey articles, the index is an essential element in this encyclopedia. To the editors' credit it is an exhaustive and well-compiled reference, with 400,000 entries annotated to distinguish similar entries, and with references to maps, illustrations, and bibliography entries. Readers will find the index indispensable and reliable.

As an indication of the scope and style of individual entries, the reader searching for information about Marie Curie will find the following index entries:

> **CURIE** (Fr. fam.) **7**-571a
>> **Curie, Eve** (Fr. mus., au.) **7**-571c
>> **Curie, Irene** (Fr. phys.): see Joliot Curie, Irene
>> **Curie, Jacques** (Fr. phys.) **21**-223b
>> **Curie, Marie** (Pol. sci.) **7**-571a; **17**-571a, 572c; **19**-604d, 630b
>>> medicine **15**-653d—*Ill.* **7**-571
>> **Curie, Paul-Jean** (Fr. phys.) **7**-571c
>> **Curie, Pierre** (Fr. chem., phys.) **7**-571c, 571a; **17**-571a; **19**-604d
>> magnets **15**-271b
>> medicine **15**-653d
>> sound **21**-223a

These are followed by entries for **Curie** (measure), **Curie point**, **Curie's law**, **Curie temperature**, and **Curie-Weiss law**. Thus, the index is highly specific, and the reader may have to do some close reading to track down every reference to *Curie*.

IX. Special Features

A special feature of *Collier's Encyclopedia* is the annotated bibliography in Volume 24. There are 11,500 titles, numbered and arranged according to subject and in order of difficulty. This will be especially helpful to those using the encyclopedia for research.

The bibliography was compiled by 45 public and academic librarians and academic subject specialists. According to the editors, "the books listed begin at about high school level and progress through college level and beyond. All books have been selected with a view to their availability. . . . Many are books one may expect to find even in smaller libraries or are books that a small library in all probability can borrow from its state agency." Most of these claims are true most of the time. Many of the titles listed are classics that are still widely available; the bibliographies also include a significant number of books published in the 1980s.

Unlike the bibliography in FUNK & WAGNALLS, the *Collier's* bibliography is not arranged by any standard system (e.g., Dewey Decimal or Library of Congress). Rather, the titles appear under very broad subject headings such as philosophy, history, the arts, economics, and general science. All titles are listed in the index.

Altogether, the *Collier's* bibliography is more comprehensive than the separate bibliographies included at the end of selected subject entries in EN-CYCLOPEDIA AMERICANA and the NEW BRITAN-NICA MICROPAEDIA. Like those encyclopedias, however, some of the articles in *Collier's* also include brief bibliographies.

A study guide appears in Volume 24 between the bibliography and the index. It is divided into academic disciplines and within each field are listed the titles of relevant *Collier's* articles, moving from introductory to advanced material. Many critics and educators question the efficacy of such study guides, which will be useful only to the extent that they are consulted and applied by the user.

Another major feature is the index, previously discussed (see *Accessibility*). This takes up the greater portion of Volume 24.

There are 17,350 illustrations, of which 1,750 are in color. There are several color transparencies, which are attractive and show relationships between things in a dramatic way. The color plates on subjects such as Birds, Dogs, Paintings, and Shells are also beautifully produced and very effective. The black-and-white illustrations are mostly of good quality but, like those in the ENCYCLOPEDIA AMERICANA, vary widely in quality. Some of the photographs have reproduced rather dark in the current edition. A small number of photographs appear to be somewhat dated. There is also some repetition of certain subjects in illustrations, while other subjects that could benefit from illustrations are not illustrated at all. For example, there are four photographs of the Appian

Way (one each in Volumes 2, 9, 12, and 22), while there is no illustration for the article on JOHN SINGER SARGENT.

Collier's contains 1,600 maps, which were prepared by the well-known cartographer Rand McNally & Company. Articles on continents, major countries, and North American states and provinces include excellent color maps with extensive map indexes. There are also maps with topographic and economic information, rainfall, growing seasons, and other topics of interest. On the whole, *Collier's* maps are of the highest quality, and in many cases surpass those found in competing encyclopedias.

Helpful tables accompany some articles. There are tables on subjects such as "The Growth of the Old Testament," "International Atomic Weights," and "Table of the World's Languages," as well as in entries on individual states, nations, and continents. These tables present a great deal of information clearly and concisely.

X. Format

Collier's Encyclopedia includes 24 volumes of between 700 and 800 pages each (except Volume 24, which is 1,050 pages long). Like AMERICANA and BRITANNICA, *Collier's* is organized in the split-letter system. The black cloth binding with red panels and gold lettering is sturdy and attractive. The trim size is 8¼″ x 10⅝″ and the books are roughly 1⅜″ thick. The entire set takes up approximately three feet of horizontal shelf space. The two-column page layout is augmented with illustrations; the headings, running heads, and page numbers (flush with the outside margin at the top of each page) are bold and legible.

XI. Other Opinions

ARBA 82: "*Collier's* is a relatively up-to-date encyclopedia that is competitive with ENCYCLOPEDIA AMERICANA and the NEW ENCYCLOPAEDIA BRITANNICA. . . . It is carefully prepared and edited. . . . *Collier's* is suitable for general adult use, and has features particularly useful to the secondary-school and college student."

ARBA 86: "*Collier's* is one of the best encyclopedias on the market, it is readable and reasonably up-to-date. It is best suited for schools and home use and one can also recommend it for junior college level. Certainly not flashy, *Collier's* is reasonably priced and should be recommended for purchase without any serious reservations."

Booklist, November 15, 1986: "*Collier's Encyclopedia* continues to be one of the most important encyclopedias, especially for readers at the secondary-school and college levels . . . a systematic program of revision maintains excellence in readability, objectivity, scholarship, and currentness.''

XI. Summary

As a well-balanced reference source with good general coverage, *Collier's Encyclopedia* offers excellent value. It is reasonably up-to-date and well written and will serve the needs of secondary school students and adults. Strong coverage of academic disciplines makes it a good choice for school use.

The broad entry format makes *Collier's* slightly less suitable for quick-reference use than some other multivolume encyclopedias (notably ACADEMIC AMERICAN), although readers familiar with its index will have little difficulty.

Smaller and less expensive than both ENCYCLOPEDIA AMERICANA and NEW BRITANNICA, *Collier's* yields to neither in authority, accuracy, or currency. It offers scholarly articles in a clear and concise format that will serve many reference needs.

Collier's Encyclopedia costs $1,099.50 to individuals and $744 to institutions. Thus, the set is a particularly attractive purchase to schools and libraries.

Individuals wishing to purchase *Collier's Encyclopedia* may contact the publisher, Macmillan Educational Corporation, at 866 Third Avenue, New York, NY 10022, or telephone (800) 257-9500. Schools and libraries may address their orders to the same address or phone (800) 257-5755.

Compton's Encyclopedia

Facts at a Glance

Full Title: **Compton's Encyclopedia.**
Publisher: Encyclopaedia Britannica, Inc., 310 South Michigan Avenue, Chicago, IL 60604.
Editor: Dale Good.
Copyright: 1987.

Number of Volumes: 26.
Number of Contributors: 500.
Number of Article Entries: 4,300 in main text.
Number of Pages: 9,500.
Number of Words: 7,000,000.
Number of Maps: 2,000.
Number of Cross-references: not available.
Number of Indexes: 26.
Number of Index Entries: 60,000, including 7,000 "fact entries," 27,000 "capsule articles."
Number of Illustrations: 7,900 four-color, 14,600 two-color or black-and-white.

Trim Size: 7½″ × 9¹⁵⁄₁₆″.

Intended Readership: ages 8 through 18.
Price: $699 for individuals; $525 for schools and libraries—$495 school/library discount price for purchase of two or more sets.
Sold through independent distributors. (See page **595**.) ISBN 0-85229-444-1.
Revised annually.

I. Introduction

Compton's Encyclopedia is a 26-volume work designed primarily for students at the upper elementary, junior high, and high school levels. It is intended to be equally appropriate for home, school, and library use.

The editor's Preface, quoting the title page of the first edition (1922) of *Compton's*, announces the encyclopedia's intention: "To inspire ambition, to stimulate the imagination, to provide the inquiring mind with accurate information told in an interesting style. . ." Thus, *Compton's* aims to be more than simply a comprehensive source of facts and figures; in the ancient meaning of the word *encyclopedia*, it attempts to provide a full circle of learning.

II. Scope

Compton's is unique in its structure and scope. The main body of each of the set's first 25 volumes consists of extended articles on subjects that the editors believe will be of the most interest and importance to young readers. A Fact-Index at the end of each volume combines standard index features with brief dictionary-type entries that provide basic facts about the subject. These Fact-Index entries cover subjects included in the main body as well as additional subjects judged by the editors to be of lesser importance. Volume 26 consists entirely of a Fact-Index, which recapitulates the indexes contained in the first 25 volumes.

Compton's contains some 7 million words in 9,500 pages. There are 4,300 main articles—the fewest of any multivolume encyclopedia currently on the market—and 60,000 index entries, the majority of which present facts in a dictionary format. Article entries average about 1,500 words (one-and-a-half pages of text) each. Most Fact-Index entries (apart from those that are strictly index entries) are from 10 to 30 words long. Most main entries are given at least one-half page (approximately 61 lines/500 words); many are considerably longer. For example, as an indication

Compton's Encyclopedia

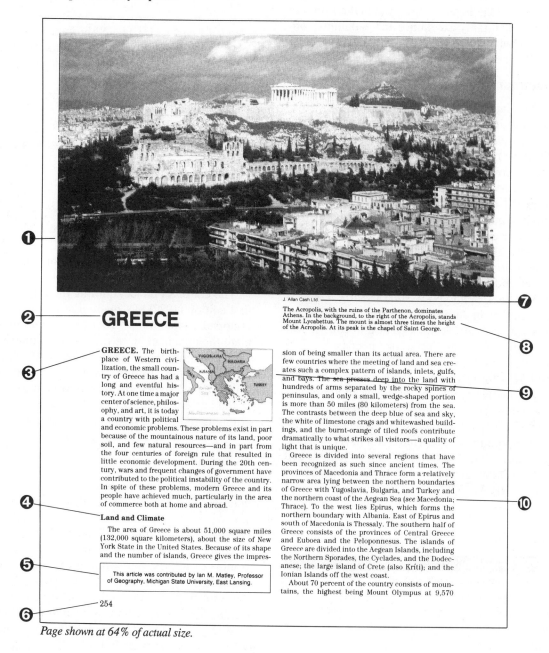

GREECE

GREECE. The birthplace of Western civilization, the small country of Greece has had a long and eventful history. At one time a major center of science, philosophy, and art, it is today a country with political and economic problems. These problems exist in part because of the mountainous nature of its land, poor soil, and few natural resources—and in part from the four centuries of foreign rule that resulted in little economic development. During the 20th century, wars and frequent changes of government have contributed to the political instability of the country. In spite of these problems, modern Greece and its people have achieved much, particularly in the area of commerce both at home and abroad.

Land and Climate

The area of Greece is about 51,000 square miles (132,000 square kilometers), about the size of New York State in the United States. Because of its shape and the number of islands, Greece gives the impres-

This article was contributed by Ian M. Matley, Professor of Geography, Michigan State University, East Lansing.

254

J. Allan Cash Ltd.

The Acropolis, with the ruins of the Parthenon, dominates Athens. In the background, to the right of the Acropolis, stands Mount Lycabettus. The mount is almost three times the height of the Acropolis. At its peak is the chapel of Saint George.

sion of being smaller than its actual area. There are few countries where the meeting of land and sea creates such a complex pattern of islands, inlets, gulfs, and bays. The sea presses deep into the land with hundreds of arms separated by the rocky spines of peninsulas, and only a small, wedge-shaped portion is more than 50 miles (80 kilometers) from the sea. The contrasts between the deep blue of sea and sky, the white of limestone crags and whitewashed buildings, and the burnt-orange of tiled roofs contribute dramatically to what strikes all visitors—a quality of light that is unique.

Greece is divided into several regions that have been recognized as such since ancient times. The provinces of Macedonia and Thrace form a relatively narrow area lying between the northern boundaries of Greece with Yugoslavia, Bulgaria, and Turkey and the northern coast of the Aegean Sea (*see* Macedonia; Thrace). To the west lies Epirus, which forms the northern boundary with Albania. East of Epirus and south of Macedonia is Thessaly. The southern half of Greece consists of the provinces of Central Greece and Euboea and the Peloponnesus. The islands of Greece are divided into the Aegean Islands, including the Northern Sporades, the Cyclades, and the Dodecanese; the large island of Crete (also Kríti); and the Ionian Islands off the west coast.

About 70 percent of the country consists of mountains, the highest being Mount Olympus at 9,570

Page shown at 64% of actual size.

❶ Illustration: Compton's includes 17,500 photographs, of which one-third are four-color and two-thirds two-color or black-and-white.

❷ Display title

❸ Main entry: Compton's contains about 4,300 articles, arranged alphabetically letter-by-letter, in addition to 27,000 capsule articles and 7,000 fact entries in the Fact-Index.

❹ Subhead

❺ Contributor information box: Compton's has about 500 contributors.

❻ Page number

❼ Photo credit

❽ Caption

❾ Locator map: Compton's contains about 2,000 maps, including locator maps, physical maps, and one- and two-page maps in four-color.

❿ Cross-reference: Cross-references to other entries are indicated by the words *see* or *see also* in parentheses.

of how space is apportioned among different subjects, **Ray Charles** gets 24 words in the Fact-Index but is not covered in the main section. **Charlemagne** is covered in a full page in the main section. The main article on **Ty Cobb** is about one-fourth of a page, while his Fact-Index entry is shorter than one dozen words. **Konstantin Chernenko**, featured in the main section, gets nearly one-half page. **Cleveland** (Ohio) is two-and-a-half pages long; the article on the **American Civil War** is 15 pages long; the main entry on **Christianity** is covered in five full pages; and **China** is discussed in 50 pages. (Although most of *Compton's* articles are of a general survey nature, the set also contains specific-entry articles. Thus, there are additional entries for particular subjects related to the Civil War, China, and Christianity both in the main body and in the Fact-Index. See *Accessibility*.)

Geared primarily to the needs of school students, *Compton's* subject matter is largely (though not consistently) tied to school curricula. Subjects covered in a random 50-page spread (pages 587-637) include **Samuel Colt, John Coltrane, Columbia** (S.C.), **Columbia River, Columbine, Christopher Columbus, Columbus** (GA), **coma, John Comenius, comet, commodity exchange, The** (British) **Commonwealth, communal living, communication, communication skills, Communism, Comoros, compass, compass plants, compost, Compromise of 1850, Arthur Holly Compton, computer, August Comte, Conakry,** (Guinea), and **James Bryant Conant.**

The publisher has not provided a percentage breakdown of subject areas covered in *Compton's*. Our own breakdown of a volume chosen at random (Volume 19—*Phill* through *Pytho*) indicates that 25 percent of the main articles are in the area of natural sciences or natural history. About 21 percent of the entries are biographical, and 15 percent cover what may be considered broad, non-academic topics of general interest (e.g., **photography, postal service, public speaking**). Only 12 percent of the main entries in this volume concern geography, while 7 percent deal with history, and another 7 percent with social sciences. Subjects in the arts and literature, religion and philosophy, technology, and abstract sciences are each allotted less than 5 percent of the entries.

Compton's is written for a North American readership, but the rest of the world is not ignored. The reader will find that many of the general-interest articles contain fascinating sections on how that particular subject (e.g., **postal service**) applies in foreign countries. As an indication of how *Compton's* apportions space among American and non-American subjects, 20 pages are devoted to the state of **South Carolina**, while the nation of **South Africa** is covered in only five pages. On the other hand, the continent of **South America** receives fairly extensive coverage, with a 39-page article.

III. Authority

Compton's has a long and generally distinguished history. The set's original predecessor, *Compton's Pictured Encyclopedia*, was published in 1922 by the F. E. Compton Company of Chicago. This eight-volume set for young adults contained more illustrations than any comparable encyclopedia of its time, and is believed to have been the first encyclopedia with color photographs. For this reason, and because of its reputation for accuracy and clarity, it was enormously popular with librarians and the public alike. The set was revised annually, a policy that continued without interruption through the Great Depression and World War II. *Compton's* also continued to grow in size, nearly doubling in number of volumes in the first ten years of its existence. Since 1961, when the F. E. Compton Company became a division of Encyclopaedia Britannica, Inc., *Compton's* has served as an intermediate encyclopedia between COMPTON'S PRECYCLOPEDIA and the ENCYCLOPAEDIA BRITANNICA. The word *Pictured* was dropped from the title in 1969. At that time, when all encyclopedias were illustrated, *Compton's* still led the field in the extent and calibre of its illustrations. However, with a series of cuts in staff and budget during the 1970s, it failed to maintain its high standards and lost its lead in the intermediate encyclopedia market to MERIT STUDENTS ENCYCLOPEDIA and WORLD BOOK. The publisher has made an effort to upgrade the set in the 1980s, but the *Compton's* has not regained its prestige.

Dale Good, formerly Senior Editor, now serves as *Compton's* Editor-in-Chief. The editorial staff, small by any standards and certainly small for a multivolume encyclopedia that is revised annually, consists of the Editor, a Planning Editor, two Senior Editors, a Staff Writer, two Assistant Editors, two Editorial Assistants, and a small art department. Eighteen "editorial advisors," mainly college and university professors, are also listed.

The front matter also identifies about 425 "editorial consultants and contributors," with their credentials and the articles to which they have contributed. While few of the consultants have big name recognition, most of them hold major academic posts or are leading professionals in their fields; however, a significant number are reported as retired or deceased. Moreover, as all but a few articles are unsigned, it is impossible to tell what input, if any, these individuals have had in the current edition. One suspects that in many cases the contributors are no longer actively affiliated with the encyclopedia. With such a relatively small editorial staff, one also wonders how thorough the annual revision can be.

IV. Currency

The publisher reports that the 1987 edition of *Compton's Encyclopedia* contains 229 new articles, 430 revised or rewritten articles, and 107 updated articles. Among the new subjects covered are **Corazon Aquino, electronic games, electronic instruments, epidemiology, espionage, exercise, genetic disorders, God, Great Depression, Grenada, guerrilla warfare, Mother Teresa, technology, telecommunication, Torah,** and **transistor**. Interestingly, virtually all the new or rewritten articles are for subjects beginning with E, G, or T, which are found in Volumes 7, 9, and 23.

Although it reportedly undergoes a 19-percent revision each year, a high figure by any standard, *Compton's* unfortunately cannot be considered reasonably up-to-date. Throughout the set, our reviewers found many obvious instances of inadequate coverage of recent trends and events. A few examples should suffice to illustrate this point.

The article on **New York** notes that "famous transatlantic liners dock along the Hudson River." Alas, the transatlantic liners have been gone for some years, and many piers stand derelict and rotting. **Great Britain** asserts that "little crude petroleum is produced in Great Britain," a statement that completely ignores the North Sea oil fields that have been operating since the 1970s. By contrast, however, the newly rewritten entry on **England** informs the reader that "As a result of the North Sea petroleum fields, Britain is now self-sufficient in oil and produces more than 75 percent of its natural gas requirements."

South Africa is up-to-date as far as 1983, but the subsection on "Events After World War II" contains fairly little recent "hard" information. It accurately notes that "In the 1970s . . . black African governments joined those of the West in condemning the policy of apartheid. And South African blacks began to demand political power. Racial disturbances in black townships were widespread and frequent. In reaction South Africa made some concessions, relaxing discrimination in employment and public facilities, but remained committed to white rule. . . . In 1983 a referendum approved a constitutional change conceding limited political power to coloreds and Asians, but none to blacks." However, there is no mention by name of any individual leaders, black or white, since Jan Christiaan Smuts, nor of the in-

creasing international economic pressure on the government in the 1980s.

Zimbabwe is discussed under the entry **Rhodesia**, although the country has been known officially as *Zimbabwe* since 1980. Throughout the article it is called Rhodesia; the article ends with the 1980 elections that transferred power to a black government under Robert Mugabe. Evidently the article has not been revised at all since that time.

Even in some articles where there has been an obvious attempt to update, the update has not been comprehensive. For example, although **Nicaragua** mentions that "the United States' relations with the Sandinista government worsened during the 1980s" and that "Daniel Ortega Saavedra . . . was sworn in as president . . . on Jan. 10, 1985," there is no mention of the anti-Sandinista Contra movement.

Space travel contains information on the subject through early 1984.

There are also some notable omissions that may make the reader question *Compton's* currency. For example, the 1987 edition includes an entry for **AIDS** in the Fact-Index but not in the main text. The syndrome is included in a table on "Some Notable Infectious Diseases" in the article on **Human Disease**. (The same table also contains information on Legionnaire's Disease and Toxic Shock Syndrome, among others.)

Compton's uses terminology that has not been standard since the 1960s. For example, the word *Negro* appears in contexts in which most contemporary American writers use the word *black*. Harlem is called "New York's Negro community"; elsewhere, one reads that "Negros make up more than two thirds of South Africa's people." *Compton's* also uses language that many critics would consider "sexist," although for the most part this is being eliminated as entire volumes are revised.

The most immediately apparent indication of the set's lack of currency is the age of its photographs. For example, an aerial shot of "contemporary" midtown Manhattan on page 268 of Volume 16 was taken before the construction of most of the skyscrapers that now occupy the area. In many photos, hairstyles and clothing date from the 1950s or 1960s, as do automobile models. Most of the photos in **police**, to take a random entry, seem to have been taken in the mid-1950s, as do the illustrations in **prisons**. While many of these photos would be effective as period illustrations, clearly they do not represent current conditions.

Admittedly, some articles and photographs are more up-to-date. The entry on **terrorism**, for example, discusses a number of international terrorist incidents that occurred during one week in June 1985. And the article on **dance** is well illustrated with contemporary photographs. However, such examples are the exception rather than the rule. On the whole, despite major revisions in three volumes of the 1987 edition, Funk & Wagnalls, Merit, and World Book are all considerably more up-to-date than *Compton's*.

V. Accuracy

Compton's failure to maintain adequate currency adversely affects the encyclopedia's accuracy. This is particularly evident when the set deals with recent events or with subject areas in which changes are ongoing. Statistics throughout the set are not to be trusted. For example, in a chart comparing the population of the Soviet Union with that of the United States, *Compton's* reports a figure of 203,000,000 people in the U.S. compared to 242,000,000 in the U.S.S.R. according to the "latest census." However, in 1983 the population of the United States was more than 234,000,000, and that of the Soviet Union over 273,000,000. Given that this edition has a 1987 copyright date, the information provided here is woefully inaccurate. The information *Compton's* provides about national and local economies is also questionable.

Compton's also tends to make unsupported generalizations, or to present theory as fact. (See also *Objectivity*.) This is especially true in the coverage of the social sciences. For example, the article on **Maturity** declares that "Criteria for maturity has [sic] been established in seven different areas. . . . These criteria are based on observations of people and not on armchair speculation." In fact, the topic is highly subjective and speculative, and psychologists and child development specialists do not agree on such standard criteria for measuring maturity.

Even in dealing with subjects in which facts have been well documented, *Compton's* perpetuates some popular fallacies and misconceptions. The article on **Henry the Navigator** says that the 15th century Portugese prince "set up an observatory, a naval arsenal, and a school where young men could study." Although Henry favored the idea of such a school, he was not personally involved in establishing it.

Many of the set's inaccuracies and distortions result from the omission of significant information. For example, **drama** mentions neither Samuel Beckett nor the Theatre of the Absurd. The same article, in discussing the plays of Harold Pinter, lists some of his lesser-known plays but neglects his most significant and characteristic ones (e.g., *The Homecoming, The Caretaker, The Birthday Party, Old Times, Be-*

trayal). While such figures as Beckett and Pinter will not be of interest to younger readers, certainly high school students studying drama should be aware of their accomplishments.

Our subject specialists' reviews suggest that the set's articles are of varying quality. A number of the inaccuracies in **Saturn** are probably the result of outdated information.

The new entry on **transistors** is a marked improvement on the article it replaces, which was sorely out of date. The article gives a brief but clear and accurate description of how transistors work. Both bipolar junction transistors and metal-oxide-semiconductor field effect transistors, and their uses, are mentioned. The importance of silicon as a semiconductor is also discussed. The final paragraph deals with integrated circuits. There is also a section on "Semiconducting Devices" in the **electronics** article.

The entry on **money**, containing little worthwhile economic information, compares unfavorably with the treatment of the subject in *Compton's* competitors (World Book, for example). The explanation of inflation is not wholly accurate, the currency and exchange table is outdated and misleading, and the "cute" illustrations are not particularly helpful. But the article on the **brain** is well organized and accurate.

In terms of accuracy and comprehensiveness, *Compton's* greatest strength is perhaps its fine coverage of subjects in botany, zoology, and natural history. Here *Compton's* bears comparison with its direct competitors. But overall, Merit, World Book, and Funk & Wagnalls all provide more reliable information.

VI. Clarity

Compton's is written in a manner intended to make the subject as interesting as possible to the young reader. Thus, many articles begin not with a definition of the subject, as in most secondary-level encyclopedias, but with a general statement or an anecdote about the subject. For example, the opening sentence in **varnish** reads: "When mummy cases of Egyptian kings are removed from their tombs, the cases are usually found to be coated with varnish." The article on **spiders** begins:

> The spinners, weavers, and civil engineers of the world of nature are the spiders. Few creatures have more interesting habits. Their silken webs are marvels of geometric design and workmanship. Spiders swing suspension bridges across streams and other obstacles. They travel great distances through the air on filmy balloons.

When they want to return to earth they drop a landing 'cable' and slowly descend.

Compared with Funk & Wagnalls which is dry and factual, *Compton's* is deliberately colloquial and engaging. At times, the writing can be considered quaint and old-fashioned. Our reviewers note a similarity in tone to that of Compton's Precyclopedia, a set for younger readers reviewed on page 000.

Some articles have titles in addition to their entry words. Thus, for example, the entry for **Poland** is titled "Poland's Tragic Story and Loyal People." **Portugal** is called "The Tiny Nation with the Last Big Empire," and **Prisons** is "Where Society Sends Its Lawbreakers." However, this style is being phased out as individual volumes are revised.

The extended articles in *Compton's* utilize the so-called "pyramid" style. That is, the articles begin with the simplest or general facts and progress to the more complex or specific facts. The following extract from the opening of **lighthouse** illustrates the style of a typical entry in *Compton's*.

Lighthouse. To help those on ships determine location and to warn of potential hazards, lighthouses have been built for centuries in areas where naval or commercial vessels sail. The history of lighthouses is filled with tales of lighthouse keepers, the men who once lived in or near the lighthouse whose light it was their responsibility to keep burning. Most modern lighthouses, however, have automatic lights that need little tending.

Some few lighthouses have become quite famous. The one built on the island of Pharos, near Alexandria, Egypt, about 280 BC was regarded as one of the seven wonders of the ancient world. Along the Hudson River in New York City, under the George Washington Bridge, stands a small lighthouse about which a children's book was written—'The Little Red Lighthouse and the Great Grey Bridge' by W. H. Swift and Lynd Ward. But the best known of all is the Eddystone Lighthouse on a reef 14 miles (22.5 kilometers) off the shore of Plymouth, England. Celebrated in ballad and folklore, it has had a long and sometimes tragic history. Four successive lighthouses have stood at this location. The first, opened in 1699, was swept out to sea only four years later. Its replacement was destroyed by fire in 1755. The third was replaced by the present tower in 1882.

VII. Objectivity

As one may infer from some of the examples cited under *Currency*, *Compton's* presents a world that is mostly sweetness and light. For instance, from reading **Liverpool**, the reader would have no idea that the city's port traffic has declined precipitously in the last twenty years, giving way to high unemployment and urban blight. The article on **New York City** proclaims that "magnificent highways cross the Bronx into Westchester County. . .", perhaps true at one time, but certainly no longer the case.

Whereas New Standard takes a positive tone toward some subjects and a negative tone toward others, *Compton's* usually ignores most controversial areas, and incidents of obvious political bias are rare. One notable exception is the coverage of the Soviet Union. **Union of Soviet Socialist Republics** contains the statement that "[the Soviet] government is a ruthless Communist dictatorship." While there are indeed many facts that could be used to justify this assertion, the article does not cite any. In **Russia**, where most of the information on the Soviet Union is found, a Cold War viewpoint prevails. A two-page spread of charts and tables at the end of the article, titled "How Russia and the United States Compare," seems intended to illustrate how much better life is in the United States than in the Soviet Union. The article itself contains remarks that verge on editorial comment. For example, the introduction to the section on "Soviet Science" declares that "Soviet leaders persuade the Russian people to believe that everything 'scientific' is good, beneficial, and the only answer to all the ills of the individual and thus of mankind. Science is also used as a vehicle for anti-religious propaganda." Actually, this attitude is not confined to the Soviet Union, but is also popular in the West. The article also contains a subsection on corruption in the Soviet economy; another section, headed "The Well-Paid Bureaucracy," describes how Party members take advantage of their position. While this information may be true and is certainly interesting, it is presented in a manner that seems intended not so much to convey facts as to persuade the reader of the Soviet system's flaws.

Compton's coverage of **South Africa** is more even-handed, certainly in comparison to the coverage that the subject gets in the New Standard Encyclopedia. However, the *Compton's* article is sketchy on the nation's history, and does not illuminate the Afrikaner mentality or explain how apartheid evolved.

In discussing the career of **Andrew Jackson**, *Compton's* skims over some of his more controversial actions, but does mention some of the contradictions of his personality:

Through his stormy life Jackson acted in many opposite ways. . . . He hanged two men as spies, ordered six soldiers shot for mutiny, killed one man in a duel and wounded others, yet spoiled his little adopted son. He swore, gambled, owned fighting cocks, and raced horses, yet built a church for his wife and he deeply revered God. . . . He insisted that others obey, yet broke the law whenever he pleased. He flew into rages when anger suited his purpose, yet showed the greatest patience with his slaves, his family, and his friends.

Yet in all, the article paints a flattering portrait of a dashing if rather rough-hewn hero. While mentioning some of Jackson's character flaws, the article clearly sides with him, depicting his presidency in a positive light. His pro-slavery views go unmentioned, as do his forcible removal of Indians from their own lands, his abuse of patronage, and his disdain for the Supreme Court. The implications of his bank policy are never discussed.

Abortion gives some idea of the controversy surrounding abortion, but does not really explain the full moral and political implications of the issue from either side:

> Induced abortion is regarded as a moral issue in some cultures. In others it is seen as a perfectly acceptable method of birth control. . . . In the United States abortion was made legal in 1971 [*sic*—it was actually 1973] over the objection of some groups, the Roman Catholic Church in particular. Those opposed to abortion feel it is the taking of a human life. Those in favor of legalized abortion cite overpopulation, the problems of unwanted children, and the dangers of illegal abortion.

The article on **evolution**, prepared by a University of Texas zoologist and a Fellow of San Diego's Salk Institute, is one of the few signed articles in *Compton's*. Although it describes religious and mythical views of the origin of life, the article assumes that **evolution** has been proven. There is no separate entry on creationism.

Compton's coverage of the social sciences also tends to be unacceptably biased. The encyclopedia is highly prescriptive in its broad assertions. For example, in the article on **Maturity** cited in *Accuracy*, one reads that "The emotionally mature person is free from moodiness. He is also free from sentimentality, although he is not lacking in love, patriotism, or loyalty to family or friends. He simply does not allow his sentiments to sweep him off his feet." The subsection on "Social Maturity" comments that "a mature citizen does not . . . limit his part in the government to paying taxes, voting, and obeying the laws." The implication of the article is that character idiosyncrasies or deviations from some ideal middle class norm are evidence of immaturity.

In other subject areas, *Compton's* is usually objective. The article on **pollution**, to name one, is exceptional. The Fact-Index entries are entirely factual and objective. Once again, however, *Compton's* does not measure up to its competitors.

VIII. Accessibility

Compton's structure should pose no undue difficulty for the intended user. The frontmatter in Volume 1 includes one page on "How to Use *Compton's Encyclopedia*," which explains the organization of the articles and of the Fact-Index. The editors advise, "Always consult the Fact-Index first. You may have to go no further. . . . If you need more [information], the Fact-Index tells you where to look in *Compton's*." This claim is well-founded.

For example, suppose the student is looking for information about Marie Curie. The student can consult either the Fact-Index for Volume 5 (Chile-Czech) or the Master Fact-Index in Volume 26, where the same information is duplicated. The entry reads:

Curie, **Marie**, or **Manya Skodowska** (1867–1934), French physicist C-806, *picture* R-70
   nuclear physics N-378g
   radium R-63
   term "radioactivity" B-123

This entry shows that, as the editors claim, "the Fact-Index is both a source of information in its own right and a guide to the information in all the rest of *Compton's*. . . ."

Each volume also contains a table of contents, titled "Here and There in Volume _____." In this table of contents, subject entries are listed alphabetically under several subject area headings: *Arts, Physical Science, Living Things, Medicine, Technology and Business, Geography, History, Social and Political Science,* and *Potpourri*. The editors note, however, that "While [the subject-area outline] may serve as a study guide, a specialized learning experience, or simply a key for browsing, it is not a complete table of contents." Still, in conjunction with the Fact-Index, the contents outline will enhance the set's accessibility for most readers.

Entries in *Compton's* are arranged alphabetically, letter by letter. Following standard indexing practice, names beginning with *Mc* are treated as though they begin with *Mac;* the same rule applies to the use of the abbreviation *St.* for *Saint*.

Guide words at the top of each page indicate the first entry on the left-hand page and the last entry on the right-hand page. Page numbers are located at the bottom of each page, flush with the outside margin. Entry headings are printed in large capitals in boldface type. Subheads within articles are also printed in boldface and are easy to locate.

Cross-references in *Compton's* are in the form of parenthetical *See also . . .* notes placed within the text. The publisher has not made a count of the number of cross-entries, but estimates that there are "thousands." Our examination of the encyclopedia indicates that *Compton's* contains far fewer cross-references than WORLD BOOK, for example, which has 100,000. It is quite evident that *Compton's* cross-referencing system is not comprehensive.

IX. Special Features

In addition to the Fact-Index, which is not a standard feature in any other general multivolume encyclopedia, *Compton's* includes several interesting and helpful features. The "Here and There" contents pages at the beginning of each volume have already been mentioned. Following each "Here and There" section is a feature titled "Exploring Volume ____," consisting of a two-page spread with several four-color illustrations directly related to articles in the volume. Accompanying each illustration is a caption asking a question intended to spark the reader's curiosity about the subject. The caption also gives the page number on which the answer can be found. For example, one of the photographs in "Exploring Volume 12" shows a jaguar; the caption asks, "Which is the largest member of the cat family to be found on the American continents?" and refers the reader to page 12. This feature is not crucial, but it does add some interest and color to the set, especially for younger readers.

Most articles on individual continents, nations, American states, and Canadian provinces are accompanied by "Fact Summaries" which give basic information about the subject. These summaries often include tables, charts, and graphs containing information about economy, natural resources, population growth, etc. There may also be a page devoted to "Notable Events" in the history of the nation or state, in addition to "Profile" pages illustrated with four-color photographs. Articles on individual presidents include time lines noting significant events during that presidency, as well as maps that show locations of major world events in this period. These features are all well designed and present important information in a clear and straightforward manner. However, as already noted, many of the facts and statistics are outdated and thus no longer accurate.

Some articles about foreign countries and scientific or technical subjects include short pedagogical sections ("Words to Know" and "Questions to Think About"). These features do not appear consistently from article to article, and are generally too brief and random to be useful. Similar features are presented much more effectively in WORLD BOOK.

Bibliographies appear at the conclusion of many (though not all) of the more extensive articles. Unlike those in FUNK & WAGNALLS, *Compton's* are not annotated. Moreover, a significant proportion of the titles listed have copyright dates from the 1960s or earlier; most of these books are out of print, although many may be found in the collections of larger libraries. The bibliographies are helpful in that they are divided into "Books for Children" and "Books for Young Adults and Teachers."

Most of *Compton's* 2,000 maps are in four-color and were prepared by the well-known cartographic firm of Hammond, Inc. In general, these maps are well drawn, and are usually large enough to be read easily. Political, physical, and special land-use maps are included. Two-color maps are used to indicate voyages of discovery. *Compton's* maps compare favorably with those in FUNK & WAGNALLS and NEW STANDARD; while not quite up to the excellent standard set in WORLD BOOK, they are far more appealing than those in MERIT.

As previously noted, *Compton's* first gained fame through its extensive use of stunning illustrations. In recent years the publisher has failed to maintain its original high standard, and many of the illustrations are now quite noticeably dated. The publisher claims that about one-third of *Compton's* illustrations are in four-color, but these are not spread evenly throughout the set. Thus, most of the pages are visually drab.

X. Format

Compton's Encyclopedia comes in one format—the 26-volume print edition. Most volumes contain all the entries beginning with one letter, though entries for subjects beginning with certain letters (e.g., A, C, P, S) are spread over two volumes. All volumes are not of equal length, but the variation in the number of pages between one volume and another is much smaller than is the case in NEW STANDARD and WORLD BOOK. Each volume is about an inch thick, lightweight, and easy to handle.

The books are bound in sturdy, attractive red-and-black synthetic covers with embossed gold lettering. They should stand up to frequent, repeated use. The entire set takes up about two feet of horizontal shelf space.

XI. Other Opinions

Marda Woodbury, *ARBA 82*—review of 1981 edition: "*Compton's*, though attractive, relatively comprehensive, essentially fair and factual, and superbly organized, qualitatively falls behind both the MERIT STUDENTS ENCYCLOPEDIA and the WORLD BOOK, although it excels in some respects. . . . The set . . . is basically slanted for grades 5 through high school but is considered suitable for general family use.

"General assets of the set include high-quality layout and graphics, good typography, and readability. The overall organization and layout facilitate individual reading and browsing. . . . *Compton's*, though outdated in some respects, has kept its science articles (particularly its biology and physics), very current. . . . In some cases—not all—its historic content is superior."

Kenneth Kister, *Best Encyclopedias* (Oryx, 1986): "*Compton's* . . . provides especially strong coverage in the area of science and technology. The encyclopedia is normally reliable and interestingly written. On the negative side, it sometimes avoids controversial issues, is not always up-to-date, and its illustrations, once the set's greatest strength, are now often too dark and old."

Booklist/Reference Books Bulletin, November 15, 1986: "*Compton's* contains many current, authoritative, well-written and well-illustrated articles, especially in the area of science, and has the potential to be an excellent encyclopedia for children and young adults. Libraries that own several encyclopedias may find *Compton's* useful for supplemental information. However, before it can serve as the only encyclopedia in a home or library, the set will need extensive revision."

XII. Summary

In many respects, *Compton's* is an interesting, even fascinating, encyclopedia. Its articles are designed to spark the reader's curiosity, and its unique Fact-Index gives it a high degree of accessibility. But while the Fact-Index provides many additional entries, their usefulness is extremely limited. At the same time, the set's omissions can be frustrating. In the final analysis, because many of its articles rely on 1950s middle class assumptions and attitudes, *Compton's* cannot be considered a mainstream contemporary encyclopedia. The publisher is apparently making a concerted effort to update the set—an examination of Volumes 7, 9, and 23 illustrates this—but for the time being, other volumes remain extremely out of date. It may be some years before *Compton's* is restored to its former high standing. As *Booklist* points out, *Compton's* is an adequate supplemental encyclopedia for libraries with several multivolume titles, but makes a questionable first choice for families.

Individuals wishing to purchase *Compton's* may phone Britannica's Customer Service Department at (312) 347-7298; the publisher will arrange for a local distributor to deliver the set. Institutions can order the set from Britannica Educational Corporation at (800) 554-9862.

Compton's Precyclopedia

Facts at a Glance

Full Title: **Compton's Precyclopedia.**
Former Title: Compton's Young Children's Precyclopedia.
Publisher: Encyclopaedia Britannica, Inc.
Editor: Howard L. Goodkind.
Copyright: 1985.

Number of Volumes: 16.
Number of Entries: 642.
Number of Pages: 2,944.
Number of Maps: 18.
Number of Indexes: 1.
Number of Index Entries: 2,700.
Number of Cross-references: 1,321.
Number of Illustrations: 3,423.
Trim Size: $7\frac{3}{4}'' \times 9\frac{3}{16}''$.

Intended Readership: 4- to 8-year-olds.
Price: $249 retail, $239 to schools and libraries.
Sold directly to individuals and institutions by the publisher; also marketed at conferences and exhibits, and in malls. ISBN 0-85229-427-1.
Revised "as needed."

I. Introduction

Compton's Precyclopedia, a 16-volume collection of stories, poems, riddles, articles, and activities, is intended to "instruct as well as entertain the young child." The publisher describes a precyclopedia as a "trainer encyclopedia specifically designed for preschool and early school children—to turn the preschooler into pre-scholar."

Published by the F. E. Compton division of Encyclopaedia Britannica, Inc., *Compton's* first appeared in 1971 as *Compton's Young Children's Pre-cyclopedia*. Two years later the title was shortened to *Compton's Precyclopedia*. As the subtitle ("Based on the YOUNG CHILDREN'S ENCYCLOPEDIA") suggests, its contents are virtually identical to those of the *YCE*. Whereas the *YCE* is sold only to the home market, the *Precyclopedia* is available to schools and libraries. Moreover, each volume of *Compton's* includes a 24-page "Things To Do" section, and the set comes with a 110-page Teaching Guide and Index. Authority, scope, currency, accuracy, clarity, accessibility, and objectivity are discussed in the review of the YOUNG CHILDREN'S ENCYCLOPEDIA on pages 205-09.

II. Special Features

Each volume is prefaced by "Things to Do," a 24-page section of text-related activities. According to the editors, "some stories and articles lend themselves to activities more than others. [We] have chosen for additional emphasis only those articles that are 'activity oriented.' Some of these activities are for very young children, while others are for older children."

For example, the suggested follow-up activity for the story "Big Winds" tells how to record each day's weather by placing symbols on an ordinary calendar. Many of the activities—such as learning the alphabet through games—are both entertaining and educationally sound. Often, however, the follow-up activity is simply a quiz for older children, with instructions to see *Compton's Encyclopedia* for the answers. A typical activity for the older reader looks like this:

About Myths

Read "Gods of Fire" on page 39.
Ancient peoples believed that the gods controlled nature.
Here is a myth quiz for the older child.*
1. Who was the greatest of the gods?
2. Who was the god of the sea?
3. Which god rode in a sun chariot?
4. Who was the god of the underworld?
*For answers see Compton's Encyclopedia article on "Mythology."

The reader who does not have *Compton's Encyclopedia* will be frustrated. Moreover, the *Encyclopedia* is not a companion set to the *Precyclopedia*.

The Teaching Guide and Index is a self-contained 110-page paperback volume. The index provides a comprehensive listing of the subjects covered in the *Precyclopedia*; the teaching guide breaks the *Pre-*

cyclopedia's contents into 13 "topics most frequently taught in early school grades": *about make-believe*; *being me*; *pioneers*; *home, school, and family*; *health and safety*; *the community is people*; *communication*; *transportation*; *exploring*; *our earth*; *animals*; *plants*; and *getting ready for mathematics*.

Teaching guide topics are listed in boldface, preceded by a shaded square and numeral indicating where they are found in the teaching guide. Most of the subjects covered in the text are also printed in boldface, with volume and page numbers. Subjects mentioned within a major article are in regular type, with volume and page numbers. Entries from the "Things To Do" sections are preceded by "ballot boxes." A typical index entry follows:

7 Communication
Communication

Letter Writing **9**-58-61
Newspapers **11**-52-57
☐ pantomime game **4**-xviii
☐ picture quizzes **10**-xv; **4**-xviii
Radio **13**-26-29; **14**-87
Telegraphs **3**-116
Television **15**-24-33; **6**-158
See also Language, Signs and signals, Telephones

The teaching guide subdivides each topic into a number of possible study units. For example, the subtopics listed under *communication* include *developments in communication*, *communication with language*, *signs and signals*, *how we communicate through art*, and *how animals communicate*. The subtopic *developments in communication* refers to eight articles, including "The First Telephone" and "How a Television Show Is Made," as well as several "Things To Do" activities.

Although designated as a teaching guide, this section is in fact an index, with topical rather than alphabetic listings. It offers no teaching suggestions but refers the reader to related "Things To Do" activities.

III. Summary

Compton's Precyclopedia, an augmented version of the YOUNG CHILDREN'S ENCYCLOPEDIA, is a 16-volume set designed to stimulate a young child's curiosity and to provide preliminary experience in using an encyclopedia. *Compton's* is enhanced by two special features not available in the *YCE*: "Things To Do," and the Teaching Guide and Index. *Compton's* benefits from an extra-heavy-duty binding that enhances the set's durability for library use. In other respects, the two sets share the same strengths and weaknesses. Information is accessible, the scope of coverage wide though uneven, the reading level appropriate to the intended readership, and the illustrations appealing but uninspired. Factual articles tend to be vague, and much of the textual material of indifferent quality. Like the *YCE*, *Compton's* lacks bibliographies for further reading on topics of special interest.

Compton's Precyclopedia retails for $249—considerably more than the *YCE*. Individuals may find that the Teaching Guide and Index and the additional 24-page "Things To Do" featured in each volume are not worth an additional $100. The publisher offers a modest $10 discount to schools and libraries.

Individuals wishing to purchase *Compton's Precyclopedia* may contact the publisher, Encyclopaedia Britannica, Inc., at Britannica Centre, Customer Service Department, 310 South Michigan Avenue, Chicago, IL 60604, or telephone (312) 347-7298. Schools and libraries may order from the Britannica Educational Corporation at the same address, or phone (800) 554-9862.

Concise Columbia Encyclopedia

Facts at a Glance

Full Title: **The Concise Columbia Encyclopedia**.
Publisher: Columbia University Press, 562 West 113 Street, New York, NY 10025 (hardcover and large-print editions); Avon Books, 1790 Broadway, New York, NY 10019 (paperback edition).
Editors: Judith S. Levey and Agnes Greenhall.
Copyright: 1983.

Number of Volumes: 1. (18 volumes in large print edition.)
Number of Contributors: 33.
Number of Entries: 15,000.
Number of Pages: 943.
Number of Words: 1,000,000.
Number of Maps: 73.
Number of Cross-references: 50,000.
Number of Illustrations: 117, black-and-white only.
Trim Size: 7¼″ × 10¼″.

Intended Readership: secondary and above.
Price: $29.95, cloth; $14.95, paper; $275, large-print.
Sold in bookstores and by direct mail. ISBN 0-231-05678-8.
No revision policy; no scheduled revision.

I. Introduction

The Concise Columbia Encyclopedia, published in 1983, is a single-volume general encyclopedia intended for adult and secondary-level readers. As its title implies, the volume aims to be concise and yet truly encyclopedic—no easy task, given the immense body of knowledge that is condensed into so small a space. In their preface, the editors claim that to achieve this end they have made "scrupulous efforts to avoid distortion and to maintain readability without sacrificing grace of expression." However, they do not give details of their selection criteria, beyond saying that they "did not include articles that would be simply definitions available in a dictionary, not certain survey articles . . . on subjects whose depth and breadth precludes adequate treatment in a short-entry encyclopedia."

II. Scope

The Concise Columbia Encyclopedia contains 15,000 entries, each an average length of 70 words. Thus, the entire volume contains slightly more than one million words.

According to the editors, approximately one third of the entries are biographical. A spot-check by our reviewers bears this out. Place names and historical topics and events are also given prominent attention, but the *CCE* covers a wide range of subjects in all the traditional academic disciplines. The jacket blurb also asserts that over 3,000 articles deal with "up-to-date scientific and technical subjects." Relatively few entries relate to contemporary popular culture, and the book scrupulously avoids topics of merely passing interest or ephemeral quality in favor of mainstream subjects in the humanities and natural sciences. Such contemporary figures from the world of sports and entertainment who are included are those whose accomplishments in their fields, from the vantage point of 1982, seemed likely to have more than a passing impact. Among such entries are **Woody Allen**, **Henry Fonda**, **Jane Fonda**, and **Jack Nicklaus**.

In their preface, the editors explain that "subjects of approximately equal importance [sometimes] required different treatment. . . . Explanations in some detail proved to be necessary for an understanding of certain technical subjects, and some controversial topics required mention of several points of view. . . . The length of an article does not necessarily indicate the importance of a subject." Entries for complex scientific concepts or major historical movements are generally longer than those for biographical subjects.

Concise Columbia Encyclopedia

❶ 369

❸ HEART

Hazlitt, William, 1778-1830, English essayist and critic. His penetrating literary criticism is collected in *Characters of Shakespeare's Plays* (1817), *Lectures on the English Poets* (1818), *Lectures on the English Comic Writers* (1819), *Table Talk* (1821-22), and *The Spirit of the Age* (1825). His *Dramatic Literature of the Age of Elizabeth* (1820) renewed interest in SHAKESPEARE and Elizabethan drama. Among his masterful essays are "On Going a Journey," "My First Acquaintance with Poets," and "On the Feeling of Immortality in Youth."

Hazzard, Shirley, 1931-, Australian novelist. She has lived in the U.S. since 1951. Noted for her insight, sensitivity, and poetic style, she has published two collections of short stories and three novels, *The Evening of the Holiday* (1966), *The Bay of Noon* (1970), and *The Transit of Venus* (1980).

❷ **H.D.:** see DOOLITTLE, HILDA.

He, chemical symbol of the element HELIUM.

Head, Edith: see FASHION (table).

Head, Sir Francis Bond, 1793-1875, British lieutenant governor of Upper Canada (1835-37). He allied himself with the FAMILY COMPACT clique and drove radical reformers to revolt (1837). He quelled the revolt but was forced to leave (1838) Canada.

head-hunting, widespread practice of taking and preserving the head of a slain enemy, occurring from ancient times into the 20th cent. It may have evolved from CANNIBALISM. Taking a head was believed to strengthen one's own tribe and weaken the enemy's. Heads were also secured as tokens of courage and manhood. North American Indians took the scalp; the JIVARO of South America preserve the skin to make so-called shrunken heads.

Head Start, U.S. educational program for disadvantaged preschool children, established under the Economic Opportunity Act of 1964. The program was initially aimed at preparing poor children for elementary school, but it was later extended to children above the poverty level, whose parents paid according to their income.

Health and Human Services, United States Department of, federal executive department that administers government health and SOCIAL SECURITY programs. It is the reorganized successor (1979) to the Dept. of Health, Education, and Welfare. It includes the Public Health Service, the Office of Child Support Enforcement, the Social Security Administration, and the Health Care Financing Administration, which administers the Medicare and Medicaid programs.

Health, Education, and Welfare, United States Department of: see EDUCATION, UNITED STATES DEPARTMENT OF; HEALTH AND HUMAN SERVICES, UNITED STATES DEPARTMENT OF.

health insurance, prepayment plan providing medical services or cash indemnities for medical care; it may be voluntary or compulsory. Compulsory accident and sickness insurance was initiated (1883-84) in Germany by Bismarck and adopted by Britain, France, Chile, the USSR, and other nations after World War I. In 1948 Britain instituted the most comprehensive compulsory health plan to date, including free medical care from any doctor participating in the system; a small charge for some services has been instituted since then. Canada has provided nearly free hospital service since 1958 and more comprehensive coverage since 1967. National health insurance has been widely adopted in Europe and parts of Asia. In the U.S., where the medical profession opposed government health insurance, voluntary cooperative or commercial programs developed, offering limited benefits to group or individual subscribers. Blue Cross and Blue Shield, the largest such insurers, covering hospital care and doctors' fees respectively, are community-sponsored, nonprofit agencies. In 1965 the federal government established two plans: Medicare, for persons age 65 and over, providing basic hospital insurance and supplementary insurance for doctors' and other health-care bills; and Medicaid, for low-income persons, operated by the states and covering hospital, physician, and other services. The U.S. is the only Western industrial nation without some form of comprehensive national health insurance.

Health Maintenance Organization (HMO), type of prepaid medical service in which members pay a monthly or yearly fee for all health care, including hospitalization. Most

HMOs involve physicians engaged in group practice. Because costs to patients are fixed in advance, preventive medicine is stressed to avoid costly hospitalization. HMOs experienced some growth in the U.S. in the 1970s but, as late as 1982, covered less than 5% of the population. **❹**

Heaney, Seamus (hē'nē), 1939-, Northern Irish poet. Rooted in his own life and in that of Ireland, balanced between the personal and the topical, Heaney's carefully crafted poems are extremely evocative, yet clear and direct. His volumes of verse include *Door into the Dark* (1969), *North* (1975), and *Field Work* (1979). Many of his critical and autobiographical pieces in prose were collected in *Preoccupations* (1980).

hearing: see EAR.

Hearn, Lafcadio, 1850-1904, American author; b. Ionian Islands; came to U.S., 1869. Partially blind and morbidly discontented, he was skilled at writing about the macabre and exotic, e.g., *Stray Leaves from Strange Literature* (1884). In 1890 he went to Japan, where he became a citizen and wrote 12 books, e.g., *Japan: An Attempt at Interpretation* (1904).

Hearne, Samuel, 1745-92, British fur trader and explorer of N Canada. Working for the HUDSON'S BAY COMPANY, he explored the Coppermine River area in 1770. He opened up unknown territory and proved that there was no short NORTHWEST PASSAGE. **❺**

Hearst, William Randolph, 1863-1951, American journalist and publisher; b. San Francisco. During his lifetime Hearst established a vast publishing empire that included 18 newspapers in 12 cities and 9 successful magazines (including *Good Housekeeping* and *Harper's Bazaar*). His use of flamboyant pictures, shrieking typography, and earthy, mass-appeal news coverage, together with a policy of buying distinctive talent from other papers and selling papers at a penny, made him the leader in "penny journalism" by 1900. His papers' wild reports of Cuba's struggle for independence from Spain helped bring about the SPANISH-AMERICAN WAR. A flamboyant figure, he later in life became stridently conservative. His huge castle at San Simeon, Calif., is now a state museum.

heart, muscular organ that pumps blood to all parts of the body. The pear-shaped human heart is about the size of a fist and lies just left of center within the chest cavity. The contractions of heart muscle, or myocardium, are entirely self-stimulated. The heart is divided into two cavities by a wall of muscle; each cavity is divided in turn into two

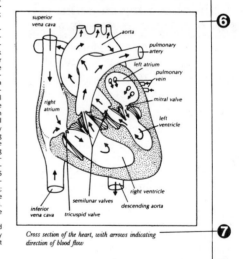

❻

superior vena cava

aorta

pulmonary artery

left atrium

pulmonary vein

mitral valve

right atrium

left ventricle

right ventricle

inferior vena cava

semilunar valves

tricuspid valve

descending aorta

Cross section of the heart, with arrows indicating direction of blood flow   **❼**

Cross-references are indicated by SMALL CAPITALS.   **❽**

Page shown at 70% of actual size.

❶ Page number

❷ Cross-reference entries

❸ Guide word

❹ Main entry: Concise Columbia contains 15,000 entries, arranged alphabetically, letter-by-letter. Entry words are printed in boldface type, and may be followed by a phonetic pronunciation.

❺ Cross-references: Concise Columbia contains 50,000 cross-references, printed in small capital letters.

❻ Illustration: Concise Columbia contains 117 illustrations, most of which are annotated. All illustrations are in black-and-white.

❼ Caption

❽ Annotation repeated on every right-hand page reminds user about cross-references. Annotation in corresponding position on left-hand pages reminds user about pronunciation guide in the front matter.

As an indication of how space is apportioned among different historical figures, a sampling of biographical entries on a page taken at random (page 240) shows the following: **John Dos Passos** is accorded 10 lines; **Fedor Dostoevski**, 32 lines; **Gerard Dou**, 4; **Abner Doubleday**, 7; **Charles Doughty**, 3; **Sir James Douglas**, 6; **Sir James de Douglas**, 8; **Stephen Douglas**, 15; **William Douglas**, 8; **Sir Alec Douglas-Home**, 6; and **Frederick Douglass**, 10.

The *CCE* is also notable for its coverage of non-American, non-British topics. For example, out of 19 people and place entries on a random page (page 473), 14 are non-American and non-British. Another random page (page 330) includes such entries as **Gezira** (a region in the Sudan), **Ghana** (separate articles on the ancient African empire and the modern African nation), the **Ghats** mountain ranges in India, the Islamic philosopher **al-Ghazali**, the 20th century Belgian dramatist **Michel de Ghelderode**, the Belgian city of **Ghent**, the Rumanian Communist leader **Gheorghe Gheorghiu-Dej**, the Florentine artists **Lorenzo Ghiberti** and **Domenico Ghirlandaio**, and the Indian mystic **Aurobindo Ghose**.

As already mentioned, a preponderance of the articles are specific-entry rather than general-survey. However, the encyclopedia does include "articles on many specific aspects of these broad topics." Only rarely does the *CCE* depart from this scheme, as in the articles on the **French Revolution**, the **Renaissance**, and **Renaissance art and architecture**. Such longer articles tend to be brief chronological sketches, and rely heavily on a system of extensive cross-references. Generally, however, the specific entries are only several sentences long.

With 117 line drawings and 73 maps accompanying nearly 1000 pages of text, the *CCE* is sparsely illustrated. There are no photographs. The line drawings, many of which are annotated diagrams, pertain almost exclusively to technical subjects (e.g., **circulatory system**, **ear**, **jet propulsion engines**, **reproductive system**), and thus add to the encyclopedia's conciseness. Here, the *CCE* has a distinct advantage over the NEW AMERICAN DESK ENCYCLOPEDIA, which has no illustrations and only rudimentary maps. At the same time, because the *CCE* does not contain photographs or color illustrations, the publisher is still able to sell the book at a reasonable price.

III. Authority

Over the last half century, the Columbia University Press has established a solid reputation as a leading publisher of both general and topical reference works. *The Concise Columbia Encyclopedia* carries on the tradition of excellence begun in 1935 with the *Columbia Encyclopedia* and continued with subsequent editions of that work, including the celebrated 1963 edition and the extensively revised *New Columbia Encyclopedia* (1975). Some users may also be familiar with the one-volume *Columbia-Viking Desk Encyclopedia* and the 22-volume *Illustrated Columbia Encyclopedia* (1967). All these titles are currently out of print.

The work's joint editors, Judith S. Levey and Agnes Greenhall, bring impressive credentials to the book. Levey, now Editor-in-Chief at Macmillan, held that position at Columbia University Press and has edited a number of other reference works. Greenhall was Senior Editor, Humanities, for the *New Columbia Encyclopedia*; Associate Editor, Humanities, for COLLIER'S ENCYCLOPEDIA and MERIT STUDENTS ENCYCLOPEDIA; and Managing Editor of *The Columbia Dictionary of Modern European Literature*. The editors were assisted by the reference staff of the Columbia University Press.

Nineteen of the book's 33 consultants are affiliated with Columbia University; most of the remaining consultants hold posts at other universities, museums, or on periodicals. The extent of the consultants' participation is not clear, though the generally high quality and factual accuracy of the individual entries would seem to indicate that the articles were carefully checked by content specialists.

The editors acknowledge that "although the articles have been prepared especially for the *Concise* encyclopedia, much of the information derives from its predecessors—especially *The New Columbia Encyclopedia*." Direct comparison of entries in the two books gives clear evidence that many of the *Concise Columbia*'s articles are basically adaptations of longer articles that appeared in the earlier volume. At the same time, about 500 new entries were written especially for this volume, and articles adapted from *New Columbia* have been revised to bring them up-to-date.

The individual contributors—the writers who actually wrote the articles—are listed in the front of the book. However, their credentials, affiliations, and areas of expertise are not given. All articles are unsigned.

IV. Currency

Published in 1983, *The Concise Columbia Encyclopedia* differs significantly from most other single- and multivolume encyclopedias in that it is not periodically revised, but is rather a one-time publication. This puts it at an automatic disadvantage when compared with other small volume encyclopedias for currency.

The editors claim that "many of our articles reflect the enormous changes that have taken place worldwide during the past five years" (i.e., 1978–83). The preface states that "the articles are up to date as of January 1, 1983," an assertion that seems justified, for the most part. The articles on **Ronald Reagan**, **Margaret Thatcher**, and **South Africa**, for example, include information on those subjects through 1982. One subject conspicuous by its omission, however, is AIDS, which was first identified in 1980.

The publisher's policy of not revising the book periodically does pose certain limitations on the encyclopedia's currency, limitations that will become increasingly apparent with the passage of time. For example, while the article on **nuclear disarmament** ends with mention of the 1982 Strategic Arms Reduction Talks, there can obviously be no mention of President Reagan's 1983 Strategic Defense Initiative—the kind of information that one would expect to be included were the book revised on a regular cycle. Nor can one expect any mention of the Bhopal, Challenger, Chernobyl, and Rhine disasters, which would also have to be incorporated in a revision. Thus, in terms of currency, *The Concise Columbia Encyclopedia* will become increasingly weak in its coverage of current events; however, its coverage of pre-1983 events is reliably up-to-date and, in subject areas where no new findings or interpretations are expected, should remain authoritative.

V. Accuracy

The highly condensed articles that make up the *CCE* are comprised largely of straightforward statements of facts and figures. Indeed, with its experienced editors and team of distinguished consultants, this reference work sets high standards for factual accuracy. A great deal of meticulous scholarship has evidently gone into the preparation of this volume.

Factual errors do occasionally occur, however. For example, the article on **herpes simplex** reports that: "Genital herpes, a type of VENEREAL DISEASE, can be treated with the drug acyclovir." The article does not mention that this drug treats only the symptoms of the infection, and that, as of January 1983, genital herpes was incurable.

Our subject specialists note that the *CCE*'s entries on **money** and **Saturn** are both brief but accurate. The encyclopedia's coverage of the **Bill of Rights** is somewhat cursory, but correct as far as it goes. **Transistors** is brief and discusses only bipolar transistors; however, it does contain important cross-references

to entries on **integrated circuits** and **microelectronics**, which help give the reader a more complete picture of the subject.

On the whole, such sins of omission that occur from time to time seem to be the unavoidable consequence of this encyclopedia's concise approach—in which complex topics must necessarily be reduced to their bare essentials—rather than of editorial carelessness. Such omissions will rarely affect the value of the work for the high school student. The *CCE* can generally be counted on to provide accurate factual information, and the reader need have little hesitation in trusting the facts presented in this work.

VI. Clarity

Many of the *CCE*'s articles are abridged versions of articles from *New Columbia*. With the average length of an entry a mere 70 words, clarity was obviously a prime concern. The articles are straightforward and to the point. Scholarship is evident in the writing, but the scholarly quality does not intrude on presentation of the subject. *CCE*'s straightforward prose presents a clear contrast to LINCOLN LIBRARY, which is sometimes pedantic and tends to rely on generalities in many of its articles. The tone and style of the NEW AMERICAN DESK ENCYCLOPEDIA is more directly comparable.

In general, entries in the *CCE* assume that although the reader may have heard of the particular subject, he or she has no previous knowledge of that subject. The purpose of this encyclopedia is to present basic facts about the subjects rather than to give specialist information that may not be available elsewhere. Throughout the work, our reviewers found no condescension or unnecessary explanation.

A few examples will illustrate the style of the entries in the *CCE*. The entries are quoted in full.

Muses, in Greek mythology, the nine patron goddesses of the arts; daughters of ZEUS and Mnemosyne, a TITAN who personified memory. They were: Calliope (epic poetry and eloquence), Euterpe (music and lyric poetry), Erato (love poetry), Polyhymnia (oratory or sacred poetry), Clio (history), Melpomene (tragedy), Thalia (comedy), Terpsichore (choral song and dance), and Urania (astronomy).

Lena, river, easternmost of the great rivers of Siberia, USSR, c. 2,670 mi (4,300 km) long. It flows generally north, then northeast, from a source near Lake BAYKAL to empty into the ARCTIC OCEAN through a delta c. 250 mi (400 km) wide. The river, which is navigable for 2,135 mi (3,436 km) in summer, is frozen at its mouth from Oct. to June.

gadolinium (GD), metallic element, extracted in oxide form by J.C.G. de Marignac in 1880. This silver-white malleable, ductile, lustrous RARE-EARTH METAL is found in gadolinite, MONAZITE, and bastnasite. It is paramagnetic at room temperature but becomes strongly ferromagnetic when cooled. See ELEMENT (table); PERIODIC TABLE.

While these entries are straightforward, they require at least a passing familiarity with Greek mythology, Asian geography, and chemistry, respectively. Some readers may find that they will also need to consult a dictionary. Also, contrary to the editors' stated intention, some of the articles (such as the one on gadolinium) are only one step removed from being dictionary definitions. As you can see, while these articles are clear and precise as far as they go, they are little more than thumbnail sketches. The article on the **Muses**, for example, neither explains the implications of their parentage nor indicates their mythological and historical significance. The **gadolinium** article gives the reader no idea of the metal's uses, if any.

The articles in the *Concise Columbia Encyclopedia* conform to a strict house style. The entire book reads like the work of a single author, or of a handful of experienced authors who are all the product of the same intellectual environment. While this is not necessarily desirable (or even possible to achieve) in a general multivolume encyclopedia, it brings particular benefits to a concise one-volume reference work. For one thing, the articles are structured in such a way that, after using this encyclopedia a few times, the reader knows what to look for and what to expect in an entry. Rarely are these expectations disappointed. While technical terms are not defined in the context of an entry, the reader is frequently directed, via a cross-reference, to a separate entry for that term. On the whole, the entries in the *CCE* are models of brevity and precision. However, as the publisher acknowledges, the book is not suitable for students below high school level.

VII. Objectivity

In its tone and in the balance with which it presents information on a wide range of subjects, *The Concise Columbia Encyclopedia* is scholarly and objective. The article on **homosexuality** notes that "Medical and psychological research has yielded little evidence that homosexuality is caused by either biological predisposition or feelings that one belongs to the opposite sex. No theory is conclusive but many have been proposed. . . ." The concluding sentence in **Republic of South Africa** reports that "South Africa's refusal to yield control over Namibia, its creation of bantustans, and its rigid support of apartheid has led to growing international ostracism of the country." The entry on **Ronald Wilson Reagan** gives factual information about his presidency through 1982 without editorial comment.

In articles dealing with political or religious subjects (or subjects which may be the focus of political or religious controversy), the encyclopedia's tone is rigorously neutral. It presents known facts as such, and identifies theory as such. For example, the article on **evolution** describes the concept and dispassionately states the grounds on which it rests. It also notes that "[evolution] has been challenged by those believing in the creation theory of the universe (see **CREATIONISM**)." The article on **creationism** describes it as "belief in the biblical account of the creation of the world," and notes that its advocates dispute the theory of evolution. The articles make no value judgments on either subject.

As previously noted, the *CCE* does an admirable job of avoiding, as far as is possible in a work of its size and scope, an undue American bias in its contents. (See *Scope*.)

VIII. Accessibility

With space limitations making conciseness a major concern, the editors appear to have given careful thought to the book's layout and to the arrangement of the articles. A one-and-a-half-page introduction, "How to Use *The Concise Columbia Encyclopedia*," systematically explains all the elements and variations of style that are encountered in the body of this volume. However, the explanations are not as clear as they might be.

All article heads are in boldface type, making them easy to distinguish and identify at a glance. Entries are arranged alphabetically by word. Headnotes indicate the first entry on the left-hand page and the last entry on the right-hand page. Page numbers are located at the top of the page, but flush with the inside, not the outside, margin of the page—a format that makes them less easy to see as the reader thumbs through the book.

Given the number of entries and the complexity of some of the subjects, it was probably inevitable that the arrangement of the entries could not be as obvious or as clear-cut as the user might wish. While the editors have attempted to come up with a logical system for arranging the entries, they have not been entirely consistent, and there are some puzzling exceptions to each rule they have made.

For example, when several items have the same heading, they are arranged in order of persons, places, and things. Thus, **McKinley, William** comes before **McKinley, Mount**. However, **Paris**, the city, precedes **Paris**, the character whose abduction of Helen precipitated the Trojan War. The reason for this deviation is unclear, unless the second Paris, being mythological, is classified as a thing rather than as a person. Such apparent inconsistencies mean that the reader may not initially find a particular article where he or she expected to find it, and that it may be necessary to look in other likely locations.

There are several other departures from strict alphabetic order when the encyclopedia deals with proper names. Although most biographical headings are inverted and alphabetized by the subject's last name (e.g., **Bunyan, Paul**), some mythological or folkloric figures are entered with their first name first (e.g., **John Henry**). The rationale for this is not made clear. Names with *de*, *van*, *von*, or other prefixes are entered according to what the editors regard as the most common form of the name in general use. Thus, the *CCE* gives us **Beauvoir, Simone de**; **Teilhard de Chardin, Pierre**; and **von Neuman, John**; there are no cross-reference entries for possible variations, such as "**de Beauvoir, Simone**: see BEAUVOIR." This can make certain entries difficult to find, and may be frustrating to the reader who is unfamiliar with the common form of a particular name, or when there are several commonly used forms. The reader has better luck finding articles on people who are best known by their pseudonyms: the entry for **Evans, Mary Ann**, for example, refers the reader to **Eliot, George** for information about the famous Victorian novelist.

Names beginning with *Mc* are treated as though they begin with *Mac*. A similar rule applies to the use of the abbreviation *St.* for *Saint*.

Members of the same family are generally grouped together under the family name. Monarchs are grouped together under their given name by nationality. Thus, the *CCE* gives us "**Henry**, rulers of the Holy Roman Empire"; "**Henry**, kings of England"; and "**Henry**, kings of France." The individual rulers are treated in succession within the appropriate article.

While such treatment of proper name entries may seem like excessive scholarly scruple, and may occasionally confuse or even intimidate some readers, the system is not difficult to master. The boldface type makes entries easy to spot, and with a little practice in thumbing through the volume, users can find subjects in the *CCE* as easily as they can find words in a dictionary.

The real key to the accessibility of the *CCE* is the volume's extensive system of cross-references, of which there are some 50,000. It is this system that helps the book achieve its conciseness. Cross-references occur in the text of individual articles, at the conclusion of articles, and immediately after a heading when the subject is actually discussed under a different heading (such as "**peat moss**: see SPHAGNUM"). In all cases, cross-reference indications are printed in small capitals, making them, like the entry headings, immediately identifiable.

Occasionally, some articles seem to be little more than lists of cross-references. The 32-line article on **drugs**, for instance, refers the reader to 29 different articles. There is a danger that an article will rely so heavily on cross-references that the reader will be unable to comprehend the subject without reading the related entries. Also, the potential purchaser should be aware that *The Concise Columbia Encyclopedia* does not contain an index. This is a distinct drawback, especially in light of the inconsistencies in the arrangement of entries as already noted. Without an index, the user has no easy and reliable way of knowing whether a certain topic is included in the *CCE* or, if it is, on what page it is discussed.

Regardless of these criticisms, however, in the vast majority of cases the use of cross-references greatly enhances the value of a particular article. Indeed, the careful and comprehensive cross-referencing throughout *The Concise Columbia Encyclopedia* is indispensable to the volume's conciseness. And the book's alphabetical arrangement makes it more accessible and far less complicated to the average reader than is The LINCOLN LIBRARY OF ESSENTIAL INFORMATION.

IX. Special Features

As a basic single-volume desk encyclopedia, *The Concise Columbia Encyclopedia* does not boast any unusual special features. Many of its features, such as metric equivalents for measurements and pronunciations for some foreign-name entries, are standard for any encyclopedia of this size and scope. The book is significantly enhanced, however, by the clear line drawings that illustrate subjects not easily explained in the text. (For more on the illustrations, see *Scope*.)

Equally helpful are 37 tables which accompany corresponding entries. While some of these tables (e.g., **Constitution of the United States, Rulers of England and Great Britain, Nobel Prizes**) are fairly standard and will be found in any decent encyclopedia, others are quite surprising and provide interesting factual information not readily accessible in other general reference sources. Among such tables are **African Languages**, **American Indian Languages**, **Dance Companies**, **Music Festivals**, **National Parks of the United States**, and **Shakespeare's Plays**. Many of these tables are by no means all-inclusive and comprehensive, but they do give the reader a handy, compact outline, providing good starting points for further study. Like the text, the tables also make extensive use of cross-referencing.

X. Format

The Concise Columbia Encyclopedia is available in hardcover and paperback. The hardcover edition is priced at $29.95; the paperback, distributed by Avon Books, retails for $14.95. The paperback version is a photo-reduced copy of the hardcover edition, which means that the print in the paperback version is noticeably smaller. The text of both editions is identical. There is also an eight-volume large print edition for $275.

The hardcover edition does have the advantage of a 16-page, four-color world atlas provided by Rand McNally, which appears in the middle of the book. Though the map scales are small and not consistent throughout the atlas, the overall quality of these maps is very good indeed. The paperback edition includes seven maps of the continents. These black-and-white maps, which appear in the back of the volume, are rudimentary and cannot compare in quality to the color atlas in the hardcover version.

The other main difference between the hardcover and paperback versions is durability. While the paperback is half the price of the hardcover edition, it may become worn much more quickly. Libraries will certainly prefer the more durable hardcover edition. Both formats are certainly more suitable for school and library use than is the format of the NEW AMERICAN DESK ENCYCLOPEDIA. At the same time, the *CCE* is easier to handle than the two large books that comprise THE LINCOLN LIBRARY.

XI. Other Opinions

Harry E. Whitmore, *Library Journal* (December 15, 1983): "The *Concise Columbia* continues the high standards of its predecessors and is a useful ready reference and supplementary information source. There is no comparable work within its price range."

Wilson Library Bulletin (December 1983): "Giving balanced subject coverage in clear, objective articles, the *Concise Columbia* merits accolades and frequent use as a desk reference."

Reference Books Bulletin (March 1, 1984): "The *Concise Columbia* covers a broad range of historical and contemporary topics. . . . There are some inconsistencies in coverage. . . . Articles include facts and brief explanations; they generally lack the historical coverage and detail found in the *New Columbia*, [but] the level of accuracy is high. . . . The encyclopedia is both current and objective. . . . [It] is a reasonably priced reference tool for all types of libraries and for home use as well . . . an attractive alternative to other . . . one-volume encyclopedias [for] ready reference."

School Library Journal (May 1984): "Within its limitations of brevity, this is a useful, ready-reference tool for junior high and up."

Samuel Rothstein, *ARBA 84*: "For clarity, coverage, ease of use, and low cost, *CCE* ranks very high indeed. It should be a top priority for the home reference library, and even in institutional collections its up-to-dateness and conciseness will make it welcome."

XII. Summary

The Bowker library survey indicates that while many librarians continue to find the *New Columbia Encyclopedia* a useful single-volume reference work, patrons consult the *Concise Columbia Encyclopedia* much less frequently. The book's relatively compact format, reasonable price, and wide availability—it is stocked in many bookstores—would seem to indicate that the *CCE* is intended primarily for purchase by individuals for use in the home, rather than as a major library reference resource. However, it may also be a particularly attractive purchase to high school libraries and small public libraries with limited budgets.

The *CCE* provides concise, accurate, and fairly accessible answers to such questions as, What islands make up the nation of The Comoros, and where are they located? When were seeing-eye guide dogs first used? What happens in a cell during meiosis? What is a mirage? While it obviously cannot compete with multivolume encyclopedias in providing in-depth discussions of these topics, and indeed contains less detailed information than the competing small-volume encyclopedias, for its size and price it is a remarkable value. Keeping in mind its limitations, it can be highly recommended to the adult or high school reader looking for a handy desk-top single-volume encyclopedia for personal use.

The Encyclopedia Americana

Facts at a Glance

Full Title: **The Encyclopedia Americana**.
Publisher: Grolier Incorporated, Sherman Turnpike, Danbury, CT 06816.
Editors: Bernard S. Cayne, Editorial Director; David T. Holland, Editor-in-Chief.
Copyright: 1987.

Number of Volumes: 30.
Number of Entries: 52,000.
Number of Pages: 26,965.
Number of Words: 30,800,000.
Number of Maps: 1,279.
Number of Cross-references: 40,000.
Number of Indexes: 1.
Number of Index Entries: 353,000.
Number of Illustrations: 3,184 four-color; 19,468 black-and-white.
Trim Size: 7¼" × 10".

Intended Readership: upper elementary through adult.
Price: $1,200 plus shipping and handling for individuals; $869 plus shipping and handling school/library discount.
Sold directly by the publisher and door-to-door. ISBN 0-7172-0118-X.
Revised annually.

I. Introduction

The Encyclopedia Americana is a 30-volume work written for "a wide range of readers . . . [including] young students, teachers, librarians, and adults. . . . The content," the publisher claims, "reflects the curriculum in the upper elementary and secondary grades, and covers subjects of general interest to the family." Today, the *Americana* is regarded as one of the "big three" scholarly encyclopedias on the market—the other two being COLLIER'S ENCYCLOPEDIA and NEW ENCYCLOPAEDIA BRITANNICA. To some degree, as its title indicates, the *Americana* is designed to emulate the *Britannica* and to challenge it as the preeminent encyclopedia in the United States.

II. Scope

With some 52,000 articles, the *Americana* is one of the most wide-ranging of all multivolume encyclopedias, second only to BRITANNICA, which contains approximately 11,000 more entries. Like both BRI-

TANNICA and COLLIER'S, the *Americana* includes a mix of general survey and specific-entry articles. As the publisher notes, the short articles are designed for ready reference; "when further expansion is needed," the articles are somewhat longer; and very long articles allow major subjects to be covered at some length. "Many of the short articles are 20 lines or less and are structured to answer specific questions on a subject. Every short article is designed at least to define, describe, and provide the significance of the subject it covers," the publisher adds. On the whole, these claims are justified. In effect, *Americana*'s extended general-subject entries serve much the same function as NEW BRITANNICA'S Macropaedia entries, although *Americana* does not segregate these entries from the rest of the text.

As an indication of how space is apportioned among different subjects, **Charlemagne** receives two-and-one-half pages; **Konstantin Chernenko** gets just over one-half page (including a family photograph); **Ty Cobb** also receives one-half page, with a photograph. The article on the American **Civil War** is 38 pages long; 17 pages are devoted to **Christianity**; and **China** is treated in 106 pages.

Although the set is geared to the American reader, Grolier reports—not without justification—that the *Americana*'s "coverage of foreign topics, such as foreign cities, artists, and politicians, is in most cases at least as great as that of American topics and in some cases greater."

As an indication of the attention *Americana* gives to non-American subjects, the encyclopedia's entries from **Bartolome Mitre** to **Mohammed**, inclusive, include the following articles: **Mitre** (Argentine statesman), **Dimitri Mitropoulos** (Greek-born American orchestral conductor), **Eilhard Mitscherlich** (19th century German chemist), **Francois Mitterand** (French president), **Mixtec Indians, Miyagi** (Japanese prefecture), **Miyazaki** (Japanese city), **Mizoram** (territory in India), **Mo Tzu** (ancient Chinese philosopher), **Moab** (ancient Near Eastern Kingdom), **Vilhelm Moberg** (20th century Swedish author), **Mobutu Sese Seko** (Zairian president), **Moche** (Peruvian valley), **Modena** (Italian city), **modernismo** (Latin American literary movement), **Modigliani** (Italian artist), **Thomas Mofolo** (African writer), **Mogadishu** (Somalian capital), **Mogilev** (Russian city), **Mohacs** (Hungarian town), and **Mohammed**. These represent 21 entries out of a total of 58 in this span.

III. Authority

The *Americana* has the distinction of being the first encyclopedia published in the United States. The initial volumes were issued in 1829, and the first set

The Encyclopedia Americana

1 — 420 KHOMEINI–KHORRAMSHAHR — 5

2 —

LEDRU/PAVLOVSKY/SYGMA

3 — Ayatollah Ruhollah Khomeini, inspirer and symbol of Iran's successful revolution in 1979 against the shah.

4 — **KHOMEINI,** KHŌ-mä'nē, **Ruhollah** (1900–), Iranian religious leader, known by the Islamic title of *ayatollah,* who directed the overthrow of the shah in January 1979 and became the source of political authority in succeeding governments.

Ruhollah was born in the town of Khomein (Khumain) in west central Iran. His family name was Hendi, but he later assumed the name Khomeini from his birthplace. He attended religious schools and then became a teacher of religion and philosophy. Outspoken in his opposition to the shah for adulterating Islam and weakening the religious community by his secularizing policies, he received the religious title of ayotollah by popular acclaim in the 1950's. His criticisms of the shah led to imprisonment and then in 1964 to exile in Najaf, Iraq. When his denunciations of the shah caused difficulties in Iraq, he was expelled from that country and settled with his second wife near Paris in October 1978.

The ayatollah directed the movement to overthrow the shah by smuggling into Iran taped messages that were then broadcast by religious leaders to the faithful. He called for a general strike in October 1978, which was followed by a crippling strike in the oil fields in November. Strikes led to riots, and finally on Jan. 16, 1979, the shah went into exile. Khomeini returned to Iran in triumph on February 1.

The ayatollah took no office for himself but retired to the holy city of Qum. From there he directed the revival of traditionalist Islamic values, customs, laws, and legal procedures, detailing how they were to affect all activities, public and private. All matters of importance, including the handling of the American hostages taken from the U.S. embassy when it was seized by Iranian militants in November 1979 and the drafting of a new constitution, were referred to him for final decision. He acted as arbiter among the various feuding secular and religious groups that struggled for power in the revolutionary state, playing off one faction against another. But his most faithful supporters, chiefly peasants who had gained control of parliament, opposed the revolution's more conservative factions by favoring land redistribution.

In 1979 the ailing ayatollah assumed the all-powerful role of Fagih, or Religious Guide. As Fagih he was commander in chief of the army, which succeeded in 1982 in rolling back an Iraqi invasion that had begun two years before.

KHONE FALLS, kô-nä', a cataract on the Mekong — 6 River where it crosses the Laos-Kampuchea (Cambodia) border near Voun Kham, Kampuchea. Here, about 180 miles (290 km) above Phnom Penh, the Mekong flows around Khone Island, and the branches rejoin. Although the Khone drops only 70 feet (21 meters), it has the second-largest volume of all waterfalls, with an average discharge of about 400,000 cubic feet (11,325 cu meters). Only the Guairá Falls on the Paraná River in South America is larger.

Khone Falls, also known as Chute des Khone, makes the Mekong River unnavigable and is a factor in dividing the economies of Laos and Kampuchea.

KHORASAN. See KHURASAN, a province in Iran; — 7 and KHURASAN, a historical region.

KHOREZM OBLAST, kō-rezm', a major civil division of the Uzbek republic of the Soviet Union. With an area of 1,730 square miles (4,480 sq km), it lies on the left bank of the Amu-Darya in the southeast half of Khorezm (Khiva) oasis. The name Khorezm is a Russian variant of Khwarizm. (See KHWARIZM.) Cotton, grown in irrigated fields, is the chief crop of this densely populated — 8 oblast. The main towns are Urgench, the capital; Khiva, the old regional center; and Druzhba, at the Tyuya-Muyun irrigation dam on the Amu-Darya. The Uzbeks account for 93% of the population. Population: (1979) 747,011.

THEODORE SHABAD — 9
Editor, "Soviet Geography" Magazine

KHORRAMSHAHR, khŏŏr-räm-shär, a city in southwestern Iran in a hot and humid lowland region in the province of Khuzistan. The present settlement on the Karun River where it enters the Shatt al-Arab is the most recent of several to have been established in the Karun-Tigris-Euphrates confluence area.

In the early 19th century it appears as Mohammerah (the "red fort") and was governed by an Arab sheikh under Iranian suzerainty. It was brought under Teheran's direct control in 1925 and was renamed Khorramshahr (also transliterated Khurramshahr), the "fortunate city." During World War II it expanded as a commercial port, with a link to the Trans-Iranian railway, and became a major port of entry to the Persian Gulf. It saw heavy fighting in the Iraq-Iran war that broke out in 1980 and was held by Iraq from 1980 to 1982. The carnage there led the Iranians to refer to it as Khuninshahr, "bloody city." Population: (1976) 146,709.

C. E. BOSWORTH, *University of Manchester*

Page shown at 71% of actual size.

1. Page number
2. Illustration: Encyclopedia Americana contains 22,650 illustrations, of which nearly 3,200 are in color.
3. Caption
4. Main entry: Encyclopedia Americana contains 52,000 entries, the second-largest amount of any multivolume general encyclopedia. Entries are arranged alphabetically word-by-word.
5. Guide words
6. Pronunciation: Foreign or other difficult entry words are followed by phonetic pronunciation.
7. Cross-reference: Encyclopedia Americana contains 40,000 cross-references.
8. Cross-reference
9. Contributor's credit: Encyclopedia Americana has 6,460 contributors. On signed articles, the contributor's authority is frequently cited.

was completed four years later with the publication of Volume 13. By 1850 the *Americana* was a standard feature in many American homes—the publishers claim that it was included in Abraham Lincoln's small collection of books.

Since 1930, *Americana* has been published by Grolier Inc., a major publisher of encyclopedias and educational material. Grolier also publishes the ACADEMIC AMERICAN ENCYCLOPEDIA and THE NEW BOOK OF KNOWLEDGE, both of which are reviewed in this Buying Guide.

A staff of eight editors, 16 associate editors, and other researchers and editorial assistants works under the direction of Bernard S. Cayne, Editorial Director (who is also responsible for Grolier's other two encyclopedias) and David T. Holland, Editor-in-Chief. Some 6,460 contributors, most of whom are affiliated with colleges, universities, museums, or professional journals, are listed in the frontmatter. Articles are signed, and the end-of-article credits frequently cite a major book on the subject by the contributor, thereby establishing the writer's authority. Among well-known names in the contributors' list are Isaac Asimov, Jacques Barzun, Eric Bentley, Asa Briggs, Henry Steele Commager, Norman Cousins, Richard Ellmann, Thor Heyerdahl, Alan Hodgkin, Edward Teller, Carl Van Doren, and Martin Williams. However, a considerable percentage of the contributors have since moved on to institutions other than the ones to which they are identified as belonging, and some, like Van Doren, have been deceased for several years.

According to the Preface, "Distinguished advisors have assisted the editors in organizing the information in their fields into convenient forms of presentation. . . . The advisors have also assisted the editors in choosing leading authorities in each field to write the articles. After the expert is selected . . . he or she is reminded of the need to write for the unspecialized reader. The author is asked not to 'write down,' but to present facts and interpretations in an orderly way and in a direct style, and to explain technical terms when they are used." On the whole, the contributors seem to have adhered to this dictum, although technical terms are not always defined. (See also *Clarity*.)

IV. Currency

Like virtually all general multivolume encyclopedias on the market, *The Encyclopedia Americana* is revised and reprinted annually. While the publisher does not give a specific figure as to the percentage of pages handled in each revision, it does remark that "thousands of pages . . . are revised each year to reflect new developments in the modern world and fresh discoveries about the past." In this process, new entries have been added; outdated existing articles have been replaced by newly written ones on the same subject; major changes have been made within articles when the subject (or human knowledge about it) has changed significantly; and minor revisions have been made when recent developments warrant them.

Among new biographical entries added to the 1987 *Americana* are those for **Benigno Aquino**, **Corazon Aquino**, **Steve Carlton**, **Jane Goodall**, **Antonin Scalia**, **Stevie Smith**, **Alice Walker**, and **Elie Wiesel**. The 1987 edition includes 42 new entries in all. In light of recent or ongoing developments, 71 existing articles were replaced. These include **Extinct and Endangered Species**, **Health Insurance**, **Hong Kong**, **Ferdinand Marcos**, **Imelda Marcos**, **Nuclear Energy**, and **Uranus**. Important chapters within the long entries on **Brazil**, **Chile**, and **Colombia** were also replaced. An additional 60 articles underwent major revision, while minor changes were made in yet another 950 entries.

Significant as these revisions are, however, our reviewers found that the *Americana* is not consistently up-to-date. Some articles are very current, while others (sometimes dealing with a closely related topic) are out of date. For example, the article **Afrikaners** ends: "After 1948, the NP [National Party] was in power successively under D. F. Malan (1948-1954), J. G. Strijdom (1954-1958), H. F. Verwoerd (1958-1966), and B. J. Vorster (1966-)." P. W. Botha, who became head of the South African government following Vorster's resignation in 1978, is not mentioned, nor is there a biographical entry for him. Yet he is named in the **South Africa** article, which also describes the main provisions of the 1984 constitution but does not note that international sanctions were applied against the nation in the mid-1980s in an effort to change the government's apartheid policy.

Titanic reports that "on September 1, 1985, the *Titanic* was located on the ocean floor upright and mostly intact by a U.S.–French team of oceanographers." Yet the article on **sound recording and reproduction** makes no note of digital recording or compact discs; in fact, the last innovation it mentions is the introduction of quadraphonic recording, which occurred in 1971. Nor is there any indication that the quadraphonic technique failed to catch on and that the record industry abandoned quadraphonic recording by 1980.

The entry on **Ronald Reagan** is reasonably up-to-date. It mentions the ouster of the Marcos regime and the recognition of the Aquino government in the Philippines (February 1986), the U. S. raids on Libya (April 1986), and the passage of tax reform (October 1986). On the other hand, the entry on **Margaret Thatcher** ends with the Conservative Party's victory in the election of May 1979, providing no information about her subsequent long and often controversial tenure as Prime Minister of Great Britain. Yet the entry on **Great Britain** follows developments during her government through the 1983 election.

Coverage of notable contemporary figures is also uneven. For example, the *Americana* includes entries for **Geraldine Ferraro**, **Gary Hart**, **Barbara McClintock**, and **Brian Mulroney**, but none for Brazilian President Jose Sarney or 1984 and 1985 Nobel (literature) Prize winners Jaroslav Seifert and Claude Simone. The omission of Sarney is particularly curious, since the article on **Brazil** concludes with five paragraphs about his administration. Seifert and Simone are listed in the encyclopedia's roster of **Nobel Prize** winners.

The publisher reports that United States population figures are based on the 1980 census. Those for Canada are based on the 1981 Canadian census. For other nations, the publisher claims that "every effort is made to provide the latest available figures or the most recent reliable estimates." In fact, however, these statistics frequently are not as current as they could be. For example, *Americana*'s entry on the **Union of Soviet Socialist Republics** gives the nation's 1970 census figure (241,720,134) and the 1977 estimated figure (257,900,000). By contrast, the 1987 ACADEMIC AMERICANA gives a 1986 estimate (279,904,000); the 1986 BRITANNICA gives a 1984 estimate (274,492,000); the 1986 COLLIER'S gives the 1983 figure (273,000,000); and the 1987 WORLD BOOK gives a 1987 estimate (283,620,000).

According to the publisher, "the encyclopedia has been engaged in a program through which entire volumes are completely rebuilt. In the rebuild program the alphabetical span covered by an entire volume is examined as though a totally new work were being created." Grolier reports that Volumes 1 through 19 and 21 through 26 have already been "rebuilt," and that "the program is continuing." This undertaking is certainly ambitious, and is made all the more difficult by the sheer size of the set. It remains to be seen if the program will ultimately result in an encyclopedia that is as comprehensively and consistently up-to-date as Grolier's other fine encyclopedias, the ACADEMIC AMERICAN and THE NEW BOOK OF KNOWLEDGE.

V. Accuracy

With its many distinguished contributors, one can expect a high degree of accuracy in the *Americana*'s articles. Indeed, this is the case more often than not, especially when significant facts are concerned. However, our reviewers did encounter a number of factual errors that cast doubt on the set's consistency.

For example, the article on the **symphony** tells us that Dimitri Shostakovich "wrote 14 symphonies," and refers to "the six symphonies of the English composer Ralph Vaughan Williams." In fact, Shostakovich composed 15 symphonies, while Vaughan Williams wrote nine. The entry for **John Le Carre** reports that this is the nom de plume of David Cromwell, when in fact the author's name is *Cornwell*.

Other distortions or misinterpretations also occur. For example, the entry on **Ty Cobb** asserts that "his father, a respected educator and state senator, was fatally shot by his mother, who supposedly had mistaken him for an intruder." It has been generally established that his mother shot Cobb's father in a fit of rage because of his infidelity. It must be stressed, however, that for the general reader such minor inaccuracies will not detrimentally affect the overall usefulness and reliability of the set.

The *Americana*'s article on Prince **Henry** the Navigator gives a fuller and more truthful account of his motives than is found in either BRITANNICA or COLLIER'S:

> In 1418 he settled at the Vila do Infante near Sagres, where he built an observatory and attracted to his palace adventurers as well as astronomers and others involved in the study of navigation. . . . Although he had a scientific interest in navigation, he also hoped that these voyages would expand Portuguese trade in African gold and slaves. . . . Henry won lasting fame by encouraging voyages of exploration and the scientific study of navigation, although he himself did not travel farther than North Africa.

Americana's entry on **Saturn** is complete and up-to-date. **Bill of Rights** presents a clear account of that subject, combining the historical and analytical approaches. In contrast to these entries, the article on **money** is poorly written and organized, making it difficult for the average reader to follow. Moreover its errors and biases make it of a significantly lower standard than its counterparts in COLLIER'S and NEW BRITANNICA. The entry on the **brain** also suffers from poor organization, and is not up-to-date. Overly detailed in some areas, it is skimpy in others. Among its major omissions, it does not mention the different functions of the left and right hemispheres of the brain, and its discussion of consciousness is also weak. *Americana*'s description of how **transistors** work is also accurate but probably more detailed than it needs to be. For example, the discussion of various wiring configurations used with bipolar transistors will be of interest mainly to the specialist and is more pertinent to an article on electronics than to one limited to transistors. At the same time, the article barely mentions integrated circuits; the reader is referred to the section *microelectronics* in the **electronics** article.

VI. Clarity

According to Grolier, the *Americana*'s "level of readability . . . is as carefully planned and controlled as the content. Each article is written at a level that seems appropriate for those most likely to consult the article. Technical vocabulary is kept to a minimum, and no article is written at a higher level than it need be. . . . Where technical terms cannot be avoided, they are defined when introduced into the text."

However, our reviewers have found that these claims are not always justified. Contrary to the publisher's claim, difficult or technical terms are not consistently explained in context. This is particularly evident in articles on scientific or technical subjects. For example, the first paragraph of **electron** reads as follows:

> **ELECTRON**, an elementary particle carrying a unit negative charge of electricity. The charges of all other particles are positive or negative integral multiples of the unit charge of the electron. The rest mass of the electron is 9.11×10^{-28} gram, about 1/1836 the mass of the proton or neutron.

This definition is so abstruse as to be virtually meaningless to the average reader who has little or no previous knowledge of the subject. At the same time, however, it does allow for a more highly sophisticated discussion of this complex subject than would otherwise be possible.

Like NEW BRITANNICA, the *Americana* allows its contributors a good deal of leeway. As in NEW BRITANNICA and, to a lesser degree, COLLIER'S, many of the *Americana*'s non-science articles are also pervaded by a scholarly and sometimes idiosyncratic writing style. While the writing is often distinguished and rarely "talks down" to the reader, it makes few concessions to the average adult reader, much less to the average student. For example, we read in the entry on **Unitarianism** that "In England, in the turmoil of the 17th century, Socinianism made an appeal to several Anglican and Nonconformist circles as a rational, irenic expression of Christianity, tolerant of nonessential variations." Even though Socinianism is defined earlier in the article, this sentence may puzzle many readers. Nor is this an isolated example. Articles by specialist contributors in philosophy, history, and the social sciences often make liberal use of the particular language of that discipline.

The following extract from **lighthouse** illustrates the style of a typical entry in *The Encyclopedia Americana*:

> **lighthouse**, a tower or other high structure topped by a powerful light for guiding mariners. Lighthouses are erected at port entrances on prominent headlands, or on other danger points. A lightship is an anchored ship serving as a lighthouse in an exposed location where it is impractical to build a fixed structure.
>
> History. Early navigators in the Mediterranean area may have been guided by fires lighted on the tops of hills along the shore. As ship traffic increased, it became necessary to put up lights in the entrances to the major ports. The first real lighthouse was the Pharos of Alexandria, one of the Seven Wonders of the World. Designed by Sostratus of Cnidos about 280 B.C., it was at least 85 meters (280 feet) high and rested on a tall square base. Reflectors were used to concentrate the light from its wood fires so that it was visible from a distance of about 56 km (35 miles).
>
> The largest lighthouse in ancient Italy was at Portus, the port of Rome, and was built about 46 A.D. The Romans built other lighthouses, including one at Boulogne, France, that stood until the mid-17th century. This lighthouse was probably built by Emperor Caligula to commemorate his attempted invasion of Britain. The Romans also built two lighthouses at Dover, England, one of which is still standing. . . .

VII. Objectivity

In describing the encyclopedia's objectivity, the Preface to the 1986 edition of *Americana* quotes the editor of the first (1829) edition: "My wish has been not to obtrude opinions, but to furnish facts." However, as in NEW BRITANNICA, contributors are often allowed considerable latitude in expressing personal opinions or venturing speculative surmises. There is much to be said in favor of this essay-style approach to encyclopedia article-writing. Certainly, it makes for more interesting reading, and gives the reader a more human perspective on the particular subject than is possible in an article that attempts only to recite facts. It also assumes that the reader is able to exercise critical judgment about the writer's interpretation.

For example, the general introduction to the **United States** article, contributed by a Princeton University historian, is a rather subjective and freewheeling exploration of the contradictions of contemporary American society. The first sentence reads: "The United States entered its third century the richest nation in history, secure in its broadly democratic structure, brilliant in the application of techniques for mastering land, sea, and water—and deeply troubled." Various sections of the article, written by other historians, seem less like standard encyclopedia articles than personal essays in which the historian is at liberty to argue a thesis. Facts are presented selectively; occasionally, more attention is devoted to certain points than seems warranted. For example, President Jimmy Carter is characterized as "a 'born-again Christian' " and "a self-proclaimed expert on efficiency in government," and the writer refers to "his ostentatious Baptist faith." While these references may be accurate, they are made in a context that suggests a biased, not necessarily central, point of view.

In many survey articles, speculative statements are not uncommon. For example, we read in **London** that "Great cities rarely change fundamentally in a short time, but those who knew the London of the empire, of extremes of wealth and poverty, and of a concentration on commerce have wondered if they were witnessing a historic transitional period in the life of the 1,900-year-old city." Such speculative remarks may stimulate the reader to think about the subject in a more imaginative way, rather than just trying to memorize facts and figures.

Entries on social issues and scientific concepts occasionally present a one-sided, doctrinaire view of the subject without mentioning other valid points of view. For example, the eleven-and-a-half page article on **prejudice and discrimination**, while generally accurate, often takes a moralistic, moralizing tone. The article seeks not simply to inform but also to persuade. The four-and-a-half pages it devotes to *sexism* takes a strongly feminist view of the issue and imply that those who do not actively share feminist views, goals, or methods contribute to the exploitation of women. The article ends with the exhortation that "contemporary societies must make an attempt to [eliminate sexism]. If this effort is to succeed, it must incorporate all of the available approaches." One may agree or disagree; the point is, this type of writing is more appropriate to a newspaper editorial or political essay than to an encyclopedia, and cannot be considered objective. Such instances of overtly

polemical writing in *The Encyclopedia Americana* are relatively rare, however.

The more objective article on **abortion** is divided into two sections of roughly equal length. The first is a discussion of the moral, religious, legal, and political issues surrounding the topic; the second is a discussion of its medical aspects. Under the subhead "The Moral Issue," the article states that "The basic problem is the moral or religious one relating to the rights of the fetus. One answers the question according to the conclusion one wishes to reach. . . ." The article then summarizes the major arguments both pro and con. However, it does not mention the common pro-abortion view that the fetus is part of the mother's body and that women should have the right to control their bodies.

The *Americana*'s comprehensive and well-balanced coverage of **evolution** includes a discussion of pre-Darwinian beliefs and theories. The article notes that "some people have always preferred to believe that the world is stable and unchanging, while others have thought that it is changing." It also reports on post-Darwinian theories of evolution, and on opposition to Darwin both from within and without the scientific community. The article assumes, however, that evolution is "the only scientifically tenable explanation of organic diversity and of adaptedness," and that "species have not always existed in their present state but have evolved from different ancestral species."

A one-page article on **creationism** recounts the history of the movement from Darwin's day through the Scopes trial and up to the present, summarizing the main creationist arguments. While the article is factually sound, the reader might infer from its tone that the contributor, identified as the chairman of the Department of the History of Medicine at the University of Wisconsin, is dismissive of the creationists' claims. The article notes creationists' efforts to pass state laws "requiring a balanced treatment of creation and evolution" in the schools. However, the claim that "they also convinced a majority of Americans that evolution should not be taught exclusively" is unsubstantiated and questionable.

The five-page article on **Andrew Jackson** is highly objective, reporting all the major achievements and controversies in a fair and straightforward manner. The article mentions that the duel in which he killed another lawyer "gave wide fame to Jackson's iron will but also provided his enemies with the claim that he took pleasure in violence and brutality." The entry ends with a paragraph on *Historical Interpretation* of his presidency, noting that "historians have debated the significance of Jacksonian Democracy for many decades" and presenting some major interpretations. The article concludes that "it is likely that succeeding generations will make their own judgments on the Age of Jackson."

VIII. Accessibility

Entries are arranged alphabetically, word by word. When several items have the same heading, they are arranged in the customary order of people, places, and things. Names beginning with *Mc* are alphabetized as though they began with *Mac*; names beginning with *St.* are likewise alphabetized as though *Saint* were spelled out.

According to the publisher, *Americana*'s index of more than 350,000 entries "provides a complete guide to the contents of the encyclopedia." The index is extremely useful and comprehensive. It not only includes entry subjects, but also refers the reader to instances where subjects not covered under their own entries are discussed in other articles.

As an indication of the scope and style of individual entries, the reader searching for information about Marie Curie will find the following index entry:

> **CURIE, Marie** (Fr. phys.) 8-331
> Polonium 22-362
> Radioactivity 23-186
> Radium 23-199

(Information pertaining to Irène, Jacques, and Pierre Curie is indexed under separate entries for each of these individuals.)

The *Americana* makes use of several types of cross-references. In addition to *g.v.* or *gg.v.* notations, articles incorporate "See also" entries within the text or at the end of the article. However, the end-of-article cross-references are sparser and less comprehensive than those found in the NEW STANDARD ENCYCLOPEDIA and in WORLD BOOK. Like all other encyclopedias, *Americana* also makes use of cross-reference entries.

Nevertheless, although the publisher reports some 40,000 cross-references (an average of two per page), our reviewers found that the cross-referencing in the *Americana* is sometimes inadequate. For example, the half-page article on **Mount Everest** contains no cross-references, even though Edmund Hillary and Tenzing Norkay, who are mentioned, receive separate biographical entries. Readers looking for more information under *Norkay*, where one might expect to find the climber's biography, will not find a cross-reference entry directing them to the entry **Tenzing Norkay**, where his entry is actually located. (In fair-

ness, neither BRITANNICA nor COLLIER'S include a cross-reference entry under *Norkay*, although WORLD BOOK does.) Without adequate cross-referencing, it is difficult for the lay reader to appreciate the entire scope of a given subject and the interrelationships within that subject.

Structurally, the articles in *Americana* are clearly organized. In long survey articles, readers are aided by a paginated "table of contents" printed on the first page of the article. The contents table for **United States**, for example, shows that the article is organized into eight main sections: introduction, the land, the people, culture and the arts, government, national defense, the economy, and history. These sections are divided further into 30 major subsections; in fact, the article makes use of four levels of subheads. Only BRITANNICA (Macropaedia), NEW STANDARD ENCYCLOPEDIA, and WORLD BOOK provide comparable structure. Such organization makes the articles extremely easy to follow, and enables students to see at a glance the relationships among the different aspects of a complex topic.

IX. Special Features

The Encyclopedia Americana contains a number of standard special features common to most multivolume general encyclopedias, including illustrations, bibliographies, tables, charts, graphs, and maps. There are more than 22,500 illustrations, of which a little more than 3,000—only about 14 percent—are in color. This is a greater number of illustrations, overall, than in COLLIER'S, and almost as many as in NEW BRITANNICA—but the *Americana*'s illustrations are larger than BRITANNICA's.

The illustrations are generally adequate but not outstanding. Occasionally, hairstyles, dress, automobiles, or other incidental features betray the age of a particular photograph. In this respect, however, the *Americana*'s photos are usually on a par with those in COLLIER'S, and are certainly more current than those found in COMPTON'S. The photos bear out Grolier's claim that they have been "carefully chosen to complement the text." More than 5,000 drawings and diagrams, about 10 percent of them in color, were commissioned for the *Americana*. Of particular interest are the simplified schematic diagrams that accompany many of the articles on technical subjects. The *Americana*'s anatomical drawings and diagrams are also clear and useful.

Three hundred of *Americana*'s 1,279 maps are in full color, and many are full-page or double-page in size. Designed by the respected cartographic firm of Hammond Incorporated, these maps are generally clear, accurate, and up-to-date, and are as fine as those found in any other contemporary encyclopedia. There are maps for the continents, most major countries, and all 50 states, as well as many special-purpose topical maps.

Bibliographies are provided for articles "when there are works of value to cite that can be used as a starting point for further study." The publisher claims that works listed in the various bibliographies "are known to be authoritative and are at the appropriate level for the user." For the 1987 edition of *Americana*, important new titles were added to more than 550 existing bibliographies, thereby enhancing these bibliographies' value. Classic texts are still included regardless of their age or current print status. However, the bibliographies do not distinguish between books for adults and books for younger readers. Moreover, many of the books cited (apart from these "classics") are now quite dated and out of print, and may not be available in many small school and public libraries. The bibliographies function as "starting points for further study," but the student will probably need to consult the library catalogue for a more comprehensive listing of pertinent titles.

As previously noted (see *Accessibility*), long survey articles are headed by excellent tables of contents.

X. Format

The 30-volume *Encyclopedia Americana* comes in a standard green McCain Sewn Lexotone II binding, which should stand up well under heavy, repeated use. The volumes, using the split-letter system, are of approximately equal length, generally about 800 pages each. (The shortest, Volume 9, is 761 pages long, while Volume 14, at 965 pages, is the longest.) A single volume does not contain all the entries beginning with a particular letter. For example, Volume 26 contains all the entries from **Sumatra** to **trampoline**, while the next volume contains all the entries from **trance** to **venial sin**. The volume number and the titles of the first and last entries are stamped in clear gold lettering on red bands on the spine.

With a smaller trim size than either COLLIER'S or NEW BRITANNICA, the individual volumes of the *Americana* are fairly easy to handle. However, the entire set takes up nearly four-and-a-half feet of horizontal shelf space, making it physically the longest of all general multivolume encyclopedias.

XI. Other Opinions

ARBA 82 (Susan C. Holte, Bohdan S. Wynar): "In terms of statistics (number of words and articles, quantity of illustrations, number of contributors),

Americana ranks as one of the most comprehensive general encyclopedia. . . . Readability is quite evident in such areas as medicine and technology, where technical terms are introduced into most of the articles with definitions that are adequate for the nonspecialist."

ARBA 84 (Bohdan S. Wynar): "*The Encyclopedia Americana* is a well-balanced and clearly written authoritative work prepared by an experienced editorial staff, with an excellent index and well-designed illustrations. . . . In spite of certain shortcomings, *Americana* remains a well-edited and comprehensive work, which is highly recommended to all types of libraries as well as for home use."

Booklist (Reference Books Bulletin), November 15, 1986: "Today's *Americana* is international in coverage and scope. It is outstanding for its detailed coverage of U.S. and Canadian history and geography; its biographical, scientific, and technical articles; and its extensive treatment of literature, art, and music of every century. It is written in language easily comprehended by nonspecialists from junior high upwards. *Americana* maintains a high level of accuracy and authority. . . . *Americana*'s index is extremely detailed, with citations to illustrations and maps. . . . The 1986 edition lives up to the good reputation for informative, unbiased, authoritative articles established by earlier editions of the *Encyclopedia Americana* and [is recommended] for home and library use by both adults and students beyond the level of the elementary grades."

XII. Summary

As a comprehensive multivolume reference set, *The Encyclopedia Americana* can be classified in the mainstream of contemporary American reference books. The set will be of interest to a wide range of adults and high school students. Its usefulness for upper elementary and middle school students is questionable, however.

The *Americana*'s main strengths are its wide scope and its comprehensive and detailed articles. The short specific-entry articles are excellent for ready reference, while the longer survey articles often are more informative than textbooks on the same subject. On the whole, *Americana* provides more information than Collier's; many of its individual entries give more information than their counterparts in NEW BRITANNICA. *Americana*'s articles also more closely reflect the curricula of American schools, though not as closely as do those in WORLD BOOK. *Americana*'s biographical articles are generally first-rate, and its coverage of science and technology is also outstanding (even though many of the entries in these areas are written at a higher level of complexity than they need to be).

Against these considerable strengths, the potential purchaser needs to weigh *Americana*'s defects. Although particular articles are sufficiently up-to-date, the set is not consistently current, and the user cannot assume that any given article will give a contemporary account of the subject. This lack of currency often adversely affects the set's accuracy. Moreover, the encyclopedia is dotted with many instances of obvious factual errors that, while relatively minor, could and should have been prevented. Certain articles evidence an occasional lack of objectivity and reflect the contributor's personal biases. The inadequate cross-referencing system is a more serious weakness that will prevent many readers from taking full advantage of the wealth of information that the *Americana* does contain. And finally, the preponderance of black-and-white illustrations (of which a number are noticeably outdated) give the set a somewhat drab, unappealing look.

The Encyclopedia Americana costs $1,200 to individuals and $869 to institutions. The disparity between the two prices may make the set a much more attractive purchase to libraries than to private collectors.

Individuals wishing to purchase *The Encyclopedia Americana* may contact the publisher, Grolier Incorporated, at Sherman Turnpike, Danbury, CT 06816, or telephone (800) 243-7256. Schools and libraries should address their orders to Grolier Educational Corporation at the same address and phone number.

Everyman's Encyclopaedia Online

Facts at a Glance

Full Title: **Everyman's Encyclopaedia** (online version).
Publisher: J. M. Dent & Sons Ltd., 33 Welbeck St., London W1M 8LX, England.
Editor: David A. Girling.
Online Vendor: Dialog Information Services, Inc., 3460 Hillview Avenue, Palo Alto, CA 94304.
Copyright: 1978.

Number of Volumes: 12 (print edition; not applicable to online version).
Number of Entries: 50,000.
Number of Words: 8,000,000.
Number of Cross-references: 15,000.
No index.

Intended Users: upper grades through adult.
Price: by subscription to vendor and online charges.
Revised infrequently.

I. Introduction

The online version of *Everyman's Encyclopaedia* derives from a respected multivolume British encyclopedia published by J. M. Dent & Sons, Ltd. since 1913-14. The 12 volumes of the most recent print edition (1978) contain almost 9,000 pages, 50,000 entries, and eight million words, along with 5,600 black-and-white illustrations. Most of the 350 contributors are British academics, and the set was clearly designed to meet the needs of British readers.

Revised infrequently—once every ten years or so—the print version of *Everyman's* has been withdrawn from the American market in the face of stiff competition from more up-to-date American encyclopedias. Today, the set is something of a rarity in American libraries, although it is available in Canada from Fitzhenry & Whiteside Publishers.

II. Accessibility

Online, *Everyman's Encyclopaedia* is accessible only through Dialog Information Services, Inc., a vendor of online database services; a user cannot access *Everyman's* directly. With Dialog, the search routine is in two parts: first, boot the system, load the communications program, dial the vendor, and when connected give the user ID. Second, select the database, give the search word(s), conduct the database search, display the text of the desired entry, and finally respond to the prompt for the next action. Each part usually takes at least two minutes, though the second can take far longer.

The command-driven Dialog search method is complex but very efficient once mastered. It was designed, however, for bibliographical databases such as Georef ("Surveys of worldwide technical literature on geology and geophysics from the American Geological Institute") and the Federal Index, so is only moderately suitable for searching an encyclopedia. A Dialog search makes much use of abstracts, for example, and abstracts do not appear in encyclopedias. As a result, online search of *Everyman's* can seem slow compared with direct consultation of the print edition, even though Dialog uses a well-designed search method and the ten-volume print edition lacks an index.

III. Locating Information

The Dialog search method attempts to match search words, which may be connected by logical operators such as AND, OR, and NOT, with text in the *Everyman's Encyclopaedia* entries themselves, not simply with the entry titles. Because the search method was designed for use with abstracts, the user cannot always narrow the search sufficiently without seeing the full entry. A search for "Menière's Disease" or "Menière's Syndrome" found no matches ("hits"), but a search for "Menière" alone reported several; without abstracts, only by displaying the full entry on the screen could the user see which if any of these would be pertinent. "Menière" might figure in the title of a lengthy entry, or it might be part of a passing mention. An alternative strategy, searching for "ears AND disease," elicited among other things a lengthy entry on the history of grain cultivation.

Copious capitalized cross-references to other entries enable the user to extend the search beyond the target entry. The excellent 2,900-word entry on **Spanish-American Literature** encourages the reader to "see also BRAZIL, CENTRAL AMERICA, MEXICAN AND CENTRAL AMERICAN NATIVE LANGUAGES, PORTUGAL, ROMANCE LANGUAGES, SOUTH AMERICA and SOUTH AMERICAN NATIVE LANGUAGES" generically, along with specific individuals from **Cortes** to **Borges**.

IV. Cost

A search in *Everyman's* via Dialog need not prove costly, assuming the user already subscribes to the vendor's service. If the search makes an immediate hit—that is, if the service reports that it has only one match for the search word(s)—the entry can be displayed and the search concluded in less than a minute, which with Dialog means less than a dollar's cost. The connect time through a local node of Tymnet or Telenet would increase that figure only by pennies (the short entry on **Ronald Reagan** quoted in the following text cost about 57 cents to retrieve).

Search and connect costs rise, however, if the user fails to make a hit or makes more than one and has to renew the search on a more specific set of words or, worse still, has to review a large number of entries on the screen to discover which one is relevant to the search.

When the desired entry has been found, the user can obtain a hard copy in three ways: by ordering it from the vendor; by storing the incoming file in the computer memory (floppy or hard disk) and printing it later when off-line; or by outputting it directly to the home printer. Because most printers cannot keep up with the incoming data, the last option is the least economical, and causes the online charges to burgeon.

V. Currency

The online *Everyman's Encyclopaedia* is not at all up-to-date. In July 1987 the entry on **Ronald Reagan** read as follows in its entirety:

> **Reagan, Ronald Wilson** (1911-), US politician, born at Tampico, Illinois; educated Eureka College (1932). He was a sports announcer in Des Moines, Iowa (1932-37) and a motion picture actor in Hollywood (1937-54), becoming president of the Screen Actors Guild (1947-52 and 1959-60). Later he became a TV actor and producer, and in 1964 he became active in Republican politics in California. In 1966 he was elected governor of California, serving until 1974. He became a possible presidential or vice-presidential candidate in 1968, and again in 1972. He is active in Republican national politics and especially popular among conservatives.
>
> BIOGRAPHY
>
>   United States; 19th [sic] Century A.D.
> History; North America

The two entries that include material on the space shuttle, **Rocket** and **Space Travel**, make no reference to events after 1976, and their bibliography also stops at that year. The entry on the British **Conservative party** mentions Margaret Thatcher only once:

> The party was again defeated in October 1974 and in February 1975 Heath was defeated in the leadership election by Mrs Margaret Thatcher, who thus became the first woman to lead a major party in Western Europe or North America.

As Mrs. Thatcher has become, since the 1987 British General Election, the senior national leader in the Western alliance, the entry is obviously long out of date.

The encyclopedia also lacks any reference to such current concerns as AIDS, privatization, or Chernobyl. Neither Corazon Aquino nor Armand Hammer have entries. When dealing with timeless topics, such as Thomas Aquinas, the encyclopedia's out-of-dateness is less vital. However, the bibliography for this entry lists no books written after 1962. Judging from the entries scanned in this review, the online version of the mid-1980s is no more up-to-date than the 1978 print edition. Online *Everyman's* severely undermines its authority by its lack of timeliness. Timeliness should be the salient quality of an online reference work.

VI. Accuracy, Objectivity, and Clarity

The academic background of its contributors has served *Everyman's Encyclopaedia* well. To the extent that any entry a decade out of date can be accurate and authoritative, these appear to be. And by the same token, they are objective. At something over 1,200 words, the entry on the **Conservative party** shows the British origins of the work but, allowing for the British viewpoint, it is even-handed, although because of the passage of time certain facts no longer hold true. It concludes:

> The modern Conservative party, while opposed to any extension of state ownership, has not, when in power, repealed the nationalisation acts of its Labour predecessors except in the cases of road transport and steel. Its general economic outlook remains bound up with free enterprise, though it has in fact increasingly acknowledged that in the modern state this must operate within the framework of much state planning. Its progressive policies today differ from those of its principal opponents largely on points of emphasis. Despite its verbal insistence on tradition, the Conservative party has been able to absorb new ideas and policies, and to adapt itself to changing conditions, both domestic and international.

The bibliography for this entry includes books by Hailsham on the right and Harrington on the left, among others.

VII. Summary

Everyman's Encyclopaedia is a large-scale reference work especially valuable for its coverage of British and other European subjects. The astute cross-references adapt it readily to the user's needs. As long as the user makes an immediate "hit" and does not need to output a hard copy directly to the printer, *Everyman's* is relatively inexpensive to use. Unfortunately the version accessible online in mid-1987 was so out of date that information taken from it could be used with confidence only after checking and supplementation elsewhere. Until and unless *Everyman's* undergoes a thorough revision, its usefulness will remain limited.

Individuals and institutions interested in subscribing to the online version of *Everyman's Encyclopaedia* may contact the vendor, Dialog Information Services, Inc., 3460 Hillview Avenue, Palo Alto, CA 94304, telephone (415) 858-2700.

Funk & Wagnalls New Encyclopedia

Facts at a Glance

Full Title: **Funk & Wagnalls New Encyclopedia**.
Publisher: Funk & Wagnalls, Inc., 70 Hilltop Road, Ramsey, NJ 07746.
Editors: Leon L. Bram, Editorial Director; Norma H. Dickey, Editor-in Chief.
Copyright: 1986.

Number of Volumes: 29.
Number of Contributors: 1,033.
Number of Entries: 25,000.
Number of Pages: 13,024.
Number of Words: 9,000,000.
Number of Maps: 317.
Number of Cross-references: 85,000.
Number of Indexes: 1.
Number of Illustrations: 3,332 four-color; 5,849 two-color or black-and-white.
Trim Size: 6″ × 9″.

Intended Readership: grade 5 through adult.
Price: $139.81.
Sold in supermarkets; only schools and libraries may order direct from distributor. (See page 596.) ISBN 0-8343-0072-9.
Revised twice a year, with twice-yearly printings.

I. Introduction

Funk & Wagnalls New Encyclopedia is a 29-volume work designed primarily for household use. The publisher's promotional brochure boasts that it is "the wisest investment you'll ever make for your family," and that it provides "a wealth of information that doesn't cost a fortune." Moreover, in the words of the publishing firm's chairman, James L. Stoltzfus, the set is a "valuable . . . learning resource . . . in the educational development of children. This great learning tool will stimulate your children's curiosity about all kinds of subjects. It will also help them get high grades in school by encouraging good study habits and by serving as a source for term papers and reports and as an aid in preparing for exams."

While such claims may be dismissed as advertising hyperbole, they do indicate the publisher's desire to challenge other encyclopedias in the lucrative home encyclopedia market.

Funk & Wagnalls New Encyclopedia

LAURIER ➋

Self-Portrait, by Marie Laurencin.

rhythms that they and other leaders of modern art had introduced. Her subject matter, as in *Mother and Child* (Detroit Institute of Arts), was often of single or grouped female figures, frail and distant, clothed in pastel pink and blue. Her paintings have a dreamlike atmosphere, and their tones are as charmingly flat as those of early Persian miniatures. She was also a printmaker and a theatrical designer.

LAURENS, Henry (1724-92), American colonial statesman, born in Charleston, S.C., where he was educated. He was a successful merchant of Charleston until 1764, when he became a planter. He served almost continuously in the colonial assembly from 1757 to 1774. In 1775 he was president of the first provincial congress and was vice-president of South Carolina from 1776 to 1777. In 1777 he became a member of the Continental Congress, serving as president in 1777 and 1778. In 1779 Congress appointed him envoy to negotiate a treaty with the Dutch, but he was captured at sea by the British and imprisoned in the Tower of London. In December 1781 he was exchanged for the British general Charles Cornwallis, who had surrendered to the Americans. Late in 1782 Laurens was a signer of the preliminary peace treaty ending the American Revolution. He later returned to South Carolina.

LAURENTIAN MOUNTAINS, also Laurentides, upland area underlain by ancient rocks, S Québec Province, Canada, part of the Canadian ➊ Shield (q.v.) geological region. The heavily forested Laurentians support a large lumbering industry and are a popular year-round recreation

area for residents of Ottawa, Montréal, and Québec City. The highest point is atop Mont-Tremblant (968 m/3176 ft). ➌

LAURENTIAN PLATEAU. *See* CANADIAN SHIELD.

LAURIER, Sir Wilfrid (1841-1919), Canadian statesman, of French-Canadian parentage, born Nov. 20, 1841, in Saint Lin (now Laurentides, Qué.), and educated at L'Assomption College and at McGill University. After being admitted to the bar in 1864, he practiced law first in Montréal and later at Arthabaskaville (now Arthabaska). In 1871 he was elected as a Liberal to the Québec provincial legislature, and in 1874 he was elected to the Canadian House of Commons. While in the House he advocated a closer bond between the French- and English-speaking peoples of Canada. In 1877 he served briefly as minister of inland revenue, and in 1896 he became the first French-Canadian prime minister of Canada. The following year he was knighted. His government was notable for the expansion of Canadian trade, the construction of the transcontinental Grand Trunk and Canadian Northern railway companies (now the Canadian National Railways), the solution of the boundary dispute between Alaska and British Columbia, the development of Canadian resources and agriculture, and the establishment of closer ties with Great Britain. Although his party lost the elections in 1911, he continued to lead the Liberal opposition in the House of Commons. In World War I he supported the Conservative policy of extending aid to Great ➏ ➍ ➎

Sir Wilfrid Laurier Public Archives of Canada ➐

➑

445 ➒

Page shown at 75% of actual size.

➊ *q.v.* cross-reference: Cross-references are indicated in several ways, including the initials q.v. in parentheses. Other cross-references are distinguished by the words "see also." In all, Funk & Wagnalls contains some 85,000 cross-references.

➋ Guide word

➌ Measurements are given in both metric and English systems.

➍ Cross-reference entry

➎ Main entry: Funk & Wagnalls New Encyclopedia contains 25,000 entries, arranged alphabetically, letter-by-letter. Entry words are printed in boldface capitals.

➏ Caption

➐ Photo credit

➑ Illustration: Funk & Wagnalls contains more than 9,000 illustrations, of which one-third are in color.

➒ Page number

II. Scope

Funk & Wagnalls New Encyclopedia contains some 25,000 entries at an average length of 360 words, for a total word count of 9 million. Actual article length varies considerably, from a few lines for minor biographical entries and geographical locations to upwards of 30 pages or more for general survey articles on continents, nations, and other broad subjects. For example, as an indication of how space is apportioned among different subjects, **Ray Charles, Konstantin Chernenko,** and **Ty Cobb** each get about one-sixth of a page; **Cleveland** (Ohio), one-and-a-half pages; the article on the American **Civil War** is 11 pages long; **Christianity** is treated in just under 12 pages; and **China** receives 47 pages of coverage. (Individual Civil War battles are accorded separate entries, where they are treated in more depth; subjects such as Chinese art and architecture, literature, music, and philosophy are also treated in separate entries, where they receive a combined 25 pages of coverage. For a discussion of article arrangements and structure, see *Accessibility*.)

In their preface, the editors write that "the organization and selection of information in all major areas of knowledge and activity . . . must create a network of articles interrelated in such a way that no area is omitted or inadvertantly isolated." For the purposes of compiling the encyclopedia, subjects were broken down into ten major categories. According to the publisher, 20 percent of the text space is devoted to history, and an almost equal amount to geography. The physical sciences get 12 percent; the life sciences, 11 percent; and the social sciences slightly more than 9 percent. The remaining 25 percent of text space is accorded to coverage of religion and philosophy (8 percent), language and literature (6¾ percent), the visual arts (nearly 6 percent), the performing arts (3½ percent), and miscellaneous subjects such as sports, hobbies, and military affairs. About 40 percent of all entries (*not* text space) are biographical; in the breakdown given above, the publisher has counted the space in biographical articles toward the subject area in which the person worked.

From this breakdown, the coverage of literature and the arts seems rather weak. The publisher claims, however, that "the subject-area proportions of FWNE historically reflect the needs of its users, as demonstrated in the marketplace since 1971. . . ." Nonetheless, the content of such survey articles as the **Novel, Music,** and **Painting** is sketchy at best. Information given in articles on particular authors and artists also tends to be superficial.

The company points to "a concerted effort to increase the scope of the encyclopedia's international coverage," and claims that although the encyclopedia is still designed primarily for the U.S. and Canadian markets, "every feasible effort has been made to escape Anglo-American bias." The results of these efforts are readily apparent. As an indication of the scope and depth of its coverage of non-American/British subjects, a random page spread in Volume 1 (pages 260-261) contains the following 16 entries: **Aguadilla** (town in Puerto Rico), **Emilio Aguinaldo** (historic Filipino leader), **Lope de Aguirre** (Spanish colonial adventurer), **Cape Agulhas** (Africa), **Ahab** (king of ancient Israel), **Ahad Ha-am** (Russian-Jewish writer, **Ahaggar Mountains** (Algeria), **Ahasuerus** (Old Testament character), **Ahaz** (king of ancient Judah), **Ahmadou Ahidjo** (first president of Cameroon), **Ahithophel** (Old Testament character), **Ahmadabad** (city in India), **Ahmad Shah** (first emir of Afghanistan), **Ahmadu** (African Islamic leader), and **Fakhruddin Ali Ahmed** (fifth president of India).

With the major 1983 revision, *Funk & Wagnalls* added "new history articles treating a number of vanished ancient African and Asian states" in addition to its coverage of contemporary nations on those continents. Coverage of Islamic religion, culture, and politics has also been greatly expanded. Indeed, the attention to non-American and non-Western subject matter is impressive.

III. Authority

The name Funk & Wagnalls has long been synonymous with encyclopedias and dictionaries. The company originated in 1875, when Isaac Kaufmann Funk, a Lutheran pastor turned editor and publisher, started the firm of I. K. Funk & Co. in New York City. A year later he was joined by clergyman Adam Willis Wagnalls, and the company was renamed Funk & Wagnalls. Originally a publisher of religious books and periodicals, the company issued its first general reference encyclopedia, the 25-volume *Funk & Wagnalls Standard Encyclopedia*, in 1912. This set formed the basis for all subsequent editions, although the firm and the rights to the Funk & Wagnalls name have changed hands several times since the 1940s.

In the early 1950s, the publisher began selling the encyclopedia in supermarkets. From a marketing standpoint, this practice was highly successful but was frowned on by librarians, educators, and other publishers, who tended to regard any encyclopedia sold by such methods as inherently inferior.

In 1971, the company undertook a major revision of the set, issued in 1972 as *Funk & Wagnalls New*

Encyclopedia. The set underwent another overhaul in 1983. Every article was studied by staff editors and outside consultants for accuracy, objectivity, and currency, and nearly two-thirds of the content was revised. Outdated articles were dropped or thoroughly rewritten; new articles were commissioned; the number of four-color illustrations was almost doubled; all the maps were revised and most converted to four-color; a new index was created; and a comprehensive bibliography was compiled. The publisher now incorporates ongoing revisions into the set with each biannual printing.

To keep the encyclopedia up-to-date, the firm maintains a large and experienced editorial staff, led since 1974 by Vice President and Editorial Director Leon Bram. Previously Executive Editor of F. E. Compton, Bram has worked in the reference publishing field since 1955.

The Editor-in-Chief, Norma H. Dickey, was Editor-in-Chief of the Bibliography and Index of the spring 1983 edition, and has held editorial posts with Macmillan and other educational and reference publishers. For the autumn 1986 edition reviewed here, the credits page lists an editorial staff of 45 people, many of whom have previously worked for such major reference publishers as Columbia University Press, Encyclopaedia Britannica, Grolier, and Macmillan.

In addition to these individuals, Funk & Wagnalls employs a separate staff of some 20 people responsible for the bibliography and index. Barbara M. Preschel, the Index Manager, formerly held the same post on the ACADEMIC AMERICAN ENCYCLOPEDIA and has also taught library and information science. Bibliography Editor Rachel Shor Donner has edited three catalogues for the H. W. Wilson Company.

The frontmatter lists 73 consultants along with their credentials and areas of expertise. Although drawn primarily from the academic community, some are affiliated with museums or professional organizations or are editors of journals. Familiar names include literary biographers Denis Donoghue and Leon Edel and the paleontologist Stephen Jay Gould. The publisher states that the consultants "made recommendations on coverage, proportions, and contributors" in planning the 1983 edition; their participation in the subsequent biannual revisions is unclear.

Many of the 1,000 contributors are prominent academics or practicing specialists. Among the names on this roster are economist and social scientist Kenneth Boulding, heart surgeons Denton Cooley and Michael DeBakey, religion scholar Mircea Eliade,

writer-broadcaster Magnus Magnusson, and critic Lionel Trilling. However, the fact that a number of these contributors have been deceased for several years throws some doubt on the extent of the contributors' participation in the autumn 1986 revision. Fewer than half of the articles are signed (with initials only, keyed to the initials given in the list of contributors). The publisher explains that "unsigned articles are either house-written or are house-reviewed and approved texts, the contributors of which are now deceased." The editorial staff includes 11 writers.

IV. Currency

With its policy of ongoing revisions incorporated in each biannual printing, *Funk & Wagnalls* is quite up-to-date. Within already existing articles, the editors make an effort to include recent developments. For example, the entry on **Saturn** is up-to-date in all respects except in its breakdown of the planet's atmosphere, and there only minor revision is necessary. **Union of Soviet Socialist Republics** mentions the 1986 accident at the nuclear power plant in Chernobyl. The entry on **South Africa** concludes: "In the mid-1980s continued unrest and rising black militancy resulted in international pressure, a state of emergency, restriction of press freedoms, and abolition of pass laws." Given the volatility of the situation, this is a fair contemporary assessment. The article also includes a photograph showing two prominent black figures of the mid-1980s, Winnie Mandela and the Reverend Allan Boesak.

However, in articles on other nations, our reviewers did find some examples of important recent developments that went unmentioned. For example, although the article on **Nicaragua** states that in the 1980s "the U. S. . . . began to support an anti-Sandinist guerrilla movement," it does not mention the Contras by name, nor does it supply any details about that movement or the nature of the U. S. support, although this information was available at the time. The article on **Northern Ireland** fails to report the significant 1985 agreement between Great Britain and the Republic of Ireland giving the Republic a formal voice in the governing of the province, although this agreement is referred to in both the articles on **Great Britain** and the **Republic of Ireland**.

Evidence of the set's currency is found in articles in other subject areas. For example, **space exploration** not only reports the January 1986 Challenger disaster and its cause, but also notes the findings of the Presidential Commission on the tragedy and discusses the implications for the future of the American space program. **History of Motion Pictures** discusses the impact of cable television and the video rental business on both the film industry and the nature of the movie-watching experience. **Advertising** includes a four-color still photo from a 1986 television commercial that was airing at the time of this review, and the caption describes the commercial.

According to the publisher, "population and economic statistics throughout the set are as current as available international source material allow." However, this is not always the case. For example, the population figures given for the U.S.S.R. are 1983 estimates; those for the United States are from the 1980 census. At the time of publication, more recent accurate estimates were available.

As well as updating existing articles, the publisher has added new articles on subjects that have been the focus of increasing attention in the 1980s. Among these articles are **AIDS**, **Employment of Women**, **International Terrorism**, **Sports Medicine**, and **Video Recording**.

While pursuing this aggressive updating policy, the publisher also notes that "despite the desire to present the state of human knowledge in a recognizably contemporary form, the editors in general favor proved topics over 'hot' or trendy ones, preferring to err in the direction of caution rather than of mere topicality. Some ephemeral topics—mostly in the area commonly described as popular culture—that are judged to have journalistic rather than permanent importance are set aside to be treated in the encyclopedia's yearbook until such time as a clearly permanent pattern is discernable." By generally accepted encyclopedia publishing standards, this is a sound practice.

V. Accuracy

Funk & Wagnalls' promotional literature states: "Factual accuracy ranks, along with consistency and balance, as one of the three overriding editorial concerns." In the course of the editorial process, each article undergoes scrutiny by at least six people; in fact, the publisher claims that some articles were reviewed 15 times or more before they were approved for publication.

On the whole, the editors have done an admirable job of ensuring the set's accuracy. Occasional errors do creep in, however. For example, the article on **Gerard Manley Hopkins** refers to him as "a Victorian poet whose work was not introduced to the world until 1981." Here a minor typographical transposition that slipped past the copy editors misleads the

reader. Hopkin's work, in fact, was first published in 1918.

A caption in Volume 19, page 188, reads: "Belfast is the focus of political and religious strife between Great Britain and Northern Ireland." This is not so: the strife is not between Great Britain and Northern Ireland, but between the Protestant and Catholic communities in the province, and between the IRA and their supporters on the one hand and government forces on the other.

The article on **Henry the Navigator** perpetuates the popular but erroneous belief that he "established an observatory and the first school for navigators in Europe." Although Henry supported such efforts, he himself did not found any institutions.

Such instances suggest that although *Funk & Wagnalls* is broadly accurate, specific details are not as precise as they might be. Beyond the question of simple accuracy lies that of comprehensiveness and oversimplification. While this encyclopedia's content is generally accurate, it is not always as thorough as one might wish. For example, the article on **Ronald Reagan**, which is fairly brief, does not name his vice president or cabinet members, nor describe any of the controversies that have involved officials in his administration. (See *Objectivity*.)

The general survey articles also present accurate facts, but again the question of comprehensiveness and simplification arises. For example, while **American Literature** provides basic factual information about major movements, authors, and works, it rarely discusses a particular aspect of the subject in detail. About Mark Twain, for instance, it makes the sweeping statement that "[his] genius . . . was that he understood the moral realism of childhood," but the statement is never amplified.

Similar lack of detail was noted in two of the entries examined by our subject specialists. **Money**, through reasonably clear and accurate, has a narrow focus and touches on only a few aspects of the subject. **Bill of Rights** is short, omits some basic information, and is potentially misleading.

VI. Clarity

According to the publisher, *Funk & Wagnalls* is suitable for fifth-grade readers through adults. However, unlike several other encyclopedias—most notably, WORLD BOOK—its vocabulary is not geared to a specific grade level. Nor is its content geared to specific school curricula. The reading level is best suited to students at the middle and high school grades. The articles do not assume that the reader has any previous familiarity with the subject.

Writing style varies considerably from article to article. Scientific subjects, for example, are usually written at a higher level of sophistication than, say, articles on general interest subjects. In such technical subjects, the encyclopedia uses the so-called "pyramid approach," in which the article begins by presenting the most basic facts and works up to more complex information, or begins with a general description of the subject before dealing with specific aspects. Technical terms are usually defined when they are first used: however, the editors sometimes assume that the context provides an adequate definition, and in such cases do not provide a further definition. The reader may be referred to articles on related subjects by means of cross-references. (See *Accessibility*.)

The editors claim to have striven for "an encyclopedia style that was clear, concise, direct, and as lively as possible." However, while the writing in *Funk & Wagnalls* is straightforward, it is generally dry and unlikely to evoke enthusiasm in the indifferent reader. The reader often encounters overuse of the passive voice, vague generalizations and imprecise words, repetition, and choppy sentence structure, as in this paragraph from **South Africa**:

> In general, the rivers of the country are irregular in flow. Many are dry during much of the year. Consequently, the rivers are of little use for navigation or hydroelectric power but are of some use for navigation.

This awkwardness may be a consequence of the limited space available. In the process of revision, when additional information is added to one part of an article but the overall space allotted to that article is not increased, part of the article may be cut and condensed.

Yet it must be said that some individual entries are very well written indeed. For example, the encyclopedia's articles on the **Strategic Defense Initiative** and on **evolution** present information on those complex subjects in a clear and interesting manner.

The following extract from **lighthouse** illustrates the style of a typical entry in *Funk & Wagnalls*:

> **LIGHTHOUSE**, structure from which light is projected at night, or which serves as a marker by day, to guide ships sailing in coastal waters. Constructed at important points on a coastline, on isolated or sunken rocks or shoals, and at entrances to harbors and estuaries, lighthouses have been employed to safeguard coast-faring mariners since early times. The earliest known, built on the Mediterranean Sea, were constructed in the 7th century BC. Perhaps, [sic] the most monumental light-

house built in ancient times, one of the so-called Seven Wonders of the Ancient World, was the Pharos at Alexandria. Ancient lighthouses were simple structures surmounted by a beacon fire. Modern lights are powered by electricity and are frequently equipped with various types of electrically powered fog signals and auxiliary radio navigation systems (*see* NAVIGATION; RADIO). Lights used may vary in power from 10 candlepower to 28 million candlepower, depending on the importance of the traffic they serve, customary weather conditions, and the requirements of visibility. In areas where it is impractical to construct buildings to house a beacon, lightships and lighted buoys are often used (*see* BUOY).

VII. Objectivity

During the 1950s and 1960s, Funk & Wagnalls encyclopedias generally ignored controversial subjects or controversial aspects of more conventional subjects. However, since the early 1970s, the editors have made a conscious effort to provide a more balanced view of such subjects. The publisher's press release for the major 1983 revision states that "In the treatment of controversial subjects, FWNE strives for fairness by presenting all major shades of opinion in as balanced a fashion as possible."

This effort has been largely successful. For example, the article on **abortion** devotes considerable attention to the controversy over its legalization, discussing several court cases challenging its constitutionality, and concluding that "As both proponents and opponents of abortion carry on their fight, it appears that the political and social controversy engendered by legal abortion will concern the nation for years to come."

The article on **evolution** does not take Darwin's account as a necessarily correct view of existence, but does assume that living organisms "have been diversified and modified through sustained changes in form and function." The only controversy it describes is that among scientists who have proposed differing theories of evolution. It does not refer specifically to fundamentalist objections to general scientific evolutionary theory, but concludes with the note, "For a theological interpretation of the origin of life, *see* CREATION." **Creation** describes the challenges to a literal interpretation of the biblical account of the Creation that have taken place since the Renaissance, and notes that contemporary "creationists claim that the evidence for evolutionary science is flawed, that the biblical account of creation can be proved scientifically, and that either both theories should be taught in American schools or neither should be." It also mentions court cases brought by fundamentalists in various states over the teaching of evolution in public schools.

Biographical entries in *Funk & Wagnalls* also cite controversial facts or apparent contradictions when they are pertinent to a balanced understanding of an individual's life. However, except in the cases of extremely significant historical figures, the article generally does not attempt to evaluate the individual's accomplishments.

The article on **Andrew Jackson** presents an even and balanced view of the man, mentioning some controversial aspects of his career: his ownership of large numbers of slaves, his proslavery views, his forcible removal of American Indians from lands that had been promised to them by federal treaties and Supreme Court decisions, his abuse of patronage, his misuse of the presidential veto, and his highhanded attitude toward the banking system. His achievements are also reported.

VIII. Accessibility

On the whole, *Funk & Wagnalls* is a well designed and organized encyclopedia, and includes a number of features that enhance its accessibility. Entries are arranged letter by letter rather than word by word. When several items have the same heading, they are arranged in order of persons, places, and things. Following standard library practice, names beginning with *Mc* are treated as though they begin with *Mac*; the same rule applies to the use of the abbreviation *St.* for *Saint*.

Running heads indicate the first entry on the left-hand page and the last entry on the right-hand page. Page numbers are located at the bottom of each page, flush with the outside margin. For pagination purposes, each volume is treated as a separate book: pages are numbered 1 through 448 (apart from volume 29), regardless of the volume. The text is printed in two columns per page.

Entry headings are in boldface type, but some readers may find that they do not stand out conspicuously. Moreover, there is no additional space between the end of one article and the beginning of the next; this may make it difficult for some readers to locate a specific entry quickly.

Internally, articles may follow one of several set structures, depending upon the length of the article and the nature of the subject. Brief articles (generally one text column or less) are usually written as running text, without subheads. Longer, more detailed biographical entries may contain subheads that break the treatment of the subject into chronological pe-

riods and, for extremely significant figures whose accomplishments may be varied and complex, sometimes include separate subhead sections under which a particular work is discussed. Longer geographical articles—in particular, those treating continents, nation, and states—generally contain both A-heads (main heads) and B-heads (secondary subheads).

As previously noted (see *Scope*), subjects related to a broad survey entry are generally treated under separate, individual entries, not in the survey article. Thus, for example, there are separate entries for **Russia, Russian Language, Russian Literature, Russian Revolution, Russo-Finnish War**, and **Russo-Japanese War**. The article **Russia** includes cross-references to these entries where appropriate.

The most significant finding aid in *Funk & Wagnalls New Encyclopedia* is the index, which takes up all of volume 29 and contains some 130,000 entries. This means that, on average, there are more than five index entries for every article, or one per every 70 words of text. Each article is cited under its own title, as well as under other appropriate headings. The index also contains a number of standardized subheads that are used whenever appropriate in referring the reader to articles on continents and nations, and for certain types of historical events, such as wars. These subheads allow the reader to find the specific page within an article that contains information on the specific subject the reader is seeking.

In addition to cross-reference entries, several types of cross-references are used within individual articles. Some cross-references are indicated by the abbreviation q.v. (for the Latin *quod vide*, "which see") printed in parentheses immediately after the name of a subject that is treated in a separate article. In other cases, a parenthetical note in the text directs the reader to "*see. . .* [article title]." *See* notations may also be given at the end of an article in the form, "*See also* [article titles]," or "For further information on this topic, see. . . [article titles]." When a person's name is mentioned in an article without life dates following, there is a separate entry for that person.

IX. Special Features

A basic, low-cost general reference work, *Funk & Wagnalls* is not known for outstanding special features. However, it does have a substantial annotated, fairly up-to-date bibliography organized in 1,255 numbered subject areas (corresponding to the Dewey decimal system), plus a separate section for biographies. Altogether, some 9,000 titles are listed. Cross-reference notations at the end of individual articles refer the reader to the appropriate section of the bibliography. For example, the article on Zaire ends with the note, "*For further information on this topic, see the Bibliography in volume 28, section 1031.*" Section 1031 lists ten books on the region.

Chosen by 21 librarians and subject specialists, the books in the bibliography are generally appropriate for students, although most date from the 1970s and many are out of print. Some older books which have attained classic status are listed, as are some technical or scholarly books. According to the bibliography editors, "dull treatments of subjects have been avoided as much as possible. Opposing points of view on controversial topics are represented." A brief annotation for each title should help the reader decide whether that book will be useful for the reader's purpose.

Other special features include three-page articles on "How to Use the Library" and on "How to Write a Term Paper," located just before the bibliography in Volume 28. While these articles provide some useful information, they are rather cursory and cannot take the place of a more detailed orientation. The front matter in Volume 1 includes a profusely illustrated 18-page essay titled "In the Course of Human Affairs. . ." The essay describes seven general ways of explaining history; while intriguing, it is highly idiosyncratic and has no evident relation to the encyclopedia as a whole.

Approximately one-third of the 9,181 illustrations in *Funk & Wagnalls New Encyclopedia* are four-color. The color photographs are generally adequate, but it should be pointed out that they have not reproduced well on the paper, and in both reproduction quality and in overall attractiveness cannot match the photographs in WORLD BOOK ENCYCLOPEDIA. Some of the black-and-white photographs are reproductions of color artwork; apart from this drawback, many of the illustrations lack clarity and definition. Still, considering the set's very low price, one cannot expect the kind of illustrations one would find in a "coffee-table" artbook.

The encyclopedia also contains 317 maps, provided by Hammond, which accompany the respective articles on continents, nations, and states. More than 250 of these maps are one-half page or longer (including a significant number of two-page spreads), and these are all in color.

X. Format

Funk & Wagnalls New Encyclopedia is available in only one format—the 29-volume edition. Each volume is 448 pages long, except for Volume 29, which is 496 pages. With a trim size of 6″ × 9″, these one-inch-thick books should be easy to handle by users of all ages. While the binding and cover material is not as sturdy as that used in comparable encyclopedias, it should prove adequate for home use. The entire set will take up a little more than two-and-a-half feet of shelf space.

XI. Other Opinions

Reference Books Bulletin 1983-1984: "[*Funk & Wagnalls New Encyclopedia*] offers excellent value for its price. While certainly not as scholarly and as detailed as ENCYCLOPEDIA AMERICANA, COLLIER'S ENCYCLOPEDIA, or NEW ENCYCLOPAEDIA BRITANNICA, it offers global coverage of all fields of knowledge. . . ."

Reference Books Bulletin (Nov. 15, 1986): "While not as comprehensive as the largest English-language encyclopedias, *Funk & Wagnalls New Encyclopedia* presents facts on people, places, and things in a straightforward manner offering global coverage of all fields of knowledge. . . . The set continues to provide fine value for its price and remains an excellent choice for homes, useful for both adults and older children."

XII. Summary

Even at a higher price than its present $139.81, *Funk & Wagnalls New Encyclopedia* would still be a good bargain. For many families on a restricted budget, it will be the first choice. It is reasonably up-to-date, accurate, objective, and well-written.

Where *Funk & Wagnalls* falls short is in the depth of its coverage. Here it certainly cannot compare with such multivolume reference works as NEW BRITANNICA and COLLIER'S—but at a small fraction of their cost, it is not intended to. It will not be the choice of the scholar, and advanced-level students in the higher grades will usually consult another set before they consult this one. However, for average students and for the adult who consults an encyclopedia as a general source of basic information rather than as a sophisticated research tool, *Funk & Wagnalls* will be quite adequate. And while it is designed primarily for home use, libraries with very small reference budgets may be well satisfied and well served with this set.

Individuals can only purchase *Funk & Wagnalls New Encyclopedia* at supermarkets, one volume per week. Unfortunately, the publisher cannot give out information about when the set will be sold in a particular supermarket, but individual store managers may be able to let interested consumers know ahead of time if and when the set will be available. Otherwise, prospective purchasers should stay alert when they shop and make sure that they begin collecting the set during the first week it is offered.

Schools and libraries should be able to purchase the entire set through a distributor. The general distributor for the school and library market is Proteus Enterprises, Inc., 961 West Thorndale, Bensenville, IL 60106; telephone (312) 766-5544.

Kussmaul Encyclopedia

Facts at a Glance

Full Title: **Kussmaul Encyclopedia**.
Former Title: Cadillac Modern Encyclopedia (one volume, 1973, out of print).
Publisher: General Videotex Corporation, 3 Blackstone Street, Cambridge, MA 02139.
Editor: J. Wesley Kussmaul, Editorial Director.
Online Vendor: Delphi (a service of General Videotex).
Copyright: 1981 through 1987.

Number of Entries: 20,000.
Number of Words: 3,000,000.
Number of Cross-references: 50,000.
No index.

Intended Users: upper grades through adult.
Price: $49.95 for permanent subscription to Delphi, plus online charges.
Revised irregularly.

I. Introduction

The *Kussmaul Encyclopedia* is an online general reference encyclopedia derived from the single-volume *Cadillac Modern Encyclopedia*, which was published in 1973 and is now out of print. Updated and put into online form in 1980 by J. Wesley Kussmaul, for whom it was renamed, *Kussmaul* is one of several features of Delphi, a service of General Videotex Corporation that provides online information and communications.

II. Accessibility

Delphi is available through many local nodes of packet-switching networks such as Telenet and Tymnet. Subscribers to Delphi can readily read the *Kussmaul Encyclopedia* articles, or "files," with a home computer or an office terminal. Unlike other online encyclopedias, *Kussmaul* has no available related print version and is accessible through only one online information service.

Because *Kussmaul* is part of the larger Delphi package, subscribers have automatic access to a wide range of information and communications databases. Among these, *The Research Library* (described as "a collection of 200 separate databases with comprehensive information on just about everything") will be of particular interest to library reference departments.

III. Locating Information

First-time Delphi users get a tour of the service from a genial monologuist named "Max;" well-designed menus then take over to locate the "Library" feature of Delphi and within it, the encyclopedia. More experienced users can opt for a faster command-driven path to the feature. In response to the plain English "Search for:" prompts, the user simply enters the subject and the program searches for an article (called here a "file") with that assigned title.

If the program finds more than one title that fits, it displays them all in a numbered list and asks which number the user wants to see. Because the program lists all titles that include the search string, the lists can be surprising: a search for "ear" found the sought-for string along with **Ear Training**, **Earle, John**, **Earth** and seven other "earth" titles from **Earth Quake** to **Earthworm**, culminating in **Earwig**. The effect nicely reproduces the serendipity of leafing through a print encyclopedia and happening on articles only alphabetically akin to the one sought.

If the program cannot match the entire string, it automatically tries again with strings incrementally shortened from the end. Thus when no "Chernobyl" was found, the program tried "Chernoby," "Chernob," and finally "Cherno," which it found in the longer string:

CHERNOZEM (cher'-no-zem), a black SOIL of alluvial origin rich in humus and with a loose crumbly texture. It is found wherever the original vegetation cover was natural grassland, and it is one of the most productive soils in the world. The largest expanse of chernozem is found in a zone stretching from E. Siberia west to Hungary and Romania and in the U.S. and Canada, where it is coextensive with the former natural prairie grassland from Manitoba south to Texas.

In the same fashion the search word "Aquino" garnered only an article on **St. Thomas Aquinas**, and "privatization" came up with a numbered list of the titles **Private Bank**, **Private Enterprise**, **Private Property**, and **Privateering**.

Because the program searches titles rather than full text, the listed search item "Private Enterprise" did not find the phrase where it appeared in the article on **Margaret Thatcher** (see *Currency*.)

Most articles in the *Kussmaul Encyclopedia* include several cross-references, set in capital letters. For convenience, these are repeated in a numbered list at the end of the article, enabling the user to pursue the reference simply by typing the desired number. The pursuit, however, involves occasional wild geese: the cross-reference HEARING in the article on **Ear** turned out to concern judicial, not sensory, hearing.

Most articles in the encyclopedia do not include bibliographical references.

IV. Cost

Subscription to Delphi costs $49.95; online charges are $16.00 per hour at peak times and $6.00 per hour off-peak (evenings, weekends, and holidays). Use of a local node of Tymnet incurs little or no charge. Delphi is operational 24 hours a day, but even a peak-time search can cost well under a dollar, because the menu and search features of the program are notably brisk, the articles are usually short, and the faster 1200- or 2400-baud modems are supported without surcharge.

V. Currency

Wes Kussmaul's original intention to update the *Kussmaul Encyclopedia* by adding current news to the articles inherited from *Cadillac* did not prove practical in the long run. Consequently, in mid-1987 many of the articles were badly behind the times, as the lack of articles on Corazon Aquino, Armand Hammer, Chernobyl, and AIDS suggests.

The article on **Margaret Thatcher**, for example, contains no information after 1981; that on **Ronald Reagan** none after 1980. The entry **Space Shuttle** also contains no information after 1981. Among the technical and scientific articles in which the *Kussmaul Encyclopedia* excels, the lengthy article on **superconductivity** is of limited use because it omits any reference to the important research discoveries published during 1986 and 1987. Lack of currency in a rapidly evolving scientific field such as this one is tantamount to lack of accuracy.

VI. Accuracy, Objectivity, and Clarity

The article on **Margaret Thatcher** begins

THATCHER, MARGARET HILDA (1925-) became the first woman prime minister of Great Britain in May, 1979. A member of the Conservative party, Thatcher espoused the belief that the lessening of inflation of prices and the economic revitalization of Great Britain could be achieved through a policy of reducing government expenditures and tight control of the nation's money supply. Thatcher's steadfastness in pursuing this policy, which is known as monetarism, in the face of a severe economic slump earned her the epithet, "Iron Lady."

The paragraph and especially the second sentence are rather loose. Sharpening the sentence to read "Thatcher believed that price inflation could be lessened and the British economy revitalized through tight control of government spending and the nation's money supply," 24 words instead of 35, would bring the passage back into focus.

The account of Thatcher emphasizes her distinction as a woman prime minister and quotes a popular epithet that also refers to her sex. But the article avoids the more scurrilous politico-sexist epithets (such as "Attila the Hen") frequently applied to Thatcher in popular journalism, and uses terms like "steadfastness" and elsewhere "leading challenger," "break decisively," "embarked boldly," "held firm," that treat the subject as a resolute political leader, not merely as a historical curiosity.

VII. Summary

The *Kussmaul Encyclopedia* is a distinctive online-only general reference work with concise articles appropriate for upper grade and adult users. Without question the most accessible and easiest to use of the online encyclopedias, the user-friendly features inherent in the Delphi system will make it especially attractive to home, school, office, and library users. Although it does not have full-text searching capabilities, its search procedures and cross-references are usually comprehensive enough to enable the user to make the most of its contents.

Although charges vary from vendor to vendor, and direct, consistent comparisons are difficult to make, in the long run *Kussmaul* would seem to be considerably cheaper to access than ACADEMIC AMERICAN online. It may well be substantially more cost-effective to use than EVERYMAN'S online. However, despite the addition of some 2,000 articles not in the 1973 *Cadillac Modern Encyclopedia* on which it is largely based, *Kussmaul* is badly out of date. This unfortunately negates some of its more admirable qualities. Prospective users are also reminded that it contains only about half as many entries as either ACADEMIC AMERICAN or EVERYMAN'S. But subscribers do get automatic access to Delphi's *Re-*

search Library, a useful bonus. Subscribers can even communicate online with Wes Kussmaul himself.

Individuals and institutions interested in the *Kussmaul Encyclopedia* should contact General Videotex Corporation, 3 Blackstone Street, Cambridge, MA 02139. General Videotex's toll-free number is (800) 544-4005; in Massachusetts the number is (617) 491-3393. Friendly company representatives are most helpful in answering questions and arranging demonstrations.

The Lincoln Library of Essential Information

Facts at a Glance

Full Title: **The Lincoln Library of Essential Information**.

Publisher: Frontier Press Company, P.O. Box 1098, Columbus, Ohio 43216.

Editor-in-Chief: William H. Seibert.

Copyright: 1985.

Number of Volumes: 2.
Number of Contributors: 125.
Number of Entries: 26,000.
Number of Pages: 2,323.
Number of Index Entries: 26,000.
Number of Cross-references: 8,800.
Number of Indexes: 1.
Number of Illustrations: 800 black-and-white, 145 color.
Trim Size: 9″ × 11½″.

Intended Readership: secondary and above.
Price: $139.95, hardcover only.
Sold in bookstores, and by direct mail to libraries and schools. ISBN 0-912168-12-9.
Generally revised biannually; extent of revisions varies. *Next Scheduled Revision*: 1988.

I. Introduction

The Lincoln Library of Essential Information is a two-volume general encyclopedia written for secondary-level student and average adult readers. First produced in 1924, the most recent edition was published in 1985. According to the Preface, a main purpose of the *Lincoln Library* is "to embody in two volumes the greatest amount of useful information for the average reader that could reasonably be placed in one work." The Preface goes on to say that "this work contains from twice to many times as much

information as the average work of many volumes." This seemingly vast quantity of information has been arranged within 11 subject areas, called "departments," plus a Miscellany department. This approach was chosen for its merits of grouping related material and avoiding repetition. The editors do not explain how the 11 departments (Geography, Economics, History, Government, Education, English, Literature, Fine Arts, Mathematics, Science, and Biography) were chosen.

The *Lincoln Library* is designed for the reader involved in self-education—hence the titular reference to Abraham Lincoln. The topical structure of the work is intended to give the reader a thorough overview of selected branches of learning. The material is "based upon primary sources and . . . has been subjected to intense verification." With its voluminous information, thematic arrangement, and pedagogical outlook, *Lincoln Library* combines many of the functions of reference works and textbooks.

II. Scope

There are approximately 3.5 million words in the *Lincoln Library*, and 26,000 entries in the index. Much of the material is organized to proceed from the general to the specific (a survey article on Geography is followed by a section on the geography of North America, with subsections on New England, the Middle Atlantic, and so on). The length of entries or articles varies widely, from two-line entries under "Meanings of Place Names" to a 74-page article on "American History."

At 333 pages, Biography is the largest department, with over 4,000 profiles arranged alphabetically. History, geography, and the humanities receive broad but not particularly consistent coverage. All of the physical sciences are combined in one department of 289 pages, not much longer than the 223 pages devoted to the fine arts. There are no departments for religion, philosophy, or some of the other social sciences. Thus, the coverage of various branches of study is at best uneven.

Within the departments the choice of subjects receiving detailed discussion is also idiosyncratic. For example, the Science department includes 51 pages on **botany** but fewer than four pages on **microbiology**. The Education department contains 12 pages on **intelligence testing** (with several pages on World War I, U. S. Army test questions reproduced in full), where only six pages are devoted to **modern school systems of world countries**.

As mentioned above, the editors do not outline in the Preface the rationale for selecting material,

Lincoln Library

❶ **264**

❷ **Economics**

news sheet to appear in the Western Hemisphere was the *Relación*, issued in 1594 at Lima, Peru, but it was not until 1620 that a regular newspaper was published there. The first regular newspaper in British America was *The Boston News-Letter*, begun in 1704.

Before the days of the telegraph, enterprising newsmen employed carrier pigeons, fast ships, pony expresses, and even semaphore signaling systems for gathering news. With the rise of telegraph and telephone systems, this task was greatly simplified and was put on an organized basis. See *Newspaper Press Associations*. With the development of phototelegraphy, it has become possible to transmit news in picture form with practically the same speed as verbal messages. Improvements in printing presses make it possible now to issue editions containing latest news within a few minutes.

❹ **Radio.** Within the decade 1920–30, a second means of rapid dissemination of information grew into effective rivalry with newspapers. This was the system of radio broadcasting.

Experimental dissemination of speech and music from a central sending station to owners of receiving sets began some years prior to 1920. Lee De Forest was one of the leaders in this development. Station KDKA, operated by the Westinghouse Electric and Manufacturing Company at East Pittsburgh, Pa., broadcast the presidential election returns in 1920. The popularity of this broadcast led the way for a phenomenal increase in the number of receiving sets owned and for a corresponding increase in broadcasting stations. By 1940, there was an average of one radio receiving set for each 2.4 persons in the United States, and programs for every taste and purpose had become routine.

By utilizing telephone wires, chains of stations may be connected so as to send out identical programs. In this manner, nationwide and worldwide "hook-ups" afford opportunities for statesmen, entertainers, or advertisers to reach the ears of millions of listeners. By 1940, there were 675 radio stations in the United States; by 1980, there were well over 8000. In 1980, there were almost a half a billion radios in operation in the United States—more than two per person. The Soviet Union was second in total numbers with some 130 million radios in operation.

One reason for the great increase in radio use in the United States, despite the great rise in television viewing, is that a radio became standard equipment in every automobile. As the television and other video components gained center stage for home entertainment, the car radio allowed the radio-broadcasting industry to continue to thrive. At first the car radio could only receive the AM (Amplitude Modulation) band. But by the 1970's, most car radios could also receive the better-quality FM (Frequency Modulation) band. As a consequence, the number of FM stations, many of which broadcast in stereo, multiplied tremendously in that decade.

Television. The technology behind the electrical transmission of visual images with accompanying sound (that is, video with audio) was developed in the late 19th century. In 1884, the German Paul Nipkow invented the Nipkow disk, a primitive scanner consisting of a circular disk with a number of apertures, or holes. Other developments that contributed to the development of television were the invention of the cathode-ray tube by Ferdinand Braun in 1897 and the invention of a primitive camera tube (the iconoscope) by Vladimir Zworykin in 1923. The first televised images were sent from New York to Philadelphia in 1923. Over the next two decades, the technology was greatly improved. The first regularly scheduled telecasts occurred in London, England, in 1936. The first American station began operating in Schenectady, N.Y., in 1939. But it was not until after World War II that television became a significant part of American life. U.S.

television stations increased from 50 in 1950 to some 1000 in 1980. There were many more throughout the world, though the great majority operated in the industrialized countries. Television sets were likewise unevenly distributed. For example, in 1980 there were about 142 million sets in use in the United States; whereas there were only about 1.2 million sets in use in India, a country of much greater population.

In the United States, the telecasting of programs nationwide was early dominated by the three networks that had developed in the radio-broadcasting industry: the Columbia Broadcasting System (CBS), the National Broadcasting Company (NBC), and the American Broadcasting Company (ABC). The three networks financed their programming by the sale of time for advertising. Each network owned and operated only a few local stations, though each telecast through hundreds of affiliated stations. There also developed numerous independent stations and a loose network of public (noncommercial) stations. The television industry saw significant change in the 1970's and 1980's, when cable television and video tapedecks became widespread. Viewers were able to buy cable packages that included specialized programming, such as sports, religion, news, and music channels. They could also purchase video cassettes of their favorite programs.

Within a few decades, television had become a tremendous force in the world. Television's significance as a tool of communication is just beginning to be understood.

COMMUNICATIONS IN SELECTED COUNTRIES
(figures per 1000 persons in 1980)

❺

Country	Telephones	Televisions	Radios
Australia	489	378	1,026
Bangladesh	1*	1	8
Brazil	63	122	284
Canada	686	471	1,109
China	4	4	57
Egypt	12	33	143
India	4*	2	45
Japan	460	539	678
Mexico	72	104	285
Poland	95	224	295*
Soviet Union	89	303*	490
United Kingdom	477	404	947
United States	788	624	2,099

Source: *Statistical Abstract of the U.S.*, 1984.
*In 1979.

Communications Satellites. The instantaneous communication between practically any two points in the world is a function of the earth-orbiting communications satellites. They are generally of two types: the *passive communications satellites* simply reflect signals from one part of the globe to another; the *active communications satellites* receive and amplify such signals back to earth. Most communications satellites are deployed in a *geosynchronous orbit*; that is, their revolutions around the earth are synchronized with the earth's orbit in such a way that each satellite remains in the same place relative to a point on earth. Such satellites relay television programs, radio broadcasts, and telephone conversations from one end of the earth to the other. Such a transmission of the 1964 Olympics from Japan to America was an event; within a few years satellite communication became commonplace. Many countries have deployed these satellites. In 1960, the United States launched the first, called Echo 1. The first commercial communications satellite was Early Bird, launched in 1965 by the Communications Satellite Corporation (COMSAT), a part of the International Telecommunications Satellite Consortium (INTELSAT). The tremendous advances in computer technology have made satellite operations manageable.

Page shown at 87% of actual size.

❶ Page number

❷ Guide word

❸ Cross-reference: The Lincoln Library contains nearly 9,000 cross-references.

❹ Level 2 subhead: The Lincoln Library uses up to two subhead levels within main entries.

❺ Statistical table: The Lincoln Library contains 275 tables and charts, some of which are a full page or more in length.

saying only that "This work . . . offers a vast array of practical information on subjects that are fundamental." In particular, subjects that have grown in importance since the *Lincoln Library* was first compiled in 1924 seem to be sparsely covered. **Computers**, for example, are discussed in less than one page in the Miscellany department; **psychiatry** is also dealt with under Miscellany, appearing between **religious bodies** and **design and drawing**.

While the Biography department emphasizes historical subjects, it also includes some more varied and more current entries than found elsewhere in this encyclopedia. For example, there are entries for such figures as **Yasir Arafat**, **James Baldwin**, and **Robert Dole**. Space seems to be apportioned according to relative importance of the subjects, from four lines for **Jean Baptiste Biot** (1774-1862), a French astronomer and physicist, to 80 lines for **Beethoven**.

Lincoln includes photographs, maps, drawings, paintings, and diagrams. Of these, 800 are black-and-white and 145 are in color. There is a detailed 48-page color atlas in Volume 1 which is quite useful, although dated (the nation of Zimbabwe is labeled Rhodesia). The illustrations in the Science and Fine Arts departments are also helpful and informative, while many of the others are less integral to the text. However, the editors make plain in the Preface that "it has not been the aim to provide a heavily illustrated reference work."

III. Authority

The Lincoln Library of Essential Information was first compiled in 1924 under the direction of M. J. Kinsella, founder of the Frontier Press Company. From 1978 to 1981 the work was known as *The New Lincoln Library Encyclopedia*, and has occasionally appeared in three rather than two volumes. Now in its 43rd edition, the work has reverted to two volumes, and the original title has been restored. Some readers may also be familiar with the *Encyclopedia of World Knowledge*, a 14-volume version of the *Lincoln Library* that was available in supermarkets at one time.

The current editor-in-chief is William H. Seibert, president of Frontier Press. The frontmatter of Volume 1 lists a staff of 15 editors. Also included is a partial list of contributors, with annotations identifying those sections for which each contributor was responsible, and specifying whether the individual wrote, reviewed, or revised the material. The contributors' affiliations are also listed; most are (or were) university-level academics in relevant fields from a wide variety of institutions. However, none of the

contributors is identified as having been specifically involved subsequent to the 34th edition. Moreover, at least 16 contributors are deceased.

Sources are provided for most of the tables, particularly those involving statistics. The maps in the set's 48-page color atlas were prepared by the well-known cartographic firm of C. S. Hammond and Company.

IV. Currency

It is readily apparent that *Lincoln Library* is badly out of date in some areas. Indeed, this constitutes a serious problem with the encyclopedia as a whole. Although the current edition has a 1985 copyright date, much of the material clearly has remained unchanged from earlier editions. Dated material is not confined to scattered sentences, but rather occupies large blocks of space throughout the encyclopedia. For example, over half of page 899 is occupied by tables of 1967 and 1968 school enrollment statistics.

According to the editors, the *Lincoln Library* is revised continuously, and "at each new printing those portions which are affected by the passage of events are thoroughly revised." Yet in many cases new information has simply been added at the end of an article, without any clear relation to the paragraphs that precede it. For example, the Mulroney administration in Canada is mentioned fleetingly under a bold heading **The Trudeau Era**. Following 16 lines on Mr. Trudeau's term in office, the section ends as follows:

> Trudeau resigned in 1984 and was succeeded for two months by the liberal John Turner. In new elections, Brian Mulroney and the Progressive Conservatives won a landslide victory.

Similarly the article in the Miscellany department on **aeronautics and space exploration** treats in-depth the Apollo missions (including details of handshakes and ceremonial gestures exchanged in the Apollo-Soyuz mission, 1975). The article ends with two brief paragraphs on the Space Shuttle and a paragraph on The Future in Space. The chart following page 1600, on Recent U.S. Space Flights, lists missions only up to Viking 2 (Sept. 9, 1975). Elsewhere the *Lincoln Library's* information on the moons of **Saturn** was already out of date some 13 years before the first Voyager mission.

According to our physics reviewer, the article on **transistors** is at least 20 years old. It mentions neither the use of silicon in transistors nor of integrated circuits, and the current dimensions of transistors are far smaller than those described in the article. Similarly, the entry on **money** is filled with anachronisms, and its tables present no data later than 1974.

A few examples will illustrate the fact that the text needs more than updating additions. The following paragraph appears under the heading Radio and Television in Education:

A recent invention enables television pictures to be recorded on tape, called "Video tape." This tape is usable for delayed re-broadcasting. Like radio tape recording, it can be edited and used by schools when the recording fits into the curriculum. At the present time, this invention is considered too costly to be practical for extensive school use.

Under the heading **computer** is the following passage:

Its more sanguine spokesmen foresee the use of the "home computer" by which a person can push a selected button and obtain almost any desired item of information through a telephone circuit. . .

As mentioned above, some of the Biography entries have been more thoroughly updated or more recently written. Biographies for **Ronald Reagan** and **Margaret Thatcher**, for example, are reasonably current up to 1983 or 1984.

Many of the illustrations show signs of age. For example, a page on sports figures includes youthful portraits of Peggy Fleming, James Brown, Gary Player, Arnold Palmer, and Jack Nicklaus. The **sculpture** article, with over 50 illustrations of 20th century works, includes no pieces more recent than 1972. The Fine Arts section as a whole, however, presents such instructive analyses of works that it is still of considerable value. In general, those illustrations intended as historical documents remain useful.

V. Accuracy

As mentioned, the *Lincoln Library* contains a vast quantity of specific factual information, particularly statistics. The tables were carefully compiled and in general appear accurate up to the time at which they were prepared. The same is generally true of the articles. However, the presence of out-of-date material is at times confusing and frequently misleading. Indeed, this is the source of most of the inaccuracies in this encyclopedia.

For example, entries appear on pages 215 and 663, discussing, respectively, the geography and history of **Rhodesia**. In neither case is there any mention of Zimbabwe. Separate articles about **Zimbabwe** appear on pages 540 and 804. A reader encountering

the first two entries mentioned would be unaware of the major political changes in that country since the late 1970s, including the new names of the nation and its capital city. A reader encountering all four references might find them perplexing. Similarly, the information on the **European Economic Community** is incomplete, and no mention is made of the memberships of Ireland, Greece, Spain, or Portugal, all of whom were admitted after the 1957 treaty agreement. The memberships of Great Britain and Denmark are mentioned only in passing elsewhere in the volume.

Several of our content specialists noted serious inaccuracies in entries in their respective fields. For example, *Lincoln*'s 17-sentence entry on **Saturn** contains at least four minor errors and three major ones. It is, on the whole, the least satisfactory article on the subject in all the encyclopedias reviewed in this Buying Guide. Similarly, *Lincoln*'s entry on **money** cannot be considered reasonably accurate. The encyclopedia's information on **transistors** is generally inaccurate because the article is seriously out of date.

VI. Clarity

Entries in the *Lincoln Library* are generally clear and suited to the intended readership level of secondary school students. The writing varies from the more discursive style used in the background articles to more concise language used to report factual information.

The tone of the articles more often resembles that of a textbook than a reference book. As an example, the introduction to the History department begins as follows:

The word history is sometimes used to mean all that has happened in the past. In this sense we speak of the history of the earth, of rocks, or of plants, as well as of the history of man. In the narrower sense, however, history is an account of the actions and the fortunes of mankind. Such an account must be based upon reliable records which can be understood and interpreted by the writers of history.

An example of the more condensed language used for specific subjects would be this entry from the section on American History:

Ordinance of 1787. An act of the Congress of the Confederation making provision for the government of the Northwest Territory, providing for religious toleration and popular education, and forbidding slavery in the territory.

The style of the Mathematics department is entirely that of a textbook. Moreover, the language is noticeably dated, as in the following example from page 1479:

(1) to multiply an integer by 10, 100, 1000, etc.
Annex to the multiplicand as many ciphers as there are ciphers in the multiplier.
Problem. Multiply 28 by 1000.
Solution.—Three ciphers annexed to 28 gives 28,000, which is the product required.

In a random review of individual pages, certain stylistic inconsistencies were noted. An entry on **John Dewey** (page 860) is written in the present tense. The first heading in the Government department is "Introductory," while the heading beginning the Economics department is "Introduction." The metric system is not used consistently for scientific material. However, these are minor matters and do not tend to distort the sense of the text.

VII. Objectivity

The presentation of the information in *The Lincoln Library of Essential Information* is generally balanced and objective. An attempt is made to mirror the complexity of issues and to represent varying points of view. The biography of **Ronald Reagan** states that "The combination of tax cuts and tremendous increase in defense spending fueled an economic recovery toward the end of his first term. But the federal deficit under Reagan grew to almost 200 billion dollars a year." The article on **South Africa** notes that its government's "policies of racial segregation won the antipathy of much of the world. . . . South Africa became the most prosperous country of southern Africa. Yet political turmoil was constant." The biography of **James Joyce** says of *Ulysses*, "Couched in expressive but often difficult language forms and complicated by the author's erudition, it expressed the thoughts of the characters with a freedom of inhibition unexampled in English literature. Its influence on other authors was widely felt."

Lincoln Library covers a few controversial subjects. There are no articles on homosexuality, racism, contraception, drug abuse, or nuclear disarmament. The article on **evolution** asserts, "This has established practically universal acceptance by the scientific world of the general theory of evolution as a cosmic process." There is no article on creationism. While the omission of these subjects leaves gaps in the comprehensiveness of this encyclopedia, those subjects

that are discussed are treated impartially and without distortion.

VIII. Accessibility

The organizational structure of the *Lincoln Library* works well for readers interested in studying one of the large subject areas covered by a department. The encyclopedia begins with an atlas, followed by the subject departments and a comprehensive index. Each department opens with some background material on the particular discipline, followed by articles exploring the subject in detail. Each main article begins with an uppercase heading, with subsections introduced by boldface headings. Glossaries of terms in relevant subject areas are included, with entries appearing in boldface. The tables are organized in logical fashion, often chronological, and are positioned close to relevant text. Where the material is grouped according to national boundaries (as in History and Government), the United States is discussed first, followed by other countries in alphabetical order. Historical subjects are treated chronologically.

The title page of each department provides a table of contents to assist the reader in locating information. The best aid to locating material is the detailed index, which is printed in full at the end of both volumes.

One drawback of the division of the books into departments is that information on a particular subject may be dispersed throughout the two volumes. For example, information on Iran is found in the departments of Geography, Economics, History, Fine Arts, Government, and Miscellany. In order to find this information the reader would consult the index where there are 14 subentries under **Iran**, as well as entries for **Iranians** and **Iran-Iraq War**. This process is avoided in THE CONCISE COLUMBIA ENCYCLOPEDIA and in all the other single and multivolume general encyclopedias, which are arranged alphabetically. A review in *Booklist* (January 1, 1979) noted, "Persons used to the simple alphabetical arrangement of most American encyclopedias will find more disadvantage than advantage in the *Lincoln*'s structure." The *Lincoln* system might be useful for a reader wishing particularly to compare the government of Iran with those of Indonesia, Iraq, Israel, and Italy, which are discussed on facing pages.

As noted, the index is the key to locating information in the *Lincoln Library*. Subentries are arranged alphabetically under the main entry, so that references for a single key word are in one place. Cross-references are italicized. Occasionally, related entries are not arranged together. "Letters of

Marque" falls between "Letters: Words and Phrases Frequently Misused in" and "Letter Writing." Arrangement of entries beginning with the same word is strictly alphabetical, as in "Adams, John; Adams, John Couch; Adams, John Q."

Some individuals with pseudonyms are listed under their real names while others are listed under their pseudonyms. There is a biography for **Lewis Carroll** and a cross-reference for **Charles Dodgson** but no index entry for Dodgson. Conversely, **Mark Twain** appears under **Samuel Langhorne Clemens**, with a cross-reference under his pseudonym. He is listed under both names in the index. **George Eliot** is treated in the same manner as Lewis Carroll, with no index entry for Mary Ann Evans. Some names beginning with prefixes are listed both under the prefix and under the main portion of the name, as "Da Vinci, "Vinci," Leonardo da" and "Vinci, Leonardo da." Others appear in only one form, as "Balzac, Honore de," for which there is no cross-reference.

Names beginning with *Mc* are alphabetized as though they began with *Mac*. The abbreviation *St.* is always spelled as *Saint* in the index; in the Biography department, it is abbreviated but alphabetized as *Saint*. Monarchs with the same name are grouped according to country and in the order of their succession.

While the division of the work into departments results in repetition of some information and separates related material, it also brings some related material together; moreover, frequent reference to the index can aid the reader. Also of help are the cross-references, of which there are some 8,800. These are italicized and often preceded by "see" in the text and in the index. The arrangement of the *Lincoln Library* is complex, but with an awareness of the topical, alphabetical, and chronological systems employed most information can be readily located.

IX. Special Features

The *Lincoln Library* provides several special features not found in similar works. One such feature is the 48-page color atlas of maps of the world. While the scale of the maps is necessarily small, national boundaries are distinguished in color, and small land masses, secondary cities, and provincial boundaries are represented in detailed fashion.

Another feature is the glossaries, called Dictionaries, included in most of the departments. These are alphabetical lists of identifications and definitions of terms relevant to the field. Some of the dictionary entries are longer than some articles in the CONCISE COLUMBIA or the NEW AMERICAN DESK ENCYCLOPEDIA. There are over 60 dictionaries on subjects such as Art Terms and Subjects; Business, Banking, and Legal Terms; Chemical Substances; Popular Names of Cities; and Literary Plots, Characters, and Allusions. The Dictionaries are printed in a typeface smaller than that of the text, thus condensing the information further.

One of *Lincoln*'s most useful features is its tables. A great deal of thought seems to have gone into organizing these and positioning them near relevant articles. Subjects treated in tables include Abdications; Air Pollution; Cabinet Members; Bacterial Diseases; Federal Reserve System; Historical Periods, Events, and Movements in the New World; Common Logarithms; Mythological Associations; Nobel Prize Winners; Presidents of the United States; and United Nations. As already mentioned, there is a problem with out-of-date information in some of the tables, but others deal with information unaffected by the passage of time. Some tables have been brought up to date, such as the table of Presidents of the United States and the table of Nobel Prize Winners (both current to 1984). Like the Dictionaries, the tables are concise vehicles for conveying a great deal of information. In addition, they help to show linear and tabular relationships between facts. According to the editors, "Many, if expanded into descriptive text, would each provide material for a substantial volume."

Yet another special feature is the Review Questions section included at the end of each department. Numerous questions are posed (seven full pages of questions at the end of Economics) to assist the reader in reviewing the material. The questions are challenging, as, for example, "Summarize the history of popular ratification of state constitutions" and "What kind of words were brought into the English language by the introduction of Christianity?" In the Mathematics section, answers to numerical problems are supplied. According to the Preface, "In all, there are 10,000 such questions, the answers to which, in themselves, constitute the foundations of a liberal education." Among secondary-level encyclopedias, only the multivolume WORLD BOOK includes a similar feature.

Bibliographies are included at the end of each department. These have apparently been updated at various times. The references in Geography and History are to works published up to 1966, while the references in Economics date from 1969 to 1976. The Education and English Language departments contain *no dates*—a distinct drawback. Author, title, and publisher are supplied for each work, and works are listed under bold headings corresponding to portions of the text. Neither of the single-volume encyclopedias (CONCISE COLUMBIA, NEW AMERICAN DESK ENCYCLOPEDIA) include bibliographies.

X. Format

The *Lincoln Library of Essential Information* is available only in a two-volume hardcover edition. The sturdy Black Wolf Grain binding is suitable for school and library use. Both volumes are thumb-indexed for easy access to the subject departments, which are also embossed on the spines in gold.

XI. Other Opinions

Booklist, January 1, 1979 (reviewing the 36th edition, pub. 1974): ". . .those who wish to explore independently the subjects covered in *Lincoln* will find its arrangement effective. Others may find it arbitrary and complicated. . . . The most successfully handled topics are in the sciences, history, and mathematics. . . . The social sciences are less well treated. . . . Because *Lincoln Library* does not treat turbulent and controversial subjects—or those aspects of well-known subjects—its fairness in handling topics of this sort is seldom questioned. . . . Bibliographies are not a strong feature of the *Lincoln Library*. . . . The maps . . . are small but have excellent definition."

Katz, William A., *Introduction to Reference Work*: "The index is detailed enough to overcome the basic problem of arrangement, which is not ideal for ready-reference work. Among its many good features are its several hundred charts and tables, bibliographies, quality illustrations, a good atlas of the world, and broad coverage of general knowledge. The articles are well written and can be easily understood by a junior high or high school student. As the material is arranged under broad sections with over 25,000 different entries, coverage tends to be brief, factual, and unopinionated.

"The difficulty with the *Lincoln* is its revision policy. Although it claims a policy of constant revision, a cursory glance at the 1980 printing will show it is best on current events, but slower on updating standard material in the social sciences, arts, and humanities."

XII. Summary

The Lincoln Library of Essential Information has much to offer as a reference resource. It provides good background introductions and abundant information on some subjects. Both its price (higher than other works in this category) and its large two-volume for-

mat suggest that it would be more suited to libraries than to individual purchasers.

As a general library reference work, however, the *Lincoln Library* is not of consistently high quality in all fields. Some subjects are sparsely covered, controversial material is avoided, and much of the information is out of date. It is also not the most accessible work in this category. It would be most suited to libraries that also include other ready reference works, rather than as the sole work of its type in collection. Librarians seeking a two-volume general reference work for ready reference may wish to investigate THE VOLUME LIBRARY.

The *Lincoln Library* costs $139.95. It is carried by some bookstores; individuals and institutions wishing to order the set may contact the publisher, Frontier Press, at P. O. Box 1098, Columbus, OH 43216, or phone (614) 864-3737.

Merit Students Encyclopedia

Facts at a Glance

Full Title: **Merit Students Encyclopedia.**
Publisher: Macmillan Educational Company, 866 Third Avenue, New York, NY 10022.
Editors: William D. Halsey, Editorial Director; Emanuel Friedman, Editor-in-Chief.
Copyright: 1986.

Number of Volumes: 20.
Number of Contributors: 2,300.
Number of Entries: 21,000.
Number of Pages: 12,300.
Number of Words: 9,000,000.
Number of Maps: 1,570.
Number of Cross-references: 11,000.
Number of Indexes: 1.
Number of Illustrations: 5,000 color, 15,000 black-and-white.
Trim Size: $8\frac{1}{4}'' \times 10\frac{5}{8}''$.

Intended Readership: Elementary through high school.
Price: $1099.50 to individuals; $525 plus $16 shipping ($489 plus shipping for two or more sets) to schools and libraries.
Sold door-to-door, directly to libraries and schools, and by direct mail. ISBN 0-02-943200-6.
Revised annually.

I. Introduction

Merit Students Encyclopedia is a 20-volume work intended primarily for students from grade five through

Merit Students Encyclopedia

① 378   **frostbite**

②

③

Robert Frost, one of the leading American poets, was presented with the Congressional Medal by President John F. Kennedy in 1962. ⑤

WIDE WORLD

merous colleges and universities. Texts of some of his lectures are represented, along with reviews and other of his critical writings, in *Robert Frost on Writing* (1974), edited by Elaine Barry.

Among Frost's beautiful nature poems with philosophic overtones is *Birches,* which describes the poet's growth from a young "swinger of birches" to an old man contemplating the meaning of death and eternity. *The Road Not Taken* and *Stopping by Woods on a Snowy Evening* are typical of his lyrics, in which a few well-chosen words and images express a great deal of meaning and emotion.

Although Frost's verse is lyrical, he is often considered an essentially dramatic poet. One of his most admired poems, *Mending Wall,* describes the conflict that arises between the poem's narrator and his neighbor over rebuilding a wall that separates their farms. The neighbor holds the traditional opinion that "Good fences make good neighbors," but the narrator believes that walls are unnecessary and unnatural between people who should trust each other. *The Death of the Hired Man* is a dramatic dialogue which shows Frost's skill at setting up a conflict and revealing the paradoxes of life. Frost also wrote two verse dramas, *A Masque of Reason* (1945) and *A Masque of Mercy* (1947), based on Biblical stories.

During his lifetime, Frost was the American equivalent of a poet laureate. In 1950 the United States Senate passed a resolution in honor of his 75th birthday, stating that his poems "have helped to guide American thought with humor and wisdom." At the inauguration of President John F. Kennedy in 1961, Frost read his poem *The Gift Outright,* about America's gaining of independence through its devotion to the land. Frost's own love of the soil, his quiet humor and subtle insights, and his simple but moving language made him one of the most respected poets of his generation.

Books for Further Study
Robert Frost: The Work of Knowing by Richard Poirier (Oxford U. P., 1977).
Robert Frost: A Pictorial Chronicle by Kathleen Morrison (Holt, 1974). ④

Robert Frost by Lawrance Thompson (rev. ed., Minnesota 1964).
Introduction to Robert Frost by Elizabeth Isaacs (Haskell, 1962).

Marta Gurtoff
Reviewed by *Walter B. Rideout* ⑥

frostbite (frôst′bīt), a condition in which a part of the body freezes, turns yellowish white, and becomes numb. Frostbite usually occurs in the extremities of the body, such as the toes, the fingers, the tip of the nose, and the ears. In extreme cold the small blood vessels that carry blood to these areas constrict, and blood circulates at a slower than normal rate. As a result, eventually the body fluids in the affected areas may freeze. ⑦

The condition is treated by rapidly warming the frostbitten part back to normal body temperature. This may be done by placing the person in a warm room and bathing the affected area in warm water. Removing tight clothing helps restore circulation. To prevent injury to tissues, a frostbitten area should never be massaged or rubbed with snow.

Mild frostbite is not serious. However, if frostbite is not treated early, the tissues may be so seriously damaged that gangrene may result, and it may be necessary to amputate the frostbitten part. Frostbite can be prevented by wearing warm clothing that is not tight or binding. It is especially important to keep the clothing dry.   *Louis J. Vorhaus, M.D.*

Frostburg State College, an accredited, coeducational, state college in Frostburg, Md. The school offers undergraduate courses of study in teacher education and in the arts and sciences. Graduate work on the master's level is offered in education. Affiliated with the college is a laboratory school that comprises kindergarten through the seventh grade. The institution was founded in 1898 and adopted its present name in 1963. *See also* SCHOOLS, COLLEGES, AND UNIVERSITIES.   *R. Bowen Hardesty* ⑧ ⑨

frozen custard. *See under* ICE CREAM. ⑩

Page shown at 67% of actual size.

① Page number
② Guide word
③ Illustration: Merit Students Encyclopedia contains some 20,000 illustrations, of which one-quarter are in color.
④ Bibliography: Many articles also contain a separate list of books for younger readers.
⑤ Caption
⑥ Contributor and reviewer credits: Merit has 2,300 contributors. Most articles are signed by the contributor and/or a reviewer.
⑦ Pronunciation for entry word
⑧ Main entry: Merit contains 21,000 entries, arranged alphabetically, letter-by-letter. Entry words are printed in boldface.
⑨ "See also" cross-reference: Merit includes about 11,000 cross-references in all.
⑩ Cross-reference entry

high school. The encyclopedia's purpose, as summarized in the Preface, is "to meet the educational and informational demands brought about by the changes that have taken place in our society and our schools since the advent of the space age."

The subjects covered in *Merit* were chosen according to curricula taught in North American schools. "The scope and content of the encyclopedia were developed after analysis of the published curriculum material available from all the states of the United States, from the provinces of Canada, and from parochial school systems." (Preface) The use of the word "students" in the title indicates that this work is intended primarily for student use as a resource for school work.

II. Scope

Merit Students Encyclopedia contains some 21,000 articles and 9 million words, with an average of 429 words per article. The actual length of articles varies widely, more or less according to the importance of the subject. As an example of how space is apportioned, **Prince Charles** gets about one-sixth of a page, **Anton Pavlovich Chekhov** about two-thirds of a page, and **Konstantin Ustinovich Chernenko** about one-third of a page. **China** receives 20 and one-half pages of coverage, **Christianity** six and one-half pages, and the **Civil War** 30 pages. The school-oriented approach is evident here, since the Civil War looms large in the curricula of schools in the U.S., and receives considerable space in this work.

American history is especially well covered, with long articles on topics such as **colonial life in the Americas** (28 pages) and **American Indians** (38 pages), plus long articles on each U. S. president and Canadian prime minister, all written to a similar format. Articles on each state and province of North America also include history sections.

Geography is well covered, with articles on all continents and countries as well as the states and provinces just mentioned. Most of these articles are accompanied by maps and illustrations, and consider various aspects of each region, such as physical geography, economy, people, religion, government, and history.

Most of the sciences are well represented, as least through an introductory level. The botanical entries are accompanied by excellent drawings showing species characteristics, in addition to articles such as **leaf**, which discusses the functions of leaves and their comparative anatomy. In addition to a general article on **mathematics**, *Merit* also includes more detailed articles on specific subjects such as **algebra**, **analytic**

geometry, and **calculus**. In the same way, there is a general article on **William Shakespeare** and separate articles on each of Shakespeare's major plays. Important literary characters, such as **Desdemona** and **D'Artagnan**, also receive individual entries.

Merit's content reflects young people's interests beyond the school curriculum as well. For example, it includes fairly extensive articles on youth organizations such as the **Boy Scouts** (five and three-quarters pages); sports, hobbies, and other leisure activities such as **bowling** (three and one-quarter pages) and **camping** (six pages), and **careers in** . . . major professional fields such as **architecture**, **banking**, **music**, and **veterinary medicine** (each about one-half page). Sensitive topics such as **adolescence** and **anorexia nervosa** are also covered.

One limitation arising from the emphasis on subjects in the school curriculum and those related to leisure interests is that more specialized subjects often receive sparse coverage that bears no direct relation to their overall importance. For example, various branches of medicine are covered in individual entries, but some of these entries, such as **pediatrics** and **internal medicine**, are only a few lines long.

III. Authority

Merit Students Encyclopedia is published by the Macmillan Educational Company (MEC), a division of the Macmillan Publishing Company, one of the largest, oldest, and most respected publishers of trade, text, and reference books in the United States. In fact, Macmillan is today regarded as one of the four major publishers of general encyclopedias in the country—the other three being Encyclopaedia Britannica, Grolier, and World Book.

The second newest of all general multivolume encyclopedias (predating only the ACADEMIC AMERICAN), *Merit* first appeared in 1967 and has been reissued with revisions every year since. Although the set is ostensibly independent from MEC's COLLIER'S ENCYCLOPEDIA, it is clearly modeled on COLLIER'S, and a small but significant portion of its articles are abridged versions of entries initially written for COLLIER'S.

William D. Halsey serves as Editorial Director for both encyclopedias, while Emanuel Friedman similarly serves in a dual capacity as Editor-in-Chief for the two sets. A staff of 23 editors is credited in *Merit*'s frontmatter, which also lists two Advisory Boards (Library and International) and a Board of Special Editors who "participated in the development of this encyclopedia." The latter list gives the full credentials of each advisory editor and the subject area in *Merit* with which he or she assisted.

As previously mentioned, there are several similarities between *Merit* and COLLIER'S. A number of Macmillan editors have worked on both encyclopedias. Many of the illustrations used in COLLIER'S also appear in *Merit*. Moreover, about one-fifth of *Merit*'s articles are clearly derived from material in COLLIER'S. But there are significant differences between the two encyclopedias and each has clearly been compiled with a different purpose in mind.

The Preface to *Merit* states that "Each article in *Merit Students Encyclopedia* was written or reviewed by a subject-matter expert." Many articles are signed and, in cases where the contributor reviewed, but did not write, an article, the signature is preceded by an asterisk. A list of contributors and reviewers appears in Volume 20, providing affiliations for each contributor at the time of his or her contribution. Most of the contributors are American academics, with public officials, journalists, librarians, and other specialists also represented. With each revision of the encyclopedia, new articles are added and others are revised; the list of contributors and reviewers is accordingly updated, as is evident in the 1986 edition.

IV. Currency

Merit Students Encyclopedia is revised annually. According to the publisher, each of the last five revisions has involved changes to some 1600 pages. This ambitious policy has resulted in an encyclopedia that is reasonably up-to-date in most areas, as a random sample of articles will illustrate.

For example, the article on South Africa reports events of 1985 such as the state of emergency declared by the South African government and the temporary freeze on repayments of loan principal, as well as the activities of Desmond Tutu and Allan Boesak. The entry for **space flight** reports the January 1986 Challenger space shuttle explosion. The article on **acquired immune deficiency syndrome** explains the current understanding about the AIDS virus and reports the approximate number of deaths caused by the disease up to the mid-1980s. The article on **Nicaragua** is current to 1984, giving information on the election of Daniel Ortega Saavedra as president.

Significant recent events are missing from some articles, however. For example, the article on **Northern Ireland** fails to mention the 1985 agreement between the United Kingdom and the Republic of Ireland giving the Republic a voice in governing Northern Ireland. Tables of ongoing information, such as heads of state or recipients of awards are up-to-date, but tables of statistics such as industrial production of some regions often date from the mid-1970s. For example, in **U.S.S.R.**, tables of crop and livestock production give figures from 1976. The nation's population reported at the head of the article is a 1983 estimate; a 1988 projection is also given. Thus, current events seem to be well recorded in *Merit* while gradual change in some fields may not be incorporated until somewhat later in the revision process.

The 1986 edition of *Merit* includes new entries on **Rajiv Gandhi**, **Mikhail Sergevich Gorbachev**, **Ted Hughes**, **ibuprofen**, **kiwifruit**, and **Shimon Peres**. Articles on **alcoholism**, **apartheid**, **Harry Blackmun**, **China: economic activities** and **cocaine** have all been completely rewritten. These and many other articles on topics of current interest provide up-to-date information for students of current affairs.

An attempt is made to keep the illustrations in the text up-to-date and here, too, there are only occasional lapses. The article on **clothing**, for example, includes color plates of styles, the most recent of which date from the 1960s. But the 1986 edition of the encyclopedia does include some 40 new illustrations and 21 revised maps, demonstrating the commitment to updating the work as a whole on an ongoing basis.

V. Accuracy

Like most general reference encyclopedias, careful attention is paid to the accuracy of information in *Merit Students Encyclopedia*. In the Preface the editors state that "The articles are written to satisfy the educator who teaches in today's schools as well as the scholar." Reviewers are said to have vouched "for the accuracy and completeness of the article" (List of Contributors and Reviewers). The standard thus set out is high and the text achieves it for the most part, given the scope and level of the material.

One limitation already mentioned is that some articles are not as comprehensive or as detailed as their subjects might warrant (see *Scope*). The coverage of medical specialties is one example of this. In some cases, the brevity of articles results in oversimplification or in the omission of significant information. For example, *Merit*'s article on the **brain** does not discuss neurotransmitters, a significant element that has improved our understanding of the brain. The discussion of the basal ganglia is dated and in some respects incorrect. The encyclopedia's coverage of **transistors** is generally good, but similarly suffers from occasional mistakes. For example, the explanation of current flow is inaccurate, and the discussion of semiconductor types is misleading. **Saturn** also has two major flaws (relating to the planet's thermal radiation and the diameter of the rings). On the other hand, the coverage of the U. S. **Bill of Rights** is both extensive and objective. And *Merit*'s entry on **money** is the best and most clearly written article on the subject to be found in any encyclopedia for this age group—including COMPTON'S ENCYCLOPEDIA, the NEW BOOK OF KNOWLEDGE, and WORLD BOOK. On the whole, for student use *Merit* is sufficiently comprehensive and reliable.

VI. Clarity

The writing style and the structure of the articles in *Merit Students Encyclopedia* is simple and clear. The text is not written to a particular reading level throughout, but rather, as the Preface reports, "individual articles were designed and written primarily at the grade level at which they are taught. Material for younger students is included at the beginning of an article. As the content of the article is developed, more advanced material is incorporated for the many students who are able to go beyond their grade level." This policy is evident in the longer articles, where there is sufficient space to distinguish the introductory material from the more advanced discussion. In general the style of the text seems rather challenging for fifth-grade readers, but should be well within the range of junior high and high school students.

Entries on people, places, minerals, and chemical elements begin with basic identification information in italics. For example, the entry for **Henry David Thoreau** identifies him as an "*American writer, philosopher, and naturalist. Born Concord, Mass., July 12, 1817. Died Concord, May 6, 1862.*" This helps readers to determine whether the article is the one they are seeking; for younger readers, this opening section may provide much of the information they need. Other articles begin with a brief definition, such as "**marathon**, a long-distance run, or footrace, introduced at the first modern Olympic Games in 1896, in Athens, Greece. . . ." Technical terms are often defined in context, as in this excerpt from the article on **marine biology**: "One of the most important activities of marine biologists is to determine the *biogeography*, or distribution of marine organisms. . . ."

Biographical articles often depart from a strict chronological sequence of events, presenting major accomplishments of the subject's life first. The article on **Harold Macmillan** begins: "Harold Macmillan became prime minister and leader of the Conservative Party in January 1957 . . ." and discusses the events of his term as prime minister. The final paragraph of the entry goes back in time to Macmillan's education and his early political life. This can be confusing for those attempting to follow the course of an individual's development, but has the advantage of highlighting significant activities, particularly for those readers who may find it difficult to complete some of the longer articles.

Helpful stylistic features include pronunciation supplied for many key words, including foreign entry words; metric equivalents provided for all measurements; and lists of key facts appearing at the beginning of many major articles. Articles on similar subjects (such as animals, presidents, and countries) follow standard formats, helping to make them readable and clear.

The following extract from **lighthouse** illustrates the style of a typical entry in *Merit Students Encyclopedia*:

> **lighthouse** (līt′hous′), a structure in or near the water, illuminated to warn and guide ships at sea. Lighthouses are often built in the shape of a tower, usually on or near points dangerous to navigation. In addition to lights, modern lighthouses also have sound fog signals, radio and radar beacons, and other equipment for transmitting electronic signals. Structures that are built inland and along much traveled air routes for the guidance of airplanes are called aerial lighthouses.
>
> **Lighthouses and Lightships.** Lighthouses are built either on rocks or other sites exposed to the sea, or on land. Towers built open to the sea are made of masonry and concrete or of openwork steel and iron-framed materials. They may be located on rocks or built on pilings or a caisson or cylinder foundation. They are circular in form, with a low center of gravity. Special skills are needed to construct open-to-the-sea towers. The actual building is complex and slow, and provisions must be made to protect the structure from the battering waves. Lighthouses built on land are easier to construct, and are usually in stone, brick, or reinforced concrete.

VII. Objectivity

Merit Students Encyclopedia does not avoid controversial issues. According to the Preface, "Controversial issues are treated in an honest and reasonable manner. . . . In every case where more than one point of view exists or where research has developed conflicting data, various points of view are given and the fact that differences of opinion exist is clearly pointed out." A random survey confirms that opposing views are mentioned, although they may not always be explained in full.

Merit's article on **evolution** briefly describes pre-Darwinian beliefs. It then asserts that "in the opinion of almost all biologists the matter was finally settled by . . . Darwin." Present-day objections to the theory of evolution by "creationists" are not mentioned, and the encyclopedia does not include a separate entry for scientific creationism.

The article on **abortion** briefly mentions moral and religious opposition and discusses legal restrictions, as well as arguments in favor of permitting abortion. It also notes varying attitudes in different countries, and reports on changes in United States abortion laws during the 1970s. However, it does not mention developments during the 1980s.

While the brevity of some *Merit* articles may curtail the full presentation of opposing views, a few controversial subjects of particular importance for students are treated with great sensitivity. For example, the entry on **suicide** presents a well-balanced discussion of causes, methods, statistics, and prevention.

Controversial aspects of important careers are also touched on in biographical entries. The article on **Andrew Jackson** mentions a number of the flaws in his character and his career, such as his harsh treatment of Indians. A few of these flaws are, if not excused, then presented in the best possible light. For example, we read that "Jackson owned 20 slaves, but it was said that 'He was a kind master, governing his slaves more as a Scotch chieftain his clan, or a Hebrew patriarch his tribe, than as a driver. . . .' " About Jackson's use of the spoils system, the article states: "The custom of rewarding political supporters with public office had existed since the founding of the Republic" and "Jackson used it to prevent the growth of an entrenched bureaucracy."

VIII. Accessibility

The entries in *Merit Students Encyclopedia* are arranged alphabetically, letter by letter. A full explanation of the alphabetical system appears at the beginning of each volume. Entry headings appear in boldface type with subheadings also in boldface; two levels of subheadings are frequently used in longer, more detailed entries. Each volume is paginated separately and the page numbers and running heads are printed in the outside corners of the upper margins. All of these elements are clear and easy to read.

Articles of a similar nature follow a set format, facilitating both quick reference and comparative study. Major geographic articles make consistent use of maps and statistics that can form the basis for comparison with other articles. Biographical articles

of similar figures (such as presidents) present comparable details (such as election results and cabinet members). There are some survey articles, such as **agriculture** and **American literature**, but most articles are of the specific-entry type. Thus major agricultural products are subjects of separate articles, as are major American authors.

A special feature in the longer articles is the Student's Guide, a box containing an explanation of the way in which the article is organized, and references to other articles in the encyclopedia where related information can be found. This not only helps the reader to locate specific information quickly, but also helps in researching a broad topic.

There are 11,000 cross-references, directing the reader from one article to others on similar topics. The use of these is somewhat inconsistent; it is unclear why some articles include several cross-references while others lack even the obvious ones. For example, there are separate articles on each of Shakespeare's major plays, but there are no cross-references in the articles on **As You Like It** or **Othello** to the **William Shakespeare** article. Those cross-references that do appear are of two main types: those that send the reader from one heading to another where the relevant article is found (such as "**asymptote**. *See under* HYPERBOLA"), and those that suggest related articles for further reading (such as "*See also* GALAXY; QUASAR; UNIVERSE" in the **astronomy** article). As just noted, the Student's Guide boxes contain cross-references to related articles. While these are useful, more are needed—particularly for younger readers who may have less experience in investigating many sides of a topic.

The index in *Merit* is most thorough, with over 140,000 entries, or an average of seven entries for every article. The index helps to overcome any difficulties that may be found in locating information through the alphabetical arrangement of articles or the cross-references. Brief annotations distinguish similar entries, and topics to which an article is devoted appear in boldface capital letters. Pictures, maps, and diagrams are all noted in the index. As an indication of the scope and style of individual entries, the reader searching for information about Marie Curie will find the following index entry:

CURIE, MARIE SKLODOWSKA
(Pol.-Fr. sci.) **5**-382 *with picture;* **15**-44 *with picture;* **16**-449 *with picture*
polonium **15**-191
radioactivity **15**-475

Taken together, all of the aids mentioned here help to make information in *Merit* readily accessible, for quick reference or extensive research.

IX. Special Features

Various special features enhance the usefulness and appearance of this well-rounded encyclopedia. There are 20,000 illustrations in *Merit*, of which 5,000 are in color. The editors explain that "In each case the type of illustration was selected to provide the best visual communication" (Preface) and most of the illustrations are indeed very effective. Clothing, hair styles, and automobiles mark some of the black-and-white photographs as from the 1960s and 1970s, but these anachronisms rarely contradict the sense of the text. There are very attractive color plates on subjects such as **birds**, **fishes**, and **ships**, and color transparencies on **camouflage**, **human anatomy**, and **printing in color**. The 60-page article on **painting** is printed on coated paper to accommodate the many excellent reproductions of paintings that appear throughout.

Merit contains nearly 1,600 maps, which accompany all of the major geographic articles and appear in other pertinent entries. While this is several hundred fewer than the number in WORLD BOOK, those in *Merit* are comparable in quality, and there are no serious omissions. State, province, country, and continent maps (all prepared by Rand McNally) occupy two-page spreads and show boundaries, bodies of water, and primary and secondary cities in appropriate detail. Indexes to these maps are also thorough. Smaller thematic maps, prepared by *Merit*'s cartographic staff, are also of high quality and will be useful to students.

Bibliographies are appended to some major articles, and books for younger readers or for advanced students are occasionally annotated as such. Some of these lists have been updated, but others include no books more recent than the 1970s. Since the majority of the articles have no bibliographies, *Merit* will not be the preferred encyclopedia for sources of further information.

X. Format

Merit Students Encyclopedia comprises 20 volumes, each approximately 600 pages long. (Volume 20, at 648 pages, is the longest.) Unlike WORLD BOOK, *Merit* utilizes the split-letter system. The complete set occupies approximately two feet two inches of horizontal shelf space. The red cloth binding with gold lettering and black-and-gold panels is sturdy and attractive, and suitable for school and library use.

The two-column page design is clear, well-illustrated, and generally inviting.

XI. Other Opinions

ARBA 82: "While *Merit Students Encyclopedia* is on the whole a well-indexed, well-illustrated, and well-written work, treating the broad range of young adults' interests, we were disappointed at times with the unevenness of revision. . . ."

ARBA 86: ". . . *Merit* was found to be especially useful for curriculum backup and objective articles on controversial topics. The bibliographies are useful, but sparse. Though obvious effort has been put into updating, there are disappointing omissions in this area. It is an attractive set, with well-placed and generally eye-catching graphics. . . ."

Reference Books Bulletin (November 15, 1986): ". . . The 1986 edition of *Merit Students Encyclopedia* continues to provide solid, objective, generally well illustrated articles for young people through high school. Although articles dealing with current events are usually up-to-date, there is a need for examination and revision of some material, especially photographs, in order to maintain *Merit*'s timeliness."

XII. Summary

Merit Students Encyclopedia is a valuable general reference work for young adults. Covering a wide selection of topics, it is reasonably accurate, objective, and up-to-date, despite the occasional errors, omissions, and anachronisms mentioned in this review.

While the publisher claims that *Merit* is suitable for students in the elementary through high school grades, the set will have little utility for children in the lower elementary grades. Its usefulness rises as students progress through middle school into high school.

Merit's main competitors are COMPTON'S ENCYCLOPEDIA and WORLD BOOK. *Merit* is generally more sophisticated than COMPTON'S and other comparable sets such as FUNK & WAGNALLS NEW ENCYCLOPEDIA and NEW STANDARD ENCYCLOPEDIA. On the other hand, its graphics are dull in comparison with those in the popular WORLD BOOK, which may mean that some children will be less inclined to consult this set.

On balance, *Merit* is a good though not outstanding encyclopedia. It works well as a ready reference tool, and is also a useful resource for beginning research into subjects related to most school curricula.

For individuals, *Merit*'s price of $1099.50 is considerably more expensive than the cost of both COMPTON'S and WORLD BOOK. On the other hand, the generous discount that the publisher extends to schools and librarians ($525 for one set, $489 each for purchases of two or more sets) is comparable to the school/library price of these two competitors. Individuals may order from the Macmillan Educational Corporation at (800) 257-9500. Institutions may order by dialing another toll-free number, (800) 257-5755.

The New American Desk Encyclopedia

Facts at a Glance

Full Title: **The New American Desk Encyclopedia**.
Publisher: New American Library, 1633 Broadway, New York, NY 10019.
Editor-in-Chief: Robert A. Rosenbaum.
Copyright: 1984.

Number of Volumes: 1.
Number of Articles: 13,000.
Number of Pages: 1,305.
Number of Words: 1,000,000.
Number of Maps: 225.
Number of Illustrations: 35 four-color.
Trim Size: 4¼" x 7".

Intended Readership: junior high school and above.
Price: $6.95.
Sold in bookstores and supermarkets, and by direct mail. ISBN 0-451-14289-6.
Revision of not less than 10 percent every 4 to 5 years.
Next Scheduled Revision: 1989.

I. Introduction

The New American Desk Encyclopedia is a one-volume general encyclopedia intended for secondary-level and adult readers. Available in a compact, mass-market paperback edition, this encyclopedia aims to cover a full range of subjects in an extremely limited amount of space. The book claims to be "the only one-volume pocket-size paperback guide that combines information on all major fields of knowledge with up-to-the-minute coverage of the contemporary world scene." It is designed for home, school, and office use.

There is no preface to the book, and thus no explanation of how the subjects were chosen or the entries compiled and edited.

II. Scope

The New American Desk Encyclopedia (NADE) contains 13,000 entries and approximately one million words. Thus, the average length of an article is 77 words, roughly the same as for the entries in the CONCISE COLUMBIA ENCYCLOPEDIA, although the *CCE* contains 2,000 more entries.

Entries are arranged alphabetically, letter by letter. Some entries are only a few lines long, such as those for **Muslims** (two lines) and for the aviatrix **Amelia Earhart** (eight lines). Others go into greater depth and length, including more detailed technical explorations (such as the 106-line entry for **heart**) or historical information (such as the 86-line entry for **immigration**). There are 175 articles about individual countries, as well as separate entries for each of the 50 states of the United States. Geographical entries follow a format distinct from that of other subjects. They are introduced by a list of general facts about the region, such as area and population, as well as a small regional map with the relevant country or state highlighted. The remainder of the article is subdivided by boldface subheadings such as *Land*, *People*, *Economy*, and *History*. As a result, these are among the longer articles in the book; taken together, they give the *NADE* a consistently broad, but succinct, coverage of political geography.

Many of the brief entries serve primarily as definitions or identifications. Entries for individuals typically supply dates of birth and death, nationality, position or occupation, and the bare outlines of significant activities or accomplishments. Cross-references direct the reader to further information in order to avoid repetition of definitions. All efforts seem to have been made to use the available space in this compact book economically.

In light of the variety of subjects covered, *NADE*'s claim to include "all major fields of knowledge" is justified. Major historical figures and events are well represented, as are many of their present-day counterparts. As an indication of *NADE*'s range, there are entries for **Mozart**, **Benjamin Britten**, **Coriolanus**, **Fidel Castro**, the **astrolabe**, and the **electron microscope**. Contemporary popular subjects of importance are covered, as in the entries on **bluegrass music** and **Humphrey Bogart**. Issues of current social concern, such as **Baby Boom**, are also included. While considerable space is devoted to coverage of the United States, international subjects are not neglected (for

The New American Desk Encyclopedia

❶ **312**   **CUYP**

❷ renowned and respected French scientist in the early 19th century.

❸ CUYP, Aelbert (1620–1691), outstanding member of a family of Dutch painters. His glowing river scenes with cattle are particularly fine, but he also painted portraits, still lifes and seascapes. He influenced later English landscape artists, and many of his best works are in Britain.

CYANIDES, compounds containing the CN group. Organic cyanides are called nitriles. Inorganic cyanides are salts of **hydrocyanic acid** (HCN), a volatile weak ACID; both are highly toxic. Sodium cyanide is made by the Castner process: ammonia is passed through a mixture of carbon and fused sodium. The cyanide ion (CN⁻) is a pseudohalogen, and forms many complexes. Cyanides are used in the extraction of GOLD and SILVER.

CYBERNETICS, a field of science which compares the communication and control systems built into mechanical and other man-made devices with those present in biological organisms. For example, fruitful comparisons may be made between data **❹** processing in COMPUTERS and various functions of the BRAIN; and the fundamental theories of cybernetics may be applied with equal validity to both.

CYCLONE, a low-pressure atmospheric disturbance (see ATMOSPHERE; METEOROLOGY) of a roughly circular form, a center towards which ground WINDS move, and at which there is an upward air movement, usually spiraling. Above the center, in the upper troposphere, there is a general outward movement. The direction of spiraling is counterclockwise in the N Hemisphere, clockwise in the S Hemisphere, owing to the CORIOLIS EFFECT. **Anticyclones,** by contrast, are high-pressure atmospheric disturbances characterized by out-blowing winds and a clockwise circulation in the N Hemisphere (counterclockwise in the S Hemisphere). (See also HURRICANE; TORNADO.)

CYNICS, members of an ascetic Greek philosophical sect following DIOGENES (4th century BC), and influenced by SOCRATES. They ignored conventional standards, preached self-control, condemned immorality and renounced worldly comfort, living as simply as animals (hence, probably, their name: *kynikos* means "doglike"). Their movement influenced STOICISM but vanished in imperial Roman times.

CYPRIAN, Saint (Thascius Caecilianus Cyprianus; c200–258 AD), bishop of Carthage (248–258) and martyr, one of the CHURCH FATHERS. Converted to Christianity c246, Cyprian wrote and spoke influentially

on order and conduct in the Church, stressing Church unity and episcopal authority. Feast day: Sept. 16.

CYPRUS, island republic in the NE Mediterranean, about 40mi from the S Turkish coast. It is the third-largest island in the Mediterranean after Sicily and Sardinia.

❺

Official name: The Republic of Cyprus
Capital: Nicosia
Area: 3,572sq mi
Population: 630,000
Languages: Greek, Turkish
Religions: Greek Orthodox, Turkish Muslim
Monetary unit(s): 1 Cyprus pound=1,000 mils

❻

Land. The island consists of fertile central lowlands with rugged mountains to the N and S. The N range comprises the Kyrenia and Karpas mountains (Akromandra, 3,357ft). In the SW, the Troodos massif has Mt Olympus (6,403ft), the island's highest peak. On the Mesaoria lowland between the mountain systems is Nicosia, the capital. The mountains are partly forested (pine, cypress, and juniper) and have much poor pasture. The climate is typically E Mediterranean.

People. The population is about 80% Greek and 20% Turkish. Both Greek and Turkish are official languages and English is widely spoken. In 1973 nearly 37% of the people lived in the six district capitals: Nicosia, Limassol, Famagusta, Larnaca, Paphos and Kyrenia, but recent events have changed the pattern.

❼

The economy normally depends heavily upon irrigated agriculture (citrus fruits, vines, tobacco, cereals and vegetables). Mineral resources include cupreous and iron pyrites, asbestos, chromite and gypsum. Tourism was formerly important.

History. Ruled successively by the Ottoman Turks (1570–1878) and Great Britain, Cyprus became an independent republic, with Archbishop Makarios III as president, in 1960. But strife between Greek and Turkish Cypriots continued, and in 1974 a

Page shown at 107% of actual size.

❶ Page number
❷ Guide word
❸ Main entry: New American Desk Encyclopedia contains 13,000 entries, arranged alphabetically, letter-by-letter. Entry words are printed in boldface type.

❹ Cross-references are indicated by words printed in small capital letters.
❺ Location map: New American Desk Encyclopedia includes 225 maps in all.

❻ Nation and state entries include a "fact table" giving basic statistics about geography, population, etc.
❼ Subheads: Nation and state entries are divided into sections by subheads.

comparison, the article on **Idaho** is slightly longer than the article on **Iceland**). Although names of people and places predominate, there is excellent coverage of scientific and technical subjects, and wide coverage of other subjects of general interest such as **integration**, **intelligence**, **interior decoration**, and **international law**.

Illustrations are not a strong feature of this encyclopedia. In addition to the small black-and-white maps in the geographical articles, there is a 16-page color atlas section with illustrations relating to geology, geography, and astronomy. This is positioned near the beginning of the work and does not illustrate any particular article. There are no other illustrations in the volume.

III. Authority

The current edition of the *NADE* was issued in 1984 by New American Library, a leading publisher of mass-market paperbacks. According to the publisher, the *NADE* is a "derivation and adaptation of the *University Desk Encyclopedia*," which was published jointly by E. P. Dutton & Company and the Dutch publisher Elsevier in 1977. That work was never revised and is now out of print. In 1981 a three-volume edition was published by Concord Reference Books, Inc., as the *Concord Encyclopedia*; this is also now out of print.

The *NADE* differs from the *UDE* in several respects. It includes half as many entries and half as many words as the older book, which was heavily illustrated and produced in a large hardcover format. The *NADE*'s entries have been updated through 1983 (see also *Currency*), and it costs less than its older cousin did.

The nine-person editorial staff for this edition was headed by Robert A. Rosenbaum, the editor-in-chief. In addition, the credits list 31 contributing editors although their affiliations and areas of specialization are not identified. All of the articles are unsigned.

IV. Currency

As mentioned above, since *The New American Desk Encyclopedia* was first produced in the early 1980s, both the choice of subjects and the content of the articles are generally current to that time. Where articles have been adapted from the *University Desk Encyclopedia* they have often been updated, and subjects missing from the earlier work appear in the *NADE*. For example, the article on **Margaret Thatcher** mentions her party's electoral victory in 1983, while the article on **Ronald Reagan** mentions his 1984 election campaign. The article on **South Africa**, however,

mentions none of the recent political upheaval in that country, and ends "In 1961 this country became a republic and left the Commonwealth largely because of differences over its apartheid policies." The article on **disarmament** ends with mention of the 1975 arms limitations agreement but makes no mention of either the 1982 Strategic Arms Reduction Talks or Ronald Reagan's 1983 Strategic Defense Initiative, although there is a separate article on the former. The entry on **transistors** is, on the whole, quite dated.

Brevity of the articles sometimes limits the amount of current information, since details beyond a certain level of significance are not included. Thus an article on the **Iraqi-Iranian War** states that "Sporadic fighting, without military distinction, led to a stalemate that continued through the early 1980s." The growing implications of this conflict, for the Middle East and the entire world, are not incorporated in the space available for the entry.

Many subjects that have only recently achieved prominence are covered, as in the articles on **AIDS** and **Boat People**. According to the publisher, the *NADE* will be revised every four to five years, with at least 10 percent of the material revised each time. The next scheduled revision will appear in 1989. This policy shows a promising intention to keep the encyclopedia more or less up-to-date and to incorporate new material as developments warrant.

V. Accuracy

The majority of the entries in the *NADE* are reliably correct and the level of detail is consistent. However, because the articles are so brief, unavoidable choices have been made in selecting information to include. On the whole, important facts are given appropriate weight, but occasionally significant information has been omitted. For example, **AIDS** fails to mention the high incidence of the disease in Africa; instead statistics are given for high risk groups, presumably in the United States although this is not made clear. The article on **Robert Byrd** identifies him as a "U.S. legislator" but fails to mention the state (West Virginia) that he represents. The article on **Isaac Bashevis Singer** mentions his 1978 Nobel Prize for Literature, yet the article on **Saul Bellow** does not mention his (awarded in 1976). There is no entry at all for **Eugenio Montale**, recipient of the 1975 Nobel Prize. These omissions can be misleading for a reader looking to rely upon the encyclopedia's consistent and accurate presentation of information.

The article on **money** contains several mistakes and oversimplifications. The entry on **Saturn** is generally accurate.

On the whole, the inaccuracies noted here are not so significant as to cast doubt upon the *NADE*'s overall authority. Since the entries consist largely of salient, well-confirmed facts, this is not a great problem.

VI. Clarity

In order to cover 13,000 subjects in one paperback volume, the articles are extremely condensed. Many of the entries are basically definitions or identifications, with perhaps a small amount of background information. While not dictionary definitions, they may be only a few sentences in length. The following entry for **Bobwhite** (quoted in full) is an example of this:

> BOBWHITE, *Colinus virginiarus*, North American gamebird related to the **QUAIL** and **PARTRIDGE**. It is about 10 in. long and reddish brown in color. Bobwhites feed on insects and seeds and keep within a group or covey.

Certain complex subjects are treated in longer articles written in a less truncated style. The tone is still direct, scholarly without being pedantic, and easily understood by the average reader. The following passage from the article on **economics** illustrates this:

> Under the influence of **KEYNESIAN ECONOMICS**, US government policies from the 1950s emphasized increasing demand by both manipulating tax rates and increasing the money supply. However, starting in the 1970s, inflation and a stagnating or decreasing gross national product brought these fiscal policies under question, strengthening the influence of non-Keynesian economists.

Alternate forms of scientific or technical terms are sometimes supplied, which is most helpful, as in the case of "**ASPIRIN**, or **acetylsalicylic acid**," but technical terms are not always defined in context. The article on **artificial respiration** begins: "the means of inducing **RESPIRATION** when it has ceased, as after drowning, asphyxia, in coma or respiratory paralysis." Some readers may need to consult a dictionary for the meaning of *asphyxia*. Similarly, the entry for **hunchback** includes the terms *ankylosing spondylitis* and *vertebral collapse*, without defining them. The article on **Saturn** uses units of measurement designed as *Mm* and *Gm*, but these are not explained in the list of abbreviations in the frontmatter. In general, the more technical articles are written at a higher reading level than the rest of the *NADE*.

As previously mentioned, the *NADE* contains few illustrations other than its maps. The maps are very small black-and-white outline drawings, with no labeling or scale and with the state or country under discussion colored in black. For regions whose outlines are familiar to the reader these maps give an idea of general location, but for unfamiliar regions they are only marginally helpful.

The lack of illustrations is sometimes a drawback. For example, the text must cope with the task of describing the periodic table of the elements ("arranged in rows and columns to illustrate periodic similarities"). This could be much more clearly depicted with an illustration of the table accompanying the entry.

VII. Objectivity

The articles in *The New American Desk Encyclopedia* are predominantly factual rather than interpretive, and the presentation of facts is generally objective. Information is given emphasis and space in accordance with its relative importance, and multiple points of view are suggested for complex issues. The article on **capital punishment**, for example, states that "Capital punishment has long been a center of debate as to whether it deters serious crime or is only a form of revenge."

There are a few exceptions to this rule, in the form of subjects receiving an insufficient or inordinate amount of space, or biased coverage. One of the longest articles is that on the **Women's Movement**, which is twice as long as articles on similarly important subjects such as **Civil Rights** or **Slavery**. In discussing legislation concerning women, the article includes this barbed statement: "Chivalrous legislators still exempted them from certain responsibilities of citizenship, such as jury duty and poll and property taxes." The article on **family planning** states that with modern methods of contraception "unwanted **PREGNANCY** should be a rarity. However, ignorance and neglect have prevented the realization of this ideal." The article does not mention the social and political controversy surrounding this issue, although there is a separate entry treating the **abortion controversy**.

NADE's entry on **evolution** describes several evolutionist theories, and gives examples of the process. It concludes that "today, the evidence for evolution is overwhelming and comes from many branches of biology." It also declares that "**LIFE** probably first evolved from the primeval soup some 3–4 billion years ago, when the first organic chemicals were synthesized due to the effect of lightning." The entry on **creationism** treats the subject in a somewhat dismissive tone. Creationism is identified as a "theory held by fundamentalist Christians that the Earth and living beings were created as described in Genesis rather than through a process of evolution, such as is accepted in modern geology and biology." The article goes on to note that "espousing supposedly nonreligious 'scientific creationism,' creationists of the 1970s pressured textbook publishers and science teachers nationwide into equivocating with regard to the validity of scientific knowledge."

In spite of these examples, the encyclopedia's overall tone is one of balanced objectivity. The *NADE* can be consulted for a reasonable presentation of most issues.

VIII. Accessibility

Entries in the *NADE* are arranged alphabetically, letter by letter. At the beginning of the volume is a helpful section entitled "How to Use *The New American Desk Encyclopedia*," which explains the system of alphabetization in simple terms. This is followed by a section explaining the use of "Subheadings and Cross-References," and a list of abbreviations. However, this list is not comprehensive, since some abbreviations (such as *mp* and *bp*, used in the entries for chemical elements) are not listed.

Entry titles appear in bold capital letters, with subheads in bold upper- and lowercase letters. The editors' notes indicate that subheads are used for divisions of longer entries as well as "subjects that might otherwise appear as entries in their own right in a larger encyclopedia." Guide words showing the first and last entries in each spread provide a quick means of locating articles. According to the editors, "Keywords [entry titles] appear in the form most familiar to the majority of readers . . . Where the keyword is a pseudonym the real name will appear either in this way or in the text if less well known." Thus there are entries under **George Eliot** and **Mark Twain**, with cross-references under **Mary Ann Evans** and **Samuel Langhorne Clemens**.

As in the CONCISE COLUMBIA ENCYCLOPEDIA, a complex system of cross-references is provided, which is essential since information on a broad subject is often dispersed under various keywords with little repetition. Cross-references appear either within the articles or at the end of an article, in small capital letters. Some articles contain a considerable number of cross-references (there are 35 in the article on **Philosophy**) and they can be distracting, but they are an invaluable and necessary means of locating related material.

This is even more true as the *NADE*, again in common with the *CCE*, contains no index. The lack of an index is a disadvantage since, by choosing the wrong keyword, a reader can fail to locate information that may actually exist elsewhere in the volume. An index with subheads listed under major entries might have brought related keywords together to show at a glance all of the entries in a field. However, the logical alphabetical format, the lucid editors' notes on organization, and the extensive cross-references all come to the reader's aid in making information in the *NADE* readily accessible.

IX. Special Features

Few special features are incorporated in *The New American Desk Encyclopedia* which, because of its small size, devotes all available space to subject entries. The rudimentary black-and-white location maps enhance the articles on countries and states but do not provide much detail. The 16-page color section, titled "An Atlas of the Earth and Universe" includes color drawings and maps, and a chart offering information on astronomy, geology, and geography. These illustrations are not linked to the text or mentioned in cross-references, but they are interesting and attractive and the extensive captions are informative. On the whole, the maps and illustrations in the *CCE* give that desk encyclopedia an advantage over the *NADE*.

X. Format

The *NADE* is available in paperback form only. This form has the advantages of light weight and low price, since at $6.95 this is the least expensive encyclopedia in this category. It is "pocket-size" (4¼″ × 7″) and can easily be held in one hand.

The paper binding is not very durable and would not be suitable for libraries. Nor does the volume lie flat when open. However, it should be sufficiently durable for use by individuals when purchased for personal use.

XI. Other Opinions

The Los Angeles Times Book Review (April 22, 1984): ". . .Adapted from the 'University Desk Encyclopedia,' this truly portable version offers good general coverage of basic reference subjects, plus some rather contemporary entries: not only Archimedes, Atomic Clock, and Maple Syrup, but AIDS, Agent Orange, and the Moral Majority too."

XII. Summary

The New American Desk Encyclopedia is a good general reference book, covering a wide variety of topics. As a successor to the *University Desk Encyclo-*

pedia, which was becoming dated and is now out of print, the *NADE* offers the benefit of up-to-date information and new subject coverage. The format is convenient, easy to use, and works well as a quick reference source.

The small size of this encyclopedia, however, means that the length and scope of the articles are limited. Few subjects are explored in depth. The fact that there are few illustrations and tables also limits the comprehensiveness of the work as compared with the CONCISE COLUMBIA ENCYCLOPEDIA, which does include these features.

While *The New American Desk Encyclopedia* is less suitable for libraries because of its paperback format, it is a convenient reference for individual use and, at $6.95, offers good value.

The *NADE* is available in the reference section of many bookstores. If it is out of stock, most stores can order it from the publishers. Individuals and institutions wishing to order directly should send their order, with $6.95 plus $1.00 to cover postage and handling, to New American Library, P.O. Box 999, Bergenfield, NJ 07621. It will normally take from four to six weeks for the order to be processed.

The New Book of Knowledge

Facts at a Glance

Full Title: **The New Book of Knowledge**.
Publisher: Grolier Incorporated, Sherman Turnpike, Danbury, CT 06816.
Editors: Bernard S. Cayne, Editorial Director; Jean E. Reynolds, Editor-in-Chief.
Copyright: 1987.

Number of Volumes: 21.
Number of Contributors: 1,506.
Number of Entries: 9,002.
Number of Pages: 10,540.
Number of Words: 6,800,000.
Number of Maps: 1,062.
Number of Cross-references: 4,000.
Number of Indexes: 21.
Number of Illustrations: 20,300 color; 2,200 black-and-white.
Trim Size: 7⅜″ × 10″.

Intended Readership: grades 2 through 8.
Price: $800 plus shipping and handling ($529.50 plus shipping and handling to schools and libraries).
Sold door-to-door, by direct mail to individuals,

and directly to libraries and schools. ISBN 0-7172-0518-5.
Revised annually.

I. Introduction

The New Book of Knowledge is a 21-volume encyclopedia for home and school use. It is intended as a general reference work for students in second through eighth grades. According to the promotional brochure, "This is not a junior version of an adult encyclopedia but one created especially for the elementary-grade student" and "The topics span the full range of children's in-school and out-of-school interests. . . ." The editorial policy revolves around these central aims.

For younger children this encyclopedia offers games, activities, stories, and engaging illustrations. The Preface suggests that "Parents will find material to read aloud to preschool children, both for pleasure and as answers to their questions." At the other end of the readership range, numerous topics in the junior high school curriculum are covered. But the primary emphasis is on the elementary school curriculum and the research needs of children at this level. The subjects, reading level, illustrations, and overall organization have been prepared with this group primarily in mind.

II. Scope

The New Book of Knowledge contains some 9,000 entries; of these, 4,000 are text articles and the remainder are brief dictionary index entries. There is a total of 6,800,000 words, with an average of 755 words per article. The articles fall into three types: broad survey articles on general topics, shorter articles on specific topics, and index entries providing brief information on specific topics.

As already noted, the emphasis in the selection of subjects is on the elementary school curriculum. In addition, the set attempts to cover many extra-curricular interests of children. Thus both the subjects and the priorities according to which space is allotted differ considerably from an adult or secondary level encyclopedia. Certain subjects of particular interest to school children, such as **book reports and reviews, bulletin boards, marbles,** and **experiments and other science activities** would probably not appear in an adult encyclopedia.

There is a good balance of academic subjects and space seems to be assigned according to a subject's prominence in the North American school curriculum. Geography is covered thoroughly, with articles

The New Book of Knowledge

❶

WOODCUT PRINTING

Woodcut, or wood-block, printing is one of the oldest of printmaking techniques. The first prints were probably made by the Chinese in the 8th century. From China the craft spread to Korea and Japan, where it was an art of great importance. Most Oriental woodcuts with which the Western world is familiar are Japanese.

No wood-block prints dated earlier than the beginning of the 15th century survive. But there is reason to believe that the technique was used for royal stamps and textile printing before then.

After the invention of the modern printing press, with movable type, in the 15th century, woodcut printing became the method used to reproduce drawings for printed books. At this time, woodcutting was considered a technique for reproducing drawings, not a creative art. Therefore, skillful artists like Albrecht Dürer (1471–1528) only designed the woodcut print; the actual cutting was left to an artisan.

In the 16th century, metal engraving and etching became the most important printmaking techniques in Europe. For the next several centuries, woodcut printing was not very popular. The art was not revived until the middle of the 19th century, when manufacturers of beautiful books began to return to the woodcut print for illustrations.

❷ ▶ **HOW WOODCUT PRINTS ARE MADE**

Wood-block printing is a **relief** method. This means that the uncut surface of the block will print and the cut-away areas will not.

To make a print the artist cuts a piece of softwood, such as pine or fir, to a desired size. In order to see the area that will be printed, the artist may first paint the block of wood with India ink. The contrast between the color of the ink and the color of the bare wood shows the artist which areas will print and which will not.

❸

Some artists trace a drawing or draw directly on the wood with chalk, while others cut directly without following a sketch. In either case, the artist cuts the design with a knife and a tool called a **gouge.** Then tacky ink is applied to the surface of the block with a roller. Next the artist carefully places a piece of very absorbent paper—such as Japanese rice or

In relief printing, the uncut surface of a block of wood will print, while cut-away areas will not. This woodcut, *Fishing* (1912), is by French artist Raoul Dufy.   ❺

❹

mulberry paper—on the inked block. When the paper is rubbed with a hard, smooth instrument (many artists use the back of a wooden spoon), the inked image on the block is transferred to the paper. The artist then inks the block again and makes any number of prints. To make a print of many colors, the artist follows the same steps; but a different block is needed for each color.

Traditionally, woodcut prints have been divided into two types: black-line cuts and white-line cuts. In a black-line cut, the surface areas that print form the main shapes of the design. In a white-line cut—the more popular form—the shapes of the design are cut away. Therefore, the areas that print are actually the background of the design.

▶ **WOOD ENGRAVING**

A wood engraving differs slightly from a woodcut print, although the two have much in common. Harder wood is used for wood engraving—usually box or cherry—and the wood is cut on the edge (cross grain) instead of in plank form, as in woodcut printing. A tool called a **burin** is used. It cuts very fine lines. Wood engravings are usually printed on a letterpress, but hand-printing methods may be used.

Reviewed by JOHN SPARKS
Maryland Institute, College of Art

See also GRAPHIC ARTS.

WOODWIND INSTRUMENTS. See WIND INSTRUMENTS.

❻

❼

❽

❾

WOODWIND INSTRUMENTS · 229   ❿

Page shown at 70% of actual size.

❶ Main entry: The New Book of Knowledge contains 4,000 text articles, arranged alphabetically letter-by-letter.

❷ Subhead: Lengthy articles are divided into sections under subheadings.

❸ Technical terms are highlighted in boldface type and defined in context.

❹ Illustration: New Book of Knowledge contains 22,500 illustrations, of which 20,300 are in full color.

❺ Caption: Captions in The New Book of Knowledge often add to the information presented in the main text.

❻ Reviewer's credit: All articles are signed by an author and/or a

reviewer. There are 1,500 contributors to The New Book of Knowledge.

❼ End-of-article cross-reference

❽ Cross-reference entry: The New Book of Knowledge contains 4,000 cross-references.

❾ Guide words

❿ Page number

on continents, regions, countries, U. S. states, Canadian provinces and major cities, as well as features such as mountains and rivers. These articles follow standard formats, with consistent use of maps, fact boxes, and varied illustrations showing many aspects of each region and its inhabitants. As an example of the North American emphasis, the article on **Arizona**, at 16 pages, is longer than the article on **Argentina**, which encompasses eight-and-one-half pages.

Biographical articles are included for individuals from many fields. American presidents are covered in depth. Many of the biographical articles include portraits, and each biography of an artist includes an illustration of the artist's work. For example, the article on **John James Audubon** includes a portrait of Audubon as well as two of his bird paintings. Articles on literary figures of interest to children often include an excerpt from the writer's work. Less important figures, such as marathon runner **Grete Waitz** and composer **John Williams**, receive brief entries in the text or in the dictionary index.

History is covered in the geographical articles, often under a subheading for History and Government. There are also many separate articles on historical subjects such as **American colonies**, **Byzantine Empire**, and **battles important in world history**. As with geography subjects, the emphasis is on North American history, although the rest of the world is not slighted, and coverage of foreign history is adequate for the intended readership.

Articles on scientific subjects cover all of the major fields of science and technology and most are extremely well illustrated. The article on the **human body**, for example, includes diagrams of various body systems on 18 of its 22 pages. The illustrations are clear and well labeled and make use of color to highlight details. Since the language is kept within the overall reading level for the set, the diagrams are especially helpful in elucidating complex concepts. The articles on mathematics, such as **algebra** and **arithmetic**, introduce concepts and work through sample problems to demonstrate solutions. They are a useful review or study guide that might supplement classroom work.

The humanities are covered in a broad variety of articles. In addition to the biographical articles on literary and artistic figures, survey articles cover such topics as **American literature**, **art**, and **music**. There are articles on more specific aspects of art such as **needlecraft** and **music festivals**. And there are regional articles such as **Oriental art and architecture** and **Oriental literature**. Writers in English, and particularly writers of children's literature, receive the most coverage.

As an example of how space is apportioned among subjects, the article on **Charlemagne** is one-and-one-half pages long, the article on **Chaucer** is one page, and the article on **chemistry** is nine-and-one-half pages, with separate articles on **history of chemistry** (seven-and-one-half pages) and **some terms of chemistry** (two-and-one-half pages). **Chicago** receives four pages, as does **child development**; **China** is the subject of an 18-page entry, and the U. S. **Civil War** is covered in 11 pages.

As the examples cited here indicate, the articles cover all of the major fields of study. *The New Book of Knowledge* lives up to its claim that the topics span the full range of children's interests.

III. Authority

The New Book of Knowledge has been published by Grolier Incorporated since 1966. Its predecessor, *The Book of Knowledge*, was a topically arranged children's encyclopedia published between 1912 and 1965. Grolier has a well-established reputation as a publisher of a variety of reference works, including ENCYCLOPEDIA AMERICANA and ACADEMIC AMERICAN ENCYCLOPEDIA. Grolier's editorial director, Bernard S. Cayne, brings a wide-ranging background in reference book publishing to the task of overseeing the preparation of all the company's general reference works. Editor-in-Chief Jean E. Reynolds also brings extensive experience to the work, particularly in children's publications. She heads a staff of 9 editors and 13 associate editors. In addition to those editors, the credits pages in Volume 1 also list the full staff for the first edition. A list of 31 advisers and consultants (librarians, educators, and subject specialists) is also provided.

More than 1,500 authors, consultants, and reviewers are cited in the contributors list in Volume 20. Among these are many whose names will be familiar to adult readers, such as Jeanne Chall, Aba Eban, Ira Gershwin, Walter Gropius, Eugene Ormandy, and Morris Udall. The identification information listed for the contributors shows that many of them possess strong academic credentials and all are authorities in their subjects. As with most encyclopedias, a small percentage of the contributors are deceased.

All articles are signed by an author, a reviewer, or both, along with brief identifications. This meticulous documentation is unusual and is a reminder of the careful editorial work that is evident throughout the set.

More than 45 new contributors were involved in the preparation of the 1987 edition. They include

Helen K. Wright, of the American Library Association Publishing Services section, who reviewed and updated the article on **the modern library and its services**; John H. Ostrom, Professor of Geology at Yale University, who reviewed **dinosaurs**; and Kenneth W. Miller, President and Dean of the Albany College of Pharmacy, who wrote the article on **drugs**.

IV. Currency

The New Book of Knowledge is revised annually. According to the editors, for the 1987 edition nearly 1,000 pages, or 10 percent of the total, were revised. The revisions include 50 newly written text articles, 86 text articles with major revisions, 516 new photographs, and 210 new pieces of color artwork. The set has a fresh and contemporary look and the search for current illustrations has resulted in artwork and photography of a very high standard.

Equally important is the inclusion of current information, particularly for subjects in which events are in constant flux. Recent events through 1986 are included in many articles. For example, the article on **Libya** mentions the 1986 bombing by the United States in response to Libya's terrorist activities. The article on **drug abuse** discusses the increasing use of crack, and places it in context in a discussion of other abused drugs, from nicotine and alcohol to heroin.

The 1986 nuclear power plant accident at Chernobyl is discussed in **nuclear energy**. The article on **Ronald Reagan** mentions a variety of recent events, including the approval of economic sanctions against South Africa over the President's veto, the appointments of Chief Justice Rehnquist and Associate Justice Antonin Scalia, the Reykjavik summit, and the Iran arms sale controversy.

In addition to current events, coverage of new trends and concepts was expanded, often in dictionary index entries. These are brief entries appearing in the alphabetical index for subjects not covered by an article in the main text. Entries on topics of current concern include **homeless people**, **homosexuality**, and **surrogate parent**. Since they are brief, these entries are limited in scope and depth. This portion of the set is used to reflect current trends by adding or deleting any such entries as the changing times require. A random check of the dictionary index entries in Volume 20 reveals references to events of 1986 in entries for **John David Waihee III** (newly elected governor of Hawaii), **Kurt Waldheim**, **Elie Wiesel**, and **Andrew Newell Wyeth**.

V. Accuracy

The information contained in *The New Book of Knowledge* is reliable and consistent. Since some of its articles are briefer than those in adult encyclopedias, there is limited space for extensive detailed discussion. Yet a considerable degree of detail is condensed into many of the articles. For example, the article on **racket sports** describes squash and racquetball courts and equipment, providing dimensions in both metric and English measures for each. Scale diagrams of both courts, labeled with all dimensions, accompany the text. Enough information is presented to assist the reader in planning and designing a court.

The article on **Renaissance art and architecture** recounts the competition for the bronze doors of the Baptistery in Florence. The text describes Ghiberti's second set of doors as follows, "The reliefs on the Gates of Paradise look much more realistic and are done in perspective. The human figures look more like classical sculptures." On the facing page there is a color photograph of the Gates of Paradise, as well as a close-up color photograph of one of the panels, so that the reader may see clearly the characteristics that are described. This level of detail is typical of many of the articles.

Sources of statistical data are not provided in the text, but the editors claim that they use primary, rather than secondary sources and that they try to use statistics that are consistent for purposes of comparison. Population statistics based upon estimates are noted accordingly. However, occasional inconsistencies appear. For example, on page 263 of Volume 3 the population of the People's Republic of China is given as 1,040,000,000 (estimate), while on page 446 the population given is 1,008,000,000 (estimate). Such inconsistencies are few and do not cast doubt on the general reliability of the set although they may cause some confusion.

Our subject specialists report that *The New Book of Knowledge* usually presents accurate and unbiased information in the articles reviewed. **Bill of rights** discusses not only the U. S. Bill of Rights, but also the English, French, Canadian and U. N. bills of rights. It also includes a brief summary of each of the ten amendments. The entry on **money** is well written and gives a clear history of money integrated into a theoretical discussion of the uses of money. There is, however, one notable error: the article states that most countries went off the gold standard in 1933, when in fact the U. S. was the only major industrial nation to do so. The article on the **brain**, says our reviewer, is "excellent for young readers—straightforward, well organized, enjoyable, and easy to read." The entry on **Saturn** is also reported to be a good reference for young readers, despite several numeric differences from currently accepted figures.

There are no errors in the article on **transistors**, although the entry is by no means comprehensive.

VI. Clarity

The New Book of Knowledge is intended for children in the second through eighth grades. Articles are written for the grade level at which the subject is usually introduced. Thus, technical subjects or complex concepts are discussed at a more advanced level than basic subjects. Most articles will be best suited to children in the upper elementary grades. According to the Preface, "The Dale-Chall readability formula is used to test the reading level of every article." However, the editors add that "prescribed word lists are not used, as writing to a formula is inhibiting and tends to make writing stiff and colorless."

Another technique at work is the use of a pyramid structure, in which articles begin at a simple level and increase in difficulty in subsequent sections. **Optical instruments** begins "**Optics** is the science of light and vision." More complex sentences appear further in the article, such as "The power of a compound microscope is found by multiplying the power of the objective lens by the power of the eyepiece." Students may thus read that portion of each article that is suited to their reading skills. In addition, a number of articles begin in such a way as to catch the reader's attention. For example, the biography of **Marian Anderson** begins "Visitors to a small church in Philadelphia, Pennsylvania, were amazed by the beautiful voice of a 6-year-old girl singing in the choir."

Articles are subdivided by bold subheadings that indicate how information is organized. Technical terms are printed in boldface type and defined in context. The writing style is lucid and often lively, and the articles are arranged logically so that children should have little difficulty in following them.

The following extract from **lighthouses** illustrates the style of a typical entry in *The New Book of Knowledge*:

> Thousands of years ago, the Egyptians kindled fires on high hilltops to guide their ships at night. As water traffic increased on the Nile River, the Egyptians built stone towers to serve as lighthouses. Priests tended the flames that burned all night in the towers. The priests and guiding fires were both considered holy by the ancient Egyptian mariners.
>
> About 280 B.C. the Egyptians began to construct the tallest lighthouse ever built in ancient—or modern—times. This was the Pharos of Alexandria, one of the seven wonders of the ancient world. The lighthouse, built on the island of Pharos near Alexandria, was over 120 meters (400 feet) high. At the top of the tower,

open fires were kept burning. They served as a beacon for Mediterranean voyagers for about 1,500 years.

> Today most nations operate some form of lighthouse, to help mariners at night determine the positions of their ships. Lighthouses are located in fixed positions at known locations. Each lighthouse has its own identifying flashing signal. Lighthouse engineers know the amount of pressure that winds and waves cause on any surface area. They erect buildings and beacons that can outlast the pounding of seas and the battering of storms.

VII. Objectivity

The editors of *The New Book of Knowledge* claim that, where authorities disagree on an issue, "the reader is so informed." This is generally true, and a balanced view of controversial matters prevails. Controversy is not avoided, although some subjects, such as **abortion** and **homosexuality**, are not entered in the main text but rather in the dictionary index. Readers not using the index may not find these.

All of the articles in this set have been written with young readers in mind. But even in the dictionary index complex concepts are included, albeit in simplified fashion. The entry for **abortion** states two of the commonly held positions, but does not recount the arguments of opposing groups. "Some people believe that elective abortion is murder. Others say that it is a private matter between a woman and her doctor." The entry for **homosexuality** mentions laws governing the practice but does not mention moral opposition to it. In the new edition there seems to be a greater effort to include such controversial topics; among the dictionary index entries added in the 1987 edition are **Greenpeace**, **living will**, **meltdown**, and **Right to Die**.

In the main portion of the text, where articles are longer, diverse points of view tend to be more fully represented. The article on **segregation** makes a useful distinction between *de jure* and *de facto* segregation, citing modern examples of both. The article on **Andrew Jackson** says of Jackson's treatment of Indians, "The Indian resettlement policy was tragic for thousands of Indians, though it was popular with the settlers in the South and the West." The article on **science and society** reminds the reader that "the power that scientific knowledge gives us can be used for good or bad purposes." Such discussions tend to focus upon fact, rather than opinion, and are handled objectively.

VIII. Accessibility

The New Book of Knowledge is well organized. A number of features help make it easy for children to use. Volumes 1 through 20 are arranged alphabetically and paginated separately. Volumes are divided by the letter-unit system; some volumes contain all the entries for more than one letter. Entries are arranged alphabetically, letter by letter. Page numbers and guide words appear at the foot of the page towards the outside margin, where they are easily seen.

Subheadings are used in longer articles that discuss many smaller topics. For example, geographical articles on countries are often divided into sections titled The People, The Land, The Economy, and Government and History. These sections are further subdivided as necessary.

When two articles appear on a page, a rule is used to separate them. Occasionally, a rule also separates different sections within an article, as in the article **Bible**. This may be slightly confusing, since it gives the impression that a new article is beginning. Also slightly confusing is that titles of articles are sometimes printed in different sizes and different typefaces. Still, most readers will not have any difficulty with this, and there is no question that the page design is attractive.

Study outline boxes appear at the beginning of some longer articles, describing what is covered in the article and listing related articles in the set. Fact summaries, chronologies, tables, and lists of technical terms are examples of other features that help highlight significant material.

There are 4,000 cross-references in *The New Book of Knowledge*. These are mainly of two types: "see" references to alternative article titles, and "see also" references at the ends of articles indicating related information located elsewhere. These are a valuable aid for children whose research skills are still developing.

The extensive index is one of the best features of *The New Book of Knowledge*, and certainly its most valuable aid for locating information. The full A to Z index appears in Volume 21. In each of the other volumes, that part of the index relating to the volume is included and printed on pages tinted blue to distinguish it from the normal text. In addition, these portions of the index include the dictionary index entries, of which there are some 5,000. These entries fill the useful role of concisely presenting material that falls outside the areas covered by the text but is still of interest, such as biographical data on minor individuals or definitions of unusual terms. Readers will find that it is often necessary to consult the index in order to locate information, and it is a great convenience to have the relevant section included in each volume. For broader research the full A to Z index in Volume 21 should be used, although this volume does not include the dictionary index entries

that are found in the separate volume indexes. The print in both indexes is extremely legible.

IX. Special Features

Several special features help make *The New Book of Knowledge* an attractive, informative, and exciting encyclopedia for young readers. Volumes 1 and 21 each include a section titled How to Use the Index (both virtually identical) that uses a question-and-answer format to clarify the system. A Pronunciation Guide is also included in Volume 21, explaining the Minimal Change System of pronunciation used in the set.

In addition to the fact boxes and study guides already mentioned (see *Accessibility*), other boxes also supplement the text. Wonder Questions, such as "Why were some of the early bridges in America covered?" are posed to stimulate inquiry. An explanation is supplied for each question. Projects and Experiments, such as "How to Build a Birdhouse" are outlined in precise detail, to enable readers to apply new knowledge and investigate a subject.

The most striking feature of *The New Book of Knowledge* is its excellent illustration program. Of its 22,500 illustrations, 20,300 are in color. There are 1,062 maps. Especially designed for *The New Book of Knowledge*, these clear and uncluttered maps can easily be read by young students. The artwork and photographs are unfailingly excellent and well reproduced, and they are well chosen to illustrate specific points in the text. Captions often point out details and comparisons, thereby enhancing the text. Color is used profusely, making the volumes highly appealing.

Supplemental materials available include a yearbook, *The New Book of Knowledge Annual*, issued in February of each year in English, French, and Spanish. The English edition sells for $17.45 in the United States. A separate paperbound volume titled *The Home and School Reading and Study Guides* is available as a supplement to the 21-volume set. It includes a bibliography and a study guide as aids for parents and teachers working with children. Note, however, that these works bear little direct relation to the encyclopedia itself.

X. Format

The 21 volumes of *The New Book of Knowledge* are bound in a durable hardcover Lexotone II binding. The bright blue covers are stamped in silver and gold, with Grolier's tree motif on the front, and volume number and letter and year of publication on the spine. The entire set takes up about two feet of horizontal shelf space.

Pages are arranged in a two-column format. The page design is clear and attractive; the typefaces are easily legible. Overall, the encyclopedia is handsome and will be sturdy enough for heavy use.

XI. Other Opinions

ARBA 82: "Some of the subject headings are difficult to locate and to understand, and there are a few voids in the cross-references, but the wide range of subjects, the colorful illustrations, and the numerous games, stories, and puzzles make this an excellent home and school encyclopedia for elementary children."

Reference Books Bulletin (November 15, 1986): "Organized to meet the needs of today's youngsters from primary age to junior high, *The New Book of Knowledge* maintains its high standards of reliability, currentness, accessibility, accuracy, and design. It is recommended for homes and for school and public libraries."

XII. Summary

The New Book of Knowledge has a reputation as an excellent children's encyclopedia, which the 1987 edition shows to be well deserved in all respects. The material is reliable, up-to-date, and clearly written. The set is beautifully designed and the illustrations are superb. Children should be able to familiarize themselves with the encyclopedia with very little effort, and then locate information easily.

Every effort has been made in this set to keep in mind the needs of children. It neither mirrors the contents of an adult encyclopedia nor devotes much coverage to topics that might be of greater interest to adults than to children. Topics that are important to children, in connection with their studies or with myriad other interests, are explained and brought to life. This work is a fine resource for home, school, or library.

The main competitors to *The New Book of Knowledge* are COMPTON'S ENCYCLOPEDIA and WORLD BOOK. All three gear their content to the needs of the school student. In terms of accuracy, currency, clarity, and objectivity, both *The New Book of Knowledge* and WORLD BOOK maintain an extremely high standard. *The New Book of Knowledge* is more suitable for younger (i.e., elementary-age) children, while WORLD BOOK will be more useful for those in middle school as well as for some high school students. In each of the criteria listed above, *The New Book of Knowledge* is superior to COMPTON'S ENCYCLOPEDIA. However, COMPTON'S 1988 edition (not available as this Buying Guide went to press) is ex-

pected to be considerably improved over previous editions of that work.

Prospective purchasers should note that, for both individuals and institutions, *The New Book of Knowledge* is slightly more expensive than these two alternatives. But because of the work's quality, the higher cost may not be a significant factor in deciding which set to purchase.

Individuals wishing to order *The New Book of Knowledge* may phone Grolier Inc., toll-free at (800) 243-3356. Institutions may order from Grolier Educational Corporation at (800) 243-7256 or, in Connecticut, 797-3500.

New Encyclopaedia Britannica

°Facts at a Glance

Full Title: **New Encyclopaedia Britannica**.
Publisher: Encyclopaedia Britannica, Inc., Britannica Centre, 310 South Michigan Avenue, Chicago, IL 60604.
Editors: Philip W. Goetz, Editor-in-Chief, Margaret Sutton, Executive Editor.
Copyright: 1986. 15th edition,

Number of Volumes: 32 (1 Propaedia, 12 Micropaedia, 17 Macropaedia, 2 index).
Number of Contributors: more than 4,000.
Number of Entries: 61,000 (Micropaedia); 680 (Macropaedia).
Number of Pages: 32,000.
Number of Words: 44,000,000.
Number of Maps: 1,000.
Number of Cross-references: 25,000.
Number of Indexes: 1 (two volumes).
Number of Index Entries: 400,000.
Number of Illustrations: 8,000 color, plus 164 color plates; 16,000 black-and-white.
Trim Size: 8¾″ × 10¹³⁄₁₆″.

Intended Readership: high school through adult.
Price: $1,249 for individuals, $999 school/library discount.
Sold directly by publisher, through distributors, at conventions, in selected bookstores, and in some supermarkets. ISBN 0-85229-434-4.
Revised annually.

I. Introduction

The *New Encyclopaedia Britannica* is a 32-volume general reference work designed to offer "a truly remarkable range of valuable information . . . in a highly-acclaimed four-part structure." In a brochure

New Encyclopaedia Britannica

lished black leaders, including labour leader A. Philip Randolph and W.E.B. Du Bois, head of the National Association for the Advancement of Colored People (NAACP). Garvey's influence declined rapidly when he and other UNIA members were indicted for mail fraud in 1922 in connection with the sale of stock for the Black Star Line. He served two years of a five-year prison term, but in 1927 his sentence was commuted by Pres. Calvin Coolidge, and he was deported as an undesirable alien. He was never able to revive the movement abroad, and he died in virtual obscurity. Edmund David Cronon's biography *Black Moses* appeared in 1955.

Gary, city, Lake County, extreme northwest Indiana, U.S., at the southern end of Lake Michigan in the Calumet district east of Chicago. In 1906 the town (named for Elbert H. Gary, chief organizer of the United States Steel Corporation) was laid out as an adjunct of the company's vast new manufacturing complex. The site was chosen because it lay on navigable water midway between the iron ore beds to the north and the coal region to the south. Large areas were drained, a meandering river was rerouted, and sand dunes were removed. Steelworks were then built along the lake shore, with the city to the south. The Gary Land Company, a U.S. Steel subsidiary, laid out its part of the city, constructed the streets and sidewalks, installed the sewage system, and built the waterworks and electric plant. The first blast furnace was fired in December 1908, and steel production began early the following year. Although Gary has some diversified manufacturing, it is essentially a one-industry city and has periodically suffered from declines in steel production and labour disputes. During World War I a sizable number of blacks came to work in Gary and comprised one-sixth of the population in the 1930s. World War II drew many more, and in 1967 Richard G. Hatcher was one of the first blacks to be elected mayor of a major U.S. city. Gary was the scene of a significant early 20th-century development in public education when William A. Wirt established the work–study–play school, popularly known as the platoon school, designed to attract underprivileged children. Construction of a new civic centre in the city's downtown area was begun in 1979. Gary is the seat of Indiana University Northwest (1948). Inc. town, 1906; city, 1909. Pop. (1980) city, 151,953; Gary–Hammond–East Chicago metropolitan area (SMSA), 642,-781.

Gary, Elbert Henry (b. Oct. 8, 1846, near Wheaton, Ill., U.S.—d. Aug. 15, 1927, New York City), U.S. jurist and chief organizer of the United States Steel Corporation.

In 1871 Gary entered law practice in Chicago. He served as judge of Du Page County, Ill., from 1882 to 1890 and was president of the Chicago Bar Association from 1893 to 1894.

Elbert H. Gary
U S Steel Photo

A leader and an authority in corporate law and the insurance business, Gary became general counsel and a director in a number of

large railroads, banks, and industrial corporations. In 1898 he became the first president of the newly organized Federal Steel Company, which was backed by the financier J.P. Morgan. Federal Steel merged with the U.S. Steel Corporation in 1901. Gary was elected chairman of the board of directors and was the corporation's chief executive officer during 26 years of remarkable development and growth of the steel industry.

As chairman of U.S. Steel, Gary helped improve the workers' conditions by promoting stock ownership and profit sharing by the employees, higher wages, and safe, sanitary working conditions. He was a firm advocate of the open shop, however, and his unwillingness to negotiate that issue led to the steel strike of 1919–20. The strike forced him to give his support to abolishing the 7-day week and the 12-hour day in the steel mills. The town of Gary, Ind., named in his honour, was laid out in 1906 by U.S. Steel.

Gary, Romain, original name ROMAIN KACEW (b. May 8, 1914, Vilnius, Lithuania, Russian Empire—d. Dec. 2, 1980, Paris), French novelist whose first work, *L'Éducation européenne* (1945; *Forest of Anger,* 1944), won him immediate acclaim. Humanistic and optimistic despite its graphic depictions of the horrors of World War II, the novel was later revised and reissued in English as *Nothing Important Ever Dies* (1960).

Gary's novels mix humour with tragedy and faith with cynicism. *Les Couleurs du jour* (1952; *The Colors of the Day,* 1953), set in Nice at carnival, and *La Danse de Gengis Cohn* (1967; *The Dance of Genghis Cohn,* 1968), in which the ghost of a Jewish stand-up comedian takes possession of his Nazi executioner, are comic novels nonetheless informed by serious moral considerations. *Les Racines du ciel* (1956; *The Roots of Heaven,* 1958), winner of the Prix Goncourt, balances a visionary conception of freedom and justice against a pessimistic comprehension of man's cruelty and greed. Other works by Gary include *Le Grand Vestiaire* (1948; *The Company of Men,* 1950), a novel set in postwar Paris; *Lady L* (French and English versions, 1959), a social satire; *La Promesse de l'aube* (1960; *Promise at Dawn,* 1962), an autobiography; *Clair de femme* (1977; "The Light of a Woman"); and *Les Cerf-volants* (1980; "The Kite").

During World War II Gary joined Gen. Charles de Gaulle in London. Already trained as an aviator, he served with the Free French Forces in Europe and North Africa, earning the Croix de Guerre and Compagnon de la Libération. For 20 years following the war, he served in French diplomatic service. From 1956 to 1960 he was French consul general in Los Angeles.

Garyān (Libya): *see* Gharyān.

gas, one of the three fundamental states of matter. It has distinctly different properties from the liquid and solid states.

A brief treatment of gas follows. For full treatment, *see* MACROPAEDIA: Matter: Its Properties, States, Varieties, and Behaviour.

A gas has no definite shape and exhibits high fluidity. It tends to expand indefinitely and readily fills any container into which it is introduced. Gases are highly compressible, and under ordinary conditions they have a density approximately 1,000 times less than that of liquids. A small change in temperature or pressure generally produces a substantial change in the volume of a gas. The relationships between the temperature, pressure, and volume of gases have been deduced and expressed in the form of equations known as the gas laws (*see* Boyle's law; Charles's law; Avogadro's law).

Gases were studied as early as antiquity, but an understanding of the gaseous state, as of the other basic states of matter, came only

with the development of the kinetic molecular theory in the 19th century. According to this theory, all matter is composed of particles (atoms or molecules or mixtures of both) in constant motion. In a gas, the particles are far enough apart and are moving fast enough to escape each other's influence (*e.g.,* attraction or repulsion due to electrical charges). The freely moving particles constantly collide with one another, but the collisions result in no loss of energy. When a gas is cooled, its particles move more slowly, and those that are slow enough to linger in each other's vicinity tend to coalesce because a force of attraction overcomes their lowered kinetic energy—*i.e.,* energy of motion. Each particle, when it joins the liquid state with others, gives up a measure of heat called the latent heat of liquefaction, but each continues to move at the same speed within the liquid so long as the temperature remains at the condensation point. Warming up a liquid, by contrast, provides constituent particles with heat of evaporation, which enables them to escape each other and form the vapour of the liquid—namely, the gaseous state.

gas, natural: *see* natural gas.

gas, perfect (physics): *see* perfect gas.

gas burner, heating device in which natural gas is used for fuel. Gas may be supplied to the burner prior to combustion at a pressure sufficient to induce a supply of air to mix with it; the mixture passes through several long narrow openings or a nozzle to mix with additional air in the combustion chamber. Metal surfaces supply the means of heat transfer to circulating water or air.

gas chamber, method of executing condemned prisoners by lethal gas. It was first used in the U.S. state of Nevada in 1924 in an effort to provide a more humane form of capital punishment. The prisoner is strapped in a chair in a sealed chamber in which poisonous fumes, such as cyanide, are released. If the prisoner breathes deeply, death is almost instantaneous and painless. By the second half of the 20th century, 11 U.S. states had adopted the gas chamber as the method of execution.

During the Holocaust (*q.v.*) in Nazi Germany during World War II, gas chambers were employed for the purpose of killing Jews and other unwanted minorities. They were established at concentration camps and usually disguised as bathhouses. Men, women, and children were herded naked into the chambers after being told that they were going to take showers. The doors were closed, and poison gas was injected.

gas chromatography, in analytical chemistry, technique for separating chemical substances in which the sample is carried by a moving gas stream through a tube packed with a finely divided solid that may be coated with a film of a liquid. Because of its simplicity, sensitivity, and effectiveness in separating components of mixtures, gas chromatography is one of the most important tools in chemistry. It is widely used for quantitative and qualitative analysis of mixtures, for the purification of compounds, and for the determination of such thermochemical constants as heats of solution and vaporization, vapour pressure, and activity coefficients. Gas chromatography is also used to monitor industrial processes automatically: gas streams are analyzed periodically, and manual or automatic responses are made to counteract undesirable variations. Many routine analyses are performed rapidly in medical and other fields. For example, by the use of only 0.1 cubic centimetre (0.003 ounce) of blood, it is possible to determine

Page shown at 66% of actual size.

1 Illustration: New Britannica has some 24,000 illustrations, of which one-third are in color.
2 Caption
3 Photo credit
4 Page number
5 Guide words

6 Cross-reference entries: The Micropaedia contains 25,000 cross-reference entries.
7 Main entry: The Micropaedia contains 61,000 entries, arranged alphabetically, word-by-word. Printed in boldface.

8 q.v. cross-reference
9 Cross-reference to Macropaedia: Refers reader to a more extensive discussion of the subject in the Macropaedia.

accompanying the set, the publisher assures that "your family will find it an invaluable source of reference and learning for years to come."

The largest and most ambitious reference work on the market today (and a direct descendant of the most venerated encyclopedia in the English language), *New Britannica* has inspired both widespread acclaim and vituperous criticism from reviewers, librarians, and general users alike. Many critics have disputed the publisher's claims about accessibility and suitability, while others have expressed admiration for the breadth and depth of learning that the set embodies.

New Britannica aims to accomplish three things: to supply an easy-to-use source of basic facts (the Micropaedia), to provide a scholarly presentation of "knowledge in depth" (the Macropaedia), and to present an organized plan for self-education (the Propaedia). Thus, *New Britannica* can be viewed as three (or four, counting the index) distinct but interrelated sets of reference tools, each serving a different but complementary purpose.

II. Scope

Any useful discussion of the scope of *New Britannica* must first take into account the encyclopedia's unique structure. Otherwise, a count of number of articles, article lengths, number of words, and so forth would be rendered meaningless.

New Britannica's four parts are: (1) the Propaedia, or "Outline of Knowledge," one unnumbered volume; (2) the Micropaedia, or "Ready Reference," 12 volumes numbered 1 through 12; (3) the Macropaedia, or "Knowledge in Depth," 17 volumes numbered 13 through 29; (4) the index, two unnumbered volumes.

In the words of Mortimer Adler, who planned its concept and directed its execution, the single-volume Propaedia is intended to provide "an orderly topical outline of the whole of human knowledge, in the form of the circle of learning that is an *en-cyclo-paedia*." The publisher claims that the 744-page Propaedia "sets up major fields of knowledge in an outline sequence that enables you to learn on your own, at your own pace, using the pages of Britannica as your personal tutors."

The ten areas outlined in the Propaedia are: (1) Matter and Energy; (2) The Earth; (3) Life on Earth; (4) Human Life; (5) Human Society; (6) Art; (7) Technology; (8) Religion; (9) The History of Mankind; (10) The Branches of Knowledge (logic, mathematics, science, history and the humanities, and philosophy). Each outline is preceded by a prefatory

essay or overview by a noted authority in that field. At the end of each section of the outlines are lists of related articles in the Macropaedia and Micropaedia. Finally, the Propaedia also contains a complete list of all contributors to *New Britannica*, giving their credits and credentials.

The 12-volume Micropaedia is the part of *New Britannica* that most closely resembles other standard multivolume general encyclopedias. Its more than 11,800 pages contain some 61,000 specific-entry factual articles, in addition to 25,000 cross-reference entries. When *New Britannica* was first issued in 1974, articles in the Micropaedia were never longer than 750 words. Editorial policy has since changed, however, and some articles are now several times that length. Nevertheless, the general average remains around 300–400 words, and some Micropaedia articles are as brief as 50 words.

The 17-volume, 23,000,000-word Macropaedia contains more than 17,000 pages, and includes in-depth discussions of 680 subjects—an average of 25 pages per article. Actual article length ranges from fewer than three pages for such entries as **Beirut** and **Barcelona**, to 90 pages or more for subjects such as **Australia**, **Animal Behaviour**, and **Biblical Literature and its Critical Interpretations**. At 323 pages, the entry for **United States of America** is truly book-length. As the page lengths and subject titles indicate, Macropaedia articles are generally of the broad-entry type.

Whereas the Micropaedia intends to be encyclopedic in its breadth of coverage, entries in the Macropaedia are much more selective, and therefore more arbitrary. (Moreover, the Macropaedia's articles are often written from a highly personal or idiosyncratic viewpoint. See also *Objectivity*.) Mortimer Adler's influence on the Macropaedia may be seen in the coverage extended to philosophy and subjects with some philosophical content. In Volume 24, for example, at least 12 out of 48 entries touch on aspects of philosophy or involve a substantial degree of discussion of theory as well as practice: **Metaphysics**, **Ancient Middle Eastern Religions**, **John Stuart Mill**, **Milton**, **Philosophy of Mind**, **Modernization and Urbanization**, **Mystery Religions**, **Motion Pictures**, **Myth and Mythology**, **Names**, **Newton**, and **Nietzsche**. Indeed, the Macropaedia is highly philosophical throughout, not merely in the popular sense meaning "thoughtful" or "contemplative," but also in the sense of teasing out various meanings, possible causes, and consequences. The purpose of the Macropaedia is not only to present facts, but also to engage in substantial philosophical speculation or to discuss possible interpretations in a philosophical manner. In this sense, Macropaedia articles may be said to resemble university seminars.

The Micropaedia is printed in a format of three columns per page; the Macropaedia has two columns per page. As an indication of how space is apportioned among different subjects, **Charlemagne** is covered in 47 lines in the Micropaedia and three-and-a-half pages in the Macropaedia. **Konstantin Chernenko** receives 49 lines in the Micropaedia; **Ty Cobb** is covered in 34 lines in the same volume. *New Britannica*'s coverage of the **American Civil War** consists of about two-thirds of a page in the Micropaedia, more than eight pages in the Macropaedia article **United States of America**, and several dozen Micropaedia entries on individual figures, battles, and issues. **Christianity** occupies two-thirds of a page in the Micropaedia, but the reader is referred to the Macropaedia, which devotes 115 pages to the subject. The nine-and-a-half page Micropaedia entry of **China** includes a seven-page table of major Chinese dynasties; the nation and its history receive 222 pages in the Macropaedia.

Britannica encyclopedias have long been noted for their extensive coverage in the areas of geography and biography. The 15th edition maintains this reputation and also provides strong coverage of literature, the arts, and the humanities, while scientific and technological subjects now make up close to two-fifths of the encyclopedia's entries. Although the publisher has not provided this Buying Guide with a percentage breakdown of subject areas covered in *New Britannica*, the cross-reference entry lists in the Propaedia outlines give a good clue to the scope of the encyclopedia's overall coverage. Using the Propaedia's subject classifications, our reviewers arrived at the following approximate breakdown for entries in the Micropaedia:

Matter and Energy (physics, astrophysics, chemistry): 6 percent

The Earth (geology, physical geography, climatology): 4.5 percent

Life on Earth (life sciences, nature): 13.33 percent

Human Life (evolution, heredity, health and disease, behavior and experience): 5.5 percent

Human Society (social and political science): 10.5 percent

Art (literature, fine and performing arts): 17 percent

Technology: 7.5 percent

Religion: 13 percent

History: 23 percent

The Branches of Knowledge: 5.5 percent

Because a number of entries are classified under more than one subject area, percentages add up to more than 100 percent. Biographical entries have not been counted as a separate category.

With its scholarly perspective, *New Britannica* gives short shrift to fads and to contemporary figures who, from the present perspective, may not be likely to have more than a passing influence on our culture and society. (For example, there are entries for **Elvis Presley** and the **Beatles**, but none for Michael Jackson, who is included in ACADEMIC AMERICAN and COLLIER'S.) This policy is generally a sound one. *New Britannica* also disdains the sort of "how-to" subjects covered in most general multivolume encyclopedias. Presumably, such subjects do not fall within the purview of the "Outline of Knowledge" presented in the Propaedia, and would conflict with the set's scholarly tone. However, in the view of our reviewers, this intellectual fastidiousness may make *New Britannica* less competitive with the ENCYCLOPEDIA AMERICANA and COLLIER'S, which otherwise also set high standards of scholarship.

Writing in the *Encyclopedia Buying Guide* (R. R. Bowker, 1981), critic Kenneth Kister pinpointed one of the major strengths of the 1980 version of *New Britannica*: "Considerably more attention is given to non-Western languages, and social systems than has ever been attempted by a general encyclopedia." This assessment holds true for the 1986-copyright edition as well. *New Britannica*'s coverage of foreign, non-American subject matter is indeed second to none. While the set may have a predominantly Anglo-American tone, its coverage is by no means Anglo-centric or parochial.

As an indication of the attention *New Britannica* gives to non-American subjects, 74 of the encyclopedia's 150 Micropaedia entries in the span from **Bartolome Mitre** to **Mohammed** concern foreign subjects. There are too many to list here, but the following examples will give an idea of the range of subjects *Britannica* covers: **Magnus Gosta Mittag-Leffler** (Swedish mathematician), **Mittenwald** (Bavarian village), **Mmabatho** (town in Bophuthatswana), **Mocamedes** (province in Angola), **Pavel Mockalov** (Russian actor), **Leone Modena** (Jewish Venetian writer), **Moesia** (a province of the Roman Empire), **Thomas Mokopu** (African writer), **Mogi das Cruzes** (Brazilian city), and **Peter Mogila** (17th century Moldavian theologian).

Note that *New Britannica* contains more total entries in this span than do either AMERICANA or COL-

LIER'S, and that a higher proportion of them (49.3 percent) deal with foreign subjects.

There is a very small degree of overlap (though not duplication) between the Micropaedia and the Macropaedia, in that particular subjects included in the Micropaedia are also covered in greater detail in the Macropaedia. As already noted, the Micropaedia is intended to be consulted as a source of major facts, while the Macropaedia articles give in-depth, large-scale overviews of broad subjects. (See also *Accessibility.*) Suffice it to say that *New Britannica*'s coverage is exceptionally well-balanced, and that no other encyclopedia can rival its broad scope.

III. Authority

For many people, the name Britannica is virtually synonymous with encyclopedias. Now in its 15th edition, *Britannica* is the oldest and largest English-language general encyclopedia on the market, and is considered by many to be the most authoritative. This authority derives largely from the set's distinguished history.

The first edition was published in 1768–71 in Edinburgh under the auspices of editor William Smellie, engraver Andrew Bell, and printer Colin Macfarquhar. (For more of *Britannica*'s early history, see Chapter 1: "The History of Reference Works.") In 1901, a group of American investors purchased the rights to the set, and although it has been published in the United States ever since that time, the *Britannica* has preserved much of its British flavor. Many critics regard the 11th edition, in print from 1910 to 1922, as possibly the most comprehensive and most perfect encyclopedia ever published in the English language (if, indeed, any encyclopedia can be said to approach perfection). In 1936, the editors began the policy, maintained ever since, of annual revision.

The 14th edition was in print from 1929 through 1973. In the late 1950s, *Britannica*'s editorial board, under the aegis of businessman and former U. S. Senator William Benton, decided to launch an entirely new edition. The significance of this 15th edition was not simply its unprecedented length, or even the fact that it was an entirely new encyclopedia in which every article was written from scratch. Rather, it was the radically different structure of the set, in which the editors attempted not only to list all subjects, but to relate all subjects to each other in a grand scheme—in other words, to provide a full circle of learning. The 15th edition was conceived as a comprehensive general reference encyclopedia that would provide a structured pedagogical function akin to that available in a good university. Thus was born the concept of the tripartite encyclopedia: the Propaedia (Outline of Knowledge), the Macropaedia (Knowledge in Depth), and the Micropaedia (Ready Reference and Index). This 30-volume edition cost the publisher an estimated $32 million, not including printing costs, and is said to have involved 2.5 million man-hours. The work was such a radical departure from previous editions that the publisher added the word *New* to the title. Interestingly, the Britannica company managed to keep the development of this massive new edition a secret not only from other publishers but from Britannica's own salespeople as well.

Upon its publication in 1974, the *New Encyclopaedia Britannica* (popularly dubbed *Britannica 3*, because of its three-part structure) generated a good deal of controversy. It was greeted with some scathing reviews not only in professional journals but also in a number of respected mass-circulation periodicals, notably the *Atlantic* and the *New York Times Book Review*. Critics particularly bemoaned the lack of any index in such a complex multivolume work. In response, the publisher undertook a major overhaul of the set in an attempt to make it more accessible. Among other changes, a two-volume index was added, bringing the set to 32 volumes. Several hundred Macropaedia articles were shortened and transferred to the Micropaedia. This extensive restructuring, first evident in the 1985 edition, cost Britannica, Inc., an estimated $24 million.

While some critics have also called the encyclopedia's accuracy into question, it is hard to deny that among the many contributors to *New Britannica* are some of the world's most distinguished contemporary writers, historians, biographers, and scientists, including a number of Nobel Prize winners. Among the more than 6,500 contributors and consultants of international repute are astronomer Carl Sagan; biologist Sir Peter Medawar; cardiologist Michael DeBakey; historians Frank Friedel and A. J. P. Taylor; novelists Anthony Burgess, Anthony Powell, and Isaac Bashevis Singer; economists Kenneth Boulding, Arthur Burns, and Milton Friedman; musicologist H. C. Robbins Landon; social critics Asa Briggs (Lord Briggs), Jacques Barzun, and Conor Cruise O'Brien; and former U. S. Senator and Secretary of State Edmund S. Muskie. A large majority of the contributors hold prestigious posts at major universities and other important institutions (e.g., museums, observatories, hospitals, journals, newspapers, and professional organizations). Indeed, the lengthy credits in *New Britannica* read like a Who's Who of world intellectuals. (Articles are unsigned, but the writers' initials are given and are keyed to the credits list in the Propaedia.)

As the names above suggest, *New Britannica*'s contributors include a large proportion of British academics—about 25 percent, by one estimate. An examination of the full list of contributors also reveals a sizeable proportion of contributors from other parts of the globe. Indeed, the encyclopedia's editorial board maintains formal affiliations with the universities of Oxford, Cambridge, London, and Edinburgh, as well as with the University of Chicago, the University of Tokyo, and the Australian National University.

Philosopher and educator Mortimer Adler served as Director of Planning for the 15th edition, and is at present Chairman of the Board of Editors. The overall scheme of *New Britannica* was largely his inspiration. Philip W. Goetz, who served as Executive Editor during the period of *New Britannica*'s genesis, is now Editor-in-Chief. Otherwise, the editorial staff remains anonymous. (During the encyclopedia's development in the early 1970s, some 360 editors were reportedly employed in-house. Presumably, that number has dropped considerably.)

IV. Currency

Like most general multivolume encyclopedias on the market, *New Britannica* is revised annually. As already noted, the 1985 revision was a major one, affecting not only individual articles but the entire structure and organization of the encyclopedia. According to the publisher, the 1986 revision involved changes on 2,000 pages in the Macropaedia, 1,300 pages in the Micropaedia, and 800 pages in the Propaedia. Furthermore, the index was entirely revised and reset. Not counting the index and Propaedia, this amounts to roughly a ten-percent revision. The 1986 Macropaedia added one new article (**Humanism**) and revised 79 from the 1985 edition, mostly in the areas of science, technology, and foreign nations and cities. Some 90 new articles were added to the Micropaedia; most of these were biographies, but some covered topics in the sciences and technology.

This rate of revision represents a considerable improvement over the rate of revision between 1974 and 1984, estimated in that period to have been less than four percent per year. Nonetheless, the 1986 Macropaedia still cannot be considered sufficiently up-to-date.

For example, articles on nations often end with the advice, "For current political history, see the annual issues of *Britannica Book of the Year*." The "Northern Ireland" section of **United Kingdom** (Ma-

cropaedia) concludes with a summary of crucial events in 1972 (the shooting of 13 Catholic protestors in Derry by British soldiers, the suspension of the Northern Ireland parliament and the institution of direct rule by Westminster); the article's final sentence reads, "Violence continued for the rest of the decade and beyond." The last election mentioned in **Ireland** (Macropaedia) is that of 1973, and none of the subsequent prime ministers is ever referred to.

South Africa (Macropaedia) is somewhat more current. Here, the "History" section ends with a description of the 1984 constitution. However, the international economic and political pressure against that nation are not mentioned, and the reader is again advised to "see the annual issues of the *Britannica Book of the Year*." The final sentence in **Nicaragua** (Macropaedia) reads: "The forced relocation of 10,000 Miskito Indians in 1982 and the defection of non-Communist revolutionaries from the junta and the FSLN stimulated increased internal opposition to the Sandinistas." Sandinista leader and national president Daniel Ortega is not mentioned, nor are the "non-Communist revolutionaries" identified as the Contras. Furthermore, while noting that the United States cut off aid to Nicaragua in 1981, the article does not mention the Reagan administration's overt and covert support of the Contras.

Micropaedia entries are generally more up-to-date than those in the Macropaedia. (The publisher sets the Micropaedia on computer tape, thus facilitating revision and resetting.) However, while many individual Micropaedia articles are reasonably up-to-date, our reviewers found that there are too many omissions (both in terms of entries, and of recent developments reported in articles) for this portion of *New Britannica* to be considered consistently current.

Ronald Reagan receives a cursory entry in the Micropaedia (about 300 words). The last of three paragraphs notes his 1984 electoral landslide, but does not name his opponent. The article is current as of late 1985, but tends to deal with events and issues in general, not specific, terms: "Reagan presented the Congress with a program of political and economic changes designed to reduce government spending, government activism, and the national inflation rate." It reports his hard line toward the Soviet Union and other communist nations, and his administration's efforts "through military and economic means to counteract what was perceived as the threat of Communist advances in the Middle East and Latin America." However, Lebanon, Nicaragua, and Grenada are not mentioned by name. Nor is there any mention of the record budget deficits that mounted during his administration, or of the controversies surrounding some of his cabinet members and advisors even during his first term.

The Micropaedia entry on **acquired immune deficiency syndrome** was current through 1985, but subsequent developments have already necessitated a thorough revision in future printings. The article also neglects to report the number of individuals affected by the syndrome, nor does it explain (except by implication) how the AIDS virus is transmitted.

Terrorism gives a good historical overview, and refers to a number of recent and contemporary terrorist organizations. It also notes the way in which the ubiquitous presence of the mass media has changed the methods used by modern terrorists.

The entry on **Bhopal** includes a paragraph on the 1984 gas leak at the Union Carbide plant that killed or injured several thousand residents.

The Micropaedia also includes up-to-date entries on such subjects of contemporary interest as **sports medicine**, **video disc**, **videotape recorder**, **video telephone**; the cross-reference entry for **video cassette** refers the reader to **cassette**. The digital compact disc is discussed in the article **sound recording**. However, all these articles tend to concentrate on the technical aspects of these subjects, and largely ignore their social implications.

The rapidly changing roles of women and adolescents are discussed at some length in the Macropaedia article **Social Differentiation**, although much of the coverage here relates to conditions in Britain. The extensive article **Work and Employment** contains little reference to women in the workplace and the effect this has had on society.

The currency of statistics in *Britannica* varies. As a rule, figures given in the Micropaedia are more up-to-date than those in the Macropaedia. The 1986 Micropaedia entries on the **Union of Soviet Socialist Republics**, **United Kingdom**, and **United States** all give 1984 population estimates. These figures are reasonably current.

As previously noted, *New Britannica* is not entirely consistent in its inclusion or omission of current events and personalities. For example, the 1986 Micropaedia contains entries for such recent or contemporary political luminaries as **Howard Baker**, **Tony Benn**, **Geraldine Ferraro**, and **Helmut Kohl**, but none for (former) Irish prime minister Garret Fitzgerald, former Senator and sometime presidential candidate Gary Hart, Brazilian president Jose Sarney, or long-time British Liberal party leader David Steel. (See also *Scope*.)

On the whole, *New Britannica* is not the encyclopedia to consult for information about recent trends, issues, and events. Its strength lies rather in the other direction—that of the more obscure movements and figures of history.

V. Accuracy

Britannica encyclopedias have long been venerated as impeccable sources of truth and wisdom. Indeed, in discussing the present (15th) edition, it is often difficult to distinguish between authority and accuracy.

While our content experts have noted occasional errors, omissions, and instances of bias in *New Britannica*, in toto they have found the entries they have examined to be of exceptional quality.

For example, the Micropaedia article on **Henry the Navigator** gives the fullest, most detailed account of his life and career of any of the multivolume encyclopedias in this Buying Guide. It cuts through many of the myths that surround the man and his career. At one point, the article notes that:

> When Duarte [Henry's oldest brother] succeeded King John in 1433, he did not hesitate to lecture and reprove Henry for such shortcomings as extravagance, unmethodical habits, failure to keep promises, and lack of scruples in the raising of money. This rebuke is not supported by the traditional account of the Navigator as a lofty, ascetic person, indifferent to all but religion and the furtherance of his mission of discovery.

The article clearly delineates the complexity of Henry's motives in sponsoring Portugal's voyages of trade and discovery, and in his dealings with the rest of the royal family.

Our economics consultant reports that the Macropaedia entry on **money**, written by Noble Prize-winning economist Milton Friedman, is far and away the strongest entry on this subject of those in all multivolume encyclopedias. The article is comprehensive in scope and written clearly for the lay reader. Friedman's views, as one might expect, are biased in favor of monetarism, and the editors have let his biases stand, making no serious attempt to treat alternative approaches to monetary policy. Like all other encyclopedia articles on this subject, Friedman's assumes that money circulates within a "closed economy," and does not take into account such major influences as foreign trade and international political considerations. Nevertheless, despite these flaws, the article is recommended to any high school student or adult interested in getting an intelligent introduction to money and monetary policy.

Britannica's Micropaedia entry on **Saturn** is one of the better articles on the subject in all the encyclopedias considered in this Buying Guide. The entry is brief but accurate, complete, and up-to-date in all important respects. However, the longer Macropaedia article on **Saturn** is less satisfactory. Many basic statistics, such as the planet's distance from Earth, its mass, and its albedo (the measure of a planet's brightness), have not been revised in light of recent findings, and are therefore inaccurate.

The Micropaedia entry on **transistors** is accurate as far as it goes; but in the opinion of our reviewer it does not go quite far enough, and there are some crucial omissions. For example, there is no discussion of the different types of transistors, and only one sentence on the development of integrated circuits. Much of the information presented in the Macropaedia entry is very dated and therefore no longer accurate. The article states that bipolar transistors are the only type of transistor (this is no longer true), and it fails to mention any of the applications made possible by integrated circuits. Moreover, the article, written at an advanced level, assumes that the reader is familiar with device physics. On the whole, this article is not sufficiently accurate to be recommended.

The entry on the **brain** in the Micropaedia contains a good deal of material, and for the most part is presented in a clear, straightforward manner. However, the first several paragraphs jump from species to species, making it difficult to tell when the writer is talking about the human brain as opposed to the brains of animals. The reference to brain scanning methods is not quite contemporary. The Macropaedia article gives an accurate and detailed account of the structure and function of the brain and the central nervous system. Although the article touches on the function of the different lobes, it fails to mention the specialized functions of the brain's right and left hemispheres. But this is the only notable deficiency in this article.

Britannica's Micropaedia includes individual entries for the British and U. S. **Bill of Rights** and the French **Declaration of the Rights of Man and of the Citizen**. All three entries are accurate, concise, clearly written, and useful, covering all major points. The article on the U. S. Bill combines historical and analytical approaches. The entries on the British Bill of Rights and French Declaration of Rights are accompanied by the complete texts of these documents, printed as separate boxes. The text of the U. S. Bill of Rights is printed in the Micropaedia entry **Constitution of the United States of America**.

VI. Clarity

Britannica encyclopedias have long and justly been admired by many readers for the scholarly and often colorful, idiosyncratic qualities inherent in the writing. These same qualities are apparent in *New Britannica*, where the tone continues to be scholarly and the prose can often be characterized as elegant.

The generally high reading level and the sophistication with which difficult concepts are presented certainly make *New Britannica* unsuitable for elementary and junior high school students. Even among high school students, one may surmise that only more advanced students will be able to take full advantage of the wealth of information that *New Britannica* offers. Moreover, the longer Macropaedia entries generally require more intellectual stamina and more sustained attention than many students (even at the college undergraduate level) are able to muster. Readers should also be aware that, unlike most general multivolume encyclopedias (notably WORLD BOOK), *New Britannica* does not define difficult terms in context. Even highly technical terms and concepts, such as those occurring in physics, are used without comment. The majority of articles are written at a college reading level (and many are suitable for postgraduate students), and it is generally assumed that the reader will already possess some familiarity with the subject and any special terms relating to it.

Another notable quirk (seen by some readers as an annoying affectation, but regarded by others with affection) is *New Britannica*'s continued insistence on using British spellings (e.g., *colour*, *theatre*, and *encyclopaedia*). This accounts, in part, for the general public perception that Britannica is still a British publication. A rather high-toned and sometimes willfully archaic writing style (today rarely encountered outside the Oxbridge academic establishment) is also evident in many articles, further contributing to this perception. In other words, much of *New Britannica*—particularly the Macropaedia—reads the way many Americans like to imagine that the British write and speak. While our reviewers do not regard this in itself as a serious drawback, this style frequently stands in the way of clarity. What is the average American reader to make, for example, of this sentence from **Southern Africa** in the Macropaedia: "Health services were biased toward curative medicine in central hospitals." Or this, from the Macropaedia article on **birds**: "It is hoped that these developments will encourage taxonomists to abandon some of their more tenacious opinions—*e.g.*, that the crows represent the apex of passerine evolution." Although admittedly these sentences are quoted out of context, surely the observations they are meant to convey could be expressed in a simpler, more straightforward manner.

Elsewhere, articles display a propensity for understatement—another characteristic commonly associated with British English. For example, in **United Kingdom** (Macropaedia), we are told that "Northern Ireland's climate is temperate and maritime: most of its weather comes from the southwest in a series of lows bringing the rain and cloud that often lend character to the landscape." What this means is that the generally overcast skies and frequent rain make everything seem dreary and depressing. One may read this as the writer's personal tongue-in-cheek comment. (See also *Objectivity*.)

And yet, many readers will admire *New Britannica*'s elegance and subtlety of argument. In the Micropaedia article on **censorship**, for example, one reads: "Whereas it could once be maintained that the law forbids whatever it does not permit, it is now generally accepted—at least wherever Western liberalism is in the ascendancy—that one may do whatever is not forbidden by law." Such delightful prose and subtle distinctions are rare in modern general reference works, where the demand for utilitarian information usually outweighs concern for the elegance with which that information is presented.

The following extract from **lighthouse** illustrates the style of a typical entry in the Micropaedia of *New Britannica*. The reader should be aware, however, that this encyclopedia more than in any other set currently on the market contains a wide variety of styles, and that the degree of clarity varies from article to article. No single excerpt can be taken as the norm for the entire set.

lighthouse, structure, usually with a tower, built on shore or in shallow water to support a light used as an aid to maritime coastal navigation. From the sea a lighthouse may be identified by day by the distinctive painting of the structure and at night by the colour coding, flashing, or occulting of its light.

A brief history of the history, construction, and equipment of lighthouses follows. For a full treatment, *see* MACROPAEDIA: Public Works.

The first known lighthouse was the Pharos of Alexandria, which stood some 350 feet (110 metres) high. During the first few centuries A.D. the Phoenicians and Romans also built lighthouses at numerous sites, ranging from the Black Sea, along the Mediterranean and Atlantic Coasts, to Britain. After the fall of the Roman Empire, there was little maritime trade or travel, and no lighthouses were built in Europe until the revival of commerce in the 12th century. The French and Italians built the earliest of these lighthouses, followed by the Hanseatic League, which constructed a number of such structures along the Scandinavian and German coasts. By the end of the 16th century, there were at least 30 lighthouses marking the European coastline. . . .

Finally, a word must be said about the clarity of the Propaedia. It is no easy task to classify all the information contained in a multivolume encyclopedia of *Britannica*'s scope into a single volume outline of knowledge. But while admiring the Propaedia's comprehensiveness, our reviewers believe that the publisher's claims for this volume are grossly exaggerated. For the average reader—and even for many of above-average ability and curiosity—the Propaedia will remain difficult to use and to comprehend, and its value will remain limited.

VII. Objectivity

In presenting differing points of view on sensitive issues, *New Britannica* is impeccably objective. The Micropaedia generally presents known facts as such without editorial comment; it is also careful to identify theory, belief, and opinions as such, though rarely goes into detail in explaining these. The generous space in the Macropaedia affords writers the opportunity to expand upon various theories and suppositions at some length. Here, the writing is often less objective, in the sense that writers can and do indulge their personal tastes and pursue byways and eddies of thought that would not enter a more straightforward encyclopedia. This same subjective quality also informs most of the essays that precede the Propaedia outlines. It should be stressed, however, that in both cases this "subjectivity" is virtually always well-informed, not narrow or partisan. The tone of such articles is one of scholarly enthusiasm, not of dry pedantry or of propagandizing.

New Britannica offers an excellent presentation of **Sex and Sexuality** (Macropaedia), where, under the heading "Psychological Aspects," a full page is devoted to "Effects of early conditioning." "Social and Cultural Aspects" of sexuality and "Homosexuality" each receive two-and-a-half pages of thorough and highly objective coverage.

New Britannica approaches the highly sensitive issue of **abortion** in an exemplary manner. The Micropaedia article on the subject makes clear that "whether and to what extent induced abortions should be permitted, encouraged, or severely repressed is a social issue that has divided theologians, philosophers, and legislators for centuries." After a brief overview of attitudes towards abortion in various cultures and at various times in history, the article describes the ongoing debate in the United States and presents lucid summaries of the major arguments, both pro and con. It concludes that "the public debate . . . has demonstrated the enormous difficulties experienced by political institutions in grappling with moral and ethical problems."

The Macropaedia contains extensive, highly technical articles on **The Theory of Evolution** and **Human Evolution**. Both articles assume that the "main hypothesis of organic evolution" has been accepted by the scientific community and by society as a whole, although **Human Evolution** notes widespread opposition to the theory in Darwin's day, and remarks that "misconceptions . . . still arise . . . from the use and misuse of the colloquial terms man and human in the discussion of evolutionary origins." **Theory of Evolution** contains a brief section on "The Acceptance of Evolution," which mentions the 1925 Scopes trial and states that "in 1968, the United States Supreme Court ruled that anti-evolution laws were unconstitutional." However, subsequent (and ongoing) opposition by certain fundamentalist religious groups to the teaching of evolution in public schools goes unmentioned. Nor are there any articles on creationism or scientific creationism in either the Micropaedia or the Macropaedia.

The 3,000-word Micropaedia article on **Andrew Jackson** is straightforward and generally objective. However, unlike most of the rival multivolume encyclopedias (including AMERICANA and COLLIER'S), the *Britannica* article does not mention his early rambunctiousness—his duels, gambling, and hot temper. Nor does it describe the fierce attacks on Jackson's wife by his political opponents. More importantly, there is nothing about his ownership of slaves; his policy towards the Indians is alluded to but not fully spelled out in any detail. In recounting his activities as president, the article does deal with the issues of patronage, nullification, and the national bank. It notes quite objectively that the spoils system "did not begin with Jackson, nor did he utilize this practice as extensively as was charged. Jackson removed fewer than one-fifth of all federal officeholders."

VIII. Accessibility

In the past, the main criticisms of *New Britannica* have centered on the set's accessibility, or lack thereof. In 1985, with the introduction of the two-volume index, the encyclopedia's accessibility was improved considerably. Many of the problems the critics had complained about were rectified. (See also *Other Opinions*.)

As previously discussed, both the Macropaedia and the Micropaedia may be regarded as self-contained sets. Entries in each are arranged alphabetically, word by word. Names beginning with *Mc* are treated as though they begin with *Mac*; the same rule applies to the use of the abbreviation *St.* for *Saint*.

Running heads (guide words) at the top of each page indicate the first entry on the left-hand page and the last entry on the right-hand page. Page numbers are located next to the guide words.

In the Micropaedia, entry headings are printed in boldface type, and individual articles are separated by a line space. Subheads are used only in longer articles; in such cases, subsections are identified by a word or words in italics at the beginning of a paragraph. Since these words are in the same typesize as the main text, it is difficult for the reader to readily distinguish such subsections.

Macropaedia articles usually begin on a new page; the title is printed in large boldface type. Most Macropaedia entries begin with a brief overview of the subject. A "table of contents" or outline is also usually given near the beginning of the entry, followed by the main article text. Three levels of subheads may be used.

New Britannica contains the most extensive index of any multivolume encyclopedia, with nearly 400,000 entries spread over two volumes. As an indication of the scope and style of individual entries, the reader searching for information about Marie Curie will find the following index entry:

Curie, Marie, *or* Manya Sklodowska (Fr. phys.) **3**:798:3a
   association with Becquerel **2**:35:3b
   discovery of
      polonium **9**:574:2b; **15**:990:2b
      radium **15**:969:1b
   naming of curie **3**:798:3a

Each citation contains three elements, identifying the volume, the page number, and the section of the page on which the item occurs. For example, in the example above, the first reference occurs in Volume 3, page 798, in the upper half of the third column.

Several critics reviewing the 1985 *New Britannica*—the first printing to contain the index—noted that the index was by no means comprehensive or consistent. For example, several index entries referred to the Macropaedia but did not note that the subject was also covered in the Micropaedia. In checking these specific examples, our reviewers found that in every case these omissions had been rectified in the 1986 edition, and did not find any other obvious oversights. There is no guarantee that the index is now complete and accurate, but it does seem to have been improved from the 1985 version. Since the entire index is revised and reset annually, we may hope that each successive printing will result in further refinements.

Cross-references also play an important role in enhancing *New Britannica*'s accessibility. The Micropaedia contains some 25,000 cross-reference entries; in addition, both the Micropaedia and Macropaedia contain an unspecified number of "see" cross-references within individual entries.

IX. Special Features

Apart from its unique four-part organization, *New Britannica* does not boast any special features to speak of. Many users consider the Propaedia as a special feature, as it contains elements (e.g., the comprehensive outlines of human knowledge) not found in any other encyclopedia. The essays that precede each outline may also be of interest to some readers. The section on "The Human Body" contains two sets of detailed transparent overlays, identifying the principal parts of the male and female anatomy. Mortimer Adler's explication of the Propaedia, "The Circle of Learning," will be useful only to those interested in Adler's epistemological theories.

The publisher claims 24,000 illustrations in the set, of which 8,000 are in full color (in addition to 164 color plates). The prospective purchaser should be aware that the vast majority of these illustrations are little larger than postage-stamp size, and as a whole *New Britannica* is graphically dull. There are no illustrations in the Propaedia (apart from the physiology color transparencies); the majority of illustrations occur in the Micropaedia. In the Macropaedia, a handful of articles, such as that on the **Decorative Arts**, are accompanied by color plates. But otherwise, many consecutive pages of text go unrelieved by illustrations of any kind. Nevertheless, most photographs and art reproductions for biographical entries are interesting and give an adequate representation of the subject; the same is true for photographs illustrating various flora and fauna. Technical diagrams are also generally clear and functional.

New Britannica contains about 1,000 maps, most of which occupy only a fraction of a page and are in black-and-white. A number of the maps, particularly the historical maps, were not designed for *Britannica* but have been reprinted from other sources. (For a review of the separate atlas published by Britannica, Inc., see *Britannica Atlas* in the atlas review section of this Buying Guide.)

Like its competitors, *New Britannica* contains extensive bibliographies. These are found at the end of selected articles in the Micropaedia, and at the end of each article in the Macropaedia. Bibliographies in the Micropaedia are the exception rather than the rule. The Micropaedia bibliographies are generally quite brief, but they are up-to-date.

Macropaedia bibliographies are often extensive, sometimes running over two entire pages or more. However, all too often they are seriously out of date. For example, an overwhelming majority of titles in the half-page bibliography at the conclusion of **Endocrine Systems** were published in the 1960s; the most recent are from 1971. A spot check reveals that this is also the case in the bibliographies for **Human Emotion and Motivation**, **Human Evolution**, and **The Theory of Evolution**. Incidentally, many of the Macropaedia bibliographies, especially those pertaining to scientific or technical subjects, list foreign-language works without English translations.

It seems to our reviewers that the value of the Propaedia could have been enhanced by the placement of comprehensive bibliographies in this section. However, the publisher has not chosen to arrange the set this way.

For the most part, the bibliographies are highly specialized and will be of more use to the scholar than to the general reader.

X. Format

The 32-volume *New Britannica* comes in a standard heavy-duty simulated brown leather binding with embossed gold lettering on the spine. Colored bands on the spine identify each volume as part of the Propaedia, Micropaedia, Macropaedia, or index. The titles of the first and last entries in the volume are also stamped on the spine, enabling the user to identify and retrieve the pertinent volume easily. Volumes are of roughly equal length (generally from 950 to 1050 pages each), and therefore a single volume does not contain all the entries beginning with a particular letter. (For example, Volume 8 of the Micropaedia contains the entries **Menage** through **Ottawa**; Volume 9 contains **Otter** through **Rethimnon**.) The entire set takes up slightly more than four feet of horizontal shelf space.

Macropaedia pages are printed in a two-column format. Micropaedia pages use a format of three columns per page.

XI. Other Opinions

Geoffrey Wolff, "Britannica 3, Failures Of," *Atlantic*, November 1976: "There . . . seems no justification for the segregation of long articles (arranged alphabetically rather than topically) from short, save the economic convenience to [the publisher]."

Newsweek, May 6, 1985: "The addition of a two-volume index is a signal improvement; the new Britannica is far more accessible than its predecessor. And yet, welcome as it is, this index needs work."

ARBA, 1986: "Without question, the restructuring and refinements [reflected in the 1985 revision] have drastically improved the accessibility and convenience of the set. The Micropaedia can now stand alone as an impressive one-stop source of factual information. The Macropaedia's and Propaedia's changes further enhance the set's educational objectives. . . . The real key to this revision, however, is the two-volume index. While applauding the tremendous improvement it brings to the set, we cannot overlook its numerous flaws . . . We found again and again . . . that important references were omitted. . . . *See also* references are used unevenly. . . .

"We might have hoped for more currency. Some [Macropaedia] articles are woefully out-of-date, making the Micropaedia articles which are derived from them also dated. . . ."

"[A]ccessibility and currency [are] two persistent weaknesses in an otherwise outstanding encyclopedia, arguably the very best English-language general adult set available."

Booklist (*Reference Books Bulletin*), November 15, 1986: "The 1986 printing retains the international coverage and impressive list of contributors commended earlier by the Board. . . . While most of the bibliographies in the Macropaedia are current, some need updating . . . illustrations are adequate. . . . [T]he attention to biographies and current topics and additions to the index are evidence that continuous revision remains *NEB*'s policy. It can be recommended to serious high school, college and adult readers for its scholarly, exhaustive articles on a wide range of subjects."

Harvey Einbinder, "The New Britannica: Pro: Depth and Detail by Design," *Library Journal*, April 15, 1987: "The primary achievement of the *New Britannica* is to provide an editorial plan that efficiently furnishes factual information and effectively deals with ideas. This has been accomplished by utilizing two sharply separated sets of alphabetic entries supplemented by a two-volume index and a volume that contains a guide to related articles in the set. Although the titles and contents of individual articles will change in future editions, this editorial plan will assist the editors in maintaining the *Britannica*'s position as the leading general encyclopedia in the English language."

Harvey Einbinder, "The New Britannica: Con: The Not-So-Perfect Britannica," *Library Journal*, April 15, 1987: "Twenty years ago I demonstrated in *The Myth of the Britannica* the danger of retaining old articles for decades. Nevertheless, this hazardous policy has been adopted in the 1985 edition, despite an editorial budget of $24 million dollars. . . . Important medical developments are slighted. . . . Similar omissions occur in treating technological subjects. . . . Major advances in mathematics are neglected because the *Britannica*'s mathematical articles consist almost entirely of material taken from the 1974 edition. . . . Much material has been taken from the 1974 edition without critical scrutiny. . . . The large number of old bibliographies diminishes the *Britannica*'s utility as a reliable guide to outside sources of information. Yet its annotated bibliographies are potentially a valuable aid for students and librarians because they contain a convenient, detailed compilation of printed sources on an extremely wide range of subjects. But their utility is severely impaired when they neglect references published in the last decade. . . . The large amount of material taken from the 1974 edition seriously undermines the many outstanding innovations and improvements introduced in the latest edition."

XII. Summary

Without question, *New Encyclopaedia Britannica* is the most fascinating general multivolume encyclopedia on the market today. It is also the quirkiest, and has aroused the passions of both its admirers and its detractors. Many libraries will find it indispensable for their reference collections, as it provides a greater range and depth of knowledge than is available in any other encyclopedia. No other set approaches *New Britannica*'s Macropaedia in the amount of attention devoted to a selection of "large" subjects. However, the Macropaedia is recommended primarily for those who desire a detailed overview of these subjects; it is of considerably less value to those seeking basic facts and figures. It is also considerably less up-to-date than one would wish. The specific-entry Micropaedia is admirably concise, clear, and accurate. But the Propaedia will be of limited value to all but a handful of users. Moreover, despite the two-volume index, *New Britannica* remains arguably the most difficult encyclopedia to use. Many patrons will require the assistance of an experienced reference librarian to find the information they need, and even for experienced users the index is not foolproof.

In the final analysis, the *New Britannica* succeeds more as an intelligent browser's encyclopedia than as a basic reference source. It will be of most use to college-level users, to writers and other professionals, and to well-educated, well-informed laypeople who have frequent need for a sophisticated general encyclopedia. High school students at more advanced levels will also find the set useful. However, any claim that *New Britannica* is suitable for grade-school children and junior high students is patently false.

Considering the high costs involved in producing an encyclopedia of such size and complexity as *New Britannica*, this set offers good value. Its price ($1,249 for individuals, $999 for institutions) is only marginally higher than that of its major competitors, COLLIER'S, which has eight fewer volumes, and ENCYCLOPEDIA AMERICANA, a 30-volume set. The yearbook, *Britannica World Data Annual*, will probably be useful for libraries, but is less crucial to individuals.

Individuals wishing to purchase *New Britannica* may contact the local distributor listed under "Encyclopaedia Britannica, Inc." in the "Encyclopedia" section of the Yellow Pages. The company offers a modest trade-in allowance on previous *Britannica* editions and on major encyclopedias of other publishers. This offer is available to individuals only, not to institutions.

For school and library purchases, phone the Britannica Educational Corporation at (800) 554-9862.

New Standard Encyclopedia

Facts at a Glance

Full Title: **New Standard Encyclopedia**.
Publisher: Standard Educational Corporation, 600 West Monroe, Chicago, IL 60606.
Editor-in-Chief: Douglas W. Downey.
Copyright: 1986.

Number of Volumes: 17.
Number of Contributors: 700.
Number of Entries: 30,960 entries for 17,394 articles.
Number of Pages: 10,100.
Number of Words: 6,400,000.
Number of Maps: 642.
Number of Cross-references: 40,000.
Number of Indexes: none.
Number of Illustrations: 2,300 four-color; 9,700 two-color or black-and-white.
Trim Size: 6¾″ × 9¼″.

Intended Readership: junior high and high school.
Price: $649.50 publisher's suggested retail price to individuals; $422.50 discount price to schools and libraries.
Sold only through independent distributors.
ISBN 0-87392-191-7.
Revised annually.

I. Introduction

The *New Standard Encyclopedia* is a 17-volume work designed for home, school, and library use. "Although children as young as nine or ten can understand much of the material," the publisher claims, "the content is not juvenile and the level of detail is sufficient for basic reference use by persons of any age." The set's primary function, in the editor's words, is "to provide as much information of interest to the general reader as is possible within an illustrated set selling for a moderate price."

New Standard can serve as a general reference work for the adult layperson whose interests may be wide-ranging but not necessarily scholarly. It will also be of particular usefulness to the junior high or high school student who is not necessarily college bound.

II. Scope

The *New Standard Encyclopedia* contains 17,394 articles, in addition to some 13,500 "See" entries that serve solely as cross-references. With a total word count of approximately 6,400,000 spread over its 10,100 pages, the average article length is about 375 words. Actual article length in *New Standard* varies considerably, from a half dozen lines (45 words) for minor biographical figures to as much as 90 pages for **United States**. As a rule, however, the majority of articles are shorter than the 375-word average.

As an indication of how space is apportioned among different subjects, **Charlemagne** receives about one-and-one-sixth pages (including a map and bibliography); **Konstantin Chernenko** receives about one-third of a page (including a small photograph), and **Ty Cobb** gets 11 lines (about one-tenth of a page). The article on the **American Civil War** is nine-and-a-half pages long (including maps, illustrations, cross-references, and bibliography); the entry for **Christianity** is shorter than two-and-a-half pages; and **China** is treated in 22 pages.

Because *New Standard* is a specific-entry encyclopedia, individual Civil War battles are accorded separate entries, as are individual figures from the Civil War. The same is true for different Christian reli-

New Standard Encyclopedia

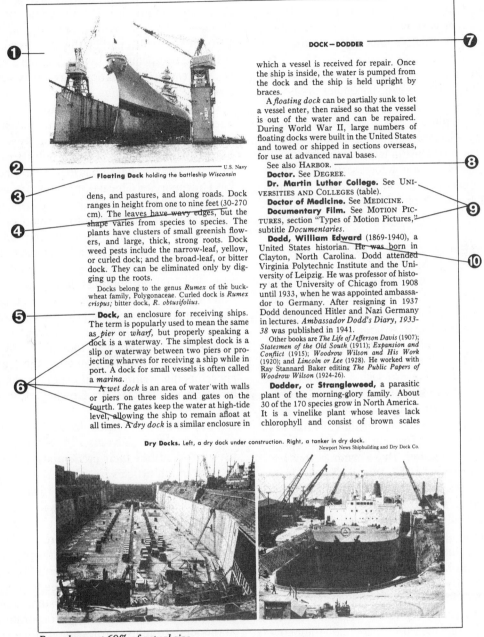

DOCK — DODDER

U.S. Navy
Floating Dock holding the battleship *Wisconsin*

which a vessel is received for repair. Once the ship is inside, the water is pumped from the dock and the ship is held upright by braces.

A *floating dock* can be partially sunk to let a vessel enter, then raised so that the vessel is out of the water and can be repaired. During World War II, large numbers of floating docks were built in the United States and towed or shipped in sections overseas, for use at advanced naval bases.

See also HARBOR.

Doctor. See DEGREE.

Dr. Martin Luther College. See UNIVERSITIES AND COLLEGES (table).

Doctor of Medicine. See MEDICINE.

Documentary Film. See MOTION PICTURES, section "Types of Motion Pictures," subtitle *Documentaries*.

Dodd, William Edward (1869-1940), a United States historian. He was born in Clayton, North Carolina. Dodd attended Virginia Polytechnic Institute and the University of Leipzig. He was professor of history at the University of Chicago from 1908 until 1933, when he was appointed ambassador to Germany. After resigning in 1937 Dodd denounced Hitler and Nazi Germany in lectures. *Ambassador Dodd's Diary, 1933-38* was published in 1941.

Other books are *The Life of Jefferson Davis* (1907); *Statesmen of the Old South* (1911); *Expansion and Conflict* (1915); *Woodrow Wilson and His Work* (1920); and *Lincoln or Lee* (1928). He worked with Ray Stannard Baker editing *The Public Papers of Woodrow Wilson* (1924-26).

Dodder, or **Strangleweed,** a parasitic plant of the morning-glory family. About 30 of the 170 species grow in North America. It is a vinelike plant whose leaves lack chlorophyll and consist of brown scales

dens, and pastures, and along roads. Dock ranges in height from one to nine feet (30-270 cm). The leaves have wavy edges, but the shape varies from species to species. The plants have clusters of small greenish flowers, and large, thick, strong roots. Dock weed pests include the narrow-leaf, yellow, or curled dock; and the broad-leaf, or bitter dock. They can be eliminated only by digging up the roots.

Docks belong to the genus *Rumex* of the buckwheat family, Polygonaceae. Curled dock is *Rumex crispus;* bitter dock, *R. obtusifolius.*

Dock, an enclosure for receiving ships. The term is popularly used to mean the same as *pier* or *wharf,* but properly speaking a dock is a waterway. The simplest dock is a slip or waterway between two piers or projecting wharves for receiving a ship while in port. A dock for small vessels is often called a *marina.*

A *wet dock* is an area of water with walls or piers on three sides and gates on the fourth. The gates keep the water at high-tide level, allowing the ship to remain afloat at all times. A *dry dock* is a similar enclosure in

Dry Docks. Left, a dry dock under construction. Right, a tanker in dry dock.
Newport News Shipbuilding and Dry Dock Co.

Page shown at 69% of actual size.

❶ Illustration: New Standard contains 12,000 illustrations, of which 2,300 are four-color.

❷ Photo credit

❸ Caption

❹ Metric approximations are given for standard measures.

❺ Endnotes to articles on fauna and flora give scientific classifications.

❻ Italics indicate that the term is defined in context.

❼ Guide words indicate the first and last entries on the page.

❽ "See also" cross-reference: New Standard includes 40,000 cross-references in article text.

❾ New Standard contains 13,500 cross-reference entries. The

encyclopedia lacks an index and relies on cross-references to provide accessibility.

❿ Main entry: New Standard contains more than 17,000 articles. Entries are arranged alphabetically, word-by-word. Some articles include bibliographies.

gious figures, denominations, movements, and practices, and for specific aspects of a nation's geography. As this Buying Guide reader may infer, there is not necessarily a direct correlation between the length of an article and the relative importance of the subject it covers.

The publisher has not provided this Buying Guide with a percentage breakdown of subject areas. By our reviewers' estimates, roughly one-third of the articles are biographical, and about one-fifth deal with geography. Science subjects generally receive adequate coverage, at least in terms of the frequency of science entries (though not necessarily in terms of the space devoted to a particular subject). The arts, literature, religion, and philosophy seem underrepresented both in number of entries and in percentage of space.

As a general-interest encyclopedia for the non-academic lay reader, *New Standard* covers a wide range of subjects not usually found in more scholarly reference works. For example, there are entries for many legal terms, such as **abandonment**, **alias**, **easement**, **negligence**, and **tort**. A large number of corporations, professional associations, government agencies, and public service organizations are also the subjects of individual articles. A random sampling of entry titles taken from Volume 5, pages D286b–D327 will illustrate the extensiveness of general-interest subjects: **Drills and Drilling, Driver Education, Driver's License, Drought, Drowning, Drum, Drury Lane, Dry Cleaning, Dry Farming, Dry Ice, Dry Rot,** *The Duchess of Malfi*, **Ducking Stool, Duckbill Platypus, Duckweed, Ductility, Duel, Dugong, Duke, Duke University, Dukhobors, Dulcimer, Dumas, Dumdum Bullet, The Dun & Bradstreet Corporation, Duplicating and Copying Machines, Du Pont Company, Dust, Dust Bowl, Dust Counter, Dust Explosion, Dutch Elm Disease, Dutch Reformed Church, Dwarf, Dyes and Dyeing, Dynamite, Dynamometer**.

Compared to competing encyclopedias (FUNK & WAGNALLS NEW ENCYCLOPEDIA, for example) that have taken deliberate measures to increase their coverage of non-American subjects, *New Standard* shows evident weakness in this aspect. Nearly 19 pages are devoted to the state of **South Carolina**, for example, while **South Africa** gets 13 pages.

III. Authority

Although the name *New Standard* and the Standard Educational Corporation may not be as familiar to most readers as those of other encyclopedias and their publishers, the *New Standard Encyclopedia* is by no means a newcomer to the reference publishing market. Its forerunner, the five-volume *Aiton's En-*cyclopedia, was published in 1910 and achieved some popularity at the time. It was reissued in an expanded six-volume edition in 1912, under the title *Standard Reference Work for Home, School, and Library*. In 1930 the set, which had by this time expanded to ten volumes, was acquired by the Standard Educational Society (now Corporation), and was retitled *New Standard Encyclopedia*.

As its former title implies, the *New Standard*'s intellectual aims have always been modest, and it has never been regarded as a particularly authoritative source of information. Unlike NEW ENCYCLOPAEDIA BRITANNICA, which has long-established ties with the University of Chicago, or the CONCISE COLUMBIA ENCYCLOPEDIA and its predecessors, which drew many advisors and contributors from Columbia University, *New Standard* does not rely on a pool of scholars for its authority. Rather, most of the articles are written by an in-house editorial staff; the credits page lists 30 "contributing editors" in addition to 50 other editors, designers, cartographers, and general consultants. In explaining how the encyclopedia has been put together, the foreword notes that "staff members are qualified in their fields by education and experience and are trained in the techniques of encyclopedia writing." This staff works under the direction of Douglas W. Downey, Editor-in-Chief since 1964.

An additional 700 people are listed as "contributors, consultants, advisers, and authenticators"; this list also identifies their credentials and affiliations, as well as the articles on which they have worked. The term "authenticator" is used to describe the subject specialist who is responsible for an article's accuracy. The foreword states that "each article . . . has been reviewed by five or more persons. At least one of these is a recognized authority in the field being covered." However, the term "recognized authority" is vague; the skeptical reader may well ask, "recognized by whom?" A substantial number of these people are employed by corporate public relations departments, professional organizations, or government agencies. While these individuals may well have a more thorough practical knowledge of their particular subject than do many academics, their objectivity may be called into question. (See *Accuracy* and *Objectivity*.) Only a very small number of these consultants (such as the former astronaut Neil Armstrong and the linguist Mario Pei) have achieved wide recognition outside their fields of specialization. Simply in terms of name recognition, *New Standard* would seem to have the weakest consulting staff of any encyclopedia on the market today. Moreover, a number of these individuals are deceased.

Apart from the subject notations given in the list of consultants, it is difficult to trace responsibility for individual articles. As the publisher notes, "since each article is the work of several persons, the articles are not signed."

IV. Currency

The *New Standard Encyclopedia* is revised and reprinted annually. Although the publisher claims that 23 percent of the pages in the 1986 edition were revised from the previous edition, it is difficult to judge the extent of actual revision. The publisher states: "Each year major sections within volumes are completely revised; all material is reevaluated and many articles are rewritten or reillustrated to assure a contemporary approach to the subjects involved." However, it is difficult to verify this claim.

According to the publisher, "graphs, bibliographies, and statistics are reviewed for revision at least once every four or five years." While some new articles have been added, most updating seems to be in the form of new figures (e.g., recent death dates) and a sentence or two added to the ends of articles (usually articles on nations) to give the reader some notion of recent developments.

Apparently the galleys of the 1986 *New Standard* were set near the end of 1985. The article on the **United States** (subsection: *History*) concludes by mentioning that "a summit meeting between President Reagan and the Soviet leader was arranged for November, 1985." The article on the **Union of Soviet Socialist Republics** ends with the sentence: "[Chernenko] died in March, 1985, and was succeeded as party chief by Mikhail S. Gorbachev." Again, as the 1986 edition of *New Standard* went to press, it was probably too early to assess how the new leadership might affect Soviet society.

New Standard does include reasonably up-to-date entries on such subjects of contemporary interest as **AIDS**, **compact disc player**, and **Mikhail Gorbachev**. Yet, there is no entry for the American filmmaker **Woody Allen**. The entry on **computers** discusses in some detail the growing use of personal computers in the 1980s, as well as their applications.

The article on **terrorism**, however, is badly dated. It includes mentions of the Mau Mau, the Irish Republican Army, the Ku Klux Klan, the Mafia, and "various Palestinian groups" as organizations that have used terror tactics, but gives no specific historical examples of any terrorist acts perpetrated by these groups. Furthermore, the article gives no sense of the rising tide of terrorism in the 1970s and 1980s, or of counterterrorist measures taken by various gov-

ernments. Similarly, the article on **sports medicine**, a booming field in the 1980s, is extremely sketchy and generalized and gives no examples of sports medicine's contemporary applications. There is no entry for **employment of women**; the article titled **affirmative action** does not give the reader a sense of how women's roles in the workplace have changed over the last 20 years or of how these changes have affected the rest of society. Nor does the article include any recent statistics about the number of women now working full time in the United States and other nations. FUNK & WAGNALLS provides a much fuller and more up-to-date account of all these subjects.

Illustrations (apart from those chosen for historical interest) are sometimes dated. For example, the most recent photos in **advertising** seem to date from the 1950s or early 1960s. (The text of the article itself is badly out of date. The only sentence on the history of television advertising states that "the use of television for advertising purposes began shortly before the end of World War II, and grew rapidly in the postwar period.")

The overall impression one gets is that while many of the articles are up-to-date, revision is spotty and seemingly random.

V. Accuracy

New Standard generally maintains a reasonable standard of accuracy. However, our reviewers note that the set has a tendency to make unsubstantiated generalizations. For example, a caption of a photo in the **Europe** article (Volume 5, page E-246) declares that "Ancient European Civilization reached its apex under Marcus Aurelius. . ." In the same article, one reads that "No other continent has produced so many great artists, musicians, writers, philosophers, and scientists." In **Stalin**, the terms "Russia" and "Soviet Union" are often used interchangeably, and no distinction is made between Russians and other ethnic groups within the Soviet Union. Such instances of editorial carelessness and generalization are not confined to these articles or to entries in particular subject areas. One can find similar minor but misleading lapses throughout the set. For example, the article on **Henry the Navigator** remarks that the 15th century Portuguese prince "held an informal school of navigation at his court in Sagres. . . ." This is a popular misconception; although he favored the idea of such a school, he was not personally involved in this work.

Yet in many respects *New Standard* is remarkably informative. The entry on **Ronald Reagan**, for example, presents a good deal of accurate factual information about the man and his presidency. It includes details of his early radio and film careers, and his first marriage, although it is vague on his activities as head of the Screen Actors Guild in the late 1940s. It gives an accurate account of his entry into politics, his terms as governor of California, and the major events of his presidency up to November 1985.

New Standard's entry on **Saturn** is generally accurate, although the information it gives about the planet's moons is out of date. The information contained in the several articles on **bills of rights** is, by and large, accurate, but the discussions are too brief to be particularly illuminating. The **money** article is narrower in scope than other encyclopedias' entries on this subject, but the information given (apart from the dated exchange rates) is accurate. The coverage of **transistors** is extremely dated; most importantly, there is no explanation of how transistors work, while integrated circuits are only mentioned in passing.

VI. Clarity

A major strength of *New Standard*—indeed, perhaps its most attractive feature—is its generally colloquial, non-technical writing style. While this sometimes resembles textbook style, it is never dry or pedantic. The general-interest survey articles (e.g., **airplane**) in particular should stimulate and satisfy the curiosity of the average student. Even such complex subjects as the **theory of relativity** are explained in lucid, easy-to-understand language. However, unlike WORLD BOOK, *New Standard* does not use a controlled reading level vocabulary. Application of the Fry Readability Scale shows that **lighthouse** is written at ninth-grade level, **relativity** at twelfth-grade level, and **Union of Soviet Socialist Republics** at a college freshman/sophomore level. Thus, although the writing style is generally attractive, many of the articles may be written at too high a level for the intended readership.

New Standard contains particularly well-written articles in several subject areas. The user will find excellent, well-organized, well-illustrated, and useful articles on certain animals (e.g., **dog** and **horse**), which give detailed breakdowns and descriptions of different breeds. There are also good though brief articles on classical music performers, giving thumbnail characterizations in addition to the standard biographical data. Readers who possess only a rudimentary grasp of science and scientific principles should find the science entries interesting and easy to understand.

The following extract from **lighthouse** illustrates the style of a typical entry in *New Standard*.

Lighthouse, a structure provided with a powerful light to warn or guide ships. Lighthouses are built on coasts, islands, reefs, and shoals, sometimes far from shore. Some warn ships of hazards. Others help ships determine their position, or guide them along coasts, through channels, or into harbors.

The light must be high above the water, not only to protect it from waves, which in some places reach great heights, but also so that the light may be seen from far away. Lighthouses therefore are tall structures or are erected on high land close to the water. Many lighthouses have lights that can be seen for 20 miles (32 km) or more on a clear night.

VII. Objectivity

New Standard is not afraid to make broad value judgments or characterize major historical figures when such judgments are supported by historical evidence. For example, the article on **Joseph Stalin** asserts that "[in transforming Russia] from an underdeveloped land into an industrial and military power . . . he drove the Russian people ruthlessly, and millions suffered and died. Although outwardly mild-mannered, Stalin annihilated all opposition and turned Russia into a police state."

Assessing **Andrew Jackson**'s personality, *New Standard* says: "Jackson was neither an original nor a profound thinker, and did not always follow or understand the principles of 'Jacksonian democracy' that bears his name. . . . Jackson's hot temper frequently caused him to act in a hasty or injudicious manner, and he was often swayed by personal prejudices." According to current historical interpretations of the man and his presidency, this is a fair and even-handed assessment.

In many instances, however, articles tend to skim over controversial issues and downplay or ignore disturbing facts. For example, although the article on **drugs** contains a section on "the drug problem," cocaine is not mentioned, and the article does not include any facts or figures about contemporary drug abuse in America.

Often, the writers seem to take information provided by official sources at face value, as in the article on **South Africa**. For example, in describing the four ethnic groups differentiated by the South African government, the article reports that "under the policy of *apartheid* ('apartness'), each group is to develop separately, the official goal being a number of autonomous states based on racial and cultural identity." There is no comment on what apartheid means in practice, or on the political and economic inequality that the system is intended to perpetuate. This section simply notes, in describing the "Bantu" population, that "in urban areas they must live in separate communities called townships. In some cases their families do not live with them but reside in the Bantu homelands and states." In the subsection *government*, *New Standard* notes that "the Bantu homelands, called Bantustans, are largely self-governing and some are nominally independent." Later in the *history* section, the article reports that "In 1976 Transkei was granted independence. However, no foreign government recognized it as a separate nation, the feeling being that it was independent in name only." The article concludes with a mention of the new constitution that came into force in 1984, and which "for the first time gave some political power to the Colored and Asian populations." There is no mention of any black political groups, nor are the names of any prominent black leaders given, although the caption to a photo of Desmond Tutu notes that he "was awarded the 1984 Nobel Peace Prize for his outspoken opposition to apartheid. . ." These statements may be true as far as they go, but certainly they do not tell the whole story, and cannot be considered objective.

A glowing tone pervades many of the articles on individual nations, corporations, professional organizations, and government agencies. For example, the entry on the **Union Carbide Corporation** makes no mention of the 1984 chemical leak at the company's plant in Bhopal, India, that killed and injured hundreds of people.

By the same token, *New Standard* often adopts a negative tone toward many subjects that do not conform to a mainstream American view of contemporary affairs. For example, the entry on **Socialism** generalizes: "All socialists . . . hold certain fundamental beliefs in common. They believe that the existing capitalist society is unjust, that a new society can be created that will improve mankind, and that what is required is a fundamental transformation amounting to a revolution." While some socialists may feel this, certainly the experience of Western European nations with democratic socialist parties in power does not bear this out; in such countries, mixed economies (i.e., a combination of government ownership and private enterprise) have been the rule. The conclusion of the article does note that in the United States "public policy has been influenced to a considerable extent by socialistic ideas, and many early socialist proposals, such as a social security system, have been adopted by the two major political parties." Even this statement, however, is a simplification.

The second sentence in **evolution** states that "some religious groups deny that evolution exists, but most scientists accept it as fact." The article also points out that, contrary to a popular misconception, "the theory states that man and apes had a common ancestor that was neither man nor ape." It acknowledges that "most religious denominations now accept the theory, but in varying degrees," and mentions the ongoing campaign by creationists to teach creationist theory along with evolution theory in public schools. There is no separate article dealing with creationism.

The article on **abortion** fails to mention the intense ongoing debate over the morality of abortion. It simply states that "abortions . . . long were illegal in most of the United States. However, a 1973 decision of the U. S. Supreme Court held that the right of privacy covered a woman's right to end an unwanted pregnancy in the early stages." **Homosexuality** notes that "among psychologists and other experts, much controversy exists as to whether homosexuality is a mental illness," but does not mention the 1974 decision by the American Psychiatric Association to remove homosexuality from its official list of mental disorders.

VIII. Accessibility

New Standard contains a number of basic finding aids that should make it readily accessible to the average intended user. A two-page article in the frontmatter, "Suggestions on How to Use *New Standard Encyclopedia*," with a section on "Finding What You Want Quickly," explains the article's setup clearly and simply.

Entries are arranged alphabetically, word by word. The single exception to this rule is for hyphenated entry words, which are treated as a single word. When several items have the same heading, they are arranged in order of persons, places, and things or ideas. Following standard indexing practice, names beginning with *Mc* are treated as though they begin with *Mac*; the same rule applies to the use of the abbreviation *St.* for *Saint*.

Nevertheless, despite these standard features, the user will encounter some peculiar entry arrangements. A notable example is the arrangement of articles on national literatures. The reader searching for information on American Literature, for example, will find the article not in the A-AND volume, but in the KL volume under **Literature, American**, following the entry for **Literature, African**. The following pages contain articles on **Literature, Arabic**; **Literature, Australian**; **Literature, Babylonian and Assyrian**, and so on. However, this type of article arrangement is not consistent for all national and ethnic literatures. For instance, the entry for **Literature, Anglo-Saxon** instructs the reader to "See LITERATURE, ENGLISH, subtitle *Old English*"; **Literature, Austrian** refers the reader to **Literature, German**; **Literature, Brazilian** sends the user to **Literature, Portugese**, and so forth. *New Standard* is the only general multivolume encyclopedia currently in print that uses this arrangement; every other encyclopedia reviewed in this Buying Guide contains the articles under their normal headings.

Guide words at the top of each page indicate the first and last entries on that page. Page numbers are located at the bottom of each page, flush with the outside margin. (See also *Format*.)

Entry headings are printed in boldface type. There are 13,500 "See" entries which serve only as cross-references. In addition, there are 40,000 cross-references within the text. According to the publisher, these cross-references make the set entirely "self-indexing," and dispense with the need for a general index. Regardless of the quality of the internal cross-referencing features, an index would help readers locate information more efficiently. COMPTON'S, FUNK & WAGNALLS, MERIT, and WORLD BOOK all include full indexes.

IX. Special Features

New Standard includes few special features. Most useful for students will be the bibliographies that follow many of the longer articles, under the heading "Books about [subject]." Many of the bibliographies contain a section devoted to books "For Younger Readers." While the bibliographies are neither extensive nor definitive, they will help lead the reader to additional basic information on the subject. Unlike those in FUNK & WAGNALLS, the bibliographies in *New Standard* do not key individual titles to Dewey Decimal numbers. However, since *New Standard*'s bibliographies are located at the ends of the relevant articles, rather than in a separate volume, they will certainly be much easier for readers to consult than those in FUNK & WAGNALLS.

New Standard's illustrations are of varying quality. Many are too small to give an adequate representation of their subject, and some are outdated. A large number were provided by government tourist agencies or corporate public relations departments; while these photos may be of high technical quality, they do not always give an objective impression of the subject. For example, most of the photographs in *South Africa* were provided by Satour, the official South African tourist authority. Those that illustrate

the country's landscape are attractive and accurate; however, those that show people portray an idyllic society.

Most of the 642 maps in the encyclopedia were prepared by the respected cartographic firm of Rand McNally. However, these maps are not of even quality. American states have full-page (and often two-page spread), full-color maps, whereas many articles on large nations are accompanied by half-page (or smaller) two-color maps that show little detail. In addition, so-called "fact boxes" accompany articles on states and nations, giving basic statistics about those subjects.

X. Format

New Standard Encyclopedia comes in one format—the 17-volume edition. Unlike most general multivolume encyclopedias on the market today, the volumes in *NSE* are not of equal length. Rather (with the exception of *A* and *S*, which are each spread over two volumes), each volume contains all the entries for one, two, three, or four letters. (e.g., Volume 7 contains all the entries beginning with H, I, and J, while Volume 17 contains all the entries beginning with W, X, Y, and Z.) This means that volumes are not equal in length. Volume 16 (U, V) containing 410 pages is shortest, while the longest volume, 6 (F, G) contains 716 pages. The main advantage of this system (which WORLD BOOK also uses) is that the user can know immediately which volume to consult to find a particular entry.

Each volume is bound in a bright red Sturdite binding that should stand up to repeated use over a long period of time. The entire set will take up just under two feet of shelf length, making *New Standard* the most compact multivolume encyclopedia reviewed in this section of the Buying Guide.

XI. Other Opinions

Kenneth Kister, *Encyclopedia Buying Guide* (R. R. Bowker, 1981)—review of 1980 edition: "*New Standard* is a decent but not outstanding encyclopedia that can adequately serve the needs of students and adults, especially those with a limited educational and intellectual background."

Frances Neel Cheney, *ARBA 84*—review of 1983 edition: "[Earlier ARBA reviews of previous editions] noted that treatment of subjects was satisfactory for home use, with some exceptions, showing much improvement in such areas as technology, literature, and certain aspects of the fine arts; that controversial subjects were handled objectively and that there was good coverage of practical information; that illustrations were adequate and generally well integrated with the text; that difficult words in the text were defined, with separate glossaries as needed; and that there was an adequate revision program. Weak points mentioned were the lack of a general index and that from the standpoint of younger users, articles were not related directly to school curricula. Also noted were inadequate treatment of certain specific articles. . . .

"In subject emphasis, biographies are well covered, with the exception of some contemporary figures. Geographical entries give more space to some U. S. states than to some foreign countries . . . Science and technology receive adequate treatment. . . .

"However, libraries will continue to prefer encyclopedias that treat their subjects more fully or that are aimed more directly at the school curriculum, while the increased price [then $559] may make the set less attractive for home purchase."

Booklist (*Reference Books Bulletin*), November 15, 1986: "*New Standard* aims to serve a broad audience. . . . The editors do not use a controlled vocabulary list nor do they subject articles to formal reading-level tests. *New Standard* employs a matter-of-fact, reportorial style throughout. Even in articles on controversial subjects . . . the editors choose merely to summarize opposing viewpoints. *New Standard* has long had a reputation for meeting high standards in both objectivity and accuracy. . . .

"The quality of updating of text varies. . . . As strong as *New Standard* is on recent facts, it is weak in analyzing recent social trends. . . .

"[The] cross-references are integral to the encyclopedia's functioning. . . .

"Overall, the *New Standard Encyclopedia* meets its goal of providing current, accurate basic information about a wide range of topics for readers from middle grades through adult level. . . ."

XII. Summary

While the *New Standard Encyclopedia* is generally well-written, its articles easy to comprehend, and its format easy to use, prospective purchasers should carefully consider its deficiencies in currency and objectivity. Families requiring a simple, straightforward source of practical information may be satisfied with this set. On the other hand, they may find that such competing sets as FUNK & WAGNALLS NEW ENCYCLOPEDIA (at a fraction of the cost) will provide them with a somewhat more balanced, objective, and comprehensive overview of the same information, although on the whole the writing style in FUNK & WAGNALLS may not appeal to students with average or below-average reading ability. WORLD BOOK, by far the most popular encyclopedia for students, according to this Buying Guide's survey of school and public libraries, uses a controlled vocabulary, has a greater array of study aids, is more accessible, and has better illustrations. However, it costs considerably more than *New Standard*.

The *New Standard Encyclopedia* is sold only through independent distributors. Interested individuals should contact Standard Educational Corporation, 200 West Monroe, Chicago, IL 60606; telephone (312) 346-7440. The publisher's suggested retail price for individuals is $649.50. A discount price of $422.50 is available for schools and libraries.

New Talking Cassette Encyclopedia

Facts at a Glance

Full Title: **New Talking Cassette Encyclopedia**.
Former Title: Talking Cassette Encyclopedia.
Publisher: Troll Associates, 320 Route 17, Mahwah, NJ 07430.
Editors: not identified.
Copyright: 1984.

Number of Volumes: 10 albums, each containing 10 cassettes.
Number of Entries: 100.
Number of Indexes: 1 one-page volume guide, with 100 entries.
Cross-references: cross-reference subject guide listing 22 subject categories.
Running Time: approximately 10 minutes per subject (single side of cassette); approximately 16 hours 40 minutes total time.

Intended Audience: grades 2 through 6
Price: $695.
Sold by direct mail and directly from the publisher to libraries and schools.

I. Introduction

The *New Talking Cassette Encyclopedia* is a set of 100 audio cassettes, each devoted to a different subject. All the programs use a single male narrator, with background music and occasional sound effects. However, there are no dramatizations or use of documentary source recordings. The set is designed primarily for elementary school classroom use, and is also suitable as a supplementary resource for elementary libraries. It is not directed toward the blind or visually impaired, although the set will be of interest to such children.

II. Scope and Format

The 100 cassettes are arranged alphabetically by topic into ten "volumes." Each cassette runs for approximately ten minutes; thus, it would take 16 hours and 40 minutes to listen to the entire encyclopedia.

The cassettes can be grouped into several subject areas. For example, eight deal with *American Indians*, seven with *animals*, seven with *astronomy*, fourteen with *famous people*, nine with *geography and foreign lands*, six with *health and safety*, thirteen with *history*, twelve with *land formations and geology*, nine with *nature studies*, and sixteen with *science and technology*. (Several cassettes can be grouped in two or more areas—for example, some belong both to *animals* and to *nature studies*, while some of the *famous people* are also covered under *history* or *science and technology*.) In virtually all instances, tapes are geared to the upper elementary and middle school curriculum. For example, among the subjects covered are **Colonial Life in America**, **American Revolution**, **Oregon Trail**, **George Washington**, **Helen Keller**, **Martin Luther King**, the **Human Body**, **Health and Hygiene**, **Microbes and Bacteria**, **Birds**, **Insects**, the **Seasons**, **Light**, **Water**, **Music**, **Rockets and Satellites**, **Space Exploration and Travel**, and **Computers**. Individual cassettes are also devoted to all the continents as well as to several nations. However, there is no coverage of subjects in language, literature, or mathematics.

III. Authority

Troll Associates is a New Jersey-based producer of educational audiovisual and text materials. The company also publishes juvenile books on sports and hobbies. Troll's first *Talking Cassette Encyclopedia* was released in 1971. The *New Talking Cassette Encyclopedia*, based on this set, was issued in 1984.

According to the publisher, the scripts for the cassettes were written by "experts in the various fields." However, these contributors are not identified, and it is therefore impossible to assess precisely the authority of the *NTCE*.

IV. Currency

Currency is rarely an issue in *NTCE*. The purpose of the set is not to present the latest developments in space exploration, say, or in computers, but to give a general overview of the subject. **Space Exploration and Travel**, produced before the 1986 Challenger explosion, assumes that the shuttle missions have been continuing without any problems. The cassette ends with the sanguine observation that "each [space shuttle] flight brought us closer to the possibility of permanent orbiting space stations and of flights to the stars. And this is just the beginning. Someday, great spacecraft may carry humans to other galaxies in the limitless universe around us." (See also *Objectivity*.)

Other tapes on scientific or technical subjects, such as **Computers**, **Microbes and Bacteria**, **Molecules and Atoms**, are reasonably up-to-date from a 1984 vantage point. Again, the purpose of each tape is to describe the subject in general terms, not to give details of contemporary research. The degree of currency in these tapes is appropriate for the grade level.

V. Accuracy

On the whole, the information provided in *NTCE* is accurate. However, there is a tendency to rely on generalizations that occasionally misrepresent reality.

For example, in **Europe** we are told that "A narrow waterway called the English Channel separates the British Isles from the rest of the continent." It is not altogether accurate to describe the English Channel as "a narrow waterway"—it is narrow relative to an ocean, but considerably wider than a river or canal implied by the term "waterway."

The same article also tells us that "The Western European countries are linked together in an organization called the Common Market. . . . By simplifying trade, the Common Market has done a lot to reduce tensions that caused war in Europe over hundreds of years." The passage implies that all Western European nations belong to the Common Market—they do not. Moreover, a sizeable number of politicians and other informed observers in member nations strongly question whether the EEC indeed "simplifies trade"; in some cases, Common Market rulings have caused tensions between some member nations.

Finally, the tape asserts that "Most of the people of Europe also enjoy a decent standard of living, good housing, and medical care." This statement is the sort of vague generalization that occasionally mars an otherwise acceptable presentation. (See also *Objectivity*.) At any rate, by contemporary American standards, the economic status of many Europeans would be considered substandard.

In **Canada**, we hear that "A number of harbors dot the coast because fishing and shipbuilding have long been the major industries here." This is clearly a non sequitur.

Our reviewers also found some errors. **Space Exploration and Travel** states that the Apollo 11 mission "was followed by five more United States moon shots. On every American lunar mission, a lunar module made a soft landing on the moon's surface." In fact, there were *six* subsequent lunar missions. Because of technical difficulties, one (Apollo 13) did not land on the moon, but returned to earth after circling the moon.

Discussing the influence of Henry David Thoreau on **Martin Luther King, Jr.**, the King tape says that "Thoreau refused to pay a church tax . . . because the United States constitution provides for the separation of church and state." Actually, Thoreau refused to pay a poll tax because he objected to the American war against Mexico. The tape also gives the false impression that King fought against segregation and discrimination simply by preaching: "He was jailed many times for disobeying unjust laws, but he continued to preach love and nonviolence. In this way, he inspired the civil rights movement, and the segregationist structure throughout the nation began to crumble." There is no mention of the many protest campaigns he deliberately organized to challenge segregation laws.

Despite these errors and omissions, it can be fairly argued that, given the level of the intended audience and the brevity of the tapes, some simplification and generalization is necessary and acceptable. Many of the subjects presented in *NTCE* are quite complex, and to explore all their subtleties would require longer tapes. Moreover, to dwell on controversy and to go into full detail would defeat the purpose of the set, which is to provide interesting introductions to selected topics rather than comprehensive fact-filled treatises.

VI. Clarity

Although the narrative on the tapes cannot be described as lively, it is generally interesting and should attract and hold children's attention (provided that the child is not made to listen to several tapes in a row, in which case the material could quickly become boring). The narrator speaks clearly and distinctly, and the background music and occasional sound effects do not overpower the narration. Moreover, the information in each tape is well organized. There is a set structure for each subject category. For example, the **Canada** cassette begins

by telling where Canada is and what it is. The narrator explains the origin of the nation's name: "In the language of the Iroquois Indians, the word Canada means 'a group of huts, or a village." The tape then proceeds with a discussion of five broad aspects of Canada: geography, the provinces and territories, government, history, and the ethnic groups that make up the population of contemporary Canada.

Although the tapes are intended for children, there has apparently been no effort to use a controlled vocabulary. For example, the cassette on **Forests and Jungles** includes the words *tropical, temperate, conifers, deciduous, naturalist, canopy, photosynthesis,* and *understory,* all of which, according to *The Living Word* vocabulary list by Dale and O'Roarke, are well above sixth-grade level. However, it should be stated that many such words are briefly defined in context. Among phrases used to define some of the above words are "conifers, or evergreen trees," "deciduous trees . . . shed their leaves in the autumn," and "photosynthesis, the process by which green plants make food." One disadvantage to the tape format is that the listener cannot see how the word is spelled, nor in a classroom is there always an opportunity to study and memorize the definition before continuing. Here, the lack of a classroom guide with a vocabulary list is a distinct disadvantage.

VII. Objectivity

Perhaps *NTCE*'s most noticeable flaw is its tendency to make sweeping generalizations, broad assumptions, and glowing predictions. For example, the tape on **computers** ends with this statement: "In the future, computers will have an even greater influence on our lives, on technology, indeed on virtually every phase of existence." The implication is that this influence is desirable and will be entirely beneficial. The tape on **Australia** concludes by saying that "For all the growth Australia has already experienced, there is plenty of room for more expansion. . . . Of course, much of [the outback] has not been fit to live on, but as the land is improved by irrigation, and as electric power becomes available to these open areas, all that will change. And as it does, not only Australia but the entire world will profit from it." This conclusion is both vague and highly speculative.

Similarly, the **Canada** tape tells us that "For [all Canadians] the future is filled with the promise of greater prosperity and even greater growth." There is no suggestion that the country has been experiencing serious economic and social difficulties for a number of years. Nor is there any mention of Canada's complex and sometimes uneasy relationship with the United States, or of occasional tensions between the French- and English-speaking populations. On the other hand, the narrator does talk about the disruption of Indian and Eskimo life and culture by the arrival of white Canadians.

VIII. Accessibility

As mentioned, *NTCE*'s tapes come in a package of ten cassette albums, each holding ten tapes. The tapes are arranged alphabetically by subject. The set is accompanied by a one-page volume guide, listing all the tapes album by album, and a two-page "cross-reference subject guide," listing 22 subject categories and the tapes appropriate to each. These guides serve as a table of contents rather than as an index.

Obviously, the tape format has at least one disadvantage in comparison to the printed page. One cannot "skim through" a tape to find a particular bit of information as one can skim through an article. The user simply has to listen to a tape from beginning to end in order not to miss anything. But as has already been mentioned, this is not the sort of reference work intended to be consulted for an answer to a specific question. Conveniently, each subject is presented complete on a single side of a cassette; the other side is a duplication of the first. Therefore, the user does not have to rewind a cassette after use, but can simply play the other side from the beginning and hear the same "article." Of course, the drawback of this format is that using the same number of tapes it could provide twice as much information, or information on twice as many topics.

IX. Special Features

The only special feature associated with *NTCE* is a set of 100 duplicating spirit masters, each containing about a dozen test questions on the subject of one tape. The questions are of the true/false and multiple choice variety; an answer key is provided. Although some teachers may find these questions useful, they in no way enhance the set's encyclopedic qualities, and they do not provide an adequate substitute for a discussion guide.

X. Other Opinions

Booklist (July 1985): "Like a good elementary encyclopedia, these recordings reflect careful consideration of the common science and social studies curricula and condense and present their information in a straightforward manner. This self-contained reference set, however, is not nearly as comprehensive as the smallest one-volume encyclopedia. . . . Ten minutes does not seem to be much time to cover such broad topics as agriculture and the Renaissance, but on these and all other tapes the producers have managed to cover the most important concepts and facts in a logical and interesting way. . . . It would be helpful to have a guide with suggestions for managing and utilizing the materials creatively. For those schools able to afford the cost, these recordings provide good audio materials for library and media center use."

XI. Summary

New Talking Cassette Encyclopedia serves a useful purpose if one recognizes that it is neither an encyclopedia as such, nor a substitute for an encyclopedia. It is not designed to be consulted for specific information, but the tapes do provide users with interesting, well-organized overviews of selected topics, primarily in the natural sciences and social studies. As the *Booklist* review points out, the lack of a user's guide is a major drawback.

There are several inherent disadvantages to an audio format. One of the reasons that these cassettes treat their topics in broad, sweeping terms is that it is impossible to go into much detail in a ten-minute audio presentation. Since all the cassette programs are of roughly equal length, there is no correspondence between the subject's importance and the amount of coverage it receives. Obviously, a ten-minute tape on **Harriet Tubman** can be more comprehensive and specific than can a ten-minute tape on **The Renaissance**—another way of saying that "specific-entry" subjects fare better in this format than do "broad" subjects.

Against these limitations, the *New Talking Cassette Encyclopedia* does have certain advantages over the conventional printed encyclopedia. Like old radio programs, an audio presentation, with its more dramatic script and appropriate sound effects, may arouse some children's imaginations and curiosity more effectively than the printed word can do. It may also be of some benefit to "reluctant readers." Ultimately, however, at a price of $695 the *New Talking Cassette Encyclopedia* cannot be considered competitive with print encyclopedias for the home, school, and library markets.

Individuals and institutions wishing to purchase the *New Talking Cassette Encyclopedia* may order directly from the producer, Troll Associates, 320 Route 17, Mahwah, NJ 07430; telephone (201) 529-4000, or (800) 526-5289.

Tell Me Why

Facts at a Glance

Full Title: **Tell Me Why: Answers to Hundreds of Questions Children Ask.**
Publisher: Grosset & Dunlap.
Author: Arkady Leokum.
Copyright: 1986.

Number of Volumes: 4.
Number of Entries: 900 (225 per volume).
Number of Words: 360,000 (90,000 per volume).
Number of Pages: 832 (208 per volume).
Number of Indexes: 4 (1 per volume).
Number of Index Entries: 2,600 (650 per volume).
Number of Illustrations: 400 (100 per volume),
    black-and-white only.
Trim Size: 7″ × 9″.

Intended Readership: 7- through 14-year-olds.
Price: $9.95 per volume.
Volumes sold individually in bookstores. ISBN 0-448-22501-8; 0-448-22502-6; 0-448-22503-4; 0-448-22504-2.
No scheduled revisions.

I. Introduction

Tell Me Why, a four-volume reference set for readers ages 7 through 14, is designed to provide "brief, accurate answers to hundreds of questions children ask about Our World, How Things Began, The Human Body, How Other Creatures Live, and How Things Are Made." Although *Tell Me Why* is actually a trade book rather than a reference encyclopedia, the publisher describes it as "encyclopedic in scope." Its question-and-answer format is intended to encourage "browsing in specific areas of interest to young readers."

II. Authority

Tell Me Why is published by Grosset & Dunlap, a division of the Putnam Publishing Group, known for a wide range of adult and juvenile trade books. Written by Arkady Leokum, an advertising executive who is also the author of several novels, plays, and children's books, the set derives from Leokum's syndicated newspaper column.

The volumes were originally published as *Tell Me Why* (1965), *More Tell Me Why* (1967), *Still More Tell Me Why* (1967), and *Lots More Tell Me Why* (1972). In 1986 the books were abridged and reissued, with new illustrations and cover design, as *Tell Me Why #1*, *#2*, *#3*, and *#4*.

III. Scope

Each volume is divided into five chapters, the first of which, titled "Our World," covers the natural and social sciences. Among the questions answered in these sections are "What is pollination?" "How do tornadoes start?" "How are caves formed?" "Who was Leonardo da Vinci?" and "Who were the mound builders?"

"How Other Creatures Live" (Chapter 2 in Volumes 2 and 3, and Chapter 4 in Volumes 1 and 4) deals with biology and zoology, answering such questions as, "Can dogs see colors?" "Are rats of any use to man?" "What are nitrogen-fixing bacteria?" and "How do frogs croak?"

Chapter 3 in all the books is titled "The Human Body" and answers such questions as, "Why are there different types of hair?" "What is the RH factor?" "Why do onions make us cry?" and "What is cancer?"

"How Things Began" (Chapter 4 in Volumes 2 and 3, and Chapter 2 in Volumes 1 and 4) concerns "firsts": the first settlers in Canada; first coins, photographs, and records; the inventors of skating, stockings, brooms, and helicopters; the start of kissing, haircutting, fingerprinting, medicine, and religion.

The final chapter of each volume, "How Things Are Made," concerns the physical sciences. Some questions included in these sections are "What is a micrometer?" "What is an atom smasher?" "How do eyeglasses correct vision?" "How does a camera take pictures?" and "How are tunnels built?"

Coverage of topics is often wide-ranging. A typical entry contains about 350 words and answers a specific question. For example, "Who was Hippocrates?" begins with a definition of the Hippocratic oath and a description of the changes in medicine from the early forms that depended on witch doctors, magicians, prayers, and sacrifices, to the beginning of scientific medicine in ancient India, Egypt, and Greece. The article describes Hippocrates' method, and concludes with an excerpt from the Hippocratic oath.

The set is illustrated with 200 black-and-white illustrations—about one every four text pages. Unlike the other encyclopedias for young readers reviewed in this Guide, *Tell Me Why* contains no color illustrations.

IV. Currency

Currency is not a critical issue with a set of this type, since few of the topics included are affected by the passage of time. A comparison of the 1967 and 1986 editions of Volume 2 shows that half the articles from the earlier book were dropped and the remaining articles reprinted verbatim in the current edition without revision. Children seeking answers to questions about nuclear energy, computers, space exploration, or black holes will be not find them in *TMW*. Very few recent developments are mentioned. For example, the article on radio telescopes describes the telescope but none of the discoveries scientists have made using it. The article on the Nobel Prize discusses the awards for work in chemistry, physics, medicine, literature, and peace but fails to mention the prize for economic sciences which was established in 1968 and was first awarded in 1969.

The two-color illustrations of the previous edition have been replaced by black-and-white drawings which lack detail and appeal. Although the illustrations are new, many have a dated look. For example, the drawing accompanying an article on fashion in Volume 4 shows two models with somewhat old-fashioned clothing and hair styles. Similarly, an illustration of a baseball game in Volume 1 shows a batter wearing a cloth cap instead of the regulation batting helmet which has been required since the 1950s.

V. Accuracy

Although much of the content is reasonably accurate, the series is marred by incorrect, misleading, or speculative information. For example, in the article titled **What Was the Industrial Revolution?**, machines are defined as follows: "A machine is like a tool, except that it does nearly all the work and supplies nearly all the power." A machine, in fact, does not supply power but rather needs power supplied to it in order to work.

An entry about the Nobel Prize wrongly implies that Alfred Nobel set out to "help the science of destruction" when, in fact, his intention was to make a smokeless and better explosive. Nobel's fortune was made largely from TNT's commercial rather than its military uses during the period of rapid industrial growth in the latter half of the nineteenth century. Names of two of the prize-winning organizations are cited incorrectly, which reflects a tendency to be careless with facts.

Several articles present speculation as fact. For example, answering the question **How did music begin?** the author writes that "Eventually, man learned to sing, and this was the first man-made music. What do you think would be the first thing man would want to express in song? Happiness? Yes, the happiness of love. The first songs ever sung were love songs."

In the article **Can Animals See in Color?**, the reader is told that "the reason for color-blindness in mammals is connected with the fact that most of them hunt by night and don't depend on color, and also that they themselves are usually dull in color, so it isn't important in their lives." The former is a reasonable assumption, but there is no logical connection between the claim that most mammals are "dull in color" and the conclusion that "color . . . isn't important in their lives." Moreover, this vague assertion does not satisfactorily explain why mammals are color-blind.

VI. Accessibility

Although articles in each volume are arranged under five general categories—Our World, How Things Began, The Human Body, How Other Creatures Live, and How Things Are Made—they are not arranged alphabetically within the category. Nor is there an obvious rationale for locating individual articles in one volume rather than another. In its organization, *Tell Me Why* bears only superficial resemblance to a general multivolume encyclopedia.

Readers can locate specific information in *Tell Me Why* either by browsing through the table of contents in each volume or by consulting each of the four indexes. The table of contents lists chapter number, title, and all the questions contained in the chapter in the order in which they appear in the text. The following listing from Volume 1 is typical:

Chapter 3

The Human Body

How do we grow? 106
Why do we stop growing? 107
What makes us hungry? 108
How do we digest food? 109
What is a calorie? 110

The index at the back of each book alphabetically lists the topics contained in that volume only. There is no index to the set as a whole. To locate all information on **color**, for example, readers must consult the indexes in each of the four books. Unlike CHILDCRAFT, which provides a comprehensive index to the entire set, accessibility in *Tell Me Why* is limited.

When a topic has multiple listings, index entries are descriptive:

Color:

> in birds, 141–142
> of flowers, 51
> in human skin, 117–118
> in leaves, 52
> vision, in animals, 135–136

Some index entries are misleading. For example, the index reference to *space exploration* in Volume 4 directs the reader to the article **Why Do All the Planets Look Different?** Yet the only comment on the topic in that article is this: "We actually know very little about what the planets are made of, and this is one of the questions man hopes to answer with the space explorations that are presently going on and those that are being planned for the future."

Accessibility is enhanced by occasional cross-indexing. For example, readers can find endocrine glands under E (Endocrine glands, 107-8), or under G (Glands, endocrine, 107-8). The indexes also make some use of "see also" references; for example, the index entry for *coins* in Volume 1 directs the reader to "See also *Money*."

VII. Clarity

Tell Me Why is frequently marred by awkward, ungrammatical writing. Consider the following examples: "A person has to be predisposed to epilepsy to have such reactions, because other people may undergo the same chemical changes and not have convulsions. There is a possibility that it is hereditary." "Winning the Nobel Prize is considered by most people the highest honor that can be achieved in certain particular fields such as chemistry, physics, medicine, and literature." "As to how the asteroids were formed, the theory is that a satellite of Jupiter exploded and created these fragments."

Although the questions that serve as occasions for individual articles are usually concise and well-focused, too often the answers are vague and poorly organized. For example, the first paragraph in the article **How Was the Telephone Invented?** reads: "The story of the invention of the telephone is a very dramatic one. (No wonder they were able to make a movie of it!) But first let's make sure we understand the principle of how a telephone works." The article **Who Invented the Camera?** mentions some early steps, but then hedges by saying that "more and more developments were contributed by individuals all over the world as time went on. Many of them are too technical to discuss here, but as you can see, it was

a long slow process of growth." The excerpt on color-blindness in animals already cited (see *Accuracy*) is another illustration of Leokum's loose, often rambling style.

Difficult and unfamiliar words are often used without any attempt to define or clarify them. For example, the reader looking for the answer to **What is the F.B.I.** will encounter the following explanation: "The F.B.I. has authority to investigate violations of Federal laws and matters in which the United States is, or may be, a party in interest. . . . In June, 1939, the President of the United States selected the F.B.I. as the agency responsible for the investigation of espionage, sabotage, and other national matters." According to the *Living Word Vocabulary* by Dale and O'Rourke, most of the intended audience for the set would not know the words *authority*, *investigate*, *violations*, *federal*, *espionage*, or *sabotage*. The legalistic syntax further complicates the passage. This is not an isolated example.

VIII. Objectivity

As the previous excerpt suggests (see *Clarity*), Arkady Leokum takes a highly idiosyncratic, often quirky approach to many of the subjects he treats. This unabashed individuality marks *Tell Me Why* as a trade rather than a general reference title. Suppositions and opinions are sometimes presented as facts without any supporting evidence. For example, the article **When Did Automobile Racing Begin?** asserts that the Indianapolis 500 is "the best-attended sporting event in the whole world." An article about the planets states that "the reason each of the planets looks different to us is that each one seems to be made up of different substances."

Tell Me Why deals with very few potentially controversial subjects. When it does, the treatment is generally evenhanded if cursory. For example, in **What is Evolution?**, the author notes that "While most scientists accept this theory, many people do not. They feel it goes against what is written in the Bible." The article **What Are UFO's?** notes that "no matter what scientific investigations reveal, there will still be people who believe they exist."

Almost without exception, *Tell Me Why* displays a white, middle class, male bias. The words *man* or *men* are invariably used when people are referred to in generic terms, as in the following excerpts: "Men of all races, religions, and degrees of wealth must be treated as equal before the law." "Man has always known that fire can be his friend and servant..."

"Man for a long time has been trying to create a universal language that would serve all men..."

There is an entry about the Boy Scouts but none about Girl Scouts. Names of 142 men are listed in the indexes, but only eight women are listed, although more than eight appear in the text. This, however, may be a consequence of poor indexing rather than of overt sexism.

The accomplishments of women are often trivialized. For example, Hatshepsut is cited as the Egyptian queen who had her likeness carved on a sphinx, while Cleopatra "carried the use of cosmetics to new heights." Joan of Arc, referred to as Joan, is the only woman who is the subject of a biographical article. Marie Curie, with her husband, receives a short paragraph describing their discovery of radium. Clearly, these citations emphasize the stereotypical traits and interests of women and ignore their substantial achievements.

George Washington Carver and Booker T. Washington are the only two blacks represented in biographical articles. Both articles are straightforward and unbiased.

IX. Special Features

Although the publisher describes *Tell Me Why*'s format of questions and answers as a special feature, it is nothing more than a format. The set has no special features.

X. Other Opinions

Upon its publication, *Still More Tell Me Why* (now Volume 3) was called "the kind of book to enrage purists and absorb children" by a reviewer in the [London] *Times Literary Supplement* (July 2, 1971). The review goes on to say that "adults will see it as a heterogeneous collection of facts, poorly organized and with signs that inspiration is running out. . . ." A second *TLS* review (July 14, 1972) notes that "the producers of *Tell Me Why*, realizing they have hit a winning formula, continue to develop it in this companion volume [*More Tell Me Why*, now Volume 2], first published in 1967 and now in its third impression with no signs of revision."

Library Journal (May 15, 1973) characterized *Lots More Tell Me Why* (Volume 4 of the current edition) as a "dull compilation of questions which children supposedly ask" and that "the information it contains can be found more easily in any standard encyclopedia."

XI. Summary

Tell Me Why is based on a sound concept: to provide children with answers to some of the questions they ask about the world. Indeed, the abundant factual tidbits scattered throughout the set provide useful information on many topics. However, the execution rarely matches the concept; the set is poorly edited, and while the content is interesting and entertaining it is often trivial. Although a series such as this could serve as a useful first reference resource, the poor organization and absence of special features greatly diminish its value. Librarians and parents considering this set should be aware that it is not suitable for genuine reference work—nor is it intended to be. For younger children (preschool-grade 3) learning to use encyclopedias, CHILDCRAFT or COMPTON'S PRE-CYCLOPEDIA would be a better choice. For older children (grades 4–8), student encyclopedias such as WORLD BOOK or NEW BOOK OF KNOWLEDGE should be considered.

Volume Library

Facts at a Glance

Full Title: **The Volume Library.**
Publisher: The Southwestern Company, Nashville, Tennessee.
Editors: The Hudson Group, Inc., Pleasantville, NY. Gorton Carruth, Editor-in-Chief; Hayden Carruth, Managing Editor; Courtlandt Canby, Bryan Bunch, and Lawrence T. Lorimer, Editors.
Copyright: 1986.

Number of Volumes: 2.
Number of Contributors: 208.
Number of Pages: 2,519.
Number of Entries: not available.
Number of Words: 2.5 million.
Number of Maps: 200+.
Number of Cross-references: not known.
Number of Indexes: 1.
Number of Index Entries: 22,000 (estimated).
Number of Illustrations: not known.
Trim Size: 11" × 9".

Intended Readership: high school through adult.
Price: $145.
Sold in bookstores and directly by the publisher.
ISBN 0-87197-208-5.
Revised periodically.

I. Introduction

The Volume Library is a two-volume general reference encyclopedia intended for "home and school use." According to the publisher, the work is "designed for interested, well-informed people—students and adults who need a convenient reference book on their home bookshelves, and parents who want to keep up with the subjects their children are studying in school." The work's text and illustrations are intended to "provide clear introductions to all major fields of study and bring together in one convenient volume [sic] much important and hard-to-find information." The editors add that "Only you, the reader, can decide which of the many attractive features of the Volume Library makes it most useful for your purposes."

The publisher further identifies four broad purposes for which *The Volume Library* will be useful: learning, reference, research, and browsing. Thus, its function is not only to serve as a general reference; it is also intended as a pedagogical tool in self-education.

II. Scope

The Volume Library contains some two and a half million words and an unspecified number of entries. Because the encyclopedia is arranged topically rather than alphabetically, and because individual subjects within a section tend to be treated as subsections of longer articles rather than as separate entries, there is no way to obtain a consistent count of the number of entries. (This arrangement is similar to that of the LINCOLN LIBRARY.)

The Volume Library is organized into 26 topical departments (called "volumes" by the publisher, although they are not separate volumes in any common sense of the word). These give an indication of the range of subjects covered by the set, and the amount of space devoted to each. These departments, and the number of pages included in each, are as follows. Book One: **Animals** (66 pages), **Art** (66 pages), **Asia and Australasia** (82 pages), **Astronomy and Space** (50 pages), **Business and Finance** (82 pages), **Computers** (50 pages), **Chemistry and Physics** (82 pages), **Child and Family** (66 pages), **Earth Sciences** (82 pages), **Europe** (145 pages), **Food and Agriculture** (51 pages), **Government and Law** (98 pages), **Health and Life Sciences** (82 pages), **Industry and Technology** (104 pages), **Language** (96 pages). Book Two: **Literature** (130 pages), **Mathematics** (114 pages), **Middle East and Africa** (98 pages), **People** [biographies] (178 pages), **Performing Arts** (66 pages), **Plants** (66 pages), **Religion and Philosophy** (50 pages), **Social Sciences** (66 pages), **South and Central America** (82 pages), **Sports and Recreation** (50 pages), **United States and Canada** (146 pages).

The publisher notes that the subjects included in *Volume Library* can be categorized into six broad areas: History and Geography, Social Studies, Arts and Letters, The Sciences, Practical Arts, and Practical Skills.

III. Authority

Although *The Volume Library* is not a household name in the reference world, it actually has the longest history of all American small-volume general reference encyclopedias. It was first published in a single-volume edition in 1917 by Educators Association, which subsequently issued the book in annual editions through 1962. As the 1981 Bowker *Encyclopedia Buying Guide* notes, the first editor, Henry Woldmar Ruoff, also compiled the 800-page *Standard Dictionary of Facts* (1908-1927), upon which much of the first edition of THE LINCOLN LIBRARY OF ESSENTIAL INFORMATION was based. The close resemblance between THE LINCOLN LIBRARY and *Volume Library* continues to this day.

In 1963, rights to the book were acquired by Cowles Book Company, Inc., and it was retitled *Cowles Comprehensive Encyclopedia: the Volume Library*. A few years later this was abbreviated to *Cowles Volume Library*. The Southwestern Company of Nashville, Tennessee, purchased the book in 1970 and brought it out under the original title. In 1985, because its contents had expanded to well over 2,000 pages, *Volume* was issued in two volumes to facilitate easier handling.

Southwestern (not to be confused with South-Western Publishing Company of Cincinnati, Ohio, which publishes textbooks) also markets popular how-to books (e.g., cookbooks, home decorating books), and does not have wide recognition in the library reference field.

The frontmatter also lists some 200 contributors to the 1986 edition, their credentials, and the subject departments to which they contributed. Our reviewers did not recognize any of the contributors' names. About one-quarter hold positions at universities or institutions, including the Massachusetts Institute of Technology, Princeton University, and the Smithsonian Institution. However, the vast majority are identified simply as freelance writers and editors, or are affiliated with corporations or professional and industry associations. As is the case with the contributors to COMPTON'S ENCYCLOPEDIA, this may affect the objectivity of *Volume Library*. (See also *Objectivity*.)

Based solely on the names and credentials of their respective contributors, *The Volume Library* would appear to be neither more nor less authoritative than Lincoln Library. However, most of its contributors are living, while a high proportion of Lincoln's are deceased. And, more significantly, *Volume* is edited by a highly experienced staff.

IV. Currency

During the 1970s and early 1980s, *The Volume Library* became so severely out-of-date in many subject areas that it could no longer be taken very seriously as a general reference work. Under the aegis of The Hudson Group, however, there has apparently been a concerted effort to substantially revise the encyclopedia. The results of this effort can clearly be seen in this edition.

One notable example is the **Computers** department, which contains a wealth of up-to-the-minute information on different types of computers, their various features and components, and their applications. In fact, this section is as up-to-date as any of the computer and computer-related entries in any of the encyclopedias reviewed in this Buying Guide. The **Computers** department concludes with a highly current and comprehensive "Glossary of Computer Terms" and a bibliography in which virtually all the listed titles were published after 1982.

However, some other departments have been picked up and carried over from the previous editions with only minimal changes. This is evident not only from the content but also from the typeface, graphics, and design, which differ noticeably from those in the newer departments, having a distinctly dated look. (At the same time, the use of a new design in the newer departments may well be a signal that the publisher eventually intends to replace or rewrite all the departments. If this is the case, future editions of *The Volume Library* may be consistently current.) Among the most evidently dated departments in the 1986 edition are **Business and Finance** and **Industry and Technology**, whereas the aforementioned **Computers** is exceptionally recent. Incidentally, in contrast to the **Computers** bibliography mentioned above, the **Business and Finance** bibliography lists two 1975 titles and one 1962 title under "Business and the Computer." Departments on regions of the world (**Asia and Australasia**, **Europe**, **Middle East and Africa**, **South and Central America**, and **United States and Canada**) are generally current through the early 1980s. Population figures for individual nations, for

the most part, are for 1980. As a rule, like the Lincoln Library, *Volume*'s coverage of recent events in nations is not as consistent as the coverage provided by multivolume encyclopedias.

While much of the set is up-to-date, the revision is uneven. Apart from the aforementioned **Computers** department, and the very up-to-date **Health and Life Sciences**, the editors seem to have concentrated on humanities and social science subjects rather than on science and technology in their revisions. Presumably, these areas will be revised in future editions. At any rate, suffice it to say that *Volume Library* is already far more up-to-date than its main competitor, Lincoln Library.

V. Accuracy

Overall, *The Volume Library* is a reasonably accurate and reliable reference work. Much of the inaccuracy that does exist in this encyclopedia is a consequence of outdated information. Some of it, however, seems to be a result of lack of adequate research and editorial carelessness. For example, the entry for the American poet **Theodore Roethke** in the **People** department erroneously reports that his poems are "often based on his Pennsylvania childhood...." Roethke actually spent his entire childhood in Michigan, a fact that the briefest of research would have easily uncovered or that an authority on 20th century American literature would be expected to know. The brief entry for **William Butler Yeats** in the same department rightly describes him as "one of the outstanding figures in 20th-century poetry"; but of the nine works mentioned by title, only two of them are poetry collections, and both are from the early phase of his career. From reading the entry on **Ralph Vaughan Williams**, the reader would not get an inkling of the fact that this 20th century composer wrote nine symphonies.

While it may be unfair to pick on such isolated examples as these, the fact remains that students looking up information on these figures would be misinformed in the first instance and underinformed and misled in the second and third.

The brief entry on **Saturn** states that the planet's atmosphere is composed of 80 percent hydrogen and 18 percent helium; these figures are substantially off from the currently accepted figure of 90 percent hydrogen and approximately 8 percent helium. But the reference to the number of moons ("21 or 23") is accurate according to our present knowledge.

The portion of the article on **semiconductors** that deals with **transistors** is generally accurate and up-to-date. It discusses different types of transistors (including integrated circuits), briefly describing the characteristics and applications of each. The importance of silicon and germanium in semiconductors is also noted.

The article on **money** explains the significance of money as a standard medium of exchange. It also describes the private banking system (and how money "grows") in some detail. The Federal Reserve system, monetary policy, and international trade are also among the related subjects covered. This article is highly technical, and portions may be too advanced for many high school students and adult lay readers. In general, though, *Volume Library* offers a very good and comprehensive treatment of this difficult subject.

Information on the U.S. Bill of Rights is scattered throughout the **Government and Law** department of this encyclopedia, but there is no single entry on the subject. However, the Amendments to the Constitution are printed in their entirety, with brief but helpful marginal annotations.

VI. Clarity

Volume Library contains a fairly wide variety of writing styles, ranging from the scholarly to the popular ("how to"). There seems to have been little editorial effort to achieve a consistency of tone from department to department, although this is not necessarily a negative criticism. Difficult or technical terms are rarely defined in context, but most of the departments conclude with a glossary of commonly-used terms in that subject area.

Although most longer entries in *Volume Library* do not formally follow a "pyramid" style, individual articles are usually well organized. Extended articles often use up to three levels of subheads.

Users will find that some departments are exceptionally clear and well written, while others leave something to be desired in this category. **Literature**, for example, is extremely well-organized. It begins with a 47-page narrative, **History of Literature**. This is followed by an 80-page **Literature Glossary** containing entries for genres (e.g., **biography, epic, fairy tales**), classical and mythological characters (e.g., **Charon, Circe, Furies**), movements (e.g., **angry young men, Irish renaissance, New Criticism**), and specific literary works (e.g., **The Canterbury Tales, The Raven, Wuthering Heights**). These brief entries are ideal for ready reference; they are generally sophisticated for their length and indeed are more comparable to similar entries in the CONCISE COLUMBIA ENCYCLOPEDIA than those in LINCOLN LIBRARY. Incidentally, this department does not contain entries for individ-

ual authors; these may be located in the department **People**.

The following extract from **lighthouse** (in **Communications and Transportation**) illustrates the style of a typical entry in the *Volume Library*:

> **Lighthouse**, a structure surmounted by a powerful light, used in marine navigation. Since the earliest days, the concept of a bright fire on a hill as a warning to ships at sea has been an accepted navigation and warning device. Whether it was recognized or not, the principle that the higher the light is situated the farther it will be visible, was an early proof that the Earth was round.
>
> The earliest harbor planners knew that two lights were highly desirable for a safe entrance, for with two lights on which to base his position, the mariner by triangulation could know definitely where he was. Harbor lighthouses are known as *making lights* because they are the ones the ship's officer sees when he is "making" land.
>
> Another type of light is the *warning light*, such as the famous Eddystone Lighthouse, which is used to mark an especially dangerous spot. *Coasting lights*, which lead the sailor along a coast, are still another type. *Leading lights* lead a ship up a channel or into a harbor. . . .

VII. Objectivity

On the whole, *The Volume Library* is an objective and well-balanced reference work. Although space is limited in this two-volume encyclopedia, the combination of survey articles and specific subject entries allows the editors to address a number of controversial topics.

The department **Religion and Philosophy** includes straightforward, evenhanded descriptions of virtually all religions, religious denominations, and sects.

Evolution is discussed in **The Origin of Life and Life Processes**, part of the **Life Sciences** section in the **Health and Nutrition** department. Various hypotheses are described, but scientific creationism is not among them. Nor is there a separate entry for scientific creationism anywhere in *Volume Library*.

Homosexuality is discussed briefly in the **Marriage and Family** section of the **Child and Family** department. The discussion notes that

> Even though many societies (including our own) have discouraged homosexual behavior, it continues to exist. . . . There is no general agreement on what causes homosexuality. Evidence suggests that certain people

may have a biological predisposition. Other evidence suggests that a homosexual orientation may be fostered by experiences in early childhood. . . . Most psychologists agree that homosexuality is not an emotional illness but a part of some people's makeup that is unlikely to change.

Addressed primarily to parents and adolescents, the **Child and Family** department in particular largely adopts a textbook tone. The writers take particular pains to avoid offending any readers who may hold differing points of view. For example, **Dating and Sex** (part of the **Adolescence** section of this department) contains the following paragraph:

It seems clear that parents must offer their teenage children a clear explanation of their own moral and religious beliefs about sex and dating. They need also to set certain limits on the activities of teenagers, if for no other reason than to express concern for the child's well-being. At the same time, the parent must realize that the child has, in fact, the ability to act according to his own wishes and desires. Moreover, the time is approaching when the child will be an adult who must negotiate the world of sex and dating without any parental intervention. It is the parents' job, then, to offer guidelines and assistance where necessary, with the goal of having the adolescent develop his own rational and coherent set of moral standards.

Clearly this passage is prescriptive, not descriptive. This illustrates the educational, as opposed to strictly reference, function of *Volume Library*.

VIII. Accessibility

Volume Library is a highly accessible and easy-to-use reference work. Accessibility is facilitated by the work's straightforward organization into 26 clear-cut topical departments (see *Scope*), the table of contents, and the 159-page index. Moreover, sections, subsections, and specific entries within individual departments are clearly identified.

There is a thumb index for each department, making it easy for both the casual browser and the serious researcher to locate a particular topical section quickly. (LINCOLN LIBRARY also includes thumb indexes, but has only 13 compared to *Volume*'s 28.) Guide words at the top of each page also alert the reader to the nature of the topical section.

The only major impediment to accessibility is the general lack of cross-references, which are found only in the introductions to individual departments. Printed in small capitals, these tend to direct the reader to

general sections elsewhere in *Volume Library* rather than to specific entries.

Volume's index contains some 22,000 entries, making it quite comprehensive for an encyclopedia of this size. Entries are arranged alphabetically, letter by letter, regardless of punctuation. Names beginning with *Mac* or *Mc* are arranged as they are actually spelled. Entry words are printed in boldface type, making them easy to locate on the index page. Page numbers are followed by *a*, *b*, or *c*, indicating the column on the page where the pertinent information will be found. The index is preceded by a concise section on "How to Use the Index" and by a list of abbreviations.

IX. Special Features

Perhaps the most noteworthy special feature is the 55-page **Atlas** department, which in comprehensiveness and overall quality rivals some of the atlases reviewed in the atlas section of this Buying Guide. There are 31 four-color maps, the majority of them two-page spreads and many containing insets, as well as two pages of illustrated information on map projections. The cartography was produced by Rand McNally and is up to their generally high standard. Useful indexes for each map are printed on the outside margin of the page on which the map is located. The **Atlas** section is printed on glossary, heavy stock paper.

Volume's glossaries are also worthy of comment. They are extensive, accurate, and (especially in the **Health and Life Sciences** department), generally up-to-date. Many of the glossary entries rival the general content entries in the entry-specific single volume CONCISE COLUMBIA and NEW AMERICAN DESK encyclopedias.

There are an unspecified number of illustrations. Each department opens with a full-page, four-color photograph. These are designed to identify the department rather than to illustrate a particular aspect of the broad subject covered in that department. These photos are clear, dramatic, and up-to-date. Other color photos are included in plates in **Animals, Art, Astronomy and Space, Earth Sciences, Performing Arts, Plants, Sports and Recreation,** and **United States and Canada**. There are also eight pages of **Human Anatomy** color plates in **Health and Life Sciences**. The great majority of illustrations, however, are in black-and-white. Some show signs of age, but most that are intended to illustrate contemporary situations do so. It seems clear that as some of the less up-to-date departments are revised in future editions, old illustrations in these departments will be replaced. At any rate, the illustrations in the 1986 *Volume Library* are already unquestionably more extensive than, and superior to, those in LINCOLN LIBRARY.

X. Summary

The Volume Library makes for interesting and often edifying reading. As the publisher intends, it is effective for browsing and will also provide answers to some ready-reference questions.

Volume's price of $145 is similar to the cost of LINCOLN LIBRARY ($139.95), so price will not be a decisive factor in choosing between the two sets. Despite occasional lapses, *Volume* is to be preferred in terms of scope, clarity and currency. It is easily more accessible, and on the whole maintains a higher degree of accuracy. Neither set can claim outstanding authority, but here *Volume* would also seem to have the edge over its main competitor. In short, *The Volume Library* is a pleasantly surprising find, and it is hoped that future editions will continue to improve on the quality of the current set.

Like the other small-volume encyclopedias reviewed in this Buying Guide, *Volume Library* is sold in some bookstores. It can also be ordered directly from the publisher, Southwestern Company, Box 810, Nashville, TN 37202, telephone (615) 790-4000.

[Note: As this Buying Guide was in production, a revised edition of *Volume Library* was in preparation and due to be issued in late 1987 or early 1988.]

Webster's Beginning Book of Facts

Facts at a Glance

Full Title: **Webster's Beginning Book of Facts.**
Publisher: Merriam-Webster Inc.
Copyright: 1978 by Encyclopaedia Britannica, Inc.

Number of Volumes: 1.
Number of Entries: 88.
Number of Pages: 384.
Number of Illustrations: approximately 400.
Trim Size: 7¾" × 9⅛".

Intended Readership: 4- to 8-year-olds.
Price: $9.95
Sold in bookstores; also available directly from the publisher. ISBN 0-87779-074-4.
No revision policy; no scheduled revision.

I. Introduction

Published and distributed by the well-known dictionary maker Merriam-Webster Inc., *Webster's Be-*

ginning Book of Facts is a single-volume abridgement of the YOUNG CHILDREN'S ENCYCLOPEDIA for preschool and beginning readers. Arranged alphabetically, it is described as "a collection of articles covering a variety of popular topics" intended "to stimulate and entertain, to amuse and inform, and, while satisfying a child's curiosity, to demonstrate that reading and learning are fun." Like the other books for this age group reviewed in this Buying Guide, *Webster's Beginning Book of Facts* does not purport to be an encyclopedia, per se.

Authority, currency, accuracy, clarity, and objectivity are discussed in the review of the YOUNG CHILDREN'S ENCYCLOPEDIA on pages 206-10.

II. Scope

The publisher states that *Webster*'s 88 articles, chosen from the 642 in the *YCE*, "represent the kinds of things that young children find endlessly fascinating." This claim is generally justified. Topics such as airplanes, crocodiles, eclipses, fireflies, insect-eating plants, raisins, volcanoes, and zippers have been included. More than 60 articles deal with science and nature. There are five articles each on geography and transportation and four about food. Articles average 400 words and cover about four pages with illustrations.

Like the *YCE*, *Webster*'s rarely deals with the sort of precise facts that one would expect to find in a more advanced encyclopedia. Time and quantity, for example, are written as "long, long ago" and "billions of tiny droplets." However, despite this occasional vagueness, the articles generally provide useful, comprehensible information. For example, in the article "What's a Cloud?" the reader is told that "it takes billions of tiny droplets to make a big cloud.... Sometimes the water droplets form around tiny pieces of dust in the air. These droplets with dust in them get bigger and bigger as they join together until they become too heavy to float and they fall... And that's rain!"

Full-color illustrations accompany each entry, adding to the visual appeal and instructional value of the book. These illustrations are identical to those found in the same entries in the *YCE* and in COMPTON'S PRECYCLOPEDIA.

III. Accessibility

Webster's generic entries are listed alphabetically in a clear, easy-to-use two-page table of contents at the beginning of the book. The book does not contain any indexes or cross-references; in any event, such features would be largely superfluous in a book of this size and scope. Guide words, corresponding to the listings in the table of contents, appear at the beginning of each article. In addition to its generic subject title, each entry also has a descriptive title. For example, the entry on **dinosaurs** is called "Monsters of the Past."

IV. Summary

Webster's Beginning Book of Facts is a colorful, well-illustrated collection of articles on a variety of popular topics. Although the coverage is somewhat arbitrary and incomplete, the choice of topics is good, and should prove interesting to preschool children. The stories and descriptive articles are sufficiently detailed yet brief enough to gain and hold the preschooler's attention when read aloud by a parent or older sibling or friend. Children in grades 3-5 would benefit more from a multivolume set more akin to a standard encyclopedia, such as CHILDCRAFT, COMPTON'S PRECYCLOPEDIA, or the YOUNG CHILDREN'S ENCYCLOPEDIA. At $9.95, *Webster's Beginning Book of Facts* performs its functions well and is recommended for families with young children and a limited budget. It is also appropriate for the circulating portion of a library's young readers' reference collection.

World Book Encyclopedia

Facts at a Glance

Full Title: **The World Book Encyclopedia**.
Publisher: World Book, Inc., 510 Merchandise Mart Plaza, Chicago, IL 60654.
Editors: William H. Nault, Publisher; Robert O. Zeleny, Editor-in-Chief; A. Richard Harmet, Executive Editor.
Copyright: 1987.

Number of Volumes: 22.
Number of Contributors: more than 3,000.
Number of Entries: 18,300.
Number of Pages: 14,000.
Number of Words: 10,000,000.
Number of Maps: 2,350.
Number of Cross-references: 100,000.
Number of Indexes: 1.
Number of Index Entries: 150,000.
Number of Illustrations: 14,500 four-color; 14,500 black-and-white.
Trim Size: 7¼″ × 9¾″.

Intended Readership: elementary through general adult.
Price: $599 plus $29 shipping and handling; $499 (including delivery) to schools and libraries.

Sold through local representatives, or direct from World Book, Inc. ISBN 0-7166-0087-0. Revised annually.

I. Introduction

World Book is a 22-volume general encyclopedia whose purpose, in the words of the publisher, is fourfold:

(1) To select information from the vast reservoir of knowledge about humanity, the world, and the universe of which we are a part; (2) To provide for the general dissemination of this knowledge in the most accessible and usable form possible for homes, schools, and libraries; (3) To meet the reference and study needs of students in elementary school, junior high school, and high school—as well as other members of the family, at a level of understanding appropriate to the user; and (4) To provide an everyday reference tool for librarians, teachers, business and professional men and women, and the general public.

II. Scope

World Book contains more than 18,300 entries. With some ten million words spread over more than 14,000 pages, articles in the set average about 550 words. Minor subjects such as **Navajo National Monument** may be treated in only a half-dozen lines (about 45 words), whereas more complex and more important subjects such as **United States History** may have upwards of 50 pages. The length of a particular article generally reflects the emphasis that the subject receives in American school curricula. Different facets of some broad subjects are also discussed under separate entries. For example, *World Book* devotes separate articles to the **United States** (38 pages), **United States Government** (10 pages), and **United States History** (53 pages).

World Book includes a combination of short, specific-entry articles and longer survey articles. Therefore, information found in a specific-entry article will also be found in a related broad survey entry. For example, the article on **plants** contains a section about algae. The reader will also find information on this subject by consulting the entry for **algae**.

Article lengths are usually in proportion to the subject's relative importance; only occasionally do article lengths seem out of proportion. The most notable example of this our reviewers found concerns the entry for **Henry Wadsworth Longfellow**, to whom *World Book* devotes three full pages. By contrast, **Emily Dickinson**, a far more significant figure in

World Book Encyclopedia

must be moved rapidly from one target to the next.

During the late 1960's, physicists perfected the *laser*, a complex device that produces an intense beam of light. Their work resulted in the development of optical radars, which operate at the high frequencies of laser light. This type of radar requires an antenna only about the size of a thumbtack to send out an extremely narrow signal beam.

❶ Radar in the Future. Researchers today are seeking ways to reduce the size of microwave radars and to manufacture them at low cost. They expect to produce inexpensive, pocket-sized units by using integrated circuits, microprocessors, and other miniature electronic equipment. These radar units could be widely used as aids for blind people and as collision-warning devices in cars. Compact radar sets might also be carried in spacecraft to study the earth's atmosphere in greater detail and to make weather predictions more accurate. In addition, large radars might be built in space to track ship and air traffic over half the earth from one point.   G. D. Thome

❷ Related Articles in World Book include:

Airport	Microwave	Range Finder
DEW Line	Navigation	Shoran
Electronics	Radio	Watson-Watt,
Guided Missile	Rain (Measuring	Sir Robert A.
Laser	Rainfall)	

Outline

❸
I. **The Uses of Radar**
  A. In Aviation
  B. In Ship Navigation
  C. In the Military
  D. In Controlling Automobile Speed and Traffic
  E. In Weather Observation and Forecasting
  F. In Scientific Research
  G. In Space Travel
II. **How Radar Works**
  A. Pulse Radar
  B. Continuous-Wave Radar
III. **The Parts of a Radar Set**
  A. The Oscillator   F. The Receiver
  B. The Modulator   G. The Signal Processor
  C. The Transmitter   H. The Display
  D. The Duplexer   I. The Timer
  E. The Antenna
IV. **The Development of Radar**

Questions

❹
What are some uses of radar in scientific research?
Why was the magnetron important in the development of radar?
How does pulse radar find the distance to an object?
What is a Plan Position Indicator?
What are some military uses of radar?
What is the special feature of phased array radar?
How does radar help weather forecasters?
What is Doppler radar? How is it used?
Why is radar an effective aid in ship navigation?
What is a duplexer? Why is it important?

Additional Resources

❺
Battan, Louis J. *Radar Observation of the Atmosphere*. Rev. ed. Univ. of Chicago Press, 1973.
Coombs, Charles I. *Spacetrack, Watchdog of the Skies*. Morrow, 1969. For younger readers. Explains various types of radar installations and operations circling the North American continent.
Jones, Raymond F. *Radar: How It Works*. Putnam, 1972.
Page, Robert Morris. *The Origin of Radar*. Greenwood, 1979.

RADCLIFFE-BROWN, A. R. (1881-1955), a British anthropologist, helped develop present-day American

❻ RADIANT HEATING

and British anthropological theories. Alfred Reginald Radcliffe-Brown was born in England and was graduated from Cambridge University. After many years of research and teaching in London, Australia, and the Union of South Africa, he taught at the University of Chicago from 1931 to 1937. Radcliffe-Brown then became the first professor of social anthropology at Oxford University.   David B. Stout ❼

RADCLIFFE COLLEGE is a private liberal arts college for women in Cambridge, Mass. It is affiliated with Harvard University, and Radcliffe students are the women undergraduates at Harvard. Radcliffe is a separate institution with its own board of trustees. But at the undergraduate level, it shares classes, housing, and other facilities with Harvard. The Harvard faculty provides all instruction for Radcliffe undergraduates. Radcliffe operates its own program of continuing education and a fellowship program for advanced study.

Radcliffe was founded in 1879. In 1943, Radcliffe made an agreement with Harvard that all courses offered by Harvard's Faculty of Arts and Sciences would be open to Radcliffe students. Since 1963, Radcliffe graduates have received degrees from Harvard. See also ❽ HARVARD UNIVERSITY.   Matina S. Horner

RADFORD, ARTHUR WILLIAM (1896-1973), an admiral in the United States Navy, served from 1953 to 1957 as chairman of the Joint Chiefs of Staff. Born in Chicago, he graduated from the U.S. Naval Academy, and served during World Wars I and II. Radford won recognition as an expert on naval aviation and aircraft-carrier warfare. He was commander in chief of the U.S. Pacific Fleet from 1949 to 1953.   Donald W. Mitchell ❾

RADIAN is a metric unit used to measure angles. Engineers and scientists frequently measure angles in radians because the unit simplifies many of their calculations. Navigators, surveyors, and most other people measure angles in degrees. One radian equals an angle of 57.29578 degrees.

An angle of 1 radian is formed between two radii of

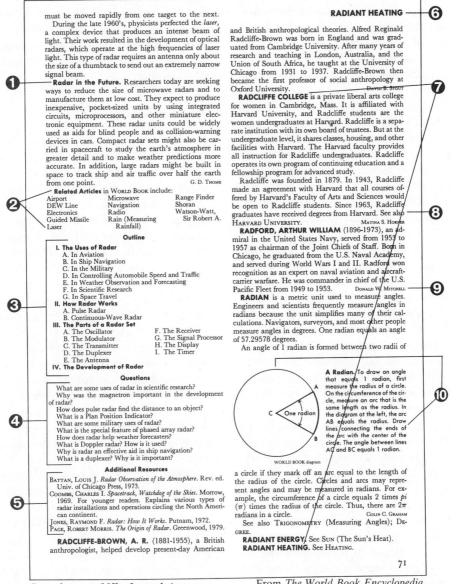

A Radian. To draw an angle that equals 1 radian, first measure the radius of a circle. On the circumference of the circle, measure an arc that is the same length as the radius. In the diagram at the left, the arc AB equals the radius. Draw lines connecting the ends of the arc with the center of the circle. The angle between lines AC and BC equals 1 radian.

WORLD BOOK diagram

a circle if they mark off an arc equal to the length of the radius of the circle. Circles and arcs may represent angles and may be measured in radians. For example, the circumference of a circle equals 2 times *pi* (π) times the radius of the circle. Thus, there are 2π radians in a circle.   Colin C. Graham

See also Trigonometry (Measuring Angles); Degree.

RADIANT ENERGY. See Sun (The Sun's Heat).
RADIANT HEATING. See Heating.

71

Page shown at 66% of actual size.

From *The World Book Encyclopedia*.
© 1987 World Book, Inc.

❶ Article subhead

❷ "Related articles" cross-references: Handy lists suggest further readings about related subjects in World Book.

❸ Article outline: Outlines of extended articles give an overview of the subject and help the reader see the relationship of different parts.

❹ Review questions: Extended articles are followed by review questions that help users determine how much they have learned.

❺ Bibliography: More than 1,500 articles are accompanied by reading lists. Some titles are annotated.

❻ Guide word

❼ Main entry: World Book contains 18,300 articles, arranged alphabetically, word-by-word, plus extensive cross-reference entries. Entry words are printed in boldface capitals.

❽ "See also" cross-reference: World Book includes more than 100,000 cross-references in all.

❾ Contributor's credit: World Book has more than 3,000 contributors. All articles, except those written by World Book Staff, are signed.

❿ Illustration and caption: World Book contains more than 29,000 illustrations, about half of them in color. Captions in World Book often provide specific factual information.

American literature, is given only a half page; even **Charles Dickens** gets less space than **Longfellow**. (On the other hand, 29 pages are devoted to **Shakespeare**, a major subject of study in high school English classes.)

As an indication of how space is apportioned among different subjects, **Charlemagne** receives about two-and-a-half pages (including a map); **Konstatin Chernenko** receives about one-quarter of a page, as does **Ty Cobb**. The article on the **Civil War** occupies 22 pages; the entry for **Christianity** contains about three-and-a-third pages; and **China** is covered in 34 pages.

World Book provides well-balanced if not comprehensive coverage of topics in all major subject areas. While the editors are justly proud of the encyclopedia's readability and of its suitability for use by students, prospective purchasers should be aware that *World Book* is not merely a "school encyclopedia." It covers a wealth of subjects that are not, strictly speaking, part of any school curricula but that will be of interest and importance to students and adults alike. Particular attention is given to subjects in which students may have frequent need for research information (e.g., **American Indians**, 49 pages; **cell**, 13½ pages; **insects**, 24 pages).

While the publisher has not provided this Buying Guide with a percentage breakdown of subject areas, our examination of the 1987 set indicates that all major subject areas receive more than adequate coverage, and that there are no obvious serious weaknesses in the coverage of any particular area. Topics in geography, history, natural sciences, physical sciences, the arts, literature, and language all receive a fair amount of exposure. In addition, the encyclopedia has good coverage of non-academic, general-interest subjects. Based on a random sampling of entries throughout the set, this Buying Guide estimates that about 25 percent of the articles are biographies, while an equal number deal with natural history, the natural sciences, or medicine. Some 20 percent discuss nations or geographical features. The remaining articles seem to be divided equally among the other subject areas.

Entries dealing strictly with history seem less numerous than those in other subject areas. However, the reader should note that many of the entries in the biography and geography categories, among others, contain a good deal of historical information. Furthermore, a large portion of the history entries tends to be longer than the 550-word average entry length.

World Book, like Compton's Encyclopedia, emphasizes American and Canadian history, geography, and culture. For example, more than 23 pages are devoted to the state of **South Carolina**, whereas the nation of **South Africa** is covered in 14 pages. The entire continent of **South America** is dispatched in 17 pages. Individual South American nations do receive generous coverage in their own entries, however: **Argentina** gets 14 pages, **Brazil**, 20, and **Columbia**, 7. This coverage seems quite adequate and appropriate.

III. Authority

World Book has been published in one form or another since 1917, when it first appeared in eight volumes. The encyclopedia quickly grew in both size and reputation. By 1933, the set had been expanded to 19 volumes. No less important, its first editor, Michael Vincent O'Shea, a former education professor at the University of Wisconsin, established high standards of accuracy, clarity, and accessibility. These standards were upheld by his successor, John Morris Jones, who assumed the editorship in the 1940s. Dr. William H. Nault, who succeeded Jones in 1962, has continued to be active in the planning and managing of the set.

World Book was owned by a variety of Chicago-based companies until 1978, when it was bought by the Scott Fetzer Company, an Ohio firm known primarily as a manufacturer of household appliances. Despite this unlikely ownership, however, the encyclopedia seems to operate with a high degree of editorial independence under the aegis of World Book, Inc.

While Dr. Nault serves as Publisher and as General Chairman of the Editorial Advisory Boards, *World Book*'s editorial staff is headed by Robert O. Zeleny as Editor-in-Chief. Some 40 editors are employed in-house, and the publisher also keeps additional art, research, and production staff on hand.

The staff is supported by an extensive and highly structured network of advisors, consultants, and contributors, who are scholars or specialists in their fields. These individuals not only approve article revisions, but also alert editors to areas in which recent developments necessitate revision or the addition of new articles. In all, the set boasts more than 3,000 authors, authenticators, illustrators, reviewers, and consultants.

The frontmatter lists contributors and consultants, noting their credentials and the articles to which they have contributed. The majority hold impressive posts at major colleges and universities, while others are prominent in professional organizations and publications. Among well-known names on the list are Isaac Asimov, Samuel Eliot Morison, Arthur Schlesinger, Jr., and Werner von Braun. Whereas some other encyclopedia publishers may be seen to use "big names" primarily to give prestige to the product, judging by the credits pages and by the quality of individual articles, the specialists who contributed to *World Book* seem to have been well-chosen and to have fulfilled their assignments most conscientiously.

Most articles are signed. Brief, unsigned articles dealing with particular organizations or with historic sites have frequently been authenticated by officials of these organizations. For example, the article **Camp David** was critically reviewed by the Military Office of the White House, while that on the **Camp Fire** organization was critically reviewed by Camp Fire, Incorporated. By and large, this practice does not seem to have affected the objectivity of these articles. (See also *Objectivity*.)

IV. Currency

With its experienced staff and extensive network of consultants and content experts, *World Book* is able to remain admirably up-to-date. The encyclopedia is revised annually. In the period from 1982 to 1987, an average of 5,100 pages (more than one-third of the set) underwent partial or complete revision each year. During this time, more than 450 new articles were added to *World Book*, and over 9,000 existing articles were completely or partially revised. Based on a comparison of the revision figures we have received from the publishers of the encyclopedias reviewed in this Buying Guide, *World Book* undergoes a more extensive annual revision than any other encyclopedia now on the market. In the publisher's words, "*World Book* makes revisions in every field of knowledge or activity whenever developments make it appropriate to do so. Every subject in the volume is under continuing surveillance. The revision program is never confined to any one area or to any one volume."

As well as updating and adding text where necessary, *World Book* also ensures that the statistical information it provides is the most recent available. Population data are always drawn from the most recent census available, the publisher claims; this appears to be true. Furthermore, whenever possible the encyclopedia also gives population figures for 1987 (the year of publication) and projected figures for the near future. For example, **South Africa** reports the nation's 1980 census figures, plus estimates of the 1987 and 1992 population.

Sports tables are updated annually to include the winners of major national and international championship events. Other articles in subject areas in which statistics change rapidly, such as the economy, also receive annual updates. For example, **money** includes a table of currency exchange rates for February 28, 1986.

World Book's comprehensive revision policy is evident in the text of individual articles. The article on **Ronald Reagan**, for example, is as current as could be expected for an encyclopedia available for distribution in early 1987, mentioning the U. S. air strikes against Libya in April 1986, and the Reykjavik summit meeting that took place in October of that year. Other articles on important subjects are equally up-to-date. **United States History** contains a half-page discussion of events and issues in the 1980s within the subsection "Recent Developments." **Russia** concludes by mentioning the accident at the nuclear power plant in Chernobyl. Information about the Chernobyl accident has also been incorporated into *World Book*'s articles on **nuclear energy** and the **nuclear reactor**.

South Africa describes the constitution adopted in 1984 and renewed outbreaks of violence. It ends: "In July 1985 and again in June 1986, the government declared states of emergency in large black areas. Under the states of emergency, the government was allowed to arrest and hold people without a charge." However, there is no mention of the trade sanctions imposed on South Africa by other nations in an attempt to persuade the South African government to abandon its policy of apartheid. Similarly, **space travel** ends with a mention of the *Challenger* explosion, but does not discuss the causes or consequences of the tragedy.

World Book also includes a significant number of new or thoroughly revised articles in science and technology. The articles on **biology** and **chemistry** were revised and re-illustrated for the 1987 edition. New articles have been added to deal with such highly specialized subjects as the **artificial heart**, **Grand Unified Theories**, and **Magellanic Clouds**, among others. *World Book*'s coverage of **AIDS** is as up-to-date as that of any encyclopedia reviewed in this Buying Guide.

Spot checks of less significant subjects indicate that revision has not been limited to the more obvious entries. For example, the biographical entry for **Woody Allen** has added the 1986 film *Hannah and Her Sisters* to the list of his pictures. The article on **recording** mentions the compact disc and some of its advantages. And **Statue of Liberty** describes in detail the restoration of the statue, and also includes several photographs and diagrams illustrating how the restoration was carried out.

World Book does include up-to-date entries on such subjects of contemporary interest as **sports medicine** and **terrorism**. **Corazon Aquino** is among the contemporary figures who gets a biographical entry for the first time in the 1987 edition. The four-page article **woman** contains an extensive section on "Women's Roles Today," which discusses the impact of legislation and the women's liberation movement as well as employment and the roles of women in other countries.

World Book's thorough revision policy applies to illustrations as well as text and statistical material. Throughout the set, photos are up-to-date; those intended to depict contemporary scenes indeed show no signs of anachronism. In terms of currency, *World Book*'s illustrations are second to none.

V. Accuracy

The same attention to detail evidenced by *World Book*'s revision policy also helps ensure that the facts presented in the encyclopedia are accurate. Contributors, reviewers, and editors have evidently done their jobs well. Our reviewers found few factual errors, and those mostly insignificant.

Among the more notable errors is the statement in **religion** that "Christianity was founded by Jesus Christ..." In fact, Jesus did not found an organized religion; rather, his early followers founded a church based on his teachings.

On a more worldly scale, **Henry the Navigator** states that in planning Portugese expeditions the 15th-century prince "was aided by mapmakers, astronomers, and mathematicians of many nationalities, whom he gathered together at Sagres. . . ." This is true, but fails to mention that Henry sponsored voyages to Africa primarily to extend Portugal's trade rather than to discover new territories or advance European knowledge.

Our subject specialists found that *World Book* entries are generally sound and reliable, if occasionally superficial. For instance, the information in **brain** is well organized and relatively complete, and the illustrations complement the text nicely. **Money** provides an accurate history of U. S. currency, although the exchange-rate table is poorly designed. **Saturn** is reliable, even though it fails to incorporate some recent findings. On the other hand, *World Book*'s accurate entry on transistors is marred by some out-of-date information and an obsolete illustration. The encyclopedia covers a wide range of **bills of rights**, but its discussion of the American Bill of Rights is extremely short and not especially useful.

Some articles do display a tendency to stereotype or to make generalizations which, while true in some respects, may oversimplify the truth. An obvious instance of this occurs in the discussion of national cultures and way of life. This may be a consequence of the editors' attempt to make the articles in *World Book* accessible and interesting to a wide range of readers. (For an example of this, see the reference to **Ireland** in *Objectivity*.)

On the whole, *World Book* remains a remarkably accurate and informative source of information. What it sometimes lacks in depth, it makes up for in breadth.

VI. Clarity

One of *World Book*'s major strengths is its readability. According to the publisher, each article in *World Book* is the result of curriculum analysis, classroom research, and "an elaborate procedure of editing, copy editing, and review" designed to ensure "that information is presented in a simple, direct style that meets the most exacting standards of readability."

Additionally, the publisher states that "the editors establish an appropriate age level or levels for most *World Book* articles by using information from the curriculum analysis and classroom research programs. Vocabulary is geared to the proper age group . . . *World Book* editors use words that can be understood at the grade level of the article. . . ." In other words, articles on simple subjects dealt with in elementary schools (e.g., **lion**) are written at grade-school reading level. More complex subjects that will only be encountered by advanced students at higher grades (e.g., **physics**) are discussed on a more sophisticated level. Many longer articles use the "pyramid" approach, presenting simpler concepts in easy language at the beginning of the article and gradually building toward more complex concepts and more sophisticated language as the article progresses.

The publisher determines the appropriate reading level for individual articles from an ongoing survey of 400 classrooms throughout the United States and Canada. World Book, Inc. also conducts an extensive analysis of school curricula. Editors verify the reading level in each article by applying readability guidelines developed by Dr. Edgar Dale, the noted reading authority. Overall, *World Book*'s attention to school curricula and the school student's research needs is second to none.

The following extract from **lighthouse** illustrates the style of a typical entry in *World Book*:

Lighthouse is a tower with an extremely strong light that serves as a navigational aid for mariners. Lighthouses help sailors determine their position, inform them that land is near, and warn them of dangerous rocks and reefs. Lighthouses are built at ports and harbors, on capes and peninsulas, and on isolated rocks. Some are built in the sea itself, with their foundations sunk into rock or coral beneath the water.

Lighthouses have been used as navigational aids for thousands of years. Since the 1940's, however, they have declined in importance because of the development of advanced navigational aids (see NAVIGATION [Electronic Navigation]). As a result, the number of lighthouses operated in the United States has declined from about 1,500 in the early 1900's to about 340 today. In fact, there are only about 1,400 lighthouses currently in use worldwide.

VII. Objectivity

In nearly every respect, *World Book* adheres to high standards of objectivity. The encyclopedia does not avoid dealing frankly with controversy, but neither does it sensationalize or give more attention to unpleasant facts than is necessary to give the reader a fair understanding of the subject. Throughout the set, in articles dealing with controversial or potentially controversial issues, the writers are careful to maintain an impartial tone.

For example, in assessing **Andrew Jackson's** career and personality, *World Book* does not overlook his flaws, but does not draw undue attention to them. It mentions his "hair-trigger temper," his removal of the Indians to the West, and his use of the spoils system, but in general portrays Jackson as an energetic, forward-looking president.

World Book's coverage of **South Africa** is admirably objective. The encyclopedia is especially strong in delineating the various complex strands that have formed South Africa's history and its present social structure. For example, the article does not take the government's race classifications at face value, pointing out that each race is not a homogenous community:

Each group's way of life... reflects not only its inherited traditions but also the fact that it must associate with other groups in economic activities. Differences exist within each racial group as well as between the groups. In each group, some people have better jobs and make more money than others. Even in the black, Asian, and Colored communities—which have many very poor people—there are successful executives and professional persons. Political differences also exist within the groups. For example, most whites vote for politicians

who support apartheid, but some vote for candidates who oppose the policy. Some blacks would like to drive whites out of the country. Yet other blacks believe in cooperating with whites to build a new society without racial bars.

The article also reports on differences between Afrikaners and English-speaking whites.

Evolution is described as "a process of gradual change," then discussed as the theory that "living things evolved from non-living matter and changed through the ages..." The article also states that "although the theory of evolution is supported by a vast amount of scientific evidence, it is not universally accepted." There are subsections on "Acceptance of Evolution" and "Evolution and Religion." These discussions not only present religious objections to evolution, but also note that evolution and religious beliefs are not necessarily incompatible. The article mentions court cases in the 1970s and 1980s in which religious groups sued to have creation theory taught in the public schools.

A separate article on **scientific creationism** notes among other arguments for this belief that existing fossil evidence is incomplete and "fails to show any kind of organism in transition to any other kind of organism." Throughout both these articles, the tone is evenhanded and scrupulously objective: the writers present the case for each argument without passing judgment on its merits. They are careful to distinguish between theory, belief, evidence, and fact.

The encyclopedia is also judicious in its presentation of **abortion**, reporting that "for years, abortion has been an extremely controversial subject. One important aspect of the controversy is whether a woman should be permitted by law to have an abortion and, if so, under what circumstances. Another is whether, and to what extent, laws should protect the unborn child's right to life." A significant portion of the article is devoted to "Arguments Against Abortion" and "Arguments for Abortion"; both cases are presented in an unemotional, well-reasoned manner. The subsection "Abortion Laws" discusses particular legislation and court cases, and also describes abortion laws in other countries.

World Book's treatment of **homosexuality** is similarly evenhanded. The article remarks that "causes of homosexuality are not fully understood," and while presenting several theories notes that "the evidence for each of these... is contradictory and confusing. Many experts feel that a number of different factors can lead to homosexuality in different people." The article also includes a brief discussion of attitudes toward homosexuality in different cultures.

As noted in the section on *Accuracy*, some *World Book* articles occasionally give the appearance of perpetuating stereotypes. Statements on particular nations or American states sometimes read like tourist brochures. This may be a consequence of the editors' attempt to make the articles in *World Book* accessible and interesting to a wide range of readers. For example, in **Ireland**, under the subsection "Way of Life," we are told that "many of the Irish... enjoy visiting their neighborhood *pub* (public house). People gather in their favorite pubs to drink beer and whiskey, talk with friends, and play darts." Yet, while these statements may oversimplify, none of them is untrue, and considering the objectivity evident in *World Book*'s overall presentation, these are minor quibbles.

VIII. Accessibility

World Book is an exceptionally well-organized and well-designed encyclopedia that contains a variety of useful finding aids. A nine-page article in the front-matter, "How to Get the Most Out of *World Book*," explains the set's arrangement clearly, simply, and in detail.

Entries are arranged alphabetically, word by word. However, some foreign proper names (such as De Gaulle) are alphabetized as if they were a single word. Unlike most other encyclopedias, *World Book* treats names beginning with *Mc* as they are actually spelled, not as though they began with *Mac*. Younger readers especially should find this system less confusing than the usual library practice of alphabetizing *Mc* as *Mac*. The word-by-word arrangement is also easier for many students to follow than is the letter-by-letter scheme.

Running heads at the top of each page indicate the first entry on the left-hand page and the last entry on the right-hand page. Page numbers are located at the bottom of each page, flush with the outside margin. Entry headings are printed in large boldface capital letters. Subheads within articles are also printed in boldface type and stand out clearly.

Many longer survey articles in *World Book* are organized into sections called "topical units." The publisher notes that "each topical unit stands on its own as a reference unit within the context of the larger article." Topical units are self-contained and always occupy a complete page or pages for easy reference. Each topical unit is broken down into subsections, identified by subheads. This arrangement enables students to easily find and consult specific information on the aspect of the topic in which they are interested.

World Book's comprehensive index, consisting of more than 150,000 entries, occupies most of Volume 22. As an indication of the scope and style of individual entries, the reader searching for information about **Marie Curie** will find the following index entry:

Curie, Marie Sklodowska [Polish-French physicist] **Ci:950**
Curie, Pierre **Ci:950** *with picture*
Medicine (The Medical Revolution) **M:306e**;
  picture on **M306c**
Nobel Prizes (Physics) N:340 *with*
  picture; (Chemistry) **N:342**
Physics *picture on* **P:393**
Radiation (Early Theories and
  Discoveries) **R:75–76**
Radium **R:98** *with picture*

World Book contains an estimated 100,000 cross-references, which appear in several forms. These include entry cross-references (e.g., **RHODESIA**. See ZIMBABWE) as well as "see" and "see also" cross-references within the text. All cross-references are printed in small caps and are thus immediately noticeable. Most helpful of all are the lists at the end of many articles under the heading, "Related Articles in WORLD BOOK include:..." These enable the reader to tell at a glance what other articles in the encyclopedia may contain relevant information. This feature is unique to *World Book*.

IX. Special Features

World Book contains a number of special features that enhance its accessibility and usefulness for the student and general reader alike. Of special interest to students are the "Study Aids" sections that follow major survey articles. The "Study Aids" page contains a list of *Related Articles* (described in *Accessibility*, above); an *Outline* of the article; a series of *Questions* that tests readers' knowledge; and *Additional Resources*—a bibliography, usually divided into "Level I" (books for younger readers) and "Level II" (books for more advanced readers).

Students may also benefit from the "Research Guide" in Volume 22. Essays on writing, speaking, and research skills provide basic practical information in a well-organized, straightforward, and easily understandable fashion. Special "Reading and Study Guides" throughout the index suggest report topics and provide biographical information. In addition, a number of science articles in the first 21 volumes contain detailed ideas for science projects.

Individual articles may also contain special tables which give the reader quick access to basic factual information. "Facts in Brief" tables, located in state, province, country, continent, and other articles provide statistics about government, population, economy, and geographic features. "Tables of Terms" are glossaries that define words or phrases used in technical subjects. "Tables of Important Dates" help the reader to place certain subjects in historical perspective.

Survey articles in the sciences or other specialized areas of knowledge often include charts and diagrams that highlight particular facts. For example, the article **animal** includes separate tables on "Comparative Speeds of Animals," "A Classification of the Animal Kingdom," "Animals and Their Young," and several pages devoted to animals of different regions. Many of these features include four-color illustrations and maps.

With half of its nearly 30,000 illustrations in four-color, *World Book* is the most profusely illustrated encyclopedia on the market today. Moreover, the set's color photographs and commissioned illustrations are of exceptionally high quality. They are generally bright, lively, and interesting; moreover, they bear a close relation to the articles they are intended to illustrate. For example, the 30-page article on **architecture** contains 43 four-color photographs (in addition to several black-and-white photos and two-color illustrations) that amply illustrate the wide range of concepts and styles discussed in the text.

World Book's maps are similarly distinguished. Most state, nation, and continent articles include full-page physical and political maps. Other maps give details of climate, natural resources, economic activity, historic explorations, and shifts in borders. Some of the maps have been provided by Rand McNally, while others have been prepared in conjunction with *World Book*'s own cartographic staff. Overall, the maps in *World Book* compare favorably with those in all other encyclopedias on the market.

X. Format

The 22-volume edition of *World Book* is available in four different bindings, known as Standard, School/ Library, Aristocrat, and Classical. All bindings embody the same production features; there is apparently no substantial qualitative difference between any one binding and another, although the Standard binding costs $50 less ($549) than the other three.

Regardless of binding style, the books are designed to stand up to heavy use.

Most volumes contain all the entries beginning with one letter; the exceptions are the C and S entries, which are each spread over two volumes. Thus, the number of pages in each volume varies. The entire set takes up just over two feet of horizontal shelf space.

(See also *Summary*, below, for information about foreign-language and recorded editions of *World Book*.)

XI. Other Opinions

Booklist (Reference Books Bulletin), November 15, 1986—review of the 1986 edition: "The set is curriculum oriented and has consistently garnered the Board's high praise for readability, authority, accuracy, and outstanding graphics. It is well edited and produced to meet the reference and leisure informational needs of students from grade four through high school. It is also an excellent source for adults."

Kenneth Kister, *Best Encyclopedias* (Oryx, 1986): "...[A] reference work of prominently high quality.... noteworthy for its readability, ease of use, broad and balanced coverage, accurate and up-to-date articles, and appealing illustrations and layout."

XII. Summary

It is not without cause that *World Book* is the best selling encyclopedia on the market today. Its easy-to-use format, excellent readability, scrupulous objectivity, high degree of currency, and almost impeccable authority and accuracy make it by far the favorite general reference encyclopedia among librarians, as our survey indicates. Librarians and teachers report that the set is immensely popular with students as well. As previously mentioned, *World Book* is also suitable for adults seeking a general reference encyclopedia. Its price of $599 (plus shipping and handling) to individuals, $499 to schools and libraries (including shipping and handling) compares favorably with that of its major competitors (COMPTON'S, MERIT, NEW BOOK OF KNOWLEDGE, and NEW STANDARD); only FUNK & WAGNALLS is less expensive.

Individuals and institutions wishing to purchase *World Book* may contact the local distributor listed under "Encyclopedias" in the Yellow Pages, or phone World Book, Inc., toll free at (800) 621-8202. The publisher offers individuals a discount for trade-ins of previous *World Book* editions.

Consumers should note that foreign-language editions of *World Book* are also sometimes available; these sets may or may not be in print at any given time. Interested individuals may contact the publisher for more information. The American Printing House for the Blind (1839 Frankfort Avenue, Box 6349, Louisville, KY 40206—telephone [502] 895-2405) distributes a massive 219-tape recorded edition of *World Book*, priced at $1,176.

Young Children's Encyclopedia

Facts at a Glance

Full Title: **The Young Children's Encyclopedia.**
Publisher: Encyclopaedia Britannica, Inc.
Editor: Howard L. Goodkind.
Copyright: 1985.

Number of Volumes: 16.
Number of Entries: 642.
Number of Pages: 2,560.
Number of Words: 339,000.
Number of Maps: 17.
Number of Cross-references: 1,114.
Number of Indexes: 0.
Number of Illustrations: 2,675, color; 48, black-and-white.
Trim Size: 7¾″ × 9³⁄₁₆″.

Intended Readership: 4- to 8-year-olds.
Price: $149.50
Sold directly by publisher to individuals only.
    ISBN 0-85229-426-3.
Revised "as needed."

I. Introduction

The 16-volume *Young Children's Encyclopedia*, published in 1985, is less a conventional encyclopedia than a collection of poems, stories, riddles, activities, and factual articles for four- to eight-year-olds. Designed primarily for browsing and for stimulating a young child's curiosity, it was also created as a "training" encyclopedia to help young children learn what an encyclopedia is and how it can be used.

II. Authority

Young Children's Encyclopedia is published by Encyclopaedia Britannica, Inc., best known as the publisher of the NEW ENCYCLOPAEDIA BRITANNICA and its predecessors. The Chicago-based firm publishes other reference works for young readers, including

COMPTON'S PRECYCLOPEDIA and COMPTON'S ENCYCLOPEDIA, reviewed in this Buying Guide.

The *YCE* was first published in 1970 for the supermarket and mail-order trade. The following year, under the aegis of Britannica's F. E. Compton division, it was reissued as *Compton's Young Children's Precyclopedia*. Both sets were minimally reviewed in 1977 and again in 1985, the date of the current edition.

YCE's editorial staff of 36 is headed by Editor-in Chief Howard L. Goodkind. In addition to this staff, some 150 individuals are listed as staff writers, contributing writers, or artists. The set's small roster of consultants includes author and critic Clifton Fadiman, former Library of Congress Poetry Consultant Gwendolyn Brooks, and Robert Hess, Professor of History at the University of Illinois. A six-member advisory board includes educators affiliated with the Early Childhood Center of Sarah Lawrence College, Bank Street College of Education, and Child Study Association of America.

III. Scope

The *Young Children's Encyclopedia* contains 642 entries (arranged alphabetically), each averaging 500 words, or five full pages with illustrations. The reading level ranges from third through sixth grades. Broad topics are often treated in a series of articles or a combination of articles, stories, and poems, each of which has its own title. The generic entry **nature**, for example, contains a story about a farm attacked by locusts ("Insect Armies") as well as articles on animal parks ("Animals at Home"), ecology ("Why Animals and Plants Live Where They Do"), and pond life ("Free Aquarium").

More specific entries, such as biographies, average 300 words and take up two illustrated pages. Approximately 50 entries are followed by a "More About... " section, intended for older children who are able to absorb more information. In these sections the print size is smaller than that of the main text, and the pictures more technical, extending the age range of the intended readership.

Approximately 40 percent of the entries cover nature and science topics. Geography (13 percent), biography (11 percent), everyday life (8 percent), and fantasy and imagination (5 percent) also receive significant attention. Other subjects include work, recreation, history, transportation, mathematics, and the arts.

The treatment of geography and mathematics is sound and closely related to the curriculum in the early grades. For example, there are 28 features titled "Where Am I?" which teach geography lessons in the form of a guessing game. The place is named at the end of the article and the reader is referred to the world map in Volume 16 to find its location. More than 75 percent of the places in these features are in foreign countries. They include well-known cities like Moscow and Tokyo; sites of historic or cultural interest, such as the Taj Mahal; and little-known villages. As a further indication of the geographic coverage in the *YCE*, Volume 8 (I-K) includes entries about **India**, **Israel**, **Italy**, and **Japan**.

Mathematical concepts are presented through games and activities. Concepts such as set theory, one-on-one relationships, measurement, and infinity are explained simply and clearly.

Occasionally, the choice of topics and the scope with which they are treated are somewhat arbitrary. For example, **baseball** is the only sport covered. There is an article on marsupials, but none on mammals, amphibians, or reptiles. The article on **snakes** makes no reference to the reptile family.

Biographical entries are also limited. **George Washington** and **Abraham Lincoln** are the only U. S. presidents covered, and there are no entries for contemporary figures. However, as mentioned, the *Young Children's Encyclopedia* is not intended to be comprehensive, and given its limitations, the set seems reasonably well balanced in coverage.

Throughout the set, text is often superimposed over illustrations. Overall, color illustrations account for about half of the actual page space.

IV. Currency

The 1985 edition of *YCE* does not differ significantly from the 1977 edition. However, currency is not nearly as critical in children's encyclopedias as it is in student and adult encyclopedias, and most of the entries in this set require little updating.

A few new articles, all dealing with famous women (for example, **Louisa May Alcott** and **Emily Dickenson**), have been added to the 1985 edition. Some articles from the previous set have been rewritten and reillustrated. Regardless of this revision, however, some of the material in the set may be of limited interest to children. For example, of the 50 biographical entries, only six—**Salvador Dali**, **Albert Einstein**, **Mahatma Gandhi**, **Pablo Picasso**, **Albert Schweitzer**, and **Igor Stravinsky**—lived during the twentieth century. Although these are useful and appropriate entries, the inclusion of important recent figures would give the set a more contemporary flavor.

Many of the illustrations in *YCE* are noticeably dated, as indicated by the clothing and hairstyles of many of the people depicted. For example, the entry on "The Two-Way Radio" is accompanied by an illustration of a taxi driver and a dispatcher, both of whom are wearing white shirts and ties; the driver is also wearing an old-fashioned cabbie's hat.

V. Accuracy

Although the *YCE* is not a fact-oriented work, the information it furnishes is generally accurate and objective. Nevertheless, the set tends to deal in vague generalities rather than in specifics, particularly in articles on historical events and actual locations. For example, the entry on **Richard the Lionhearted** reports that he "lived in the days when soldiers in armor fought with spears and bows and arrows."

As the foregoing example suggests, many of *YCE*'s articles on famous people treat their subjects in anecdotal form. The entry on **Ludwig van Beethoven**, "The Lonely Giant," for example, is typically incomplete, fictionalized, and sentimental. It opens with a group of Viennese schoolboys making fun of an eccentric. One of the boys, who is named Franz, remembers that his parents have promised to take him to a concert by "the great composer Ludwig van Beethoven... if he practiced [the piano] every day." On the night of the concert, Franz realizes that "the crazy man" is "the great Beethoven" himself. This concert is the premier of Beethoven's Ninth Symphony; the only factual information in the article is that at the end of the concert "one of the performers gently turned [Beethoven] around so that he could see the people clapping." It is apparently implied that the boy "Franz" is Franz Schubert. In fact, although Schubert was a devoted admirer of Beethoven and did attend the premier, he was in his mid-twenties at the time.

Another criticism of the *YCE* involves the inaccurate use of certain terminology. For example, the article "The Bear That Isn't a Bear," explains that the koala is not a bear, but is found under the heading **koala bears**. Moreover, the article refers to koalas as "pouch animals," rather than *marsupials*, even though marsupial is used in the entry **kangaroos** in the same volume.

Our reviewers also pinpointed several more obvious errors. A 6-page article on **ants** describes the insects as able to "talk with other... ants by tapping them with their feelers." In fact, insects' antennae are sensory receptors; they do not emit signals. The entry on **islands** mentions "the island of New Zealand." New Zealand is not an island, however, but a nation that occupies several islands, the two largest of which are called North Island and South Island.

By comparison, the articles in CHILDCRAFT provide far more factual information, and are generally more precise and reliable than those in the *Young Children's Encyclopedia.*

VI. Accessibility

Because the set is not indexed, its accessibility is limited. To find information on a particular subject, users must check the table of contents at the beginning of each volume, where subject entries are listed alphabetically in red. Under each heading, titles and page numbers of individual articles, stories, verses, and activities appear in black type and are frequently accompanied by a description of the article.

Unlike CHILDCRAFT, the *Young Children's Encyclopedia* does not provide guide words at the top of the page. This omission makes it difficult for readers to find an entry by leafing through the book.

The generic headings in the table of contents are sometimes misleading. For example, the entry **automobiles** is not about cars but about transportation before the information age; **parents** describes how human and animal babies travel; and **swimming** discusses scuba diving. When considering the *YCE* for purchase, however, keep in mind that the set was designed for four- to eight-year-olds, who may enjoy browsing but are not ready to do research. The titles of individual articles are colorful and should pique a child's curiosity. For example, "The Airplane That Wouldn't Stay Down" is about Charles Lindbergh's transatlantic flight; "Insect Armies" is about locusts; and "Music with Strings and Hammers" is about pianos.

The *Young Children's Encyclopedia* provides an excellent two-part cross-referencing system. The equivalent of "see also" references are printed in italics at the end of articles. For example, the article "Inside the Earth" is followed by the note, *Want to know more? Read* "Fossils" *in Volume 6 and* "Volcanoes" *in Volume 16.* The cross-reference at the end of "How to Catch a Giraffe" says, *If you liked this story, read* "Animals at Home" *under* Nature *in Volume 11.* The other type of cross-reference occurs following the table of contents in each volume. The reader is given a list of subjects under the heading, *Here are more words beginning with...* The words in this list are followed by the actual entry heading and the volume and page number where the pertinent article can be found.

The 1977 edition of the *Young Children's Encyclopedia* included a 144-page parents' manual. However, no manual or user's guide is offered with the 1985 edition.

VII. Clarity

More than 50 writers contributed to the *YCE.* Although the writing styles are often uneven, most of the articles are clear and conversational in tone. Reading levels range from third through sixth grade, as measured on the Fry Readability Scale.

As indicated under *Accuracy,* some articles seem to take key information for granted, leaving important points unexplained. For example, "The Boy Who Conquered a Horse," an article about **Alexander the Great**, begins with young Alexander taming a wild horse, which he names Bucephalus. Although the name is repeated several times in the article, we are never told what it means, nor how it is pronounced. Similarly, although Alexander's home is identified as Macedonia, the reader never learns where it is. Toward the end of the article we are told: "Bucephalus died. Alexander built another new city . . . and named it Bucephalus after his horse." By this point, the article has strayed rather far from the premise of its title, but the reader has not been given a context for Alexander's achievement.

As in the **Beethoven** entry cited previously (see *Accuracy*), many articles tend to be cloying and sentimental. For example, "Friends or Enemies," an article on **insects**, declares that "the next time you are annoyed by the insects that visit your picnic, you'll shoo them away. But if you remember all the good things insects do, you may be shooing away a *friend. . . .*" The reader is told that the **koala bear** "looks so much like a toy bear that you want to turn it around to see if it has a key in its back so you can wind it up." This type of writing, apparently designed to appeal to the young reader, smacks of condescension; moreover, it stands in the way of a simple, straightforward discussion of the subject.

This "cute" tone pervades the first of the set's two entries on **lighthouses**, "The Light That Saves Lives," written in a somewhat graceless irregular verse form. The final stanza reads, in part:

If you're ever the captain of a ship
   and it's as dark as a closet
      some night,
      look for those ribbons
      that circle above the sea
      like a merry-go-round of light!
(And that's the lighthouse light.). . .

The second entry on the subject, "More About Lighthouses," is introduced by a two-paragraph story about a teen-age girl who runs an island lighthouse while her parents visit the mainland. The article then gives basic factual information about the history and operation of lighthouses. A typical paragraph reads:

> Wood-burning lighthouses could not send their lights very far. Lighthouse lamps that burned oil were better. And the bright electric lights seen in some of today's lighthouses can be seen by sailors 30 miles away. Each lighthouse blinks its light in a special way, on and off, long and short, so that sailors will know which lighthouse is sending out the light. Each is also painted in a different way so that sailors can tell where they are when they see the lighthouse in the daytime. . . .

Each entry is illustrated profusely in full color. The set also includes a limited number of color photographs, and a handful of reproductions of works by Leonardo da Vinci, Rembrandt, and other famous artists. With nearly 90 contributing artists, the illustrations vary widely in style and quality. Most of the illustrations are rendered in traditional children's book style. Cartoons, line drawings, and Oriental-style pictures are also included. Although competent and varied, the quality of *YCE*'s artwork does not match that found in CHILDCRAFT.

VIII. Objectivity

The *YCE*'s articles and illustrations depict a wide variety of ethnic and racial groups. For example, "Looking for a Hideout," a story in Volume 1, tells about a Puerto Rican boy. One of the entries under **Africa** tells about Amos Biwott, an Olympic gold medalist from Kenya. Pictures showing groups of people also include a fair racial and ethnic balance.

The *YCE* is generally less successful in avoiding sexist stereotypes. For example, one illustration in the entry **alone** shows three women "hanging out their wash and talking about what their husbands liked for dinner." In a number of illustrations of mixed groups of males and females, men and boys are often pictured in active roles while women and girls are onlookers.

This is not always the case, however. For example, the entry on **jobs** shows that both men and women can do many types of work. The article asks "Who fixes things around the house?" It answers "Father does. But sometimes Mother might. Many mothers are good at fixing things. They can hammer, saw, or figure out why a window shade won't work or why the drain won't drain. They think it's fun to be able to fix these things." The article also reports that "it's handy for Father to know how to iron or sew."

While only 15 percent of the biographical entries are about women, the set includes some important and interesting women with whom children in this age group may not be familiar. Among these subjects are **Elizabeth Blackwell** ("The First Woman Doctor") and the **Brontë Sisters**.

As noted, the *YCE* includes entries on a wide range of nations. However, life in these countries is sometimes misrepresented through one-sided or overly sanguine accounts. Of particular interest are two entries on the **U.S.S.R.**: "Leaving Moscow" (a story about a family that moves from Moscow to a provincial town in Siberia, where the father will work at a hydroelectric plant and the mother will work as a pediatrician); and "More About the U.S.S.R.", a two-page article about the land, climate, and history. The former portrays ordinary Russians as people very much like Americans. The latter is also generally objective, although some American parents may take issue with the article's characterization of Lenin as a leader who "was always careful to teach that no one country or race of people was better than any other. All men, he said, deserved the same chance in life." The article is more objective when it states that "after Lenin died, the Soviet Union had a leader who became as cruel as the czars," and that "in some ways people are still not as free in the Soviet Union as they would like to be. They are not as free to travel or to change their jobs, to read all the things they may wish to, to choose their leaders, or to talk about different ideas." The article's final claim that "things keep changing and getting better" is dubious.

IX. Summary

The 16-volume *Young Children's Encyclopedia* (also sold in a slightly different format as COMPTON'S PRE-CYCLOPEDIA) is the main competitor to *Childcraft, the How and Why Library* in the young children's encyclopedia home market. Although neither set is an encyclopedia in the strict sense of the word, both offer attractive features for beginning readers. While both are appropriate for "reference," they also encourage browsing and general reading.

Like CHILDCRAFT, the *YCE* contains a varied mixture of stories, verses, activities, and factual articles written at a level appropriate to its intended readership. Whereas CHILDCRAFT's entries are organized in topical volumes, the *YCE*'s entries follow a strict alphabetic arrangement similar to that found in an adult general encyclopedia. Moreover, entries in the *YCE* are given both a generic subject designation and a more specific descriptive title. *YCE*'s cross-referencing system should stimulate readers to explore in the set at length.

Although it is profusely illustrated, *YCE*'s pictures are not quite on a par with those in CHILD-

CRAFT. The most obvious difference between the two sets, however, is the quality of their text. Both sets can fairly be described as "high interest"; however, the *YCE* does not include traditional or classic poems and stories but relies upon anonymous contributions from staff and freelance writers, much of which our reviewers found inferior to the material available in CHILDCRAFT. Similarly, the *YCE*'s science, history, and biographical articles tend to be less specific and factual.

Individuals wishing to purchase the *Young Children's Encyclopedia* may contact the publisher, Encyclopaedia Britannica, Inc., at Britannica Centre, Customer Service Department, 310 South Michigan Avenue, Chicago, IL 60604, or telephone (312) 347-7298. The set retails for $149.50. Note that the *YCE* is not sold to schools and libraries; institutions should consult the review of COMPTON'S PRECYCLOPEDIA that begins on page 113.

PART THREE

Atlases

Chapter 7
What to Look for
in Atlases

Atlases are indispensable aids to understanding the many facets of our complex planet. As such, they are essential assets to library collections, particularly those serving young people. An atlas is a collection of general reference maps and thematic maps (those that depict a particular subject or group of related subjects, such as energy resources, along with related graphic and statistical data, bound together in book format. Individual atlases differ in their content, both in the information shown on the general reference maps and in the choice of subject maps. Choosing the appropriate atlas for your particular needs, then, is a more complex process than it might appear at first glance. Each atlas is designed for a particular audience and purpose.

Selecting an atlas—whether for use in the formal setting of a school classroom, school library, or public library, or more informally at home—will depend on the intended user's level of skill, knowledge of and interest in geography, as well as specific study or leisure needs.

This section of the Buying Guide covers reviews for general atlases intended for readers from preschool and elementary school age to college. The reviews were written from the perspective of the intended readership of each atlas. The range of map-reading skills and comprehension that are needed to use the contents of an atlas effectively was also considered. The reviews in this section of the Buying Guide describe atlases in much more depth than those written for geographers or map librarians because

they assume that the readers of this guide are not as familiar with selecting atlases as are specialists in the fields of geography and mapping. The reviews attempt to explain and illustrate specific features, wherever possible, so that buyers can acquire a balanced view of each atlas's contents.

Each evaluation is preceded by a summary of factual information about the atlas, provided by the publishers at the Buying Guide's request. This information includes the full title of the work, the publisher's formal name, the editor or editorial staff, the copyright date, the publication date of the edition reviewed, the number of pages, and the trim size of the volume. This is followed by a brief description of the intended readership (usually written by the publisher), the price, and kind of binding, plus any pertinent information supplied to us by the publishers on their revision policy. When the publishers have specified the extent of revisions, this information is included.

In many cases, you will note a discrepancy between the atlas's copyright date and its publication date (that is, the edition reviewed). Although some atlases are revised annually, the amount of material revised is often not sufficient to warrant a new copyright. Thus, for example, an atlas may have a 1984 copyright even though it was printed in 1987 and reflects post-1984 revision.

The reviews describe each atlas, using the aspects of format, special features, geographical balance, scale and projections, accuracy, recency, legibility, accessibility, and price. How these aspects are treated in the reviews is described in more detail below.

Introduction. This section provides a brief general description of the atlas reviewed and its relation to other works by the same publisher, a description of the work's purpose and intended readership, and an identification of the cartographers and consultants, and their qualifications. Pertinent statements about the purposes or content by the editors, from the preface or directly from the publisher, are often quoted.

Format. The specific purpose of an atlas has a direct influence on the content, physical organization and arrangement of its maps. Some contain primarily physical maps; others, political maps. In some atlases, the maps cover one page; whereas in others, the maps are double-page spreads. The intended purpose of atlases also affects their size. Some are large in order to accommodate large-scale maps of large areas; others are small so that they can be conveniently carried. When appraising each atlas's format, reviewers have evaluated its ease of handling, the relationship of its size to the type of maps it contains, and the convenience of its size for the intended readership.

The bindings used for atlases also affect their uses. If the maps are double-page spreads, for example, the atlas should lie flat when opened without breaking the binding. If it will not lie flat, information will be lost in the gutter (the adjoining inside margins of two facing pages), or the spine will soon break from users pressing down on it in attempts to see the information.

Reviewers have also described the map legends used in each atlas, how they are set up, and which elements or symbols they include. Every map should have a legend that explains the symbols used; the explanations are clearer in some atlases than they are in others. The location of the legend is also important. It should be convenient and easily used and related to the map. Some atlases include the legend on each page; others put it on a page preceding the maps, and others print it on a card that can be consulted beside each map. Some legends include all the symbols used; others omit some symbols that the compilers believe are self-explanatory.

Special Features. Many atlases contain special features. These may be a section of thematic maps, or tables of political and socioeconomic information, or encyclopedic information, such as descriptions of weather patterns, man's pollution of the earth, or the solar system, and so on. In some atlases, these sections are well written and quite informative, whereas in others the maps are not well made or useful, the tables are inaccurate, or encyclopedic information is irrelevant. The reviewers have described these special features where they exist, and commented on their cartographic quality, accuracy, relevancy, or usefulness.

Geographical Balance. One extremely important question addressed by the reviewers is how adequate and balanced the atlas's representation is of all regions of the world. Some atlases show the United States in great detail whereas the Third World is shown in very little detail; other atlases use consistent scales for all parts of the world. This is not to say that an atlas with a marked American bias is nec-

essarily bad; it all depends on its intended audience. If an atlas does have a bias toward one geographic area, and gives it disproportionate coverage, the reviewer has commented on whether or not this occurs at the expense of other regions.

Scale and Projections. Every map has a scale and projection which need to be appropriately chosen for the area depicted and the size of the page on which it is printed. Maps must necessarily be smaller than the areas they depict, and the proportional relationship or ratio between the distance or area on the map and the distance or area on the ground is called the map scale. It can be represented in three ways: (1) as a simple fraction or ratio, called the representative fraction or RF; (2) as a verbal or written statement of map distance in relation to earth distance; and (3) as a graphic representation or a bar scale.

The representative fraction is usually written as 1:100,000, where 1 always refers to a unit of distance on the map and the 100,000 (or any other number) refers to the number of the same units it takes to cover the same distance on the ground. The written or verbal statement expresses distances in terms more easily comprehended by map readers, such as "one inch equals one mile." The graphic representation, or bar scale, is usually a line placed on the map that has been subdivided to show the lengths of units of earth distance.

Many maps include all three types of scale statements. The RF and the verbal statement are used to compare scales of two or more maps in close proximity and the bar scale is used to estimate or measure distances on the map itself. It is also the only type of scale statement which remains accurate when the map is enlarged or reduced while being photocopied. The RF or verbal statement may also be used alone.

There are three basic types of projections in use today: cylinders, cones, and planes. All three geometric shapes are related mathematically (the surface of a sphere is equal to the area of an enveloping cylinder, a cone elongated sufficiently becomes a cylinder, both the cone and cylinder can be cut and laid flat). They are, therefore, suitable for transferring information from the earth's spherical surface to a flat plane.

Any method of map projection must involve relative shrinking or stretching of portions of the spherical earth in the projection's representation on a flat surface. The cartographer has the choice of either retaining some kinds of comparable angular relationships (bearings or directions), *or* retaining comparable areas or distances. The cartographer chooses the appropriate projection and scale according to the information he or she wishes to present with the least distortion. Some projections can preserve direction and distance only from a single point. Such projections are called "equidistant." If directions at any point on the projection are preserved (if angles and shapes at any point are as they are on the globe) the projection is called "conformal" (or "orthomorphic"). If a projection preserves comparable areas (only at the expense of conformality and equidistance), it is called "equal-area." No projection can possess more than one of the three qualities; some possess none.

The earth's grid of lines of latitude and longitude can be projected perspectively or mathematically to give conformal or equidistant representation on a plane, a cone, or a cylinder. Each property, conformality, equidistance, or equal-area, can be attained by projection onto all three projection surfaces. To extend the range of area they cover, or to minimize some of the defects inherent in them, the basic principles are modified or the characteristics of one are combined with another.

The choice of projection depends on a number of factors, including the purpose of the map, the area covered, and the ease of construction. The reviewers have indicated whether or not the map scales used are reasonable for the size of the area being shown on the map and for the size of the page, as well as to what extent the scales for comparable-size areas are consistent. They have also discussed the advantages and disadvantages of the projections used for the various areas mapped, and have pointed out any unacceptable or potentially misleading distortions caused by using the "wrong" projections in any of the maps.

Accuracy. The names of places and their positioning on the maps are the bases for comments on accuracy. Place names must be spelled correctly according to national or international standards. Spellings must be consistent. The introduction of a good atlas will explain its standards of place name spelling.

Place names must also be accurately located. This can be tricky when many location names are placed close together and when large physical areas, like mountain ranges, are presented, and the name needs to convey the extent as well as the location. The reviewers have evaluated each atlas for the spelling and positioning of place names.

Currency. Unless one is specifically looking for an historical atlas, the natural assumption is that a recently published atlas has information that is as up-to-date as possible. Any atlas being considered for purchase should be evaluated as to the dating of the political changes it reflects. A current copyright date does not guarantee that all the information contained

in an atlas is as recent as that. The reviewers have evaluated recency by looking to see if the latest name changes are reflected in the names printed on the maps. Another way they have evaluated recency is to examine any photographs or text description of a place to determine if they are up-to-date or contemporary.

Legibility. Perhaps no element of a map is so important in conveying an impression of quality as the lettering or typefaces used and the manner in which they are positioned on the map. Readers of all ages are unlikely to trust a map that has poorly designed and positioned lettering, for the utility of a reference map depends to a great extent on these characteristics. The recognition of the feature to which a name applies, the "search time" necessary to find names, and the ease with which the lettering can be read are all important to the function of the map.

Like all other marks on a map, the type functions as a graphic symbol. By its position within the structural framework of the map, it helps to indicate the location of points. By its spacing and array, it more directly shows such things as linear or areal extent, for instance, of mountain ranges or political units. By its arrangement with respect to the latitude and longitude grid, the type can clearly indicate orientation.

The systematic employment of distinctions of style, form, and color in type enables the cartographer to show nominal classes to which labeled features belong. For example, blue type is typically used to identify all hydrographic features, and within that general class, open water may be labeled with all-capital letters, and running water by capitals and lowercase letters. Type-size variations can indicate the ordinal characteristics of geographical phenomena, ranking them, for example, in terms of relative area or importance.

In a more subtle way, type serves as an indication of scale. Size contrasts with respect to other factors, such as line width and symbol size, can give the impression that one map is a larger or smaller scale than another. If the cartographer has not been careful, this important impression can be lost or even reversed.

Typically, different styles of typeface are used to differentiate between different types of geographic information, such as names of physical features and names of populated places. Not only do the typefaces have to be legible, but they must be sufficiently differentiated so that it is easy to distinguish among the various place-name categories of different types of geographic information.

When many place names need to be positioned in a small area on the map, the cartographer has to make decisions concerning type size and styles in order to fit all the names in legibly. If he does a poor job, the map will look cluttered and individual names will be hard to find. Symbols used to delineate rivers, roads, railroads, and so forth, also need to be clearly distinguishable from each other.

When judging the legibility of maps in an atlas, the reviewers evaluated the type for style, form, size, and color, as well as lettering for the contrast between it and its background, and for its positioning.

Accessibility. One of the greatest assets of an atlas should be its index of the place names that appear on its maps. The best index is one that, at a minimum, lists every name that appears on all the general maps. The spelling in the index should be consistent with that on the maps. Ideally, there should be cross-references to popular or variant spellings of names. Most atlas compilers index names to the largest scale map on which they appear. Sometimes, however, the compiler will index names to all maps on which they appear.

After each name in an index, either a number/letter grid coordinate or latitude/longitude reference is used to locate it on the map. The best and most accurate method is to use latitude/longitude, expressed in degrees and minutes, or degrees and fractions of a degree. With the grid-coordinate system, there is usually a one- to four-square-inch area in which to search for the name.

Another aspect of accessibility is the indexing of map insets. A good atlas index will list the place names in these, also.

The reviewers have evaluated these aspects of accessibility and have made comments accordingly.

Summary. Certainly every user wants to get the best value possible when purchasing an atlas, but content alone is not necessarily a basis for deciding whether or not an atlas is priced fairly. Overall quality as well as content should be the bases for judging the reasonableness of price. Price comparisons of several similar atlases are also useful determinants for choosing the one that serves your needs at an affordable price.

Whenever possible, the summary makes broad comparisons between the atlas under review and similar competing atlases. It weighs the merits and drawbacks of the atlas, and gives an overview that can help guide the reader to a decision.

Few buyers have the chance to examine a number of atlases before making a purchase. The reviews included on the following pages have been prepared using the criteria described above, and their detailed descriptions should help you to choose an appropriate atlas for your library, classroom, or home.

Glossary

In the event that the users of this guide are unfamiliar with the cartographic terms employed in these reviews, a glossary of these terms is provided below:

aerial chart. *See* **aeronautical chart**.

aerial photograph. A photograph of the surface of the earth taken downward from the air.

aeronautical chart. A map designed to assist navigation in the air.

air photo. *See* **aerial photograph**.

altitude tint. *See* **hypsometric tint**.

ancillary map. A small supplementary or secondary map outside the neat line of the principal or main map. *See also* **inset**.

azimuthal projection. *See* **plane projection**.

bar scale. A subdivided line which shows the lengths of units of earth distance.

base map. A map used as a framework on which to depict other information.

bathymetric tint. A color applied to the area between selected depth contours to depict the physical relief of the floor of a body of water. *See also* **hypsometric tint.**

bleeding edge. An edge of a map to which printed detail extends after the paper has been trimmed.

block diagram. A representation of the landscape in either perspective or isometric projection, usually with some vertical exaggeration.

Bonne projection. A conic, equal-area projection in which distances are true along all parallels and the central meridian.

cadastral map. A map which delineates property boundaries. *See also* **plat.**

cardinal directions. The four principal directions: north, south, east, and west.

cartogram. A map with areas or distances distorted to promote communication of a concept.

cartographic material. Any material representing, in whole or in part, the earth or any celestial body at any scale.

cartouche. A panel on a map, often with decoration, enclosing the title, legends, and/or scale.

celestial chart. A map representing the heavens.

chart. A map designed primarily for navigation.

cholopleth map. A map with areal units colored or shaded so that the brightness of each symbolized area represents its numerical value for the distribution mapped.

conic projection. Any **map projection** in which the parallels and meridians appear as they would if a cone were laid over a globe and touched it along one or two parallels.

contour. A line joining points of equal elevation on a surface.

contour interval. The difference in elevation between adjacent contour lines.

contour map. A map which uses contour lines to portray relief.

cylindrical projection. Any map projection in which the parallels and meridians appear as they would if a cylinder was wrapped around the globe, touching it at the equator.

dot distribution map. A map in which each discrete dot represents a set number of the objects comprising the distribution displayed on the map.

elevation tint. *See* **hypsometric tint.**

equal-area projection. Any **plane** (or **azimuthal**) **projection** that shows land areas in their correct proportions.

equivalent scale. *See* **verbal scale.**

facsimile map. A printed reproduction of a map identical with the original.

format. The general physical organization of a publication.

form lines. Lines, resembling contour lines but drawn without regard to regular spacing, which present the shape of the terrain.

gazetteer. A list of geographic names, together with descriptive information and/or references to their geographic location.

geographic coordinates. A system which expresses the position of points in terms of latitude and longitude.

geographic pole. Either of the two points of intersection of the surface of the earth with its axis, where all meridians meet.

Goode's interrupted homolosine projection. An **equal-area projection** that produces an oval-shaped map, often used for world distribution maps.

gradient tint. *See* **hypsometric tint.**

graphic scale. A drawing or diagram which enables quantitative measurements to be read. *See also* **bar scale.**

graticule. A network of lines on a map which represents meridians and parallels. *See also* **grid.**

Greenwich meridian. *See* **prime meridian.**

grid. Network of two sets of uniformly spaced parallel lines, one set intersecting the other at right angles. When superimposed on a map, it usually carries the name of the projection used for the map.

hachures. Short lines, following the direction of maximum slope, which indicate relief.

hill shading. Shading employed to create a three-dimensional impression of relief. *See also* **shaded relief.**

historical map. A map which represents features or phenomena which existed, or which are believed to have existed, in some past period of time.

hydrographic chart. A chart designed to assist navigation at sea or on other waterways.

hypsometric layer. A uniform tint or shade covering the area between two successive isolines.

hypsometric map. *See* **relief map.**

hypsometric tint. A color applied to the area between two selected contours when relief is depicted by a system of layers.

index map. An index, usually based on an outline map, which shows the layout and numbering system of map sheets which cover an area.

inset map. A separate map positioned within the neat line of a larger map.

isoline map. A map which represents a continuous distribution by means of lines (called *isolines*) along which values are constant.

key map. *See* **index map.**

Lambert azimuthal equal-area projection. A **plane projection** used for mapping polar regions or other circular areas.

Lambert conformal conic projection. A **conic projection** that uses two standard parallels instead of

(*continued on page 222*)

Political Maps

General non-thematic maps in an atlas may be either **political** or **physical** maps. Political maps highlight nations as distinct political entities. They also present information about man-made (artificial) entities on the earth, using a variety of symbols. These symbols are described in a map key or legend, which may be located in the front of the atlas as well as, in an abbreviated form, on each map page.

Typically, political maps depict the following features: 1) political boundaries (national, and often state or provincial; disputed boundaries or territories may also be indicated). 2) Cities. Depending upon the level of detail and the map scale, these symbols may distinguish the size of the city. Extremely large or densely populated urban areas may be shown by a mark that indicates the actual extent of the area. Otherwise, dots of different sizes or configurations may be used to distinguish different levels of population. Capital cities are frequently marked by a star-shaped symbol. City symbols are invariably printed in black.

Political maps also designate elements of the transportation system: major highways, railroads, and international airports. Sea shipping lanes may be indicated as well. On most four-color maps, colors are used to identify different types of routes. Railway lines are usually gray or black, while roads are customarily red. As with city symbols,

Physical Maps

these are frequently varied to identify different types of roads.

Equally important in helping the user distinguish among varying features are the typefaces in which the labels appear. Ideally, different typefaces and type sizes are used to identify nations, provinces, and cities, or other population areas. Political maps often show limited physical features as well—primarily important bodies of water such as lakes, rivers, and oceans. The presence of extensive landforms such as deserts and mountain ranges is sometimes designated by name labels, but political maps rarely indicate the actual natural boundaries of such areas.

For these, readers turn to physical maps. Some physical maps use color, shades of color, or relief to indicate altitude. Others use color or shading to depict actual land types such as forest, desert, or tundra.

Few maps are purely political or purely physical. Physical maps, for example, may or may not show national borders. Like political maps, they may show roads and cities and distinguish among population centers. As a rule, physical maps are more complex than their political counterparts: they endeavor to interpret the relationship between society and environment.

Projection Types—World Maps

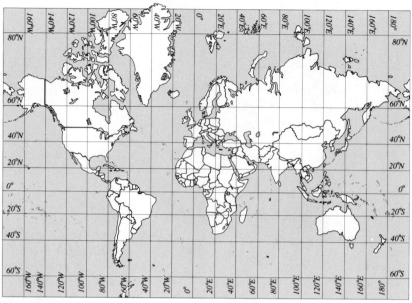

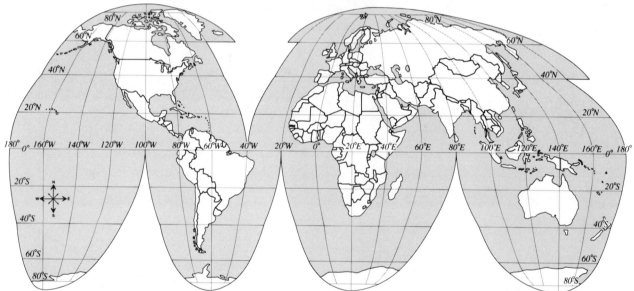

The maps on this page illustrate two types of projections (**Mercator** and **Goode's Interrupted**) and the kinds of distortions that can occur on world maps. Note that virtually all world maps are made from some type of cylindrical projection.

The Mercator projection shows the correct shape of land masses, but distorts their area (that is, their size). This distortion is minimal in equatorial regions, but increases near the poles. As a result, Greenland appears larger than South America. In fact, Greenland's area is only 840,000 square miles, whereas that of South America is 7 million square miles. The Mercator projection is used for ocean navigation because a line drawn between any two points on this map gives the true compass direction from one point to the other. Mercator maps are especially popular in young readers' atlases because they are easy for children to interpret. But they can also easily mislead children about the relative sizes of land areas.

A more complex projection for world maps found in a number of atlases for high school students and adults is Goode's Interrupted Homolosine projection. Combining the features of two other projections (the **Mollweide Homolographic** and the **Sinusoidal,** or **Sanson-Flamsteed,** projections), it allows fairly faithful representation of both the shape and size of large land masses. Its major distortions—the interruptions—occur in ocean areas. Goode's Homolosine projection is useful for population distribution and other thematic world maps as well as for political and physical world maps.

Projection Types—Regional Maps

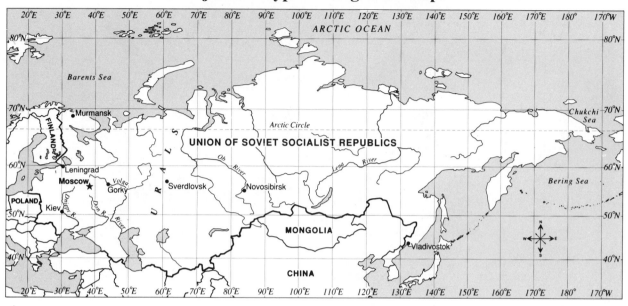

A

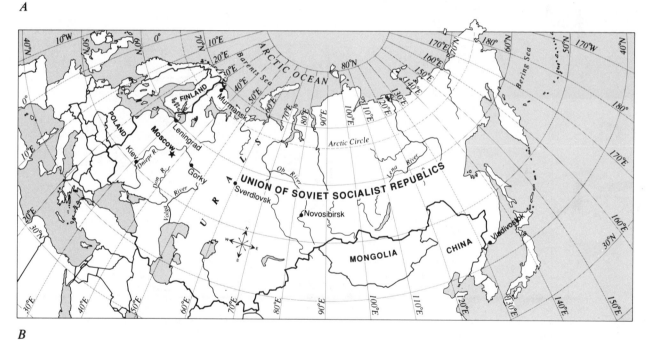

B

The larger the area covered in a map, the greater the distortion will be, regardless of the type of projection used. Thus, while distortions on a map of a continent are not as severe as on a map of the entire world, the choice of projection still affects the accuracy of size, shape, or direction. To produce national and continental maps, cartographers can use conic or plane as well as cylindrical projections. Their preference depends largely on the size, shape, and location of the nation or continent.

Two different projection types are used in the maps on this page. Map A depicts the U.S.S.R. in the Miller projection, a cylindrical projection similar to the Mercator projection. It shows shapes less accurately than does the Mercator projection, but it also distorts sizes less severely. Map B shows the U.S.S.R. in the Lambert azimuthal projection, a plane projection. In this projection, a straight line shows the shortest distance between any two points. This projection is ideal for plotting airline routes. However, both shape and distance are increasingly distorted away from the center of this map.

Large Scale and Small Scale

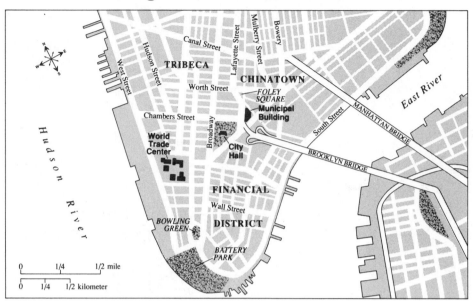

A

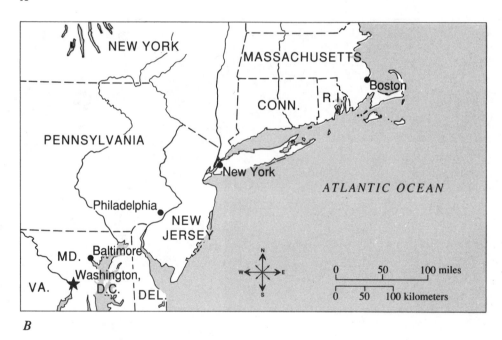

B

*Many readers are confused by the terms **large scale** and **small scale**. These expressions refer not to the size of a map, but rather to the area that is included in the map. The larger the scale, the greater the amount of detail that can be presented but the smaller the area that can be covered. Different scales are used for different purposes. Each has its advantages and disadvantages.*

The two maps on this page are both the same size, but each is drawn to a different scale. On Map A (Lower Manhattan), a large-scale map, one inch equals ½ mile. On Map B (the Eastern seaboard of the United States), a

relatively small-scale map, one inch equals 100 miles.

Map A depicts streets, rivers, parks, and other major features of Lower Manhattan. This map would be useful for a visitor who might need detailed information about this section of New York. Map B covers a much larger area, allowing the reader to see New York's location relative to other cities along the Eastern seaboard. At the same time, however, it does not render the features of New York City in the kind of detail that is possible only in the larger-scale map.

Thematic Maps

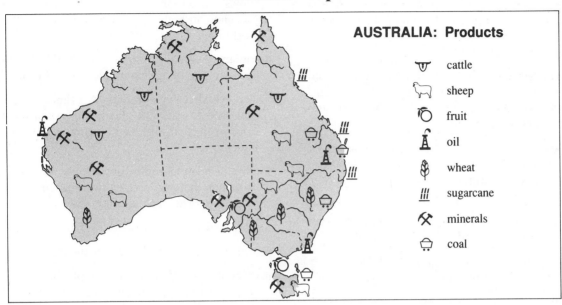

AUSTRALIA: Products

cattle	
sheep	
fruit	
oil	
wheat	
sugarcane	
minerals	
coal	

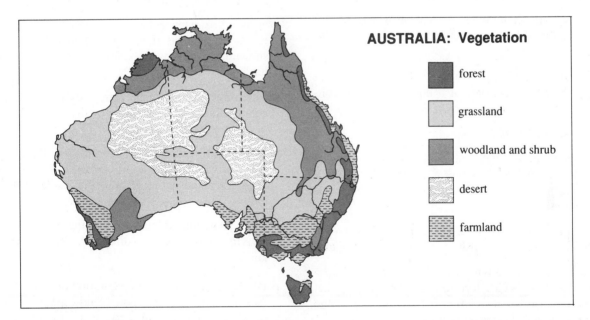

AUSTRALIA: Vegetation

- forest
- grassland
- woodland and shrub
- desert
- farmland

Thematic maps present information about a single aspect of geography, the environment, or society. They can be used to show agricultural patterns, industry, income, life expectancy, geological structures, military alliances, or a myriad of other details. The two thematic maps on this page are typical of product and vegetation maps found in many atlases for young readers.

Product maps may use a variety of pictorial symbols to show what kind of products are produced in a particular nation or region. For example, to indicate mining activity, a cartographer may use a pick axe, shovel, or other logo commonly associated with mining. Word labels or keyed numbers may also be used to indicate the material that is mined in a particular area. Other typical pictograms may include sheep and cattle to indicate ranching, oil rigs for petroleum production, cars for automobile manufacturing, and so on.

Vegetation maps may also use standard symbols to approximate actual conditions. The Australia vegetation map on this page shows five different types of vegetation that occur on this continent. In addition to giving direct information about vegetation, such maps often give clues about population distribution and climate. For example, the reader can infer that because much of central Australia is desert, it receives little rainfall and is sparsely populated.

(*continued from page 215*)

the single parallel used in most conic projections. Because distortions of shape and size are minimal, this projection is useful for mapping regions in middle latitudes with extended east-west areas, such as the United States or Asia.

landform drawing. A small-scale map showing landforms by the systematic application of a standardized set of simplified pictorial symbols. *See also* **pictorial relief map.**

Landsat. One of a series of Earth-observation satellites in a near-polar orbit designed to cover almost the entire earth, with repeated coverage every 18 days.

landscape map. A topographic map made to a relatively large scale and showing all details.

latitude. Angular distance on a meridian measured north or south of the equator.

layer tint. *See* **hypsometric tint.**

layered (relief hair) map. A map on which relief is represented by hypsometric layers. *See also* **relief map.**

leaf. One of the units into which the original sheet is folded to form part of a book, each leaf consisting of two pages, one on each side.

linear scale. *See* **bar scale.**

location map. A small-scale map inset in, or placed in the margin of, a map at a larger scale, to show the location of the area represented by the large-scale map.

longitude. The angular distance east or west of a reference meridian, usually the prime meridian.

map. A representation, normally to scale and on a flat medium, of a selection of material or abstract features on, or in relation to, the surface of the earth or other celestial body.

map profile. *See* **profile.**

map projection. Any systematic arrangement of meridians and parallels, portraying the curved surface of the earth upon a plane.

map section. A scaled representation of a vertical surface displaying both the profile where it intersects the surface of the ground and the underlying structures along the plane of intersection.

marginal information. Information which appears in the margin of a map.

marginal map. *See* **ancillary map.**

Mercator projection. A **cylindrical projection** that shows correct land shapes but distorts land areas, especially in higher latitudes. Frequently used for world maps.

meridian. A great circle arc of 180 degrees terminated by the geographic poles. *See also* **parallel.**

Miller cylindrical projection. A **cylindrical projection** used for showing the world. As in the **Mercator projection**, distortion increases in higher latitudes.

Mollweide homolographic projection. An **equal-area projection** that produces an oval-shaped map, often used for world distribution maps.

natural scale. *See* **representative fraction.**

neat line. A line which encloses the detail of a map.

orthophotomap. A map with a planimetrically accurate photograph image and some symbolized terrain and man-made features.

overlay. A transparent sheet containing matter, at the same scale as the map to which it is keyed, showing detail that does not appear on the original.

outline map. A map which presents just sufficient geographic information to permit the correlation of additional data placed over it.

panorama. A perspective representation of the landscape in which the detail is shown as if projected onto a vertical plane or onto the inside of a cylinder.

parallel. Any line of latitude, running parallel to the equator in an east-west direction. *See also* **meridian.**

perspective view. The representation on a plane surface of the three-dimensional landscape, using lines of projection converging to a central point, as the landscape might appear to the eye. Also called **worm's-eye view.**

photomap. A reproduction of an aerial photograph, to which names, symbols, grid lines have been added.

pictorial map. A map in which features are represented by individual pictures in elevation, or perspective, rather than by conventionalized cartographic symbols.

pictorial relief map. A map on which landforms and other topographic features are shown in their correct planimetric position by pictorial symbols representing their appearance from a high oblique view. *See also* **landform drawing.**

plane projection. Any **map projection** in which the parallels and meridians appear as if the surface of a globe was projected onto a flat surface (a plane) touching the globe at a single point.

planimetric map. A large-scale, detailed map, in which the outlines of buildings, roads, and other man-made features are shown to scale with little generalization.

plat. A scale diagram of political, subdivision, and property boundaries, as well as some physical features designed to provide a frame of reference for the purpose of recording ownership of land, mineral claims, or other property rights.

plate. A page or leaf containing illustrative matter, with or without explanatory text, that does not form part of either the preliminary or the main sequences of pages or leaves.

prime meridian. The meridian on the earth's surface from which longitude is measured. Since 1884, the meridian passing through Greenwich, England, has been recognized as the prime meridian.

profile. A scale representation of the intersection of a vertical surface with the surface of the ground.

recto. The right-hand page of a book; or the side of a map sheet intended to be read first.

relief. The collective elevations or inequalities of a land surface, represented on maps by contours, hypsometric tints, shading, spot elevations, hachures, etc.

relief map. A map produced primarily to represent the physical configuration of the landscape, often with hypsometric tints.

remote sensing. The measurement of surface characteristics from a distant aerial or satellite platform with an electronic or optical device for measuring or recording electromagnetic radiation.

representative fraction. The scale of a map expressed as a fraction or ratio which relates unit distance on the map to distance, measured in the same units, on the ground.

scale. The ratio of distances on a map to the actual distances they represent.

schematic map. A map representing features in a much simplified or diagrammatic form.

segment. A part of a map where, because of physical limitations, the area being portrayed has been divided to fit on the sheet.

shaded relief. A cartographic technique that provides an apparent three-dimensional configuration of the terrain on maps by the use of graded shadows that would be cast by high ground if light were shining from the northwest.

sounding. The measured or charted depth of water, expressed in feet or fathoms.

spot height. A point on a map whose elevation above sea level is noted, usually by a dot and the elevation value.

thematic map. A map portraying information on a specific topic, such as geology, agriculture, or demography, rather than general geographic distributions.

topographic map. A map designed to portray and identify the features of the earth's surface as precisely as possible within the limitations imposed by scale.

Universal Transverse Mercator (UTM) grid. A widely used plane-coordinate system, based on the transverse Mercator projection and employing 60 zones worldwide, extending from 80 degrees south to 84 degrees north, with each zone covering 6 degrees of longitude.

verbal scale. The relationship which a small distance on a map bears to the corresponding distance on the earth, expressed as an equivalence, such as 1 inch (on the map) equals 1 mile (on the ground).

verso. The left-hand page of a book.

vertical exaggeration. The ratio of the vertical to the horizontal scale.

view. A perspective representation of the landscape in which detail is shown as if projected onto an oblique plane.

worm's-eye view. *See* **perspective view.**

Chapter 8
Evaluations of
Atlases

Ambassador World Atlas

Facts at a Glance

Full Title: **Ambassador World Atlas.**
Publisher: Hammond Incorporated.
Editors: Martin A. Bacheller, Editor-in-Chief, and
the Hammond staff.
Copyright: 1986.

Edition Reviewed: 1986.
Number of Volumes: 1.
Number of Pages: 500.
Number of Maps: 415.
Number of Indexes: 1 master index, plus individual
same-page indexes accompanying all map
areas.
Number of Index Entries: 100,000 in master index;
48,000 in same-page indexes.
Trim Size: 9½″ × 12½″.
Binding: cloth.

Intended Readership: grade 9 and up.
Price: $39.95. 15 percent discount to schools and
libraries. ISBN 0-8437-1251-1.
Revised annually or twice a year as necessary.

I. Introduction

The Hammond *Ambassador World Atlas*, published
in 1984, incorporates the same cartography as the
Hammond's 1986 CITATION WORLD ATLAS and is
identical in trim size. Two additional features and a
greatly expanded index add 164 pages to the *Ambassador* edition. This review considers only those
features unique to the *Ambassador World Atlas*; for
a complete review, refer to the evaluation of the
CITATION WORLD ATLAS on page 231.

The *Ambassador* is indended for readers in grade
nine and above, although it may have more appeal
to adult users, primarily because of its indexes.

II. Format

Unlike its companion volume, the *Ambassador World
Atlas* is available only in a hardcover edition, al-

though it shares the same convenient 9½″ × 12½″ trim size. Its sturdy binding, durable cover, and heavy paper will stand up to extensive use in the library and classroom.

In format, the arrangement of maps corresponds exactly to that of the CITATION.

III. Special Features

In addition to all the features found in the CITATION, this work includes two special sections on weather. The first provides two pages of charts on "Foreign City Weather," listing average daily high and low temperatures for each month, together with the average number of days with rain. These well-organized, highly readable charts furnish useful information not only for travelers but also for students of world geography.

The second section, "U.S. City Weather," lists data on annual precipitation, wind speeds, record high and low temperatures (without dates), the elevations of weather stations, and average monthly temperature. Our reviewers found the information in this section too incomplete to be of significant value either to travelers or students.

IV. Currency

Map contents in the *Ambassador World Atlas* are as current as its 1984 copyright date. According to the publisher, the atlas is updated annually or twice yearly to incorporate changes in political boundaries, place names, and statistical data. A revised edition is scheduled for 1987 but was not reviewed for the Buying Guide.

V. Accessibility

The major difference between the *Ambassador* and CITATION editions is the master index of the place names in each volume. The *Ambassador*'s index of some 100,000 entries occupies more than 140 pages; the CITATION has 25,000 entries on 24 pages. According to the publisher, the master index cites all place names found in the atlas, including those not listed in the same-page indexes that accompany the maps. The entries themselves are more complete than those in the CITATION and enable the reader to locate a place name in only one step. ZIP codes for U.S. cities are also given in the master index, which may please librarians and businesspeople but will be of less use in the classroom.

In principle, the master index gives a citation for every map on which a given place name appears, which makes this edition much more accessible than the CITATION. Since each name is given a separate entry for each map, however, this system tends to inflate the total number of index entries. Nevertheless, there are problems. For example, the city of Bombay is listed three times in the master index. The first citation is given as "54/J8," Bombay's correct location on a map of Asia on page 54. The second citation is "2/N5." Although the grid "N5" is correct, this location is actually on page 3, not 2, of a two-page world map. (Bombay's location on a world map on page 1 is not cited in the index.) The final map location is given as "Bombay (harb.), India 68/B7." This gives the mistaken impression that the location is for the harbor rather than for the city itself. Moreover, the grid location "B7" refers to an inset map, not to Bombay's location on the map of India. (Similarly, the same-page index for India gives the single map reference "B7.") Although rare, such lapses pose pitfalls for the reader.

As in the CITATION, four large-scale maps of U.S. cities are included in neither the master index nor the table of contents, and are effectively lost to users.

A "Gazetteer-Index of the World" appears at the front of the volume. This list, which includes more place names than does its counterpart in the CITATION, also privides the "Sources of Population Data," thus allowing the user to check the date and reliability of statistics. This feature is important for serious researchers, though it is not relevant to the needs of most high school students.

VI. Summary

The *Ambassador World Atlas* is the largest atlas in Hammond's INTERNATIONAL/CITATION/AMBASSADOR series, and is priced accordingly. As does the CITATION, the *Ambassador* contains individual maps of all 50 U.S. states, and a same-page index for each map in the atlas. It also contains thematic maps for different nations and regions, as well as basic population statistics that accompany each main map. These features are all decided pluses, and $39.95 is a fair price to pay for the greater accessibility offered by the *Ambassador* edition—but only if this is the primary world atlas in a library's collection. Users requiring less emphasis on the United States, and/or more information about the physical world, may prefer the PRENTICE-HALL NEW WORLD ATLAS or RAND MCNALLY GOODE'S WORLD ATLAS.

Background Notes

Facts at a Glance

Full Title: **Background Notes on the Countries of the World**.

Publisher: U.S. Department of State; distributed by the Superintendent of Documents, U.S. Government Printing Office, Washington, D.C. 20402.

Editors: Juanita Adams, Joan Reppert Reams, and other State Department officers.

Copyright: 1984–1987.

Number of Volumes: series of 160 looseleaf pamphlets; two-piece binder available separately.

Number of Indexes: 1.

Number of Index Entries: 160.

Intended Readership: general.

Price: $70.00 for complete set; individual pamphlets $1.00 or $2.00.

Ongoing revision; yearly subscription to revised pamphlets as issued, $32.00.

I. Introduction

Background Notes consists of more than 160 "short, authoritative pamphlets about various countries; territories, and international organizations." Although not an atlas per se, each pamphlet in the set combines a number of encyclopedic and atlas-like features, and is designed to serve the needs of a wide variety of users, including students, teachers, librarians, writers, travelers, and businesspeople.

Background Notes is issued by the U.S. State Department. According to the Department, each pamphlet is "written by officers in the Department of State's geographic and functional bureaus" and edited by the Department's Editorial Division, a branch of its Bureau of Public Affairs.

II. Format

Each *Background Notes* pamphlet consists of four or eight 8½″ × 11″ pages devoted to a particular nation. (A few, such as China, are 16 pages long.) The self-contained pamphlets are perforated for insertion in a ring binder, and because each follows the same internal format, the entire series can be arranged to form an international atlas-gazetteer.

Each pamphlet provides informative text, a small location or orientation map, and a full national map. All maps are black-and-white and show political rather than topographical detail; the level of detail varies from one map to another.

The text is divided into several sections: Profile (including statistics on population, geography, government, and economy), People, Geography, History, Government, Political Conditions, Economy, Foreign Relations, Defense, and Relations with the U.S. A "Travel Notes" sidebar gives pertinent information for travelers to the country. Principal Government Officials are also listed, as are Principal U.S. Officials at the American Embassy and consulates in the country. In addition, many of the *Background Notes* include a bibliography.

The full-page black-and-white nation map included in each *Background Notes* is suitable for photocopying. All material in the pamphlets is in the public domain and may be reproduced without permission. These political maps show international boundaries, national capitals, major cities and towns, roads, railroads, international airports, and rivers. A handful of maps also depict state or provincial boundaries as well as major natural features other than rivers (for example, mountain ranges and deserts). All maps include a symbol key and scale.

A ring binder is not provided, but the pamphlets can be used with any two- or three-ring notebook binder. Because the complete set of *Background Notes* amounts to roughly 1,000 pages, at least two notebooks are needed to hold the set.

III. Special Features

Apart from the elements just mentioned, *Background Notes* contains no special features per se. However, since much of the information included in the pamphlets—in particular, the lists of government officials, embassies, and consulates—is not available in most general atlases or encyclopedias, these may be regarded as special features. The location or orientation maps, printed on the first page of each pamphlet, which show the nation in relation to its neighbors, are also useful.

IV. Geographical Balance

Because virtually every nation, including such small or little-known countries as Andorra, Bhutan, the Comoros, Liechtenstein, Monaco, Nauru, San Marino, São Tomé and Principe, and Seychelles, is the subject of an individual pamphlet, *Background Notes* can be said to have excellent geographical balance. Each nation, regardless of its size, is given a fairly detailed map; the size of the map seems to be determined by the nation's size and shape. In general, the maps are large enough to clearly show major cities, roads, and other important features.

The text provides a level of attention appropriate to each nation's importance and to the reader's potential requirements. Smaller nations are covered in four pages, larger or more complex ones in eight, and a few, such as China, in sixteen. Nations whose governments are out of favor with the United States government (such as Cuba, Kampuchea, and Nicaragua) receive the same dispassionate attention accorded to America's closest allies. In cases where relations with the U.S. are either particularly warm or especially strained, this is noted in the section on U.S. relations. However, the nature of the relationship does not seem to have prejudiced the information presented in the rest of the text.

V. Scale and Projections

Each map in *Background Notes* has been drawn to a different scale. As with the map sizes, scale is determined to a large degree by the size and shape of the nation and by the amount of detail needed to make the map accurate and useful. To determine the relative sizes of several different nations at a glance, the user must consult another source, since *Background Notes* does not contain a world map. However, the orientation map on the first page of each pamphlet is useful for comparing the size of a nation with that of its neighbors.

The map scales are not reported as fractional representations. However, each main map is accompanied by a bar scale that gives both metric and standard measures. The following examples indicate the general range of scales used in *Background Notes* maps: Iran, $9/10''$ = 150 miles; Iraq, $1/10''$ = 100 miles; Indonesia, $1''$ = 400 miles; Ireland, $1\frac{1}{2}''$ = 50 miles; Italy, $1''$ = 100 miles. At opposite extremes of the spectrum are the map of Canada, where $1''$ = 500 miles, and San Marino, where $4/5''$ = 1 mile. Although they exhibit a wide range, the scales are generally appropriate to the size of the country.

The projections used in the various maps are not identified. Because each map covers a single nation, where distortions are not as apparent as in area, continent, or world maps, this is not a serious omission. (It should be noted, however, that optimum projection types vary according to the size and location of the area depicted. For example, an ideal projection for representing an equatorial nation would

cause unacceptable distortions if used to represent a nation in the high latitudes.) On the whole, *Background Notes* seems to use projections that cause the least distortion to the area represented.

VI. Accuracy

Background Notes maps reflect official United States government policy. Therefore, each map carries the disclaimer that "boundary representation is not necessarily authoritative." The maps also note when U.S. government policy differs from the policy of other nations regarding political boundaries. For example, the maps of Finland, Poland, and the Soviet Union remind the reader that "the United States Government has not recognized the incorporation of Estonia, Latvia, and Lithuania into the Soviet Union. Names and boundary representation are not necessarily authoritative." The map of the Federal Republic of Germany includes the German Democratic Republic; the border between the two is shown but is not represented as an international boundary. A footnote on the map comments that the "final borders of Germany have not been established."

Even though the amount of detail is limited by the size and nature of the maps, in all other respects, the information appears to be definitive. Place names are spelled with consistent accuracy, and spelling follows generally accepted contemporary practice. Anglicized spellings are used for major cities (for example, *Warsaw*) with the vernacular spelling in parentheses (*Warszawa*).

Although all maps in the set are rendered in black-and-white, cartographic detail is clear. The quality is far superior to that found in MAPS ON FILE and is often comparable to that of political maps found in many commercial atlases. Occasionally, nation maps show less detail than the user might wish. For example, while the United Kingdom map shows such major cities as London, Bristol, Birmingham, Manchester, Liverpool, and Leeds, it excludes others such as Portsmouth, Sheffield, Bradford, and York. On the whole, however, users will be well served with the accuracy of the maps.

Since more pages of *Background Notes* are occupied by text than by maps, the accuracy of the text is also an important consideration. Text (including nation statistics) has been compiled by area specialists in the State Department. Our reviewers found the information about people, geography, history, government, political conditions, economy, and other aspects to be highly reliable. Although this material makes no effort to be comprehensive, it nevertheless provides an accurate, well organized introduction to each nation akin in many respects to that found in a good encyclopedia.

VIII. Currency

Background Notes is available as a complete set but each pamphlet is published separately and is updated on an individual basis. The title page of each pamphlet includes the month and year in which it was published. Because the State Department issues updated versions of approximately 75 *Background Notes* each year, the currency of an entire set will vary. Text and maps are revised to reflect conditions at the time of publication. Institutions and individuals can take out annual subscriptions to all the *Background Notes* pamphlets published during that year. (See also *Summary*.) This revision and subscription procedure helps ensure that a collection's set of *Background Notes* is as up-to-date as possible.

VIII. Legibility

All maps and text in the *Background Notes* series are in the public domain and may be reproduced without permission and at no fee. Although the maps are not specifically designed for photocopying, our tests indicate that most of them will produce satisfactory copies, depending on the quality of the machine.

The maps generally display a high graphic quality. For the most part, place names are legible although the small type used for place names on many maps may discourage younger students and the visually impaired. It may also adversely affect the quality of photocopies. Similarly, detail on some of the maps (for example, the Bahamas and Fiji) is also too small to reproduce clearly. Lines representing roads and rivers are faint and may not reproduce on some machines. The dark shading of neighboring nations may also be obscured on photocopies. (The main nation covered on these maps is always unshaded so that place names and other symbols appear on a plain white background.) Nevertheless, the overall legibility of the maps is adequate for their intended purpose.

IX. Summary

Background Notes is a concise, accurate, and authoritative source of maps and basic information about the world's nations. The series should serve the needs of a wide variety of users. Students at the junior high school and high school levels will find the material especially helpful when they need to research facts or prepare social studies reports about specific na-

tions. Teachers can use the series to supplement social studies lessons and to provide definitive national statistics, or to add to their resource collection. Librarians will also find many uses for the series in response to their patrons' ready reference requests; in addition, libraries will welcome the fact that the pamphlets can be copied without permission. Travelers, writers, and journalists may also find these publications useful for many purposes.

In many respects, *Background Notes* is a direct if unintended competitor to MAPS ON FILE. Although not appropriate for elementary students, the series will serve a wider range of students in the higher grades than will MAPS ON FILE, and will provide much factual information that is not offered by MAPS ON FILE. MAPS ON FILE yields clearer photocopies, but in virtually every other respect *Background Notes* is a superior and more professional source of geographic information.

Background Notes are available individually at $1 or $2 each, depending on the title. The complete set, which costs $70, represents a considerable savings over the cumulative price of individual pamphlets. An annual subscription, costing $32, ensures that the subscriber automatically receives revised pamphlets upon publication. Roughly 75 titles are updated and reissued each year.

Interested individuals or institutions may order *Background Notes* through the Superintendent of Documents, U.S. Government Printing Office, Washington, D.C. 20402.

Britannica Atlas

Facts at a Glance

Full Title: **Britannica Atlas**.
Publisher: Encyclopaedia Britannica, Inc.
Copyright: 1986.

Edition Reviewed: 1986.
Number of Volumes: 1.
Number of Pages: 568.
Number of Maps: 301.
Number of Indexes: 1.
Number of Index Entries: 160,000.
Trim Size: 11" × 14¾".
Binding: cloth.

Intended Readership: general.
Price: $79.50.
Sold door-to-door, by direct mail, and in combination with NEW ENCYCLOPAEDIA

BRITANNICA. ISBN 0-85229-436-0.
Revised every two years.

I. Introduction

The *Britannica Atlas* is a large-size (11″ × 14¾″) general world atlas that was compiled and published in a joint effort with Rand McNally. The contents of this atlas, except for slight variations in the foreword, are taken directly from *The New International Atlas* published by Rand McNally and reviewed in Bowker's *General Reference Books for Adults*.

The maps were compiled by the cartographic firms of Rand McNally & Co. (Chicago), Mondadori-McNally GmbH (Stuttgart), Cartographia (Budapest), Esselte Map Service (Stockholm), George Philip & Son Limited (London), and Teikoku-Shoin Co., Ltd. (Tokyo), under the direction of an eight-member International Planning Conference, and assisted by a team of map advisors and contributors from academic and government institutions. The maps for the "World Scene" section were designed by David L. Burke, with the help of a team of contributors from American universities.

II. Format

The *Britannica Atlas* is arranged in six distinct sections: introductory material (contents, index maps, and legend); general reference maps; world thematic maps ("World Scene"); lists of geographic terms and name changes; statistical information; and an index to place names. The general reference maps occupy nearly 300 pages; the index is 200 pages long.

Almost all of the maps spread across both open pages. Because the pages lie flat (without breaking the spine), no information is lost in the gutter.

On maps of the oceans and continents, the colors used correspond to broad ecosystem types, such as tundra, grassland, or desert. The regional maps at 1:3,000,000 and 1:6,000,000 use colors to show elevation with hypsometric tints. The regional maps at 1:12,000,000 and 1:1,000,000 show international boundaries with colors, as well as internal political boundaries.

III. Special Features

The main special feature of this atlas is its "internationalness." The foreword and other text is in five languages: English, German, Spanish, French, and Portuguese. The local spelling of place names is used on the maps. For names in non-roman alphabets, an internationally accepted transliteration is used. This is a generally sound practice, but may cause some confusion for American users. Transliterations for place names in the Soviet Union in particular will look odd to most Americans. In the case of extremely unfamiliar local names of prominent cities and natural features, English translation is provided.

A glossary, arranged alphabetically by local spelling of place names, follows the map section. Each term is translated in each of the five languages.

Following the glossary are tables showing place name changes since 1969; area and population data for continents, countries, and administrative subdivisions; and the population of cities and towns. The international effort is clearly evident, as every country and its capital city are listed, as well as all urban centers with 50,000 or more inhabitants.

The "World Scene" section contains double-page world maps showing 24 subjects related to cultural and physical geography. Among the topics covered in these thematic maps are population, religions, languages, agricultural regions, minerals, energy production and consumption, time zones, climate regions, and natural vegetation. Tables, graphs, and inset maps help describe each subject. This section of world thematic maps is much more extensive and detailed than comparable sections in other atlases.

The index is quite helpful. In addition to listing the page and location of each place name, it uses symbols to indicate the type of feature (political unit, mountain, swamp, island, etc.) associated with all names other than populated places.

An especially useful feature is the listing of adjoining map page numbers in the borders of each regional map.

IV. Geographical Balance

The collaborative efforts of an international team of distinguished cartographers, and the cartographic capabilities of respected mapmaking concerns in five countries, have helped ensure that the *Britannica Atlas* is the most balanced atlas on the market today. There is no evident bias toward any region or nation as there is in most U.S., Canadian, and British atlases of otherwise high quality. All areas of the earth receive adequate coverage, with an appropriate level of detail.

V. Scale and Projections

In an effort to provide valid area comparisons of world regions, consistent map scales have been used throughout this atlas. Maps of the oceans are at a scale of 1:48,000,000; continents are shown at 1:24,000,000; and regions are at 1:12,000,000.

Most inhabited areas of the world are mapped at either 1:6,000,000 (for less populous areas such as South America, Africa, and Australia) or 1:3,000,000 (for more populous areas such as Anglo-America, Europe, and parts of Asia). Regions with high population or significant economic activity are shown again at 1:1,000,000, and selected metropolitan areas at 1:300,000.

On all maps, scales are given as ratios and also shown in bar scales (in both kilometers and statute miles).

VI. Accuracy

The *Britannica Atlas* is noted for its precision and accuracy. However, there are at least two blemishes—minor but noteworthy—on its reputation.

The first of these concerns the now-celebrated identification of a nonexistent town in the North of England, "Wansbeck." This "town" appears on both the British Isles map and on the more detailed Dublin-Manchester-Newcastle upon Tyne map, which were compiled by the highly respected firm of George Philip & Son. Wansbeck's population is supposedly between 25,000 and 100,000 people. The placement of this imaginary town on maps of such otherwise impeccable quality is either a major gaffe, a tongue-in-cheek joke, or an efficient method of copyright protection.

The second inaccuracy concerns the omission of a well-known town in the Soviet Union—namely, Chernobyl—from the detailed map of the Ukraine. This map was compiled by the Hungarian mapmaker Cartographia of Budapest. Soviet authorities have been known to prohibit sensitive sites, such as towns with military installations or advanced research facilities, from appearing on their own or other Eastern-bloc maps. One can presume that Chernobyl was omitted for a similar reason. (*Not* because of the accident that occurred at the nuclear power plant there, which in any event postdates this map, but simply because Chernobyl was the site of a nuclear power plant.) Chernobyl does appear on maps of similar or even less detail produced by other cartographers whose atlases are reviewed in this Buying Guide. This omission may lead the reader to wonder whether other Soviet towns have been omitted on similar grounds.

VII. Currency

The copyright date of this atlas is 1986. It contains information as current as 1985. The census date or estimate date is indicated for each country in the city population section. The populations listed in the World

Information Table are 1985 estimates by Rand McNally.

VIII. Legibility

Typefaces on the maps are neat and legible, although some users may have difficulty reading the 3-point type used for some small towns and natural features. Place-name categories are easily differentiated by typeface and are explained extensively in the legend. On the maps, land areas are shown in a fairly dark tint, while bodies of water are in shades of blue. Though shaded relief is used extensively, this does not interfere with legibility. Name labels are well placed, and it is easy to identify the features to which they refer.

Political boundaries are pastel colored on the 1:12,000,000 scale maps and red on the other scale maps. One of the drawbacks of this atlas is that on the other scale maps, the province or state names are sometimes placed along the borders, sometimes placed in the center of the unit, and appear in either red or black type. This is quite confusing, as there is no explanation on the map pages and it is not adequately explained in the legend.

Different symbols are used to indicate the size of cities, and different sizes of type are used to indicate their economic and political importance. These are all readily distinguishable.

IX. Accessibility

To find the location of a place name, the user can look in the index under its local language spelling or under the English equivalent name. For example, the location of Vienna, Austria, can be found by looking under "Vienna" or "Wien." Most place names are indexed to the largest-scale map on which they appear.

Degrees of longitude and latitude, rather than the letter-number grid common to other atlases, are used to locate a place. Because the coordinates of each place are given in degrees and seconds in the index, places can be located much more accurately.

X. Summary

The *Britannica Atlas* is without question the most comprehensive and authoritative of all the atlases reviewed in this Buying Guide. It features the best geographic balance, an extensive index, and up-to-date thematic maps. Its outstanding, highly detailed general maps contain a wealth of information about every region of the globe.

At $79.95, it is also the most expensive of the atlases in this Buying Guide. It should also be noted that it is not a "children's" atlas, and is not suitable for use in the elementary or middle school grades. Nor does it have—despite its title and the fact that it is sold by Encyclopaedia Britannica, Inc.—any direct connection to the NEW ENCYCLOPAEDIA BRITANNICA or any other encyclopedia. Rather, it is a much lower-priced edition of the *New International Atlas* published by Rand McNally and reviewed in Bowker's *General Reference Books for Adults*.

The *Britannica Atlas* would be the flagship atlas of any collection. However, libraries that do not require so comprehensive or expensive an atlas might be just as well served by the NATIONAL GEOGRAPHIC ATLAS OF THE WORLD, the PRENTICE-HALL NEW WORLD ATLAS, or RAND MCNALLY GOODE'S WORLD ATLAS.

Citation World Atlas

Facts at a Glance

Full Title: **Citation World Atlas**.
Publisher: Hammond Incorporated.
Editors: Martin A. Bacheller, Editor-in-Chief, and the Hammond staff.
Copyright: 1986.

Edition Reviewed: 1986.
Number of Volumes: 1.
Number of Pages: 364.
Number of Maps: 400.
Number of Indexes: 1 master index, plus 400 individual map indexes.
Number of Index Entries: 25,000.
Trim Size: 9½″ × 12½″.
Binding: Available in cloth or paper.

Intended Readership: high school through adult.
Price: $24.95 cloth, $15.95 paper. 15 percent discount to schools and libraries.
ISBN 0-8437-1254-6.
Revised annually or twice a year as necessary.

I. Introduction

The Hammond *Citation World Atlas* is a general world atlas intended for readers in grades nine and above. This 364-page volume, featuring 400 maps, was edited by the Hammond staff, with an advisory board composed of thirteen notable specialists in geography and related fields. The selected list of source materials includes the best available government documents for statistics and place names, although with a heavy bias toward United States sources. The *Citation* is intended for the high school through adult level.

II. Format

Physically, the atlas will hold up well in a classroom or library setting. The sturdy hardcover binding holds the pages firmly and does not crack with repeated use. The paperbound edition of the *Citation* was not examined by reviewers.

The maps in this volume are divided into nine geographic sections: World and Polar Regions, Europe, Asia, Pacific Ocean and Australia, Africa, South America, North America, Canada, and the United States. The largest scale map for every continent, region, country, province, or state is a political map, followed by smaller-scale thematic maps depicting such topics as population distribution and climate. A physical map is also provided for each region.

Most maps fit on one full page or less. Some maps extend to a second page, but this does not pose a problem, as the contents do not run into the gutter and the pages lie flat when the book is opened. The size of the atlas is ideal for student and library users.

Map legends, which appear under the title of each political map, provide bar scales in miles and kilometers and the scale as a fractional representation, but only a few of the symbols that are found on the maps. Symbols used on the political maps (including those for rivers, mountain peaks, marshlands, urban areas, and cities other than capitals) are not described anywhere in the atlas. Although experienced map users will not find this omission a drawback, younger readers or anyone unfamiliar with the conventions of cartography will require some assistance in interpreting the maps. For example, on the map of Central Africa, students may not be able to identify the unexplained symbol for swamps that is used along the Congo-Zaire border or, on the map of Southern Africa, the dots spread along the southern coast of Namibia. Knowledgeable readers may correctly assume that these dots represent the desert but will be left to wonder why the name "Namib Desert" extends well beyond the dots along the entire coast.

Each thematic map is accompanied by its own legend, which adequately explains the meaning of the colors and symbols employed.

III. Special Features

Each political map in the *Citation World Atlas* is accompanied by a brief fact table listing the area, population, largest city, and highest and lowest points for every continent. The same information is provided for individual nations, in addition to their capital cities, monetary units, major languages, and major religions. Additional data are provided for the United States. A color illustration of the country's national flag adjoins each fact list. Population figures appear in each political map's list of place names, as do ZIP codes for U.S. cities. These features will be useful for ready reference as well as for classroom work on world geography.

A two-page introduction clearly explains the scope, organization, and use of the atlas but fails to provide an adequate guide to map reading. In the section titled "Indexes—Pinpointing a Location," the text and two illustrations are particularly misleading and confusing. Students who are unfamiliar with map grid systems will need special assistance to understand their use.

Seven pages of special features appear at the end of the atlas. Airline distances are provided in five separate tables. Two pages of world statistical tables offer useful data on the solar system, the earth, continents, oceans, canals, islands, mountains, rivers, and natural lakes. An illustrated article on map projections by the noted cartographer Erwin Raisz completes the atlas and adds a noteworthy dimension to the work. True geographic awareness requires knowledge of the uses and limitations of map projections. This three-page article is a good, authoritative introduction to the subject. For librarians, these pages of special features are clearly organized for ready reference work.

IV. Geographical Balance

The *Citation World Atlas* includes maps of all nations, although half of the volume is devoted to the United States and Canada. Canada is covered in 26 pages, for example, and the entire continent of Africa in only 18. Not a single African country is given an individual map. Countries on other continents appear in groups, pairs, or individually. The introduction explains that several nations are shown on a single map if "they are of lesser relative importance" as separate entities. As examples, the following four areas are listed with their largest scale maps: Ohio (1:1,800,000), Denmark (1:2,300,000), Argentina (1:13,000,000), and Western Africa (1:15,200,000). For school studies on North America and Europe, the map scales are good; for developing countries, they are inadequate. Geographic imbalance limits the usefulness of the *Citation*, as a world atlas should serve as a primary source of information on those areas which are least familiar to the user.

V. Scale and Projections

A variety of scales are employed in the *Citation World Atlas* depending on the nation or area depicted. The choice of scales reflects the editors' appraisal of a given area's relative importance, a judgment that may not always coincide with the specific needs of the reader.

The name of the map projection used for each political map appears with the map's title. The projections are the most common ones used to depict areas of the size and shape under consideration. Southeast Asia, for example, is shown on an azimuthal equal-area projection. Smaller areas, such as Scandinavia and the Indian Subcontinent, use a conic projection, while many individual countries are shown on the Mercator projection. The use of these projections ensures that the shapes and sizes of continents, countries, and states will be familiar to students.

VI. Accuracy

Place names appear in the local official spellings—a sound practice which conforms to international cartographic trends—with the exception of major names, which follow conventional anglicized spellings. According to the introduction, the complete form of a place name can be found in the index when there is not sufficient space on the map itself. Likewise, alternate names or spellings of a place appear only in the index, not on the maps. This system can present problems to the reader who consults a map without looking at the index. For example, no cross-reference is given in the text from *Cambodia* to *Kampuchea*, or from *East Germany* to its official name, the *German Democratic Republic*. In the maps of China, *Peking* is given preference over *Beijing*, although the majority of names are spelled according to the official Pinyin system.

The placement of names on the maps is accurate. Locations of physical features, such as mountain ranges, are clear when they are labeled, although the physical maps fail to add a generic description to names of physical features. *El Djouf*, for example, is identified as a desert only in the index, not on the map itself.

VII. Currency

With a few exceptions, most of the *Citation*'s data are as current as its 1986 copyright date. The nation of Brunei is not described as a member of the United Nations, even though it joined the UN in 1984. The Byelorussian S.S.R. is not listed in the gazetteer-index of "grand divisions" and countries, although it is a member of the UN, as is the Ukrainian S.S.R., which does appear on the list. Changes rendered to the flags of Egypt, Haiti, and St. Vincent prior to or during 1986 are not reflected in the atlas.

VIII. Legibility

Typefaces used on the maps are neat and legible. Place-name categories are clearly differentiated by typefaces, although these categories are not delineated in the legend. Individual maps of the U.S. states (each on one or two pages) have the greatest number and density of place names, but towns and geographic features are easy to locate. The use of different colors to highlight international and internal boundary lines is an immense help to the reader. In fact, it is the generous and clear use of color that makes this atlas especially suitable for student use.

IX. Accessibility

Individual political maps are accompanied by an index of place names that appear on their pages together with a key to each map's local grid system. Although inset maps of urban areas do not appear in the table of contents, they are included in the individual indexes, but at the expense of their locations on the primary political maps. For example, the index for the map of India refers the reader only to the inset map of Bombay. To find Bombay's location within the country as a whole, the reader must scan the map of India.

A complete index of place names is found at the end of the volume. This 25,000-item master index cites the larger political division for each entry, with the page number for the largest-scale map on which the place appears. A reader must then turn to the map's individual index (which is not always on the same page as the map) to obtain the precise location. Latitudes and longitudes are not given.

A major fault with this "complete" index is the practice of citing only one map for each place name, even when the name appears on several maps. Furthermore, four large-scale maps of United States cities which appear at the end of the U.S. section, are not listed in either individual indexes or the complete index. This incomplete and often cumbersome indexing system limits access to the *Citation World Atlas* and will doubtless prove frustrating not only to the beginning but also the experienced atlas user.

X. Summary

The *Citation World Atlas* is priced at $24.95 and $15.95 for the cloth and paperbound editions, respectively. These prices are very reasonable for the generous size of the text. However, prospective purchasers should be aware of some major limitations in considering this a true world atlas: the excess coverage of the United States and Canada, to the detriment of coverage of important developing areas, like Africa, and the inadequacies of the indexing system already described are two significant limitations. Despite its faults, the atlas remains a useful, reasonably current reference tool in schools and libraries. Comparable atlases include the RAND McNALLY FAMILY WORLD ATLAS, RAND McNALLY GOODE'S WORLD ATLAS, and the PRENTICE-HALL NEW WORLD ATLAS.

Colorprint Scholastic World Atlas

Facts at a Glance

Full Title: **Colorprint Scholastic World Atlas**.
Publisher: American Map Corporation.
Copyright: none given.

Number of Volumes: 1.
Number of Pages: 46.
Number of Maps: 36.
Number of Indexes: 1.
Number of Index Entries: approximately 2,400.
Intended Readership: grade 3 and up.
Trim Size: 9¼" × 12¼".
Binding: paper.

Price: $2.95, with a 20-percent discount to schools and libraries on orders of $250 or more. Sold in bookstores and direct from publisher. ISBN 0-8416-9552-0.

I. Introduction

The *Colorprint Scholastic World Atlas* is a 46-page paperback published by American Map Corporation of Maspeth, NY. American Map Corporation has been producing maps and atlases for 60 years and prides itself on its "ability to combine cartographic excellence with affordability."

II. Format

The atlas is divided into maps of the world, continents, groups of countries (for example, the Scandinavian countries), and individual countries. These are all political maps.

The maps generally cover one full page with the exceptions of the maps of the world, the United States, and the Soviet Union. Although these maps are two-page spreads, this presents no problems in reading them since the pages lie flat when opened. Bar scales, in miles and kilometers, appear under the title of each map. Two symbols are used throughout the atlas, small circles for cities and stars for capitals, but they are not explained in the book. The atlas is a convenient size for classroom use and suitable for studying basic political geography as well as for locating places discussed in a current events class. The atlas is unsatisfactory for teaching physical geography, however, since it provides too few physical features.

III. Special Features

Information on the solar system, including the planets' relative diameters and distances from the sun, is located inside the front cover of the atlas, along with a table that provides information about each planet's eccentricity of orbit, period of rotation, volume, mass, density, and so on. Although this information may be interesting to a select few, it seems only marginally useful or comprehensible to most students. The page also includes some "Facts About the Earth," for example, land area, ocean area, the lengths of a degree of latitude and longitude at the equator.

Users will find "Some Geographical Comparisons" of the world's largest islands and lakes, the longest rivers, and the highest and lowest points on continents inside the back cover.

IV. Geographical Balance

The atlas covers all the countries of the world. Of the 36 maps in the book, 2 are world maps, 12 cover Europe, 7 cover Asia, 2 cover Africa, 4 cover North America, 3 Central America, and 3 South America.

Several areas are featured in insets. For example, the two-page map of the United States includes insets of the areas surrounding several major cities such as San Francisco, Los Angeles, Chicago, St. Louis, Detroit, New York, and others. The map of France includes an inset of Paris and its surrounding area.

One map, titled "Israel, Jordan, Lebanon, Syria," shows only Israel in its entirety. And, because of its long and narrow shape, that country is shown in two parts: the major portion of the country and an inset of the Negev Desert.

V. Scale and Projections

Scale is shown on bar scales in both miles and kilometers. These appear beneath the title of each map and vary from about 1:3,800,600 on a map of Haiti and the Dominican Republic to approximately 1:50,700,000 on a map of Asia. Several standard pro-

jections are used, for example, polar and Mercator for the world maps and sinusoidal for Africa. These are listed under the map title.

VI. Accuracy

The placement of names on the map is accurate. Locations of physical features, such as lakes and rivers, are reasonably clear. In some instances, however, mountain ranges appear as shadings with no labels, or labeled with no shadings, resulting in some confusion.

Place names appear with conventional anglicized spellings. The preferred Pinyin spellings for place names in China are not used here; the capital is, therefore, labeled as *Peking*, not *Beijing*. Occasionally, alternate or local spellings are provided in parentheses as in *Riyadh (Ar Riyad)* and *Beirut (Beyrouth)*.

VII. Currency

Although no copyright date appears in the atlas, there is evidence of revisions made after 1984. Kenneth Kister noted in the *Atlas Buying Guide* (1984) that Kampuchea and Zimbabwe were referred to by their old names, *Cambodia* and *Rhodesia*. This edition reflects these name changes. Similarly, Vietnam is shown as the unified country it has been since 1976. However, the southern capital of Vietnam, renamed Ho Chi Minh City, is still called *Saigon*, and Upper Volta, which has been Burkina Faso for years, is still *Upper Volta*.

VIII. Legibility

Several typefaces are used to differentiate place-name categories, though these are not explained. International boundary lines are shown by broken black lines and are highlighted in different colors on the maps of continents. On maps showing groups of countries, as well as on the map of the United States, political boundaries are indicated by broken gray lines.

Boundary lines and labels are clear and legible. Some users may find the shading somewhat faint.

IX. Accessibility

A seven-page "Glossary and Index" is included at the back of the atlas but, in fact, this is an index only. The listings are alphabetical with countries in boldface type, political divisions in uppercase letters, and capitals or chief cities are followed by a dot in a small circle. Physical features, such as islands, mountains, lakes, and rivers, are in italics. Page number and grid location are provided in the index. Area and/or population figures are given. In many instances where only one number follows an entry, young users may be confused about whether this is an area or a population figure. Because the atlas provides no explanations, its accessibility is limited.

Although the publisher claims to have included more than 2,400 entries in the index, a spot-check revealed many omissions. In addition, several map revisions are not reflected in the index. For example, *Bulawayo* is listed as a city in *Rhodesia* instead of in *Zimbabwe*, the current name of the country formerly called *Rhodesia*.

X. Summary

Colorprint Scholastic World Atlas is priced at $2.95, with discounts for bulk orders. The atlas is reasonably up-to-date, accurate, and legible. Although the index and special features are only marginally helpful, the low price makes it a good buy for teaching basic map skills without having to share books.

Colorprint Student's Atlas of the World

Facts at a Glance

Title: **Colorprint Student's Atlas of the World.**
Publisher: American Map Corporation.
Copyright: 1963.

Number of Volumes: 1.
Number of Pages: 22.
Number of Maps: 15.
Number of Indexes: 1.
Number of Index Entries: approximately 2,400.
Intended Readership: grade 3 and up.
Trim Size: 9¼″ × 12¼″.
Binding: paper.

Price: $2.25, with a 20-percent discount to schools and libraries on orders of $250 or more. Sold in bookstores and directly from the publisher. ISBN 8416-9551-2.

I. Introduction

Student's Atlas of the World is another title in the *Colorprint* series published by American Map Corporation. It is a 22-page paperback atlas containing 14 color maps and one black-and-white polar-projection world map. American Map Corporation has been publishing maps and atlases for 60 years and they have tried to provide an "accurate, authorita-

tive, up-to-date atlas" at a very modest price. The atlas is intended for classroom use in grades 3 and above.

For a discussion of Scale and Projections, Accuracy, Currency, Legibility, and Accessibility see the review of the COLORPRINT SCHOLASTIC WORLD ATLAS on pages 233-34 of this Buying Guide.

II. Format

Student's Atlas of the World contains no table of contents. Of the 15 maps included, two cover the world and six cover the continents. The remaining seven include the following: the United States; Canada; the United Kingdom and Ireland; Mexico, Central America, and the Caribbean Area; Western Europe (highlighting the Common Market); the Philippines; and Japan and Korea. Similar to SCHOLASTIC WORLD ATLAS, the limited size of the volume allows it to lie flat when opened. Therefore, no information is lost in the inner margins of the two-page maps.

Most of the maps cover a full page. The exceptions include two 2-page maps of the world and Europe, as well as three small maps (Western Europe, the Philippines, Japan and Korea) that appear on one page.

The index, described by the publisher as "detailed," is located in the middle of the atlas. This placement is somewhat inconvenient since most users would expect to find an index at the back of the book.

III. Geographical Balance

Of the 15 maps included, seven cover countries on the European and North American continents. The remaining eight include two world maps, Africa, Asia, Australia, the Philippines, and a map of Japan and Korea. Overall, the coverage is skimpy, considering the publisher's claims for it.

IV. Summary

The *Colorprint Student's Atlas of the World*, priced at $2.25, offers half as many maps as the SCHOLASTIC WORLD ATLAS at much more than half the price. *Student's Atlas of the World* contains no special features and little else to recommend it, especially as it is not up-to-date. It does not reflect the many name changes of developing countries. Those in need of an inexpensive atlas should consider the SCHOLASTIC WORLD ATLAS or the RAND MCNALLY QUICK REFERENCE WORLD ATLAS (at only $2.95, with 48 pages). If, however, a comprehensive world atlas in paperback is desired, several are available, such as the Hammond CITATION WORLD ATLAS.

Colorprint World Atlas

Facts at a Glance

Full Title: **Colorprint World Atlas**.
Publisher: American Map Corporation.
Copyright: 1959.

Number of Volumes: 1.
Number of Pages: 14.
Number of Maps: 13.
Number of Indexes: none.
Intended Readership: grade 3 and up.
Trim Size: 9¼″ × 12¼″.
Binding: paper.

Price: $1.50, with discounts of 20 percent to
schools and libraries on orders of $250 or more.
Sold in bookstores, through newspaper advertising,
and direct from publisher. ISBN 8416-9550-4.

I. Introduction

Colorprint World Atlas is a 14-page volume of color
maps published by American Map Corporation.
American Map Corporation has been publishing maps
and atlases for 60 years. According to the publisher,
the *Colorprint* series is designed to combine "cartographic excellence with affordability." The *World
Atlas* is intended for classroom use from third grade
and above.

II. Format

World Atlas contains 13 color maps. Six of these
cover the continents: North America, South America, Europe, Africa, Australia, and Asia. The remaining seven include the United States, Mexico and
Central America, Canada, The World, Alaska, Philippines, and a map of Japan and Korea.

The atlas lacks both a table of contents and an
index, and contains no special features. The front
and back covers show the flags of 101 countries. A
spot-check of these revealed that several were incorrect and the pale colors somewhat misleading.

Because of the thinness of the atlas, the pages lie
flat and no information is lost in the inner margins.

III. Geographical Balance

Of the 13 maps included, three cover two pages
(United States, The World, Europe), seven are full-
page maps (Mexico and Central America, Canada,
North America, South America, Africa, Australia,
and Asia), and the remaining three are on one page
(Alaska, Philippines, Japan, and Korea).

IV. Accessibility

The atlas lacks a table of contents and an index. In
consequence, the accessibility of the information is
severely limited.

V. Summary

The *Colorprint World Atlas* has little more than its
very low price of $1.50 to recommend it. It contains
no special features and even lacks some regular features, as previously mentioned. Several other inexpensive atlases are available that provide more at a
relatively small cost increase, for example, COLOR-
PRINT SCHOLASTIC WORLD ATLAS and RAND
MCNALLY QUICK REFERENCE WORLD ATLAS (both
$2.95).

Comparative World Atlas

Facts at a Glance

Full Title: **Comparative World Atlas**.
Publisher: Hammond Incorporated.
Editor: Martin A. Bacheller.
Copyright: 1985.

Number of Volumes: 1.
Number of Pages: 60.
Number of Maps: 84.
Number of Indexes: 2.
Number of Illustrations: 35.
Trim Size: 9⅜″ × 12¼″.
Binding: paper.

Intended Readership: grades 8 through 12.
Price: $3.75.
Sold in bookstores. ISBN 0-8437-7110-0.
Revised annually.

I. Introduction

The *Comparative World Atlas* is a 60-page paperback
reference appropriate for use by high school students. Its purpose is threefold: to present cartographic material on major world regions; to provide
comparative map data; and to explain selected geographic information through illustrations and text.

II. Format

The *Comparative World Atlas* contains a wide variety
of maps whose organization is not always logically
apparent. A political map of the world is followed
by a series of both physical and political maps on

regions and subregions of the world, each usually one page in size. Interspersed among these are smaller maps which present data on the temperature and rainfall, vegetation, population distribution, and physical features of most continents.

Except for scale information, the legends on political maps vary. Some include symbols for capitals, canals, railroads, and international boundaries. Others use a different symbol for capitals or include symbols for provincial boundaries, administrative centers, or mountain peaks. Moreover, on physical maps the color gradients for elevation are not consistent. Because every map has a legend, each one is individualized. This inconsistency may prove troublesome to inexperienced map users.

Unlike other Hammond student atlases, this paperback is larger than the customary notebook size— 9⅜″ × 12¼″. Although it is less convenient to carry or store than a smaller book, its larger maps are easier to read.

III. Special Features

This atlas has many special features. On the inside front cover is a list of geographic terms. A gazetteer index follows the table of contents. The cartography is introduced by a section of illustrated text explaining the world's variety of landforms, such as tundra, desert, and boreal forest.

There is a series of comparative world maps in a section following maps of the earth's major regions. They present data on such topics as major religions, languages, population distribution, climate, and agricultural regions. Maps showing the raw material production of such minerals as petroleum, coal, iron, and nickel are also included, as are those of major crops like wheat and barley. Last is a series of comparative maps illustrating temperature, rainfall, wind, and ocean-current patterns.

The end of the atlas contains an extensive latitude-longitude index (some 6,500 entries) and an illustrated section explaining various map projections. A set of statistical tables on principal rivers, islands, and lakes, located on the inside back cover, completes the special material.

The special features in this atlas offer many opportunities for classroom study. The imaginative teacher can build a variety of activities around these special sections, thus making the atlas valuable beyond its basic use as a general reference tool.

IV. Geographical Balance

With the exception of Antarctica, which is shown only as part of a world map, all major regions of the world are included in this atlas. Greatest emphasis

is given the continents of North America, Europe, and Asia, which include maps of subregional areas. The placement of maps of the Near and Middle East, as well as the Soviet Union, in the section under Europe may be confusing to the reader.

V. Scale and Projections

Bar scales both in miles and kilometers appear beneath the title of every political map. A variety of scales is used throughout the cartography section; however, the same scales are applied to the physical and political maps of the same area, which usually face each other. The scales are geared for maximum readability on a page and are usually reasonable for the size of the area being represented.

The atlas also uses a variety of projections, including conic, polyconic, and Lambert-Azimuthal equal-area projections, which are so labeled on the maps.

VI. Accuracy

Place names appear to be spelled accurately. The map of the Soviet Union, however, does not label the Ural Mountains, and on the physical map of Europe, they are labeled *Urals* without any identification of the kind of feature they are.

The atlas uses generic titles, such as *China, East Germany, Ireland*, and *South Korea* on its maps. However, the maps do not consistently provide official names for these nations in the index. For example, although the official names for East and West Germany are listed, those for Ireland and North and South Korea are not.

Areas in dispute are not always so indicated. These include the Falkland Islands, Gibraltar, and areas in the Middle East and Southern Asia.

VII. Currency

With minor exceptions, this atlas provides current, up-to-date data. Vietnam is shown unified, with *Saigon* correctly replaced by *Ho Chi Minh City*. Zimbabwe is similarly up-to-date. The island of Greenland is still so labeled; however, *Kalaallit Nunaat* is given in parentheses.

VIII. Legibility

For the most part, typefaces on the maps are clear and legible. Place-name categories are usually differentiated by a variety of consistent typefaces. The world map is the most difficult to read, not only because of the density of information, but because of the addition of occasional physical feature data to the map. The density of political information provided for the western Soviet Union also makes it difficult to read.

The national title of the United Kingdom may be confusing to readers. On the political map of Europe, both *United Kingdom* and *British Isles* appear as printed titles. On the physical map of Europe the title listed is *Great Britain*. Finally, on the political map of Western and Central Europe, *United Kingdom* is used along with *Great Britain*; many students may not understand these distinctions. Moreover, *Scotland* appears in lighter typeface than the names of some major Scottish cities; whereas the typeface for *London* is the same as that used for *Great Britain*. In a small-scale map like this the profusion of place names makes the map cluttered and confusing.

IX. Accessibility

This atlas has the best access to information of any of the Hammond student publications. It has two indexes, a comprehensive latitude-longitude index of the world in the back, and a gazetteer-index of the world in the front. The former is extensive and includes countries, cities, regions, political divisions, and physical features. Latitude-longitude coordinates (these are clearly depicted on the maps) are given for each entry, as well as a page number for the map on which the entry appears to the best advantage. Capitals are designated by asterisks.

The gazetteer index focuses on political data. It gives the area in square miles, population, and alphanumeric grid coordinates and page number on which places are shown on the largest scale. An asterisk indicates membership in the United Nations.

X. Summary

This atlas is priced at $3.75, a reasonable amount for such a comprehensive work. Its basic cartography is derived from other Hammond large-format atlases. The results are mixed. Though packed with information, this atlas attempts too much in too few pages. Of the Hammond atlases reviewed, however, it contains the most thorough index. It also allows the best opportunity for understanding the earth holistically and making comparisons among its various divisions. Thus, if purchased as a comparative reference tool, it is a reasonable buy for the price, for high school student use. However, a comparable volume such as the SCOTT, FORESMAN WORLD ATLAS presents similar information much more clearly and with better cartography to boot.

Concise Earthbook

Facts at a Glance

Full Title: **Concise Earthbook**.
Publisher: Graphic Learning International Publishing Corporation.
Copyright: ©1987 by Esselte Map Service AB, Stockholm.

Edition Reviewed: First edition, 1987.
Number of Volumes: 1.
Number of Pages: 215.
Number of Maps: 70.
Number of Indexes: 1.
Number of Index Entries: 20,000.
Trim Size: 5¼″ × 7¼″.
Binding: hardcover.

Intended Readership: high school through adult.
Price: $12.95.
Sold in stores and directly to schools and libraries.
ISBN 0-87746-101-5.
No revision policy.

I. Introduction

The *Concise Earthbook* world atlas is a 215-page, small format (19 × 14 cm.) general world atlas intended to be a portable ready-reference source of geographic information. It has 70 color maps, a 48-page statistical section, and a 78-page index. It was designed, edited, drawn, and copyrighted in 1987 by the well-known Esselte Map Service of Sweden, and published in the United States by Graphic Learning International of Boulder, Colorado. The cartography is similar to that in the larger EARTHBOOK published by the same firm. James E. Davis and Sharryl Davis Hawke are credited as consultants for this edition.

II. Format

Most of the maps in the *Concise Earthbook* are physical, with shading to indicate relief and coloring to indicate the types of land cover, such as tundra, sand desert, or cultivated land. The maps spread over both open pages. The tightly sewn binding prevents the pages from lying flat when opened, but loss of information in the gutter is minimal.

The maps are arranged by continent in a west-to-east, north-to-south order, starting with North America and ending with Australasia. Each continent section begins with a physical map of the continent accompanied by flags of the countries included, then covers the continent in west-to-east, north-to-south order, from the northwest corner to the southeast. Following these are maps of the polar regions, world thematic maps, a section of continent and country statistics, and finally, the index.

The maps are preceded by a master legend (called "Reader Information"), which includes a sample map with annotations explaining the meaning of selected symbols and abbreviations, and a table of explanations of symbols and colors used on the maps.

The maps themselves do not include legends. Most of them do include the scale expressed as a representational fraction and a bar scale, but others lack any indication of scale.

III. Special Features

Inside the front cover is a world political map, accompanied by a list of countries and the page numbers on which their map coverage can be found. The countries on each continent map are keyed numerically to flags in the margin, as well as to their location in the statistical section. The maps that include a bar scale also feature an airplane symbol indicating the distance covered by "modern passenger aircraft" in one hour or one-half hour.

One feature not found in any other atlas allows the user to compare the latitudes of cities on any map with cities in other parts of the world whose names are printed at their appropriate latitudes in the right-hand margin. Thus, for example, a user looking at the map of North America can see at a glance that Rome is at approximately the same latitude as New York. This feature helps the reader put the rest of the world in perspective. However, only a limited number of off-map names are used, and they are not used consistently. Incidentally, *Ottawa* is frequently misprinted in these marginal notes as *Ottava*.

The section of world thematic maps includes a political, a physical, and a time zone map, in addition to a map showing the location of 21 animals "on the edge of extinction."

The statistical section includes basic statistics (including area, population, population density, and physical feature notes) for each continent. The section also reports the following information for each country: the official name, area, population, annual population growth, life expectancy, literacy rate, capital city with population, other important cities with population, language, religion, and currency. A brief thumbnail description is also included for each.

Inside the back cover is another copy of the world time zone map, accompanied by a table of interna-

tional telephone dialing codes and toll-free numbers for airlines. Given the volatility of the airline industry, however, this latter information is apt to date quickly.

IV. Geographical Balance

This atlas gives adequate representation to all populated regions of the world. While there is no marked North American or European bias, it is unfortunate that the populous areas of eastern and southern Asia are shown at a scale smaller than that accorded to the populous areas of Europe and the United States. Maps of this small scale cannot comfortably accommodate the number of place names that this region warrants.

V. Scale and Projections

The map scales are reasonable for the areas represented on the maps and for the page size. For the most part they were well chosen and are consistent for each continent. The notable exception is for the coverage of eastern and southern Asia already mentioned.

Europe and the Middle East are shown at a scale of 1:10,000,000; North America is at 1:13,500,000; South America, Asia, Africa, and Australasia at 1:20,000,000; and the polar regions at 1:60,000,000. The world maps are at 1:180,000,000 and the continent maps are at 1:50,000,000, with the exceptions of Europe at 1:30,000,000 and Asia at 1:75,000,000.

The type of map projections are not indicated, except on the political and time zone maps of the world, and on the South American continent map. Despite this inconsistency, the projections used are appropriate. These maps appear to be on the same projections as those in the full-size EARTHBOOK, which identifies them as the Miller bipolar and the Lambert azimuthal equal-area projections.

VI. Accuracy

The inaccuracies in this atlas are numerous and detract significantly from its usefulness. There are word misspellings, for example (such as *Ottava* for *Ottawa*, as already noted) and dot symbols indicating the location of populated places without an adjacent name label. The names of some physical areas do not accurately indicate their extent, a problem compounded by use of the same type style for physical names and political subunits, and because no explanation is offered in the legend.

The choice of place names, at least for the United States, is questionable. For example, the town of

Champaign-Urbana, Illinois (population 100,000) does not appear on the largest scale maps, while smaller Illinois towns such as Anna (pop. 5,400) and Taylorville (pop. 11,000) do.

In the master legend, six sizes of type and five different symbols are listed for populated places. The symbol for the smallest population category is not used on the maps, however.

These inaccuracies do not appear in the full-size edition, in part because of the larger scale of the maps.

Local spellings are used on the maps for foreign names, with popular, anglicized names in parentheses. The indexing of these names is inconsistent, though. *Cairo* is in the index, even though it is in parentheses beneath *Al Qahirah*. *Aden* is not in the index; its local spelling *Baladiyat Adan* is the only index listing. *Jerusalem* is in the index, but its reference is to a 1:20,000,000-scale map of the Nile Valley and Arabia, while the reference for the city's local name, *Yerushalayim* is to the 1:10,000,000-scale map of the Middle East.

VII. Currency

In general, the information in this atlas is as up-to-date as its copyright date. It includes recent boundary and place name changes, including the 1986 boundary claims of Libya. The only bit of out-of-date information is the inclusion of the American bison in the "animals on the edge of extinction" map.

VIII. Legibility

The typefaces on the maps are legible, with the exception of the smallest population category names on the large-scale maps. These are too small and faint to be easily deciphered, particularly when superimposed over relief shading.

Only two styles of type are used: one for populated places and another for all other place names. These two type styles are quite similar, and differentiating between types of place names is difficult, particularly where many names are close together.

On the positive side, rivers, roads, railroads, borders, and natural features are clearly distinguishable. Also, the colors used for land cover types are in register and give the maps a high-quality appearance.

IX. Accessibility

The index in this atlas is extensive. Place names are located by alphanumeric grid coordinates which are integrated into the latitude-longitude grid on the maps. Most of the inset maps have separate grid coordi-

nates, and the names included in them are accurately indexed.

There are many discrepancies and inaccuracies in the index, however, in addition to the ones already mentioned. Names are missing, for example, such as *Manila* and other cities in the Philippines. The Soviet Union cannot be found under any of its common names (*U.S.S.R.*, *Russia*, or *Soviet Union*).

There are inaccuracies on the contents page, also. French Guiana is not listed at all, for example. Panama is listed with other South American countries, but is included in the North American section of flags and statistics. Again, these inaccuracies do not appear in the full-size edition.

X. Summary

The price of the *Concise Earthbook* world atlas is $12.95 retail, which is somewhat expensive compared to the price of similar atlases, such as the RANDOM HOUSE CONCISE WORLD ATLAS which contains many of the same features and larger scale, better detailed maps. The *Concise Earthbook* is worth the selling price, but users will become frustrated with its inaccuracies sooner or later.

Diplomat World Atlas

Facts at a Glance

Full Title: **Diplomat World Atlas**.
Publisher: Hammond Incorporated.
Copyright: 1984.

Edition Reviewed: 1986 printing.
Number of Volumes: 1.
Number of Maps: 302.
Number of Indexes: 1 master index, plus same-page indexes for each map.
Number of Index Entries: 5,000 in master index.
Trim Size: 8½″ × 11″.
Binding: cloth.

Intended Readership: grade 9 and up.
Price: $24.95; 15 percent school and library discount. Sold in bookstores and direct to schools and libraries. ISBN 0-8437-1260-0. Revised annually.

I. Scope and Format

The Hammond *Diplomat World Atlas* is a deluxe edition of Hammond's NEW HORIZON WORLD ATLAS. The contents of the two atlases are identical.

The *Diplomat* is bound in maroon leather, with the title stamped in large gold lettering on the front cover and spine. The pages are gilt-edged, and the volume has a clear acetate jacket. For a full description of the maps and other features of this atlas, see the review of the NEW HORIZON WORLD ATLAS on page 259.

Earthbook

Facts at a Glance

Full Title: **Earthbook**.
Publisher: Graphic Learning International
   Publishing Corporation.
Copyright: ©1987 by Esselte Map Service AB,
   Stockholm.

Edition Reviewed: first edition, 1987.
Number of Volumes: 1.
Number of Pages: 327.
Number of Maps: 185.
Number of Indexes: 1.
Number of Index Entries: 46,000.
Number of Illustrations: 240, color.
Trim Size: 10″ × 13¼″.
Binding: cloth.

Intended Readership: high school through adult.
Price: $65.50.
Sold in stores and directly to schools and libraries.
   ISBN 0-87746-100-7.
No revision policy.

I. Introduction

Earthbook is a general world atlas accompanied by an encyclopedic section of earth science information. The atlas section features maps with colors representing natural environments. The 96-page encyclopedic section provides scientific information in text, photos, and illustrations which describe the complex interrelationships of humanity's impact on each of the four classical elements—air, water, fire, and earth. The publisher included this section in an attempt to raise users' "geographic consciousness." The level of information is appropriate for secondary schools, as well as for the home, office, and library.

The maps were designed, drawn, edited, reproduced, and copyrighted in 1987 by the well-known Esselte Map Service in Stockholm, Sweden. For the United States edition, base material for the large-

scale U.S. maps was supplied by the U.S. Geological Survey.

The atlas was printed in Sweden, and published by Graphic Learning International in Boulder, Colorado. Consultants for the U.S. edition are Sharryl Davis Hawke and James E. Davis. Their credentials are not listed.

II. Format

The maps in *Earthbook* spread to the edge of both open pages, except along the bottom edge, where a border is provided for the title and scale. The colors used on the maps correspond to various physical environments, such as tundra, sand desert, and arable land. Shading is used to portray relief.

Earthbook is small enough for users to handle easily but large enough to provide large-scale maps covering broad areas. It is a well made atlas, with a binding sewn loose enough to let the atlas lay flat when opened. The two halves of each map join accurately and no information is lost in the gutter.

Preceding the section of maps is a master legend describing the colors used to represent various environments. It is set up quite nicely, with a sample environmental map of Asia surrounded by examples of each type of environment, a small map indicating where on the continent that environment exists, and a photograph depicting the environment. A note on this page directs readers to the legend inside the back cover, which includes a table of the symbols used on the medium-scale maps, the symbols used on the small-scale maps, a color key to the environment colors, and a table of the symbols and colors used on the large-scale United States maps. These two legends are not identified on the contents page, but users will remember where they are after they initially stumble onto them.

The maps themselves do not contain legends. Most of them include the map scale indicated as a representative fraction and a bar scale expressed in kilometers and miles. Some maps, however, lack scale statements and even titles.

III. Special Features

This atlas contains a 96-page section of reference material called "Encyclopedia of the Earth." It is divided into four sections, each corresponding to one of the four classical elements. Each section begins with a basic description of the element, then discusses its dynamics and interactions, and ends with a description of man's impact on and use of it. The text, photographs, and illustrations are well done and do a wonderful job of describing the current state of the planet.

There is a special section of thematic maps for each continent which includes, in addition to a general map, maps showing political divisions, population distribution, relief, rainfall and ocean currents, temperature and winds, climate, soils, organic (agricultural) production, and inorganic (energy and mineral resources) production.

The bar scales on the general continent maps feature an airplane symbol and a time unit (i.e., 1 hour). Unfortunately this is not explained. The same symbol is used in the *Concise Earthbook*, where the legend explains that it indicates the distance covered by "modern passenger aircraft" in the time unit specified.

There is also a section of thematic maps of the world, which includes maps on the themes of environment types, climate, oceans, population, political divisions, energy, and ethnology.

IV. Geographical Balance

Although its cartography is Swedish, *Earthbook* was designed specifically for sale in the United States, and has a marked bias toward this country. The United States maps are the largest scale maps in the atlas. They are prominently listed first in the contents and have a separate legend of symbols and colors inside the back cover.

Adequate representation is given to the rest of the world; the extensive coverage given to the United States is not at the expense of other regions. It is unfortunate, however, that the populous areas of Asia are not shown at the same scale as the populous areas of Europe.

V. Scale and Projections

In general, the map scales and projections used were well chosen for the size of areas represented in relation to the page size. All areas of the world are shown at the consistent scale of 1:10,000,000, with the exceptions of the polar regions, which are shown at 1:30,000,000, and Oceania, which is shown at 1:27,000,000. Europe and the Middle East are shown again at the larger scale of 1:5,000,000 and the United States is shown again at 1:3,000,000.

Each continent is shown on a two-page spread at a scale of 1:25,000,000, with the exception of Europe, which is at 1:15,000,000. The largest scale map of the world is at a scale of 1:90,000,000; the smallest scale is 1:220,000.000.

Map projections are identified only on the general continent maps. The projections used are Miller's bipolar for North and South America, Miller's stereographic for Africa, Lambert's conformal conic for

Europe, Lambert's azimuthal equal-area for Asia and Australasia, Mercator for Oceania and the small-scale world maps, azimuthal equidistant for the polar regions, and Van der Grinten for the large-scale world maps. These projections are appropriately chosen, as they are the same or similar to those used for the same areas by other atlas producers.

There are a few unfortunate cases of inappropriate scale choice. The coverage of the populous areas of Asia already mentioned should be at 1:5,000,000 for comparability to the Europe maps. Oceania is shown at 1:27,000,000 to make it fit on the page, compromising the amount of detail that could be shown. The largest scale coverage of New Zealand is on a 1:10,000,000 scale map which also includes the southeastern portion of Australia and a lot of empty space (in the form of the Tasman Sea). The only incidence of misleading distortion caused by the use of the "wrong" projection is on a world physical map depicting the ocean floor, which uses the Mercator projection.

VI. Accuracy

Generally, the information in this atlas is accurate. Place names are spelled correctly and consistently, and are accurately placed on the maps.

There are discrepancies concerning "local" and "generic" names, however. For countries, the generic name is listed first, with the local name below it in parentheses, while for cities, the local name is first and the generic name is in parentheses.

It is unfortunate that political unit names are sometimes shown with compact letter spacing and other times with expanded spacing. The names of physical features are also shown with expanded lettering and use the same type style, making it hard to differentiate between political and physical names.

Other inaccuracies include the listing of Panama in the contents as a South American country rather than a Central American country; the presence on the 1:3,000,000 scale map of California of a permanent lake in Death Valley National Monument, rather than the dry lake bed that actually exists there; and the presence of what appears to be a strip of prairie west of St. Louis on the 1:10,000,000 scale map of the United States. This prairie, which does not actually exist, does not appear on the 1:3,000,000 scale map of the area.

VII. Currency

The information in this atlas is as up-to-date as its copyright date. Recent boundary and place name changes are included, such as the 1986 boundary claims of Libya, and Panama's joint ownership of the Panama Canal. The publisher claims that *Earthbook*'s maps are more current than all of the competition.''

The text, illustrations, and photographs in the "Encyclopedia of the Earth" section are up-to-date and contemporary. Nothing in this atlas gives it a dated appearance.

VIII. Legibility

In general, the typefaces on the maps are legible. The exception is the names for the smallest population category on all large-scale maps other than the 1:3,000,000 scale United States maps. The type used for these names is too small and faint, particularly when superimposed over relief shading.

While many sizes of type are used, there are only two styles of type—one for populated places and another for all other names. As already mentioned, the same style is used for both political and physical names, making it difficult to differentiate between the two. Similarly, some of the colors used to depict types of environment are quite similar, making it hard to differentiate between them.

On the positive side, rivers, roads, railroads, and borders are clearly distinguishable. Also, the use of color to depict types of environment gives a much higher quality appearance to the maps than do the traditional hypsometric tints, which show the low-lying Sahara desert in green.

IX. Accessibility

The index in this atlas is extensive, and includes all names on the maps. Place names are located by alphanumeric grid coordinates, which are integrated into the latitude-longitude grid on the maps. Most of the inset maps have separate grid coordinates, and the names on them are accurately indexed. Both "generic" and "local" name spellings are listed in the index, but they are listed separately, with no cross-referencing.

Unfortunately, there are discrepancies and inaccuracies in the index. Names of United States cities are identified by state, but foreign cities are not followed by the name of the country in which they are located. There is also no note indicating what type of feature the names correspond to. The result is that the same name appears in the index two or more times, forcing the user to peruse the list in order to locate the right one. This happens on almost every index page.

Another problem with accessibility is that the grid boundaries on the large-scale Europe maps are quite large, so that the user has an 8- to 14-square-inch area in which to search for the name. For most of

Europe, quite a few names are packed into each grid square.

X. Summary

The price of this edition of *Earthbook* is $65.50, which the publisher says is "strategically positioned in between the most expensive (yet popular) atlases and the lesser quality atlases." Its price is reasonable, based on its content and overall quality. *Earthbook*'s currency and its "Encyclopedia of the Earth" section make it a highly attractive purchase for libraries needing a large-format atlas. On the other hand, other comparably priced atlases, particularly the NATIONAL GEOGRAPHIC ATLAS OF THE WORLD, offer larger-scale maps showing more detail, along with more indexed place names.

Gage Atlas of the World

Facts at a Glance

Full Title: **Gage Atlas of the World**.
Publisher: Gage Educational Publishing Limited.
Copyright: 1985.

Edition Reviewed: 1985.
Number of Pages: 192.
Number of Maps: 170.
Number of Indexes: 2.
Number of Index Entries: 10,500.
Number of Illustrations: 72.
Trim Size: 8½" × 11".
Binding: hardcover.

Intended Readership: grades 7 through 12.
Price: $17.25. ISBN 0-7715-8162-9.
Revised every ten years.

I. Introduction

The *Gage Atlas of the World* is intended for Canadian high school students. It is divided into three sections. The first part focuses on both physical and human patterns of the world, including the solar system, population density, occupations, and food resources. Continental and regional studies comprise the second section, which features a variety of political, topographical, and thematic maps. Tables of meteorological statistics for the countries of the world follow the map section of the atlas. A major portion of this third and final section profiles Canada's economic and social features.

According to the preface, the *Gage Atlas* is designed to help students understand the complex relationship between people and their environment; to appreciate the implications of this relationship throughout the world; and to identify and structure data with which to make informed assessments of local, regional, and global issues. Because these goals require advanced skills in geography, the *Gage Atlas* is appropriate for students in grades 7 through 12.

The maps and index were prepared by George Philip and Son, Ltd., a London cartographic service. Founded in 1834, George Philip is well known in Europe as a producer of quality map products. Gage Publishing Limited, which issues this book in North America, also publishes THE MACMILLAN SCHOOL ATLAS for younger students.

II. Format

The atlas contains a wide variety of maps. Separate physical and political maps accompany sections on the world, North America, Central and South America, Europe, Africa, Asia, and Australasia; except for the world and Australasia, the other five sections also include an economic map. These major maps all occupy one page.

Subregional political/physical maps, both one- and two-page spreads, supplement the continental cartography. These sections also feature a variety of smaller thematic maps on climate, vegetation, population, and trade.

Nearly a fourth of the atlas is devoted to a detailed examination of Canada. The maps in this special section cover subregions and major cities of Canada, as well as specialized thematic maps depicting landforms, agriculture, fisheries, energy, trade, and other topics.

The atlas is 8½″ × 11″, a size that is convenient and easy to handle for a high school student. Most maps fit the page well; some, however, such as the Middle United States, occupy so much of the page that bodies of nearby water are cut off or seem smaller than they really are. Moreover, not all maps facing each other are consistently placed in a horizontal or vertical position.

The atlas is a well bound hardcover book. Most pages lie flat when open, although a few maps, such as the Atlantic Provinces of Canada, lose information in the gutter.

Map legends vary in the data they provide. All maps include a scale and an elevation code, when appropriate. The scale is presented in bar form of kilometers. The elevation is shown as a series of colored rectangles with a kilometer notation for each level, so that each color represents an altitude above sea level or a depth below sea level. Political maps provide only a scale, but a master key to both po-

litical and physical features is provided in the front of the book. The key includes symbols for such features as settlements, boundaries, communications, and topographical characteristics. Thematic maps on the economy, climate, or a specific city carry detailed legends on each page.

III. Special Features

An important strength of this atlas is its special features. In addition to the master key, the introductory material includes diagrams of map projections, an illustrated explanation of the solar system, and a two-page spread on time and distance. A 27-page section on the world completes the introduction. It presents comparative maps of evolution, diagrams of landscapes, graphs of metropolitan climates, photographs of vegetation types, studies of population trends, and other useful information.

Each regional section contains an economic map as well as smaller thematic maps on climate, vegetation, and population. In addition, special features on Canada provide detailed maps with data concerning the nation's geology, landforms, vegetation and soils, agriculture, fisheries, energy, trade, and specific provinces and cities.

The back of the atlas contains statistical tables and two indexes. The tables, which provide pertinent data on both the world and Canada, lend themselves well to graph making and other classroom activities.

The front endpapers of the atlas feature eight photographs of various parts of Canada from space. The back endpapers do the same for various parts of the earth. An informative caption accompanies each picture.

IV. Geographical Balance

The *Gage Atlas* adequately represents all regions of the world, although some of its geographical categories depart from traditional divisions found in many atlases. For example, the U.S.S.R. is treated as an entity entirely within Asia. Turkey, however, is shown twice: as part of Europe's Mediterranean Lands, and as part of Southwest Asia.

The atlas has a deliberate Canadian bias. Cartography of Canada, its provinces, and its cities occupies nearly a fourth of the book. Likewise, a majority of the statistical data in the back of the atlas are devoted to information about Canada.

V. Scale and Projections

Map scales are usually reasonable for the size of the area being represented. Notable exceptions are the subregional maps of the United States, which are poorly scaled to fit their pages. For example, the Eastern United States requires a map insert to show Maine, and the Middle United States barely shows Lake Michigan and requires a map insert for southeastern Texas.

The atlas uses a variety of scales expressed in kilometers. They range from 1:250,000 for such cities as Vancouver to 1:54,000,000 for the Pacific Ocean to 1:80,000,000 for the world. Sometimes the same scale is applied to areas of differing size: for example, the scale 1:4,000,000 is used to represent the British Isles as well as France and the Low Countries.

Projections appear in small print at the bottom left of each map. The cartographers have used a variety of projections, including Bonne, zenithal equidistant, conical with two standard parallels, and Lambert's conformal conic.

VI. Accuracy

Place names are spelled correctly. Spellings of Canadian names are consistent with those given in the *Gazetteer of Canada*. Other names conform to the rules established by the Permanent Committee on Geographical Names and the United States Board on Geographic Names.

The atlas is not always consistent in its use of place names. For example, *United Kingdom* appears as the title on the political map of Europe, but *British Isles* is the title used on the subregional map. Although both headings appear in the index, only the *United Kingdom* is listed on the statistical table of principal countries of the world. Furthermore, *Ireland* is the place name used on the map and in the index, whereas *Irish Republic* appears as the title in the listing of principal countries.

One notable omission is the state of Alaska from the map of the United States. Although this map includes an inset of Hawaii, Alaska is shown only on the political map of North America.

The atlas uses generic rather than official political names. For example, the political map of Europe gives one color to divided Germany and titles the area *Germany*, with *East* and *West* designations in smaller print. A map of Central Europe follows this same pattern. In the index, the two nations are listed separately under their unofficial names. The map of Korea, however, uses different shadings for North and South, and labels each separately. The People's Republic of China is labeled *China*, both on the map and in the index. An insert on the map of Northern Africa, titled *Palestine* (not found in the index), can be a source of confusion.

Rival claims to territory are not indicated on maps. Rather, international boundaries show the *de facto* situation when differences remain unresolved. This is the case with such territories as the Falkland Islands, Gibraltar, and parts of Israel.

VII. Currency

The *Gage Atlas* reflects recent political changes, showing the unification of Vietnam and using the new names of *Zimbabwe*, *Brunei*, and *Burkina Faso*. The atlas also reflects an awareness of current world problems. For example, one of the thematic maps in the introductory section is titled "Man-made Problems" and shows, among other things, oil spills, areas affected by acid rain, and recent conflicts in such places as El Salvador and the Falkland Islands. A few minor exceptions include the use of *Peking* rather than *Beijing* as the capital of the People's Republic of China, and *Greenland* instead of the now-favored *Kalaalit Nunaat*. In addition, the statistical information given in the tables at the end of the atlas ranges from 1980 to 1982, although the book carries a 1985 copyright.

The atlas uses very few photographs. Although contemporary, they are disappointingly small and the captions furnish only minimal information.

VIII. Legibility

Legibility is not one of this atlas's strong features. The type is often too thin to read easily. For example, state names on subregional maps of the United States are hard to locate and read. Likewise, the names of physical features are not always easy to distinguish. For instance, the title of *Wales* overlaps with *Cambrian Mts.* and the labels of various physical features in France are not neatly placed.

Most maps are not overcrowded with data, and features in areas of low density are easy to locate and read. A few subregional maps, such as Eastern Canada, Northern South America, or Ontario—South include more data than other dense locales and thus take longer to read.

Boundary lines are another weak feature. International boundaries, internal boundaries, freeways, and roads are all printed in red, which often makes it difficult to distinguish state lines from highways, province lines from freeways, or national state borders from roads. In the British Isles, for example, it is almost impossible to distinguish between the boundaries of England, Scotland, and Wales. Similarly, it is difficult to distinguish the various nations of South America, the states of the United States, and the provinces of Canada.

On relief maps, the colors used to show altitude are easy to read and altitude numbers are legible. In areas such as Southern South America, however, the names of physical features are difficult to read. For example, to locate the Parana River a reader would have to consult the physical map of South America, even though the Parana is indexed to the crowded physical-political map of Southern South America.

IX. Accessibility

The *Gage Atlas* has two indexes, one for Canada and a second for the rest of the world. Since a large segment of cartography is devoted to Canada, the decision to provide two indexes has the advantage of ease of access, especially if a student is using the atlas primarily for Canadian studies.

Both indexes are long, but the twelve-page Canadian index contains a disproportionate number of entries when compared to the eight-page world index. Each entry provides a single page reference, followed by its geographical coordinates in latitude and longitude.

A two-page introduction precedes the indexes. One page explains how to use the index and what abbreviations were used. The second page provides a diagrammed explanation of latitude and longitude.

A few maps contain insets, often to show map material that did not fit on the page, as with Japan, Texas, and Maine. It is not immediately clear where these areas belong with respect to the map as a whole. Other insets show islands, and a few represent major cities located on the larger map.

X. Summary

This atlas has many worthwhile features. It has a variety of finely executed maps which extend beyond the traditional emphasis on political and physical features. It includes an in-depth focus on the world and provides valuable comparative data on social issues such as the Third World population explosion, illiteracy, urbanization, nutrition, and standards of living. Statistical tables in the back of the atlas are detailed and complement the cartography in ways useful to the advanced learner. Despite its coverage of all world regions, this atlas is particularly suitable for students of Canadian geography but of less value to students in the United States. Nonetheless, the *Gage Atlas of the World* ably fulfills its stated purposes. The imaginative teacher will find that it offers a wealth of information for drawing conclusions about people, their environment, and how their interaction has produced a variety of world problems.

Hammond Headline World Atlas

Facts at a Glance

Full Title: **Hammond Headline World Atlas**.
Publisher: Hammond Incorporated.
Editor: Martin A. Bacheller.
Copyright: 1986.

Number of Volumes: 1.
Number of Pages: 48.
Number of Maps: 59.
Number of Indexes: 1.
Trim Size: 8½″ × 11″.
Binding: paper.

Intended Readership: grade 9 and up.
Price: $2.95 with a 15 percent discount for schools and libraries.
Sold in bookstores and supermarkets, and direct to libraries and schools.
ISBN 0-8437-2505-2.
Updated annually.

I. Introduction

The *Hammond Headline World Atlas* is a 48-page paperback reference intended for high school students, with the same cartographic base as that of other large-format Hammond atlases. Because it does not have a table of contents, the order and nature of its maps is not immediately apparent. Some maps are regional, followed by maps of subregional areas; other maps confine themselves to one particular region without further cartography. No explanatory text, instructional material, or skill activities are included.

II. Format

The atlas contains a variety of world, regional, and subregional maps. It begins with a one-page political map of the world. One- or two-page spreads of political maps of the world's continents are interspersed throughout, with the exception of a smaller map of Antarctica. In selected instances, some of these maps are also followed by political maps of subregional areas, such as the United States, Central America, or Italy.

In addition to political maps, selected regions and subregions also provide a physical map as well as a land-use map illustrating agriculture, industry, and resources. These maps vary in size from one-half to one page.

The atlas is paperback with a saddle-stitched binding, published in a convenient, easy-to-handle notebook size. It lies flat when opened, with no loss of detail in the gutter. Most political maps occupy one page.

Each political map includes a title, projection, bar scale in miles and kilometers, and explanation of symbols. These include symbols for capitals, administrative centers, international boundaries, and internal borders. Relief is indicated on special maps by hypsometric tinting, and a consistent legend of color gradients for elevation is applied throughout. Each agriculture, industry, and resource map is accompanied by a legend indicating dominant land use and major mineral sources, although the number of symbols used on a given map varies.

Most maps contain insets of islands, special divisions like the Vatican, major cities, or areas of density, such as the New York-Philadelphia axis. Many are poorly labeled and confusing, as in the case of Australia and New Zealand. A student could not interpret the political status of Berlin, either from the map of Germany or its accompanying inset.

III. Special Features

The maps depicting relief and agriculture, industry, and resources also include the flags of the nations shown. To save space, however, these flags are sometimes imposed on the political map; in other instances, as with Africa, the flags share a page with a map of Antarctica. A small global illustration of part of the earth also highlights the map area being illustrated, so that the reader can see, for example, the size of the West Indies relative to the rest of the Western Hemisphere.

The back cover of this atlas contains a table of world statistics on the surface area of the earth, continents, and oceans; the height of major mountains in feet and meters; the length of major rivers in miles and kilometers; and the area in square miles and square kilometers of the world's largest islands and lakes.

Likewise, the gazetteer-index which serves as the table of contents provides information on continents, countries, states, and colonial divisions. The data provided give area, population, and capital or chief town, along with an index reference and page number.

IV. Geographical Balance

The selection of countries in this atlas is arbitrary and lacks geographical balance. It has a marked North American, European, and Asian bias. For example,

subregional maps of North America include Canada, Mexico, Central America, the West Indies, and a two-page spread of the United States. On the other hand, South America is allotted only two pages.

Europe commands the greatest share of map space, with eight subregional maps, including two maps of the Soviet Union.

The best Third World coverage is given to Asia, with five subregional maps. Two of these, titled Southeast Asia and the Indochinese and Malay Peninsulas, present similar data. Like South America, Africa has no subregional maps. The marked western bias in map selection makes this atlas questionable for use in courses which include study of these two major continents.

V. Scale and Projections

The map projection and a bar scale in miles and kilometers appear below the title of most political maps; a few omit the projection. A variety of map scales and projections are used. For example, the world map uses a modified Mercator projection, the United States uses a polyconic projection, and the United Kingdom a Bonne projection. Scales vary widely, and give misconceptions of relative size and shape. This is particularly misleading when two areas, such as Germany and the Scandinavian countries, are placed on opposing pages with different scales.

VI. Accuracy

Place names are accurately and consistently spelled. However, some of the relief maps fail to show geographical features in their entirety. For example, with no relief map of North America, the reader is likely to miss the fact that some features, such as the Rocky Mountains, are common to Canada, the United States, and Mexico, even though they are correctly placed on the three individual topographical maps of each country.

VII. Currency

With a few exceptions, the data in this atlas are in line with its 1986 copyright. The place name of *Cambodia*, with *Kampuchea* in parentheses, is used in the gazetteer, as well as on the three maps where it is featured. The index also uses the generic terms for East and West Germany, with official names in parentheses, whereas the same data is not provided for North and South Korea, or Ireland. Changes in Vietnam and the status of Zimbabwe are also up-to-date. The capital of the People's Republic of China retains its name of *Peking*, rather than *Beijing*.

VIII. Legibility

Typefaces on the maps are inconsistent in their clarity and legibility. Place-name categories are differentiated by typefaces, although the density of names on some maps is confusing. This stems from the fact that many of the maps are reduced-size maps taken from Hammond's large-format atlases. The cities included on the map of England, for example, are unnecessarily numerous and clutter the cartography. The fact that Dublin is the capital of the Republic of Ireland is not readily apparent. The map of the United States is similarly crowded, so that the names of some states are difficult to read.

The density of data provided on these maps varies widely, so that some are more difficult to read than others. The small, land-use map of Europe, for example, is extremely compact and crowded.

International borders are not always clearly apparent. For example, the borders between East and West Germany and other nations, and smaller political divisions within each of the two nations confuse the reader. The conflicting claims of two nations are not always acknowledged; whereas the Falklands is indicated as being claimed by Argentina, Gibraltar is not so noted with respect to Spain. Conflicting claims over parts of Israel are also not noted, and the borders of that nation are confusing to interpret.

Agriculture, industry, and resource maps convey only general information, such as the dominant land use and the location of major minerals. No statistical information accompanies the symbols. For example, the reader can tell that gas and petroleum are located in Venezuela, but cannot ascertain the volume of production or the relative importance of these products with respect to others in the nation.

IX. Accessibility

Accessibility to information in this atlas is limited. There is no table of contents; a gazetteer-index has been placed in the front of the atlas as a substitute. It includes continents and other major divisions, but does not list the cities, counties, provinces, or minor political areas shown on many maps. Rivers, mountains, and other physical features are omitted altogether. Moreover, for countries, states, and other divisions, the gazetteer lists only the page number on which these places are shown on the largest scale. This one index notation shows the alphanumeric reference (e.g., C-4) on the respective map in which each place is located.

X. Summary

At $2.95 this atlas would seem to be a bargain. Even at this low price, however, it has limitations as an easy reference source. A student would be better served in the long run to invest in a more carefully executed atlas than the *Headline World Atlas*. It is not recommended for librarians as an appropriate source because of its limitations in coverage, clarity, and index.

Hammond World Atlas: Gemini Edition

Facts at a Glance

Full Title: **Hammond World Atlas: Gemini Edition**.
Publisher: Hammond Incorporated.
Copyright: 1985.

Edition Reviewed: 1986 printing.
Number of Volumes: 1.
Number of Pages: 200.
Number of Maps: 265.
Number of Indexes: No master index, but same-page indexes accompany all map areas.
Trim Size: 9½" × 12½".
Binding: paper.

Intended Readership: grade 7 and up.
Price: $9.95.
Sold in bookstores and directly to schools and libraries. ISBN 0-8437-1135-3.
Revised annually.

I. Scope and Format

The *Hammond World Atlas: Gemini Edition* is a paperbound version of Hammond's INTERNATIONAL WORLD ATLAS, which in turn is an abridgement of the publisher's CITATION WORLD ATLAS. Apart from the matter of the binding, it is identical to the INTERNATIONAL in every respect save one. Whereas the frontmatter of the INTERNATIONAL includes a one-page Introduction to Maps and Indexes and another page listing Sources and Acknowledgements, the *Gemini Edition* instead provides two pages of World Statistics. The statistical tables, identical in every respect to those found in the inside covers of the WHOLE EARTH ATLAS, are also published by Hammond.

The washable paper cover of the *Gemini Edition* is thick and sturdy. Priced at $9.95, compared to

$14.95 for the hardcover INTERNATIONAL, this is a suitable purchase for reference libraries.

For complete information about the maps and other features of this atlas, see the reviews of the CITATION WORLD ATLAS on page 231 and the INTERNATIONAL WORLD ATLAS on page 251.

The Intermediate World Atlas

Facts at a Glance

Full Title: **The Intermediate World Atlas: A Map Study Book.**
Publisher: Hammond Incorporated.
Editor: Martin A. Bacheller.
Copyright: 1984. Maps updated to 1986.

Number of Volumes: 1.
Number of Pages: 80.
Number of Maps: 80.
Number of Indexes: 2.
Trim Size: 8½" × 11".
Binding: paper.

Intended Readership: grades 7 and 8.
Price: $3.95.
Sold directly to schools. ISBN 0-8437-7466-5.
Revised annually.

I. Introduction

The Intermediate World Atlas is a paperback text intended for junior high students at the seventh- and eighth-grade levels. Described by the publisher as a "map study book," it uses different cartography from that found in most Hammond student atlases. Its material is organized around the world and its ten regions: North America, Central America, the West Indies, South America, Africa, Europe, Asia, Australia and New Zealand, Oceania, and Antarctica. From one-half to one page of explanatory text accompanies the introductory map on each of these regions, which is followed by a series of subregional maps. The atlas assumes a basic knowledge of geographic skills, and it focuses instead on providing information rather than on teaching students how to improve their map-reading skills. It could be used in the classroom both as a ready reference for individual students and as supplemental material for geography texts.

II. Format

The maps in this atlas are one page or smaller in size. It is unusual for a student atlas not to have two-page spreads covering large areas with much detail. This causes crowding in maps like those of the United States and Europe. Except for the world maps, which treat political, topographical, population, and land-use features on four separate maps, the remaining cartography combines political and physical features into a single map. Maps of certain regions, such as South America, are supplemented by maps of subregions, such as Peru and Chile. Small maps depicting temperature, rainfall, and vegetation are also provided for each region.

Map legends are complete only with reference to physical features. A consistent color scheme for elevation is used on all maps and explained in all legends. However, no explanation of the political symbols for international boundaries, state boundaries, cities, or capitals is provided. Boundaries between nations are indicated by a red line, which is also used to demarcate the boundaries between states of the United States. However, there is no master legend for these political symbols.

The atlas is a convenient notebook size (8½" × 11"). Many maps are positioned horizontally on the page, however, requiring the student to turn the atlas sideways.

III. Special Features

The Intermediate World Atlas has several interesting features. One of the world maps shows population density, but although it locates cities with over 4 million inhabitants, their names are not provided. Another world map illustrates land use, enabling the student to identify areas where forestry, ranching, farming, and other economic activities are concentrated.

Special maps also accompany each full-page regional map. These include four maps on one page: two for January-June average temperatures, one for annual average rainfall, and one for vegetation patterns. These maps are small, with complicated accompanying legends.

An explanatory text of one page or less accompanies each of the world and ten regional maps. This material does not always face the regional map being discussed; thus, references or directions to the reader require turning the page to follow the discussion. In all cases, the material would have been improved by involving the reader, either by asking questions within the body of the text or by having students locate areas being described. The end of each description includes several review questions; these usually require recall of data rather than analysis, synthesis, or comparison of information.

The atlas includes a glossary of geographical terms, a glossary of abbreviations, and a gazetteer-index which lists the areas of countries and states in square miles and square kilometers. The back cover of the book contains useful statistical world tables covering such topics as the earth's dimensions, heights of mountains, lengths of rivers, and areas of islands and lakes.

IV. Geographical Balance

This atlas has a marked Western bias. Although it is geographically the second-smallest continent, Europe is allotted more maps of individual areas than any other region. Italy, Poland, and Switzerland, for example, each have full one-page maps. Asia, however, which is the world's largest continent, has fewer subregional maps, each of which combines at least two or more nations. Likewise, the United States coverage includes nine subregional maps, whereas one each is devoted to Canada and Mexico. Not only does the United States predominate in map coverage over its North American neighbors, but its map space is more than double that allotted to Africa.

V. Scale and Projections

Bar scales in both miles and kilometers appear beneath the title of every political map. Because various map scales are used, relative size is sometimes difficult to appreciate. For example, looking at the individual maps of Switzerland, Poland, and China, students might assume that they are about equal in area. Only experience in interpreting map scales—or the data in the gazetteer—would enable them to obtain a correct impression. Moreover, standard scales are not applied to the ten major regional maps; a page showing the comparative sizes of these regions would have been a useful corrective for students as a summary at the conclusion of the atlas. Projections are not noted on the maps.

VI. Accuracy

The placement of names on the maps is usually accurate. The political world map is crowded and difficult to read, however, and would have been improved as a two-page spread. In contrast, omission is a problem on other maps. The regional map of North America, for example, does not label the Rocky Mountains so that the reader can know that they begin in Canada and extend southward into Mexico.

This map also includes many major U.S. cities, whereas only the capital of Mexico is indicated. On the regional map of Europe, the labels of physical features are often incomplete, so that places say *Alps*, *Danube*, or *Latvia*, without additional identification.

Areas in dispute are not always indicated. These include the Falkland Islands, Gibraltar, and areas in the Middle East and Southern Asia. The map of Israel and Jordan is confusing, for it shows boundaries within boundaries whose occupation is not clear.

In the interest of space, the names of some countries do not bear their official title. These include East and West Germany, North and South Korea, China, and Cambodia. Moreover, in the gazetteer-index, official names of only some of these nations are given in parentheses. In the maps of China, the name *Peking* is given preference over *Beijing*.

The treatment of the Soviet Union may confuse some readers. On the regional maps of both Europe and Asia, it is shown as part of each continent, divided at the Ural Mountains. The subregional map of the Soviet Union is placed in the section covering Europe, however, and includes the entire nation eastward to the Bering Sea. The map provides no information to remind the reader that this nation spans the landmass known as Eurasia, or that the continents "divide" at the Urals. Since most of the Soviet Union is in Asia, this is a serious oversight.

VII. Currency

With minor exceptions, the edition of *The Intermediate World Atlas* considered in this review provides data as current up to 1986 copyright. The newly named nations of Zimbabwe and Burkina Faso are so indicated. The nation of Kampuchea is labeled *Cambodia* on all maps where it is shown, however, although its new name is listed in parentheses in the gazetteer. The omission of Brunei from the United Nations is another oversight. There are, however, few such errors.

VIII. Legibility

Typefaces on the maps are neat and legible. Place-name categories are clearly differentiated by typefaces, although some maps, such as those of the world and Europe, are overly crowded and might be difficult to use. International and internal boundary lines are both indicated in red ink, which is also confusing. On the map of North America, for example, a red line demarcates the border between Mexico, the United States, and Canada; at the same time, this map uses red lines to distinguish the various Canadian provinces, even though U.S. and Mexican subdivisions are not shown. On other maps, such as those for the Indochinese and Malayan Peninsulas, the red ink is so pale that it fails to accentuate the borders between Vietnam and Laos, or between Malaya, Thailand, and Burma with sufficient clarity.

IX. Accessibility

This atlas has a general index and a gazetteer. They provide only a one-page reference to a place name, even though it might appear on more than one map. Neither index provides latitudes or longitudes, nor are the maps coded so that place names can be located by a grid system. Thus, a student trying to find *Baku* in the U.S.S.R. must peruse the entire map to locate it; conversely, not all cities shown on the map of the Soviet Union are listed in the index.

None of the place names in either index has reference pages to the explanatory material accompanying each regional map. For example, although the Andes Mountains are described in some detail in the explanatory material introducing South America, no page reference to the Andes other than the regional map where they are located is provided in the index.

The gazetteer is more complete than the index. For each nation, state, or province in the atlas it lists the area in miles and kilometers and gives the population.

X. Summary

The atlas is priced at $3.95, a reasonable cost for a paperbound volume of this size. As a reference for librarians and a supplemental geography tool for classroom teachers, the atlas provides basic, useful information for the junior high student. However, it has important limitations, which should be noted in judging whether or not to purchase it. These revolve primarily around its sparse index coverage both so far as number of entries and data included are concerned. In addition, the crowded one-page maps, with extensive detail, may limit maximum utility of this reference work. Institutions and individuals requiring an atlas at this age level may also wish to consider the RAND MCNALLY CLASSROOM ATLAS.

International World Atlas

Facts at a Glance

Full Title: **International World Atlas.**
Publisher: Hammond Incorporated.
Editors: Martin A. Bacheller, Editor-in-Chief, and the Hammond staff.
Copyright: 1986.

Edition Reviewed: 1986.
Number of Volumes: 1.
Number of Pages: 200.
Number of Maps: 265.
Number of Indexes: No master index, but same-page indexes accompany all map areas.
Trim Size: 9½″ × 12½″.
Binding: cloth.

Intended Readership: grade 7 and up.
Price: $14.95. 15 percent discount to schools and libraries. ISBN 0-8437-1237-6.
Revised annually.

I. Introduction

The current edition of the Hammond *International World Atlas* was published in 1984. Its contents were taken entirely from the Hammond CITATION WORLD ATLAS. The reader should refer to the evaluation of that title on page 231 for a complete description of the maps. A paperbound edition of the *International World Atlas* is published as the HAMMOND WORLD ATLAS: GEMINI EDITION.

The *International World Atlas* is intended for readers in grades seven and above.

II. Format

The *International World Atlas* is a slimmer version of the CITATION. It measures 9½″ × 12½″ which is a convenient size for desktop work. The binding is sturdy and will withstand regular use in schools and libraries. Unlike most student atlases, it also has a book jacket.

The arrangement of maps corresponds exactly to the CITATION's format. The main difference, to be discussed more fully in sections below, is the elimination of United States maps and a master index.

III. Special Features

The same features that accompany the maps in the CITATION WORLD ATLAS appear here. Other features of the CITATION which appear in separate sections have been eliminated outright or reduced in length. The CITATION's one-and-a-half-page introduction has been cut to one page in the *International*. This cut was minor and will have no significant impact on atlas use.

IV. Geographical Balance

All maps of the 50 United States have been eliminated from the CITATION for this atlas, thereby creating—in theory—a more balanced international world atlas. This cut in itself is not a problem, but it has created the unusual situation of Canada's having more coverage and detailed maps than does the United States (Canada has 26 pages; the U.S., 5). Readers will find this atlas useful for research on non-U.S. countries, but they will have to look elsewhere for information at the state level for the United States.

V. Currency

As with other Hammond atlases, the contents are as current as the copyright date. This particular title is updated annually but, as usual with Hammond atlases, the copyright is only changed every few years.

VI. Accessibility

There is no master index of place names. Readers must depend upon the same-page indexes which accompany each individual political map. These indexes, as in the CITATION, are somewhat incomplete. In order to find a place name, the reader must first know the name of the country or region in which the place appears. If a student is trying to find Managua on a map, for example, he or she must first consult another source to learn that Managua is in Nicaragua. But if the student does not also know that Nicaragua is in Central America, he or she would have to hunt through the gazetteer-index, not the contents, to learn this. The publisher considers this atlas suitable for lower grades than the CITATION. It is difficult to comprehend how eliminating a locator aid makes an atlas more accessible for readers of any age. Other reference works will be needed to supplement this atlas if independent study is encouraged, and instructors will be required to answer more questions.

The "Gazetteer-Index of the World" at the front of the volume is identical to the one in the CITATION.

VII. Summary

The hardbound *International* costs $14.95; the paperbound GEMINI, $9.95. These prices are good when one considers the overall quality and recency of the atlases. However, one must also consider that other atlases may be needed to supplement either of these editions; the relatively low prices were achieved by eliminating a comprehensive index and maps of the United States.

The Macmillan School Atlas

Facts at a Glance

Full Title: **The Macmillan School Atlas.**
Publisher: Gage Educational Publishing Company.
Copyright: 1982.

Edition Reviewed: Revised Metric Edition.
Number of Pages: 128.
Number of Maps: 105.
Number of Indexes: 2.
Number of Illustrations: 23 color.
Trim Size: 8½″ x 11″.
Binding: hardcover.

Intended Readership: grades 4 through 8.
Price: $10.75. ISBN 0-7715-8268-4.
Revised every ten years.

I. Introduction

The Macmillan School Atlas is a handsome hardbound reference work intended for middle-level Canadian students. There is only minimal map content focus on continents outside the Western Hemisphere. Within this area, most of the maps concentrate on Canada, its provinces, and its historical development (shown cartographically). The atlas begins with a review of basic geographic concepts, moves on to the world and North America, and then studies Canada in depth. Twelve sections are devoted to the transportation systems, landforms, farming, and economic resources of the provinces. The remainder of the atlas presents maps of the United States, Mexico, Central America, the Caribbean Islands, and South America, as well as six regional areas outside the Western Hemisphere. The atlas concludes with a section on explorations, again focusing primarily on Canada.

The purpose of the book appears to be to provide the student with an intermediate-level reference on Canadian geography. The introductory material on maps and how to use them also gives the atlas a useful secondary purpose. Because coverage outside Canada is limited, the book has only marginal reference value as a world atlas for students in the United States.

The maps and illustrations were drawn by John R. Waller. The introductory text was written by Ronald C. Daly. Gage Publishing Limited, which issues this book, also publishes the GAGE ATLAS OF THE WORLD for middle school and high school students.

II. Format

The maps in *The Macmillan School Atlas* are clearly executed and easy to read. Except for the polar regions, every continent has one map showing political divisions and a second illustrating physical features. Special maps of North and South America also provide data on climate, rainfall, land use, and vegetation. In addition, Canada's coverage includes thematic maps on transportation, natural resources, and settled areas, as well as a series of historical maps tracing the routes of explorers and locating the settlements of native Americans. Except for several two-page spreads of the world, most maps occupy one page.

The atlas is a convenient, easy-to-use 8¼″ × 10 ½″ notebook size. Maps fit well on the page, usually leaving enough space so that the reader has a good sense of the surrounding contextual area, that is, surrounding bodies of water or landforms.

The atlas is sturdily bound and uses an excellent quality paper. Its washable cover features a bright blue relief map of the Western Hemisphere as seen from space. Most maps leave enough margins so that no data are lost in the gutter, although two-page world maps in the introductory section cannot be completely read near the binding.

Map legends include place name, title, explanation of symbols, and bar scale in kilometers. Political maps include international boundaries, state and provincial boundaries, and capitals. Topographical maps show three consistent elevations: lowlands, middlelands, and highlands.

Each map has its own legend. The introduction also includes a one-page description explaining the use of legends and scales on maps.

III. Special Features

The atlas has a variety of special features that are particularly useful for the middle-grade student. The introduction includes a series of one-page illustrated lessons on the world and how to read maps of the earth. It discusses such concepts as diameter, hemisphere, latitude, and longitude. Diagrammed lessons explain the earth and moon, night and day, and the change of seasons. The section on map reading explains how projections are used to draw maps and reviews legends, symbols, bar scales, direction signs, and methods of indicating elevation.

A special section at the end of the atlas features historical maps of explorations, including not only Canadian ventures, but also expeditions to South America, Africa, and the two Poles. Other historical maps include North American native peoples in 1500,

North American colonial claims in 1664, and the political development of Canada.

Statistical tables are noticeably absent from the atlas. The book would have been improved by relevant summaries of some of the cartographic data it features.

IV. Geographical Balance

The atlas gives minimal representation to the world's regions. With the exception of the polar regions and the Western Hemisphere, each continent receives only two maps of political divisions and landforms. For that reason, it cannot be considered a balanced world atlas.

The Macmillan School Atlas has a marked—and quite intentional—Canadian bias. In the main body of the work, 45 pages are devoted to maps of Canada and its provinces. Likewise, nearly half the special section on exploration features developments in Canada. This atlas would, therefore, best serve the student of Canadian history or geography.

V. Scale and Projections

The maps in this atlas are reasonable in size for the pages on which they appear. Bar scales expressed in kilometers appear below the title of each map. Neither the map projection used nor the scale expressed in fractional terms is provided.

The atlas uses different scales for different maps; however, most maps that face each other employ the same scale. Scales range from 120 to 600 kilometers per half-inch for small areas to 1,200 and 6,000 kilometers per quarter-inch for large landforms. In fact, "kilometer" is spelled the British way—*kilometre*—and it is confusing to have the metric scale relate to the inch scale for comparison, although there is a variety of relationships. It seems inconsistent not to have uniform measurements. Further, there are many instances where the unit is not a full centimeter or half-centimeter, or full half-inch, and so on, which would make it very hard to use the scale.

VI. Accuracy

Place names are correctly and consistently spelled. In accord with the expectation of use primarily by Canadian students, differences in spelling follow British practice, as in "kilometres." Elevations are not shown except on landform maps.

Official political names are not used on their respective maps. For example, *Ireland* and *China* are used instead of *Republic of Ireland* and *People's Republic of China*. In addition, the names *Germany* and *Korea* span both territories, with *East* and *West*, *North* and *South*, shown separately from the titles. Likewise, the index lists only one Korea, and Germany is completely omitted.

Large physical areas are not always represented accurately. For example, the relief map of North America does not show the full extent of the Rocky Mountains, which stretch from Canada to Mexico.

Sometimes the maps are inconsistent or confusing. For example, a student who sees *Denmark* in parentheses after the place name of *Greenland* might conclude that *Denmark* is an alternate name for the island. On the political map of North America, data are not consistently presented. For example, Alaska is the only U. S. state that is labeled, whereas all the Canadian provinces are titled. Likewise, only capitals of the United States, Mexico, and Central America are given, although Canada includes a sprinkling of cities in addition to its capital, Ottawa.

As stated in the legend, the political map of the United States excludes Alaska and Hawaii. Hawaii is shown only on the introductory political map of the world.

VII. Currency

This atlas needs updating to reflect recent political changes. Greenland lacks its new name of *Kalaalit Nunaat*. Although Zimbabwe is correctly labeled, its capital is given as *Salisbury* instead of *Harare*, and the book is too old to incorporate the recent names for Brunei and Burkina Faso. *Peking* is shown as the capital of China, rather than the preferred Pinyin spelling of *Beijing*.

VIII. Legibility

The typefaces used in *The Macmillan School Atlas* are clearly differentiated so that national names, subdivisions, and cities are easily distinguishable. None of the maps is cluttered or overcrowded with excess data.

National borders, however, are not always easy to discern. A red line, differing only in boldness, is used to distinguish both international and state-provincial boundaries. It would have been an improvement to use symbols that were more clearly differentiated.

The colors used on these maps are bright and appealing. Only three colors for elevation are used on topographical maps, and they are consistently applied throughout the atlas.

IX. Accessibility

The gazetteer is divided into two parts: one for Canada and another for the rest of the world. It also includes an introduction explaining how to use the gazetteer, as well as a list of abbreviations found throughout the index.

Place names as well as physical features are included in the gazetteer. Names that appear more than once are indexed only once, to the map on which they are most easily located. Each item in the gazetteer is followed by the page number and grid coordinates that help the reader locate the place quickly. Data such as latitude, longitude, population, and area are not provided.

The index omits some important entries. Many capitals of African and South American nations, such as Buenos Aires, Nairobi, and Cairo, are missing. Although cities like Berlin and Stuttgart are indexed, Germany itself is not.

X. Summary

This atlas ably fulfills its purpose so far as maps of Canada are concerned. Attractively bound with clear, well-executed maps, it best serves the intermediate student of Canadian history or geography. However, even a Canadian student would not get a well-rounded world view from its use. The introductory material presents an adequate review of map reading and basic geographic concepts.

The Macmillan School Atlas is not recommended for use in a context of study beyond North America. It lacks a world perspective, and maps of regions outside the Western Hemisphere are minimal. The atlas also needs revision to bring it up to date, and the index lacks access to important references outside Canada. Despite its Canadian focus, this atlas would benefit from statistical tables that would enable the student to make comparisons and that would furnish additional data to supplement the maps.

Maps on File

Facts at a Glance
Full Title: **Maps on File.**
Publisher: Facts on File, Inc., 460 Park Avenue South, New York, N.Y. 10016.
Editor: Eleanora Schoenbaum.
Copyright: 1984, 1986.

Number of Volumes: 2.
Number of Maps: 400.
Number of Indexes: 1.

Number of Index Entries: 1,400.

Intended Readership: general.
Price: $145.00. ISBN 0-8160-1685-2.
Ongoing revision; yearly update available for
   $47.95.

I. Introduction

Maps on File is a set of approximately 400 looseleaf
maps designed specifically for photocopying. The
publisher, Facts on File, intends the maps to be used
by "the student, librarian, or researcher" as a map
reference source or, more appropriately, as worksheets for map-skills exercises. The set is not an atlas
in the conventional sense.

Facts on File, known primarily for its wide range
of topical reference books, also publishes *State Maps
on File* and *Historical Maps on File*, both in a loose-
leaf format, but does not publish conventional atlases. The maps in this set are copyrighted by Martin
Greenwald Associates; Mr. Greenwald is the Vice
President and Marketing Director of Facts on File.
Previous editions of *Maps on File* were edited by
Lester A. Sobel, a Facts on File editor since 1946;
the current edition was edited by Eleanora Schoenbaum. According to credits listed on individual maps,
some information incorporated on the maps has been
provided by national governments and by a number
of international organizations, including the United
Nations and the World Bank.

II. Format

Maps on File is published in a two-volume format.
Volume One contains some 260 regional and national
maps; Volume Two is comprised of about 135 specialized maps. (See also *Special Features*.) Although
each map is titled and numbered, there is no table
of contents or complete map list. Maps are arranged
alphabetically by title within the following sections:
Volume One: The World and Regions, Africa, Asia,
Australia and Oceania, Europe, North and Central
America and the Caribbean, South America, Canadian Provinces, and U.S. States. Volume Two:
Demographic and Medical Maps; Natural and Energy Resource Maps; Political, Economic, and Military Maps; Social and Educational Maps; Historical
Maps; Outline Maps.

Each volume consists of a three-ring notebook
binder. The maps, drawn in black and white, are
printed on ultra-heavy 8½" × 11" stock and can be
removed from the binder to be photocopied. Maps
are drawn in outline form, with rudimentary detail.

Dots, hatch marks, and a handful of symbols show
specific details.

A brief "Key to Symbols" has been inserted at
the beginning of the first volume. This key explains
symbols used to represent major roads; major railways; national boundaries; international airports;
national, state, and provincial capitals; major sea-
ports, mountains; and oilfields. The same symbol is
employed for each type of capital (misspelled *capitol*
in the key). When additional symbols are used on
the topical maps, separate map legends are usually
provided.

Each map includes a bar scale. However, not only
are the scales inconsistent from map to map, but the
systems used to indicate scale are also inconsistent.
(See *Scale and Projections*.)

Although the binder format is convenient, particularly for classroom use, the binders can be a source
of frustration. The pages do not turn easily, and the
binders are difficult to close. The looseleaf format
means that individual maps are apt to be lost or
misplaced. Moreover, because of their large size (the
spine of each is four inches wide), the volumes are
unwieldy, and users with small hands will probably
experience some difficulty handling them.

III. Special Features

As already mentioned, Volume Two consists entirely
of specialized maps. Like the maps in Volume One,
these are also "black-line" maps that make use of
hatch marks to indicate population distribution, per-
capita income, and other statistical information.
However, in no other way can these maps be considered "special," as they are qualitatively identical
to the maps in Volume One and are designed for the
same purpose.

The publisher also regards the "tab cards" that
identify each section to be special features. These
will be considered under *Accessibility*.

IV. Geographical Balance

Virtually every nation, including Equatorial Guinea,
Lesotho, Bhutan, Vanuatu, and Liechtenstein (but
not Andorra or San Marino) is given an individual
map, and in this respect *Maps on File* displays excellent geographical balance. In addition to these
national maps, the set contains individual maps for
all 50 states of the United States, the Canadian provinces and territories, and the Australian states and
territories.

V. Scale and Projections

Each map has been drawn to a different scale, with no attempt at consistency. None of the maps gives scale as a fractional representation which is standard practice in quality atlases. Although each map provides a bar scale, the graphic device used to represent bar scales varies from one map to another. For example, on map #4.015 (Ireland), there is a single bar, $7/10''$ in length. The scale indicates that this represents 40 km/25 miles.

On map #2.023 (Nepal), the user will find two bars: on one, $1\frac{1}{2}''$ represents 200 km; on the other, $1\frac{1}{5}''$ represents 100 miles. Elsewhere, the user will find yet a third system for showing distances. Map #4.029 (United Kingdom), for example, presents two lines. The $2''$ line represents 200 miles; the $1\frac{1}{5}''$ line represents 200 km.

There is no sound reason for using three different types of bar scales in a single volume. Moreover, because the choice of scale system seems to be entirely random, the user never knows which system will occur in the next map.

Projections are not identified in *Maps on File*. It may be argued that the type of projection is of little significance in maps of this type. Nevertheless, labeling the projections can alert the user to inherent distortions. This is especially important for area and continent maps, in which distortions increase with the size of area depicted.

VI. Accuracy

Because the maps in *Maps on File* are designed to be photocopied, the amount of detail that can be shown is necessarily limited. The format also imposes restrictions on the style of the maps. For example, place names must be a certain minimum size in order to reproduce well; likewise, lines for boundaries, roads, and rivers must be thicker than they would normally be. The lack of color also reduces the amount of information that can be depicted. As a result, for certain purposes the maps are neither as fine nor as comprehensive as the user might wish.

The graphic techniques used to produce the maps also results in loss of information. For example, many place names were apparently affixed to the map by simple cut-and-paste, camera-ready methods, leaving a blank area around the place names. It is often difficult to tell what location the name refers to, and in many cases the blank area covers other details on the map. For example, place name labels on the map of Indonesia (map #2.009) obscure many of the cities and islands they are intended to identify. Similarly, on the map of India (map #2.008), the Ganges River

is labeled, but the river itself is partially covered by other place names and by lines representing roads and other rivers.

Frequently, it is difficult to determine the precise location of cities, especially when they are on a coast. In these instances, the black dot used to mark the city overlaps the thick black line that marks the coastline and is rendered all but indistinguishable.

Poor graphics and design present additional drawbacks. For example, although a page is devoted to the Hawaiian Islands (map #8.011), the islands are drawn to such a small scale that no significant detail can be shown. The smaller islands are mere specks. The island of Oahu, measuring about $\frac{1}{4}''$ square, is overwhelmed by the names of four towns, a harbor symbol, and an airport symbol. Another anomaly on the map of Oahu is the omission of mountains or mountainous areas, although mountain hachures are used on other maps. On map #8.019 (Maine), the thick boundary line cannot accurately depict the many harbors and indentations of the state's coastline; offshore islands also lack meaningful detail. This problem occurs on almost all maps of states or nations with irregular coastlines.

From these maps, it is also difficult to pinpoint the precise locations of deserts and other natural features. For example, the words *Air Massif Region* appear on the map of Niger (map #1.033) to show roughly where this region is located, but no markings indicate how extensive the region actually is.

Finally, it must be noted that all maps, including the world and regional maps, lack latitude and longitude lines. This is a decided drawback and further hampers the set's accuracy and comprehensiveness. On the whole, the maps in *Facts on File* cannot be considered accurate except in superficial details.

VII. Currency

A yearly update is available from the publisher at a cost of $47.95. The information in the set reviewed by this Buying Guide is fairly up-to-date. For example, the set uses the current names *Kampuchea*, *Ho Chi Minh City*, *Zimbabwe*, and *Harare* as well as the currently accepted Pinyin transliteration of Chinese place names. However, *Burkina Faso* appears under its pre-1984 name of *Upper Volta* on several maps, including those of Africa (map #1.000), Ghana (map #1.017—incorrectly numbered as 0.017), Ivory Coast (map #1.020), Mali (map #1.028), Niger (map #1.033), Togo (map #1.044), and on several of the specialized maps. However, it is identified as *Burkina Faso* on the map of the nation itself (map #1.005.1).

The thematic maps in Volume Two give information current from different dates. For example: Population: Asia (map #9.008) gives figures from January 1980. Incomes: U. S. (map #11.012) states that the figures are "for 1978 unless otherwise indicated." The several maps showing Military Manpower of countries in different regions (maps #11.013-#11.018) do not identify the year in which the figures were compiled, and there is no copyright date on any of these maps.

The prospective purchaser should note that most maps in the set have copyright dates of either 1984 or 1986. A substantial number, however, bear no copyright date.

VIII. Legibility

In *Maps on File*, legibility is a particular concern, for its maps must not only be legible but also capable of yielding legible photocopies. Naturally, the quality of the photocopy will depend upon the quality of the machine that is used. Our tests on several machines showed a wide variation in the quality of the photocopies, from very good to poor. Prospective purchasers should consider whether their library's machine makes sufficiently good copies for them to be able to take full advantage of the purpose for which *Maps on File* is intended.

As previously mentioned (see *Accuracy*), many of the maps in this set are marred by inferior graphics. Many place names are poorly positioned, and it is often difficult to see the precise location of cities, particularly in the maps of small islands or island chains (for example, Hawaii, Indonesia, Japan, and the Philippines). Readers should also note that there is no correspondence between the importance of a particular nation (for example, the number of cities it contains) and the scale on which it is rendered. Rather, the scale is usually determined by the largest area that will fit on a page. For example, the small Caribbean islands of Nevis and St. Kitts are depicted on a scale of about 2½" to 10 miles and the Philippines on a scale of 1" to 150 miles. Clearly, the scales for these two maps were not chosen according to the significance and geographical complexity of the areas they represent.

IX. Accessibility

Accessibility to *Maps on File* is through a 19-page bound index containing some 1,400 entries. Each entry word is printed in bold-face, identified by classification (for example, town, city, seaport, province, country), and labeled according to the state, country, or continent to which it belongs, followed by the number of each map on which the location appears. Specialized maps are also identified by title.

The index is generally accurate and comprehensive, despite occasional errors and inconsistencies. For example, there are separate entries for Burkina Faso and Upper Volta; the two are treated as though they were separate nations. (For a discussion of the general treatment of this nation, see *Currency*.) The index contains no cross-references or cross-reference entries. (Incidentally, in the Upper Volta entry, the Africa map [map #1.000] is misnumbered as 1.00.)

In general, however, the index is trustworthy and should serve as a useful guide to the contents of the two volumes. As an extra finding aid, small protruding tabs act as thumb indexes and mark the beginning of each section within the two volumes.

X. Summary

Maps on File is a two-volume set of reproducible black-and-white outline maps intended for general use but geared to the needs of elementary and junior high school grades. The concept of a reproducible map series is sound; social studies teachers especially would find many uses for such a set. However, the poor quality of the graphics and cartography in *Maps on File* poses serious drawbacks. Other than as a source of worksheets for map exercises in which students are required to write directly on the photocopied map, this set is of very limited value. As a rule, readers will be better served by BACKGROUND NOTES, the series of reproducible maps and fact sheets issued by the U.S. State Department and reviewed on page 226. In addition to its higher quality, the BACKGROUND NOTES series is available at about half the price of *Maps on File*.

Maps on File costs $145; a yearly update service is available for an additional $47.95. Interested individuals and institutions may order from the publisher, Facts on File, 460 Park Avenue South, New York, NY 10016; telephone (212) 683-2244 or (800) 322-8755. In Canada, contact the Canadian Manda Group, P.O. Box 920, Station "U," Toronto, Ontario M8Z 5P9.

National Geographic Atlas of the World

Facts at a Glance

Full Title: **National Geographic Atlas of the World.**

Publisher: National Geographic Society, Washington, D.C.

Editors: Wilbur E. Garrett, Editor; Joseph Judge, Associate Editor.

Copyright: 1981.

Edition Reviewed: Fifth Edition.
Number of Volumes: 1.
Number of Pages: 385.
Number of Maps: 172.
Number of Indexes: 1.
Number of Index Entries: 155,000.
Number of Illustrations: 36 four-color.
Trim Size: 12½″ × 18¼″.
Binding: cloth.

Intended Readership: upper elementary school
    through adult.
Price: $44.95.
Sold through direct-mail advertising.
    ISBN 0-87044-347-X.
Revised every ten years. Next scheduled revision
    1991–92.

I. Introduction

The *National Geographic Atlas of the World* is a folio-sized (12½″ × 18¼″) general world atlas intended for readers in grades 3 through 12, as well as for adults. It was compiled by National Geographic Society staff, with the help of scientific contributors and geographic consultants from American universities, cartographic consultants from U. S. and foreign government agencies, and editorial consultants from government, academic, and private organizations, all of whom are named on the copyright page of the volume.

II. Format

The atlas contains seven types of information: encyclopedic descriptions of the universe, solar system, and planet earth; physical maps of continents and ocean floors; thematic maps of the world; political/physical maps of the United States and foreign countries; statistical data; a glossary; and a place-name index.

There is a handy "Key to Atlas Maps" inside the front and back covers, which consists of a world map showing the page number and coverage of each physical and political/physical map. A card containing map symbols, table of contents, and metric conversion tables is stored in a pocket attached to the inside back cover. This card is intended to help interpret the political/physical maps.

Almost all of the maps are double-page spreads with no margins. Unfortunately, information is lost in the gutter because the pages do not lie flat when opened. Librarians will quickly find that readers will break the spine while attempting to see that information.

III. Special Features

Annual updates to this atlas, which are formatted so that they can also be stored in the back-cover pocket, are automatically sent to atlas owners. These describe changes in political boundaries, flag designs, and place-name spellings.

The encyclopedic section begins with the society's unique graphic description of the size and scope of the known universe, called "The Universe through Time and Space." This is the same graphic issued with the June 1983 issue of National Geographic Magazine. It is followed in the atlas by maps of the heavens, and graphic descriptions of the solar system and earth's near-space environment, atmosphere, and crust. These are all depicted in an easy-to-understand fashion.

The world thematic section features a two-page text and three maps of resources: one of food, one of energy, and one of minerals. Each includes three small inset maps showing related subjects.

Each section of political/physical maps is preceded by two to four pages of text describing the history of each U. S. state or foreign country, depending on the map content, and tables listing its area, population, capital, and economy. For U.S. states, state nickname and date of admission to the Union are included. For foreign countries, the official language(s), religion, and literacy rate are listed.

Two to four pages of urban regional insets follow each section. These are not detailed street maps, but they do locate suburbs, outlying towns, and main roads.

The statistical data section includes geographic comparisons; airline distances; a time zone map; metric conversion tables; monthly climatic data for 320 places around the world; 1980 populations of U.S. cities; "latest estimate" populations of foreign cities; and a list of foreign terms (glossary).

IV. Geographical Balance

This atlas has a fairly good geographical balance. Of the 168 pages of political/physical maps, 40 pages are devoted to North and Central America (28 of these to the United States), 32 to Europe, 28 to Asia, 12 to Africa, 10 to South America, 10 to the oceans, and 6 to Australasia and Antarctica.

The maps of heavily populated and/or industrialized regions are shown in the larger scales and the Third World is shown with smaller scales. This typical but unfortunate treatment of underdeveloped countries might result from the lack of large-scale source maps.

V. Scale and Projections

The scale expressed as a representative fraction, the map projection, and a bar scale appear below the title of each map. A variety of map scales and projections are used, and are apparently determined by what it takes to fit the named area onto the two-page spread with the most detail and least distortion. The variety of projections and scales creates a problem because they are misleading about relative size and shape when comparing two areas. Fortunately, there are other ways to compare area, such as the statistical data in this atlas or a terrestrial globe.

VI. Accuracy

Names on the maps are placed quite accurately. Although there is no generic description of foreign terms for physical features on the maps themselves, they are easily interpreted with the general legend and glossary.

International boundaries, shown with dotted lines and tasteful pastel colors, are designated as either defined or undefined. The claims of both nations are shown where boundaries are in dispute.

The maps in the world thematic section are valuable only for conveying general information. No statistical information is attached to the symbols used. For example, one can see that South Africa is a source of diamonds, but the volume of production is not given.

VII. Currency

With the exception of changes which occurred as the atlas was going to press, the data is as current as its 1981 copyright date. The annual supplements keep the atlas up to date, although no means are provided to coordinate the new information into the existing text.

VIII. Legibility

The legibility of the maps in this atlas are what helped to establish the National Geographic Society's fine cartographic reputation. The typefaces are neat, legible, and clearly differentiate place-name categories. The Society's subtle portrayal of shaded relief and use of color only at boundaries greatly enhances place-name legibility.

IX. Accessibility

The gazetteer, or place-name index, occupies the last third of the atlas. The listing for each place includes the larger political division it belongs to, the page number and alphanumeric coordinates for the largest-scale map on which the place appears, and if applicable, the same for an urban regional map or physical map.

Latitudes, longitudes, populations, and elevations are not listed for place names in the index. Latitude and longitude lines are printed on the maps, so the coordinates of a particular place can be interpolated. Elevations are not given. Different sizes of type are used for towns, but there is no explanation of the population categories to which they correspond, if that is indeed the intent. There is no means in this atlas of determining the elevations of towns.

X. Summary

The *National Geographic Atlas of the World* is priced at $44.95, which is quite reasonable considering the wealth of information contained within its covers. There are some drawbacks, such as the loss of detail in the gutters and the absence of some kinds of information, but these are more than offset by this atlas's many strengths.

The publisher's claim that the *National Geographic Atlas* is suitable for third-graders seems exaggerated, as few children at this age will have mastered the map-reading skills required to use such a large and detailed atlas without adult supervision. By no stretch of the imagination is this a "children's" atlas. However, as this Buying Guide's library survey indicates, the *National Geographic Atlas* is a mainstay of many elementary, middle, and high school library atlas collections.

The *National Geographic Atlas* competes effectively against such other large atlases as AMBASSADOR WORLD ATLAS and the RAND MCNALLY COSMOPOLITAN ATLAS OF THE WORLD and is a useful alternative or supplement to RAND MCNALLY GOODE'S WORLD ATLAS and the PRENTICE-HALL NEW WORLD ATLAS when a very-large-page atlas is called for.

New Horizon World Atlas

Facts at a Glance

Full Title: **New Horizon World Atlas.**
Publisher: Hammond Incorporated.
Copyright: 1984.

Edition Reviewed: 1986 printing.
Number of Volumes: 1.
Number of Pages: 272.
Number of Maps: 302.
Number of Indexes: One master index, plus same-page indexes for each map.
Number of Index Entries: 5,000 in master index.
Trim Size: 8½″ × 11″.
Binding: cloth.

Intended Readership: grade 9 and up.
Price: $13.95; 15 percent school and library discount. Sold in bookstores and direct to schools and libraries. ISBN 0-8437-1225-2. Revised annually.

I. Introduction

The Hammond *New Horizon World Atlas* under review was published in 1984. Its contents are based entirely on maps from Hammond's CITATION WORLD ATLAS. (Refer to the evaluation of that reference work on page 231 for a full description of the maps.) An edition of the *New Horizon World Atlas* is also published with a different cloth binding as the DIPLOMAT WORLD ATLAS.

The *New Horizon World Atlas* is intended for readers in grades 9 and above. Its format and scope make it more acceptable for general home use than for schools or libraries.

II. Format

The *New Horizon* is 8½ × 11 inches, a smaller size than the CITATION. Its binding is not as sturdy as the CITATION or INTERNATIONAL atlases, and may not withstand regular library use. However, it will do well in homes or as a student's individual volume. It lies fairly flat when opened, but many of the maps bleed to the center so that text is lost in the gutters.

In general, map arrangement follows that used in the CITATION atlas. Some sections have been inexplicably rearranged. The section on North America, for example, begins with Canada, and is followed by Mexico, Central America, the West Indies, and finally, the United States. This lack of a clear geographic arrangement is a drawback because the atlas has no table of contents; therefore, readers cannot logically search through the volume for a country or region as the presentation sequence is arbitrary. Readers would have to work backward from the index to locate general regions they want to study.

Numerous CITATION maps have been eliminated from this atlas. In particular, relief and other the-

matic maps of continents are gone, as are provincial maps of Australia. Maps of Africa and South America have been reduced to two for each continent—the northern and southern parts. These omissions not only limit utility in general, but eliminate the opportunity to give students exposure to a wide variety of map types and the chance to understand and work with them. They also reduce the volume's value as a reference tool.

III. Special Features

The same features that accompany maps in CITATION appear here. However, all features appearing as separate sections in CITATION have been eliminated from *New Horizon*, including the introduction on the arrangement and use of the atlas. Without this introductory information, the atlas is inappropriate for library or classroom use. This exacerbates the limitations already mentioned.

IV. Geographical Balance

Although this is a world atlas, the reduced number of African and South American maps emphasizes coverage of the United States and Canada more than in the *Citation*.

V. Scale and Projections

All maps are reduced versions of the ones that appear in CITATION; that is, the map scales have been made smaller. Each map's bar scale reflects this reduction, but the representative fraction (for example, 1:10,000,000) is no longer provided.

The map projections remain the same. Their names are provided on the legend of each political map.

VI. Currency

As with other Hammond atlases, the contents are as current as the copyright date. This particular atlas is updated annually.

VII. Legibility

Although the size of the typefaces has been reduced on each map, the type remains clear and the maps remain relatively uncluttered. However, the small type will be difficult for many users to read. Some type is also lost in the gutters.

VIII. Accessibility

The *New Horizon World Atlas* does not contain a table of contents. The "Gazetteer-Index of the World" at the front of the volume is nearly identical to the list in CITATION. Each political map's same-page index has fewer entries than the CITATION's equivalent indexes. The volume's master index contains only 5,000 entries, as compared to CITATION's 25,000. Oddly enough, however, the *New Horizon*'s master index provides more complete information for each entry than does the CITATION. Not only is a page number given, but a grid locater reference is given as well. However, other problems with the CITATION's index are repeated here.

Accessibility is a severe problem with this atlas. Without proper indexes, it can be used only for the most general or casual purposes.

IX. Summary

The *New Horizon World Atlas* is an abridged version of Hammond's CITATION WORLD ATLAS. It is suitable for home browsing, but is not particularly useful for school or library use. It is also available in a version sold as the DIPLOMAT WORLD ATLAS, which is identical to *New Horizon* in every respect except binding and price. The DIPLOMAT edition features a bonded maroon leather binding with the title embossed in gold, gilt-edged pages, and a transparent acetate jacket. For most consumers, these features do not justify the price of $24.95, almost double that of *New Horizon*.

The RAND MCNALLY FAMILY WORLD ATLAS is a direct competitor at $12.95; it is a handy size and has the advantage of a comprehensive, well-organized index, but suffers from small, cluttered maps. At $22.95, the RAND MCNALLY GOODE'S WORLD ATLAS contains clear maps, and its useful special features are an added bonus that make GOODE'S a high recommendation for schools and libraries.

New Penguin World Atlas

Facts at a Glance
Full Title: **New Penguin World Atlas.**
Former Title: The Penguin World Atlas.
Publisher: Penguin Books, Harmondsworth, Middlesex, England.
Editor: Peter Hall.
Copyright: 1979.

Number of Volumes: 1.
Number of Pages: 96.
Number of Maps: 44.
Number of Indexes: 1.
Number of Index Entries: 17,000.
Trim Size: 7½" × 10".
Binding: paper.

Intended Readership: high school through adult.
Price: $9.95.
Sold in bookstores. ISBN 0-14051-196-6.
No revision scheduled.

I. Introduction

The *New Penguin World Atlas*, which was compiled by Oxford University Press, is a revision of the 1974 *Penguin World Atlas*, redesigned to be "even more accessible to the general reader." Physical, economic, and political data are presented in it. Peter Hall, editor of the atlas, is Professor of Geography at the University of Reading. The maps themselves are attributed to the Oxford University Press.

II. Format

The atlas contains 44 physical maps superimposed with political information. Twenty-nine of these are two-page spreads. The paperback volume is slim, easy to hold, and will stay flat when opened. The text paper is of good quality and opacity and the cover stock is of normal weight for paperback volumes. The binding is sturdily sewn, and should stand up well to normal use.

Each map has a title and an indication of scale, projection, and elevation (in meters). A legend is provided for most, but not all, maps and typically includes symbols for boundaries, roads, railways, airports, canals, seasonal rivers and lakes, marshes, salt pans, ice caps, sand deserts, and national parks. Ocean maps show currents.

Maps extend to page edges without neat lines. Two-page maps tend to lose detail and information in the gutter.

III. Special Features

Several continental maps show rainfall, bedrock geology, minerals, and population on a very small scale (for example, 1:110,000,000 for Eurasia and 1:190,000,000 for Africa). Inset maps represent population density and power resources of the British Isles, as well as monsoon rainfall in India and neighboring countries. These special maps do not have much detail but are useful for an overview. Also included is an easy-to-read two-page table listing capital cities, population, and other statistics for the world's states and dependencies. Another page lists populations of major urban areas and basic geographic figures for the continents, like land areas, longest rivers, highest peaks, largest lakes.

IV. Geographical Balance

The publisher states that maps have been selected to "focus maximum attention on those parts of the world likely to attract the average reader's interest." This includes primarily the British Isles, Western Europe, and North America. Special coverage is supposed to be provided for those parts of the world "likely to appear in the world news," such as the Middle East and southern Africa, but neither of these areas has above-average coverage in terms of numbers of maps or amount of detail except for the Suez Canal, whose map is at a 1:1,500,000 scale. Coverage of most of South America and the eastern U.S.S.R. is disappointingly sparse. There is no map of Antarctica in its entirety.

V. Scale and Projections

Scales are noted in the table of contents as well as on each map. Scales vary widely, ranging from 1:1,500,000 for certain areas, such as the Suez and Panama canals, to the 1:165,000,000 world map (the table of contents lists this scale as 1:163,000,000). Scales are roughly consistent for areas of comparable size, although the bias toward Great Britain and Europe means that these areas are represented at somewhat larger scales than are others.

Throughout the atlas, distances on bar scales are given in kilometers only, never in miles. This may limit this atlas's usefulness for American readers who are not fully conversant with metric measurement.

Projections are identified on most maps. In all, seven standard projections have been used.

VI. Accuracy

Geographic names appear in their conventional anglicized forms when these exist. For example, *Moscow* is used rather than the vernacular Russian *Moskva*. The alternate vernacular name is frequently given in parentheses on the map, and a cross-reference appears in the index from the alternate name to the familiar one.

Names and their locations are for the most part accurate, although some inconsistent spellings are given for West Germany. For example, the town of *Giessen* is incorrectly spelled *Geissen* on the main map on page 24 and in the index (thus hindering the reader who looks for it under its correct spelling in the index), but is spelled correctly on the map on page 20. Likewise, *Schwabisch Hall* is incorrectly spelled *Schwarbisch Hall* on the map on page 24 and in the index. Both German nations are labeled with their official names rather than simply *West Germany* and *East Germany*.

VII. Currency

With its 1979 copyright date and apparent lack of subsequent revision, the *New Penguin World Atlas* is not as current in some areas as most comparable atlases with later copyright dates. This is reflected in population statistics given in tables at the beginning of the book. The publisher states that they are "based on the latest available United Nations figures," but obviously these no longer are the "latest" figures.

Lack of currency is also reflected in certain place names. For example, although Zimbabwe is labeled with its current name, the capital, now called *Harare*, is identified by its old name of *Salisbury*. Burkina Faso appears as *Upper Volta*, and all Chinese place names are spelled in the Wade-Gilles style of transliteration rather than in the Pinyin style that has generally superceded it. But the country formerly known as *Cambodia* is labeled by its more current appellation, *Kampuchea*. The label *Ho Chi Minh City* is followed by *Saigon* in parentheses.

VIII. Legibility

None of the maps appears cluttered with too many place names; in fact, there is plenty space for additional place names on most maps.

Typefaces are legible and are differentiated to indicate various sorts of political and physical features. Although these distinctions are not explained in any legend, most of them become obvious as one uses the atlas. Some differences in typeface are not clear, however. For instance, on some maps most town and city names are slightly italicized, but others (apparently the largest) are not. On other maps, only names of natural features are italicized. The various city symbols used do not make the distinction any clearer, as they are also not explained. Mantua and Cremona in Italy, for example, are represented on page 25 with what appears to be the same symbol; *Mantua*, however, is printed in heavy italics and *Cremona* is in a thinner, regular typeface.

Various boundaries, roads, railways, canals, and rivers are clearly distinguishable from one another. Natural features, shaded relief, and spot heights are likewise clear. Elevations are in meters. Colors are sufficiently strong and in register.

IX. Accessibility

The index endeavors to list every name shown on the maps, unlike some small atlases which omit some less important names. The index is easy to use, although abbreviations are not explained. Alphanumeric grid coordinates are included for easy place location. Latitude and longitude are not given in the index but do appear on the maps. The grid areas are too large on some maps, which may make finding a particular place difficult. To pinpoint the small city of Herisau, Switzerland, for example, one has to comb an area of 4¾″ × 7″ spanning two pages.

Numerous inset maps supplement the main ones. Most have no title, but they are clearly marked with latitude, longitude, and indication of scale. Inset maps are indexed.

X. Summary

This is a good, basic, concise atlas. It does not contain as much information as the VNR POCKET ATLAS, nor is it as easy to interpret as the RANDOM HOUSE CONCISE WORLD ATLAS; its price of $9.95 is comparable to or higher than either of these. Its high quality cartography, large physical map format, and pleasing visual impact are pluses that make it a possible candidate for basic student classroom use, or for general adult use. However, its British orientation, emphasis on Great Britain and Europe in the maps, out-of-date information in certain instances, and strictly metric bar scales will keep it from being the first choice among paperback atlases for the typical American.

Prentice-Hall New World Atlas

Facts at a Glance

Full Title: **Prentice-Hall New World Atlas.**
Publisher: Prentice-Hall, Inc., Englewood Cliffs, NJ.
Editors: B. M. Willett, Harold Fullard.
Copyright: 1984.

Edition Reviewed: 1st edition, 1984.
Number of Volumes: 1.
Number of Pages: 284.
Number of Maps: 100.
Number of Indexes: 1.
Number of Index Entries: 45,000.
Number of Illustrations: 200, color.
Trim Size: 8¾″ × 11″.
Binding: cloth.

Intended Readership: high school through adult.
Price: $16.95. Fifteen-percent discount on prepaid orders of one to nine books; fifteen percent on orders of ten or more books.
Sold in bookstores, supermarkets, and by direct mail and newspaper and magazine advertising. ISBN 0-13-695867-2.

Revised periodically.

I. Introduction

The *Prentice-Hall New World Atlas* is a general reference atlas first issued in the United States in 1984. It is intended for high school through adult readers. The maps have been provided by George Philip and Son, a leading British cartographic firm, which also produces atlases under its own name. The publishers state that it has been designed to provide a compact and convenient reference book which is easy to handle and consult.

II. Format

The atlas contains political maps with shaded relief, the majority of which are two-page spreads, in the general reference section. There is an adequate though not generous gutter along the spine edges of the pages. There is also a large selection of world thematic maps, most of which are on single pages.

With a 9″ × 12″ cover, the atlas is a convenient size, and allows for maps with a fair amount of detail.

There is a master legend at the front of the reference section. Each map in this section includes a bar scale and a representative fraction scale, and a scale showing relief (elevation) coloring used. Each thematic map includes a clear, well-located legend.

The volume has a well-finished cloth binding, and a sewn spine. The map section is produced on heavy paper; the index is on lighter weight matte paper with poor opacity. The volume is sturdily produced. It also has an attractive full-color jacket.

III. Special Features

The atlas begins with a 48-page section of world thematic maps, which includes: Chart of the Stars; Solar System; Time; Atmosphere and Clouds; Climate and Weather; Earth from Space; Evolution of the Continents; Unstable Earth; Making of Landscape, Earth: Physical Dimensions; Distances; Water Resources and Vegetation; Population; Languages; Religion; Growth of Cities; Food Resources; Nutrition; Mineral Resources; Fuel and Energy; Occupations; Industry; Transport; Trade; and Wealth. Each section includes one or several clear, well-made maps, which are often supplemented by graphs, text, and photographs.

The reference maps section covers 128 pages, and generally includes political relief maps, with several solely political or physical maps for each continent.

IV. Geographical Balance

This atlas was produced in Great Britain by a British cartographer; thus, its marked European bias is to be expected. Of the 128 pages of reference maps, 52 are of Europe; 18 are of Asia; 16 of Africa; 8 of Australia/Oceania; 20 of North America; and 7 of South America. There are maps of administrative divisions of Great Britain, a detail not repeated for other countries. Maps of Europe also appear most consistently at the largest scale available in the atlas, 1:2,500,000, as compared to 1:6,000,000 to 1:10,000,000 for Asia; 1:8,000,000 for Africa; 1:4,500,000 to 1:12,000,000 for Australia/Oceania; 1:6,000,000 to 1:12,000,000 for North America; and 1:8,000,000 to 1:16,000,000 for South America. The thematic world maps also frequently include insets of Europe which are the same size as the world maps; however, this actually presents a clearer picture of what would otherwise be an overcrowded map.

V. Scale and Projections

The atlas uses a wide range of scales, 1:1,000,000 to 1:50,000,000. The choice of scales is appropriate to the size of the pages and provides maps of good detail. There is fairly good consistency in presenting adjacent areas at similar scales, particularly in the maps of Europe, Africa, Canada, and the United States. However, the range of scales for Asia, at 1:1,000,000 to 1:20,000,000, may be too wide, and may confuse some users about the relative sizes of areas.

Although not confusing, the presentation of South America in northern and southern halves at 1:16,000,000, with an enlarged map of central South America at 1:8,000,000 is an unfortunate inconsistency.

Many of the maps are drawn using a conical projection with two standard parallels, an excellent choice for equal-area representation with a minimum of distortion. Other projections used in the atlas, such as Bonne, Lambert's equivalent azimuthal, and Mercator, are less frequently seen. However, they are adequate for their purposes, with the exception of the Hammer equal area and Mollweide's homolographic projections, used for the World and Pacific Ocean maps, respectively, which are unusual and distortive.

VI. Accuracy

Place names are consistently presented in their respective languages, with English versions given in parentheses for important or otherwise unrecognizable place names. New version (Pinyin) Chinese place names are used consistently. Great care is evident in placing names in their proper locations, clearly adjacent to appropriate symbols.

VII. Currency

Recent name changes (*Belize, Vanuatu, Vietnam, Zimbabwe*) are presented correctly, although Kampuchea is labeled *Cambodia*.

Text and photographs are contemporary, and should not appear dated for some time.

VIII. Legibility

Typefaces are legible and sufficiently varied to distinguish different types of features and sizes of towns. Most of the maps are clear, and show good detail without appearing overcrowded. The relief colors are well distinguished, although print in mountainous areas is occasionally hard to read. Color reproduction is excellent and in register.

The typeface used in the index is very small, and may prove difficult for many readers.

IX. Accessibility

The table of contents covers seven pages. It is divided into continents, and includes a list of maps, their pages, and scales; numbered inset on each two-page spread showing the regions listed in the contents pages; and an appropriate photograph. It is a worthwhile feature, but contains a serious flaw: it includes only the maps in the main reference section. Although the main title of the thematic maps section is given at the top of the table of contents, there is no listing of topics or page numbers. The same is true of the index. In addition, each of the three sections (thematic maps, main maps, index) is paginated separately (a frequent problem in atlases), so there is virtually no access to the thematic maps and index, and the situation is confusing.

There is a 96-page index, including 45,000 entries, and a table of recent name changes of places in India, Iran, Mozambique, and Zimbabwe. The index is prefaced with a short but sufficient explanation of its use, and a list of abbreviations. Symbols are included with entries for rivers, countries, and administrative subdivisions. Unfortunately, countries are not given in entries for cities, towns, etc., unless they are needed to distinguish between identical entries. Entries give page numbers and latitude and longitude in degrees and minutes. A spot check shows that even small towns on the maps are included in the index, and entries in the index were found on the maps with reasonable ease, although some confusion resulted when the place name appeared in an inset instead of in the main map.

There are several clearly labeled, easily distinguished insets.

X. Summary

The *Prentice-Hall New World Atlas* is attractive and well presented, and the opening section of thematic maps is a valuable asset. The maps are very good, but American users may find the European emphasis and lack of detailed maps of the United States a deficiency.

This atlas is appropriate for secondary, college, and public libraries, and would be a good general reference atlas for home or office. Although it is a fairly new title, the *Prentice-Hall New World Atlas* is an authoritative alternative to the well-established RAND MCNALLY GOODE'S WORLD ATLAS, which costs six dollars more. In sum, at $16.95 this atlas is a splendid value.

The Prentice-Hall Pocket Atlas of the World

Facts at a Glance

Full Title: **The Prentice-Hall Pocket Atlas of the World.**
Publisher: Prentice-Hall, Inc.
Editor: Howard Fullard.
Copyright: 1983.

Number of Volumes: 1.
Number of Pages: 120.
Number of Maps: 55.
Number of Indexes: 1.
Number of Index Entries: 11,000.
Trim Size: 4½″ × 7½″.
Binding: paper.

Intended Readership: elementary school through general adult.
Price: $2.95.
Sold in bookstores and through direct mail and magazine and newspaper advertising.
    ISBN 0-13-697045-1.
Revised periodically.

I. Introduction

The Prentice-Hall Pocket Atlas of the World offers a basic collection of maps in a handy pocket size (4½″ × 7½″). The maps combine political and physical features. The publisher has stated that this volume is suitable for use by elementary and high school

students as well as for general readers. The editor and director of cartography is Howard Fullard. The maps were created by George Philip and Son, Ltd., a prestigious and respected cartographic firm.

II. Format

A political map format is used throughout, with some physical features identified by name or symbol. There are 14 one-page maps and 41 two-page maps.

The atlas is easy to hold and flip through, though it does not lie flat by itself when opened. The paperback binding is sewn and the text paper is good quality and reasonably opaque. The attractive full-color cover is standard cover stock. The cover is also scored to minimize damage to the binding from repeated use. All in all, it is a well made book for its type. The book's size is suitable for the types of maps included.

Legends are sparse. Instead of a master legend in a small atlas such as this, each map has an inset containing a title (a feature lacking in many pocket atlases), a scale, and a few symbols. Most legends show, at most, symbols for railways, canals, and altitudes. Several legends indicate oil pipelines, and a few show other miscellaneous symbols. Principal roads—a feature not usually shown on pocket atlas maps—are indicated in the legends for maps of New Zealand and the central Middle East, although there is no apparent reason why only these two maps were chosen for this feature.

Maps are contained within neat border lines. Two-page maps are separated in the center by a small margin so that nothing is lost in the gutter of the book. Some effort has been made to ensure that words spanning two pages are not inconveniently cut in half, but this is not always true.

III. Special Features

The only special feature is a small-scale world air routes map which provides an adequate overview of routes. The table of contents lists the scale for each map, thus enabling the reader to compare scales at a glance for various areas. The individual map legends give scale not only in ratio and bar-scale form, but also in miles per inch, a useful aid found in very few atlases.

IV. Geographical Balance

Western Europe is somewhat better represented than the rest of the world, with generally larger-scale maps. Japan's map is at a 1:8,500,000 scale, although Japan is bigger and has almost double the population of Italy, which has a larger-scale map at 1:6,000,000.

V. Scale and Projections

Scales vary throughout the atlas, from the smallest-scale world air routes map (1:250,000,000) to the largest-scale map, the Suez Canal (1:1,000,000). Continental maps of Asia and Africa are represented at much smaller scales (1:60,000,000 and 1:45,000,000, respectively) than are Europe and Australia, continents much smaller in size (1:27,500,000 and 1:22,500,000, respectively). Scales are given in fractional, verbal, and bar form; bar-form scales are in miles and kilometers.

An unusual feature for an atlas of this size is the inclusion of the map projection under the legend inset. In all, ten projections are used, generally well chosen for the area represented. On the world map, the continents and other land areas would have been more accurately represented had a projection other than Mercator been used. Greenland is smaller than South America, not larger, as appears on a Mercator projection. The world map also fails to show the Pacific Ocean south of the Aleutian Islands between about 185°E and 135°W, an area which encompasses Hawaii and several other islands. Although this area is shown on another map, it is misleading to omit it from a "world" map.

VI. Accuracy

It is convenient for the average American reader that place names are given in conventional anglicized spellings. Although no symbols are used to denote natural features, such as mountains, deserts, or plateaus, many such areas are indicated by their names on the maps. Some names include the generic term to describe the feature, but many do not; the lack of both a generic term and a descriptive symbol on the map and in the index may leave a reader with no idea about the type of feature shown. El Djouf, for example, a desert in Mauritania, is not described or symbolized as such on the map or in the index, although the list of index abbreviations includes *des.* for "desert."

Placement of names on the maps is generally accurate, although the town of Rehoboth is located in two different places on the map of Namibia on page 74, and indexed for only one placement.

VII. Currency

Geographic names are relatively current with the 1983 publication date of this atlas. *Cambodia*, however, is referred to by that name, rather than by *Kampuchea*, the current name, which appears widely in many other atlases.

VIII. Legibility

In general, colors are adequate and in register, but a few of the maps have a "washed out" appearance; their colors and print are somewhat weak. A few maps, such as that of eastern France, Switzerland, and northwest Italy (pages 20–21), appear slightly cluttered because numerous places are shown and the print is not very strong. Close inspection, however, reveals this map to be accurate and remarkably full of information, considering the small page size. However, not all areas of the world enjoy such detailed coverage as this.

Typefaces are differentiated for various place categories, but no legends indicate what these are. In most cases, the experienced reader can deduce from typeface and location to what a particular name refers, and can judge the comparative sizes of towns and cities by symbols and typeface. Capital cities are not distinguished from other cities, either on the maps or in the index.

Rivers are drawn and labeled clearly. Borders are also drawn clearly but again, because there is no legend, the reader must deduce whether some boundaries are local or national. The map of Germany and Austria, for example (pages 16–17), is confusing as both West and East Germany are colored the same shade of tan, with the word *Germany* spanning both parts. The only indications that they are somehow separate are the *West* and *East* labels and a fine-line yellow border. Some readers, especially younger ones, could be misled into thinking that these are not actually two autonomous countries.

Other than river and a few other symbols which appear on the maps without explanation, physical features are distinguishable only when they are labeled with a name. Readers familiar with standard map symbols may be able to recognize some of the unexplained symbols used on these maps, but inexperienced readers could not. Elevations are not depicted, although most map legends have a statement that appears to indicate height in feet for the highest area on it.

IX. Accessibility

This atlas index contains about 11,000 entries, compared with 20,000 for a similar size pocket atlas such as the RANDOM HOUSE MINI WORLD ATLAS. The index is adequate, though not all names shown on the maps are indexed. The Eifel mountains in West Germany, for example, are not indexed, although the Ardennes mountains, 50 miles to the west in France, are. A bigger deterrent to easy use is the index format, which is not only presented in small, hard-to-read type, but in columns in which the reference page precedes the name so that it almost appears to "belong" to the item in the column to the left. The locations on the maps are indicated by letter designations (Bd, Ce, etc.) rather than by the more commonly used alphanumeric grid system. Latitude and longitude are not given.

X. Summary

The maps in the *Prentice-Hall Pocket Atlas of the World* are generally of high quality, especially for their size and scale, and the price of $2.95 is a true bargain. However, the limited features of this atlas, and the peculiarly formatted index, make this a questionable choice for students and adults alike. Despite the publisher's claim, this atlas is really not appropriate for the needs and map-reading skills of most elementary and middle school students. At best, this work would come in handy for a traveler (particularly one whose business may involve frequent international travel) who might need a convenient pocket-size world atlas. This atlas is generally preferable to THE RANDOM HOUSE MINI WORLD ATLAS, which costs two dollars more. Those seeking a small paperback atlas might investigate the VNR POCKET ATLAS ($8.95) or THE RANDOM HOUSE CONCISE WORLD ATLAS ($7.95), although both are significantly more expensive.

Rand McNally Children's Atlas of the World

Facts at a Glance

Full Title: **Rand McNally Children's Atlas of the World.**
Publisher: Rand McNally & Company.
Authors: Bruce Ogilvie and Douglas Waitley.
Copyright: 1985.

Number of Volumes: 1.
Number of Pages: 96.
Number of Maps: 34.
Number of Indexes: 1.
Number of Index Entries: 500.
Number of Illustrations: 120 color.
Trim Size: 10¼" × 12¼".
Binding: hardcover.

Intended Readership: elementary school children.
Price: $11.95, with a 25 percent discount for schools and libraries.

Sold in bookstores and by direct mail. ISBN 0-528-82418-X. Updated every three years, with major map revisions.

I. Introduction

The *Rand McNally Children's Atlas of the World* is a brief (96 pages), oversized (9" × 12") book containing some maps and much interesting, well organized, and readable text on geographical subjects. Intended for primary grade students, the *Children's Atlas* is not an atlas *per se* but rather, in the publisher's words, "a pictorial introduction to the planet Earth." Authorship is credited to Bruce Ogilvie, formerly of the University of Chicago Department of Geography, and Douglas Waitley. Rand McNally is a preeminent and well respected cartographic publisher. The volume reviewed here is the 1985 revised edition (updated from 1979). It is priced at $11.95.

II. Format

The atlas contains simple physical, political, thematic, and pictorial maps. Maps appear on both single pages, and on two-page spreads. Most maps are smaller than a full page, and share the space with text, illustrations, or both.

The atlas uses heavy, semigloss paper; reproduction is good. The spine is sewn, and the cover is well finished, paper over heavy boards, with a textured, washable surface. The atlas has the appearance of a children's picture book, is easy to handle, and should be fairly durable.

Only a few of the thematic maps have legends. These are simple and appear adjacent to the appropriate map. The remaining maps do not have legends.

III. Special Features

The atlas begins with 37 pages of text which discuss topics such as the earth in space, origins of maps, sky and oceans, agriculture, energy, and population. Each topic is covered in two pages and includes a good deal of information presented in a simple easy-to-understand manner, well illustrated with drawings, photographs, and maps. Eight-page continental sections follow. Exceptions are six pages for Australia/Oceania and two pages for Antarctica. Major continent sections include two pages each for "Terrain;" "Countries and Cities"; "Life on the Land;" and "Its Animals." Terrain includes a physical map, text, photograph(s), and box of facts; Countries and

Cities includes a political map, text, and photographs; Life on the Land includes a pictorial map, text, and drawings; Its Animals includes a pictorial map, text, and drawings. Four pages of "Other Kinds of Maps" follow the continent sections, and include seasonal temperature and land use thematic maps; small illustrations of types of map projections; text; and drawings. The two-page glossary, titled "Those Hard Words," contains more than 140 geography terms. A four-page index concludes the volume. Physical and political world maps are found on the endpapers. The text is well written and effectively presented, as well as being enhanced by attractive and relevant full-color photographs and drawings.

IV. Geographical Balance

Each continent is given equal and uniform treatment, with the exceptions already mentioned.

Illustrations in the text tend to deal more with North America and Europe than with other parts of the world.

V. Scale and Projections

Scale is given only for the endpaper maps and the final thematic maps, although there is a two-paragraph discussion of scale in the introductory text. For the most part, the maps are sized appropriately to fit the pages; however, the physical maps in the Terrain sections are small considering the large areas they cover. Even though scale is not given, except for the terrain maps, adequate space is given to the map depictions so that their details are easily visible.

Projections are not given at all, except in the Other Kinds of Maps text, which includes illustrations of Mercator, Goode's, and polar projections. The maps appearing in the text and continental sections do not display any noticeable distortions.

VI. Accuracy

Because of the small sizes of maps, not all political entities are named. Those names that do appear are accurate and properly placed.

The text, although relatively brief, is accurate, and shows an effort to avoid sexual and racial stereotypes.

A caption on page 7 describing the tilt of the earth's axis incorrectly reads $23\frac{1}{2}^2$ rather than $23\frac{1}{2}°$, and might possibly be a typographical error.

VII. Currency

Recent name changes (*Belize, Kampuchea, Zimbabwe*) are represented correctly.

The illustrations are well chosen and avoid giving the volume a dated look.

VIII. Legibility

The typefaces are clearly legible. The text print is fairly large, and very readable for children. The well-illustrated pictorial maps, all in full color, appear somewhat crowded, but not overly so. Their colors are solid and distinctive.

IX. Accessibility

The table of contents is clear, comprehensive, and easy to use. The index, containing approximately 1,000 entries, refers to the text rather than to the maps. However, this is not a serious liability in a book of this kind for young readers, in which the maps are designed as accompaniment for the text rather than vice-versa. Accessibility is enhanced by the fact that each topical section is presented as a self-contained two-page spread and opens on the left-hand page. The title, or subject heading, of each section is printed in large type in the upper left-hand corner of the left-page, so that the reader can see the subject at a glance.

X. Summary

The price of $11.95 is reasonable for this well-designed, durable volume, which introduces the young reader to a wide spectrum about the world, its natural resources, and its people. Much of the text in this atlas is duplicated in the RAND MCNALLY STUDENT'S ATLAS, which is designed for slightly older students and contains more detailed, more sophisticated maps. The *Rand McNally Children's Atlas of the World* is clearly superior in every respect to the VIKING CHILDREN'S WORLD ATLAS, which is intended for the same readership. It is better organized; has a livelier, more informative text; its maps are more accurate; and elementary-age children will find its illustrations more appealing.

Rand McNally Classroom Atlas

Facts at a Glance

Title: **Rand McNally Classroom Atlas.**
Publisher: Rand McNally.
Copyright: 1986.

Edition Reviewed: Eighth Edition, 1987.
Number of Volumes: 1.
Number of Pages: 96.
Number of Maps: 59.
Number of Indexes: 1.
Number of Index Entries: 2,000.
Number of Illustrations: 9 four-color.

Trim Size: 7¼″ × 10″.
Binding: paper.

Intended Readership: lower elementary through
    junior high school.
Price: $3.95. Twenty-five percent discount to
    schools and libraries.
Sold in bookstores and direct from publisher.
    ISBN 528-17720-6.
Revised annually.

I. Introduction

The *Rand McNally Classroom Atlas* is a small (7¼″
× 10″), brief (96 pages), paperbound atlas containing
59 maps in full color, intended for classroom use by
elementary through high school students. The "1987
edition" is the eighth of a well-received work, although its copyright page indicates only six prior ones,
and the latest date is 1986. Although there is no
authorship credited, Rand McNally is a well-respected cartographic publisher.

II. Format

Easy to handle and convenient to use, even for small
hands, the atlas is produced on medium-weight paper
and has a saddle-stitched stapled binding. Each page
is packed with maps and information, including the
back and inside covers.

The atlas contains physical, political, and thematic
maps. The physical and thematic maps have clear,
straightforward legends on each page; the political
map symbols key appears only at the beginning of
the volume. There are both one- and two-page map
spreads.

III. Special Features

The atlas begins with well-illustrated sections on geographic features, including a brief glossary, and instructions for using the atlas, including how to locate
places using the index, how to measure distances,
latitude and longitude, and map symbols. These sections are clear and useful, although a few problems
are evident. For example, in the very small illustrations of latitude and longitude, the prime meridian
does not pass through England, and the Equator is
a little too far north. Also, geographic terms are
illustrated which are not defined in the glossary, such
as *shoal, gulch,* and *reservoir.*

Physical and political maps of the world are followed by a selection of thematic maps, including climates, natural vegetation, economic activities, population, languages, and settlement.

Continental maps include merged relief, political,
environments, rainfall and temperature, natural vegetation, physical-political, and density of population.

The index has approximately 2,000 entries. There
is a world information table, including area, population, and population density; a page of United States
geographical and historical facts; and world facts and
comparisons.

IV. Geographical Balance

The geographical presentation is fairly well balanced.
As with virtually all American-produced atlases for
children, however, the United States receives the
most attention. There are separate maps of the United
States, including four regional physical maps, and
merged relief, political, and highway maps; there are
also separate merged relief and political maps of
Canada. The Australia-New Zealand area lacks environmental, rainfall/temperature, and physical/po-
litical thematic maps. In addition, a separate political
map for Central America is not included.

V. Scale and Projections

The scales are large and thus show little detail, but
fit the size of the pages and the purpose of the atlas.
Many of the maps give only bar scales, which are
useful for learning to measure distances on maps.
However, verbal or representative fraction scales
would have been an additional useful feature. Many
of the world thematic maps give no scale; however,
their sizes on the page allow the clear depiction of a
good amount of detail. There is some inconsistency
in scales used (United States, Canada, Europe, Australia all at or near 1:16,000,000, but South America
at 1:29,000,000, Africa at 1:36,000,000, and Asia at
1:42,000,000), which could lead to misinterpretation
of relative sizes unless the student is taught that different scales are needed for different-sized areas to
be covered in the same space.

Projections are identified for about half of the
maps. The standard equal area, conic, and sinusoidal
projections are used. A Miller cylindrical projection
of the world is present for studying latitude, longitude, and direction, although this type of projection
greatly distorts the areas of polar regions. A somewhat unusual azimuthal equidistant polar projection
centered on the North Pole with an inset of the South
Pole is a good illustration of a different type of projection, but the Southern Hemisphere distortion is
very misleading. This would be more appropriate in
a larger atlas with a discussion of map projections.

Elevations are included in insets on the merged
relief maps. They are in the form of mountain ranges

with color variations indicating altitude and they are both attractive and easily understood.

VI. Accuracy

Place names are spelled consistently and correctly, and are printed in their proper locations. Occasionally, the city symbols are placed improperly (Tijuana, Mexico, appears on, rather than next to, the border). Physical areas and borders are represented appropriately.

VII. Currency

Recent place name changes (*Vietnam, Belize, Zimbabwe*) are presented correctly. The World Information Table contains area and estimated population figures as of January 1, 1986, which makes this quite up-to-date.

Although the atlas does not really appear to be dated, the merged relief maps in particular are printed in the heavily colored fashion generally associated with atlases for children. The environment maps, however, have a much more modern appearance, with colors that are less intense but still distinctive.

VIII. Legibility

The typefaces are clear and legible, although they are a bit too light for easy reading on the environment maps. Generally, the maps avoid overcrowding by showing only the largest cities and towns, and most important physical features. Colors used on thematic maps and to show relief are sufficiently distinctive to avoid confusion. Color reproduction is very good, and the colors are generally in register.

IX. Accessibility

There is a clear, well-organized table of contents.

The easy-to-read index includes over 2,000 entries. It refers to page number and simple location grid, the use of which is explained in the introductory text. Unfortunately, a spot check reveals that not all place names shown on the maps are listed in the index. In addition, the page given in the index is sometimes the incorrect page of a two-page spread.

Most of the United States maps include insets to show Alaska and Hawaii.

X. Summary

The currency, compact size, variety of maps, good introductory material, and modest price combine to make the *Rand McNally Classroom Atlas* an excellent value. Home users will find this a quick and handy reference tool. Teachers may wish to have multiple copies for classroom use, as this atlas would make a good basis for increasing geography awareness in both elementary and secondary schools. School libraries can consider this an inexpensive way to provide circulating copies of atlases; public libraries may also consider it for this use. The generous 25-percent discount offered to institutions for bulk purchases is a further incentive.

Its cartography is without question superior to that found in the American Map Corporation's Colorprint series (not to mention the Sharon STUDENTS' WORLD ATLAS). While the *Classroom Atlas* contains much less text and explanatory material than some of the larger atlases in its class (notably the VIKING STUDENT ATLAS), it compares favorably with Hammond's INTERMEDIATE WORLD ATLAS, a "map study book" for the junior high school grades that retails for the same price.

Rand McNally Family World Atlas

Facts at a Glance

Full Title: **Rand McNally Family World Atlas.**
Former Title: Worldmaster.
Publisher: Rand McNally & Company.
Copyright: 1984.

Edition Reviewed: 1985 revision.
Number of Volumes: 1.
Number of Pages: 256.
Number of Maps: 216.
Number of Indexes: 1.
Number of Index Entries: 30,000.
Number of Illustrations: 16.
Trim Size: 9″ × 11″.
Binding: cloth.

Intended Readership: elementary school and up.
Price: $14.95.
Sold in bookstores, by direct mail, and directly to schools and libraries. ISBN 0-528-83145-3.
Revised annually.

I. Introduction

The *Rand McNally Family World Atlas* is a small format (9″ × 11″) atlas of 256 pages. It is intended as a reference tool for use by the entire family, from child through adult, and is based on the Rand McNally map series.

II. Format

The atlas consists primarily of one-page political maps, and includes a section of continental theme maps.

The pages are printed on fairly lightweight paper, with good nonglossy color reproduction but poor opacity, so that there is a fair amount of show-through of dark colors. The volume has a sewn spine with a heavy, well-finished cover. The binding has been scored for ease of opening and lying flat, a worthwhile practice for a big volume. It has an attractive and expensive looking jacket. The volume, which is virtually identical in size to the RAND MCNALLY GOODE'S WORLD ATLAS, is fairly easy to handle, although younger children will find it heavy.

A master legend precedes the political maps elsewhere and is not repeated. Although straightforward, it does not include actual population figures in its explanation of relative sizes of city symbols.

III. Special Features

The atlas begins with a 26-page section titled "Today's World in Maps." Each continent is represented by introductory text, a global view showing relief, a location map, and several small thematic maps. The thematic maps include subjects like rainfall, vegetation, population, minerals, and energy. Each continent is covered by six or eight maps.

The next section, "The Political World in Maps," includes 90 pages of political maps. "World Tables and Facts" includes 9 pages of political information, comparisons, and populations, while "United States Tables and Facts" covers 34 pages, and includes for the most part populations of cities, towns, counties, and states.

A table of abbreviations precedes the 75-page index.

IV. Geographical Balance

North America, South America, and Africa fare best in the opening section of thematic maps, each with eight maps, as compared to six each for Europe, Asia, and Australia/Oceania.

In the main section of political maps, a North American bias is evident. North America has 57 pages of coverage, of which 9 are on Canada and 45 are on the United States. Europe has 12 pages; Asia, 6 pages; Africa, 4 pages; Australia/Oceania, 2 pages; and South America, 6 pages. Each U. S. state and Canadian province is given a full page, with the space-saving exceptions of 12 states which appear two on a page.

V. Scale and Projections

Only bar scales are given for most maps, making comparison of areas difficult. The scales of maps in the main political section range from approximately 1:950,000 to 1:52,000,000. These very small scales are inappropriate for the size of the pages and the amount of detail the maps attempt to show. The maps are crowded and cluttered in appearance, and difficult to use. The individual state maps vary widely in scale. Texas actually looks smaller than New Jersey, as each fills the page on which it appears. This distortion may be misleading to younger readers.

The thematic maps are small but usable, although several have such wide margins that they could have been made larger. They would then have been able to cover more area or, even better, to have been reproduced in a larger, more readable scale.

The standard azimuthal, conic, and cylindrical projections have been used, and no serious distortions in shape or area caused by projection are evident. However, a polar azimuthal projection is used to show the North Pole and air distances, and a Miller cylindrical projection is used for the map of the world; both result in considerable distortion at their edges.

VI. Accuracy

Place names appear to be spelled accurately, with anglicized versions given preference over vernacular names. Vernacular versions are included in parentheses for important entries. For example, *Riyadh* (*Ar Riyad*), *Ruse* (*Ruschuk*), *Rio Grande* (*Rio Bravo del Norte*), and so on. Considerable care is evident in printing names in proper correlation to their symbols. This is always important, but all the more so when the maps are of such small scale and include so many place names.

Except for rivers and lakes, most physical features are labeled but not represented on the maps by any symbols or relief. Borders are fairly clear. They are somewhat heavier than usual on most maps, but this makes them easy to locate.

VII. Currency

Recent name changes (*Belize, Vanuatu, Kampuchea, Vietnam, Zimbabwe*) are represented correctly.

As in the *Rand McNally Cosmopolitan World Atlas* (reviewed in *General Reference Books for Adults*), the figures given in the Populations of Foreign Cities and Towns table are not recent. At least half of the figures are from the early 1970s, with some as early as 1962. The revision of this atlas is inconsistent, as the population figures in the World Political Information Table are 1984 estimates, and comparisons between the two sources of figures show considerable differences. U. S. figures are from the 1980 Census.

VIII. Legibility

Typefaces are clear and sufficiently varied to distinguish between political units and physical features.

Because they are relatively small, most maps appear very cluttered. Print size is also quite small, of necessity, thus adding to the confusion. On the U. S. state maps, county borders are represented by a blue broken line over a gray solid line; often, these colors are not in register, which further detracts from the appearance of the maps and adds to the confusion. Adults with poor eyesight may have trouble with the size of the print; younger readers, with the cluttered appearance.

Though fairly dark, the colors reproduce well.

IX. Accessibility

The table of contents is clear and comprehensive, making it easy for users to locate particular maps and tables.

The index includes over 30,000 entries and gives page and alphanumeric grid locators. The grid squares are small enough for easy location. However, the marginal grid markings are very small and light and are themselves hard to see and keep in view. The introduction to the index is thorough and concise, and states that "all important names that appear on the reference maps" are included. A spot check shows that most of the smallest towns on the maps do not appear in the index, which is consistent with their not being important enough for inclusion. Each entry includes a descriptive term, such as "co" for county, "is" for island, and so on, for entries other than cities, and the state or country. Several entries cite appearances of names on both main maps and insets.

Abundant insets show important urban areas or extensions of areas from the main maps. The insets are clearly distinguishable from the main maps; however, because they are tucked into much of the available space on pages, their inclusion adds to the clutter.

X. Summary

The great advantage of the *Rand McNally Family World Atlas* is its price, which, at $12.95, makes it one of the least expensive hardcover atlases available. The handiness of size and reference value of its good index makes the atlas useful to school and public libraries and home users. However, its dis-

advantages, primarily the small size of maps and resultant clutter, make this atlas a questionable value even at this low price. Both libraries and home users would be substantially better served by the clear maps and special features of the RAND MCNALLY GOODE'S WORLD ATLAS at $22.95, or by the PRENTICE-HALL NEW WORLD ATLAS at $16.95.

Rand McNally Goode's World Atlas

Facts at a Glance

Full Title: **Rand McNally Goode's World Atlas, 17th edition.**
Publisher: Rand McNally & Company.
Editors: Edward B. Espenshade, Jr. and Joel L. Morrison.
Copyright: 1986.

Edition Reviewed: 17th edition, revised second printing, 1986.
Number of Volumes: 1.
Number of Pages: 384.
Number of Maps: 396.
Number of Indexes: 1.
Number of Index Entries: 36,000.
Number of Illustrations: 43, color.
Trim Size: 8½″ × 11″.
Binding: cloth.

Intended Readership: high school and college.
Price: $22.95.
Sold in bookstores and directly to schools and libraries. Discount of 25 percent to schools and libraries. ISBN 0-528-83127-5.
Major revisions on reference maps for each printing; statistical thematic maps revised every four years.

I. Introduction

The *Rand McNally Goode's World Atlas* is a medium-size (8½″ × 11″) atlas intended for high school and college students. It contains six sections: "Introduction: Maps and Imagery;" "World Thematic Maps;" "Major Cities;" "Regional Section;" "Plate Tectonics and Ocean Floor Maps;" and "Geographic Tables and Indexes." Its editor is Edward B. Espenshade, Jr., Professor Emeritus of Geography at Northwestern University; Joel L. Morrison, Senior Consultant, is affiliated with the United States Geological Survey. The atlas, which still carries the name of its original compiler, the American cartographer J. Paul Goode, is now in its 17th edition; the first edition was issued in 1922.

II. Format

The atlas is printed using a good medium-weight paper which provides excellent color reproduction and opacity. The spine is sewn, and the binding is well-finished and durable. It has an attractive full-color jacket. The size of the atlas makes it easy to handle and convenient to store, but also leads to overcrowding on its maps and elimination of worthwhile detail. Many maps are two-page spreads, but a gutter along the spine edge makes reading their centers easy. Maps often "escape" their neat lines and this, combined with the many insets, gives some pages a cluttered look, as on page 200. Full legends appear only at the beginnings of the Regional and Major Cities sections, requiring awkward consultation. Scale, relief, and population symbols conveniently appear on most pages.

III. Special Features

Each of the six sections of *Goode's World Atlas* may be considered a special feature.

Introduction: Maps and Imagery (nine pages) contains a basic discussion of maps and mapmaking, including map scales and projections, and recent technological advances. The text materials are brief, basic and good, but are fairly technical and might be difficult for the layman to read and/or comprehend. For example, the explanation of Mercator projection says in part: "Thus, for every point on the map, the angles shown are correct in every direction within a limited area. To achieve this, the projection increases latitudinal and longitudinal distances away from the equator." Without an explanation of latitude this is hardly clear.

World Thematic Maps (52 pages) includes maps on a wide variety of subjects, including political and physical maps, climate, weather, vegetation, soils, population, health, economics, industry, agriculture, minerals, and transportation. Many of these maps are accompanied by statistical graphs. The thematic maps are an excellent ready source of basic information.

Major Cities (28 pages) includes 62 maps of the world's most populous metropolitan areas, all depicted at the same scale and in a standardized and comparable format.

The Regional Section (160 pages) is divided into standard continental areas. A selection of thematic maps precedes the general physical/political maps of

each area. Many insets highlight important population centers throughout this section. Plate Tectonics and Ocean Floor Maps (seven pages) includes text, diagrams, and maps.

Geographic Tables and Indexes (126 pages) has an unusual feature in an atlas—for the most part, entries have a pronunciation key, which is missing only with repetition of a first part. For example, when a word like "Valley" or "Pine" is repeated, the phonetic spelling is not given twice, although frequently it appears in the second entry, not the first. There are also tables of political information, comparisons, principal cities, and foreign geographical terms. The pronouncing feature of the index is both unusual and quite helpful.

IV. Geographical Balance

This atlas is heavily weighted toward the United States and Canada. Of 160 pages in the Regional Section, 60 represent North America, 37 Europe, 25 Asia, 7 Australia, and only 14 show Africa and 8 South America. The Major Cities section is slightly better; 14 of the 62 maps show U. S. or Canadian cities, and several more unusual cities are represented, such as Brazzaville, Manila, and Teheran. The thematic maps preceding the North America regional section are far more extensive than in any other section.

V. Scale and Projections

Scales for the most detailed maps in the Regional Section are 1:4,000,000, which provides a good overall picture, although at the cost of some detail. Conic projections, which represent areas equally and with a minimum of distortion, are used for the majority of maps in this section. The world thematic maps generally use a Goode's homolosine equal area (condensed) projection, which is standard in this type of map. One unfortunate problem occurs in the Landforms map, where the interruption, which removes the center portion of the Atlantic Ocean to save space on the page, actually causes the deletion of the Mid-Atlantic Ridge, which is precisely the type of feature being shown on this map. Most of the small world thematic maps try to show more detail than their scales will allow with clarity. A few of these maps require insets to show adequate detail; this is confusing. All Major Cities maps are at the scale of 1:300,000, making comparison easy. However, this scale allows little detail beyond major through routes, extent of urbanization, boundaries, and some local names. A larger scale would show less of the cities' surroundings, but could give greater detail more clearly presented.

VI. Accuracy

Considerable effort is evident in trying to print place names in their proper relationship to symbols. Unfortunately, confusion and overcrowding occasionally result from the small size and large scale of maps, combined with the variety of information which the cartographers are trying to include, often in several different typefaces, such as the names (sometimes in two languages) of countries, cities, towns, rivers, physical features, regions, states, and so forth. A few problems in accuracy appear. One problem is an inconsistent use of conventional and new forms in Chinese names. The capital of China is given as *Peking* (*Beijing*), with preference to the conventional form, whereas another label says *Xizang* (*Tibet*), giving preference to the new Pinyin form. On two maps, the English resort towns of Torquay and Torbay appear as one city. The New York City metropolitan map lists *Passaic Expwy* as an alternate name for Interstate 80, although this name is not in common usage locally.

VII. Currency

Rand McNally's excellent revision policy includes major revisions of the reference maps for each printing, and revisions of the statistical thematic maps every four years as new data becomes available. This assures that the most recent geographic information will appear in each printing of the atlas. In spot checks, recent name and/or boundary changes for the following were shown correctly in the atlas: Salisbury, Rhodesia now *Harare*, *Zimbabwe*; North Vietnam and South Vietnam now *Vietnam*; Cambodia now *Kampuchea*; British Honduras now *Belize*.

VIII. Legibility

The typefaces used on the maps are legible; however, their size, combined with the range of information being portrayed, sometimes results in an overcrowded map which is difficult to read. The use of shaded gradient tints enhances the depiction of relief, but it also hinders the readability of the print. The city maps portray roads with a yellow line against a dark background. This is unusual and can confuse readers, as roads are more generally depicted in a dark color against a lighter background. This is also inconsistent with road symbols used on the regional maps, which show roads in red against a light green or light brown background.

IX. Accessibility

The extensive index refers to pages and gives latitude and longitude for locating places. Having coordinates appear here provides valuable additional information; however, this requires some practice to use for locating places. A brief explanation of latitude and longitude would be a welcome addition. It must be noted that the presentation of coordinates in an alternate style, for example *53.37 N* rather than *53° 37' N*, requires some familiarity with this system, or some practice on the part of a new user. The detailed table of contents is an important and necessary asset, as many insets may appear out of strict geographic order, and most thematic maps appear two on a page.

X. Summary

Public libraries may prefer to use a large-format atlas for primary research work, but the *Rand McNally Goode's World Atlas* is an excellent quick reference source with particularly helpful features in the thematic maps and pronouncing index. School libraries will also find these features useful, and may prefer its size. However, students less familiar with atlas use may be confused by some overcrowded pages, the small sizes of most thematic maps, and the inconsistent use of road symbols. Shaded relief, though, is usually a popular visual device with younger students. Home users will be well served by this atlas, and may prefer its format.

In either case, the volume's price of $22.95 is quite reasonable for the amount of information provided, making this an excellent value. Its longevity (17 editions since 1922) is a clear indication that it has found acceptance by a substantial buying public. In short, few atlases of this size are in *Goode's* class. The PRENTICE-HALL NEW WORLD ATLAS is one title that may prove a less expensive, high quality alternative, but although its thematic maps are good, they are much less extensive than *Goode's*.

Rand McNally Images of the World: An Atlas of Satellite Imagery and Maps

Facts at a Glance

Full Title: **Rand McNally Images of the World: An Atlas of Satellite Imagery and Maps.**
Former Title: Diercke Weltraumbild-Atlas.
Publisher: Rand McNally & Company.
Editor: Christopher Mueller-Wille.
Copyright: 1983.

Number of Volumes: 1.
Number of Pages: 160.
Number of Maps: 151.
Number of Illustrations: 112 satellite images
    (photographs).
Trim Size: 8¾″ × 11¾″.
Binding: hardcover.

Intended Readership: high school through adult.
Price: $24.95; 25-percent discount to schools and
    libraries.
Sold in bookstores and through direct-mail
    advertising. ISBN 0-528-63002-4.
No scheduled revision.

I. Introduction.

Rand McNally Images of the World, an Atlas of Satellite Imagery and Maps is a compilation of high-altitude photographs and corresponding maps of areas of agricultural, geologic, industrial, and urban development interest throughout the world. It is a specialized work, intended for high school and college students, and should not be mistaken for a traditional atlas. Its editor states that "its concept of clearly focused regional emphasis makes it a perfect companion to other atlas and geographic texts, as well as a valuable, independent fact-providing and fact-finding volume."

II. Format

Each two-page grouping contains one or more large satellite-image photographs and one or more corresponding maps, depicting the same area with emphasis on a particular theme, such as delta environments, flooding, economy, etc. In a relatively few cases, photographs bleed into the page gutters, thus losing some of the image.

The paper stock is lightweight and glossy, and this glossiness enhances the photographic printing. Color reproduction is excellent. Although the pages are sewn and reinforced with headbands and footbands, the full-color paper-over-boards binding appears to be weak. The front endpapers and cover were already torn in our review copy. The volume will probably not hold up well with moderate use.

III. Special Features

Three sections of introductory text discuss "Concepts and Technical Foundations of Remote Sensing," "Uses and Applications of Spaceborne Remote Sending," and "Image Processing and Cartographic Prepara-

tion." Although the text is fairly technical, these well-illustrated sections provide a solid basic knowledge of satellite imagery. The introduction concludes with a glossary of foreign terms, abbreviations, a metric conversion chart, and a table of imagery sources and dates of photographs used in the volume.

The subjects of photo/map groupings consist of: Coastal Forms/Estuaries/Land Reclamation (13 groupings); Geology/Tectonic Structure/Natural Catastrophes/Natural Events (6 groupings); Vegetational Succession/Vegetational and Climatic Zonation (7 groups); Agriculture/Agricultural Development (8 groupings); Irrigation Agriculture/Oases/Arid Lands (10 groupings); Subarctic and Arctic Zones/Tundra/Taiga (6 groupings); Industrial Production and Energy/Mineral Extraction (8 groupings); and Urban Agglomerations (9 groupings).

An appendix includes nine images of Munich, West Germany, which illustrate different data collection and reproduction techniques. This might have been better integrated into the introductory material, which deals with the technical aspects of satellite photography.

IV. Geographical Balance

The geographical balance is somewhat weighted toward Europe, with 34 groupings, as compared to 20 for North America, 24 for Asia, 10 for Africa, 4 for Australia, and 5 for South America. However, this should not be considered a serious problem as the purpose of this atlas is not to attempt to represent the entire world, but rather to use a variety of images to illustrate the versatility of satellite photography. The editor states that photographs for inclusion were selected on the basis of quality.

V. Scale and Projections

Scale information appears for most maps and photographs are representative fractions.

The photographs are given larger scales, with ones usually of 1:1,500,000 or larger. The scales of the urban photographs for New York, Washington, D.C., and San Francisco are particularly impressive. At 1:50,000, the reader can clearly see the World Trade Center, the White House, and the towers of the Golden Gate Bridge.

The scales of the maps are often smaller, and there are many examples of maps at scales more than half that of the corresponding photographs. In fact, most of the groupings have photographs and maps which are not at the same scale. This makes it difficult to interpret the photographs, a task already unfamiliar to most readers. Only rarely is a box provided on a map to outline the area shown in the photograph, and the photographs are never labeled with the area shown on the map.

Several examples of photographs and corresponding maps are presented in a misoriented fashion; that is, with north-south alignments that do not match. Although this does not seriously hamper the reader's ability to interpret the photograph, it is careless and should have been avoided.

Projections used for the maps are not stated; however, given the purpose of the volume, this is not troublesome.

VI. Accuracy

Two obvious inaccuracies are present. On the map of New York City, one of the most detailed maps in the atlas, ferry lines that did not exist at the time of publication are incorrectly shown crossing the Hudson River. On the photograph of California a straight line represents the state's border. A less-experienced reader might interpret this to mean that this man-made feature actually occurs in nature, particularly as no other photograph includes any superimposed label. Although neither is a glaring error, they bring into question the accuracy of depictions of other less-familiar areas.

A more subtle but also more frequent inaccuracy is the presence of several maps which do not properly match their corresponding photographs. This is often caused by misorientation or greatly differing scales, and may cause difficulty in interpreting the photographs. Examples include the groupings for the Rhone Valley, France (page 38); Fujiyama, Japan (page 63); Elburz Mountains, Iran (pages 64–65); and Argolis, Greece (page 93).

VII. Currency

It is difficult to judge the currency of the material, as the volume does not present the standard benchmarks against which to judge. Most of the photography was done in the 1970s, which is sufficiently recent for the stated purpose of depicting thematic features of the earth's surface. Similarly, only major changes in satellite technology would cause the introductory materials to become outdated. It was copyrighted in West Germany in 1981, and again in 1983 when the American edition was published. There probably were no revisions between the two dates.

VIII. Legibility

The volume boasts excellent color reproduction. The photographs are very well reproduced, and the maps are clearly legible. Symbols used on maps are well differentiated, easy to interpret, and appropriate to the purpose of each map.

IX. Accessibility

The detailed table of contents takes up two pages, and the two color-coded index maps that appear early in the volume indicate the subject and geographic coverage provided in the atlas.

Unfortunately, there is no index. However, there are illustrated introductory sections on: Concepts and Technical Foundations of Remote Sensing; Uses and Applications of Spaceborne Remote Sensing; and Image Processing and Cartographic Preparation.

X. Summary

Despite some problems, *Rand McNally Images of the World* is a handsome volume which is well worth its $24.95 price, if only for its uniqueness. However, besides this, it is an excellent value, and would be well used as a text that illustrates new ways to learn about our planet, if not at least as required additional reading for high school and college students in geography and geology courses. Although it has little reference value for libraries, it does provide much worthwhile and often hard-to-find, satellite imagery in one place. It should also prove fascinating browsing material for public, school, and college libraries, and in homes where there is special interest in such materials.

Rand McNally Quick Reference World Atlas

Facts at a Glance

Full Title: **Rand McNally Quick Reference World Atlas.**
Publisher: Rand McNally & Company.
Copyright: 1977.

Edition Reviewed: 1985.
Number of Volumes: 1.
Number of Pages: 48.
Number of Maps: 45.
Trim Size: $8\frac{3}{4}'' \times 10\frac{7}{8}''$.
Binding: paper.

Intended Readership: general.
Price: $3.95.
Sold in bookstores. ISBN 0-528-83226-3.
Revised annually.

I. Introduction

The *Rand McNally Quick Reference Atlas* is a small (about 9″ x 11″), brief (48 pages) paperbound atlas intended for general ready reference use by students and adults. Its cartography follows the style of other Rand McNally atlases and uses maps also found in other Rand McNally publications.

II. Format

The atlas contains political maps with shaded relief. All but one of the 45 in the atlas are two-page spreads, with sufficient gutter space to avoid loss of information.

The binding material is heavy coated paper, and the binding is stapled. It is easy to handle, with maps large enough to contain a basic level of information. It is sturdy enough for general use.

At the front of the atlas are a master legend and a brief explanation of map symbols. City symbols, which are designated by community size, are repeated at the bottom of many pages.

III. Special Features

The inside front cover contains a list of principal countries and regions of the world, including their areas in square miles, populations, and population per square mile. The inside back cover lists principal cities of the world and their populations. There is a world map with a graph showing comparative land areas and populations. The atlas contains 45 pages of regional maps. There is no index.

IV. Geographical Balance

Of the 45 pages of maps in the atlas, more than one-third (16 pages) show the United States. These maps are also presented at the best scales used in the atlas (1:4,000,000). Of the remaining maps, the geographical representation is fairly well distributed, although Africa receives only four pages and South America three pages.

V. Scale and Projections

Scales are given on every map in the forms of representative fraction, verbal statement, and bar scale. Each map also contains a small diagram showing area represented in square miles.

The scales used in the atlas, ranging from 1:4,000,000 to 1:40,000,000, with most at 1:16,000,000, do not allow the depiction of a great deal of detail, but do result in a clear map that avoids cluttering and overcrowding. By presenting maps of adjacent areas at the same scale (for example, Africa on several pages all at 1:16,000,000), the editors have given a degree of consistency.

Standard conic, azimuthal, and sinusoidal projections are used to show equal area representation with a minimum of distortion. Projections are identified on each map. There is a statement on each map that "elevations and depressions are given in feet," but no keys or legends indicate these.

VI. Accuracy

Greater care could have been given to the placement of names on maps in order to provide a clearer connection with the appropriate city symbols. There are several examples in urban areas of confusion in determining which names match which symbols. In addition, on the 1:4,000,000 map of the northeastern U. S., the symbol for Burlington, Vermont, is incorrectly the same size as those for its much smaller neighbors, Essex and Winooski. Although symbols are available on the legend for cities of 1,000,000+ population, most large urban areas are represented instead by a red area that shows the extent of urbanization, a practice that introduces occasional distortions. For example, on the 1:12,000,000 U. S. map, Miami appears to occupy the lower third of Florida's east coast.

VII. Currency

Population figures in the World Political Information Table are estimates for 1985. Recent name changes (such as *Belize, Zimbabwe, Vanuatu,* and *Kampuchea*) are represented correctly. There is a small table converting conventional Chinese place names to the new Pinyin versions. However, the presentation of Chinese place names on the maps themselves is inconsistent. For example, the capital city is identified as *Peking (Beijing)*, but *Xizang (Tibet)* is the way the former Himalayan nation is labeled.

VIII. Legibility

Typefaces are legible and clear, with sufficient differentiation to distinguish political units from physical features. However, names printed over dark relief shading are difficult to read. Only the Western Europe map suffers from serious overcrowding. Colors are varied and well produced, without giving the appearance of overcoloring.

IX. Accessibility

There is no index in this atlas, which is a serious flaw. The listings on the inside front and back covers could have been set up to include these important data, which would have made this a far more useful volume.

There are several insets, which are readily distinguished from the main maps. The selection of areas to be shown in insets, other than areas off the main maps, is not always consistent. For instance, there are three insets showing South Africa; in the United States, there are insets only for Houston and San Diego.

X. Summary

The *Quick Reference Atlas*, priced at $3.95, provides good value as a convenient, quick-reference (as its name implies) atlas for basic home use, although it is lacking in detail. It is probably too basic for school, college, or public libraries, and its lack of an index of any sort seriously limits its accessibility.

Rand McNally Student's World Atlas

Facts at a Glance
Full Title: **Rand McNally Student's World Atlas**.
Former Title: Young Student's Atlas.
Publisher: Rand McNally.
Copyright: 1982.

Edition Reviewed: 1986 revised edition.
Number of Volumes: 1.
Number of Pages: 96.
Number of Maps: 60.
Number of Indexes: 1.
Number of Index Entries: 500.
Number of Illustrations: 70.
Trim Size: 8¼″ × 11″.
Binding: paper.

Intended Readership: elementary through high school.
Price: $3.95.
Sold in bookstores and directly to schools and libraries. ISBN 0-528-83140-2.
Revised annually.

I. Introduction

The *Rand McNally Student's World Atlas* is an 8¼″ x 11″, 96-page atlas intended as a beginning volume for students from elementary through high school. Authorship is unattributed; the maps were created by the Rand McNally Company, a respected cartographic firm. It contains an introductory section on

the earth in space, planets and earth movements, the concepts of mapping, scale, latitude and longitude, projections, kinds of maps, and an explanation of map legends. This is followed by seven map sections and a section on geographical tables and the index.

II. Format

The atlas is small and light enough to be easily handled by children. The pages are made of relatively lightweight paper, with good color reproduction but only fair opacity; there is see-through of heavily inked text and art. The binding is glued, with normal cover stock. The atlas seems to be fairly durable.

The atlas contains physical, political, thematic, and pictorial maps. Almost all are two-page spreads; unfortunately, there are no spine edge gutters on the map pages, so there is loss of information in the gutters. The pressure required to open the atlas well enough to see into the spine areas will probably damage the binding.

There are master legends in the introductory material for both the environment and physical-political maps. The appropriate legend is repeated on each environment map, but no legends are repeated on the physical-political maps.

III. Special Features

Because the atlas is intended as an instructional tool for young readers, it contains a good deal of well-illustrated, simplified introductory material. This includes: The Nine Planets and Earth Movements; Mapping the World (includes map scale and latitude and longitude); The Round Earth on Flat Paper (map projections); Imagery and Maps (remote sensing and satellite imagery); Kinds of Maps and Legends and What They Mean. The illustrations in this section include maps and drawings. The text is clear and straightforward, and is well fashioned for elementary and intermediate students; it may also be adequate for secondary students. Continental sections follow. Each opens with two pages on Terrain, including text, physical map, photographs, and a box of facts with location map. The Rand McNally environment map used in many of its atlases follows, on two pages. The next two pages discuss animals, with text, drawings, and pictorial map with many illustrations. Countries and Cities covers two pages, with text, simple political map, and photographs, and discusses briefly such topics as history, geographical influences on culture and settlement, languages, and population. Two to six pages of physical-political maps, often with insets of areas of interest, conclude each continental section.

There is a glossary and list of map and geographical terms (130 entries); map names and abbreviations, including foreign terms (50 entries); one page of world facts and comparisons; one page of principal cities of the world; and an index of major places on the physical-political maps (500 entries).

IV. Geographical Balance

Each continent is represented in the atlas with a complete selection of features, including Terrain, Environment, Animals, and Countries and Cities. Each feature is covered in two pages for each continent, with the exception of the Asia environment map, which covers four pages.

The number of pages of political maps that conclude each continental presentation varies, although not unreasonably. Maps of North America cover six pages; Europe and Africa have four pages each; South America has three pages; Asia and Australia/Oceania have two pages each.

Antarctica is not presented with all the listed features, but instead is covered in one page, which includes text, a physical-political map, a photograph, and a box of facts.

V. Scale and Projections

Only the environment and physical-political maps include scale and projection labels. Where labeled, the scale is indicated with representative fraction, verbal statement, and bar scale.

The scales of the environment maps range from 1:16,000,000 to 1:28,000,000, sufficient to fill the two-page spread for these maps and to show fair to good amounts of detail. The physical-political maps vary in scale from 1:12,000,000 to 1:42,000,000, although all but one are at scales of 1:21,000,000 or better. The maps of the United States and Canada show the best detail, although all of the maps are at scales adequate for the purpose of the atlas.

The standard conic, sinusoidal, and azimuthal projections are used to provide equal area representation with the least distortion.

VI. Accuracy

For the most part, place names are spelled and placed correctly. There is an extra unlabeled city symbol in the San Francisco area on page 74 of the United States map. There is some inconsistency in the use of anglicized and local versions of place names. The capital of Egypt is presented as *Cairo* (*Al Qahirah*), giving preference to the Anglicized version, whereas the capital of Sudan is given as *Al Khartum* (*Khar-*

toum), giving preference to the local version. The smaller political map on Africa's Countries and Cities pages uses *Cairo* and *Khartoum*.

VII. Currency

Recent name changes are presented correctly. For example, the atlas identifies *Belize*, *Zimbabwe*, and *Vanuatu*.

Traditional Wade-Giles versions of Chinese place names are used, rather than the Pinyin versions. However, because of the small size of the China map, few Chinese place names are given.

VIII. Legibility

The typefaces are clearly legible, although some names on the environment and pictorial maps are difficult to see against dark backgrounds.

Too many different typefaces are used to represent different categories of political and physical features. Several maps show labels not connected to city, feature, or boundary symbols, and are not otherwise explained on the legend, nor listed in the index with a descriptive term.

Colors are well chosen and well reproduced.

IX. Accessibility

There is a good table of contents, which delineates all the maps and text features.

The index includes only about 500 names found on the physical-political maps; thus, many names shown on the maps are not listed in the index. The index gives either the name of the state or country for city entries, or a descriptive term for countries or features, and gives page and grid locators.

Several of the physical-political maps include well-placed, clearly distinguishable insets. Some of these show extensions of areas not on the main map, whereas others are quite interesting for their inclusion; for example, there are three insets of South Africa; one of the vicinity of Bogota, Colombia; another of Caracas, Venezuela; and one of the Malaysian Peninsula.

The index and insets can be effectively used as teaching aids.

X. Summary

Although it has some minor flaws, this is a well presented and nicely balanced volume, and can be an effective beginner's atlas for younger students. It can serve equally well in the classroom, as a homework resource, and as a home reference book for students.

At $3.95, the *Rand McNally Student's World Atlas* is an excellent value.

By comparison, the RAND MCNALLY CLASSROOM ATLAS, whose appearance implies use by younger readers because of its size and heavily colored maps, actually serves as a small reference atlas, and less a beginner's atlas, than the *Rand McNally Student's World Atlas*. The *Student's World Atlas* is more appropriate as a teaching aid than the RAND MCNALLY CHILDREN'S ATLAS OF THE WORLD. The text in the CHILDREN'S ATLAS is longer, but very similar to that in the *Student's World Atlas*. However, the CHILDREN'S ATLAS does not contain the physical-political maps or the map index found in the *Student's World Atlas*.

The Random House Concise World Atlas

Facts at a Glance

Full Title: **The Random House Concise World Atlas.**
Publisher: Random House, Inc.
Editors: staff of John Bartholomew & Son Ltd.
Copyright: ©1984 by John Bartholomew & Son Ltd.

Number of Volumes: 1.
Number of Pages: 208.
Number of Maps: 120.
Number of Indexes: 1.
Number of Index Entries: 20,000.
Trim Size: 6″ × 8⅝″.
Binding: laminated paper.

Intended Readership: general.
Price: $7.95.
Sold in bookstores and directly to schools and libraries. ISBN 0-394-74007-6.
Revised as needed.

I. Introduction

The maps contained in *The Random House Concise World Atlas* were compiled by John Bartholomew & Son, the same respected Edinburgh-based cartographers responsible for the *Times Atlas of the World*. The atlas is intended to provide the general reader with basic physical and political maps of the world in a convenient format.

II. Format

The atlas consists predominantly of physical maps of regions and countries, interspersed with smaller-scale political maps of the continents. Over half of the maps are two-page spreads, but these are generally separated by a narrow space so that the contents are not swallowed in the gutter. In the center of a few maps, however, names are cut off and boundary lines and other features do not match exactly. Each map is contained within neat lines. Occasionally, part of a map spills over the neat line in order to show an important detail that might otherwise be cut off.

There is both a print and graphic table of contents. Every continent but Antarctica is shown in outline form overlaid with index maps which are labeled with page numbers.

The atlas opens fully but does not lay flat. The size is adequate for the types of maps included, and is convenient both for desktop use and storage on library shelves. The sewn paperback binding is sturdy. Pages are heavy and nonglossy.

A master legend is located near the front of the atlas; the relatively small page size precludes a legend on each map. The symbols describe various types of boundaries, transportation elements, and landscape and miscellaneous features. The legend ranks eight levels of population centers, and uses various typefaces to describe political and other features. The only features described in the atlas that relate to economic geography are oil and gas fields and pipelines.

Two British usages in the legend may be drawbacks for the general American reader: the numbers describing various sizes of population centers are printed with a space instead of a comma to denote thousands. Also, physical relief is recorded in meters only and no indication is provided to show that "m" means meters.

III. Special Features

Three special two-page thematic maps complement the political and physical maps. The world physical map, at a 1:150,000,000 scale, is very general but does show major air travel routes. On the same two pages is a comparative cross-sectional diagram of major mountain peaks and their elevations. The world time zones map, a desirable atlas feature, has a slightly larger scale with national boundaries delineated. Major ocean shipping lanes are also shown. However, the use of 24-hour clock readings rather than "a. m." and "p. m." might be a drawback for many American readers.

The world environment map, at a larger scale than the previous two maps, shows general relief, river systems, vegetation, major ocean currents, continental and ice shelves, and a few extreme weather records. Eight vegetation types are shown in color and are explained succinctly in a legend. Specific rainfall figures are not given.

Two two-page bathymetric maps show the Atlantic Ocean in its entirety and most of the Pacific Ocean, with special emphasis on the maritime boundaries of Australasia. The latter map includes only those areas between about 45°N and 55°S. Some of the other maps provide information about the parts excluded from this map, but part of the area directly south of the Bering Strait, including the southwestern Aleutian Islands, is omitted from this atlas.

IV. Geographical Balance

Most of the world is well represented in this atlas, although there are gaps such as those already noted. There is slightly better coverage of the United States and Western Europe than of any other regions, both in terms of scale size and number of maps. Great Britain has six pages of maps while all of Africa has only seven. Most countries appear in groups, although that is not a major disadvantage in an atlas of this size.

V. Scale and Projections

Various scales are used throughout the atlas, presented both as representative fractions and as bar scales (kilometers and miles). The capital letter "M" is used after the representative fraction to denote "million," but nowhere is this explained. The use of 1:2.5M in place of 1:2,500,000 with no explanation might be confusing to American readers.

In general, densely populated areas have been selected for detailed representation. The slight Anglo-American geographical bias, however, leads to such instances as a two-page map of New Zealand at 1:5,000,000 and a one-page map of the Philippines (which has a larger population and total land area) at 1:10,000,000. The smallest scale used (least detailed) is the 1:150,000,000 world physical map. The largest is 1:2,500,000, used for Europe, parts of the United States, and Israel and Lebanon. The most typical scale is 1:20,000,000.

Town and city symbols are generally clear. It is ambitious for an atlas of this size to distinguish between towns above and below 10,000 inhabitants, and in fact, the distinction between these two symbols is often difficult to see on the maps.

Projections are not specified, although they appear to be standard ones suitable for the areas represented.

VI. Accuracy

Names of countries appear in their conventional Anglicized forms. Other place names are usually spelled according to the official language(s) of each country. Alternate spellings are included in parentheses for places commonly known by conventional spellings. On the map of Central European Russia, for example, *Warsaw* appears in parentheses as the alternate name for *Warszawa*. However, *Warsaw* as an alternate spelling does not appear on the larger scale map of east-central Europe. Similarly, the Carpathian Mountains appear on the former map only as *Carpathians* but on the latter only as *Carpatii Orientali*.

Names are generally well placed on the maps. Generic terms describing physical features do not always appear together with the proper name, nor are symbols or shading always sufficient to indicate the nature of a physical feature. For example, the map of England gives no indication as to what kind of feature *The Weald* is. This information can be found in the index, however.

VII. Currency

Place names and international borders are up-to-date. A notable exception is the use of *Cambodia*—both on maps and in the index—in place of the currently universally accepted *Kampuchea*, which was adopted by the government of that country in 1977. However, this atlas does use the name *Zimbabwe*, which was adopted in 1980.

VIII. Legibility

Typefaces on the maps are legible and sufficiently differentiated to distinguish categories. The number of place names that appear is suited to the size of the map to avoid a cluttered appearance. Major transportation routes, physical features, and borders are clearly marked and distinguishable from one another.

Nine levels of shading, for which the key appears in the introductory section, indicating relief above sea level are sharp and easily distinguishable. Six levels of shading are used for below-sea-level elevations, but the color for one category did not match the legend, so differences between it and the next elevation are not easily apparent. Colors are registered and consistent throughout.

IX. Accessibility

The 20,000-entry index lists only the vernacular spelling, if used, of place names; there are no cross-references from common conventional spellings. The reader who is not familiar with the vernacular spellings might not find in the index such major places as Copenhagen (København), Vienna (Wien), and Sardinia (Sardegna). Names in the index are followed by the name or abbreviation of the country in which they are located. The names of physical features are clarified by one of 21 categories. The index is extensive, although the countries of Mauritius and Zimbabwe have been omitted from the index (but not from the maps). Because the index is otherwise so complete, it would appear that these are typographic oversights, and do not reflect intent.

The index indicates map page number and on the page, location by the alphanumeric grid system. Latitude and longitude coordinates are not used. Perhaps to save space, not all occurrences of a place are listed in the index. The map listed for Papua New Guinea, for example, actually shows less of that country than does another unindexed map at the same scale. The contents feature of numbered areas of an inset map correlated with the printed text is a helpful ready-reference guide.

There are over 20 inset maps, each clearly marked, including indication of scale.

X. Summary

At $7.95, *The Random House Concise World Atlas* compares favorably in price with similar atlases, such as the CONCISE EARTHBOOK. Its overall quality, despite some shortcomings, is very good. Its manageable size—slightly larger than the typical "pocket" atlas—is an added attraction for both library and personal use.

The Random House Mini World Atlas

Facts at a Glance
Full Title: **The Random House Mini World Atlas.**
Publisher: Random House.
Editors: staff of John Bartholomew & Son Ltd.
Copyright: 1984 by John Bartholomew & Son Ltd.

Number of Volumes: 1.
Number of Pages: 208.
Number of Maps: 120.
Number of Indexes: 1.
Number of Index Entries: 20,000.

Trim Size: 4″ × 6″.
Binding: laminated paper.

Intended Readership: general.
Price: $4.95.
Sold in bookstores and directly to schools and libraries. ISBN 0-394-74008-4.
Revised as needed.

I. Introduction

The Random House Mini World Atlas is a smaller, more compact version of THE RANDOM HOUSE CONCISE WORLD ATLAS. Some minor deletions have been made because of space considerations. For complete information about the basic material common to both atlases, see the review of THE RANDOM HOUSE CONCISE WORLD ATLAS that begins on page 280 of this Buying Guide.

II. Format

Format and pagination are the same as in the *Concise* version, but the maps differ; what were physical maps in the *Concise* version have been rendered here as simple political maps. Shaded relief is not shown and shaded ocean depths are shown on only a few maps. Everything is on a reduced scale from the *Concise* version; dimensions have been reduced by 2¾ inches in height and 2 inches in width to produce a compact, easily held size. As a result, there is less content of several symbols from the master legend; for example, maritime boundaries and roads have been eliminated. The only landscape-feature symbols retained are rivers and permanent and seasonal lakes.

The neat borders enclosing the maps in the *Concise* version have been omitted, so that maps extend to the edge of the page; much of the content is lost in the gutter of the book. This was not a major problem in the *Concise* atlas, but will frustrate any serious atlas user. Occasionally a name has been cut in half at the page edge, which leaves the reader wondering what is missing.

The table of contents lacks the extremely useful index maps found in the *Concise* atlas.

III. Special Features

The special features of the *Mini World Atlas* are essentially the same as those in the *Concise* version, which are described in detail on page 280 of this Buying Guide.

IV. Geographical Balance

Like THE RANDOM HOUSE CONCISE WORLD ATLAS, this atlas gives greater and more detailed coverage to Europe and the United States than to other regions of the world. Given the limited size of this atlas, however, the balance is adequate.

V. Scale and Projections

The *Concise* atlas presents most scales in both fractional and bar-scale form. Because the same base maps are used in both versions, however, the scale of maps in the *Mini* atlas is necessarily reduced in order to incorporate the same information onto a smaller page. Thus, the representative fraction scales no longer apply to the scaled-down version and have, therefore, been omitted. However, since these are still relevant, bar scales calibrated in kilometers and miles remain for most of the maps. The four world maps have only fractional scales in the *Concise* version, which means that no scales appear at all for these maps in the *Mini* version. Most users will find this a drawback.

VI. Accuracy

This is the same as in the *Concise* version, on the whole acceptable, particularly for an atlas this small.

VII. Currency

This is the same as in the *Concise* version, usually reflecting place names and borders current in the early 1980s.

VIII. Legibility

Despite the reduction of typefaces to accommodate the smaller page size, names remain legible and the various typefaces and borders are still easily distinguished. Names of natural features are shown. Colors are good and in register.

IX. Accessibility

A few place names which appeared in the *Concise* version have been omitted, but these tend to be located at the page edges. Papua New Guinea, for example, lost several towns on its eastern coast. This would not be a significant problem except that the indexes for both versions contain the same entries, resulting in blind index references in the *Mini* atlas. The town of Finschhafen in Papua New Guinea, for instance, is listed in both indexes but appears on the indicated map only in the *Concise* atlas.

X. Summary

The publisher tried to adapt an existing small atlas to an even smaller format rather than produce a new atlas with features and scale more suitable to the reduced format. The publisher describes *The Random House Mini World Atlas* as "small enough for ready reference, detailed enough for essential information," but THE RANDOM HOUSE CONCISE WORLD ATLAS is not much bigger or much more expensive and is a good deal more useful. The PRENTICE-HALL POCKET ATLAS OF THE WORLD is almost as small as the *Mini* atlas, is reasonably good, and costs less. The *Mini* atlas could be useful for basic reference and easy desk-drawer storage, but its flaws and few advantages make it a poor choice for either a school library or a serious adult reader.

Scott, Foresman World Atlas

Facts at a Glance

Full Title: **Scott, Foresman World Atlas.**
Publisher: Scott, Foresman and Company, Glenview, Illinois.
Editor: Mary Chase.
Copyright: 1982.

Number of Volumes: 1.
Number of Pages: 128.
Number of Maps: 139.
Number of Indexes: 1.
Number of Illustrations: 70 color.
Trim Size: 8¾" × 11".
Binding: paper.

Intended Readership: grades 7 through 12.
Price: $5.80.
Sold in stores and directly by the publisher.
   ISBN 0-673-13356-7.
Revised as needed. Current edition, 1985.
Next Scheduled Revision: 1987.

I. Introduction

The *Scott, Foresman World Atlas* is a comprehensive paperback volume of general reference and thematic maps of the world, its continents, regions, and nations. A brief introduction explaining map symbols and projections is followed by the first quarter of the atlas, which focuses on general information about the world. This includes such topics as the theory of continental drift, temperature and ocean currents, climate regions, and world food resources. The remainder of the atlas is organized around eight regions or continents. These sections present both physical and political maps of each region, as well as thematic maps depicting climate, population density, vegetation, and other specialized information. Detailed physical-political maps of smaller subregions are included in most of the eight divisions. Series of diagrams, drawings, graphs, photographs, tables, and explanatory text supplement the map illustrations throughout.

Because this atlas is "designed for people living in North America," the first and longest of the eight sections covers this region. This bias makes the *Scott, Foresman World Atlas* particularly useful for intermediate-level classes or for students studying American history. In addition, the long section on the world gives the book a unique global focus in contrast to other map-study books for students at the high school level.

The maps were prepared by George Phillip and Son, Ltd., a London cartographic firm founded in 1834. It is well-known in Europe as a publisher of quality maps and atlases.

II. Format

The *Scott, Foresman World Atlas* strikes an even balance between general reference and thematic maps. Most of its global maps are devoted to the world's languages, population, minerals, and other specialized information. The introductory maps of each region combine physical and political data on one- or two-page spreads. Some map details of two-page spreads are lost in the gutters unless the binding is forced down flat by hand. Maps of subregions include physical and political data on the same map. Except for Australia, Oceania, and the Polar Regions, the regional sections also include thematic maps illustrating oil production, exports, transportation, metropolitan areas, and other features.

The atlas is a convenient, easy-to-use $8\frac{3}{4}'' \times 11''$ size. It is a sturdily bound paperback, with a Landsat image of California's Imperial Valley on its cover.

The map legends, however, are not easy to identify. For each physical-political map, a bar scale in miles and kilometers is shown at the top of the page. The color code for elevation is usually shown separately at the side or bottom of the page. Borders between states or countries or provinces are fine red lines, not appreciably different, when all together on a map, from the red lines denoting roads and highways. A great many place names are included, and it is not always possible to locate them close to their sites or to separate many very close together. Al-

though none of the maps provides an explanation of the political symbols used, a master key to all symbols is located in the front of the atlas; it includes cities, boundaries, transportation routes, and water forms. No symbol for capitals is shown on the master legend; moreover, the symbol used for particular cities depends on each settlement's population, and these parameters vary from one map to another. This is another source of confusion in using these maps.

The series of thematic maps for each region has its own individual legend that varies with the information being described. Circle graphs, diagrams, and other comparative data often supplement these legends.

III. Special Features

The *Scott, Foresman World Atlas* contains a variety of special features. The book has a detailed table of contents (with topographical maps indicated by a blue dot); a key to symbols; an illustrated text on map projections; and a section on how to use the atlas.

The special maps in the world section make this atlas particularly useful. There are maps of the solar system, the terrestrial zone, the earth's orbit, the phases of the moon, annual precipitation, climate regions, minerals, population, and energy resources. This section also includes text explaining the world's major languages, principal religions, and major food resources. Statistical tables provide data on the earth's dimensions, comparisons of continents, oceans, seas, rivers, lakes, and inland bodies of water. A diagram of the hydrological cycle accompanies an illustrated description of the world's vegetation. In all cases, the text and accompanying materials are contained on one or two pages so that the reader can refer to the illustrations while reading the description.

Special maps also accompany each regional section of the atlas. These thematic maps vary from section to section and include such topics as types of farming, urban density, rainfall, agricultural production, and mineral distribution.

The back of the atlas contains a variety of useful tables. One provides the area, population density, and capitals of the world's countries and dependencies. Others cover gross domestic products, international trade, climatic data, and a glossary of geographical terms. An extensive index concludes the atlas.

IV. Geographical Balance

The atlas adequately represents all regions of the world. An organizational decision to devote one section of the atlas to the Soviet Union solves the traditional problem of dividing the U.S.S.R. between Europe and Asia. By putting this section between the two regions, the editor has clarified the Soviet Union's geographic position as a nation that straddles Eurasia.

Although the atlas devotes nearly one-fourth of its space to North America, it was the stated intention of the publisher to do so. About equal space is given to Europe, Asia, and Africa. South America receives the least attention of the Third World areas.

V. Scale and Projections

Scales expressed as a representative fraction and a bar scale in miles and kilometers appear at the tops of most maps. The placement of some scales is inconsistent and therefore may be initially confusing to the reader. Map projections are not identified.

Map scales vary, depending on the size of the area and the space allowed for its projection. In addition, different scales are applied to the same area, such as the one-page maps of the Soviet Union on pages 72–75. To some extent, these misconceptions of relative size and shape are corrected by the data provided in the index and in statistical tables.

VI. Accuracy

Place names are usually spelled accurately. Generic names, such as *China*, *Ireland*, or *East* and *West Germany*, are used both on the maps and in the index; official political names are not provided. Former names, however, are given in both locations; for example, Kampuchea shows *Cambodia* in parentheses on the map and lists both place names in the index. The claims of two countries for the same territory are usually not indicated, as in the case of the Falkland Islands, the West Bank of Israel, or Gibraltar.

Locations of physical features, such as mountain ranges, are clearly marked on the physical-political maps. In some instances, however, the maps fail to include a generic description with names of physical features. Mississippi, for example, is identified as a river in the index but not on the map itself.

The arbitrary division of South America into two parts, north and south, distorts both its physical and political continuity. Parts of Chile, Argentina, Paraguay, and Brazil lie on both maps. Likewise, the Andes Mountain range is bisected. A better division of subregions is needed to improve this section of the atlas.

VII. Currency

For the most part, the *Scott, Foresman World Atlas* reflects current realities in the world's political status. Vietnam is united, with *Ho Chi Minh City* replacing *Saigon*. The newly named nation of Zimbabwe correctly identifies *Harare*, not *Salisbury*, as its capital. The capital of China is still named *Peking* and not *Beijing*, however, and Greenland is not given its more recent name of *Kalaalit Nunaat*.

VIII. Legibility

The typefaces on maps are clear and for the most part easy to read. The practice of combining physical and political data on each regional map, however, sometimes creates a cluttered look, particularly with the maps of Europe and the United States, which are densely populated and settled areas. The abbreviations for nearly 100 French departments, for example, are difficult to decipher. However, the map of the Soviet Union is not overcrowded with data. These regions would have benefited from the separate physical and political cartography accorded Africa.

Boundary lines are indicated by red lines that are not always sufficiently thick and bold. The map of the United States, for example, does not clearly demarcate states, nor does the international boundary separating it from Canada or Mexico look any different from the state boundary lines. Despite an inset of the Palestine area on the map of Northern Africa, it still remains difficult to tell which nation occupies which territory. In fact, this inset denotes Roman Palestine, which includes Syria and Lebanon as well as the current states of Jordan, Lebanon, and Israel. This entity has not existed since before World War I, and it is confusing to have included it.

Some two-page maps are not bound evenly. The two maps of Northern Africa, for example, do not mesh correctly. Parts of other maps, such as northern South America, the eastern United States, and Canada, are lost in the gutter unless one forces the book flat with one's hand.

The photos, although recent, are very small. The captions, like those accompanying the pictures on page 81, are also small and very difficult to read.

IX. Accessibility

An 18-page index containing approximately 7,400 entries is located at the end of the atlas. It is one of the most thorough and extensive provided in a student atlas, and includes political and physical place names. In addition to a page number, each reference is followed by its geographic coordinates of latitude and longitude. Although these coordinates are sometimes only approximate, they are close enough to locate the place name. Names of countries are so indicated by an appropriate symbol which, along with other information, is explained in an introductory section on how to use the index.

Many of the maps contain insets. Some are small photos. Some of these insets fail to show the location of the area being shown. For example, in an inset on the map of the middle United States, part of Texas is shown on page 51, but it is not clearly identified as to location. Corsica's physical relation to France is likewise unclear. There is no inset for Hawaii on the map of the United States, although these islands along with Alaska, the Aleutians, Puerto Rico, and the Virgin Islands are shown on another page.

X. Summary

The *Scott, Foresman World Atlas* is clearly organized and its information easy to locate. Although scales vary, the maps are beautifully rendered and, for the most part, easy to read and interpret. Other strengths of this atlas include its variety of special features, an excellent index, and a comprehensive section on physical and political features of the world.

Its bias in the cartography of North America may make this atlas less appealing for use in world-history classrooms. With the exception of South America, however, all regions of the world receive adequate coverage, particularly the Soviet Union. This atlas is not only an excellent reference tool, but also uses a holistic approach which lends itself well to comparisons among the world's regions.

In addition to its excellent cartography, the lightweight but durable paperback format of the *Scott, Foresman World Atlas* helps make this volume an attractive alternative to some of the more expensive hardcover atlases published by Hammond and Rand McNally. The *Scott, Foresman World Atlas* holds its own against its direct competitors.

The Simon & Schuster Young Readers' Atlas

Facts at a Glance

Full Title: **The Simon & Schuster Young Readers' Atlas.**
Publisher: Wanderer Books, a division of Simon & Schuster.
Authors: Jill and David Wright.
Copyright: 1983.

Number of Volumes: 1.
Number of Entries: 50.
Number of Pages: 189.
Number of Maps: 40.
Number of Indexes: 2.
Number of Illustrations: 200 color.
Trim Size: 4¾" × 7⅜".
Binding: paper.

Intended Readership: grades 4 through 9.
Price: $6.95, paper.
Sold in bookstores. ISBN 0-671-50657-9.
Updated with each reprint.

I. Introduction

The Simon & Schuster Young Readers' Atlas is a pocket-size reference work divided into 11 color-coded sections. The first three parts focus on using maps, map making, and understanding the world. The remaining sections cover the six major continents, as well as Antarctica and the Arctic. Each division consists of simple relief maps of the continent, followed by political-physical subregional maps of one page or smaller. Interspersed with the cartography is a wide variety of data: explanatory text describing subregions, national flags, color photographs, tables of facts and figures, interesting historical tidbits, and summaries of climate, farming, industry, languages, religion, and other pertinent data. In this respect, the *YRA* can be considered an almanac as well as an atlas.

This book is appropriate for middle-grade students. Its purpose is twofold: to provide the reader with clear, easily read maps, and to present significant factual data through the use of charts, graphs, tables, diagrams, and narrative text.

Originally published in Great Britain, the atlas uses English cartography produced by Product Support Limited and Malcolm Porter. The text by Jill and David Wright has been modified with American spellings.

II. Format

The maps of major continents are half-page or smaller in size, executed in simple relief. Subregional areas combine political and physical data on maps that vary in size from one to two pages. Two maps of the world, both two-page spreads, show topography and political divisions.

The atlas is slightly larger than a mass-market paperback. It is easy to carry, but the pages do not lie flat for convenient use. Moreover, the book's sturdy binding is a disadvantage for two-page maps, which lose some cartographic data in the gutters.

Map legends of subregions provide only a title, directional symbol, and bar scale in kilometers and miles. Continental maps lack any legends, as do the two world maps. A key to the symbols used, found in the introduction, includes natural features such as rivers, lakes, and mountains, as well as symbols for countries, capitals, cities, and boundaries. Topographical features are italicized, whereas cultural features appear in non-italic letters.

III. Special Features

The chief strength of the *Young Readers' Atlas* is its special features. Besides the conventional cartography, additional maps show administrative subdivisions within nations, such as counties, provinces, or republics. In addition, near each regional map is a smaller map which illustrates in red the location of that particular area in relation to the rest of the world. The only thematic maps are those showing the earth's climate and vegetation, its population, and the division between industrialized and developing parts of the world.

The atlas provides a wealth of statistical information. Tables summarize vital information about individual nations, graphs chart weather patterns, and diagrams illustrate dams, landforms, and rain forests. Interspersed throughout are a variety of colorful flags and photographs.

Explanatory text accompanies the maps of each continent and subregion. These narratives are informative and well-written. Additional text, such as features on the Lapps, on Italy for Tourists, or on the Japanese Bullet Train, enliven the preponderance of statistical information.

The first part of the atlas includes an explanation about using maps, a diagram of the solar system, and summaries of world facts and figures. A description of mapmaking shows a variety of map projections and explains latitude, longitude, and earth time. In addition to the index, the back of the atlas features a glossary of geographical terms, some illustrated by diagram or photograph. The world relief map shown at the beginning of the atlas is conveniently repeated at the end of the book.

IV. Geographical Balance

The *Young Readers' Atlas* represents all regions of the world adequately. It seems not to have an intended geographical market and therefore is not purposely biased toward a particular area. Nonetheless, nearly one-fourth of the atlas is devoted to Europe,

nearly three times the space allotted South America. There is no other specific western bias since Asia and Africa both command greater coverage than North America.

V. Scale and Projections

Map scales are reasonable for the size of an area being represented. Scale information is not provided on the world, thematic, or continental maps. On other maps, it is located on differing parts of the page, always presented in bar scales showing both kilometers and miles.

A variety of scales are used to represent subregional areas. These vary from 50 to 2,000 kilometers per centimeter. Because many of these maps are usually a page or so in size, they may convey a misleading impression of areas which seem comparable in size but in fact vary significantly. Therefore, careful attention to and understanding of scale variations is important.

The symbol for cities is uniform throughout the cartography and gives no indication of population or size.

Although map projections are explained in the introduction to the *YRA*, no information on individual maps indicates the actual projection used.

VI. Accuracy

Place names are correctly and consistently spelled and for the most part appear in their proper locations. Perhaps the most glaring error is the failure to indicate on the map that the U.S.S.R. is part of both Europe and Asia. The first statement in the text indicates this fact, however, and the editor has organized the book so that the U.S.S.R. is strategically placed between Europe and Asia.

The atlas uses generic rather than official political designations. For example, *China*, *East* and *West Germany*, and *North* and *South Korea* are the designations given, both on the cartography and in the map index. One exception is the use of *Republic of Ireland* (*Eire*) rather than simply *Ireland*.

Physical areas are sparingly noted and confined to mountains, rivers, lakes, and other bodies of water. Places like the Grand Canyon or the Great Barrier Reef are not included.

Two glaring omissions from the United States map are Alaska, which is only partially shown on the map of Canada, and Hawaii, which is also missing and appears instead on the map of the Pacific Islands. Alaska does not appear in the map index either, but this is unrelated to its map placement, as other states have also been omitted.

VII. Currency

Despite its 1983 copyright, the *YRA* is cartographically up-to-date. Vietnam is shown as a unified nation. Zimbabwe, Brunei, and Kampuchea are properly named. On the map of China, *Beijing* and other spellings in the Pinyin system are used. The name changes from *Upper Volta* to *Burkina Faso* in 1984, and from *Greenland* to *Kalaalit Nunaat* took place too recently to be included.

Borders are current, though conflicting claims are not so indicated on maps. Rather, in places like Israel, borders reflect the *de facto* situation.

This atlas is updated with each reprint. Given the amount of statistical data it includes, this is extremely important. Nonetheless, facts and figures, such as population, are not the most recent available because the atlas has not been revised since 1983.

VIII. Legibility

Typefaces on the maps are neat and legible. Country names appear in bold capital letters, whereas capitals and cities are marked in smaller print. Physical features, limited to mountains and bodies of water, are recognizable by their italicized print.

Places are clearly distinguishable from each other. Even maps of dense areas in Europe are uncluttered and easy to read. When county and administrative data are furnished, they appear on separate thematic maps with a number system and name referent given in the legend. State or provincial borders are never confused with national boundaries because they are not shown together when two or more nations appear on the same map.

Rather than a complex system of color tints for elevation, the maps show five simple types of vegetation. In addition to white for mountains, the colors are pale green, tan, or yellow. Except where mountain areas are indicated, the reader has no notion of varying altitudes.

IX. Accessibility

There are two indexes. One is a two-page guide to the text material, which is too short and inadequate because it omits many topics discussed in the body of the atlas, such as canals (Suez, 111, and Panama, 139), Arabic (108–09), Sikhs (94), or trains (85). It also omits page numbers on which indexed information appears, such as the failure to include page 162 under geysers, page 147 under rain forest, or page 90 under colonies.

The map index is six pages long and contains approximately 1,160 entries. Rivers, mountains, and islands are so indicated after the name listing, and the appropriate nation or political subdivision is given following the entry of every city. Unlike many atlas indexes, more than one page referent is provided for a specific entry.

Except for the map of Southern Africa, which includes an inset for Madagascar, the cartography has no insets.

X. Summary

This atlas is an extremely useful reference work for the middle-grade student. The maps are simple and easy to read. The appealing layout features colorful flags, interesting diagrams, informative pictures, and special inserts discussing original topics. The well-written text is geographically focused and informative. Tables and charts include a wealth of statistical data. Teachers desiring more sophisticated cartography may be disappointed at the scarcity of data provided, the failure to show elevation, and the lack of latitude-longitude lines. There are very few thematic maps. Moreover, the binding on this small book is not conducive to easy use or to locating information on two-page map spreads. Nonetheless, this atlas has achieved its two aims well, and students will find it a useful reference beyond its intended classroom use. It is currently the only atlas that combines descriptive text, photographs, and easy-to-read maps in a pocket-size format.

Students' World Atlas

Facts at a Glance

Full Title: **Students' World Atlas.**
Publisher: Sharon Publications, Inc.
Copyright: none given; 1984 printing date.

Number of Volumes: 1.
Number of Pages: 48.
Number of Maps: 55.
Number of Indexes: 1.
Number of Index Entries: 286.
Intended Readership: grades 2 through 9.
Trim Size: 8″ × 11″.
Binding: paper.

Price: $3.95 in U.S., $4.95 in Canada, 25 percent discount to schools and libraries.
Sold by direct mail, through magazine/newspaper advertising, in bookstores, and in supermarkets.
Updated annually.

I. Introduction

The *Students' World Atlas* is a 48-page paperback atlas published by Sharon Publications, Inc. of Teaneck, N.J., a subsidiary of Edrei Communications. The book has no copyright attribution, and no credit is given for authorship or cartography. Further, neither Sharon nor Edrei has any reputation in the field of cartography. The atlas is intended for classroom use in grades 2 through 9.

II. Format

Students' World Atlas includes political maps, topographical maps, and maps showing industrial/agricultural and other resources. Each map group (political, topographical, resources) also includes an inset map of the world with the subject area shown in red.

The political maps occupy one or two pages, depending on the area they depict. Part of all the two-page maps has been lost, not because it disappears into the gutter of the book, but because a one-inch margin separating the pages (to accommodate loose-leaf use) cuts a swath through the maps. Thus, the two-page spread for the United States omits a thin section running from western Minnesota through eastern Texas. Readers will not find Tulsa, Oklahoma; Sioux City, Iowa; Emporia, Kansas, and many other smaller cities. This gap is quite arbitrary and produces such labels as HUN RY for Hungary and SAS CITY for Kansas City.

Bar scales, in miles and kilometers, appear in the key under the title of each political map, together with a key to the seven symbols employed. A broken line interspersed with single dots indicates internal boundaries; when interspersed with double dots, it represents international boundaries. Large, medium, and small dots indicate capitals, major cities, and cities, respectively. This system proves troublesome in distinguishing city dots from boundary line dots.

Generally, the topographical, resources, and inset maps follow the political map. In a few instances, such as the United States and South America, one or all of the special maps precede the political map of the subject area.

Lines of latitude and longitude are labeled on most maps, though generally not on all four sides of the map. In a few instances, such as South America, these figures were cut off when the book was trimmed.

The atlas is a convenient size for classroom use and is five-hole-punched for easy insertion into a student's notebook. The paper on which it is printed is an inexpensive, ground wood quality; the cover is dull and uninteresting.

III. Special Features

Unlike the Colorprint atlas series (see pages 233–236), the *Students' World Atlas* provides topographical, resource, and inset maps. Tables on the inside front cover furnish statistical information about major oceans and seas, lakes, rivers, islands, and mountains of the world. All figures are in miles and feet with no metric equivalents. The source of these figures is not identified, although there are close resemblances to similar data in the Hammond WORLD ATLAS FOR STUDENTS.

IV. Geographical Balance

The atlas covers all the countries of the world. Of the 55 maps included, 14 cover North America, 13 Asia, 12 Europe, 3 each for Australia and New Zealand, Africa, South America, and the Soviet Union, 2 polar maps (North and South Poles), one map of the Pacific Ocean, and one map of the world.

V. Scale and Projections

Two types of projections appear to be used for political maps in this volume, although neither is identified. A Miller cylindrical projection is used for the world map that appears on page 1. This modified Mercator projection, which bears a close resemblance to that used in several Hammond atlases, distorts areas at high latitudes in much the same way but does not show compass directions as straight lines—a peculiar choice since this map shows shipping lanes and air routes. A type of polyconic projection has been used for the remaining political maps. Areas or nations close to the equator display only minimal distortion, but at high latitudes distortion increases progressively as lines of latitude diverge.

Bar scales are shown in both miles and kilometers but not in representative fractions. The choice of scales seems random and unsystematic, with little thought for purposes of geographic comparison. The two polar maps, for example, are at widely different scales (approximately 1:38,000,000 for the Antarctic, 1:95,000,000 for the Arctic regions), even though they appear on the same page. The map for the United Kingdom and Ireland (approximately 1:5,400,000) faces a map of France (approximately 1:6,400,000). These and other variations can be confusing to many students who do not understand that size variations make such scale variations necessary. Small scale maps in this volume are difficult to read and sometimes omit important information. The map of the world, for example (approximately 1:58,400,000), provides a place-name label for West Germany but neither label nor national boundaries for East Germany. This scale also requires highly abbreviated names in some instances, to the detriment of students who may not associate "Rum" with Rumania, "Bulg" with Bulgaria, or "Camb" with Cambodia. (See *Legibility* for a further discussion.)

VI. Accuracy

A certain carelessness about factual details is evident throughout the *Students' World Atlas*. Placement of major cities seems to be a particular problem. Kisangani, a city in Zaire, is placed almost 400 miles south of the equator in the map of Africa when in fact it is located about 25 miles north of the equator. Possibly the editors confused it with another Zairian city, Kananga, which does not appear. Other omissions are equally troublesome. Leicester, England, is not shown, although several smaller cities in the same vicinity do appear. Strasbourg has been omitted from the map of France, and West Virginia is not labeled. Suva, the capital of Fiji, is labeled *Sava* on the world map but does not appear in the map of the Pacific Ocean. Taiwan appears as *China (Taiwan)* in the index but as *Taiwan* on the maps of Southeast Asia and East Asia.

The figures provided on the inside front cover of the atlas are not entirely reliable and in some instances seem to have been rounded off from more precise numbers to simpler units. The area in square miles of the Caspian Sea, for example, is given as 168,500 but appears as 143,550 in *Webster's New Geographical Dictionary* and as "approximately 143,000" in the NEW ENCYCLOPAEDIA BRITANNICA. Both *Webster's* and *Britannica* agree on an altitude of 20,561 for Mount Chimborazo in Ecuador, which is listed in the *Students' World Atlas* as 20,700.

The misspelling of place names casts further doubt on this work's accuracy. *Cameron* instead of *Cameroon* (Africa) and the state of *Main* rather than *Maine* (index) are only two instances of the inaccuracies that our reviewers found in this volume.

VII. Currency

Although the editors state that the copyright is 1984, it appears not to be up-to-date as of that year. Further, although the editors also state that it is updated annually, as of 1987, only the 1984 edition was available for review. Zimbabwe is listed as *Rhodesia*, although it does appear both ways in the index. Kampuchea retains its old name of *Cambodia*, yet Saigon is listed as *Ho Chi Minh City*. The preferred Pinyin spellings are not used; therefore, *Peking*, not *Beijing* is listed as the capital of China.

VIII. Legibility

Because many of the maps appear to have been reduced from larger versions, legibility is a problem throughout the *Students' World Atlas*. Two sizes of type differentiate between larger and smaller cities. The ones for smaller cities, in fly-speck size, break up and almost disappear in certain maps. Most place names in the maps of Asia and Southwest Asia, for example, are illegible in the copy available to our reviewers. Some topographic maps (the Soviet Union, for instance) are printed out of register and cannot be read.

The use of three different sized dots for capitals, major cities, and cities is another source of confusion since they are often difficult to distinguish among, especially when labels have been placed in ambiguous positions. In the map of the United States, for example, five dots of virtually identical size are found in the vicinity of Dallas and Fort Worth, but the reader has no way to tell which place names belong with them.

Large light blue capital letters identify nations on some maps of Europe but not on others. On page 22, for example, East Germany and West Germany are clearly labeled. On the facing page, however, which shows Scandinavia and Finland, no nation is identified. Elsewhere, the light blue labels are sometimes obscured when printed over darker type. The occasional use of dark colors for national boundaries also makes some place names difficult to read.

IX. Accessibility

Access is limited by lack of a table of contents. The two-page index, located at the back of the atlas, provides very limited assistance with a total of only 286 place-name entries, 50 of which are states of the United States. Only nations and U. S. states appear in the index. No cities have been included. Entries provide page numbers where the maps can be found, location by grid, population, and area in square miles. Grid numbers and letters on many maps are small and difficult to locate. Some locations are inaccurate. According to the index, Fiji is located in the wrong grid, but in fact the name does not appear even in its correct location on the map of the Pacific Ocean. The name of the state of West Virginia is listed in the index, placed in the area where Georgia and South Carolina are located, and omitted from the map of the United States. Even students with a detailed knowledge of geography will find it difficult to locate places in this atlas.

X. Summary

Students' World Atlas is a 48-page atlas for classroom use in grades 2 through 9. It sells for $3.95 in the United States and $4.95 in Canada. Although its low price and five-hole punch make it attractive for classroom resource centers or for individual student use, this work is inferior to the Colorprint series (see pages 233–236), the HAMMOND WORLD ATLAS FOR STUDENTS (after which it seems patterned), the RAND McNALLY STUDENTS' WORLD ATLAS, and several of the pocket atlases reviewed in this Buying Guide. Its numerous factual errors, instances of out-of-date place names, highly limited access, and the illegibility of many place names are decided liabilities at any price. Under no circumstances is this atlas recommended.

The Viking Children's World Atlas

Facts at a Glance

Full Title: **The Viking Children's World Atlas: An Introductory Atlas for Young People.**
Publisher: The Viking Press.
Editor: Regina Hayes.
Copyright: 1983.

Number of Volumes: 1.
Number of Pages: 48.
Number of Maps: 20.
Number of Indexes: none.
Number of Illustrations: 48 color.
Trim Size: 8″ × 11½″.

Intended Readership: children ages 5 through 12.
Price: $8.95 hardcover, $4.95 paper.
Sold through magazine/newspaper advertising, and in bookstores. ISBN 0-670-21791-3.
No scheduled revision.

I. Introduction

This beginning atlas, which is written for children ages 5 through 12, introduces the reader to maps and the data they represent. The atlas starts with illustrations of two young children next to their home, then moves in expanding territorial circles from street, to town, to country, to the world, and finally to the earth as part of the solar system. A series of pictorial maps colorfully illustrates boundaries, capitals, vegetation areas, crops, kinds of work, and vacation places. Some maps, like that of South America, are regional, but others consist of subregions or nations, such as Western Europe or Japan. The atlas concludes with a picture of the earth in space, the solar system, and an illustrated diagram summarizing what is called the ages of life on earth, but which really depicts the eras, in 100-million-year spans, from the earliest assumed life form appearance some 500 million years ago.

According to the editor, the purpose of this atlas is "to lead children from their familiar local environments, through the concept of maps of the continents, and on to the idea of the world as a planet in space." The authors assume a knowledge on the part of their audience of certain basic concepts, such as what a map is, how symbols on maps represent certain data, and the differences between continents, nations, and states. For that reason, the atlas is more appropriate for an older child than one who is five or six.

The text was written by Jacqueline Tivers and Michael Day. No information is given concerning their educational qualifications. The respected British cartographer John Bartholomew & Son, Ltd., is also credited on the copyright page.

II. Format

Each map combines political, physical, and economic data. These chiefly illustrate national capitals, state and national boundaries, types of vegetation, large bodies of water, crops, livestock, and occupations. Most maps are two-page spreads of continents or large subregions. Nations like Japan and New Zealand are shown on one page.

The atlas is 8″ × 11½″, a bit larger than the standard-size elementary textbook. The maps are large and invite the reader's attention. The pages lie flat and the atlas is easy to handle.

The hardcover book is well bound and uses an excellent grade of paper. The washable cover features a multiracial group of children pinning symbols on a large wall map; readers may like the focus on children without immediately recognizing what they are doing. The atlas is also available in a paperback edition at a lower price.

None of the maps includes a legend. Two pages at the beginning of the book explain some of the symbols used on the maps, such as vegetation, crops, livestock, and kinds of work. Although a caption on the United States map explains the symbol used for state capitals, there is no explanation of how international boundaries, state boundaries, national capitals, cities, or rivers are represented. Mountains are not identified. Large bodies of water surrounding territory are not always labeled. Thus, this book cannot be used as a definitive locator of places.

III. Special Features

This atlas contains no specifically thematic maps or statistical tables, and has few special features. Each map is surrounded by a series of captioned photographs which highlight some of the physical, economic, and cultural features of the area. Sometimes the captioned material is too difficult for younger readers; for example, references to Aborigines, Lapps, Incas, and the Berlin Wall. Each page includes a small inset map of the world, which shows in red the area featured on the large map.

The authors have attempted to gear the explanatory text to the elementary-age child. They begin the narration in a way that arouses the reader's curiosity by presenting two children, showing their home, and by asking the reader questions. The children disappear from the text almost immediately, however, and these original and stimulating techniques are not used throughout the rest of the book. Instead, the narration reverts to a traditional approach which is not always clear or easy to understand. For example, the explanation of the colors used to indicate types of land forms fails to make a crucial point: that the different colors used on the maps stand for the pictures shown on the legend. In other instances, unfamiliar terms or phrases are not defined; for instance, it is doubtful that the reader will know what *the continental United States*, *oil refineries*, *densely populated*, or *ice cap* mean. In contrast, some explanations are simplified to the point of distortion; for example, "A geyser is a hot water fountain."

Some text concentrates on narrowly focused material; for example most of the description of Canada is devoted to the tundra. Other explanations are so short as to be misleading; the summary of Japan, for example, consists of a mere two sentences. Little attempt is made to connect the text to the map, and only a few questions encourage the reader to interpret the material that is presented visually. On the whole, the text is so fragmented and skimpy that it creates misleading impressions of many areas.

IV. Geographical Balance

Except for the Pacific Islands, the atlas gives adequate representation to all regions of the world. Although two maps of the United States are included as opposed to one for other areas, no other bias is evident.

V. Scale and Projections

The concepts of scale and projection are not introduced in this atlas, and none of the maps provide scale information. Because there is no way to judge relative size, the reader cannot accurately compare different areas. Compass directions are also lacking on all maps.

The map of the continental United States is drawn on a different scale from that for the inset one of Alaska. Consequently, Texas appears to be the largest state in the union.

VI. Accuracy

Place names are correctly and consistently spelled, although official political names are not given for such nations as China, North and South Korea, East and West Germany, and Ireland.

Place names are not always put in proper position. The titles of *Vietnam*, *Malaysia*, and *Indonesia* do not make clear the area they represent. Likewise, the label for New Guinea is placed so that a reader might wonder if another nation owns the western part of the island.

The cartography is inconsistent about labeling bodies of water. Some maps clearly identify surrounding bodies of water; others, such as the ones for Japan, Australia, New Zealand, and China, fail to provide the names of seas and oceans.

Some physical features are not accurately represented. For example, the Ural Mountains do not extend far enough south, nor are they properly identified. The Andes Mountains are not labeled. The extent and location of the Rocky Mountains are poorly depicted on the United States map, and they are not labeled on any map. Some physical features not identified in the master legend appear sporadically on certain maps, such as the Great Barrier Reef and the Grand Canyon.

VII. Currency

Boundaries and place names on this atlas are fairly up-to-date. The maps reflect the unification of Vietnam and the change in Rhodesia's name to *Zimbabwe*. *Cambodia* is still used, although *Kampuchea* is indicated in parentheses. *Peking* is used for the capital of China rather than *Beijing*.

For the most part, the text and photographs are contemporary. Some of the text tends to rely on dated impressions and oversimplified generalizations. For example, the description of the Middle East focuses on oil, aridity, desert nomads, and holy cities. Moreover, the editor had a tendency to choose photographs that stress the exotic or stereotypic. For example, one of the Western European illustrations shows a Spanish couple in a flamenco costume, and the feature on New Zealand shows Maoris in native dress.

VIII. Legibility

Typefaces on the maps are legible and bold. Place names are clearly differentiated so that cities and nations cannot be confused. Names of islands like Sicily, Sardinia, and Corsica, however, use the same typeface as cities. The maps are not cluttered with too much data.

Physical features are not always completely labeled. For example, the Amazon, Colorado, and MacKenzie do not have "river" following their names, nor is this physical feature identified in the discussion of symbols at the start of the atlas.

Borders are clearly marked in bold red lines. The nationality of islands like Majorca and Sicily, however, is not clear.

IX. Accessibility

Although some of the blank pages in the back of the book could have been used for this purpose, this atlas has no index. Therefore, access to place names, as well as to data in the text, is completely lacking. This is a serious drawback to the use of the atlas, particularly in the classroom.

X. Summary

This is an introductory atlas for children ages 5 through 12. It moves the young child from the local and familiar to the universal and unfamiliar. Through the use of colorful maps and pictures, it introduces children to important features of the world's major regions and subregions.

By assuming too much knowledge on the part of the reader, however, the authors fail to convey basic map concepts in a clear way. They seem well aware of this shortcoming. "We have tried to make the book as self-explanatory as possible," they write in a note to parents and teachers, "but some words and concepts may need further elaboration." Unfortunately, the text often fails to explain adequately the ideas it presents. Nor is the reader given any opportunity, either through the use of questions, review, or skill activities, to apply new concepts and ideas to the cartographic data. Despite the authors' intentions, this atlas is not appropriate for the five- or six-year-old child. It is further hampered by the lack of an index, uneven summaries of the area shown

on the map, and poor linkage between the master legend and the symbols featured on the maps. Parents, teachers, and librarians requiring an introductory learning atlas for elementary school children may wish to consider THE WONDERFUL WORLD OF MAPS, published by Hammond and reviewed on page 298 of this Buying Guide.

The Viking Children's World Atlas is available in bookstores. The paperback format costs $4.95, while the hardcover version is $8.95.

The Viking Student World Atlas

Facts at a Glance

Full Title: **The Viking Student World Atlas.**
Publisher: Viking Penguin, Inc.
Editor: Regina Hayes.
Copyright: 1986.

Number of Volumes: 1.
Number of Pages: 64.
Number of Maps: 31.
Number of Indexes: 1.
Number of Index Entries: approximately 1,800.
Number of Illustrations: 64 color.
Trim Size: 9″ × 12½″.

Intended Readership: ages 8 through 13.
Price: $9.95.
Sold by magazine/newspaper advertising, and in bookstores. ISBN 0-670-81122-X.
No scheduled revision.

I. Introduction

The Viking Student World Atlas is divided into five parts. Each section features a political map of a world region, followed by subregional maps which combine political and physical data. Smaller thematic maps representing population, vegetation, and products supplement the principal cartography. A "Did You Know That?" column highlights interesting details of the area shown, and gazetteers headed by flags of some of the larger countries list pertinent statistical data. Every spread includes a location globe which pinpoints the featured map in red. Color photographs supplement the introductory political maps of continents.

The purpose of this atlas is to provide the 8- to 13-year-old student with simplified maps of the world's regions. The editor describes it as bridging "the gap between pictorial atlases intended for young children and the much more complex atlases published for adults." In addition, this atlas provides the reader with an introductory lesson on how to read maps, as well as supplementary information on continents and individual nations.

The cartographer of this atlas is not named. Four geography specialists from Edinburgh, Scotland, however, have provided assistance in the preparation of the publication. The atlas was first published in Great Britain as *The Illustrated Reference Atlas of the World* by John Bartholomew & Son, Ltd., who provided the cartography.

II. Format

This atlas contains six political maps of Europe, Africa, Asia, Australia, North America, and South America, rendered in pastel hues. Maps of subcontinents and nations combine political and topographical data in soft shades of green and brown. Maps consist of both one- and two-page spreads. The binding opens flat so that no map part is lost in the gutters.

The atlas is large but easy to use. The pages lie flat wherever the book is opened.

This hardcover atlas is sturdily bound and is printed on high-quality coated paper. The washable cover features a NASA photograph of the earth from space.

The large maps include only a title, representative fraction, and bar scale at the top of each page. A master legend in the introduction provides a Key to Symbols that explains lettering styles, lake shadings, landscape features, boundaries, elevation colors, and the symbols for towns and cities, as well as rivers, dams, waterfalls, aqueducts, reefs, and mountain peaks.

Thematic maps carry their own legends. These include symbols for vegetation, products, and population distribution.

III. Special Features

This atlas contains a wide variety of special features. The introductory text explains the concept of scale, map projections, and the world's eight climatic zones, using color photos, diagrams, and maps. A map key to the main part of the atlas and a master legend complete the introduction.

The large regional maps are supplemented by two smaller maps depicting natural vegetation, products, and population. Pertinent statistical data on individual nations is headed by colorful flags of each country. In addition, a globe inset highlights in red the region's location relative to the rest of the world.

A numbered list of facts gives additional data about the featured region. These facts are keyed with numbers to their location on the political map, as well as to color photos in selected instances. This text is interesting and well-written. Some of the topics include a description of the Great Barrier Reef, identification of the tallest geyser, a discussion of the Great Wall of China, and a capsule narrative on Incan civilization.

IV. Geographical Balance

This atlas adequately represents all regions of the world, which are color-coded by continent in the Contents, with the color carrying over in the map borders for that continent. Although no bias is shown, for some reason the editor put Asia and Australia in one division along with the Polar regions, so that they all have the same color key (yellow). The reader may conclude that the earth consists of only five continents.

V. Scale and Projections

The scale, expressed as a representative fraction and a bar scale in kilometers and miles, appears at the top of each regional and subregional map, next to the title. A variety of map scales are used, ranging from 1.5M to 60,000,000. The scales are presented in very fine, difficult-to-read lines and numbers.

The same scale is sometimes applied to areas that are not comparable. For example, 5,000,000 is used for both Spain-Portugal and New Zealand, even though New Zealand is less than half the size of Spain and Portugal. The map of the continental United States, however, is drawn on a different scale from that of the inset of Alaska. As a result, Texas appears to be the largest state in the Union.

VI. Accuracy

Place names are correctly and consistently spelled. Conventional Anglicized spellings are usually given, with vernacular spellings given in parentheses. Place-name titles are occasionally placed in a confusing manner, however. For example, the labels for Newfoundland, Japan, North Korea, South Korea, Madagascar, and Java are shown in the water, instead of being located within the territory, as with other areas. New Guinea is also titled in such a way as to confuse the reader, as the name is spread across the middle of the island and also repeated for Papua New Guinea, a separate republic. Irian Jaya is the other half of the island of New Guinea and it is a province of Indonesia.

Official place names are not always treated consistently. For example, *United Kingdom of Great Britain and Northern Ireland* appears on the political map of Europe, whereas only *England*, *Wales*, *Scotland*, and *Northern Ireland* appear on the subregional map of Great Britain and Ireland. Likewise, *Ireland* is used on one map, *Republic of Ireland* on another. Unofficial titles are used in other instances, as with China, East and West Germany, and North and South Korea.

The locations of physical features such as rivers are clear when they are labeled on subregional maps. In some cases, such as the Ural Mountains, the maps fail to include a generic description with the names of physical features.

VII. Currency

The atlas is fairly current, although some changes are needed to bring it fully up-to-date. *Cambodia* is the name used for that country, with *Kampuchea* shown in parentheses. Though Vietnam is united, *Saigon* is used in preference to *Ho Chi Minh City*. In the maps of China, the name *Peking* is used; *Beijing* and other place names spelled in the official Pinyin system are given in parentheses. The current *Kalaalit Nunaat* has not replaced *Greenland* as the name for Denmark's dependency.

VIII. Legibility

Typefaces in the atlas are neat and legible. Place-name categories are distinguished clearly by typefaces. Moreover, a section on lettering style in the Key to Symbols explains the various categories used on maps.

On the political maps of principal continents, nations are differentiated by colors rather than by boldly marked boundary lines. On subregional maps, however, a pale gray line is used to demarcate borders, which are not always readily apparent. For example, administrative divisions of the Soviet Union, such as Kazakhskaya and Ukraninskaya, are very difficult to distinguish.

IX. Accessibility

The index is quite extensive and contains approximately 1,800 entries. After each name, the country name or other data (e.g., province of, or state in, and so on) is given; a list of abbreviations is given at the beginning of the index. The next item in the entry is the name of the country in which the place is located. Finally, a reference number, for example, **16C3**, which represents the page and grid coordi-

nates, tells where the place can be found. The grids are suitable in size for fairly easy location of the places being found. Latitudes and longitudes are not provided.

Some important data shown on the maps have been omitted from the index. Neither the Byelorussian S.S.R. or the Ukrainian S.S.R. are indexed, although both are members of the United Nations. Physical entities, such as Victoria Island, are likewise occasionally omitted.

Subregional maps are not crowded with too many insets. Map insets are restricted to Alaska and several islands in the Indian, South Pacific, Arctic, and Atlantic Oceans, and Caribbean Sea. Their relations to the larger map can only be ascertained by referring to the continent's political map.

X. Summary

This is a fine atlas for intermediate-grade students to use as a supplemental text. It would also serve as a useful library reference. The maps are handsomely rendered in soft, pastel hues. The "Did You Know That. . . ?" feature is original and well-written. The color photographs, most of which are keyed to the text, are contemporary and informative. Instead of listing data in tables at the end of the atlas, useful statistical information appears next to the political map of each region. The index contains an extensive listing of place names and physical features. This atlas does not attempt to include more data than a reader can comfortably absorb. Its uncluttered appearance and lack of extraneous material give it a consistency of purpose lacking in many atlases designed for the intermediate-age child.

VNR Pocket Atlas

Facts at a Glance
Full Title: **VNR Pocket Atlas.**
Publisher: Van Nostrand Reinhold Company Inc.
Editors: RNDr. Jiří Novotný, Cartographic Editor; Marie Pánková, Technical Editor.
Copyright: 1981 by Kartografie, Prague.

Edition Reviewed: First United States edition, 1983.
Number of Volumes: 1.
Number of Pages: 236.
Number of Maps: 80, including inserts.
Number of Indexes: 1.
Number of Index Entries: 13,500.
Trim Size: 4½″ × 6⅝″.

Binding: laminated paper.
Intended Readership: general.
Price: $8.95.
Sold in bookshops and by direct mail.
  ISBN 0-442-29661-4.
No scheduled revision.

I. Introduction

The *VNR Pocket Atlas* is a concise pocket-sized work of 236 pages that provides 80 full-color maps as well as information on the political, economic, and physical geography of the world. Designed for students and the general reader, it was published in 1983 by Van Nostrand Reinhold, using maps and text prepared in 1981 by Kartografie of Czechoslovakia. It was also printed in Czechoslovakia.

II. Format

The *VNR Pocket Atlas* measures 4½″ × 6⅝″, and fits easily in a student's pocket or bookbag. Its sturdy paperback binding opens flat without cracking and should withstand heavy use, although like any paperback, the corners of the cover can quickly become dog-eared. The matte-finish text stock has good opacity.

Maps cover one or two pages, except for 11 gatefold pages for maps of the world, Northern and Central Africa, and several other areas. Political maps, which predominate in the work, are far more detailed than physical maps. Most maps are not contained within neat lines and bleed to the edges of the page. The master legend at the front of the atlas includes symbols for cities, boundaries, railway lines, train ferry routes, ten types of physical features, relative sizes of cities, relief above sea level, ocean depths, and typographic conventions for place name categories. Metric measurements are used throughout the atlas, supplemented with a simple metric conversion table at the front of the book.

Each two-page map spread is interspersed with an additional two pages of text that provides a succinct description of the history, political administration, geography, population, and economy of each continent and nation. Much of the statistical data are organized in convenient tabular form, which facilitates access. A color illustration of each nation's flag appears in the text pages. Although not intended as a substitute for an encyclopedia or comprehensive almanac, the text is nevertheless remarkably informative and furnishes far more data than do many larger atlases.

III. Special Features

In addition to the text material described, the *VNR Pocket Atlas* includes a number of special maps and tables. A world time zone map identifies not only standard time zones but also those zones that vary from the standard. Tabular data about the planets provides such information as mean distance from the sun, sidereal period, diameter, mass, rotational period, and number of satellites. The sky maps of the Northern and Southern Hemispheres include codes for the spectral classes and magnitudes of stars. There is also a table of satellites (some of it outdated since the Mariner and Voyager flights), a map of the moon, a map of Mars, and statistical data about the Earth.

Two interesting physical maps of Antarctica and the Arctic show routes taken by more than 20 polar expeditions, as well as the location and nationality of recent scientific research stations.

IV. Geographical Balance

In terms of coverage, the *VNR* atlas is decidedly biased toward the United Kingdom. European and English-speaking nations in general receive more coverage than do other areas, with an average of half a page of text per country. Many countries in Asia, Africa, Central America, and Oceania, however, receive as little as one-sixth of a page of text. The United Kingdom enjoys by far the most coverage, with 14 pages of maps and text. The Soviet Union also reaps a bumper harvest, with nine pages of text and map material.

V. Scale and Projections

Although map projections are not identified in the *VNR Pocket Atlas*, our reviewers found them appropriate for the size of the maps and the areas represented.

In an atlas of such small dimensions, map scales tend to be small of necessity. Each map labels the scale as a representative fraction and a bar scale, shown in both meters and miles. By far the smallest scale maps (those showing largest area and least detail) are those of the world (1:150,000,000). Many large regions are rendered at 1:50,000,000 (for example, North America or Australia and the Pacific) or 1:65,000,000 (for example, Asia and Europe). Australia, South America, Canada, China, and similar areas are shown at a scale of 1:25,000,000, whereas individual nations or small groups of countries range from 1:3,500,000 (England) to 1:10,000,000 (Scandinavia). The choice of scales is appropriate and enables the reader to make ready comparisons among various parts of the globe.

VI. Accuracy

Place names are generally spelled according to local vernacular usage. Alternate conventional Anglicized spellings for well-known places are listed on many maps and appear in the index with a cross-reference to the vernacular spelling. Physical and political features are accurately represented and labeled, although the Laurentian Plateau in Canada is misspelled *Laurentin* both on the map and in the index.

West Berlin is listed in the text with its own entry, separate from West Germany. It is merely described as being "administered by the Senate," with no explanation that this is the West Germany Senate, or that it is a state of West Germany.

VII. Currency

The maps and text are relatively current with the 1983 publication date. The latest date cited for statistics is 1982, although the average date for national statistics, such as population, is about 1978; 1970 rather than 1980 figures for U.S. population are given, but the date cited for the name of the U.S. President is 1981. The use of what has by now become badly dated statistical information undermines the value of this portion of the book, particularly for students of economic geography and current events.

VIII. Legibility

Typefaces on the maps are legible and serve to differentiate among place-name categories. Although there are only a few small-scale physical maps, several types of natural features are shown, identified either by symbol or typeface. However, because deserts, lowlands, plateaus, and plains are all labeled in the same typeface, the reader can easily become confused, especially when the map does not label the type of feature. If the name is in English or has been Anglicized, the generic English term is usually provided—for example, the Great Victoria Desert. If the name is given in the vernacular, however, the generic English term is often omitted. For example, the Deccan Plateau in India is described on the physical map of India only as "Deccan." The reader must consult the index to learn that Deccan is a plateau.

Physical maps label some cities and altitudes but not international boundaries. On political maps the five types of political boundaries are often difficult to distinguish because, like rivers, they are printed in blue. Town and city symbols, however, are very easy to distinguish. Six symbols are used for towns and cities of Great Britain, and five for the rest of the world. Colors are strong and are in register, al-

though they are not always used to advantage. For example, on the maps of Africa and southern Africa, the bordering nations of Botswana, Zimbabwe, Zambia, Malawi, Tanzania, Kenya, and Uganda are all shaded pink, even though as many as eight colors and shades are used elsewhere and could have been used for clearer differentiation.

States or provinces are shown on the political maps for selected countries. For some countries they are labeled directly; on others, they are indicated by numbers, with the individual names in an inset legend.

Even though type size ranges from 8 points to as small as 3 points, place-name labels are remarkably easy to read, although very young readers and the visually impaired would find them difficult. Compared to their counterparts in THE PRENTICE-HALL POCKET ATLAS OF THE WORLD, political maps in *VNR* are much more legible, primarily because there is less background detail. Legibility becomes a noticeable problem in the text pages, where dense blocks of small type discourage the eye; in the index the near-flyspeck type presents serious obstacles to efficient use.

IX. Accessibility

The table of contents lists each map alphabetically and refers the reader to text page, map number, and the page on which the map can be found. The system is not without its pitfalls. Because maps bleed to the edge of the page, only text pages are numbered, which can make locating maps a nuisance. Moreover, it is left to the reader to figure out that map numbers are given on text pages; the running head on the left-hand page usually refers to the map on the preceding page; the running head on the right-hand side to the map on the following page. Even then, the running heads may trip the unwary reader. The text material for Yemen, for example, appears on a page with the running head "map 25" (Southeast Asia), whereas Yemen is located on maps 26 and 28. The table of contents refers the reader to map 28 only; likewise, Singapore is found on more than one map but listed only once in the table of contents. This system is sure to defeat all but the most persistent reader.

The comprehensive 49-page index lists all geographical names used in the maps, in alphabetical order, followed by the map rather than the page number. Alphanumeric grid coordinates are used for locator references, but these also present pitfalls. Since there are no neat line borders on the maps, the letter and number coordinates fall on the maps themselves and are not always easily located mixed in with place names, and so on. Text entries are not indexed.

Many index entries are accompanied by one of 25 abbreviations for such features as channels, hills, lakes, rivers, reservoirs, swamps, and volcanoes. The index is preceded by a clear explanation of entry notations and abbreviations.

Although all main entries are in the vernacular form, cross-references guide the reader from well-known conventional anglicized versions to the vernacular.

X. Summary

The *VNR Pocket Atlas* is a well-designed, easy-to-read, highly portable reference source for students and general readers. Despite its small size, it furnishes a surprising amount of information, although much of its statistical data are now out of date.

For a true pocket atlas, the *VNR* is extremely legible (the index excepted). Maps are attractive and uncluttered and will serve the needs of young readers who want a convenient quick reference source that can be kept in their desk or bookbag. It is unfortunate that the index makes it so difficult to locate place names, for in almost every other respect this is a superior pocket-sized atlas.

Whole Earth Atlas

Facts at a Glance
Full Title: **Whole Earth Atlas**.
Publisher: Hammond Incorporated.
Copyright: 1984.

Edition Reviewed: 1986 printing.
Number of Volumes: 1.
Number of Pages: 256.
Number of Maps: 302.
Number of Indexes: 302 same-page indexes; no master index.
Trim Size: 8½" × 11".
Binding: paper.

Intended Readership: grade 9 and up.
Price: $8.95; 15-percent school and library discount.
Sold in bookstores and direct to schools and libraries. ISBN 0-8437-2499-4.
Revised annually or every two years, as necessary.

I. Scope and Format

The Hammond *Whole Earth Atlas* is a paperbound version of Hammond's NEW HORIZON and DIPLOMAT world atlases, containing the same maps in the same sequence as those atlases. Apart from the binding and price, it differs in only two respects from those volumes. First, a series of "World Statistical Tables" are printed on the inside front and inside back covers of the book. These deal with such items as Elements of the Solar System, Dimensions of the Earth, Oceans and Major Seas, Largest Islands, Principal Mountains of the World, and Longest Rivers of the World. Second, the *Whole Earth Atlas* does not contain a master index, but does include identical same-page indexes to those found in NEW HORIZON and DIPLOMAT. For complete information about the maps and other features of this atlas, see the review of the NEW HORIZON WORLD ATLAS on page 259.

The Wonderful World of Maps

Facts at a Glance
Full Title: **The Wonderful World of Maps**.
Publisher: Hammond Incorporated.
Author: James F. Madden.
Editor: Martin A. Bacheller.
Copyright: 1986.

Number of Volumes: 1.
Number of Pages: 64.
Number of Maps: 48.
Number of Indexes: 1.
Trim Size: 8½" × 11".

Intended Readership: grades 3 and 4.
Price: $8.95 to individuals; 15 percent discount for schools and libraries.
Sold in bookstores. ISBN 0-8437-3411-6.
Revised approximately every two years.

I. Introduction

The Wonderful World of Maps is a beginning world atlas intended for third and fourth grade students. James F. Madden, a school principal, is the author of this appealing reference work that introduces basic concepts of map-reading to the elementary-school child. The book is divided into three parts: a section on how to read maps, a section of illustrated maps, and a short section of skill-building activities.

II. Format

The first part of *The Wonderful World of Maps* teaches the student how to read and interpret maps. It includes such information as facts about the earth, what data a map provides, the meaning of direction, and the use of symbols.

The map section includes 12 geographic areas and a total of 48 maps. The largest is a two-page political map of the world. Other areas, such as North America, show a physical map on one full page and a political map on the facing page. Smaller-scale thematic maps depicting vegetation, population, and leading products of each of the seven continents are also found in the second section.

Map legends are inconsistently provided. The legends of each physical map provide bar scales in miles and kilometers, and appropriate explanation of the use of colors. Vegetation, population, and product maps are also adequately coded. The legends of political maps, however, include only bar scales of miles and kilometers; other symbols used on the political maps, such as capitals, boundaries, cities, and rivers are not provided, though they are explained in the introductory section of the atlas.

The third section of this atlas contains skill-builder activities designed to reinforce the material presented in the first section of the book. The activities are self-contained, and do not require use of the maps in the second section.

The atlas is a convenient notebook size. It is hardbound, with a sturdy, washable cover, clever diagrams, and interesting photo illustrations that will appeal to young readers.

III. Special Features

This atlas contains a variety of imaginative special features. The first section of the atlas introduces the elementary-school child to the basics of map-reading. Starting with a brief review of the planet Earth, it explains what a map is, and how information from symbols, direction, and distance is shown on a map. This section clearly explains such basic terms as orbit, scale, latitude, longitude, routes, boundaries, and time zones. It uses a variety of illustrative techniques to convey information, including diagrams, photographs, and maps. The data are clearly organized, so that a single topic, such as distance or scale, is explained on a two-page spread. Some, though not all, of these topics refer the reader to a page on which an appropriate skill-builder activity can be used to reinforce the lesson.

The skill-builder section at the end of the atlas is very short and provides only five activities. Each is one page long, and calls for the student to apply some of the map-reading skills introduced earlier. For example, one activity tests the student's knowledge of latitude and longitude.

Other special features include a comparative map of the world's continents by size, as well as photographs which supplement the vegetation, population, and product map pages. The inside front cover of the atlas features a set of World Fact Tables, including data on oceans and seas, lakes and inland seas, and famous islands, mountains, and rivers. A map index is provided on the inside back cover; an index to the terms and concepts discussed in the first section is not included.

IV. Geographical Balance

The atlas provides maps of the world, the seven continents, and the Pacific Ocean Island area. Maps of Canada and the United States supplement that of North America, indicating some bias toward that region. Also, Antarctica does not receive the standard one-page illustration given other continents. With these exceptions, however, the atlas is evenhanded in its coverage of the continents.

V. Scale and Projections

A bar scale in both miles and kilometers appears below the title of every physical and political map. The scales used are not consistent, and are apparently intended to provide the largest scale possible in the available space. As a result, the primary-grade student comparing the United States map to that of North America might conclude that the former is greater in size. The only material that might correct such misconceptions is the page comparing the world's continents by size. However, this problem can be overcome if the student is made aware of the scale variations and learns to judge size by scale rather than by appearance. Projection is not indicated in this book.

VI. Accuracy

Names on the maps are accurately placed. In the case of the world map, however, a combination of names and numbers is used to identify countries, and this system is confusing. For example, Poland and Iceland are labeled by name, whereas Afghanistan and Botswana have only a number which must be referred to in the legend for identification.

In other instances, bias is reflected in the place names chosen for inclusion. In the political map of North America, for example, over a dozen cities are identified in the United States, whereas Quebec is not even included among the sprinkling of Canadian cities located, and Mexico City is the only city identified in Mexico. No capitals of any Central American country are provided. In addition, Communist nations are not always given complete names. China is not labeled as the *People's Republic of China*. The German Democratic Republic has been given its generic title of *East Germany*. Other bias is reflected in the failure to include the capital of North Korea, whereas that of South Korea is included. Finally, territories such as the Falkland Islands or Gibraltar are not identified as areas in dispute.

VII. Currency

The material in this atlas is up-to-date. Such recent discoveries as the North Sea oil off the coast of Great Britain are shown in the product map of Europe. Vietnam is shown as one nation with *Ho Chi Minh City* replacing *Saigon* as the name of the south's major city. Zimbabwe and Burkina Faso are given their proper names. However, *Peking* rather than *Beijing* is still the name used to identify the capital of the People's Republic of China.

VIII. Legibility

Typefaces on the maps in this atlas are unusually clear and legible. Place-name categories on political maps are clearly differentiated by typefaces, although different categories are not explained in the legend. National and state boundary lines are indicated by a system of dots and dashes (—•—) so that it is difficult to distinguish between international and state boundaries. This may cause some confusion, since a lesson in the introductory section of the atlas deals only with the symbol for international boundary lines. A judicious use of color helps compensate for this problem.

IX. Accessibility

The map index is limited to one page with 165 entries on the inside back cover and is not adequate for the material presented. Not all nations, such as Nepal, Sri Lanka, or Bhutan, are included. Rivers such as the Volga or Yukon are listed, but the Mississippi is omitted. For each listing, both a page reference and grid coordinates are provided, although latitudes and longitudes are not. If a place name, such as *Chicago*, appears on more than one map, only one reference to its location appears in the index. None of the terms and concepts discussed in the introductory section is included in the index.

Several of the maps contain inserts which are clearly marked. For the young reader, however, the location of these inserts relative to the rest of the data on the map may not be clear. This would hold true for the location of New Zealand vis-a-vis Australia, for example, as well as for the location of Hawaii and Alaska with respect to the continental United States.

X. Summary

The Wonderful World of Maps is well worth its retail price of $8.95. On the whole, it is preferable to its main competitor, THE VIKING CHILDREN'S WORLD ATLAS. It offers the elementary student a superior introduction to the basic concepts of geography and map-reading. It is a good reference for librarians; however, it would have better served the classroom teacher if more skill-building activities had been included in the text. An expanded index, including not only complete place coverage but also data coverage of the text, would have added greatly to the utility of this work.

World Atlas for Students

Facts at a Glance

Title: **World Atlas for Students**.
Publisher: Hammond Incorporated.
Editor: Martin A. Bacheller.
Copyright: 1985.

Number of Volumes: 1.
Number of Pages: 53.
Number of Maps: 83.
Number of Indexes: 1.
Number of Index Entries: 300.
Trim Size: 8½″ × 11″.

Intended Readership: grades 8 through 12.
Price: $3.45.
Sold in bookstores, and direct to schools and libraries. ISBN 0-8437-7820-2.
Revised annually.

I. Introduction

The Hammond *World Atlas for Students* is a general world atlas intended for students in grades eight and above. It contains 83 map entries; the principal color maps include political data on the chief regions and nations of the world. Smaller maps illustrating topographical features and agricultural, industrial, and mineral data accompany the political maps. The cartographic contents of this atlas are exactly the same as those found in the HAMMOND HEADLINE WORLD ATLAS, with one exception. The back of this atlas includes 24 small black-and-white maps which provide such information as the earth's natural vegetation, political associations of the world, the worldwide distribution of mineral resources, and the production of corn, rice, and other crops. Because no explanatory text or skill activities are included, this atlas will serve primarily as a reference tool to supplement classroom use. Although the editors claim that it is revised annually to include the most recent changes, they also state that the copyright, which is easily changed, is updated only every few years.

II. Format

This atlas is similar in format to the HAMMOND HEADLINE WORLD ATLAS. It contains a variety of world, regional, and subregional maps. Beginning with a one-page world map, it features one- or two-page spreads of political maps of the world's continents. In selected instances, some of these maps are followed by political maps of subregional areas, such as the United States, Central America, the United Kingdom, and Ireland. (For further information, see the description in the format section of the HAMMOND HEADLINE WORLD ATLAS.) This volume is paperbound, with saddle-stitched pages, so that it lies flat when opened, resulting in no loss of content in the gutters.

III. Special Features

This atlas contains several features that the cartographically similar HEADLINE WORLD ATLAS lacks. The front cover illustrates the population distribution of the world, and the back cover shows diagrams of the seasons of the year and the world's time zones. On the inside front cover are statistical tables of the earth's dimensions, mountains, rivers, islands, and lakes. Four black-and-white maps in the front illustrate various transportation systems throughout the world, occupational patterns, religious concentrations, and predominant languages spoken. Twenty-four small black-and-white maps at the back of the atlas illustrate the world's vegetation, political associations, mineral distribution, and the production of various crops; the insets and graphs in these maps are small and very difficult to read.

The topographical, agriculture, industry, and resource maps include flags of the nations depicted. Because of a lack of space, however, these flags are sometimes imposed on the political map; in other instances, as with Africa, the flags share a page with the map of Antarctica. A small global illustration of part of the earth also highlights the map area being illustrated, so that the reader can see the size of the area relative to the rest of the world.

IV. Geographical Balance

The selection of countries in this atlas is arbitrary and geographically unbalanced. North America, Europe, and Asia are featured in the majority of the map illustrations. For example, subregional maps of North America include Canada, Mexico, Central America, the West Indies, and a two-page spread of the United States. South America, however, is allotted only two pages for its principal regional map. Of all continents, Europe commands the greatest share of map space, with eight subregional maps. These include two maps of the Soviet Union.

The most thorough Third World coverage is given to Asia, with five subregional maps. Two of these, titled Southeast Asia and the Indochinese and Malay Peninsulas, overlap with similar data. Like South America, Africa too has no subregional maps. The marked western bias in the map selection makes this atlas of questionable value for use in courses which include study of Africa and South America.

V. Scale and Projections

The map projection and a bar scale in miles and kilometers appear below the title of most political maps. A variety of map scales and projections are used, including a modified Mercator projection, a polyconic projection, and a Bonne projection. Scales vary widely; however, because a majority of the maps feature vast land areas on a single page, small-scale maps predominate. The mix of small- and medium-scale maps occasionally gives rise to misconceptions of relative size and shape. This variation is particularly misleading when two areas, such as Germany and the Scandinavian countries, are placed on facing pages with different scales. Elevations are not included.

VI. Accuracy

Place names are accurately and consistently spelled. However, some of the topographical maps fail to show geographical features in their entirety. For example, there is no topographical map of North America, so the reader may miss the fact that some features, such as the Rocky Mountains, are common to Canada, the United States, and Mexico, even though they are correctly placed on the three separate topographical maps of each country.

The atlas is not consistent in its use of generic and official names. For example, the gazetteer indexes East and West Germany and the two Chinas, with official names given in parentheses; unofficial names are used on the maps. Official titles are not provided for North Korea, South Korea, or Ireland. Another inaccuracy is the gazetteer's listing of *Kampuchea*, which is then shown as *Cambodia* on the map. Also confusing is the indexing of *Kalaalit Nunaat*, which is titled *Greenland* on the map. It appears that the index has been updated to include the current names, but the maps remain untouched.

VII. Currency

With few exceptions, the information in this atlas is current and reflects up-to-date revisions. The former *Saigon* is labeled as *Ho Chi Minh City*. The new nations of Burkina Faso and Brunei are indexed and mapped. However, the capital of the People's Republic of China is still shown as *Peking*, not *Beijing*.

VIII. Legibility

Typefaces on the maps are inconsistent in their clarity and legibility. Place name categories are differentiated by typefaces, although the density of names on some maps is confusing. Too many cities are included on the map of England, for example; this clutters the cartography. The map of the United States is similarly crowded, so that even some state names are difficult to read.

International borders do not always stand out clearly. For example, the boundaries between East and West Germany and other nations, and smaller political divisions within each of the two nations can be confusing. The conflicting claims of two nations are not consistently noted, particularly in the case of Israel, whose borders are also difficult to locate.

The small black-and-white maps in the back of the atlas have insets that are particularly difficult to read.

For example, the map showing the production of various raw materials includes pie graphs which show how these resources are allocated among the world's nations. However, these pie graphs are quite small, difficult to read, and have no indications as to percentages of the totals that can be attributed to the countries shown.

IX. Accessibility

The index gazetteer at the front of the book provides extremely limited access to cartographic information. Although it includes continents and other major divisions, it does not list cities, counties, provinces, and minor political areas that are shown on the political maps. Rivers, mountains, deserts, and other topographical data are omitted altogether. Moreover, for countries, states, and other divisions, the gazetteer lists only the page number on which these places are shown on the largest scale, and its grid coordinates. Further, the gazetteer-index is located two pages into the book—not at the direct front, and not at the back where it is normally found. Consequently, it is not as accessible as it could or should be.

X. Summary

For $3.45, this atlas provides slightly more data than the HAMMOND HEADLINE WORLD ATLAS. Cartographically, however, it has the same biases as the *Headline Atlas*, and thus the same limitations for classroom use. It is not inclusive enough to recommend for libraries, and students would be better served by a more carefully planned atlas, such as the RAND MCNALLY QUICK REFERENCE WORLD ATLAS. The value of the *Hammond World Atlas for Students* is limited by its skimpy index with the confusing inclusion of gazetteer data, and it offers no skill-building challenges to students.

PART FOUR

Dictionaries and Word Books

Chapter 9
What to Look for in Dictionaries and in Word Books

Selecting a dictionary—whether for use in the formal setting of a school classroom, a school library, or a public library, or more informally at home—involves a number of considerations. One's choice will depend on the student's level of skill and interest in language, as well as specific study or leisure needs.

Most dictionaries range beyond the basic purpose of presenting an alphabetical register of the words and meanings of a given language. As young readers progress through school, they need and expect more detailed information and guidance on language from the dictionaries they consult.

General dictionaries are more complex and individual than may be apparent at first glance. The reviews in this guide, therefore, describe the similarities and differences among the individual works and briefly analyze the features they offer in addition to the main vocabulary and definitions.

Chapter 2, "Choosing General Reference Books for Young Readers," describes the general classifications and basic features of dictionaries. But to help in selecting specific dictionaries, readers of this guide need

- to know how the team of reviewers, editors, and consultants approached the task of evaluation;

- to be aware of the specific issue of *currency* in dictionaries, especially of scientific and technical words; and

- to understand how the dictionary reviews in the guide are presented, as well as the kinds of features that reviewers commonly selected for comment or illustration.

General approach to evaluations. The reviews were prepared with an overriding awareness of each dictionary's intended readership—the range of reading levels and language skills that might be necessary to use the contents effectively. Wherever possible, the reviews explain and illustrate specific features so that potential buyers acquire a balanced view of a dictionary's contents. This will help readers of the Buying Guide to select dictionaries that meet the needs of young people from preschool through the high school years.

Currency of scientific and technical words. Apart from the explicit criteria represented by the numbered sections of the evaluations, there is one aspect of dictionaries that is widely discussed, cited in review periodicals, and featured in publishers' promotional materials. This is the *currency* of words and meanings, how up-to-date a work is. Although currency affects the quality and usefulness of a dictionary's general vocabulary, scientific and technical terms, and their special or professional meanings, are the most obvious signs of a dictionary's currency. Dictionaries that are used by readers from junior high level upward need to reflect the burgeoning scientific and technical meanings of words, *at least* to the extent that these enter into everyday vocabulary. Works for younger readers, who are still acquiring basic vocabulary, are less directly affected.

Increasingly, publishers emphasize the *quantity* of new scientific and technical words and meanings included in their dictionaries—even in concise or paperback editions. Accordingly, prospective buyers tend to seek examples of such words in assessing the latest edition of a work. To a certain degree, scientific and technical currency indicates the choices a dictionary's editors make about which terms they consider to be most frequently used or needed by the intended readers.

In evaluating currency, the reviewers have generally tried to judge the dictionaries from the perspective of general-purpose use; that is, how clear the definitions of scientific and technical terms will be to readers who do not have special knowledge of the fields the terms cover. We notice, for example, a trend in some college dictionaries that are considered suitable for high school readers toward defining terms (for example, in biochemistry and mathematics) in formal scientific terms rather than in language that can be readily understood by a general reader. Nevertheless, many dictionaries do make a strenuous effort to define all words, including scientific and technological ones, and to discriminate among meanings, so that readers with general high school or adult-level reading skills can readily understand them.

The basic lexicon of modern dictionaries remains current for perhaps ten years; after that a portion of the vocabulary begins to date, even if some annual revision is undertaken. Thus, for instance, as yet, few dictionaries include the acronym *AIDS* (1982 is the usual date given for the term's emergence into the general vocabulary); but general dictionaries, even those labeled concise or condensed, include both a noun and a verb sense of *program*, as it is used in computer science, unless they are very out-of-date.

In many cases, the reviews give examples of scientific and technical definitions, to show a work's currency or lack of updating. When considering any dictionary for purchase, however, buyers themselves should research for a sample of words from medicine, science, and technology to judge whether the inclusions and defined senses of such words are, in fact, likely to be useful for the intended reader. School librarians, and others serving children and young adults, will naturally consider whether the textbooks that students use have up-to-date subject matter glossaries. This factor may well then lead them to conclude that a basic dictionary with an appropriate age or reading-skill level is more useful to some students than a higher-level dictionary that has more contemporary scientific vocabulary.

The structure of reviews. For the convenience of readers of this Buying Guide, each review of a dictionary or word book is divided into numbered sections, so that the evaluations of specific features are readily accessible. Furthermore, there are two basic formats for the reviews that reflect either the relative complexity of works according to intended readership or their potential use:

Preschool and Elementary Dictionaries

   I.   Scope and Format
  II.   Authority
 III.   Quality and Currency of Entries
 IV.   Illustrations
  V.   Summary

Middle School, Junior High,
  and High School Dictionaries

    I.   Introduction
   II.   Authority
  III.   Comprehensiveness
  IV.   Quality and Currency of Entries
   V.   Syllabication and Pronunciation
  VI.   Special Features
 VII.   Accessibility
VIII.   Graphics and Format
  IX.   Summary

Word Books and Large-Print Works

  I.   Introduction and Scope
 II.   Format
III.   Quality and Currency of Entries
IV.   Accessibility
 V.   Summary

The following paragraphs explain some considerations and detail the criteria for each section of the dictionary and word book evaluations that appear in chapters 10, 11, and 12. Describing the criteria will give the reader of this guide a sound basis for making a personal evaluation of the works reviewed, and will highlight some of the features of general dictionaries and word books suitable for young readers that a prospective purchaser will need to consider.

Facts at a Glance. Each evaluation is preceded by a boxed insert of factual information about the dictionary provided by the publishers. This information includes the full title of the work and occasionally alternate or previous titles; the publisher's formal name; the author, compiler, editor or, in some cases, the senior lexicographic staff; the date of the edition reviewed and the printing in some cases (where this date is not the original copyright, reviews briefly explain the earlier dates); the number of volumes; the number of definitions or entries as specified by the publisher (where publishers have not given this information, the Buying Guide's editorial staff has supplied an estimate of main boldface entry words based either on a hand count or on the sampling procedures described in the "Federal Specification—Dictionaries, English: G-D-331D, 28 June 1974); the number of pages (usually the last numbered page in the work); the number of indexes; the number and a brief description of the kinds of illustrations; the trim size of the volume(s); the kind of binding (occasionally more than one binding is listed) and the price(s). This is followed by a brief description of the intended readership (usually the publisher's own description, but occasionally expanded—note that dictionaries suitable for adults as well as younger readers are *not* so designated in this guide); and a general note on where the dictionary is sold.

Introduction. This section provides an overview of the edition of the dictionary reviewed, its relation to other works by the same publisher, and a description of the work's purpose and intended readership. Pertinent quotations about the purposes or content by the editors, from the introduction or preface, or directly from the publisher are often included.

In addition, a statement is usually included about the extent of the vocabulary, any additional features, and the approach taken by the dictionary's compilers to the vocabulary and other lexicographic features.

A special note: In some cases, the evaluations of dictionaries or word books consist only of "Facts at a Glance" and an introductory section entitled, "I. Scope and Format." This occurs when a book is, for example, a slightly different version of a work reviewed fully in another edition, or when a book is an exact or close replica of a title that exists in another format (such as a paperback edition and a hardbound edition from the same publisher).

Authority. This section gives a brief summary of the generally acknowledged reputation of the dictionary's publisher, including other dictionaries currently or previously published. If the edition reviewed is a revision of an earlier edition, occasional critical opinions may be cited on the original work, if they are considered especially useful to readers of this guide.

When available, information is provided about the editors, the publisher's lexicographic staff, and whether that staff has been involved in the preparation of other dictionaries.

Information is also supplied on the academic, linguistic, and lexicographic qualifications, or other expertise, of consultants and of usage experts. If there are special sources for vocabulary, etymologies, usage, or other features, which might include citation files or a previous dictionary's word bank or databases, this information is noted.

Every dictionary of quality needs to have experienced, trained lexicographers and editors. Authoritative consultants in etymology, linguistics, and in subject matter are also necessary to insure a quality product. Describing the authority of a dictionary gives buyers some basis on which to judge its contents.

But as buyers will realize, the recognized authority of a dictionary cannot substitute for careful analysis of the actual work. Buyers should also be aware that there are many dictionaries on the market whose original staffs and consultants were extremely authoritative, but which have not been well revised or brought up-to-date in accordance with the initial standards. For younger readers, there are also some illustrated picture "dictionaries" written by people with little expertise in linguistics or lexicography. In general, authority can guide the buyer in the initial selection of a work and may be a final deciding factor, but reputation should not take the place of assessment of a work's contents.

Comprehensiveness. In these reviews, the category of comprehensiveness is viewed from several perspectives. One is the relative comprehensiveness of the vocabulary, linguistic data, and information on the history and use of language as measured ultimately against such monuments of lexicography as the multivolume *Oxford English Dictionary* or other unabridged adult dictionaries. A second view is the relative comprehensiveness of a dictionary when compared to another in the same—or similar—category, such as preschool, middle school, college, or concise dictionaries.

The reviewers have not criticized dictionaries for a lack of comprehensiveness when that is not appropriate to either the category of a work or its purpose. For instance, a pocket dictionary intended for quick checks on spelling, hyphenation, and basic meanings may be sufficiently comprehensive for those purposes without extensive lists of synonyms or usage notes. Many student readers will need no more than brief etymologies, even in works with more extensive vocabularies.

The specific features considered under this section are the inclusion of etymologies and their treatment, lists of combining forms, quotations and usage examples, and notes and prescriptive guidance on language. Synonym treatment is also occasionally discussed in this section (in addition to the information in the definitions section). Readers' needs are a prime consideration here and, of course, vary widely according to age level and course of studies.

Etymologies are of interest not only as background to the meanings of words, but as part of cultural history. Usage examples and prescriptive guidance are particularly important for students who write extensively. Synonym lists and discriminations of meaning and usage in context are also important to student writers and to those seeking to increase their vocabularies.

This section includes a generous number of brief examples of the various features; these are used to offer both criticisms and compliments. In addition, the section often includes comments on the currency of the dictionary's vocabulary (in addition to the information given in the section on entries that describes the entries in more specific detail), with examples of words included or omitted in the dictionary's lexicon.

Quality and Currency of Entries. These evaluations are intended to characterize the entries and definitions included in a dictionary—their extent, quality, and usefulness. The reviewers also assess whether or not the definitions are appropriate for the designated age and reading level of intended readers.

Some of the questions that reviewers asked about each work were: Are the definitions generally accurate and to the point? Are they adequate, given the intended scope of the work, or too concise? Are the meanings carefully discriminated and are special senses labeled when necessary? Are useful cross-references included?

Reviews describe the general sequence of information in the entries (main word, pronunciations, parts of speech, labels, etymologies, and so forth) and note how senses and homographs are ordered. In part, the sequence of information presented in dictionaries depends on custom: a bold main entry word is usually followed by its respelled pronunciation; thereafter, the sequence varies considerably. Buyers will want to look at the sequence of information given in several short and longer entries, to judge whether or not such items as the part of speech, field label, or word history (etymology) can be located easily. When etymologies, for example, are not considered an important feature for the intended reader, they are often shortened or placed at the end of an entry, or sometimes omitted. Dictionaries for very young readers may omit the part of speech or place it after a definition. Buyers should also check on the discriminated senses of words: Are they numbered within entries or otherwise handled appropriately for the age group? Are phrases or sentences given that show clearly how different meanings are used? Are homographs (two words spelled alike but with different etymologies and meanings) omitted, or run into an entry, or are they numbered and placed as separate entries?

Other questions answered by the reviews include: Are words defined in historical order or is current usage placed first? Often a dictionary's preface will describe the order of defined senses. But buyers will need to consider whether or not younger readers,

for example, might be confused by the order: Could they mistake a traditional common meaning for a more current usage they require or vice versa? If more current usage is emphasized, a buyer needs to consider whether or not a more traditional but widely used sense of a word has been sacrificed for currency.

For dictionaries prepared especially for younger readers, the reviews describe whether words are defined descriptively or analytically or whether meanings are implied from the context of short, illustrative sentences and pictures. Reviews often indicate whether synonyms are used to define meanings, are separately listed, and are exemplified, discriminated, or cross-referenced.

The selection of dictionaries to suit younger readers is extremely important because young children are still in the process of acquiring basic language skills. One general method of judging the differences and the quality of meanings in dictionaries is to compare the entries for a common word with Old English origins, such as **game**. This comparison will quickly reveal whether the sequence of information and the definitions—even the typographic conventions (the typefaces, spacing, and punctuation, etc.) used to distinguish the kinds of information supplied under a main entry word—will be suitable for the intended readership.

Consider the differences in the entries for **game** from two respected children's "intermediate" dictionaries:

Example 1:
> **game**[1] (gām), **1** way of playing; pastime; amusement: *a game of tag, a game with bat and ball.* **2** things needed to play a game: *This store sells games.* **3** contest with certain rules: *a football game.* One person or side tries to win it. **4** number of points that wins a game: *In volleyball, a game is fifteen points.* **5** plan; scheme: *She tried to trick us, but we saw through her game.* **6** wild animals, birds, or fish hunted or caught for sport or for food. **7** flesh of wild animals or birds used for food. **8** having to do with game, hunting, or fishing: *Game laws protect wildlife.* **9** brave; plucky: *The losing team put up a game fight.* **10** having spirit or will enough: *The children were game for any adventure.* **11** to gamble. 1–7 *n.,* 8–10 *adj.* **gam er, gam est**; 11 *v.,* **gamed, gam ing**. [*Game*[1] comes from Old English *ga-men*, meaning "joy."]—**game′ly**, *adv.*—**game′ness**, *n.*

(from Scott, Foresman's *Intermediate Dictionary*)

Example 2:

> ¹**game** \ˈgam\ *n* **1 a** : AMUSEMENT 1, DIVER-
> SION   **b** : ¹FUN 1, SPORT ⟨make *game* of a
> nervous player⟩   **2 a** : ¹PLAN 2, STRATA-
> GEM   **b** : a line of work : PROFESSION
> **3 a** : a contest carried on following set rules
> for amusement, exercise, or reward   **b** : a
> division of a larger contest   **c** : the number
> of points necessary to win   **d** : the manner
> of playing in a contest **4 a** : animals pursued
> or taken by hunting   **b** : the flesh of game
> animals   **c** : an object of ridicule or at-
> tack—often used in the phrase *fair game*
> ²**game** *vb* **gamed; gam·ing** : ¹GAMBLE 1a
> ³**game** *adj* **gam·er; gam·est**   **1** : full of spirit
> or eagerness : DETERMINED ⟨*game* to the
> end⟩   **2** : of or relating to animals that are
> hunted ⟨the *game* laws⟩—**game·ly** *adv*—
> **game·ness** *n*

(from *Webster's Intermediate Dictionary*)

At this upper elementary reading level (approximately, grades five through eight) the main lexicographic features and techniques for conveying information about language—those used in adult
dictionaries—appear in simpler form. Making a choice
between these dictionaries would involve not only
the specific features of the definitions, but also the
style of writing: the former is more flowing in style,
the latter more compact, although it could be more
difficult for some readers.

A noticeable feature is that the first example numbers the meanings separately and provides fuller illustrative sentences. The second entry subsumes discriminated meanings under four numbers representing
the main senses of the word and also includes more
discriminated meanings (for example, see **1 b**, **2 b**,
3 b), although it omits the sense of **2** given in the
first example. In the first, the abbreviations for parts
of speech follow the meanings; in the second, the **n**
for noun follows the pronunciation. The typography
is plainer in the first, but dots for syllable divisions
are absent. The second follows the more complex
typography of the Merriam-Webster dictionary family: a colon (:) precedes all definitions; superior numbering is used for homographs (which are positioned
as indented subentries under the main entry word)
and also for definitions cross-referenced to other main
entries (note ¹PLAN 2, for example); small capital
letters are used for defining words that also appear
as main entries. The first example, however, contains
a simplified etymology that may be helpful to young
readers in understanding **game**; the second omits this.

Description of these kinds of features is included
in the reviews to help the buyer acquire a feel for
the quality as well as the style of the definitions and
to guide in purchase selection. In each review, short
examples are frequent and brief comparisons are usually given—especially when a "family" of related
dictionaries is published, in varying lengths and formats for different audiences, as with desk, condensed, or paperback editions, or when a publisher
offers a range of dictionaries for many age levels.

Reviewers examined the methods of conveying
usage information. They also often commented on
prescriptive guidance, such as the explanations of
how to use grammar or disputed words, given within
the main vocabulary. They assessed the usefulness
of context, field, style, and temporal labels.

The reviewers have attempted to present a balanced judgment of each work's entries. For any dictionary, this is a time-consuming task, one that becomes more complex as the age and reading skill of
its intended readers increase. A central purpose of
this section, therefore, is to judge whether entries
contain sufficient descriptive and analytic information on words to satisfy the younger readers most
likely to consult the dictionary.

Syllabication and Pronunciation. How the main
entry words and variants are divided into syllables
and the practice this is based upon are briefly noted
in this section of the reviews. Because readers often
seek guidance on hyphenation of words, a dictionary
needs a clear system that conforms to current printing practice.

Information on the pronunciations is often more
detailed because each dictionary varies in how it re-
spells words for pronunciations and conveys the sounds
of spoken language. With the exception of dictionaries for very young children, most use a range of
symbols from the International Phonetic Alphabet
for English (IPA) rather than just alphabet respellings. Each review describes the system used and indicates whether or not there are adequate pronunciation charts and keys as well as clear explanations
of the phonetic symbols for young readers. Where
the information is pertinent, reviews comment on
the level of difficulty of the pronunciations and the
symbols.

If pronunciations are important to users, then buyers need to examine carefully the respellings and
symbols to see if they are suited to the intended
readers' skills and previous study in phonetics, as
well as experience in recognizing diacritical marks
that represent sounds.

The following short list shows some of the variations that appear in respellings and symbols, even

in dictionaries for younger readers. For the main entry word, **exact**, these pronunciations are used:

eg zakt′	Macmillan *Beginning Dictionary*
ĭg **zăkt′**	*American Heritage Children's Dictionary*
ig zakt′	*Webster's II Riverside Children's Dictionary*
ĭg- **zăkt′**	*Webster's Intermediate Dictionary*
ig- ′zaht	*Webster's School Dictionary*
ig zaht	*The Random House School Dictionary*
ig zakt′	*American Heritage Student's Dictionary*

Because pronunciation systems vary, the best system is one that the potential reader will be most at ease using. These sample keys below represent, in general, some basic methods of treating pronunciations in dictionaries for a younger audience:

Example 1:

ă	pat	ĭ	pit	oi	oil	th	bath
ā	pay	ī	ride	o͞o	book	*th*	bathe
â	care	î	fierce	o͞o	boot	ə	ago, item
ä	father	ŏ	pot	ou	out		pencil
ĕ	pet	ō	go	ŭ	cut		atom
ē	be	ô	paw, for	û	fur		circus

(from *The American Heritage Children's Dictionary*)

Example 2:

at; āpe; cär; end; mē; it; īce; hot; ōld;
fôrk; wood; f͞ool; oil; out; up; turn; sing;
thin; this; hw in white; zh in treasure.
ə stands for **a** in about, **e** in taken,
i in pencil, **o** in lemon, and **u** in circus.

(from the Macmillan *Dictionary for Children*)

Example 3:

a hat	**i** it	**oi** oil	**ch** child		a in about
ā age	**ī** ice	**ou** out	**ng** long		e in taken
ä far	**o** hot	**u** cup	**sh** she	ə =	i in pencil
e let	**ō** open	**ů** put	**th** thin		o in lemon
ē equal	**ô** order	**ü** rule	**ŦH** then		u in circus
ėr term			**zh** measure		

(from Scott, Foresman's *Intermediate Dictionary*)

If elementary and middle school students, for example, have only had instruction in using simplified phonetic respellings with a minimum of diacritical marks (for example, the —, as in mo͞on, and the ˘, as in păt), they may find many of the less familiar IPA symbols difficult to remember and to use. Older students may be familiar with a wide range of symbols from the IPA or be able to use them by reading a dictionary's introductory explanations. School librarians, teachers, and parents can judge whether young readers will have difficulty with such symbols as the schwa ə, representing the sound of "uh" in vowels occurring in unaccented syllables, or the ŋ representing the **ng** sound in dri**nk** or si**ng**, or ŦH for the sound in **th**is.

In dictionaries suitable for junior high school readers and up, an imbalance between the use of more complex pronunciation symbols and the simplified definitions often appears in condensed, desk, or paperback dictionaries, especially in those derived from or related to the standard college dictionaries.

The reviews also explain a dictionary's method of recording acceptable alternate pronunciations; and they describe information given on regional variations in pronunciations.

Special Features. Dictionary publishers frequently emphasize, or advertise, a work's "special features." The range of such features, in addition to a dictionary's main lexicon or vocabulary, may be narrow or fairly extensive. A few dictionaries include the kind of reference matter that might be found in an encyclopedia; others have separate "encyclopedic" supplements; some contain almanac-type listings.

The purpose of this section is to point out the additional kinds of information available and to assess its quality, currency (when appropriate), and usefulness to a student reader. Reviews often note when "special features" seem to be merely tacked on to a dictionary or when they do not match the quality or currency of the main vocabulary.

Readers' needs for such additional material will vary. In general, biographical and geographical lists are useful for quick checking of unfamiliar names or places, although readers should not rely on the dates in such sections as few dictionaries are revised frequently enough to be current. Many country entries, especially for the Third World, are also not current in the majority of dictionaries. So-called "college" dictionaries usually include lists of colleges and universities in the United States, but the usefulness of this conventional tally is debatable. Full, up-to-date separate listings of abbreviations are always useful to students in junior high and high school, especially because abbreviation and acronym use is increasing. Guidance on usage can be valuable from the middle school years and up. Students do seek and expect to find this kind of information in dictionaries, both in the main lexicon and in its supplements. Guidance on punctuation is also useful. When dictionaries do not have a full index of tables and charts, reviews especially try to point out the variety of this information. Lists of currencies, alphabets, measurements, planets, elements, and so forth can be very helpful—in a dictionary—to students and may save them research time when only small bits of information need to be checked.

As a general rule, dictionaries for classroom use will be more valuable if they include supplementary special features. Among the items found in dictionaries that may be reviewed in this section are lists in the main vocabulary related to entry words (kinds of animals or insects); separate A to Z abbreviations, biographical, college and university, and geographic lists; essays on the spoken and written use of language, its pronunciations, or its history; style manuals; advice to students on how to write research papers; guidance on preparing footnotes and bibliographies; examples of forms of address and of letters; and appendixes of various information, such as measurements and symbols and signs used in a variety of fields. In addition to this sort of feature, the reviews survey any specific features that characterize a particular dictionary. These may appear as appendixes or in the main vocabulary and might include special paragraphs on word usage, special kinds of synonym treatment, and so forth.

Accessibility. In these reviews, accessibility refers to how information is physically placed on a dictionary's pages and the specific aids to finding the information entries appearing in the main A to Z vocabulary, as well as in the introductory and supplementary sections. In brief, accessibility means the ease with which a reader can locate the required information within the dictionary.

This section describes the sequence and the methods of alphabetizing words. Letter-by-letter sequence is usual and many dictionaries for younger readers contain clear explanations and even practice examples that will help them learn how to find the words and other information in the pages.

Other features that help a reader find words are described, such as the guide words at the top of pages and thumb indexes. Pairs of guide words at the top of pages are most useful in finding the range of entries on a dictionary's page. But some works for younger students have only a single bold guide word, which is sufficient when the typeface is large and there are only a few words on a page. In larger dictionaries, readers may find thumb-index tabs helpful in getting to the general alphabetical vicinity of a sought-for entry quickly. Other readers find thumb indexes unnecessary. Buyers should be aware that tabs with more than one letter of the alphabet on them guide a reader only to the approximate center of the range of entries between, for example, *M* and *N*.

A description of any introductory explanation or guide to using the contents of the dictionary is included in each review. These are important sections and should be well spaced, have clearly delineated subheads, and very specific instructions with exam-

ples. Reviews often comment on essays that precede the vocabulary because many are extremely useful, especially in the more advanced or college dictionaries. They may provide a wealth of background on the history and use of language as well as on variations in pronunciations; they often serve as excellent introductions to the kinds of information that can be accessed in dictionaries.

In addition, reviews comment on the accessibility of material in appendixes, such as biographical and geographic listings, abbreviations lists, and the usefulness of indexes if they are included. Occasionally, a review mentions the accessibility of additional tabular or chart material appearing within the main vocabulary at specific entries. Finally, it is useful to the reader to have a separate index of this material, especially if it is extensive.

Graphics and Format. The illustrations, general appearance, and physical format are important features of any dictionary. Because a dictionary must stand up to frequent use, a sturdy binding and good quality paper, preferably with high opacity, are necessary. Durability is especially important for any dictionary that will be consulted by many students in classrooms or libraries, or used extensively in the home. All these features are assessed in this section, as well as the suitability of format—whether paperback, desk-size, or oversized—to the work's contents and purpose.

The reviews often provide fairly extensive descriptive assessments of illustrations and captions, tables, and charts in relation to the definitions—especially for those dictionaries prepared for younger readers and for older-age readers when drawings or photographs are featured. For younger readers, the reviews assess whether the pictures are well-drawn, suitable and appealing to the potential readers' ages, and useful as extensions of brief definitions. One question the reviews answer is, Do the illustrations help a reader to understand specific meanings or are they merely decorative? For older students, reviews assess whether or not illustrations attempt to illustrate difficult discriminated meanings that might not be easy to understand from a definition. Captions and labels are assessed as to whether or not they add information. Signs and symbols are judged for clarity.

The general appearance of the typeface of various elements, such as the main entry word, run-on entries, guide words, and text is described. These basic elements need to be clear and readable. Reviews describe whether or not there are sufficient margins and enough leading (white space between text lines) to make reading relatively easy for the intended readership. In cases where the specific format or size of a dictionary is especially important, reviews offer special notes, for example, on whether or not a so-called "pocket" dictionary will actually fit into a pocket or whether the size of a large-print text can be easily read by visually impaired readers.

Summary. The summary of each dictionary's evaluation coordinates the main points made in the individual sections of the reviews. The strengths and weaknesses of each work are balanced and a general judgment as to the overall quality and specific usefulness of the dictionary is given. The buyer may wish to compare the general characteristics and qualities of several dictionaries by reading their review summaries first and then proceeding to read the entire reviews of those that seem likely to be of most value to the potential younger reader.

Facsimile entries. For the dictionary reviews, facsimiles that show representative entries, illustrations, and occasional special features of over sixty of the dictionaries and word books reviewed in this guide have been included. These will help buyers to judge the type of features and qualities they may specifically require in a dictionary. The facsimiles will help readers using this guide to comparison-shop prior to purchasing a dictionary. The facsimile examples were chosen from as wide a range of titles as possible so that Buying Guide readers could acquire an overview of the whole category of general dictionaries available for young readers. Each facsimile has explanatory captions keyed by number to specific items.

These numbered captions clearly identify particular features, most related to the text of a dictionary's review.

Often, especially in school or larger adult dictionaries, publishers themselves include partial or extensive full-page facsimile illustrations with labels. These are printed in the introductory material and sometimes on the back of a title's dust jacket, and are often valuable guides to a work's format and content for those buyers who have a chance to inspect titles before purchase.

Above all, the reviewers, consultants, and editors of this guide have attempted to provide as much information on the qualities and characteristics of the dictionaries included for review as possible, given the space limitations. No dictionary is perfect but many are superior to others in a similar category in one or another or even many aspects. The reviews, in effect, attempt to define and describe each dictionary in as helpful a manner as possible for potential buyers. The Buying Guide reviewers of dictionaries and word books have judiciously kept in mind Sidney I. Landau's comment in *The Art and Craft of Lexicography* that "it will not do to give a pure definition that does not answer the basic need of many readers."

The glossary following this chapter contains many terms that may be unfamiliar to some readers, but will be encountered in the prefaces or introductions to many dictionaries as well as in many of the reviews in this guide.

The International Phonetic Alphabet and the Trager-Smith Phonemic Alphabet for Standard American English

	IPA Symbol	Sound Represented	Trager-Smith Symbol
Consonants	[p]	*p*arson, u*p*	/p/
	[b]	*b*ill, sla*b*	/b/
	[t]	*t*ry, po*t*	/t/
	[d]	*d*ark, en*d*ure	/d/
	[k]	*c*at, qui*ck*	/k/
	[g]	*g*aze, pi*g*	/g/
	[f]	*f*law, enou*gh*	/f/
	[v]	*v*ain, re*v*eal	/v/
	[θ]	*th*in, *th*rough	/θ/
	[ð]	*th*is, *th*erefore	/ð/
	[s]	*s*eal, re*c*eive	/s/
	[z]	*z*ebra, ea*s*ed	/z/
	[ʃ]	*sh*ip, *s*ure	/š/
	[ʒ]	mea*s*ure, sei*z*ure	/ž/
	[tʃ]	*ch*urch, *ch*atter	/č/
	[dʒ]	*j*ud*g*e, *j*angle	/ǰ/
	[m]	*m*ain, sta*mm*er	/m/
	[n]	*n*eon, differe*nt*	/n/

	IPA Symbol	Sound Represented	Trager-Smith Symbol
Consonants	[ŋ]	si*ng*, a*n*xious	/ŋ/
Liquids	[l]	*l*eap, rumb*l*e	/l/
	[r]	*r*anch, sc*r*atchy	/r/
Glides	[j]	*y*et, *u*niversity	/y/
	[w]	*w*ander, q*u*ick	/w/
	[h]	*h*elp, thresh*h*old	/h/
Vowels	[ɪ]	*i*ndex, p*i*t	/i/
	[ɛ]	*e*ver, tr*e*mble	/e/
	[æ]	*a*fter, c*a*n	/æ/
	[ə]	*a*bout, ros*e*s	/ə/
	[ʌ]	j*u*st, th*u*nder	/ə/
	[ɑ]	f*a*ther, b*o*ther	/a/
	[ʊ]	b*oo*k, p*u*t	/u/
	[o]	(no example in English)	/o/
	[ɔ]	l*a*w, bl*o*nde	/ɔ/
	[a]	*au*nt (some dialects)	—
Diphthongs	[i]	s*ee*, cl*e*an	/iy/
	[ɛɪ]	w*ay*, bl*a*me	/ey/
	[aɪ]	fl*y*, b*i*nd	/ay/
	[ɔɪ]	n*oise*, b*oy*	/ɔy/
	[u]	m*oo*n, bl*ue*	/uw/
	[oʊ]	t*oe*, m*o*tor	/ow/
	[aʊ]	h*ow*, r*ou*nd	/aw/
	[ɛh]	*yeah*, *e*ver	/eh/
Post-Diphthong [r] *or* /r/	[ɚ]	f*ear*, f*air*, f*ar*, tou*r*	/hr/

Chart from *How Language Works* (p. 41) by Madelon E. Heatherington.

Glossary

abridged A category of adult dictionary based on size; a dictionary of about 50,000 to 130,000 entries; condensed, shortened, or reduced from a larger or longer work.

antonym A word that has an opposite or nearly opposite meaning to another. *See also* **synonym**.

authority The experience, expertise, and reputation of a dictionary's publisher, professional lexicographers, editorial staff, and consultants, as well as a work's generally acknowledged critical reputation (if the edition reviewed is not the first).

citation(s) The source(s) of definitions; quotations in the context of actual usage used to provide a basis for defining new words and new meanings or senses of established words.

citation file A collection of illustrative quotations, usually from newspapers, magazines, or books with a wide reading public, in the context of actual usage that is used to develop lexical matter.

college (dictionary) Often called a **semi-abridged dictionary**, a category of dictionary usually containing from 130,000 to 170,000 entries, desk-sized and directed toward the vocabulary needs of the college community; also, a dictionary with fewer entries than an unabridged dictionary, but with more than a **desk** dictionary.

collegiate *See* **college**.

colloquial Informal style of expression; a phrase or term not considered appropriate in standard formal contexts.

concise Abridged or condensed (a dictionary with little detail).

condensed Also **concise**, **abridged**; shortened definitions or versions of a text; compact is sometimes used as a description in place of condensed.

connotation The attributes of a word or phrase derived from use and custom; the associated emotional or attitudinal meaning of a word or phrase;

beyond the essential meaning; how a word fits into the social context in which it is used.

cross-reference A key word or phrase directing the reader from one entry or word in the dictionary to another.

definition Information a reader must have to understand the meaning of a word. A definition tells what a word means rather than describing its concept or illustrating its use.

D'Nealian Alphabet Oval, slanted letters, introduced in 1978, into the elementary schools, that are more like cursive writing than traditional manuscript. D'Nealian handwriting is intended to make cursive easier for children to learn.

desk (dictionary) A category of dictionary containing 50,000 or 60,000 to 100,000 words, conveniently sized for home or office use; sometimes called an **abridged** or **concise** dictionary.

denotation The exact, or literal, meaning of a word or phrase.

dictionary A reference work that lists words in alphabetical order and describes their meanings, and often other information related to words, such as usage, pronunciation, etymology, synonyms; a work that serves as a record of, and often a standard for, the language it records.

discrimination(s, -ed) The careful distinguishing of the various meanings and usage of words; separating and identifying the subtle shades of synonyms and antonym meanings.

entry A word or phrase identified or defined in a dictionary, usually set off by boldface type. Also called a *main entry*. *See also* **headword** and **run-on entry**.

entry term The key element that comprises the dictionary entry. Also called a *main entry*.

entry word A synonym for **entry term**.

etymon A root word, from the Greek for "true meaning."

etymology(ies) The study of word origins, their history, and their development.

field label A qualifying term that restricts a word's meaning to its use in a specific area in a scientific, technical, or applied field, such as music, physics, biology, engineering, law, philosophy, and so forth; a term for the field of work or study in which a

word or phrase has a special meaning; used for identification and clarification.

finding aid Any device that helps a reader to find information in a dictionary or thesaurus, such as **guide words**, **thumb indexes**, or printed **thumb tabs**. Cross-references are often considered such aids.

glossary An alphabetically listed vocabulary of specialized terms, with brief definitions. A glossary is usually restricted to one subject.

guide word(s) A word at the head of a column or a page which repeats the first, or the last entry on that page. Guide words often appear in pairs at the top of a page, indicating the first and last entries on that page.

headword The main **entry**; the alphabetized listing by which the word or expression that is being defined is identified; it indicates preferred spelling, capitalization, and syllabication.

homograph(s) Words that are spelled the same way but often pronounced differently, and that have different meanings and different **etymologies.**

homonym *See* **homophone**.

homophone(s) Sometimes called **homonyms**, especially in the elementary grades; words that are written differently, and that often have different meanings, but which sound alike.

idiom(s) An expression, the meaning of which cannot be worked out from its separate parts; an expression, usually of two or more words, that functions as a single unit and that conveys distinctive meanings in a particular language.

inflected form(s) The alteration of a word to show a change in meaning or grammatical function (such as number, person, tense, etc.).

inflection Changing a word in some way according to the rules of grammar.

IPA International Phonetic Association; also International Phonetic Alphabet. IPA designates a phonetic pronunciation system (often used in ESL, bi-dialectic, and bilingual dictionaries, as well as in general dictionaries).

key *See* **pronunciation key**.

label A brief caption for an illustration. *See also* **field label**; **style label**; **usage label**.

lexicographer One who compiles or writes a dictionary.

lexicon A dictionary; the set (collection) of all the words and idioms of a language; also refers to a dictionary's main (A to Z) **vocabulary.**

linguistics The science of language; the study of the nature and structure of human speech and communication.

main entry *See* **entry** and **entry term.**

meaning That which the language in general, or a word in particular, represents or expresses.

nonstandard A label used in some dictionaries to indicate words or usage not considered acceptable in all circumstances, or that are regionalisms, slang, colloquialisms, vulgarisms, or taboo.

phonemic Notation of the smallest speech units that may be pronounced differently by different people. The phonemic alphabet, developed by George L. Trager and Henry L. Smith, Jr., is often called the Trager-Smith or T-S system. *See* chart in this chapter.

phonetic Notation of actual speech sounds with a distinct set of symbols, each representing a particular sound or articulation. American English has about forty-five distinctive speech sounds. *See* chart in this chapter.

pronunciation(s) The way sounds of speech are produced and the way these are symbolized in the dictionary, either in **phonetic** or **phonemic** system.

pronunciation key A guide to pronunciation used in a particular dictionary.

respelling Spelling a word again using letters or symbols to represent a phonetic alphabet.

run-on entry(ies) Also called *run-on derivatives* or *run-on(s)*. A word added to the end of an entry that is related to the main term, usually one. Created by adding or dropping suffixes (such as *-ly, -er, -tion, -ness, -ity, -ment*, etc.), the meaning of which is understood from the form of the word to which it is added; a subordinate entry to the main **entry.**

semi-abridged A category of adult dictionary, intermediate in size between **college** and **unabridged** dictionaries, having approximately 250,000 or slightly more entries.

standard A label that refers to words or usage generally recognized and accepted as correct by all native speakers of the language.

style label A term which denotes a level (social or cultural) of usage.

syllabication Word division; the division of a word into syllables to show spelling, hyphenation at the end of lines of writing or printing, or pronunciation; usually denoted by a centered period, a space, or other symbol.

synonym A word that can be substituted for another word that is very close in meaning. **Discrimination** of synonyms involves describing the context in which words with near but not exact meanings are used.

synonym study A longer descriptive paragraph in a dictionary or thesaurus that lists and illustrates a variety of synonyms; **antonyms** are often included.

thumb index or **thumb tab** A finding aid in larger dictionaries.

unabridged Not condensed; a category of dictionary of over 300,000 and up to about 600,000 entries that provides full coverage of the lexicon of a language that is in general use; quotations are provided to support definitions and to illustrate context and varieties of usage.

usage How a language is actually used; the ways people write or speak a language; also, more loosely, a prescriptive indication of how to use or when to use designated grammar, meanings, idioms, or other forms of language.

usage label Information given in dictionaries to identify restrictive or special usage of a particular word or phrase; usage labels can show regional, technical, temporal, or cultural, or other restrictions of a word.

vocabulary A **glossary** or **lexicon**; a list of words arranged and defined in alphabetical order; all the words and **idioms** of a language. *See also* **lexicon.**

variant(s) A slight difference in the form of a word, such as a different spelling or pronunciation.

word history A term used often in elementary dictionaries for a short "biography" of a word; also an **etymology.**

Chapter 10
Evaluations of Dictionaries

The American Heritage Children's Dictionary

Facts at a Glance

Full Title: **The American Heritage Children's Dictionary.**

Former Title: Children's Dictionary, An American Heritage Dictionary.

Publisher: Houghton Mifflin Company.

Editors: Anne H. Soukhanov, Pamela B. DeVinne, and Kaethe Ellis.

Edition Reviewed: © 1986.

Number of Volumes: 1.

Number of Entries: 36,000.

Number of Pages: 864.

Number of Illustrations: 1,500 in full color.

Number of Maps: 5 in full color.

Trim Size: 7½″ × 9⅞″.

Binding: cloth.

Price: $13.95.

Intended Readership: grades 3 through 6; ages 8 through 12.

Sold in bookstores and other outlets; also sold to libraries and schools. ISBN 0-395-42529-8.

I. Introduction

The American Heritage Children's Dictionary is one of a series of four dictionaries designed for preschool through ninth grade from Houghton Mifflin. This one follows THE AMERICAN HERITAGE FIRST DICTIONARY (also reviewed in this Buying Guide) and is intended for students in third to sixth grade, with particular emphasis on imparting skills in dictionary use. It is a substantial dictionary for this age level with 36,000 entry words and definitions, enhanced by 1,500 full color photographs and drawings. In addition, many special features are incorporated into the body of the dictionary.

The American Heritage Children's Dictionary

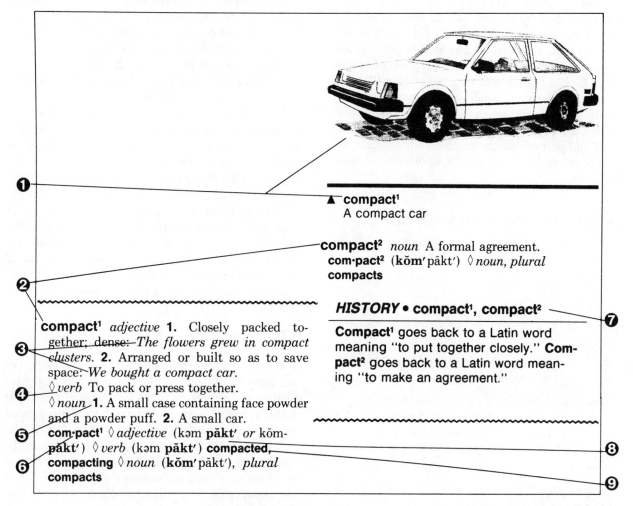

▲ **compact¹**
A compact car

compact² *noun* A formal agreement.
com·pact² (kŏm′pākt′) ◊ *noun, plural*
compacts

compact¹ *adjective* **1.** Closely packed together; dense: *The flowers grew in compact
clusters.* **2.** Arranged or built so as to save
space: *We bought a compact car.*
◊ *verb* To pack or press together.
◊ *noun* **1.** A small case containing face powder
and a powder puff. **2.** A small car.
com·pact¹ ◊ *adjective* (kəm **pākt′** *or* kŏm-
pākt′) ◊ *verb* (kəm **pākt′**) **compacted,
compacting** ◊ *noun* (**kŏm′**pākt′), *plural*
compacts

HISTORY • compact¹, compact²

Compact¹ goes back to a Latin word
meaning "to put together closely." **Compact²** goes back to a Latin word meaning "to make an agreement."

❶ Full color illustration of a first definition's second sense
❷ Main entries are in boldface type; homographs are indicated by superior numbers
❸ Sample sentences show how an entry word is used
❹ Part of speech, in italic, is spelled out
❺ Each part of speech is followed by a definition; separate meanings are introduced with boldface numbers
❻ Syllables are divided by boldface dots
❼ Simple etymology is given in a "Word History" paragraph for
all homographs; each meaning is indicated by superior numbers
❽ Pronunciations are given in parentheses, with the stressed syllable in boldface type
❾ Inflected forms are shown in boldface

II. Authority

Houghton Mifflin Company is the publisher of the highly acclaimed adult dictionary, *The American Heritage Dictionary of the English Language.* The editors of the *Children's Dictionary* are members of the publisher's permanent lexicographic staff. According to the publisher, "the word list is based on a computerized study of the words that children need and use."

III. Comprehensiveness

The dictionary seems to be fairly up-to-date, with many computer words and space science terms included; for example, **disk (2.), input, astronautics,** and **lunar module**. States of the United States are excluded as main entries; however, their standard and ZIP code abbreviations are included, as are many other abbreviations students might seek, such as **etc.**, **R.R.**, and **St.** Information provided is, for this age level, comprehensive. Entries include part of speech labels (in italics), the meaning and often a sentence of extra information, usually an illustrative sentence (in italics). Where appropriate, idioms and homophones are provided. At the end of the entry, the word and part of speech are repeated, and pronunciation, syllabication, and plurals, or other word forms are given.

IV. Quality and Currency of Entries

Definitions are accurate, concise, and clear. Technical terms are clarified for the general reader, for example:

> **disk**. . . 2. A flexible circular plate coated with magnetic material on which computer programs and data can be stored.

Emotions and terms dealing with religion are particularly well defined, for example:

> **fear** *noun* A feeling caused by a sense of danger or the expectation that something harmful or evil may happen. ◇ *verb* 1. To be afraid of: *You have nothing to fear*. 2. To have a very uneasy feeling: *I feared that you were lost*.

> **heaven** *noun* 1. Often **heavens** The sky over the earth; upper regions of the air: *Stars twinkled in the heavens*. 2. Often **Heaven** In Christianity and some other religions, the dwelling place of God and the angels. 3. A place of great happiness: *The cool forest was heaven on a hot day*.

V. Syllabication and Pronunciation

Syllabication is clearly indicated with heavy, dark dots. Pronunciation is explained in a full key as well as in short keys, emphasizing vowels, on all left-hand pages. Age-appropriate sample words make the keys easy to follow. Alternative pronunciations are provided following the presentation of standard American pronunciation.

VI. Special Features

Many special features can be found throughout the book, and they are presented in a clearly labeled guide, written for students, in the introduction. Within the dictionary itself are many color-coded boxes that contain synonyms, word histories, "Vocabulary Builders," i.e., prefixes and suffixes, such as **re-** for words that are not in the dictionary, and "Language Detective" discussions of regional variations in vocabulary. Color coding enables the interested student to seek out particular types of information, and the concise presentation will stimulate interest in language and language acquisition. The short key to pronunciation on left-hand pages will be especially useful to the young student unaccustomed to seeking such information elsewhere in a dictionary. Appended to the dictionary is a very brief thesaurus of synonyms and antonyms that are appropriate for the age group. There is also a short listing of facts about each U.S. state presented in a color box with the state flag printed in color, as well as five clear, attractive maps: one double-page map of the world with subsidiary maps of Europe and the Middle East, and a United States map with a subsidiary map of Alaska.

VII. Accessibility

A magenta-colored strip along the outside margin of the right-hand pages contains the letters of the alphabet and serves as a kind of thumb index, but without perforations. For letters *A* to *G* it is printed on the upper third of the pages, *H* to *Q* is in the middle, and *R* to *Z* is at the lower third. Guide words, the first and last word defined on the page, are printed in white on a magenta border that stretches across the top of pages, as "dignified·dinner." Alphabetization is letter by letter, not word by word, which results in such sequences as **point . . . pointer . . . point of view** and **Romance language . . . Roman numeral**. Entry words and subentries are in bold sans serif, word forms and subentries are in italics, pronunciation is in parentheses, and the definition is in roman type. The typographic design facilitates access to the variety of information, enabling students quickly to locate the information they need. The sequence of information in entries is problematic in its placement of pronunciation at the end of the entry. Students must read, in order, the word as a main entry, the sentence of further explanation, and the illustrative sentence before they learn how the word is pronounced. An example of this is

> **monopoly** *noun* 1. Complete control over a product or service: *The electric company has a monopoly on electricity*. 2. A group or person having a monopoly.
>
> **mo·nop·o·ly** (mə **nŏp′** ə lē) ◇ *noun, plural* **monopolies**.

VIII. Graphics and Format

Each page of the dictionary is divided into two distinct columns. Special features are blocked off and color coded. Illustrations and photographs are labeled with main entry words. The illustrations are colorful, relevant, and of an appropriate size, as are the very sharp photographs. Racial and gender bias have been avoided. Examples are: a man and two women, comprising three racial types, wearing **helmets**; a black female **shortstop**. Typefaces are easy to read, and print is sufficiently large. The book is printed on coated white paper with minimal show-through of text. Boldfaced main entry words overhang the text. The book is sturdily bound and will hold up well to steady use by students.

IX. Summary

The American Heritage Children's Dictionary contains solid information in an attractive format that encourages browsing. Special features throughout will facilitate elementary students' language acquisition as well as their awareness of and interest in language. This should be a standard reference work in public and school libraries and is also a good home desk dictionary for elementary school age children.

The American Heritage Desk Dictionary

Facts at a Glance

Full Title: **The American Heritage Desk Dictionary.**
Publisher: Houghton Mifflin Company.
Editors: Fernando de Mello Vianna, Editor-in-Chief; Anne D. Steinhardt and Mark Boyer.
Edition Reviewed: © 1981.

Number of Volumes: 1.
Number of Entries: more than 100,000.
Number of Pages: 1,184.
Number of Illustrations: more than 1,500 black-and-white photographs and line drawings.
Trim Size: $6\frac{3}{4}'' \times 9\frac{9}{16}''$.
Binding: cloth.

Price: $10.95.
Intended Readership: high school, college, and up.
Sold in bookstores and other outlets; also sold to libraries and schools. ISBN 0-395-31256-6.

I. Introduction

The American Heritage Desk Dictionary, published in 1981, is the second largest of the dictionaries in the American Heritage "family." The publishers describe the desk version as "an entirely new comprehensive dictionary for home, school, and office . . . that reflects the basic lexicographic approach" of THE AMERICAN HERITAGE DICTIONARY. The main features of that approach were: (a) an attempt to place the most current central meaning of a word first in a definition and then to add other meanings in logical sequence; and (b) guidance on using words according to "educated" speech with "grace and precision." Both approaches are evident in this desk dictionary, and "Usage Notes," based on the opinions of the celebrated Usage Panel for the parent work are included.

The vocabulary consists of more than 100,000 entries, plus 2,500 biographical and geographic entries. According to the publisher, the synonym paragraphs reflect the extensive work that went into the preparation of the ROGET'S II: THE NEW THESAURUS (1980), published by the same company.

The desk dictionary's design and page layout differ considerably from the other American Heritage dictionaries, although similar, extensive use is made of photographs. In this desk volume, they are larger, printed more clearly, and hence more useful.

II. Authority

Houghton Mifflin's lexicographic staff prepared this desk dictionary under the guidance of Fernando de Mello Vianna, who was also Editor-in-Chief of the publisher's respected ROGET'S II: THE NEW THESAURUS. The American Heritage family of dictionaries is well known, and the dictionaries have generally received excellent reviews.

Considerable effort has been made to reflect contemporary usage and meaning in this, as in other American Heritage dictionaries. In appearance, this desk dictionary is a model of contemporary, accessible design; the many photographs are generally good and appropriate for the entries.

III. Comprehensiveness

For an abridged work with a typeface large enough to be read with ease, the desk dictionary is comprehensive enough for most students as a general, everyday reference. The dictionary does not have the extensive number of scientific and technological terms

The American Heritage Desk Dictionary

❶ Definitions are ordered with most current, central meaning first

❷ Usage labels are spelled out in italics

❸ Idioms are labeled in boldface and defined

❹ Line drawing illustrates second homograph

❺ Example phrases or sentence are italicized

❻ Etymologies, with terms spelled out, included in brackets

date¹ (dāt) *n.* **1. a.** Time stated in terms of the month, day, and year or any of these: *The date was May 13, 1851.* **b.** A statement of calendar time, as on a document. **2.** The day of the month. **3.** The time when something happened or is to happen. **4.** A time or period in history: *Egyptian tombs of an early date.* **5. dates.** The years of a person's birth and death. **6.** *Informal.* **a.** An appointment, esp. an engagement to go out socially with a member of the opposite sex. **b.** A person's companion on a date. —*v.* **dat·ed, dat·ing.** —*tr.v.* **1.** To mark or supply with a date: *to date a letter.* **2.** To determine the age, time, or origin of; assign a date to: *date a fossil.* **3.** To betray the age of. **4.** *Informal.* To go on a date with. —*intr.v.* **1.** To have origin in a particular time in the past: *This statue dates from 500 B.C.* **2.** To become old-fashioned. **3.** *Informal.* To go on dates with a companion or as a couple. —*idioms.* **out of date.** No longer current, valid, or useful. **to date.** Up to the present time. **up to date.** In line with current knowledge, modern methods, or recent styles. [Middle English, from Old French, from Medieval Latin *data*, "given," "issued" (as a letter) from Latin, *dare, to give.*]
date² (dāt) *n.* The sweet, oblong, edible fruit of the date palm tree that contains a narrow, hard seed. [Middle English, from Old French, from Latin *dactylus*, from Greek *daktulos*, "finger."]

date²

---

included in the AMERICAN HERITAGE DICTIONARY: SECOND COLLEGE EDITION. There are, for example, fewer medical terms, and the level of many of them, such as **laryngectomy** (a surgical procedure), is probably more specialized than the majority of people need. If this level of vocabulary in the sciences and technologies is required, student readers will be better served with textbook or special glossaries.

A comparison of a representative segment of entries from **paprika** to **parachute** shows that the AMERICAN HERITAGE DICTIONARY: SECOND COLLEGE EDITION included 22 separate entry words, while the desk dictionary has nine. In the *Second College Edition*, however, seven of the 22 separate entries are variants of **par**, **par-**, or **para**, while in the desk dictionary several of those diverse meanings are included under the entries for **par** *n.* and **para-** or **par-**. Neither the desk dictionary nor the CONCISE AMERICAN HERITAGE DICTIONARY (reviewed later in this Buying Guide) include the following entries between **paprika** and **parachute**: *Papuan n., papule, papyrika, papyrology, paraaminobenzoic acid, parabiosis, parablast,* or *paraboloid.*

Although *The American Heritage Desk Dictionary* is comprehensive for an abridged dictionary, some words that are commonly used are missing, such as *videocassette* and *aerobics.*

IV. Quality and Currency of Entries

Entries include: boldface syllabication, pronunciation with abbreviated variations given in parentheses, italicized part-of-speech, abbreviation, definitions, variant word forms with the parts of speech indicated, usage information for some entries, and etymology or source.

Definitions are, in general, concise and easy to understand. Frequent italicized short examples (phrases or brief sentences) immediately following many of the meanings will be especially helpful to students just beginning to use an adult dictionary. These examples are often lively and contemporary. For example, see:

> **fend** *tr. v.* To keep off; repel. *He used an oar to fend off the sharks,*

or

> **a·bol·ish** *tr. v.* To do away with; put an end to: *We must abolish sexism.*

When such examples are quotations, the author is cited.

The order of defined meanings tends to present the most widely used meaning first, as in:

ab·ra·ca·dab·ra *n*. **1**. A word once held to possess magical powers to ward off disease or disaster. **2**. Jargon; gibberish.

The terms in the etymologies are spelled out in full and, therefore, will probably be read even by younger students, as, for example, the one for **abracadabra**:

[Late Latin, from late Greek *abrasadebra*, a magic word used by an ancient religious sect.]

Where necessary, words that are, in fact, short forms are noted: **graph**, for example, is defined as "short for graphic formula." Synonyms are listed after the appropriate meaning or cross-referenced. For **lapse**, the cross reference is "—See Syns at **error**." Then, at **error**, a synonym list appears that includes a fuller definition of **slip-up**:

(*Informal*) *n. Core meaning:* An unintentional deviation from what is correct, right, or true (*an error in judgment*).

The "core meaning" is derived from the first definition of a word appearing in ROGET'S II: THE NEW THESAURUS, and differs from the main entry for **slip-up**:

n. Informal:

An error; oversight; mistake. —See Syns at error.

The insertion of the core meanings for selected synonyms is one method this work uses for condensing material. But it also helps the reader who is searching for a more complete definition of the word or a synonym.

Several other features are especially helpful to students, including the identification of homographs, listing of prefixes and suffixes, and listing of plural forms of verbs.

Homographs, words that have distinct meanings but that are spelled alike, such as **lark**, a bird, or **lark**, a carefree adventure, are included as separate numbered entries. Prefixes and suffixes (**-ish**, etc.) are also separate entries with definitions and etymologies. For more complete spelling reference, plural forms of words follow main entry words, but are *also* listed separately if they are variant forms. Compare "**lar·ynx** *n*. pl. **larynges** or **-ynxes**" with the sep-

arate entry, "**laryn·ges** *n*. A plural of **larynx**." Similarly, prefixes and prefix variant forms appear as separate bold entries: "**laryng-**. Var. of **laryngo-**."

Idiomatic usage is clearly labeled and defined, with multiple meanings when necessary. For the entry **large**, under the label **-idioms.**, the idiomatic phrase **at large** has four defined meanings followed by a definition of **by and large**.

The usage notes following definitions seem up-to-date and useful in the desk dictionary. Under the entry **chair**, for example, a usage note appears:

chair, chairman, chairperson. These three nouns are interchangeably used to refer to one who presides over a group. The terms chair and chairman can also be used as verbs.

This usage note is absent in THE AMERICAN HERITAGE DICTIONARY: SECOND COLLEGE EDITION.

A comparison of particular definitions, from the desk dictionary and the college work may be of special interest to potential buyers:

From the desk dictionary:
fem·i·nism *n*. **1**. A doctrine that advocates the political, social, and economic equality of men and women. **2**. Activity undertaken in support of the doctrine of feminism.

From the college dictionary:
fem·i·nism *n*. **1**. A doctrine that advocates or demands for women the same rights granted men, as in political and economic status. **2**. The movement in support of feminism.

From the desk dictionary:
rac·ism *n*. Racial prejudice or discrimination.

From the college dictionary:
rac·ism *n*. **1**. The notion that one's own ethnic stock is superior. **2**. Discrimination or prejudice based on racism.

As the reviewer for *American Reference Books Annual 1983* commented, "Naturally, this variant [the desk dictionary] relies heavily on *AHD* . . . the reductions in entries and definitions produced some cases of circularity [but] on the whole, a solid piece of work. . . ." The vocabulary and phrasing of many entries in the *Desk Dictionary* does rely on THE AMERICAN HERITAGE DICTIONARY: SECOND COLLEGE EDITION, as a comparison of one brief segment of entries (chosen at random)—from **paprika** to **parachute**—shows. Some entries in the desk version have been shortened by omission of secondary meanings, or a few words. In the desk dictionary, **paprika** is defined as "A mild, powdered seasoning made from sweet red peppers." In the college dictionary, that is the first meaning, followed by a second, which is omitted in the desk version: "A dark to deep or vivid reddish orange."

Another representative entry, **Pap test**, shows how the two dictionaries define an entry from a specialist field such as medicine. In the *Desk*, **Pap test** is defined:

A test in which a smear of bodily secretion is immediately fixed and examined to detect cancer in an early stage. Also called **Pap smear**. [Invented by George Papanicolaou (1883–1962), American scientist.]

In the college dictionary, **Pap smear** is a separate entry word, the definition of **Pap test** is more detailed and includes a field label:

A test in which a smear of a bodily secretion, esp. from the cervix or vagina, is immediately fixed and examined for exfoliated cells to detect cancer in an early stage or to evaluate hormonal condition. [After George Papanicolaou (1883–1962), its inventor.]

This simple comparison shows that the desk version is especially helpful for students who are beginning to use an adult dictionary and for readers who need a quick, understandable definition, but not necessarily the scientific detail of a phrase such as "exfoliated cells."

V. Syllabication and Pronunciation

As in other American Heritage dictionaries, centered bold dots divide syllables in all the main entries: **mor·a·to·ri·um**. Hyphens in compound words are retained, but syllable division is not if a word in a compound appears elsewhere as a separate entry: an example is **bituminous coal**. Syllable divisions follow modern printing and editorial practice.

Pronunciation symbols are given for all main entries and other forms as required. The pronunciation key appears in a large chart with a good explanation at the front of the dictionary. The symbols used are "designed to enable the reader to reproduce a satisfactory pronunciation with no more than a quick reference to the key." A shortened form of the key is printed at the bottom of each page of the dictionary for quick reference. The system of symbols is common to all the American Heritage dictionaries, and the publisher states that "all pronunciations given

are acceptable in all circumstances," meaning in formal as well as in informal circumstances. If more than one pronunciation is listed for a word, the first is assumed to be more common:

pan·zer (păn′zər, păn′sər, pänt′sər).

In addition, there are clear notes on special symbols that may be less familiar, such as the schwa: ə. Primary and secondary stress is indicated with bold and lighter face marks: "păn′tə-mīm′."

VI. Special Features

Tables are located at the end of the dictionary's entries and include: a "Guide to the Metric System," a "Periodic Table of Elements," proofreaders' marks, symbols and signs, and alphabets.

Following the tables are separate sections of biographical and geographic entries, totaling approximately 2,500 entries. These are set in three columns of type per page and are easy to read and very brief. Biographical entries include appropriate part-of-speech labels (**Chaucerian** is identified as both an adjective and a noun). The names of popes and kings, such as Pius and George, which are differentiated only by roman numerals, are listed as separate entries. Variant spellings are entered for geographic names. Neither section is current for dates or population figures after the early 1980s.

The ready accessibility of the special features at the end of the *Desk Dictionary* make it useful for quick reference; however, for more in-depth research, the reader would require specialized sources.

A brief list of standard abbreviations is included at the end of the book, as well as an extensive, separate listing of abbreviations used in the dictionary's entries of field labels, and of abbreviations used in the etymologies and in the biographical and geographic entries. This gathering of all abbreviations used in the dictionary is an excellent idea, providing users with an easily accessible reference page.

Other special features, conveniently explained in "How to Use Your Dictionary" at the front of the volume, include:

(1) *Synonym Studies*, both short and long paragraphs listing parts of speech, core meaning, and giving examples;

(2) *Usage Notes*, based on the opinions of the Usage Panel for the parent work whose members are listed at the front of the desk edition. These notes are not, the publisher says, "prescriptions. . . . Rather

they reflect standard American English as it is written and spoken by educated users today." The publisher also indicates that these notes "are designed to help you express yourself fluently, clearly, and concisely in formal and informal settings—and in such a way as to avoid criticism"—clearly, a rather large claim; and, in addition;

(3) *Alphabet Letter Histories*, which appear on the first page of each alphabetical sequence, tracing the 3,000 or so years of a letter's past. These are condensed versions of a feature in THE AMERICAN HERITAGE DICTIONARY: SECOND COLLEGE EDITION; in the desk volume, they are more a narrative than an orthographical history.

Another feature is the eight-page "Manual of Style" with four main sections: punctuation, capitalization, use of italics, and business letters. There are brief examples covering most typical problems in the first three sections and four styles of business letter formats used in current correspondence—all will be useful for students.

VII. Accessibility

All entries, including compound words, are arranged in strict letter-by-letter alphabetical order. The two-column format with boldface main entries—printed in a readable size overhanging the text—makes this dictionary easy to read. Inflected forms of a word, numbers preceding definitions with an entry, cross-referenced words, and labels for phrasal, modifying, and idiomatic examples (—**phrasal verbs,** —**modifier,** —**idiom**) are printed in sans-serif bold type and are easily found within entries. Synonym lists are placed in separate paragraphs following the main body of an entry.

The use of easily readable type plus the listing of special features such as synonyms and idiomatic examples within each entry makes it easier for a user to find cross-references and variant forms of words.

A special effort has been made in the "How to . . ." section to define and to explain what a dictionary is and what its various parts are intended to do—in general and in this volume in particular. This section will be especially useful to teachers and to those students who study it.

A brief contents appears immediately after the title page and lists the tables in the appendix except for "Symbols and Signs" (presumably an oversight). The separate biographical and geographic entries follow the tables, and the list of abbreviations is located handily at the extreme back of the book.

VIII. Graphics and Format

The quality varies among the over 1,500 captioned illustrations, all in the main vocabulary. Some pictures appear "muddy," but most are clear and useful. The size of the illustrations ranges from 2¼ inches wide and 1½ inches high to slightly larger. This means that the objects in the pictures are much more visible than in other illustrated American Heritage dictionaries. Furthermore, the white, relatively opaque paper makes the photographs seem clearer in contrast.

The drawings of human anatomy are simple and clear, many with small, but readable labels. The line drawings of flowers and of birds are exceptionally clear and detailed. Many photographs are excellent (e.g., that of screech owls). The pictures have been well cropped, generally, so that the detail intended to illustrate an entry is apparent (there are, of course, exceptions, the **hookah** cannot be seen in one photo). Occasionally drawings and up-to-date photographs illustrate several kinds of a defined object (e.g., **nail** and **triangle**) or variations in meaning (**afghan rug** and **afghan hound**). There are no portraits included in the biographical section nor maps in the geographic section.

The overall graphic design of the dictionary is attractive—with the notable exception of the "Style Manual" at the front of the book. This displays too much white space between letters, which distracts readers. To be fair, the "Style Manual" design is a minor aberration in an otherwise easy-to-read book.

IX. Summary

The American Heritage Desk Dictionary is a useful dictionary with fewer special features than its larger, but complementary companion, THE AMERICAN HERITAGE DICTIONARY: SECOND COLLEGE EDITION. For everyday use, many students will find this a good choice because access is easy, the typeface is readable, the paper quality is good, the ink does not smear or rub off, and the binding is sturdy. The generous number of illustrations, well spaced in the two columns of entries, gives the pages a more open and attractive look than is usual in dictionaries. In addition to its physical features, the simplified definitions are clear and well written. The synonym paragraphs may be especially useful for students writing letters or high school level papers. The introductory matter is condensed but, nevertheless, useful for most everyday questions about how to use this dictionary or matters of writing style such as capitalization. College preparatory students will need a more extensive dictionary, despite this volume's merits.

The American Heritage Dictionary

❶ Pronunciation of irregular inflected form provided in parentheses

❷ Usage labels are spelled out in italics

❸ A paragraph of usage notes follows the definitions

❹ Illustrative phrases in italics give examples of usage

❺ Phrasal verbs and idioms, in bold, are introduced by bold, italic labels

❻ Etymology provided within square brackets

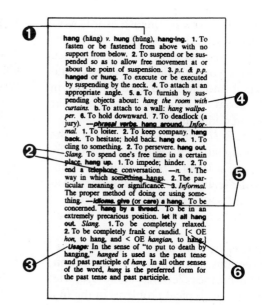

The American Heritage Desk Dictionary is generally recommended for student use in the classroom or the home, and also for school libraries, as a concise, accurate, desk-top reference volume.

The American Heritage Dictionary

Facts at a Glance

Full Title: **The American Heritage Dictionary.**
Publisher: Dell Publishing Co.
Editors: Susan Moldow (Dell); Mark Boyer, Kaethe Ellis, Dolores R. Harris, and Anne H. Soukanov (Houghton Mifflin).
Edition Reviewed: © 1983; July 1985 printing.

Number of Volumes: 1.
Number of Definitions: about 60,000.
Number of Pages: 880.
Number of Illustrations: over 415.
Trim Size: 4¾″ × 6¾″.
Binding: paperback.

Price: $4.95.
Intended Readership: junior high school through adult.
Sold in bookstores and other outlets; also sold to libraries and schools. ISBN 0-440-10068-2.

I. Introduction

The 1983 Dell paperback edition of *The American Heritage Dictionary* is based on THE AMERICAN HERITAGE DICTIONARY: SECOND COLLEGE EDITION, published in 1983 by Houghton Mifflin. The preface to the Dell edition states that "it is an independent reference work embodying in smaller form the additions of the parent *Second College Edition* book." This refers to the general and technical words that were added to the AHD: SECOND COLLEGE EDITION to reflect more current vocabulary and use. The vocabulary and length of entries in the Dell edition are more like those in the desk-size CONCISE AMERICAN HERITAGE DICTIONARY, although there are some differences. (The etymologies and word sources, for example, are even shorter in the paperback than in the *Concise AHD*).

The Dell version, however, readily serves as a portable, simplified version of its parent dictionary. Although the type size is very small, entries are suitable for most readers from junior high level to adult. Some brief usage notes, based on the opinions of *The American Heritage Dictionary*'s Usage Panel, are included. There are approximately 60,000 definitions and more than 415 photographs and line drawings. Separate biographical and geographic entries appear at the back of the book.

II. Authority

Dell, a publisher of several quality paperback imprints, began publishing paperback editions of the American Heritage family of dictionaries in 1970, a year after the original work appeared. As with the previous paperbacks, this edition was prepared by Houghton Mifflin's *American Heritage Dictionary* staff. Even though no paperback abridgment can substitute for its larger parent work, the Dell dictionary's editors have produced carefully condensed and rewritten definitions that are generally reliable. Given the size limitations of the format, this dictionary manages to retain a family resemblance to the respected parent work.

III. Comprehensiveness

The 60,000 definitions, claimed by the publisher, are not the equivalent of main entries. The number of main boldface entry words and terms is slightly over 31,300. The quantity of entries and definitions is probably sufficient for most junior high school students and for quick, everyday high school and adult reference purposes, depending on the extent of the reader's needs.

Separate lists of words derived from combined forms do incorporate more vocabulary and spellings. Placed on the lower half of pages and separated from the text by rules, these lists include the common compound words formed from: **de-, dis-, -mania, non-over-, phobia-, re-, un-**. The word lists for **-mania** and **-phobia** also include brief meanings.

The publisher claims that the dictionary includes "10,000 new words and meanings from business, science, and technology." But a comparison of all entries between **paprika** and **parachute** (a sample segment chosen arbitrarily) from the paperback and from the AHD: SECOND COLLEGE EDITION shows that the paperback *excludes* most current and more advanced medical, chemical, economic, and geographic words, and also omits taxonomy and field labels. In this sample section, there are fourteen *more* main entry items in the college dictionary than in the paperback. The paperback entries in this sample sequence include

> **paprika**, **Pap test**, **papyrus**, **par**, **para**, **para-** or **par**, **parable**, **parabola**, **parachute**

(all these words are in the larger work, too). The following entries from the college edition are omitted in the paper edition:

> **Pap smear**, **Papuan**, **papule**, **papyri**, **papyrology**, several forms of **par/-para**, **paraaminobenzoic acid**, **parabiosis**, **parablast**, **parabolic**, and **paraboloid**.

High school and adult users may need a larger dictionary for science entries, but junior high school readers may find this paperback sufficient.

The approximately 1,000 biographical and 1,500 geographic entries may serve for minimal quick reference in everyday contexts. The list of abbreviations needs revision. It includes a selected range, from those most frequently encountered, such as **a.k.a.** (also known as), to some not so frequent, such as **LOOM** (Loyal Order of Moose). Some areas of abbreviations are not well covered: the titles of "**Mdm.** Madam" and "**Mr.** Mister" are included, but not *Mrs.*, or *Ms.*

IV. Quality and Currency of Entries

The entries appear in strict letter-by-letter alphabetical order. The general sequence of information in the entries is: boldface main word; pronunciation(s); part of speech; inflected form(s); stylistic or field label; definition (numbered, when necessary); very brief etymology or source; other parts of speech; verbal phrases; and idioms. A cross-reference is substituted in some cases for a definition: "**par·a** *n*. See table at **currency**. [Turk.]." The definitions are generally clear, and often considerably shorter than in the parent work. Occasionally, an explanation of the source words for entries, such as **gerrymander** and **hobby**, is omitted. In other cases, only the source language is cited; for example, [F.] French or [G.] German. The shortened usage notes are sometimes less confusing than the extended examples in the larger work. One example of improvement in the Dell edition is the briefer explanation of **who**: because it is more concise, the explanation makes the difference between **who** and **whom** clearer for students.

There are fewer stylistic and field labels in the paperback. Regional *area* labels are simplified to one term: "regional." Poetic use of words such as **o'er** is labeled. Some meanings of a few words are labeled *Chiefly Brit.* when appropriate, but this is not indicated in the "Guide to the Dictionary." Some field labels such as *Math.* or *Mus.* (music) are included. Special use in a field is indicated, if necessary, in the definitions: **neoclassicism** is described by the phrase "esp. in art, music, and literature." Words or senses that are idiomatic or capitalized in special senses are labeled and briefly defined. Entries for verbs such as **be** include a chart of tenses.

The first definition of a word is the "central meaning about which the other senses can be logically organized," according to the "Guide to the Dictionary." This order is not necessarily historical or the most current. Examples of numbered, different meanings in definitions are usually phrases. Chemical symbols are included as separate entries and are also labeled within entries: "**ne·on** *n.* *Symbol* Ne." The synonym paragraphs, which had examples in the larger work, are cut to occasional brief lists, but the synonyms do appear as separate entry words.

The publisher states that "10,000 new words and meanings from business, science, and technology" are included, but some words in current use are not entered, such as *heuristic*, *modem*, and *mainframe*, as well as computer science meanings for the terms *disc*, *disk*, or *floppy*. **Software** is included. Most advanced terms in the sciences are absent, as noted earlier.

The definitions, as simplified or rewritten, may be more useful or immediately understandable to a wider audience. An example is the entry **papyrus**. In the college work, the first entry reads:

> **pa·py·rus 1**. A tall aquatic sedge, *Cyperus papyrus*, of southern Europe and northern Africa.

The Dell paperback version reads:

> **pa·py·rus 1**. A tall, grasslike water plant of northern Africa.

V. Syllabication and Pronunciation

All main entries are divided into syllables, by centered dots as in "**hin·ter·land**," which represents current printing practice. As in the parent work, entries consisting of more than one word are not broken into syllables or given pronunciations if the separate words appear as main entries themselves.

Pronunciations, based on THE AMERICAN HERITAGE DICTIONARY's clear, phonetic system—intended to reflect "educated" speech—follow all main entries and are given for other word forms as needed: see the entry for "**sto·ic** (stō·ĭk) *n.*" as well as for its adjective form, "-*adj.* Also **sto·i·cal** (-ĭ-kol)." For many junior high age readers, the pronunciation symbols will seem complex, but most high school students will find them useful. Additionally, the pronunciations are briefly but clearly explained in the "Guide to the Dictionary" preceding the alphabetical entries, where a pronunciation key appears with clear notes on the symbols used. Two lines of this key appear throughout the dictionary at the foot of left-hand pages—both handy and useful for readers. Primary and secondary stresses are marked, and variant pronunciations are included, as in "**il·lus·trate** (ĭl'ə-strāt', ĭ-lŭs' trāt')."

VI. Special Features

The dictionary includes nine tables at appropriate alphabetical entries. These are a table of alphabets, books of the bible, months of three principal calendars (Gregorian, Hebrew, Moslem), currency (5⅓ pages of the text), a periodic table of the elements, guide to the metric system, proofreaders' marks, roman numerals, and symbols and signs.

The 1,000 biographical entries appear in a separate appendix, illustrated with forty-one portraits of Americans and four non-Americans (J. S. Bach, Fidel Castro, Winston Churchill, and Henry VIII). Seven of the portraits are of women; three are of blacks. The usefulness of such a section is questionable and some of the identifying information is less than helpful: St. Bede's traditional epithet, "The Venerable," is omitted; James Boswell, biographer of Samuel Johnson, is listed as Scottish lawyer and writer; W. H. Auden is listed as an author, but not as a poet.

The geographic section, following the biographies, has no maps. Entries, including capital cities, are identified briefly, although some of the most recent name changes have not been included, such as Burkina Faso for Upper Volta; population figures are given but are not current. Pronunciations are included.

VII. Accessibility

The dictionary's inside back cover has an "Easy Reference Index" that shows at a glance on which page each letter of the alphabet begins. All main entries, including prefixes such as **ab-** and **post-**, appear in alphabetical order, letter by letter. Particles such as **dis-**, **-phobia**, and others appear in the main lexicon and the separate lists of compound words from which they derive are printed close by.

Italicized, succinct examples of usage are readily apparent within definitions. See, for example, under the phrasal verbs of the main entry **call**:

> **call off. 1**. To cancel or postpone. **2**. To recall; restrain: *Call off your hounds!*

Variant forms of words are printed in bold type and are easy to distinguish in the entries.

A pair of guide words is located at the top of each page, representing the first and last main entries: **culvert | curium**. Readable page numbers appear at the top of each page near the inner margins. When a usage note follows a definition, it is printed as a separate paragraph with the word "**Usage:**" in bold type.

The brief "Table of Contents" and "Guide to the Dictionary" are easily located at the front of the work. The 8½-page guide contains clearly labeled short sections that provide an overview of the dictionary and explain the parts of definitions and the information they contain. It is easy to leaf through the guide to find, for example, the list of abbreviations used in etymologies. All style labels are noted in the guide, but the one sentence explaining the field labels is not accompanied by a list or examples (buyers might be interested to know, for example, that **cricket** as well as **baseball** terms are included).

In general, the small type requires more concentration in scanning for the required entry word than is usual in dictionaries with larger type.

VIII. Graphics and Format

The entries are printed in two columns with adequate margins. The main entry words are printed in sans serif bold type overhanging the small-size text set in Times Roman. The illustrations are good, in general—often better, in fact, than those in the parent dictionary. It is interesting, for a change, to see **embryo** illustrated with a cow embryo rather than a human one. There are at least 309 photographs. Small, useful line drawings are scattered throughout the word list; some illustrate, for example, three different meanings of a word, such as those for **fluke**, **graft**, **spring**, and **splice**. The pictures have been chosen with care to illustrate words that may not be immediately recognizable from a written definition, especially to younger readers.

The captions often contain additional, useful historical or other specific information. However, some of the captions—photoreduced along with the illustrations—are flyspeck size. **Mallet**, **oil well**, **tooth**, and **thalamus** are examples of clear line drawings with almost unreadable tiny labels.

The general appearance of the dictionary is pleasant, and the pictures help to make the text look less dense on the pages. The paper is good quality newsprint stock; there is some show-through of text and pictures as in most dictionaries, but this is not obtrusive. In repeated use, ink rubs off the page onto the fingers. The attractive cover design, in a rich dark blue with red and white, emphasizes the "American Heritage" of the title. For a paperback, the laminated cover is sturdy. And even after extensive use, with deliberate "cracking" of the spine to facilitate opening the pages, the text signatures did not become detached from the spine (which is about 1½″ thick). This dictionary should stand up to repeated home or classroom use fairly well; libraries may want to rebind the work for their paperback collections.

IX. Summary

Dell's *The American Heritage Dictionary* is widely available, very popular in terms of sales figures, and is a handy, much-condensed paperback version of a respected college dictionary. Buyers should be aware

that the extensive, up-to-date vocabulary in the sciences and technology that the publisher claims is not readily apparent in the paperback. Students preparing for college will need a larger desk dictionary with fuller entries. However, this is good value for a school or classroom library's paperback collection, or for home use when students need brief guidance on spelling and meaning, or in some cases on usage and pronunciation—and when price and size are primary considerations.

The American Heritage Dictionary: Second College Edition

Facts at a Glance

Full Title: **The American Heritage Dictionary: Second College Edition.**
Publisher: Houghton Mifflin Company.
Editors: Mark Boyer, Pamela B. DeVinne, Kaethe Ellis, Dolores R. Harris, Anne H. Soukhanov, and Anne D. Steinhardt.
Edition Reviewed: © 1985.

Number of Volumes: 1.
Number of Entries: 200,000.
Number of Pages: 1,600.
Number of Indexes: 1.
Number of Illustrations: 3,000 black-and-white photographs and line drawings.
Number of Maps: 152.
Trim Size: 6¾″ × 9⁹⁄₁₆″.
Binding and Price: Cloth, thumb indexed (price: $15.95). Deluxe edition, kivar bound (price: $18.95). Large format edition (price: $24.95).

Intended Readership: high school and up.
Sold in bookstores and other outlets; also sold to libraries and schools. ISBN 0-395-32944-2.

I. Introduction

The 1985 printing of the *Second College Edition* of *The American Heritage Dictionary* is substantially the same as the 1982 version, which was the "first complete revision" of the dictionary since its original publication in 1969. The *Second College Edition* acknowledges the AHD's original purpose, in the words of former editor William Morris, "to create a new dictionary that would not only faithfully record our language but also add the sensible dimension of guidance toward grace and precision in the use of our language."

The American Heritage Dictionary:
Second College Edition

❶ Usage labels are spelled out in italics

❷ Cross-reference to usage note at other entries

❸ Credited quotations or illustrative phrases and sentences are presented in italics

❹ Usage notes provide detailed descriptive guidance and examples

❺ Illustration provided for the third defined meaning of the homograph **or³**

❻ Formal etymologies presented in brackets

or¹ (ôr; *unstressed* ər) *conj.* Used to indicate: **1. a.** An alternative, usually only before the last term of a series: *hot or cold; this, that, or the other.* **b.** The second of two alternatives, the first being preceded by *either* or *whether:* Your answer is either *ingenuous or wrong.* She didn't know whether *to laugh or cry.* **c.** Archaic. Either. **2.** A synonymous or equivalent expression: *acrophobia, or fear of great heights.* **3.** Uncertainty or indefiniteness: *two or three.* [ME, contraction of *other,* perh. < OE *oðδe.*]
  Usage: When all the elements in a series connected by *or* are singular, the verb they govern is singular: *Tom or Jack is coming. Beer, ale, or wine is included in the charge.* When all the elements are plural, the verb is plural. When the elements do not agree in number, some have suggested that the verb be governed by the element to which it is nearer: *Tom or his sisters are coming. The girls or their brother is coming. Cold symptoms or headache is the usual first sign.* Other grammarians, however, have argued that such constructions must be avoided and that substitutes be found in which the problem of agreement does not arise: *Either Tom is coming or his sisters are. The usual first sign may be either cold symptoms or a headache.* See also Usage notes at **and/or** and **no².**
or² (ôr) *Archaic.* —*conj.* Before. Followed by *ever* or *ere:* "*I doubt he will be dead or ere I come*" (Shakespeare). —*prep.* Before. [ME < OE *ǣr* and ON *ār.*]
or³ (ôr) *n.* Gold, represented in heraldic engraving by a white field sprinkled with small dots. [OFr. < Lat. *aurum.*]

or³

The basic lexicon of some "200,000 precise definitions" (according to the book jacket), is appropriate for an abridged, or desk, dictionary, is intended for "the well-informed, contemporary adult"— but is certainly suitable for high-school-age readers as well. The AHD's contemporary emphasis is apparent in the entries, definitions, and reference sections; in the special articles on language as it is used, spoken, and structured; and in the members of the Usage Panel, representing the arts, sciences, entertainment, business, industry, and politics.

More than 10,000 general vocabulary words and 5,000 scientific and technical terms were added to the AHD in 1982. The illustrations, numbering several thousand and including photographs and line drawings, have been augmented with 3,000 photographs. Separate biographical and geographic sections appear at the back of the work, with approximately 5,000 new entries apiece.

II. Authority

Houghton Mifflin is the respected publisher of *The American Heritage Dictionary*, its *Second College Edition*, and other dictionaries derived from the AHD. The original edition and its successors were well received, recommended by librarians and other knowledgeable reviewers, and have since become standard—and popular—dictionaries. Like its predecessors, the *Second College Edition* is known for distinguishing nonstandard, regional, dialect, slang, idiomatic, colloquial, vulgar, and obscene usages from standard, or educated, use.

Many eminent writers, language scholars, and men and women from a wide variety of fields are associated with this dictionary. The name of William Morris, editor of the AHD and its New College Edition, no longer appears, but two of the original staff, Anne D. Steinhardt (editor, definitions) and Kaethe Ellis (editor, biographical and geographic entries), are still listed. The credentials of the more than fifty editorial staff members are not provided, although those of the Usage Panel, chaired by Edwin P. Newman, and of the consultants are. Among the well-known members of the Usage Panel, Maya Angelou, Isaac Asimov, Daniel J. Boorstin, Dr. Robin Cook, Vine DeLoria, Jr., S. I. Hayakawa, Ismael Reed, Gloria Steinem, and William Zinsser are only a sampling. The panel members, according to the dictionary's introduction, responded to usage questions and "after careful tabulation and analysis" of their responses, the staff editors prepared more than 400 usage notes. The etymologies were "researched and evaluated" by Professor Calvert Watkins and members of Harvard University's Department of Linguistics.

Listed among the special staff consultants are Geoffrey Nunberg of Stanford University and Dwight Bolinger, both of whom contributed introductory essays on issues concerning the use of language. Lee Pedersen of Emory University wrote the opening article, a survey of the historical and cultural backgrounds of American speech and writing.

III. Comprehensiveness

As a standard college and adult desk dictionary, the

AHD is comprehensive enough to serve most general purposes. The range of words included from specialized fields, such as medicine and computer science, is more than adequate for general needs.

Along with the emphasis on contemporary vocabulary, definitions, and usage, the prescriptive features of this dictionary are a distinguishing mark; they are clear, useful, and add a considerable amount of lexicographic and stylistic information to the work. These features include labels for stylistic, field, and geographic usage; notes on preferred current usage; a "Style Manual" which is functional and brief; and short essays describing American language and its use in speech and writing. Additionally, guidance on syllabication, pronunciation, spelling variants, and synonym nuances is easy to understand, as are the brief etymologies.

The list of general abbreviations in current use and the separate geographic section with its locator maps are both helpful, although some geographical place names have not been updated: for example, *Burkina Faso* appears as **Upper Volta**, and *Harare*, the capital of Zimbabwe, appears as **Salisbury**. The biographical section can only serve as a quick reference because of the brevity of its entries; some are cryptic, at best: see, "**Grasso, Ella**. 1919–81. Amer. public official," and **Onassis**. . . . 2. **Jacqueline Bouvier Kennedy**. b. 1929. Amer. socialite and editor.

IV. Quality and Currency of Entries

The general order for entries is: boldface word; pronunciation; part of speech; inflected forms; stylistic or field label (if applicable); the definitions themselves; notes on word form, source, or etymology in square brackets; variant form(s); part(s) of speech of the variant forms (with label, such as *idiom.*, or - *phrasal verb*). Examples are interspersed in the entries as appropriate. Synonyms and usage notes follow in separate paragraphs; both often include extensive examples. The usage notes contain prescriptive opinions of the Usage Panel.

The definitions present "the most prevalent, contemporary sense of meaning of a word first"—this is not, however, as claimed by the publisher, "unique" to the AHD; the feature emphasizes currency, and is also used in, for example, THE RANDOM HOUSE COLLEGE DICTIONARY. In general, the definitions are understandable, accurate, and cover an accepted range of meanings. Occasionally, the necessity for being concise leads to cursory definitions that assume background knowledge on the part of the reader; however, the intended readership *is* designated as "well-informed." Although the small typeface indicates a college or adult level reader, most entries could be read with little difficulty by students from ninth grade upwards, for example:

> **lift·off** *n.* The initial movement by which or instant in which a rocket or other craft commences flight.

When a word has *more* than one sense, the succeeding definitions are ordered analytically, rather than historically or by frequency of use, and go from a central meaning to related or separate senses. A short example is:

> **cyn·i·cal** *adj.* **1.** Scornful of the motives or virtue of others. **2.** Bitterly mocking; sneering.

Italicized words, phrases, or sentences are often used to demonstrate a particular meaning; the source of some, but not all, examples is cited.

One entry from the 1982 edition, cited by ALA *Booklist* (August 1983), was "**channel bass** *n.* A fish, the red drum" has become less clear in the revised *Second College Edition*: "**channel bass** *n.* The red drum." A reader who does not realize that bass refers to a fish, will have to look up "**red drum** *n.* A food fish, etc.," or remain puzzled. Although few entries are as brief as channel bass, some do suffer from brevity. **Blue point**, for example, is defined as a noun (an oyster), but not as an adjective referring to a type of domestic cat. Although cross-referenced to who, **whom** is defined merely as "*pron.* The objective case of **who**." The use of whom is troublesome for many students. Even though there are good usage examples under the **who** headword, with explanations of the grammatical difficulties, readers would be more readily served with some guidance at **whom**.

Brevity appears to be the culprit in other representative cases of less than satisfactory definitions. There is a tendency toward circularity, a hazard in all dictionaries where space is at a premium. The definition of **black comedy**, for example, reads "Comedy that uses **black humor**," which requires the reader to consult the entry on **black humor** to complete the definition. Similarly, **mesmerism**, defined in the first instance as "Hypnotic induction believed to involve animal magnetism," is not clarified by looking up "**animal magnetism** *n.* **1.** Hypnotism or mesmerism." Another problem involves the presumed knowledge of contexts that are not explained in a brief definition. For example, the entry "**Bunyanesque** *adj.*" refers to John Bunyan's allegorical style as well as to Paul Bunyan. John Bunyan's work, *The Pilgrim's Progress*, is not mentioned, and it is arguable whether the majority of students today will grasp the meaning of Bunyanesque from the word "allegorical" in the brief definition.

The claim that words are first defined according to their "most prevalent, contemporary sense," is broadly accurate. For example, the first definition of **believe** (transitive verb) is given as "To accept as true or real." **Skirmish** is first defined as "A minor encounter in war between small bodies of troops, often as part of larger movement," and then as a "minor or preliminary conflict or dispute." But there are enough instances of first definitions that seem unlikely to strike a student as current to suggest that the claim needs qualification. Compare the sequence of definitions for **ben·e·fit of cler·gy**:

> *n.* 1. Exemption from trial or punishment in a civil court given to clergy in the Middle Ages. 2. The authorized sanction of a religious rite: *co-habiting without benefit of clergy.*

Or **skinny**, first defined as "Of, pertaining to, or resembling skin," and secondly, as "very thin." And will readers consider "parched with the heat of the sun" the most prevalent, or current, definition of **torrid**?

V. Syllabication and Pronunciation

Entry words as well as inflected and derived forms are divided into syllables, indicated by centered dots: **fly·a·way**. The syllables represent the "established practice of printers and editors" in breaking words that fall at the end of a printed line. Entries of more than one word are not divided into syllables, for example, **dust jacket**, if the divisible word, or words, appears elsewhere as a separate entry, such as **jack·et**.

Pronunciations of words are also divided "for the sake of clarity" according to phonetic rules. The division of syllables (marked by stress marks and hyphens), following how a word is pronounced, often differs from written division, as in **or·di·nar·y** (ôr′ dn-ĕr′ ē).

There is an admirably clear description of the pronunciation symbols, ones that should be "familiar to the reader untrained in phonetics." Pronunciation is thus relatively easy to determine. The editors state simply that the pronunciations recorded are "exclusively those of educated speech," not those of social dialects, although the guide to pronunciation recognizes the "great variety" of American speech sounds and regional intonations. A table of sound-speech correspondences is included with an explanation to help readers find words they can pronounce but not spell:

> *sound:* **church** *spelling:* **cz** *sample word:* **Cz**ech.

Additionally, a formal pronunciation key lists word spellings with both the AHD symbols and those of the International Phonetic Alphabet (IPA), noted as being "widely used by scholars." Three common French sounds (**feu, tu,** and bo**n**), three common German (sch**ö**n, **ü**ber, i**ch**), and one Scottish (lo**ch**) are also keyed. So too are primary stress (indicated by a boldface mark) and secondary stress (a lightface mark): *bi′ o-mas′*. Two-line examples of keyed pronunciations are printed for quick reference at the bottom of each dictionary page.

VI. Special Features

The AHD's special features range from usage notes to a substantial list of abbreviations and a table of chemical elements. The front right-hand endpaper lists, alphabetically, twenty-three reference features, including the tables (of alphabets, calendars, the elements mentioned above, currency, geologic time, Morse code, proofreaders' marks, Roman numerals, signs and symbols, subatomic particles, taxonomy, and common weights and measures). It also directs the reader to the "Explanations of the Color Definitions," an illustrated mini-essay, accompanying the entries on color, that explains the technical basis of terms such as **hue, lightness,** and **saturation,** and includes 267 standard color names.

An index list appears on the left-hand back endpaper. Included are the main sections of the dictionary, the items in the frontmatter (for example, the "Style Manual" and Usage Panel), and the formal titles of tables. Appendixes include A to Z biographical entries with 217 small but excellent portraits (including those of twenty-five American minority group members). Syllabication and pronunciation of names is indicated. Historical dynasties are included and variant spellings of names are listed. The section of A to Z geographical entries contains 152 clear, small locator maps of countries and islands. Entries are identified as city, lake, and so forth. Population figures are included: U.S. towns and cities follow 1980 U.S. census figures, but the populations given for countries predate reliable 1983 estimates. Occasional tidbits of identifying historical information are included, as well as variant spellings, alternate names (**Porto** *Portuguese* **Oporto**), and former names (Belgian East Africa for Rwanda and Burundi). Adjectival and noun forms of geographic names are noted. Additionally, there are lists of four-year and two-year colleges and universities (the latter lists institutions as small as twenty students and includes technical and vocational schools as well as selected "for profit" business schools [Katherine Gibbs is one]).

The "Style Manual" is concise and gives clear, brief directions with examples; but the sample footnote and bibliographic styles should not be relied on—especially by students: the examples are outdated and the editions of the standard style manuals recommended in the section have been superseded by new editions with significant changes.

Four special articles give an excellent view of contemporary thought about language. Professor Lee Pederson's opening essay, "Language, Culture, and the American Heritage," is notable for its succinct and authoritative overview of the diversity in the American language. Included in the essay is brief, useful information on topics such as gullah, bilingualism, social dialects, and regional variants in pronunciation. The essay-debate—between Dwight Bolinger (for) and William Buckley (against)—on "Resolved: The prevailing usage of its speakers should be the chief determinant of acceptability in language" is perhaps more informative on the current state of rhetorical argument than it is on the set topic. Henry Kučera's "The Mathematics of Language" is superb and could be read with pleasure by many students, whether or not their main fields of interest are mathematics or language.

VII. Accessibility

Familiarity with alphabetizing is the only knowledge required to use the *Second College Edition* of the AHD. All entries are listed in strict letter by letter alphabetical order. Each letter section of the dictionary is preceded by a single page of graphic examples of the letter, a device that also provides helpful spatial separation of letters. The thumb-index tabs available in one edition are attractive and sturdy.

Alternate spellings are generally treated thoroughly, avoiding confusion and needless speculation for the student. They appear as variants in an entry and also alphabetically as entry words. For example, there is the entry, "na·if or na·ïf *adj. & n.* Variants of **naive**;" then its main entry, "na·ive or na·ïve also na·if or na·ïf," is followed by the definitions. Inflected forms of a word are printed in boldface and are easily found, even in longer entries. Sometimes cognate words, for example, **naiveté** for **naive**, are referred to under the synonym example (*unaffected*

in the case of naiveté) and then also appear as an entry. Words spelled alike that have different etymologies are listed as separate entries with superior numbers, making them easy to scan.

In thirteen pages, the "Guide to the Dictionary" explains in clear language how to find specific information within an entry. The heads and subheads in the guide are in large type, which is fortunate because there is no key or outline for the section and, therefore, a reader has to leaf through it to discover where to find synonyms, or cross-references, undefined forms of a word, or the abbreviations and labels used in the dictionary. More sophisticated high school students familiar with the general structure of entries in adult or college-level dictionaries will find information more quickly; others might ignore this section.

At the top of each page, a pair of guide words separated by a vertical line, for example, **interferometer | internal**, indicates the first and last entry words on the page. One word of each pair extends into the white space of the illustration column and is readily visible. This adds to the ease of finding a word and, when the dictionary lies open, allows the reader to see at a glance the inclusive contents of a double-page spread. Small page numbers are printed at the top of the text near the inside margins.

The location of pictures in the outside margins on each page is a handy way for a reader to check if he or she is close to locating a required word.

On the back left-hand endpaper there is a brief index, in larger type than the text, to the special sections and the tables in the dictionary.

VIII. Graphics and Format

The *Second College Edition* has several notable graphics features. The sturdy white paper does not crease or tear easily, an important element in a dictionary that must sustain frequent use. In common with many other dictionaries, there is noticeable show-through of text and pictures, although this is more obvious in the AHD because of the illustrations column on each page.

For a desk dictionary, the AHD devotes an unusual amount of space to illustrations. These are printed in the outside margin of each page and contribute to a feeling of space. Frequently, the pictures illustrate the different meanings of a word. (There are photographs, for example, of an Afghan rug and an Afghan hound.) An estimated three-fifths of the illustrations are photographs, which adds a contemporary feeling to the pages. Perhaps as many as a third of the photographs, however, show too much surrounding detail, making it difficult to determine which object is intended to illustrate the entry. The bird drawings by George Miksch Sutton are outstanding; line drawings of plants and medical subjects vary in quality; the many photographs of tools and mechanical devices add interest to a usually dull category of dictionary illustration; geometric and architectural drawings are clear. There is little question that the illustrations enhance the AHD's value as a reference source. One reviewer quibbled that some illustrations are placed too far away from relevant entries on a page, although many have brief captions.

Useful, and decorative, features include the separate page preceding each letter of the alphabet with large examples of how the letter is printed in different typefaces, accompanied by a brief orthographical history.

All entries, inflected forms, variant forms and spellings, and the word "Usage" preceding the paragraphs explaining usage, as well as numbers for different meanings, are printed in bold sans-serif, easily readable type. Main entry words overhang the text for easier visual access. The guide words are printed in a larger bold sans-serif face. The text is printed in a two-column format, allowing for a third but narrower column for all illustrations. Although the typeface is small, there is sufficient white space between lines for readability. A far-sighted person, however, may not find the text comfortable to read.

IX. Summary

The American Heritage Dictionary: Second College Edition, as claimed, "covers the vocabulary ranging from the language of Shakespeare to the idiom of the present day." Although some definitions are cursory, its coverage of contemporary language—especially the developments of the 1970s in the sciences and technology—is extensive. The quantity of illustrations adds an extra dimension to the dictionary as do the paragraphs on contemporary usage in the entries.

The *Second College Edition* is attractively and sturdily bound; its pages lie flat when opened; and it feels substantial but not uncomfortably heavy when picked up. The heavy endpapers are solidly reinforced.

Numerous recognizable and some world-famous names are associated with the *Second College Edition*; many, but certainly *not* all, are experts in the fields of language and lexicography. This dictionary has been recommended by reliable reviewers as a good desk reference in each succeeding edition. ALA *Booklist* concluded its mostly favorable review of the 1982 edition: "*The American Heritage Dictionary*

continues, in its College Edition, to be a credit to its publishers, editors, and contributors. . . ." In his *Dictionaries: The Art and Craft of Lexicography* (1984, p. 74), Sidney F. Landau provided an interesting highlight: the *AHD* reintroduced taboo words [in 1969] . . . excluded from general dictionaries . . . since the eighteenth century. This was an important and courageous step in reporting the actual usage of commonly used words, and every other college dictionary with the exception of *World* soon followed suit." *Library Journal*, in a short review (1 November 1982, p. 2086), wrote: "Although this dictionary has been published in a number of editions . . . the same high standards prevail as in previous editions . . . labeling is firmer and more precise . . . the volume generally fulfills its stated purpose and will meet the needs of most dictionary users."

The reader may want to compare the *AHD: Second College Edition* with the WEBSTER'S NINTH NEW COLLEGIATE DICTIONARY, another widely used dictionary for the same readership. One main difference between these two excellent reference works lies in the use of extensive marginal illustrations by the *AHD*. The *AHD* also places greater emphasis on contemporary usage and scientific terms. The *Webster's*, however, appears to offer more precisely worded definitions and a more accessible vocabulary, for example, in mathematics. The *Webster's* is also more linguistically advanced and uses a complicated set of symbols for pronunciation, features that many high school students may find somewhat difficult to master. The two dictionaries have similar useful introductory and appendix material, with *Webster's* providing, in addition, a Language Research Service for individual written inquiries.

For the reader from high school up, who wants a dictionary that distinguishes educated from other use and that provides guidance to usage—as well as generally solid definitions, standard, scientific, and technical, the *Second College Edition* of *The American Heritage Dictionary* is a good choice at a reasonable price.

The American Heritage First Dictionary

Facts at a Glance

Full Title: **The American Heritage First Dictionary.**
Former Title: My First Dictionary.
Publisher: Houghton Mifflin Company.
Editors: Fernando de Mello Vianna, Editorial Director; Stephen Kreusky, Definitions Editor; Vivian Fueyo, Contributing Editor.
Edition Reviewed: © 1986.

Number of Pages: 340.
Number of Entries: 1,700.
Number of Illustrations: 600 in full color.
Trim Size: $7\frac{7}{8}'' \times 10\frac{13}{16}''$.

Intended Readership: ages 5 through 8; grades K
    through 3.
Price: $10.95.
Sold in bookstores and other outlets; also sold to
    libraries and schools. ISBN 0-395-42530-1.

I. Scope and Format

This dictionary is a part of a series of four American
Heritage dictionaries intended for children from preschool through ninth grade. *The American Heritage
First Dictionary* is a revised edition of the 1980 book,
My First Dictionary. Only the introduction and the
appendix appear to be revised, however; the main
body remains the same.

Geared to primary grade students, nearly one-
third of its 1,700 words are found in readers and in
the everyday language of six- and seven-year-olds.
The *First Dictionary*—with colorful illustrations and
definitions consisting of a few short sentences—acts
as a bridge between a picture dictionary and one with
a more complex vocabulary that can be used by a
student having more advanced reading skills.

The book is attractively printed on a coated, ivory
stock with minimal show-through. It is bound with
heavy board covers and should withstand normal
classroom and library use.

II. Authority

Houghton Mifflin Company is the publisher of the
highly respected parent work, *The American Heritage Dictionary of the English Language*. The editorial director of that work, plus Houghton Mifflin
staff lexicographers, joined a special contributing editor and educational consultants in the preparation
of the *First Dictionary*.

III. Quality and Currency of Entries

According to the preface, 500 of the main entry words
"are those found most frequently in children's first
primers and reading textbooks. The remainder of the

vocabulary is a broad selection of other words children see and use every day." Our reviewers compared the dictionary's vocabulary with several books
currently read by a wide range of beginning readers
and the inclusion of such contractions as **aren't**, **can't**,
I'm, and **I'll**, for example, supports this claim.

The extremely brief definitions are written with a
controlled vocabulary; every word in a definition is
also an entry word. The preface states, "Every word
is defined, either directly by telling what it is or in-
directly by building such a strong context that the
meaning cannot escape understanding." This works
well, as the following examples show:

however
The ghost stopped in front of a door. The door was
locked. The ghost, **however**, did not need a key. It just
went through the door like smoke through a fence.

borrow
Jane takes books from the library. She returns them a
few days later. She **borrows** the books to read. Last
week she **borrowed** five of them.

number
1. A **number** is a symbol for an amount of things.

seven
Seven is a number. It is written **7. 6 + 1 = 7.**

The definitions are written in such a way that they
will have great appeal to primary grade school children and thus impart early on the benefits and en-
joyment of using books, as an earlier review noted:
"[The] illustrative sentences match the reading level
and the interests of the intended audience" (*Reference Books Bulletin, 1981–82*, p. 149).

Plurals of nouns are given. Present and past tenses
of verbs are presented in boldface:

Words having more than one meaning have several definitions given; the most frequently used one
is placed first. Homonyms are treated as separate
entries numbered with superscripts, thus showing a
relationship:

ring[1]
A **ring** is a circle with an empty center. The circus tiger
jumped through **rings** of fire.
2. Jane wears a gold circle on her finger. Her finger fits
through the middle of a narrow gold **ring**.

ring[2]
A bell makes a sound when it is hit. It **rings**. The bell
rang when school began.

The American Heritage First Dictionary

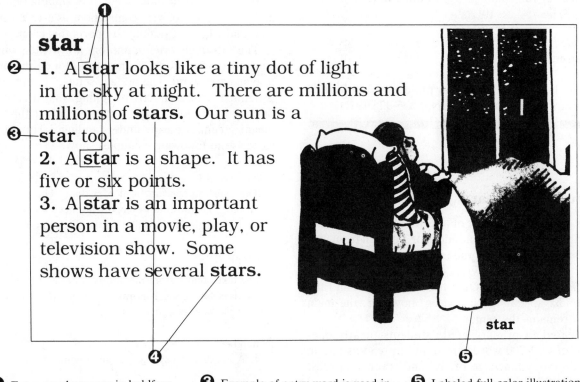

1 Entry word appears in boldface type within the definition

2 Each definition is numbered with boldface numeral under a main entry word

3 Example of entry word is used in a sentence

4 The plural form of entry word is in boldface type

5 Labeled full-color illustration of the entry word's first meaning

Irregular verbs are acknowledged by a sentence following the definitions. For example:

Am, is, are, was, were and **been** are forms of **be**.

The *First Dictionary* does not include words associated with computers; those can be found in THE AMERICAN HERITAGE CHILDREN'S DICTIONARY, a book for somewhat older children. Parts of speech, syllabication, pronunciation, and etymologies are not given, since these features are unnecessary for the intended young readers.

Access to the words is alphabetical and is facilitated by a deep pink rectangle located on the upper outside margin of each page. Within the rectangle is a white letter of the alphabet signifying the letter with which the words on that page begin. Since each pink rectangle "bleeds" off the edge of the page, the resulting color at the same place on the edge of all the pages acts as a kind of thumb index (without the indentations) to the location of letters of the alphabet

throughout the book. A child can quickly flip through the pages to find the desired letter.

Each new letter is introduced by a part title page of illustrations of objects that begin with the letter and an alphabet all in black letters except for the featured one, which is printed in bright pink. On the following pages of definitions, the word defined is in large lowercase bold type with the definitions in a smaller yet very easy-to-read roman type suitable for beginning readers. The definition begins on the line beneath the entry word, making that word very visible. There are about seven entry words per page.

IV. Illustrations

Many of the definitions are accompanied by full-color, captioned illustrations that "are used to enhance definitions, not to convey abstract ideas" (*Reference Books Bulletin, 1981–82*, p. 149). The illustrations include much detail that will encourage browsing. Children pictured are representative of various ethnic groups. At least one picture appears on every page. The book shows a pleasing variety of graphic layouts.

V. Summary

The dictionary is prefaced by four pages of instructions and four double spreads of games called "Words About . . . ," designed to encourage children to use the dictionary. The introduction is written to the level of the child who would use the dictionary, and the activities are fun and easy to follow. The four games are intriguing for the young student and provide excellent, subtle lessons in beginning reference skills. For example, "Words About the City" asks the reader to put various buildings or places in alphabetical order. In addition, a three-page section of homophones entitled "Words that Sound Alike but are Spelled Differently," is appended at the end of the main vocabulary. The homophones are defined and illustrated; this section will be an especially useful reference for children studying word sounds.

The American Heritage First Dictionary is a cheerful beginning reference book that will be useful in public, school, and home libraries where children are first introduced to reading and understanding the written word. Especially noteworthy is the way the use of the dictionary is introduced and the way in which the controlled vocabulary of the definitions is handled so that it appeals directly to the interests of children in the primary grades.

The American Heritage Picture Dictionary

Facts at a Glance

Full Title: **The American Heritage Picture Dictionary.**
Publisher: Houghton Mifflin Company.
Compiler: Robert L. Hillerich.
Illustrator: Maggie Swanson.
Edition Reviewed: © 1986.

Number of Volumes: 1.
Number of Entries: 600.
Number of Words: 900.
Number of Pages: 144.
Number of Illustrations: 649 in full color.
Trim Size: 8½″ × 11″.
Binding: hardbound.

Price: $7.95.
Intended Readership: grades K through 1.

Sold in bookstores and other outlets; also sold to libraries and schools. ISBN 0-395-42531-X.

I. Scope and Format

The American Heritage Picture Dictionary is the first in a series of four dictionaries from Houghton Mifflin intended for children from preschool through ninth grade. The preface states that it is "designed to provide the help and encouragement young children need now, in the preschool and early primary years, as well as to provide the readiness that will be needed in the future for more advanced levels of dictionary use." Visual representations are given for most of the main entry words, and a simple sentence using the word in context accompanies many illustrations.

II. Authority

Houghton Mifflin is the publisher of the highly respected family of American Heritage dictionaries. In this series of children's dictionaries, the American Heritage editors have maintained their high lexicographic standards. The prefatory note to parents and teachers indicates that the dictionary is based on ten different word counts; among them are "words common to first-grade reading programs . . . as well as words used by first graders in speaking . . . and writing, and words used in elementary school materials of all kinds." Of these, words that could be simply defined or whose meaning could be clearly understood from an illustration were used.

The compiler, Robert L. Hillerich, has published several well-known pedagogical works, including the *Pacemaker Core Vocabularies, One & Two* (1980), *The Principal's Guide to Improving Reading Instruction* (1983), and *A Writing Vocabulary of Elementary Children* (1978), the latter cited by the editors in the *Picture Dictionary*'s preface.

III. Quality and Currency of Entries

With the exception of **first grade** and **how many**, all main entries are single words, or variant forms, such as **fish · fishes**. The entries are accompanied by an illustration that visually identifies the word. Many entries also have a simple sentence or two that clarifies one meaning of the word. Examples are, **line** accompanied by an illustration of five children (one with leg braces and crutches) standing and the sentence: "We stand in a **line**." For the word **was**, the illustration is of two boys waiting on the baseball mound for a girl who is coming to replace the pitcher: "Ching Wah **was** the pitcher." This is also an example of how the dictionary avoids stereotypes.

The American Heritage Picture Dictionary

❶ A proper name identifies the child in the illustration

❷ Four-color drawings illustrate a cast of children and adults from different ethnic backgrounds

❸ The entry word is printed in blue and used in a sentence

❹ The illustration identifies the entry word

The exceptions to this format are the nine words that are each illustrated on a full- or double-page spread at the end of the book: astronaut, body, classroom, dinosaur, farm, games and fun, supermarket, and word. This section expands the meaning of a key word by including many related words that are labeled as well as pictured. In keeping with the intended readership, parts of speech, syllabication, pronunciation, and etymology are not given.

Access to the words is by alphabetical order. The plural of a word is given when it varies from adding an s, for example, **children**, **ladies**, **leaves**, and **sheep**, and an illustration reinforces the plural concept.

IV. Illustrations

Maggie Swanson's four-color, realistic art presents clear-cut, easily accessible meanings in pictures and is delightfully appealing for young readers. The artist has included a cast of children and adults from different ethnic backgrounds. They reappear with their pets and friends in a variety of simple, homey settings.

Handsomely designed for clarity and balance, the book presents two to four illustrated words on each page in two columns on a white background. The columns are set off by thin blue rules and the entry words are set off by thin black lines. Each letter of the alphabet appears in capital and lowercase form in black on a large block of bright color at the top of the page or pages it introduces. An illustration appears alongside the letter, for example, a pig for *Pp*, a kite for *Kk*. Each entry word is printed in bold blue sans-serif type, and the example sentences are in black with the entry word or a simple variant form repeated in blue.

One feature of the design is not completely successful. The nine words illustrated at the end of the book are introduced in their proper alphabetical position in a band of color. The preface tells us that the word's color is cross-referenced in the border surrounding the illustration in the back of the book and thus to the related words. Without the explanation in the preface, however, the mechanism is not immediately obvious and, without adult explanation, will be lost on many young readers.

V. Summary

The American Heritage Picture Dictionary has much quieter illustrations and its definitions are far more serious, helpful—and current—for the beginning dictionary user than THE CAT IN THE HAT BEGINNER BOOK DICTIONARY, for example. Both have merit for public and school library and home use. *The American Heritage Picture Dictionary* will serve especially well to teach younger readers the skills they need to begin using "real" dictionaries.

The American Heritage Student's Dictionary

Facts at a Glance

Full Title: **The American Heritage Student's Dictionary.**

Former Title: The American Heritage School Dictionary.

Publisher: Houghton Mifflin Company.

Editors: Peter Davies, Editor-in-Chief; Barry Richman, Executive Editor; Fernando de Mello Vianna, Managing Editor.

Edition Reviewed: © 1986.

Number of Volumes: 1.

Number of Entries: more than 70,000.

Number of Pages: 992.

Number of Illustrations: 2,000 in black and white.

Trim Size: 7½" × 9¼".

Binding: laminated paper over boards.

Price: $11.95.

Intended Readership: grades 7 through 10; ages 12 through 15.

Sold in bookstores; also sold to libraries and schools. ISBN 0-395-40417-7.

I. Introduction

The American Heritage Student's Dictionary is the most advanced in a series of four dictionaries from Houghton Mifflin intended for children from preschool through ninth or tenth grades. The earlier volumes are THE AMERICAN HERITAGE PICTURE DICTIONARY, THE AMERICAN HERITAGE FIRST DICTIONARY, and THE AMERICAN HERITAGE CHILDREN'S DICTIONARY.

This dictionary is an updating of a work originally published in 1972 and revised in 1977, titled *The American Heritage School Dictionary*. The introduction states that the *Student's Dictionary* "embodies the many innovations in lexicography introduced by *The American Heritage Dictionary of the English Language*, principally in areas of design and illustrations and guidance on matters of usage." Indeed, the two are very similar in appearance, and the younger reader familiar with the *Student's Dictionary* will move with ease to the second college edition of THE AMERICAN HERITAGE DICTIONARY. There are 35,000 main entries, and about 70,000 separately defined meanings and uses.

The work's introduction states that the dictionary is "intended for use in American schools in grades 6 through 9," although a sales sticker on the front

notes: "Revised! For students ages 12–15 in grades 7–10."

II. Authority

Peter Davies, Editor-in-Chief for this dictionary, was Executive Editor of the parent dictionary, THE AMERICAN HERITAGE DICTIONARY OF THE ENGLISH LANGUAGE. The editors of the *Student's Dictionary* are members of the publisher's permanent lexicographic staff. Seven of the eleven people who worked on the definitions were also involved in the same activity in the parent dictionary. The Advisory Board and the Consultants are experts in the fields of education, psychology, mathematics, the environment, and language arts. Words were selected by computerized research and were based on "textbooks, magazines, encyclopedias, workbooks, and other printed materials that are used in schools," according to the editors; thus, the dictionary will harmonize well with junior high students' overall academic experience.

III. Comprehensiveness

The 35,000 entry words are likely to be familiar, through the printed word, to the sixth through ninth grader. Not all of the words are common, for some are, as the introduction points out, "important [in] specialized ways—in science or mathematics, for example." So, while students will be familiar with many of the words, there are still many new ones to learn.

Geographic and biographical entries are incorporated in the main alphabetical vocabulary. This feature is especially helpful in that student users often will not know that the word they are seeking is the name of a person or a place and might not search for it in a separate listing. Words as well as phrases are included as main entries; for example, **first base**, **petty larceny**, and **square root** are main entries. Many words recently added to current usage are included, particularly from computer and other science fields; for example,

file[1] . . . **2.** A collection of related data for a computer

and also **floppy disk**, and **space shuttle**. However, *AIDS*, *cursor*, and *modem* are among the words omitted.

IV. Quality and Currency of Entries

The definitions are accurate, clear, and appropriate in their level of complexity to the intended audience.

The American Heritage
Student's Dictionary

❶ Variant spellings and pronunciations are given

❷ Pronunciations are enclosed in vertical bars. The syllable(s) with primary stress appears in boldface type

❸ Variant forms, inflections, and phrases are boldfaced

❹ Illustrative sentences show the use of entry word in context

❺ The cross-reference in brackets, draws attention to the informal etymology note

❻ Etymology, set in italics, is placed in the margin, with entry word boldfaced throughout

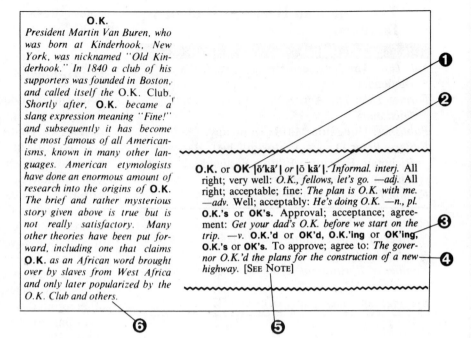

O.K.
*President Martin Van Buren, who was born at Kinderhook, New York, was nicknamed "Old Kinderhook." In 1840 a club of his supporters was founded in Boston, and called itself the O.K. Club. Shortly after, **O.K.** became a slang expression meaning "Fine!" and subsequently it has become the most famous of all Americanisms, known in many other languages. American etymologists have done an enormous amount of research into the origins of **O.K.** The brief and rather mysterious story given above is true but is not really satisfactory. Many other theories have been put forward, including one that claims **O.K.** as an African word brought over by slaves from West Africa and only later popularized by the O.K. Club and others.*

O.K. or **OK** |ō′kā′| *or* |ō kā′|. *Informal. interj.* All right; very well: *O.K., fellows, let's go.* —*adj.* All right; acceptable; fine: *The plan is O.K. with me.* —*adv.* Well; acceptably: *He's doing O.K.* —*n., pl.* **O.K.'s** or **OK's.** Approval; acceptance; agreement: *Get your dad's O.K. before we start on the trip.* —*v.* **O.K.'d** or **OK'd, O.K.'ing** or **OK'ing, O.K.'s** or **OK's.** To approve; agree to: *The governor O.K.'d the plans for the construction of a new highway.* [SEE NOTE]

For example, the first meaning given for the word **definition** is

    a statement of the precise meaning or meanings of a word, phrase, etc.

In the margin, where, in italicized passages, meanings sometimes receive more elaboration, we find

    Definitions in dictionaries cannot be truly precise. Meaning is still mysterious, and every word is unique. Most dictionaries, including this one, define a word by a phrase or another word that seems to mean the same thing. But a phrase cannot have exactly the same meaning as a single word. . . .

This is an impressively clear statement of the complex nature of meaning, well suited to the intended student audience.

    The definitions are brief, in general, with the most common meaning given first. Illustrative sentences are frequently used to put the word in context, and occasional black and white illustrations and photographs in the margin give visual meaning to the entry words. Synonyms are not given as such, although they may be derived in many cases from the statements of definition. The definitions also include parts of speech, modifiers, run-on entries, phrasal verbs, inflected forms, variants, and homophones, providing students with information that will complement their increasing knowledge of English grammar and, to some extent, their foreign language studies.

Meanings of abstract words and concepts are also well handled. Compare the definition of **heaven** in this volume with that in the dictionary preceding this one in level, THE AMERICAN HERITAGE CHILDREN'S DICTIONARY:

CHILDREN'S DICTIONARY

heaven *noun* 1. Often **heavens** The sky over the earth; upper regions of the air: *Stars twinkled in the heavens.* 2. Often **Heaven** In Christianity and some other religions, the dwelling place of God and the angels. 3. A place of great happiness: *The cool forest was heaven on a hot day.* . . . .

STUDENT'S DICTIONARY

heav·en . . . 1. Often **heavens**. The sky or universe as seen from the earth. 2. In many religions, the abode of God, holy celestial beings, and the blessed dead. 3. **Heaven**. The divine Providence; God: *Thank Heaven for your safety.* 4. Often **heavens**. Used in exclamations: *Good heavens! Look at that crowd!* 5.a. Great happiness; bliss: *It'll be heaven to visit that park.* b. A wonderful thing or place; a delight: *Her kitchen, fragrant from baking, was heaven.*

    Idioms. *in seventh heaven*. Supremely happy: *She is in seventh heaven now that she has a piano.* **move heaven and earth**. To do everything possible: *He'll move heaven and earth in order to find the lost letter.*

The definition is broader in scope: it closely parallels the definition in the parent work and obviously goes far beyond that given in the *Children's Dictionary*. It provides students with a wider awareness, appropriate to the increasing linguistic sophistication of the age group, of the word's connotative values and idiomatic usage.

V. Syllabication and Pronunciation

Syllabication is provided for every word of two or more syllables. Pronunciation is included for every word or abbreviation that is part of the spoken language. For example, the dictionary gives **PG** | **pē′jē′** | for the PG rating of the film industry, but **Cl**, the symbol for the element chlorine, receives no pronunciation. Alternative pronunciations are provided following standard American English pronunciation. A full pronunciation guide is given in the "How to Use Your Dictionary" section and repeated on the right side of the front endpapers, seen when the front cover is opened. For quick reference, an abbreviated pronunciation guide, focused primarily on vowels, is also given at the lower left corner of each double spread. Diacritical marks and phonetic spellings are effectively used.

VI. Special Features

Two special features written for student readers precede the dictionary. One is an excellent comprehensive introduction to the use of the dictionary where each part of the entry is carefully and clearly described. There is also a "Style Guide" that shows uses of punctuation, capitalization, and italics. Within the dictionary, in the outer margins of the pages, usage notes, etymology, and additional information are provided for some words. At the end of the volume are also charts on weights and measures and the metric system, valuable adjuncts to students' math and science studies.

VII. Accessibility

Access to the information is strictly alphabetical. No thumb index is provided. Two guidewords, such as **boll weevil** | **bonehead**, appear at the top of each page, giving the first and last words defined on the page. The sequence of information under each main entry, beginning with pronunciation and part of speech, is clear and easy to follow.

Alternative spellings are included in bold type after main entries, and distinguished according to relative frequency or preference. Examples are **cat·a·log** or **cat·a·logue** (words occurring with the same degree of frequency) and **lunch·room**, also **lunch-room** (first form preferred). The dictionary's special features are listed in the contents and thereby are easily found.

VIII. Graphics and Format

The text is printed in two columns; the entry word in bold sans-serif type overhangs the text; the definition is in roman, the part of speech and illustrative sentences in italic, and word variants in small bold sans-serif. These typefaces are all easy to read, and their variety will enable students to pick out the information in which they are particularly interested.

Two thousand drawings, all placed in the outside margins of the pages, and all black and white, serve to increase knowledge of a word and to encourage the student reader to browse. (The same device is used effectively in the parent dictionary.) There are, however, no maps. The attention to detail in graphics can be seen in the photograph illustrating **handlebar**: the man riding a bike, holding onto the handlebars, has a handlebar mustache.

The book is sturdily bound and will withstand heavy use.

IX. Summary

The American Heritage Student's Dictionary is a well-crafted dictionary, designed so that students who learn to use it will be prepared to understand the layout of THE AMERICAN HERITAGE DICTIONARY: SECOND COLLEGE EDITION, a standard college and adult reference work. The four books in this series should be considered standard reference sources for children's use in the home, and for school and public library collections.

Beginning Dictionary

Facts at a Glance

Full Title: **Beginning Dictionary.**
Publisher: Macmillan.
Editors: William D. Halsey, Editorial Director;
    Phyllis R. Winant, Supervising Editor.
Edition Reviewed: © 1987.

Number of Volumes: 1.
Number of Entries: 30,000.
Number of Pages: 816.
Number of Illustrations: 1,200 in full color.
Number of Maps: 4 pages in full color.
Trim Size: 8″ × 10″.
Binding: hardcover.

Price: list $22.00; school $16.50.
Intended Readership: grades 3 through 5.
Sold to libraries and schools. ISBN 0-02-195370-8.

Beginning Dictionary

❶ Example sentences show the entry word in context, sometimes using inflected forms

❷ Pronunciation, parts of speech, and inflections are set off at end of an entry

❸ Informal etymologies or language notes are marked with a small solid blue triangle, and set apart from the text with blue rules above and below the paragraph

❹ Four-color illustration of meaning **1**.

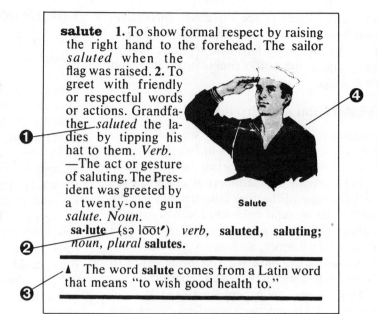

salute   **1.** To show formal respect by raising the right hand to the forehead. The sailor *saluted* when the flag was raised. **2.** To greet with friendly or respectful words or actions. Grandfather *saluted* the ladies by tipping his hat to them. *Verb.*
—The act or gesture of saluting. The President was greeted by a twenty-one gun *salute. Noun.*
   sa·lute (sə lōōt′) *verb,* **saluted, saluting;** *noun, plural* **salutes.**

▲ The word **salute** comes from a Latin word that means "to wish good health to."

Salute

I. Scope and Format

Macmillan's *Beginning Dictionary* identically reproduces the 724-page word list and the pronunciation key found in the MACMILLAN DICTIONARY FOR CHILDREN, reviewed in this Buying Guide. While both volumes are intended for use in the elementary grades, they differ substantially in the special features they include.

The *Beginning Dictionary* begins with a full listing of the volume's contents, while the *Macmillan Dictionary for Children* provides a contents listing, after the word list, covering only the reference sections in the back of the volume. While the *Macmillan Dictionary for Children* addresses its preface, "Welcome to Your Dictionary" to children, the preface to the *Beginning Dictionary* is directed to adults, especially teachers, and defines the book specifically as a school dictionary, "intended to be the first real dictionary that students use in the classroom."

Both volumes contain explanations of the dictionary and its use. This section in the *Macmillan Dictionary for Children* is clear, but brief. In the *Beginning Dictionary*, an expanded "Guide to the Dictionary" begins with a useful sample page keyed to the guide. The guide uses text, illustrations, and examples to lead students through the process of finding a word and to introduce the many kinds of information—such as spelling, pronunciation, and usage—available in the dictionary. A particularly valuable feature for classroom use is the inclusion of "Try This" exercise sections within the guide: these provide stu-

dents with practice of such skills as alphabetizing, forming words with suffixes and prefixes, and selecting correct verb forms. The *Beginning Dictionary* also contains a useful "Table of English Spellings," enabling students to locate words which they know how to pronounce but not spell. The *Macmillan Dictionary for Children* omits this feature, although it contains an interesting article titled "The Story of English" that is not included in the other volume.

A number of special features also appear in the backs of these dictionaries, again with significant differences. Both volumes contain a glossary of computer terms. They have similar illustrated listings of events in United States history through 1976, but the *Macmillan Dictionary for Children* also adds a listing of significant events in twentieth-century American technological progress through 1981. Portraits of United States presidents appear in both volumes; some differences appear in the portraits themselves, and while the *Beginning Dictionary* provides only the presidents' dates, the *Macmillan Dictionary for Children* also adds their vice presidents. Tables of measure are included in both, and the *Beginning Dictionary* has the advantage of providing metric system information on the same page with customary units rather than elsewhere in the volume. Geographic information in the *Beginning Dictionary* is limited to two double-spread maps— the world and the United States—while the *Macmillan Dictionary for Children* contains a ten-page atlas. "Flags of the United States and Outlying Areas" appears in the *Macmillan Dictionary for Children*; its counterpart illustrates maps of the world. The *Macmillan Dictionary for Children* contains one additional feature omitted from the *Macmillan Beginning Dictionary*: a two-page spread, including photographs, on the solar system. However, the *Beginning Dictionary* includes one especially useful feature for its intended readers: a 29-page supplement, "Practice Pages," further reinforcing information and skills presented in the guide.

Although the *Macmillan Dictionary for Children* provides many valuable features at an attractive price, the publisher's *Beginning Dictionary* justifies its higher cost because of its own special features. Its expanded "Guide to the Dictionary" and its practice exercises make it especially applicable to its intended use in schools.

The Cat in the Hat Beginner Book Dictionary

Facts at a Glance

Full Title: **The Cat in the Hat Beginner Book Dictionary.**
Publisher: Random House (Beginner Books).
Authors: Dr. Seuss and P. D. Eastman.
Edition Reviewed: © 1964.

Number of Volumes: 1.
Number of Words: 1,350.
Number of Pages: 133.
Number of Illustrations: 132 pages in full color.
Trim Size: 8″ × 11″.
Binding: Paper over boards.

Price: $7.95.
Intended Readership: Beginning readers.
Sold in bookstores and other outlets. ISBN 0-394-81009-0.

I. Scope and Format

The Cat in the Hat Beginner Book Dictionary "by the Cat himself and P. D. Eastman" is a beginning dictionary of 1,350 words defined by simple text and full-color illustrations. The editors, according to the preface by Dr. Seuss, "decided they could be serious . . . and still avoid being stuffy. So they made this book of words just as funny as they could make it . . . . [because] The average child, we've discovered, seems to like things just that way . . . . It helps us to focus the child's attention . . . to make him recognize, remember, *and really enjoy* a basic elemen-

tary vocabulary." Strictly speaking, however, this is not a dictionary in the traditional sense; it is an illustrated word book that defines primarily by picturing selected word meanings.

II. Authority

In 1957 Dr. Seuss's *The Cat in the Hat* was published and, thereafter, stories could be silly, characters could be cartoonlike and ridiculous, and children could belly laugh while learning to read. That same approach is used in this dictionary, which is part of the Beginner Books series.

III. Quality and Currency of Entries

Each entry word is, in effect, a separate illustration, placed on a white block of space (three to seven blocks per page) and captioned with the entry word and a brief definition. The "definitions" are amazingly clear, even though they are seldom more than a simple phrase. The sparse text relies heavily on the illustrations. For example: **empty Empty bed**. The drawing shows a bed with covers thrown back, and we see a bare foot walking off the page. At the entry **late Late for school**, there is a picture of a child rushing up the walk to a schoolhouse with the hands of the school clock pointing to a few minutes past nine. **Numbers** has no text for definition, just a dog on a stepladder writing numbers: **39, 570, 686, 2, 33⅓, 100**, and so on. Sometimes root words are used. For example: **cook A cook cooking a cookie** (although the joke strains good word usage here: a cookie is "baked," not "cooked"). The entry for **do** shows a dog tacking up signs of **The "do" words: did, does, doing, doesn't, don't, done.** Superlatives are depicted; for example, **loud: loud, louder, loudest** are portrayed by a crying baby whose mouth opens wider and wider with each word.

No parts of speech are defined, and no syllabication, pronunciation, or etymologies are provided. The book has not been revised since its original 1964 publication, so no computer or space terms are included.

The arrangement is strictly alphabetical. The only way to tell which letter you are on is to look at the words on the page and to note the color of the bars separating the definitions. A different color is introduced as background color for the illustrations on the several pages devoted to each letter. There are no top-of-the-page guide words, but this is a book that will be used for browsing or reading aloud as much as, or more than, for definitions, so alphabetical access is not a major concern.

The Cat in the Hat Beginner Book Dictionary

❶ Large boldface entry word
❷ Phrase emphasizes the first letter of the entry word, using humorous alliteration
❸ Words defined by illustration in four-color
❹ Illustrative phrase uses entry word highlighted in contrasting type color

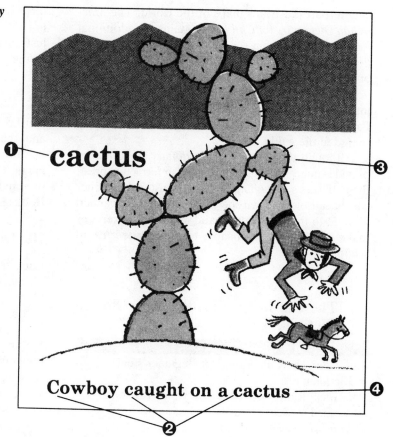

IV. Illustrations

The illustrations by P. D. Eastman are delightful. Aaron the Alligator is the first character we meet. He is green and appears confident and inquisitive. He is seen at least once on every double-page spread, always involved in the visual interpretation of a word. Abigail and her Aunt Ada, the humans, also occur frequently, as do the humanized brown dogs and bears and the quadruplet boys, Jack, James, Jerry, and Joe, who come to the fore in the words that begin with letter **J**. Except for an Eskimo, an American Indian, and an Indian from India there is no serious attempt to portray various ethnic groups.

The graphic layout is simple and clear. Each letter of the alphabet is given at least a half page introduction on which the white 2½″ uppercase and 1¾″ lowercase letters appear on a field of color, a new color for each letter of the alphabet. That color is then used in the wide horizontal and vertical bars that divide the following pages into two columns and separate each definition. Roman type is used throughout.

V. Summary

The famous Cat in the Hat is the only illustration on the cover of *The Cat in the Hat Beginner Book Dictionary*, and young readers may recognize it as a symbol of a book that they will derive great pleasure from reading. (The Cat does not appear inside the book.) This dictionary is an old favorite, almost old enough to be considered a modern classic. It subtly plays with interrelationships of words, has clear definitions, and the funny characters that are seen throughout the pages have the silliness and earnestness of the universal child.

Purists might argue that this is out of date, omits ethnic variations in its art (it was completed before such concerns became the important part of American education that they are today), and defines more with pictures than with words. However, it does convey that learning can be fun and painless. For that reason, it is as suitable for a home or library picture-book collection as it is for the younger elementary classroom.

Childcraft Dictionary

❶ Homophone is marked by a
black triangle

❷ Syllabication, pronunciation,
parts of speech (spelled out),
and inflected forms all follow the
definition

❸ Word history is marked by a
blue triangle and is printed
between blue rules

❹ Labeled four-color illustration
identifies entry word

---

gorilla / governor

gorilla   A large, very strong animal that is a
kind of monkey. Gorillas have big, heavy
bodies, short legs, and long arms. They live in
~~Africa.~~ ▲ Another word that sounds like this
is **guerrilla.**
go·ril·la (gə ril′ə) *noun, plural* **gorillas.**

▲   The word **gorilla** comes from a Greek
word that means "wild, hairy person." Some
early explorers in Africa thought that the
gorillas were wild people instead of animals.

Gorilla

Childcraft Dictionary

Facts at a Glance

Full Title: **Childcraft Dictionary.**
Publisher: World Book, Inc.
Editor: William D. Halsey.
Edition Reviewed: 1982.

Number of Volumes: 1.
Number of Entries: 30,000.
Number of Pages: 800.
Number of Illustrations: 1,000 in full color.
Trim Size: 7¼″ × 9¾″.
Binding: cloth.

Price: $25.00.
Intended Readership: grades 3 through 6.
Sold door-to-door and by direct mail. ISBN 0-
7166-3170-9.

I. Scope and Format

The *Childcraft Dictionary* identically reproduces the
724-page word list and pronunciation key found in
the MACMILLAN DICTIONARY FOR CHILDREN reviewed elsewhere in this Buying Guide. Both contain
the same clear, brief guide, "How to Use Your Dictionary," although with different illustrations. Both
volumes are intended for use by children in the elementary grades.

A primary difference between the two volumes is
that the *Childcraft Dictionary* does not purport to be
a comprehensive reference source. While the MAC-
MILLAN DICTIONARY FOR CHILDREN includes an article titled "The Story of English" and a substantial
reference section, presenting geographic, historical,
and scientific information, the *Childcraft Dictionary*
contains no analogous features.

What the *Childcraft Dictionary* does contain, in
addition to a complete contents listing that its counterpart lacks, is a 61-page feature titled "The Magic
of Words," which is reprinted from *The Magic of
Words—The 1975 Childcraft Annual* (© 1975). En-
gagingly written at a reading level accessible to the
intended audience, this section serves to stimulate
children's interest in language and is likely to encourage them to browse through the word list itself.
A section titled "Fun with Words" presents various
forms of wordplay, including rebuses, tongue twist-
ers, riddles, puns, palindromes, and anagrams, as
well as more formal word games. Children will enjoy
this section and will be encouraged to look further
into the volume. Although most of the activities have

no didactic content, it is probable that children who become interested in riddles and puns will also be intrigued by varied definitions and usages as presented within the word list.

Another section, titled "Names are Words," lists the meanings of many common given names and explains the origin of surnames in familial relationships, occupations, physical features, character traits, and places of residence. Children will eagerly seek their own names and names of family members and friends. Again, while the primary value of the material is its power to interest and entertain children, it also introduces the idea of etymology in a particularly accessible way.

Etymology is itself the topic of the final subsection, "Word Stories." Appealing to children's interests, this section begins with a presentation of etymologies of food terms, such as **sundae** and **hamburger**. Etymologies are provided for animal names, house parts, meal names, clothing terms, and words related to school and to occupations: all of these words are within the scope and interest of children of the intended ages. Also discussed are words coined as abbreviations of longer forms (for example, **cab** from **cabriolet**), shifts in words' meanings through history, invented words, and onomatopoeia.

The *Childcraft Dictionary* is well designed for home use by elementary school children. The other dictionaries incorporating the same word list, the MACMILLAN DICTIONARY FOR CHILDREN and Macmillan BEGINNING DICTIONARY, have a more studious tone as well as some direct classroom applications; the *Childcraft Dictionary* is designed for children's entertainment as well as edification, and they will have no difficulty reading and browsing through it independently. However, the *Childcraft Dictionary* omits the glossary of computer terms appended to the other dictionaries, and potential purchasers may wish to delay acquisition of the dictionary in the hope that a later edition will incorporate, preferably within the main word list, computer terminology.

The Christian Student Dictionary

Facts at a Glance

Full Title: **The Christian Student Dictionary.**
Publisher: Bob Jones University Press.
Editor: Grace C. Collins.
Edition Reviewed: ©1982.

Number of Volumes: 1.
Number of Entries: 13,000.
Number of Pages: 864.

Number of Illustrations: 1,400 (700 in full color; 700 in black and white).
Trim Size: 8″ × 10″.
Binding: paper over boards.

Price: $16.90.
Intended Readership: grades 2 through 5.
Sold in bookstores and other outlets; also sold to schools. ISBN 0-89084-172-1.

I. Introduction

This is the first edition of a work described by its publishers as "a *complete* up-to-date dictionary reflecting a Christian world view." It is designed to be used for school and home reference by students in elementary school. In the preface, the publishers provide their rationale for the compilation of this work:

> *The Christian Student Dictionary* was conceived following a thorough review of the most highly regarded student dictionaries. This review provided ample evidence that not one of these dictionaries could be whole-heartedly recommended for use by Christian young people. Many key definitions reflected a skeptical or humanistic bias about the existence of God, about the life and redemptive work of Jesus Christ, and about the important doctrines of the Christian faith. Illustrative sentences . . . presented examples of dishonesty, disrespect for authority, disregard for Sunday as the Lord's day, humanism, role reversal in the home, magic and the occult, and objectionable activities.

The stated purpose of the dictionary is to replace these "objectionable features" with entries that reflect a biblical perspective. While the preface takes a doctrinaire fundamentalist position, much of the text is not couched in religious terms. The "Guide to the Dictionary," for example, includes no religious content, and most of the entries within the word list are comparable to those of other children's dictionaries. However, selected entries within the word list *are* dominated by a fundamentalist view. These entries in many instances define words related to what the fundamentalist would term "secular humanism." In some instances, the text's emphasis on a specific sectarian Christian usage of a term obscures its other meanings. As one would expect, fundamentalism also

The Christian Student Dictionary

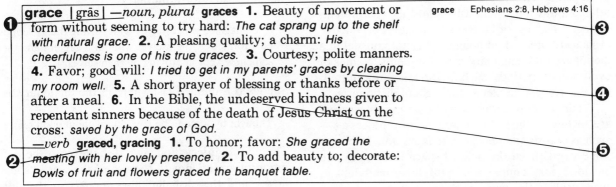

grace |grās| —*noun, plural* **graces** **1.** Beauty of movement or form without seeming to try hard: *The cat sprang up to the shelf with natural grace.* **2.** A pleasing quality; a charm: *His cheerfulness is one of his true graces.* **3.** Courtesy; polite manners. **4.** Favor; good will: *I tried to get in my parents' graces by cleaning my room well.* **5.** A short prayer of blessing or thanks before or after a meal. **6.** In the Bible, the undeserved kindness given to repentant sinners because of the death of Jesus Christ on the cross: *saved by the grace of God.* —*verb* **graced, gracing** **1.** To honor; favor: *She graced the meeting with her lovely presence.* **2.** To add beauty to; decorate: *Bowls of fruit and flowers graced the banquet table.*

grace   Ephesians 2:8, Hebrews 4:16

❶ Part of speech is spelled out and listed with its separate numbered definitions

❷ Inflected forms follow the part-of-speech label

❸ Brief cross-references from an entry word to scriptural passages appear in the margins

❹ Illustrative sentences follow some definitions

❺ Some meanings are specific to fundamentalist Christian doctrine

appears directly in definitions of religious terms, such as **Bible**:

> The 39 books of the Old Testament and the 27 books of the New Testament, which together make up the complete revelation from God to man and which is the final authority for the Christian's faith and practice. The Bible is also called the Scriptures or the Word of God.

Other children's dictionaries define the word more broadly and reveal its use by more than one religion or sect. The definition provided in THE AMERICAN HERITAGE CHILDREN'S DICTIONARY is representative:

> **1.** The book of the sacred writings of the Christian religion that includes the Old and New Testaments. **2.** The sacred book of Judaism, consisting of the Old Testament. **3.** A book containing the sacred writings of any religion.

Adult dictionary buyers *outside* the specific, sectarian group for which this work is intended would find it limited and clearly biased. Elementary readers would not be capable of distinguishing the bias.

II. Authority

The Christian Student Dictionary's word list is based on the lexical database of the 1981 Houghton Mifflin CHILDREN'S DICTIONARY. The choice of words is based on their inclusion in *The American Heritage Word Frequency Book* (Houghton Mifflin, 1971)—

a compilation of the words most frequently used in books and periodicals for students of different ages—and *The Living Word Vocabulary*, by Edgar Dale and Joseph O'Rourke (Field Enterprises Educational Corp., 1976), a vocabulary inventory reflecting word recognition at various age levels. Both these sources are reliable, but dated.

To ensure the dictionary's comprehensive inclusion of religious terms, its compilers included words related to biblical Christianity regardless of whether or not they appeared in word frequency listings. Sources consulted for the selection of these terms included, according to the publishers, "Bible glossaries, Bible dictionaries, and basic word lists for Bible study."

Bob Jones University Press is affiliated with Bob Jones University in Greenville, South Carolina. Founded by evangelist Bob Jones in 1927, the accredited university has an enrollment of over 4,000 and also runs schools for grades K through 12. Grace Collins, the dictionary's editor and consultant for lexicography and linguistics, chairs the university's Department of Linguistics.

III. Comprehensiveness

The Christian Student Dictionary includes most words that students in grades two through five might encounter in school and private reading; main entry words are comparable to those found in such standard student dictionaries as WEBSTER'S ELEMENTARY DICTIONARY and the MACMILLAN DICTIONARY FOR CHILDREN.

The effort to make certain definitions reflect fundamentalist Christian views, together with certain related omissions, seriously limits its comprehensiveness. Names for human sexual and reproductive organs are omitted, although this is not unusual in a dictionary for elementary school students. Names of evolutionary periods, such as *Jurassic*, are omitted, but this is usual in elementary school dictionaries.

While scientific terms such as **gene** and **chlorophyll** are included, those for most scientific processes—such as *mitosis* and *photosynthesis* are not. Although some words from the field of space technology are included (for example, **astronaut**, **lunar module**, and **space walk**), the work excludes computer science terms—such as *floppy disk* and the computer-related meanings of *disk*, *file*, and *terminal*—that would be appropriately included in a dictionary for this age group and are included, for example, in the Macmillan Dictionary for Children.

There are etymologies for some words; these appear as boxed items in the wide outer margin of the page. Interestingly written, they often present the history of more than one sense of a word. For example, in the margin next to two main entries for **content** appears the following:

Content[1] and **content**[2] both come from the same Latin word, which originally meant "to hold together." But the word also meant "to contain or hold" and then "something contained" (**content**[1]). And it meant "to restrain, hold back" and then "restrained, satisfied" (**content**[2]).

Also included are homophones, homographs, verb forms, phrasal verbs, illustrative phrases and sentences, and—in the margins—biblical references for selected words. These enable children to refer to the Bible to see the word used in context; they are based on the Revised Standard Version. Biographical entries are excluded, but brief geographical entries appear, including U.S. states, with location and capital, and major foreign countries.

IV. Quality and Currency of Entries

Entries are generally clearly written at an appropriate reading level for the intended audience. The vocabulary is controlled on both religious and linguistic principles. Terms inconsistent with the publishers' interpretation of the Bible are avoided; words that might be unfamiliar are defined in their own entries.

The publishers' avowed objectives result in a number of definitions that will be unacceptable to a non-

fundamentalist reader. For example, the second meaning listed for **evolution** is

The imagined processes by which living things supposedly formed by themselves without a Creator and then somehow kept improving by themselves.

Supposed is defined elsewhere in the dictionary as

Thought by some to be true, but without good reason.

The editors inject their own disbelief into the definition of **evolution** with the use of the word "somehow," and this disbelief also appears in the third definition provided for **evolve**:

To undergo the imagined evolution of living things: *How could birds evolve from reptiles?*

The repetition of the adjective "imagined" in the definitions for **evolve** and **evolution** violates a basic principle of good lexicography: to describe what a word means, not to characterize its concept—especially from a limited point of view and for children at a formative stage of intellectual development.

Definitions of some words not directly related to religion or so-called secular humanism are also influenced by fundamentalist authoritarian thought as well as questionable lexicography. For example, **definition** is defined as

An explanation of the exact meaning or meanings of a word or phrase.

Definitions in comparable dictionaries avoid such terms as "exact." *The Christian Student Dictionary* offers the following as a second definition for **role**:

A proper or usual part played by someone or something: *Mothers have important roles in children's lives.*

Fundamentalist bias is subtly reflected in the use of "proper" and overtly in the illustrative sentence.

In some instances, especially in the case of words with religious usages, some important senses of the word are not defined. For example, **heaven** is defined as

1. Often **heavens** The sky or universe as seen from the earth. 2. The eternal place of God, the angels, and those who are saved; the place of complete happiness.

This definition does not indicate that *many* world religions share a belief in an "eternal" heaven, nor does it reflect the metaphorical, nonreligious use of the word to mean "a pleasant place." In some instances in which more than one definition is given, a doctrinaire preference is expressed. For example, **Christianity** is defined as

> The religion based upon the person and teachings of Jesus Christ as found in the Bible. 2. Very loosely, all religions that claim to worship Christ. Bible-believing Christians usually do not use the word this way.

The last sentence implies a very restricted definition of *belief* that may confuse young readers.

V. Syllabication and Pronunciation

Syllabication is indicated by centered bold dots within the main entry word. Pronunciation is given for each word, following the main entry word. Stressed syllables are indicated by boldface type and accent marks, and phonetic spelling and diacritical marks indicate pronunciation. A full pronunciation key appears at the front of the volume; an abbreviated key, for quick reference, appears at the bottom left of each double spread. Variant pronunciations are rare—for example, **creek** |krēk| or |krĭk| —but the choices are appropriate for use at this level.

VI. Special Features

Special features within the word list include a brief visual history, heading each section, of the letter of the alphabet, as well as the boxed etymologies and the scriptural references already discussed. The work also includes a detailed "Guide to the Dictionary," clearly written for children, that introduces them to the information found in the dictionary and the skills required to locate it. Exercises, suitable for individual or classroom use, are interspersed within the guide and are well designed to give children practice with dictionary skills. A "Spelling Table" presents the varied ways in which sounds are spelled in English and enables students to look up words they know how to pronounce but not how to spell.

VII. Accessibility

Entry words are alphabetized letter by letter. Some alternative spellings are provided, with the most common American spelling given first, as for **catalog**
or **catalogue**. Occasionally the variant spelling is given in bold type at the end of the entry; for example, the conclusion of the entry for **Chanukah** (which provides an accurate but sketchy definition) reads "Another form of this word is **Hanukkah**." The words shown with variant spellings are primarily those borrowed from other languages and those British spellings that are acceptable in the United States.

The book is not thumb indexed, but colored bars, with the letter appearing in white, are printed near the top of each page. All of the bars are in the same color and are located at the same spot on pages. Because there is no clear demarcation between sections, this feature will be of limited use to novice dictionary users. More helpful are the pairs of guide words at the top of each page that enable a reader to narrow the search for a word. A table of contents at the beginning of the volume lists the work's special features, ensuring that they will not be overlooked.

VIII. Graphics and Format

The Christian Student Dictionary is profusely illustrated in color and has line drawings and photographs, both black and white and toned. Illustrations appear next to their entries and are captioned with the main entry word and sometimes a brief phrase of further clarification. For example, an explanatory caption accompanies a two-part drawing illustrating **potato** as both a plant and a vegetable. A good ethnic balance is evident in the illustrations. However, in keeping with its stated opposition to "role reversal in the home," the dictionary depicts men and women *exclusively* in traditional roles. Illustrations are attractive and generally helpful adjuncts to the verbal definitions. Some drawings, however, such as the anatomical diagrams illustrating body organs, are sketchy; the drawings of plants and animals are more detailed.

The pages are attractively laid out, with bright blue rules guiding the eye to the two-thirds width of each page devoted to text. The remaining one-third serves as a wide margin, providing uncrowded space for illustrations, etymology boxes, scriptural references, and brief pronunciation keys. Main entry words appear in boldface type overhanging the text. Also boldfaced are variant and derived forms; part-of-speech labels and illustrative sentences are italicized. The print is of appropriate size for a work at this level, and variations in typeface help a student reader to locate information. The paper is bright white and of high quality with minimal show-through. The laminated washable cover is sturdy, and the pages are securely bound.

IX. Summary

In those private school and home settings where conservative Christian fundamentalism is the ruling world view, this dictionary will serve to teach children new words, show them how to use words in context, and provide practice with dictionary skills. Although the work is similar in format to high quality nonsectarian dictionaries, such as THE AMERICAN HERITAGE CHILDREN'S DICTIONARY and the MACMILLAN DICTIONARY FOR CHILDREN, public schools will find the focus of *The Christian Student Dictionary* unsuited to the typical reference needs of students; the clientele of some public libraries, however, may include patrons who would elect to use just such a work.

The Concise American Heritage Dictionary

Facts at a Glance

Full Title: **The Concise American Heritage Dictionary.**
Publisher: Houghton Mifflin Company.
Editors: Staff of *The American Heritage Dictionary.*
Edition Reviewed: © 1980.

Number of Volumes: 1.
Number of Definitions: about 55,000.
Number of Pages: 820.
Number of Illustrations: nearly 300.
Trim Size: 6⅛″ × 9¾″.
Binding: hardcover.

Price: $7.95.
Intended Readership: junior high and high school through adult.
Sold in bookstores and other outlets. ISBN 0-395-24522-2.

I. Introduction

The *Concise American Heritage Dictionary*, a heavily abridged version of the original AMERICAN HERITAGE DICTIONARY OF THE ENGLISH LANGUAGE (© 1969), contains approximately 55,000 entries. Although the definitions in the *Concise* have been specially revised to be simpler and easier to read, the editors have retained many features—in condensed form—that are characteristic of the parent work. The preface to the *Concise* summarizes these: "*The American Heritage Dictionary of the English Language* [1969], edited by William Morris, presented several innovations in lexicography, princi-

pally in the areas of design and illustration, guidance on matters of usage, and etymology." One much-praised feature of the parent work, the tracing of words to their Indo-European roots in the etymologies, has been retained as a separate appendix for this dictionary.

The *Concise*'s typeface is slightly larger than that in THE AMERICAN HERITAGE DESK DICTIONARY. The nearly 300 illustrations, including maps and portraits, are also considerably larger than those in other American Heritage dictionaries. Biographical and geographic entries are included in the main alphabetical sections. In the preface, the publisher notes that a paperback edition of this work, simply titled THE AMERICAN HERITAGE DICTIONARY, is available from Dell Publishing Company (the Dell edition is reviewed elsewhere in this Buying Guide).

II. Authority

The Concise American Heritage Dictionary is published by Houghton Mifflin, publisher of the American Heritage family of dictionaries and other respected language reference books for adults and students. The dictionary was prepared by the *American Heritage Dictionary* editorial staff, none of whom are listed in the current printing.

The preface explains that the more than 100 usage notes in the text "are derived from the deliberations of the American Heritage Panel on English Usage over a period of four years." No formal list of the panel's members appears, but the back cover mentions that they include some of "America's most famous writers, editors, and speakers—including Isaac Asimov, Cleveland Amory, Barbara W. Tuchman, David Ogilvy, Walter W. (Red) Smith—led by Edwin Newman, the distinguished commentator and writer."

As in the other American Heritage dictionaries, the etymologies are based on those prepared for the parent work by Professor Calvert Watkins and other members of Harvard University's linguistics department.

III. Comprehensiveness

The *Concise* has an acceptable number of entries for an abridged school or everyday dictionary and does not claim to be "comprehensive." A brief comparison of the number of entries between **largess** and **lasagna** shows that the *Concise AHD* has 12 entries compared to the *AHD Desk Dictionary*'s 18. The words not in the *Concise* are: **larghetto, laryng-, laryngeal, larynges, laryngo-** or **laryng,** and **laryngo-**

The Concise American Heritage Dictionary

❶ Boldface guide words in upper right or left corner of each page, indicating first and last words listed on the page

❷ Part of speech is indicated in italic abbreviation

❸ Chemical symbols are presented in boldface type

❹ Definitions with closely related senses are marked with boldface lower case letters

❺ Etymology is bracketed and includes a cross reference to the appendix for more detailed information

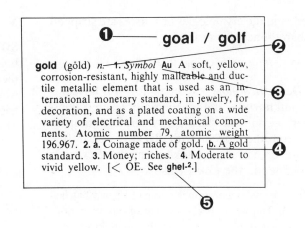

scope. In the section of entries from **paprika** to **parachute**, the *Concise* and the *Desk* both have nine entries, eight of them alike: for the ninth entry, *Desk* includes the adjective **parabolic**, and *Concise* includes the abbreviation **par** (which is not labeled as an abbreviation, incidentally).

All words have etymologies or sources; there is also a generous use of short examples, and quotations with attributions, but only 100 words have usage notes.

Lists of compound words formed from **de-**, **dis-**, **non-**, **over-**, and **re-** are included and so are English meanings for a list of words combined with **-mania**, such as **heliomania** (sunbathing) and **sitomania** (food). There are also a considerable number of illustrations with caption labels, as well as charts and tables that add to the reader's understanding of words (see the section below on "Special Features" of this dictionary).

In general, the dictionary is very complete for a concise edition, although many *advanced* scientific and technical terms are excluded from the *Concise*, as they are from the *Desk*. In the *Concise*, fewer meanings are included and these are considerably rewritten and condensed.

IV. Quality and Currency of Entries

The publisher's claim that the definitions have been "selected, and rewritten or edited, to be as accurately lucid and useful as possible" is generally true. The reviewer of the *Concise AHD* for *American Refer-*

ence Books Annual 1982 stated that this dictionary "approaches language sensibly" but cited an example of "inevitable inconsistencies and lapses:" for example, "The entry *prior* is labeled an adjective, its accepted usage; but in the definition of *premature*—'occurring . . . prior to the customary or correct time'—*prior* functions in its prevalent but questionable role as a preposition."

The information in the entries follows the usual *American Heritage Dictionary* sequence: bold main entry word divided into syllables; pronunciation(s); part of speech; inflected forms; definitions, numbered when necessary and often accompanied by short examples of use; brief etymology, source, or indication that an entry is a short form—"**em·cee** . . . [short for *M(aster of) C(eremonies)*.]"—and alternate forms and their parts of speech. In some cases, variant forms or spellings follow the entry word. Field or style labels occur before meanings, but apart from the label "*Informal*," these appear less frequently than in other abridged versions of the parent work. Synonyms are not labeled or listed. All this information under each entry is helpful to users, since they do not have to search in the appendixes or in other reference books for specifics.

A comparison of several definitions between the entries for **largess** and **lasagna**, from the AMERICAN HERITAGE DESK DICTIONARY and the *Concise* reveals considerable differences in how these abridged works define terms. In almost all cases, the language of the *Concise* is simpler and more direct. Taxonomy is omitted, only the most common field labels are included, and the etymologies or sources are stripped to the bare bones, for example:

> **lar·rup** *v. Informal.* To flog; thrash; beat. [?].

In the *Desk Dictionary*, the etymology for **larrup** is "[Orig. unknown.]," rather than a bracketed question mark. Compare "**lark**[2] *n.* A carefree romp or prank" from the *Concise* with "**lark**[2] *n.* A carefree adventure or harmless prank" from the *Desk*. Or **larva**, defined in the *Concise* as

> **1.** The wingless, often wormlike form of a newly hatched insect. **2.** The newly hatched stage of any of various animals that differ markedly in the adult form, as a tadpole.

In the *Desk* version, **larva** is defined as

> **1.** The wingless, often wormlike form, such as a caterpillar, of a newly hatched insect before undergoing metamorphosis.
> **2.** The newly hatched, earliest stage of any of various animals that undergo metamorphosis, differing markedly in form and appearance from the adult.

As these examples show, for general school use in junior high and up, the *Concise* is an adult dictionary with normal lexicographic apparatus that can be understood by younger readers with unsophisticated, or limited, vocabularies.

The order of defined meanings is not necessarily the historical order, as explained in the "Guide to the Dictionary." Rather, it is the central meaning with other meanings added in logical order. This order is clearer for the reader, and it is also the form many younger dictionaries use. The guide specifically notes that the organization of meanings under an entry "seeks to clarify the fact that, despite its various meanings, the entry is a single 'word' and not a number of separate words that happen to be spelled the same way." This goal is usually achieved in the simplified definitions of the *Concise*, as the example for **larva** shows. Occasionally the condensation does leave out a useful sense, but the *Concise* is sometimes more efficient at including senses than the slightly larger AHD Desk Dictionary. For example, under the prefix **para-**, which is widely used, the *Concise* includes the meaning of "subsidiary to," whereas the *Desk* does not.

Since this dictionary's most recent copyright date is 1980, many words in common use today are also not included. The omission of advanced technical terms and of words such as *aerobics*, *byte*, and *videocassette*, limits the overall usefulness of this dictionary.

V. Syllabication and Pronunciation

Syllables in the *Concise*'s entry words are divided by bold centered dots, as in other American Heritage dictionaries: **da·ta** or **pro·cess·ing**. However, when words in phrasal entries also appear as separate entries, they are not divided: **data processing**; another example is **cir·cu·la·tory system**, but the adjective *circulatory* does not appear as a main entry. The breaking of words into syllables follows standard editorial and printing practice.

The pronunciation also follows the standard American Heritage system and is intended to help readers reproduce a satisfactory pronunciation acceptable in "all circumstances," although the editors acknowledge that regional sounds will vary. A brief key to pronunciations, with a typical word that demonstrates the sound accompanied by *The American Heritage Dictionary* sound symbol appears in the "Guide to the Dictionary." Two lines of this pronunciation key appear at the bottom of each page in the dictionary. Special vowel sounds, such as the *schwa* (ə) in **telegraph** (**tĕl′ ə-grăf′**), and *l* and *n* (the syllabic consonants) are explained, as are nine foreign sounds common in English, including the French sound of *gn* in compiègne. Primary and secondary stress are shown with bold and lighter face stress marks: **beau′ti·fi·ca′tion**. These pronunciation guides are very useful to the reader who takes the time to read them, as are the pronunciation guides at the bottom of each page.

VI. Special Features

Within the alphabetical sections of the *Concise* are numerous excellent charts, lists, and tables presented in larger formats than in the other American Heritage dictionaries. These include: a table of alphabets (Arabic, Hebrew, Greek, and Russian), a list of 26 common bacteria (clearly illustrated, with Latin names), books of the Bible (Hebrew Scriptures, Douay, King James Version, and New Testament, accompanied by a handsome facsimile of a page from a fourteenth-century Spanish Hebrew text), the Braille alphabet, months of three principal calendars (Gregorian, Hebrew, and Moslem), a table of currencies (with exchange rates for August 1975), a periodical table of elements, international code flags, Morse code, a full-page chart of geologic time scales, a chart of the Indo-European family of languages, the manual alphabet, a table of measurement units, proofreaders' marks, roman and arabic numerals, and even a chart of the 24 basic Germanic and two later English alphabetic runes, plus symbols and signs. Since there is no table of contents, and no appendixes, readers who are used to finding these tables at the back of a dictionary (where they are placed in many other dictionaries) may have difficulty finding them within the alphabetical listing—until they become familiar with the text.

Apart from these, two other features are the opening "Guide to the Dictionary" and the alphabetic listing of Indo-European roots, a feature of the original AMERICAN HERITAGE DICTIONARY. The guide has helpful subheads for its explanatory paragraphs, for example, "Idioms," but rather surprisingly the whole section has not been revised so that its language matches the simpler definitions and text in the *Concise*. The etymologies of the parent work traced words to their Indo-European roots. This material is placed in an appendix in the *Concise*. There is no question that it is scholarly and excellent lexicographic material, but it does seem too advanced for the level of the *Concise*'s definitions, which were specially revised, according to the publisher, to be easy to read.

Usage notes, which were featured in the original AMERICAN HERITAGE DICTIONARY and its subsequent college editions, are much condensed here and accompany the most basic words such as **affect**[1] *v.*, **comprise**, **convince**, **foot**, **help**, **influence**, **who**, and so forth. A particularly useful note distinguishes the use of **bimonthly** from **semimonthly**. The majority of definitions feature very brief, italicized examples of a word's use.

VII. Accessibility

At first glance, the most notable feature of this dictionary is the generous size of its typeface, which is a relief from the eye-straining print in many dictionaries. Also, the generous white space between lines makes scanning the text and head words easier. In addition, the pair of guide words at the top of each page is printed in large bold type. This is helpful, since the dictionary is not thumb-indexed. For students with some visual impairment, this dictionary could be useful.

All entries occur in letter-by-letter alphabetical order. This includes compound words, biographical names, geographic entries, and standard abbreviations. For example: **kt.**, **Kuala Lumpur**, **Kublai Khan**, **kudos**. Alternative spellings and inflections are printed in boldface type. In the definitions, cross-references are indicated in bold type:

net·ton. See **ton**.
New Greek. **Modern Greek**.

mold[3] *n.* Also chiefly Brit. **mould**.
mould. Chief Brit. Variant of **mold**.

The five-page "Guide to the Dictionary" is printed immediately before the main entries and has clear subheads for its explanatory paragraphs such as "Idioms," "Numbers and Letters," "Main Entry Words Having Meaning Only in a Phrase," and so forth. The pronunciation key list is easily deciphered, and the explanatory notes are clear, but may be difficult for users below high school age. A list of abbreviations and symbols appearing in the dictionary's etymologies faces the first page of entries for the letter **Aa**.

The appendix of Indo-European roots appears after **Zz** entries and includes a brief explanation of the root entries. Again, this will be difficult for younger students.

Special charts and tables, such as currencies, appear in the main alphabetic sections, but are not listed elsewhere. There is, in fact, no table of contents, a regrettable omission.

VIII. Graphics and Format

Although there are only approximately 300 illustrations, many of them photographs, they are large enough to see clearly and are generally excellent. In its original 1979 review of THE AMERICAN HERITAGE DICTIONARY abridged versions, *Library Journal* noted that the publicity on the illustrations (especially for the paperback abridgment) was "more a promotional gimmick than a vocabulary aid." In the case of this hardbound abridgment, the opposite is true. The pictures, especially those with extensive labels such as the anatomy drawings, add considerably to the reader's understanding of words. There are even clear line drawings for the entries **beef**, **lamb**, and **pork** that label cuts of meat.

The maps are large enough to show geographic locations and areas clearly; capital cities are indicated on them with bold stars. The portraits are also large and clear, although only two women (Elizabeth I and Queen Victoria) appear out of 70. Charts, tables, and lists such as Morse code are well designed. The heavy white paper and sturdy binding with plain dark blue laminated cover are attractive and will withstand heavy use.

IX. Summary

The *Concise American Heritage Dictionary* is a generally reliable, much condensed, and easier to read variation of the respected AMERICAN HERITAGE DICTIONARY, now in its *Second College Edi-*

tion. For a "budget-priced dictionary," as the publisher calls it, the work is good value for the money. Many readers will appreciate the large, informative pictures; they are much more than just a gimmick. Readers should be aware that the current edition does not have a large vocabulary of highly scientific or technical words and that some dates, such as population figures in the geographic entries or recent death dates are either not current or absent.

Obscene and vulgar words are omitted here as in other abridged versions of the parent work. While usage is explained and demonstrated, the dictionary is less prescriptive in its condensed form here than in other versions; only basic style labels such as **informal** and **poetic** are included, and the special field labels are less evident.

This edition is very thorough for a concise dictionary. In some areas it gives more information than is needed in a concise edition; however, it is easy to use. For this reason, *The Concise American Heritage Dictionary* will be a useful work for junior high and high school libraries as well as for classrooms and for home use.

The Doubleday Children's Picture Dictionary

Facts at a Glance

Full Title: **The Doubleday Children's Picture Dictionary**.
Publisher: Doubleday & Company.
Compiler: Felicia Law.
Illustrator: Carol Holmes.
Current Edition: © 1986.

Number of Volumes: 1.
Number of Entries: over 1,500.
Number of Pages: 199.
Number of Illustrations: 199 pages in full color.
Number of Maps: 6 in full color.
Trim Size: 9″ × 10¾″.
Binding: paper over boards.

Price: $11.95.
Intended Readership: early elementary grades.
Sold in bookstores and other outlets; and also to libraries and schools. ISBN 0-385-23711-1.

I. Scope and Format

The Doubleday Children's Picture Dictionary is an illustrated dictionary of over 1,500 words. The language used in the definitions is comprehensible by children in the primary grades. This book advances beyond the word-picture identification dictionaries in that there is an average of nine definitions per page and only one or two illustrations to a page.

Originally published in the United Kingdom under the title *Kingfisher First Dictionary*, the book provides, in its introduction, a global view of the English language. According to the introduction, "In ordinary life few people use more than 1,500 to 3,000 words. . . . [This dictionary] will tell you about 1,500 of these English words."

Arrangement of the entry words is alphabetical with two guide words at the top of each page that indicate the first and last words defined on it. Big bold black roman type identifies the entry word on the line above the definition. When the word or a form of it is repeated in the definition, it is also highlighted with a heavier type than the rest of the sentence. When more than one definition is provided, the meanings are numbered. Because of the clear graphic layout, access is quite easy. Each page is divided into two columns with wide margins. Definitions are distinctly set apart with white space. The letters of the alphabet are introduced on the appropriate page in 1¾″ upper and lowercase blue letters.

A special feature of the dictionary is a spelling list of 3,000 words, almost half of which are not defined in the volume. The copy on the back cover calls this a "300-word 'speller,'" an obvious numerical typographical error. Words that are considered difficult to spell are in bold print.

A second special feature is a map section at the end of the volume, which begins with a map of the world. However, what follows immediately is a map of the British Isles succeeded by maps of the United States, Canada, Australia, and New Zealand. Thus, the British origin of the book is obvious, and young Americans might be confused to see a map of their country relegated to second place behind that of Britain. And, while the map of Canada might be relevant for this age level, those of Britain, Australia, and New Zealand do not seem appropriate.

II. Authority

Although the introduction implies that the words included in the dictionary constitute approximately half of the most commonly used English words, no authority for the selection is cited. The compiler's credentials are not listed.

III. Quality and Currency of Entries

Many of the definitions are inadequate, inconsistent, or in need of a clarifying illustration. For example, "**A** is used a lot in talking and writing. It is often

The Doubleday Children's Picture Dictionary

❶ Entry word appears in boldface type, with senses numbered

❷ The entry's plural form, in boldface, is used in a sentence

❸ Four-color illustration aids in understanding meaning of the entry word

❹ Entry word in definition also bold

❺ Illustrative sentences explain meaning

Lucy **likes** playing with her toys.

like

1. I **like** all my toys. I enjoy playing with them. I **like** people I enjoy spending time with.
2. If one thing is **like** another, they are similar. Tom is just **like** his twin sister.

used before the name of a thing. We say, 'a ball can bounce,' or 'I saw a bird fly.' The word *a* is used five times in the entry, yet it has not been defined, only talked about. Of the numbers zero (0) through ten (10), only eight are identified in the text as numbers; three (3) is defined as "a small number."

Surprisingly, in a book for this age group, an attempt is made to define some religious words. This may be the result of the book's English origin: it may have been intended for use in Church of England schools. Dictionaries for primary-grade children usually do not define these, because at this age children do not yet have the cognitive skills to understand such concepts. When reduced to limited vocabulary, the "definitions" become simplistic, even misleading: for example, "Many people believe that **God** made the world. We can read about **God** in religious books"; "Christians believe they will go to heaven when they die." These are not really definitions, and in a pluralistic society such as that in the United States, it is offputting to see the concept of Heaven limited to one of Christian belief when it is shared by many other religions.

There are also errors in the definitions that will prove confusing to young readers. For example, under the entry word **quick**, not the adjective but the related adverb is defined: "things done **quickly** take only a short time. We ran **quickly**."

Pronunciation is given for some words. However, the selection is erratic and without an apparent rationale; it will certainly leave the young reader with inadequate information. For example, pronunciation is provided for **captain**, **cough**, **gnome**, the *kn* words, and for **listen**, **loose**, and **lose**, but not for **champion**, **couple**, **dwarf**, **leopard**, **restaurant**, or **soldier**. Parts of speech, syllabication, and etymology are not given for any words. Although this may be appropriate for the youngest intended users, the complete omission of information in these categories renders the book inadequate for even a slightly older audience.

IV. Illustrations

The full-color illustrations are pleasing and add to the graphic design. Unfortunately, some words whose definitions *should* have been reinforced visually were not, and words not especially in need of such clarification are sometimes illustrated. For example, on the page containing the entry **lasso**, no illustration is provided for that word, but an illustration depicting three men in a boat is provided to amplify definitions of **large**, **lake**, and **land**. The first picture within the word list is a poor choice: it portrays a child who looks ill and illustrates the sentence "John ate **about** fifteen chocolates." This is a dubious way to excite children and get them interested in browsing through the rest of the dictionary, and it certainly does not explain the word **about**. On the other hand, the drawings manifest good minority representation, and illustrator Carol Holmes added interest to the pictures by using a variety of artistic styles and by often working an interpretation of two or more words into a single scene.

V. Summary

The Doubleday Children's Picture Dictionary falls below standard. It is inconsistent and suffers from poor editing; it will not adequately serve the needs of young dictionary users. Home, public, and school libraries would do well to pass this one up.

The Doubleday Dictionary for Home, School, and Office

Facts at a Glance

Full Title: **The Doubleday Dictionary for Home, School, and Office.**
Publisher: Doubleday & Company.
Editor: Sidney I. Landau, Editor-in-Chief.
Edition Reviewed: © 1975.

Volumes: 1.
Number of Entries: 85,000.
Number of Pages: 906.
Number of Illustrations: 970 black-and-white line drawings, maps, tables, and charts.
Trim Size: $5\frac{1}{2}'' \times 8\frac{1}{8}''$.
Binding: hardcover.

Price: $11.95; thumb-indexed, $12.95.
Intended Readership: junior high school students and up.
Sold in bookstores and other outlets; also sold to libraries and schools. ISBN 0-385-04099-7; 0-385-03368-0.

I. Introduction

Originally published in 1975, *The Doubleday Dictionary* was designed as a general purpose work ranging between concise dictionaries of about 55,000 entries and the more extensive, abridged works of 100,000 and up. At the time of publication, it was claimed by the editor to be the first entirely new dictionary in its class for almost a decade. Subsequently, other new dictionaries of approximately comparable size were published. These included THE SCRIBNER-BANTAM ENGLISH DICTIONARY in 1977 and the 1980 OXFORD AMERICAN DICTIONARY.

Sidney I. Landau states in his preface that *The Doubleday Dictionary* was intended to be compact but comparable "in coverage of the general vocabulary with much larger dictionaries." To achieve this goal, many obsolete and archaic terms are excluded and etymologies have been condensed. Technical terms are included only if they require definition apart from that encompassed by the general vocabulary's meanings. Hence, terms such as *database* and *ion exchange* are omitted because their meanings can be derived from the definitions of their component words. The dictionary also excludes racial and religious epithets, although certain words usually considered taboo are entered, such as **fuck** and **shit**. Distinctively Canadian terms are included as is an essay describing Canadian English.

II. Authority

Doubleday & Company are well-known publishers whose titles include several special-feature dictionaries (such as crossword puzzle dictionaries). Sidney I. Landau was editor-in-chief of *The Doubleday Dictionary*, of THE DOUBLEDAY ROGET'S THESAURUS, and of several Funk & Wagnall's dictionaries, including their *Standard Dictionary of the English Language*. The editor notes in the preface that the staff "had the use of an extensive citation file" of usage quotations.

The five distinguished members of the Dictionary Advisory Committee were Albert H. Marckwardt, its chairman, professor emeritus of English and linguistics, Princeton University; Harold B. Allen, professor emeritus of English and linguistics, University of Minnesota; S. I. Hayakawa, president emeritus, San Francisco State University; Rudolph C. Troike, former director of the Center for Applied Linguistics, Washington, D.C.; and H. Rex Wilson, associate professor of English (linguistics), University of Western Ontario. These scholars' names often appear on dictionaries incorporating Funk & Wagnall's lexicographical material.

The Doubleday Dictionary for Home, School, and Office

❶ Synonym cross-reference to a main entry word appears in small capitals

❷ Idioms are printed in boldface type and defined

❸ Etymology is bracketed and includes a meaning for the source word

❹ Usage labels are spelled out and in italic type

❺ Illustrative phrases and sentences show usage of the defined sense

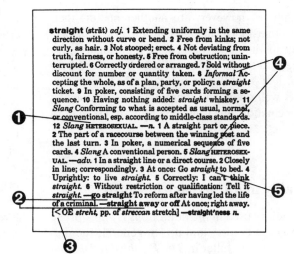

III. Comprehensiveness

Because the stated original purpose of *The Doubleday Dictionary* was to provide general vocabulary coverage comparable to much larger dictionaries, the buyer needs to weigh this claim, as well as the relative comprehensiveness of this compact, midsize work, against the claims of other dictionaries of similar size and, now, more up-to-date vocabularies.

One technique used by the editors was to omit entries for technical terms that could be understood from component words. Terms such as **data processing** and **software**, however, are included because their technical meanings cannot be gleaned by combining the definitions of **data** with **processing** or of **soft** with **ware**. A random check of other words that an up-to-date dictionary of this size should include shows that **bit**, for example, and computer science meanings for **program** are included. Missing words include: *ayatollah*, *baud*, *bluepoint* (a variety of oyster and of domestic cat), and *byte*. Some definitions need additional meanings, such as **Orthodox**, which refers only to the Eastern Orthodox Church.

A comparative check of more difficult but not commonly used words, such as

sternutation *n*. The act of sneezing

shows that *The Doubleday Dictionary* compares well with others such as WEBSTER'S NINTH, and THE AMERICAN HERITAGE SECOND COLLEGE EDITION.

Occasionally, *The Doubleday Dictionary* provides fuller coverage with more extensive examples that will be especially useful to younger readers. The following is an example, from assorted entries for **gob·ble·dy·gook**:

WEBSTER'S NINTH NEW COLLEGIATE DICTIONARY

n. [irreg. fr. *gobble*, *n*. (1944)]: wordy and generally unintelligible jargon

THE RANDOM HOUSE COLLEGE DICTIONARY

n. language characterized by circumlocution and jargon: *the gobbledygook of government reports* . . . [fanciful formation from GOBBLE[2]]

THE AMERICAN HERITAGE DICTIONARY: SECOND COLLEGE EDITION

n. unclear wordy jargon. [Coined by Maury Maverick (1895–1954).]

THE DOUBLEDAY DICTIONARY

n. *Informal* Involved, pedantic, and pompous talk or writing. Also gob'·ble·de·gook[1]. *Gobbledygook* usually refers to wordiness, the unnecessary use of long words, and a stuffy style often encountered in bureaucratic memoranda. "The writer is disposed to regard as contrary to efficient office procedure the utilization of governmental communications apparatus to conduct nongovernmental business," for example, means "Don't use our phones to conduct your personal business."

Perhaps unfairly, many earlier reviews of the dictionary expressed reservations about its claims to comparison with larger works. For example, *Library Journal* (15 January 1975) wrote that "a random survey of their entries (not only in the text but also in the useful gazetteer and biographies sections) does support their claim that they have truly reexamined the language.

. . . Definitions, however, are another matter: their efforts to cram much into little result in a terseness which defeats the major purpose of a dictionary. . . . Recommended for limited purposes." The *Wilson Library Bulletin* (April 1975) noted that "the 'how to use' material is well done, and there are brief sections on usage, punctuation, and Canadian English. Definitions are very brief. . . ."

IV. Quality and Currency of Entries

The vocabulary used in the definitions is appropriate for ninth grade readers and up. In general, the definitions are slightly fuller in *The Doubleday Dictionary* than in other compact dictionaries of a similar size.

The basic sequence of information is: main entry word; pronunciation; part of speech; inflected or alternative forms, or comparative forms of adjectives and adverbs; definitions (numbered and labeled when appropriate, or cross-referenced to a main entry variant spelling or synonym, as in "barrel organ HAND ORGAN"); etymologies; run-in derivatives; and occasional synonym lists appended to entries:

e·vent . . . -Syn. 1 occurrence, happening, episode, incident.

Brief guidance on usage appears in definitions as illustrative phrases or prescriptive instruction:

who . . . 1 Which or what person or persons: *Who is she?* . . . 3 That: used as a relative to introduce a clause: the man *who* mows our lawn.

No guidance appears at whom, unfortunately.

Meanings are ordered according to frequency of use, not semantic evolution, as in sabotage:

n. 1 A wasting of materials or damage to machinery, tools, etc., by workmen to make management comply with their demands. 2 The destruction of bridges, railroads, supply depots, etc., either by enemy agents or by underground resisters. 3 Any deliberate effort to obstruct plans or aims.

The restrictive labels in this dictionary are useful and they indicate (a) usage: *Slang, Informal* (for colloquial use), and *Nonstand.* (for usage not accepted as standard by most native speakers of English); (b) localization: *Regional* for a particular U.S. region, *Brit.* (British), *Can.* (Canadian), *Austral.*, and oc-

casionally *U.S.* when a meaning of a word differs from that understood in the larger English-speaking world. Fields and subjects, for example, *Med.* (medicine), *Ecol.* (ecology), and *Geom.* (geometry), are used. Language of origin, *French, German,* and *Latin,* is indicated for words often italicized in writing that have not been Anglicized; for example, Weltschmerz [G. Lit., world pain]; par excellence [F. Lit., by way of excellence].

In a selected segment of entries, paprika to parachute, both the Doubleday and Scribner-Bantam dictionaries contain 11 entries, with some minor differences. The Doubleday work uses Pap smear; Scribner-Bantam, Pap test. The Scribner-Bantam includes geographic entries, such as Papua New Guinea, while the Doubleday lists geographic terms in a separate alphabetical appendix.

THE SCRIBNER-BANTAM ENGLISH DICTIONARY includes papule; *The Doubleday Dictionary* does not, but it adds the abbreviation par., defined, and the combining form para-^{2}, defined separately from the prefix form entered as para-^{1}. Etymologies for both are included selectively, for example: in the Scribner-Bantam work, para- [Gk = besides]; in Doubleday, para^1 [<Gk. *para* besides] and para^2 [<Ital. *parare* defend]. The Doubleday etymologies, although brief, include the source word as well as the language.

The following comparisons of the definitions for helix will give the reader a sense of the style and fullness of the Doubleday work:

THE DOUBLEDAY DICTIONARY
1 *Geom.* A curve lying on the surface of a cone or cylinder and cutting each element at a constant angle greater than 0° and less than 90°. 2 Any spiral. 3 *Anat.* The spiral cartilage of the external ear. 4 *Archit.* A small volute.

THE AMERICAN HERITAGE DICTIONARY: SECOND COLLEGE EDITION
1. *Math.* A three-dimensional curve that lies on a cylinder or cone and cuts the elements at a constant angle. 2. A spiral form or structure. 3. *Anat.* The folded rim of skin and cartilage around the outer ear. 4. *Archit.* A volute on a Corinthian or Ionic capital.

OXFORD AMERICAN DICTIONARY
a spiral with a diminishing circumference (like a corkscrew) or a constant circumference (like a watch spring).

THE SCRIBNER-BANTAM DICTIONARY
Anything in the shape of the thread of a screw or a spiral.

V. Syllabication and Pronunciation

Syllables are indicated by centered dots to show where words may be hyphenated at the end of a line: **pa·trol**. In general, words in phrases or in special terms are not syllabicated if the words appear separately in the vocabulary as main entries: **patrol wagon**. Exceptions, however, do occur: *rheumatoid* is neither a separate syllabicated entry nor is it divided in **rheumatoid arthritis**. A reader will have to judge its correct syllabication from **rheu·ma·tic** and similar entries.

A "Pronunciation Key" appears on the front, right-hand endpaper and following the preface. The pronunciations use the letters of the alphabet and the more familiar diacritical marks for vowels (â, ä, ē, ī, ō ô, o͞o, o͞o, û, yo͞o), plus th for *th*is, a superscript ʰ (**whale** ʰwāl) and superscript ʸ (**due** dʸo͞o), and the schwa (ə) for the six unstressed vowel sounds in *a*bove, sick*e*n, clar*i*ty, mel*o*n, and foc*u*s. There are brief but useful instructions on pronouncing six foreign sounds frequently encountered in English: à *ami*; oe *peu* or *schön*, ü *vue* or *grün*, kh *ach* or *loch*, and ṅ indicating a preceding nasal sound; and · a voiceless *l* or *r* as in the French *débâcle* (dā·bä′kl′) or a consonant *y* pronounced as a separate syllable with a slight schwa sound following, as the French *fille* (fē′ʸ·). A handy, brief reference chart of vowel signs appears at the bottom of each right-hand page in the book. This chart also explains the signs < derived from; ? origin uncertain or unknown.

VI. Special Features

The introductory material includes two essays and an article on punctuation that are regularly reprinted in other dictionaries derived from *The Doubleday Dictionary* and from former Funk & Wagnall's dictionaries now published by J. G. Ferguson, formerly a part of the Doubleday publishing operation.

Professor Marckwardt's interesting and informative opening essay on "Usage" appears in several works, including the WEBSTER ILLUSTRATED CONTEMPORARY DICTIONARY and the WEBSTER COMPREHENSIVE DICTIONARY (international and encyclopedic editions), that also incorporate *The Doubleday Dictionary* entries. His useful analysis of some of the well-known objections to the use of "hopefully" is also included. The article on "Punctuation" by Professor Allen and that on "Canadian English" by Professor Wilson also appear in the dictionaries cited above (see reviews of them in this book for further description).

Other special features are the separate gazetteer that includes all U.S. and Canadian towns and cities with a population over 15,000 and a list of post office

ZIP codes. As would be expected in a book with a 1975 copyright date, American population and world population figures are not current, and some country names are not up-to-date. Most readers would be better served by a current almanac for this information.

VII. Accessibility

All main words, including abbreviations, appear in strict letter-by-letter alphabetical order. The lower-case form of a word usually precedes the capitalized form, but abbreviations show the most common form first. In the following representative sequence of main entries, note the two entries for **loyalist** and for **Ltd.**, for example:

loy·al·ist, Loy·al·ist, loy·al·ty, loz·enge, LP, Lr, L.s.c., LSD, £.s.d., Lt., l.t., l.tn., Ltd., ltd., Lu, lub·ber.

Main entry words are printed in bold type overhanging the text. Within entries, inflected and alternative forms of words, idioms, and run-in derivations appear in smaller bold type. Two bold guide words appear at the top of each page with a centered page number.

A contents page lists the features including the appendix of measures and weights, which is also reprinted on the back endpapers, the alphabetical gazetteer and the separate biographies, as well as the special essays on language by the chairman and two advisory committee members, the pronunciation key, and a half-page note on the "Formation of Plurals and Participles." Preceding the "Guide to the Dictionary" is a page containing a sample column of text with exceptionally clear call-out labels that point to the special terms used in the guide's eighteen numbered sections. The instructions, running little more than two pages, are clear; their brevity certainly makes them accessible to many readers. The examples given in the guide are short but sufficient. A "List of Abbreviations and Symbols Used in This Dictionary" precedes the main word list vocabulary and is also printed along with the pronunciation key on the front endpapers.

Black thumb-index tabs with gold letters are available; there are no index tabs to the gazetteer or biographical sections.

VIII. Graphics and Format

The dictionary includes about 970 black-and-white line illustrations, including tables, charts, and some fifty locator maps within the 863-page main vocabulary. The maps range in size from ¾" x ¾" to 3¼" x 4½", in the case of the United States. In general, the pictures are well selected to illustrate less familiar terms or meanings, especially those that might not readily be visualized by younger readers. For example, "**ac·co·lade . . . 2** *Archit.* A curved ornamental molding" is accompanied by a clear drawing. Pictures are labeled with a cross-reference to a numbered meaning (*def. 2*) or to a numbered homograph (spats⁴). Cross-references to pictures also appear under definitions:

Fal·lo·pi·an tube. . . . See OVARY.

Mathematics, anatomy, and mechanical diagrams are especially clear, and many have useful labels (**airplane** has 16, for example). A generous proportion of drawings illustrate several varieties of a term: there are three kinds of **adze** shown and three different **acorns**. Smaller, explanatory drawings of the **date line**, **meridians**, and a **mercator projection** will be useful to younger readers.

The tables and charts, which are useful but not always up-to-date, include: the Braille alphabet, a chess game in progress, constellations, chemical elements, geologic time scale, comparative grades in the United States Armed Services, the Jewish calendar, phases of the moon, and the teeth of an adult human, as well as a periodic table of elements, a table of planets, proofreader's marks, a temperature conversion table, and signs of the zodiac. (More description of these appears in the section on "Graphics and Format" in the review of the WEBSTER COMPREHENSIVE DICTIONARY.)

The general typography in *The Doubleday Dictionary*'s two-column text is clear and pleasantly free of distracting gimmicks. The margins are adequate, and there is sufficient white space between lines of text, although the print is *very small*. Most earlier reviews commented on the text size unfavorably; buyers will want to consider this factor.

The ivory paper is sturdy and the pages lie flat when the dictionary is opened, but in the copy examined by this buying guide's reviewers, some signatures separated from the spine's reinforcement. Although the dictionary is hard bound in gold and black simulated leather paper, the meager reinforcement at the spine, despite its top headband, will not withstand even moderate library use without rebinding. The rounding of the spine allows too flexible a gap; hence the dictionary's bottom and top spine edges develop noticeable fraying and some cracks after even a few sessions of use. If the dictionary is

for the home, buyers will want to consider how much use it will need to sustain.

IX. Summary

A high school student preparing for college will need a larger dictionary, but many students in junior high and high school might find the size of *The Doubleday Dictionary*'s general vocabulary more satisfactory than those of smaller desk dictionaries and its style of writing and less complex lexicographic apparatus readily accessible.

This dictionary is now more than a decade old, and it has not been revised to keep pace with technical, scientific, or newer meanings of common words; its main strength lies in its accessible general definitions. There are also many readers who do not require the level of scientific and technical definition, written in special terminology by specialist definers, that appears increasingly frequent in larger, newer dictionaries. This work might well suit their needs. School libraries will probably find other dictionaries more useful for their young readers, as well as more physically durable, but home buyers might want to consider this work, depending upon the potential reader's reaction to its very small print.

English Picture Dictionary

Facts at a Glance

Full Title: **English Picture Dictionary**.
Publisher: National Textbook Company (Passport Books).
Compiler: Angela Wilkes.
Illustrator: Colin King.
Edition Reviewed: © 1986.

Number of Volumes: 1.
Number of Entries: over 1,200.
Number of Pages: 82.
Number of Illustrations: 80 pages in full color.
Trim Size: 7½" × 10¼".
Binding: laminated paper over boards.

Price: $7.95.
Intended Readership: beginning readers through young elementary.
Sold in bookstores and other outlets; also sold to libraries and schools. ISBN 0-8442-5447-9.

I. Scope and Format

The *English Picture Dictionary* is an alphabetical listing of words whose meanings are intended to be clarified by pictures and sentences that include the word or a paraphrase of its meaning. Only 25 letters of the alphabet are included: *x* is omitted with no explanation, and there is no full listing of the alphabet. This could prove confusing to the very young beginning readers for whom the book is designed.

According to the preface, "Not only is it an effective vocabulary builder and spelling book, but also an entertaining picture book-reader that will encourage children to develop their language skills as they learn to use simple reference books." As this review will describe, the claim is not fulfilled.

The dictionary is one in a series of this publisher's picture dictionaries; others are available in French, German, and Spanish—all with English translations.

Each page within the word list is divided by blue lines into 15 equal-sized boxes: three across and five running down the page. Each section of the alphabet begins with a box containing the appropriate letter in uppercase (red) and lowercase (yellow) form. A drawing of one or more objects whose name begins with the letter appears in the box. In the boxes, each entry word appears in large bold type in the upper left-hand corner. Most boxes contain a sentence in smaller, lightfaced type using a form of the entry word and, in some cases, an additional illustrated sentence. For words difficult to illustrate, such as **afternoon**, **Easter**, **learn**, **or**, and **since**, several sentences use and paraphrase the entry word.

No guide words are provided, and new letter sections often begin in midpage, so access is not particularly easy.

Two special features included at the end of the book are "Parts of Speech" and "Useful Words." In the former, the eight main parts of speech are listed, defined, and exemplified. The lists of words that are considered useful include cardinal and ordinal numbers (numerals and words), the days of the week, the months of the year, and the seasons. There is also a selected list of 32 geographic names (countries and the continents) that could be useful for young readers beginning to study areas of the world, except that there is no indication of which names are countries and which are continents.

The pages are good quality white paper with excellent opacity, so there is little show-through of text or pictures. However, the signatures are center-sewn; heavy use may loosen the threads.

II. Authority

Compiler Angela Wilkes is the author and editor of other books designed for young readers. Betty Root, listed as consultant, is associated with the Center for the Teaching of Reading at the University of Read-

ing, England. The dictionary's originators, London-based Usborne Publishing, have produced other heavily illustrated supplementary educational books for young readers.

III. Quality and Currency of Entries

Little attempt is made to define entry words. The entry sentences tend to be captions for the illustrations that show the words in a selected context or sometimes provide a synonym or paraphrase. This attempt to show meaning rather than to define has two major drawbacks. First, in many instances the sentences emphasize the context *more* than the entry word. For example, **arrow** is illustrated with a drawing of a man in a Sherlock Holmes outfit using a magnifying glass to examine an arrow painted on the sidewalk, while the painter lurks behind a nearby wall. The sentence reads:

Sherlock Holmes has found an arrow.

In both the drawing and the sentence, the emphasis is on Sherlock Holmes, not on the word **arrow**. Here, and in other instances, the grammatical subject of the "defining" sentence captures the child's interest, while the entry word is relegated to a subsidiary level.

A second drawback is that the word often appears in the sentence in a different form from that of the main entry: For example:

fry   Ben is frying an egg.
pinch Bill pinches Ben.
plant He is planting it in the garden.

Young readers, who are only beginning to develop word recognition skills, may find this arbitrary use of variant forms and inflections difficult. Another difficulty for the audience is the advanced vocabulary, such as

capital Rome is the capital of Italy. It is the country's main city. Paris is the capital of France. 'A' is a capital letter and 'a' is a small letter.

The several undiscriminated meanings are not helpful for young readers. In the few instances where two entry boxes are used to illustrate a word's variant meanings (as for **fly** and **fish**), no reason is given for their selection, when comparable words have not been so treated. In general, the meanings given for entry words and the illustrative sentences are uneven and inconsistent.

IV. Illustrations

The cartoon-style full-color drawings pack much detail into relatively small spaces, sometimes obscuring the meaning of entry words, as in the entry for **arrow** just described. Children will also notice discrepancies between text and pictures, for example, when pigs appear tan colored but are called "pink" and when brown mice are shown but are called "gray."

A group of characters that first appear on the end papers provides continuity throughout the text, and their antics may often amuse children. All of the characters are Caucasian, only three of the nine are female, and all are adults except for "Zizi." Zizi appears in a sleep suit through the dictionary, as an infant in a crib, a toddler, and a young child. Having central characters that children can identify with participate in activities suitable for a variety of age levels is often an appealing device to engage young readers' attention, especially when the character is an animal (for example, Richard Scarry's squiggly worm). Zizi is obviously designed to perform the same function, but it is more likely that children will find her activities inconsistent with her appearance.

V. Summary

Unlike many picture-book dictionaries that are mainly intended for home use but that also can be used effectively in more formal educational settings, the *English Picture Dictionary*'s treatment of words is too inconsistent to be useful. Librarians, teachers, and parents should look for other early dictionary-word books, such as the American Heritage or Macmillan titles reviewed in this Buying Guide.

Everyday American English Dictionary

Facts at a Glance

Full Title: **Everyday American English Dictionary**.
Publisher: Voluntad Publishers/National Textbook Company.
Editors: Richard A. Spears, Linda Schinke-Llano, Betty Kirkpatrick.
Edition Reviewed: © 1984; 1987 printing.

Number of Volumes: 1.
Number of Entries: 5,500.
Number of Pages: 400.
Trim Size: 5¼" × 7½".
Binding: paperback; hardbound.

Price: $4.95; $7.95 hardbound.

Intended Readership: beginning and intermediate students of English as a second language.
Sold in bookstores and other outlets; also sold to libraries and schools. ISBN 0-8325-0337-1.

I. Introduction

The *Everyday American English Dictionary*, subtitled *A Basic Dictionary for English Language Learning*, was first published in 1984. It is designed to be a first English-to-English dictionary for use by students of English as a Second Language. According to the publishers, the work will aid students in learning to speak and write English well. It will also teach the student "the basic methods of finding dictionary information with ease and confidence."

In the preface, the publishers note that the work is intended to serve as either a portable dictionary or an educational text. However, the selection of entries, the notes to the instructor, and the accompanying workbook all suggest that the primary use of the work will be in connection with *formal* ESL instruction.

The 5,500 entries in the dictionary reflect the vocabulary level at which second language students begin independent reading of works intended for native speakers. The work incorporates "school and community 'survival' word lists" and focuses on the language associated with basic daily living experiences.

II. Authority

The dictionary is published by Voluntad Publishers, a subsidiary of the National Textbook Company, which has gained recognition as a publisher of books for English-Spanish bilingual programs. The work is partially based on *Chambers First Learners' Dictionary*, published by the British firm of W & R Chambers. Richard A. Spears, the editor, is an associate professor of linguistics at Northwestern University and a specialist in lexicography, ESL, American culture, and several areas of linguistics. The associate editor and primary writer of the companion workbook is Linda Schinke-Llano, a lecturer in linguistics at Northwestern University and ESL specialist. Betty Kirkpatrick, Editorial Director and Dictionaries Editor at Chambers, served as a consulting editor on the work.

III. Comprehensiveness

The scope of the work is purposely limited to words that the beginning and intermediate ESL student is likely to encounter in everyday life. However, the word list more closely reflects the vocabulary of ESL texts at this level than the spoken or written vocabulary the student may actually need. For example, although **cash** and **charge** both appear in the word list, there is nothing in these entries that will enable the student to make sense of the common question, "Cash or charge?" Idioms are also excluded. While these omissions will not undercut the dictionary's value as a classroom text, they do limit its usefulness as a portable dictionary for independent use by the non-native English speaker.

IV. Quality and Currency of Entries

Typical entries include the entry word in boldface, a pronunciation guide in brackets, an italicized part-of-speech abbreviation, and the definition(s). When more than one meaning of a word is given, boldfaced numerals precede each definition, and the part-of-speech designation follows each numeral. In about ten percent of the entries, an illustrative sentence follows the definition. The sentence is introduced by the signal *Ex.* For irregular verbs, inflected forms are given after the definitions. The forms are identified with abbreviated tense labels that are explained in the front of the volume.

Although the book is intended for use in everyday situations as well as in the classroom, its definitions are not well designed to teach "survival" English. For example, a "survival" definition of **egg** would be "something that one buys, cooks, or eats"; this work defines **egg** as

> an oval object with a thin shell which holds a baby bird, fish, or reptile.

Similarly, the higher-level word **summon** would first be encountered in daily living in its inflected form, *summons*. In this dictionary, only **summon** is included; it is defined as

> to send for someone.

The definitions are written with a controlled vocabulary, and terms used in the definitions are given their own main entries. However, in some cases the student looking up a secondary word will be baffled by an inadequate definition. For example, **pasta** is defined as

> foods made from flour paste, such as macaroni, spaghetti, lasagne, and ravioli.

The student seeking a definition of the word **paste**, used in this entry, will find the unhelpful phrase:

> a thick white glue used to stick paper and other things together.

When more than one definition is given for a word, the dictionary appears to follow the pattern of adult native language dictionaries that list definitions in order of historical use rather than in order of frequency of use. **Patch**, for example, is defined first as

> a small piece of ground.

The sense of a cloth patch for clothing follows, and the verb form is defined last. **Patter**, in itself a questionable choice for inclusion, is defined first as

> to tap lightly and quickly

and then as

> the sound of light tapping.

ESL students and new speakers of English would be better served by an ordering based on frequency.

An ESL dictionary is not expected to adhere to the standards of currency usual in a dictionary for native speakers. However, this dictionary's failure to cover some common conversational applications of words, as well as specific idiomatic usage, limits its usefulness. Overall, the work's entries render it adequate for classroom use but not for independent use in everyday life.

V. Syllabication and Pronunciation

Syllable breaks are not shown in either the entry word or in the phonetic respelling provided as a pronunciation guide. Although stress marks indicate stressed syllables, the absence of full syllabication is a serious drawback, especially in a work designed to help its readers speak English correctly.

The dictionary uses International Phonetic Alphabet (IPA) phonetic transcriptions to indicate pronunciation. Standard American English pronunciations are given, and no variants are provided. A full pronunciation guide appears in the introductory section of the volume. This guide lists sample words showing the various ways each sound may be spelled. Exercises in the companion workbook will also help the student learn correct pronunciation. There are no abbreviated pronunciation keys within the word list, which—like the absence of syllabication—will prove inconvenient to the reader.

VI. Special Features

The volume's introduction addressed "To the User" provides keys to abbreviations and to pronunciation. A section addressed "To the Instructor" explains the work's organization, selection of entries, and pronunciation system. It also provides a table of irregular verbs, with their past tenses and past participles.

An appendix at the back of the book lists U.S. states with their postal abbreviations, capitals, and largest cities. U.S. presidents through Ronald Reagan are listed, with their dates in office. There are also listings of U.S. national holidays (excluding Martin Luther King, Jr., Day and Presidents' Day), cardinal and ordinal numbers, and common fractions. Also included in the appendix is a map of the United States, showing states and capitals. Large secondary cities are shown, as are surrounding bodies of water and neighboring countries.

The 40-page companion workbook gives a series of lessons and exercises that can be used for building vocabulary, as well as for practice in using the dictionary. Topics covered include alphabetizing, pronunciation, parts of speech, irregular plurals, verb forms, synonyms and antonyms, and others. Well-designed practice exercises in each section require students to use the dictionary to locate correct answers. A number of the exercises valuably require students to write full-sentence answers. The workbook significantly enhances the dictionary's value as a text for formal ESL instruction.

VII. Accessibility

Two large, boldfaced guide words appear on each spread, indicating the first and last words entered on the spread. A ruled line sets off the guide words, along with the page number, at the top of the page, so page numbers are easy to spot. This is important because the workbook often refers to page numbers.

Within the entry, entry words recurring in illustrative sentences, and inflected forms, are neither italicized nor boldfaced: the reader will therefore find these difficult to distinguish from other parts of the entry. Another confusing feature is the absence of periods after abbreviations. Non-native speakers might naturally attach an *n*, *v*, or *Ex* to the beginning of an unfamiliar word.

Because no table of contents is provided, the volume's appended special features may be overlooked.

VIII. Graphics and Format

The dictionary is very readable, with only one column of type on each page. Main entry words appear in boldface overhanging the text. Both the dictionary and the workbook are paperbound, with heavily varnished and colorful covers. The paper is off-white with no distracting show-through. The typeface in both books is larger than usual for books of this genre, and the layout of each page is inviting and easy to read. Refreshingly, the answer lines provided in the workbook are long enough and separated with enough leading for the student to write in the answer easily.

IX. Summary

The *Everyday American English Dictionary* is a clearly formatted, easy-to-read reference source. Its most advantageous use would be in a classroom setting with high school or adult students in a formal ESL program. The dictionary is not well designed to be used independently by non-native speakers in everyday situations. However, in a classroom setting, the words to be looked up could be controlled. Students who found definitions difficult or perplexing could raise questions in class discussion. This would be particularly useful when students looked up a word used within an entry and found its definition inapplicable to the sense they needed to know. Students could also raise questions in class when the work's lack of syllabication caused them problems.

Native speakers, who would already be familiar with the words, would not be confused by incomplete definitions or the lack of syllabication. The dictionary and workbook would therefore be suitable for basic or remedial classes of native speakers. The books would be useful in teaching dictionary use skills, and the workbook exercises would be of value in such a class. School and public libraries serving ESL and remedial student populations will want to consider this work.

Fearon New School Dictionary

Facts at a Glance

Full Title: **Fearon New School Dictionary**.
Publisher: David S. Lake Publishers.
Editors: Alvin Granowsky and Ken Weber.
Edition Reviewed: © 1987.

Number of Volumes: 1.
Number of Entries: approximately 70,000.
Number of Pages: 1,267.

Trim Size: 4¼" × 7".
Binding: cloth.

Price: $12.75.
Intended Readership: junior high through high school.
Sold in bookstores and other outlets; also sold to libraries and schools. ISBN 0-8224-3049-5.

I. Introduction

The *Fearon New School Dictionary* was created for use "in school, at the office, and at home. . . . Sophisticated enough for all but the most scholarly use, yet friendly enough to be a constant companion." According to the publisher, the dictionary contains 70,000 entries; however, an informal count by our reviewers produced less than half that figure. This suggests that the publisher's count includes variant forms.

II. Authority

The editorial staff is identified by name, but their credentials are not included. A quick search through standard biographical reference sources yielded no information. No consultants are identified, and there is no mention of a citation file or of the books, periodicals, or media used in drawing up the volume's word list. This edition appears to be drawn from 1976 and 1978 volumes published by Heinemann Educational Australia and a 1984 edition from Globe Modern Curriculum Press. However, the authorities and sources for these preceding dictionaries and their relationship to the current *Fearon New School Dictionary* is not made clear in its brief preface. Therefore, it is impossible to determine whether or not this dictionary was compiled according to reliable and acceptable standards.

III. Comprehensiveness

This relatively short dictionary adequately covers current American English as it is used in popular media and speech. Although some important new words such as *AIDS, CAT scan, sonogram,* and *ayatollah* are omitted, many other words, such as **chemotherapy, terrorist, test tube baby, rack and pinion**, and **videodisk** are included. Particular attention has been paid to computer terms, including **mainframe, FORTRAN, modem, parity bit**, and **byte**.

This dictionary also includes a number of slang and informal words, related phrases, and idiomatic expressions. Words and phrases such as **busman's holiday, burnout, hang-up, under the hammer, hand in glove, deck out, cut in**, and **take to heart** are included. Furthermore, this dictionary is not as sanitized as many other school dictionaries. Words such as **penis, vagina, copulation, pornography, prostitute, striptease**, and **syphilis** are included.

Etymologies are not consistently provided but often appear with foreign words—words from Latin, Greek, French origins, among others. The etymologies are very simple and informal, providing almost no scholarly apparatus. Here is a brief list of entry words with their complete etymologies:

neglect [Latin *neglectus* unheeded]
reverie [French *rêver* to dream]
resent [Re- + Latin *sentire* to feel] (the prefix re- is defined at its proper place in the main alphabet)
Gestapo [German GE(heime) STA(ats) PO(lizei) secret state police]
micro- [Greek *mikros* small]

Other words with complicated histories are well explained. For example:

gerrymander (JERRi-mander) *verb*
1. *Politics:* to arrange the boundaries of a constituency, a riding, etc. to the advantage of a particular party or candidate. [*Riding* refers to a Canadian constituency.]
2. to manipulate unfairly *Word Family:* gerrymander, *noun*
[from *E. Gerry*, a governor of Massachusetts who created new boundaries there in 1812 + sala(MANDER), which animal the rearranged map was considered to resemble]

Although the etymologies provide addition information, and students may enjoy reading that **blunderbuss** is derived from "thundergun" and **hara-kiri** is Japanese for "belly cut" the information is not systematically provided in a form suitable for students to gain proper knowledge about the origins of our language.

The word "synonym" is used neither in the prefatory remarks nor the user key. Nevertheless, alternative words are used to describe entries and convey meaning. **Authentic** is described as "genuine, believable"; **august** as "imposing, majestic." However, these words, and many others in a variety of entries, could have been labeled as synonyms, a more appropriate and instructive usage for younger readers. While the broad and current word coverage in the *Fearon New School Dictionary* forms a distinct advantage, inconsistencies in etymological presentation and the lack of a clear explanation of synonyms

Fearon New School Dictionary

❶ Part of speech, in italics, is followed by numbered definitions

❷ Brief etymology provided in brackets

❸ Usage or field label is in italics

❹ Illustrative sentence (here employing inflected form of main entry) clarifies usage

❺ Words related to the main entry are provided in the Word Family section

❻ Pronunciation is given for some entries; presented as phonetic respellings with the stressed syllable in capital letters

---

fiddle *noun*
1. *Music:* a violin.
2. *(informal)* an underhand or illegal enterprise.
Phrases:
fit as a fiddle, very healthy.
play second fiddle, She dislikes playing second fiddle to her sister. (= taking second place)
fiddle *verb*
1. to play a violin.
2. to move the hands restlessly or aimlessly.
3. *(informal)* to distort or falsify dishonestly: The clerk *fiddled* the accounts.
fiddle about, to waste time.
Word Family: **fiddly**, *adverb*, intricate and difficult; **fiddler**, *noun*.

fidelity (fid–DELL-i–tee) *noun*
1. loyalty: The king rewarded his old servant for his *fidelity*.
2. exactness or accuracy: The *fidelity* of sound produced by a radio.
[Latin *fides* trust]

---

tend to make this dictionary insufficient for youngsters in their preparation of many school assignments.

IV. Quality and Currency of Entries

Each entry includes the word being defined in boldface, its part of speech, a definition, and usually a list of related words and inflected forms. Usage notes and examples are often provided for informal, slang, and idiomatic expressions and for related phrases. Pronunciations, alternate spellings, plural spellings, and etymologies are included, but sparingly. Different meanings are separately numbered and variant usages are separately lettered within each entry. Subject labels are provided for words used in a special field.

The prefatory material does not specify the order used in presenting multiple definitions. Therefore, the reader does not know which definitions are provided for historic coverage and which are provided for current usage. In general, definitions are short and uneven. **Hanukkah**, for example, is defined as "an eight-day Jewish festival in December." But what does the festival celebrate? The entry for **intercourse** defines the word in its sexual connotation as "sexual intercourse," offering no definition and failing to cross-reference to the entry **sexual intercourse**. The entry **homosexual** makes no reference to the currently preferred term *gay*, yet the entry **gay** is defined, secondarily, in its homosexual sense. A similar problem arises with the entries for **Black** and **Negro**, which make no reference to each other, while the term

Afro-American is omitted. The entry **caper** does not include a definition relating to illegal activity; **hospice** fails to mention a home for the sick and dying.

Another problem is that several different parts of speech may be included in an entry, but they are not always defined. For example, **prostitution**, *noun* appears under **prostitute**, *noun*; **orate**, *verb*; **orator**, *noun*, and **oratorical**, *adjective* appear under **oration**, *noun*. However, under **prostrate**, *adjective*, appears

prostrate, *verb*, to cast oneself down, in adoration or pleading; **prostration**, *noun*, a) the act of prostrating, b) extreme weakness or helplessness.

Since the parts of speech appear under the heading "Word Family," however, their relation to the main entry is usually clear, and it may be inferred that only the more difficult or complex words receive more complete definitions in their other forms. Nevertheless, the very informality of this system requires a degree of sophistication and familiarity with the English language that the reader may not have.

Many entries are also quite informative. The definition of **whist** describes the game and states that "bridge developed from whist." The entries for **who** and **whom** include illustrative sentences to help explain proper usage. The entry for **Mohs scale** names the minerals at both ends of the scale and includes the name and dates for the mineralogist who devised it.

Plural spellings are a major problem. The introductory remarks and user key provide no information as to when plural spellings are provided, although some irregular forms are given under the main entry, such as **tomatoes**, plural of **tomato**, and **sheep**, plural of **sheep**. This means that readers must remember rules such as changing *y* to *i* before adding *es* (babies). Readers also have to remember exceptions, such as *hellos*. Dictionaries should provide this type of information; readers—especially students—should not be presumed to know it.

Slang meanings, idiomatic expressions, and related phrases are explained clearly and with usage examples. Each example consists of sentences in which the entry word is used and is followed by an explanatory synonym or descriptive phrase. Illustrative sentences and phrases are included in other parts of the definition as well. These features make the senses easy to understand for most high school and junior high school students.

V. Syllabication and Pronunciation

Entry words are presented without syllable breaks, and the word divisions used in the pronunciations provided often include more than one syllable. This is a serious drawback since all users need some guidance for dividing a word at the end of a written line.

In *Fearon*, pronunciations are given "where necessary," surprisingly often, but not often enough. Neither a chart of pronunciation symbols nor a pronunciation key is provided, and IPA symbols are not used. Their absence calls into question many of the pronunciations that are provided. The entries **probable** and **probate**, for instance, show the same pronunciation for the letter *a*, even though their sound is different. The effective use of these phonetic respellings depends on the reader's knowledge of such phonetic rules as that vowels are long when followed by a single consonant and an *e* in the final syllable. Many readers—young and old—may not know these rules and will have no standard by which to relate one sound to another. Nonetheless, in a strictly informal way, readers may well find this simplified pronunciation system helpful. One unquestionably helpful element for the reader is the printing of the accented syllables in capital letters. This visual aid highlights the stress and makes the sound easier to "hear." In conclusion, however, since most readers depend on a dictionary for authoritative information on pronunciation, the *Fearon New School Dictionary*'s inconsistent and sometimes misleading approach to pronunciation represents a serious drawback to its usefulness in schools.

VI. Special Features

All the special features of the *Fearon New School Dictionary* are contained in the appendixes. These include lists of the planets, continents, islands, countries, oceans, lakes, rivers, Canadian provinces, states of the U.S., prime ministers of Canada, presidents of the U.S., fathers of the Confederation (Canada), and signers of the Declaration of Independence. There is also a guide to the metric system. Each list contains other information related to the main topic, such as capitals of states and terms of office. This information is available in other reference sources, but at home or in the office other reference sources are not always available. It is particularly refreshing to find the special information for Canada.

Entries for plants and animals do not include Latin names. Entries for chemical elements provide atomic numbers but not atomic weights or symbols.

There are no maps, charts, tables, biographical entries, or essays. Another omission is prefix tables. These are helpful to all readers, but especially to students, who need to know when the addition of *re-*, *im-*, and *un-* and other such prefixes is appropriate. (Prefixes are listed, however, in the main alphabet.)

VII. Accessibility

Alternative spellings of words are listed in the main alphabet as separate entries that refer readers to the more generally accepted spelling where full explication is given. Some variant spellings, such as *Chanukah*, are omitted, however.

All entries are arranged letter by letter within a single alphabet. Guide words are included on each page, but there is no thumb indexing. The dictionary does have a convenient table of contents for the appendixes and a user key that is printed on the endpapers in the front and back of the book where it is easy to find. All labels and parts of speech that appear in the entries are spelled out.

VIII. Graphics and Format

Fearon New School Dictionary is a pocket-sized hardback dictionary with sewn signatures. The binding is sturdy and durable and should hold up under heavy use. The paper is strong and there is little show-through from one side of the page to the other. The print is small, but precise and clear. Most people will have little trouble reading the print for short periods of time. On the other hand, the lack of illustrations is a drawback, especially for students, since pictures can be extremely useful in elucidating the meaning of many words. For example, the entry **graph** would be enhanced by a diagram, and an annotated drawing of a **column** would supply additional information.

IX. Summary

The *Fearon New School Dictionary* has a number of positive attributes: it is easy to use, its general range of words is relatively broad and broad-minded, it includes informative appendixes, and it provides substantial coverage of contemporary slang and idiomatic expression. However, its deficiencies seriously affect its usefulness in a school, office, or home setting. Unlike slang dictionaries, it does not include extensive information on the origin and development of the idiomatic words, which is what students often need. By excluding abbreviations, symbols, and diacritical marks, the editors have also excluded a wealth of standard dictionary information. No systems for syllabication, pronunciation, plural forms, etymologies, and synonyms have been provided, and this leaves the young reader with too many misconceptions about dictionaries and all readers with too little information. This dictionary is not recommended as a primary acquisition for library or classroom use.

The First Thousand Words: A Picture Word Book

Facts at a Glance

Full Title: **The First Thousand Words: A Picture Word Book.**
Publisher: EDC Publishing.
Compiler: Heather Amery.
Illustrator: Stephen Cartwright.
Edition Reviewed: © 1983.

Number of Volumes: 1.
Number of Words: over 1,000.
Number of Pages: 63.
Number of Indexes: 1.
Number of Illustrations: 55 pages in full color.
Trim Size: 12⅛″ × 9⅛″.
Binding: laminated paper over boards.

Price: $10.95.
Intended Readership: ages 2 through 12.
Sold in bookstores and other outlets; also sold to schools and libraries. ISBN 0-86020-266-6.

I. Scope and Format

The First Thousand Words is a picture word book, not a dictionary. Designed to help children improve their vocabularies, it provides lively illustrations for 1,000 words. They are grouped into 29 subjects such as **hospital**, **me** (body parts), **doing things**, **opposite words**, **storybook words**, and **school**. The publishers indicate that the book will be suitable for age levels ranging from two to twelve. The book is really only suitable for preschool to about second grade readers, although according to the introduction, "older children will be able to use this book when writing their own stories. It will provide them with ideas, new words and correct spellings."

Originally published in England in 1979, the text has been adapted for an American audience, yet a few British spellings remain such as *aeroplane* (on the cover art and in the text). Special editions of the book are also available in French, German, Spanish, Italian, Russian, and Hebrew. The words are not alphabetically arranged, but are presented in thematic groups. No criteria for the selection of words are given, although the objects and words presented are those with which young children are likely to have some familiarity.

II. Authority

The book was created by Usborne Publishing Ltd., a British firm. Betty Root, of the Center for the Teaching of Reading at the University of Reading in England, served as consultant to *The First Thousand Words* and provided a brief introduction, "About this book," for parents and teachers.

III. Quality and Currency of Entries

Two techniques are used to present the words. Fifteen scenes are presented on double-page spreads; then around the outside margins of these scenes, individual objects are shown, redrawn, and labeled. The child has the enjoyable opportunity of hunting for the labeled object somewhere in the scene. This gamelike aspect of the book encourages the development of the skills of matching and identifying.

For example, the workshop scene shows the interior of a cluttered workshop. No electrical equipment is shown, but plenty of nuts, bolts, screws, and nails are spread around. A guilty-looking boy is dumping a box of tacks onto the workbench, while a frowning father, a grinning sister, and a pet duck peer at him from behind a doorway. Items drawn and labeled in the margins include **barrel**, **axe**, **tape measure**, **ladder**, **vise**, **plane**, **jars**, **penknife**, **shavings**, and **screwdriver**. All of these objects are easy to locate in the workshop. The matching is of *similar* rather than identical objects. The redrawings of the objects do not alter their basic shape and are unlikely to confuse children.

The First Thousand Words: A Picture Word Book

❶ Words are organized by theme under a subject heading

❷ Humorous color pictures illustrate concepts and encourage browsing

The second technique uses the 20 pages following the scenes to depict and label many related objects against a white background. Each of these pages and, in some cases, double-page spreads, has a category name, such as **food**, **people**, and **sports**.

Arrangement is by subject, but subjects must be found by browsing through the book rather than looking up words—an appropriate task for the young reader. There is no table of contents.

An index titled "Words in order" is preceded by a five-sentence explanation written for young readers. The index provides the quickest method of accessing a particular word, but does not designate which words are used as the main topic subjects. Obviously, many younger readers will not be able to use the index. Each letter of the alphabet in the index is an oversize lowercase letter accompanied by a line drawing of one object listed under the letter. Page numbers (some incorrect) follow each word in the list.

Immediately preceding the index is a single page, titled "Words without pictures," that provides an alphabetical list of words suggested for reading, saying aloud, and spelling. This appears to be an extra practice feature, for the words are not defined nor

do they appear elsewhere in the book. The words are common ones that children need to communicate on an everyday basis, such as days of the week, months, pronouns, simple adverbs, and so on. Although no rationale is given for the inclusion of this list, it may facilitate the child's transition from the picture word book to an elementary dictionary.

IV. Illustrations

The two techniques used to introduce the words call for two distinct graphic designs. The double-page spreads are always filled with comfortably messy, and gently humorous, scenes of human activity. Bold black lines confine the scenes and leave wide margins for the labeled objects. The other technique uses either single objects or small scenes. These appear in a wide variety of layouts, all with a sense of order. The one jarring note is the inclusion of the zoo scene among the double-spread scenes. The animals are presented as individual objects and are in a different and more realistic style than those in the rest of Stephen Cartwright's bright, cheerful, and predominantly yellow drawings. As a special feature, explained on the inside front cover, a yellow duck lurks on every double-page spread, waiting to be found. This feature enhances the gamelike quality of the book and will make it especially enjoyable to the youngest users, especially those familiar with Richard Scarry's books.

Although some effort is made to avoid sexist bias in the illustrations—a man is washing dishes in the kitchen scene—many of them manifest sex role stereotyping. For example, the hospital scene depicts only male doctors and female nurses. Almost all of the figures associated with sports are male. Some flaws in the book's adaptation for American users include a **pram** and an **aeroplane** (British spelling), for example, and these are pictured on the cover, as are ice cream cones labeled **ices**. The bathroom depicted is certainly not a typical American one, and there are other minor details that adults but probably not children will notice. The most confusing of these, perhaps, is the illustration for the letter *v* in the index. This depicts a girl holding her undershirt (*vest* in British usage) extended toward the viewer.

V. Summary

Over half of *The First Thousand Words* offers an innovative game of matching and identifying as an approach to vocabulary building. Children up to about age six or seven could enjoy this book on their own, but those from preschool to first grade sharing the book with an adult will benefit most. This will be marginally suitable as an additional book for a home library or young elementary school classroom, but it is not for the circulating shelves of public libraries.

The Grosset-Webster Dictionary

Facts at a Glance

Full Title: **The Grosset-Webster Dictionary**.
Former Title: Words: The New Dictionary.
Publisher: Putnam (Grosset & Dunlap).
Editors: Charles P. Chadsey and Harold
  Wentworth.
Edition Reviewed: © 1978; 1985 printing.

Number of Volumes: 1.
Number of Entries: 75,000.
Number of Words: 800,000.
Number of Pages: 648.
Number of Illustrations: 1,000 in black and white.
Trim Size: 7" × 9¼".
Binding: paperback.

Price: $6.95.
Intended Readership: elementary students and up.

Sold in bookstores and other outlets. ISBN 0-448-16264-4.

I. Introduction

This large format paperback dictionary is intended for use by a wide range of students. It has two distinctive features: the first is its large type; the second, its pronunciations shown by phonetic respelling without diacritical markings. The system is similar to that used in the *NBC Handbook of Pronunciation* and language handbooks prepared by the American armed forces during World War II.

II. Authority

The Grosset-Webster Dictionary was edited by Charles P. Chadsey and Harold Wentworth "with a staff of language experts." The work was first published in 1947 as *Words: The New Dictionary*. In 1960, it was retitled and edited by Chadsey and William Morris; it was withdrawn from the market in the early 1970s. It has subsequently been updated and was reissued in 1985. First published as both a dictionary and a quick-reference source for students and adults, the book in its current form omits many of the original special features, such as a biographical dictionary, lists of U.S. presidents, foreign phrases, abbreviations, and maps.

III. Comprehensiveness

Most of this dictionary's entries are words used in everyday speech, but there are also some scientific and technical terms, including entries for **arcology**, **ballistic missile**, and **chemosphere**. Proper nouns are included within the main alphabet, with capitalization indicated, but personal names are excluded except for a selection from the Bible and Greek mythology. Some geographical entries are included within the word list, and a brief pronouncing gazetteer appended to the back of this dictionary includes additional geographic information. Usage notes are provided, but etymology, synonyms, and antonyms are not, and these omissions are disadvantageous. Abbreviations appear only in the new words section of the dictionary and are limited to acronyms.

IV. Quality and Currency of Entries

Definitions are clear and concise and generally explain the meaning of the word rather than relying on synonymous terms, as do many less effective abridged dictionaries. The reading level of the definitions may be somewhat advanced for the dictionary's youngest users. For example, **chain reaction** is defined as

> A series, esp. of nuclear fissions, in which each reaction actuates other reactions with the result that the series is self-sustaining.

However, for the majority of intended users, definitions—including those of scientific and technical terms—are accessible and accurate. Multiple definitions including specialized meanings are provided as needed. For example, the entry for **foot** contains six meanings for the noun and three for the verb. Specialized meanings include the military, the poetic, and the colloquial. Compound words are also noted. Those for **foot** range from **footband** to **foot-worn** with thirty examples given. Up-to-date scientific and technical words, along with other words recently incorporated into the language such as **angry young man**, **gamesmanship**, and **zilch** appear not in the main word list but in a separate section, "How Words Change," at the beginning of the book. This will make them less readily accessible.

V. Syllabication and Pronunciation

Entry words are divided by heavy dots into syllables, and hyphenated words are clearly indicated. Pronunciation is shown by a distinctive system of phonetic respellings without diacritical marks. The stressed syllable is printed in italics. When appropriate, two different pronunciations are provided, but preference for one or the other is not indicated. Pronunciation is not given for simple words, but the approach used in this dictionary makes even difficult terms such as **caoutchouc** or **flautist** easy to sound out as "*koo*-chook" and *flawt*-ist."

VI. Special Features

A pronunciation quiz, included in the preface, is designed to help students make use of the phonetic pronunciation system used in the dictionary. There is also an eight-page pronouncing gazetteer appended to the back of the book. Information given in this section includes location, population, capital (when appropriate), and, for countries, area in square miles. This addendum is limited in its usefulness. Most readers' needs would be better served by *Webster's Biographical Dictionary* or the *Columbia Lippincott Gazetteer of the World*.

VII. Accessibility

Variants in spelling appear directly after the main entry word; for example, **lagniappe**, **lagnappe**; **bastille**, **bastile**. No preferred spelling is indicated. Entries are easily located in the *Grosset Webster Dictionary* with the aid of guide words at the top of each page and oversize letters, in the far right margin of each double-page spread, specifying the alphabetic section. Students must remember to search "How Words Change" for some terms or additional meanings of older words. This is awkward and time consuming and may discourage the younger user. The presence of the gazetteer is not noted in the contents, which renders this feature less accessible.

VIII. Graphics and Format

The Grosset Webster Dictionary contains 1,000 black line drawings, with several appearing on almost every page. They are large enough to show reasonable detail and, for the most part, enhance the definitions they illustrate.

This paperbound dictionary is larger than most abridged works, and it will lie flat when it is opened. The paper quality is marginal; pages will discolor and tear easily. The narrow margins at the spine make rebinding impossible. The book would not stand up to heavy library use for long. It would be more appropriate for home use than for libraries or classrooms.

IX. Summary

The two qualities that distinguish this dictionary from other abridged paperbacks are its large print and its phonetic pronunciation system. Although students should at some point become familiar with the diacritical markings found in most dictionaries, this book serves a useful purpose in simplifying the pronunciation of difficult words. The price for its size is reasonable. Nevertheless, the poor quality of the paper and the narrow margins at the gutter suggest that this volume is not practical for libraries.

HBJ School Dictionary

Facts at a Glance

Full Title: **HBJ School Dictionary**.
Publisher: Harcourt Brace Jovanovich.
Editors: Sidney Landau (first edition); Ronald Bogus (second edition).
Edition Reviewed: © 1985.

Number of Volumes: 1.

Number of Entries: 65,000.
Number of Words: 1.4 million.
Number of Pages: 1,100.
Number of Cross-References: 1,800.
Number of Illustrations: 2,075: 150 in full color;
    975 in two colors; 950 in black and white.
Number of Maps: 13 pages in full color.
Trim Size: 8″ × 10″.
Binding: cloth.

Price: $17.97.
Intended Readership: elementary school students.
Sold in bookstores; also sold to libraries and
    schools. ISBN 0-15-321135-0.

I. Introduction

The *HBJ School Dictionary* is designed to serve as both a school textbook and a home reference work for elementary school children. The publishers stress that the dictionary, as a reference tool, should answer questions children have about words and that, as a textbook it should provide ample material for the study of words and usage.

Some material in the volume originally appeared in editions of 1968, 1972, and 1977; the current edition was published in 1985. The approximately 65,000 entries have been gathered from textbooks, magazines, newspapers, and works of juvenile fiction. A significant feature of the work, and one that fits with its stated purpose as a text, is an introductory 54-page guide, including exercises, to dictionary use. The publishers indicate that revision takes place as needed to maintain the dictionary's currency.

II. Authority

The original editor of the dictionary was Sidney Landau, a respected lexicographer and the author of *The Art and Craft of Lexicography*. The current format, structure, and tone of the entries reflect Landau's belief that a dictionary for young readers should be as clear as possible and that etymology should be included only as a natural extension of a definition.

The current version of the dictionary is based on the citation files of Harcourt Brace Jovanovich, a well-known publisher of textbooks and juvenile literature. The Advisory Board for the dictionary includes such experts as John Warriner, author of the widely used *English Grammar and Composition* series, and university professors of English, education, science, geography, mathematics, music, as well as health, physical education, and recreation.

III. Comprehensiveness

Although an effort has been made to include words used in contemporary technology, the dictionary is significantly less comprehensive than other student dictionaries, such as the Scott, Foresman Intermediate Dictionary, which is geared to the same age group. The *HBJ School Dictionary* includes entries for **disk**, **diskette**, **BASIC**, and **LOGO**, as well as computer-related definitions for such words as **input**, **program**, **network**, **hardware**, and **dish**. *Disk drive*, however, is omitted, and the definition of **computer** does not refer to programmability, stating that computers "are widely used to solve mathematical and logical problems quickly and accurately." Words such as **compatible** and **file** do not include computer-related definitions. Also omitted are current definitions for *arcade*, *mouse*, and *hack*.

Other omissions include such popular terms as *gridlock*, *U-turn*, *Kwanza*, *UPC*, *triathlete*, *yuppie*, and *hacker*—all words included in many other dictionaries intended for use at this level. Medical terms (for example, *strep throat* and the more recent *AIDS*) are not included; but the names for the reproductive organs and terms such as **self-image** are entered, which will prove useful to the student working within health education curricula. Overall, the recent copyright date and the policy of revisions lead the user to expect that the dictionary will be more up-to-date than it in fact is.

The definitions in the *HBJ School Dictionary* are frequently clarified by an illustrative sentence or phrase. Synonyms, variant spellings, prefixes and suffixes, and irregular inflections are cross-referenced. They appear in small capitals with a brief explanation; for instance, the definition for **eglantine** states, "Another name for SWEETBRIER." This simple cross-reference system is well suited for students in this age group. Some etymologies are included, although the etymological root is not always given in the original language. For instance, the etymology of **delicatessen** only states that it "comes from a German word meaning *delicacies*"; the German word is not given. The young student might find this information interesting and enriching. The Scott, Foresman Intermediate Dictionary, for example, supplies expanded etymologies for its young users.

IV. Quality and Currency of Entries

The definitions have been written using the simple vocabulary generally found in fourth to sixth grade texts. In most cases the words used in the definitions are at a lower reading level than the main entry word.

HBJ School Dictionary

❶ Boldface entry word is followed by pronunciation in brackets and a part-of-speech abbreviation

❷ Illustrative sentence or phrase shows how an entry word is used in context

❸ Usage notes appear in italics

❹ Cross-references to main entry words are indicated by a blue diamond

❺ Labeled illustration

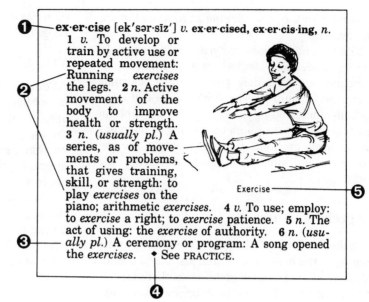

❶ **ex·er·cise** [ek′sər·sīz′] *v.* **ex·er·cised, ex·er·cis·ing,** *n.*
1 *v.* To develop or train by active use or repeated movement: Running *exercises* the legs. 2 *n.* Active movement of the body to improve health or strength. 3 *n.* (*usually pl.*) A series, as of movements or problems, that gives training, skill, or strength: to play *exercises* on the piano; arithmetic *exercises.* 4 *v.* To use; employ: to *exercise* a right; to *exercise* patience. 5 *n.* The act of using: the *exercise* of authority. 6 *n.* (*usually pl.*) A ceremony or program: A song opened the *exercises.* ♦ See PRACTICE.

Exercise ❺

When more difficult words are necessary, an illustrative phrase is provided, or the defining word is given its own main entry. For example, the entry **community** has as its first definition, "a group of people living together in one locality: a rural *community*," and **locality** is also a main entry word. Where an illustrative phrase would not be helpful, as in the definition of **computerized axial tomography**

tomography in which a computerized combination of tomograms form a three-dimensional image

the student would find the unfamiliar words **tomography**, **tomogram**, **computerized**, and **three-dimensional** in the dictionary.

The illustrative phrases or sentences are useful for showing the entry word in context, but the printing style may confuse a young reader. Following a colon at the end of the definition, the illustrative phrases appear in roman type with only the target word italicized. A student might find it difficult to separate the illustrating example from the definition proper. Most other student dictionaries helpfully italicize the whole illustrative example.

In typical entries, the boldfaced main entry word is followed by pronunciation in brackets, part of speech, boldface inflected forms, and the definitions. When the word functions as only one part of speech, the part-of-speech abbreviation precedes the definition or numbered definitions, which appear in order of frequency. When the word operates as more than one part of speech, the abbreviated designation is included after the numeral in each definition. Subentries are boldfaced and placed in parentheses as

part of the appropriate definition; boldfaced run-on entries with part-of-speech designations follow a dash at the end of the entry.

A typical entry (with both a subentry and a run-on entry) is the following:

cru·sade [kroo̅ · sād′] *n.*, *v.* **cru·sad·ed, cru·sad·ing** 1 *n.* (*often written* **Crusade**) One of a series of wars fought by European Christians during the Middle Ages in an attempt to capture the Holy Land from the Muslims. 2 *n.* A vigorous struggle against an evil or in favor of a cause. 3 *v.* To take part in a crusade.— **cru·sad′er** *n.*

In general, the young student should have little difficulty in interpreting the entries and understanding the definitions, especially if he or she follows the instructions given in the guide at the beginning of the volume.

V. Syllabication and Pronunciation

Pronunciation, with syllable breaks and light and heavy stress marks, is given in brackets immediately after the entry word. The main entry word is also syllabified. Syllable divisions are demarcated by centered dots or stress marks.

Forty-three symbols with four diacritical marks are used in the pronunciation key. The full key, appearing only deep within the introductory guide, is not readily accessible; however, extensive practice exercises are usefully provided at this point in the volume. Abbreviated keys, showing vowel sounds and four consonant digraphs are given on the lower right-hand corner of each double-page spread in the main vocabulary.

Variant pronunciations are given in two ways. In the more easily used method, both pronunciations are spelled out separately (for example, **carmine** [kär′min *or* kär′min′]). The other method used is potentially confusing to young readers: a symbol in parentheses within the phonetic spelling of the entry shows a variant pronunciation; for example, the two possible pronunciations of **duet** are given as: [d(y)o͞o, · et].

VI. Special Features

"Using the Dictionary," the guide for students at the beginning of the book, is comprehensive and sound. An overview outlines each component that may appear in an entry. Following the overview, each component is discussed separately. The discussions begin with an example in large type set off in a rectangle at the head of the page. The component is then identified, its function is explained, and several examples are given. The discussions are reinforced by clear, useful exercises that students can complete at home or in class. "Using the Dictionary" also contains a spelling chart that will enable students to find words they cannot spell.

In the main vocabulary, the page on which each letter section begins features a history of that letter, tracing its development from ancient to modern forms.

An extensive appendix includes biographical information on world leaders, noted historical figures, and Nobel prize winners; geographical information; maps; and a wide range of charts useful for math, science, and social studies projects, such as "Customary Weights and Measures," "Mathematical Formulas and Symbols," and "Presidents of the United States." The biographical entries are up-to-date (**Margaret Thatcher** and **Ronald Reagan** are included); women are also well represented here (**Georgia O'Keefe**, **Nikki Giovanni**, and **Karen Horney**, among others). Many of the entries are accompanied by small photographs or portraits. The section on twentieth-century leaders lists them country by country in a time-line format that shows who was the U.S. president during the tenure of each foreign leader. This excellent format for showing world leaders, however, is marred by the fact that only one year after publication, six out of thirteen leaders shown as current were no longer in power and, further, by incorrect spelling, such as **Murtado** as a surname for Mexican President Miguel de la Madrid Hurtado.

The special features are generally strong, well designed to supplement curricula, and extensive enough

to serve as the first source for research projects in geography or history.

VII. Accessibility

Alternative spellings are easily located. They appear in boldface following the main entry word; for example, **cat·a·log** or **cat·a·logue**. Two guide words at the top of each page indicate the first and last words on that page. Although the volume is not thumb indexed, printed thumb-size tabs on the right-hand pages show a section's letter—in white on a black background—and make it easy for users to turn to the section they are seeking. These are easily seen on the pages and visible when the volume is closed. The book's special features, fully listed in the contents at the beginning of the volume, are also easily located.

VIII. Graphics and Format

Illustration is not a major strength of this work. Line drawings and photographs, with captions that refer to the headword, are used mainly to relieve the text and do not play a major role in defining words. Captions do not indicate which of multiple definitions is illustrated. Ethnic diversity is shown in the drawings, and women are shown as military officers and athletes, but a noticeable preponderance of the illustrations show males.

Illustrations in the biographical, geographic, and map sections at the back of the book are well chosen, balanced, and of high quality, in marked contrast to the rest of the dictionary.

The print in the *HBJ School Dictionary* is clear and easily read. Boldfaced main entry words overhang the text. Columns of text are justified both right and left, but hyphenated words, which impede readability, are kept to a minimum by variable spacing. The heavy white paper permits a minimum of show-through. The gutter margin is, unfortunately, rather narrow and there is no curvature binding. The cover is brightly colored and attractive.

IX. Summary

The major drawback of the *HBJ School Dictionary* is its omission of a significant number of current popular and technological terms—terms that are found in comparable dictionaries, such as the Scott, Foresman Intermediate Dictionary. In considering this dictionary, the buyer will have to determine if the subject-area textbooks that the children will use with the dictionary have glossaries that will cover the omission of so many contemporary words.

The major strength of this dictionary is the ease with which its definitions can be understood. Thus the *HBJ School Dictionary* can be used profitably by elementary school students as a companion to textbook and recreational reading and as a reference resource for school projects.

As a text, the *HBJ School Dictionary* could be well used by classroom teachers as the core of a curricular unit on dictionary skills and by librarians helping students use the dictionary on their own.

Holt School Dictionary of American English

Facts at a Glance
Full Title: **Holt School Dictionary of American English**.
Publisher: Holt, Rinehart and Winston.
Edition Reviewed: © 1981.

Number of Volumes: 1.
Number of Pages: 1,056.
Number of Illustrations: approximately 1,450 black-and-white line drawings, plus a 32-page insert in full color.
Trim Size: 7½" × 9³⁄₁₆".
Binding: hardcover.

Price: $22.64.
Intended Readership: ages 9 and up.
Sold to schools and libraries. ISBN 0-03-058999-1.

I. Introduction

This 1981 edition of the *Holt School Dictionary of American English*, previously copyrighted in 1966 and 1967, is "a completely revised edition," according to the editor's preface, "to include new scientific and mathematical terms and to update word meanings which have changed." It contains over 40,000 definitions and over 1,450 illustrations. The work is an abridged dictionary designed specifically for students of age nine and up, or for any novice who needs a basic introduction on how to use a dictionary. The special features of this edition include a 24-page introduction, "You and Your Dictionary," and a 28-page section of exercises geared toward building dictionary skills.

II. Authority

The editors' preface lists the "distinguished linguists and educators" who were consulted in the preparation of the HOLT INTERMEDIATE DICTIONARY OF AMERICAN ENGLISH (on which the *Holt School Dictionary of American English* is based and which is

now out of print), including S. I. Hayakawa, Hans Kurath, Helen F. Olson, James Sledd, and other special consultants and contributors. The editors of the present edition, however, have not been identified, although Holt, Rinehart and Winston were once well regarded for their line of Winston dictionaries (now out of print).

III. Comprehensiveness

Readers will find that some of the newer computer and science technology terms, as well as other new words of the 1980s, are represented. For example, **data bank**, **data processing**, and the particular meaning of **program** as it relates to computers are included. However, the "Periodic Table of the Elements" needs updating.

Brief illustrative sentences or phrases are sometimes provided to help distinguish among similar meanings of the same word; however, examples are not always given. This omission is unfortunate since concrete examples help to clarify a word's meaning, particularly for young readers. For instance, although the entry **catchy** is illustrated with a phrase ("quick to win popular fancy; a catchy tune"), the word **catty** is not given similar treatment ("sly and malicious; spiteful").

Irregular inflected forms are fully indicated in brackets following the part-of-speech label. The etymology of the word appears at the end of the entry in brackets, as in the following case:

> **to·ma·to** (tə mā′tō, -mä′tō) **n-** pl. **to·ma·toes 1** red or yellow juicy fruit, widely eaten as a vegetable. **2** the plant bearing this fruit. [American word from American Spanish tomate, from Nahuatl Indian tomatl.]

Etymologies are not provided for every word, which could be a problem for students completing assignments on word origins.

Not only are common prefixes and suffixes such as **dis-**, **-able**, and **-ful** entered and labeled as separate entries, but countless idioms and slang terms are also included; however, these are placed after the definition of the key word in the idiom, for example: **fat of the land** is found under the noun **fat**; **so far so good** is listed under the adverb entry **far**; **hang heavy** is located under the adjective entry **heavy**; and a whole series of idioms is enumerated in alphabetical order under the verb entry **run**. Although the listing of idioms is useful to the student, he or she may find difficulty in determining the key word for some expressions.

Holt School Dictionary of American English

❶ Cross-reference to a related main entry, in italics, is enclosed in parentheses

❷ The main entry's homophone is cross-referenced

❸ Idiomatic phrases, in boldface, are listed separately and defined at the end of an entry

❹ Irregular inflected forms are given in boldface type within brackets

❺ Illustration of animal species is labeled with the length or height of the animal

❻ Illustrative sentences, printed in italics, show the entry word in roman type

❼ Etymology, provided within brackets, with word sources in boldface type

¹bear (bâr) *n-* **1** large animal with long shaggy hair and a very short tail. **2** rough surly person. **3** on the stock exchange, one who tries to lower prices for his own advantage (see also *¹bull*). [from Old English **bera**.] *Hom-* bare. —*adj-* **bear′like′**.

²bear (bâr) *vt-* [**bore, borne, bear·ing**] **1** to support; hold up; sustain: *The pillars* bear *the weight of the roof.* **2** to carry or convey; transport: *The letter* bears *good news.* **3** to stand up under; endure; abide: *He has* borne *much pain. That will* not bear *scrutiny.* **4** to have on one's person, or mind, or feelings: *to* bear *a scar; to* bear *a grudge.* **5** to bring forth; produce: *to* bear *young; to* bear *fruit. vi-* **1** to produce or be able to produce fruit, young, etc.: *This tree* bore *heavily last year.* **2** to move toward or be situated on a certain point of the compass: *We were* bearing *due north.* [from Old English **beran**.] *Hom-* bare.

bear away to change (a ship's course) away from the wind.

Black bear.
about 5 ft. long

IV. Quality and Currency of Entries

Overall, the definitions are clearly stated and offer multiple meanings of the word; occasionally, however, a word that is derived from the base word of an entry previously defined merely restates the base word in its definition. For example, the entry word **corrode** is defined as meaning

> to eat away or destroy gradually by or as if by chemical action; *some acids* corrode *metal.*

Yet, the same sense of the word in the entry **corrosive** is merely defined as

> corroding or tending to corrode other substances.

This dictionary is intended for use by elementary school students, and this type of definition is not the most useful for them.

When definitions within an entry are distinctly different, they are introduced by boldface numerals; however, related meanings are indicated by lighter numbers in parentheses and are generally rendered in order of their frequency of use—with the most common meaning first. If a word has a scientific meaning, however, it appears first because, according to the introduction, the scientific sense of the word "is the meaning that most students will be look-

ing up." For example, the ordering of the three definitions under **energy** begins with the most scientific explanation ("**1** material power of the universe") and ends with the more general sense of the word ("**3** mental or physical force.") Although a student may be seeking only the general meaning of a word, having the scientific definition appear first will increase his or her understanding.

The use of abbreviations is often questionable, for example, the entry word **Abdia** is defined as

> the CCD Bible name for Obadiah.

CCD is not defined. Elsewhere abbreviations such as **A.A.**, **AAA**, **CNS**, and **PC** are either not defined, or their definitions or referents must be sought elsewhere in the volume. Again, in a dictionary for students, this practice is a drawback.

V. Syllabication and Pronunciation

The syllables within each main entry word are separated by centered dots: **em·u·la·tive**. Pronunciations are indicated by accent marks, diacritical marks, and phonetic respellings; they are enclosed in parentheses and follow the entry word, or wherever else pronunciation is needed—for example, after inflected forms. A pronunciation key is fully and clearly described in the introduction. The system, according to the editors, uses symbols that can fit the speech sounds of speakers of different regions. The key is reproduced immediately preceding the main text and is subsequently presented in an abridged form at the bottom of each right-hand page. With this quick access to the key, the student may be apt to use it more often. Although the pronunciations are based on standard phonetics and IPA symbols (including the schwa ə), the markings are fairly sophisticated for young readers; beginners will need time to learn how to use them.

VI. Special Features

This book serves the twofold purpose of providing young readers with a comprehensive reference guide and a tool for developing dictionary skills. Therefore, a generous assortment of special features is included. The comprehensive introduction, "You and Your Dictionary," discusses the features of the dictionary in clear language that young readers will understand. This section also offers valuable pronunciation, spelling, and usage guides.

The introduction is followed by a 32-page full-color illustrated section containing a view of the earth from space, various maps of the world, a chart of Indian cultures of the Americas, portraits of U.S. Presidents, U.S. flags, illustrated word histories and examples of U.S. regional word variations, the solar system, human body systems, and rock types.

In addition to the "Skills Practice Pages," which provide exercises to enhance dictionary skills, the material appended following the main vocabulary provides a glossary of "Persons and Places in Mythology and Folklore," and lists tables of "The Nations of the World," "The Presidents of the United States," including Ronald Reagan, the "States of the United States," "The Provinces and Territories of Canada," "Sixty Indian Tribes of North America," and "Domestic Weights and Measures." It also charts "The Metric System" and includes a page designating common signs and symbols.

Each of these special features should prove handy for both students and teachers.

VII. Accessibility

Pairs of boldface guide words in the upper margins identify the first and last word on each page. The main vocabulary is alphabetized letter by letter. There are no thumb indexes, but strategies on how to open the book to the approximate location of the word

sought are given in the introduction. This section is clear and well written but will probably be used only if the teacher guides the students through it.

Homographs are listed separately and are indicated by superior numbers to the left of the entry words. When more than one spelling occurs, the more common rendering is offered first; the alternative spelling is then noted at the end of the entry. Homophones of certain words are also noted at the end of the entries. For example:

> **des·sert . . . n-** a course of fruits, pastry, pudding, etc., served at the end of a meal.
> **Homs-** [1]desert, [3]desert.

All of the special features included in the dictionary are listed in the "Table of Contents," which makes the different parts of the book very accessible to the student.

VIII. Graphics and Format

There are almost 1,500 spot illustrations in the dictionary, in addition to the color insert. Most are well detailed and serve to enhance word meanings, although in general the black-and-white presentation may not be particularly appealing to young readers. For geographic entries, small locator maps are scattered throughout the dictionary.

Entry words are printed in boldface type, overhanging the text. The text type size is clear and easy to read. The paper is white with little show-through. The binding is sturdy, and the book should survive fairly strenuous use.

IX. Summary

The *Holt School Dictionary* contains a number of special features: it is a dictionary, a reference book, and a teaching tool all in one. The definitions are clear, fairly comprehensive, and for the most part relevant to the 1980s, although an updating would be helpful. This dictionary, however, does not include etymologies or illustrative sentences for every word, and it often restates the base word as the definition of a derived word. Students in elementary school will not be best served by these inconsistencies and might find The American Heritage, Scott, Foresman, Macmillan, or Random House elementary-level dictionaries more appropriate for their needs. School librarians might also prefer other elementary dictionaries unless the Holt volume is a specific choice of teachers within their schools.

The Little Oxford Dictionary of Current English

Facts at a Glance

Full Title: **The Little Oxford Dictionary of Current English**.
Publisher: Oxford University Press.
Editor: Julia Swannell.
Edition Reviewed: © 1986.

Number of Volumes: 1.
Number of Entries: 25,000.
Number of Words: 34,000.
Number of Pages: 720.
Trim Size: 4″ × 6″.
Binding: paper over boards.

Price: $9.95.
Intended Readership: high school and up.
Sold in bookstores and by direct mail; also sold to libraries and schools. ISBN 0-19-861188-9.

I. Introduction

The Little Oxford Dictionary of Current English is a British English dictionary intended for a general audience, but it would also be suitable for high school and college students, particularly those intending to travel to Great Britain and those studying contemporary British humanities subjects (for example, history, journalism, literature, and so forth). It is important to keep in mind that this dictionary is a British publication and that its spellings, the guide to pronunciations, and the specialized meanings reflect its origins.

The publisher states that the work, first published in 1930, has been thoroughly revised for this sixth edition. There is an emphasis on quick and easy reference, and many new words have been added.

II. Authority

Published by the highly reputable Clarendon Press of Oxford University, the dictionary's first edition appeared in 1930 under the editorship of George Ostler. The second through fourth editions were edited by Jessie Coulson, a member of the editorial staff of the *Oxford English Dictionary*. Julia Swannell edited the fifth and also the current sixth edition, with the assistance of members of Oxford University Press's Oxford English Dictionary department.

III. Comprehensiveness

The book jacket lists among the work's important features its broad range of contemporary English and the special attention paid to the vocabulary of new technology. The computer-related definition of **bit** is included; some terms dealing with the new video technologies are not. Also well represented are popular new words and phrases, such as **ageism**, **aikido**, **allergenic**, **futon**, **privatize**, **surrogate mother**, **tofu**, and **user-friendly**.

Foreign words that are not fully assimilated into English appear as main entries in bold italics, and their language is noted in abbreviated form in square brackets; for example, [F] for French.

Parts of speech are indicated immediately following the entry word. There are some usage labels, such as *colloq.* for colloquialisms and *sl.* for slang words. Field labels, such as *law*, are provided to identify other specialized word uses. Irregular inflected forms are provided. For example, under **lie** (*v.i.*) appears this clarification of inflections:

(*past* **lay**; *p.p.* **lain**; *partic.* **lying**).

Similarly, the forms **better** and **best** are listed under **good**.

There are no illustrative phrases or sentences to enhance definitions such as can be found in many other pocket dictionaries. For American students seeking to understand unfamiliar British usages, this omission is a drawback. Etymologies, synonyms, and antonyms are excluded, but these omissions are not unusual in a work of this scope.

IV. Quality and Currency of Entries

The definitions are concise and clearly written. They could be understood by bright seventh graders, although it is unlikely that young American students would have a need for such a dictionary, unless they were visiting Great Britain. Senses of words are arranged by frequency of use in Great Britain and are numbered consecutively. Specialized uses are introduced by an abbreviated, italicized label. For example, the third entry for the noun **bill** indicates that the word historically (*hist.*) meant

weapon with hook-shaped blade.

The verb form as well as phrases and compound words are listed under the first and most common sense; these include **bill of exchange** and **billposter**.

The Little Oxford Dictionary
of Current English

❶ Boldface main entry with superior number indicating homograph

❷ Part of speech given in italic preceded by boldface number when a main entry exists as more than one part of speech

❸ Plural form of an entry word is indicated by *pl.* set in italics

❹ An additional pronunciation with a specific meaning is shown between slashes and followed by its definition

❺ Definitions ordered according to most common usage

❻ Idiomatic use, or phrases and combinations using main entry word, are included in boldface and listed in alphabetical order

fer (person) temporarily to another department etc. **4 second-best** next after the best; **second class** second-best group or category or accommodation; **second cousin** child of parent's first cousin; **second fiddle** subordinate position; **second-hand** (of goods) bought after use etc. by previous owner, (of information etc.) obtained from others and not by original observation etc.; **second nature** acquired tendency that has become instinctive; **second-rate** inferior; **second sight** supposed power of perceiving future events; **second string** person or thing kept in reserve; **second thoughts** new opinion reached after consideration; **second wind** renewed capacity for effort after tiredness.
second² /'sekənd/ *n.* sixtieth part of minute of time or angle.

second¹ /'sekənd/ **1** *a.* next after first; other, another, additional; of subordinate importance or value; inferior. **2** *n.* second person or class etc.; supporter or helper esp. of boxer or duellist; in *pl.* goods of second quality; second helping of food. **3** *v.t.* back up, give one's support to; /sɪ'kɒnd/ trans

Adjectives are most often defined by the use of synonymous words rather than a sentence or phrase of definition. For example, **steely** is defined as:

of or like steel; inflexible, obdurate.

V. Syllabication and Pronunciation

The work uses the International Phonetic Alphabet to indicate pronunciations, and it adds marks for nasalization and an *x* for the Scottish *ch* (pronounced as the *k* in "lock"), as in **loch**. The pronunciation key appears at the front of the volume. Set off by slash marks, pronunciation is noted immediately following the entry word for most but not all words. For example, **bleach** is pronounced, but **bleak**, **bleed**, and **bleep** are not. Accent marks indicate stressed syllables within the pronunciations, but syllabication is not noted. This omission is a drawback for student readers of the dictionary. The pronunciations provided are those of southern England, not standard American English. Only the preferred form of pronunciation is given.

VI. Special Features

The dictionary's introduction provides a helpful explanation to the reader on how to use the contents effectively. Also provided at the front of the book are a full pronunciation key, a list of abbreviations, are a full pronunciation key, a list of abbreviations, and a note on proprietary terms and trade marks. There are three appendixes: I. "Some points of English usage"; II. "Countries of the world and related adjectives"; and III. "The metric system of weights and measures." These features take up only ten pages and are especially useful for students.

VII. Accessibility

Main entry words appear in boldface type and overhang the text; capital letters are used as appropriate, as for abbreviations and proper nouns. Subsenses are easily located with their boldfaced numbers, and run-in entries and compounds also appear in boldface.

The dictionary has paired bold guide words at the top of each double-columned page, with a centered page number. This is helpful because some of the work's cross-references cite page numbers. A table of contents lists the dictionary's special features, so the reader will not overlook them.

VIII. Graphics and Format

There are no illustrations provided in this dictionary. The overall layout of each page is good for a book of this size. The margins are narrow, but the typeface is strong and clear. The board cover, stitching, and headband make this a sturdy volume that would withstand travel and frequent consultation.

IX. Summary

The Little Oxford Dictionary accomplishes what it sets out to do—provide a quick reference source for precise definitions in the *English*—British, not American—language. Although the editors have made an effort to include new words that often do not appear even in recently published larger volumes, their success is somewhat uneven. For students and travelers who need a small dictionary that reflects the British use of words, this one is a good buy. The authority behind the book is trustworthy. For a library, the volume's small size may pose something of a shelving problem, but it is sufficiently sturdy for reference use.

The Little Webster

Facts at a Glance
Full Title: **The Little Webster (Langenscheidt Lilliput Webster English Dictionary).**
Publisher: Langenscheidt, New York.
Compiler: Sidney Fuller.
Edition Reviewed: © by Langenscheidt KG, n.d.

Number of Volumes: 1.
Number of Entries: more than 7,000.
Number of Pages: 640.
Trim Size: 1½" × 2".
Binding: paper with flexible vinyl cover.

Price: $2.00.
Intended Readership: junior high school through adult.
Sold in bookstores and other outlets; available direct from the publisher. ISBN 3-468-96519-2.

I. Introduction

In an unusual departure from other dictionaries, *The Little Webster*, a tiny novelty dictionary, has chosen to eliminate common well-known words in favor of over 7,000 "relatively rare and difficult words," according to the preface. The reasoning behind this is that most people turn to pocket dictionaries for definitions of words that they do *not* know, rather than ones they do know.

II. Authority

The Langenscheidt Lilliput dictionary has been in print for about 78 years. This edition is the only one of the publisher's volumes devoted exclusively to the English language. The 15 other small-size works are bilingual (English-French, English-German, and so forth).

III. Comprehensiveness

Given its stated rationale for eliminating common words, the word list takes on a decidedly different character from those of most dictionaries. For example, here is a list of all of the words defined on one randomly selected page: **fatigue, fatuous, faun, fauna, feasible, feature, febrile, feces, fecund.** This list of relatively rare and difficult words eliminates such common words as *fault, favor, fear, feast,* and *February.* Because of the criterion for selection and the lack of a date on the copyright notice, it is difficult to evaluate the word list's currency.

IV. Quality and Currency of Entries

Most small dictionaries, according to the preface, provide definitions in "words similar or nearly equal in meaning to the head entry," based on the theory that the user will know at least one of the words. *The Little Webster*, where possible, has used words in the definition that are simpler than the main entry word, clear, and easy to understand. For example,

roustabout dock worker
zombi(e) dead person said to be brought to life by witchcraft.

To save space, partial definitions from previous or succeeding entries flow over into what otherwise would have been empty space. This is sometimes confusing to the reader. Word forms are occasionally included; etymology, synonyms, and antonyms are not.

V. Syllabication and Pronunciation

Syllabication is indicated by a dot between syllables of the main entry words. Stressed syllables are indicated. Pronunciation is clarified using only the macron to denote long vowel sounds and by phonetic respelling. There is no pronunciation key.

VI. Special Features

The special feature of this dictionary is its unusually diminutive size.

The Little Webster

❶ Definitions are simple words or phrases

❷ Main entries, in boldface, are divided into syllables; primary stress is marked

❸ Space is conserved by use of bracketed words placed in available line space above the pertinent entry word

❹ Pronunciations or partial pronunciations are provided for those words that might present special difficulty

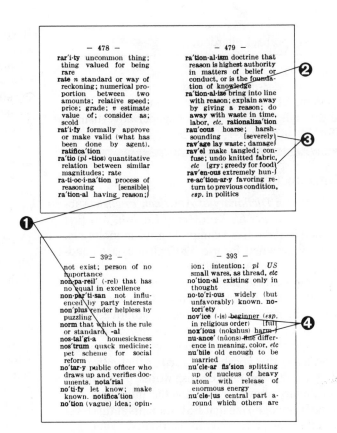

VII. Accessibility

Access is by alphabetical order; to save space, there are no guide words. When searching for a word users must, therefore, stop every few pages and read a main entry word to locate their place. Page numbers are centered at the top of each text page.

VIII. Graphics and Format

This lilliputian dictionary is the size of a fat matchbox—1½″ x 1¾″ x ¾″; therefore, the typography and design are as simple as possible. The main entry is in bold print; the definitions are indented one space and run across the entire page. The printed text on each page runs 1″ horizontally and 1½″ vertically; the ⅛″ margins and gutter provide a generous amount of white space given the book's size. The entries are in small type that is clearly printed on a smooth, white paper. The cover is wipe-clean flexible dark blue plastic with gold lettering.

IX. Summary

The Little Webster dictionary is a delightful novelty gift item. In its miniature form, it is unique as a dictionary of curiosity appeal. Adults will find that it fulfills its purpose, as stated in the preface, "of

telling the user, in a quick, clear and economical manner, things he does not know and wants to know," and they will find that it easily slips into a purse or pocket. Students from junior high school and up will welcome this as a gift that, because of its uniqueness, will spur them on to browse through the words. School and public libraries may wish to purchase this, not as a reference item, but for display.

Longman Dictionary of American English

Facts at a Glance

Full Title: **Longman Dictionary of American English**.

Publisher: Longman, Inc.

Editors: Arley Gray, Della Summers, Adrian Stenton, and Leah Berkowitz.

Edition Reviewed: © 1983.

Number of Volumes: 1.

Number of Entries: 38,000.

Number of Pages: 792.

Number of Illustrations: 15 pages in black and white.

Trim Size: 5³⁄₁₀″ × 8½″.

Binding: paperback; hardbound.

Prices: $7.95; $12.95.
Intended Readership: intermediate and advanced
  students of English as a second language.
Sold through magazine and newspaper advertising.
  ISBN 0-582-79797-7; 0-582-906113.

I. Introduction

The *Longman Dictionary of American English*, subtitled *A Dictionary for Learners of English*, was first
published in 1983. It is a comprehensive monolingual
dictionary designed for use by English-as-a-second-
language students with full literacy skills and comprehension skills at the intermediate and advanced
levels. It moves the student away from the use of
bilingual dictionaries by showing connotative values
and usage of words and expressions in English.

Although the dictionary includes 38,000 entry words
and phrases, the vocabulary used in definitions is
limited to 2,000 common English words. This control
of vocabulary shows respect for the intelligence of
the reader, recognizing that ESL students at this level
have full language capacity in their native languages
and can understand the concept behind any lexical
item. The goal is to help the student identify the
lexical item and then express it in English.

II. Authority

Longman is a highly regarded publisher of texts for
ESL instruction as well as for the training of ESL
teachers. Consultants for the project include Virginia
French Allen, William Crawford, and other recognized authorities in the field, representing major U.S.
centers for ESL research and instruction.

Both the selection of main entry words and the
controlled vocabulary used in the definitions are based
on the publisher's established list of words most frequently used in spoken as well as written English.

III. Comprehensiveness

The dictionary's word list is appropriate for the student of English at the intermediate and advanced
levels and for high school and college students using
English in mainstream (as opposed to bilingual or
remedial) content courses. The list contains a balance
of words that students will encounter in formal and
informal speech and reading. The jargon of language
instruction, used in the introductory exercises and
the "Study Notes," is incorporated into the word list.

The list provides full coverage of standard "survival" words and expressions common to ESL texts.

It gives equal attention to the words that students
will encounter in the speech and writings of native
speakers. The work includes over 5,000 idioms and
figurative expressions. For example, the expressions
lay off, **psych out**, **brand new**, and **mess up** are given,
as are such words as **mess**, **junket**, **snack**, **tease**, and
(sports) **fan**. The financial-transaction definitions for
credit, **interest**, **deposit**, and **reduce** are included, enhancing the work's practical value.

Variant forms and comparable and contrasting
forms are given and illustrated, expanding the range
of the word list still further.

IV. Quality and Currency of Entries

The information is ordered within entries according
to the following basic sequence: entry word or phrase;
pronunciations, set off by virgules; the part-of-speech
label; British spelling or other variant, as appropriate; boldfaced inflected forms, when irregular or requiring consonant doubling; a boldfaced numeral,
when more than one meaning is defined; the grammar code (explained in the introduction); definition;
illustrative sentence or phrase, in italics; synonyms;
boldfaced run-ins; cross-references to related words,
"Study Notes," and illustrations; and sometimes a
paragraph of usage notes, also cross-referenced. Many
entries also include cross-references for comparison
of words that are logically equal in deep structure
but not interchangeable in surface structure, for example, HOMEWORK and HOUSEWORK.

An important feature of the entries, second in
importance to the well-controlled vocabulary, is the
usage instructions. Codes and symbols are used to
show such language features as noun countability and
the objects of phrasal verbs. These points of syntax
are essential to native-level language use. Step-by-
step instructions in the introduction and a series of
thorough "Study Notes" explain the use of these
guides. Both the introduction and the "Study Notes"
are cross-referenced in the entries.

Another key feature of the entries is the extensive
use of illustrative phrases and sentences, at a ratio
of 55,000 illustrations of context for 38,000 entry
words.

The work's currency is strong in the area of contemporary idiom, as is appropriate to an ESL dictionary.

V. Syllabication and Pronunciation

Entry words are syllabified by centered dots; inflected forms and run-ins are not syllabified.

Each entry word is followed by a pronunciation
guide enclosed within virgules. The guide takes the

form of a respelling in the International Phonetic Alphabet (IPA). In international ESL instruction, the IPA is the pronunciation code of choice. Students initially instructed by U.S.-educated teachers without professional ESL training may not have encountered the IPA symbols. However, foreign-born or educated students and those who have used standard ESL beginning texts will find the symbols familiar. In any case, the symbols are fully explained in the introduction, where a full pronunciation key is provided. In acknowledgment of the sometimes tenuous links between English pronunciation and spelling, "Spelling Notes" are provided that outline the varying ways in which a sound may be spelled.

VI. Special Features

A thorough introduction explains the work's features. It is based on the assumption that the literate student will know how to use a general dictionary, and it builds on this knowledge with careful directions for using a study dictionary of usage. Also included is a 38-page "Dictionary Skills Workbook," which is cross-referenced throughout the text. The workbook provides exercises for using the dictionary to illustrate the features of grammar and usage that are discussed. Answers are provided at the end of the section.

Affixes are explained, and separate listings for prefixes and suffixes are appended in a section called "Word Building." Explanations and examples are given for ways to change a word's meaning and/or part of speech by using affixes. This is a key skill for the student to master in gaining linguistic fluency. Also provided is a listing of irregular verb forms.

VII. Accessibility

Boldfaced guide words are provided for each spread and are set off by rules. The work is heavily cross-referenced, and the "Spelling Notes" offer tips to aid students in finding words they may never have seen or may have only partially heard.

Homographs are listed separately and are designated by superscript numerals following the entry word.

VIII. Graphics and Format

The entries are easy to read with their clear typeface and adequate leading. The paper is bright white with no show-through. The margins are narrow, but the entry words are clearly legible, printed in a larger type, boldfaced, and overhanging the text.

There are no illustrations for individual entries. However, concepts in the "Study Notes" are illus-

trated with line drawings, and fifteen full-page drawings are provided. These drawings are in the realistic cartooning style used in most adult ESL texts. They identify objects related to everyday experience and travel. For example, one illustration features items and fixtures in a clothing store; another shows a doctor's office. The illustrations are captioned with the most common spoken variant for each object. The illustration pages are placed adjacent to the page where the relevant main entry appears—that is, the entry for the location (airport, kitchen) or general grouping (electronic items, car parts) illustrated. All the captions are themselves main entry words, and cross-references to the drawings are provided in their entries.

IX. Summary

The *Longman Dictionary of American English* is both a dictionary and an active learning text for intermediate and advanced students of English as a second or foreign language. It is appropriate for adult learners and secondary school students. It is designed as a self-study text and yet could serve as a valuable auxiliary text for formal instruction.

The dictionary contains the vocabulary necessary for oral and literate fluency both in intake and in production. Although the work presumes on the inherent diligence of the second language student, native speakers interested in the study of English grammar and teachers of basic grammar would find the work valuable as well. The work is recommended for acquisition by school and public libraries serving these populations.

Macmillan Dictionary

Facts at a Glance

Full Title: **Macmillan Dictionary**.
Publisher: Macmillan.
Editor: William D. Halsey.
Edition Reviewed: © 1987.

Number of Volumes: 1.
Number of Entries: 90,000.
Number of Definitions: 120,000.
Number of Pages: 1,232.
Number of Illustrations: 1,800 in black and white, some with one added color.
Number of Maps: 13 pages in full color.
Trim Size: 8″ × 10″.
Binding: hardcover.

Price: list $22.68; school $17.01.

Intended Readership: grades 8 and up.
Sold in bookstores and other outlets; also sold to schools and libraries. ISBN 0-02-195390-2.

I. Introduction

The *Macmillan Dictionary* is intended for home, classroom, or library use by students in grades eight and above. It is designed to function, according to the editors, as "a comprehensive reference source to help you learn about the English language." An abridged dictionary, its 120,000 definitions "reflect current American usage." The volume also contains special features that enhance its value as a reference source for students. The *Macmillan Dictionary* is the most advanced of a series of four Macmillan dictionaries for students; the series also comprises the MACMILLAN DICTIONARY FOR CHILDREN, MACMILLAN SCHOOL DICTIONARY, and MACMILLAN DICTIONARY FOR STUDENTS.

II. Authority

The dictionary's publisher, Macmillan, is well known for its reference materials and educational books. William D. Halsey, the series' editorial director, has been senior vice president at Macmillan since 1968 and has served as the editorial director of the MERIT STUDENTS ENCYCLOPEDIA and COLLIER'S ENCYCLOPEDIA (published by Crowell-Collier). Consultants for the *Macmillan Dictionary* include, for etymology, Ralph L. Ward, Professor of Classics, Hunter College. According to the editors, words included in the dictionary have been drawn from "two primary sources: (1) the language of literature, history, and science that you study in school; and (2) the language of everyday speech and conversation."

III. Comprehensiveness

A number of words that should appear in a dictionary with a 1987 copyright have been omitted from the *Macmillan Dictionary*. These terms, recent additions to current usage, include *aerobics, ayatollah, compact disk,* and *videocassette.* A glossary of computer terms is included among the special features at the end of the volume, but the exclusion of these terms from the main word list will create difficulties for students trying to locate their meanings. Biological terms for sexual and reproductive organs are included in the dictionary, as are the words **homosexual** and **lesbian**. None of the definitions for **gay**, however, includes reference to homosexuality, nor is *AIDS* included in the word list.

Etymological notes appear in brackets at the end of the entry. Although etymological information is not provided for *all* entries, the amount and selection appear adequate for the dictionary's intended audience and purpose. The derivation of **mascot**, for example is traced:

[French *mascotte*, from Provençal *mascoto* sorcery, from *masco* witch; of uncertain origin.]

In a few instances, full etymological information is provided in anecdotal form. For example, under **red tape** appears the clarification:

[From the practice that began in the seventeenth century in England of using *red tape* to tie official documents.]

Synonyms, included for some entries, are introduced by the abbreviation **Syn.** and appear in a separate paragraph at the end of the entry. In some cases, a synonym given is cross-referenced to its own entry: for example, under **constrain** the reader is directed to "see **force**." More detailed information is provided for some synonymous words. Under **droop** the differences between the synonyms **wilt** and **sag** are carefully explained and illustrated with sentences including the words.

Extensive usage notes, marked by a boldface triangle, appear in many entries. For example, **ain't**, often simply designated in dictionaries as nonstandard or colloquial, is clarified by the following usage note:

This form is now frowned on in any use except where the aim is deliberately to show departure from standard speech as for humor or characterization: *We ain't got a barrel of money.*

Also included in the dictionary are abbreviations; biographical and geographic entries; combining forms; prefixes and suffixes; inflected forms of verbs, nouns, and adjectives; and irregular noun plurals.

IV. Quality and Currency of Entries

Definitions are accurate and concise, their reading level appropriate to the intended audience. Illustrative phrases and sentences that help to clarify definitions are extensively used. Some are quotations from literature, including Shakespeare and the Bible, with sources given; others are created by the lexicographers. Scientific and technical terms are made accessible to the general reader. For example, **quantum theory** is defined as

> theory, formulated by Max Planck in 1900, stating that radiant energy is emitted and absorbed in quanta, rather than in a continuous manner.

Scientific names of plants and animals appear in italics within the definitions for their common names.

Grouped according to part of speech, definitions are numbered consecutively in boldface type. The most commonly used meaning is placed first. Appropriate designations signal informal use, slang, archaic forms, and British usage. Homographs are given separate entries.

Geographical entries are concise, yet detailed. For example, **Belize** is defined as a

> country on the northeastern coast of Central America, on the Caribbean, formerly British Honduras. Capital, Belmopan. Area, 8,867 sq. mi. Pop. (1974 est.), 130,000.

A spot check indicated that many of the population figures in the geographic entries are estimates dating from the late 1960s and early 1970s. Updating of these numbers would make the valuable geographic feature more helpful for today's students. Biographical entries, although often very brief, will also prove useful to students.

V. Syllabication and Pronunciation

Dots are used to divide words into syllables, and dashes mark a hyphenated entry: dot and dash are clearly distinguishable and will not be mistaken for one another. Accent marks indicate stressed syllables; phonetic respelling and simple diacritical marks represent pronunciation. The system is explained in the "Guide to the Dictionary" and in the "Pronunciation Key" at the front of the volume. An abbreviated pronunciation key is also provided, for quick reference, at the bottom of every page. Pronunciation is given in parentheses immediately following each main entry word. Alternative pronunciations are provided for many words; for example, **Don Quixote**, **Illinois**, **nauseous**, **tomato**, and **vase**. If one pronunciation is more common than others, it is listed first. All pronunciations given are accepted in current American English usage.

VI. Special Features

One of the outstanding special features of this work is its introductory "Guide to the Dictionary." It is detailed, clearly written, and well designed as a finding aid to all elements in the dictionary. It is preceded by a well-marked sample page, which is numerically coded and keyed to sections in the guide. A "List of Abbreviations Used in This Dictionary," a "Table of English Spellings," and the pronunciation follow the guide; all of these features are indispensable to the student.

At the back of the book the student will find 13 pages of full-color maps. These may be generally useful but lack detail. A one-page chart lists U.S. states with their postal abbreviations, capitals, dates admitted to the Union, and state mottoes. This is followed by a chart depicting the interrelationships among the Indo-European languages and a very brief history of the English language. Next come four pages of portraits of U.S. presidents (through Reagan) with their dates of office and names of vice presidents. A chronology of historical events in the U.S. through 1981 is followed by tables of measure and chemical elements. Although these brief, quick-reference guides lack depth of detail, they are extremely useful features in a student dictionary.

Perhaps the finest special feature in the dictionary is the supplement that provides follow-up activities for students to reinforce the guide material. The supplement is not well titled, however, and is listed in the dictionary's main contents only as "Practice Pages." It would be helpful to have the supplement's existence more clearly noted in the contents and in the introductory paragraphs to the "Guide to the Dictionary."

VII. Accessibility

Alphabetization is letter by letter, with biographical entries alphabetized under the surname. Guide words, such as **novella / nuisance** indicate the first and last words defined on each page. The book is not thumb indexed, but there are black thumb tabs printed on the far right-hand margin of every double spread with the letter designation in white. These letter labels stand out clearly and make it easier for readers to find the pages they are seeking. Under words for which a full entry is not given, cross-references direct the user to appropriate main entries and definition numbers. For example, the reader looking up **giant panda** will be directed to

> panda (*def. 1*).

Alternative spellings appear after the pronunciation

and inflected forms; they are preceded by *also* and are printed in boldface type. The contents fully lists all special features, although the section titled "Practice Pages," as discussed above, might be more descriptively titled.

VIII. Graphics and Format

The *Macmillan Dictionary* is sturdy and attractive, with bright wipe-clean board covers. Because the binding is not excessively tightly stitched, the volume lies flat when opened. The paper used is heavy and allows for minimal show-through of text and pictures. The double-column pages have ample margins; main entry words, in boldface type, overhang the text. Typefaces are appropriately sized and easy to read, and the use of a variety of typefaces makes it easy for the user to locate particular kinds of information.

Illustrations are black line drawings, in some instances enhanced with either brown or green. They appear next to the words they illustrate; they are captioned and add substance to the definitions. Drawings include many plants, animals, mechanical devices, and architectural features.

IX. Summary

The *Macmillan Dictionary* compares favorably to the WORLD BOOK DICTIONARY (1983), which is also intended for junior and senior high school use. The WORLD BOOK DICTIONARY is larger, with 225,000 entries and more than 3,000 illustrations; but the *Macmillan Dictionary* is more attractive in format and contains geographical and biographical information, which the WORLD BOOK DICTIONARY lacks. The *Macmillan Dictionary* also compares favorably to the SCOTT, FORESMAN ADVANCED DICTIONARY. Particularly in its inclusion of a detailed "Guide to the Dictionary" and a supplement of follow-up activities, the *Macmillan Dictionary* is an excellent choice as a classroom dictionary. School libraries will also find it a good choice.

Macmillan Dictionary for Children

Facts at a Glance
Full Title: **Macmillan Dictionary for Children.**
Publisher: Macmillan.
Editor: William D. Halsey.
Edition Reviewed: © 1987.

Number of Volumes: 1.
Number of Entries: 30,000.

Number of Pages: 784.
Number of Illustrations: 1,200 in full color.
Number of Maps: 10 in full color.
Trim Size: 8″ × 10″.
Binding: hardcover.

Price: $13.95.
Intended Readership: ages 7 through 11.
ISBN 0-02-578790-X.

I. Introduction

The *Macmillan Dictionary for Children* is intended for students in elementary school between the ages of 7 and 11. Part of the Macmillan dictionary series, it was originally published in 1975 with a first revised edition in 1982 and the current revision in 1987. It contains 30,000 entries and 1,200 full-color illustrations. The dictionary is attractively designed for this age group, and the preface, titled "Welcome to Your Dictionary," suggests that it is not only a book to turn to for information but also a book to read for fun. There are 724 pages of words and their definitions, along with 54 pages of introductory and supplementary material.

II. Authority

The supervising editor for this book is Phyllis R. Winant, assisted by a staff of editors, consultants, and artists. The readability consultant for the dictionary is Milton D. Jacobson. *American Reference Books Annual* (ARBA–85) called the previous edition one of the most reputable for children. Other editions of this work are published under the titles MACMILLAN BEGINNING DICTIONARY and SCRIBNER BEGINNING DICTIONARY, and the text has also been licensed to Field Enterprises Education Corporation and appears under the title CHILDCRAFT DICTIONARY.

III. Comprehensiveness

There are no biographical entries, foreign words or phrases, or slang terms. Sexually oriented words are not included. There are only a few abbreviations and geographical listings, but this limitation is not a disadvantage for the intended audience. The geographical listings include U.S. states (with location and state capital given), major countries of the world (with location and capital given), and continents (location and, in some cases, relative size given). The

Macmillan Dictionary for Children

❶ Boldface guide words (with superior numbers for homographs) appear at top of each page

❷ Main entry word in boldface type is *not* divided into syllables

❸ Definitions are grouped according to the part of speech; the most commonly used meaning is placed first

❹ Part of speech is spelled out, in italic; noun plurals are indicated

❺ Illustrative sentences are provided with the entry word italicized

❻ Syllabication, in boldface, precedes pronunciation in parentheses

❼ Full-color captioned illustration of the first homograph

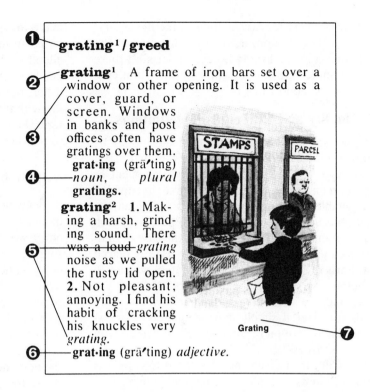

geographical information selected for presentation is stable, so that it will not become outdated. Contractions, prefixes, and suffixes are entered; synonyms and antonyms are not. Homophones are handled in an interesting and accessible way in this dictionary. They are signaled by a solid black triangle and prefaced with the statement "another word that sounds like this is. . . ." For example, under the word **bear** there is a note:

▲ Another word that sounds like this is **bare**.

Inflections of words are provided within the main entry word. A useful feature for young readers is that noun plurals are indicated even when they are formed regularly: "*noun, plural.*" When the noun plural is irregular, it is given a separate entry, as in the case of **ox** and **oxen**. When the singular and plural are the same, as with the word **moose**, the noun plural is still indicated. Verb forms are listed at the end of the main entry; for example, "beat, beaten, or beat, beating." However, the verb **be** is handled somewhat differently. "Been" and "being" are noted, but **am** and **are** have separate listings in the dictionary and are not defined; they are merely used in sentences. While this practice is probably less confusing to children, a definition indicating that these words are part

of the verb family "be" seems necessary in any dictionary, regardless of age level.

All forms of words are usually given in a single entry, and the part of speech is indicated at the end of each definition. In some cases, nouns and verbs are given separately by numbered entries. Some examples are **grating**, **fell**, and **bear**.

The history of words is indicated for some entries. These are attractively presented, varied in their focus, and likely to interest students. Called "word stories," they are set apart from the definition by bright blue borders that are signaled by a solid blue triangle. A typical word story is found after the entry for the word **garbage**:

The word **garbage** first meant "the insides of an animal used for food." These were usually eaten only by people who could not afford to eat more expensive meat, and other people threw them out. So the word *garbage* came to mean "food that is thrown out."

The history note under **academy** is less anecdotal and more historical. It explains that the word

comes from the Greek name of a place near Athens. Plato, a famous Greek teacher, had a school there more than two thousand years ago. The Romans used this name for any school like this one.

There are very few usage notes in the dictionary, but when they do appear, they are handled in the same format as the history notes. Under **ain't** there is a note indicating that the contraction is "not considered to be good English."

IV. Quality and Currency of Definitions

Entry words are arranged alphabetically, letter by letter. A unique and useful feature of this dictionary, for younger readers, is that entry words appear as they are seen in any other printed source, *not* divided into syllables. As in other Macmillan dictionaries, definitions are grouped according to part of speech and are numbered consecutively. In the case of multiple meanings, the most commonly used is placed first. Parts of speech are not abbreviated, which will be helpful to young student readers. The print is large, and the definitions, which follow the entry words, are stated simply and adequately. For example, the definition of **complacent** is "pleased with oneself; satisfied."

Many illustrative sentences are used to explain a word both in its multiple meanings and in its various parts of speech. These illustrative examples are not set off in any way and could be confused with the definitions themselves, although the entry word within them is italicized. Most entries rate only one or two definitions. Some words have three—such as **litter**, with one for a mess, a second for animals born at the same time, and a third for a stretcher—but this is not usual.

Most of the definitions are quite acceptable for the intended age group, but a few are questionable. For example, the second definition given for **colored** is "**2.** Of the Negro race." There is no usage note to indicate that **colored** is not an acceptable substitute for the word "Black." Nor is the term **black** as clearly defined as it might be in terms of current racial usage. The dictionary merely states in a second definition that a black is "A member of one of the major divisions of the human race." **Indian**, **Jew**, and **Oriental** with capital first letters are included. *Black* with a capital *B* is not. By contrast, Webster's Elementary Dictionary handles this meaning of the word **black** as follows:

> *often cap*: of or relating to the Negro race or to Afro-American people and their culture (*black* Africans) (*black* studies).

The *Dictionary for Children* has some of the same problems with currency as do the other Macmillan dictionaries. A comparison of the 1987 edition with the 1981 revealed that few, if any, changes had been made in the word section. A glossary of computer terms from *The Apple IIe User's Guide* has been added to the back of the book. This process of appending lists of new words is convenient for the publisher, but not for young readers who often will not know that the word they are seeking is a computer term. Further, not all of these definitions are geared to the dictionary's intended audience.

V. Syllabication and Pronunciation

Syllabication and pronunciation are given at the end of the entry. Although students thus see the main entry word as it would appear in any other print source, they may find it difficult to read through the entry without knowing how to pronounce the word. Syllabication appears in boldface type followed by pronunciation in parentheses "**gor·geous** (gôr′jəs) *adjective*." The format for syllabication and the key to pronunciation are the same as in the *Macmillan School Dictionary* and are thus good preparation for the more advanced work while still being age-appropriate for this work. The full pronunciation key appears prominently on the left-hand page opposite the beginning of the word list, and an abbreviated key, focused on vowel pronunciation, is provided—in the bottom right corner of all right-hand pages within the word list—for easy student access. Alternative pronunciations are given as needed to enable students to distinguish alternative meanings more easily. For example, two definitions are given for the world **contrary**. For each definition a separate pronunciation is given—one meaning "opposite," the other, "liking to argue."

VI. Special Features

The appended materials in the back of the *Dictionary for Children* are similar to those found in the Macmillan Dictionary for Students. One difference is in the maps found in the atlas section. The children's dictionary has much better quality maps, produced by Rand McNally. There is a "Flags of the World" section that will appeal to and interest young students, and in the "Presidents of the United States" section the portraits are photographs from the National Portrait Gallery, the Smithsonian Institution, and the National Geographic Society.

In the front of the book, the guide to the dictionary is well illustrated, and the material is simply and clearly presented for young readers. There also appears a rather long section on the history of English, well-written for the intended audience, followed by the pronunciation key. There are no dictionary exercises in this edition of the book; such exercises can be found in the MACMILLAN BEGINNING DICTIONARY.

VII. Accessibility

Like the other Macmillan dictionaries, the *Dictionary for Children* is not thumb indexed, but there are bright blue, thumb-shaped markings on the right hand margins of every page with the letter designation in white. Although not as prominent as a thumb index, these will aid students in locating alphabetic sections of the dictionary. Also useful are the guide words, such as "**comic strip / commissioner**," that appear at the top of each page.

Variant spellings for words are not given. While this may cause confusion for students later on when they use more advanced dictionaries, the absence here of alternative spellings is appropriate for younger readers. There are a few cross-references, carefully designed to be accessible to elementary school students. For example, under the word **convex** the reader is instructed to "Look up **concave** for a picture of this."

Access to the special features in the back of the volume is facilitated by a Contents listing between the word list and these features; however, the features preceding the word list are not listed in a contents or index.

VIII. Graphics and Format

This dictionary is very attractive and has a great deal of eye appeal with its bright cover surfaced in wipe-clean plastic. The paper is heavy, but nonglossy, and each double-column page has from one to three full-color drawings captioned with main entry words. Drawings are two to three inches in size and located immediately above or below the word they help to define. There is a good minority representation in the drawings. The sections appended to the word list also contain colorful photographs, including pictures taken from spacecraft of the sun, Jupiter, and Saturn. The history of each letter of the alphabet is described and brightly illustrated at the beginning of every letter section.

Layout and typeface are such that this book is very easy to read, and students will easily locate particular types of information. Main entry words are in boldface type overhanging the text; definitions are in roman type; illustrative sentences are in roman with the entry word italicized. Syllabication is given in boldface, followed by pronunciation in parentheses and word variants in boldface. The volume is sturdily bound and will hold up well to steady use in the home, classroom, or library.

IX. Summary

The *Macmillan Dictionary for Children* enters words in the way that they are normally seen in print. This practice makes it easier for children to locate words, but it may not prepare them well for other dictionary use as they grow older. It provides simple, clear definitions of words and uses the words in many illustrative sentences. It contains numerous colorful pictures, and the large type and layout make it easy for elementary school children to use. The *Macmillan Dictionary for Children* largely compares favorably with WEBSTER'S ELEMENTARY DICTIONARY (Merriam-Webster, 1986), although Webster's is less expensive. Both measure 8″ x 10″ and Webster's contains 2,000 more words, but it has none of the supplementary materials found in the Macmillan work. Both are well illustrated, but Webster's enters words in the traditional dictionary format by breaking entry words into syllables. The Webster guide to using the dictionary is more difficult than that in the Macmillan dictionary, which has done an excellent job of simplifying this information. Webster's is more appropriate for the upper grades of elementary school and could even be used for academically less developed students in junior high; the *Macmillan Dictionary for Children* is more appropriate for lower elementary grades but is useful for many students in the upper levels as well. Both do an excellent job of serving elementary dictionary needs and deserve a place in the school library media center. The Macmillan work fills a gap between simple picture dictionaries and the more traditional elementary word books.

Macmillan Dictionary for Students

Facts at a Glance

Full Title: **Macmillan Dictionary for Students**.
Former Title: Macmillan Contemporary Dictionary.
Publisher: Macmillan.
Editor: William D. Halsey.
Edition Reviewed: © 1984.

Number of Volumes: 1.
Number of Entries: 90,000.
Number of Definitions: 120,000.
Number of Pages: 1,190.
Number of Illustrations: 1,800.
Trim Size: 8″ × 10″.
Binding: hardcover.

Macmillan Dictionary for Students

1 Inflected forms, printed in boldface type, follow the main entry and are given pronunciations where necessary.

2 Sentences illustrating the various discriminated meanings of the main entry word are set in italic. These sentences occasionally use the inflected form of a main entry word.

3 Idiomatic phrases or common expressions are printed in boldface type so they can be seen easily; the idioms are given definitions and are used in sentences that are printed in italic type.

4 A bold upright triangle precedes a usage note that applies to a previous illustrative sentence.

5 The etymology is presented in square brackets at the end of an entry paragraph. The etymology includes meanings for the root or source word.

6 A synonym study indicated by **Syn.** briefly defines the given synonyms, explains nuances of the meanings and gives precise illustrative sentences.

hear (hĕr) **heard** (hurd), **hear·ing.** *v.t.* **1.** to be able to perceive (sound) by means of the ear. **2.** to pay attention to; listen: *We heard both sides of the argument before we made a decision.* **3.** to be informed of: *We heard the news on the radio.* **4.** to give a formal, official, or legal hearing to: *The judge heard the testimony of all the witnesses.* **5.** to listen to with compliance; accede to; grant: *His prayers were heard.* **6.** to attend and listen to as part of an audience. **7. to hear out.** to listen to until the end: *Hear me out before you decide.* —*v.i.* **1.** to perceive or be able to perceive sound by means of the ear. **2.** to receive information; be told; learn (with *of, about,* or *from*): *What have you heard about the situation? Have you ever heard of him?* **3. to hear of.** to allow, consider, or agree to: *I will not hear of your leaving.* ▲ usually with the negative. **4. to hear tell.** *Informal.* to learn: *I hear tell you're getting married.* —*interj.* **hear, hear.** well done or well spoken. [Old English *hēran* to perceive sound, listen.] —**hear′er,** *n.*
Syn. *v.i.* **1. Hear, listen** mean to perceive sound by the ear. **Hear** suggests the physical act of perceiving sound: *Deaf men cannot hear.* **Listen** implies giving heed or paying attention to what is heard: *The audience listened very carefully to the president's speech.*

Price: $16.95.
Intended Readership: grades 8 and up.
Sold in bookstores and other outlets; also sold to libraries. ISBN 0-02-761560-X.

I. Scope and Format

The *Macmillan Dictionary for Students*, a comprehensive reference source for junior and senior high school students, is in most respects identical to the MACMILLAN DICTIONARY, reviewed in this guide. These dictionaries differ in three areas. While the MACMILLAN DICTIONARY carries a copyright date of 1987 (earlier edition © 1981), the most recent copyright date for the *Macmillan Dictionary for Students* is 1984 (earlier editions © 1981, 1979, and 1973).

Differences also appear in the dictionaries' special features, although they share several excellent features, including the "Sample Page," "Guide to the Dictionary," "Abbreviations Used in This Diction-

ary," "Table of English Spellings," and "Pronunciation Key," all located at the front of the volume. At the back, both volumes contain a chart of the Indo-European languages; a history of the English language; information on U.S. presidents (through President Reagan); a listing of important events in U.S. history (with dates from the 1980s and minor variations between the lists in the different editions); and a "Glossary of Computer Terms." Included in the MACMILLAN DICTIONARY, but not in the *Macmillan Dictionary for Students*, are a 13-page atlas, facts about U.S. states and territories, portraits of the presidents, tables of measure and chemical elements, and a supplement of follow-up activities for the student.

Some features in the *Macmillan Dictionary for Students* do not appear in the *Macmillan Dictionary*: a handbook of style (punctuation, capitalization, and numbers) and a seven-page article, "The World of Computers." The features unique to the *Macmillan Dictionary for Students* enhance the book's usefulness to the intended student audience; however, this

Macmillan First Dictionary

A tiger is a **large** animal.

large
Large means very big. A tiger is a **large** animal. ☼*See the picture.*

❶ The definition is phrased as if it were an answer to a question about the word

❷ Symbol and italicized phrase refer the reader to the picture

❸ Four-color illustration helps to identify the entry word

❹ The illustrative sentence is used in the definition and repeated in the caption

volume's omission of features contained in the other dictionary, especially the tables and follow-up activities, may limit its use for classroom applications.

The final difference between the dictionaries is price: the MACMILLAN DICTIONARY lists at $22.68, with a school price of $17.01; the *Macmillan Dictionary for Students*, at $16.95, may well be a better buy for home use. Variations in the special features may determine the selection of either version for schools and libraries.

Macmillan First Dictionary

Facts at a Glance

Full Title: **Macmillan First Dictionary**.
Publisher: Macmillan.
Editor: William D. Halsey.
Edition Reviewed: © 1987.

Number of Volumes: 1.
Number of Entries: 1,500 in full color.

Number of Pages: 268.
Number of Illustrations: 500.
Trim Size: 8½″ × 11″.
Binding: hardcover.

Price: $12.57.
Intended Readership: grades 1 through 2.
Sold to schools. ISBN 0-02-195360-0.

I. Introduction and Scope

With the exceptions of the title, cover, introduction, appendix, and the standard school property stamp on the inside front cover, this book is identical to the MACMILLAN VERY FIRST DICTIONARY, which is reviewed in this buying guide. This is the school edition of that book and the next higher level after MACMILLAN PICTURE DICTIONARY, also reviewed in this guide. The preface states that the book "provides support for a basal reading program because its word list is drawn from the vocabulary used in

The Macmillan Picture Wordbook

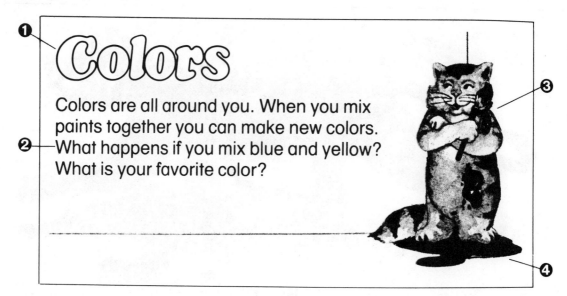

❶ Words are grouped according to topics familiar to children

❷ Reading readiness games and questions are suggested that

relate to the words and pictures in the book

❸ Pre-readers are encouraged to look at each page closely in

order to "find the cat" hiding on almost every page

❹ Four-color illustrations stimulate interest

primary-grade materials. Definitions of entries are understandable and meaningful because the reading level has been strictly controlled." In four simple steps, a "How to Use Your Book" introductory section for children explains how to use this dictionary: know the alphabet; know how to alphabetize words; read the definition; if there is an illustration, look at it. The appendix reviews these steps and describes activities to reinforce them. The book contains over 500 full-color illustrations and 1,500 words explained in context. Special features at the back of the book include "Days of the Week" and "Months of the Year," "Practice Pages on How to Find a Word," "How to Learn About a Word," "How to Learn from a Picture," and a "Review" section.

The *Macmillan First Dictionary* is the appropriate edition for school use and for school libraries because of its well-designed practical instructions supplied in the introductory section and appendixes. The *Macmillan Very First Dictionary* is better for in the home and public library collections.

The Macmillan Picture Wordbook

Facts at a Glance
Full Title: **The Macmillan Picture Wordbook**.
Publisher: Macmillan.

Compiler: Kathleen N. Daly.
Illustrator: John Wallner.
Edition Reviewed: © 1982.

Number of Volumes: 1.
Number of Categories: 44.
Number of Words: 1,500.
Number of Pages: 80.
Number of Illustrations: 80 pages in full color.
Trim Size: 8½" × 11".
Binding: hardcover.

Price: $7.95.
Intended Readership: ages 2 through 5. ·
Sold in bookstores and other outlets; also sold to libraries. ISBN 0-02-725600-6.

I. Scope and Format

The Macmillan Picture Wordbook is a word and picture identification book, not a dictionary; no definitions or sentences using words in context are given. The book consists of one- or two-page illustrations devoted to a variety of subjects, or categories of objects, people, or animals—all pictured with word labels and all falling within the range of a child's knowledge as it expands with age and experience. "The child will grasp the connection between the picture and the printed word that goes with it," according to an introductory section titled, "How to Help a Child Enjoy this Book." This introduction also states that the book is designed for "young readers-to-be." The pictures of many young children engaged in a variety of activities reinforce the book's intended audience as being preschool to kindergarten or first grade.

II. Authority

Macmillan publishes many well-regarded dictionaries for younger readers, including a series of beginning, intermediate, and school dictionaries at graduated reading levels. The publisher gives no clues in this word book as to how or why its particular categories or words were selected for young readers.

III. Quality and Currency of Entries

This book contains no real definitions, but rather words that identify people and objects. A young reader will absorb a "definition" of a labeled item from the illustrated context.

Access to the words is not alphabetical; they are grouped under 44 wide-ranging topics, accessible only through a table of contents that lists the topics in somewhat random order, beginning with the surroundings most familiar to children, **Houses**. Other topics include: **Wheels on the Road**, **People at Work**, **School**, **Your Body**, **Outer Space**, **Dinosaurs**, **Make Believe**, **Telling Time**, **Shapes**, **Colors**, **Opposites**, **Tools**, and **Musical Instruments**, and even **Manners**. Double-page spreads are used for all but 13 of these broad topics. Apart from the words, each spread contains a simple paragraph of explanation of its subject. For example, under **The Airport** is the following short paragraph:

An airport is a place where all kinds of airplanes take off and land on runways. Some carry cargo. Many of them carry hundreds of passengers. Small airplanes may hold only two people. Have you ever gone to an airport?

Some of the 44 objects labeled on the airport spread are: **wind speed**, **gauge**, **radar scanner**, **observation deck**, **automatic doors**, **baggage cart**, **luggage**, **newsstand**, **restrooms**, **telephones**, **gates**, **security check**, **pilot**, **cabin**, **flight attendant**, **fuselage**, **landing gear**, and **runway**. These words are printed in easy-to-read

sans serif type; the topic explanation is printed in larger type.

In addition, children are encouraged to play word games such as "In Grandma's Trunk" or "I Spy" or "I Remember." The introduction suggests that if children cannot find any of the words they need for these games in the book, they make up their own list from other sources, such as magazines. This guidance will be familiar to classroom teachers and librarians involved in reading readiness programs for the young.

Since access to the words in this book is limited to the broad topics listed on the contents page, the child—or adult user—will have to browse through every page in search of a particular object or word. Inclusion of an alphabetical word list index would have been more practical for users and would help children prepare to use more advanced word books.

IV. Illustrations

The artist, John Wallner, has done a fine job of presenting many details without crowding the pages. He has included various ethnic groups and, in addition to the labeled figures and objects, there is much to interest a child in the pictures. The airport scene, for example, includes a harried traveler at the check-in counter with objects spilling from his pockets and luggage, an information person helping a woman, and a child looking at a magazine at the newsstand. Young readers will pore over these pictures and enjoy making up stories while learning the proper terminology from the word labels.

V. Summary

The graphics are well designed, providing a clear layout containing full-color drawings with considerable detail. Because this word and picture identification book uses proper terminology, even such difficult words as **fuselage**, it will help expand childrens' vocabulary, although the lack of an alphabetical word list or index limits its usefulness. This picture book is a suitable choice for families, and also for school and public libraries—for children learning words and acquiring the correct words to describe the people, activities, and objects in our world. The book might also be useful for young children learning English as a second language who need to expand their vocabulary—if it is shared with an English-speaking adult. The school edition of this same book is titled Picture Dictionary; its brief review in this guide describes the minor differences between the two editions.

Macmillan School Dictionary

❶ Homographs are indicated by superior numbers

❷ Illustrative sentence or phrase provided in italics

❸ The homograph has an etymology with definitions provided within square brackets. The etymon is given a meaning

❹ Usage labels provided in italic

❺ Labeled illustration of first homograph's second meaning (with superior number and definition number)

truck¹ (truk) *n.* **1.** a motor vehicle designed to carry heavy loads, especially one with a cab in front for the driver, and a trailer or open area in the rear for freight. **2.** a low rectangular frame on four wheels, often motorized, used for moving heavy loads; dolly. **3.** a set of two or more pairs of wheels mounted closely together in a swiveling frame, as on a railroad car or locomotive. —*v.t.* to transport on a truck or trucks: *to truck fresh vegetables to market.* —*v.i.* to drive a truck or engage in trucking. [Probably from Latin *trochus* an iron hoop, from Greek *trochos* wheel.]
truck² (truk) *n.* **1.** vegetables raised for sale in a market. **2.** *Informal.* dealings: *She will have no truck with her neighbors.* **3.** *Informal.* trash or rubbish. [Old French *troquer* to barter; of uncertain origin.]

Truck¹ *(def. 2)*

Macmillan School Dictionary

Facts at a Glance

Full Title: **Macmillan School Dictionary**.
Publisher: Macmillan.
Editor: William D. Halsey.
Edition Reviewed: © 1987.

Number of Volumes: 1.
Number of Entries: 65,000.
Number of Definitions: 95,000.
Number of Pages: 1,168.
Number of Illustrations: 1,500 in two colors.
Number of Maps: 13 pages in full color.
Trim Size: 8″ × 10″.
Binding: hardcover.

Prices: list $24.32; school $18.24.
Intended Readership: grades 5 through 7.
Sold in bookstores and other outlets; also sold to libraries and schools. ISBN 0-02-195380-5.

I. Introduction

The *Macmillan School Dictionary* (originally copyrighted in 1981) is a companion to the MACMILLAN DICTIONARY and is intended for use by upper elementary students. Its editors define it as "a special book designed to help you learn about the English language and use it more effectively." In addition to its 65,000 entries, comprising 95,000 definitions, the dictionary contains special features that expand its usefulness, as both a reference source and a manual of practical skills, to the student.

II. Authority

Macmillan publishes a complete range of school dictionaries. The firm's reference works have been highly regarded by teachers and librarians for many years.

William D. Halsey, the Editorial Director, is assisted by an editorial staff and a group of consultants, including several consultants for separate academic disciplines. Senior Editors are Vesta K. Wells and Phyllis R. Winant.

According to the editors, the compilation is based on four sources, the most important of which is textbooks: "The editors studied and selected vocabulary found in the current textbooks of all major publishers." Other sources for words included are literature, current periodicals, and conversational American English.

III. Comprehensiveness

For its size and scope, the *Macmillan School Dictionary* is comprehensive. In addition to conventional definitions and part-of-speech labels, it provides 37,000 examples of words in context—that is, sentences illustrating how the word is used. For example, to explain the usage of **file** as a transitive verb, the following is given:

v.t. **1.** to keep (papers or similar items) arranged in order. **2.** to place in a file: *The clerk filed the letter in its proper alphabetical place.* **3.** to hand in legally or officially; enter on a record: *to file a report, to file one's income tax return.*

While synonyms and antonyms are excluded, many entries include usage labels, usage notes, quotations, variants, and etymological notes. When the etymology is given, it appears in brackets at the end of the entry and in some instances contains anecdotal information. For example, the definition of **decimate** is followed by

[Latin *decimātus*, the past participle of *decimāre* to select every tenth man for punishment. In ancient Rome an army revolt was punished by taking every tenth soldier and executing him.]

Under **teddy bear** appears

[From *Teddy*, a nickname of President Theodore Roosevelt; from a cartoon in which he was shown sparing the life of a bear cub while hunting.]

Included in the word list are geographic and biographical entries. Geographic entries include, as appropriate, such information as location, capital, area, and population. Population figures for U. S. states are based on 1970 estimates, despite the existence of more recent census figures; those for countries of the world range from the early 1970s to the early 1980s. Biographical entries include dates and a concise, informative phrase of identification. For example, the entry for **Susan B. Anthony** reads

1820–1906, U.S. social reformer and leader of the women's suffrage movement.

Abbreviations also appear in the word list; they include chemical elements as well as most common utility abbreviations.

Computer terms are included—not, however, in the main word list, but in an appended glossary, where they may be overlooked. Some other recent additions to the language are omitted: while **video tape** appears as a main entry, *videocassette* and *compact disk* do not. Appropriate to the intended audience are the exclusions of most archaic word meanings and of the scientific terms for plants and animals. However, while the dictionary appropriately includes the names of human and animal sexual and reproductive organs, as well as the words **homosexual** and **lesbian**, it excludes the definition of *gay* as homosexual and the term *AIDS*. These words might reasonably be expected to appear in a 1987 dictionary, one of whose word sources is the newspaper.

IV. Quality and Currency of Entries

Definitions are straightforward and easily understood. Within entries, definitions are grouped according to part of speech and are numbered consecutively. The most commonly used meaning appears first.

One of this dictionary's strengths is its frequent use of words in illustrative phrases and sentences; one of its weaknesses, however, is a tendency to oversimplify difficult terms. For example, the following definition is given for **allegory**:

a story that teaches a lesson or shows something about life by having the characters and events stand for ideas, people, or moral principles. Aesop's fables are examples of allegories.

Based on the reading level of its intended audience, this definition compares favorably to that in the MACMILLAN DICTIONARY:

literary device for presenting abstract ideas or moral principles in the form of symbolic characters, events, or objects; extended metaphor.

However, a crucial aspect of the word's meaning is not reflected in the *Macmillan School Dictionary*: that is, that allegorical narratives unfold simultaneously on two levels. THE RANDOM HOUSE SCHOOL DICTIONARY (1984), for example, provides a superior definition:

a story whose characters and events have a meaning that is deeper than it appears and that teaches a lesson or moral.

On the other hand, the *Macmillan School Dictionary* provides particularly effective definitions for the scientific terms it includes. **Alimentary canal**, for example, clearly illustrated with an anatomical diagram, is defined as

a continuous tube extending from the mouth to the anus, through which food passes as it is digested, then absorbed, and finally eliminated as waste matter.

Also commendably clear are the dictionary's distinctions between **atheist** and **agnostic**.

V. Syllabication and Pronunciation

Black dots divide words into syllables, and dashes mark a hyphenated entry. Pronunciation for each word is given in parentheses immediately following the main entry word. Alternative pronunciations are provided, with the most common appearing first. Accent marks indicate stressed syllables, while phonetic respelling and diacritical marks clarify pronunciation. A full pronunciation key appears at the front of the volume, and a shorter key, for quick reference, is located in a color block at the bottom of the right-hand column on all right hand pages. The key used in the *Macmillan School Dictionary* is slightly different from that in the MACMILLAN DICTIONARY. For example, *u* as in "usage" is indicated in the younger readers' dictionary by y$\overline{oo}$, rather than $\overline{u}$,; *hw* represents the wh sound in "white" and "which," while the adult dictionary has no representation of this sound. The pronunciation key in the *Macmillan School Dictionary* is more helpful to a novice dictionary user and is appropriately simplified by the omission of sounds found in non-English words.

VI. Special Features

Among the dictionary's special features are those designed to teach dictionary skills. A "Guide to the Dictionary" clearly explains what information appears in the dictionary and how it may be located. "Try This" practice exercises are well designed and useful; however, their placement, interspersed throughout the guide, makes the guide more difficult to use. They might be more effectively grouped in a separate section following the guide. Supplementary dictionary exercises also appear in a section called "Practice Pages" at the back of the volume. The sample dictionary page is annotated but, disappointingly, not numerically keyed to the guide.

Following the guide are three more features designed to help the student use the dictionary. In addition to a list of abbreviations used in the dictionary and the full pronunciation key is a "Table of English Spellings." This table reflects the varying ways sounds may be spelled in English; for example, the sound *k* may be spelled *c*, *k*, *ck*, *ch*, *cc*, *qu*, *q*, *cq*, *cu*, or *que*. Sample words are also given, such as **cat**, **key**, and **tack**. This table will help students locate words they know how to pronounce but not how to spell.

The reference section appended to the back of the volume is similar to that found in the MACMILLAN DICTIONARY. It includes a 13-page atlas, as well as additional geographic, historical, linguistic, and scientific information. The tables of measure found in the adult dictionary are here abbreviated, and its table of chemical elements is absent from the student work. A list of "Inventions and Inventors," however, appears only in the latter.

The "Practice Pages" supplement is a clear and thorough follow-up to information and skills imparted in the guide. It is colorfully illustrated, although some of the illustrations, such as those of the shower and the sink, seem geared to children younger than many of those who would otherwise benefit from this material.

VII. Accessibility

The *Macmillan School Dictionary* is alphabetized letter by letter. Although the volume is not thumb indexed, there are useful black thumb-shaped markings on the far right-hand margin of every double-page spread, with the letter designation in white. Two boldfaced guide words appear at the top outer margin of each page; for example, **element / elixir**. Alternative spellings, in boldface type, are easily located following the main entry word and its pronunciation. A table of contents at the front of the volume facilitates access to special features. Individual items within the reference section are not listed here; however, a detailed contents list precedes that section. Similarly, a detailed contents precedes the "Practice Pages" supplement.

VIII. Graphics and Format

The *Macmillan School Dictionary* has the same layout, paper weight, and illustrations as the MACMILLAN DICTIONARY. Each two-column page has adequate margins, and the good-quality paper allows for minimal show-through of text. The type size is, appropriately, larger than that found in the MACMILLAN DICTIONARY. Main entry words appear in boldface type overhanging the text. Boldface is also used for variants, inflected forms, cross-references, and subentries; illustrative sentences and quotations appear in italic. These variations in typeface make entries easy to read and particular types of information easy to find at a glance.

There are generally one to three illustrations on a page—line drawings, some of which have added brown or green coloring. They appear next to the words they clarify and are captioned with main entry words. They are acceptable for this age group and serve to amplify definitions. Some are additionally labeled; for example, the illustration for **derrick** labels the parts of the machine: **guy**, **hoisting tackle**, **vertical support**, and **boom**.

The book is sturdily bound in an attractive bright orange and yellow-green cover that does not look drably institutional.

IX. Summary

The strengths of the *Macmillan School Dictionary* lie in its attractive format, sturdy binding, and concise, simply stated, and well-illustrated definitions. The learning activities are well designed and make the work useful in the classroom as well as the library. The *Macmillan School Dictionary* is comparable to the SCOTT, FORESMAN INTERMEDIATE DICTIONARY, designed for grades five through nine, which is similar in size and format and contains many of the same words and supplementary materials. The latter's 57,000 entries are fewer than the Macmillan dictionary's 65,000; but the *Scott, Foresman* is more consistent in its coverage and definitions, and reviewers continue to rank it as excellent (ARBA-84). Considering its lower price, it may be a better buy than the *Macmillan School Dictionary* for school libraries with limited budgets.

Macmillan Very First Dictionary

Facts at a Glance

Full Title: **Macmillan Very First Dictionary: A Magic World of Words**.
Former Title: Macmillan Magic World of Words.
Publisher: Macmillan.
Editor: William D. Halsey.
Edition Reviewed: © 1983.

Number of Volumes: 1.
Number of Entries: nearly 1,500.
Number of Pages: 280.
Number of Illustrations: 500 in full color.
Trim Size: 8½″ × 11″.
Binding: hardcover.

Price: $10.95.
Intended Readership: ages 4 through 7.
Sold in bookstores and other outlets; also sold to libraries. ISBN 0-02-761730-0.

I. Scope and Format

The *Macmillan Very First Dictionary* (original copyright 1977) and the MACMILLAN FIRST DICTIONARY have identical texts for the dictionary portion of the work (see the review of MACMILLAN FIRST DICTIONARY in this guide); and this dictionary is the next step up in vocabulary level from the MACMILLAN PICTURE WORDBOOK. The *Macmillan Very First Dic-*

tionary is the home and library edition (the MACMILLAN FIRST DICTIONARY is the school edition) and is designed to be used by children in the primary grades to extend their vocabularies.

In the introduction, the editors state that the book "is intended to serve children at different age levels. The youngest child can learn his or her ABC's from the special pages that introduce each letter of the alphabet." These pages contain a simple depiction of the upper- and lowercase forms of each letter with some pictures of words starting with the letter on the same page. Those just beginning to read can use this dictionary, but second and third graders with a command of reading and an interest in new words will find it most useful. There are almost 1,500 words and 500 illustrations, making the dictionary a transitional step between a picture dictionary and a more advanced dictionary with the familiar two-column format and occasional illustrations. The binding is sturdy, the page well designed and easy to follow. The type is large, and the paper is opaque.

The special features include a brief introductory statement to adults explaining the purpose and scope of the book and "How to Help a Child Use This Book," followed by two brief, highly illustrated essays written for children: "How Words Came to Be" and "How Writing Came to Be." Although cursory, they are entertaining and appropriate for the age level. The "How to Use Your Book" section is helpful but needs to be read in conjunction with the labeled example of an entry, which appears on the back cover of the book. The appendix, "Our Wonderful World," is a smattering of science, exploration, and maps, with sections on "Our Earth," "Learning About Our World" (which is really about explorers and how they made maps), "Flat Maps of a Round World," and "The World." The map of the world is extremely simple, identifying the seven continents and the Pacific, Atlantic, and Indian oceans.

II. Authority

Macmillan has published many well-regarded dictionaries and word books for children, including a complete series of school dictionaries.

III. Quality and Currency of Entries

Parents and teachers are likely to appreciate the way in which the definitions are constructed. They have been carefully designed to answer a child's question, "What does _____ mean?" The answer, always in a complete sentence, responds to that silent question by placing the entry word either as the first word or very early in the sentence and defining it in terms of a child's experiences. Two or more sentences are given, usually one defining the word and one using it in an illustrative manner. For example:

number
A **number** tells you how many there are of something. 2 and 50 are **numbers**. The **number** of children in our family is three. Do you know your own telephone **number**? The pages in this book are **numbered**.

God
Many people believe that **God** is the one that made the world and everything in it. Christians, Jews, and Muslims have this idea of **God**. People show their love of **God** in many ways.

However, in some entries, none of the sentences is truly definitional, and this is at times an avoidable omission. For example:

above
The birds flew **above** the trees. The sun is shining **above**.

Many of the entry words are concept words and will need further explanation by an adult. No syllabication or pronunciation is given, which is appropriate for the readers' level.

Accessibility is strictly alphabetical with all entries consisting of only one word. The top outer margin of each page contains a guide that gives the first and last words defined on the page. Although the book has instructions to children on how to use the dictionary, it fails to mention this device. The relatively complicated explanation of guide words can be verbally transmitted by parents or teachers. The entry word is in large bold lowercase roman type. The definition begins directly under the entry.

IV. Illustrations

If the entry has an accompanying illustration elsewhere on the page, a sunburst symbol and the words "See the picture" follow the definition. The illustration is always easy to find and is captioned with a brief additional sentence that uses the entry word.

Depending on the length of the definitions and the size of the illustrations, there are four to seven definitions per page. They run across the page with the left but not the right margins justified. Each letter of the alphabet is introduced on a page with several illustrations of main entry words that can be found in the following section of the book. Each illustration has a page number next to it; on the page where the

illustration appears in its proper alphabetical position, a bright pink square follows the definition. Instructions indicating what this square means are found on each page that introduces a new letter but are not explained in the "How to Use Your Book" sections. According to the editors "a unique feature of the book is that these illustrations are used exclusively to explain conceptual words that express ideas, rather than words that describe things." For example: **Love** is illustrated by a grandfather and small boy and girl all embracing. A caption reads: Grandpa **loves** his grandchildren. However, **costume**, **horse**, and **milk** might well be considered "things" rather than "ideas" and *are* illustrated, while many of the conceptual words in the book, such as **famous**, **hate**, and **selfish**, *are not* illustrated. *Reference Books Bulletin, 1981–1982* described the pictures as "very attractive, with excellent color and composition."

V. Summary

While the definitions in the *Macmillan Very First Dictionary* are usually adequate and the overall book quite attractive, the book lacks the complete and realistic introductory remarks and well-designed introductory sections that would give it maximum value for young children.

The Merriam-Webster Dictionary

Facts at a Glance

Full Title: **The Merriam-Webster Dictionary**.
Publisher: Pocket Books.
Editor: Henry Bosley Woolf, Editor-in-Chief.
Edition Reviewed: © 1974; 39th printing.

Number of Volumes: 1.
Number of Entries: 57,000.
Number of Pages: 848.
Trim Size: $4\frac{1}{8}'' \times 6\frac{3}{4}''$.
Binding: paperback.

Price: $3.95.
Intended Readership: young adults and adults.
Sold in bookstores and other outlets; also sold to libraries and schools. ISBN 0-671-53088-7.

I. Introduction

This paperback dictionary is a reformatted edition of the MERRIAM-WEBSTER CONCISE FAMILY DICTIONARY, prepared by the lexicographic staff of the Merriam-Webster Company. In paperback, it has been published since 1947. A second edition appeared in 1964. This edition, the third, was first published in 1974 after *Merriam-Webster's New Collegiate Dictionary* (the *eighth*, not the current ninth, edition) appeared in 1973. In the preface to this paperback edition, the editors state that a new edition became "necessary" after the *New Collegiate* was published to meet "the needs of those who want an up-to-date record of present-day English in compact form." With its core vocabulary of some 57,000 words, Pocket Books' edition has been selling steadily for thirteen years, at this writing. While the work is no longer "up-to-date," as the preface still claims, it is a condensed, but substantial paperback compilation equivalent to the category of dictionaries normally labeled "concise" in hardback. It is designed, the publisher states, "for home and school use."

II. Authority

Pocket Books, now a paperback publishing division of Simon & Schuster, Inc., has published the current edition of this dictionary, by arrangement with G. & C. Merriam Co. (now Merriam-Webster Inc.), since 1964.

Merriam publishes the family of highly respected Merriam-Webster® dictionaries that includes the authoritative *Webster's Third New International Dictionary* and WEBSTER'S NINTH NEW COLLEGIATE DICTIONARY. This paperback is a photoreduced edition of the MERRIAM-WEBSTER CONCISE FAMILY DICTIONARY, which, in the hardbound version, is printed in a larger typeface than is usual in adult dictionaries.

The paperback and its companion were prepared by Merriam-Webster's staff of lexicographers, using the publisher's own continuously updated citation files that then numbered some 11,500,000 entries. The Editor-in-Chief, Henry Bosley Woolf, and the staff—from senior editors to typists, as well as the librarian—are credited.

III. Comprehensiveness

The *Merriam-Webster Dictionary* has about two thousand more entries than THE CONCISE AMERICAN HERITAGE DICTIONARY, and about three thousand less than THE AMERICAN HERITAGE DICTIONARY paper edition. The *Merriam-Webster Dictionary*'s 57,000 entries include an estimated 36,000 main vocabulary words with the remainder being variant spellings, variant forms, and run-on entries. Under **doghouse**, for example, the run-on entry is "—**in the doghouse**: in a state of disfavor."

A large number of main entries contain self-explanatory single words or sequences of words as definitions. Multiple definitions and senses are handled fairly extensively for a condensed work. In a 1979 review of this edition, a *Library Journal* reviewer correctly noted that although "the definitions are normally very brief and verbal illustrations few and far between . . . synonyms are fairly plentiful, however, as are helpful cross-references."

Included within the main entries are common abbreviations such as the two-letter postal state codes, the languages used in the etymologies, symbols of chemical elements, and so forth. An example of a naturally occurring alphabetical sequence includes **LF**, **lg**, **LGk**, **LH**, **LHD**, **li**, **Li**, and **LI**, all with brief definitions. Abbreviations appear in only one form. Many contain brief numbered meanings.

The opening notes indicate that etymologies are given for "a number" of words, but not how these sparse selections were chosen. Some are for words derived from foreign languages; an etymology is given for **Khaki**:

. . . Hindi *Khaki* dust-colored, fr. *Khāk* for dust, fr. Per,

but not for **kibbutz**. This inconsistency is a severe disadvantage to the student who is searching for an etymology that is not included.

Within the alphabetical entries, ten common prefixes have additional lists of undefined compound words showing hyphenation where appropriate. At the entry for **anti-** there are 22 words listed; **non-** has a list of 224 additional combinations.

IV. Quality and Currency of Entries

The definitions, based on citations in Merriam-Webster's extensive files, present condensed meanings of what the preface calls "the core of the English language."

The explanatory notes detail the information and typographic conventions used in the entries with examples (for example, all definitions are preceded by a bold colon :). The overall sequence of information in the entries is main bold face entry, pronunciation(s), part of speech, etymology, inflected forms, and definitions. An example of the method used to teach pronunciation is given in the explanatory notes:

vol·ca·no \völ-'kā-nō\.

The symbols between the reversed virgules show the pronunciation, which is based on the key inside the

The Merriam-Webster Dictionary

❶ Pronunciation, within back slashes, follows the boldface entry word which is divided into syllables by centered dots

❷ Illustrative phrases are placed within angle brackets; the entry word is replaced by a swung dash

❸ Variant word forms in boldface are run-in to the entry with the part of speech abbreviated

❹ Synonym cross-references, in small capital letters are preceded by a boldface colon

❺ Synonyms are introduced by **syn** in boldface near end of entry

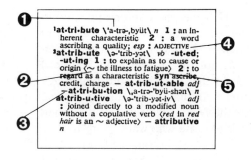

back cover. The definitions include necessary labels (temporal, regional, or stylistic):

kick in *vb* **1:** CONTRIBUTE **2** *slang* : DIE.

Entries often contain more than one definition of a single sense, frequently a synonym, as in

²**flat** *n* **1** : a level surface of land : PLAIN.

Usage examples are shown at the appropriate senses within angled brackets:

³**flat** *adv* **1** : FLATLY **2** :EXACTLY < in one minute~>

Multiple meanings in entries are numbered and variant forms follow with pronunciations for appropriate syllables and with parts of speech.

Several additional labels may be of special use to younger readers, including *often cap* (for capitalization), *abbr* (for all abbreviations appearing as main entries), and the spelling out in full of some parts of speech: *indefinite article*, *conjunction*, *past of* ("¹**lit** . . . *past of* light"), *pron*, *objective case of*, and so forth.

The definitions, in general, are good for quick reference and the use of synonym cross references will appeal to many readers. A comparison of a randomly chosen segment of entries, **paprika** to **parachute**, shows that the *Merriam-Webster Dictionary* contains eleven entries to the nine included in this segment in the paperback AMERICAN HERITAGE

DICTIONARY. There are minor differences in the entries. The Merriam-Webster work contains no etymologies in this section, whereas all entries have abbreviated ones in the American Heritage work. Merriam-Webster's contains **Pap smear** in addition to **Pap test** (defined much more simply than in the other dictionary). Merriam-Webster's other addition is an entry for

pap·ule . . . *n* : a small solid usu. conical lesion of the skin.

Because these two paperbacks are similar in size, length of definitions, and have vocabularies relatively similar in length, as well as authoritative reputations, the following representative comparison of an entry may help demonstrate the difference between THE AMERICAN HERITAGE DICTIONARY (based on a larger *college* dictionary) and the *Merriam-Webster Dictionary*, presented as suitable for *family* and *school* use.

From the *Merriam-Webster Dictionary* paperback:

pa·rab·o·la \pə-ʹrab-ə-lə\ *n* : a curve formed by the intersection of a cone with a plane parallel to its side— **par·a·bol·ic** \par-ə-ʹbäl-ik\ *adj*.

From THE AMERICAN HERITAGE DICTIONARY paperback:

pa·rab·o·la (pə-răbʹa-lə) *n.* A plane curve formed by the locus of points equidistant from a fixed line and a fixed point not on the line. [<Gk. *parabolē*.] — **par′·a·bolic** (par′ -ə-bŏl ĭk) *adj.*

In general, the *Merriam-Webster Dictionary*'s definitions are simpler and more accessible to younger readers as well as to adults not especially familiar with technical and scientific language.

The dictionary does not include the many terms that have gained popular currency within the last decade. The word **aerobic** (*adj.*) is in, but not the prevalent noun *aerobics*; *ayatollah, baud, byte,* and *mainframe*. But established, standard terms are, such as the computer sense of **bit, program** as a verb form used in computer science, and even **immunosuppressive** with an example of use,

<techniques for kidney transplants>.

The general definitions are helpful with only minor exceptions (the noun **killing**, for example, needs an additional sense besides "a sudden notable gain or profit"). The young adult will find these clear definitions adequate for most purposes. For scholarly pursuits he or she may need to use other references.

V. Syllabication and Pronunciation

Entry words are divided into syllables by centered dots, indicating the point(s) where a hyphen may be inserted at the end of a line of print or writing. The explanatory notes print an example of the three ways that **res·er·va·tion**, for example, can be hyphenated. Single letter syllables at the front or end of words are not divided by dots because printers rarely break words at syllables such as the *a* in **abet**, the *o*'s in **oleo**, or the *y* in **tributary**. Syllable divisions are shown for the first, but not the succeeding homographs:

¹**of·fi·cial**, ²**official**.

Inflected and variant forms, as well as run-in entries are divided:

¹**old** . . . —**old·ish**.

The dictionary employs a useful typographic convention—the stacked, double hyphen (=) to distinguish those words in the definitions that fall at the end of a line but that are normally hyphened. In pronunciations, syllable division is shown by a normal hyphen. The following example shows syllable division in (a) a main entry, (b) in an entry's pronunciation, and (c) with the double hyphen:

pitch·fork ′pich-₁fork *n* : a long = handled fork used esp. in pitching hay.

The pronunciations are derived from the system used in the *Webster's Third New International Dictionary*, although simplified. Based on the symbols used in the scholarly International Pronunciation Alphabet (IPA), the pronunciations are, relatively, much more sophisticated than the condensed vocabulary definitions. Readers unfamiliar with IPA symbols or the pronunciations in the larger Merriam-Webster dictionaries will need to study those used here carefully before they become as easy to use as the vocabulary.

A brief explanation of the pronunciation respellings with clear examples appears in the explanatory notes at the front of the dictionary. The notes indicate that the chart of pronunciation symbols is "printed inside the front and back covers," but it is only printed on the inside back cover of the paperback. In addition, there is no pronunciation key at the bottom of each page. Students could use this extra help to guide them through the complex system of pronunciation.

Merriam-Webster pronunciation editors base the given pronunciations on a continuously updated citation file, and the publisher indicates that "all of the variants fall within the range of acceptable variation." Occasionally, area labels, such as *Brit.* (British) or *Southern*, indicate special regional pronunciations.

The pronunciation chart contains brief examples of explanations of fifty symbols based on alphabetic letters and three standard diacritical marks: ā, ä, and à plus *th*, and a superior ⁿ and ʸ. The symbols are keyed to short words with corresponding bold face letters: "**zh** . . . vision, pleasure." In addition, five special symbols are used. These include the syllable hyphen and reversed virgules, or slant lines, enclosing pronunciations:

′**may·fly** \mā-flī\.

Stress marks precede syllables. A "high-set mark" shows primary stress; a "low-set mark" indicates secondary stress:

pol·i·ti·cian \päl-ə-′tish-ən\.

Parentheses enclose letters or symbols for sounds that are sometimes not pronounced:

leg·horn \′leg-₁ (h)órn\.

There is no question that even in simplified form these pronunciations are authoritative (with minor errors such as a primary stress mark on the last syllable of **po·et·ic** \pō′et-′ik\). The range of diacritical marks, however, coupled with other typographic symbols plus various ligatures, such as oe, $\overline{oe}$, ue, $\overline{ue}$,, will make the pronunciations less accessible for many school students.

VI. Special Features

Immediately following the main vocabulary, there are seven short reference lists. The first is an eleven-page dictionary of foreign words and phrases often encountered in English speech and writing. Latin and French phrases predominate (mostly aphorisms and mottoes—all U.S. state ones are included); but German, Greek, Italian, Spanish, and even the Chinook **al-ki**, Japanese **sayonara**, and Russian **nyet** appear. Pronunciations are included for each phrase and a key to the symbols appears on each double-page spread.

There are also lists of nations of the world (with pronunciations and outdated population figures), population of places in the U.S. (with 12,000 or more inhabitants as of 1970—also outdated), plus brief outdated population lists of U.S. states, Canadian places, provinces, and territories. The ten groups of common symbols and signs (astronomy, business, mathematics, medicine, apothecaries' measures and weights, miscellaneous, reference marks, stamps, and weather) are clear and useful. Since much of this supplementary material is outdated, however, students will find it necessary to use other, more recent resources.

VII. Accessibility

The main text is printed in very small type. The main entry words are in clear bold type overhanging the text, which is printed in two columns. The entry words as well as the variant forms of words and run-on entry words and phrases appear in bold type and are easy to distinguish on a page. Each letter of the alphabet begins with a large capital letter enclosed in a bold decorative square. Two boldfaced guide words appear at the top outer margin on each page; readable page numbers appear at the top inner margins. The inner, top, outer and bottom margins are generous.

The explanatory notes appear in separate sections with appropriate subheads and are readily accessible at the front of the book. There is no separate list of the appendix sections, although these are mentioned in the preface. The text entries also refer to the metric system tables, and these appear on pp. 440–41, almost in the center of the book. The weights and measures equivalent tables are found in the *W* vocabulary at **weight**. It is unlikely that students will use these tables unless they find them by chance or perseverance.

VIII. Graphics and Format

This paperback has no illustrations apart from the separate signs and symbols lists. These are generously spaced out on the pages and are easy to read. The opening explanatory notes are similarly well spaced. The text appears to be a reduction of about 30% of the text size in the *Webster*'s *Concise Family Dictionary*. There is noticeable blurring of letters and some of the diacritical marks in the pronunciations cannot be distinguished. When multiple lines in successive entries run to the full column width, the text appears uncomfortably dense on a page. The bold figures for numbered meanings and bold colons preceding definitions are visually helpful. Within definitions, small capital letters indicate cross references and are readily apparent.

The book's design, in general, is clear. The newsprint quality paper reveals scant show-through. The dictionary is excellently bound; pages open easily and seem to withstand use even when the spine is cracked. The pages are tipped in lemon yellow to coordinate with the dictionary's front cover, which contains an attractive full-color photomontage of various items a reader might expect to find defined—arbitrarily rather than alphabetically arranged.

IX. Summary

As a review in *Library Journal* (15 November 1979) pointed out, for years this work has been one of the leading, authoritative abridged paperback dictionaries and "many consumers will continue to buy Merriam-Webster, if for no other reason than that it represents the best known name in American lexicography."

With its excellent core definitions, this is a useful, smaller dictionary to have at hand, especially for upper junior high school and high school students (and for adults) who prefer a dictionary with less lexicographical apparatus and who do not require etymologies for most words. The pronunciations will not be used easily without some study by many students and even adults, but they are useful for sounding out foreign words and phrases in English.

As is typical of Merriam-Webster dictionaries, the explanatory notes are especially good. The separate alphabetical listing of foreign words and phrases is also useful. However, this fine dictionary, printed in 1974, is dated; many new ideas and terms are absent. Finally, the random etymologies are too few for students searching for the origin and history of words.

My First Picture Dictionary

Facts at a Glance

Full Title: **My First Picture Dictionary**.
Publisher: Random House.
Editor: Katherine Howard.
Illustrator: Howard (Huck) Scarry.
Edition Reviewed: © 1978.

Number of Volumes: 1.
Number of Entries: 233.
Number of Words: over 500.
Number of Pages: 32.
Number of Illustrations: over 250 in full color.
Trim Size: 8″ × 8″.
Bindings: paper over boards (side-sewn); paper-bound (saddle-stitched).

Prices: $4.99; $1.95.
Intended Readership: preschoolers.
Sold in bookstores and other outlets; also sold to libraries and schools. ISBN 0-394-83486-0; ISBN 0-394-93486-5.

I. Scope and Format

My First Picture Dictionary is a very brief dictionary for preschoolers and early elementary school children. It contains 233 entry words, predominantly about animals and vehicles, all in very small print for the intended audience of preschoolers. In addition, labels on the illustrations look handwritten and are even smaller; they may be difficult for young children to read.

The hardcover edition is side-sewn for library durability. The paperback edition is stapled and would have a short shelf life if handled by many children.

II. Authority

Random House publishes other dictionaries for young children, including the popular THE CAT IN THE HAT BEGINNER BOOK DICTIONARY, which is also reviewed in this Buying Guide.

My First Picture Dictionary has no introductory statements; and no criteria are listed to tell how the words were selected: **astronaut** is included but not *pilot*; **yolk** is an entry word, but *egg* is not. Over a quarter of the word list is about the animal kingdom.

III. Quality and Currency of Entries

Every entry is defined by a sentence or a phrase or two. The vocabulary used to define or describe entry words is not controlled or always appropriate for the intended age group. For example:

> **Ball**—A round, or almost round, object used to play games.

This entry is accompanied by illustrations with labels of a **soccer ball**, **baseball**, **basketball**, and **football**.
Another example is:

> **Rice**—A kind of grain that grows in shallow water. Rice is the most important food in Asia.

Illustrated and labeled are **rice plant**, **head**, **grains**, and **kernels**. Of all the words in the definition, only **rice** and **food** are main entry words. Definitions, such as **rice**, that contain difficult words, concepts, and geographic references will be strange, at best, or even meaningless to very young children. How many preschoolers would know what **grain** is, or where or what **Asia** is? In this and other cases, the compiler has overlooked the possibilities of relating the definitions to known things in children's lives. For example, the test could have simply stated that rice is a kind of food like potatoes or spaghetti.

Many entry words are supplemented with labels in drawings that show relationships to the main word. Very few sentences are given to illustrate the entry word in context. In a dictionary for this age level, the sample sentence is needed to reinforce the meaning of the word. Although all the words used are nouns, this is never stated.

The words are in alphabetical order. An alphabet runs vertically along the outer margin of each page, and the letter or letters being featured on any given page appear in that margin in a colored block. A column-wide band of the same color introduces each

My First Picture Dictionary

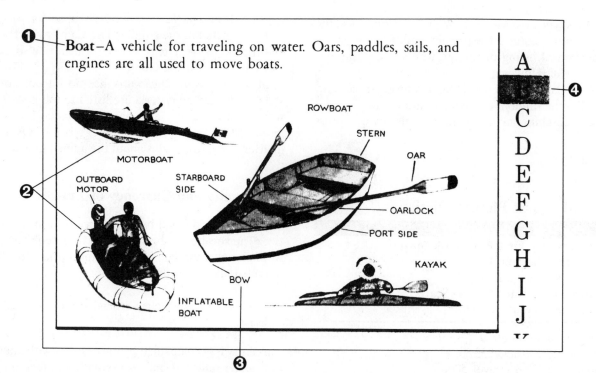

❶ Boat–A vehicle for traveling on water. Oars, paddles, sails, and engines are all used to move boats.

ROWBOAT

STERN

OAR

OARLOCK

PORT SIDE

KAYAK

BOW

INFLATABLE BOAT

STARBOARD SIDE

MOTORBOAT

OUTBOARD MOTOR

A
C
D
E
F
G
H
I
J

❹

❶ Each boldface entry word is defined by a sentence

❷ Labeled four-color illustrations aid in understanding the varied contexts of an entry word

❸ Labels within drawings present additional vocabulary related to main word

❹ The alphabet, with the featured letter in a color block, runs down the outer margin of each page

letter in capital and lowercase form when it first appears on the page. This helpful repetition of the letter is graphically pleasing and a useful locator for the young reader.

IV. Illustrations

Illustrations by Huck Scarry have long delighted children. He has an ability to portray sharply clear miniature scenes that definitely attract the attention of child readers. The many extra labeled illustrations that often appear with the main word are a special feature of the book. The word **train** shows seven different kinds of railroad cars, including a **locomotive** and a **caboose**. **Harbor** has nine words related to the accompanying illustration. Scarry's drawing for the word **farm** is 4¾″ x 3½″ and includes a farm scene with these labeled objects: **field**, **barn**, **pigpen**, **silo**, **manure**, **hens**, **farmer**, **orchard**, and **farmhouse**. Also pictured, but not labeled, are a tractor, fence, pig, trees, wheelbarrow, bucket, pitchfork, horse-

shoes, weathervane, and a basket of apples. Despite all this detail, the picture is still crisp and each item is clearly visible.

Every page of the book is divided into three columns with about eight words per page. Many of the illustrations cover two columns' width or depth, and some stretch across the inner margins.

V. Summary

My First Picture Dictionary is very brief and its purpose is unclear. As a dictionary, it has drawbacks. Full sentences are often not used to convey the meaning of the words and the text's vocabulary is often far beyond a preschooler's grasp. The print is too small for easy use by the preschooler or the beginning reader. Although these drawbacks (including a scant 233-word entry list) limit its use in a public or school library, the illustrations are charming enough to capture a place in the home library.

My First Picture Dictionary

Facts at a Glance

Full Title: **My First Picture Dictionary**.
Publisher: Scott, Foresman.
Editors: William A. Jenkins, Andrew Schiller.
Edition Reviewed: © 1987.

Number of Volumes: 1.
Number of Entries: 914.
Number of Pages: 192.
Number of Indexes: 1.
Number of Illustrations: 770 in four colors.
Trim Size: 7½″ × 9³⁄₁₆″.
Bindings: paper over boards; hardbound.

Prices: $8.81; $10.81.
Intended Readership: grade 1.
Sold to schools. ISBN 0-673-12482-7; ISBN 0-673-12483-5.

I. Scope and Format

My First Picture Dictionary is the second word and picture book in a three-book word study series published by Scott, Foresman (see the reviews of MY PICTIONARY and MY SECOND PICTURE DICTIONARY). It contains 914 words with definitions and 770 illustrations. Introductory pages include a table of contents that color-codes seven of the book's word sections ("Words That Name . . . People," "Animals," "Storybook Characters," "Things," and "Places," plus "Action Words" and "Words That Help"). Seven further categories are listed: "Words That Tell . . . What Kind," "What Color," "How Much or How Many," "How," "When," "Where," and "Which One." This is followed by two pages depicting the letters of the alphabet in large-size uppercase and lowercase letters. An index, the D'Nealian Alphabet, and numerals appear at the end of the book. There is no note to the teacher or student about how to use the dictionary, which may be a drawback for teachers needing guidance to the material. The inside front cover has the "This Book is the Property of . . . " box usual in textbooks.

II. Authority

Scott, Foresman is a well-regarded publisher of school texts and reference books, including the series of word books to which this volume (originally published in 1970) belongs.

III. Quality and Currency of Entries

The book page is divided into two columns separated by white space, with the illustration on the left and the words and their "definitions" to the right of the illustration. The singular and plural forms of nouns appear above a sentence (often two or three sentences) using the noun in context. Some words are listed without illustrations; some words have no formal definitions, for example, **superintendent**. Pictured on the left is a woman on a TV screen. On the right, following the singular and plural forms of the entry word, is one sentence: "The superintendent of schools is speaking on TV today." The word **name**, for example, appears without an illustration, but with the sentences: "Everyone has a name. Some names are short." Young readers may have difficulty understanding such "definitions."

One particularly difficult concept is attempted by the editors under the word **family**. A simplified genealogical chart has been indicated with lines joining different colored human figures to each other. The figures all have names, for example, **Aunt Alice and Uncle Jim Smith** and **Cousin Jane Jones**. However, it would take a very sophisticated first-grader to understand the relationships of this family group. Other words with pictures of human figures are introduced on other pages, for example, **nephew**, and **niece** are cross-referenced to, say, **Cousin Jane Jones** (who is, however, not labeled as a niece), and are similarly difficult to fit into the family group. "Action Words" appear in the same format, in the infinitive (but without the *to*). The sentences explaining verbs use the verb in different forms from the entry word, but an accompanying picture shows the action. An example of such a verb is:

dig
The dog is digging a hole. It dug two holes yesterday. It has dug holes all over the yard.

The key entry word in the explanatory sentences is not italicized or boldfaced and thus the word appears naturally in context for the young reader. This is in keeping with the level of the book, which has advanced from the very simple stage of MY PICTIONARY, the first book in this series, which is also reviewed in this guide.

IV. Illustrations

The four-color illustrations are realistic and for the most part show accurate renderings of their words, although some may need adult explanation, such as the architect's blueprint that illustrates **plan**. The objects are drawn with greater detail than the people, who are very stylized and flat, with the simplest of faces and features. Care has been given to include different ethnic groups. The front cover makes attractive use of paper sculptures of a clown, giraffe, monkey, and a climbing vine, while the back cover shows bright bands of color.

V. Summary

My First Picture Dictionary will make many new words available to young readers and successfully introduces new dictionary skills to those who have completed MY PICTIONARY. Teacher or parent guidance is necessary for young students to use and enjoy the book to the fullest. This dictionary will be most useful in classroom libraries, and school libraries may wish to buy it too, especially if recommended by a teacher.

My Pictionary

Facts at a Glance

Full Title: **My Pictionary**.
Publisher: Scott, Foresman.
Editors: Marion Monroe and Andrew Schiller.
Edition Reviewed: © 1987.

Number of Volumes: 1.
Number of Illustrations: 476 in four colors.
Number of Pages: 96.
Trim Size: 7½″ × 9³⁄₁₆″.
Bindings: hardbound; paperback.

Prices: $9.12; $6.29.
Intended Readership: grades K through 1.
Sold to schools. ISBN 0-673-12480-0; ISBN 0-673-12481-9.

I. Scope and Format

My Pictionary, first published in 1970, is a word and picture book that includes 548 words without definitions. In an introductory note "To the Teacher," the book states that it "will aid children in their reading, writing, and spelling, and it will help enlarge their vocabulary."

The words, most of which are nouns, are grouped according to categories of meanings, with small color-coded marginal blocks in each category referring back to a corresponding color in the table of contents. Categories include "People," "Animals," "Storybook Characters," "What We Do," "Things,"

"Places," "Colors," "Numbers," and "Words That Help." Some confusion may arise when the teacher refers to the color "blue" assigned to the category "People"; it is very purple in hue and may be confused with the actual purple color used for "Colors." A two-page spread of upper- and lowercase letters of the alphabet precede the main part of the *Pictionary*, and an index and page containing the D'Nealian Alphabet follow it.

II. Authority

Scott, Foresman is a well-regarded publisher of schoolbooks, and this series of word study books includes two additional titles: MY FIRST PICTURE DICTIONARY and MY SECOND PICTURE DICTIONARY. According to the publisher: "Together these three books provide children with the solid, step-by-step preparation necessary for use of a full-fledged beginning dictionary."

III. Quality and Currency of Entries

Words are not presented in alphabetical order, but within categories. Families of words are often grouped together for easy comprehension and remembering; for example: under "Things": fruits, vegetables, clothes, and so forth. The book contains a large variety of simple nouns, including irregular plurals, as well as a few action verbs, adjectives, and prepositions, all providing a solid vocabulary of familiar people, objects, and actions. "Storybook Characters" are somewhat more fanciful and assume some prior knowledge of fairy tales. No pronunciation or syllabication is given, but this is not a flaw for the intended age level. This is strictly a word and picture book, and its most effective use may be as a lap book for interaction between an adult and a child.

IV. Illustrations

The illustrations are four-color, realistic renderings, with up to about a dozen on a page. They are sometimes fuzzy and not very exciting, but they successfully picture the words. Objects are crisper and more successfully printed than the people, who, despite their obvious ethnic differences, tend to look alike. The words stand out clearly in lowercase, sans-serif type beneath the illustrations.

The cover makes attractive use of colorful paper art, and plain horizontal strips of color are carried over onto the back cover. These will be useful for young children practicing color discrimination and learning color names.

V. Summary

My Pictionary adequately presents a useful vocabulary resource for the home. The contents, index, and color-coding give it classroom applicability since they are good tools for the beginning dictionary user to learn, but they must be presented with the help of an adult and the instructions in the introductory note. *My Pictionary* is preferable to Silver, Burdett & Ginn's MY PICTURE DICTIONARY, intended for the same age level but with a smaller vocabulary and less-inspired art than this Scott, Foresman book. Children will get the most benefit from *My Pictionary* in a dialogue situation in classrooms or at home, where words are discussed in relation to personal knowledge and experience. Schools and public libraries might want a copy to circulate to teachers or parents.

My Picture Dictionary

Facts at a Glance

Full Title: **My Picture Dictionary**.
Publisher: Silver, Burdett & Ginn.
Editors: Hale C. Reid and Helen W. Crane.
Edition Reviewed: © 1985.

Number of Volumes: 1.
Number of Words: 624.
Number of Pages: 48 in total.
Number of Illustrations: about 277 in full color.
Trim Size: 6½″ × 9″.
Binding: cloth.

Price: $5.99.
Intended Readership: grades K through 1.
Sold to schools and other markets. ISBN 0-663-42378-3.

I. Scope and Format

My Picture Dictionary is a word and picture book that includes about 175 illustrated words in alphabetical order (primarily nouns) with no further text. Under each letter of the alphabet, an additional unillustrated word list adds 274 further words (nouns, pronouns, prepositions, adjectives, and verbs in different forms). The "Note to Parents and Teachers," at the back of the book, states that "the entire word list has been closely correlated with the vocabulary of the early books in the Ginn reading program." This program was first published some 20 or more years ago. Selection of the 175 illustrated nouns, ac-

cording to the note, was based on "2,800 different words found in 4,500 independently written compositions of 1,500 first-grade children. The additional 274 words found in the body of the dictionary are among those that appeared with high frequency in these compositions." The criteria for the final selection of nouns are not stated.

II. Authority

Ginn and Company, now part of Silver, Burdett & Ginn, are well-known publishers of textbooks and educational materials. This book was originally included in Ginn's *Elementary English Series*; its previous copyright date was 1963. The words were selected from the author's analysis of compositions written by students in first grade classes.

III. Quality and Currency of Entries

The arrangement is alphabetical for the illustrated words as well as for the listed ones, with the illustrated words appearing first. Large, clear uppercase and lowercase examples of the letters of the alphabet are printed on the back of the title page. The appropriate letter is printed in dark pink at the center top of each page or occasionally at other points on a page where a new letter commences, providing easy access to the words beginning with that letter.

The vocabulary words are printed in large, thin sans-serif type. There is a small airport scene for the word **airport**, a red apple for **apple**. These are the only two words visually depicted of the 21 words that are included for the letter *A*. For *E*, the only illustrated word is **eggs**, with two more words in the separate boxed list: **eat** and **every**. Obviously, this is not a comprehensive book. *S* has 11 illustrations and 22 listed words. No other formal elements of lexicography—definitions, parts of speech, syllabication, pronunciations, or etymology—are provided.

Appended to the main vocabulary are 16 pages containing 175 vocabulary words that are classified under the headings: "Action Words," "Parts of the Body," "The Family," "Toys," "Helpful Little Words," "Farm," "City," "Fruits," "Vegetables," and so forth. In this section, illustrations are not in alphabetical order, but the words are labeled. Some show scenes; others show individual objects. There are no guidelines for using these words and no reasons given for separating them from the main body of the dictionary, although each page does group a related "family" of words.

My Picture Dictionary

❶ Main entry word with illustration   **❷** Guide letters in capital and lower-case letters   **❸** Boxed list of additional vocabulary words

IV. Illustrations

Overall, the book has a clean, uncluttered—and uncreative—appearance. The realistic illustrations are small and look washed out; many appear fuzzy. They are also pedestrian, although they do show ethnic variety. The listed words are neatly confined to boxed columns, and there is a great deal of white space around each word.

V. Summary

My Picture Dictionary is an uninspired word and picture book that is designed to be used with the Ginn reading programs. Its use will be confined to schools, but it will require a persuasive teacher to spark a child to use it. It fails both as a bona fide dictionary and as a pleasing picture book. *My Picture Dictionary* is not a suitable purchase for use in the home or in public libraries.

My Second Picture Dictionary

Facts at a Glance

Full Title: **My Second Picture Dictionary**.
Publisher: Scott, Foresman.
Editors: William A. Jenkins and Andrew Schiller.
Edition Reviewed: © 1987.

Number of Volumes: 1.
Number of Entries: 4,099.
Number of Pages: 384.
Number of Illustrations: 1,178 in full color.
Trim Size: 7½″ × 9³⁄₁₆″.
Binding: hardcover; paperback.

Prices: $11.01; $13.54.

Intended Readership: grade 2.
Sold to schools. ISBN 0-673-12484-3; 0-673-12485-1.

I. Scope and Format

My Second Picture Dictionary is the third book in a series that includes MY PICTIONARY and MY FIRST DICTIONARY. The second dictionary was published in 1971 and the current edition has a 1987 copyright date. The vocabulary has over 4,000 entries with numbered definitions, example sentences showing the word in context, noun plurals, past and present participles of verbs, and word phrases. About one quarter of the words are illustrated in full color, and the attractive and sturdy book seems durable and inviting for children to use.

No directions for use of the dictionary are given; however, the book is clearly divided into two parts, as shown in the contents, lexicon and gazetteer. The gazetteer takes up the last 58 pages of the volume. In it the U.S. states are presented alphabetically, one to a page, and are illustrated with the state flag, tree, bird, flower, sometimes fish, and a simple, color silhouette map of the state with its name and location of the capital marked. The same sort of maps, with bare outlines of countries, states, or provinces, are provided for North America, the United States, Canada, and Mexico.

II. Authority

Scott, Foresman is a well-regarded publisher of school texts and reference books. No criteria are presented for the choice of words included in the dictionary, but a note indicates that the "contents of the dictionary entries in this book have been adapted from the *Thorndike Barnhart Beginning Dictionary*, copyright © 1979, 1974 by Scott, Foresman and Company." As librarians and teachers know, the Thorndike-Barnhart approach to dictionaries for young readers is that all main entry words should be defined in words simpler than the entry, so that children can readily grasp the meanings.

III. Quality and Currency of Entries

The entries in this second-grade dictionary are appropriately more difficult than the two earlier books, and the format begins to look like an adult dictionary, thus capping off a well-planned progression.

Main entry words often are defined very briefly or with synonyms, for example:

fierce wild
fifteen five more than ten
same not another
tall high

Other words have more lengthy definitions when necessary. For example:

mumps a disease that puts your neck and face out of shape and makes it hard for you to swallow.
tar a black, sticky material taken from wood or coal

Words with numbered definitions thoroughly distinguish among meanings with the help of example sentences and sometimes are followed up by a second entry word (with a superscript number) using the original word in a different form, or by a word phrase. For example:

miss[1] 1. fail to hit: *He shot twice but missed.* 2. fail to get: *Don't miss the train.* 3. Leave out or skip. *She missed a word when she read this sentence.* 4. notice or feel bad because something is gone. *I did not miss my glove till I got home. We miss you.* **missed, missing.**

Miss[2] a title given to a girl or to a woman who is not married. **Miss es**

The form **Ms.** with its plural **Ms es** also appears as a main entry.

taste 1. what makes something special when you put it in your mouth. The taste of sugar is sweet. 2. The one of your five senses that tells the difference between things when you put them in your mouth. 3. knowing what is excellent: *She has very good taste in*

books. **4.** try by taking a little into the mouth: *Taste this orange sauce.* **tastes; tast ed, tast ing.**

taste buds tiny bumps on your tongue that let you taste.

Or, a more simple example:

compute count or figure up
computer a machine that computes

The circular quality of some of the definitions (**computer . . . computes**) is not ideal.

Entries include only a few abbreviations (**Mr., Mrs., Ms., U.S., U.S.A.**) and a minimum of specialized words in current usage—**astronaut, computer, jet, launching pad, module,** and **pollution),** for example. Among the entries not included that today's children should know are **freezer, atom, countdown, program** (in the computer sense), or **blast off.** In general, the selection of words seems somewhat arbitrary and out of keeping with words young students recognize.

Syllables are indicated by spaces in the words. No pronunciation guides or symbols are given, nor are parts of speech; this is in keeping with the intended grade level of readers. Entry words are in bold, large-size sans-serif type and overhang the main text; plurals and verb forms also appear in boldface. Illustrative sentences appear in italics. The variation in type, plus the generous leading provided, makes the page very easy to read.

IV. Illustrations

Approximately one-quarter of the entries are illustrated with clear, crisp four-color drawings in the margin near the proper entry. The direction **See the picture** is sometimes given in the entry. The illustrations are all captioned and include a reference to the particular numbered entry, if necessary. The maps in the gazetteer are rudimentary and without much appeal, although children may learn capital cities and the shape of states, as well as their location in the country. While birds, fish, and flowers are clearly represented, all the trees tend to have a similar, fuzzy look.

The cover and title page use an especially effective set of cut-out or relief letters, with vivid colors.

V. Summary

The attractiveness and accessibility of this dictionary probably outweighs an arguable lack of up-to-date words included in an otherwise useful and appropriate vocabulary for the intended grade level. Although the maps are extremely simplified, the gazetteer section may be useful in familiarizing children with the basic outlines of their states and the country's position in North America. Other dictionaries at this level, for example, Silver, Burdett and Ginn's *My Second Picture Dictionary*, introduce the young reader to stress marks and such formally-named word groups as synonyms, antonyms, homonyms, and compound words. Nevertheless, Scott, Foresman's *My Second Picture Dictionary* will be useful in school classrooms and libraries, especially with initial guidance from an adult.

My Second Picture Dictionary

Facts at a Glance

Full Title: **My Second Picture Dictionary**.
Publisher: Silver, Burdett and Ginn.
Editors: Hale C. Reid, Helen W. Crane, and Betty Ellen Jenkins.
Illustrators: Tom Cooke and Bea Holmes.
Edition Reviewed: © 1985.

Number of Volumes: 1.
Number of Entries: 1,060.
Number of Words: 1,110.
Number of Pages: 220.
Number of Cross-references: nearly 200.
Number of Illustrations: 790 in full color.
Trim Size: 7″ × 9″.
Binding: cloth.

Price: $10.25.
Intended Readership: grades 1 through 2.
Sold to schools and through other outlets.
    ISBN 0-663-42380-5.

I. Scope and Format

My Second Picture Dictionary, published in 1964, and reviewed in an edition copyrighted in 1985, is a primary-grade-level dictionary that defines 1,060 words with sample sentences that show the word used in context; many of the words are illustrated in color, which should attract the attention of young readers. The size of the book makes it comfortable for children to hold and use, and the quality of the cover and binding makes the book appear very durable.

Special features include several word lists. The introductory notes to the students say "Find page 189. What lists follow this page?" The very first list is of "Words for the Space Age." But none of the 24 words listed is defined here, and only two of them

are found in the dictionary. This seems to be a method to update the book—by adding lists of new words, rather than integrating them throughout. This same method, using the same words, was used in the 1976 edition. There are also lists of compound words, antonyms, homonyms, and 12 groupings of words that are illustrated and labeled.

II. Authority

Ginn, who are well known as publishers of textbooks, are now part of Silver, Burdett, also well known educational publishers.

A message to parents and teachers at the end of the book states: "The words in the dictionary were selected on the basis of word studies by Horn, Rinsland and Buckingham-Dolch. . . . Another important source was the authors' study of high frequency words from the compositions of primary-grade children." The studies cited are now over four decades old; Rinsland, for example, published *A Basic Vocabulary of Elementary Children* in 1945. Given these criteria, it is surprising that words such as **antelope** and **hibiscus** are included.

III. Quality and Currency Entries

The definitions—about six per page—are adequate for the most part, although some cannot stand on their own and only become clear when the illustrative sentences are used: "**thin** not thick or fat; growing far apart; like water." Without the sample sentences, "Grandfather has *thin* hair" and "I made the paste *thinner* by adding water," these meanings would be difficult to understand. Even with illustrative sentences, some meanings are still not clear. Other definitions have broad appeal to children, for example: "**pass** to go by. I *pass* the fire station on my way to school." The illustration is of a jaunty little boy walking past a fire station. Many entry words have subentry words that show word relationship or irregular formations. Under the main word **meet**, the subentries are **met** and **meeting**. The entry word is defined, and it and the subentries have illustrative sentences.

There are *see* references for irregular verbs and for many, but not all, of the words in the separate word lists that are appended. Syllabication is shown by spaces unless it would result in a letter standing alone at the beginning or end of the word (**about** is an example). Diacritical marks are used to aid pronunciation.

It is surprising that in a book with a 1985 copyright no computer terms and few space terms are defined in the main vocabulary, since these are so much a part of even very young children's vocabularies. Parts

My Second Picture Dictionary

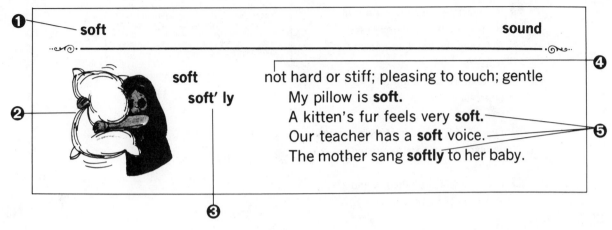

❶ Left-hand guide word indicates the first main entry on a page

❷ Four-color illustration of first descriptive sentence

❸ Subentry shows adverb, also in boldface type, with primary stress and syllable division

❹ Brief statements give a word's meanings in context

❺ Entry word and variant are used in descriptive sentences

of speech and etymology are not included. The entry words, in alphabetical order, are in bold lowercase sans-serif type. The definition begins on the same line, and several spaces separate it from the entry word. Subentries are in the same bold type and are indented under the entry word. Illustrative sentences are indented three spaces under the definition. When they appear, illustrations are placed to the left of the entry word. Guide words are used at the upper left and right margins of each page, making for quick and easy accessibility.

IV. Illustrations

The overall page design with no columns is pleasant. Decorative blue rules at the top and bottom of each page separate the guide words and the page numbers from the text. Wide margins and well-placed type lend an open and easily readable appearance to the pages. The miniature and highly detailed full-color illustrations appear in the left-hand margins of each page. There are never fewer than two or more than four to a page. They are attractive and reflect ethnic and socioeconomic diversity.

V. Summary

Although *My Second Picture Dictionary* is a more lively dictionary than the younger work that precedes it (MY PICTURE DICTIONARY), it has major flaws. One is the separate list of "Words for the Space Age" that is appended. These words are part of a child's vocabulary and should be defined and incorporated into the main word list.

Some of the appended word lists run on for several pages, but only the first page of each has a heading. Thus, children turning the pages can easily forget the category into which the words fall. The inconsistency of including some but not all of the appended word lists as *see* references in the main text needs to be corrected.

This dictionary has some excellent basic characteristics. However, its flaws—a need for further updating, inconsistencies, poor integration of some materials—interfere with its effective use in home, school, or public libraries.

New American Webster Handy College Dictionary

Facts at a Glance

Full Title: **New American Webster Handy College Dictionary**.

Former Title: The New American Webster Dictionary.

Publisher: New American Library.

Editors: Albert and Loy Morehead, Phillip D. Morehead, and Andrew T. Morehead.

Edition Reviewed: © 1981.

Number of Volumes: 1.
Number of Entries: more than 115,000.
Number of Pages: 640.
Number of Indexes: 2.
Trim Size: 4¼" × 7".
Binding: paperback.

New American Webster Handy College Dictionary

❶ Pronunciation for the noun sense is provided within parentheses following the boldface entry word

❷ Second pronunciation follows the abbreviated part of speech (transitive verb) in italics

❸ Definitions, in order of most common usage, are numbered in boldface

❹ Usage labels are italicized and appear in parentheses

❶ ❸
❷ ❹

con′tract (kon′trakt) *n.* **1,** a legal or business agreement. **2,** in certain games, the highest bid. **3,** (*Slang*) an agreement for murder. —*v.t.* (kən-trakt′) **1,** make smaller; condense; abridge. **2,** acquire (a habit, disease, etc.); incur; enter into. —*v.i.* **1,** enter into an agreement. **2,** shrink.

Price: $2.95.
Intended Readership: middle school and up.
Sold in bookstores and other outlets; also sold to libraries and schools. ISBN 0-451-12537-1.

I. Introduction

This dictionary first appeared in 1951 and has had numerous successive printings. An expanded edition was published in 1972. According to the introduction, the work "supplies the spelling, syllabication, pronunciation, and meaning of the most useful words in the English language as it is spoken in the United States." This revised and updated edition contains more than 115,000 definitions and includes abbreviations, geographic names, foreign words and phrases, and forms of address.

II. Authority

The dictionary was prepared and edited by an organization that calls itself the "National Lexicographic Board." This group has no apparent formal connection to recognized scholarly associations or to those groups within the government that promote language studies. The late Albert H. Morehead is listed as Chairman and General Editor. A large number of consultants and their positions are listed; most are affiliated with universities, but companies such as Corning Glass Works and General Electric are also represented. The consultants' fields are wide ranging and include art education, theology, sports editing, bacteriology, and electronics. No information is given on the criteria for inclusion of words nor on any sources used to compile the work.

III. Comprehensiveness

Comprehensiveness is a primary criterion for a small pocket dictionary; however, users' expectations for comprehensiveness will be met in part by this dictionary's inclusion of special feature listings at the back of the volume, such as a gazetteer, an abbreviations list, forms of address, and weights and measures, plus signs and symbols.

Within the main word list, some slang and colloquialisms and a few abbreviations are included. Particularly full coverage is given to irregular verbs. For example, under **be** appear the following forms:

present indicative: **I am**; **you are** (*Archaic,* **thou art**); **he is**; **we, you, they are**; *pret.* **I, he was**; **we, you, they were**; *p.p.* **been** (bin); **be′ing.**

Biographical entries appear rarely in the dictionary. A few historically significant people, such as **Caesar**, are entered; names of gods and goddesses and of literary figures are not. Some proper nouns are entered, such as names of movements (**Black Power**), trade names (**Magicube**), and holidays (**Quinquagesima**).

No etymology is given, and regularly formed inflections do not appear. Illustrative sentences or phrases are not provided.

IV. Quality and Currency of Entries

Definitions are brief and to the point. Entries include italicized part-of-speech abbreviations, pronunciation, and usage labels. A representative entry is the following:

die (di) *v.i.* [**died, dy′ing,**] **1,** cease to live; expire. **2,** come to an end. **3,** (with *away* or *out*) fade away. **4,**

(with *for*) (*Colloq.*) desire keenly.—*n.* **1**, an engraved stamp used for impressing a design. **2**, any of various mechanical devices, as a tool for cutting the threads of screws. **3**, sing. of *dice.*

Definitions are generally more concise than those in the comparable WEBSTER'S NEW WORLD COMPACT SCHOOL AND OFFICE DICTIONARY. For example, under **contempt**, the first definition listed in the *Compact* is: "the feeling of a person toward someone or something he considers low, worthless." In the *Handy College Dictionary*, the first meaning reads: "the act of despising." For a second definition, the *Compact* lists "the condition of being despised"; the *Handy College Dictionary* provides "a feeling of disdain." In both dictionaries, the final meaning listed is the word's specialized usage in law. The *Compact*'s definition is "a showing of disrespect for the dignity of a court (or legislature)"; the *Handy College Dictionary*'s is "defiance of a court, etc." Although the *Handy College Dictionary* provides very brief definitions, they are adequate for a work of this size. For many entries, several meanings are listed.

Homographs, such as **fair** (beautiful) and **fair** (bazaar) are generally grouped within a single entry. This practice is likely to prove confusing for students, who may expect to find homographs separately listed.

The volume's size and scope limits its inclusion of new words, although a number do appear. Included in the word list are **byte**, **videodisc**, **tofu**, and **afterburner**; excluded are, for example, *surrogate mother* and *videocassette*. While such omissions might be expected of a compact dictionary, purchasers will have to determine whether this level of currency meets their needs.

V. Syllabication and Pronunciation

Pronunciation is given in parentheses immediately following the entry word. The key to pronunciation is located at the front of the volume in the guide to the dictionary, and there is also an abbreviated guide at the bottom of each page. All of the symbols are standard ones, except for three not commonly found in small dictionaries: **ngg** as in *finger*, **nk** as in *ink*, and **kh** as in *blockhouse*. One German and two French sounds are indicated. Only one pronunciation is given for each entry word, and it is based, according to the editors, on "normal conversation rather than . . . formal speech."

Syllabication is indicated in the entry word with stress marks or centered dots. A single accent mark indicates primary stress, and paired accent marks indicate secondary stress, as in **smor'gas·bord"**. These

procedures are similar to those used in other dictionaries, and students should have little difficulty with them here.

VI. Special Features

For a dictionary of its size, *The New American Webster Handy College Dictionary* has a number of interesting features. It includes a five-page guide to the use of the dictionary, which presents rules for forming inflections. Appended to the lexicon is a list of abbreviations, which adds considerably to the few included in the main word list. Its wide range of entries includes **AP** (Associated Press), **BLT** (bacon, lettuce, and tomato sandwich), **SALT** (strategic arms limitation treaty), **Thurs.** (Thursday), and **ult.** (last month). While the list itself may be helpful to students, having some abbreviations located only in the main word list (not all appear in *both* places) may be inconvenient and misleading for the user.

Also included in the volume is a pronouncing gazetteer with population figures from the late 1970s and early 1980s. There is a three-page list of foreign words and phrases, including many from the Latin. Each entry provides pronunciation, a language label, and a translation. Other features are a list of forms of address, tables of weights and measures (including a metric conversion chart), and a list of signs and symbols. This last includes symbols used in punctuation, business and finance, weather, mathematics, medicine, and other fields.

VII. Accessibility

The boldface type makes entries fairly easy to locate; however, the fact that the dictionary does not provide separate entries for homographs and does not set main entry words overhanging the text requires more painstaking searching for words. Guide words on each page indicate the first and last entries on the page. These are boldfaced but in rather small type.

Occasionally, an alternative spelling is noted at the end of an entry. Under **catalog**, for example, appears "Also **cat'a·logue**." For the most part, however, alternative spellings are not given. The guide to the dictionary notes that "The user of this dictionary may rely upon finding a correct way to spell his word, but it will not necessarily be *the only* correct way." Given the limited scope of the dictionary, this should suffice.

VIII. Graphics and Format

Entry words are boldfaced and set flush with succeeding lines of the entry. This format may pose problems, since it is always easier for the eye to locate words when entries overhang the text. Pages are double-column, and the layout and spacing are very tight. The paper is stock newsprint, but it is sufficiently heavy so that type from one side does not show through to the other. Pages separate easily from the volume's binding, and this paperback is unlikely to withstand heavy use.

IX. Summary

The New American Webster Handy College Dictionary is a serviceable and inexpensive pocket dictionary. The currency of the word list is adequate and the definitions are extremely brief; its main use would be as a guide to spelling, syllabication, pronunciation, and identifying parts of speech. Appended materials are useful, and the guide to the dictionary is full for a small paperback. The binding and paper quality are poor. The dictionary can be compared to WEBSTER'S NEW WORLD COMPACT SCHOOL AND OFFICE DICTIONARY, which provides etymology and has a format that makes words easier to locate. *The Compact* also has better quality paper and is large enough and sturdy enough to withstand moderate library circulation. Personal names are included, and all abbreviations appear in the main word list. While the *Handy College Dictionary* is more limited in use than WEBSTER'S NEW WORLD COMPACT, it is also less expensive, has more new words, and would serve as a handy reference tool for occasional home and office use.

New Century Vest-Pocket Webster Dictionary

Facts at a Glance

Full Title: **New Century Vest-Pocket Webster Dictionary**.
Publisher: New Century Publishers, Inc.
Editors: Arthur Norman and Robert E. Allen.
Edition Reviewed: 1975.

Number of Volumes: 1.
Number of Entries: Approximately 21,000.
Number of Pages: 304.
Number of Illustrations: Approximately 300.
Trim Size: 3″ × 5⅜″.
Binding: paperback.

Price: $2.95.
Intended Readership: high school through adult.
Sold in bookstores and directly to schools and libraries. ISBN 0-8329-1536-X.

I. Introduction

The *New Century Vest-Pocket Webster Dictionary* is a small, brief-entry format dictionary similar in size and purpose to other "vest pocket" books such as THE RANDOM HOUSE AMERICAN DICTIONARY, Simon & Schuster's WEBSTER'S NEW WORLD VEST POCKET DICTIONARY, and Merriam-Webster's VEST POCKET DICTIONARY. Revised by Arthur Norman, associate professor of English at the University of Texas, and Robert E. Allen, professor of English at Colorado State University, this dictionary bears a copyright date of 1975.

According to the preface, dictionary users "rarely or never look up the meaning or spelling of common, everyday words like *be, and, is, not, of, or,* etc." Therefore, in order to make the best use of limited space, many such words are not included in this edition. They are also omitted, states the publisher, in order to make room "for thousands of modern terms and definitions not usually included in a dictionary of this size"—many of these inclusions, however, are now out-of-date.

II. Authority

Although this dictionary was revised by two English professors, no information is given about any previous edition of this work, nor are the original editors identified. Moreover, no information is provided regarding the word lists or sources used in compiling the work.

III. Comprehensiveness

Our reviewers estimate that the *New Century Vest-Pocket Webster Dictionary* contains some 21,000 main entries, a relatively large number for so small and compact a book. However, due to space limitations, the entries are far from comprehensive. Verbal illustrations have been omitted and discriminated meanings for the same word are not identified by numerals.

The *New Century Vest-Pocket Webster Dictionary* has not been updated since 1975. Therefore, the statement made in the preface that certain common terms were excluded for the purpose of adding recent terms is no longer of much significance. Examples of the more recent but common technology words that are not included are *videocassette, video disc, video tape, modem, database, data bank* (although **data processing** is included), and *disc/k drive* (the only reference to **disc** applies to a phonograph).

IV. Quality and Currency of Entries

A typical entry appears in the following sequence in the *New Century Vest-Pocket Webster Dictionary*: boldface, syllabified entry word; pronunciations in parentheses (when given); italicized part-of-speech label; principal verb form endings in parentheses (where appropriate) synonymous meanings, divided by commas, plus the various definitions, divided by semicolons; and any idioms or colloquialisms. Note the entry format in the following examples:

odd *a.* not paired with another, single; left over; not exactly dividable by two; strange; **-I·TY** *n.* strangeness; strange person or thing; *-s n. pl.* difference in flavor of one against another; advantage

o'cean *n.* vast expanse of salt water that covers the greater part of the globe

op·pro'bri·um (ə·pro'bre-əm) *n.* disgrace, shame; OP·PRO'BRI·OUS *a.*

Some arbitrary decisions have been made regarding the "common, everyday words" not listed in the *New Century Vest-Pocket Webster Dictionary*. As noted above, the simple entry **odd** is included, but there is no listing for **fast**, whereas most abridged paperback dictionaries offer several entries for **fast** and note its homograph distinction.

Definitions are not always adequate. For example, the definition for **extrasensory** merely states: "gotten by some means other than normal senses (as *extrasensory perception*)." This gives little indication of *what* is "gotten by . . . other than normal senses," nor does the example "extrasensory perception" help to further qualify the meaning in any substantial way.

V. Syllabication and Pronunciation

Entry word syllabication is indicated by centered dots, except where stress is shown by an accent mark. Only problematic pronunciations are phonetically respelled (see **opprobrium**, in the previous section, as compared to **odd** and **ocean**). A "Key to Pronunciation" in the front section of the book describes the 41 phonetic symbols used in this dictionary. According to the editor, the key is based on the Midwestern dialect, "regarded by linguists as the nearest thing to a general standard of English pronunciation that the United States is likely to have." The pronunciation key is not duplicated elsewhere in the dictionary, a distinct drawback for students.

VI. Special Features

In addition to the pronunciation key, which gives 41 phonetic symbols for vowels and consonants, the front matter provides an explanatory page that clearly outlines the structure of the book's definitions and gives an annotated example of each entry's component parts. There is also a listing of the 22 abbreviations used in the dictionary.

Appendixes include short essays that provide rules for punctuation, abbreviations and contractions, capitalization, spelling, and letter writing. By and large, this section is too general and condensed to substantially assist users. The back matter also contains a two-page map with time zones indicated and twenty pages of statistical tables on such subjects as population, food, industrial production, United States and world cities, U. S. presidents, and weights and measures. Many of these statistics are badly outdated and of little practical value, while others remain marginally useful.

VII. Accessibility

Entries in the *New Century Vest-Pocket Dictionary* are reasonably accessible. Boldface guide words appear at the top outer corner of each page, indicating the first entry on the left-hand page and the last entry on the right-hand page. No thumb indexes or other finding aids are provided. Alternate spellings of words are included as part of the main entry heading (**crit'i·cize**, **crit-i·cise**).

VIII. Graphics and Format

The print in this pocket edition is extremely small, and it is almost impossible to read the supplementary back sections without the aid of a magnifying lens.

The black-and-white line drawings that are scattered throughout this dictionary are too small and rudimentary to be of much value. Sometimes these illustrations are irrelevant simply because the definition is not stated clearly enough to show the intent of the drawing—for example, **esophagus** is defined as "gullet." However, the illustration diagrams the outline of a human figure and the passageway from the mouth to the large intestine. Although one section of the internal structure is distinguished by a solid line (as opposed to the other sections, roughly sketched by a broken line), there is nothing to indicate which part is the esophagus.

IX. Summary

Prospective purchasers should be aware that the *New Century Vest-Pocket Webster Dictionary* is limited in its scope and comprehensiveness, and its often outdated entries will not always be useful for today's student. While this true "pocket" dictionary will fit conveniently in even the smallest pocket and is extremely handy to carry about, it provides minimal information about those words it does include. Readers requiring a dictionary in this format will be better served by WEBSTER'S VEST POCKET DICTIONARY, published by Merriam-Webster.

The New Color-Picture Dictionary for Children

Facts at a Glance

Full Title: **The New Color-Picture Dictionary for Children**.
Publisher: Delair.
Compiler: Archie Bennett.
Illustrator: Nancy Sears.
Edition Reviewed: © 1977.

Number of Volumes: 1.
Number of Entries: over 1,500.
Number of Pages: 256.
Number of Illustrations: 800 in full color.
Trim Size: 8″ × 10⅞″.
Binding: paper over boards.

Prices: $14.95 to schools and libraries; $19.93 to individuals.
Intended Readership: ages 5 through 9.
Sold in bookstores and other outlets; also sold to libraries and schools. ISBN 0-516-00820-X.

I. Scope and Format

In a note to parents and teachers, which calls this work "a first step into the world of dictionaries," the publishers of *The New Color-Picture Dictionary for Children* states that imitation, repetition, substitution, and fascination with color are "among the most important tools for learning words your child has." Calling on adults to supply imitation by reading this dictionary aloud to children, the publishers claim that the book supplies the other three tools for learning the more than 1,500 words included. Their claim that the dictionary enhances the development of skill in substituting one word for another is valid in that the words are often defined in terms of synonyms and phrases that can be substituted for the entry word.

Access to the words is easy. There is a guide letter at the top left of the left-hand pages and one at the top right of the right-hand pages. The entry words are in oversize boldface roman letters and are on the left-hand side of the page. There are about six entry words to a page.

The graphic design is simple. Each entry word begins at the left margin; the definition sentences start exactly one-half inch away from the entry word: thus the margins for the definitions are not even down the page. A fine blue horizontal line that stretches across the page separates entries from one another.

After page 12 the quality of the paper changes from a good-quality white stock to a poor-quality grayish-tan. Words and illustrations show up less effectively on this darker paper, which tends to discolor around the edges. The side-sewn reinforced binding appears to be of sturdy and durable quality.

The dictionary's only special feature is the inclusion within the word list of 100 words marked with an asterisk indicating that they are relatively difficult to spell or understand. The introductory "Note to Parents and Teachers" suggests that they "spend some extra time with your child on these words."

II. Authority

The publisher's note states, "We have taken 1500 words and definitions from our *New Webster's Dictionary of the English Language* and presented them in a way that matches your child's natural tools of learning." The source dictionary cited was published by Consolidated Book Publishers in 1975 and is an adult semi-abridged volume, a reprint of *The Living Webster Encyclopedic Dictionary of the English Language* (© 1971), described by Kristo (1977) as not authoritative. Sidney R. Berquist, Ph.D., Northwestern University, is listed as the consultant to *The New Color-Picture Dictionary*, but his field is not indicated.

III. Quality and Currency of Entries

The "definitions," which are not actually definitions, are simplistic and pedestrian. For example:

> **everybody** Tom gave **everybody** a piece of candy.
> Tom gave **everyone** a piece of candy.
> Tom gave **each person** a piece of candy.

> **prompt** Jane is always **prompt**.
> Jane is always **on time**.

> **weary** Mother worked all day and she is **weary**.
> Mother worked all day and she is **tired**.

Some definitions have as many as four sentences that "define" the word in this manner. Differences between parts of speech are not explained or noted,

The New Color-Picture Dictionary for Children

pen

We write with a **pen.**
The **pen** makes marks with ink.

The farmer keeps his pigs in a **pen.**
The farmer keeps the pigs in a **yard with a fence around it.**
A **pen** for pigs is also called a **sty.**

❶ Entry word in large bold type is set off from the text

❷ A space sets off different meanings of the homographs

❸ Bold entry word is used in sentences that define in context or by description

❹ Four-color illustration aids in understanding the second meaning of the entry word

which could result in confusion to the young reader. For example:

> **lead** Would you **lead** me to the lunchroom?Would you **guide** me to the lunchroom?I would like to **lead** the band.I would like to **conduct** the band.**Lead** is a heavy metal.The black stick in a pencil is called the **lead.**

Conduct, used in the entry above, is not an entry word, although **conductor** is. The heavy hand of didacticism hangs over many of these definitions, reducing their interest value for children. Irregular forms of verbs are sometimes, but not always, listed as subentries. Parts of speech, syllabication, pronunciation, and etymology are not given but are also not really necessary or customarily included at this age level.

IV. Illustrations

Illustrations tend to be as simplistic and pedestrian as the entries. Each page displays about three full-

color drawings; drawings illustrate only one meaning of a word when multiple meanings are listed. While a few minority children are depicted, and the illustration for **land** shows a jumbo jet, most of the drawings look as if they came out of a basal reader of the 1950s. For example, the illustration for **flash** shows a 1950s-style police car. Sex role stereotyping is evident; women are drawn bathing babies (under **bath**) and setting tables (under **china**); men are portrayed as police officers (under **brave**), mail carriers (under **bring**), and fire fighters (under **fireman**).

V. Summary

The New Color-Picture Dictionary for Children fails to respond to the creative and imaginative needs of children. Although the only copyright date listed is 1977, the whole volume (text and illustrations) seems considerably older. Definitions are didactic and boring. This book would have very limited usefulness in homes or libraries today.

New Scholastic Dictionary of American English

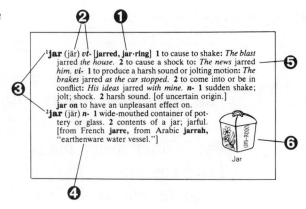

❶ Inflected forms, in boldface type, are bracketed; syllabication is indicated by a centered dot

❷ Pronunciation appears in parentheses followed by abbreviated part of speech in boldface italic

❸ Homographs are indicated by superior numbers in front of the main entry words

❹ Informal etymology includes a definition of the source word

❺ Illustrative sentences appear in italic, with entry word and inflected forms in roman type

❻ Line drawing illustrates the second homograph

New Scholastic Dictionary of American English

Facts at a Glance

Full Title: **New Scholastic Dictionary of American English**.
Publisher: Scholastic Inc.
Edition Reviewed: © 1981.

Number of Volumes: 1.
Number of Entries: over 40,000.
Number of Pages: 1,024.
Number of Illustrations: approximately 1,450 black-and-white line drawings.
Trim Size: 5¼″ × 7⅝″.
Binding: paperback.

Price: $6.95.
Intended Readership: ages 9 and up.
Sold in bookstores; also sold to schools. ISBN 0-590-40415-6.

I. Introduction and Scope

This 1981 edition of the *New Scholastic Dictionary of American English* is the paperback edition of the HOLT SCHOOL DICTIONARY OF AMERICAN ENG-LISH, which is reviewed elsewhere in this Buying Guide. It contains over 40,000 definitions and over 1,450 illustrations. Presented in an oversize paperback format, the work is designed specifically for students of age nine and up, or for any novice who needs a basic introduction on how to use a dictionary. The special features of this edition include a 24-page introduction, "You and Your Dictionary," and a 28-page section of exercises geared toward building dictionary skills.

The volume is, for the most part, a photographic reproduction in smaller format of the parent Holt book; but it is distinctly less attractive. The text is extremely small and printed on coated newsprint stock. The text also appears to have been taken from an earlier edition of the Holt book that does not contain a few of the features of the revised hardcover edition. The main vocabulary, however, is the same. The paperback edition lacks the 32-page color insert and contains a significantly shorter list of "Persons and Places" in the appendix material; there are other slight differences in the appendixes. The preface in the hardcover Holt edition does not appear here. The hardbound book and the paperback are, however, for all intents and purposes the same book. See the review of the HOLT SCHOOL DICTIONARY OF AMERICAN ENGLISH for a more complete description.

Open Sesame Picture Dictionary

❶ The right-hand page has numbered pictures with accompanying vocabulary words

❷ The word index at back of book includes an alphabetical listing of all words in the dictionary, keyed to a page number and item number.

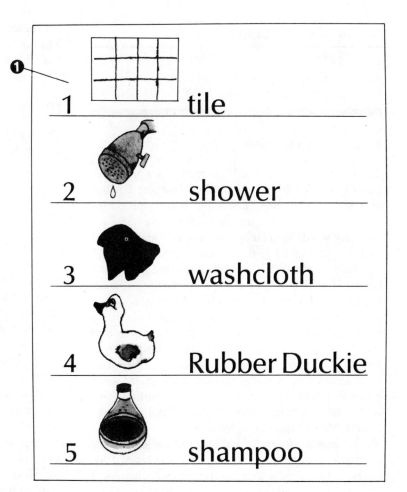

Open Sesame Picture Dictionary

Facts at a Glance

Full Title: **Open Sesame Picture Dictionary** (Open Sesame English as a Second Language Series).
Publisher: Oxford University Press.
Author: Jill Wagner Schimpff.
Illustrator: Tom Cooke.

Edition Reviewed: © 1982.

Number of Words: over 550.
Number of Pages: 83.
Number of Indexes: 1.
Number of Illustrations: 68 pages in full color.
Trim Size: 8½″ × 11″.

Binding: laminated paper over boards.

Price: $4.95.
Intended Readership: elementary school children.
Sold to libraries and schools. ISBN 0-19-503201-2.

I. Scope and Format

The *Open Sesame Picture Dictionary* is designed specifically for use by young children learning English as a Second Language (ESL), but is appropriate for use by any young beginning reader. Over 550 vocabulary words are categorized and introduced in 34 units, covering such topics as "Verbs," "Fruit," "Months of the Year," and items found in specific rooms of a house. Each unit comprises two consecutive full-color pages. The left-hand page is a full-page illustration presenting the target vocabulary words (identified with numbers) in a contextualized setting. The facing right-hand page features picture lists of the target words in isolation together with their identifying numbers and the appropriate word written in bold, lowercase letters. This format reinforces the vocabulary since the reader can recognize items both in context and individually.

The words chosen for inclusion in the dictionary are those usually taught in the early lessons of ESL courses. They deal with items students will encounter in everyday situations in a typical Western (i.e., American or European) middle-class cultural setting, such as food, clothing, and neighborhood settings. The words are indexed by page number and word number in an alphabetical word list at the back of the book and the word category for each unit is given in the table of contents.

In general, left to right progression along horizontal planes is followed in the placement of identifying numbers on the contextualized illustration. The numeration, however, is not consistent. This may be a problem for young readers who are looking for a specific word in context and have to scan the whole page to find the item rather than following the numbers to the item they seek.

II. Authority

The *Open Sesame Picture Dictionary* is part of an "Oxford American English" list of books and belongs to an elementary school English as a Second Language (ESL) series from Oxford University Press. OUP is an international leader in the creation of English language material for use by non-native speakers. The author of the dictionary is an ESL instructor at Pitzer College in Claremont, California. The book and series were created in cooperation with the Childrens' Television Workshop, the producers of "Sesame Street."

III. Quality and Currency of Entries

The words used in the *Open Sesame Picture Dictionary* have been selected because of their high frequency use in everyday contexts. The illustrations, used in this dictionary to define words and their contextual use, are clear and simple and would be easily recognized by the reader who is familiar with the item being shown. In cases where the student may not have lived long enough in a mainstream American or European culture to be familiar with a particular item of food or home furnishing, the illustrations may be too general. **Cheese** and **butter**, for instance, are both shown as sticks of yellowish food and **ice cream** is shown in a dish rather than in a more recognizable cone. Also, sizes are shown out of proportion, as is common in popular children's illustrations. On the full page illustrations, confusion would probably not occur. However, readers who are unfamiliar with the items would not necessarily interpret new lexical items correctly when shown the corresponding numbered lists in which a domesticated **cat**, a **seal**, a **parrot** and a **pony**, for example, are all drawn to the same small size. Because the book is clearly designed to be used in an instructional setting, problems with the illustrations could be overcome by the teacher who is aware of the possibility for confusion.

Only in one unit, the category of names for relationships among family members, are the illustrated definitions actually inaccurate. The words are presented in the context of a stylized family tree that so confuses the relationships of **uncle**, **aunt**, and **cousin** that a non-native reader could not infer the meanings of these English words.

The units on verbs are particularly strong. In cases where a single illustration might leave some confusion, such as with the words **catch** and **throw**, two sets of actions are shown, each clearly defining only one word.

IV. Illustrations

The items are shown in realistic, if fantasized, settings with Muppet characters as the "human" components. Appropriately, the only illustrations showing humans are in the unit naming the parts of the body.

The numerals indicating the item being named are clear and are enclosed in circles. A small line from the circle to the exact item being named is used, if for the purposes of clarity the circle is not placed directly on the item.

V. Summary

The *Open Sesame Picture Dictionary* is designed for use in an elementary English as a Second Language class and is appropriate for this use. The picture pages can be a catalyst for conversation lessons as well as grammar, reading, and writing lessons. The word list contains enough nouns, verbs, and adjectives to cover all the sentence patterns used in the first levels of ESL instruction. The book has an attractive, easy-to-follow format that capitalizes on the international appeal of the Muppet characters.

The dictionary could also be used to great advantage in general English language instruction to suggest ideas for telling or writing stories and for spelling work in remedial as well as in developmental settings.

Because of the book's appealing format and clear labeling system, the *Open Sesame Picture Dictionary* is preferable to works such as MY FIRST PICTURE DICTIONARY or MY PICTURE DICTIONARY—and is a very good choice for a preschool child's first home dictionary or word book.

Oxford Children's Dictionary: Second Edition

Facts at a Glance

Full Title: **Oxford Children's Dictionary: Second Edition.**
Publisher: Oxford University Press.
Compilers: Alan Spooner and John Weston.
Illustrators: Bill le Fever and Paul Thomas.
Edition Reviewed: © 1985.

Number of Volumes: 1.
Number of Entries: 12,000.
Number of Pages: 322.
Number of Illustrations: approximately 215 in full color.
Trim Size: 5″ × 7¾″.
Binding: hardbound.

Price: $11.95.
Intended Readership: elementary and middle school students.

Sold in bookstores; also sold to libraries and schools. ISBN 0-19-861183-8.

I. Introduction

According to the preface to the second edition, this is a thoroughly revised and redesigned edition of the OXFORD CHILDREN'S DICTIONARY, originally published in 1976. It includes "many new words in the areas of technology, sport, and other aspects of modern society." The two principles upon which the original dictionary were based remain the same: "that young readers and writers should find the dictionary self-explanatory and easy to use, and that it should be a real dictionary which prepares children for the use of more adult dictionaries in due course." The dictionary has 12,000 main entries and is illustrated with drawings in full color.

Although the age level is not specifically stated, the dictionary appears to be intended for use by elementary and middle school students. However, since the vocabulary and spelling used in the dictionary are strictly British, the dictionary will be of little use to American schoolchildren.

II. Authority

This edition was overseen by the staff of the Oxford Dictionaries and published by the distinguished reference book publisher, Oxford University Press.

III. Comprehensiveness

With 12,000 entries, the dictionary contains less than twenty percent of the number contained in the SCOTT, FORESMAN INTERMEDIATE DICTIONARY. And since the vocabulary and the spellings are entirely British, American children would not find this dictionary useful unless they were planning a trip to Great Britain or studying British usage. Examples of words that have specific British definitions include:

bonnet, lorry, cheeky, jumper, dustbin, fly-over, football, conker, lift, subway, pram, swot, boot, and **pavement**.

In addition, exclusively British terms such as **MOT test, lbw, Venture Scout,** and **ITV** have no American counterparts. Words spelled in the British way include **colour, honour, centre, gaol,** and **programme**.

Although the dictionary includes some up-to-date technical words, especially those associated with computers, such as **bit, word processor, bug, cursor,**

microchip, and the British **VDU** (visual display unit), it does not include *database*, *modem*, *byte*, or *access* (as a verb). **Cosmonaut**, **satellite**, **space shuttle**, **microwave oven**, **compact disc**, and **Kung Fu** appear, but *blastoff*, *ICBM*, *AIDS*, the names of sex organs, and the slang use of *sting*, *flaky*, and *stoned* do not.

The work contains no geographic terms (other than adjectives denoting nationality, such as **American**, **English**, **French**), and no biographical entries. There are few abbreviations; foreign words (**sari**) are included as main entries. The dictionary consists solely of the main vocabulary, plus two brief prefatory pages. There is no table of contents and no pronunciation guide.

IV. Quality and Currency of Entries

Entries consist of the main word in large blue type and brief definitions in smaller black type. Definitions are often reinforced with sentences or phrases to show how the word is used. When multiple definitions are presented, they are numbered. Plurals and verb forms are given in parentheses, as are comparative and superlative forms of adjectives; none of these forms is labeled. Some inflections are separate main entries cross-referenced to the verb's main form: **sung** See **sing**. Additional forms of the main entry appear in boldface blue type at the end of the entry. No pronunciations, syllabications, etymologies, or parts of speech are indicated.

Words appearing, for example, as both a noun and a verb are marked by a small superior number for each form; for example:

> **cool**[1] (cooler, coolest) **1.** Fairly cold, **2.** Calm. *Keep cool, don't panic!* **3.** Not enthusiastic. **coolly**, **coolness**.
> **cool**[2] (cools, cooling, cooled) To become cool, to make cool. **cooler**.

Note that the forms *coolly*, *coolness*, and *cooler* do not appear as main entries and thus are not formally defined. This could be confusing for a student.

There are no abbreviations used in the entries. Occasionally words are indicated as informal, but no field labels are used. Definitions are extremely brief, but usually accurate. Many, however, deserve fuller explanations, for example:

> **football** A game played with a large, air-filled ball.

This definition is hardly exclusive to British football (called *soccer* in the United States) and would benefit from further description.

Sometimes the definition is circular. For example:

> **Mohammedan** A muslim.

But:

> **Muslim** A believer in Islam, a follower of Muhammed.

Muhammed is not entered, but:

> **Muhammedan** A muslim.

Finally:

> **Islam** The religion of Muslims.

Variant forms appear immediately following the main entry and do not appear as main entries themselves. For example:

> **coppice** (coppices) **copse** (copses) A clump of trees.

The entries are built on a rational system that may become easier for a child following instruction from an adult or with some practice. However, by failing to use punctuation, syllabication, parts of speech, and etymologies, the dictionary—contrary to statements in the preface—is *not* "a real dictionary which prepares children for the use of adult dictionaries." The lack of many words in current usage also makes the dictionary less accommodating to children who may be expected to be familiar with them.

V. Syllabication and Pronunciation

As mentioned, no syllabication is indicated, and no pronunciation system (including stress marks) is used. Very occasionally unusual pronunciations are indicated with the stressed syllable in italic type:

> **contest**[1] (pronounced con*test*) To contend, to fight
> **contest**[2] (pronounced *con*test) A fight, a competition

Many children will have serious difficulty with the lack of help in these areas.

VI. Special Features

There are no special features in the volume.

VII. Accessibility

Entry words appear in boldface in blue and overhang the definition. Guide words appear at the top left and right of each double-page spread. Words are easily accessible in general.

VIII. Graphics and Format

Clear but undistinguished full-color illustrations are used sparingly throughout the volume. They have no captions but appear directly above the word they illustrate. The drawings are helpful, but no criteria are stated for the selection of particular words illustrated.

The general format of the page is very clear, with two columns of text placed within generous white space. Guide words and page numbers appear at the top of pages separated from the text by a thin, horizontal rule.

The attractive laminated cover is placed over sturdy boards. The size and feel of the book are very handy, and the book will stand up to strenuous use.

IX. Summary

Apart from its crisp, attractive format, the *Oxford Children's Dictionary* has little to offer American children. The British vocabulary and spellings, the lack of formal pronunciations, syllabication, parts of speech, and other useful dictionary aids, and the absence of special features severely limit its usefulness, except for the traveler to Great Britain.

Oxford Student's Dictionary of American English

Facts at a Glance

Full Title: **Oxford Student's Dictionary of American English**.

Publisher: Oxford University Press.

Editors: A. S. Hornby, with Christina A. Ruse; Dolores Harris and William A. Stewart (American edition).

Edition Reviewed: second edition, © 1986.

Number of Volumes: 1.
Number of Words: over 20,000 words and phrases.
Number of Pages: 714.
Number of Illustrations: 142 in black and white.
Trim Size: 5¼″ × 8¼″.
Binding: hardcover; paperback.

Prices: $15.95; $5.95.
Intended Readership: intermediate students of English as a Second or Foreign Language.
Sold in bookstores; also sold to libraries and schools. ISBN 0-19-431194-5.

I. Introduction

Adapted from the OXFORD STUDENT'S DICTIONARY OF CURRENT ENGLISH, this American English edition of the *Oxford Student's Dictionary* will be particularly useful for teachers and librarians who serve populations of students speaking English-based creole dialects, such as Jamaican Creole or Hawaiian Creole. Because this dictionary was conceived for users who have a bidialectal orientation, it crosses the boundaries of typical lexicons. Its purpose is to emphasize the differences between British and American English, rather than to merely offer lexical studies. For this reason, the work focuses on the more common words and expressions that the beginner to American English will hear in everyday conversation or will see in written material, excluding the most technical or literary terms. Sample verbal illustrations frequently show usage distinctions or clarify difficult points of spelling, pronunciation, and meaning. Occasional black-and-white line drawings and photographs (an average of one every five pages), with labels, also help to illustrate entry terms.

Although the section, "Using the Dictionary," is written for a fairly sophisticated readership and is not designed to serve *younger* students, it may prove helpful for most beginners to American English, if the material is covered with the assistance of a knowledgeable instructor. For example, several pages devoted to both inflections and contractions not only emphasize usage rules but include an extensive discussion on pronunciation.

Also included in this reference book are six brief appendixes that contain the following information: a list and discussion of numerical expressions (cardinal and ordinal numbers and also house numbers, postal zip codes, and telephone numbers); brief material on the ways in which the time of day, dates, and money are depicted, pronounced and written about in American English; a table showing the Greek alphabet and its use in American contexts; and a list of the names and postal abbreviations of the states. With the exception of the cardinal and ordinal numerical expressions (appendix 1, section 1), each appendix is limited to a single page.

II. Authority

Not only is this work an adaptation of the original *Oxford Student's Dictionary of Current English* but, as the preface notes, material from the *Oxford Advanced Learner's Dictionary of Current English* has also been incorporated "to serve learners of American English through the Intermediate level." The *Oxford Student's Dictionary of American English* was

Oxford Student's Dictionary of American English

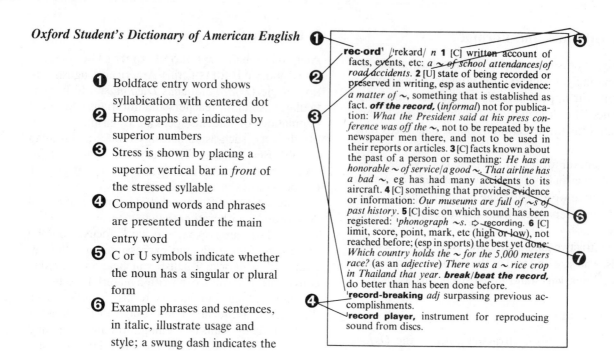

❶ Boldface entry word shows syllabication with centered dot

❷ Homographs are indicated by superior numbers

❸ Stress is shown by placing a superior vertical bar in *front* of the stressed syllable

❹ Compound words and phrases are presented under the main entry word

❺ C or U symbols indicate whether the noun has a singular or plural form

❻ Example phrases and sentences, in italic, illustrate usage and style; a swung dash indicates the entry word

❼ Cross-reference is indicated by an open right arrow

compiled by the highly reputable Oxford University Press staff, and the American editors, who adapted the earlier A. S. Hornby *Current English* for this work, are Dolores Harris and William A. Stewart.

III. Comprehensiveness

In the words of the editors, "there has been no attempt (in this dictionary) to include the considerable body of slang, which varies from place to place and is always changing." Further, because this dictionary serves the dual purpose of acting as a lexicon and as a learning tool, this edition should not be judged wholly on how inclusive or up-to-date entries are. Readers will want to be aware that the following are *not* included: the noun sense of *aerobics*; *crack*, as the word refers to cocaine; *Dolby*; *free base*; *fast track*; *sitcom*; *meltdown*; *gridlock*; and *modem*. The slang term **hippie**, **hippy** is included, but the more recent term *yuppie* (yuppiey) is not.

Other current listings seem to have been selected arbitrarily. For example, such computer and technical terms as **data processing**, **data bank**, **programming** (as it relates to the computer), **video recorder**, and **video tape** are included; but *database*, *video cassette*, *video disc/k*, and *disc/k drive* are omitted. **Gay**, in its homosexual sense, is included. The dictionary is not completely successful in its attempt to hone in on "everyday" language.

IV. Quality and Currency of Entries

The typical entry is presented as follows: the boldface entry word divided into syllables, overhanging the text at the left of each column; the pronunciation(s), enclosed in diagonal bars; the italicized part-of-speech label; and in the case of noun entries, stylistic usage labels. [C] stands for "countable" and indicates that a noun has both a singular and plural form; [U] indicates an "uncountable" noun, one that does not have a plural form; [C,U] indicates that a noun can be used either as a countable or uncountable word. Thus, **kumquat** is designated with a [C]; **kinship** is designated with a [U]; and **coin** is designated with a [C,U]. In the case of irregular verb entries, the present participle, the past participle, and inflected forms appear in parentheses. In the case of adjectives or adverbs, irregular comparisons appear in parentheses. Boldface numerals introduce the various meanings and, when applicable, boldface lowercase letters signal subtle shades of meaning. The definitions then appear, followed by verbal instructions in italics; language labels in italics, when indicated; an open, small box symbol (□) to denote when a main entry word changes from one part of speech to another, where applicable; idiomatic expressions in bold italic type, listed alphabetically; and occasionally, an arrow sign (⇔), indicating cross-references to other entries (the word cross-referenced appears in sans serif type).

Consider the following main entry with its subsidiary entries:

> **boat** /bout/ *n* [C] small open vessel traveling in on water, esp the kind with oars ('row ~), sails ('sail −) engines ('motor −); also used of fishing vessel small steamers: *We crossed the river by ~/in a~.* ↻ *illus at* ship *be (all) in the same boat* have the same problems to face □ *vi* travel in a boat, esp for pleasure: *We~ed down the river.* ↻ *also* ferry, house[1], life.
>> **'boat·house** . . .
>> **'boat·man** . . .
>> **'boat race** . . .
>> **'boat·swain** . . .

As a space-saving device, note that the editors insert a tilde (~), rather than repeatedly restate the headword; this shortcut is especially useful in the longer entries.

It will take the user some time to become familiar with the various labels, symbols, abbreviations, and different type faces used throughout this dictionary. This reference guide is obviously not designed for a novice to the use of a dictionary. For instance, a user will need to know how to find a key or an explanation to understand the meaning of such symbols as the bracketed *C*, the tilde, the arrow, and the numbers in parentheses in the example shown. Although this information can be gleaned from the introductory "Using the Dictionary" section, and a chart of symbols and abbreviations used in the volume appears on the inside back cover, specific material is not easy to locate. However, this dictionary was *never* meant to act as a quick-and-handy reference guide, but as a *learning* device. Regular users are forced to become familiar with the information section of the book, and to refer to it frequently.

Definitions are listed in order of meaning, from the most common or simple sense first to the most uncommon or complex meaning. As in the example shown, word derivatives are alphabetically listed in conjunction with the main root word entry (**boat-house; boatman; boat race**); whereas **boatswain** is listed as a separate entry, and overhangs the text as do other main entry words.

Derivatives, or truncated forms, are not as fully defined as their root word and tend to restate the previous derivative, as in the following example:

> **im·mo·bile** /i'moubəl/ *adj* not able to move or be moved; motionless.
>> **im·mo·bil·ity** /,imou'bɪləti/ *n* [U] state of being immobile

> **im·mo·bi·lize** /i'moubə,laiz/ *vt* make immobile.
>> **im·mo·bi·liz·ation** /i'moubə,li'zeiʃən/ *n* [U]

Note that there is no meaning given for the noun **immobilization**: this may cause confusion to users.

V. Syllabication and Pronunciation

Entry word syllables are indicated by boldface centered dots. The phonetic symbols in this dictionary are the ones designated by the International Phonetic Association, although the shift from British to American English necessitated some changes in the use of certain symbols and in the indication of stress and length. These changes are detailed in the preface, following a brief discussion on converting British to American spelling, or vice versa. Pronunciations and spellings are not presented in key form on the lexicon's page. A chart of phonetic symbols does appear on the inside front cover. Since pronunciation is one of the most significant differences between British and American English, this omission may detract from the usefulness of this work—especially for younger users or those with poor language skills.

VI. Special Features

Generally, the appendixes are functional and help to educate the reader about some of the subtler nuances that differentiate American English from British English, particularly from a pragmatic, "everyday" perspective. For instance, one appendix discusses how numerical expressions are handled in American English, pointing out the discrepancies with British English. Appendixes on dates, the time of day, and money serve the same function. The list of names and postal abbreviations of the states will be helpful to readers as a quick reference. The appendix on the Greek alphabet is introduced by a brief statement that relates the Greek alphabet to mathematical symbols and to sorority and fraternity use. For Jamaican students, who have been educated in the British examination system and who are college bound in America, this is a small but useful plus.

VII. Accessibility

Guide-word pairs, divided by a diagonal bar, appear in the upper, inner margin of each page—for example, **cow/craft; craftsman/crawl**. These guide words are not much larger than the entry words themselves. This small size, combined with their close proximity to the inner margins of the book, make them difficult to read; users must turn the pages individually and spread the book flat to see them clearly. There are no thumb tabs or other location devices to help the user find specific terms.

VIII. Graphics and Format

The black-and-white line drawings scattered throughout the volume are well conceived and labeled, and quite attractive. Some illustrations fill a considerable amount of the page—for example, one drawing not only depicts various types of fruit but labels the different parts (skin or peel, core, seed, pip (a Britishism for seeds, as in the orange, which is illustrated) rind, section, and so on). Another drawing diagrams several flowers and their parts in a similar manner. The editors have also included photographs, some of which depict uniquely "American" scenes—for example, one photograph shows a duplex house (for the entry **duplex**); another pictures the Washington Monument (for the entry **monument**). However, in many instances, the illustration captions, which are set in all small boldface capitals not appreciably larger than the entry words, are placed at the side of the column very close to entry words, and it is hard to see them easily.

This dictionary has a sturdy sewn binding that should withstand extensive use. Although the inking is generally sharp, the typeface is small, but the white space, or leading, helps to make the text more readable. The paper is thin, but fairly white and of good opacity so that there is little show-through.

IX. Summary

The *Oxford Student's Dictionary of American English* has several points to recommend it. Like the comparable LONGMAN DICTIONARY OF AMERICAN ENGLISH (Longman, 1983), it is a portable reference work, providing simply stated definitions that beginners in American English will grasp and focusing on the language of everyday American living. While the latter puts a somewhat greater emphasis on providing illustrative phrases and sentences, the Oxford work is more fully illustrated with photographs and line drawings throughout the text.

The Oxford work may cause difficulties for some users in the complexity of its format and coding systems. For example, users who require a well-annotated pronunciation key will be lost in this volume; these students would be better served by the Longman volume. Because of this difficulty, some students may not benefit from the Oxford work's bidialectal orientation. Most newcomers to American English, unless they are well educated and already-fluent readers, will also have difficulty in making their way through the fairly technical introductory

explanations about its use. Therefore, this dictionary will find maximum utility in a classroom setting in which a teacher interprets this material for students, whereas the LONGMAN DICTIONARY OF AMERICAN ENGLISH is designed to function effectively as a self-study tool. In a library setting, the Oxford work demands the librarian's assistance with the junior high, high school, or young adult population whose English is not American-based. Buyers should also be aware that this dictionary does not incorporate many current words and slang expressions in American English. However, given these caveats, this is a useful work for bidialectal students who are serious about learning formal American English.

Picture Dictionary

Facts at a Glance

Full Title: **Picture Dictionary**.
Publisher: Macmillan.
Edition Reviewed: © 1983.

Number of Volumes: 1.
Number of Categories: 46.
Number of Words: 1,500.
Number of Pages: 80.
Number of Illustrations: 80 in full color.
Trim Size: 8½″ × 11″.
Binding: cloth.

Prices: $13.17; $9.87.
Intended Readership: ages 2 through 5.
Sold to schools and libraries. ISBN 0-02-195120-9.

I. Scope and Format

The Macmillan *Picture Dictionary* is the school edition of THE MACMILLAN PICTURE WORDBOOK. The differences between the two editions are that the *Picture Dictionary* has a new title, cover design, and reformatted table of contents. The text and illustrations remain the same. The introduction is retitled, "How To Help Your Students Use This Book," and the words "a child" are replaced with "your students." The standard textbook boxed-in form, "This book is the property of . . . ," is printed on the inside front cover of the book.

The term *dictionary* in this title is misleading. This is really a series of theme pages (the publisher calls them "categories") with illustrations depicting the themes. (Neither the author, Kathleen N. Daly, nor the illustrator, John Wallner, are credited in this edition.) Occasionally, the theme word is explained, but that is as far as the text goes toward defining.

A full review of text of THE MACMILLAN PICTURE WORDBOOK appears elsewhere in this Buying Guide. School librarians will want this edition.

The Random House American Dictionary: New Revised Edition

Facts at a Glance

Full Title: **The Random House American Dictionary: New Revised Edition**.
Publisher: Random House.
Editor: Stuart B. Flexner, Editor-in-Chief.
Edition Reviewed: © 1983.

Number of Volumes: 1.
Number of Entries: 30,000.
Number of Pages: 315.
Trim Size: $2^7/8'' \times 5^3/8''$.
Binding: paper with flexible vinyl cover.

Price: $2.95.
Intended Readership: junior high and up.
Sold in bookstores and office supply stores; also sold to schools. Licensed to Wang Laboratories for a variety of software formats and widely used by Wang sublicensees as a spelling checker. ISBN 0-394-52900-6.

I. Introduction

The Random House American Dictionary: New Revised Edition, the smallest dictionary in the Random House line, contains some 30,000 entries. Its tiny size, identical to that of THE RANDOM HOUSE THESAURUS: A DICTIONARY OF SYNONYMS AND ANTONYMS, puts it in the "vest pocket" category. The publisher describes it as "a handy reference book for the student or business person who requires a small format dictionary offering reliable guidance in spelling, pronunciation, and word meanings, plus a host of useful and up-to-date encyclopedic supplements."

II. Authority

The dictionary's primary editor, Stuart Berg Flexner, and its editorial consultant, Jess Stein, are both experienced, highly regarded lexicographers. Both have worked on a number of Random House dictionaries, including the 1966 edition of *The Random House Dictionary of the English Language: Unabridged Edi-*

tion—Flexner as Senior Editor and Stein as Editor-in-Chief.

III. Comprehensiveness

With only 30,000 entries included in the dictionary, many common words are excluded. For example, while the unabridged *Random House Dictionary of the English Language* has 46 entries between **dizzy** and **do**, *The Random House American Dictionary* has none.

Few proper names and abbreviations are listed. Names of nations are not included as entries, but some words relating to continents and countries are. Thus, **African, French, German**, and **Russian** can be found, but not *Africa, France, Germany*, or *Russia*. Idioms, synonyms, and antonyms are not given; nor are etymologies. However, entries do identify part of speech, and some include usage labels (such as *informal*). Alternative spellings are given where appropriate, but phonetic pronunciations are given only in rare instances.

IV. Quality and Currency of Entries

As is the standard practice in vest-pocket dictionaries, definitions in *The Random House American Dictionary* are compressed, often into a single word or phrase. For the most part, however, definitions in this dictionary are succinct and to the point. As far as is possible within the limitations of the vest-pocket format, multiple meanings are given. Word forms are always given, and variations of the word are found at the end of the entry.

Brief as the definitions usually are, they remain clear and direct. For example, **caffeine** is identified as a noun and defined as "chemical in coffee, etc., used as stimulant." **Myopia** is defined simply as "near-sightedness," while **visible** is labeled as an adjective and given three definitions: "1. capable of being seen. 2. perceptible. 3. manifest."

The dictionary's coverage of technologically current terms is uneven. Although **byte, videodisk**, and **videocassette** are included, *cursor* and the computer-related meanings of *file* and *program* are not.

V. Syllabication and Pronunciation

Dots indicate syllabications, and diacritical marks distinguish phonetic values in main entry words. If further pronunciation guides are needed, they follow the main entry word in parentheses. For example: ar·te′sian (-zhən) well.

The dictionary lacks a pronunciation key, but readers who are familiar with standard pronunciation symbols should have no difficulty.

VI. Special Features

Despite its very small size, *The Random House American Dictionary* contains 22 useful tables in a ready-reference appendix. Among these are "Major Nations of the World," "World Time Differences," "Distances Between U.S. Cities," and "The Metric System." More directly relevant to language and grammar are such features as "Forms of Address," "Rules of Spelling," "Rules of Punctuation," and "Words Most Often Misspelled." These features enhance the value of this dictionary for students and other readers.

VII. Accessibility

With one reservation, accessibility is not a problem in this little dictionary. Entries are arranged alphabetically, letter by letter. Two guide words at the top of each page identify the first and last entries on the page.

The sole reservation concerns the type size, which can only be described as miniscule. Any user with less-than-perfect vision will probably experience some difficulty in locating a particular word and in reading the print, and extended reading would doubtless cause severe eye strain.

VIII. Graphics and Format

Entry words and variant forms and endings are printed in boldface, distinguishing them from the definitions, which appear in the same type size but in light print. Although the print is extremely small, the typeface is otherwise legible. Entry words overhang the text by one character space. A thin vertical line divides each page into two columns, giving the book a look of clean organization. There are no illustrations. The red, white, and blue cover of the book is flexible, washable vinyl.

IX. Summary

The Random House American Dictionary is intended as a vest-pocket dictionary for quick reference by an individual rather than for research. Because it has 30,000 entries, a fairly large number for a dictionary of this size and format, the print is uncomfortably small. Home, school, and public libraries will doubtless require larger, more comprehensive dictionaries. However, the definitions are concise, and the volume will be useful to individuals who need a handy reference work of this nature.

The Random House College Dictionary: Revised Edition

Facts at a Glance

Full Title: **The Random House College Dictionary: Revised Edition**.
Publisher: Random House.
Editors: Jess Stein, Editor-in-Chief Emeritus; Stuart B. Flexner, Editor-in-Chief; Leonore C. Hauck, Managing Editor; P. Y. Su, Senior Defining Editor.
Edition Reviewed: © 1984.

Number of Volumes: 1.
Number of Entries: 170,000.
Number of Pages: 1,600.
Number of Illustrations: 1,500.
Number of Maps: 200.
Trim Size: $6\frac{9}{16}'' \times 9\frac{5}{8}''$.
Binding: cloth.

Prices: $15.95 (thumb indexed); $14.95 (plain).
Intended Readership: high school and up.
Sold in bookstores, office supply stores, and other outlets; also sold to libraries and schools. ISBN 0-394-43600-8.

I. Introduction

The Random House College Dictionary: Revised Edition is an abridgement of the first edition of *The Random House Dictionary of the English Language: Unabridged Edition*. It has been available since the mid-1960s; its previous edition was copyrighted in 1975. The current edition includes approximately 170,000 entries. The editors state that "the function of a dictionary [is] to provide the user with an exact record of the language he sees and hears. That record must be *fully* descriptive." This dictionary is intended to meet the needs of advanced high school students, as well as college students, and adults.

II. Authority

The editor-in-chief, Stuart B. Flexner, is a respected authority who has long been associated with a variety of respected general and special dictionaries, most recently of the revised, unabridged edition of *The Random House Dictionary*. Noted lexicographers Jess Stein and Laurence Urdang have also contributed to this work. Other members of the editorial and consultant staffs are listed along with their credentials.

The Random House College Dictionary: Revised Edition

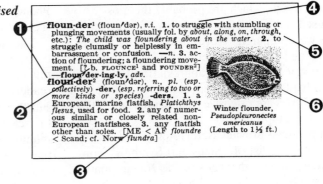

Winter flounder,
*Pseudopleuronectes
americanus*
(Length to 1½ ft.)

❶ Homographs are indicated by superior numbers

❷ Lower case b. indicates a possible *blend* (of flounce and flounder); the preceding ? indicates the etymology is uncertain

❸ Etymology is given in square brackets

❹ Definitions are ordered according to the most common part of speech, followed by the most frequently encountered meaning

❺ Common use is stated in parentheses, followed by a form of the entry word used in a sentence

❻ Illustration of a second homograph, labeled with its English and Latin classification in italics and the length of the species in parentheses

Among the more than 200 consultants specialists from a wide variety of fields are Craig Claiborne, Erik Erikson, Andreas Feininger, Toni Morrison, Richard Sennett, and James D. Watson.

Random House, a major trade book publisher, is no stranger to the reference book field; in 1947 they published the *American College Dictionary*. In the past ten years, through the use of electronic data processing, the firm's dictionary editors have been able to research "texts of every written material imaginable—newspaper and magazine articles, stories, textbooks, novels, even specialized texts ranging from parts catalogs through articles in technical and scholarly journals to court decisions." Tape recordings of radio and television programs have been analyzed for pronunciation.

III. Comprehensiveness

The editors' goal in preparing this dictionary has been to provide "judicious selectivity." Such contemporary words as **AIDS**, **ayatollah**, **chemotherapy**, **modem**, **Heimlich maneuver**, and **freebasing**, are included; however, other such current terms as *Alzheimer's disease*, *laparoscopy*, *redshirt*, and *arthroscope* are not. Curiously, every breed of dog checked by the reviewers was provided, but only **Siamese** and **Manx** cat breeds were found. Cats are so generally excluded that **blue point** is defined as an oyster but not as a type of cat. However, although the general selection sometimes appears limited in certain subject areas, the dictionary is more than adequate in its coverage of present-day American English.

The editors have also provided excellent usage notes and synonym lists. The entry **because**, for instance, includes a long usage note that explains the difference in meaning among its synonyms **as**, **since**, **for**, **inasmuch as** and gives an example for the proper use of each synonym. Each synonym in the dictionary is cross-referenced, and synonyms are provided whenever possible. The reader, therefore, has the greatest chance of choosing the proper word. Quotations from literature and the sciences are not included. But, in view of the extensivje usage notes and synonym lists, this is not a serious drawback.

Etymologies are included at the end of each entry, allowing the reader to concentrate on spelling, definition, and usage, which are probably the most frequently used feature of the dictionary. The etymologies are well prepared. Words are carefully traced from one language and time period to another. The etymology key and language abbreviation table are conveniently placed on the front end paper. The bibliographic entries are extensive (numbering some 700) but far from comprehensive.

The appendixes provide useful reference material. For example, the list of "Signs and Symbols" contains, among others, the signs of the zodiac, mathematical symbols, and musical notation.

IV. Quality and Currency of Entries

Entries consist of main entry word (in boldface), pronunciation, part of speech, restrictive label (if applicable), inflected forms, definitions, etymology, and synonyms. Antonyms and usage notes for many words are included.

High school seniors and graduates should be able to understand the definitions with little difficulty. The definitions are thorough, detailed, and descriptive. The entry **farm**, for example, includes reference to "farm teams" in baseball, as well as historical and obscure meanings. The entries **wave** and **vector** explain the scientific meanings in intelligible and precise language. The entry **double-time** includes the number of paces a marching troop takes in one minute at this speed. The **fandango** is described as a "lively Spanish or Spanish American dance . . . performed (while) playing castanets," and the **Charleston** is described as "vigorous."

The most common part of speech is listed first, and for each part the definitions are numbered in order of frequency. Idiomatic meanings and phrases are defined. When necessary, a definition is clarified by a sentence that demonstrates its use. For example, the definition of **whiz** includes one sentence to clarify its meaning as a sound and movement and another sentence for the colloquial meaning ("expert at a particular activity").

V. Syllabication and Pronunciation

Syllabication is provided as a guide for both pronunciation and written word breaks. Main entries are syllabicated by centered dots "according to the usual American principles of word division, as observed . . . in printing and typing." Pronunciations are syllabicated to provide "a visual aid in sounding out a word." For quick reference, a shortened pronunciation table is included at the bottom of every page. The table refers to the full key printed in large type on the front flyleaf. In place of the International

Phonetic Alphabet symbols, 47 phonetic symbols with six diacritical marks are used.

The guide to the dictionary explains both syllabication and pronunciation, although it assumes a full understanding of phonetics on the part of the reader. While it will not always be necessary to consult the pronunciation guide, some symbols such as the schwa (ə), "th" variant, and a, ā, ä, and â may require further explanation, which can be found in the key. The pronunciation most frequently used among educated speakers is given first. Permissible variants are also included.

VI. Special Features

The work has a number of special features that merit discussion. Most important are the prefix tables for **re-**, **pro-**, **well-**, **un-**, **over-**, etc. that appear in their respective alphabetical sections. The periodic table of elements is included, as is the International Phonetics Alphabet. The appendixes include a list of U.S. and Canadian colleges and universities, a list of English given names, and a manual of style. The final endpapers contain weight and measurement tables and a list of five foreign alphabets and their transliterations.

Entries for plants and animals include the Latin names, and entries for chemical elements include symbols, atomic weights, and numbers. Biographies are also included within the alphabetical list. Aside from U.S. presidents, the twentieth-century names listed include **Camus**, **DiMaggio**, **Einstein**, **Garbo**, **Giraudoux**, **Heifetz**, **Hitler**, **Fulbright**, **Van Doren**, **Van Vechten**, and others. Each entry includes birth and death dates and a brief descriptive phrase. These biographical entries are useful mainly for spelling purposes. Finally, the guide to the dictionary includes a few essays on language that will be of interest to scholarly readers.

VII. Accessibility

The volume includes a brief but useful table of contents that directs readers to the dictionary's charts, special features, and items in the appendixes. The dictionary is also thumb-indexed (two letters per tab). Each thumb tab is midway between the letters. There are no tabs for the introductory material or the appendixes.

Page numbers are centered at the top of the page between the two columns. There are also two guide words at the top of each page, allowing the reader to see at a glance the range of entries on the particular page.

Variant spellings are cross-referenced to the most common spelling. This permits the user to establish the preferred spelling and to distinguish misspellings from variants.

VIII. Graphics and Format

The volume contains approximately 1,500 illustrations, all clear black-and-white line drawings or diagrams. Definitions for many entries such as **graph**, **geodesic dome**, **lantern**, and **water gauge** are graphically explained through illustration. Some other entries, such as **cross** and **vault**, include multiple illustrations for various types of the item. Illustrations do not always show variations, however. The entry for **column**, for example, illustrates the parts of a Roman column but not the five orders; they are depicted at the entry **order** but without cross-reference. Informative maps are included for a variety of geographic regions and countries, both modern and historical.

The dictionary has a bold red dust jacket that describes some of its more important features. The cover is also red with gold letters on the spine. The hardback curvature spine is tight and durable enough to withstand repeated use in a library or at home. There is sufficient gutter margin to permit the reader to see the full page without straining the binding. The paper is white, but rather thin, with some showthrough. The publisher has used a variety of typefaces within each entry: boldface, italic, roman. Each is clear and precise but small.

IX. Summary

On the whole, *The Random House College Dictionary: Revised Edition* is an exceptionally good dictionary. The definitions are substantial and easy to understand. The usage notes, synonym lists, graphics, and some special features are genuine aids to the everyday user. The "Guide to the Dictionary" is detailed and clear, but it does assume some sophistication on the part of the reader. The two areas of concern are minor. A few contemporary words, such as *downlink* and *null-modem* have been omitted. The typeface is somewhat small. But these problems do not substantially diminish the many strengths of this dictionary. Because it supplies not only a variety of definitions for each entry, but information on usage and etymological history, as well as other encyclopedic information, the dictionary would be very useful for a library, a high school or college student, or a general reader.

The Random House Dictionary

Facts at a Glance

Full Title: **The Random House Dictionary.**
Publisher: Ballantine Books.
Editors: Jess Stein, Editor-in-Chief; P. Y. Su.
Copyright: © 1980.

Number of Volumes: 1.
Number of Entries: approximately 74,000.
Number of Pages: 1,072.
Trim Size: $4\frac{1}{8}'' \times 6\frac{7}{8}''$.
Binding: paperback.

Price: $3.50.
Intended Readership: high school and up.
Sold in bookstores and other outlets; also sold to libraries and schools. ISBN 0-345-32298-3.

I. Introduction

The Random House Dictionary is a paperback edition of the hardcover RANDOM HOUSE DICTIONARY: CONCISE EDITION. The publisher's jacket blurbs proclaim this as "the finest, most useful paperback dictionary" and "the largest dictionary of its kind." While such statements may be regarded as advertising hyperbole, *The Random House Dictionary* is a major work in the paperback dictionary category.

II. Authority

The Random House Dictionary was prepared by Random House's permanent lexicographic staff under the direction of Stuart Berg Flexner and Jess Stein, both of whom are distinguished lexicographers. Flexner, noted for his studies of American slang, was also a moving force behind the OXFORD AMERICAN DICTIONARY. Random House has an established reputation as a leading dictionary publisher. Ballantine, who publish this paperback edition, are a division of Random House.

The publisher notes that in compiling this dictionary, its staff lexicographers were assisted by "many hundreds of scholars, educators, and specialists"; none, however, are identified.

III. Comprehensiveness

The Random House Dictionary contains slightly over 74,000 entries, compared to 60,000 in the Dell AMERICAN HERITAGE DICTIONARY, 57,000 in the MERRIAM-WEBSTER DICTIONARY, and 82,000 in FUNK & WAGNALLS STANDARD DICTIONARY. The

The Random House Dictionary

❶ Homographs are marked by
superior numbers

❷ Irregularly spelled inflected
forms are followed by defined
parts of speech for the main
entry. Illustrative phrases or
sentences are italicized

❸ Usage labels are provided in
italics

❹ Idioms, in boldface, are given
style labels and defined

❶ **stick¹** (stik), *n.* **1.** a twig or branch cut
or broken off. **2.** any slender, long
piece of wood, as a club or drumstick.
3. *Brit.* cane (def. 1). **4.** anything
resembling a stick in shape. **5.** *Informal.* an unenthusiastic person. **6. the ❸
sticks,** *Informal.* rural districts.
stick² (stik), *v.,* **stuck, stick·ing,** *n.*
—*v.t.* **1.** to pierce or puncture with
something pointed. **2.** to thrust in
(something pointed) so as to pierce or
puncture. **3.** to fix in position. **4.** to
fasten or attach by glue, moisture, etc.
5. to render unable to proceed or go
back: *The car was stuck in the mud.*
6. to confuse or puzzle. **7.** *Informal.* to
impose something disagreeable upon.
—*v.i.* **8.** to have the point or points
embedded. **9.** to remain attached by
adhesion. **10.** to remain firm, as in resolution. **11.** to keep or remain steadily
or unremittingly, as to a task. **12.** to
become fastened or stationary by some
obstruction. **13.** to be embarrassed or
puzzled. **14.** to hesitate or scruple.
15. to extend or protrude. **16. stick ❹
around,** *Slang.* to remain or linger.
17. stick by or **to,** to remain faithful
to. **18. stick up,** *Slang.* to rob, esp. at
gunpoint. **19. stick up for,** *Informal.*
to support or defend. —*n.* **20.** a
thrust with or as with a pointed object.

word list was compiled from the Random House citation file, which is based on such sources as books,
periodicals, special vocabulary lists, and radio and
television broadcasts. The publisher claims that among
these entries are "thousands . . . not found in any
other paperback dictionary." This book, however,
has not been revised since 1980.

Given the 1980 copyright, this paperback still provides reasonably adequate coverage of contemporary
American English. Many computer terms, such as
floppy disk, **mainframe**, and **modem** are included.
The computer language **COBOL** is listed, but **FOR-
TRAN** is excluded. There is an entry for **videodisc**,
but none for *compact disc*. *AIDS*, which had not
entered the vocabulary in 1980, is obviously not included in this dictionary; nor is *CAT scan*, which
had. Other words entered in *The Random House
Dictionary* include **chemotherapy**, **ophthalmoscope**,
nosh (Yiddish), and **joie de vivre** (French).

The "Guide to the Dictionary" in the front matter
notes that usage labels, usage notes, etymologies,
and synonyms are given for many of the entries. For
example, the entry for **among** includes a long usage
note that compares the word to *between*; the entry
for **alright** states that the word is usually unacceptable, and refers readers to alternatives. The entry
for **Negro** reports that "Many people today consider
Negro to be derogatory and offensive, preferring the
use of *black*." Usage labels in other entries may note
slang, archaic, and informal expressions. These notes
and labels are standard features and provide the reader
with genuine aids to proper and accurate use of the
language. (Field labels, however, are not included.)

Etymologies are included only intermittently, and,
in fact, are not given for most entries. (An etymology
key is printed on the inside of the back cover.) The
same holds true for synonyms.

IV. Quality and Currency of Entries

As already mentioned, definitions in *The Random
House Dictionary* are concise and economical but by
no means simplistic. Many entries include a phrase
or sentence to illustrate different meanings of a particular word.

The "Guide to the Dictionary" in the front matter
explains clearly how entries are arranged: "Definitions within an entry are individually numbered in a
single sequence, regardless of the groupings according to part of speech. In general, the most common
part of speech is listed first, and the most frequent
meaning appears as the first definition for each part
of speech." Idiomatic expressions are entered in
boldface type under the main entry word to which
they are most closely related, following the definitions for the main entry word.

The following is representative of the entries in
The Random House Dictionary:

de·liv·er (di·liv′ər), *v.t.* **1.** to carry (letters, goods, etc.)
to the intended recipient. 2. to give into another's
possession or keeping. 3. to utter or pronounce: *to
deliver a speech.* 4. to strike or throw: *to deliver a
blow.* 5. to set free. 6. to assist at the birth of.—*v.i.*
8. to give birth. 9. to provide delivery service.—
de·liv′er·er, *n.*

This entry compares favorably with entries for the same word in WEBSTER'S NEW WORLD DICTIONARY and WEBSTER'S II NEW RIVERSIDE DICTIONARY.

Other entries are equally detailed. The word **go**, for example, has 61 separate definitions. Fifteen definitions are given for **hot**, including:

4. having or showing intense or violent feeling: *hot temper*. 5. lustful or lascivious. 6. violent, furious, or intense: *the hottest battle of the war*. 7. absolutely new: *hot from the press*. 8. *Slang*. following very closely: *hot pursuit*. 9. *Slang*. extremely lucky: *a hot crap shooter*. 10. *Slang*. sensational or scandalous: *a hot news story*. 11. *Slang*. stolen recently. 12. actively conducting an electric current: *a hot wire*.

The idiomatic expression **make it hot for** is listed for definition number 14, but the slang term **hot air** is a separate entry. Homographs, such as **content**[1] (matter contained in a book or speech) and **content**[2] (satisfied) are listed as separate entries, distinguished from one another by superscript numbers.

The Random House Dictionary, with a 1980 copyright date, can no longer be considered absolutely current. In 1987, this dictionary could benefit from some revision, given Random House's commitment to high quality dictionaries, and the fact that in 1987 Random House issued a new (second) edition of the unabridged *Random House Dictionary of the English Language*.

V. Syllabication and Pronunciation

Entry words are divided into syllables by centered periods. Pronunciation is given immediately following the entry word. A full-page pronunciation key in the front matter spells out the dictionary's pronunciation system. The system makes use primarily of phonetic respelling, with a minimum of diacritical marks. Long and short vowels are indicated by the traditional marks; the *schwa* (ə) is also used to indicate the sound of vowels in unaccented syllables. Altogether, the dictionary makes use of 45 different symbols.

As a sample of pronunciation respellings that occur in *The Random House Dictionary*, consider:

a·ban·doned (ə ban′dən)
ac·tu·al (ak′cho͞o əl)
de·lin·quent (di ling′kwənt)
flau·tist (flô′tist, flou′-)

There is also a pronunciation key for foreign sounds, employing seven symbols. These apply mainly to

French words (such as **fait accompli**), but also to German, Italian, Spanish, and Scottish pronunciations. Unlike WEBSTER'S NEW WORLD DICTIONARY, for one, *The Random House Dictionary* does not include an abbreviated pronunciation key on each page spread.

VI. Special Features

The Random House Dictionary includes a number of special features that are standard in many paperback dictionaries. Foremost among these is a twenty-page "Basic Manual of Style" appended to the lexicon. The manual attends to such matters of usage as punctuation, division of words, abbreviation, capitalization, and footnotes and endnotes. This section will be particularly useful to students as a quick reference source on style.

Other special features include a three-and-a-half page table of common signs and symbols (used in astronomy, mathematics, medicine, religion, and other fields), proofreaders' marks, forms of address, and weights and measures. These basic, straightforward features all provide useful ready-reference information and enhance the value of this dictionary, especially for students.

VII. Accessibility

Entry words are set in boldface type, making them readily accessible. Inflected forms, variant spellings, and idioms are also printed in boldface, which makes them immediately distinguishable from the rest of the text. The number preceding each definition is boldface as well. Note, however, that main entry words overhang the text by only one character.

Guide words at the top of each page indicate the first and last entry on that page. The table of contents makes the special features accessible at a glance.

VIII. Graphics and Format

In graphics and format, *The Random House Dictionary* is a match for any other paperback dictionary currently before the public. The book has been thoughtfully designed to enhance accessibility. The typeface is clean, and the type itself large and dark enough to avoid straining the reader's eyes.

The paperback book itself is fairly sturdy although, as one would expect from any paperback with more than 1,000 pages, the spine will break down with regular use, and after a while pages will begin to break away. In this respect, *The Random House Dictionary* is virtually identical to WEBSTER'S NEW WORLD DICTIONARY, WEBSTER'S II NEW RIVERSIDE DICTIONARY, and other books in paperback format.

IX. Summary

The Random House Dictionary is a first-rate paperback dictionary in most respects. It is organized for maximum clarity and accessibility. The definitions are concise and yet express the nuances of meaning that make English such a rich and varied language. Users will find some omissions of recent words, but apart from this drawback, this dictionary will serve the high school student well.

The Random House Dictionary: Concise Edition

Facts at a Glance

Full Title: **The Random House Dictionary: Concise Edition**.
Publisher: Random House.
Editors: Stuart Berg Flexner, Editor-in-Chief; Jess Stein, P. Y. Su.
Edition Reviewed © 1983.

Number of Volumes: 1.
Number of Entries: approximately 74,000.
Number of Pages: 1,072.
Trim Size: 4⅛″ × 6⅞″.
Binding: hardcover.

Price: $5.95.
Intended Readership: high school and up.
Sold in bookstores and other outlets; also sold to libraries and schools. ISBN 0-394-51200-6.

I. Introduction and Scope

The Random House Dictionary: Concise Edition is a hardcover edition of THE RANDOM HOUSE DICTIONARY's paperback edition. Except for the different bindings, copyright dates, and extraneous information on the covers and flyleaves of the paperback, these two dictionaries are identical. Although the *Concise Edition* bears a later copyright date than its paperback sibling, our reviewers are unable to find any revisions or additions in this version.

With its red, simulated-leather cover embossed in gold with the title and the Random House logo, the

Concise Edition would seem to be specially designed for school and library collections. Certainly the hardcover format is much more durable than the paperback. However, this format also presents several problems not evident in the paperback. The pages do not lie flat when the book is opened. The inner margin is scant, and the text tends to spill into the gutter. In short, the cover looks impressive, but this version offers nothing that is not available in the less expensive and more handy paperback edition.

For complete information about the contents of this dictionary, consult the review of THE RANDOM HOUSE DICTIONARY in this Buying Guide.

The Random House School Dictionary

Facts at a Glance

Full Title: **The Random House School Dictionary**.
Alternative Title: The Random House Dictionary of the English Language: School Edition.
Editor: Stuart Berg Flexner, Editor-in-Chief.
Edition Reviewed: © 1984.

Number of Volumes: 1.
Number of Entries: estimated 24,500.
Number of Pages: 908.
Number of Indexes: 1 for a world atlas section.
Number of Illustrations: black-and-white line drawings plus 14-page full-color atlas.
Trim Size: 6⁹⁄₁₆″ × 9⅝″.
Binding: paper over boards.

Price: $15.99.
Intended Readership: high school and up.
Sold in bookstores; also sold to libraries and schools. ISBN 0-676-39289-X.

I. Introduction

Although the publisher intends it for use by older students and adults, *The Random House School Dictionary* could also be used by advanced junior high school students. Originally published in 1970, and subsequently revised in 1971, 1973, and 1978, the work's current edition has a 1984 copyright. It is based on the Random House unabridged (not the new 1987 edition, of course) and college dictionaries. The publisher does not state the number of entries included, but an estimate based on five percent of the pages suggests that the book contains approximately 24,500 main entry words. This school dic-

The Random House School Dictionary

❶ Pronunciation appears in parentheses

❷ Special use is stated in parentheses

❸ Both homographs have a formal etymology, with etymon given a meaning

❹ Definitions are specially ordered according to current, but not necessarily the most common, usage

❺ Additional part of speech and idiomatic use are included in numbered discrimination of meanings of an entry word

❻ Example of a common idiom, defined

> ❶ ❹
>
> **fair¹** (fâr), *adj.* **1.** free from dishonesty or prejudice; just: *The judge made a fair decision.* **2.** according to the rules: *a fair fight.* **3.** moderate or reasonable; average: *a fair amount of money; fair health.* **4.** sunny and fine; not stormy: *fair weather.* **5.** of a light color; not dark: *a fair complexion.* **6.** pleasing in appearance; attractive: *a fair young maiden.* **7.** without mistakes or faults: *to make a fair copy of one's homework to hand in.* **8.** polite or well-spoken: *a fair speech of welcome.* **9.** (in sports) not foul; within the foul lines: *a fair ball.* —*adv.* **10.** in a fair manner: *to play fair.* **11. fair and square,** honestly; justly: *She won the contest fair and square.* [from the Old English word *fæger*] —**fair′ness,** *n.*
>
> **fair²** (fâr), *n.* **1.** an exhibition of farm products and farm animals, with contests to pick the best entries and various kinds of entertainment. **2.** any large exhibition of products: *a trade fair.* **3.** an exhibition and sale of articles to raise money, often for a charitable purpose: *a church fair.* **4.** *Chiefly British.* a gathering of buyers and sellers. [from an Old French word, which comes from Latin *fēria* "holiday"]
>
> ❷ ❸ ❺ ❻

tionary contains approximately 15 percent of the entries found in the publisher's college dictionary and about ten percent of the entries in the previous unabridged work. *The Random House School Dictionary*'s lexicon is intended to reflect current American usage.

II. Authority

Stuart Berg Flexner is the Editor-in-Chief for this school dictionary as well as for the college work. His involvement with the authoritative Random House adult dictionaries helps to ensure editorial consistency. The other members of the editorial staff are identified, but no specific educational consultants are listed, although—according to the preface—this edition was "specially compiled with the assistance of many teachers, principals, linguists, textbook editors and consultants."

The preface further states that the *School Dictionary* makes full use of the parent volumes' "word frequency studies, citation files, and other scholarly resources." The word list is based on the occurrence of words in U.S. school textbooks, works of children's literature, popular magazines, and newspapers recommended for students, as well as on conversational English that students are likely to encounter.

III. Comprehensiveness

This is a relatively brief dictionary, but, as such, it is just comprehensive enough to meet most of its objectives in satisfying its intended readers. How-

ever, certain omissions will limit the work's usefulness to that audience.

The treatment of contemporary computer terms is too haphazard to supplement textbooks. The words **terminal** and **floppy disk** are included, but the words *mainframe, modem,* and *FORTRAN* are excluded. Similar inconsistency in coverage of the vocabulary is evident throughout. *Heimlich maneuver, chemotherapy, Fifth Amendment,* and *pinball* are omitted; **ayatollah, videocassette,** and **electron microscope** are included.

The treatment of sex-related colloquial and formal language is less than adequate, even for a school dictionary. Of course, the "four-letter words" are absent, but so are *pornography, homosexual, lesbian,* the sexual connotation of the word *intercourse,* and *gay* in its homosexual sense. These omissions are not warranted by the work's intended audience or its stated objectives: even conversational English that students are likely to encounter is not as sanitized as this dictionary's lexicon implies. Comparable dictionaries for students at this level, such as THE AMERICAN HERITAGE STUDENT'S DICTIONARY, contain many of the words this work omits; dictionaries for the older audiences the publisher intends to reach include most or all of them.

Geographic and biographical entries are incorporated into the word list. The former include location and, as appropriate, area in square miles, capital, and former name or status. Some information is outdated; for example, **Cambodia** is listed as a main entry, and no reference is made to *Kampuchea*. Biographical entries include dates and a brief identification. Women and minorities are not adequately represented. Although **Martin Luther King** is included, *Frederick Douglass, James Baldwin, Dred Scott, Desmond Tutu, Ralph Bunche, Duke Ellington*, and *Langston Hughes* are not. The work omits *Susan B. Anthony, Elizabeth Stanton, Rachel Carson* (although **Kit Carson** is included), *Amelia Earhart* (**Charles Lindbergh** is included), *Betty Friedan*, and *Harriet Beecher Stowe*.

Occasional entries include synonyms (in some instances a substantial number of them), placed after the definition(s) and separated by semicolons. For example, under **angry**, the first definition, with synonyms, appears as follows:

> 1. feeling anger; furious; enraged; infuriated: *I was very angry at him for coming so late.*

Under **sweet**, the final definition given is:

> 8. a beloved person; dear; darling.

Although the location of these synonyms is described in the work's introductory guide, this format and the absence of labels makes it difficult for novice dictionary users to locate them.

Etymologies are included in some entries. They are located at the end of the entry in brackets, but they do not include any symbols or special notations. Although etymologies are condensed in this dictionary, those provided for **cue**, **limerick**, and **spell**, for example, are quite informative. The editors state, in the guide, that histories are given only for homographs and "words of unusual interest." Finally, some entries include usage notes and labels to show the proper grammatical use of words such as **altogether**, or to prevent offensive improper use, as with **Asiatic** and **Negro**. These notes and labels will be of particular help to young readers who need guidance in effectively using language.

IV. Quality and Currency of Entries

Definitions include entry word, in boldface; pronunciation; part of speech; inflected forms; definition; illustrative sentences or phrases, in italics; idiomatic phrases, etymology; run-in entries; and usage notes. The common meaning of a word is usually given first and the other meanings are given in decreasing order of frequency. Each definition is detailed, specific, and written in a style that can be easily understood by most young readers. For example, the entry **in-**

tolerance refers to beliefs, races, and background. The entry for **power** includes eight different meanings for the noun, plus additional meanings for the verb and the adjective. The word **positive** is provided with 13 definitions, including its specialized uses in grammar, mathematics, and testing.

Each entry contains at least one use of the word in a sentence or a phrase for each definition. In fact, the work relies heavily, and successfully, on these sentences and phrases to reveal meaning. The entry for **equestrian**, for example, gives four definitions with useful illustrative sentences and phrases:

> . . . *adj.* **1.** of or referring to horsemen or horsemanship: *He doesn't ride well enough to compete in the equestrian events.* **2.** mounted on horseback: *equestrian knights.* **3.** showing a person mounted on horseback: *an equestrian statue.* —*n.* **4.** a person who rides horses.

These illustrative phrases are particularly effective for the clarification of idioms and slang. The entry for **pick** includes four idiomatic and two slang uses of the word.

V. Syllabication and Pronunciation

It is easy to use the dictionary to syllabicate words for writing and speaking. Syllables are divided by centered dots; stress marks are used in entries consisting of more than one word. The student guide includes simple rules for dividing words at the end of a line. Pronunciation, too, is easy to understand and a table is included at the bottom of each page. A valuable reference guide for students, and a full pronunciation key with 46 pronunciation symbols, appears on the flyleaf of the front cover. The treatment of pronunciation in the student guide is detailed and readable, but not necessary for casual use. Of particular merit, however, is the full discussion of the schwa (ə) as it is used in phonetics.

VI. Special Features

In addition to the table of weights and measures on the flyleaf of the back cover, the dictionary offers two special features. The first is the "Student's Guide to the Dictionary," designed to teach students how to use a dictionary. The guide—with its series of activities that demonstrate multiple aspects of words and their meanings such as pronunciation, syllabication, combinations, stress marks, dialects, and definitions—helps to develop students' sensitivity to language. It includes exercises that can be used by teachers as homework assignments and as tests.

Used either in the home or in the classroom, this feature will help students make effective use of the dictionary.

The second special feature is an atlas of the world found at the end of the volume. It is colorful and very detailed, but also very hard to read. The type is small, and some of the colors used for print do not contrast properly with other colors on the page, making reading difficult. The light blue type superimposed on a darker shade of blue that represents water is almost unreadable.

VII. Accessibility

Guide words referring to the first and last word on a page are printed in boldface, but there are neither thumb tabs nor thumb indexing, resulting in a volume that is cumbersome to use. Alternative spellings are usefully cross-referenced to the common spelling where most readers would look first. Moreover, a strict letter-by-letter arrangement and a table of contents make it easy to locate various sections.

VIII. Graphics and Format

The illustrations in this dictionary are not as elaborate as those in the publisher's college dictionary, although they remain useful adjuncts to the definitions. The entry for **column**, in the college work is accompanied by a fully annotated drawing of a Roman Doric column. But in the school dictionary, the illustration lacks much of the detail as well as the annotation. The entry for **cross** in the college work is accompanied by drawings of thirteen different crosses; in the school volume there are only four drawings. The illustrations accompanying **graph**, **water gauge**, **electromagnetic**, and other technical terms have, however, been retained. Informative maps of geographical regions, cities, points of interest, and antiquity have also been retained. Illustrations are captioned with main entry words and occasionally with additional phrases of clarification.

The dictionary will prove durable. The hardback binding is tight and the paper is much thicker than that used in most dictionaries. This dictionary should hold up under repeated use in the home and the library. The type is also large, clear, and easy to read, and the boldfaced main entry words overhang the text.

IX. Summary

The Random House School Dictionary is a good beginner's dictionary. Its main problem is its limited coverage of the language and the "squeaky clean"

vocabulary that includes few controversial words. Entries that are included, however, are thoroughly explained. The type size, paper, binding, and introductory guide make the work especially suitable for junior high or middle school students.

Although the comparable AMERICAN HERITAGE STUDENT'S DICTIONARY is more comprehensive and better illustrated—with photographs as well as drawings in its wide outer margins—*The Random House School Dictionary* would be a good purchase for the school library and for the classroom, where the student guide could be put to its best use. Parents should purchase this dictionary with the knowledge that their children will soon outgrow it. Nevertheless, for quick, concise explanations of a wide range of meanings, this work is a valuable addition to the library.

Scott, Foresman Advanced Dictionary

Facts at a Glance

Full Title: **Scott, Foresman Advanced Dictionary**.
Former Title: Thorndike-Barnhart Advanced Dictionary.
Publisher: Scott, Foresman.
Editors: Scott, Foresman dictionary staff.
Edition Reviewed: © 1988.

Number of Volumes: 1.
Number of Entries: 100,000.
Number of Pages: 1,328.
Number of Illustrations: 1,500 (40 percent with second color added).
Trim Size: $7\frac{5}{8}'' \times 9\frac{3}{16}''$.
Binding: hardbound.

Price: $16.94.
Intended Readership: grades 7 through 12.
Sold in bookstores; also sold to libraries and schools. ISBN 0-673-12385-5.

I. Introduction

The *Scott, Foresman Advanced Dictionary*, continuously in print since 1945, is the highest level in the series of dictionaries for younger readers based on the pioneering work of Edward L. Thorndike and Clarence L. Barnhart. This work is written for high school and mature junior high school students, and is designed as a text of essential information about English vocabulary as well as a reference work for use in interpreting other works.

The 100,000 main entry words in this 1988 revised edition (reviewed in an advance copy provided by the publisher) include some 7,500 new words and definitions. This high percentage of new items qualifies the work to be considered as one of the most up-to-date and comprehensive dictionaries available for students at this level, especially since the work was revised only about five years earlier. The current revision has also changed scientific entries to reflect recent scholarship and updated the names of nations and cities, although former names are retained so that the dictionary will be useful as a supplement to older history books and other reference works.

The publishers note that the entries are chosen to help students in reading, writing, listening, and speaking. This reflects the facts that in junior high and high school, students are exposed to more complex information and are speaking and writing at a higher level.

II. Authority

Scott, Foresman, the publisher of the *Advanced Dictionary*, was the first publisher of the Thorndike-Barnhart pioneering youth dictionary in 1929. Since that time, it has maintained an in-house editorial dictionary staff. The authority of the work is further backed by the publisher's extensive citation files, used in the preparation of this dictionary—400,000 citations have been added to the files in the last decade.

III. Comprehensiveness

This dictionary is particularly strong as a support for the reading skills required from the 7th through 12th grades. Outside reading and the use of texts with minimal glossaries are characteristic of instruction at this level, so it is important that terms in the natural and social sciences be given major attention. In the areas of health sciences, for example, entries include such terms as **AIDS**, **interferon**, **monoclonal antibody**, **retrovirus**, **herpes**, and **pacemaker**. In the social sciences, such terms as **client state** and **dialectical materialism** are included, as are U.N. agencies. Coverage of computer terms is excellent: entries include **byte**, **cursor**, **modem**, **mouse**, and such computer languages as **COBOL** and **FORTRAN**.

In a departure from the practice of most high school-level dictionaries, linguistic terms, such as **diphthong** and **inflection**, are included as main entries to help students study the nature of written and spoken language in greater detail. And, as should be expected of a work at this level, terms related to sexual intercourse, procreation, and abortion are defined.

Appropriately differing from more adult dictionaries, the *Scott, Foresman Advanced Dictionary* does not include inflected variants as separate headwords, nor does it include most obsolete terms. Those few obsolete and archaic usages that are included appear as the last of multiple definitions within an entry. For example, the final definition for **nice** appears as

ARCHAIC. affectedly modest; coyly reserved.

Restrictive labels are used for these words as well as for items of slang, dialect, informal usage, and foreign borrowings.

IV. Quality and Currency of Entries

Definitions are brief, lucid, and clarified by excellent illustrative phrases or sentences. In writing the definitions, the dictionary staff has adhered to Thorndike and Barnhart's principles of (a) using words that are simpler than the main entry word and of (b) including all key words in a definition as separate headwords. Scientific and technical terms are made particularly accessible in this manner. For example, **interferon** is defined as

a protein produced by animal cells infected by a virus to protect similar types of cells from infection by the same or other viruses.

Synonyms, parts of speech, and inflected forms, as well as etymologies and pronunciation are also included in the definitions.

In a typical entry, the headword is boldfaced and followed by pronunciation in parentheses, the parts of speech that the word can assume, and inflected verb forms. Multiple definitions of words are given in descending order of frequency of use and divided by parts of speech. Each time a new part of speech is presented, the abbreviation for the part of speech is repeated at the left-hand column and the definitions then follow. Illustrative sentences or phrases are italicized and appear after the meaning of the word they clarify. Etymologies appear in brackets following the definitions. Next may appear inflected forms that are a different part of speech from the words defined, together with an abbreviated part of speech designation. Synonym studies appear last; they give synonyms in boldface and then explain the connotative value of each synonym and how usage varies. All of this information is particularly well suited to the needs of students at the secondary level.

V. Syllabication and Pronunciation

Respellings of words, showing syllable breaks as well as light and heavy stress, are given in parentheses after the main entry word. Syllable breaks are also given for the boldfaced inflected forms wherever they appear in the entry. Syllables are separated by spaces.

The pronunciation system uses 41 symbols. Pronunciation keys showing vowel sounds and consonant digraphs are given on each double-spread, providing quick access for the reader. Full pronunciation keys, including guides to some foreign pronunciations, are given inside the back and front covers.

Variant pronunciations are given in parentheses with the most commonly used pronunciation given first, for example: **greas y** (grē′sē, grē′zē). In the study notes at the beginning of the book, the user is told that when variant pronunciations are included, both are considered equally acceptable. When variant pronunciations are dictated by differing usage, abbreviated part-of-speech designations are given, but all pronunciations are still given after the head word, for example:

sep a rate (*v.* sep′ə rāt′; *adj.*, *n.* sep′ər it).

Foreign pronunciations of borrowings are also given in the initial pronunciation guide, even if they are defined only in the bracketed etymology at the end of the definitions. The symbol for derivation is included in the pronunciation key on each spread. The logic and consistency of this format make it especially effective for the intended audience.

VI. Special Features

A self-study guide to dictionary use appears at the beginning of the book. In this section, students are led through an intensive series of exercises well designed to help them use the dictionary to their best advantage. A second kind of guide appears at the back of the book: a sixteen-page style guide listing details of standard typescript format; rules of capitalization, punctuation, spelling, and word division; and proofreader's marks, all of which will aid students in their report-writing efforts.

VII. Accessibility

The boldfaced entries are printed in slightly larger type overhanging the text. Other than the main entry word, columns are justified right and left. Boldfaced type is also used for all inflected forms, for the synonym designation (**Syn.**) and for each time the syn-

onyms appear in the synonym study. Italics are used for part-of-speech designations and for illustrating sentences and phrases.

Wide side margins and colored rules to set off pronunciation keys and any special charts make the blocks of text easy to read, although the typeface is smaller than those students will normally encounter in their school reading.

Guide words appear on the top outside corners of every page to help locate entries in the lexicon. A detailed contents page makes the main entries of the dictionary easy to find; however, a thumb index has not been provided.

VIII. Graphics and Format

The dictionary is physically well-designed, with sturdy covers that lie flat when opened. The paper is a light cream color with no bleed-through.

Numerous well-chosen graphics are spread evenly throughout the text. The black-and-white illustrations are from one-third to one-half column in width, are carefully captioned, and have lexicon text wrapped around the left of the illustration only. Illustrations include scientific diagrams, drawings, photographs, art reproductions, and movie stills.

Although they also have the effect of breaking up the text, the primary effect of the illustrations is to enhance the definitions. In some cases, the entry definition will give one example of that definition and an illustration will give another. **Reticulate**, for example, uses the idea of reticulated leaves in the definition and an illustration of reticulated markings on a giraffe to expand the definition.

Special charts illustrating such diverse topics as the Richter Scale and Indo-European language families are placed close to appropriate main entry words and are of either half- or full-column width. These charts are listed in the table of contents.

Two kinds of etymological references appear in boxes throughout the text. These are **Word Sources** (lists of English words from a particular language, placed after the main entry word for the name of the language) and **Word Families** (related English words from a common foreign language root).

IX. Summary

The new revision of the *Scott, Foresman Advanced Dictionary* has expanded the comprehensiveness of the dictionary to such an extent that it can now be used by adult students for most private reading and as a writing tool for undergraduate students. However, strict control over the definitions and the careful use of both graphic and text illustration have kept it well within the intellectual reach of the target users in junior high and especially high school. The dictionary can be used in private study as well as in a classroom setting. As a resource for completing classroom assignments, this work would probably be the only outside reference book a high school student would need for daily work.

Many will prefer this work to the standard "college" dictionaries because of the accessible definitions in all areas. It is an exceptionally useful dictionary for all libraries serving student patrons. It is a preferable dictionary for most high school students—even given the high quality of its competitors. THE RANDOM HOUSE SCHOOL DICTIONARY, for instance, has far fewer entries. The *Scott, Foresman Advanced Dictionary* is probably also the preferred choice over WEBSTER'S SCHOOL DICTIONARY for high school students, since it is now more current.

Scott, Foresman Beginning Dictionary

Facts at a Glance

Full Title: **Scott, Foresman Beginning Dictionary**.
Former Title: *Thorndike-Barnhart Beginning Dictionary*.
Publisher: Scott, Foresman.
Editors: E. L. Thorndike, Clarence L. Barnhart, and the Scott, Foresman dictionary staff.
Edition Reviewed: advance folded and gathered sheets of the new edition, © 1988.

Number of Volumes: 1.
Number of Entries: 28,000.
Number of Pages: 832.
Number of Illustrations: 1,275 (75 percent in color).
Trim Size: 8" × 10".
Binding: cloth.

Price: $16.49.
Intended Readership: grades 3 through 5.
Sold in bookstores and other outlets; also sold to libraries and schools. ISBN 0-673-12383-9.

I. Introduction

The *Scott, Foresman Beginning Dictionary* is part of a series of dictionaries, in continuous publication since 1945, designed for children that includes *Intermediate* and *Advanced* editions. At the core of the development of this dictionary is the publisher's intent to capitalize on the fact that children enjoy using words in conversation and writing and learning about words. The new edition is also an excellent example of the key concept pioneered by Edward L. Thorndike and Clarence L. Barnhart: that books for children be created specifically *for* children and not be watered-down versions of adult ones. The 1988 edition of the *Beginning Dictionary* is completely revised and reset, with over 200 new entries that reflect the changing nature of English as well as the changing educational expectations for grades three through five. The dictionary is designed for use in schools and libraries and can be used for personal research or in classroom settings.

II. Authority

The Thorndike-Barnhart series, which Scott, Foresman began publishing in 1929, and to which this dictionary belongs, is highly regarded—not only because it is based on the seminal work of the original compilers, but also because of the strength of the publisher's in-house dictionary staff. The selection of entries for the dictionary is based on continuous reading of current children's literature and texts, as well as on the extensive Scott, Foresman citation files, in which over one and a quarter million examples of words in use are maintained. The dictionary staff also conducts frequency-use and readability studies so that the entries and definitions will be appropriate for the designated grade levels.

III. Comprehensiveness

The entries contain most of the words that young readers in grades three through five might encounter in their personal or classroom reading. The 28,000 entries include a comprehensive group of words related to modern technology, particularly words related to the space program and computer use, which are interesting to contemporary students. Definitions that reflect new uses for words like **shuttle** and **menu** have been added.

One major exception to the comprehensiveness of the work is the exclusion of words for sex organs or references to sexuality and sexual reproduction. For example, even words taught in health classes, such as *fetus*, are excluded. It must be assumed that this omission is deliberate, possibly to avoid antagonizing the conservative school and community markets that object to such realism, because words less likely to occur in texts or books for students of this age, such as **meander**, **peal**, and **utter** are included.

Another area of deficiency is in terms used in general science classes at this level. Words such as *osmosis* and *phloem* are not included. Their absence, and that of the biology terms, might not be noted in a classroom, since they might be included in the glossaries of science texts, but for use in a library or at home, the exclusions limit the value of the dictionary. The next higher level in the Scott, Foresman series, the *Intermediate Dictionary*, does include all of the terms that might appear in fourth and fifth grade science and health texts that are absent from this version.

Etymologies are given by two methods: (1) printed in blue in brackets after the entry, or (2) placed in illustrated boxes that are captioned "Word History." In order not to confuse the young learner with foreign language terms, the base language and the meaning of the original term, rather than the term itself, are given. Exceptions are made for words like **post meridian** that are in current usage. Etymologies are also part of the "Student's Reference Section" in the back of the dictionary, where four pages are devoted to listing borrowings used in English, including those from Mexican Spanish and Native American languages. The percentage of words for which derivation is given is very small and usually revolves around an interesting anecdote.

The selection reflected in the dictionary is well balanced. It covers curricular disciplines and a variety of parts of speech. The balance in parts of speech is especially well suited for students of this age because most younger dictionaries concentrate on verbs and nouns, which can be fairly easily defined. At this age, however, students are expanding their use of concrete adjectives and adverbs in speech as well as in reading and writing, so they need to be able to look up, identify, and absorb many of these abstract terms: this dictionary is an excellent tool for this purpose.

IV. Quality and Currency of Entries

Typical entries include the main entry word in boldface; the respelling of the word showing pronunciation, syllabication, and stress; the definition with an illustrative sentence; and the part of speech. The part of speech is sometimes omitted, for no apparent reason. When a word has more than one definition, each is preceded by boldface numerals; definitions are presented in descending order of frequency of use. If the different meanings of the words reflect different parts of speech, the numerals are used at the end of the entry to indicate the part of speech for each entry: for example,

pock·et (pok′it), **1** a small bag sewed into clothing for carrying money or other small articles. **2** to put in one's pocket. **3** meant to be carried in a pocket: *a pocket handkerchief.* **4** small enough to go in a pocket: *a pocket camera.* **5** an airpocket. **1,5** *noun*, **2** *verb*, **3,4** *adjective*.

Homographs, such as **pawn**, are treated as separate entries.

The definitions are concise, crisp, and simple, reflecting Thorndike's premise that definitions for children should explain the main entry word in language that is simpler than the entry word itself. Where words of equal difficulty are used, the illustrative sentence or phrase attempts to teach the young reader how to use the main entry word.

V. Syllabication and Pronunciation

Main entry words are divided into syllables, shown by centered dots, and followed by pronunciations that appear in parentheses. Variant word forms are also syllabicated. A key to 23 pronunciation symbols appears in the upper right-hand corner of each double-page spread, and all of the pronunciation symbols are clearly explained in the introduction to the dictionary. Heavy and light stress marks are used to show emphasis.

When a word has more than one meaning and differing pronunciations are used, all pronunciations are still given right after the main entry word and the bold numbers that precede each of the definitions are used to match up correct pronunciations: for example, **re · fill** (rē′fil for *1*; rē′fil′ for *2 and 3*). A few variant pronunciations are given: nü mō′nyə *or* nyü mō′nyə for **pneumonia**; but most entries show only one pronunciation, that of standard American English. One interesting change in pronunciation in this edition is the inclusion of the current as well as the traditional pronunciation of **Uranus** (yùr′a nəs *or* yə rā′nəs); in the advanced level of the dictionary series, only the first, the current scientific pronunciation, is given.

VI. Special Features

Self-teaching lessons on how to use the dictionary are included in the first section of the book. These are well chosen and are interesting as well as informative. Exercises are included. Although permission to reproduce the exercises is given and students are told to copy items such as crossword puzzle grids, students will be tempted to fill in some of the answers in the lessons, making for greatly reduced value to the next student using the book.

A special 32-page "Student's Reference Section" at the back of the lexicon includes astronomical and world maps as well as other research tools for studying curriculum-related topics, such as the water cycle, food groups, the earth, and so forth.

VII. Accessibility

The boldface main entry words are in slightly larger type than the definitions. The variant forms of words appear in smaller bold type at the end of entries where they can be readily seen. The ragged-right edge of each column of type forces the eye to the left and is an aid in finding main entry words.

Guide words for the first and last words are in large boldface type at the outer top corners of each page; their use is carefully explained in the introductory material.

Italic print is used to set off illustrative sentences and phrases. Unfortunately, italic is also used for the next item in the entry, the part of speech (which is spelled out rather than abbreviated); the juxtaposition does not detract from the example sentence, but it does make it harder to distinguish a word's part of speech.

Vertical bars of color about 2¾″ long are printed at the right-hand margins of all pages with the letter of the alphabet appearing in white—a kind of thumb-indexing system. The colors also divide the dictionary into three main parts for easier accessibility: red bars are used for the letters *A* through *F*; blue bars for *G* through *P*; and teal green for *Q* through *Z*. Students of this age are just learning to find words in alphabetical order, so these techniques are appropriate and also helpful.

VIII. Graphics and Format

The graphics in this dictionary are excellent. All illustrations are full-column width and are placed close to the appropriate main entry word, usually right after it or directly opposite. As with the word list and the definitions, the illustrations are up-to-date, with Darth Vader illustrating the word **sinister** and an orange, spiked punk hairdo illustrating **conspicuous**. Cartoons, diagrams, classic photographs, famous paintings, and sculpture are used as illustrations as well as the more usual photographs and line drawings. Illustrations are used to best advantage in this dictionary when they depict the emotional aspects of adjectives, or abstract ideas, or actions, or when they depict a useful but less familiar second or third meaning of a word.

The number of a particular word meaning in an entry is included in the caption of the illustration.

Both English and metric size measurements are given in captions to pictures of animals.

Care has been taken to include photographs that are ethnically balanced and ones that show both females and males in active, passive, and caregiving roles.

Overall, the dictionary is colorful and appealing with appropriately sized type. The paper is bright white and of heavy stock with good opacity.

IX. Summary

The *Scott, Foresman Beginning Dictionary* is an excellent resource tool for students in the third through fifth grades. The quality of the word list and definitions is exceptional, and the attractive format makes the content accessible to the reader. The illustrations are not only attractive but also are a useful adjunct in clarifying definitions. The publishers have not rested on the laurels of past successes but have created a work that is in every way up-to-date.

Although it is designed for young readers, this dictionary is broadly based enough to make it appropriate for use with adult students of English as a second language or in developmental reading classes for adolescents or adults. It is a worthwhile addition to home, school, or public library collections.

Scott, Foresman Intermediate Dictionary

Facts at a Glance

Full Title: **Scott, Foresman Intermediate Dictionary.**
Former Title: Thorndike-Barnhart Intermediate Dictionary.
Publisher: Scott, Foresman and Company.
Editors: E. L. Thorndike and Clarence L. Barnhart.
Edition Reviewed: © 1988.

Number of Volumes: 1.
Number of Entries: 68,700.
Number of Pages: 1,136.
Number of Illustrations: 1,700 (40 percent in two colors).
Number of Maps: 6 pages in full color.
Trim Size: 8″ × 10″.
Binding: cloth.

Price: $16.69.
Intended Readership: grades 5 through 8.

Sold to libraries and schools; also sold through magazine and newspaper advertising. ISBN 0-673-12384-7.

I. Introduction

The *Scott, Foresman Intermediate Dictionary* is the middle volume in the publisher's excellent series of dictionaries for young readers. Developed by E. L. Thorndike and Clarence L. Barnhart, the series has evolved for over six decades under a policy of continuous revision and improvement. (The edition reviewed was available in February 1987, carrying a 1988 copyright.) The work is intended for both home study and school use by students in middle and junior high schools. The editors define the work's audience as "young people who are passing from the simple curriculum of the lower elementary grades to the more complex studies of high school." In addition to fifth- through eighth-graders, the work's audience will include mature or gifted elementary students and older students in English as a Second Language courses and adult education programs.

The dictionary is designed to serve as a companion to reading as well as a source of vocabulary for writing. It is also intended as a broader-ranging educational tool, a source of encouragement to young people to seek out and retain interesting linguistic information.

The 68,700 entries in this revised edition reflect a thorough updating of previous works, both in the addition of new entries and in the revision of existing entries to reflect current usage.

II. Authority

Editorial responsibilities for this work were assigned to Scott, Foresman's respected in-house dictionary staff. Their work is based on the extensive (over one and a quarter million entries) citation files maintained by the staff and on current word frequency studies done by the publisher's reading departments. A wide variety of contemporary textbooks and other literature was also studied in the search for new words and meanings.

III. Comprehensiveness

The major strength of this dictionary lies in its comprehensiveness. Entries thoroughly reflect not only the textbook language that students of this level will encounter but also the vocabulary to which they will be exposed in oral classroom instruction and in their private reading.

The additions appearing in this volume include words related to computer science (**byte**, **debug**, the names of major computer languages, and eighty other terms); names of newly identified diseases (**AIDS**, **Reye's syndrome**); terms related to recent and current events (new names for nations and key cities and names of recent leaders—for example, **Burkina Faso**, **Managua**, **George Bush**); and recent additions to contemporary American idiom (**kasha**, **preppie**, **sashimi**, **windshear**, **workfare**).

As in the case of words related to current events, these additions cover areas in which classroom instruction is based only partly or not at all on texts. In the absence of textbook explanations and glossaries for such curricular material, the dictionary will be an especially useful adjunct. In the areas of health and sex education, instructors will find the work comprehensive: names for sex organs, as well as health and medical terms, are included and defined in simple, yet mature terms.

Entries consist of the entry word in boldface; pronunciation; definition or numbered definitions; in some cases, an illustrative sentence; part of speech, inflected forms or plurals (with syllabication, stress marks, and part of speech); and, for some entries, etymology. A representative entry is that provided for **frisk**:

(frisk), **1** run and jump about playfully; dance and skip joyously: *Our lively puppy frisks all over the house.* **2** search for concealed weapons or stolen goods by running a hand quickly over a person's clothes. *v.* —**frisk'-er**, *n.*

Etymologies are presented in two ways. In some cases, the word is presented in a "Word History" box set off by a colored frame. The language and definition of the root word is given along with a statement explaining how the word came to be given its present meaning. For example, **pedometer** is defined as an

instrument for recording the number of steps taken and thus measuring the distance traveled.

The etymology beneath this entry explains that

Pedometer is from French *pédomètre*, which came from Latin *pedem*, meaning "foot," and Greek *metron*, meaning "a measure."

Most etymologies, however, appear in brackets at the end of the entry. These also give the root form, its language, and its meaning, presented to clarify the evolution of a word toward its current form. For example, the first definition listed for **pelvis** is

the basin-shaped cavity formed by the hipbones and the end of the backbone.

The etymology concluding the entry explains:

[*Pelvis* comes from the Latin *pelvis*, meaning "a basin."]

The etymological information will therefore aid the student in remembering the word's meaning as well as providing insight into the history of the language. Both of these effects are further augmented by the 69 "Word Family" boxes appended to some entries. Set off by a colored frame, these indicate the root of the main entry word and list other words derived from the root. For example, the word family for **peace** consists of "appease, Pacific, pacifier, pacifist, pacify, pay."

IV. Quality and Currency of Entries

Definitions adhere to the guidelines initially established by Thorndike for youth dictionaries: the words in the definition are simpler than the main entry word; key words within the definition are themselves entry words; and definitions reflect young people's most common use of the word—in multiple senses, as necessary—rather than being simplified versions of adult definitions.

Students of this age group should have no trouble understanding the definitions, which are as clear as they are current. For example, **modem** is defined as

an electronic device that enables a computer to send or receive information or instructions by telephone lines.

If the student should require elaboration of the word "electronic," he or she would find that it is the adjectival form of **electronics**,

[the] branch of physics that deals with the production, flow, motion, and use of electrons in vacuums and gases. Electronics has made possible the development of television, radio, radar, and computers.

As in this case, the illustrative sentences are carefully designed to amplify and clarify definitions.

V. Syllabication and Pronunciation

Appropriately for this age level, syllable breaks are indicated by spaces rather than a graphic device that might interfere with students' ability to interpret diacritical marks. Pronunciation appears in parentheses after the main entry word. A simple system of 44 symbols and four diacritical marks is used. A full key appears on the inside of both covers; an abbreviated key, for quick reference, appears in the upper right corner of each double-page spread.

Variant pronunciations are given following the pronunciation most frequently used. For example, the pronunciation of **amateurish** appears as

(am′ə chur′ish *or* am′ə tyur′ish).

When variant pronunciations are dictated by varying definitions, as in the case of **separate**, numerals following each pronunciation are keyed to the appropriate definitions. Students should have no trouble using this system. Pronunciations of foreign language words found in etymologies are not given.

VI. Special Features

In addition to the valuable "Word History" and "Word Family" boxes, the dictionary contains special features that impart dictionary use skills and those that expand the work's range as a reference source. At the front of the volume appears a guide, "How to Use This Dictionary," explaining the varieties of information contained in the dictionary and how it is to be located. The guide includes clear directions and lively exercises geared to helping the user feel comfortable with the book. An answer key appears in the back of the volume. Although the student is given specific instructions to complete the exercises on a separate piece of paper, the exercises are set up in workbook form and include puzzle grids. Students will be tempted to write in the book, which may limit its repeated use in a school setting. However, permission is given by the publisher to reproduce the exercises for classroom use.

A "Table of Measures and Weights," reflecting both metric and customary U.S. systems, is incorporated in the word list. Additional information appears in the 32-page, full-color "Student's Reference Section" at the back of the dictionary. Material included in this section will apply to the user's studies in a range of subjects including geography, history, science, and mathematics, as well as language. Particularly noteworthy are sections titled "English Words Borrowed from Mexican Spanish," "English Words from Native American Words," and "Proofreading."

VII. Accessibility

Alternative spellings are easily located; they appear in boldface type after main entry words; for example, **the a ter** or **the a tre**. The dictionary is not thumb indexed, nor are colored tabs or bars used to highlight letter sections. This is acceptable in a dictionary at this level, although, given the size and weight of the volume, it may prove initially difficult to younger users. Guide words appear at the top of each page, indicating the first and last entry on the page. A table of contents at the front of the volume lists special features; the "Student's Reference Section" has its own detailed contents list.

VIII. Graphics and Format

Main entry words are boldfaced and overhang the text; their typeface is slightly larger than that used in the rest of the entry, which is itself clear and sufficiently large to be read easily. The right-hand margins are ragged; this avoids hyphenation and provides for reading ease.

The work is heavily illustrated with black and white photographs and drawings, many with a second color added. They include art reproductions, motion picture stills, cartoons, maps, and diagrams, as well as more conventional drawings and photographs. All illustrations are full-column width and are placed before, after, or across from the word they clarify. They are captioned with main entry words and, where necessary, a numeral in parentheses indicating which of several definitions is illustrated. Many captions also include a phrase or sentence using the entry word, and when an illustration defines an emotion or abstract term, such as **elation**, a statement clarifies the relationship between illustration and term.

The dictionary is physically well designed with sturdy board covers that lie flat when open. It will hold up well to heavy use. The paper is bright white; minimal bleed-through is visible only in open areas and does not impede reading.

IX. Summary

This revised edition of the *Scott, Foresman Intermediate Dictionary* manifests outstanding coverage of words likely to be encountered by middle and junior high school students. The dictionary is attractive and well designed; every feature in the text and illustrations is chosen for its value in conveying meaning and usage.

The work will prove especially valuable as a school dictionary. It is up-to-date in the words it includes and in biographical and geographic information. Special features are geared to many areas of the school curriculum. The dictionary can also be used effectively by a student working alone in a library or at home. The format encourages browsing, while the illustrations and special feature boxes entice the user to learn new words.

Scribner Beginning Dictionary

Facts at a Glance

Full Title: **Scribner Beginning Dictionary**.
Publisher: Scribner.
Editor: Phyllis R. Winant.
Edition Reviewed: © 1986.

Number of Volumes: 1.
Number of Entries: 30,000.
Number of Pages: 786.
Number of Illustrations: 1,200 in full color.
Number of Maps: 10 pages in full color.
Trim Size: 8″ × 10″.
Binding: laminated paper over boards.

Price: $18.15.
Intended Readership: grades 3 through 5.
Sold to schools only. ISBN 0-022-50870-8.

I. Scope and Format

As indicated on the copyright page of the MACMILLAN DICTIONARY FOR CHILDREN (which is a trade edition of this work), pages 1–724—the dictionary lexicon—of the MDC "are published in text editions under the titles MACMILLAN BEGINNING DICTIONARY and *Scribner Beginning Dictionary*. They have also been licensed to Field Enterprises Educational Corporation and appear in the CHILDCRAFT DICTIONARY." A full review of the MACMILLAN DICTIONARY FOR CHILDREN in this Buying Guide provides details on this volume.

School libraries will be interested in the MACMILLAN BEGINNING DICTIONARY or the Scribner edi-

The Scribner-Bantam English Dictionary

❶ Entry word is divided by dots into syllables, followed by phonetic respelling between slashes

❷ Etymology within brackets follows the pronunciation or main entry

❸ Synonyms, discriminations (usage notes), and antonyms are introduced by small capital letters preceded by parallel bars

❶ ❷ ❸

de·cep·tion /disep′shən/ [OF *decepcioun* < L *deceptus* deceived] *n* 1 act of deceiving; 2 state of being deceived; 3 that which deceives; fraud ‖ de·cep′tive *adj* ‖ SYN deceit, deceitfulness, falsehood, hypocrisy, dissimulation, guile, fraud, duplicity, delusion, untruth ‖ DISCR *Deceit* and *deception* both name the act of deceiving, but *deceit* always involves the intent to deceive; *deception*, though it may result from the intent to deceive, may also be unintentional. *Deceit* is practiced upon the understanding; *deception* may affect the senses as well. A mere false impression constitutes a *deception*; self-*deception* is common. *Deceitfulness* names the vice of, or tendency to, *deceit. Duplicity* is deliberate bad faith; it is accomplished by acting in one way while feeling, or intending to act, in another. *Guile*, as a characteristic, names a propensity to deceive that permeates the whole man; as an act, it denotes a *deception* accomplished by wiles or subtle artifice. An *untruth* is a false statement, spoken or written ‖ ANT frankness, veracity, honesty

tion, whereas public librarians will want to consider the MACMILLAN DICTIONARY FOR CHILDREN, as would parents of elementary students.

The Scribner-Bantam English Dictionary

Facts at a Glance

Full Title: **The Scribner-Bantam English Dictionary**.
Publisher: Bantam Books.
Editor: Edwin B. Williams.
Edition Reviewed: © 1979; 10th printing, 1985.

Number of Volumes: 1.
Number of Definitions: over 80,000.
Number of Pages: 1,120.
Trim Size: 4⅛″ × 6⅞″.
Binding: paperback.

Price: $3.95.
Intended Readership: high school and up.
Sold in bookstores and other outlets; also sold to libraries and schools. ISBN 0-553-24974-6.

I. Introduction and Scope

The Scribner-Bantam English Dictionary has been available since 1977. Revised in 1979, it is described by its publisher as offering over "80,000 definitions" and as being the "largest paperback dictionary of its kind." The *main* entry count, as opposed to the def-

initions, is closer to approximately 56,000 entries. This category of dictionary includes, for example, the Dell paperback edition of THE AMERICAN HERITAGE DICTIONARY and the Warner paperback edition of WEBSTER'S NEW WORLD DICTIONARY OF THE AMERICAN LANGUAGE. Although it concentrates on American English, the Scribner-Bantam lexicon includes meanings from other English-speaking countries. According to the publisher, this dictionary "leans towards being prescriptive" and it is intended to be a "teaching dictionary" that will meet the needs of students as well as adults.

II. Authority

This is the first general English-language dictionary that either Scribners or Bantam has published. General Editor Edwin B. Williams, lexicographer and former chairman of the Department of Romance Languages at the University of Pennsylvania, headed the distinguished staff of academics and lexicographers, listed in the front matter, that created this work. There is no mention of a citation file or of any word lists, and literary and scientific quotations are not included as examples of usage in the entries. Instead, the editors state that this dictionary "is based on all the English language dictionaries in print, on other printed and spoken sources and on consultation with authorities in many fields."

III. Comprehensiveness

According to the publisher, this dictionary has "more information than in any other dictionary of its kind . . . including new words and technical-scientific terms appearing in no other dictionary." The range of the dictionary is indeed wide and should well serve the student and general adult user. However, because it has not been revised since 1979, the vocabulary does not include many commonly used words found in other dictionaries of more recent date. It does contain a large number of biographical and geographic entries within the main vocabulary, which is a very useful feature for students. However, once again, the information is not up-to-date, or in the case of population figures, not dated at all. The dictionary also contains many abbreviations, chemical elements, foreign words and phrases, and slang terms (excluding the notable four-letter ones), as well as an excellent emphasis on synonyms, with distinctions between fine shades of meanings, and antonyms.

IV. Quality and Currency of Entries

Definitions are arranged according to frequency of use. They are often short and incomplete, and they rarely include a sentence to illustrate meaning. The definition of **bluepoint**, for example, refers to oysters but not Siamese cats. The entry for **orthodox** refers to the Eastern Orthodox Church but not to Judaism. The definition of **graph**, for example, is difficult to understand because the sense of a graph as a tool for making comparisons is vague:

> **graph** . . . *n* **1** diagram or curve representing the successive values of a changing quantity; **2** written symbol of a sound; **3** diagram expressing a mathematical relation *vt* **4** to represent by a graph.

The words **who** and **whom** are not defined in a way that makes their proper usage clear. **Whom** is defined as "objective case of who." The entry for **who** includes "*colloq* whom, as *who did you speak to?*" The proper use of *who* and *whom* is troublesome enough for students and many casual readers without the obfuscation that these definitions provide.

Variant spellings are usually cross-referenced, although some are included in the same entry. Synonyms are provided in many entries. They flesh out the definitions and offer a rich bounty of alternative choices for readers. Over 150 subject labels, numerous usage labels, and other qualifying terms are a genuine aid. Antonyms are also provided, but less frequently than synonyms. And, finally, the etymologies are unobtrusive and sufficient for readers who do not require a rigorous history of words. Many everyday words such as *aerobics, ayatollah, redshirt, modem, mainframe, floppy disk, bit, byte, database,*

sonogram are omitted—the dictionary is simply not up-to-date for the 1980s.

V. Syllabication and Pronunciation

At the front of the book, there is "A Guide to the Dictionary," where the editors provide a detailed, thorough discussion of syllabication. A long and thorough explanation of pronunciation also appears in the guide, followed by a pronunciation key. They help the reader to understand the respellings that are used.

VI. Special Features

Special features include, in the front matter, the lengthy "Guide to the Dictionary," pronunciation key, and a list of abbreviations used in the dictionary entries. The back matter includes a list of principal languages of the world and a chart of Indo-European languages, a foreign alphabets chart, proofreaders' marks, weights and measures, Roman numerals, and forms of address. A list of pronunciation symbols is the final item and would have been better placed in the front matter with the pronunciation key. Entries for plants and animals include the Latin names, and entries for chemical elements include atomic weights, numbers, and symbols.

VII. Accessibility

A contents page is provided to the main sections of the volume. The guide to the dictionary is well organized, but the reader must have a rigorous knowledge of grammar to appreciate it fully. Guide words listing the first and last entries on each page are included. There is no thumb index. Variant spellings are usually cross-referenced, although some are included in the same entry.

VIII. Graphics and Format

The two-column, concise page is well designed for a paperback edition. The print is small, but clear, with adequate white space. The paper is satisfactory, but the binding is not. This is a very bulky paperback that cannot contain the large number of pages: pages became loose from the binding after only two days of use by the reviewer. As a circulating dictionary, this book would not survive even occasional use in the library, not to speak of a half-dozen tosses into a book return repository.

IX. Summary

As a work that is described as "a teaching dictionary," *The Scribner-Bantam English Dictionary* falls short of providing adequate definitions for many traditional words and fails to include many words in current magazine and newspaper use. Because the paperback is not durable enough to withstand repeated use, it is not suitable for libraries, and it is unlikely to withstand classroom use. Students wishing to own a concise, up-to-date paperback dictionary would be better advised to choose another work such as the *American Heritage* (Dell) paperback or a *Webster's New World* paperback edition.

The Sesame Street Dictionary

Facts at a Glance

Full Title: **The Sesame Street Dictionary**.
Publisher: Random House.
Compiler: Linda Hayward.
Illustrator: Joe Mathieu.
Editors: Sharon Lerner, Editor-in-Chief; Janet Schulman.
Edition Reviewed: © 1980.

Number of Volumes: 1.
Number of Words: over 1,300.
Number of Pages: 253.
Number of Illustrations: full color throughout.
Trim Size: 8½" × 11".
Binding: laminated paper over boards.

Price: $12.95.
Intended Readership: ages 3 to 8; preschoolers and up.
Sold in bookstores. ISBN 0-394-84007-0.

I. Scope and Format

The exuberance of the Sesame Street television show has been translated into a comic-strip style book format in *The Sesame Street Dictionary*. Bert, Ernie, Big Bird, Cookie Monster, Oscar the Grouch, and other familiar characters are here. The Muppets maintain their well-known personalities and continue to teach children in this book of over 1,300 words. According to its preface, the book is designed for children ages three to eight and can be used in three stages: "as a word book and vocabulary builder, as a reading-readiness storybook, [and] as a first dictionary." The word selection was based, the preface states, on "several current vocabulary lists compiled by well-known educators," but these are not identified. Most of the words used are those found in beginning readers and in the everyday language of young children, but others such as **rocket**, **dinosaur**,

and **skeleton**, were chosen because "they fascinate young children," the preface notes.

This book is hardbound; however, the sheets are glued, not sewn, and the endpapers began to tear as the book was being looked at for review. Long-term durability in the hands of young children, therefore, seems unlikely.

II. Authority

The dictionary, which is published by Random House, is copyrighted by Children's Television Workshop, the producers of several television series that have been innovative and creative in educating the very young.

III. Quality and Currency of Entries

The definitions are accurate so far as they go and the vocabulary is geared to very young children and beginning readers. Each word is "defined" by an illustration with a caption—usually a statement by a Muppet—and used in one or two sentences to show context. For example:

> **have** When you have something, it belongs to you.
> **have** Have also means to be holding or keeping something for someone else.

A picture of Big Bird and Little Bird has two comic-book speech balloons:

> I think I **have** your scarf, Big Bird.
> I think I **have** yours, Little Bird.

The main entry words and definitions are in bold lowercase serif type; and the Muppets' speech is always in sans-serif type in the balloons. Many of the interpretations are funnier if the reader is familiar with the individual personalities of the Muppets, but knowledge of the characters is not necessary to enjoy them. For example, **not** is defined with the sentence "Not means in no way." Oscar, shown sitting in his garbage can with odors wafting up from the surrounding plants, says, "I love stinkweed. Stinkweed does **not** smell nice. It smells terrible. That is why I love it." **Silent** is defined by "Silent means without any sound." A huge creature is snoring under a blanket while Big Bird says, "Shhhh! we must be **silent** while Mr. Snuffle-upagus takes his nap!"

The lively interpretations and all their surrounding activity tempt the child to study everything carefully before moving on to the next word. The Amazing Mumford, who appears throughout the book, is

The Sesame Street Dictionary

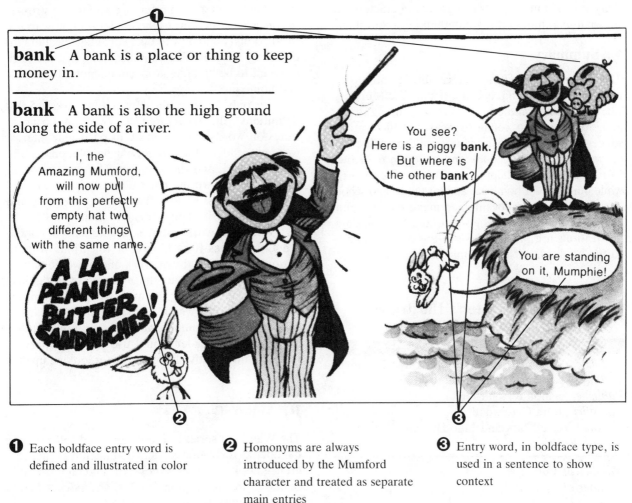

❶ Each boldface entry word is defined and illustrated in color

❷ Homonyms are always introduced by the Mumford character and treated as separate main entries

❸ Entry word, in boldface type, is used in a sentence to show context

the only one who introduces homonyms. Computer words are not defined, and parts of speech, syllabication, pronunciation, and etymology are not given. This is not a flaw, as these are seldom found and would be fairly meaningless in a volume directed toward this very young age level.

Words are in alphabetical order. Each letter of the alphabet is boisterously announced on the appropriate page: an airplane piloted by Grover flies by trailing a banner with the letter *A* in upper- and lowercase; pigs and Oscar romp around *P*; a train brings in *T*. Guide words are used inconsistently at the tops of pages. They appear only when the art does not bleed off the page.

The entry words are in bold type with the definition or descriptive sentence following on the same line. When more than one definition is given, the entry word is treated as another main entry, and occasionally the definition states that it can also mean the other definition. Access is not as easy as in other

dictionaries. The irregular layout often makes it difficult to locate and separate entry words.

IV. Illustrations

The illustrations, which feature extensive use of primary colors, are so eye-catching that one tends to look at them and forget the word being sought. The upper- and lowercase letters that begin a new letter section appear above a horizontal band of color containing all the letters of the alphabet, with the proper letter dropped out in white or printed in another color for emphasis. The color of the band is repeated in horizontal rules separating entries throughout the pages assigned to that letter. However, these are often not readily visible, and sometimes the art almost covers them, so that there is inconsistent visual separation of the boxes in which the entries appear, even though a vertical black rule consistently divides each page into two columns. Jokes, riddles, and stories abound in the brightly colored illustrations. Activity prevails in these drawings; the characters are shown *doing* things rather than thinking about them.

V. Summary

The Sesame Street Dictionary is vibrant and is sure to attract a readership because it stars the Muppets. The definitions can be read by the beginning reader and, for those too young to read, the illustrations suggest stories. Even very young children will enjoy browsing through the book and telling in their own words what they see happening. This may be a worthwhile purchase for home use and for public and school libraries because it does indeed make learning fun. However, buyers should beware of the weak binding; illustrations are printed close to the center margins so the book cannot be rebound easily.

Simon & Schuster's Illustrated Young Reader's Dictionary

Facts at a Glance

Full Title: **Simon & Schuster's Illustrated Young Reader's Dictionary** (Wanderer edition).
Publisher: Simon & Schuster.
Compiler: John Grisewood.
Editors: Grace Clark and Jane Hyman.
Edition Reviewed: © 1984.

Number of Volumes: 1.
Number of Entries: 7,700.
Number of Pages: 240.
Number of Illustrations: 100 in full color.
Trim Size: 4¾″ × 7½″.
Binding: paperback.

Price: $6.95.
Intended Readership: grades 5 through 9.
Sold in bookstores and other outlets; also sold to libraries and schools. ISBN 0-671-50821-0.

I. Introduction

This is the first American edition of *Simon & Schuster's Illustrated Young Reader's Dictionary*, originally published in England by Kingfisher Books Limited, London. The revised and expanded U.S. edition is published by Simon & Schuster's Wanderer Division, and there is a companion thesaurus and atlas in the same format.

In their introductory material, the publishers stress that this dictionary is designed to show young readers "how much fun learning new words can be." The role of a dictionary as a reference tool is also stressed in concise instructions to the reader—on how to use the dictionary and how to take advantage of standard dictionary features. The publisher states that the work is meant to be "a take-along companion" for school and home use.

With only 7,700 main entries (and about 5,000 definitions), the *Young Reader's Dictionary* concentrates on words that might be of particular interest to young readers, those involving people, places, the natural world, and the sciences. The remaining entries consist of words that students might be asked to define in class or that they might encounter and find unfamiliar in their personal reading.

Overall, the work assumes that students of middle school age (ages 10 to 12) will be as curious or more curious about how things work and how people live than they will be about the meaning of unfamiliar words. For this reason, the work is especially appropriate for the child who likes to read; hence the title's emphasis on the young *reader*. It is not unlikely that an avid young reader would use this dictionary as much for informative browsing as for looking up definitions.

II. Authority

The Wanderer series is a well-respected collection of handbooks for young readers that includes other reference books, such as a thesaurus and an atlas (also reviewed in this Buying Guide), and pocket books on such topics as the human body, aircraft, dinosaurs, and chess.

The dictionary was compiled in Great Britain by John Grisewood and edited for use in the United States by Jane Hyman, a school principal who is a trained and experienced reading specialist. The revised and expanded American edition is scrupulous in amending any lexical or syntactic items in the British version that would be even slightly unfamiliar or distracting to the American child. This is in marked contrast to American versions of other works of British origin. As a case in point: the American edition of THE OXFORD CHILDREN'S DICTIONARY defines **circulate** as "to send something round" whereas the *Young Reader's Dictionary* defines **circulate** as to "move or send something around." The adult user of standard American English would automatically substitute the structure "around" for the unfamiliar "round," but the young American reader of the Oxford work might easily be distracted by the vaguely unfamiliar structure and start to think in terms of objects that are round.

Simon & Schuster's Illustrated Young Reader's Dictionary

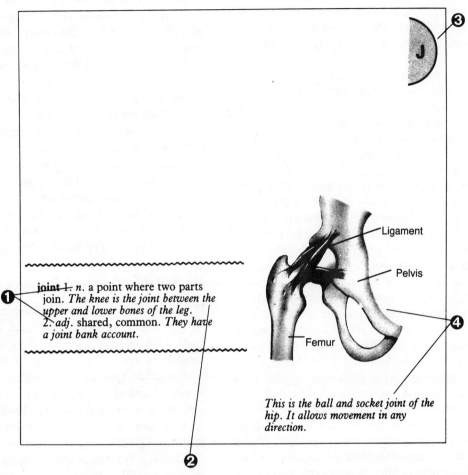

joint 1. *n.* a point where two parts join. *The knee is the joint between the upper and lower bones of the leg.* 2. *adj.* shared, common. *They have a joint bank account.*

Ligament

Pelvis

Femur

This is the ball and socket joint of the hip. It allows movement in any direction.

❶ Abbreviated parts of speech are provided for each numbered definition

❷ Sentences, in italic, assist in understanding the meaning of entry word

❸ Colored, printed thumb tabs appear at the top right-hand side of each page

❹ A four-color illustration with descriptive caption labels and illustrates new vocabulary words

In the case of words with dual British and American forms, such as **petrol** or (car) **bonnet**, the *Young Reader's Dictionary* substitutes the American term (**gasoline**) or definition (bonnet as a headcovering). The Oxford dictionary, in contrast, includes not only the word **petrol** and its British definition but also shows the preferred definition of **bonnet** to be the hood of a car.

Where a lexical item has retained a British name or definition in a significant section of the United States, the Simon & Schuster work gives both the British and American forms but does not label them as such. For example, the definition of **bin** uses the American definition of an enclosed storage space but

also includes the example of a "dustbin." Strictly American works, such as the MACMILLAN DICTIONARY FOR CHILDREN and WEBSTER'S ELEMENTARY DICTIONARY, include only the limited mainstream definition of **bin**, although both volumes are much broader in scope (30,000 and 37,000 entries, respectively).

III. Comprehensiveness

The dictionary contains no etymologies. To a limited degree, however, this work does inform the user that a particular word is derived from a foreign language, without providing the foreign form itself. For example, **boomerang** and **junk** are identified, respectively, as Australian aboriginal and Chinese terms, and a **guillotine** is said to be "named after a Dr. Guillotin" and is linked to the French Revolution. Synonyms are included with entries only as one-word definitions without being specifically identified as synonyms.

The entries include most words a reader of this age group might encounter in private reading, including names for body organs, high level descriptive words, and concrete verbs. However, subject-specific words (**mitosis**, **tangent**) are not included. This is not a serious drawback since most texts prepared for readers in this age range have controlled vocabularies, explain words in context, and provide glossaries so that students usually do not have to look up subject area terminology in dictionaries. However, if the student encounters such words in private reading, this work would provide little help.

The dictionary is also deficient in words of recent origin, particularly those associated with computer technology, an express interest of many students of this age. **Computer** is defined as "an electronic calculating machine that stores information and works with enormous speed"; **calculate** is defined as to "work out with math." Terms associated with space technology also do not appear as main entry words. This lack, however, is partially rectified by the inclusion of lavish diagrams of jet rockets and spacecraft to illustrate other terms. In the captions of these illustrations, many space-related terms (**module**, **pitch**, **roll**, **yaw**, **stages**, **thrust**, **orbits**) are labeled and illustrated rather than defined, a policy that may prove confusing to the young reader.

Since one of the stated goals of the work is to show the user how to spell words, a more serious difficulty is the omission of many simple yet often misspelled words, such as the numbers **forty** and **ninety**, as well as reflexive pronouns (**its**, **it's**, **theirs**).

Nevertheless, as already noted, the work is extremely comprehensive in terms that pertain to the social and natural world. Words associated with the three major Western religions—Christianity, Islam, and Judaism—are defined in some depth. For example, **Islam**, **Koran**, **minaret**, **mosque**, **muezzin**, and **Muslim** are all main entry words. Illustrations also help to define such entries; for example, one shows a muezzin at work and explains his task, while another explains the term **dome** by showing and identifying the Dome of the Rock in Jerusalem.

IV. Quality and Currency of Entries

Typical entries include the main entry word in boldface, an italicized abbreviation of the part of speech, and the definition. Only a few entries include pronunciation guides or examples of how the word is used in a sentence; however, each of the 100 illustrations uses the targeted word in a sentence- or paragraph-long caption. Illustrative sentences appear immediately after the definition and are italicized.

The definitions are brief, easy to understand, and include all meanings appropriate to the reading level of the designated audience. The vocabulary used in the definitions is controlled in two ways: the words used in the definitions are appropriate for fifth to ninth grade readability levels; and all new or possibly unfamiliar words in the definitions are defined by another entry, by an illustration, or within the context of the original definition.

Entries average out to a seventh grade reading level and definitions to a fifth-sixth grade level, as measured by the Fry Readability Graph.

V. Syllabication and Pronunciation

Main entry words are not divided into syllables and no pronunciation key is provided, a distinct drawback—especially in a spelling dictionary. For a small number of entries, a phonetic or rhyming pronunciation guide appears in parentheses after the head word. Sometimes the pronunciation guide gives only a rhyming word, for example, **braille** (*rhymes with sail*). In most cases, when the pronunciation is provided, the guide divides the word into syllables with the stressed syllable printed in boldface and the unstressed syllables printed in italic.

Pronunciations, when given, appear in parentheses directly after the boldface entry and before the part-of-speech designation. There is no identifiable pattern in the selection of words that receive pronunciation guides. Some words, such as **facsimile** (*fak*-**sim**-*ilee*) and **choreography** (*ko-ree*-**og**-*rafee*) are clearly chosen because they might be unfamiliar to the user. Other words, such as **perfume** (*purr* **fyoom**) and **patient** (**pay** *shent*) seem too familiar to be explained, while many words, such as **pupa** and **query**, are not given pronunciation guides.

One appropriate consideration used in choosing words with pronunciation guides was the inclusion of homographs, such as **desert**, that have different stress when used as nouns or verbs; pronunciations are provided for all such words.

The lack of variant pronunciations, however, is a drawback. Most pronunciations are for standard American usage, with a few discrepancies, perhaps never changed from the original British edition (**produce**, n. **prod**-*yous* and vb. *pro*-**dyous**).

VI. Special Features

Other than the comprehensively captioned illustrations described later (see VIII.), the only special feature of this dictionary is a two-page introduction. In clear, concise paragraphs, the introduction explains the standard features of a dictionary and details their use. Included are descriptions of alphabetical order, guide words, and typeface. The second section of the introduction describes the means of identifying parts of speech and of finding the correct definition among multiple meanings. It also tells the reader how to use the illustrating sentences and the 16 abbreviations included in the work.

VII. Accessibility

The boldface entries only slightly overhang the text but can readily be distinguished from it. Boldface variant forms of words appear within or are appended to entries; they can also be easily located. Main entries appear in strict alphabetical sequence; homographs are preceded by numbers. In the tradition of the HBJ SCHOOL DICTIONARY, the parts of speech of homographs are identified with each definition. If a word has two or more homographs that are different parts of speech, the part of speech follows the number:

> **abrasive** 1. *adj.* having the property of grinding something down. 2. *adj.* (of a person) rude, upsetting people 3. *n.* a substance that grinds or smooths.

If a word has homographs and all meanings are the same part of speech, the part of speech is noted immediately after the entry and the multiple meanings are merely numbered:

> **meal** *n.* 1. food eaten at a particular time, e.g., breakfast, lunch and dinner. *When do you have a main meal?* 2. grain ground to powder; flour.

Separate sections of the introduction explain the use of alphabetical order to find words and the means of distinguishing between homographs. Examples of homographs used in the introduction refer to entries on the first page, which faces these instructions—a subtle but insightful detail.

As previously noted, relatively few pronunciation guides and illustrative sentences are used in the dictionary, but when provided, both features are readable.

Colored thumb tabs are included. Although not cut out, they are clearly visible. All the tabs are printed at the top right-hand side of the page, about one-half inch from the top rather than spaced down the side of the page. Even though contrasting colors are used, placing all the tabs at the same level makes it hard to see where one section ends and another begins.

VIII. Graphics and Format

Physically, the volume is quite attractively designed. The typeface and size are similar to those used in paperback books designed for middle and junior high school readers. The paper is bright white and of heavy stock with virtually no show-through. The majority of copies of this dictionary are sold in paperback, although a limited quantity are available in library bindings. The signatures of the paperback version are stitched separately for durability, the books are perfect-bound, and the cover is of heavy, coated stock.

The illustrations, which include four-color drawings, photographs, and diagrams, are of outstanding quality, large, bright, and attractive. Parts of many diagrams and specific features of drawings are carefully labeled. Captions are extensive and reinforce the definitions of words described in the illustrations. In addition, captions and labels often introduce new terms that are not main entry words. For example, the illustration for **tide** illustrates and defines not only the main entry word but also **neap** and **spring** tides. The illustration of the **heart** defines **auricle** and **ventricle** as well and shows the circulation route of blood through the heart. Clearly, the illustrations demonstrate the publisher's intent to present a book that is fun and interesting to read. However, the practice of introducing new terms and concepts as a part of illustrative material rather than within definitions is not ideal for the intended readership.

IX. Summary

Simon & Schuster's Illustrated Young Reader's Dictionary is a convenient handbook for those youngsters who want to know more about words and are curious about their world. Although this work heavily emphasizes words that are related to the social and natural sciences, it is presented in an attractive format and is easily understood.

The work is most appropriate for younger middle school students but could be of interest to younger, gifted students or older, slower students. The dictionary satisfies the traditional role of the children's dictionary in helping readers acquire a more mature vocabulary by introducing words that are interesting to children. The work might have valid classroom use as an auxiliary reference or for home reading by a child who does not like to read fiction and cannot yet handle advanced prose in the sciences.

While this work is useful and extremely attractive, it also presents a number of deficiencies. It lacks etymologies and its policy regarding pronunciation guides appears extremely haphazard. The dictionary does not cover a sufficiently broad spectrum of technical and other recent terms, its range of words in several other areas is not as comprehensive as it might be, and it does not include many frequently misspelled words. Moreover, while its definitions are usually short but sufficient, the book follows the questionable practice of presenting new material as part of the illustration captions instead of introducing them in the definitions themselves. In short, while the volume has considerable merit, it is not recommended as a *primary* purchase for libraries, although many will want to consider it as a supplement to the general reference collection for younger readers.

Students' Webster Dictionary of the English Language

Facts at a Glance

Full Title: **Students' Webster Dictionary of the English Language**.
Publisher: Sharon Publications.
Edition Reviewed: © 1983.

Number of Volumes: 1.
Number of Entries: estimated 13,200.
Number of Words: approximately 10,000.
Number of Pages: 48.
Trim Size: 8″ × 11″.
Binding: paperback, with five holes for inserting into a loose-leaf ring binder.

Price: $2.95.
Intended Readership: junior high through high school.
Sold in bookstores and other outlets. ISBN 0-89531-075-9.

I. Introduction

This large format paperback dictionary is designed to be placed in a two-, three-, or five-ring notebook, as a handy, quick-reference guide for "students, typists, and for secretaries." The 48 pages of the *Students' Webster Dictionary of the English Language* lie flat when opened and, according to the editors,

its thin, manageable size ensures that users "will never be without a dictionary again."

II. Authority

This 1983 edition is published by Sharon Publications, Inc. by special arrangement with the original copyright owners, Thomas Nelson Publishers. Neither the editorial staff nor the lexicographic base is described.

III. Comprehensiveness

Omitted from this notebook dictionary are word histories, synonyms, language labels, verbal and graphic illustrations, and idioms, as well as the more subtle and varied senses of meaning for most entries. A student needing specifics such as word histories will have to consult a larger dictionary; however, students who use this work will probably only consult it for quick checks on word meaning and for spelling. Alternative spellings are occasionally offered at the end of the definition; for example, the British spelling **programme** is given under the entry for **program**. Inflected forms are included immediately following the part-of-speech label, and derived words are presented at the end of the paragraph, as in the following examples:

ad·here′, *v.i.* -hered, -hering. 1. cling. 2. be loyal or obedient. -ad·her′ent, *adj.* -ad·her′ence, ad·her′sion, *n.* -ad·he′sive, *adj., n.*

ad′e·quate, *adj.* suitable or sufficient. -ad′e·quate·ly, *adv.* -ad′e·qua·cy, *n.*

It is obvious that this edition has not been revised to include many of the new technical terms and lexical trends of the 1980s. Readers will not find such currently common words found in most similarly condensed dictionaries as *videocassette*, *videodisc*, *data processing*, or *data bank*. Apparently, the most current terms represented are space technology words, such as **space ship**, **space craft**, and **space flight**; even the more recent term, *space shuttle*, is not included. The omission of many current words that are found in other abridged dictionaries limits the use of this dictionary.

IV. Quality and Currency of Entries

The "thousands" of entries in this reference book consist of three components: the boldface entry word, slightly overhanging the text, followed by its part-of-speech label in italics; and the actual definition, numbered in boldface type when more than one sense of the word is given. The most common definition is given first. Whether the various senses within a definition are listed according to frequency of use, date of appearance in the English language, or by some other criterion is not indicated.

The brief dictionary guide's claim that users will find the definitions "concise" is accurate; however, the assertion that the entries are "comprehensive" is not: the definitions are often circular and noninclusive; for example, consider the following entry:

ec·cen'tric, *adj.* **1.** peculiar in manner. **2.** off center. -*n.* **3.** eccentric person. **4.** eccentric machine part. -ec"cen·tric'i·ty.

A number of alternative synonyms (*odd, peculiar, unconventional, departing from an established pattern*) could have been used to amplify the sense of **eccentric**. Further, a student who needs to look up this word in a dictionary may not necessarily be able to deduce that an "eccentric machine" involves a disk that is set off center on a shaft for the purpose of converting circular motion into a back-and-forth motion.

V. Syllabication and Pronunciation

The alphabetically arranged boldface entry words are broken into syllables according to standard printers' usage. An accent mark (') in the entry word notes which syllable receives the primary stress; in the case of double-stressed words, the strongest stress is indicated by double accent marks (")—otherwise, pronunciations are rarely indicated. Since no pronunciation key is offered anywhere in the work, when the pronunciation of a word is treated, many younger dictionary users may simply be left in the dark. Although the pronunciation of **pi·quant** (pē'kant) has been phonemically amplified without a key, readers will not necessarily know how to sound it out.

VI. Special Features

Included in the dictionary is a very brief discussion on "Language Origins," printed on the inside front cover of the book, and a *very* brief "Guide For Using The Sharon Dictionary," located at the top of the first page of the vocabulary. In addition, users will find on the back cover lists of "Major Nations of the World," "Chief American Holidays," "Principal Mountains of the World," "Oceans and Seas," "World Time Differences," "United States Time Differences," and "Presidents of the U.S." (including President Reagan). At the bottom of the last page are

six tables which briefly delineate "The Metric System" and the "Planets of the Solar System." Readers will find other, far more valuable and comprehensive tables in encyclopedias or in the better semiabridged dictionaries.

VII. Accessibility

Boldface guide words appear at the top right- and left-hand columns of the page. These guide words are essentially too small to catch the reader's eye and are not of much use in locating particular entries. The typeface in this dictionary is extremely small (it should be sold with a magnifying glass), and the head notes are not much larger than the individual entry words. These difficulties are compounded by the large number of entries on each page. A user must scan five narrow columns of listings to check for an entry under the guide words of a single page.

There are no index tabs, nor are there clearly defined letter sections. For instance, the letter *B* immediately follows the final entry under the letter *A*, and is found toward the bottom of the first column on page 4; the letter *C* is located toward the top of the second column several pages later (page 7); and so on.

Words with variant pronunciations or widely diverse meanings are included in the same entry. For example, consider how the homographs of **fast** are handled in the following entry:

fast, *adj.* **1.** speedy. **2.** firm, fixed. -*adv.* **3.** firmly. -*v.i.* **4.** abstain from food or drink. -*n.* **5.** act or instance of fasting.

There are obvious limitations to a dictionary that depicts such diverse, nonexemplified distinctions among meanings under the same entry word. This dictionary is not appropriate for ESL readers, nor for younger readers, who may not fully comprehend the multifaceted usage of many words in the English language.

VIII. Graphics and Format

No illustrations are provided in this abridged dictionary. The typeface is clear but extremely small, and the entries are crowded into five narrow columns per page, separated by thin bold rules. Typographic or proofreading errors are not uncommon in this dictionary. Although the user's guide states that the syllables in the entries are indicated by a half dash (-), they are actually represented by accent marks and tiny bullets: **throm·bo'sis**. Also in the user's guide, the following sentence contains a misspelling: ". . .

widely diverse meanings are included in same entrie [for entry]."

The notebook-style paper binding does make the work convenient for carrying. The gutter margin is wide enough for insertion into a standard five-, three-, or two-hole binder. The pages do open flat, thus making it easy for the user to consult this dictionary while writing a paper.

IX. Summary

Overall, school librarians and teachers should probably discourage students from using such a limited work, even given its convenient size. Students will find that the definitions in the *Students' Webster Dictionary of the English Language* are too concise and are not current enough for most dictionary needs in or out of the classroom.

The Thorndike Barnhart Handy Pocket Dictionary

Facts at a Glance

Full Title: **The Thorndike Barnhart Handy Pocket Dictionary.**
Publisher: Bantam Books.
Editors: Clarence L. Barnhart, Editor-in-Chief; W. Cabell Greet and Allan P. Hubbell.
Edition Reviewed: ©1953; 1985 printing.

Number of Volumes: 1.
Number of Entries: 36,000.
Number of Pages: 451.
Trim Size: 4¼″ × 6⅞″.
Binding: paperback.

Price: $3.50.
Intended Readership: upper elementary through high school.
Sold in bookstores and other outlets. ISBN 0-553-25664-5.

I. Introduction

Originally published in 1951, *The Thorndike Barnhart Handy Pocket Dictionary* contains 36,000 defined words, those judged most frequently used at the time of the work's first publication in 1951. It is an abridgment of the 80,000 vocabulary entries in the *Thorndike Barnhart Comprehensive Desk Dictionary*, which has been out of print for some time.

According to the editor, Clarence L. Barnhart, the dictionary was designed to be useful to "the writer who seeks a quick reminder of a correct spelling, to the speaker who wishes to verify the acceptability of a pronunciation, or to the beginner in the use of dictionaries who wants a small but trustworthy aid to the most effective use of English."

The most frequently used meanings are always placed first and are based on the *Lorge-Thorndike Semantic Count.*

II. Authority

Bantam Books, a well-known paperback company, distributes this edition for Doubleday & Company. Bantam also publishes the larger, paperback SCRIBNER-BANTAM ENGLISH DICTIONARY (also reviewed in this Buying Guide). For some years, the Thorndike Barnhart paperback was considered an outstanding smaller dictionary. Its editor, Clarence L. Barnhart, was editor of *The Thorndike Barnhart Comprehensive Desk Dictionary*, *The American College Dictionary*, the Thorndike Barnhart series of dictionaries (which currently includes THE WORLD BOOK DICTIONARY and the SCOTT, FORESMAN BEGINNING and INTERMEDIATE DICTIONARIES), as well as *The Dictionary of U.S. Army Terms.*

The twenty-seven members of the General Editorial Advisory Committee for the original edition were all distinguished experts in the field of language and linguistics. Many of them had written or edited other authoritative works on language. These experts included Professor Irving Lorge, co-author with Dr. Edward Lee Thorndike, of the *Lorge-Thorndike Semantic Count* and *Thorndike-Lorge Teacher's Word Book of 30,000 Words*; both were standard resources for judging the frequency of word usage and commonly used meanings.

Described in the preface are the methods of compiling the vocabulary and presenting its meanings that have made this work useful throughout its life. Specifically, the editors and lexicographers endeavored to explain all entries in simpler terms than the word being defined; they avoided complex constructions; they took care to order meanings of words according to their importance; and they gave "all the specific information essential to a reader's understanding." These techniques were designed to ensure that upper elementary and middle school students could use the vocabulary as readily as adults. Today's buyer, however, is advised to approach this once-authoritative compact dictionary with caution because its vocabulary is seriously dated (a factor described below).

III. Comprehensiveness

With 36,000 entry words, this dictionary is slightly more than one-half the size of the Pocket Books edition of THE MERRIAM-WEBSTER DICTIONARY. It is an extremely useful size for many readers who require a basic vocabulary in one small book.

Intended for a wide range of users, including those just beginning to look up words in adult dictionaries, *The Handy Dictionary* omits etymologies and uses compact phrases or short sentences to indicate use: "**known** . . . *Washington is known as a general*." These are justifiable practices for the beginning dictionary user, but may not serve a more knowledgeable user who wants a quick reference tool. No additional lists of combining forms are included. Synonym lists are brief: for example, "**ex·treme** . . . **—Syn.** *adj.* **1**. immoderate, excessive." Inflections and variant forms are well covered.

IV. Quality and Currency of Entries

Along with the basic vocabulary, all technical terms, proper names, geographical names, and abbreviations appear in the main lexicon. Homographs are shown by superior numbers following the bold entry words: **mint**[1] and **mint**[2], to remind the reader, as the guide to using the dictionary states, "to look at the other entries spelled in the same way if you do not find the information you are seeking under the first one."

The definitions are simple and brief, but many betray the dictionary's lack of currency. This aging of the definitions shows up in many small details, as well as in the lack of basic, contemporary meanings. Three factors combine to date the dictionary's vocabulary and definitions: the style and choice of words used to define; the acquiring of new, common meanings for many words; and the entrance of new words into frequent, everyday use—words needed even by beginning dictionary users. The *Handy Pocket Dictionary* reveals its age in each respect. For example, definitions are needed for *busing* (or *bussing*) and *data bank*, just two of the missing terms cited earlier by the Bowker *Dictionary Buying Guide* (1977). Computer meanings for a term as common as *program* are absent. **Farrier**, a term for blacksmith, is not one of the 30,000 words that might be considered most common in the American vocabulary today. It is also surprising to find **commute** still specially labeled "*Am.*" (for an Americanism), since the word is as current in the large cities of Great Britain as in the United States.

Other examples of terms or definitions that need to be updated, redefined, or omitted (in the case of archaic verb forms), especially in a very compact dictionary are: "**as·a·fet·i·da** *n.* gum resin used in medicine"; "**chaise** *n.* a lightweight carriage"; "**durst** *v.* pt. of dare"; "**ell**", which is defined only as a measurement with the example, "give him an inch and he'll take an ell (much)"; "**Kenya** *n.* British colony and protectorate in E. Africa"; "**Martian** . . . -*n.* an inhabitant of Mars"; "**mayst** *v. Archaic.* may"; "**Zionism** *n.* a plan or modern movement to colonize Jewish people in Palestine." These examples characterize the general outdatedness of this dictionary, despite the acclaim that the definitions once merited.

Below the title in bold type, the paperback's jacket still carries the words: "New Revised Edition"; buyers should note that this phrase refers to the 1955 edition.

V. Syllabication and Pronunciation

Words with more than one syllable are divided by centered dots: **got·ten**. The guide to using the dictionary notes that syllabication is determined partly by pronunciation and partly by a word's root and affixes. When more than one pronunciation is given, they ordinarily follow each word:

reb·el (n. adj. reb|el; v. ri·bel|).

According to the editors, the pronunciations are "those customarily heard from educated speakers of English in the United States," with occasional variants "sometimes not recorded elsewhere," such as

hom·i·cide (hom|ə·sīd, hō|mə-).

An explanation of the forty-three symbols used in representing the sounds of English appears in the guide to the dictionary. Since the larger number of these sounds do not require special symbols, the editors explain, only thirteen special diacritical marks are employed. This allows for an abbreviated pronunciation key that is easier to use than those in many other dictionaries. The short vowel sounds are not marked; the five long vowels are marked ā, for example. The eight remaining symbols appear as: fär, cāre tėrm, ôr, tħ as in *th*en, pùt, rüle, and the schwa for the vowel sound "uh" as in about (ə·bout). The *ng* sound in drink is represented as dri*ng*k in the pronunciations. This is easier for younger readers than the Latin alphabet's n, ŋ (used in the International Phonetic Alphabet) for ng. An abbreviated key to vowel sounds appears at the bottom of each right-hand page as a handy quick pronunciation guide for the reader.

VI. Special Features

Two clear tables, one of weights and measures and one of common signs and symbols (astronomy, chemistry, commerce, mathematics, and miscellaneous), appear after the lexicon. There are four pages of guidance on letter writing with small labeled samples of letters.

Preceding the vocabulary is a "Handy Guide to Writing English" that includes three brief but useful sections on capitalization, writing numbers, and punctuation. The latter is divided into "Punctuation That Terminates, . . . That Introduces, and . . . That Unifies." There follows a two-page chart of special forms of address, which will be useful to many readers. Opposite the first page of the main entries, is a "Common Spellings of English" chart that compares symbols of sounds with appropriate words; for example, *hw* for *wh*eat and *sh* for o*c*ean.

VII. Accessibility

Information is readily accessible in this compact dictionary, which has no distracting frills or gimmicks. Words appear in letter-by-letter alphabetical sequence. The order of information given under each main entry word is clearly listed in the first paragraph of the guide:

> (1) the word spelled in boldface type, (2) the pronunciation, (3) part of speech, (4) any irregular inflected forms (plural, past tense, etc.), (5) definitions of its meanings arranged under the appropriate parts of speech, (6) derivatives consisting of main entries, or their roots, plus the common suffixes, (7) synonyms keyed to the definitions, and (8) usage notes . . . .

The preliminary and appendix matter is brief and clearly indicated in the complete table of contents. The opening section, "How to Use This Dictionary," is a clear, numbered guide to finding information. It was designed, Clarence L. Barnhart writes in his preface, to "enable a reader to understand and use any dictionary." The instructions contain useful reminders, such as "when looking up cross references as from **bore**[3] to **bear**[1] be sure to look under the right homograph."

Under the section "How to Find a Word," instructions with useful examples are given for locating main and subordinate entries, derivatives, homographs, cross-referenced words, and idioms.

Two bold guide words with a centered page number appear at the top of each page. Printed on each right-hand page is a useful mock thumb index tab, or "speedy word finder," consisting of a pair of letters:

This shows the first letters of the first and last main entries on each double-page spread.

VIII. Graphics and Format

The text is printed in two columns of small but readable type with generous white space (for the dictionary's size) between lines. The pages appear much less cramped than in many other paperback dictionaries. The paper is good quality newsprint. Some ink adheres to the fingers when the pages are handled repeatedly.

The binding appears to hold together even when the spine is creased in use. The white laminated cover with plain black type is utilitarian but attractive. On the back cover, there appears a facsimile of a column of the vocabulary with eight identifying labels for special features of the definitions. The red arrows criss-crossing from the call-outs to the entry words are visually appealing although they obscure the matter being highlighted.

IX. Summary

This small compact dictionary has many features that have received high praise over the years of its existence. *The Handy Dictionary* was an admirable example of the art of dictionary-making but the need for updating now outweighs claims to usefulness for this work—for any age group.

Webster Comprehensive Dictionary: Encyclopedic Edition

Facts at a Glance

Full Title: **Webster Comprehensive Dictionary: Encyclopedic Edition**.

Former Title: Funk & Wagnalls Comprehensive Dictionary: Encyclopedic Edition; also *Funk & Wagnalls Standard Dictionary: Comprehensive International Edition*.

Publisher: J. G. Ferguson.

Editors: Richard Dell and E. Russell Primm.

Edition Reviewed: © 1984.

Number of Volumes: 2.
Number of Entries: 175,000.
Number of Pages: 1,725.

Number of Illustrations: 2,043 line drawings,
    including maps; and two 16-page inserts of
    black-and-white and full color
    photographs.
Trim Size: 8¼″ × 10⅞″.
Binding: hardbound.

Price: $49.95.
Intended Readership: all ages; junior high and up.
Sold door-to-door, direct mail, and as a premium
    set (e.g., with school texts and reference sets).
    ISBN 0-89434-045-X.

I. Introduction

This two-volume "encyclopedic edition" of the *Webster
Comprehensive Dictionary* (WCD) can be generally
categorized as an adult semi-abridged dictionary.
Despite this, it will be useful for students from junior
high school upward, although the publisher more
broadly designates it for "all ages." The dictionary
has been published in several editions with various
titles, but its base is the *Funk & Wagnalls Standard
Dictionary of the English Language*, first published
in 1958. The word "Standard" in the title (registered
as a trademark) was intended to reflect the dictionary's emphasis on the words considered standard in
American speech and writing in the consensus of
many authorities. Nonstandard words and usages are,
therefore, rigorously labeled as *dialect, slang, U.S.
colloq.* (colloquial), *Irish colloq.*, and so forth; vulgar
and terms considered "taboo" are excluded.

The dictionary is designed, according to the introduction, "to serve the practical and professional
needs of all who speak or use the English language."
The editors and lexicographers also attempted "to
meet the needs of foreign users and those in other
parts of the English-speaking world who want to be
at home with American literature and its idioms."

The three major objectives of the *WCD*'s staff
were first, "to present the fundamental facts and
characteristics of the language, accurately, fully, and
interestingly . . . [and second] to present adequately
the significant contributions to English made in the
United States, with requisite definitions, usage notes,
and discriminative comment," as well as other areas
of speech such as dialect and Australian and Canadian English. Their third goal was "to secure the
widest possible coverage of both the established word
stock of English and of rapidly expanding vocabularies of the arts, sciences, trades and professions."

The guiding principle in defining was "to formulate
a definition that can substitute for the word itself in
the context in which the user reads or hears it." The
appendixes and the numerous lists and charts within
the main vocabulary are intended to expand this large
dictionary's function as a general and educational
reference source.

II. Authority

The current edition of the *Webster Comprehensive
Dictionary* lists its original, distinguished three-mem-
ber editorial board: Albert H. Marckwardt, Professor Emeritus of English and Linguistics, Princeton
University; Frederick G. Cassidy, Professor of English, University of Wisconsin; and James G. Mc-
Millan, Professor of English, University of Alabama.
Its original editor-in-chief, Sidney I. Landau (see the
review of the WEBSTER ILLUSTRATED CONTEMPO-
RARY DICTIONARY) is no longer credited. Listed with
the editorial staff are numerous lexicographers, several of whom later created the next generation of
American dictionaries. The list includes *WCD*'s Con-
sulting Editor William Morris (later, editor of THE
AMERICAN HERITAGE DICTIONARY) and Laurence
Urdang (later, editor of several Random House dictionaries and other reference works).

The twenty-eight member Editorial Advisory
Board, chaired by Allen Walker Read, Professor of
English, Columbia University, includes many distin-
guished scholars: Albert C. Baugh of the University
of Pennsylvania, Arna Bontemps of Fisk University,
Margaret Bryant of Brooklyn College, and Frederick
Pottle of Yale University, among others.

III. Comprehensiveness

At approximately 175,000 entries with extensive lists,
charts, and tables of reference matter within the main
A to Z vocabulary, the *Webster Comprehensive Dictionary* encompasses the vast majority of words,
phrases, abbreviations, and names that general readers would normally encounter. Many more recent
scientific and technical word combinations (especially the neo-Latin combinations) are not included.

There are extensive additional lists of words and
particles forming combinations in English that are
useful for spelling purposes and that indicate the form
of two-word phrases. The lists indicate whether such
combining elements as **air-**, **bed**, **corn**, **fellow**, **folk**,
heart, and so forth, are written with or without
hyphens.

A brief comparison of the number of entries in
J. G. Ferguson's one-volume WEBSTER'S ILLUS-
TRATED CONTEMPORARY DICTIONARY (WICD) from

Webster Comprehensive Dictionary: Encyclopedic Edition

❶ Usage notes are preceded by colon or are marked by ◆ when more extensive notes are provided

❷ Synonym and other cross-references appear in small capitals

❸ Field labels and usage labels are abbreviated and italicized

❹ Etymology (including doublet cross-references) is provided within brackets and placed before run-on entries

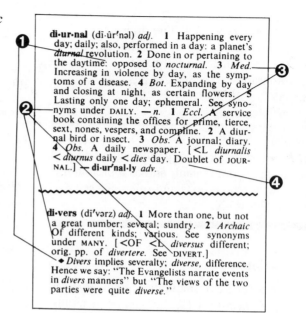

paprika to **parachute**, shows that the *WICD* contains eleven main entries in that section, whereas the *Webster Contemporary Dictionary: Encyclopedic Edition* has thirty-six main entries. Of the additional entries, six are geographic terms, one is biographical, and eleven are from specific scientific fields and carry restrictive labels (pathology, biochemistry, biology, mathematics, psychiatry, chemistry, and anatomy).

The etymologies are full; foreign words from which English words derive are given meanings so that readers can sense the evolution of language; cross-references within etymologies also are included. For example:

> **par·a·ble**, *n.* A comparison: simile; specifically, a short narrative making a moral or religious point by comparison with natural or homely things: the New Testament *parables*. See synonyms under ALLEGORY.

The etymology then reads:

> [<OF *parabole* <LL *parabola* allegory, speech <L, comparison <Gk. *parabole* a placing side by side, a comparison *para-* beside—*balein* throw. Doublet of PALAVER, PARABOLA, PAROLE.]

Under the mathematical term, **parabola**, the etymology reads:

> [<Med. L <Gk. *parabole*. Double of PALAVER, PARABLE, PAROLE.]

The dictionary's etymological information will increase the student's understanding of how scientific and non-scientific language are intertwined, and thus enhance knowledge of the actual workings and nuances of speech and writing.

Within the vocabulary, there are more than twenty-four major charts and tables, as well as numerous additional lists and illustrated, labeled charts (such as drawings of fourteen kinds of leaves, diagrams of baseball, football, and cricket fields, and a basketball court) that all add considerably to the dictionary's value as a general reference source. Students will find it especially helpful to have this information placed within the text of the dictionary rather than appended to it.

IV. Quality and Currency of Entries

The definitions, in the main, are well written, understandable, and full. There are also synonym lists for numerous main entry words, including selected cross-references to other main entries: under **error**, there are ten synonyms plus cross-references to DELUSION and FOIBLE. Many words have longer lists of synonyms with discriminated meanings plus antonyms: **equivocal** is an example, with thirteen synonyms and usage phrases, two comparative references (CLEAR, PRECARIOUS), and fifteen antonyms.

The sequence of information under the bold main entry words is: syllabicated word or phrase, pronunciation (with variants when necessary), cross reference to another main entry if no further information follows, part(s) of speech, plural or restricted forms with variant spellings in order of preferred use and pronunciations. An example is:

co·dex (kō′deks) *n. pl.* **co·di·ces** (kō′də·sēz, kod′ə-).

Restrictive field and usage labels precede a definition if the restriction applies to all senses of a word; otherwise labels follow a specific numbered definition. The labels qualify, as the editors state, "a word in terms of its relationship to standard English."

Phrasal usages and idiomatic phrases appear where appropriate in definitions:

gaul·the·ri·a . . . **2** Oil of wintergreen: also called oil of **gaultheria**.

Collateral adjectives, frequent in English, as the editors explain, because of the "grafting of Norman French and late Renaissance Latin idioms onto earlier English," are labeled and preceded by a bold diamond:

arm . . . ◆ Collateral adjective: *brachial*.

The more extended usage notes, apart from those in the definitions are also similarly marked:

la·dy . . . **2** Female; a *lady* doctor. ◆ Lady is here a genteelism, as it is in such compounds as *saleslady*. *Woman* is the more appropriate word to indicate the feminine gender . . . .

As is usual in semi-abridged dictionaries, there is extensive and varied lexicographic information provided for entries. The dictionary's explanatory notes show that thirty-six different kinds of basic information are provided, including the items described above plus homophones and homographs, as in

lox[1] (loks) *n.* Smoked salmon [<Yiddish <G *lachs* salmon]
lox[2], **LOX** (loks) *n.* Liquid oxygen.

Etymologies explain derivation and the creation of, for example, English blends and doublets; for example, as in

jour·nal . . . [<OF <L *diurnalis*. Doublet of DIURNAL.]

The extensive system of cross-references, not only for synonyms and etymologies, but to other selected items in the supplementary material and to charts and tables in the main vocabulary, increases the likelihood that readers will acquire a fuller sense of word meanings. For example:

in·de·pen·dence . . . See synonyms under LIBERTY, WEALTH. See DECLARATION OF INDEPENDENCE.

The etymology of **indenture** reads

<OF *endenture* <Med. L *indentare*. See INDENT.

The "compare" references at the end of some entries also point to definitions that will aid the reader in discriminating meanings. Examples are: **Indian tobacco** . . . Compare LOBELINE and **Orthodox Judaism** . . . Compare CONSERVATIVE JUDAISM, REFORM JUDAISM.

Trademarks and names are described, chemical and mathematical formulas are included in definitions in many cases, and there are many main entry abbreviations as well as ones appended to definitions, as for books of the Old Testament.

Biographical and geographical entries, as well as their derived adjectives, are defined, but many need updating. For example, "**Iran** A kingdom of SW Asia" is, in fact, now a republic (correctly identified as such in the dictionary's gazetteer); **Iraq** is also a republic not a kingdom as the main vocabulary defines it. Geographical definitions in the main vocabulary for **Nauru**, **Papua and New Guinea**, **Rwanda and Burundi**, and **Zimbabwe** are outdated.

Within the main vocabulary, several other kinds of definitions are useful. First names are briefly defined and their language of derivation is indicated: the Spanish **Ruiz** and the English **Rufus** are included, and so are Italian, French, and German names, plus diminutive, masculine, and feminine versions. Latin mottoes that have become familiar are given standard English translations: such as "**secundam naturam** *Latin* According to nature" or "**ars poetica** *Latin* The art of poetry." The main entries also include good definitions of mythological and folkloric terms and names (**Rumpelstiltskin**) and even famous streets, such as the **Rue de la Paix**.

Occasional definitions read oddly:

Shake·spear·i·an·ism *n.* **1** An expression peculiar to Shakespeare

or omit a standard sense, as in **Blue Point**, defined as a variety of oyster but not as a variety of domestic cat. In general, a real effort seems to have been made to define technical or scientific words so that they are relatively accessible to general readers who may not be familiar with the fields from which such terms derive. Consider:

par·a·a·mi·no·ben·zo·ic acid *Biochem.* A colorless crystalline compound, $C_7H_7NO_2$, forming part of the vitamin B complex. Present in yeast and also made synthetically: source of several local anesthetics.

Although this dictionary covers scientific and technological terms extensively, there are instances in which the definitions need updating even for a general reader. **Steroid** has a formal biochemical definition but no cross-reference to **anabolic steroid**; the definition of **mnemonic** as an adjective is "Designed to aid memory" and that of **mnemonics** as a noun is "The science of memory improvement," but there is no mention of the word's current use in either computer science or psychology. Certain terms are not included, such as *artificial intelligence* (**artificial language** is an entry, but has no computer meaning included); *modem* is not an entry. As a combining form, **brady-** is included, but not, for example, *bradykinesia*. Also, **bibliotherapy** is included with a definition under the restrictive label *Pathol.* (pathology), but since this term is used in the fields of psychology and library science, one expects further definition.

In rechecking some entries, however, that were criticized as not being up-to-date in earlier editions of the *Webster Comprehensive Dictionary*, our reviewers found that the text has been revised. **Busing** now includes a second meaning that encompasses its intent to achieve racial balance; **data bank** has been added to the entries; *deep space* is still missing; but **aesthete**, **aesthetic** now includes a philosophic sense; the definition of **radiation** has been extended beyond the field of particle radiation; and although *renovascular* is still not in, the combining forms **ren-** and **reni-** are. Apparently, a small proportion of the entries are revised as each new edition appears. A student who requires more contemporary definitions will need to consult either a special topic dictionary or a general work such as WEBSTER'S NINTH NEW COLLEGIATE or THIRD INTERNATIONAL, or the unabridged second edition of *The Random House Dictionary*, or Webster's *12,000 Words*.

V. Syllabication and Pronunciation

Syllables in main entries are divided by centered dots that indicate conventional hyphenation at the end of a line. Run-on entries and variant forms are also syllabicated, although primary and secondary stress marks supplant syllabic dots:

in·fat·u·ate *vt.* **·at·ed**, **·at·ing** . . .—**in·fat′u·at′ed** *adj.*—**in·fat′u·a′tion** *n.*

No syllables are shown for words or elements in phrasal entries that appear elsewhere, as shown in **graph·ic** and **graphic arts**.

Pronunciation(s) appear immediately after a main entry. They are also given when necessary for inflected and variant forms that appear within entries. The editors state that "all pronunciations shown are valid for educated American speech." (An exception noted is that normal American pronunciation is given for **flam·boi′ant** at the entry for **flamboyant architecture**, which—as a standard art history term—should have a French pronunciation without the heavy stress on the middle syllable.) When alternate pronunciations occur, the first is that used most widely and frequently, if known; otherwise pronunciations are equally acceptable.

According to the editors, the method of recording pronunciations "is suited to the purposes of a dictionary where the aim is to provide reference rather than extensive linguistic data." The explanation of the pronunciations used states that they "have been compiled by editors trained in phonetics and acquainted with the facts of the spoken language." Where there are *major* regional variations in pronunciations, the first pattern recorded is that of the largest region of speakers in the "great Midwestern section" of the country.

The symbols used are simple letters of the alphabet with standard diacritical marks such as the macron for long vowels, ā (pāy). The breve is only used for the vowel sound in book (bŏŏk) to avoid confusion, the editors write, with the vowel sound in *pool*. The schwa ə has been borrowed from the International Phonetic Alphabet (IPA) for unstressed neutral vowels regardless of spelling: **broil·er** (broil′ər) and **vin·di·ca·tion** (vin′də kā′shən). There is a list of words showing the range of American pronunciations with this dictionary's simplified symbols matched to those of the IPA. A brief pronunciation key is printed opposite the first page of the main vocabulary with an explanation of the most common foreign sounds used in English, a clear description of how to pronounce them, and notes on accent. In general, readers will have little trouble with the clear symbols. Those requiring more guidance will be able to use the WCD and IPA coordinating list of symbols at the front of the work quite easily.

VI. Special Features

The encyclopedic material includes extensive reference matter within the main lexicon. There are also six reference charts and tables and sixteen larger supplementary sections at the end of volume 2. Many of these are almost identical in content to those in the WEBSTER ILLUSTRATED CONTEMPORARY DICTIONARY (see the review of that work's special features for those not treated here).

The quality and usefulness of these special supplementary features varies. They have not been recently revised, in general, and much of the material duplicates information given within the main dictionary text. The gazetteer, for example, overlaps the fuller geographical entries in the main dictionary (where the black and white locator maps appear).

Albert Marckwardt's original article on improving your usage and spelling should be edited in view of the sections on spelling at the front of the dictionary; the lists of commonly misspelled words are probably still the ones most commonly misspelled.

"Abbreviations Commonly in Use," arranged in five columns per page of small type, lists some foreign abbreviations and explains capitalizations of abbreviations, as in proper names such as **Mt. Vesuvius**. There are some notable omissions, however: *AIDS* is not in, nor is *AIA* for *American Institute of Architects*; at the entry "**f.f.a., F.F.A.** free foreign agent; free from alongside" there should also be *FFA* for *free fatty acid*; *SI* for the International System of Units should also be included.

A list of 16,000 quotations under 182 main subject headings, with 30 cross-referenced terms, ranges from ABILITY to YOUTH. The section needs heavy updating and revision. Such additional information is useful to readers, who consider a large, two-volume dictionary as a source for more than just spellings or definitions, so it is unfortunate that the information here has not received the revisions needed to make it complete and up-to-date.

VII. Accessibility

At the front of volume 1, a table of contents lists the sections of information on how to use the WCD, the various usage essays in the first volume, the appendix sections to volume 2, and the titles of the sixteen "Special Supplementary Features" that follow the appendixes. The range of entries in the main dictionary is given: for volume 1—**A** through **NAME** and for volume 2—**NAME-DAY** through **Z**.

The explanatory matter in front of the dictionary is clear and detailed. A useful single page of sample entries contains 36 labels keyed to the main kinds of information available so that a reader has a visual guide to the location of specific items. This is followed by paragraphs of specific guidance on each part of the information in the entries, from syllabication to taxonomic labels to cross-references for doublets in the etymologies.

A useful small chart of the pronunciation symbols makes them easier to read than is the case in many dictionaries. A two-line pronunciation key, including the foreign language symbols and those in the etymologies, is given at the foot of each right-hand page.

The text is printed in small type in three columns per page with enough white space to make reading relatively easy. The entry words, in strict letter-by-letter alphabetical sequence, are printed in bold type overhanging the text. At the top of each page, two bold guide words are printed with a centered page number.

There is no index to the numerous additional lists, charts, and tables in the main dictionary, which are not easy to find in leafing through the work. The lists of particles and words that are combining forms stand out because they are printed in small bold type. The location of variant forms and phrasal entries is explained in the introductory matter and they are printed in bold face within entries, as are run-on entries (words derived from the entry word with the addition of a suffix or prefix).

Apart from the main dictionary, there are certain kinds of information available that the reader will only stumble on by chance, such as the map of major regional speech areas and a table of regional pronunciations, the list of words misspelled most frequently, and even the topics covered in the photographic inserts.

VIII. Graphics and Format

Black-and-white line drawings are scattered throughout the main dictionary in a proportion of one illustration to about ninety entries. The majority of drawings are clear and many captions contain further information, adding to the "encyclopedic" nature of the WCD. An attempt has been made to illustrate less familiar meanings and to provide cutaway drawings or cross sections, especially for mechanical objects and for anatomical terms.

There are two large companion drawings of thirty-three **Beneficial Insects** and fifty-two **Injurious Insects**, clear enough to be used for identification purposes, for example. Other informational charts and tables are: foreign alphabets (Arabic, Hebrew, Greek, Russian, German), tables of constellations and of chemical elements, of comparative grades in the

United States Armed Services, of mathematical and of meteorological symbols, International Morse Code (including its alpha, numeric, and punctuation symbols), a table of major planets, a list of presidents (ending with Gerald R. Ford), proofreaders' marks, standard time in principal cities, a table of principal stars and of Fahrenheit to Celsius conversion. There is a major wars of history chart with names of the contestants, notable battles, and sites of treaties, which includes the Vietnam War.

The full-page periodic table of elements is inaccurate and out of date: ten of the mass numbers need revision either for consistency of decimal place numbers or because the numbers have been adjusted (there is also no discrimination between atomic weights and mass numbers in the brief explanatory key).

The photograph pages, half in full color, printed as two separate sections on glossy paper, come from the publisher's archives—they are several decades old, but are interesting from an historical point of view. The pictures on erosion control should be replaced and the captions revised to indicate the *period* when the photographs were taken (for example, of Suez, the Manchester Ship Canal, Gatun Locks at Panama, and the Soulanges section of the St. Lawrence).

Volume 2 contains an appendix with a large type double-page spread of the metric system and equivalent units (with a ruler illustrating centimeters and inches and a thermometer illustrating °F and °C) and a two-page table of weights and measures.

The design of the book in general is attractive and readable, except for the special features printed in a wide assortment of typefaces and with page formats that are often incompatible with the main dictionary.

The dictionary's paper is white and almost opaque; the binding is reinforced and sturdy; the spine has a thickly woven head- and footband. Despite the relative bulk of these volumes, they can be handled with ease and all pages lie flat when opened.

IX. Summary

The *Webster Comprehensive Dictionary: Encyclopedic Edition* shows signs of its age—especially in the supplementary materials, in the omission of secondary meanings acquired by words in recent decades, and even in the lack of a "contemporary" tone in the articles and language. Its core lexicon, however, is still solid and definitions are written so that a reader unfamiliar with the field from which specialist terms come can readily understand the meaning.

The extensive synonyms, collateral adjectives, numerous meanings in the longer entries, etymologies,

and reference materials within the main vocabulary are generally useful. The dictionary manages to convey a feel for the English language, its evolution, and extent in a way that college dictionaries do not. The format is accessible, the pronunciations easy to understand, and the volumes are sturdy. The WCD is not appropriate for those who need the *most* current definitions available nor for readers whose interest in language is cursory, but it conveys the meanings and sense of standard language well and it is inexpensive enough to merit consideration as a second purchase in larger school libraries or for an additional reference source in classrooms.

Webster Comprehensive Dictionary: International Edition

Facts at a Glance

Full Title: **Webster Comprehensive Dictionary: International Edition**.
Former Title: Funk & Wagnalls Standard Dictionary: International Edition.
Publisher: J. G. Ferguson.
Editors: Richard Dell and E. Russell Primm.
Edition Reviewed: © 1986.

Number of Volumes: 2.
Number of Entries: 175,000.
Number of Pages: 1,536.
Number of Illustrations: more than 2,000 including maps.
Trim Size: 8½″ × 11¼″.
Binding: hardbound.

Price: $39.95.
Intended Readership: all ages; junior high school and up.
Sold door-to-door, direct mail, and as a premium set (e.g., with school texts and other reference sets).
ISBN-0-89434-054-9.

I. Introduction and Scope

The main dictionary, as well as the introductory material on language and its use, of the *International Edition* of the *Webster Comprehensive Dictionary* is the same as in the WEBSTER COMPREHENSIVE DICTIONARY: ENCYCLOPEDIC EDITION. The current edition is copyrighted 1986. Previous editions copyrighted by J. G. Ferguson go back to 1976 and the copyright page also lists dates from 1958 through 1974 in the name of Funk & Wagnalls.

The *International Edition* omits the more than 200 pages of supplementary reference material as well as the sixteen-page tipped-in section of photographs in the *Encyclopedic Edition*, and hence is less expensive. The sixteen-page color section, however, is very outdated, and its omission makes this the preferred edition of the *Webster Comprehensive*, which is reviewed in full above.

Webster Illustrated Contemporary Dictionary: Encyclopedic Edition

Facts at a Glance

Full Title: **Webster Illustrated Contemporary Dictionary: Encyclopedic Edition**.

Former Title: The Illustrated Contemporary Dictionary: Encyclopedic Edition.

Publisher: J. G. Ferguson.

Editors: Sidney I. Landau, Editor-in-Chief; Richard Dell and E. Russell Primm.

Edition Reviewed: © 1984.

Number of Volumes: 1.
Number of Entries: 85,000.
Number of Pages: 1,150.
Number of Illustrations: 970, including 8 pages in full color.
Trim Size: 7¾" × 10".
Binding: hardbound.

Price: $17.95.
Intended Readership: junior high school and up; general adult.
Sold door-to-door, direct mail, and as a premium with school texts and reference sets. ISBN 0-89434-049-2.

I. Introduction

The *Webster Illustrated Contemporary Dictionary*, formerly *The Illustrated Contemporary Dictionary*, was first published in its current format in 1975 and has since been revised and updated. Its lexicographic base includes material from THE DOUBLEDAY DICTIONARY (© 1975) and from Funk & Wagnalls dictionaries, copyrighted from 1958 to 1977, especially the retitled two-volume WEBSTER'S COMPREHENSIVE DICTIONARY, which is reviewed elsewhere in the Buying Guide.

The editors state in the preface that the dictionary was designed "to provide a compact, easy-to-use, accurate, and modern desk dictionary for home,

school, and office use." The preface also claims that the approximately 85,000 entries include "fuller coverage" than the original edition of contemporary general and scientific language. Many distinct British, Canadian, and Australian terms and usages are included. Accordingly, numerous obsolete and archaic terms have been omitted (the publishers do not indicate the extent of these) and the etymologies have been shortened. Thus the dictionary has broadened its base in the contemporary, everyday language of English as it is used around the world and has become more accessible to the general reference book reader.

A small editorial committee of preeminent language scholars advised the editors during preparations for the first edition of this work and wrote the introductory material on language and its use. The late Professor Albert H. Marckwardt of Princeton University writes in his article on "Usage" that the "editors of this dictionary have assumed that it will be used principally in the United States, by persons who are familiar with American English. Only rarely have they felt it necessary to identify features of the language which are characteristic of this country. For example, the past participial form *gotten* is identified in a note as an American usage, and the peculiarly American use of *integrate* as used in 'to integrate schools' bears the label *U.S.*"

In addition to the articles on usage in this dictionary, there are seventeen reference tables, charts, and other items, such as the Declaration of Independence and a list of the Presidents of the U.S., in the supplementary matter following the main vocabulary.

The approximately 970 illustrations include simple black-and-white line drawings for selected entries, and a tipped-in, sixteen-page section of much older photographs, on special topics such as costumes, gems, and reptiles.

II. Authority

J. G. Ferguson and Company, a former subsidiary of Doubleday, are established publishers of premium and subscription reference books, among them the two-volume WEBSTER'S COMPREHENSIVE DICTIONARY in different editions. Their one-volume WEBSTER ILLUSTRATED CONTEMPORARY DICTIONARY was prepared under Editor-in-Chief Sidney I. Landau, author of *Dictionaries: The Art and Craft of Lexicography* (Scribner's, 1984) and the former editor of Funk & Wagnalls dictionaries and THE DOUBLEDAY DICTIONARY. The name "Webster" on this dictionary has no connection to Merriam-Webster dictionaries and is used, presumably, because marketers believe the name is synonymous with "dictionary" to many American readers.

The advisory committee for all these dictionaries was chaired by Albert H. Marckwardt, Professor Emeritus of English and Linguistics at Princeton University; its other three members were Professor H. Rex Wilson (English—linguistics) of the University of Western Ontario, who contributed the Canadian terms; Harold B. Allen, Professor Emeritus of English and Linguistics, University of Minnesota; and Rudolph C. Troike, formerly Director of the Center for Applied Linguistics, Georgetown University.

III. Comprehensiveness

The approximately 85,000 entries in letter by letter alphabetical order comprise 863 pages of this desk dictionary, which is in the mid-range between, for example, THE SCRIBNER-BANTAM ENGLISH DICTIONARY (with somewhere between 60,000 and 80,000 words) and THE AMERICAN HERITAGE DESK DICTIONARY (which claims over 100,000 entries). In a review of the 1982 edition, *American Reference Books Annual* criticized the editors for claiming the *WICD* as "totally new" when it first appeared in 1975 since "it incorporates material from considerably earlier sources now under copyright by the present publishers." However, later in *ARBA 84*, it was suggested that this dictionary "should prove quite useful within its intended scope," citing updated vocabulary and the features including a gazetteer and other appendixes. The appendix material contains a sizable amount of additional information that students and teachers, especially, may find useful to have readily at hand in a classroom.

IV. Quality and Currency of Definitions

Whether one or more words, the entries appear alphabetically by letter. Within entries, the sequence of information is: bold main word(s); pronunciation(s), generally given in order of their widest use; part of speech; inflected or variant forms and/or comparative variant forms of adjectives and adverbs—small capitals indicate a cross-reference to another entry, and some synonym cross-references appear immediately after a part of speech; variant British spelling follows if it differs from the U.S. form; then definitions appear, numbered when appropriate. Homographs are entered separately with small superior numbers: **gauntlet**[1] as a glove with armor and

gauntlet[2] as in *running the gauntlet*. Idiomatic phrases are included, often with italicized usage examples (under the third meaning of **par**, for example, "**3** An accepted standard with which to compare variation: not feeling up *to par*.") Clear etymologies follow, then additional inflected forms. Synonym lists are appended to entries: for example, under **paramount**, the words are, "—**Syn**. chief, foremost, preeminent, supreme." In addition, six combining word forms have extensive lists of compound words following their entries. These are: **in-**[1], **multi-**, **non-**, **over-**, **re-**, **un-**[2].

The dictionary draws on the same lexicographic base as the larger two-volume *Webster Comprehensive* dictionaries published by J. G. Ferguson. A comparison shows that the approach and vocabulary are similar, with the definitions carefully revised or condensed in the one-volume WEBSTER ILLUSTRATED CONTEMPORARY DICTIONARY and many special field-labeled definitions omitted. For example, a representative definition from the *WICD* is:

> **par·a·chute** *n.* An apparatus of lightweight fabric that when unfurled assumes the shape of a large umbrella and acts to retard the speed of a body moving or descending through air.

The entry in the larger WEBSTER COMPREHENSIVE DICTIONARY reads:

> **par·a·chute** *n.* **1** A large, expanding, umbrella-shaped apparatus for retarding the speed of a body descending through the air, especially from an airplane[,]

which is followed by **2**, a specialized zoological definition, and an aeronautical phrase "—**pilot parachute**." Comparing the same word with another dictionary, similar in purpose and general length of entries, THE AMERICAN HERITAGE DESK DICTIONARY, shows:

> **par·a·chute** *n.* **1**. A foldable umbrella-shaped device used to slow the fall of persons or objects for vehicles. **2**. A similar device used to slow speeding vehicles.

The etymologies at the end of definitions in the *WICD* are shorter, for example, "[<F < PARA + *chute* fall]," than in the *WCD*: "[<F < *para* PARA-[2] + *chute* fall]," although both typically contain cross-references in small capital letters to another entry.

There are five categories of labels employed in the *WICD* which help the user to know exactly how to use or how *not* to use a word. These appear where entries or particular senses of words have a restricted application. The categories are: (1) level of usage such as *Slang* or *Informal* (colloquial); (2) localization—*Regional* for the U.S., *Brit.* (British), *Can.* (Canadian), and *Austral.* (Australian); (3) field or subject such as *Mus.* (music) or *Ecol.* (ecology); (4) language of origin such as *Latin* or *Spanish* for words that are not yet Anglicized; (5) *Nonstand.* (nonstandard) for words or usages not accepted as standard by most native speakers.

Included in the lexicon are such common abbreviations as "**lb., lbs., L.C., L/C, l/c, lc., LD, L.D.**," trade names, and combining forms such as "**—sophy.**" These are helpfully repeated in the list of abbreviations in the appendixes.

The definitions are adequate and well written, in general—with only minor exceptions. The first definition of **boarder**, for example, is misleading:

> *n.* **1** A person who receives regular meals, or meals and lodging, for pay. (Insert the words "in return" before "for pay" and the meaning of the definition is clear.)

The definition of **Orthodox** refers to the Eastern Orthodox Church but does not include a sense of the term as a branch of Judaism. A random check for words that are currently much used shows that the following are included with clear definitions: **aerobics**, **ayatollah**, **immunosuppressive** (but not *AIDS*), **modem**, and **software**. There is no noun sense given for **heuristic** (a term currently used in education, psychology, rhetoric, and so forth). And although there is usage guidance at the entry **who**, there are no specific examples of how to use **whom** in the *main dictionary*.

V. Syllabication and Pronunciation

Small dots divide all the bold main entry words into syllables except when phrasal words appear elsewhere as entries: "**Eng·lish**" and "**muf·fin**" are syllabicated, but not "**English muffin**." The dots indicate where it is acceptable to hyphenate words.

Immediately after the dictionary's preface, a simple, easy-to-understand pronunciation key appears. Each of the 42 main alphabetic symbols has two examples. The superscripts *h* and *y* represent sounds commonly pronounced in some regions but not in others, for example: **Tues·day** (t^{y}o͞oz′dā) or whale (^{h}wāl). The schwa (ə) represents unstressed vowel sounds, with five examples given. Foreign sounds encountered in English are described with brief guidance on pronouncing them, a useful instruction for the student or traveler. Included are four distinct

pronunciations occurring in French and German words (à as in *ami*, œ as in *peu* or *schön*, ü as in *vue* or *grün*, ṅ as in *brun*), plus the *kh* sound that is similar in German and Scottish words:

> kh as in German *ach*, Scottish *loch*. Pronounce a strongly aspirated (h) with the tongue in position for (k) as in *cool* or *keep*.
> Additionally, the symbol ′ represents the voiceless *l* or *r* in French: *debacle* (dä·bä′kl′) or the French sound of *y* as a consonant when it is followed by a slight schwa sound in a separate syllable, as in *fille* (fē′y′). Primary stress is indicated by a heavy symbol ′ and secondary stress by a lighter face ′: **e·lec·tion·eer** (i-lek′shən·ir′).
> Throughout the A to Z entries, a two-line short-form of the pronunciation key, with an explanation of two symbols in the etymologies (<derived from; ? origin uncertain or unknown), appears at the foot of all right-hand pages as a handy, quick reference for the reader.

VI. Special Features

Special features are an important part of this dictionary. The three opening essays by editorial committee members are excellent. Professor Marckwardt explains "Usage" as "one of many kinds of social behavior" and the "role of the dictionary" from the points of view of a) lexicographers who seek to record the language and b) readers who expect to find prescriptive guidance "relative to spelling, pronunciation, word division and word meaning, or grammatical form." He also describes various approaches to style, ranging from "rigid" reliance on standards (via the nineteenth century) to "nervous reluctance" to label any usage as "nonstandard." He even explains the grammatically unsound objection to *hopefully* as a verb phrase modifier, as in "Hopefully, the project will be finished by the end of the year." *Hopefully* modifies the whole clause not just the verb phrase in standard usage. Professor Allen details punctuation usage thoroughly, and Professor Wilson's brief article on Canadian English is enlightening.

Much of the more than 250 pages of reference material in the *WICD* does not date readily, which is a plus: for example, given names (male and female), Greek and Latin elements, guidance on vocabulary and spelling (part of this material is duplicated in the dictionary's preliminary material), some 1,600 quotations organized under guide words, an essay on "The World's Religions," mythology, vital facts about U.S. presidents (including Ronald W.

Reagan) and vice-presidents (including George H. Bush), the texts of the Declaration of Independence and the U.S. Constitution, with lists of signers of both documents.

Other sections *need* updating, especially the long essay on "The Library Research Paper": the advice is excellent for students, but the footnote style and the specimen bibliography are obsolete. The extensive abbreviations list needs updating, for example, "**E.R.A.** Educational Research Association; Emergency Relief Administration (ERA)" should include the Equal Rights Amendment. Signs and symbols need updating. Obviously, the editors have made some ongoing changes in the extensive gazetteer and biographical section, but many changes from the 1980s are not in the gazetteer: since 1981, **Antigua** has been Antigua and Barbuda, **St. Christopher and Nevis** became independent in 1983, and **Upper Volta** changed its name in 1984 to Burkina Faso. U.S. population figures are based on the 1980 census; those for Canada date from 1978; others are not based on even reliable estimates from ca. 1983. The biographical section contains some 1980s updating—John Lennon's death date and the inclusion of Sandra Day O'Connor. There are many popular culture figures included—Gypsy Rose Lee, labeled "U.S. stripteaser and author," Sally Rand (labeled merely as "U.S. dancer"), and even Ellen Stewart of New York City's Cafe LaMama. Standard figures are clearly identified and the major works of many authors are cited, making this section very useful to the student.

VII. Accessibility

Access to this dictionary is good in general. A contents page, printed in a larger typeface than the text, immediately follows the title page and lists (1) the preliminary sections that guide a reader in using the work, (2) the main dictionary, and (3) the supplementary, encyclopedic material. The contents do not indicate whether the special material is in the form of charts, tables, or essays, but nevertheless will help readers locate material.

Especially helpful is a two-column guide to terms used in the *WICD*, preceding the "Guide to the Use of the Dictionary." The right-hand column shows a segment of entries with twenty labels printed opposite, keyed in with a ruled line to the individual parts of entries so that a reader can recognize the typographical conventions used for run-on derivatives or cross-references to maps and so forth. (Under Switzerland, for instance, the reference "• See map at ITALY." appears.)

The chartlike format of the pronunciation key makes the symbols appear more accessible than is often the case in dictionaries. The eighteen numbered short sections that explain the terms used in the dictionary contain good, short examples, and the brief pronunciation key on every right-hand page assures quick reference ability.

Throughout the main entries, page numbers are centered above each page of text; and a large, bold guide word is printed at the top outer edge of each page.

VIII. Graphics and Format

The larger format of this desk dictionary accommodates two columns of text per page, each column approximately 2¾-inches wide by 8¾- to 9¼-inches deep. Entry words are in clear, sans-serif bold type and the text is small but readable. The top and side margins are adequate, but the text runs uncomfortably close to the bottom of the pages, and the inner margins seem narrow. The dictionary lies flat when opened. There are no thumb index guides, but the paper is heavy enough to sustain riffling through the pages without creasing or tearing.

Of the almost 900 black-and-white line drawings, most are very clear, especially the illustrations for music, architecture, anatomy, and math (the last two have labels with lines directed to the appropriate area to be identified). Among the illustrations in the main section of entries are many charts and tables, including the Braille alphabet, a list of constellations by groups, a good diagram of a solar eclipse, a table of chemical elements, a table of geological time scales with life forms, a chart of comparative grades in the U.S. Armed Services, the Jewish calendar, eleven types of leaf, almost two pages of weights and measures, phases of the moon, a table of comparative U.S. and British values (1 million to 1 decillion), a periodical table of elements, an out-of-date table of planets (Neptune has 3 satellites not 2; Pluto's mass, diameter, and rotation are not current figures, etc.), proofreaders' marks, a temperature conversion table plus a zodiac with labels and an illustration of terrestrial zones. These features are all available in other reference sources, but their inclusion here gives the dictionary's encyclopedic appellation some weight and genuine usefulness.

In general, the illustrations attempt to picture an unfamiliar or confusing sense of words. There is also a special sixteen page section of photographs printed on glossy paper that are exceptionally outdated, especially those in the sciences. The same pages are among those appearing in WEBSTER'S COMPREHEN-

Webster's Concise Family Dictionary

❶ Pronunciation between slashes follows boldface entry word printed in large type

❷ Inflected forms, in bold, are given pronunciations; alternate or irregular forms are also boldfaced

❸ The etymology in bold square brackets provides meanings for the root words

❹ Synonym cross-references (in small capital letters) are preceded by a boldface colon

❺ Phrases illustrate the use of entry word (indicated by a swung dash)

¹**show** \'shō\ *vb* **showed** \'shōd\; **shown** \'shōn\ *or* **showed**; **show-ing** [ME *shewen, showen,* fr. OE *scēawian* to look, look at, see] **1 :** to cause or permit to be seen **:** EXHIBIT ⟨~ anger⟩ **2 :** CONFER, BESTOW ⟨~ mercy⟩ **3 :** RE-VEAL, DISCLOSE ⟨~*ed* courage in battle⟩ **4 :** INSTRUCT ⟨~*ed* me how to do it⟩ **5 :** PROVE ⟨~*s* he was guilty⟩ **6 :** AP-PEAR **7 :** to be noticeable **8 :** to be third in a horse race
²**show** *n* **1 :** a demonstrative display **2 :** outward appearance ⟨a ~ of resis-tance⟩ **3 :** SPECTACLE **4 :** a theatrical presentation **5 :** a radio or television program **6 :** third place in a horse race

SIVE DICTIONARY. The reproductions of the seven wonders of the world and bridges of the world are very old-fashioned, indeed, but constitute a historical record. This section could benefit from updating and redesigning, or an explanation of the time periods being illustrated. As it stands, it serves only as a quaint relic or curio for those users who enjoy a glimpse into the past.

IX. Summary

In a short review of the 1982 edition of the *Webster Illustrated Contemporary Dictionary* (under the Dou-bleday imprint), *Library Journal* commented, "The new edition of this desk dictionary seems little changed from the 1978 edition"—and this is still true. How-ever, for its size, this dictionary has a solid base of good definitions and some useful supplementary ma-terial. Many of the more contemporary words are defined carefully and are free of assumptions about a student's or general reader's knowledge of com-puter or medical terms.

One factor that makes this dictionary appear more out-of-date than its vocabulary suggests is the sup-plementary material, some of which is very dated and some of which also appears in multiple typefaces and formats. For classroom and school library use, nevertheless, this dictionary's lexicon is useful—for junior high school and up. With more substantial revision and updating, it would be an excellent work.

Webster's Concise Family Dictionary

Facts at a Glance

Full Title: **Webster's Concise Family Dictionary**.
Publisher: Merriam-Webster.
Editor: Henry Bosley Woolf.
Edition Reviewed: © 1975.

Number of Volumes: 1.
Number of Entries: 57,000.
Number of Pages: 848.
Trim Size: 6″ × 9¼″.
Binding: cloth.

Price: $8.95.
Intended Readership: junior high and up.
Sold in bookstores and other outlets; also sold to libraries and schools. ISBN 0-87779-039-6.

I. Introduction and Scope

This dictionary's lexicon is an exact duplicate of that in the paperback THE MERRIAM-WEBSTER DICTION-ARY, except for the printing of pronunciation sym-bols at both the front and back. For a review of the contents, see the evaluation of *The Merriam-Webster Dictionary*.

The dust jacket of *Webster's Concise Family Dic-tionary* indicates that the text is set in "larger print for easier use." The print *is* larger than that in stand-

Webster's Dictionary for Everyday Use

❶ Etymology, within brackets, follows the definition

❷ Dashes indicate a compound or hyphenated subentry

❸ Entry word is divided into syllables

❹ Field label is printed in italics

❺ Guide words and printed "thumb tabs" aid accessibility

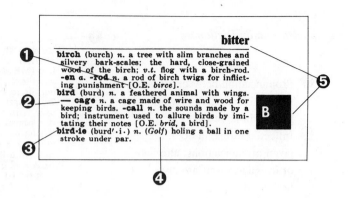

ard adult dictionaries, such as WEBSTER'S NINTH NEW COLLEGIATE, but it is still smaller than the type size used, for example, in most adult trade books. In the review copy, an unacceptable number of letters appeared broken or smudged. In many of these cases, it appeared that a quantity of ink had "lifted" from the pages before they were fully dried. Consumers should, therefore, check the printing they buy, especially by surveying the left-hand margin of the text columns where the superior numbers for successive homographs readily show these flaws.

Potential buyers should also keep in mind that this dictionary, like its paperback edition, dates from the mid-1970s; otherwise, the size of the print and the generally authoritative approach to the lexicon (although it is much condensed) may make this edition useful for students from junior high level up who have some visual impairment.

Webster's Dictionary for Everyday Use

Facts at a Glance
Full Title: **Webster's Dictionary for Everyday Use**.
Publisher: Barnes & Noble.
Edition Reviewed: © 1981; 1985 edition.

Number of Volumes: 1.
Number of Entries: over 50,000.
Number of Pages: 446.
Trim Size: 5⅜" × 7⅝".
Binding: paperback.

Price: $4.95.
Intended Readership: high school and up.

Sold in bookstores and other outlets. ISBN 0-06-463330-6.

I. Introduction and Scope

This paperback edition of a 1958 dictionary, originally compiled by John Gage Allee, professor of English philology at George Washington University, is a thoroughly out-of-date work that will be of little use to anyone. Furthermore, there is so little introductory information that students would find it very difficult to use. The shoddy printing and cheap paper combine with the other less-than-useful elements to produce a work that exemplifies the abuse of Webster's name when it is attached to a dictionary simply for marketing purposes.

Webster's Elementary Dictionary

Facts at a Glance
Full Title: **Webster's Elementary Dictionary**.
Former Title: *Webster's Beginning Dictionary*.
Publisher: Merriam-Webster Inc.
Editors: Merriam-Webster dictionary staff.
Edition Reviewed: © 1986.

Number of Volumes: 1.
Number of Entries: 32,000.
Number of Pages: 600.
Number of Illustrations: 600 in full color.
Trim Size: 8" × 10".
Binding: cloth.

Price: $10.95.
Intended Readership: elementary school students.
Sold in bookstores and other outlets; also sold to libraries and schools. ISBN 0-87779-475-8.

Webster's Elementary Dictionary

❶ Pronunciation, within slashes, is followed by the abbreviated part of speech

❷ Examples of usage appear in angle brackets

❸ Inflected forms, in bold, show syllable divisions with centered dots

❹ Synonyms in small capital letters follow some definitions and are cross-referenced to main entry words.

❺ A Word History paragraph is set off in blue type; it provides informal anecdotes that explain word origins

¹**es·cape** \is-'kāp\ *vb* **es·caped; es·cap·ing** **1** : to get away : get free or clear ⟨*escape* from a burning building⟩ **2** : to keep free of : AVOID ⟨managed to *escape* injury⟩ **3** : to fail to be noticed or remembered by ⟨the name *escapes* me⟩ **4** : to leak out from some enclosed place

Word History Picture a person who is held fast by a cape or cloak. The person being held may be able to slip out of the garment and so escape from the captor. The word *escape* is based on such a picture. The English word *escape* came from an Old French word that came from two Latin words. The first of these Latin words meant "out of" and the second meant "cloak."

²**escape** *n* **1** : the act of escaping **2** : a way of escaping

I. Introduction

Webster's Elementary Dictionary, suitable for grades four to six, is part of a series of three titles published by Merriam-Webster including WEBSTER'S INTERMEDIATE DICTIONARY and WEBSTER'S SCHOOL DICTIONARY. Originally published in 1980 and revised in 1986, the dictionary contains 32,000 entries and 600 illustrations in color. The preface to the dictionary states that words were chosen based on the frequency with which they appeared in school textbooks, in other materials that a student would normally read (these are not identified), and in everyday language use.

II. Authority

Merriam-Webster has been producing dictionaries since 1847 and is one of the most respected names in dictionary publishing. The preface states that the Merriam-Webster staff made use of the same information for this young readers' dictionary that is on file for the *Webster's Third New International* and WEBSTER'S NINTH NEW COLLEGIATE dictionaries, and that the *Elementary Dictionary* might be viewed as a "little brother or sister to those larger books."

III. Comprehensiveness

With its 32,000 words and phrases, this dictionary includes those words most students will ordinarily encounter.

Synonyms are included and identified, but anto-

nyms are not. Synonyms are dealt with in one of two ways in *Webster's Elementary Dictionary*. Synonym paragraphs are located at the end of an entry following the definition and headed with the word "**synonyms**" in bold type. Within this paragraph, the distinctions between synonymous terms are indicated. For example, under the entry for **bright**, the synonyms RADIANT and BRILLIANT are distinguished from one another and from the entry word:

BRIGHT can be used either of something that reflects a great amount of light ⟨a *bright* full moon⟩ or of something that produces much light ⟨*bright* stars⟩ RADIANT is more often used of something that sends forth its own light ⟨the sun is a *radiant* body⟩ BRILLIANT is used of something that shines with a sparkling or flashing light ⟨*brilliant* diamonds⟩.

The synonyms appear in small capital letters, indicating a cross-reference to another main entry word. Variants or inflected forms of other entries are indicated as follows: "**caught** *past of* CATCH," or "**eon** *variant of* AEON."

Webster's Elementary has separate entries for prefixes and suffixes; run-on entries follow the end of the entry for the base word and are preceded by a dash: — **hang on to** under the entry word **hang**. Run-in entries are also noted in boldface type and appear in parentheses in the middle of the definition, such as **summer solstice** under the entry word **solstice**. Some words are not defined except by a synonym. For example, under **ruckus** the reader is referred without comment to ⁴ROW, meaning the fourth definition of the entry word **row**, which is defined as "a noisy disturbance or quarrel" (students familiar with Maurice Sendak's *Where the Wild Things Are* will have no trouble with this).

This dictionary also includes usage notes, homographs, and word histories. Usage notes follow the definition and are separated from it by a dash. For example, the entry word **sonny** has the following usage note: "— used mostly to address a stranger." Homographs are given separate entries; homophones, or words that sound alike but are spelled differently, such as **bare** and **bear**, are given no special notation.

There are a substantial number of word history paragraphs in the dictionary. These are indented under the main entry, labeled "**Word History**," and printed in bright blue type. They are written in a style appropriate for children and are accurate and informative. Under the word **academy** the following word history is found:

> In ancient Greece, a wise man named Plato started a school at a gymnasium. The gymnasium was named for a hero of Greek mythology. The English word *academy* came from the name of the hero for whom Plato's school was named.

This is a more precise definition than that found for similar types of historical background on words, for example, in the MACMILLAN DICTIONARY FOR CHILDREN.

Few abbreviations are to be found in the dictionary. Some exceptions include **Mr.**, **Mrs.**, **TNT**, and **DNA**. Unfortunately, neither **TNT** nor **DNA** is spelled out, although they are defined. For example:

> **DNA** . . . *n:* a complicated organic acid that carries genetic information in the chromosomes.

Clearly, scientific terminology does not fit into a controlled vocabulary although students encounter the term in the classroom and in texts. There are, in general, very few scientific terms included, and, in random search, no archaic words were found.

Even though this reference work is intended for elementary school, the publisher did not avoid the inclusion of sex organs, although such terms as *homosexual*, *lesbian*, and the definition of *gay* as homosexual are absent. Computer terms such as *bit* and *byte* are also not included, nor are *VCR* and *videocassette*. Biographical and geographic names are not included in the main alphabet, but a separate pronouncing glossary for place names is appended to the back of the dictionary.

IV. Quality and Currency of Definitions

Main entry words are in boldface type overhanging the text; definitions are printed in a medium-weight type. A typical order for entries is: main word, pronunciation, abbreviated part of speech, definition(s), numbered and occasionally cross-referenced to other entries. For example:

> **cor·rec·tion** | kə-ʹrek-shən*ʹn* **1** : the act of correcting **2** : a change that makes something right **3** : PUNISHMENT **1**.

Definitions are clearly and simply stated and are very adequate. Several senses are given for many words and are listed in historical order. Separate, numbered entries are given for the various parts of speech, which are identified using the following abbreviations: *n* noun, *vb* verb, *adj* adjective, and *adv* adverb. Verbal illustrations are used to help define difficult words and appear in angle brackets to separate them from the definitions:

> ¹**cor·rect** . . . *vb* **1** : to make or set right <*correct* a misspelled word> . . . .

Most verbal illustrations, as in this example, are in the form of phrases or modifiers rather than complete sentences. In *Webster's Elementary* not nearly as many definitions have verbal illustrations as in the MACMILLAN DICTIONARY FOR CHILDREN, which consistently uses sentences. However, more senses of a word are given in the Merriam-Webster work than in the Macmillan. For example, in the former the adjective **crisp** has five meanings in addition to a separate entry for the verb form of the word; the Macmillan dictionary has three. Although this proliferation of meanings followed by bracketed illustrations makes for a more complete work, it might also be confusing to students in the lower elementary grades.

Students in grades five and six will surely be familiar, however, with such terms as *database* and *word processing*, in addition to other current words that are missing from the *Webster's Elementary*, and that should be included in a 1986 revision.

V. Syllabication and Pronunciation

Both syllabication and pronunciation are indicated. Entry words are given in syllables separated by bold, centered dots. Pronunciation follows and appears between back slashes: **prize·fight·er** \ ʹprīz-fīt-ərʹ \. Forty-three symbols, with diacritical marks are used in the pronunciation key, which appears on the page preceding the main body of the dictionary; accent marks indicate primary or secondary stress. There is also a useful short key to 25 of the most frequent symbols on the lower right-hand corner of each right-hand page. The key provides a quick reference for students. Variant pronunciations ("used by large numbers of educated people") are indicated, which is not always the case in children's dictionaries. For example, two pronunciations are given for **abacus** and **abdomen**; for **betroth** three variations of pronunciation are noted. Such accuracy is admirable in a children's dictionary, and although it may be confusing to some students, it will also help to explain to students the frequent inconsistencies heard in everyday speech.

VI. Special Features

The features in this dictionary include the guide and the key to pronunciation in the front, and several appendixes in the back. The guide makes use of color blocks to emphasize examples in its explanation of the parts of the dictionary. This will help young readers to understand how to use the dictionary. The appendixes are: a list of abbreviations, which includes the two-letter postal abbreviations for the states; a chart of signs and symbols; separate chronological lists for U.S. presidents and vice presidents that indicate pronunciation of name, birth and death dates, birthplace, and terms of office (Ronald Reagan and George Bush are included); and a list of geographic names that includes U.S. states, Canadian provinces and territories, nations of the world and their capitals, along with continents and oceans of the world. Each geographic name is given a pronunciation; this feature is useful for young readers, although for the presidents' and vice-presidents' names this seems superfluous since none is truly a tongue twister.

VII. Accessibility

Entries are in letter-by-letter alphabetical order, including abbreviations and disregarding spaces and hyphens. There are guide words at the top of each double-column page, but no thumb guides. Words beginning with capital letters are included as appropriate and variant spellings of words are given. However, the method of noting the preferred spelling is overly complicated for an elementary school student. When variant spellings are indicated, they are given in alphabetical order and separated by the word "*or*" to indicate that either is acceptable. When they appear out of alphabetical order (for example, "**disk** *or* **disc**"), this indicates that **disk** is more commonly

in use. A third means of indicating preference is through the use of the word "*also*." An example is "**T-shirt** *also* **tee shirt**," which tells the reader that the second spelling is not only less common, but *much* less common. Such fine shades of distinction are undoubtedly lost on all but the brightest of upper-level elementary school children.

VIII. Graphics and Format

The dictionary has 582 pages plus 18 pages of prefatory matter. There are 600 illustrations in full color. They are less cartoonlike in style and more artistically rendered than most pictures in elementary dictionaries.

Most of the illustrations depict objects rather than people; care has been taken, however, to include a variety of ethnic groups among those people illustrated. Most of the illustrations appear immediately above or below the entry word that they help to define, and all are clearly captioned in boldface. A few are placed in a different column or even on a different page, which makes them less useful to a reader. Most clearly depict the word defined, but the illustration for **transit**, a surveyor's instrument, for example, is lost in the background scene of a grassy hill and is too small to clearly identify.

The overall layout of the pages is pleasing and the text easy to read. The illustrations as well as the bright blue word histories help to break up the pages of type. The nonglare paper is sufficiently heavy to avoid show-through, but the print on some pages of the review copy was slightly blurred. The cover is made of bright yellow, cloth-covered boards that have been coated with a nonglossy acrylic. The book lies flat when opened, and the margins next to the spine are ample enough to permit rebinding. However, the binding is quite sturdy, so it will probably not be necessary to rebind for moderate use.

IX. Summary

If it is possible to put together a "scholarly" children's dictionary, then Merriam-Webster has succeeded with the *Webster's Elementary Dictionary*. Admirably, the publisher has attempted not to compromise quality for the sake of simplicity. The problem is that this is not an easy dictionary for children to use without assistance. The guide to the dictionary's use may be especially difficult to understand because of its large amount of explanatory (although excellent) text. Consider this paragraph related to variant spellings:

When variant spellings are shown at the beginning

of the entry, all of the variants are used in all meanings. If one variant form is shown at a particular definition, however, that spelling is more common for that meaning.

Many adults would need to read this paragraph more than once to make sense of it; children will need a teacher's or parent's guidance to understand the information. In comparison, the MACMILLAN DICTIONARY FOR CHILDREN has more eye appeal and is far easier to use. The Macmillan work does, however, sacrifice the detail and, sometimes, the accuracy that Merriam-Webster has tried to maintain. *Webster's Elementary Dictionary* should be available for bright students in the upper elementary grades, but even they will need assistance in understanding the finer points of its use. The work is also a possible choice for older students (junior high and high school) who need a simpler dictionary and also for those whose first language is not English. Especially useful would be the multiple senses given under an entry such as **bug**, meaning flaw as in "try to get the *bugs* out of the TV set," or a person who is enthusiastic, such as a "camera *bug*." *Webster's Elementary Dictionary* is an excellent dictionary with much to recommend it, even though it will not be *easy* for elementary students to read. However, those who do learn its intricacies will be well prepared to go on to more adult dictionaries.

Webster's Intermediate Dictionary

Facts at a Glance

Full Title: **Webster's Intermediate Dictionary**.
Publisher: Merriam-Webster Inc.
Editors: Merriam-Webster editorial staff.
Edition Reviewed: © 1986.

Number of Volumes: 1.
Number of Entries: over 65,000.
Number of Pages: 960.
Number of Illustrations: 1,000 in black and white.
Trim Size: 7⅛" × 9¼".
Binding: cloth.

Price: $9.95.
Intended Readership: grades 5 through 8.
Sold in bookstores and other outlets; also sold to libraries and schools. ISBN 0-87779-379-4.

I. Introduction

Webster's Intermediate Dictionary is the middle volume in a series of three school dictionaries published by Merriam-Webster. According to the preface, it is intended for middle and junior high school students: "The range of vocabulary covered is suited to the needs of older students, but the definitions have been written in everyday language that young students will find clear." The dictionary focuses on words that students will encounter in curricular materials, including both traditional and newer subjects. This 1986 work is a first edition, although a similar dictionary, intended for junior high and high school students, was published in 1977 under the title *Webster's New Student's Dictionary*.

II. Authority

The dictionary was compiled by Merriam-Webster's permanent staff of trained, experienced lexicographers. Entries were selected primarily on the basis of their occurrence in textbooks and other materials used in schools. In addition, the editors have consulted Merriam-Webster's extensive citation files—the files that underlie *Webster's Third New International Dictionary* and other Webster dictionaries—to ensure "that the current general vocabulary of English has received its proper share of attention."

III. Comprehensiveness

Webster's Intermediate Dictionary is comprehensive for its size and intended audience. New words are included from such fields as computer science (**byte, COBOL, floppy disk**) and video technology (**videocassette recorder**, cross-referenced to **VCR**). Terms for sexual and reproductive organs are included, with clear, brief definitions. Included are the words **homosexual** and **lesbian**; unusual, but appropriate is a synonymous cross-reference from **gay** to **homosexual**. *AIDS*, however, is excluded. Abbreviations and biographical and geographic entries appear in separate appended lists that are among the dictionary's special features.

The dictionary also includes irregularly formed plurals and inflected verbs; usage labels and notes; illustrative phrases for many common words, such as **collect, edge**, and **gather**; synonym paragraphs, which differentiate among synonyms in terms of their connotations; etymologies; and anecdotal word histories. Etymologies for main entry words provide the root word with its language and meaning and, in some cases, cross-references to related words. Names of languages are not abbreviated, which will be useful

Webster's Intermediate Dictionary

❶ Boldface entry word, divided into syllables, is followed by pronunciation within slashes

❷ Cross-reference to synonym (in small capital letters) is preceded by a colon

❸ A Word History introduces related words

❹ Etymology, within square brackets, spells out the names of languages

❺ Labeled illustration of first definition

❻ Brief illustration of use appears in angle brackets

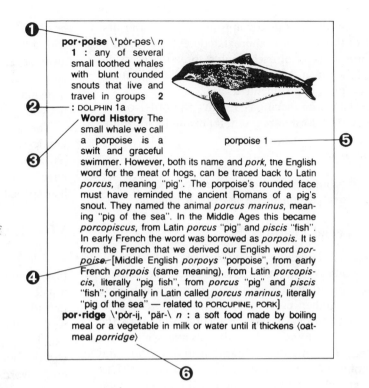

por·poise \'pȯr-pəs\ *n*
1 : any of several small toothed whales with blunt rounded snouts that live and travel in groups **2** : DOLPHIN 1a
Word History The small whale we call a porpoise is a swift and graceful swimmer. However, both its name and *pork*, the English word for the meat of hogs, can be traced back to Latin *porcus*, meaning "pig". The porpoise's rounded face must have reminded the ancient Romans of a pig's snout. They named the animal *porcus marinus*, meaning "pig of the sea". In the Middle Ages this became *porcopiscus*, from Latin *porcus* "pig" and *piscis* "fish". In early French the word was borrowed as *porpois*. It is from the French that we derived our English word *porpoise*. [Middle English *porpoys* "porpoise", from early French *porpois* (same meaning), from Latin *porcopiscis*, literally "pig fish", from *porcus* "pig" and *piscis* "fish"; originally in Latin called *porcus marinus*, literally "pig of the sea" — related to PORCUPINE, PORK]
por·ridge \'pȯr-ij, 'pär-\ *n* : a soft food made by boiling meal or a vegetable in milk or water until it thickens (oatmeal *porridge*)

porpoise 1 — ❺

to the young reader. Historical language periods are distinguished only for English. Word history paragraphs are interestingly written and amplify on the origins of words. For example, the origin of **sideburns** is explained in the following paragraph, which appears between the definition and the etymology:

> During the American Civil War, the Union general Ambrose Everett Burnside became known for the long bushy whiskers he wore on the sides of his face. Burnside was a popular figure in the city of Washington during the early days of the war. His unusual appearance caught the public eye, and other men soon began growing long whiskers like his. Such whiskers, which became the fashion throughout America, were originally called *burnsides* after the general. The modern word *sideburns* was formed by rearranging the letters of the older word *burnsides*.

The length and narrative quality of these paragraphs will encourage students to browse through the volume.

IV. Quality and Currency of Entries

Definitions are clearly stated. For example, countenance is defined as

1 a : calm expression **b** : calmness of mind **2** : ¹FACE

1, 3a; *esp* : facial expression as a sign of mood, emotion, or character **3** : a show of approval < gave no *countenance* to the plan>

When an entry contains multiple definitions, they are numbered in order of frequency of use with separate senses identified by lowercase letters. Although the illustrative phrases (provided in angle brackets) are helpful, they are less useful for students than the *full* sentences provided in other dictionaries, such as the MACMILLAN SCHOOL DICTIONARY, for this age level. Furthermore, the editors' avoidance of oversimplification is to be applauded, but they have produced a dictionary whose proliferation of definitions may occasionally overwhelm middle school and junior high school students.

Some useful adjuncts to definitions are provided. Under **bell**, for example, there is a table of a ship's bells indicating how many are tolled for each hour of the day. Under **Bible** appears a list of Old and New Testament biblical books. A table under **element** provides symbol, atomic number, and atomic weight of chemical elements.

V. Syllabication and Pronunciation

Syllabication is indicated by centered boldface dots. Pronunciation, following the main entry word, is provided for all words. The dictionary uses a pronunciation system consisting of 44 symbols and five diacritical marks. A full key appears opposite the first page of the word list; abbreviated keys are found at the bottom right of each double spread. Accessible sample words in both versions of the key will make it easy for young students to use.

Variant pronunciations are given in order of frequency. Two forms are given, for example, for **route**:

'rüt, 'raůt.

All the pronunciations given are used, according to the editors, by educated speakers of English.

VI. Special Features

Webster's Intermediate Dictionary begins with an eight-page guide, "Using Your Dictionary." The guide is thorough and written in a style appropriate for the intended audience.

Four additional reference sections appear at the back of the volume: "Abbreviations and Symbols for Chemical Elements," biographical, biblical, and mythological names, geographical names, and signs and symbols. The first of these includes most common utility abbreviations, as well as, among others, those for U.S. states, world nations, and well-known companies and organizations. The biographical and geographic lists include pronunciation. For biographical names, dates, when known, are given, as well as a brief identification. For example, for **Ronald Wilson Reagan**, the entry reads

1911— 40th president of the U.S. (1981—).

The geographic list is up-to-date. **Upper Volta**, for example, is cross-referenced to **Burkina Faso**. The final feature presents signs and symbols used in a number of fields, including astronomy, business, music, and others. All of these features make this work a more comprehensive reference source for students.

VII. Accessibility

Alphabetization is letter by letter. Variant spellings are offered according to a complex system. Equal variants—that is, two spellings that are equally acceptable in current English—are separated by the word *or*. If one of them occurs with slightly greater frequency, it is listed first; for example,

di·a·logue *or* **di·a·log**.

Unequal variants are separated by *also*; the one listed first is significantly more common. When three or more variants are presented, both *or* and *also* may

be used. An acceptable variant is given its own entry, with a cross-reference, when it appears one column away or farther from the main entry. Restricted variants, such as British spellings, appear only at their own main entry. This system may be cumbersome for young readers.

The volume has no thumb index or thumb guides. Guide words, however, appear at the top of each page indicating the first and last word defined on the page. A table of contents at the front of the book lists special features, making them easy to locate.

VIII. Graphics and Format

Webster's Intermediate Dictionary is illustrated with black line drawings. These are small, in most cases a half-column or less in width. Illustrations are not provided for many words whose meanings could be well clarified visually, such as **castanet** and **catamaran**; however, those illustrations that appear are well chosen and helpful. They are captioned with main entry words and, when applicable, definition numerals; occasionally a phrase of clarification is added to the caption.

The dictionary's print is medium-sized and easy to read. Text is printed in two columns on each page, with ample margins. Main entry words are boldfaced and overhang the text. Boldface is also used for inflected forms. Synonyms appear in block capitals. Italics are used for part-of-speech abbreviations, entry words recurring within illustrative phrases, and non-English words in etymologies. These variations facilitate the location of information; however, illustrative phrases, although they are enclosed within angle brackets, do not stand out as sharply as they would if entirely italicized, as in the MACMILLAN SCHOOL DICTIONARY. The text is printed on nonglare paper with minimal show-through. The volume lies flat when opened. Sturdily bound with an easily cleaned cover, it will hold up to heavy use.

IX. Summary

Webster's Intermediate Dictionary is a straightforward, inexpensive dictionary. It is up-to-date, and its clear definitions are accessible to middle and junior high school students, although some younger readers may find the discrimination of meaning formidable. Anecdotal etymologies add interest to the volume and encourage students to browse. The appearance of the dictionary is very sober. No color is used in the illustrations, and although the guide to the dictionary is clear, it does not invite students' interest.

The dictionary is comparable to the MACMILLAN SCHOOL DICTIONARY, which has the same number of entries, but which uses color and illustrations, and larger type advantageously. Although the Macmillan dictionary is considerably more expensive, it may be more attractive to many younger students and more easily used without adult assistance.

Webster's New Compact Dictionary for School and Office

Facts at a Glance

Full Title: **Webster's New Compact Dictionary for School and Office**.
Publisher: Thomas Nelson, Inc.
Editor: Walter C. Kidney; revised edition prepared under the direction of Laurence Urdang.
Edition Reviewed: 1985.

Number of Volumes: 1.
Number of Entries: 30,000.
Number of Pages: 313.
Trim Size: 4½″ × 6¼″.
Binding: hardbound.

Price: $2.95.
Intended Readership: middle school and up.
Sold in bookstores and other outlets; also sold to schools. ISBN 0-8407-4081-6.

I. Introduction

Webster's New Compact Dictionary for School and Office, originally published in 1978 and issued in a revised edition in 1985, is a quick-reference dictionary. As the title suggests, its compact size makes it readily portable for students or for work environments in which space is in short supply.

II. Authority

The title page credits Walter C. Kidney as editor, but adds that the dictionary was "prepared under the direction of Laurence Urdang." Urdang's credentials as a linguist and lexicographer are well-known, and one expects a dictionary bearing his name to be highly reputable. However, the full extent of his involvement in this work is not revealed, and a degree of skepticism about the dictionary's authority may be in order.

III. Comprehensiveness

Webster's New Compact Dictionary for School and Office is by no means intended to be comprehensive. Rather, as the "Foreword" notes, this dictionary is designed to provide "fingertip answers to the most frequent language puzzlers: spelling, hyphenation, and pronunciation." The parts of speech are identified, and some usage and field labels are included, but there has been no apparent effort to apply them with any regularity. Biographical and geographical names are not included, nor are synonyms, antonyms, or etymologies given.

IV. Quality and Currency of Entries

In the interest of space, the definitions given in *Webster's New Compact Dictionary* are rudimentary. They are also not necessarily succinct or clear, and do not always provide enough information to convey the essence of the word being defined. For example, **carrier** is defined as "**1**. thing or person that carries. **2**. aircraft carrier." Both definitions verge on circularity; the first gives no notion of the kind of "thing" a carrier might be (a bag, for example), while the second merely gives the full form of the expression for which it may be used as an abbreviation. Curiously, there is no entry for "aircraft carrier"; the dictionary defines **aircraft** as "flying craft." Some definitions are unduly broad and imprecise. **Cantor** is defined as "singer at a Jewish service." The definition for **destroy** ("damage so as to eliminate") in no way conveys any of this word's connotative sense.

Definitions of this sort send the reader on a frustrating wild goose chase through the dictionary. For example, the reader looking up the meaning of **handgun** will find merely "pistol." The definition for pistol is "small hand-carried firearm"; **firearm** is inadequately if not incorrectly defined as "weapon operated by explosives," and so on.

Webster's New Compact Dictionary is by no means consistent in its inclusion of commonly used words that have only recently entered the vocabulary. The reader will search in vain for such current terms as *access* in its computer sense, *acid rain*, *compact disc*, *VDT*, or *videocassette*. He or she will, however, find the computer terms **bit**, **byte**, and **diskette**, as well as such foreign words as **ayatollah**.

V. Syllabication and Pronunciation

Syllabication and pronunciation are indicated by the conventional method of dots and diacritical marks. Full phonetic pronunciation is given only in rare instances, however. Presumably, those words for which pronunciation is given are ones that may be expected to cause difficulty for many readers. However, there seems to be no particular method underlying the choice of such words. For example, phonetic pronunciation is not provided for such potentially troublesome words as **cynosure**, **dahlia**, or **ubiquity**, but is provided for **conflict**, **partial**, and **spoor**. A more serious drawback is the absence of any pronunciation key.

VI. Special Features

Webster's New Compact Dictionary contains a minimum of special features. It does include tables of weights and measures, metric equivalents, wedding anniversary symbols, birthstones, and states and territories of the United States (with post office abbreviations and capitals).

VII. Accessibility

Entry words are arranged alphabetically, letter by letter. Guide words indicate the first entry on left-hand pages and the last entry on right-hand pages. All in all, *Webster's New Compact Dictionary* is reasonably accessible.

VIII. Graphics and Format

Whatever its other deficiencies, *Webster's New Compact Dictionary* is a well-designed book. Entry words, printed in boldface type, overhang the main text. Variant forms and related words are also printed in boldface, while part-of-speech labels are italicized. The print is legible throughout.

The book is printed in two columns per page; each page is numbered at the center of the bottom margin. There are no illustrations.

IX. Summary

Webster's New Compact Dictionary for School and Office is intended primarily for quick reference. It provides spellings, some pronunciation guidance, and basic definitions—but not much more. Its definitions are often reduced to a single word, and are rarely longer than a brief phrase. Multiple meanings of a word are seldom given. Moreover, as previously noted in this review, the definitions that are given are frequently inadequate.

The bright red cover, with its embossed gold lettering, gives this dictionary an attractive appearance, and the graphics and format are appealing for a book of this size. However, even at its low price, this dictionary is no bargain. Readers seeking a simple compact dictionary might be better served by WEBSTER'S NEW WORLD HANDY POCKET DICTIONARY.

Webster's New World Compact Dictionary of American English

Facts at a Glance

Full Title: **Webster's New World Compact Dictionary of American English**.
Publisher: Prentice Hall Press.
Editor: David B. Guralnik.
Edition Reviewed: © 1981; fifth printing.

Number of Volumes: 1.
Number of Entries: over 38,000.
Number of Pages: 630.
Trim Size: 3″ × 4½″.
Binding: paper.

Price: $4.95.
Intended Readership: junior high school and up.
Sold in bookstores; also sold to libraries and schools. ISBN 0-671-41802-5.

I. Introduction

Webster's New World Compact Dictionary of American English is intended for those people who "need a simple, accurate, modern aid to a sound working knowledge of the language," according to the preface. Of the more than 38,000 entries, about 22,000 are main entries.

II. Authority

The editors based this compact dictionary on WEBSTER'S NEW WORLD DICTIONARY OF THE AMERICAN LANGUAGE: SECOND COLLEGE EDITION. The parent dictionary, also edited by David B. Guralnik, is well recognized as an authoritative dictionary.

III. Comprehensiveness

In addition to commonly used words, the preface states that the dictionary "contains hundreds of newer terms and newer senses of established terms not to be found in other dictionaries of similar scope." And indeed, such words as **ICBM**, **closed circuit**, **hardware** (the computer-related definition), and **zero population growth** are included; but *floppy disc* and *data base*, for example, are not. When slang is used, the definition is coded, as in

croak 2. [Sl.] die

IV. Quality and Currency of Entries

The definitions have been reduced to the minimum number of words possible that still allow for clarity. Many abbreviations, prefixes, and suffixes are listed in the lexicon, and idiomatic phrases are found in the definitions. Parts of speech are abbreviated and are found just following the main entry. Many colloquialisms are identified. Parts of speech are not given for foreign terms such as **bon jour** or for abbreviations such as **AM** and **A.M.** Examples of these very brief definitions are:

crackpot *n.* [Col.] an eccentric
crackup *n. 1.* crash **2.** [Col.] mental breakdown
cranberry *n.* [*pl.* -ies] sour, edible, red berry

Words or terms requiring more than a descriptive word or phrase are given longer definitions.

electoral college assembly that formally elects the U.S. president

As mentioned above, many new words and phrases have been included, although there are omissions that size alone cannot explain, for example: the verb **program**, in the sense of planning a computer program for, is included, while no verb form for **access** appears at all.

V. Syllabication and Pronunciation

Syllabication is indicated by dots and bold and light stresses between syllables in the main entry word. An abbreviated pronunciation key is provided just prior to the guide to the use of the dictionary, but pronunciations (in parentheses) are given infrequently—only when deemed necessary.

VI. Special Features

There are 21 pages appended to the dictionary that provide a variety of useful information: abbreviations; information on countries and the United States; national parks of the U.S.; the presidents of the U.S.; and weights and measures.

VII. Accessibility

Accessibility is by letter-by-letter alphabetical order. Guide words at the top of each column indicate the first and last words appearing on each page. Meanings within definitions are numbered in bold print.

VIII. Graphics and Format

Main entries overhang the definitions and are easy to find. The main entry and subentry words and part-of-speech abbreviations are in bold print. Each page contains two columns separated by a vertical black rule. There are no illustrations. The book is small and has an inch-thick spine. The flexible cover is covered with strong reinforced paper.

IX. Summary

This is a more useful small dictionary than are many of the others available. It contains numerous new terms, and it provides slang and colloquial meanings for many of the words. The limited size necessarily limits the number of main entries and the depth and completeness of the definitions. Therefore, while this is acceptable as a personal quick reference dictionary for junior high and up, public and school libraries should pass this one up.

Webster's New World Compact School and Office Dictionary

Facts at a Glance

Full Title: **Webster's New World Compact School and Office Dictionary**.
Publisher: Prentice Hall Press.
Editor: David B. Guralnik, Editor-in-Chief.
Edition Reviewed: © 1982; 12th printing.

Number of Volumes: 1.
Number of Entries: 56,000.
Number of Pages: 540.
Trim Size: 5¼" × 8".
Bindings: cloth; paperback.

Prices: $8.95; $5.95.
Intended Readership: high school and up.
Sold in bookstores and other outlets; also sold to libraries and schools. ISBN 0-671-41822-X. 0-671-44882-X.

I. Introduction

As the title suggests, this dictionary is a condensed version of the WEBSTER'S NEW WORLD DICTIONARY: SECOND COLLEGE EDITION intended for use in the home, office, and the classroom. The 56,000 entries are about average size for smaller dictionaries of this type, but its physical format is somewhat larger than the typical "pocket" dictionary. According to

Webster's New World Compact School and Office Dictionary

❶ Abbreviated usage notes, in lightface brackets, precede the meaning

❷ Idioms in boldface type are defined

❸ Brief etymology appears in bold brackets before the definitions

❹ Field labels, abbreviated, are italicized

❺ Sample phrases, with entry word in italics, are placed within slant brackets at the end of numbered meanings

num·ber (num′bər) *n.* [< L. *numerus*] **1.** a symbol or word showing how many or which one in a series (Ex.: 2, 27, four, sixth) **2.** [*pl.*] arithmetic **3.** the sum or total of persons or units **4.** *a*) [*often pl.*] many *b*) [*pl.*] numerical superiority **5.** quantity **6.** *a*) a single issue of a periodical *b*) a single song, dance, etc. in a program of entertainment **7.** [Colloq.] a person or thing singled out /a smart *number*/ **8.** *Gram.* the form of a word as indicating either singular or plural —*vt.* **1.** to count; enumerate **2.** to give a number to **3.** to include as one of a group **4.** to limit the number of **5.** to comprise; total —*vi.* to be numbered —**beyond** (or **without**) **number** too numerous to be counted —**the numbers** an illegal lottery based on certain numbers published in newspapers: also **numbers pool** (or **racket**)

the dictionary's foreword, the words entered have been carefully selected to include all the commonly used words that make up the basic vocabulary of English. In addition, the foreword states that many frequently encountered specialized terms are listed as well as abbreviations, foreign words, and phrases.

II. Authority

The primary authority for this work is the college edition of *Webster's New World Dictionary*, originally published jointly by William Collins and World Publishing, with the well-known lexicographer, David B. Guralnik, as Editor-in-Chief. According to the editor, the database for the dictionary was created and maintained by the publisher's own lexicographic staff. Many printers use the Webster New World system of hyphenation (for end-of-line word breaks) as a standard, which may be of special interest to high school students interested in journalism, communications, or writing as a profession.

III. Comprehensiveness

The *Webster's New World Compact School and Office Dictionary* gives brief etymological notes, but they are not nearly as detailed as in the parent work. As a rule only the last language prior to a word's entrance into English is noted. The practice of marking Americanisms is not used in the compact edition, as it is in the college edition. The use of a double dagger signifies a foreign word, such as **maitre d'hôtel**, but **faux pas** is not marked because it has become a part of standard English.

Biographical and geographical names are omitted from the main alphabetical listing of words. However, some personal names are included, such as Greek and Roman gods and goddesses, including **Poseidon** (Greek) and **Jupiter** (Roman). There are a surprising number of literary figures included for a compact dictionary; **Faust**, **Juliet**, and **Ali Baba** are examples of only a few.

Other features are the inclusion of parts of speech, usually abbreviated and in boldface type. Few slang terms are to be found in the dictionary, but there are quite a number of abbreviations.

IV. Quality and Currency of Entries

Main entry words are in letter-by-letter alphabetical order. Definitions are easy to understand and brief, but not so brief as to be almost meaningless, which is often the case with small dictionaries. They would be appropriate for high school and bright junior high school students as well as college students and adults. Occasionally an archaic word turns up, such as **yclept**, **ycleped** meaning "to call." **Yarmulke** or **yarmalke**, the skull cap worn by Jewish men, is included, but for the most part the words in this dictionary are those known by almost any well-read college graduate. A few current words are included, such as **videocassette**, but *futon* and *byte*, for example, are not in the dictionary.

Two, three, and sometimes more meanings are given for many words. When there is more than one meaning, they appear in chronological order, as in the parent volume. Meanings under the main entry words are separated by boldface Arabic numerals. The entry for **gauge** is an example of the definitions provided in this dictionary:

> **gauge** . . . **1.** a standard measure **2.** any device for measuring **3.** the distance between the rails of a railway

4. the size of the bore of a shotgun—**vt. gauged, gauging 1**. to measure the size, amount, etc. of **2**. to estimate; judge . . .

A comparison of the number of definitions for **gauge** with the *Second College Edition* shows that there are thirteen in the latter including a number of specialized meanings for the noun, and six meanings for the verbs. There are few specialized entries or meanings in the *Compact School and Office Dictionary* in spite of the claims made in the dictionary foreword. Homographs are given separate, numbered entries.

V. Syllabication and Pronunciation

Pronunciation and syllabication are given immediately following the entry word and appear in parentheses. The key to pronunciation appears on the inside of the front cover; it follows the same format as the parent dictionary but excludes a key to foreign sounds. Along with the key are a few explanatory notes on some of the more complex symbols from the International Phonetic Alphabet (IPA). The print on this page is not as crisp as it should be, and some symbols such as *ch*, *zh*, and *g* (the nasal sound of the -*ng* in *sing*) and the like are blurred. There are no abbreviated pronunciation keys at the bottom of the pages of the lexicon, which is something of a disadvantage to readers who may seek pronunciation guidance for unfamiliar words.

Syllables in the main entry words and run-on entries are separated by black dots. Heavy accent marks indicate the stressed syllable, and a lighter accent mark indicates secondary stress. For example: **cor-onation** is pronounced

(kôr′ə nā′shən).

VI. Special Features

Webster's New World Compact School and Office Dictionary has a number of special lists and tables appended to the back of the book. These include tables of weights and measures with a separate table of metrics and notes on how to convert U.S. measures to metric. There is a three-page manual on the correct use of punctuation marks that may be useful to students and others. Less useful is a list of presidents and vice presidents of the U.S. (including Reagan and Bush) giving their dates of office, a five-page dictionary of geographical entries, and brief lists of principal cities of the U.S. (with 1980 census population figures) and foreign countries.

VII. Accessibility

Main entry words are in letter-by-letter alphabetical order. The boldface entries overhang the text which is printed in two columns of readable text. Compared to many small dictionaries, the pages of *Webster's New World Compact* are clearly designed and hence the words are very easy to locate. There are no thumb guides, but none are really needed. Paired guide words at the top of double-column pages facilitate thumbing through the dictionary.

Alternate spellings of words are provided such as **catalog** and **catalogue**. When the alternate spelling of a word falls some distance away in the alphabet, a cross-reference is used, such as "**kerb** . . . *Brit. sp.* of CURB (n.3)." In this way, the reader is referred from a British spelling of the word to the third meaning under the main entry **curb**, which is the stone or concrete curbing along a street. Words derived from the formation of other English words are also noted, such as **movie** which clearly shows the word's derivation in bold brackets following the part of speech:

[<MOVING PICTURE] a motion picture.

VIII. Graphics and Format

There are no illustrations in this dictionary and they would serve little use, given the size and purpose of a compact dictionary. The typeface is clear, but the margins are very narrow. Page 350 of the review copy had a skewed margin so that it almost ran off the edge of the paper. In spite of its somewhat larger size for a compact dictionary, this paperback does not lie flat when opened, but it has an extra sturdy binding. Although it could not be rebound, the price is modest so it can be easily replaced after substantial use.

IX. Summary

Webster's New World Compact School and Office Dictionary is a very handy quick reference guide to words, their spelling, pronunciation, and meanings, as well as their parts of speech. The appended materials are for the most part useful, and although limited; the dictionary of geography can be an aid to the correct spelling of place names. In addition, it has a more readable, less cluttered format than many paperback dictionaries. Although mostly useful for student home reference, this could be purchased for circulation in school and in public libraries.

Webster's New World Dictionary of the American Language: Second College Edition

Facts at a Glance

Full Title: **Webster's New World Dictionary of the American Language: Second College Edition.**
Publisher: Prentice Hall Press.
Editors: David B. Guralnik, Editor-in-Chief; Samuel Solomon, Mitford M. Mathews, and William E. Umbach.
Edition Reviewed: © 1986.

Number of Volumes: 1.
Number of Entries: 160,000.
Number of Pages: 1,728.
Number of Illustrations: 1,300 in black and white.
Trim Size: $7\frac{3}{8}'' \times 9''$.
Binding: cloth.

Prices: $16.95 thumb-indexed; $15.95 plain.
Intended Readership: high school and up.
Sold in bookstores and other outlets; also sold to libraries and schools. ISBN 0-671-41809-2.

I. Introduction

Webster's New World Dictionary of the American Language: Second College Edition is the revised second edition of a work of the same title, which was first published in 1953. The second edition initially appeared in 1970, and the work has been updated biennially.

Defined by its publisher as "the world's most up-to-date and authoritative desk dictionary," the work contains over 160,000 entries. The revised edition contains more than 20,000 new words reflecting current usage. The basic lexicon is appropriate for high school, college, and adult levels. The publisher believes the work to be the most comprehensive source among college dictionaries for Americanisms: it "identifies more than 14,000 words and meanings that first became part of the English language in the United States." The work is also the first general dictionary to explain the origins of American geographic names.

II. Authority

The dictionary is published by Prentice Hall Press, a division of the highly respected Simon & Schuster, Inc. Many outstanding writers, language scholars, and expert subject consultants contributed to the work. David B. Guralnik, Editor-in-Chief, has had a long

and distinguished career as a lexicographer and publishing executive, first at World Publishing and more recently at Simon & Schuster. Other editorial luminaries include Samuel Solomon, Mitford M. Mathews, and William E. Umbach. Mathews is well known as the editor of the *Dictionary of Americanisms*.

III. Comprehensiveness

The work is highly comprehensive in its inclusion of new words and of American place names and other Americanisms, identified by stars preceding the entry word or one or more of its senses. Words identified as Americanisms include **bonanza**, **carrying charge**, **cuchifrito**, **Fletcherism**, **liftoff**, and **released time**. The date of entry into the language is not noted, but sometimes additional historical information is given. For example, under **cooper's hawk** appears a bracketed note that the bird was named after William Cooper, the nineteenth-century ornithologist. Many students will find this feature of the dictionary interesting and enriching.

Foreign words are included and are signaled by a double dagger (‡); for example ‡**mirabile dictu**. Abbreviations are incorporated into the main word list, as are biographical and geographic entries. Biographical entries are sufficiently current to include **Ronald Reagan**. They provide dates, a brief note of identification, and other names by which the figure was known. For example, the entry for **De La Warr** appears as follows:

> Baron (*Thomas West*) 1577–1618; 1st Eng. colonial governor of Virginia (1610–11); called *Lord Delaware*.

Geographic entries include countries, major cities, mountains, lakes, rivers, and other geographic landmarks. Information given includes location; date admitted to the Union (for U.S. states), capital city and area in square miles (for states and countries); and population. Also given for U.S. states are traditional and postal abbreviations and origins of the state name. Population figures are as up-to-date as one would expect to find in a dictionary and more recent than those provided in a well-known almanac, but their dates are not specified in the volume. A representative entry for a U.S. state is that given for **Vermont**:

> [< Fr. *Verd Mont* (1647), green mountain] New England State of the U.S.: admitted, 1791; 9,609 sq. mi.; pop. 511,000; cap. Montpelier; abbrev. **Vt.**, **VT**— **Ver·mont′er** *n*.

Webster's New World Dictionary of the American Language: Second College Edition

❶ Pronunciation is provided for irregularly-formed plurals

❷ Usage labels are abbreviated and italicized

❸ Formal etymology in boldface brackets shows the relationship between several word sources

❹ Illustrative examples of the entry word in context appear within slant brackets

❺ Cross-references are given in small capitals

❻ Capitalized usage is preceded by a dash

❼ Scientific name of animal species is italicized

Usage labels helpfully identify slang, colloquialisms, and other restricted usages. Field labels, such as *Linguis* (linguistics) and *Baseball*, identify other special senses. Synonyms are provided for many entries, and they are carefully and usefully discriminated. For example, the synonym paragraph under **error** begins as follows:

> **Syn.—error** implies deviation from truth, accuracy, correctness, right, etc. and is the broadest term in this comparison [an *error* in judgment, in computation, etc.]; **mistake** suggests an error resulting from carelessness, inattention, misunderstanding, etc. and does not in itself carry a strong implication of criticism [a *mistake* in reading a blueprint]; **blunder** implies stupidity, clumsiness, inefficiency, etc. and carries a suggestion of more severe criticism [a tactical *blunder* cost them the war]. . . .

This feature is particularly useful for students and writers of all levels.

Etymology is provided for many entries. The introductory guide indicates that etymology "has been made a strong feature of this dictionary because it is believed that insights into the current usage of a word can be gained from a full knowledge of the word's history." Etymologies appear in brackets after the entry's pronunciation. They indicate derivations that go back to the Latin and Greek, unlike many abridged dictionaries, which show only the more recent history of the word. Students should find this complete history especially useful.

Other inclusions in the dictionary are scientific names of plants and animals, idiomatic phrases, and inflected forms. Illustrative phrases or sentences appear only rarely. Excluded are trade names and vulgarisms.

IV. Quality and Currency of Entries

Many entries present multiple senses of the entry term. Main senses are identified by boldface numerals; subsenses are designated by italicized lowercase letters. Senses are grouped by part of speech and numbered consecutively within each part-of-speech grouping. Historically earlier senses appear before more recent ones, with specialized, restricted, and technical usages appearing last. A representative entry containing senses and subsenses begins as follows:

> **re·ac·tion** (rē ak'shən) *n.* **1.** a return or opposing action, force, influence, etc. **2.** a response, as to a stimulus or influence **3.** a movement back to a former or less advanced condition, stage, etc.; countertendency; esp. such a movement or tendency in economics or politics; extreme conservatism **4.** *Chem. a)* the mutual action of substances undergoing chemical change *b)* a process that involves changes within the nucleus of an atom *c)* the state resulting from such changes.

Definitions are clearly stated. For example, **soteriology** is defined as spiritual salvation, esp. that believed in Christian theology to have been accomplished through Jesus.

Technical terms are also clearly and simply defined: the definition provided for **magnetohydrodynamics** is

> the science that deals with the interaction of a magnetic field with an electrically conducting fluid, as a liquid metal or an ionized gas.

Although usage notes and labels are provided, some entries fail to make careful usage distinctions that would be helpful to high school and college students. For example, the dictionary may leave users confused about the frequently misused terms **further** and **farther**. Under **farther** appears the cumbersome cross-reference:

> In sense **2** of the *adj.* and senses **2** and **3** of the *adv.*, FURTHER is more commonly used.

The American Heritage Dictionary does a much better job of clarifying the distinction between the terms, noting that "farther" is normally used to refer to actual distance, "further" to degree and time, and providing illustrative sentences.

The dictionary's currency is among its strong points. New words incorporated into the word list include, for example, **AIDS**, **byte**, **futon**, **mascon**, **tofu**, **videodisc**, and **videotex**. However, unlike WEBSTER'S NINTH NEW COLLEGIATE DICTIONARY, the work does not list dates of new words' entry into American English. Definitions are also up-to-date. For example, **tofu** is defined as

> a bland, custardlike food, rich in protein, coagulated from an extract of soybeans and eaten in soups, in various cooked dishes, etc.

In comparison, *Webster's Ninth* cross-references **tofu** to **bean curd**, which it defines as

> a soft vegetable cheese prepared by treating soybean milk with coagulants (as magnesium chloride or dilute acids).

Although *Webster's Ninth* is more precise, it is less reflective of current American dietary uses of the product.

V. Syllabication and Pronunciation

Syllabication and pronunciation follow standard dictionary procedures and will present few difficulties to students. Syllabication is indicated by centered dots in the entry word and, in inflected forms, by centered dots or stress marks. Pronunciation appears in parentheses after the entry word. Boldface accent marks indicate primary stress; lighter accents show secondary stresses. Located inside the front cover, the full pronunciation key comprises 43 symbols for English sounds and ten for foreign ones. An abbreviated key appears at the bottom of all right-hand pages within the word list.

According to the volume's introductory guide, the pronunciations presented "are those used by cultivated speakers in normal, relaxed conversation." Alternative pronunciations are provided. The first listed is not necessarily the preferred, but it may be "the one most frequent in general cultivated usage" if the variants are not equally frequent. Occasionally, usage notes (*now rarely*, *occasionally*) reveal pronunciation restrictions.

VI. Special Features

A six-page guide to the use of the dictionary is clearly written and accessible to college students and adults, although high school students may have difficulty with it. The guide's format impedes readability. Headings are indented and italicized, and minimal white space separates subsections. Information would be easier to locate if headings were boldfaced and white space were more generously used.

On the inside of the front cover, there appears a map and explanation of U.S. regional dialects. Two special articles follow the guide to dictionary use: "Language and the Dictionary," by Charlton Laird, and "Etymology," by William E. Umbach. Appended at the back of the volume are listings of colleges and universities in the U.S. and Canada. These are based on "the latest information which has been supplied by the institutions themselves," and they include information on general size of enrollment, location, date founded, source of financial control, and degree programs offered. This feature will be especially useful to high school students planning college application and college students considering transfer.

Another feature useful for high school and college students is a guide to punctuation, mechanics, and manuscript form, with a discussion of the use and form of footnotes. The volume also includes a chart of proofreaders' marks and sample copy that would be helpful to the writer who needs to proof galleys. Finally, the volume includes tables of weights and measures and a listing of signs and symbols used in fields such as astronomy, commerce and finance, and medicine and pharmacy.

VII. Accessibility

Entries are arranged alphabetically, letter by letter. Homographs, such as **bat** (club), **bat** (animal), and **bat** (wink) are given separate entries, distinguished by superscript numbers. The abbreviated pronunciation key that appears at the bottom of right-hand pages also helpfully explains the symbols that identify Americanisms, foreign terms, and hypothetical etymologies, as well as the symbol meaning "derived from."

Identical biographical surnames, and geographic names that share an identical element, are grouped together under a single entry. For example, under **Washington** as a geographic entry are listed the state, the U.S. capital, and the lake and mountain of the same name. Under the biographical entry **Washington** are listed, alphabetically, Booker T. and George. Because of the subentries' brevity, the eye picks up the boldfaced secondary entries. The practice permits the inclusion of more names than could be listed in an abridged dictionary if each were given a separate entry.

The work is available in both thumb-indexed and plain editions. In both, two boldface guide words at the top of each page indicate the first and last entries on the page. Cross-references also enhance accessibility, enabling users to locate additional information about words and their synonyms and antonyms. Small capitals make cross-references easy to locate within entries.

Alternative spellings are provided. When they are alphabetically close, they appear together in boldface type at the beginning of an entry (**catalog**, **catalogue**). The spelling listed first is the more frequently used, but not to be taken as the more "correct." When variant spellings are not alphabetically close, they are cross-referenced, with the full entry provided under the spelling more frequently used.

A detailed table of contents at the front of the volume lists all special features, including the twelve subsections of the guide to dictionary use.

VIII. Graphics and Format

The dictionary is illustrated with line drawings that are of sufficient size and detail to help define the word they depict. They appear adjacent to their entries and are captioned with main entry words and, in some cases, with additional information. For example, the illustration for **cycloid** shows three different examples of this complex geometrical figure, with each separately captioned. Line drawings are provided for most plants and animals listed, and their captions include indications of size. A full page of drawings is devoted to examples of leaf forms. Small maps are provided for some geographic entries. These are limited in detail but are useful in aiding the user to locate the country depicted.

Main entry words appear in boldface type overhanging the text on double-column pages. For both the entry word and the entry itself, the type is larger than that in other college dictionaries. However, in the review copy, print on some pages was much lighter than that in the rest of the volume. The dictionary is sturdily bound and will hold up well to heavy use.

IX. Summary

Webster's New World Dictionary of the American Language: Second College Edition can be compared with Webster's Ninth New Collegiate Dictionary, The American Heritage Dictionary: Second College Edition, and The Random House College Dictionary: Revised Edition. The two Webster dictionaries have the same number of entries and include many up-to-date words. *Webster's New World Dictionary* is somewhat more current in its definitions of new words, but the *Ninth* gives dates for the words' entry into American English. Definitions in *Webster's New World Dictionary* are slightly easier to understand, but its usefulness as a high school dictionary is limited to junior and senior college-bound students. One of its drawbacks for school use is its poorly formatted guide to dictionary use. In contrast, the *Ninth* has a much longer and clearer introduction. Both Webster dictionaries provide valuable listings of and differentiations among synonyms. In pronunciation, the *Ninth* is more detailed. That dictionary makes use of 59 pronunciation symbols and a five-page explanation. The *Ninth* also provides more detailed definitions. For example, it defines **mascon** as follows:

(1968): one of the concentrations of large mass under the surface of the moon in the maria held to cause perturbations of the paths of spacecraft orbiting the moon.

Webster's New World Dictionary defines the term to mean

> a concentration of very dense material beneath the surface of the moon.

The *Ninth*'s more detailed definitions may prove to be a disadvantage for younger users but an advantage for college students and adults.

THE AMERICAN HERITAGE DICTIONARY: SECOND COLLEGE EDITION offers some useful features not provided by *Webster's New World Dictionary*. The former has superior illustrations and makes a greater effort to prescribe correct usage. Similarly, the RANDOM HOUSE COLLEGE DICTIONARY: REVISED EDITION is more extensively and more effectively illustrated, and its typefaces are darker.

Webster's New World Dictionary is neither prescriptive, like THE AMERICAN HERITAGE DICTIONARY, nor truly descriptive, like the *Ninth*. On the other hand, its comprehensive coverage of Americanisms enhances its value, especially for students. Its type is larger than that of other college dictionaries. This dictionary is slightly higher priced than the other college dictionaries, but it has much to recommend it.

Webster's New World Dictionary of the American Language: The Concise Edition

Facts at a Glance

Full Title: **Webster's New World Dictionary of the American Language: The Concise Edition**.
Alternative Title: The 100,000 Entry Edition: Webster's New World Dictionary of the American Language.
Former Title: Webster's New World Dictionary: The Concise Edition.
Publisher: NAL.
Editor: David B. Guralnik.
Edition Reviewed: © 1971.

Number of Volumes: 1.
Number of Entries: 100,000.
Number of Pages: 882.
Number of Illustrations: over 600 black-and-white line drawings.
Trim Size: 5½″ × 8½″.
Binding: paperback.

Price: $8.50.
Intended Readership: high school students and up.

Sold in bookstores and other outlets; also sold to libraries and other educational institutions. ISBN 0-452-00886-7.

I. Introduction

This paperback edition of *Webster's New World Dictionary of the American Language: The Concise Edition* is based on and includes material from *Webster's New World Dictionary: Second College Edition* © 1970. The editor's foreword indicates that the work came into being as a result of "the warm reception given its predecessor, the College Edition," and that it is designed for "professional and business people, secondary-school students, office workers, new speakers of English, and others who want a comprehensive and contemporary dictionary but who have less need for the extensive etymologies, highly technical terms, many rare and obsolete senses, and certain other features found in the College Edition." The back cover of this paperback also states more specifically that this is "a special edition for the college student . . . ."

II. Authority

The dictionary was prepared under the supervision of David B. Guralnik, general editor. The permanent lexicographic staff that developed *Webster's New World Dictionary: Second College Edition*, helped to prepare the work. Entries were selected "on the basis of how frequently they occur in contemporary newspapers, magazines, and general books of fiction and nonfiction."

III. Comprehensiveness

Many entries include idiomatic phrases. For example, under **house** are listed **bring down the house**, **keep house**, **on the house**, and **set** (or **put**) **one's house in order**. Under **snap** appear **not a snap** ("not at all"), **snap** (**a person's**) **head off**, **snap one's fingers at**, and **snap out of it**. Although some of these idioms are no longer current, their inclusion is generally an asset, especially for students and non-native American English speakers.

The word list includes a limited number of biographical and geographic entries. Their currency is limited by the work's 1971 date; population figures provided for U.S. cities are based on the 1970 census. Also incorporated into the word list are abbreviations for chemical elements, U.S. states, government agencies, academic degrees, and many others. Foreign words and phrases often used in an English context are included and identified with a double dagger (‡). For example, entries are provided for **auf Wiedersehen, fait accompli,** and **quid pro quo.** Obsolete and archaic terms are included only if they are frequently found in the Bible or in standard literary works.

Most entries include brief etymologies, which the editor believes "help one to a clearer understanding of the current meaning of these words." Some entries include illustrative phrases. Derived forms appear within entries when they are easily understood on the basis of the entry word's meaning. When inflected forms are irregular or potential spelling problems, these are provided. Specialized usage is identified with field labels, such as *in chemistry, in medicine.* Usage labels identify colloquialisms, slang, obsolete and archaic terms, poetic diction, dialect, and Britishisms.

IV. Quality and Currency of Entries

Each boldfaced main entry word is followed by pronunciation in parentheses and an italicized part-of-speech abbreviation. Where provided, the word's etymology follows, in brackets. The dictionary's definitions are concise, and multiple senses receive good coverage. Each sense is numbered, and illustrative phrases often enhance the clarification of distinct senses. Senses are ordered from the earliest in use to most recent. A representative entry begins as follows:

> **com·mand** (kə-mand′, -mänd′), v.t. [<OFr. <LL.<L. com-, intens. + mandare, to commit], 1. to give an order to; direct with authority. 2. to have authority over; control. 3. to have and be able to use: as, to command a large vocabulary. 4. to deserve and get; require as due: as, his knowledge commands respect. 5. to control (a position); overlook. v.i. to be in authority or control; act as commander.

The foreword indicates that the editors have made an effort to provide coverage of words recently introduced into the language. However, the work's 1971 date limits its currency. The foreword's examples of newer words—**desegregation, automation, einsteinium**—are no longer highly topical or unfamiliar. The word list includes such terms as **analog computer, digital computer, program** (computer sense), **spacecraft,** and **space station.** However, among the words excluded are *byte, file* (computer sense), *gay* (homosexual), and *videocassette.*

V. Syllabication and Pronunciation

Syllabication is indicated in main entry words by centered dots and, in inflected forms, by centered dots or stress marks. Pronunciation is given in parentheses after the main entry word. When that word recurs in a subsequent entry or in a phrase or hyphenated compound, the pronunciation is not repeated. A full key to pronunciation appears in the introductory "Guide to the Use of the Dictionary," and an abbreviated key is helpfully provided at the bottom of all right-hand pages.

The pronunciations given are "those observed among literate speakers of General American English." Regional variants are provided for some words, such as greasy (grēs′i, grēz′i) and route (rōot, rout). The form listed first is the one more frequently used, in most cases.

VI. Special Features

The volume's "Guide to the Use of the Dictionary" is clear and detailed and will be useful to students. It is followed by a list of abbreviations and symbols used in the dictionary. At the back of the work, several other special features are appended. A seven-page list of common given names provides pronunciation, language of origin, and meaning. Although most students are interested in the origins of their names, this feature has limited reference value. However, other features contribute substantively to the dictionary's value as a reference source. These include a chart of forms of address; tables of weights and measures; signs and symbols used in such fields as astronomy, biology, and commerce; a brief guide to punctuation; and a chart of the Indo-European family of languages.

VII. Accessibility

Two boldface guide words appear at the top of each page, indicating the first and last entries on the page; they are helpfully printed in larger type than that used for the entries. A table of contents lists all special features and ensures that they will not be overlooked. When alternative spellings are alphabetically close, they appear in boldface together at the beginning of the entry (**theater, theatre**). When they are not close (**aegis** and **egis**), each is entered separately, and the less common form is cross-referenced to the more common.

VIII. Graphics and Format

The black-and-white line drawings that illustrate the work are small, and the printing often obscures even the little detail they attempt to portray. For example, the four labels for the drawing of a flintlock are unreadable. The illustrations appear next to their entries, and they are captioned with main entry words and, at times, additional information, such as sizes for pictures of animals. In most cases, the drawings add little to the definitions.

The dictionary's print is small and cramped on the page, but readability is enhanced by the use of boldface main entry words that overhang the text. When the spine is cracked the book lies flat, and the pages do not separate easily from the binding. The book will hold up better than most paperbacks to heavy use.

IX. Summary

Webster's New World Dictionary of the American Language (*The 100,000 Entry Edition*) was a valuable reference source when it appeared in 1971. Its definitions are clear and detailed, and it provides a wide range of linguistic information, including etymology and usage and field labels. However, it is now significantly outdated, and its poor illustrations and graphics are additional drawbacks. Although it is an unusually sturdy paperback, its shelf life is limited.

A preferable alternative for many readers and for library acquisition is THE CONCISE AMERICAN HERITAGE DICTIONARY. This work is not as current as its 1980 date would suggest, and it comprises just over half the entries contained in the work reviewed here. On the other hand, the book is hardbound, well illustrated, exceptionally easy to read, and less expensive than this paperback edition *Webster's New World*.

Webster's New World Dictionary: Student Edition

Facts at a Glance

Full Title: **Webster's New World Dictionary: Student Edition**.
Publisher: Simon and Schuster.
Editor: David B. Guralnik, Editor-in-Chief.
Edition Reviewed: © 1981.

Number of Volumes: 1.
Number of Entries: 108,000.
Number of Pages: 1,152.
Number of Illustrations: 1,500 black-and-white line drawings.
Trim Size: 7⁷⁄₁₆″ × 9⁵⁄₈″.
Binding: cloth.

Price: $15.95.

Intended Readership: Secondary school students. Sold in bookstores and other outlets; also sold by direct mail and to libraries and schools. ISBN 0-671-41815-7.

I. Introduction

The *Webster's New World Dictionary: Student Edition*, designed to meet the needs of high school students, is the second in this publisher's coordinated series of dictionaries for students from elementary school through college. Its more than 108,000 main entry words have been "chosen as the ones students are most likely to come across in reading the classics, textbooks, and other classroom assignments, but also the daily newspapers and current magazines and novels." According to the foreword, the dictionary's editors "have tried to anticipate the kinds of questions students might put to a dictionary and to give the answers in the most direct form possible." The dictionary's usefulness to its intended audience is enhanced by its special features, which include an introductory guide and a variety of tables and charts. Special attention is also given to Americanisms and the origins of American place names.

II. Authority

The dictionary was prepared by the same staff who compiled the respected *Webster's New World Dictionary: Second College Edition*, and the same vast citation file was used. The editorial staff was advised by a council of teachers and educators from a range of public and private schools, colleges, universities, and libraries.

III. Comprehensiveness

The dictionary's treatment of Americanisms is especially comprehensive. Over 10,000 Americanisms are identified by a star before the main entry word or before a particular definition. For example, stars precede the main entry words **bushwhack**, **business college**, **butternut**, **death row**, **folksy**, **glassine**, **heist**, **inhalator**, and **jalopy**. Under **level**, for instance, one definition for the verb is starred:

[Slang] to be frank and honest (*with* someone).

Many scientific and popular words incorporated into American usage over the past two decades are included. Among these are **anorexia**, **data processing**, **fast food**, **gay** (in its homosexual sense), **pro-**

Webster's New World Dictionary: Student Edition

❶ Bracketed phrases illustrate the usage of an entry word (in italics) and its inflected forms

❷ Synonym studies are preceded by *SYN.* in boldface italic; synonyms are discriminated (explained)

❸ Brief etymology is provided within brackets

❹ Open stars identify Americanisms

❺ Cross-references appear in small capital letters

❻ Idioms, in boldface, defined

shake (shāk) *vt.* **shook, shak′en, shak′ing** [OE. *sceacan*] **1.** to cause to move up and down, back and forth, or from side to side with short, quick movements **2.** to bring, force, mix, scatter, etc. by short, quick movements [*shake* the medicine before taking it, *shake* salt on the steak] **3.** to cause to tremble [chills that *shook* his body] **4.** *a)* to cause to totter or become unsteady *b)* to weaken, disturb, or upset [he was *shaken* by the news] **5.** to wave in the air; brandish [he *shook* a gun in my face] **6.** to clasp (another's hand), as in greeting ☆**7.** [Colloq.] to get away from or rid of [to *shake* one's pursuers] **8.** *Music* same as TRILL —*vi.* **1.** to move quickly up and down, back and forth, etc.; vibrate **2.** to tremble, quiver, etc., as from cold or fear **3.** to become unsteady; totter **4.** to clasp each other's hand, as in greeting **5.** *Music* same as TRILL —*n.* **1.** an act of shaking [a *shake* of the fist] **2.** an unsteady or trembling movement or sound [a *shake* in his voice] **3.** a natural split in rock or timber **4.** a rough-hewn wood shingle **5.** [Colloq.] an earthquake ☆**6.** *short for* MILKSHAKE **7.** [*pl.*] [Colloq.] a violent trembling, as from chills, fear, etc. (usually with *the*) **8.** [Colloq.] a moment [be back in a *shake*] **9.** [Colloq.] a kind of treatment; deal [a fair *shake*] **10.** *Music* same as TRILL —**no great shakes** [Colloq.] not outstanding or unusual —**shake down 1.** to bring down or cause to fall by shaking **2.** to cause to settle by shaking **3.** to test or condition (new equipment, etc.) ☆**4.** [Slang] to get money from by using force or threats, as in blackmailing —**shake off** to get away from or rid of —**shake out** to make fall out, empty, straighten out, etc. by shaking —**shake up 1.** to shake, esp. so as to mix or loosen **2.** to disturb or stir up by or as by shaking **3.** to jar or shock **4.** to reorganize or redistribute by or as by shaking —**shak′a·ble, shake′a·ble** *adj.*
SYN.—shake is the general word for a moving up and down or back and forth with quick, short motions; **tremble** implies such a shaking of the body as to suggest a loss of control, as from fear, weakness, etc. [she *trembled* at the lion's roar]; **quake** usually suggests a somewhat violent trembling, as in terror [to *quake* in one's boots with dread]; **quiver** suggests a slight vibration, as of a tightly stretched string that has been plucked [the leaves *quivered* in the breeze]

gram (in its computer science sense), **snow** (as a slang term for cocaine or heroin), **space shuttle**, **space walk**, and **videocassette**. Excluded from the work are, for example, the much more recent *AIDS, crack* (in its drug sense), *fast track, freebase, holistic, modem, new wave, punk rock, reggae*. While comparable dictionaries, such the Merriam-Webster WEBSTER'S SCHOOL DICTIONARY (1986), are more comprehensive, this 1981 volume is more up-to-date than, for example, THE RANDOM HOUSE SCHOOL DICTIONARY (1984).

Foreign words included are indicated by a double dagger (‡) placed before their entries or, within entries, before a specific definition. These include, for example, **frère**, **ipse dixit**, and **señor**. Prefixes, suffixes, and combining forms are given their own main entries. Abbreviations are included in the main word list, as are biographical and geographical entries. In the case of the former, twentieth-century figures in the arts are not well represented: omissions include, for example, *Allen Ginsberg, Virginia Woolf,* and *Andrew Wyeth*. Because of the work's 1981 date, some place names do not appear in their current form. For American place names, etymologies are given. For example, the name of the city of **Buffalo**, N.Y., is derived from

the name of a Seneca Indian who lived there.

Short etymologies appear immediately before the definitions. These, designed to enhance students' comprehension of current meanings, provide information on language(s) of origin and roots, with their meanings.

At the ends of selected entries appear synonymies, paragraphs listing and distinguishing among an entry's synonyms. For example, the entry for **destroy** is amplified by a synonymy that begins:

SYN.—**destroy** implies a tearing down or bringing to an end in any of various ways, as by wrecking, spoiling, ruining, killing, etc. [to *destroy* a civilization; to *destroy* weeds; to *destroy* one's plans]; **demolish** implies such destructive force as to completely smash to pieces [the bombs *demolished* the factories]; **raze** means to level to the ground . . . .

These provide careful distinctions among synonyms in terms of both denotative and connotative values; they are well suited to the linguistic level of their intended audience.

Also included, for some entries, are antonyms, idioms, usage labels, usage notes, and field labels, demarcating usage in the specialized vocabularies of various fields. All of these inclusions are well chosen to meet the needs of high school students.

IV. Quality and Currency of Entries

Entries include pronunciation, part of speech, irregular plurals of nouns, irregular comparatives and superlatives of adjectives, inflected forms of irregular verbs, etymology, definition(s), synonyms, and antonyms. Definitions are generally clear, concise, and noncircular. The constraints of abridgment, however, have resulted in some curtailment of information. Biographical entries are especially brief, although given the decision to include these, they might have been made more substantive.

Some reduction in clarity may also be the result of the dictionary's limited length. While dictionaries of this size typically rely on cross-referencing, this work is to be commended for avoiding unduly heavy reliance on this technique. However, some entries that require extra amplification do not fully receive it. For example, the dictionary takes the reader on a word chase in the case of **who**, **whom**, and **whose**—words for which students frequently need clarification. The entry for **whom** defines the word as the

objective case of WHO: see note at WHO on the use of *who* and *whom*.

That note does not fully clarify the use of "whom." Under **whose**, there is no direct statement that the word is the possessive form of "who," nor is there a cross-reference to that word's entry. In contrast, the comparable Merriam-Webster WEBSTER'S SCHOOL DICTIONARY provides expanded entries for these words that fully explain their grammatical use and interrelationships.

Multiple definitions within an entry are designated by boldface numbers. Multiple meanings are generally further clarified by the inclusion, in brackets, of illustrative phrases and sentences.

V. Syllabication and Pronunciation

Syllabication is indicated by centered dots in main entry words and, in inflected forms, by centered dots and stress marks. Pronunciation appears in parentheses after each main entry word. Shortened pronunciations are given when a preceding entry provides some part of the necessary information. For example, the pronunciation for **digestible** is given in

full (di jes′tə b′l); that for the following entry, **digestion**, is abbreviated (-chən). Variant pronunciations are given and are, whenever possible, similarly shortened.

A full pronunciation key appears inside the volume's front cover; an abbreviated key, for quick reference, is located at the bottom of each right-hand page. Because the key uses standard symbols without abridgment and incorporates foreign sounds, some users may find the system complex. However, it is fully and clearly explained in the guide to the dictionary, and students who take the time to master this information will learn a great deal about pronunciation and dialectical differences.

VI. Special Features

The dictionary's special features are well selected for its secondary school audience. The guide, "How to Use Your Dictionary," is a thorough introduction, age-appropriate in reading level and organization. The use of subheadings, as well as indented excerpts and boldface type for the copious examples, enhances the section's readability. Included in the guide, and usefully reproduced inside the back cover, is a "Word Finder Table" showing variant spellings of sounds and enabling students to locate in the dictionary words they cannot spell.

Within the word list, there are a number of full pages devoted to tables and charts. For example, under the letter *M* is found a full-page table, "Monetary Units of All Nations"; under *G* appears a full-page geologic time chart; and under **plural** a column is devoted to rules for the formation of plurals. Other features are a table of alphabets (English, Arabic, Hebrew, Greek, Russian, German) printed inside the front cover, tables of weights and measures, and metric conversion tables. It is commendable that space is not usurped by encyclopedia material and additional appendixes of information easily located elsewhere.

VII. Accessibility

The main entry words are alphabetically arranged letter by letter. Large, boldface guide words appear at the tops of the two columns on each page: these indicate the first and last words defined on that page. As with most comparable dictionaries, there are no thumb indexes or thumb tabs. Material in the guide to the dictionary facilitates accessibility, as does the complete contents listing at the front of the volume.

Variant spellings are handled in two ways. For variants whose spelling is significantly different, definitions are given under the spelling most frequently used (such as **eon**) and variants are cross-referenced to this entry (under **aeon**, for example, *same as* EON). When the variants are spelled similarly, they appear together at the head of the entry (**caf·feine, caf·fein**) when neither is more frequent. When one form is more frequent, its alternative appears at the end of the entry.

VIII. Graphics and Format

Although the dictionary's 1,500 black-and-white line drawings may not be particularly eye-catching to the intended audience—and they are smaller than those of some comparable dictionaries—these illustrations are large enough for their details to be easily seen and are useful adjuncts to definitions. Generally one to five appear on a double-page spread. Including representational drawings, diagrams, and maps, they appear next to the entries they illustrate; they are captioned in block capitals, with main entry words and occasional brief explanatory phrases.

The dictionary is printed on white non-glare paper, with ample margins. The print is easy to read, especially the boldfaced entry words, which overhang the text. Variations in typeface (boldface, boldface italic, italic) make information easy to locate quickly. There is some show-through of text, but not enough, however, to distract a reader. The book is sturdily bound, lies flat when open, and will withstand frequent use.

IX. Summary

Certain features may limit the overall usefulness of the *Webster's New World Dictionary: Student Edition*. As a result of its 1981 date, the work does not reflect the most current language that high school students may encounter—particularly in areas of high technology, where new terms are continually being added. Occasional entries are briefer or less fully informative than would be optimal, even in an abridged dictionary.

However, although the comparable Merriam-Webster WEBSTER'S SCHOOL DICTIONARY is more comprehensive, the older dictionary offers a generous range of new and old words in a sturdy, readable volume. Its features—including its noteworthy Americanisms, synonymies, etymologies, and charts—instruct the high school student users and enhance their lexical skills. Prospective buyers, whether librarians, teachers, or parents, should find the dictionary a good value.

Webster's New World Dictionary of the American Language

Facts at a Glance

Full Title: **Webster's New World Dictionary of the American Language**.
Publisher: Warner Books.
Editor: David B. Guralnik.
Edition Reviewed: © 1984.

Number of Volumes: 1.
Number of Entries: over 59,000.
Number of Pages: 696.
Number of Illustrations: over 200.
Trim Size: 4¼" × 7".
Binding: paperback.

Price: $3.95.
Intended Readership: junior high school and up.
Sold in bookstores and other outlets. ISBN 0-446-31449-8.

I. Introduction

This abridged, illustrated pocket-size dictionary contains over 59,000 entries designed to meet the needs of students and adults. According to the foreword, the editors' intent has been "to incorporate as much useful information as possible within the available space." The work therefore includes "illustrative examples . . ., idiomatic expressions, affixes and combining forms, and other features not generally included in a paperback dictionary of this size." Among other unusual features is the inclusion of brief etymologies for most entries. A revised edition, the work includes "thousands of new terms and newer senses of established terms not found in the first edition."

II. Authority

The 1984 dictionary is an expansion and updating of a paperback dictionary first published in 1958. The current edition is based on WEBSTER'S NEW WORLD DICTIONARY: SECOND COLLEGE EDITION, first published in 1970. The work was prepared under the supervision of the Editor-in-Chief, David B. Guralnik, by members of the permanent staff that developed the *Second College Edition*. Their selection of entry words was determined on the basis of the word's "frequency of occurrence within our vast citation file and from various word-count lists."

Webster's New World Dictionary of the American Language

❶ Phrases, in parentheses, illustrate and clarify meanings

❷ Idioms are provided in boldface

❸ Related words, in boldface, are run-in to the main entry text and show stress marks and syllable breaks

❹ Etymologies are enclosed within boldface brackets

❺ Abbreviated usage labels appear within square brackets

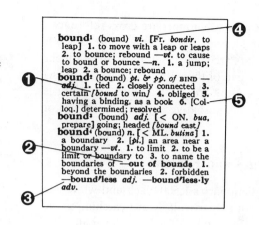

III. Comprehensiveness

The dictionary is unusually comprehensive for a volume of its size. In addition to many new words added during revision, the work incorporates selected biographical and geographic entries. Biographical entries include **Leonid Brezhnev**, **Mao Tse-Tung**, and **Ronald Reagan**. The geographic entries include world countries (with area, location, and population); major cities of the world and U.S. cities of over 100,000 inhabitants (with location and population); and other geographic landmarks. The date of the population figures is not indicated. Common abbreviations also appear as main entries. For example, **ERA** is defined both as "earned run average" in baseball and as "Equal Rights Amendment." Abbreviations listed include those for U.S. states, government agencies, chemical elements, and many others.

Brief etymologies are provided for most entries. Inflected forms are noted when they are irregular or might cause spelling difficulties. Also provided are usage labels with such identifications as slang, colloquial, archaic, poetic, dialectic, and British. Run-in entries are provided only when their meaning is readily understood on the basis of the main entry word's meaning.

Definitions of various prefixes, suffixes, and combining forms are also noted as separate entries, and lists of compound words are occasionally subsumed under affixes. For example, 64 compound words are listed under the prefix **in-** (meaning "no, not, without, non-"). Synonyms and antonyms are not provided in the dictionary. However, this omission does not detract from the volume's overall comprehensiveness and usefulness to students and adults.

IV. Quality and Currency of Entries

In general, the foreword's claim that the work provides "clear but brief" definitions is accurate. The definitions also succeed in making subtle distinctions when necessary. Multiple meanings of a word and separate entries for homographs are typically given. For example, each of the words **fast**, **mint**, **mark**, **press**, **maroon**, and **ball** has two separate entries; **desert** and **row** have three apiece; and **bay** has five. Most of these entries offer more than one sense of the word.

Each of the multiple senses in an entry is introduced by a boldfaced numeral. Slang and colloquialisms are given after more standard senses of the word and are identified with bracketed labels. Although the dictionary's obvious space limitations preclude the use of whole sentences to illustrate meanings, bracketed illustrative phrases occasionally appear to clarify distinctions among a word's senses. For example, the sense of **fast** as "nonfading" is clarified by the inclusion of the phrase "*[fast* colors]," and the meaning "ahead of time" is exemplified by "*[a fast* watch]." A representative entry is:

fat (fat) *adj.* **fat′ter, fat′test** [OE. *fætt*] **1.** containing fat; oily **2.** *a)* fleshy; plump *b)* too plump **3.** thick; broad **4.** fertile [*fat* land] **5.** profitable [a *fat* job] **6.** plentiful —*n.* **1.** an oily or greasy material found in animal tissue and plant seeds **2.** the richest part of anything **3.** superfluous part — **chew the fat** [Slang] to chat — **fat′ly** *adv.* — **fat′ness** *n.*

The entries' incorporation of multiple meanings and useful distinctions among them make the dictionary especially valuable to students.

The dictionary is current in its inclusion of new words and new senses. Among the entries are such technical and popular terms as **afterburner**, **AIDS**, **database**, **gay** (homosexual), **palimony**, **program** (computer sense), **videodisc**, **Watergate**, and **word processing**.

V. Syllabication and Pronunciation

Syllabication is indicated in main entry words by centered dots and, for words whose pronunciation is given in shortened form, by centered dots and stress marks. Pronunciation is given in parentheses immediately following the entry word; it is omitted or abbreviated for some compound main entry words. For example, pronunciation is given for **soft**, but not for such successive entries as **softball** and **soft sell**. For **software**, pronunciation appears as (-wer′).

A phonemic key appears in the introductory "Guide to the Use of the Dictionary," and an abbreviated pronunciation key appears at the bottom of all right-hand pages. This feature is not always provided in comparable dictionaries, and it will be useful to students. Although standard American English pronunciation is emphasized, some entries also provide variant pronunciations. For example, variant pronunciations are offered for **February** (feb′rə wer′ē, feb′yoo-), **boundary** (bound′drē, -dər ē), and **octave** (äk′tiv, -tāv). In most cases, the form given first is that most frequently used by American English speakers. Readers will find the inclusion of acceptable regional variants helpful.

VI. Special Features

The volume's introductory "Guide to the Use of the Dictionary" is clearly written and detailed and will be useful to students. It is followed by a list of abbreviations used in the dictionary.

VII. Accessibility

The dictionary's entries are alphabetized letter by letter. At the top of each page appear two boldface guide words, indicating the first and last entries on the page. These guide words are helpfully printed in larger type than that used for the entries. Alternative spellings of entry words are easily found. When they are alphabetically close, they are given in boldface after the main entry word (**theater**, **theatre**). When they are not close (**aegis** and **egis**), cross-references in small capitals are provided from the less to the more frequently used.

VIII. Graphics and Format

Over 200 black-and-white line drawings are spread through the entire volume, so several pages can be turned before an illustration appears. These drawings tend to look cramped on the page, and the decision to illustrate one entry as opposed to another seems arbitrary. For example, **cogwheel** is pictured,

but on the same page **colander**, which is equally hard to visualize, is not illustrated. The work's illustrations will be of minimal use to its readers.

The print in this dictionary is quite small, and the entries themselves seem cramped on the page. Although the generous gutter margin makes the pages more readable, the book does not lie flat and is cumbersome to hold. The binding also tends to tear when the book is pressed open, which means that this dictionary cannot withstand heavy use.

IX. Summary

What distinguishes *Webster's New World Dictionary of the American Language* from comparable dictionaries is the quality and comprehensiveness of its entries. The work can be compared with the paperback AMERICAN HERITAGE DICTIONARY. The latter is better illustrated and contains special features not found in the former, such as a table of chemical elements, a guide to the metric system, and a list of proofreaders' marks. However, the American Heritage work lists biographical and geographic entries separately from the main vocabulary. Many readers will appreciate the *Webster's New World Dictionary*'s incorporation of this information within the main word list.

Although the book is cumbersome to hold, and the print is small and cluttered on the page, its low price and contemporary orientation make *Webster's New World Dictionary* a good buy for occasional individual desktop use. For heavier use, the dictionary's life span will be limited. However, it merits a place in the English classroom, school library, or public library's paperback collection for younger readers.

Webster's New World Dictionary for Young Readers

Facts at a Glance

Full Title: **Webster's New World Dictionary for Young Readers**.
Publisher: Simon and Schuster.
Editor: David B. Guralnik, Editor-in-Chief.
Illustrator: Anita S. Rogoff.
Edition Reviewed: © 1983; fifth printing.

Number of Volumes: 1.
Number of Entries: 50,000.
Number of Pages: 889.
Number of Illustrations: 1,600 in black and white and two colors; 24 pages in full color.
Number of Maps: 11 pages in full color.

Webster's New World Dictionary
for Young Readers

❶ Americanisms are identified by
    an open star
❷ Italicized reference to illustration
❸ Illustrative phrases and sentences
    appear in brackets
❹ Idioms, in boldface type, are
    explained

heart (härt) *n.* **1** the hollow muscle that gets blood from the veins and sends it through the arteries by squeezing together and expanding. *See the picture.* **2** the part at the center [*hearts* of celery; the *heart* of the jungle]. **3** the main or most important part [Get to the *heart* of the matter.] **4** the human heart thought of as the part that feels love, kindness, pity, sadness, etc. [a tender *heart;* a heavy *heart*]. **5** courage or spirit [Don't lose *heart!*] **6** a person who is liked or admired [She's a brave *heart*.] **7** a figure or design shaped a little like the heart: ♡ **8** a playing card of a suit marked with this figure in red. **—after one's own heart,** that pleases one perfectly. **—at heart,** in one's truest feelings. **—break one's heart,** to cause one to feel great sorrow or disappointment. **—by heart, 1** by memorizing. **2** from memory. — ☆**change of heart,** a change of mind or feeling. **—set one's heart on,** to want very much. **—take heart,** to get courage or confidence; cheer up. **—take to heart,** to be very serious or troubled about. **—with all one's heart, 1** very sincerely. **2** very willingly; gladly.

Trim Size: 8″ × 10″.
Binding: cloth.

Price: $14.95.
Intended Readership: grades 4 through 8.
Sold in bookstores and other outlets; also sold to libraries and schools. ISBN 0-671-41821-1.

I. Introduction

The semi-abridged *Webster's New World Dictionary for Young Readers* (subtitled *New Revised Edition* on the cover and dust jacket) is designed for upper elementary and middle school students and is the first in a coordinated series of dictionaries for students from the primary grades through college. It also carries an earlier copyright of 1979, and previous editions were published by The World Publishing Company and Williams Collins + World. Also published in a *Basic School Edition* by Prentice-Hall, the work is defined by its Editor-in-Chief as "a dictionary especially prepared to answer clearly the questions about words that pupils will put to it, and one that will do so in an inviting and attractive way to excite the interest of its young readers."

In addition to its more than 50,000 entries, the attractively illustrated dictionary includes special features—many of them applicable to classroom instruction—that impart dictionary use skills and expand the work's range as a reference source.

II. Authority

The vocabulary list for the dictionary was selected, according to the foreword, "from the vast citation file of the *Webster's New World Dictionary* staff on the basis of the frequency with which these words appear in the textbooks and other reading materials" that the intended readers are likely to use. The work of an experienced lexicographic and editorial staff was complemented by the consultation of an advisory council of teachers and educators.

III. Comprehensiveness

The dictionary includes a significant number of scientific and popular words recently incorporated into current American usage. Among these are **biofeedback, data processing,** computer-related meanings of **disk** and **program, space shuttle, space walk,** and **videocassette.** Excluded—partly because of its 1983 date, and partly because of the needs of its intended audience—are such words as: *AIDS, biorhythm, byte, punk rock, workaholic.*

Many entries will be helpful adjuncts to students in their various studies. Terms for sexual and reproductive organs are included, as are the words **homosexual** and **gay** in its homosexual sense (*lesbian,* however, is omitted). Biographical and geographic entries are incorporated into the main word list. The former include historical, mythological, and biblical names, with dates, when known, and brief identifications. The entry for **Amelia Earhart**, for example, reads

> 1898–1937; early U.S. airplane pilot who set records for long-distance flying.

Many American writers are given biographical entries, but among those excluded are *Willa Cather*, *Kate Chopin*, *James Baldwin*, and *Richard Wright*. This raises questions about the balanced inclusion of women and minorities in the list as a whole, a particularly important issue in terms of this work's classroom use.

Prospective buyers also should be aware that the various biographical entries are not always fully amplified. For instance, the dust jacket claims that the biographical entries establish the importance of the individuals cited, as well as give their years of birth and death. In most cases, in addition to the birth and death dates, only the general field in which these individuals have contributed is noted. For example, it is merely commented upon that Mark Twain was a U.S. writer, who lived from 1835 to 1910, and that his real name was Samuel Langhorne Clemens. What he wrote, or the fact that he conceived the well-known characters Tom Sawyer and Huckleberry Finn—helpful information that younger students may specifically seek—is not mentioned.

Geographic entries are included for many cities and states in the U.S., for Canadian provinces, and world countries, as well as for major rivers, mountains, and other topographical features. Locations are given, but population figures are not.

Among the entries that younger users might find specifically geared toward their studies are: **Harper's Ferry**; **King Lear**; **William I** (William the Conqueror), **Louisiana Purchase**; **proportion** and **percent**; **Marx, Karl**; **Standard Time**; **Pythagoras**; **da Vinci, Leonardo**; **Napoleon Bonaparte**; **Monticello**; **Sports**; **Methuselah**; **UFO**; **Picasso**; and **Spanish-American War**. These entries are all related to the kind of basic information covered in curricula today.

Special emphasis has been given to the inclusion of more than 2,400 Americanisms, such as **hot dog**, **humongous**, and **shenanigans**. Stars identify these entries, which will interest young users and encourage them to browse.

Abbreviations, prefixes, and suffixes are given their own main entries within the word list. Also included, within the dictionary's entries, are idioms, inflected forms, usage notes, illustrative phrases and sentences, variants, cross-references, synonyms, and etymologies. Synonyms and etymologies appear in color-shaded boxes at the end of entries for which

they are provided. Etymologies generally provide the language of the root and its meaning, but not the root word itself. For example, after its definition, the following etymology is given for **hemorrhage**:

> **Hemorrhage** comes from two Greek words meaning "blood" and "burst." If a blood vessel bursts, there is much bleeding.

Students at this level could benefit from additional etymological information to broaden their language acquisition skills.

IV. Quality and Currency of Entries

The typical ordering of the entries is as follows (although not all of these categories of information are provided in each entry): syllabified entry word; variant spelling; pronunciation in parentheses; part-of-speech label; definitions, with the most common meaning listed first; illustrative phrases or sentences in brackets; usage notes, derived or inflected forms divided into syllables; idioms, variant terms, and cross-references; synonym or word history paragraphs.

Definitions are clearly stated, instructional, and age-appropriate in their reading level and orientation. For example, the entry for **emancipate**, which includes a word history paragraph, appears as follows:

> **e·man·ci·pate** (i man′ sə·pát) *v.* to set free from slavery or strict control [Lincoln *emancipated* the black slaves.] —**e·man′ ci·pat·ed, e·man′ ci·pat·ing** —**e·man′ ci·pa′ tion** *n*. —**e·man′ ci·pa·tor** *n*.
>
> **Emancipate** comes from a Latin word meaning "to take away the hand." In ancient Rome, the buyer of a slave would put a hand on that person to show that he was the master. So when a slave is emancipated, it is as though the owner has taken away his hand.

This definition is accessible to the student reader without being oversimplified or condescending. Where the WEBSTER'S NEW WORLD DICTIONARY: STUDENT EDITION—this series' dictionary for secondary school students—uses the words "bondage" and "serfdom" in its definition of **emancipate**, the younger readers' dictionary appropriately limits itself to words within the probable scope of its audience. Synonym paragraphs are also effectively geared to the audience. Under **dead** appears

> SYNONYMS: **Dead** is used of someone or something that was alive but is no longer so.

Deceased is a legal term for one who has recently died. [The property of the *deceased* is left to the church.] **Late** is used before the name of a person who is dead [the *late* Babe Ruth].

Departed and **defunct**, included in the older student's dictionary, are appropriately omitted in this work. However, while the younger readers' version makes clear and accurate denotative distinctions among synonyms, it does not introduce the connotative differences explained in the older students' version. The omission is a disservice to the dictionary's readers.

V. Syllabication and Pronunciation

Main entry words and derived and inflected forms are syllabified by centered dots. Pronunciation appears after the main entry word. A full key to the system's 44 symbols (with four diacritical marks) appears inside the front cover; an abbreviated key appears in a color-shaded box at the bottom left of each double-page spread within the word list. Easy sample words in both versions of the key will facilitate its use by young readers.

Alternative accepted pronunciations are given, with the more commonly used form appearing first. Under **either**, for example, two pronunciations are offered:

(ē′thər *or* ī′thər).

VI. Special Features

The dictionary begins with a 12-page illustrated article titled "A Story of Some American Words." Its focus on the living, evolving qualities of language and its careful selection of examples, such as **cowboy**, **bandwagon**, and **rock-and-roll**, will intrigue young readers and encourage them to browse in the dictionary, seeking both the starred Americanisms and interesting information in general. The placement of this article first, before the guide to dictionary use, is commendable: it will draw in students who might anticipate boredom or difficulty from a weighty reference book.

The guide that follows, "How to Use Your Dictionary," is a thorough and clear introduction to dictionary use. It includes well-designed practice exercises and an annotated double-spread sample page.

At the back of the volume appears a reference section. Illustrated in full color, this includes features titled "The Solar System" (including information about the planets, such as diameter, temperature, number of satellites), "Firsts in Space" (the last entry is dated

1981: launch of space shuttle *Columbia*), "Chronology of American Events" (last entry 1981: appointment to the Supreme Court of Sandra Day O'Connor), "Presidents of the United States" (through Reagan; includes portraits, with dates, parties, and vice presidents), "Facts About the Fifty States" (including, among other data, capital, date of admission to the Union, area, and 1980 population figures), "Metric Conversion Table" (with practice exercises). Also included is an 11-page atlas in full color. These reference features are clear and interesting; and they will be relevant and useful to students pursuing studies in a range of disciplines.

VII. Accessibility

Alternative spellings of words, when both are very common, appear paired at the beginning of an entry; for example,

the·a·ter *or* the·a·tre.

When the second spelling is clearly less common, it appears in boldface at the end of the entry following the italicized words *Sometimes spelled*.

Arrangement of entries is alphabetical, letter by letter. A pair of large, boldface, color-tinted guide words, indicating the first and last word defined on the page, is shown at the top of each page. No thumb index is provided, but useful color-tinted letter tabs are printed in the margin, near the bottom of each right-hand page. With the opened book laid flat, the user can easily locate letter sections by thumbing the bottom right-hand corners of the pages.

Accessibility is also enhanced by elements of the introductory guide. A "Word Finder Table," useful to the reader who is unsure of a word's spelling, offers alternative spellings for sounds. For example, if the vowel sound is "i as in *hit*," the user is instructed to try the spellings i, ie, ee, o, u, ui, y (as in the sample words **i**ll, s**ie**ve, b**ee**n, w**o**men, b**u**sy, b**ui**ld, h**y**mn). The guide's exercises are also well designed to make the work more accessible to students.

A table of contents at the front of the volume lists the dictionary's special features, including the several items that constitute the reference section. Students can thus see at a glance the full range of information the dictionary offers.

VIII. Graphics and Format

The dictionary is highly attractive in graphics and format. Although the illustrations within the word list are not in full color, the contrast and diversity provided by color-tinted drawings and black-and-white photographs will appeal to the eye and invite the young user to browse, while they also usefully clarify definitions.

The illustrations are grouped in a block at one corner of each double-page spread. Each block contains a variety of graphic forms. For example, one block within the *O* section includes drawings of an **oval** and a girl with **outstretched** arms, and photographs of an **outrigger** and a man wearing **overalls**. There is adequate representation of women and minorities in the illustrations.

Although it would be more convenient to the user to find each illustration next to its entry, captioning of the illustrations with large boldface main entry words—and, in some cases, explanatory phrases—helps to remedy the problem of their placement. Within entries, the italicized phrase *See the picture* (with a page number given if the picture is on another double-page spread) ensures that illustrations will not be overlooked.

Additional color shading highlights synonym and word history paragraphs and the pronunciation key. Ample margins also serve to make the word list appealing to the eye. Full-color illustrations, appearing within a number of the special features, are attractive and substantive.

The print is large enough for the intended audience, and typefaces are easy to read. Main entry words are in boldface and overhang the text. The use of bold type elsewhere in the entry (for example, for inflected forms), as well as italic and brackets, makes information easy to spot. Paper is of mediocre quality with some show-through; the section of special features (excluding the guide) is printed on heavier, glossy paper, adding to its attractiveness as well as its durability. The sturdy binding will withstand frequent and rugged use.

IX. Summary

The prospective buyer will find *Webster's New World Dictionary for Young Readers* attractive, easy to read, and durable. It is designed specifically for young pupils and geared toward classroom use. The entries, while sometimes brief, are age-appropriate. On the other hand, omissions among current terms and biographical entries limit the usefulness of these features. Some limitations are also manifested in etymologies and synonym paragraphs. However, the list price of this dictionary makes it an affordable as well as worthwhile investment for library, classroom, and home use.

Webster's New World Pocket Dictionary

Facts at a Glance

Full Title: **Webster's New World Pocket Dictionary**.
Alternative Title: *Webster's New World Handy Pocket Dictionary*.
Publisher: Prentice Hall Press.
Editor: Samuel Solomon, Supervising Editor.
Edition Reviewed: © 1977.

Number of Volumes: 1.
Number of Entries: 22,000.
Number of Pages: 316.
Trim size: 3″ × 5¼″.
Binding: paperback with a slip-on vinyl cover.

Price: $2.95.
Intended Readership: high school and up.
Sold in bookstores. ISBN 0-671-41826-2.

I. Introduction

Webster's New World Pocket Dictionary, also called *Webster's New World Handy Pocket Dictionary* by its publisher, was first published in 1964, revised in 1972, and is currently in a seventh printing of the 1977 edition. The book has no preface or introductory remarks. The words included appear to be those that were in common use when this edition was first published. No criteria for word selection is given. There are some 56,000 words included, with about 22,000 main entry words, accompanied by very brief definitions.

II. Authority

A notice on the copyright page states: "This book is based upon and includes material from *Webster's New World Dictionary, Second College Edition* . . . and *Webster's New World Dictionary, College Edition*." Both dictionaries have solid reputations, although the editions cited as sources for this pocketbook's entries are now outdated (the latest copyright dates listed are 1976 for the first source and 1968 for the second).

III. Comprehensiveness

The overall number of words included is extensive for such a small, compact work. But many meanings in this book do not reflect either current or common usage, and there are many important main entry words missing, as well as important additional meanings missing for those that *are* included. For example, **hardware** has only one definition: "Metal articles, as tools, nails, etc.," which ignores the word's widespread meaning in the field of computers. **Computer** is defined as "(electronic) computing machine."

A brief sample of the kinds of words that do not appear in this pocket dictionary is: *compact disc*, *highjack*, *homosexual*, and *infrastructure*. The prefixes **in-** and **un-**, however, both have additional useful lists of combined word forms that will help the reader in quick spelling checks.

IV. Quality and Currency of Entries

The definitions reflect meanings that were contemporary with the dates of publication. The selection of entries, in general, should be revised to make room for more current words and meanings. For example, **access** is defined as a noun only.

Entries are ordered as follows: bold headword divided into syllables followed by part of speech; inflections, variant forms, and plural forms; brief numbered definitions; with additional labeled parts of speech run-in to the entry. Definitions are cursory, often only a single word, and occasionally illustrative. Colloquial and slang terminology is sometimes given as well as common idioms such as "**in the light of**, considering" at the end of the entry for **light**. Word forms are given, but etymology, synonyms, and antonyms are not. This will limit this dictionary's usefulness for many school assignments.

V. Syllabication and Pronunciation

Syllabication is indicated in the main entry by a dot separating the syllables. Primary and secondary stress is indicated by dark and light accent marks. A very brief pronunciation key is found at the beginning of the book, but the symbols rarely appear as guides to words in the main alphabet. They are, however, quite simple and can be used easily.

VI. Special Features

Immediately preceding the main alphabet is a page of rules for spelling and for forming plurals. At the back of the book are punctuation rules, a list of abbreviations (which also needs updating: *a.k.a.*, for example, is not included), weights and measures, a perpetual calendar, names of U.S. states and cities with 1970 population figures, nations of the world with unspecified population figures, facts about the earth, traditional gifts for wedding anniversaries, birthstones, and a list of the members in the "Hall of Fame of Great Americans." Some of this material

may be useful, but it is also found in more detail and currency in almanacs.

VII. Accessibility

Words are entered in letter-by-letter alphabetical order. Guide word pairs with a centered page number appear at the top of each page. This small book is very easy to leaf through quickly, and the bold main entry words overhanging the text can be scanned easily.

VIII. Graphics and Format

Each page is divided into two columns by a thin vertical rule. The guide words are separated from the text by a horizontal rule. All main entry words, inflected forms, additional parts of speech, and idiomatic phrases are in clear, but small bold sans-serif type.

The print size of the text is very small and relatively hard to read. The paper is a rough white sturdy stock with little show-through. The book will fit comfortably into a pocket, and it has a flexible, washable red vinyl slip jacket for additional protection and durability. Altogether, the book's format is a neat and practical package.

IX. Summary

Webster's New World Pocket or *Handy Pocket Dictionary* is in desperate need of revision and, despite its practical, handy format, will not be the first choice in paperback pocket dictionaries. Too many words in everyday use are either not included or need to have meanings added that reflect current usage.

Webster's New World Vest Pocket Dictionary

Facts at a Glance

Full Title: **Webster's New World Vest Pocket Dictionary.**
Editor: Clark C. Livensparger.
Publisher: Simon and Schuster.
Edition Reviewed: © 1977.

Number of Volumes: 1.
Number of Entries: 15,000.
Number of Pages: 188.
Trim Size: 3″ × 5¼″.
Binding: paperback.

Price: $1.95.
Intended Readership: high school and up.

Sold in bookstores and other outlets. ISBN 0-671-41829-7.

I. Introduction and Scope

Webster's New World Vest Pocket Dictionary is a slimmer, edited version of WEBSTER'S NEW WORLD POCKET or HANDY POCKET DICTIONARY (reviewed in this Buying Guide). The number of main entries for this vest pocket work has been reduced from the pocket dictionary by about one-third. The appendix for this edition contains somewhat less information than the pocket work, and this paperback is considerably less attractive than its parent pocket edition. Like its parent dictionary, *Webster's New World Vest Pocket Dictionary* is outdated and should not be considered for purchase until it is revised.

Webster's Ninth New Collegiate Dictionary

Facts at a Glance

Full Title: **Webster's Ninth New Collegiate Dictionary.**
Publisher: Merriam-Webster.
Editor: Frederick C. Mish, Editor-in-Chief.
Edition Reviewed: © 1986.

Number of Volumes: 1.
Number of Entries: 156,000.
Number of Indexes: 1.
Number of Pages: 1,568.
Number of Illustrations: 573 black-and-white line drawings.
Trim Size: 7" × 9½".
Binding: hardcover.

Prices: hardcover: $14.95; thumb-indexed: $15.95; simulated leather: $16.95.
Intended Readership: high school and up.
Sold in bookstores; also sold to schools and libraries. ISBN 0-87779-506-8 (plain); 0-87779-509-6; 0-87779-510-x.

I. Introduction

This is Merriam-Webster's latest in their collegiate line of dictionaries published since 1898. For this volume, the editor-in-chief states that "Every entry and feature of the last edition has been reexamined so that this Collegiate offers . . . much that is new

and useful while preserving the best features of preceding editions.'' Originally published in 1983, this updated edition carries a copyright date of 1986.

Based on the publisher's continuously updated citations files of 13,000,000 examples, the collegiate is meant, according to its preface, "to serve the general public''—including school and college students, office workers, and home users—as "a reliable guide to understanding the English of our day and communicating in it.'' The English is, of course, American English.

With its "almost 160,000 entries and 200,000 definitions,'' this is a comprehensive, abridged work in which the main purpose is to describe and define the English language. A new feature in this edition is the inclusion of brief usage paragraphs to provide guidance on words whose usage is confused or disputed.

The opening essay on "The English Language in the Dictionary'' not only describes the contents, but sets the vocabulary and definitions in context, and explains the working methods of the dictionary's staff in preparing this work. There are numerous additional tables, lists, and charts, as well as appendix sections of Biographical, Geographical, and College and University names. Readers of the dictionary may also request information from the publisher's Language Research Service, which answers individual inquiries.

II. Authority

Merriam-Webster is the highly respected publisher of *Webster's Third New International Dictionary*, the authoritative unabridged work on which the *Ninth Collegiate* is based. The publisher has a permanent, trained staff of lexicographers and linguistic experts. In addition, Merriam-Webster maintains a citation file of words used in context that numbered some 13,000,000 when this dictionary was in preparation. This file was established two years after publication of the firm's original collegiate dictionary and contains citations from 1890 to the present.

In the dictionary's opening essay on language, there is an extensive list of the authoritative historical source works used in preparing the *Ninth Collegiate*. Another section in the essay, entitled, "Semantics in the Dictionary,'' explains (with precise examples) the methods used by the editors to define and write entries. This reveals the behind-the-scenes work that maintains the high reputation of the *Ninth Collegiate*, a book directly descended from Noah Webster's *American Dictionary of the English Language* (1828).

Webster's Ninth New Collegiate Dictionary

❶ Pronunciations and variants
   appear within slashes

❷ Illustrative phrase is given within
   angle brackets; the entry word is
   replaced by a swung dash

❸ Synonym paragraph is preceded
   by *syn* in boldface italics

❹ Etymology within brackets
   includes a cross-reference in
   small capital letters

❺ Date of the earliest written use
   in English of the entry word is
   enclosed in parentheses

❻ Synonym cross-references are
   given in small capital letters

III. Comprehensiveness

The preface to the dictionary states that "the treatment of words of the A–Z vocabulary section is as nearly exhaustive as the compass of the work permits."

The main vocabulary includes synonyms with subtly distinguished meanings. There are thorough etymologies, a generous amount of labels, including *ISV*, which is used by the editors to indicate "international scientific vocabulary," and dates of first recorded usage. The following examples show the form of an etymology, dating, labeling, and the form of a usage citation.

> ¹**mole** *n* [ME, fr. OE *māl*; akin to OHG *meil* spot] (bef. 12c) **:** a pigmented spot, mark, or small permanent protuberance on the human body; *esp* **:** NEVUS.
>
> **ke·tone** *n* [G *keton*, alter. of *aceton* acetone] (1851)
>
> **ke·to·ste·roid** *n* [ISV] (1939)
>
> **sci·en·tize** . . . (1917) **:** to treat with a scientific approach 〈the attempt to ~ reality, to name it and classify it —John Fowles〉.

Authoritative and relatively extensive guidance, based on the publisher's staff expertise and enormous citation files, is given in usage notes for disputed or difficult words such as **hopefully** or **whom**. For example:

> **hopefully** *adv* (1639) **1:** in a hopeful manner **2:** it is hoped

> **usage** Only the irrationally large amount of critical fire drawn by sense 2 of *hopefully* requires its particular recognition in a dictionary. Similar use of other adverbs (as *interestingly*, *presumably*, *fortunately*) as sentence modifiers is so commonplace as to excite no notice whatever. While it still arouses occasional objection, *hopefully* as a sentence modifier has been in use at least since 1932 and is well established as standard.

The dictionary also contains six additional reference sections and a style handbook.

IV. Quality and Currency of Definitions

Reviews of the definitions in the *Ninth Collegiate* when it first appeared in 1983 were favorable. The American Library Association's *Reference Books Bulletin* review (p. 31, 1983–84) of the dictionary said: "Definitions are precise and clear, with excellent synonym and usage notes. . . . Spot-checking suggests adequate currentness." Other reviews noted that the redesigned page layout allowed for the addition of "thousands" of new words and definitions, plus synonyms with discriminated senses, cross-referenced to analytical definitions, and new usage paragraphs.

All main entries appear in alphabetical sequence, letter by letter. Numerals, for example, are alphabetized as if they were spelled out. The basic sequence of information in the vocabulary is boldface main entry divided into syllables; pronunciations; part of speech, variant forms and inflections with pronunciations when necessary; the etymology is followed by the date of first recorded use; then definitions, numbered and including cross-references in small capital letters as well as sample citations in angle brackets. The senses of a word are historically ordered. The sample below shows the sequence and an example of a numbered homograph:

²**para-** \par-a*comb form* [*para*chute] **1** : parachute <*para*trooper> **2** : parachutist <*para*spotter>.

Run-on entries to the main entries, such as derivatives or phrases (defined when necessary) are preceded by a hyphen and may include pronunciation and part of speech. Under **para·bi·o·sis**, for example, the run-on entry is:

— **para·bi·ot·ic** \-'ät-ik*adj* — **para·bi·ot·i·cal·ly** \-i-k(ə-)lē *adv*.

Because the *Ninth Collegiate* emphasizes descriptive information, rather than prescriptive guidance, its labeling system, although extensive is not as obvious as, for example, that in THE AMERICAN HERITAGE DICTIONARY: SECOND COLLEGE EDITION. The *Ninth Collegiate*'s status labels include regional labels, for words or senses specific to areas of the U.S. or of the English-speaking world. Temporal labels are *obs* for obsolete and *archaic*.

Stylistic labels are *slang*, *nonstand* for nonstandard, and *substand* for substandard. *Substand* refers to use that is "disapproved of by many" or that differs substantially from that used by "the prestige group of the community" (for example, **ain't**), according to the publisher. Words generally considered vulgar are so explained within definitions. Some special subject labels are given (for example, football terminology), but generally special usage particular to a field or profession are explained in the definitions.

A randomly selected segment of entries from **paprika** through **parachute** shows twenty-two main entries in the *Ninth Collegiate*, twenty-three slightly different main entries in that segment in THE AMERICAN HERITAGE DICTIONARY; SECOND COLLEGE EDITION. A comparison of definitions for a general term from each work reveals that usually discriminations are more precise in the *Ninth Collegiate*.

From the Ninth Collegiate, compare "**par·a·ble** . . . *n* . . . : COMPARISON: *specif* : a usu. short fictitious story that illustrates a moral attitude or religious principle," with *The AHD: Second College Edition*'s: "**par·a·ble** . . . *n*. A simple story illustrating a moral or religious lesson." In other cases, such as the definition for **parachute**, the *AHD* is more scientific; in

parabola, both dictionaries are precisely scientific and both use mathematical diagrams as illustrations.

V. Syllabication and Pronunciation

The points where words may be hyphenated at the end of a line are shown for all main entries, variant forms, and inflections by centered dots: "**mach·i·nate** . . . *vb* **-nat·ed**; **-nat·ing** . . . — **mach·i·na·tor** . . . *n*." No division is indicated for single letter syllables at the beginning or end of words (**aboard**, **slith·ery**), nor for succeeding homographs (²**machine**). Within the definitions, where a hyphen within a word is normally used, a double-stacked hyphen is used at a line end: as in the compound adjective salmon=pink.

Syllabication in the pronunciation transcriptions is shown by hyphens: **nest·ed** \nes-təd\. The pronunciation system is clearly explained in the "Guide to Pronunciation" preceding the main vocabulary, where the distinguishing marks and special symbols are printed in large bold type. Three pages of "English Spelling and Sound Correspondences" follow, including a list of twenty-five letters and combinations that are often silent. The editors explain that these correspondences "are by no means exhaustive, but they should enable the user who is uncertain of the spelling to find most words in this book." They also add that "knowing the first five letters of almost any word will get the user to within a few inches of the right place in even the largest unabridged dictionaries." The spelling guide list is organized by the pronunciation symbols for vowels and diphthongs and for consonants; students used to simpler systems will need to spend a considerable amount of time becoming familiar with the extensive range of symbols before the list is useful.

The pronunciation symbols used in the transcriptions are based on the scholarly International Phonetic Alphabet (IPA); many of these will not be familiar to American students in either high schools or colleges, who generally do not receive extensive instruction in the use of various pronunciation systems. *Reference Books Bulletin* briefly summed up the *Ninth Collegiate*'s pronunciations in the review quoted earlier: "Linguistic data are very precisely displayed, with extensive (possibly to some users forbidding) use of symbols and abbreviations."

VI. Special Features

Among the additional features of the *Ninth Collegiate* are a handy list of common abbreviations normalized to one form; a list of the symbols for chemical elements, and a considerable dictionary of foreign words and phrases in common use that are not Anglicized or Americanized. These A to Z entries contain pronunciations and indicate source language. The phrases and words range from frequent Latin, Greek, and French mottoes, including those of the U.S. states, to German, Spanish, Russian, and other words. There are forty-two pages of biographical names with death dates up to about 1984–85. Edwin Meese, for example, is listed as U.S. Attorney General as of 1985; Sandra Day O'Connor is listed as an American jurist but not as a member of the Supreme Court. An extensive geographical list, with useful cross-references and alternative name forms, includes U.S. populations based on 1980 U.S. census figures and 1976 Canadian figures. The political information is generally up-to-date—for example, Harare is identified as the capital of Zimbabwe, but foreign populations are now outdated.

The remaining items are a list of colleges and universities, with zip codes that could, in many cases, be mistaken for enrollment figures; and a clearly designed style handbook with enough examples to be useful. The section on "Documentation of Sources" lists the 1982 *MLA* (Modern Language Association) guidelines but not the association's *Handbook for Writers of Research Papers* (1984, 2d ed.); otherwise, the samples of note style are up-to-date. They even compare the shorter citation style used in many professional fields with that of the humanities. A list of the various forms of address for officials and others is appended. A thorough index lists the charts and tables in the main vocabulary, the reference matter at the back of the book, and even the subsections of the style handbook.

VII. Accessibility

The boldface main entries only slightly overhang the text but can be easily distinguished from the main text. Bold variant forms appearing within or appended to entries can also be seen. Main entries appear in strict alphabetical sequence and homographs are preceded by small bold superior numbers:

drug, *n* . . . ¹drug *vb* . . . ²drug *dial past* of DRAG.

The etymologies following parts of speech are printed within square brackets, which sets them apart from the text. Clear bold page numbers appear at the outer top of margins and two bold guide words separated by a bold bullet appear next to them:

796 neutron star · newt . . . New Testament · niello 797.

Thumb index tabs are available with the clothbound edition. One of the most useful aids to accessibility is the brief, but excellent index at the back of the book. This lists specifically the many additional charts and tables within the main lexicon, as well as useful items from the front guide to the dictionary, such as "Labels, Functional," and in the style handbook at the rear, such as "Virgule, use of."

The pronunciation symbols are handily printed in bold type on the inside back cover, and a four-line pronunciation key, separated from the text by a bold rule, is printed at the foot of each recto's right-hand column.

VIII. Graphics and Format

Scattered sparsely throughout the vocabulary, the 573 captioned black-and-white line drawings are generally precise and attractive. They are also large enough so that details are not obscured, even for those illustrations with numbered labels keyed into captions (a **bird**, a human **ear**, a **fish**, a **horse**, and others).

The small but readable text is set two columns per page. The page width of the *Ninth Collegiate* was expanded about one-quarter of an inch from that in the eighth edition, which allows a slightly wider text column.

An illustrative feature at the front of the book is a double-page spread of sample text from the dictionary with some forty-six labels indicating where the features (such as etymology, or inflections, or usage illustrations in angled brackets) appear in entries. The sample text is printed in gray tone so that the items intended to help the reader find the required information, printed in solid black, can be easily spotted.

The smooth, white paper reveals minimal showthrough of text in the vocabulary section, but in the introductory section where white space abounds, showthrough is obvious. The book is sturdily bound and in general a very handsome example of reference book production.

IX. Summary

When the *Ninth Collegiate* first appeared in 1983, *Library Journal* wrote: "this is probably the best abridged dictionary available." *American Reference Books Annual* (ARBA 84) agreed: "Webster's Collegiate line is directed toward students, office employees, and home users, but, as it is one of the finest abridged dictionaries available, no respectable collection would be without it." Summing up the consensus on the work, *Reference Books Bulletin* (p. 31,

1983–84) said: "Rich not only in current English in general use but in the vocabulary of the scientific and particularly the humanistic disciplines and infused with a sense of history, *Webster's New Collegiate Dictionary* continues, in its ninth edition, to live up to its solid—and well-deserved—reputation."

This work will serve high school students (as well as college students and adults) very well. Some may find the pronunciations difficult; readers will have to decide for themselves whether they will be comfortable using these or require a more familiar and simpler system.

Webster's New School and Office Dictionary

Facts at a Glance

Full Title: **Webster's New School and Office Dictionary**.
Alternative Title: *Webster's Super New School and Office Dictionary*.
Publisher: Fawcett Crest.
Editor: Thomas Layman.
Edition Reviewed: © 1974; 1975 edition.

Number of Volumes: 1.
Number of Entries: 63,000.
Number of Pages: 888.
Trim Size: 4⅛" × 6⅞".
Binding: paperback.

Price: $3.50.
Intended Readership: junior high and up.
Sold in bookstores and other outlets; also sold to libraries and schools. ISBN 0-449-20939-3.

I. Introduction

The introduction to *Webster's New School and Office Dictionary* states that this is a revision of the original World Publishing Company edition which has "for several decades served as a helpful, economical reference book on language." The revision cited, however, was done in 1974. The book contains over 63,000 entries; its special features include a gazetteer, tables of weights and measures, a perpetual calendar, and a listing of U.S. and Canadian holidays.

II. Authority

Originally published by World, a well-known publisher of reference books, this dictionary made its first appearance in 1943. The 1974 revised edition appeared under a William Collins + World imprint.

Collins is a respected British publishing house with many quality reference works to its credit.

III. Comprehensiveness

The vocabulary in the *Webster's New School and Office Dictionary* incorporates, according to the introduction, more entries "than in any other pocket-sized paperback dictionary, including "specialized terms in the sciences and arts [and] new terms frequently encountered in newspapers, magazines, and books." However comprehensive the dictionary may have been in 1974, it has to take a back seat today to other dictionaries such as Dell's THE AMERICAN HERITAGE DICTIONARY and Warner's edition of WEBSTER'S NEW WORLD DICTIONARY OF THE AMERICAN LANGUAGE—especially in respect to technological and other terms in current usage.

Following the introduction, the *Webster's New School and Office Dictionary* contains a pronunciation key and a list of abbreviations used in the dictionary. Main entries in the word list contain few abbreviations (other than **Mr.**, **Mrs.**, **Ms.**, and **WASP**) and few biographical entries, except for some religious entries and some related adjectival terms, such as **Shakespearean** and **Freudian**. The gazetteer's entries and population figures date from the early 1970s. No formal etymological information is offered, but entries frequently provide several numbered definitions, with parts of speech and usage labels. The synonyms and antonyms included are not labeled.

IV. Quality and Currency of Entries

Entries are in alphabetical order, letter by letter, and include: main entries in boldface type that overhang the text; respelled pronunciations with simple diacritical marks in parentheses; parts of speech, irregular plural forms of nouns, and past and present participle forms of verbs; and numbered definitions with usage labels. The source of unassimilated foreign words appears after the part of speech, for example: **gemütlich**, *adj.* [German]. Definitions, although brief, differentiate clearly among meanings and are generally accurate. Slang or informal labels appear in brackets, as do rare, archaic, or special field terms. For example:

> **tongue** (tung), *n.* **1.** a fleshy, movable protrusile organ on the floor of the mouth of most vertebrates. **2.** the chief organ of speech. **3.** the power of speech. **4.** the manner of speaking. **5.** dialect; idiom. **6.** discourse. **7.** the clapper of a bell. **8.** anything resembling a tongue. **9.** a promontory: *v.t.* **tongued, tongu'ing. 1.**

to modulate or modify with the tongue. **2.** [Archaic], to scold: *v.i.* to talk; prate.

Example phrases are not given, and synonyms are not labeled but may be used as definitions. Prefixes and suffixes appear in their proper alphabetical place in the main vocabulary.

V. Syllabication and Pronunciation

Syllables are indicated by centered dots: **tooth·ache**. A pronunciation key follows the introduction, and a brief, two-line guide with examples, separated from the text by a rule, appears on the bottom of each page in the lexicon.

VI. Special Features

The gazetteer, "A Dictionary of Geography," appears following the main vocabulary, with brief, but adequate entries for cities, countries, rivers, and other features of the world. Lists of the largest cities and metropolitan areas in the United States (with 1970 population figures) are given, as is a list of principal foreign cities (with population figures that need updating).

VII. Accessibility

Bold main entry words that overhang the text, guide words at the tops of pages, and a contents page help to make the information in the dictionary accessible to the reader. However, the format, in general, is poorly designed for ease of reading.

VIII. Graphics and Format

This paperback has a cheerful bright yellow cover that will appeal to readers of all ages browsing in bookstores or at newsstands. The text, however, is printed in extremely small type, and entry words in the copy reviewed were often smudged or blurred. The diacritical marks in the pronunciations were often impossible to decipher. In addition, the poor quality of paper allows for considerable show-through of text. This dictionary is, in fact, extremely difficult to read.

The pages are very crowded, with little white space in the outer margins, between the two columns of text, or in the gutter. The print on some pages can only be read when the book is forced open by bending back the spine. This will quickly render the book unusable.

IX. Summary

There are a number of other paperback dictionaries with more up-to-date entries, better page design and printing, and more readable text than the *Webster's New School and Office Dictionary*. The narrow gutter margins that necessitate bending of the spine make it unsuitable for any library or classroom circulating paperback collection. Those students in junior high or high school who need a mass-market-size, personal paperback dictionary for quick reference should consider an *American Heritage* or *Webster New World* or *Merriam-Webster* dictionary, in preference to this volume.

Webster's Scholastic Dictionary

Facts at a Glance

Full Title: **Webster's Scholastic Dictionary**.
Publisher: Airmont Publishing Company.
Edition Reviewed: © 1985.

Number of Volumes: 1.
Number of Entries: 30,000.
Number of Pages: 416.
Number of Illustrations: 47 in black and white.
Trim Size: 4½" × 7¼".
Binding: paperback.

Price: $2.95.
Sold in bookstores and other outlets; also sold to schools. ISBN 0-8049-2001-X.

I. Introduction

As described on its cover, *Webster's Scholastic Dictionary* is a pocket-size abridged dictionary that provides "over 30,000 entries of the most commonly used words," including "most widely used slang words and expressions." The "foreword" asserts that this paperback "is designed for the use of the. pupil in schools, but it can be of equal value for everyone for general use." No age range is suggested for the intended audience. In addition to its 47 black-and-white drawings, the dictionary has an eight-page glossary of abbreviations. One additional feature, which the editors cite as rare in a dictionary of this size, is its inclusion of the British spelling following the American form of a word.

II. Authority

Published by Airmont Publishing Company, this 1985 edition gives no evidence of recent updating and appears to be simply a reprinting of the original 1966 edition. According to the "foreword," "In selecting the more than 30,000 entries, the editors have, by diligent research, retained what they consider the necessary words of the English language." However, the names and credentials of the editors are not provided, nor are any sources, such as citation files and word lists, mentioned. The title page states that the dictionary is "Based on the Lexicography of Noah Webster" and a note on the copyright page states: "This dictionary is not published by the original publishers of Webster's Dictionary, or by their successors." The minimal information provided calls the dictionary's authority into question.

III. Comprehensiveness

Users—student or adult—seeking up-to-date listings will be disappointed by this dictionary. A wide range of scientific as well as popular terms recently incorporated into American usage are omitted from the volume. These terms include *aerobics* (in its contemporary exercise sense), *Agent Orange*, *AIDS*, *anorexia*, *biofeedback*, *data processing*, *gay* (as it relates to homosexuality), *holistic*, *program* (as it relates to computer science), *space shuttle*, and *videocassette*. These omissions will put students who might use the dictionary as an adjunct to their study of recent and current events at a disadvantage.

Abbreviations appear not in the main word list, but as a separate glossary. Biographical and geographic entries do not appear. Also excluded from the dictionary are antonyms, etymologies, and usage notes, all of which may be needed by student users.

IV. Quality and Currency of Entries

In general, definitions are simple enough to be understood by readers as young as middle school students, but important senses of a word are often slighted. For example, **celibacy** is defined as

The unmarried state; a single life.

The word's more typical sense, *complete sexual abstinence*, is not included, which distorts the definition. In other instances, definitions lack the concreteness that would make them readily understandable. **Tend**, for example, is defined as:

vi. To move in or have a certain direction; to conduce; to attend. —*vt.* To attend; to guard; to take care of.

This definition needs brief illustrative phrases, such as "tend a child, tend to business."

Multiple definitions in an entry are not numbered and are linked by semicolons. The various senses of a word seem congested in the entry, and inexperienced users, particularly, will find it difficult to discern subtle variations in meaning. For example, **form** is defined as

n. Shape; manner, pattern; order; empty show; prescribed mode; ceremony; schedule; a long seat; a bench; a class; the seat or bed of a hare. —*vt.* To shape or mold; to arrange; to invent; to make up. —*vi.* To take a form.

The multiple meanings are presented in a cumbersome and arbitrary way that is likely to confuse readers. Adding to the confusion is the subsuming of derived and related words under a single main entry. For example, under the main entry **foot**, all of the following boldfaced subentries appear: **feet, football, footing, footlights, footman, footprint, footsore, footstalk,** and **footstep**. Arbitrarily, **footstool** has a separate main entry.

Although a claim, appearing on the cover, states that the dictionary provides "specific examples to explain definitions," illustrative sentences and phrases to show the use of words are not included; it is not clear what "examples" the cover alludes to. However, some clarification of word meanings is provided by synonyms. For example, **daydream** is defined vaguely as

A vision to the waking senses; a reverie.

The user who looks up **reverie** will find

A loose train of thoughts; a daydream; a visionary project.

The latter definition helps to explain the former, but no cross-referencing is provided, so many users will not reap the benefits of such clarifications.

V. Syllabication and Pronunciation

Syllabication is not indicated in the boldfaced entry word, but within the pronunciation, where syllables are separated by stress marks or hyphens. A simplified system of pronunciation, incorporating 24 symbols with four diacritical marks, should prove accessible even to younger users. The pronunciation key appears only at the front of the volume, however, which will be inconvenient for users unfamiliar with phonetic symbols.

Alternative pronunciations are provided in a few instances; for example:

dis-sern' or di-zern'.

In some instances in which a word's pronunciation varies according to part of speech, as with **separate**, only one pronunciation is given.

VI. Special Features

The dictionary's special features are its glossary of abbreviations—including, among others, abbreviations for U.S. states, world countries, units of measure, organizations and associations, titles, and degrees—and its inclusion of British spellings. This glossary appears at the front of the volume.

VII. Accessibility

Alternative spellings are given for words whose British spelling differs from the American. These appear in boldface type immediately following the main entry word:

labor, labour.

No thumb index is provided, as would be expected in a volume of this size. Guide words at the top of each page indicate the first and last word defined on the page. These are in boldface block capitals; however, in some instances the words are over-inked and difficult to decipher.

VIII. Graphics and Format

The dictionary's line drawings are small and poorly rendered. A few, such as the diagram illustrating **rhomboid** are of substantial use in clarifying definitions. Others are less useful: the illustration for **unicorn** understates the beast's characteristic horn; that for **cobra** looks more like a bird than a snake. Drawings appear next to the words they illustrate and are captioned with main entry words.

The binding is sufficiently sturdy so that pages do not easily separate from the paperback cover. The paper quality is poor, and the small-sized print and illustrations appear on some pages over-inked and blurred. The text is printed in two columns on each page, with insufficient white space between the columns for reading ease. Boldface main entry words overhang the text and are easily seen; boldfacing within entries, of derived and related words, makes these easier to locate.

IX. Summary

Despite its compact form and inexpensive price, *Webster's Scholastic Dictionary* will not meet the needs of most student users today. It does not include cur-

rent terms; and multiple definitions in entries are cluttered and hard to distinguish. The small print size and poor printing make the entries hard to read. Although the glossary of abbreviations would be useful to students and other users, the dictionary lacks many other features—such as usage notes and biographical and geographic entries—that students may require.

Webster's School Dictionary

Facts at a Glance

Full Title: **Webster's School Dictionary**.
Publisher: Merriam-Webster Inc.
Editors: Merriam-Webster editorial staff.
Edition Reviewed: © 1986.

Number of Volumes: 1.
Number of Entries: 85,000.
Number of Pages: 1,184.
Number of Illustrations: 953.
Trim Size: 8″ × 10″.
Binding: cloth.

Price: $11.95.
Intended Readership: high school students.
Sold in bookstores and other outlets; also sold to libraries and schools. ISBN 0-87779-280-1.

I. Introduction

The Preface to *Webster's School Dictionary* (*WSD*) states that it has been written especially for high school students, but the Buying Guide's reviewers feel it is also suitable for junior high readers. According to the publisher, "The range of vocabulary covered is suited to the needs of older high school students, yet the definitions are written in everyday language that will be clear to young readers." Its 85,000 entries range from scientific terms to modern idioms. This dictionary was originally published in 1980 and revised in 1986. It is one of a series of three school titles which include WEBSTER'S ELEMENTARY DICTIONARY and WEBSTER'S INTERMEDIATE DICTIONARY.

II. Authority

Although no specific credits are given, the dictionary is prepared by Merriam-Webster's highly respected dictionary staff. The entries are selected from Merriam-Webster's extensive citation files and also from appropriate school texts, according to the publisher.

Webster's School Dictionary

❶ Pronunciations and variants are given within back slashes

❷ Etymologies, within boldface brackets, spell out word sources

❸ Synonym study is preceded by boldface centered dot and **syn**

❹ Line drawing of animal species placed close to entry word

❺ Meanings cross-referenced to main entry words appear in small capital letters

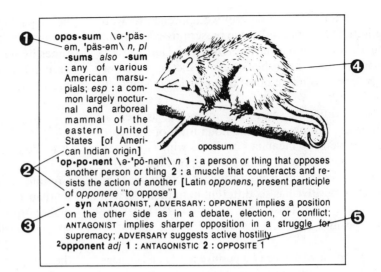

opos·sum \ə-'päs-əm, 'päs-əm\ *n, pl* **-sums** *also* **-sum** : any of various American marsupials; *esp* : a common largely nocturnal and arboreal mammal of the eastern United States [of American Indian origin]

opossum

¹**op·po·nent** \ə-'pō-nənt\ *n* **1** : a person or thing that opposes another person or thing **2** : a muscle that counteracts and resists the action of another [Latin *opponens,* present participle of *opponere* "to oppose"]

• **syn** ANTAGONIST, ADVERSARY: OPPONENT implies a position on the other side as in a debate, election, or conflict; ANTAGONIST implies sharper opposition in a struggle for supremacy; ADVERSARY suggests active hostility

²**opponent** *adj* **1** : ANTAGONISTIC **2** : OPPOSITE 1

III. Comprehensiveness

In addition to the definitions, the dictionary includes etymologies, word histories, a few usage notes, and numerous synonyms. Etymologies appear at the end of the definitions in square brackets. Word histories are longer explanatory notes and are signaled by a small triangle and the word *origin*, underlined and overhanging the following text like an entry word. Anecdotal information is often provided under these word histories. Both may appear after any given word, but the histories occur much less frequently. Synonyms, but not antonyms, are provided; these are indicated in capital letters following the entry word, for example, **FACE** for the verb **front**. There are also synonymous cross-references. In some instances, synonyms are grouped together following the abbreviation "syn." For example, under the word **opinion**, the list reads: "syn OPINION, BELIEF, CONVICTION . . . ." The different shades of meaning of each of these words are then carefully distinguished in a synonym paragraph.

There are other types of cross-references in this dictionary as well, including directional and inflectional. For example, following the entry for **Ruth** there is a dash, followed by the words "see BIBLE table," through which the reader is ultimately referred to the Book of Ruth in the Old Testament under **Roman Catholic Canon**, **Protestant Canon**, and **Jewish Scripture**. Inflectional cross-references refer the reader to the appropriate base word of an inflected entry such as, "**am** *present 1st sing of* BE." In some cases, the reader is instructed to compare one word with another for clarity. Following the definition of **altricial**, we find the reference "—compare PRECOCIAL," which has the opposite meaning.

Slang terms, such as **bennies** for amphetamine tablets, are labeled, and there are a few other kinds of usage notes throughout the dictionary. For example, the rhetorical term **asyndeton** is defined as the "omission of the connectives ordinarily expected (as in [Caesar's famous phrase] *I came, I saw, I conquered*)."

Verbal illustrations are included in the dictionary between angle brackets. For the noun **best**, the examples are:

⟨trying to be the *best*⟩, ⟨do your *best*⟩, ⟨wear your Sunday *best*⟩.

Phrases appear much more frequently than full sentences, but are adequate for the age level of the intended user. The dictionary includes capitalization when needed, both in the main entry and under senses and subsenses, if the capital only occurs with a certain meaning. Some new words are included in *Webster's School Dictionary*, but others that should be there have been omitted. **UFO**, **astronaut**, and the computer terms **bit** and **byte** are in the dictionary; however, *videodisc*, *VCR*, and *videocassette* are not found (these three video terms are included, however, in WEBSTER'S NINTH NEW COLLEGIATE).

IV. Quality and Currency of Entries

Entries in the *Webster's School Dictionary* include: boldface syllabication, pronunciation, italicized parts of speech abbreviated, numbered definitions, word origins, synonyms, and variant word forms.

The school dictionary's parent, MERRIAM-WEBSTER'S THIRD NEW INTERNATIONAL DICTIONARY, is characterized by a descriptive approach to word definitions, as opposed to the prescriptive definitions found, for example, in the American Heritage dictionaries. The publisher's school dictionary, however, contains usage notes that provide guidance to good usage.

Many different senses are indicated, as well as subsenses. For example, the noun form of the word **post** is given two meanings or senses which are numbered: one is a metal or timber support; the other is a pole or stake that is used to mark something. The adjective **positive** has six different definitions as well as numerous subsenses that are lettered. Under the noun **positive** only subsenses are defined:

> a: the positive degree or a positive form in a language
> b: a positive photograph or a print from a negative.

Subsenses deal with finer shades of meaning. Both numbers for the various senses and letters for the subsenses are in medium face type to set them apart from the text. The definitions of a word are in historical order insofar as it is possible to determine their word origins. Unless students are familiar with other Merriam-Webster dictionaries that use this order or have carefully read the front matter, they may be confused, since most dictionaries place the most commonly used definition first.

Some definitions are elaborated more than others. Under **Bible**, for example, the books of both Old and New Testaments are listed. The symbol, atomic number, and atomic weight are noted in a table for chemical elements found under **element**. Comprehensive lists of compound words are given for prefixes, such as **post**, which has 41; **super**, which has 118, and **un**, which receives three pages, each with six columns of words beginning with the **un** prefix. A few foreign words are included, such as **bête noire** and **joie de vivre**. Biographical, biblical, mythological, and geographical names are not included in the main alphabet, but are listed in separate appendixes in the back of the dictionary. These listings include boldface syllabication, pronunciation, and factual information. These appendixes are listed in the table of contents for quick reference.

V. Syllabication and Pronunciation

Centered dots indicate syllabication in the entry words. Pronunciation follows and appears between slashes. There are fifty-six pronunciation symbols used, and these appear on the page preceding the alphabet. There is also an abbreviated pronunciation key at the bottom of the right-hand column on odd numbered pages of the lexicon. Variants in pronunciation are given; they are separated by commas and sometimes by semicolons when grouped together. All the variants are considered acceptable and none is given preference.

VI. Special Features

A guide to using the dictionary is located in the front of the book and is reasonably easy to understand. Contained in the guide are clear explanations of how to read the entries in the dictionary, including explanations of: syllabication, pronunciation, parts of speech, inflected forms, definitions, cross-references, word histories, and synonyms. Under each of these topics, a short lesson is given similar to those in a grammar handbook. Suggested activities are not included, and they would be a useful addition to a school dictionary.

Appended to the back of the dictionary are abbreviations and symbols for chemical elements, signs and symbols, biographical, biblical and mythological names, geographical names, and a "Handbook of Style." Pronunciation is indicated for both biographical and geographical names, but only very brief information is given. For example, **Alcott** Louisa May is defined as "1832–88 American author." The "Handbook of Style" covers punctuation, italicization, capitalization, and plurals. This handbook section will be helpful to students proofreading and editing their papers, but it does not contain information necessary for writing a research paper, such as outlining and bibliographical formatting.

VII. Accessibility

Pairs of guide words at the top of each page facilitate locating words in the dictionary. There is no thumb indexing or thumb guides; even though the dictionary is not too large, these would still be very useful. Words in the main alphabet are listed alphabetically, letter-by-letter. Entries that are a number or an abbreviation are listed as though spelled out. To find the definition of **Dr.**, for example, a student would have to look under **doctor**. The abbreviated form is not listed as a main entry; there are no cross-references.

Variant spellings of words are separated by either the word "*or*" or "*also*." When variants follow in alphabetical order and are separated by "*or*," this indicates that they are used with a similar frequency. When one spelling is somewhat more common, the variants are separated by "*or*" but appear in reverse alphabetical order, as explained in the dictionary guide. When "*also*" separates variant spellings it means that the word that follows is much less commonly used. The dictionary guide gives the following example: **cesarean** *or* **cesarian** *also* **caesarean**. Unless the student is very familiar with this dictionary or has studied the dictionary guide, this listing format may be confusing.

VIII. Graphics and Format

The overall layout of the page design is such that the dictionary is quite easy to read, despite the large amount of information given within each entry. The dictionary is printed on non-glare paper that does not bleed through from the type on the other side of the page. Line drawings are used judiciously throughout the book. Most are adequate in size and detail for their purpose.

The book lies flat when opened, and the binding is sturdy; however, the inside margins are too narrow for the book to open flat if it is rebound. The bright green, cloth-covered board cover is attractive, but does look institutional. The review copy showed some signs of wear with limited use.

IX. Summary

Webster's School Dictionary contains over 85,000 definitions, more than 950 line drawings, over 18,000 etymologies, and some 530 synonym paragraphs. It is an authoritative work, published by Merriam-Webster. When compared to WEBSTER'S NINTH NEW COLLEGIATE DICTIONARY, however, it is hard to see that there is a strong need for the *WSD*. High school students who can use the school dictionary will, in most cases, also be able to use the *Collegiate*, which is not only more comprehensive but also more up-to-date. Junior high school readers will find the school volume very useful, especially since it benefits from somewhat larger type and more illustrations and places etymological notes at the end of the definition. Both dictionaries have very similar if not identical definitions for words. Those high school students needing an easier dictionary would fare better with the MACMILLAN DICTIONARY, which contains 120,000 definitions and is much more readable.

Webster's II New Riverside Dictionary

Facts at a Glance

Full Title: **Webster's II New Riverside Dictionary**.
Publisher: Berkley Books.
Editors: Houghton Mifflin lexicographic staff.
Edition Reviewed: © 1984; 1986 printing.

Number of Volumes: 1.
Number of Entries: 55,000 definitions.
Number of Pages: 832.
Number of Illustrations: 200 black-and-white line
    drawings.
Trim Size: 4¼" × 6⅞".
Binding: paperback.

Price: $3.95.
Intended Readership: junior high school and up.
Sold in bookstores; also sold to schools and
    libraries. ISBN 0-425-09169-4; 0-425-08298-9.

I. Introduction

Described as a "user-oriented dictionary, designed for today's school and business needs," this abridged, pocket-size paperback contains over 55,000 entries and includes "hundreds of new words not found in any other dictionary," according to the publisher. Other features include style and usage guides; word history paragraphs and synonym lists; foreign words and phrases; abbreviations and acronyms; measurement and monetary tables. According to the editors, the purpose of the *Webster's II New Riverside Dictionary* "is to mirror what our language is and to convey that information in a form appropriate to an inexpensive, fully portable dictionary."

Buyers should note that this Berkley paperback appears in two identical editions with the same price, but different covers and different ISBNs. The first ISBN in the Facts above is for a more popular— brighter—cover that indicates this work is "for successful students"; the other cover is a dark maroon.

II. Authority

Based on the first edition of WEBSTER'S II NEW RIVERSIDE UNIVERSITY DICTIONARY, this 1984 paperback abridgment was compiled by Houghton Mifflin's editorial staff. Its lexicon is drawn from Houghton Mifflin's extensive database of citations.

III. Comprehensiveness

Compared to similar paperback dictionaries, this work offers a variety of the new science, medical, computer technology, and general words of the 1980s. Some of these terms include: **biofeedback**, **video disc**, **videocassette**, **gay** (homosexual), **punk rock**, **fast-track**, **freebie**, and **AIDS**. However, obviously not all of the "25,000" new words cited in the semi-abridged uni-

Webster's II New Riverside Dictionary

❶ A dagger symbol indicates "regional" usage of an entry word

❷ Illustrative phrases are enclosed within angle brackets

❸ Synonyms in small capital letters are marked by an open star and a boldface abbreviation, **syns:**

❹ Additional forms of an entry word are run-in to the entry, divided into syllables, and listed in boldface

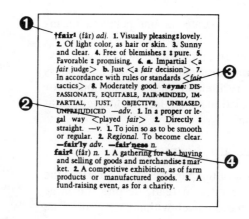

versity dictionary have been transferred to this paperback. Among the words not listed are *palimony*, *Dolby System*, *snow* (argot for "cocaine" or "heroin"), *vidicon*, *freebase*, *grid-lock*, *modem*, and *reggae*.

Word etymologies and many of the idiomatic expressions found in the university dictionary are also omitted from this edition. Many of the word history paragraphs found in the hardcover copy are given in this abridged edition. These appear at the end of the entry, and are designated by a triangle, as in the following example:

> **pi·o·neer** . . . ▲ *word history:* The word *pioneer* is derived from the French *pion*, "foot soldier." *Pioneer* orig. denoted a soldier whose task was to prepare the way for the main body of troops marching to a new area . . . .

Although they appear in fewer entries than in the parent dictionary, some word synonym lists are included. These synonyms are printed in small capital letters and are introduced by a star, as in the following example:

> **mur·der** . . . ☆ **syns:** KILL, KNOCK OFF, LIQUIDATE, RUB OUT, SLAY, WASTE, WIPE OUT, ZAP.

A variety of language labels are provided to identify a specific orientation or other qualifying sense of a meaning, including for example, subject and geographic labels, plus nonstandard, informal, archaic, and slang designations. Phrasal verbs are introduced by boldface dashes, and are defined in alphabetical sequence, as in the following case:

> **give** . . . **—give away** . . . **—give in** . . . **—give out** . . . **—give up.**

Inflected forms are either partially or fully delineated (depending on their number of syllables), and immediately follow the pronunciation of the entry word.

IV. Quality and Currency of Entries

Entry words are printed in boldface type overhanging the text columns. When entries have more than one sense, they are ordered according to clusters of related subsenses, rather than by their frequency of occurrence or by their historical meaning. These multiple senses are numbered sequentially in boldface, and subsenses are indicated by boldface letters—for example:

> **gate**[1] (gāt) *n.* **1. a.** An opening in a wall or fence. **b.** An often hinged structure that closes or blocks a gate. **2.** . . . .

A boldface colon separates two or more elements within a particular sense of a definition:

> **in·eq·ui·ty** . . . **1.** Injustice: unfairness.

Compared with other paperback dictionaries of its size and scope, the *Webster's II New Riverside Dictionary* has much to offer. Readers will find that the definitions are generally clear and concise. Although the essential meanings of the words are provided, the definitions themselves are less comprehensive than those in the hardcover edition. Other features are also either omitted or trimmed down in this work. Compare, for example, the following entries—the first entry is found in the hardcover dictionary, and the second is taken from the paperback edition:

> **cough** (kôf, kŏf) *v.* **coughed, cough·ing, coughs** [ME *coughen.*]*—vi.* **1.** to eject air from the lungs loudly

and suddenly. **2.** To produce a noise similar to that of coughing <The engine coughed and died.>—*vt.* To expel by coughing <coughed out phlegm>—**cough up.** *Slang.* To relinquish (e.g., money) often reluctantly.—*n.* **1.** an act of coughing. **2.** A condition marked by frequent coughing.

cough (kôf, kŏf) *v.* **1.** To eject air from the lungs suddenly and loudly. **2.** To make a noise similar to that of coughing. **3.** To expel by coughing.—**cough** *n.*

Although illustrative phrases are provided in many of the definitions, unfortunately, the exemplification of some abstract senses of words ("To make a noise similar to that of coughing.") is excluded in this condensed version.

V. Syllabication and Pronunciation

Syllables are separated by boldface centered dots, not only in the entry word, but in the inflected and derived forms as well, when indicated. However, syllabication of compound words is not duplicated: **dif·fer·en·tial**, but **differential calculus**, if words in the compound appear as main entries.

Pronunciations are given immediately after the entry word and are enclosed in parentheses. Based on the International Phonetic Alphabet (IPA), a pronunciation key appears in the front of the book; however, this key is not shown on any other page of the dictionary, even in a simplified form. This lack of a key throughout the dictionary may limit the paperback's usefulness for some students, but should not prove troublesome for those familiar with basic dictionary phonetics.

VI. Special Features

The appendix includes "A Concise Guide to Style and Usage," an abridged version of the guide found in the hardcover edition. The sections on capitalization, italicization, punctuation, clichés, and redundant expressions are identical to the original, but omit the section entitled "Problems in English Usage." Although the guide in this paperback edition provides some general usage rules for quick reference, it is too cursory to be of great value; a good grammar handbook would serve most students better. Measurement and currency tables are given within the dictionary's main vocabulary, under their corresponding letters in the alphabet.

VII. Accessibility

Clearly delineated boldface pairs of guide words are represented together at the top outer corner of each page, and are separated by an open square: **indolent**

□ **inevitable.** The word to the left of the square indicates the first word on the page, and the word to the right designates the last entry listed. There are no thumb indexes or other aids to help locate a particular section of the text, as is usual in paperback dictionaries. Words that have the same spelling, but are derived from a different etymology, are represented by superscript numbers which alert the user to other listings of the word.

VIII. Graphics and Format

The 200 black-and-white line drawings are fairly large and well-rendered. A rectangular border outlines each illustration, making these drawings easy to distinguish on the page. The paper is a newsprint typically used in paperbacks, and the book is not well-bound—placing the book flat, with its pages open, too often will tear them away from the spine; but, the generous amount of margin space, particularly at the gutter, means that this dictionary is easy to hold and read, even though the typeface is quite small.

IX. Summary

The *Webster's II New Riverside Dictionary* provides current, concise, and clear definitions that students will find valuable. Its small size will fit conveniently on the most cluttered desk top, but the non-durable binding is a consideration for prospective buyers who plan to use a dictionary often. For the modest price, this dictionary should serve the casual user for a number of years. However, its mediocre physical quality and the limitations of its format make it less satisfactory for classroom use or for library collections.

Webster's II Riverside Children's Dictionary

Facts at a Glance

Full Title: **Webster's II Riverside Children's Dictionary**.
Publisher: Houghton Mifflin.
Edition Reviewed: © 1984.

Number of Volumes: 1.
Number of Entries: 40,000.
Number of Pages: 800.
Number of Illustrations: over 1,200.
Number of Maps: 3.
Trim Size: 7⅞" × 9⅞".
Binding: reinforced paperback.

Webster's II Riverside Children's Dictionary

❶ Synonym box provides a cross reference and a list with explanation and examples of how meanings are used

❷ The Word History box explains the second homograph

❸ Usage examples are given in italic type

❹ The entry word is repeated before pronunciation and variant forms are listed

❺ Labeled illustration of the first homograph's fourth meaning

fair¹ *adjective* **1.** Beautiful; attractive: *a fair princess.* **2.** Light in color: *fair skin.* **3.** Clear; not cloudy: *fair skies.* **4.** Not favoring one side more than another: *a fair judge; a fair share.* **5.** Average: *The movie was only fair.* **6.** Following the rules: *fair play.*
▢*adverb* In a fair way: *She doesn't play fair.*
fair (fâr) ▢*adjective* **fairer, fairest** ▢*adverb*

SYNONYMS: **fair¹, impartial, just**
These adjectives mean not favoring one person or side more than another: *Everyone agreed that the decision was fair. All the judges in the contest were impartial. The responsibility of a jury is to give a just verdict.*

fair

fair² *noun* **1.** A gathering for the buying and selling of goods; market. **2.** A large public show of farm or industrial products, often with entertainment and contests.
fair (fâr) ▢*noun, plural* **fairs**

WORD HISTORY: **fair²**
The word *fair²* meaning "a market" comes from a Latin word that means "a holiday."

Price: $8.95.
Intended Readership: ages 8 through 12; grades 3 through 6. ISBN 0-395-37884-2.

I. Introduction

This dictionary is intended for use by elementary school children in grades 3 through 6. The Fry Readability Formula yielded an average level of fifth grade. This approximation seems quite reasonable, although the publisher's lower level of third grade seems somewhat inappropriate. No doubt a few excellent third grade students could use this dictionary, but it would be misleading to conclude that third graders in general could use it without difficulty. Students above sixth grade with below-grade reading skills could use this dictionary without being repelled by the format.

This dictionary is quite extensive: 40,000 entries, plus special features which include synonyms, word histories, and special phrase definitions, such as "in the nick of time" (which can be found by looking up the entry for the word that seems most important in each phrase). Also, a spelling table, alternative spellings of entries, and an appendix of useful encyclopedic information are included.

II. Authority

Unfortunately, other than stating on the cover that this is "a new dictionary prepared according to the principles of Noah Webster," no information on compilers, editors, or method of compilation is given.

III. Comprehensiveness

Multiple entries are included for a word that has very different meanings—"fly" for example. Current words and words pertaining to history, geography, and basic science were checked with the following results:

included	*not included*
typhoon	*words for sexual organs*
czar	*cocaine*
parliament	*DNA*
meridian	*anthropology*
Middle Ages	*mitosis*
blizzard	*vortex*
constitution	
latitude	
glacier	
lagoon	
laser	

Proper nouns such as **Moslems, Pekingese,** and **Allah** are included while personal names are not.

The dictionary includes etymologies for some words. The origin of the word is given, without either its form in the original language or a history of the development. Synonyms are given for some entries, with illustrative sentences to delineate subtle differences among the terms.

IV. Quality and Currency of Entries

Definitions are presented in the form of sentences, phrases, or single words; the majority are full sentences or phrases. The general sequence of information in each entry is: entry word in boldface type; part of speech label in italics (spelled out, not ab-

breviated); definition (numbered, when more than one); sentence or phrase in italic type that includes the entry word; syllabication and phonetic pronunciation; plural forms, if any; inflected forms, if any.

Multiple meanings are given in order of frequency of use. For the entry word **foul**, six definitions are given for the adjective, two for the noun, and three for the verb. (A ☐ indicates the next part of speech.)

A comparison of several words contained in the *Webster's II Riverside Children's Dictionary* (WII), the MACMILLAN DICTIONARY FOR CHILDREN, and the SCOTT, FORESMAN BEGINNING DICTIONARY yielded the following information:

1. **giraffe**—The *WII* describes it as "tall," but leaves out the fact that it is the tallest living animal, as well as being hoofed and cud-chewing.
2. **Doberman pinscher**—The *WII* neglects to mention that this dog has a large head, is slender, and was originally bred in Germany.
3. **fence**—The *WII* omits the definition for someone who deals in stolen goods. It neglects to include the connotation of protection and the concept of keeping people and animals in or out. Also, wood is the only building material mentioned.
4. **pendulum**—The *WII* does not mention that pendulums are often found in clocks.
5. **crawl**—The *WII* does not include the use of hands and knees.
6. **scallop**—The *WII* omits one culinary definition, and there is no verb entry.

These examples, chosen at random, suggest that at least some definitions are not as complete as they could be.

A comparison of the definitions of words chosen at random (**course, deceptive, extent**) shows that the illustrative phrases and sentences in *WII* are no better or worse than those in the Macmillan or Scott, Foresman dictionaries. The phrases or sentences are adequate.

The technical and scientific definitions are clearly stated and should be easy for students of this age to comprehend. For instance, **computer** is defined as "an electronic machine that can solve complicated problems quickly, store information, and control other machinery."

V. Syllabication and Pronunciation

Entry words divided into syllables appear in boldface after the definitions and sample sentences. The print is only slightly smaller than the original entry. Syllables are separated by dots.

The pronunciation of the entry words appears in parentheses immediately after the syllable division. The syllable or syllables to be accented are printed in boldface type within this pronunciation. Accent marks are also used. Some longer words have two kinds of accent marks—a strong one after a syllable printed in boldface and a lighter one after one or more syllables printed in regular type—**contemporary** (kən **tem′** pə rer′ ē). Hyphenated words are indicated as such.

The main pronunciation key, occupying one full page, is easily located immediately before the main part of the dictionary. A short form is boxed and shaded in the lower right-hand corners of the right-hand page, which makes consultation easy. The pronunciation key uses 35 symbols with five diacritical marks.

When an entry word has two different but acceptable pronunciations, both are shown (connected by the word "*or*"). The pronunciation given first is the most common. For example, the entry **apparatus** has the following pronunciation: "ap′ ə rā′ təs *or* ap′ ə **rat′** əs."

VI. Special Features

A four-page spelling table is included to aid the student who is not quite sure how to spell a particular word. A note of caution: use of this table will probably have to be explained by a teacher. The guide to the dictionary contains only a few brief paragraphs on the use of the spelling table.

The preview pages and the guide are both useful. Separate sections such as "More Help Pronouncing Words" with headings in large print and a contrasting color make information in the guide easy to locate. The Scott, Foresman dictionary has exercises at the end of each section of the guide to reinforce understanding; the *WII* does not. Dictionary skills exercises are in abundance elsewhere, so this is not a serious omission.

The guide does not give a very basic explanation of how to look up a word in the strict alphabetic listing but the intended audience should not need this.

An appendix located at the very end offers the following information: measurement tables, metric conversion chart, U.S. presidents, U.S. chief justices, abbreviations, manual and braille alphabets, Roman numerals, Morse code, and several basic maps (which photocopy surprisingly well).

Several pages of the appendix are devoted to a chronology of U.S. history, "Events in United States History." The chronology begins with a brief mention of pre-Columbian America and ends with the 1983 space flight of Sally Ride; it also emphasizes events that feature minorities or women. Black-and-white photographs and pictures are included in this section.

Over 250 "Word History" boxes, which provide the etymology of interesting words such as **cartoon** or **disaster**, are found after the definitions. Shaded "Synonyms" boxes are also interspersed throughout the dictionary.

The back cover claims that this volume contains "more special features than any other children's dictionary." This is doubtful, since the special features are rather typical of dictionaries intended for this age group.

VII. Accessibility

Two labeled preview pages placed at the very beginning provide a quick, visual explanation of the arrangement of the main body of the dictionary. Guide words appear in boldface at the top of every column. There is no thumb indexing but this should not be a problem for the intended age group. The sections of the appendix and of the introductory materials are all listed in the table of contents.

If a word has more than one correct spelling the most common spelling is listed first. These alternative spellings may appear in one entry, as in **pimiento** or **pimento**, or as a separate entry. In the latter case, the definition appears only in the entry for the most common spelling.

VIII. Graphics and Format

This large-format paperbound dictionary will lie flat when opened. Adequate margins, a variety of typefaces (boldface, Roman, and italics), shaded boxes, and a thick tan line under the guide words will all aid the reader.

The black, white, and tan drawings which appear on every page add interest but do not always help clarify the written material. Some less successful examples are illustrations for the words **express** (the face is not expressive); **cylinder** (the drawing is too complex); **midst** (the aerial view is confusing); and **camouflage** (Macmillan and Scott, Foresman illustrate this word much more successfully).

The *WII* is printed on white paper that is not heavy enough to prevent show-through from the reverse side. The dictionary is not curvature-bound and there is no dust jacket.

IX. Summary

The *Webster's II Riverside Children's Dictionary* is generally attractive, low priced, and accessible to the intended audience. Some special features are done well: the preview pages, the guide, and the boxed and shaded information.

However, the thin see-through paper of the text and the paper binding will prevent this book from withstanding heavy use in a classroom or library.

A major concern is the quality of definitions. Some simply are not as complete as they could be. This fact, coupled with the faults in some illustrations and the fact that the illustrative sentences are only adequate, makes this dictionary marginally acceptable and certainly not outstanding.

Webster's II New Riverside Pocket Dictionary

Facts at a Glance

Full Title: **Webster's II New Riverside Pocket Dictionary**.
Former Title: The Pocket Dictionary.
Publisher: Houghton Mifflin.
Editors: Fernando de Mello Vianna, Anne D. Steinhardt, and Pamela DeVinne.
Edition Reviewed: © 1978.

Number of Volumes: 1.
Number of Entries: 35,000.
Number of Pages: 256.
Trim Size: 3½" × 5½".
Binding: paperback.

Price: $2.95.
Intended Readership: junior high school and up.
Sold in bookstores; also sold to libraries and schools. ISBN 0-395-41822-4.

I. Introduction

Webster's II New Riverside Pocket Dictionary is a pocket-sized reference source that includes pronunciations, inflected forms, variants, and irregular plu-

rals. Its "Rapid Word Finder" index system enables the user to locate entries quickly and easily. The volume also contains several special features: a guide to the use of the dictionary and appended features covering punctuation, proofreaders' marks, weights and measures, the metric system, and U.S. states.

The work is well designed to serve an audience including both junior high and high school students and adults. While it may find its most appropriate place in the home or office library, its compact size renders it convenient for writers on the move. Its special features expand its scope as a reference source for students.

II. Authority

Editors of the volume are members of Houghton Mifflin's permanent lexicographic staff. Editorial Director Fernando de Mello Vianna has also served as an editor for the American Heritage dictionaries.

III. Comprehensiveness

With its 35,000 entries, the dictionary is considerably more comprehensive than the comparable WEBSTER'S VEST POCKET DICTIONARY. The work includes variant spellings, indicating whether two spellings are equally frequent or one is preferred. Inflected forms of verbs, adjectives, and adverbs are provided when they are irregular or may pose spelling difficulties. Irregular plurals are shown; regular plurals appear when there is an irregular variant or when the regular plural is liable to be misspelled. Part-of-speech labels are provided, as are additional grammatical labels indicating, for example, verb forms and tenses, comparatives and superlatives, and noun genders.

Excluded from the dictionary are etymologies, synonyms, abbreviations, and biographical and geographic entries. Only the omission of abbreviations is likely to present problems for the student or adult user of the work.

IV. Quality and Currency of Entries

Entries include the boldfaced, syllabified main entry word; pronunciation in parentheses; italicized part-of-speech abbreviations; boldfaced variants and inflected forms, as appropriate; and definition(s). Homographs receive separate main entries, with each distinguished by a superscript number.

Definitions are clear and concise. Multiple senses are frequently provided and are introduced with boldfaced numerals. Indeed, this work's entries often define more shades of meaning than would be expected of so compact a dictionary. A representative entry is the following:

> **a·bove** (ə-bŭv′) *adv*. **1**. Overhead. **2**. In a higher place, rank, or position.—*prep*. **1**. Over. **2**. Superior to. **3**. In preference to.—*n*. Something that is above.—*adj*. Appearing or stated earlier.

In comparison, Webster's Vest Pocket Dictionary lists only one adverbial and two prepositional senses for the word.

As is appropriate for a work of this size and scope, many technical and specialized terms are excluded. The word list includes current entries such as **astronaut**, **ecology**, **gay** (homosexual), and **program** (computer science sense). However, **computer** is listed only as a variant of **compute**, which is defined as "To calculate." Examples of words excluded, in part because of the dictionary's 1978 date, are *file* and *data* in their computer sense, *videodisc*, and *videocassette*.

V. Syllabication and Pronunciation

Syllabication is indicated in main entry words by centered dots and in inflected forms by centered dots or stress marks. Pronunciation follows a system of 45 symbols that are explained at the front of the volume in the guide to the dictionary's use. Sample words in the pronunciation key show the sound under consideration in boldface type. The symbols should not present difficulties to students or other readers.

VI. Special Features

The number of special features provided is unusual for a pocket dictionary. In addition to a brief, clear introductory guide to the use of the work, the volume includes several appended features. A brief guide to punctuation usefully covers the most important rules governing the dash, exclamation point, comma, period, colon, question mark, quotation marks, semicolon, brackets, apostrophe, and parentheses. A chart lists and illustrates the use of proofreaders' marks. Tables of weights and measures incorporate both customary U.S. and metric units, and a guide to the metric system and metric conversion table are provided. Finally, the volume includes a list of U.S. states that notes capitals, dates of admission to the Union, and population, although the date for the population figures is not indicated.

VII. Accessibility

Alternative spellings appear in boldface type. If the variants are used with roughly equal frequency, they appear together at the beginning of the entry (**ax**, **axe**). If one form is distinctly preferred, it is listed as the main entry; the variant appears after the pronunciation (Also **the·a·tre**).

Words are especially easily located with the dictionary's "Rapid Word Finder" system, which is explained on the volume's opening page. According to this system, each letter of the alphabet is assigned a number (A–1, B–2, and so on; *X*, *Y*, and *Z* have no numbers but are instead grouped together). The user refers to the chart on the first page to determine the number corresponding to the first letter of the word he or she is seeking. At the top outer margin of each page within the word list appears the appropriate letter-number designation in prominent white on a black background. The user will find it quicker to seek a number, according to this system, than to seek a letter section through the use of guide letters or guide words alone. However, each spread also is headed by two boldface guide words, indicating the first and last entries on the spread.

A table of contents at the front of the volume lists the dictionary's special features and ensures that they will not be overlooked.

VIII. Graphics and Format

Boldface main entry words overhang the text. Type is small, but readable and larger than that of Webster's Vest Pocket Dictionary. Adequate margins and white space also contribute to readability. Paper permits minimal show-through of text. When the spine is cracked to open the book flat, the pages do not separate from the binding. This paperback is sturdy enough to hold up well to frequent use.

IX. Summary

Webster's II New Riverside Pocket Dictionary can be compared to Webster's Vest Pocket Dictionary. Both are highly compact, inexpensive reference works, suitable for use by a wide student and adult audience. Webster's Vest Pocket Dictionary appends a useful list of abbreviations and has a more durable cover than *Webster's II*. However, the latter contains more entries, its entries provide more senses of words, and its print is larger and easier to read. Accessibility to the latter is enhanced by its "Rapid Word Finder" system. While both dictionaries contain useful information on punctuation, *Webster's II* contains several other special features that may be especially useful to the student user. This work warrants a place in school or English classroom library, as well as in many home and office reference collections.

Webster's Vest Pocket Dictionary

Facts at a Glance
Full Title: **Webster's Vest Pocket Dictionary**.
Publisher: Merriam-Webster.
Editor: Merriam-Webster's dictionary staff.
Edition Reviewed: © 1981.

Number of Volumes: 1.
Number of Entries: estimated at over 18,000.
Number of Pages: 380.
Trim Size: 3⅛″ × 5⅜″.
Binding: cloth (flexible simulated leather).

Price: $2.25.
Intended Readership: all ages; junior high school and up.
Sold in bookstores and other outlets; also sold to libraries and schools. ISBN 0-87779-190-2.

I. Introduction

This *Webster's Vest Pocket Dictionary* is described by the publisher as an "extremely concise reference to those words which form the very core of the English vocabulary." Despite its small, handy format, the work bears a distinct family resemblance to the larger, highly respected dictionaries in the Merriam-Webster family. The brevity of the vest pocket work's definitions will provide readers from junior high to adult level with a resource for quick, reliable checks on meaning or spelling.

II. Authority

This pocket dictionary belongs to the highly respected Merriam-Webster family of dictionaries; and it bears many resemblances to its larger companions, such as the *Webster's New Collegiate Dictionary*. Readers should be aware that this is an authoritative, although brief, book, unlike some other so-called Webster pocket dictionaries available in mass market outlets and chain stores, for instance.

III. Comprehensiveness

A rough estimate of the contents is that there are somewhere between 18,000 and 20,000 bold main entries plus twenty additional lists of words formed from the most common prefixes, such as **anti-**, **mini-**, **super-**, and **un-**. There are also many additional variant spellings, inflected forms, and run-in entries giving a term or phrase related to main entries: e.g., **sugar cane** under **sugar**, **eyeball**, **eyelashes**, and **eyelid** under **eye**.

IV. Quality and Currency of Definitions

For quick reference, these very condensed definitions provide, in general, the denotative meaning of words as defined by the editors of WEBSTER'S NINTH NEW COLLEGIATE DICTIONARY: "the direct and specific part of meaning which is sometimes indicated as the total of all referents of a word and is shared by all or most people who use the word." Two examples illustrate this well:

mne·mon·ic *adj* assisting memory

pa·ram·e·ter *n*: characteristic element.

Although secondary meanings are infrequent, essential ones are included, such as "**chin·a** *n* **1** : porcelain ware **2** : domestic pottery." In that case, the second definition covers typical everyday usage. More specialist or technical and scientific terms are usually excluded, although the third meaning of **program** is given as "coded instructions for a computer." There are other useful inclusions such as "**pro·bate** *n* : judicial determination of the validity of a will."

The lists of undefined words created by the addition of suffixes include a considerable range of words that one is likely to encounter in normal speech and writing. Under **in-**, for example, there are two brief definitions: "**1** not **2** lack of" followed by 201 words using the prefix.

The order of information under a main entry word is a simplified version of the sequence in the larger Merriam-Webster dictionaries: main entry (with variant spelling) printed in bold type and syllabicated, pronunciation(s), part of speech, inflected forms, definition, and other forms of the word and run-in entries. All entries appear in alphabetical order, including homographs of different origins indicated by superior numbers:

¹**lark** *n* : a small songbird
²**lark** *vb* or *n* : romp.

Homographs with similar origins are run-in to the main entry; succeeding ones are indicated by a swung dash ~.

V. Syllabication and Pronunciation

Main entries are syllabicated with centered dots to show where a hyphen may be used when breaking a word.

A page of pronunciation symbols, based on the system used in the larger Merriam-Webster dictionaries, is printed immediately opposite the first page of *A* entries. There are brief explanations and sample words for special symbols such as the ŋ indicating the *n* sound in "si**ng**, si**ng**er, fi**ng**er i**n**k," for example.

Primary stress is shown by a bold mark ′ before the syllable; secondary stress is shown by a ′ mark. All pronunciations appear between sets of back slashes after the bold entry: **im·por·tant** \ ′im′portənt \. Differences in pronunciations, where a syllable may not be uttered in some cases, are indicated by placing the letter(s) in parentheses, as: **lour** \ ′lau(ə)r \.

VI. Special Features

Immediately after the main vocabulary there are four pages of abbreviations, shown in one form, but with a note explaining that they often occur in other forms. There is also a brief, but very clear "Handbook of Style"—a slightly pretentious title for the brief numbered information on how to use punctuation symbols from the apostrophe to the virgule, a section on italicization (five numbered points) and on capitalization (twenty-two numbered points), plus two short paragraphs on the plurals of English words. There are useful short examples of all these items given in brackets, as

> 15. Personifications are capitalized. <She dwells with Beauty.—John Keats.>

VII. Accessibility

Although the typeface is very tiny, the main entry words are printed in bold overhanging the text. They can easily be located, as can the variant forms and run-in entries, also printed in bold type. At the top of each page toward the outer margin, two guide words are printed in bold type. A bold page number is centered over the inner column of text. Because the book is so small, it is easy to leaf through the pages to find a required word.

The main vocabulary is printed in two columns of text, with generous inner margins. There is sufficient white space so that the text does not appear dense on the pages.

VIII. Graphics and Format

There are no illustrations, but the design of the book is very attractive and the boldface vocabulary words stand out from the entry text. Occasionally the diacritical marks in the pronunciations are difficult to distinguish; this is particularly true of the umlauted vowels: ä and ü.

The paper is a smooth, white coated stock with minimal show-through.

IX. Summary

This small dictionary fits into pockets and school or handbags easily. It is derived from authoritative larger works and contains sufficient vocabulary with the most basic definitions to be useful as a check on meaning and spelling. The cloth cover is a reinforced wipe-clean simulated leather. The pages are well glued to the cover, yet they can be opened wide. All in all, this is a very good, very small dictionary that will be useful to a wide range of students, for quick reference in school and at home. In brief, it is the best of the vest-pocket dictionaries.

Webster's Vest Pocket Dictionary

Facts at a Glance

Full Title: **Webster's Vest Pocket Dictionary**.
Publisher: Thomas Nelson, Inc.
Editor: Walter C. Kidney; revised edition prepared under the direction of Laurence Urdang.
Edition Reviewed: © 1985; 3rd printing.

Number of Volumes: 1.
Number of Entries: over 10,000.
Number of Pages: 188.
Trim Size: 3″ × 5¼″.
Binding: paperback.

Price: $1.25.
Intended Readership: junior high school through adult.
Sold in bookstores and other outlets; also sold to schools. ISBN 0-8407-5991-6.

I. Introduction

Webster's Vest Pocket Dictionary: Revised Edition (published by Thomas Nelson and not to be confused with the dictionary of the same title published by Merriam-Webster) is an even more compact dictionary than Nelson's WEBSTER'S NEW COMPACT DIC-

TIONARY. About 10,000 main entry words are defined very briefly. The dictionary is paperback and the cover is designed to look as if it were brown leather with gold print; it fits easily into a shirt pocket or purse.

II. Authority

The dictionary was edited by Walter C. Kidney and its most recent revision was "prepared under the direction of Laurence Urdang," according to the title page. Urdang is the highly acclaimed linguist and lexicographer who has edited and written many books about the English language.

III. Comprehensiveness

No criteria for selection of main entry words is given, but these are words frequently used in everyday conversation. Slang, highly technical, unusual and difficult words are not included. The main entry words have definitions that are identical to those found in WEBSTER'S NEW COMPACT DICTIONARY, although this edition has fewer entries. The basis on which words were eliminated is not explained, but it appears that less common everyday words were omitted. Occasionally a new word has been added. For example, in the list of words beginning with "da," seven words were deleted and one word added to the words that are found in the WEBSTER'S NEW COMPACT DICTIONARY. Words deleted were *damper, damsel, dapple, dastard, dated, davenport,* and *daytime.* The word added was **daffodil**. Biographical and geographic names, as well as synonyms, antonyms, and etymologies are not included.

IV. Quality and Currency of Entries

Succinct, bare-boned definitions are often only one or two words, yet they convey a sense of the meaning of the word. For example:

> **gargantuan**, *adj.* gigantic.
> **gargoyle**, *n.* fantastic waterspout.
> **garish**, *adj.* vulgarly showy.

Word forms are not given although variations of the word are found in the run-on entries. The compact design of this small dictionary does not allow for expanded definitions. However, the definitions given provide a clear meaning of the word. The vocabulary contains many words in current use, such as **gay** (referring to *homosexual*), and words pertaining to computers, such as **kit**, **byte**, **database**, **program** and **modem**.

V. Syllabication and Pronunciation

Dots for syllabication and diacritical marks to distinguish phonetic values are used in the main entry word. If further pronunciation guides are needed, they follow the main entry in parentheses. For example: **as·so·ci·ate** (əs sośhē ət). However, this rarely occurs. There is no pronunciation key to explain the symbols.

VI. Special Features

In addition to its small size, which is in itself a special feature, the dictionary has tables of weights and measures, metric equivalents, birthstones, and traditional and modern gift ideas for wedding anniversaries.

VII. Accessibility

For those with vision problems, this dictionary will be difficult to read. The print used in the definitions is miniscule. Even those with excellent sight will not want to use this volume for prolonged periods of time.

Access to the material is through guide words located at the top of each page and through a letter-by-letter arrangement of the main entry words. In one case, an error occurs when **corpse** is listed before **corps**.

VIII. Graphics and Format

Entry words and related words are in small bold type, the parts of speech are abbreviated in italics, the definition is indented two spaces and is in a very small type font. Each small page is divided into two columns with an average of twenty-eight words per column. There are no illustrations.

IX. Summary

When a reader wants a pocket dictionary with many words, one sacrifices type size. *Webster's New Pocket Dictionary* possesses a currency that is not found in most other pocket dictionaries. With the inclusion of words such as **ayatollah** and **database**, the dictionary is keeping good pace with political and technical words that have entered the mainstream of everyday usage. This is a very good little dictionary, useful for both its clarity and its currency, for occasional personal use, but not for libraries.

The World Book Dictionary

Facts at a Glance

Full Title: The World Book Dictionary.
Former Title: The World Book Encyclopedia Dictionary.
Publisher: World Book.
Editors: Clarence L. Barnhart and Robert K. Barnhart; Sol Steinmetz, Chief General Editor (Barnhart Books); Robert O. Zeleny, Editor-in-Chief (World Book).
Edition Reviewed: © 1987.

Number of Volumes: 2.
Number of Entries: 225,000.
Number of Pages: 2,554.
Number of Illustrations: 3,000 in black and white.
Trim Size: 8⅜″ × 10⅞″.
Binding: hardbound.

Price: $69.00 (and various other prices when sold with the encyclopedia).
Intended Readership: elementary school age students through adult.
Sold to libraries and schools and door-to-door.
ISBN 0-7166-0287-3.

I. Introduction

The World Book Dictionary (*WBD*), a two-volume Thorndike-Barnhart work, contains over 225,000 entries and is updated each year, as appropriate, to reflect current technical and other new words and meanings. The volumes offer fuller definitions and more illustrative sentences than those found in most semi-abridged works. Although many collegiate dictionaries, for example, offer brief biographical and geographic entries, WBD does not because it was designed to complement THE WORLD BOOK ENCYCLOPEDIA and, therefore, excludes information that is better treated in a more comprehensive encyclopedic format.

The World Book Dictionary is well bound and ideally suited as both a school reference and a family dictionary. (Among the librarians surveyed in the preparation of this guide, this dictionary was extremely popular.) It is specifically designed to be accessible to a wide range of readers from those in elementary school through students in middle school, junior and senior high school—and even adults. However, despite the publisher's heroic efforts to serve this wide intended readership, elementary students could find this two-volume work formidable in several respects.

In addition to the careful attention that the 2,554 page dictionary gives to new words and phrases, it provides a generous amount of foreign words and phrases, selective etymologies, and over 3,000 line drawings. The 124 pages of front matter are organized into four main sections: "Using Your Language," "How to Write Effectively," "Using Different Languages," and "Using This Dictionary."

II. Authority

This reference book was first published in 1963 under the supervision of lexicographer Clarence L. Barnhart, and was designed as the largest work in the Thorndike-Barnhart series. It was based on the principles prepared and applied by linguist Leonard Bloomfield and psychologist Edward L. Thorndike.

In 1976, *The World Book Dictionary* was revised to include new words and meanings that had developed over the first decade of the dictionary's publication. Subsequently, each year the two-volume reference work is revised and updated to reflect what the editors call our "living language"—the working vocabulary of the most currently used words and meanings in the English language.

The trend toward excellence in the Thorndike-Barnhart tradition is clearly visible in this edition. In addition to the editors, more than 150 consultants in over seventy fields of knowledge, who constitute an international advisory committee of distinguished linguists, phoneticians, and scholars, helped in the dictionary's preparation. (These authorities are listed by name and professional affiliation along with titles of their books.) Although the firm of Barnhart Books, Inc., undertook the primary editorial work, WORLD BOOK ENCYCLOPEDIA editors evaluated the dictionary and designed the educational front matter found in *The World Book Dictionary*; thus, it is specifically meant to be used as an adjunct to that encyclopedia.

More than three million examples gathered in over twenty-five years comprise the extensive quotation file used to update the *WBD* (this is large—but not as extensive, for example, as Merriam-Webster's file).

III. Comprehensiveness

This dictionary is generally more comprehensive than other semi-abridged compilations. *The World Book Dictionary* includes a large assortment of foreign words and phrases not typically found in the main lexicons of many college-level or desk dictionaries, as well as a selection of British terms, such as **beggar-my-neighbor**, **brickie**, and **Civvy Street**. Many of these terms are unlikely to be encountered by most students in their studies or even by most families in their reading

The World Book Dictionary

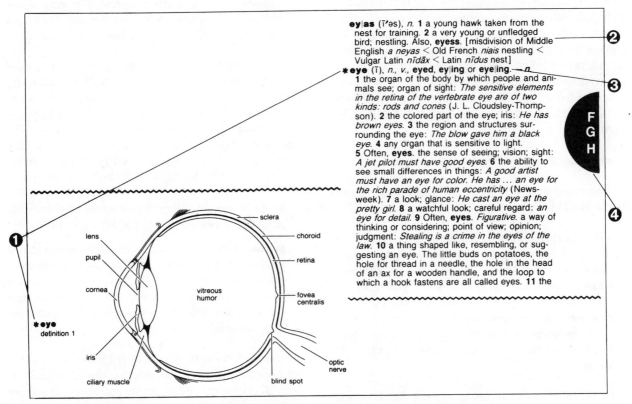

ey|as (ī′əs), *n.* **1** a young hawk taken from the nest for training. **2** a very young or unfledged bird; nestling. Also, **eyess.** [misdivision of Middle English *a neyas* < Old French *niais* nestling < Vulgar Latin *nīdāx* < Latin *nīdus* nest]

✱**eye** (ī), *n., v.,* **eyed, ey|ing** or **eye|ing.** —*n.* **1** the organ of the body by which people and animals see; organ of sight: *The sensitive elements in the retina of the vertebrate eye are of two kinds: rods and cones* (J. L. Cloudsley-Thompson). **2** the colored part of the eye; iris: *He has brown eyes.* **3** the region and structures surrounding the eye: *The blow gave him a black eye.* **4** any organ that is sensitive to light. **5** Often, **eyes.** the sense of seeing; vision; sight: *A jet pilot must have good eyes.* **6** the ability to see small differences in things: *A good artist must have an eye for color. He has ... an eye for the rich parade of human eccentricity* (Newsweek). **7** a look; glance: *He cast an eye at the pretty girl.* **8** a watchful look; careful regard: *an eye for detail.* **9** Often, **eyes.** *Figurative.* a way of thinking or considering; point of view; opinion; judgment: *Stealing is a crime in the eyes of the law.* **10** a thing shaped like, resembling, or suggesting an eye. The little buds on potatoes, the hole for thread in a needle, the hole in the head of an ax for a wooden handle, and the loop to which a hook fastens are all called eyes. **11** the

F
G
H

sclera
choroid
retina
fovea centralis

lens
pupil
cornea
vitreous humor

iris
ciliary muscle
blind spot
optic nerve

✱**eye**
definition 1

❶ Bold asterisk shows that the entry word is illustrated

❷ Etymology provided within square brackets

❸ Part of speech for main entry is followed by variant part of speech; syllable division is shown by a light vertical bar; alternate spelling is provided

❹ Simulated thumb tabs appear in the margin

for pleasure. This extensive vocabulary, however, does make *WBD* at least partially competitive with the unabridged dictionaries—for those readers who want a major dictionary that has a more accessible text and less formal lexicographic apparatus.

The examples often consist of quotations from public figures and actual writing examples. For instance, under the entry for **chafe**, one example of a figurative meaning is taken from the *Wall Street Journal* ("Missing such sales *chafes* retailers"). In another case, one meaning for the entry **alight** is illustrated by a quote from Mark Twain ("I *alighted* on just the book I needed in the library. . . . we *alighted* upon a sign which manifestly referred to billiards.").

Synonym studies immediately follow the particular definition that they are meant to amplify, and are preceded by the boldface label "SYN." in slightly smaller type size than the paragraph of text. For example, following one meaning under the entry word for **excuse** is the following synonym list:

SYN: justify, extentuate, exculpate.

Further down, following another definition under the same entry, is the following note: "**SYN.**: justification." In some cases, the reader will be referred to another entry for a synonym study: under the entry word **ethical**, a note refers the user to the synonym study under **moral**.

Regional labels are used to indicate dialectic differentiations. English-speaking variations (Australian, British, Canadian, Scottish, and the U.S.) are also identified. Language labels are used to designate foreign terms; informal, obsolete, slang, figurative, poetic, and substandard usage; prefix and suffix entries; professional terms (such as those from Biochemistry, *Medicine*, and *Photography*); trademark names; and the distinction, **Unfriendly use,** which applies to terms that belittle or insult—the latter is tactful, readily understandable, and useful.

Boldface run-on forms are syllabicated, and are shown at the end of the definition. Abbreviations are included alphabetically among the regular listings. Usage notes are indicated by boldface arrows, as seen in the example entry **can't**, previously discussed in this review. The bracketed etymologies rely on two basic symbols: the angle bracket (⟨), which means "derived from" or "taken from," and the plus symbol (+), which means "and," as in the following example:

cap|ro|lac|tam . . . [⟨capro(ic) acid + lactum].

The many new words and technical terms found in the *WBD* include:

AIDS, **biorhythm**, **bioenergetics**, **cliometrics**, **crack** (as the term relates to cocaine), **data processing/base/bank**, **disk drive**, **Dolby**, **downer**, **freebie** or **freebee**, **freebase**, **fritz out**, **fast track**, **floppy disk**, **gofer**, **grid lock**, **gay** (in its homosexual sense), **modem**, **New Wave** (but not **New Age**), **possiq**, **program** (in its computer-related sense), **palimony**, **reggae**, **sit com**, **snow** (as a drug-related term), **videocassette/disk**, and **Yuppie**, **yuppie**, or **yuppy**.

Such recently coined terms as *visually handicapped* or *hearing impaired* have not been added. Overall, the currency makes it a particularly useful language tool for users from upper elementary grades through adult levels.

IV. Quality of Definitions

The definitions are exceptionally clear, readable, and very inclusive. The basic ordering of an entry is as follows: the syllabicated boldface entry term overhanging the text; the pronunciation in parentheses; the part of speech label in italics; partially spelled inflected terms, preceded by a hyphen, and also printed in boldface type; definitions, preceded by boldface numerals (and sometimes lowercase letters) when more than one definition is given; verbal illustrations in italics, when necessary; alphabetized idioms noted after the meanings to which they refer; etymology in brackets; synonym studies; and usage notes, when applicable, in italics.

The definitions are listed with the most commonly used meaning first. Consider, for example, the following entry:

e|mit (i mit′), v.t., **-mit|ted**, **-mit|ting**. **1** to send out; give off; discharge. *The sun emits light and heat. Volcanoes*

emit lava. **SYN:** exude, expel, eject. **2** to put into circulation; issue. **3** to utter; express: *The trapped lion emitted roars of rage.* **4** to issue formally (as proper currency). [⟨Latin *ēmittere* ⟨*ex-* out + *mittere* send]

According to the editors, the various entries were written with the age level of the reader most likely to look them up in mind. For this reason, many entries have instructive notes attached at the end of the word paragraph that seem directed toward a particular user. For instance, the entry **can't**, meaning "cannot or can not," has two clarifying amendments to the definition, highlighted by boldface arrows:

▶ **can't**, **mayn't**. *Can't* almost universally takes the place of the awkward mayn't: Can't I go now?

▶ **can't help (but)**. In spite of the objection that it involves double negation, *can't* (or *cannot*) *help but* is the established informal usage: *I can't help but feel sorry about it.* In more formal usage this would be: *I cannot (or can't) help feeling sorry about it* or *I cannot but feel sorry about it.*

Students learning the basics of grammar will find the amplification, such as the one for **can't**, particularly helpful. However, many terms are aimed at a more sophisticated reader, as in the following case:

chae|to|pod (kē tə pod), **n.** any one of a group of annelid worms, having the body made up of more or less similar segments provided with muscular processes bearing setae. [⟨Greek chaitē a seta + poús, podós foot].

The definition of **chaetopod** assumes that the reader will either know what *annelid* and *setae* mean, or be capable of looking up their definitions. This might pose problems for younger readers or for those with reading-ability problems who may not have the incentive to locate two definitions or to tie them in together—a necessary process if a user wants to find a comprehensive meaning for the first entry word consulted. For the most part, however, the complexity of the definition is appropriate to the needs of the reader most likely to be researching that term.

V. Syllabication and Pronunciation

The *WBD* presents syllabication in an innovative way. It was discovered that younger readers were often confused by the centered dots and other syllabication marks and tended to include the word dividers in the actual spelling of words. In this dictionary, the syllables of entries are separated by light vertical lines.

Phrase entries that are syllabified in their own alphabetical place in the dictionary are not divided:

cer|e|bral and cor|tex; but **cerebral cortex**.

Pronunciations are given in parentheses following the main entry word. In cases where several pronunciations are possible, the preferred pronunciation is provided first, and only the syllables that differ from that preferred pronunciation are shown. For example, the entry **criss|cross** lists its two variant pronunciations: "kris′krôs" and "-kros′."

A simplified pronunciation key based on the International Phonetic Alphabet (IPA) is given on the final page of the guide to the dictionary, and on the first page of the second volume. An abridged form of this key is also found at the bottom, outer corner of every right-hand page, except in rare cases where an illustration supplants the key, as at the beginning of the letter *E*. In addition to the various diacritical marks that help to highlight specific word sounds, a boldface accent emphasizes the primary stress of each word, and, when needed, a light accent indicates syllables that have secondary stress.

VI. Special Features

A notable feature of *The World Book Dictionary* is its lengthy and comprehensive introduction, separated from the main dictionary visually as previously noted. (It is printed on buff paper.) The front matter is divided into four sections. "Using Your Language," the first section contains ten chapters:

(1) "Where English Comes From" describes the origin and development of the English language; (2) "Making Words" identifies the three elements that go into forming words (roots, affixes, and combining forms) and provides three full-page listings of prefixes, suffixes, and combining forms, their particular meanings, and word examples; (3) "Learning to Spell Correctly" gives general spelling hints and offers spelling rules along with exceptions to the rules; (4) "Common Misspellings" lists a full page of frequently misspelled words; (5) "Parts of Speech" describes the basic elements and rules of each part of speech; (6) "Capitalization"; (7) "Pronunciation"; (8) "Choosing the Right Word" distinguishes how various shades of meanings among words color language; (9) "Writing and Spelling Traps" identifies the most commonly confused words in the English language (for instance, **advice, advise; beside, besides; council, counsel**, and so on); and (10) "Increasing Your Word Power" provides hints for im-

proving vocabulary and gives vocabulary inventory lists by each age group from 3rd grade through college, a useful feature for teachers, especially.

The second section, entitled "How to Write Effectively," provides the following subsections: "Improving your Writing"; "Writing Term Papers"; "Preparing an Outline"; "Documenting Research Reports"; "Writing Book Reports"; "Preparing Manuscripts," which also lists proofreaders' marks; "Letter Writing"; and "Using the Right Forms of Address," which designates how to address, both in speaking and writing, such titled persons as the President of the United States, governors, reigning Kings and Queens, foreign ambassadors to the United States; Roman Catholic priests; rabbis with doctorate, and so on.

The third section, "Using Different Languages," provides tables of different alphabets (Braille, hand language, International Morse Code, among others); the "International Phonetic Alphabet"; describes systems of "Codes and ciphers"; and "Signs and Symbols" (those found in chemistry, plumbing, mapping, traffic, programming for computers, nautical, and so on). It also explains the purpose and development of "Slang and Jargon"; provides tables for converting measurements, including wire, lumber, time, surface or area, weight and mass measurements, among others; and gives the origins and meanings of first names (for instance, **Barbara** is Greek, meaning "stranger").

Beginning on page 113 of the introductory material is the fourth and last section, "Using This Dictionary," a guide to the general features and format of *The World Book Dictionary*. Although this section appears in the table of contents, placing this material at the end of the extensive introductory and instructional matter effectively buries this much needed information. It is also difficult to access quickly—for readers of any age or skill level—even though it does immediately precede the lexicon.

In most cases, nevertheless, students and adults will find ample use for much of the special front matter. However, some sections (many pertaining to grammar and writing) cover too much material in too few pages to be of great value; users who need more than a general survey will be better served by more comprehensive, topical reference books. Overall, most readers will learn a great deal by simply browsing through the 124-page introductory section, even if many parts are more inclusive than a typical reader will ever need. The danger is that the sheer length of this section will intimidate reluctant readers.

What sets this introduction apart from other dictionaries is its clear writing and built-in adjustments for reading levels, a technique that is also a special feature of the main lexicon. In a short review, it is very difficult to characterize this technique—and its success—effectively; however, compare part of the entry for the word **dirty** (likely to be looked up by the youngest age of reader) with the definition for **disaccharide** (a chemical term likely to be looked up by high school students or adults):

> **dirty** . . . **-adj. 1** soiled by dirt; unclean: *dirty* hands.

> **disaccharide** . . . *n.* any one of a group of carbohydrates, such as lactose, maltose, sucrose, and various other sugars, which hydrolysis changes into two simple sugars (monosaccharides): *Ordinary table sugar and milk sugar belong to the disaccharide class of sugars* (Science News Letter). . . .

Both levels of definition are clear and are amplified by well-chosen illustrative usage.

VII. Accessibility

Attractive, indented thumb tabs help readers to locate specific sections of this dictionary. Boldface guide words appear at the top, outer corner of each double-page spread. When the book is opened, the guide word on the left-hand page denotes the first listing on the spread, the guide word on the right-hand page indicates the last entry shown. Because each page contains three separate columns of entries, elementary school dictionary users may find the large number of entries that fall between the guide words too cumbersome for them to be of much practical help.

When two or more spellings of the same word are used almost interchangeably, the words appear as a single entry and are joined by "or":

> **chan|nel**[1] (chan′əl), *n., v.,* **-neled, -neling** or (*especially British*) **-nelled, -nelling.**

When there is a preferred spelling, the alternate spelling is shown at the end of the preferred spelling entry word's paragraph; alternate spellings are also cross-referenced to the preferred spelling—for example: "**col|or.** . . . Also, *especially British*, **colour**"; the entry for **colour** is then presented in its own alphabetical placement as a separate heading. Cross-references are also given for related etymologies, illustrations, equivalent terms, usage notes, synonyms, and subentries that occur under other main entries. Homographs appear as separate entries, and are indicated by superscript numerals immediately following the entry word: **crew**[1] and **crew**[2]. Users,

(especially novices to dictionary use) should find it easy to understand the etymologies studies in the *WBD*, since they do not rely heavily upon complex abbreviations:

> **game**[1] . . . [Old English *gamen* joy]

> **isologous** . . . [⟨*iso-* + Greek *lógos* word, relation + English *-ous*]

> **parabole** . . . [⟨Greek *parabolē*. See etym. of doublets **palaver, parable, parabola, parole**.].

VIII. Graphics and Format

This dictionary offers an easy-to-read modern computer-set type face (sans-serif Spectra for the main text and sans-serif Roma for the supplemental material), with generous white space. It is printed on high quality, uncoated white paper, except for the introductory section which is printed on buff.

Because of this dictionary's length (more than 2,500 pages), it is divided into two volumes: A through K, and L through Z. The binding is exceptionally sturdy and will withstand heavy use in a classroom, or school or public library. When either book is opened, the center margin is generous enough to prevent the text from disappearing into the gutter.

The over 3,000 black-and-white line drawings are distinct and well-conceived; they will be helpful in most cases to amplify entries. For example, under the entry **poultry**, there are four clear labeled drawings of a **chicken, Pekin duck, goose,** and **turkey.** Under the entry **silverware** (definition 1), there is a place setting as well as simplified drawings that are easy to identify of nine different pieces of cutlery, from **butter knife** to **teaspoon.** The publisher has taken great pains to provide appropriate illustrations for a wide range of age groups. Although young readers (who respond more fully to attractively presented, color illustrations) may not find these black-and-white drawings particularly eye-catching, they will certainly find them useful adjuncts to definitions, especially with an adult's guidance.

IX. Summary

The World Book Dictionary has much to recommend it. Its clearly delineated and updated definitions are attuned to a wide range of reading levels. Educators will value the overall comprehensiveness of the entries. Although this two-volume work is especially designed to supplement THE WORLD BOOK ENCYCLOPEDIA, it can stand alone as well.

The dictionary's sturdy, two-volume format should survive years of continued use. However, it will never be a portable companion, and its cumbersome size may be a consideration—especially for home buyers—if shelf space is limited. Young children will find these volumes particularly bulky and heavy to handle. Furthermore, users of all ages may be intimidated by the lengthy introductory section and have trouble locating immediately needed information in it.

Many younger users could be daunted when working with this dictionary, and only users at high school level or above will be comfortable with *all* the definitions. Many students in elementary and middle schools will need adult guidance to use this work effectively. Given these minor caveats, this dictionary is certainly of outstanding quality and schools and libraries will not want to be without a copy.

Chapter 11
Evaluations of Word Books

Thesauruses

The Clear and Simple Thesaurus Dictionary

Facts at a Glance

Full Title: **The Clear and Simple Thesaurus Dictionary**.

Former Title: The Young People's Thesaurus Dictionary.

Publisher: Grosset & Dunlap.

Editors: Harriet Wittels and Joan Greisman; introduction by William Morris.

Edition Reviewed: © 1971; 1986 printing.

Number of Volumes: 1.
Number of Entries: 6,500.
Number of Words: 50,000.
Number of Pages: 319.
Number of Illustrations: 200 black-and-white line drawings.
Trim Size: 6¼″ × 9¼″.
Binding: paperback.

Price: $7.95.
Intended Readership: ages 7 through 14.
Sold in bookstores and other outlets; also sold to libraries and schools. ISBN 0-448-12198-0.

I. Introduction and Scope

William Morris, the editor of the AMERICAN HER-ITAGE DICTIONARY OF THE ENGLISH LANGUAGE, wrote the introduction to this alphabetically arranged thesaurus. He tells young readers that like Mark Twain who spent his life looking for the *right* word and avoiding the *almost right* word, "that's what this book is all about." This thesaurus is intended to give "all the words which are similar in meaning," so that a reader can choose the word which seems just right and can "easily guess the meanings of unfamiliar words and thereby greatly expand" his or her vocabulary.

The book contains 50,000 words arranged under 6,500 main entries in 319 pages and is specifically aimed at a wide range of young readers age 7 through 14. The editors also note that the thesaurus dictionary is designed to help students express themselves clearly, effectively, and imaginatively.

II. Format

The Clear and Simple Thesaurus Dictionary is a sturdily bound, large-size paperback with large type and generous leading. The paper is good quality white-coated stock with little show-through. Gray and black line drawings, scattered throughout, are decorative and not designed to help young readers discriminate among synonyms.

III. Quality and Currency of Entries

The choices and method of handling synonyms often makes the lists appear dated; moreover, the inclusions are often arbitrary and occasionally inaccurate. There is no indication that the work has been updated since its appearance in 1971.

It is misleading, for example, to list **photograph** as a synonym for **X-ray**, having previously defined synonyms as words that can be substituted for each other. The synonym given for **pauper** is **poor man**; this is sexist (in addition, no antonym is listed for **pauper**). Antonyms are not provided for many other words which obviously have opposites, such as **positive** and **praise**. Some slang expressions are outdated; some inaccurate (or perhaps specially chosen in an effort to appeal directly to young readers), for example, **mastermind** is given as a synonym for **manage**.

Although **male**, **man**, and **masculine** are all listed as entry words, **feminine** is shown only as a variant form of **female**. **Woman** is listed as an entry word with no antonym, although it is given as the antonym for **man**. **Boy** and **girl** are both entry words, but neither is listed as the antonym of the other; **girlish** is a variant for **girl**—**boyish** does not appear in the listings.

IV. Accessibility

The main words in *The Clear and Simple Thesaurus Dictionary* are arranged in alphabetical order, which makes access to the vocabulary easy for students. There is a simple "How to Use . . ." section where synonyms (the error *synoyms* appears at one point in the text) are defined as words that have the same meaning and can be substituted for one another. The editors claim that "if you cannot find a word, it simply does not have synonyms." This is not only misleading, since the thesaurus includes only 6,500 entry words, but untrue. Users are also told that they must use "judgment and common sense" in choosing an appropriate synonym. Although most other thesauruses recommend using a dictionary to determine the suitability of a selected synonym, the editors of *The Clear and Simple Thesaurus Dictionary* state that readers can determine the meaning of a word they do not know by reading the synonym lists, hence they will not need to consult a dictionary at all to use this book effectively. No alphabetical list of words with selected synonyms, however, can substitute for a proper dictionary—young readers need specifically defined meanings to help them make judgments about the right word for the context.

Guide words appear at the top of each page and each entry word appears in bold type followed by a group of synonyms, listed in an apparently random order. When given, antonyms are listed at the end of an entry and are printed in light gray type. A typical entry with its antonym is:

> **above** overhead, up, aloft, on, upon below.

Sense numbers are used for entry words with more than one meaning, for example:

> **firm** 1. solid, fixed, secure, unyielding, inflexible, stationary, immovable, rigid, flexible, 2. company, business, enterprise.

An entry word that has two different pronunciations as well as different meanings is entered twice, but no pronunciation guides are provided to help students distinguish between the words. A typical entry for a word with different pronunciations is:

> 1. **minute** instant, moment, twinkle, (Slang — jiffy, sec, half a shake)
> 2. **minute** small, tiny, miniature, slight, negligible, insignificant.

Note that slang terms are listed in parentheses. Variant forms of a word are listed under the main entry word in bold capital letters:

> **happy** contented, glad, joyful, blissful, bright, radiant unhappy, sad [the antonym sad is printed in gray] **HAPPILY, HAPPINESS.**

V. Summary

Although the editors state that *The Clear and Simple Thesaurus Dictionary* is for a readership of 7- to 14-year-olds, it is appropriate for a slightly narrower range of students, those in the second through sixth grades. The vocabulary seems suitable for this target population, as well as reluctant readers in the upper elementary grades, although many fifth and sixth graders might be ready for a more sophisticated thesaurus, such as the Merriam-Webster WEBSTER'S SCHOOL THESAURUS.

There is definitely a need for a simplified easy-to-use thesaurus to introduce students to the color, variety, and excitement of the English language and to help them develop and expand their language skills. This book has a low-level vocabulary and large, primary print, plus an easy-to-use and easy-to-read format, so at first, it seems to meet this need. Nevertheless, the inconsistencies and inaccuracies could easily mislead students, especially those who have never used a thesaurus. For a young reader's first experience with this kind of word book, teachers and librarians would insist on a more consistent and flawless handling of the vocabulary. This work cannot be recommended for school and public library collections; classroom teachers and parents may find its drawback too extensive even given its format.

The Doubleday Children's Thesaurus

Facts at a Glance

Full Title: **The Doubleday Children's Thesaurus**.
Publisher: Doubleday & Company.
Editor: John Bellamy.
Illustrator: Peter Stevenson.
Edition Reviewed: © 1987.

Number of Volumes: 1.
Number of Entries: Over 6,000.
Number of Pages: 198.
Number of Illustrations: 200 in one and two colors.
Trim Size: 7⅜" × 10¼".
Binding: paper over boards.

Price: $10.95.
Intended Readership: grades 3 through 9.
Sold in bookstores and in special promotions; also sold to libraries and schools. ISBN 0-385-2383-9.

I. Introduction and Scope

The 1987 *Doubleday Children's Thesaurus* is the first American edition of a British work, the *Kingfisher Illustrated Thesaurus*. Occasional words within en-

tries and characteristics of illustrations reflect the work's British origin, but the thesaurus has been well adapted for American children, presenting American idiom and spelling.

The work is described by its publisher as a "comprehensive resource" that "allows children to speak and write in the most powerful way possible—to choose the right word." The illustrated work comprises over 6,000 alphabetized entries, with listings for synonyms, antonyms, and "homonyms" (homophones) are provided as appropriate.

The work also incorporates two special features. A one-page introduction addressed to children clearly explains the use of the thesaurus. A "Spelling Checklist" appears at the end of the volume. In five and a half double-columned pages, this section alphabetically lists words children often have difficulty spelling. A single asterisk preceding an entry in this list refers users to the main text for an explanation of differences between frequently confused word pairs. A double asterisk refers the user to a note of explanation at the end of the section. For example, two entries in sequence are

> **who's (see whose)
> **whose (see who's).

The double asterisks signal the presence of an explanation in the alphabetized notes section:

> who's: means "who is"
> whose: means "of whom."

Although useful information is provided in this section, the asterisk system may prove difficult for young users to follow.

II. Format

Within the double-columned pages of the alphabetized main text, letter sections are headed by oversize capitals printed in blue. Boldfaced main entry words overhang the text. These are followed by italicized part-of-speech labels. Where multiple senses of the entry word are reflected in the synonym listings, they are numbered, and each is given its own part-of-speech abbreviation. Rarely, illustrative sentences in italics are provided to help the reader distinguish among multiple senses. Antonyms, when provided, appear in boldfaced italics at the end of the entry or the part of the entry to which they apply. Where appropriate, homophones are given at the end of the entry in small capitals following any antonyms. Representative entries are:

free 1. *adj.* gratis, gratuitous, complimentary, without charge 2. *adj.* liberated, independent, unrestricted 3. *adj.* loose, lax, untied 4. *v.* dismiss, release, acquit *enslave*.

and

sword *n.* cutlass, blade, rapier, saber SOARED.

Peter Stevenson's blue and black drawings illustrate the text and help clarify words and distinctions among them. These are a half to a full column in width, appear adjacent to their entries, and are captioned with main entry words and their homophones. Many homophone pairs are, helpfully, illustrated. For example, **scent** and **cent** are illustrated with drawings of a penny and a skunk. The drawings often incorporate humor that will appeal to children: a drawing captioned **Teas tease** shows two cups of tea with arms, legs, and faces; one frowns and clenches its fist, the other, grinning, thumbs its nose. Other drawings illustrate, for example, a **dogged dog** and a **hoarse horse**.

Print is large and clear on heavy white paper. Adequate margins also enhance readability. The book opens flat. It is sturdily bound and will hold up well to heavy use.

III. Quality and Currency of Entries

Main entry words and vocabulary appearing in the entries will challenge young users appropriately. Although entries do not provide an exhaustive list of synonyms, those included will be interesting and useful to children. For example, synonyms listed under **cold** include **icy**, **chill**, **wintry**, **frosty**, **bleak**, and **raw**. Many entries valuably list multiple senses and, as appropriate, multiple antonyms. An especially comprehensive entry is the following:

> **praise** 1. *n.* approval, glorification, commendation, compliment *criticism, disapproval, scandal, ridicule* 2. *v.* approve, admire, commend, applaud *denounce, malign, rebuke, reprimand* PRAY, PREYS.

Illustrative sentences, although infrequent, are useful in helping children distinguish among the senses of an entry word. Under **make**, for example, the word in its sense of "perform" is illustrated by the sentence "*Next week, we shall make the first attempt to cross the river*"; the sense of "select" is illustrated by "*The school will make Sally the new sports captain.*"

Although the work has been adapted for American children, a slight British flavor remains in occasional entries. Under **cycle**, for example, the second sense listed is **bike, bicycle**. Under **cue** appears the British homophone **queue**. Under **pop**, British colloquial use appears in the synonym **slip in** and in its illustrative sentence "*While on Broadway, I popped in to see the new show*": the phrase "popped in" will certainly puzzle any young American. Although these Britishisms are not pervasive, they limit this work's usefulness.

The work reflects an effort to include some current vocabulary that is appropriate for a young audience. **Computer**, for example, is a main entry word; synonyms listed are **calculator**, **word processor**, and **microprocessor**. The drawing illustrating **invention** includes a pocket calculator. The work's currency and appropriateness to the intended audience are also enhanced by the omission of outdated and archaic synonyms.

IV. Accessibility

Entries are easily located in this alphabetized work. Two large boldface guide words appear at the top of each spread, indicating the first and last words entered on the page. However, no table of contents is provided, and the work's appended "Spelling Checklist" may be overlooked.

V. Summary

Like the comparable CLEAR AND SIMPLE THESAURUS DICTIONARY, *The Doubleday Children's Thesaurus* is alphabetically arranged and readily accessible to young readers. The Doubleday work is more current and more sturdily bound than THE CLEAR AND SIMPLE THESAURUS DICTIONARY; however, the Doubleday volume's occasional Britishisms limit its usefulness. Also comparable to the Doubleday work are the companion Scott, Foresman works IN OTHER WORDS: A BEGINNING THESAURUS (grades 3 and 4) and IN OTHER WORDS: A JUNIOR THESAURUS (grades 5 and up). Like the Doubleday work, these thesauruses provide challenging vocabulary and are well designed for young users. Although the Scott, Foresman works are designed for, and best suited for, classroom use, they are also preferable for home use. One hopes the publishers of *The Doubleday Children's Thesaurus* revise this excellent work so that it is truly suitable for young American readers.

The Doubleday Roget's Thesaurus in Dictionary Form

Facts at a Glance

Full Title: **The Doubleday Roget's Thesaurus in Dictionary Form.**

Publisher: Doubleday & Company.

Editor: Sidney I. Landau, Editor-in-Chief.

Edition Reviewed: © 1977.

Number of Volumes: 1.
Number of Entries: 17,000.
Number of Words: 250,000 synonyms and
      antonyms.
Number of Pages: 804.
Trim Size: 5⅜″ × 8″.
Binding: cloth.

Price: $12.95.
Intended Readership: high school and up.
Sold in bookstores and other outlets; also sold to
      libraries and schools. ISBN 0-385-12379-5.

I. Introduction and Scope

The preface of *The Doubleday Roget's Thesaurus in Dictionary Form* identifies the work as entirely new and not based on any other thesaurus. Entries were selected from THE DOUBLEDAY DICTIONARY, first published in 1975. It is designed to fill the gap between two types of American thesauruses: the subject-indexed variety and the brief dictionary-style work. While outdated and trite phrases are omitted, slang terms, words of recent origin, and words with new meanings have been included. Altogether, more than 250,000 synonyms and antonyms are listed in this volume. The more than 17,000 entries average ten to fifteen synonyms per entry. The work is intended for everyday use in home, school, or office.

The experienced and well-known lexicographer Sidney I. Landau served as the thesaurus's Editor-in-Chief.

II. Format

Entry words are alphabetized letter by letter. They appear in boldface type overhanging the text on double-columned pages. Homographs—that is, words spelled the same but having different meanings and roots—are entered separately and distinguished by superscript numbers. An italicized part-of-speech abbreviation follows the entry word.

The guide to the use of the thesaurus indicates that "the first few synonyms listed under each meaning are those that best distinguish it from other meanings." Thus common words appear first and are followed by more specialized terms, which are parenthetically labeled. These italicized labels follow the specialized term; for example, "Teddy Boy (*Slang*)" is offered as a synonym for **coxcomb**. Other labels include *Arch.* for archaic and *Brit.* for British.

Although most labels are easily deciphered, a key to abbreviations would be of value to the novice users.

Antonyms, when provided, follow the synonyms and are preceded by the abbreviation **ant.** in boldface type. A sample entry appears below.

> **dated** *adj.* old-fashioned, passé, antiquated, outmoded, obsolete, archaic, out of date, stale, tired, antediluvian, moth-eaten, out, old-fogeyish, old hat (*Slang*), démodé. **ant.** new, current, latest, now, fashionable, à la mode, in, hot, *au courant*.

As can be seen in this entry, foreign words are included in the lists for both synonyms and antonyms. The guide to the dictionary does not explain why some are in italics and others are not. Based on the practice in other dictionaries, it may be assumed that italicized foreign words or phrases have not been fully assimilated into the language.

III. Quality and Currency of Entries

For the most part, the entries are words used in everyday language. There are a few less common words included, such as **grandiloquent** (pompous) and **opprobrious** (abusive or offensive). Many colloquial terms, such as **frumpy** and **drubbing**, are listed as entries. Some archaic words appear among the synonyms as well: **dray** and **tumbrel** are listed as synonyms for **cart**. Occasionally there is an eponym included among the entries, such as **Cassandra** for **alarmist**. Overall, the entries are as current as the 1975 dictionary from which they were taken; a number of contemporary terms could doubtlessly be added were the thesaurus revised today.

Many slang synonyms and antonyms are included. Under **kick around** we find **bum** and **rap**; for **roost** we find **pad**; and there is also an entry for the slang term **con** with slang synonyms such as **rip off** and **psych**. These entries effectively reflect modern spoken language, even ten years after the work's latest revision date.

IV. Accessibility

Entries are easily located in this alphabetical thesaurus. The volume is thumb indexed, and there are two guide words at the top of each page indicating the first and last entries on the page. The print is clear, there is generous white space, and the text is easy to read. Cross-references, in small capitals, are easy to use. For example, "**harum-scarum** *adj.* RECKLESS" directs users to **reckless**, where they find 27 synonyms, including **harum-scarum**, and six antonyms.

Some entries provide multiple cross-references; for example, "**ego** *n.* **1** SELF. **2** EGOTISM." Cross-referenced entry words are followed by the part-of-speech abbreviation except when other labels are used. For example, the entry "**hatchet job** (*Slang*) CRITICISM," omits the part-of-speech designation.

V. Summary

The Doubleday Roget's Thesaurus in Dictionary Form fills the gap between ROGET'S INTERNATIONAL THESAURUS and WEBSTER'S NEW DICTIONARY OF SYNONYMS. Like the *Doubleday Thesaurus*, *Webster's* is alphabetical. However, *Webster's* not only provides synonyms and antonyms but distinguishes between antonyms and contrasted words as well as between synonyms and analogous words. In addition, *Webster's* is careful to draw clear distinctions in usage since no two words in the English language are true synonyms or antonyms. It is also a more recent work.

The most comprehensive lists of synonyms are to be found in ROGET'S INTERNATIONAL THESAURUS, which has an old and distinguished history. It is, however, more difficult to use than the *Doubleday* because it is arranged by categories of meaning rather than alphabetical order. This organization requires the reader to consult the index to locate a word.

A comparison of entries from the three thesauruses clearly reveals their differences. The first entry is from *The Doubleday Roget's Thesaurus:*

> **gluttonous** *adj.* voracious, insatiable, greedy, ravenous, piggish, omnivorous, swinish, edacious, hoggish, rapacious. **ant.** abstemious, temperate, moderate, abstinent, picky, anoretic.

There are also separate entries for the nouns **glutton** and **gluttony**. The entry that follows is from *Webster's:*

> **gluttonous** *voracious, ravenous, ravening, rapacious **Ana** greedy, *covetous, grasping **Ant** abstemious — **Con** temperate, *sober: dainty, finicky, fussy, fastidious, *nice.

Synonyms provided in these two entries are similar, although there are more in the *Doubleday* entry. *Webster's*, however, makes use of an asterisk to lead the reader to other entries where additional words may be located. The primary difference in this entry is in antonyms. *Webster's* lists only one and uses the designation "*Con*" for contrasting words (as opposed to antonyms, which are closer to opposite meanings). *Webster's* does not have an entry for *glutton* or *gluttony*.

The Roget work does not have a main entry for *gluttonous*; rather, the term is found under "**994.**

GLUTTONY," where eight subdivisions, including nouns, verbs, adjectives, and adverbs are listed. Antonyms for gluttony are listed immediately following the entry under "**995. FASTING.**" The numerical reference after **intemperate** refers the reader to that entry under a separate classification. The number of synonyms and antonyms in the *Roget* work is far greater than in either of the other two thesauruses; many of them are quite colorful, but, one suspects, rarely used.

The publishers of *The Doubleday Roget's Thesaurus in Dictionary Form* have succeeded in producing a comprehensive reference source that is easy to use and makes good use of contemporary language through the mid-1970s. Although it is less comprehensive and less precise than the two thesauruses with which it is compared, it will serve the purposes of many users. With its alphabetical arrangement, younger readers will find it especially easy to use. Most moderate-sized libraries that serve a general or college population will want all three.

In Other Words: A Beginning Thesaurus

Facts at a Glance

Full Title: **In Other Words: A Beginning Thesaurus**.
Publisher: Scott, Foresman.
Compilers: Andrew Schiller and William A. Jenkins.
Edition Reviewed: © 1987.

Number of Volumes: 1.
Number of Entries: 100.
Number of Synonyms and Antonyms: over 1,000.
Number of Pages: 240.
Number of Illustrations: over 300 drawings and photographs in full color.
Trim Size: 7½" × 9¼".
Binding: hardcover.

Price: $9.96.
Intended Readership: grades 3 and 4.
Sold to schools. ISBN 0-673-12486-X.

I. Introduction and Scope

This book includes 100 main entries and over 900 additional synonyms and antonyms; it is a teaching tool for introducing children to the concept of the thesaurus. The introduction has several exercises (with answers at the back of the book) designed to show elementary school users not only *how* to search for words in a thesaurus, but also *when*, as in writing letters, stories, and reports. There are no criteria stated, however, for the selection of the words.

A section at the back of the book, entitled "Sets: special names for groups of people, places, and things," is actually a picture dictionary.

II. Format

The alphabetized entry words are in bold type and have a left hand margin of 2¼ inches. Synonyms are listed under the main entry word and are distinguishable by their lighter type. Both the main entry word and the synonyms have explanations in paragraph format. These paragraphs are separated by a line of blank space. Synonyms, however, also appear in bold type as part of the alphabetical listing, followed by the words "Look up" and the main entry word under which they may be found. Antonyms, when provided, are readily recognizable at the end of the entry, printed in blue type. Every page has at least one full-color drawing or photograph that illustrates either a main entry word or a synonym described on that page.

III. Quality and Currency of Entries

Written in a popular, familiar style, the entries often speak directly to the young reader. For example:

> *Cute* is a tired word. People use it too often. Before using *cute*, look up some of these other words to see if you can find one that fits better!

A list of six sentences follows that shows the reader other synonyms: "A *cute* puppy might be *naughty, friendly, comical*." Another example is:

> . . . Here are some good words to use if you want to give poor old *awful* a rest.

The suggestions are **horrible**, **terrible**, **dreadful**, and **severe**—all with clear, full explanations.

Usually the main entry word is defined and then used in several clear sentences so that the child can grasp its meaning in several different contexts. Synonyms are discriminated in the same clear way. Sometimes the synonyms and their entries are listed by increasing degrees of intensity. The synonyms for **hate** are: **dislike**, **despise**, **detest**, and **loathe**. The first sentence of the entries for the synonyms defines the word; the other sentences use the synonym in an illustrative manner. Many words will be new to third-grade readers, but most of the words will be familiar

to fourth graders. There are a few words included that are perfectly good for this age, but that are seldom used, such as **boisterous**, **precarious**, and **woebegone**.

IV. Accessibility

Main entry words are listed alphabetically, as are synonyms and their cross-references. A cerise-colored letter on each left page guides the user who is thumbing through the book (except where an illustration interferes with the placement of this letter).

Appended to the thesaurus is an explanation of special names for groups of a variety of things: animals (**pride** of lions, **gaggle** of geese, **covey** of quail), people (**audience**, **troop**, **convention**), and trains (**caravan**, **wagon train**), for example. These are followed by specific names for individual types of things: bodies of water (**river**, **brook**, **spring**), land shapes (**mesa**, **knoll**, **mountains**). Highly illustrated pages allow each picture to play an important part in describing the words. An index would have helped students to find words and would have been an excellent teaching tool.

V. Summary

With ninety percent of this thesaurus composed of cross-reference words listed and discriminated with illustrative sentences under the main entries, *In Other Words: A Beginning Thesaurus* is an effective teaching tool. It is designed to accustom the user to searching for words in a thesaurus, and to show how synonyms differ in meaning. Once that lesson is learned, the student should quickly move on into a more advanced book, such as the publisher's IN OTHER WORDS: A JUNIOR THESAURUS. Although the book is best suited to classroom instruction at the third or fourth grade level, school libraries, and larger public libraries may want to have a copy for teacher resource or for library instruction purposes.

In Other Words: A Junior Thesaurus

Facts at a Glance

Full Title: **In Other Words: A Junior Thesaurus**.
Publisher: Scott, Foresman.
Compilers: Andrew Schiller and William A. Jenkins.
Edition Reviewed: © 1987.

Number of Volumes: 1.
Number of Entries: 324.
Number of Synonyms and Antonyms: 2,636.
Number of Pages: 447.
Number of Indexes: 1.
Number of Illustrations: over 300 illustrations and
photos in full color.
Trim Size: 7½″ × 9¼″.
Binding: hardcover.

Price: $12.67.
Intended Readership: grades five and up.
Sold to schools. ISBN 0-673-12487-8.

I. Introduction and Scope

Like IN OTHER WORDS: A BEGINNING THESAURUS, a book that precedes this one and is reviewed elsewhere in this buying guide, *In Other Words: A Junior Thesaurus* is designed for classroom use. The number of main entry words is more than triple that of the preceding volume, and the use of cross-referenced words in the main alphabet has been dropped in favor of an added index. The introduction gives no criteria for how or why the words were chosen, but it provides a series of exercises designed to familiarize the student with the organization of this thesaurus. *In Other Words: A Junior Thesaurus* appears to be geared to the upper elementary and lower middle school grades.

II. Format

The format differs only slightly from the publisher's beginning thesaurus. Main entry words are printed in boldface; synonyms and related words are listed in a column below the entry word. On the right-hand half of the page, paragraphs of explanation discriminate the synonyms, shown in italics. The print is slightly smaller, the illustrations are fewer, and related words are identifiable by a boldface bullet placed next to them. The introduction describes related words as

> different from synonyms. Both synonyms and related words are close in meaning to the entry word. But related words have an extra-added meaning.

Students may require the assistance of their teachers to understand this distinction.

III. Quality and Currency of Entries

The text of the entries in this thesaurus is more formal and less chatty and familiar than in the first book. There continues to be a very simple definition of the main entry word followed by several sentences illustrating how it can be used in various contexts. The entry for each synonym and related word follows the same pattern. The words used appear to be those that a sixth grade student is likely to encounter while reading. Words such as **appropriate**, **cumbersome**, and **inquire** are included, but not that favorite word of this age group: *gross*.

Several entry words have no synonyms and related words have been used instead. For example, **hardship**, **trouble**, **misfortune**, **predicament**, **emergency**, **annoyance**, **obstacle**, and **obstruction** are words related to **difficulty**; for **history** they are **record**, **diary**, **journal**, **log**, **chronicle**, **biography**, and **autobiography**.

IV. Accessibility

Main entry words are in alphabetical order. Occasionally, after all the synonyms and related words, one finds a "see also" cross-reference to a "related word" that is a main entry word.

An index provides page access to all main entry words, synonyms, related words, and antonyms. The same type of print is used in the index as in the text: main entries are in bold print; antonyms are in blue. The clear, well-drawn illustrations often add considerably to a synonym's discrimination. For example, for **suspicion**, a synonym under **doubt**, there is a picture of a Sherlock Holmes character looking at a pet bird in a cage with other people in the background. The caption reads: "Everyone in the room was placed under **suspicion**."

V. Summary

In Other Words: A Junior Thesaurus is a mixture of a dictionary and a thesaurus. Words are simply defined, with reliance on the illustrative sentences to convey the meaning. A distinction is made between synonyms and related words, but the explanation and examples of the differences are very weak. Without a teacher present to provide clarification, this could be a confusing book for a sixth grader to use. It was designed for classroom use where instructional help is readily available, and that is where it belongs, rather than in a home, public, or school library.

Nelson's New Compact Roget's Thesaurus

Facts at a Glance

Full Title: **Nelson's New Compact Roget's Thesaurus**.
Publisher: Thomas Nelson Publishers.
Editors: Laurence Urdang, Editor-in-Chief; Mark Boyer.
Edition Reviewed: © 1978, 7th printing.

Number of Volumes: 1.
Number of Entries: 1,000.
Number of Pages: 314.
Number of Indexes: 1.
Trim Size: 3½″ × 5¼″.
Binding: paperback.

Price: $2.45.
Intended Readership: high school through adult.
Sold in bookstores and other outlets; also sold to schools. ISBN 0-8407-5634-8.

I. Introduction and Scope

Nelson's New Compact Roget's Thesaurus, published in 1978, is a pocket-sized abridged version of Peter Mark Roget's 1852 work. Laurence Urdang, the work's Editor-in-Chief, is an authority on lexicography. According to the preface, the abridged version serves, like the original, not only as a synonym dictionary, but as "a diverse collection of associated and related words and phrases." Because of Roget's time-tested classification system, when a suitable synonym is not located under a particular entry, the user may find it under one of the nearby entries.

This pocket edition includes a comprehensive index. It retains Roget's general structure and all of the nearly one thousand "headwords" (main entries) of the original. However, antiquated language has been removed and, according to the preface, "the book has been modernized to include the most current usage and the newest developments in language." The work is relatively contemporary, but no longer as current as the preface states. Duplications have been omitted and the user is urged to seek words under associated parts of speech. The preface also contains the valuable caution:

If the word selected is not completely familiar, check its meaning and usage in a good dictionary before risking its use in an incorrect or unidiomatic context.

The work is intended for a general audience, and its compact size makes it convenient for a variety of uses. Its abridgment and emphasis on "everyday" language may render it especially accessible for the high school student to whom a larger work might seem cumbersome or confusing.

II. Format

The thesaurus is organized on the basis of Roget's six broad classes: ABSTRACT RELATIONS, SPACE, MATTER, INTELLECT, VOLITION, and AFFECTIONS. These classes are subdivided to produce 997 numbered main entries, ordered according to relationships of likeness and contrast. A typical sequence of entries, for example, is **friendship, enmity, friend, enemy, sociality, seclusion, exclusion, courtesy, discourtesy.**

Main entry numbers, in boldface, overhang the text on each page of double-column text. The entry word, also boldfaced, is followed by an italicized, abbreviated part of speech, and a list of synonyms. Where more than one part of speech is listed, each is given its own paragraph. Semicolons separate synonym lists, grouped according to shades of meaning. The word *Informal* appears in parentheses after a synonym to indicate informal usage.

Index entries are printed in three columns and appear in boldface type if they are main entry words in the text. All index entries are followed by italicized part-of-speech abbreviations and numbers that refer to the main entries under which they can be located.

The paper is white and allows minimal showthrough. Although the bold main entry words and adequate margins enhance readability, the print within entries is very small and may be difficult for some users to read. Print in the index is, however, adequate in size. The pages do not separate easily from the binding of this sturdy small paperback. The cover is brown vinyl over paper with gold lettering.

III. Quality and Currency of Entries

Entries are thorough and detailed, reflecting a wide range of senses and synonyms. A representative entry is

268 traveler *n* wayfarer, journeyer, rover, rambler, wanderer, free spirit, nomad, vagabond, bohemian, gypsy, itinerant, vagrant, tramp, hobo, straggler, waif; pilgrim, palmer, seeker, quester; voyager, passenger, tourist, sightseer, excursionist, vacationer, globetrotter, jet-setter; immigrant, emigrant, refugee, fugitive; pedestrian, walker, cyclist, biker, rider, horsewoman, horseman, equestrian, driver.

A substantial number of synonyms is included here. Closely related synonyms are placed in groups, which helps a reader to locate a precise word. To be certain of shades of meaning, connotations, and restrictions in usage, the user will require a dictionary, as the work's preface insists.

The work's inclusion of informal words and phrases is a valuable contribution to its currency. For example, **the pits** appears as an informal synonym among adjectives under **badness**. The work's currency is also reflected in its inclusion of such terms as the title **Ms.**, gender neutral terms (**letter carrier**), and female equivalents (**horsewoman**). Although the language of computer technology is not represented in the listings, terms from the fields of astronautics (**cosmonaut**, **module**) and energy (**nuclear power**, **solar energy**) are included.

IV. Accessibility

Accessibility is enhanced by the work's prefatory explanation and "Plan of Classification." The "Tabular Synopsis of Categories" permits the user a more detailed overview of the work's organization. Within the main text, boldface guide numbers appear at the top of each double-page spread to indicate the first and last numbered entries on the pages. Bold guide words at the top of each spread in the index serve the same function.

V. Summary

Nelson's New Compact Roget's Thesaurus is a small but thorough reference work. For readers and writers who seek the convenience of a pocket-sized thesaurus, this work provides the advantages of a clear format, comprehensive index, and detailed listings. Although the work is not as up-to-date as many larger thesauruses, its inclusion of informal words and phrases is useful for both a general and a student audience. The work, however, is more current, and thus more useful, than the comparable pocket-sized RANDOM HOUSE THESAURUS: A DICTIONARY OF SYNONYMS AND ANTONYMS, despite the latter's dictionary format. With its careful abridgment and focus on "everyday" language, the volume would be a worthwhile addition to a high school library's circulating paperback collection or to an English classroom collection, and the public library might well make a place for it in a circulating paperback collection, too.

The New American Roget's College Thesaurus in Dictionary Form

Facts at a Glance

Full Title: **The New American Roget's College Thesaurus in Dictionary Form**.
Publisher: Signet/New American Library.
Editor: Philip D. Morehead.
Edition Reviewed: © 1985.

Number of Volumes: 1.
Number of Entries: more than 20,000.
Number of Pages: 649.
Trim Size: 4¼" × 7"; 5¼" × 8".
Binding: paperback.

Price: $3.50; $7.95.
Intended Readership: junior high and up.
Sold in bookstores and other outlets; also sold to libraries and schools. ISBN 0-451-13474-5; 0-452-00732-1.

I. Introduction and Scope

The 1985 edition of *The New American Roget's College Thesaurus in Dictionary Form* is a revised, enlarged version of the original, first published in 1958. The thesaurus is designed for use by a wide audience ranging from junior high school students to adults. According to its editor, "this edition of ROGET'S THESAURUS is both a dictionary of synonyms and a thesaurus or 'treasury' of related words." Entries include synonyms, antonyms, and related words of other parts of speech. In addition to standard usage, entries reflect nonstandard and specialized vocabularies: colloquialism, slang, dialect, British English, and poetic and archaic usage.

Foreign words and phrases commonly used by speakers of English are not included as main entries within the body of the text, but are gathered in a separate listing at the end of the book, where they are defined and cross-referenced to English terms in the main text.

Excluded from the volume are words with no natural synonyms as well as antonyms formed with prefixes such as *un-*, *in-*, and *dis-*. Words like *unloved* that are "simple negatives" of other words are not listed, but a word like **unbearable** does appear because of the multiple meanings of **bearable**.

II. Format

The thesaurus is organized in dictionary format, which many students will find more accessible than the traditional thesaurus format. A single alphabetical listing incorporates two kinds of listings: one is a word resembling the typical thesaurus's category that shows related terms in an extensive range of parts of speech; and the second is individual words with shorter lists of their close synonyms. The larger category-type listings, headed by a main topic word in bold capitals, are printed across the full width of the page and divided by horizontal rules from the rest of the text on that page. Part-of-speech labels, in italics overhanging the text, introduce groups of related words. Boldface numbers create subcategories within these groups. At the end of the category antonyms are listed. Entries consisting of close synonyms are printed in a double-column format. Main entry words are boldfaced and followed by an abbreviated, italicized part-of-speech label.

In both kinds of entry, cross-references are provided in small capitals. Specialized usages, such as colloquialisms, are introduced by an abbreviated, italicized usage label. Within the listings, subgroupings are demarcated by semicolons.

At the end of the volume appears the alphabetical listing "Foreign Words and Phrases." Entry words are boldfaced and overhang the text. Each is followed by an italicized abbreviation indicating the word's language. A translation and cross-references (in small capitals) to the body of the text are also given.

Print is adequate in size and easy to read; judicious use of white space enhances readability. The mass market edition was examined for review: its pages do not separate easily from the binding and the volume is, for a paperback, acceptably sturdy.

III. Quality and Currency of Entries

Substantial listings, together with copious cross-references, ensure that the user will find a word's extended family in the text. The inclusion of specialized usages also broadens the entries' usefulness, especially for literary and language study.

Currency is reflected in such main entries as **astronautics** (listing, among other terms, **aerospace**, **lunar module**, **L.E.M.**, **space probe**, **escape velocity**, **launch window**, and **reentry corridor**). Although the only synonym given under **computer** is **calculator**, under **numeration**, to which the reader is cross-referred, computer-related terms listed include

> **cybernetics**, **computer**, **electronic computer** *or* **brain**, **mainframe** [**computer**], **mini-**, **micro-**, *or* **personal computer**, [**micro**]**processor**, **punch-card** *or* **-tape reader**.

Under **writing**, the user will also find the terms

printer, **dot-matrix** *or* **daisy-wheel printer**, **draft-** *or* **letter-quality printer**.

For popular terms, especially slang and colloquialisms, the thesaurus is less up-to-date. For example, in the category labeled **unconformity**, the terms **hippie** and **yippie** appear, but *punk* is absent. Under **folly** appear **jerk** and **square**, but not *turkey* or *airhead*. While the retention of dated slang terms enhances the work's value as a repository of linguistic history, its omission of more recent (post-1960s) slang limits its value for today's students.

IV. Accessibility

The alphabetical format makes the volume readily accessible to students. Cross-references, in small capitals, stand out clearly. Further, a preface titled "How to Use This Thesaurus" provides a brief but clear guide to the information included in the volume and to techniques for locating it. This feature will be especially valuable for novice thesaurus users.

Also adding to accessibility are the guide words. Two, in boldface type, appear at the top of each page within the body of the text and indicate the first and last words entered on that page. Guide words are not provided within the foreign-word list, but its brevity (five pages) renders them unnecessary.

Alternative spellings are not entered. The authority followed for preferred spellings is THE NEW AMERICAN WEBSTER HANDY COLLEGE DICTIONARY, described in the preface as a "companion volume" to the thesaurus.

V. Summary

The New American Roget's College Thesaurus in Dictionary Form is a compact, thorough reference work, well designed to meet the needs of its wide audience. Although it lacks such currency in popular terms as that provided by, for example, THE PENGUIN POCKET THESAURUS (1985), its vocabulary is American and it is current in technological terms. Further, its dictionary format and its guide to thesaurus use make the volume more accessible than the Penguin work, especially to its younger users. Its inclusion of poetic and archaic language also enhances its value to students of literature and language. The thesaurus will be useful for student's personal or classroom use, and may also be useful in libraries circulating paperback collections.

The Penguin Pocket Thesaurus

Facts at a Glance

Full Title: **The Penguin Pocket Thesaurus**.
Publisher: Penguin Books.
Editors: Faye Carney and Maurice Waite.
Edition Reviewed: © 1985.

Number of Volumes: 1.
Number of Entries: 882.
Number of Pages: 514.
Trim Size: $4\frac{3}{8}'' \times 7\frac{1}{16}''$.
Binding: paper.

Price: $3.50.
Intended Readership: grade 10 and up.
Sold in bookstores and other outlets; also sold to libraries and schools. ISBN 0-14-051.137-7.

I. Introduction and Scope

Described by its publishers as the "perfect, portable, comprehensive and up-to-date companion to the English language," *The Penguin Pocket Thesaurus* is an updated paperback version of Roget's original thesaurus. Although this 1985 copyright Penguin pocket edition is distributed in the United States, it is prepared in Great Britain for English—not American—readers: it uses British spellings and contains British slang and colloquialisms. Under **vehicle**, for example, words listed include **lorry** but not *flatbed*; under **ingestion** appear **tiffin** and **elevenses**, but not *lunch*. Indeed, the publishers note that "words and phrases current on the other side of the Atlantic are labeled as Americanisms." For American users, the work's usefulness is limited.

As noted in the preface, a paperback thesaurus cannot be as exhaustive as Roget's; therefore, some terms deemed "rare and obscure" have been omitted. Rearrangement of Roget's sequencing has been undertaken to reflect new priorities in contemporary language and the new fields of knowledge it describes. The editors' goal has been "to cover a comprehensive working vocabulary that takes in all levels of language" and is "sufficiently comprehensive to serve both as a vocabulary builder and as a source of many hours of useful browsing."

II. Format

The pocket-sized volume is alphabetically indexed. The body of its text comprises 882 main topics, consecutively numbered in boldface, grouped according to their meanings. A topic word or phrase is often related synonymically or antonymically to its predecessor. For example, the opening sequence of topic words is **existence**, **nonexistence**, **reality**, **unreality**, **essence**. Under each main topic word and phrase, cross-references (identified by the introductory *See also*, with the topic number in boldface) are followed by paragraphs, one for each part of speech illustrated, listing related words.

When the topic is a concrete term, the paragraphs, according to the preface, "list key words in that semantic area, providing a mini-vocabulary of a subject." For abstract terms, the listings incorporate related words, associations, and figurative and idiomatic usages, with the result that both formal and colloquial equivalents are provided.

Within each paragraph, words with closely related meanings are grouped. The first word in each grouping is italicized, and groups are separated by semicolons. For example, under the topic word **channel** the following paragraph appears:

n. *channel*, conduit, course, canal, waterway; *ditch*, trench, moat, riverbed, gutter, pipeline, aqueduct; *lock*, sluice, floodgate, watergate, weir, barrier; *drain*, gully, overflow, culvert, outfall, waterspout, sewer, downpipe, drainpipe.

Within the paragraphs, colloquialisms are identified, as are derogatory terms, vulgarisms, and "Americanisms."

The index is a double-column alphabetical listing of words and phrases. Part of speech is identified, and topic numbers refer the reader to the appropriate section within the text.

As in most paperbacks, the print is small, but readability is enhanced by the book's judicious use of white space and boldface type. Pages do not separate easily from the binding, and the book should prove as durable as any paperback of its size.

III. Quality and Currency of Entries

Listings are lengthy, and the editors' goal of reflecting a wide stylistic range of usage is well met. The quality of entries is compromised only by their British slant—for American users.

The thesaurus is up-to-date in its inclusion of terms recently incorporated into the language from such fields as computer science (**CPU**, **disk drive**, **information retrieval**, **machine language**, **word processing**), space technology (**astronaut**, **countdown**, **splashdown**), and contemporary music (**disco**, **new wave**, **punk**). Sexist language has been avoided in some entries (**humankind**, **spaceman/woman**), but not in others (**anchorman**, **chairman**).

IV. Accessibility

As with other thesauruses in the classic format, a user must seek a term in the index to be referred to the appropriate section in the main text. Once the reader locates that section, he or she must scan the entire entry to find the desired term. Since some of the paragraphs are lengthy, this can be a frustrating task, especially for a novice to the use of reference tools.

Accessibility is improved by the inclusion of guide words. On each double spread, at the upper right and upper left corners, two guide words appear. These identify the first and last topic entered on the spread. They are printed in boldface block capitals and are preceded by their topic numbers. Two guide words are also provided on each double-page spread within the index.

Minimal instruction in the effective use of the thesaurus is provided. The preface explains the editors' objectives and outlines the volume's format, but there is no explicit guide analogous to that provided, for example, in THE NEW AMERICAN ROGET'S COLLEGE THESAURUS IN DICTIONARY FORM. While this omission will not limit the book's accessibility for adults familiar with thesaurus use, student users may require some guidance.

V. Summary

The Penguin Pocket Thesaurus is designed to meet the needs of "commuters, crossword addicts, students, journalists, teachers, and all those who work and write on the move." An inexpensive, up-to-date, and compact volume, it probably achieves its goal quite well in Great Britain.

However, despite its currency and convenience, the thesaurus's British slant limits its usefulness, *especially* for students. British spellings would cause them confusion, and they are unlikely to have encountered in their reading or environment many of the British terms and phrases included. In some cases they will be at a loss to substitute appropriate Americanisms. For the teacher or librarian seeking an inexpensive, portable thesaurus suitable for the needs of both students and adults, a better choice would be, for example, the comparably priced NEW AMERICAN ROGET'S COLLEGE THESAURUS IN DICTIONARY FORM, with its American English focus, its dictionary format, and its guide to thesaurus use.

The Penguin Roget's Thesaurus of English Words and Phrases

Facts at a Glance

Full Title: **The Penguin Roget's Thesaurus of English Words and Phrases**.
Publisher: Penguin Books.
Editor: Susan M. Lloyd.
Edition Reviewed: 1985.

Number of Volumes: 1.
Number of Entries: 990.
Number of Pages: 776.
Trim Size: 5″ × 7¾″.
Binding: paperback.

Price: $7.95.
Intended Readership: high school through adult.
Sold in bookstores and other outlets; also sold to libraries and schools. ISBN 0-014051-155-5.

I. Introduction and Scope

The Penguin Roget's Thesaurus of English Words and Phrases traces its ancestry directly to Peter Mark Roget's original 1852 *Thesaurus of English Words and Phrases* and follows that work's organization. According to the editor's preface, "In 1952 the copyright passed to the original publishers, now known as Longman. The first Penguin edition appeared in 1953; the second, in 1966, was based by the editor, Robert A. Dutch, on his completely new edition for Longman four years earlier."

The current edition, "completely revised, updated and abridged," was designed to bring the thesaurus up-to-date: to add "the many new words and phrases which had come into circulation over the intervening twenty years as a result of rapid technological change, and the corresponding changes in our lifestyle;" and to delete material that had become outdated or ambiguous. The editor's goal, "to mirror the language and attitudes of our present society," was also met by the inclusion of alternatives to sexist usage. Published in Britain, the work retains British spellings and colloquialisms.

This paperback is an abridgment of the editor's 1982 hardbound edition of Roget's. She notes that she tried to remove wordy and peripheral material and emphasize current over outdated language, general over specific terms. Cross-references in this edition have been checked by computer, and the index is based on a computer listing of the text. The product, "a concise, practical edition which retains all the improvements made to the main edition," is intended for an audience of readers, writers, "word-lovers," and crossword puzzle fans.

II. Format

Like Roget's seminal work, the thesaurus comprises a main text, organized according to an updated version of Roget's classification scheme, and an alphabetical index. The six classes of the taxonomy are "Abstract Relations;" "Space;" "Matter;" "Intellect: the exercise of the mind;" "Volition: the exercise of the will;" and "Emotion, religion and morality." In the double-column main text, each class is divided into sections and subdivided into 990 numbered "heads" (main entries). This is, according to the editor, "a slight reduction from Roget's original 1,000." Most heads are usefully grouped in pairs representing the positive and negative aspects of an idea. **Joy**, for example, is followed by **suffering**; **pride** by **humility**.

Head words and their numbers are boldfaced, as are part-of-speech abbreviations. Entries are subdivided into paragraphs, which are grouped according to part of speech. For example, the entry for **Hope** comprises three paragraphs of nouns, two of adjectives, two of verbs, and one of interjections. Each paragraph begins with an italicized "keyword," which, according to the editor, "is both the 'key' to the rest of the paragraph, and the 'open sesame' to the whole book, being used to identify the position of other words in the index and cross-references." The keywords are indeed easily seen and useful in locating information throughout the thesaurus. Within the paragraphs, terms are grouped according to meaning or level of diction (formal, colloquial, and so forth). Cross-references are identified by head numbers and by italicized key words, enabling the user to locate them quickly without the index.

The quadruple-columned index shows alphabetized entries in boldface overhanging the text. Listed below the entry term are italicized keywords followed by head numbers and part-of-speech abbreviations. A representative index entry appears as follows:

uplift
elevate 310 vb.
make better 654 vb.
make pious 979 vb.

This format is clear and easy to use.

The newsprint-type paper used in the work is smooth and allows some show-through of text; it is also thin and may tear easily as the book ages. The print is clear and readable and use of white space on the pages is generous. Pages do not separate easily from the volume's binding.

III. Quality and Currency of Entries

The entries are extensive, with some numbered headings comprising several columns. However, the inclusion of British words and senses will prove confusing to the average American student. For example, the first paragraph under **School** contains several terms that will be unfamiliar to most Americans:

> *academy*, institute, institution; conservatoire, ballet school, art s.; academy of dramatic art; charm school, finishing school; college, university, varsity, Open University; redbrick university, Oxbridge; college of further *or* higher education; polytechnic, poly; Academy, Lyceum, Stoa; alma mater, groves of academe.

Further, although words are grouped according to diction level, no usage labels (such as "slang" or "offensive") are provided. Thus, under the entry **Female** in the paragraph headed by the key word *woman*, the user will find, among others, the terms **feminist**, **women's libber**, **wench**, **crumpet**, and **virago**, with no indications given as to their connotations or appropriate contexts. The absence of discrimination among such synonyms and related terms will be a disadvantage to a less sophisticated student.

The work's currency is strong in its inclusion of both scientific and popular terms recently incorporated into the language. Among these are **floppy disk**, **output**, **sitcom**, **telecommunication**, **teletext**, **space-time continuum**, **spacewoman**, **spaced-out**, and **cybernetics**.

IV. Accessibility

Any thesaurus such as this one, in the classic thesaurus format, will be initially more difficult for a student to use than one in dictionary form such as THE NEW AMERICAN ROGET'S COLLEGE THESAURUS. However, students who are willing to familiarize themselves with this Roget's will find it easy to use. A brief section titled "How to Use This Book" clearly explains the organization of the text and the use of the index. It is followed by an outline "Plan of Classification" that provides the user with a helpful overview of the work's structure.

At the top of the main text pages, italicized running heads on left-hand pages show the taxonomic class and, on right-hand pages, the section and head numbers. In the index, each column is headed by a three-letter guide in block capitals (for example, **POL,**

POP, **POR**). Although unusual, these guides make the index extremely useful.

V. Summary

The most valuable feature of *The Penguin Roget's Thesaurus of English Words and Phrases* is its up-to-date vocabulary. However, the work's British focus will present difficulties for American users, particularly high school students. This expensive paperback is also not sufficiently sturdy to hold up well to *heavy* classroom or library use. A better investment for a reference desk or circulating paperback collection might be a less expensive American work, such as WEBSTER'S NEW WORLD THESAURUS or THE NEW AMERICAN ROGET'S COLLEGE THESAURUS IN DICTIONARY FORM.

The Random House Thesaurus: A Dictionary of Synonyms and Antonyms

Facts at a Glance

Full Title: **The Random House Thesaurus: A Dictionary of Synonyms and Antonyms**.
Publisher: Random House.
Editor: Laurence Urdang.
Edition Reviewed: © 1960; 1985 printing.

Number of Volumes: 1.
Number of Pages: 261.
Trim Size: $2\frac{7}{8}'' \times 5\frac{3}{8}''$.
Binding: paperback with flexible vinyl cover.

Price: $2.95.
Intended Readership: general.
Sold in bookstores and office supply stores; also sold to libraries and schools. ISBN 0-394-51933-7.

I. Introduction and Scope

The Random House Thesaurus: A Dictionary of Synonyms and Antonyms, published in 1960, is a vest pocket-sized thesaurus in dictionary form. According to its preface, "judicious use of this book will more than treble the average person's . . . vocabulary." The work contains about 4,500 main entries comprising over 80,000 words. A valuable caution appears in the preface reminding the user that "there is no true synonym for any word in English," that each word has its own distinct set of meanings, and that the use of the word "must always be appropriate

to the context in which it appears." The user is urged to look up unfamiliar synonyms in a good dictionary before using them. Laurence Urdang, an authority on lexicography and author of A BASIC BOOK OF SYNONYMS AND ANTONYMS, NEW REVISED EDITION, is the editor of this Random House thesaurus. The work serves as a companion to THE RANDOM HOUSE AMERICAN DICTIONARY, NEW REVISED EDITION.

II. Format

Entries are alphabetically arranged, a feature that many students will appreciate. Main entry words are in boldface type overhanging the text. An italicized part-of-speech abbreviation follows, with synonyms listed thereafter. In instances where synonyms are provided for more than one sense of a word, the senses are numbered in boldface and listed in the order of their frequency in usage. Words with more than one part-of-speech application are separated from each other by dashes. Antonyms are provided, as appropriate, at the end of the entry, following the abbreviation *Ant*. There are no sentences to illustrate the application of the words or to demonstrate shades of meaning.

The very small type size makes the entries difficult to read, but the typeface is clear and the white paper permits minimal show-through. The pocket-sized volume has a flexible, washable vinyl cover that enables the reader to open the pages fully. The sturdy binding will stand up well to heavy use.

III. Quality and Currency of Entries

Entries are thorough in their coverage of a wide range of senses and synonyms for many words in standard English. Synonyms are ordered within their lists according to one of two principles, as the preface states:

> if the entry word is a 'strong' one, synonyms will be entered in order of decreasing intensity . . . [;] and if 'weak,' in order of increasing strength. Also, informal words have their synonyms given in the order of increasing formality . . . , while formal word synonyms go in the opposite direction.

This format will aid users in selecting a synonym with appropriate force or diction level. A representative entry, for **rich**, reads as follows:

1. well-to-do, wealthy, moneyed, opulent, affluent. **2.** abounding, abundant, bounteous, bountiful, fertile, plenteous, plentiful, copious, ample, luxuriant, productive, fruitful, prolific. **3.** valuable, valued, precious, costly, estimable, sumptuous. **4.** dear, expensive, high-priced, elegant. **5.** deep, strong, vivid, bright, gay. **6.** full, mellow, pear-shaped, harmonious, sweet. **7.** fragrant, aromatic.

Ant. poor, impoverished; scarce, barren, sterile; cheap; weak; dull; flat; noisome.

Although the latest printing of this thesaurus occurred in 1985, it was originally published in 1960. The deliberate exclusion of slang from the listings helps to minimize the work's datedness; however, recent popular coinages that have become standard are omitted, as are words that relate to astronautics, artificial intelligence, and other newly developed fields. For example, a word in such common current usage as *statistics* is not found as a main entry. Although the word **data** is listed as a synonym for **information**, it is not given the main entry status its current usage might warrant. This lack of currency could be a drawback for students who wish to be precise in their use of the most contemporary terms.

IV. Accessibility

Although the work's small print impedes accessibility, its alphabetical arrangement enables readers unfamiliar with the more traditional thesaurus format to locate entries easily. Boldfaced guide words appear at the top of each double-page spread indicating the first and last words entered on the spread. These, together with the work's flexible cover, enable users to flip quickly to the alphabetic section they are seeking.

V. Summary

The English language is not static; it is fluid. For optimal understanding and use of current language, users require good reference materials with relatively recent publication or revision dates. *The Random House Thesaurus: A Dictionary of Synonyms and Antonyms* was a useful book at its first appearance in 1960, but in the 1980s it is in need of revision and not a first choice for purchase. Those in need of a small, concise thesaurus should examine Urdang's THE BASIC BOOK OF SYNONYMS AND ANTONYMS, NEW REVISED EDITION. Although the latter contains a shorter list of main entries, it is more up-to-date, and it includes illustrative sentences to differentiate synonyms and place them in context.

The Random House Thesaurus: College Edition

Facts at a Glance

Full Title: **The Random House Thesaurus: College Edition**.
Publisher: Random House.
Editors: Jess Stein and Stuart Berg Flexner.
Edition Reviewed: © 1984.

Number of Volumes: 1.
Number of Entries: 11,000.
Number of Pages: 812.
Trim Size: $6^9/_{16}'' \times 9^5/_8''$.
Binding: cloth.

Price: $14.95.
Intended Readership: high school, college, and adult.
Sold in bookstores and other outlets; also sold to libraries and schools. ISBN 0-394-52949-9.

I. Introduction and Scope

Based on the Reader's Digest FAMILY WORD FINDER (© 1975), *The Random House Thesaurus: College Edition* contains 11,000 main entries and is intended for adult as well as high school and college audiences. Although the editors suggest that THE RANDOM HOUSE COLLEGE DICTIONARY would be a useful companion to the thesaurus, only a larger unabridged dictionary is comprehensive enough to include the many thousands of synonyms and antonyms listed under this thesaurus's main entries. In the preface, the editors suggest that the thesaurus is most effective when users "have a particular meaning or thought in mind but do not know, or cannot recall, the most effective word to express it."

II. Format

The thesaurus is arranged alphabetically with main entries in bold type. The book is bound sturdily and clearly printed on good quality ivory stock. The narrow margins are wide enough to prevent eyestrain during typical brief consultations. Some readers, however, might find the print too small if they used this book for a prolonged period.

III. Quality and Currency of Entries

Entries are thorough and well organized. Following the main entry is a standard abbreviation for the part of speech; if a word is given with more than one part of speech, each application is listed separately. When a word has more than one meaning, each is given a boldface number and a separate list of synonyms. Each meaning is introduced by at least one illustrative sentence. For example, "she gets bad grades" is one of the example sentences for **bad** (in the sense of **not good**, **poor**, **inferior**, **wretched**), while "lying is a bad thing to do" is the sentence illustrating **immoral**, **unethical**, **sinful**, **evil**, **wicked**, and so forth.

Another helpful feature, especially for student users, is that the most common synonyms and those closest in meaning (given the vagaries of usage, however, these aren't always the same) come first in the list of synonyms, so that **baneful**—quite appropriately, given its rather restricted sense—is the last in a long list of synonyms for **bad** in the sense of **not good**. (**Heinous**, curiously, does not appear as a synonym in this thesaurus under any of the twelve senses of **bad**, but it is a separate main entry.)

Italicized labels are another useful feature: users are informed, for example, that **jam** in the sense of **mess** or **trouble** is an *informal* sense of a word that can also mean **crowd**, **tie-up**, **throng**, and so forth. Sometimes the editors warn the reader to be very selective about highly specialized synonyms, which they label with the word *variously*, so that the reader does not assume, for instance, that **howitzer** is a general synonym for **gun**. This guidance will be useful to students writing papers and studying language. Although most people use thesauruses for synonyms, a list of antonyms follows many of the synonym entries. Where it is difficult or impossible to assign an antonym, as with **Holy Ghost**, none is provided. Nor do the editors enter into semantic debate about the nature of antonymy, so that, for instance, **hate** is provided as an antonym for **love**, but the less obvious but still quite defensible word, *indifference*, is not.

One does not expect a necessarily selective thesaurus with only 11,000 main entries to include a great many new and trendy words, although the editors do regard the word **trendy** as popular enough to deserve a main entry. *Pop*, on the other hand, as an adjective meaning popular is not listed either as a main entry or as a synonym for **trendy**. One might assume that the editors are conservative about admitting new words: we find **parent** as a noun, but not in its newer sense as a verb; **program** is here in the sense of schedule but not in the sense of to program a computer; **psyche** is here as a noun meaning soul or mind, but not as a verb meaning psychologically ready, a sense currently familiar to high school students. Many other newer words and meanings are also excluded, although some old-fashioned words (**balderdash** and **poppycock**) are entered. However,

without additional descriptive information, students might misapply these older terms. It seems fair to conclude that some of the most solidly established new words (including slang) have been recognized as synonyms here, although relatively few of them are included as main entries. This may be a drawback for student users.

IV. Accessibility

Alternative spellings of words are indicated in boldface at the beginning of the main entry word; for example, "**jail** Also British **gaol**." Each two-column page has a boldface guide word indicating the first word at the top of the left column and the last word at the bottom of the right column.

V. Summary

The most familiar competitor to this source is ROGET'S INTERNATIONAL THESAURUS (1984). The most obvious difference between the two is that ROGET'S synoptic arrangement of words into categories of related meanings requires the reader to look up a word in the index before lists of synonyms can be found. Because of its alphabetical arrangement, many students will find *The Random House Thesaurus* more accessible. ROGET'S includes more words and phrases, as well as numbered categories that clearly distinguish separate senses of a word, but *The Random House Thesaurus* uses sentence examples that may be of real help to student readers. Although ROGET'S offers a greater number of choices, many high school libraries will still want to offer their readers a choice, especially because many student users may find *The Random House Thesaurus* quicker and easier to use.

The Right Word II: A Concise Thesaurus

Facts at a Glance

Full Title: **The Right Word II: A Concise Thesaurus**.
Publisher: Houghton Mifflin Company.
Editor: Mark H. Boyer, Project Editor.
Edition Reviewed: © 1983.

Number of Volumes: 1.
Number of Pages: 288.
Trim Size: 4″ × 5½″.
Binding: laminated paper over boards.

Price: $3.95.
Intended Readership: junior high students and up.

Sold in bookstores; also sold to libraries and schools. ISBN 0-395-34808-0.

I. Introduction and Scope

The Right Word II: A Concise Thesaurus is based on Houghton Mifflin's AMERICAN HERITAGE DICTIONARY and replaces the publisher's *The Right Word* (© 1978). That work's space-consuming cross-references have been replaced by an index in *The Right Word II*; contents are also substantially expanded in all categories.

According to the preface, this unique work differs from a traditional thesaurus "that prints exhaustive undifferentiated synonym lists." Instead, it "provides synonym studies on the most important meanings and ideas and discriminates among many of the most frequently used—and misused—words in the English language." Thus the work serves the needs of student and adult writers, whether they are seeking a synonym to avoid repetition of a given term or looking for the "precise word to express a specific thought."

In addition to its alphabetized (and indexed) listing of words for which synonyms are provided or differentiated, the work contains four special features. The first, a prefatory article titled "How to Use This Book" defines the term *synonym*, describes the work's two kinds of synonym studies—"relatively long paragraphs that discuss the synonyms in detail and short studies that focus on one central meaning of a number of common terms"—and discusses the use of the index.

At the end of the volume appear three supplemental lists. "Collective Nouns" includes nouns applied to groups of animals or people. Seven basic terms appear at the beginning of the list; the first, for example, is

brood—young offspring under the care of the same mother; especially, birds (fowl) or fish having a common birth. Or the word can be applied to the children of a single family.

Also listed are more specialized terms, such as

shrewdness—a company of apes.

There follows a list of collateral adjectives; that is, adjectives that do not resemble the nouns to which they correspond. All nouns are listed alphabetically by category and followed by their collateral adjec-

tives: for example, **laugh**, **risible**. Categories reflected are zoology, points of the compass, parts of the body, time, seasons, celestial bodies, family, and general. Finally, a section titled "Sciences and Technology" lists major sciences and technological specialties, with field of study and activities indicated for each.

II. Format

Within the body of the text, entry words and phrases are boldfaced and overhang the text. Boldface is also used for synonyms—which are listed alphabetically, following part-of-speech abbreviation, after the entry word. Antonyms are listed at the end of the entry. Small capitals are used for the main entry word and its synonyms when these recur within a synonym study; illustrative phrases and sentences are italicized. Typefaces are clear and easy to read, and their variety enables the user to locate information quickly.

The index, in double-columned format, also uses type styles to advantage. Entries for which synonym studies are given appear in small capitals; synonyms appear in roman type with their italicized main entry words following a colon. A typical sequence is:

PASSION
passive: *submissive*
paste: *hit*
PATIENT.

Adequate margins and white space add to the work's readability, both in the main text and in the special features. The good-quality, off-white paper permits minimal show-through. The book is sturdily bound and will hold up well to heavy use.

III. Quality and Currency of Entries

Clarity and precision characterize the work's synonym studies. Two kinds of entries, both frequently including antonyms at the end, appear in the main text. The shorter synonym studies point out the common denominator of meaning among a group of terms. For example, the user seeking an alternative to the word *provoke* would find the following entry useful:

Provoke *v.* **arouse**, **excite**, **goad**, **impel**, **incite**, **inflame**, **kindle**, **motivate**, **move**, **rouse**, **spur**, **stimulate**. *Core meaning:* To stir to action or feeling (*carelessness that provoked anger*).

The second type of entry, the discriminated synonymy, distinguishes among synonyms in terms of their appropriate contexts of usage:

hard *adj.* **firm. Hard and Firm are often used interchangeably when they refer to what is resistant to pressure (a** *hard surface*; *firm ground*). ***Hard* can also suggest that something is physically toughened (a** *hard palm with calluses*), **while** *firm* **describes what shows the tone and resiliency characteristic of healthy tissue (** *firm muscles*).

Also distinguished, when appropriate, are the varying connotations of the synonyms under discussion:

Both COWARDLY and CRAVEN suggest a shameful show of fear, but *craven* implies an especially high degree of cowardice: *a cowardly lion; a craven liar.*

It is not the purpose of *The Right Word II* to provide a comprehensive overview of the English language. Therefore, its omission of terms from the field of computer science, for example, does not reflect negatively upon it, since these terms seldom have any significant range of synonyms. The work is current, however, in its careful reflection of the way words are used and distinguished in American English today, and slang and informal usage are provided as appropriate. For example, synonyms listed for **hit** include

bash (*Informal*), **belt,** (*Informal*), **clip** (*Informal*), **clobber** (*Slang*), **paste** (*Slang*) **slam, slug** (*Slang*), **smack, smash, sock** (*Slang*), **strike, swat, wallop** (*Informal*), **whack.**

Although a high school-level writer may not find in *The Right Word II* the full range of synonyms available in larger thesauruses, this work's careful groupings and distinctions make it valuable to a wide range of students. Entries are clearly and simply stated, and subtle shades of meaning are elucidated so that appropriate word choices are easily made. Its conciseness and clarity make it accessible to students, non-native speakers, and novice writers, who might be overwhelmed by a larger work lacking discriminated synonymies.

IV. Accessibility

Entries are easily located with the aid of boldface guide words. Two are located at the top of each double spread, indicating the first and last entries on the spread. The compact size of the volume makes it especially easy for the user to flip through quickly in search of an entry that has been located in the index. A contents listing at the front of the volume ensures that the work's special features will not be overlooked.

V. Summary

The Right Word II: A Concise Thesaurus is a valuable work with no truly comparable competitors. While another thesaurus, THE NEW AMERICAN ROGET'S COLLEGE THESAURUS IN DICTIONARY FORM, is similar in its accessibility to users of a wide range of age and experience, *The Right Word II* is entirely different in focus. Rather than emphasizing quantity in the numbers of entries and undifferentiated synonyms, the work both provides synonyms for its selected entries and makes careful distinctions among a great number of them. This concise thesaurus can be easily used and could serve as a fine introduction to thesauruses and synonym dictionaries for students as early as the middle school grades; it would be an ideal classroom or school library companion to the AMERICAN HERITAGE SCHOOL DICTIONARY.

Roget's International Thesaurus, Fourth Edition

Facts at a Glance

Full Title: **Roget's International Thesaurus, Fourth Edition.**
Publisher: Thomas Y. Crowell (Harper & Row, Publishers, Inc.).
Editors: Peter Mark Roget, revised by Robert L. Chapman.
Edition Reviewed: © 1977; fourth edition, 1984.

Number of Volumes: 1.
Number of Entries: 256,000.
Number of Pages: 1,318.
Number of Indexes: 1.
Trim Size: 8½″ × 11″.
Binding: cloth; thumb-indexed cloth; paper.

Price: $11.45; $12.45; $9.95.
Intended Readership: age 16 and up.
Sold in bookstores and by direct mail; also sold to libraries and schools. ISBN 0-690-00010-3; 0-690-00011-1; 0-06-091169-7.

I. Introduction and Scope

The latest edition of *Roget's International Thesaurus*, this 1984 work contains approximately 256,000 words and phrases. It follows the format developed by Peter

Mark Roget in his original 1852 thesaurus: entries are grouped in categories according to their meanings, and words are located through a comprehensive index.

The original Roget's thesaurus went through twenty-nine editions and printings before being acquired by Thomas Y. Crowell, who published his editions in 1886 and 1911. The first *Roget's International Thesaurus*, which appeared in 1922, was the product of revisions by Crowell's son, T. Irving Crowell. His grandson, Robert L. Crowell, produced a second edition in 1946; the third edition appeared in 1962. In the course of these several revisions, many expansions were made: Americanisms, foreign expressions, quotations, slang, and substandard expression were added. Reformatting was undertaken to make the work easier to use.

The fourth edition is still further improved and modernized. Combining forms, such as prefixes and suffixes, have been added, as have many words and phrases from the 1970s. This work is the definitive unabridged English-language thesaurus. According to its publishers, it contains at least 100,000 more words and phrases than any other thesaurus of the English language. Editor Robert L. Chapman states in his foreword that this edition was "published in the hope and conviction that it will be more useful than its predecessors" for "writers of all sorts."

The revision was based on the "newest and best" general dictionaries of English and of specialized subjects, new specialized encyclopedias, and reverse-indexes of English (indexes "that make the lexicon accessible in terms of sense-forming suffixes"). New words and phrases were "carefully collected for inclusion," and the "broadest possible range of levels and styles . . . has been encompassed." Computer technology was applied to ensure the accuracy of the index.

II. Format

Both index and main text are carefully formatted for optimal clarity and usability. The thesaurus's alphabetical index is printed in quadruple-column format. Boldface entry words overhang listings of subentries reflecting various senses of the entry word. Each subentry is followed by numbers referring the user to the appropriate category and paragraph within that category. For example, looking up **shapeless** in the index, the reader finds the following:

shapeless
  abnormal 85.9
  formless 247.4
  inconstant 141.7
  obscure 549.15
  ugly 899.8
  unordered 62.12
  vague 514.18

If the reader selects "formless" as the synonym closest to the meaning desired, he or she will then turn to the main text, category 247 (**FORMLESSNESS**), where the fourth paragraph enters **formless** with its synonyms. This precise decimal finding system helps readers quickly locate appropriate words and phrases. Lest the system's unfamiliarity render it confusing, an introductory guide, "How to Use This Book" clearly explains the word-finding process and provides illustrative excerpts from both the index and the main text.

The main text is organized into eight broad conceptual classes: **Abstract Relations**, **Space**, **Physics**, **Matter**, **Sensation**, **Intellect**, **Volition**, and **Affections**. These are divided and subdivided—according to an outline reproduced at the front of the volume for quick reference—to produce 1,042 numbered paragraph entries. Main entry words are printed in boldface block capitals and are grouped according to their relationships with one another. For example, the sequence of categories **HEARING**, **DEAFNESS**, **SOUND**, **SILENCE**, **FAINTNESS OF SOUND**, **LOUDNESS** is "a procession of similar, contrasting, and opposing concepts, all dealing with the perception and quality of sounds." Each numbered entry is subdivided by hanging decimal numbers (.1, .2, .3, and so on), with these subsections grouped by part of speech. Terms of greatest frequency within each sense group are boldfaced for quick location. Ordering within entries is determined by listed words' relationship to the main entry word: terms closest in meaning are listed first. Semicolons set off each subsequent cluster of terms, with each semicolon signaling a slight change in meaning or usage. Bracketed labels identify foreign words, slang terms, informal usage, and technical language. Numbered cross-references lead readers to related categories, eliminating additional trips to the index.

The paper is white and permits minimal showthrough. The print is clear and easily read, and ample white space further enhances readability. The book is sturdily bound and will hold up well to heavy use.

III. Quality and Currency of Entries

Entries are thorough and detailed. Their principles of ordering and bracketed labels markedly facilitate the reader's choice of an appropriate word, although the editor valuably stresses in the introductory guide that the work should be used in conjunction with a dictionary. Quotations that themselves serve as synonyms enhance the work's range and usefulness. For example, under **patriotism** is listed " 'the last refuge of a scoundrel' [Samuel Johnson]." Some entries are also valuably embellished with lists, often extensive, of specific terms related to the more general entry term. For example, under the main entry **SPACE TRAVEL** the subsection beginning with the term **spacecraft** includes a list of 76 names of spacecraft, including both American and Soviet vessels. Under **airplane parts** appears a list of over 200 items. Student readers will find the quotations and lists especially valuable. These additions make the thesaurus a more comprehensive reference work without compromising its primary function as a repository of synonyms and related words.

As its listing of spacecraft suggests, the work has been carefully and successfully updated. Included, for example, are many terms relating to space travel (**reaction propulsion**, **velocity peak**), telecommunications (**information theory**, **quadruplex telegraphy**), computer systems and related technologies (**digital graph plotter**, **phase discriminator**), and nuclear energy (**fusion reaction**, **reactor pile**).

IV. Accessibility

Although the classic thesaurus format of *Roget's International Thesaurus* requires a two-step process, the decimal finding system (with two decimal guide numbers at the top of each main text page) and alphabetical index (with two boldface guide words on each index page) facilitates word finding. Students, who might find a dictionary format more immediately accessible, will easily learn to use this system and will appreciate its comprehensive groupings of related words. For the few abbreviations that are used, a key is provided at the back of the volume.

V. Summary

In comparison with other available thesauruses, *Roget's International Thesaurus* contains more main entries and more synonyms and is widely considered to be the authoritative thesaurus of the English language. Its comprehensiveness, wide usefulness, and reasonable price warrant the work's inclusion in every high school library reference collection and, ideally, in every English classroom library. The work is also recommended for acquisition by public libraries and by individuals and families for their home collections.

Roget's Pocket Thesaurus

Facts at a Glance

Full Title: **Roget's Pocket Thesaurus**.
Publisher: Pocket Books.
Editors: C. O. Sylvester Mawson and Katharine Aldrich Whiting.
Edition Reviewed: © 1946, 124th printing.

Number of Volumes: 1.
Number of Pages: 479.
Trim Size: $4\frac{1}{4}'' \times 6\frac{11}{16}''$.
Binding: paperback.

Price: $3.95.
Intended Readership: high school and up.
Sold in bookstores and other outlets; also sold to libraries and schools. ISBN 0-671-53090-9.

I. Introduction and Scope

Roget's Pocket Thesaurus, which appeared in 1946, is an abridged version of ROGET'S INTERNATIONAL THESAURUS, first published in 1922 by Thomas Y. Crowell Company, which issued a second edition in 1942. Both works, according to a note at the end of the volume, "derive their extraordinary usefulness from the fidelity with which they adhere to Peter Mark Roget's original concept." Both thesauruses are expansions of Roget's work, with added divisions of knowledge, American colloquialisms, and slang. There is no indication, however, of the principles by which this abridgment was prepared, nor is there any indication that it has been updated since its original appearance in the mid-1940s.

The work begins with a brief, but still engaging introduction, written many years ago by the renowned literary critic I. A. Richards, describing the purpose and value of Roget's *Thesaurus* and cautioning against its misuse. Also included at the front of the volume are a list of abbreviations used in the work; a brief guide, "How to Use the Book"; an outline "Plan of Classification"; and a "Tabular Synopsis of Categories." Although the work is primarily intended for adult users, these special features would render it adaptable for use by most students of high school age.

Following the thesaurus and its index are two additional special features. A 16-page alphabetized listing of "Foreign Words and Phrases" includes French, German, Italian, and Latin entries. Abbreviations indicating their language are given, and the entries are defined. The foreign words and phrases are not cross-referenced to entries in the thesaurus. Finally, the work includes a 23-page alphabetized list of "Abbreviations Used in Writing and Printing." Useful common abbreviations are clarified, as are abbreviations for, among other categories, associations, titles, languages, and countries.

II. Format

The work is organized in classical thesaurus format, which many students will find difficult, especially if they have not received guidance in using this format. Large conceptual classes, such as "Abstract Relations" and "Space," are subdivided into numbered, titled sections. For example:

CLASS VI
Words Relating to the SENTIENT AND MORAL POWERS
I. AFFECTIONS IN GENERAL
820. AFFECTIONS. . . .
821. FEELING. . . .
822. SENSITIVENESS. . . .
823. INSENSITIVENESS. . . .
824. EXCITEMENT. . . .
825. [Excess of Sensitiveness] EXCITABILITY. . . .
826. INEXCITABILITY. . . .

II. PERSONAL AFFECTIONS[1]. . . .

Within these sections, boldface arabic numbers demarcate main entry words printed in bold capitals. Within entries, synonyms and related words are grouped according to part of speech, with the first word in each category boldfaced for easier location. Italicized words and phrases in parentheses are provided occasionally to refer users to other lists, which they must locate through the index. Colloquialisms, slang, and foreign language words and phrases are identified with bracketed italicized abbreviations. Occasionally, a bracketed italicized phrase is used to clarify a specialized usage; for example, under **merchant**, the term **bull** is followed by: [*Stock Exchange*].

The triple-column index shows main entry words in bold capital letters. Other index entries are in boldface lowercase letters, followed by part-of-speech abbreviations, used to distinguish multiple uses of a word, and, in many cases, a listing of italicized related words. Each entry or subentry is followed by a number referring to the section of the vocabulary where that word can be found. Section numbers are in bold type when the indexed word is a main entry or a boldfaced subentry. A representative index section is:

rotate 312

ROTATION 138, **312**
rotten *foul* 653
　　decayed 659

The type size is generally adequate; however, both within the introductory guide and within the thesaurus, some sections appear in a significantly smaller typeface. There is no clear rationale for this, and these sections are hard to read. Minimal use of white space also makes the work more difficult to read. Paper is of customary paperback quality, and the pages do not separate easily from the spine, so the work should hold up well to repeated use.

III. Quality and Currency of Entries

Entries are thorough and detailed in their presentations of semantic families. Under the main entry **drama** (noun), for example, a typical subentry reads as follows:

> **play**, drama, piece, tragedy, comedy, opera, vaudeville, curtain raiser, interlude, afterpiece, farce, extravaganza, harlequinade, pantomime, burlesque, ballet, spectacle, masque, melodrama; comedy of manners; charade, mystery, miracle play, morality play.

Separate subentries are given for **act, performance, theater, cast, actor, buffoon, company, dramatist,** and **audience**.

On the other hand, the work is markedly dated. No entries are provided for words related to *astronautics* or *computer science*. Slang and colloquialisms are frequently outdated. For example, the entry for **fool** (noun) begins with the following listing:

> idiot, tomfool, wiseacre, simpleton, Simple Simon; donkey, ass, owl, goose, dolt, booby, noodle, imbecile, nincompoop [*colloq*.], oaf, lout, blockhead, bonehead [*slang*], calf [*colloq*.], colt, numbskull [*collog*.], clod, clodhopper; soft *or* softy [*colloq. or slang*], mooncalf, saphead [*slang*], gawk, rube [*slang*].

Not only are many of these terms no longer current in standard, colloquial, or slang usage, but others— such as *jerk, turkey,* and *nerd*—are excluded. Under **place of amusement**, the dated **moving-picture theater** is listed, with the now-standard **movies** listed as a colloquialism. The book appears not to have been updated since its original appearance; and its lack of currency will limit its usefulness to students and other readers.

IV. Accessibility

Accessibility is enhanced by the inclusion of page numbers, section numbers, and categories and subcategories in the running heads of the vocabulary. An example for a double-page spread is:

Left-hand page
269a–272   SPACE   76
Right-hand page
77   MOTION   272–274

Within the index, boldface guide words in capital letters reflect the first and last entries on each spread. A table of contents helpfully lists all special features; but its placement, after the introduction rather than at the beginning of the volume, may result in its being overlooked.

The index is the primary means of access to the information in the volume. While it is not unduly difficult to use, the explanation provided in the introductory guide may hinder more than it helps the user. Students and novice users would benefit from a clearer explanation.

V. Summary

Although *Roget's Pocket Thesaurus* is a wide-ranging and detailed reference work—especially for a paperback—it is not current. Other pocket works, such as THE NEW AMERICAN ROGET'S COLLEGE THESAURUS IN DICTIONARY FORM provide more up-to-date listings and a more readable format. On the other hand, the *Roget's Pocket Thesaurus* has features that cannot be found in comparable works; for example, the thorough outlines clarifying its organization. Unfortunately, these do not compensate for its 1940s vocabulary. High school and public libraries will want to provide their patrons with more current material in their paperback collections.

Roget's II: The New Thesaurus

Facts at a Glance

Full Title: **Roget's II: The New Thesaurus.**
Publisher: Houghton Mifflin Company.
Editors: Fernando de Mello Vianna, Editorial Director, and Anne D. Steinhardt, Supervising Editor.

Number of Volumes: 1.
Number of Words: 250,000.
Number of Pages: 1,088.
Trim Size: 6¾" × 9⁹⁄₁₆".
Binding: cloth.

Price: $11.95.
Intended Readership: high school and up.
Sold in bookstores and other outlets; also sold to libraries and schools. ISBN 0-395-29605-6.

I. Introduction and Scope

Roget's II: The New Thesaurus, published in 1980, represents a departure from traditional thesaurus presentation, providing not only synonyms, but also definitions and illustrative examples. According to its preface, the work is designed to combat problems commonly faced by thesaurus users: cumbersome indexes and the indiscriminate grouping of words with vaguely related meanings. This work, by contrast, "has been carefully prepared to provide rapid access to synonyms, which are grouped by precise meanings, facilitating the choice of appropriate words to express thoughts."

Alphabetically arranged, the thesaurus contains 250,000 terms. It is intended to function as "a source of appropriate words to express thoughts or ideas, guiding the user away from the common pitfalls of selecting an unsuitable word." Definitions obviate the need to use a dictionary; usage labels identify specialized and controversial synonyms. Excluded, "for reasons of clarity and accuracy," according to the editors are related words, antonyms, and contrasting words. This may well make the work more immediately useful, but it also limits its range.

Five years of investigation preceded the publication of this volume. It was based in part on the staff's experience in compiling the American Heritage Dictionaries, and independent lexicographers aided the publisher's permanent lexicographic staff. Computer technology was applied to ensure the work's accuracy.

Designed as an adult reference work, this volume is also highly suitable for use by high school students who will benefit from its easily used format and its wide range of vocabulary, given the exclusions noted above.

II. Format

In a two-column format, the thesaurus presents five kinds of entries, all introduced by boldface "head" (main entry) words: (1) main entries with synonym lists; (2) indented subentries in smaller type that show words closely related to or derived from the main entry word; (3) secondary entries that refer the user to main-entry lists; (4) cross-references directing the user from secondary to primary variant spellings; as well as (5) cross-references from secondary entries to synonymized subentries.

Entries are listed alphabetically. In the left-hand column, each main entry word is identified by an italicized part-of-speech label. It is followed by a definition and, often, an italicized sentence or phrase using the word in context. Entries for words with multiple meanings list numbered definitions and, in many instances, multiple illustrative sentences or phrases. In the right-hand column appear the synonyms, each alphabetized group preceded by the boldface italicized abbreviation *Syns*. When necessary, synonyms are identified with temporal labels (*Archaic, Obsolete*) usage labels (*Informal, Slang, Poetic*), dialect labels (*Regional, Chiefly Regional*), language labels (*French, British*), field labels (*Law, Motion Pictures and T.V.*), or status labels (*Rare*). Idioms, when applicable, are listed after the synonyms. A representative entry shows the following definition in the left-hand column:

destroy *verb*
   1. To cause the complete ruin or wreckage of: *paintings destroyed by fire*; *drugs that destroyed her health*; *news that destroyed his hopes*.

Opposite the definition, in the right-hand column, appear the synonyms:

   1. *Syns*: demolish, destruct, dynamite, finish, ruin, ruinate (*Regional*), shatter, sink, smash, total, torpedo, undo, wrack, wreck.—*Idiom* put the kibosh on.

Secondary entries contain main entry words, italicized part-of-speech labels, definition(s), and cross-references to main entries. Cross-references to subentries and to variant spellings are identified by the word SEE.

aeon *noun*   SEE **eon**.

Cross-references to main entries are printed in small capitals:

ghoul *noun*   FIEND.
   A perversely bad, cruel,
   or wicked person.

Turning to FIEND, the user would find it listed as a main entry with seven synonyms—**archfiend**, **beast**, **ghoul**, **monster**, **ogre**, **tiger**, **vampire**—and the synonymous idiom **devil incarnate**.

The work's white paper permits some show-through but not enough to impede readability. Print is clear and adequate in size; white space is used advantageously. The sturdily bound volume will hold up well to heavy use in a classroom or library.

III. Quality and Currency of Entries

Definitions are clearly and concisely—although not simply—written, and multiple senses receive appropriate coverage. Illustrative sentences and phrases complement definitions usefully. For example, the entry for **humanitarian** includes the following:

   1. Concerned with human welfare and the alleviation of suffering: *The governor spared the prisoner out of humanitarian considerations*.
   2. Characterized by kindness and concern for others.

The separate listing of synonyms for each sense of the word helps to ensure that users will select a denotatively valid synonym, and the many restrictive labels provided facilitate the selection of a word with the appropriate connotative value.

The inclusion of slang and informal language brings currency to the work. **Hang around**, for example, is offered as an informal synonym for **frequent**; **freebie** appears as a main entry. Excluded are many contemporary terms such as *anchorperson*, *computer*, *ecology*, *meltdown*, *nuclear*, *program* (in its computer science application), *spacecraft*, and *telecommunications*, although such terms do not have a significant range of synonyms. Although this work falls short of ROGET'S INTERNATIONAL THESAURUS, Fourth Edition, which includes all these words, students will find *Roget's II* sufficiently comprehensive to meet most of their school-related needs.

IV. Accessibility

An introductory guide, "How to Use This Book," makes good use of illustrative excerpts and examples. A clearly labeled sample page on the back of the dust jacket also provides useful information. Students, who probably will not read the introductory guide unless assigned to do so, may not readily recognize cross-references that are not introduced with SEE. However, this is not a major flaw, since its other features make the thesaurus easy to use without formal instruction.

Boldface guide words at the top of each page identify the first entry on the left-hand page and the last on the right-hand page. A thumb index, with shiny gold-on-blue letter tabs, makes the location of alphabet sections easy. The few abbreviations used in the work are explained in the introductory guide. Variant spellings are easily located through the cross-referencing system.

V. Summary

Roget's II: The New Thesaurus would be a good supplement to the high school library reference collection or the English classroom. Lacking the comprehensiveness and currency of ROGET'S INTERNATIONAL THESAURUS, Fourth Edition, it will not replace this standard. Further, users may be disappointed to discover that, unlike most thesauruses, *Roget's II* does not include antonyms. However, its alphabetical arrangement, dictionary-style definitions with illustrative sentences and phrases, and its easily read double-column format make it accessible to students.

The Simon & Schuster Young Readers' Thesaurus

Facts at a Glance

Full Title: **The Simon & Schuster Young Readers' Thesaurus.**
Publisher: Simon & Schuster/Wanderer Books.
Compiler: George Beal.
Edition Reviewed: © 1984.

Number of Volumes: 1.
Number of Entries: approximately 6,000.
Number of Pages: 192.
Number of Cross-references: 5,700.
Number of Illustrations: approximately 115, most in two colors.
Trim Size: 4¾" × 7⅜".
Binding: paperback.

Price: $6.95.
Intended Readership: students in grades 5 through 9.
Sold in bookstores and other outlets; also sold to libraries and schools. ISBN 0-671-50816-4.

I. Introduction and Scope

The Simon & Schuster Young Readers' Thesaurus is a handy paperback thesaurus specifically designed for students in the upper elementary grades through junior high school. It has a colorful cover and blue, black, and white drawings scattered among its pages, ones that are mostly decorative rather than aids to understanding the synonyms.

According to its publishers, *The Young Readers' Thesaurus* can help "students and word lovers of all ages!!" And they explain that with this book, "Now you the reader can expand your vocabulary, learn to express yourself more clearly and creatively, and have loads of fun doing it!"

II. Format

Arranged in alphabetical order, *The Young Readers' Thesaurus* entries are placed in double columns of text, with each entry identified by its letter and a number: for example, the main entries under the letter *A* are numbered A1 through A186 (**abandon** through **awkward**). Entry words are in boldface type, labeled for part of speech, and followed by a list of synonyms.

When an entry word has more than one meaning, each sense is numbered and appropriate synonyms are provided. Cross-references are indicated by the use of italic type. Synonyms listed in italicized type are also main entry words. The section headed "Further Synonyms," in the introductory pages, explains this concept, although the phrase "cross-reference" is not used. Antonyms, placed in parentheses, are given reference numbers in the synonym lists. A sample entry appears thus:

> C418   **correct 1**. *adj.* faultless, exact, precise, *accurate*, true (E126, F59, I93, I127, W121) **2**. *v.* rectify, amend, set right (E123) *n.* **correction** (E127) *n.* **correctness** (M187).

Note that the entry word **correct** has a reference number, C418. For the first meaning of **correct** as an adjective, there are five synonyms given; the fourth synonym, *accurate*, appears in italics and is, therefore, also a main entry where further synonyms appear. However, the synonyms given for *accurate* at A36 are **correct**, **exact**, and **precise**—(E126, M188, W121)—and those are words already found under **correct**, so the cross-reference provides no additional information. The entry shows that antonyms are cross-referenced by their main entry number and placed in parentheses. The second meaning group given for **correct** lists it as a verb and provides three synonyms. Word variations of the entry word follow (see **correction** and **correctness**) with their antonym references, but no synonyms.

The back cover states that homonyms are printed all in blue, but they are, in fact, shown in full capital letters at the end of entries, for example:

> P317 **pour** *v.* flow, emit, issue, stream discharge. PORE.

When meanings are obscure, example sentences are provided and italicized. Pronunciation is also given when necessary, as in meanings one and three below, which show the syllable to be stressed in boldface type:

> M161 **minute 1**. (**min**-it) *n.* sixty seconds **2**. *n.* jiffy, instant **3**. (my-**nute**) *adj.* little, tiny, small, wee, microscopic (G54, H192, V22).

Guide words appear at the top of each page. Guide letters printed on a blue half-circle at the outside margins of pages simulate thumb indexes and will help students to locate appropriate pages in the book quickly.

III. Quality and Currency of Entries

The Young Readers' Thesaurus provides an acceptable range of vocabulary for its intended audience. Its introduction explains synonyms and demonstrates that there are no *exact* synonyms—but does not emphasize that readers will need to use a dictionary to discriminate meanings more closely or to choose the most precise meanings for the context.

The vocabulary is, in general, that of a standard or basic lexicon, and specialist meanings are, therefore, omitted. In some cases, this may not satisfy the needs of contemporary elementary and older students. For example, P416 **program** lists only standard noun synonyms (**schedule**, **record**, **plan**, **list**, **calendar**, **agenda**) and does not include either a noun or verb sense of **program** in its widely used computer sense. The entries for **compute** (C287) and **computer** (C288) are not adequate even for today's young readers:

> **compute** *v.* reckon, calculate, estimate, count.

> **computer** *n.* calculator, word processor, microprocessor.

A small black-and-white line drawing illustrates an old-style mainframe computer captioned "Electronic computer, 1946"—a simplified thesaurus is not an ideal place to provide historical information.

The entry for **protest** is another example of limited currency:

> P448 **protest 1**. (proh-**test**) *v.* object, dispute, challenge, demur (A135) **2**. (**proh**-test) *n.* complaint, objection.

Students will be most familiar with this word as a noun or verb in a social or political context, and an illustrative sentence would help to make this kind of meaning clear.

IV. Accessibility

Without a careful reading of the introductory pages (which fifth through ninth graders may not do on their own), students will probably not be able to take full advantage of the features in this thesaurus, beyond the identification of synonyms, without adult help. It could be difficult for many students to figure out the cross-referencing or the antonym references by looking at the text. Another drawback is that some of the vocabulary in the introductory material might be difficult for the intended readers, as in: "Here is a specimen entry from the book."

In some cases, the instructions on using the book are inaccurate. For example, in explaining that entries can have more than one meaning, the word "hand" is used as an example (as a body part, as in "farm hand," and as in "hand" someone an object, or give a "hand" to someone). In describing the first meaning, "hand" is defined as ". . . the appendage with four fingers at the end of our arms." Students might correctly argue that hands have five fingers, or four fingers and a thumb. In a section called "Key to the Entries," references to antonyms are incorrectly identified as synonym references.

While the book is very sturdily bound for a paperback, this results in making the book difficult to open and impossible to place flat on a surface. It is very hard to copy out words while either writing or working at a typewriter or word processor; it is also difficult to read the text that is closest to the gutter.

V. Summary

The Simon & Schuster Young Readers' Thesaurus sets out to provide students with a ". . . comprehensive, organized way to find synonyms." There is, indeed, a need for a simple-to-use thesaurus that younger students in the upper elementary, middle school, and junior high school can use independently or with minimal assistance. This thesaurus's complex arrangement of cross-references and difficult-to-understand directions, however, do not meet the need adequately—at least without adult assistance. Of all the thesauruses examined for this volume, Merriam-Webster's WEBSTER'S SCHOOL THESAURUS, although primarily intended for older students, comes closest to filling the need for an excellent thesaurus for student readers. For those teachers and parents who can spend the time explaining the system in *The Simon & Schuster Young Readers' Thesaurus*, however, it might well serve as a useful, inexpensive adjunct to writing assignments.

Webster's New World Thesaurus

Facts at a Glance

Full Title: **Webster's New World Thesaurus**.
Publisher: Simon and Schuster.
Editor: Charlton Laird; updated by William D. Lutz.
Edition Reviewed: © 1985.

Number of Volumes: 1.
Number of Entries: more than 30,000.
Number of Pages: 854.
Trim Size: 6½″ × 9½″.
Binding: paper over boards.

Price: $14.95 thumb-indexed, $13.95 plain.
Intended Readership: high school and up.
Sold in bookstores and other outlets; also sold to libraries and schools. ISBN 0-671-60437-6; 0-671-60738-3.

I. Introduction and Scope

Webster's New World Thesaurus was first published in 1971. The work was revised and updated in 1985 to include 7,000 additional new entries. Charlton Laird, who prepared the original work, is the author of works including *The Miracle of Language*, *Language in America*, and *Modern English Handbook*. In his words, this book "is intended to help writers and speakers in search of a better way to say what they want to." This alphabetically arranged thesaurus lists synonyms and antonyms. It differs both from Roget's original and from recastings of Roget's work in dictionary form. The differences are based on its adherence to the principle that a thesaurus should not be a book about the classification of words; rather, it should be a practical book designed to satisfy the needs of writers and speakers. The editor stresses that the words that "send" readers to a thesaurus are the everyday locutions that come readily to mind. Thus, this thesaurus is "organized on the basis of the commonest words in the language, whatever their standing in respectability, the words that most readily occur to a user of the book."

To put this principle into practice, the editors selected approximately 30,000 main entries that reflected what they deemed to be the most common groupings of synonyms in the language. To check word frequency, they made use of Henry Kučera and

W. Nelson Francis's *Computational Analysis of Present-Day American English* (1967), a computer-based study of Brown University's Standard Corpus of the Present-Day American English. Modern American usage is therefore more comprehensively covered in this volume than in its predecessors. The editors have also recognized the value to the writer of specific equivalents (such as **biceps** for **muscle**) of words for which there are no true synonyms, where an earlier thesaurus editor would have excluded the word.

Appended at the back of the work is an eleven-page alphabetized listing of synonymies, selected and adapted from WEBSTER'S NEW WORLD DICTIONARY: SECOND COLLEGE EDITION. These paragraphs discuss and illustrate "the subtle differences that distinguish . . . synonyms." This is a useful feature especially for students, supplementing the main text. Under each word, italicized, discriminated terms refer to main entries in the thesaurus's vocabulary.

II. Format

The alphabetized main entry words are boldfaced and overhang the text printed in two columns. An italicized part-of-speech abbreviation follows the main entry word. Boldfaced numbers introduce separate uses of the entry word, and a bracketed word or phrase identifies the use under consideration. Synonyms are listed for each use. For the briefer entries of less common words, bold cross-references are introduced by the word "see" and are followed by a number identifying the relevant part of the entry referred to. "See also" cross-references within the longer entries suggest other meanings of the word that the reader should consider in the search for a synonym. Where applicable, antonyms follow synonyms, are identified with an asterisk, and have their own main entries. (D) identifies words whose diction level restricts use. A representative entry is the following:

> **shown**, *mod*. **1**. [Put on display]—*Syn*. displayed, demonstrated, advertised, exposed, set out, presented, exhibited, delineated, laid out, put up for sale; *both* (D): put up, put on the block.—*Ant*. withdrawn*, concealed, held back.
> **2**. [Proved]—*Syn*. demonstrated, determined, made clear; see **established** 3, **obvious** 2.

At the conclusions of some entries, idioms incorporating the main entry word are alphabetically listed. For example, under **mind** are listed such idioms as **be in one's right mind**, **have half a mind to**, and **take one's mind off**. These appear in boldface type; synonyms and cross-references are provided for each.

The type is clear and its size in the main text is readable, although the type used in the appended synonymies is too small to be read easily. The paper permits minimal show-through, and there is adequate white space with good margins. The volume is sturdily bound and will hold up well to heavy use.

III. Quality and Currency of Entries

The entries are selected and designed to make the volume quick and easy to use. According to the foreword, "usually the commonest set of synonyms carries the main entry; uses of a word are arranged roughly by frequency of use, from common to uncommon." The same principle determines ordering within the lists of synonyms.

The detailed entries include useful features not found in most thesauruses. One of these is the appearance of bracketed phrases identifying separate uses of an entry word. Although these are not—and are not intended to be—definitions, they will assist readers in quickly finding the subentry they need.

Another valuable feature is the inclusion of many idioms; those incorporating a main entry word are listed at the conclusions of entries (under **corner**, for example, **around the corner** is one of several idiomatic phrases). Idioms sharing the same first word receive separate main entries (**hit it off**, **hit on**, **hit or miss**, **hit the jackpot**, **hit the hay**). The inclusion of idioms as main entries serves the editors' purpose of listing common words for which readers are most likely to seek synonyms.

The editors' desire to provide specific equivalents for general terms results in some extensive entries. For example, under **Europe** appears an entry of over half a column listing the countries of Europe. Shorter listings of specific equivalents also appear. The entry for **tool** includes:

> common tools include the following—can opener, hammer, knife, jack, crank, pulley, wheel, bar, crowbar, lever, sledge, winch, cam, loom, shuttle, chisel, plane, screw, brace, bit, file, saw, screwdriver, wrench, pliers, ax, hatchet, corkscrew, jimmy.

Such lists are not found in most thesauruses, and they expand the work's application as a reference source. They enable readers to locate specific names and terms for both factual and descriptive purposes.

The work's currency is also strong, in keeping with its editors' concern with making the volume practically useful. Under **computer**, for example, the following appears:

> *Syn.* electronic *or* electric brain, electrocomputer, thinking machine, IBM (trademark), microcomputer, minicomputer, mainframe, personal computer, calculator, master control, high-speed data processor, electronic circuit, number cruncher (D), cybernetic organism, analog computer, digital computer.

There follows a list of computer brand names. Space technology receives good coverage under the entries **space**, **space-age**, **spacecraft**, and **space platform**.

Some aspects of the entries are less specific than the reader may need or expect. For example, the abbreviation *mod.* (for modifier) is used to identify adjectives, adverbs, and articles: this is a drawback, especially for students. Only one usage label (D) is provided in the work. This identifies the diction level of words that may be slang, colloquial, or vulgar, and alerts a reader to consult a dictionary. The editorial decision to employ a single label was made on the sound basis that usage of these kinds can be only loosely and temporarily defined in more specific ways. However, some readers will prefer a thesaurus that offers more specific usage labels before sending its readers to the dictionary.

IV. Accessibility

Because the volume lacks a table of contents, the appended synonymies are likely to be overlooked. Cross-references are usefully provided to refer readers from one entry to others within the main text. The absence of a key to abbreviations is an irritating omission and may cause difficulties for the user because of the unusual part-of-speech abbreviation *mod.* and the (D) label, for example, although these are explained in the volume's foreword.

Two boldfaced guide words appear at the top of each page in both sections, indicating the first and last entries on the page. The volume is available in both thumb-indexed and plain editions.

V. Summary

Webster's New World Thesaurus is a valuable, up-to-date reference source. It is more current and comprehensive than either THE DOUBLEDAY ROGET'S THESAURUS IN DICTIONARY FORM or THE RANDOM HOUSE THESAURUS: COLLEGE EDITION. Although not as extensively detailed as the definitive ROGET'S INTERNATIONAL THESAURUS, it is also less overwhelming and easier to use than that work and may therefore be preferable for high school use. Its organization on the basis of the most common words in the language will also enhance its usefulness to students. The work's minor drawbacks are its blanket use of the part-of-speech abbreviation *mod.* and the diction label (D). *Webster's New World Thesaurus* would be a worthy addition to any high school library's collection and useful for most student's home reference library.

Webster's New World Thesaurus

Facts at a Glance

Full Title: **Webster's New World Thesaurus**.
Publisher: Warner Books.
Editor: Charlton Laird.
Edition Reviewed: © 1974.

Number of Volumes: 1.
Number of Entries: 30,000.
Number of Pages: 530.
Trim Size: 4″ × 7″; 5½″ × 8″.
Binding: paperback.

Price: $3.50; $8.95.
Intended Readership: grade 6 and up.
Sold in bookstores and other outlets; also sold to libraries and schools. ISBN 0-446-37053-3; 0-446-31203-7.

I. Introduction and Scope

This 1974 thesaurus is the Warner paperback edition of the 1971 WEBSTER'S NEW WORLD THESAURUS. The 1985 updating of that hardbound work, published by Simon and Schuster is reviewed in this Buying Guide. The Warner paperback does not reflect that updating, yet it does incorporate many new words from such fields as computer science and space technology. The paperback's introduction is at a lower reading level than that in the hardbound volume, and it provides a step-by-step guide to the use of the book.

Although its publishers assert that its intended audience is grade 6 and up, this work will find few readers younger than high school age. The very small print of the mass market edition will be a drawback for many readers. However, the work is easy to use, comprehensive, and fairly up-to-date. It is appropriate for the high school or English classroom library, as well as for the circulating paperback collection of the public library.

Webster's School Thesaurus

Facts at a Glance

Full Title: **Webster's School Thesaurus**.
Publisher: Merriam-Webster Inc.
Editor: Kathleen M. Doherty.

Edition Reviewed: © 1978.

Number of Volumes: 1.
Number of Entries: over 43,000.
Number of Pages: 512.
Number of Cross-references: over 18,000.
Trim Size: 8″ × 10″.
Binding: cloth.

Price: $9.95.
Intended Readership: high school.
Sold to libraries and schools; also sold in bookstores and other outlets. ISBN 0-877-79178-3.

I. Introduction and Scope

According to its preface, *Webster's School Thesaurus* is "designed for young people who want to enlarge their vocabulary and acquaint themselves with the rich variety of the English language." First published in 1978, this alphabetically arranged thesaurus is intended for a high school audience but will meet the needs of some younger students and of adults as well.

The work is based primarily on WEBSTER'S THIRD NEW INTERNATIONAL DICTIONARY. Other sources consulted by the editor include WEBSTER'S NEW COLLEGIATE DICTIONARY, existing thesauruses, and the extensive Merriam-Webster citation files.

The publisher states that this thesaurus is designed to be easy to use and "to provide real help in vocabulary building and word selection." Cartoons, illustrations, and overly large print have been avoided; the main consideration of the editor was "to afford the reader access to a usable thesaurus." Introductory features, the introduction and "Explanatory Notes," provide helpful information for the user, including readable and detailed definitions of such terms as "synonym" and "antonym" and a practical guide to the effective use of the thesaurus, illustrated with copious examples. These sections are well designed to serve as teaching tools for the classroom teacher or librarian.

II. Format

Entries are arranged alphabetically on double-column pages. Main entry words are boldfaced and overhang the text. The main entry word is followed by an italicized part-of-speech label. Where multiple senses of an entry word are listed, these are identified with boldfaced numbers. For each sense, a brief definition is provided, followed by an illustrative phrase or sentence in angle brackets, with the entry word italicized. Also provided, as appropriate, are alphabetically listed synonyms (*syn*), related words (*rel*), idiomatic equivalents (*idiom*), contrasted words (*con*), and antonyms (*ant*). A representative entry begins as follows:

> **calm** *adj* **1** free from storm or rough activity ⟨the wind died and the sea became *calm*⟩
> *syn* halcyon, hushed, placid, quiet, still, stilly, untroubled
> *rel* inactive, quiescent, reposing, resting; pacific, smooth, tranquil, unruffled
> *idiom* calm as a millpond, still as death
> *con* agitated, disturbed, perturbed, restless, turbulent, uneasy
> *ant* stormy.

Secondary entries provide a part-of-speech abbreviation and a cross-reference to the appropriate main entry:

> **convoluted** *adj syn*   SEE WINDING.

Print is small but readable, and white space is used well to enhance readability. The white paper permits minimal show-through. The sturdily bound book opens flat and will withstand heavy use.

III. Quality and Currency of Entries

Entries are thorough and detailed in general. Definitions are clear and concise, and bracketed illustrative phrases and sentences provide useful clarifications. Explanatory material is included when necessary:

> **express** *vb* . . . **2** to give expression to (as a thought, an opinion, or an emotion);

and usage notes provide further information or commentary as required:

> **yet** *adv* **1** beyond this—used as an intensive to stress the comparative degree.

Although the work provides definitions, the "Explanatory Notes" urge readers to consult a dictionary as the final authority in determining the suitability of a selected term. This is a helpful reminder to students of the complexity and subtlety of the English language.

Synonym lists are extensive and age-appropriate. A "compare cross-reference" appears at the end of a synonym list when two or more synonyms are closely related and the editor wishes to direct the user's attention to additional lists. For example, the user benefits from cross-references between **assassin** and **murderer**:

> **assassin** *n* a person hired or hirable to commit murder ⟨found out who paid the *assassin*⟩
> *syn* bravo, cutthroat, gun, gunman, ‖gunsel, gunslinger, hatchet man, hit man, torpedo, triggerman; *compare* MURDERER
>
> **murderer** *n* one who kills a human being ⟨a murderer who wouldn't hesitate to kill in cold blood⟩
> *syn* homicide, killer, manslayer, slayer; *compare* ASSASSIN.

As in the case of "gunsel" in the entry for **assassin**, double bars (‖) placed before a word alert users to some restriction, indicating that the word may be slang, regional, or in some other way limited in usage. This feature is especially appropriate to the work's educational purpose: according to the editors, such words have been included to "introduce you to the extensive range of the English language and to help you stretch your vocabulary." The editors suggest that users consult a dictionary to determine proper usage in such cases.

Although a search for current vocabulary revealed some gaps (*anchorperson*, *astronaut*, *computer*, *meltdown*, *space shuttle*), the number and range of words included make this a comprehensive resource for advanced upper elementary, junior high school, and high school students. While the vocabulary of this thesaurus is well suited to the needs of the junior and senior high school curriculum, adults will also find this a useful reference tool and readable.

Most obsolete, archaic, and highly technical words have been omitted. However, the editors believe they have included a sufficient number of out-of-the-ordinary terms to satisfy students looking for the unusual word. A random search for "unusual" words turned up **Tartarean**, **Tartuffism**, **lares and penates**, **popsy**, and **demirep**.

IV. Accessibility

Two boldfaced guide words appear at the top of each page, indicating the first and last words entered on that page. Accessibility is also enhanced by the inclusion of a key to the five main abbreviations and symbols used in the text that appears on all right-hand pages. This will prove especially useful to students.

V. Summary

Brodart's *Elementary School Library Collection* (15th edition) recommends *Webster's School Thesaurus* for advanced elementary students, and *Publishers Weekly* (19 June 1978) calls the work an "extremely valuable volume," "intelligently designed," and recommends it for ages 12 and up. Another dictionary-format thesaurus, *The New Roget's Thesaurus* (Putnam, 1978) has only 17,000 plus entries in comparison to Webster's over 43,000; the former work does not contain Webster's special vocabulary-building features. The inclusion of terms with restricted usage, as well as related and contrasted words, idioms, and antonyms for most main entries, make *Webster's School Thesaurus* an especially useful tool in vocabulary development.

Webster's School Thesaurus is a comprehensive, inexpensive, and well-planned and executed reference work. It is a first choice purchase for a school or public library's reference collection, and an excellent addition to the classroom or even a home reference collection.

Synonym, Antonym, and Other Word Books

Allen's Synonyms and Antonyms

Facts at a Glance

Full Title: **Allen's Synonyms and Antonyms**.
Publisher: Barnes & Noble.
Compiler: F. Sturges Allen.
Editor: T. H. Van Motter.
Edition Reviewed: © 1949; 1985, 14th printing of this paperback edition.

Number of Volumes: 1.
Number of Entries: approximately 12,000.
Number of Pages: 427.
Number of Cross-references: 5,000.
Trim Size: 5⅛" × 8".
Binding: Paperback.

Price: $4.95.
Intended Readership: high school and up.
Sold in bookstores and also through direct mail.
    ISBN 0-064-63328-4.

I. Introduction and Scope

The late F. Sturges Allen, general editor of WEBSTER'S NEW INTERNATIONAL DICTIONARY, prepared the text for the original 1921 edition of *Allen's Synonyms and Antonyms*, published by Harper & Row. The book was revised by T. H. Van Motter in 1949, who increased the number of main entries by about one-third. Motter included words that, he explained, "have not appeared in dictionaries in general use" and he also added "sense discriminations" and the context in which many of the words might be most appropriately used.

The edition reviewed here is the 14th printing of the 1972 paperback edition, which is essentially a reprint of the Harper & Row edition. (Only this paperback edition is still in print.)

The work contains approximately 12,000 main entries and 5,000 cross-references. The publisher claims that *Allen's* "supplies all the synonyms, antonyms, and related words that a thesaurus does, but goes beyond a thesaurus; it tells just how the words differ, makes clear their various shades of meanings, explains their distinctions, and suggests nuances that the writer and reader need to know." That claim is no longer valid in the 1980s.

The volume's word list encompasses English language words and terms from the Victorian era through the first half of the twentieth century. Although the text is specifically intended for an American audience, the words and terms identified include British, Scots, Irish, North American, Canadian, Anglo-Indian, slang, rare, colloquial, poetic, affected, and obsolete items. Words deriving from the sciences and technologies have such dated synonyms that their chief merit now is to charm or surprise the reader. For example, under the main entry **engineer**, the synonyms listed are: **machinist** . . . **driver** . . . **hydraulician**, **mechanician**, **pioneer**. For younger readers, this lack of currency will simply be confusing.

II. Format

This volume is printed in rather small, but readable type. The paper quality is unusually good for an inexpensive paperback and has little show-through. Moreover, it is sturdily bound and should be able to survive frequent use.

A preface, explanatory remarks entitled "How Shall I Say It?", and lists of explanatory terms and abbreviations, for example, (*A*) for archaic and (*R*) for rare, introduce the book. The main vocabulary is ordered alphabetically. For main entries, which appear in boldface, the parts of speech are given, followed by numbered lists of related synonyms with the "sense discrimination" or advice on meaning and usage given in parentheses. Often a "*see*" reference for at least one of the clusters of meaning is given, referring the reader to another main entry word or words where possible synonyms may be found. For example:

> **dependence**, *n*. **1**. hanging, suspension.
> **2**. hinging, turning, hanging, resting.
> **3**. *See* RELIANCE, SUPPORT.

Antonyms or other cross-references, when provided, follow the numbered section of each entry according to the sense of the word grouping that the editor deems most acceptable.

A condensed, supplementary word list appears at the foot of each page in smaller type. Each main entry in this list has one or more cross-references to entries in the main text. For example: **noiseless**: *silent*. The reader can look up the word **silent** in the main vocabulary, where **noiseless** appears among a more extensive list of synonyms. This device, according to the editor, "eliminate[s] space-consuming duplication of word-groups under separate entries for each component of a group. A maximum amount of space is therefore devoted to non-recurring items, and unavoidable duplications are minimized." Despite this explanation, the system appears cumbersome, and students, again, could be confused by it.

III. Quality and Currency of Entries

The book contains a large and relatively complicated primary word list, and its synonyms are varied and often voluminous. However, the discrimination of meanings is nearly 40 years out of date. For example, under **entertainer**, the synonyms are

> **hospitator** (*R*) **harborer** (*A*) **host, hostess**

with no mention of *actor, singer, dancer, raconteur*, or *comedian*.

In addition, many entries are either insufficiently broad for today's reader or idiosyncratic. For example, Allen and Motter provide ominous warnings about the noun **enthusiast** in their comments following that noun's synonyms:

> fanatic (*although an enthusiast is often carried beyond reason*, a fanatic *is most extreme, esp. in religion*), bigot (*one filled not only with enthusiasm, esp. in the realm of religion, but obstinately inaccessible to other views*),

zealot (*a fanatical partisan*); booster (*C* [colloquial] *U.S.*), fan (*S* [slang], *U.S.*).

Although the discriminations are well done, the main entry word no longer has the general connotation implied. In contrast with this entry, THE DOUBLEDAY ROGET'S THESAURUS IN DICTIONARY FORM simply lists with no discrimination of meanings the following synonyms:

> fan, afficionado, devotee, supporter, buff, booster, faddist, fanatic, follower, disciple, amateur, freak (slang), nut (slang).

This list would be easier for students to use with the aid of a dictionary.

IV. Accessibility

The double columns, the boldface guide words in the top margins, and the boldface main entry words overhanging the text are helpful to the reader. Finding main entries in this alphabetical thesaurus is a straightforward procedure. However, because so many cross-references are used both after the main entry words and at the foot of the page, the user must search back and forth many times. Furthermore, the complicated instructions in the prefatory pages must be read and followed before the contents of the book can be fully explored and appreciated. As the editor states in the preface, "One cannot push a button and produce the desired word."

Because this work includes many rare, archaic, and obsolete words, a contemporary high school student will find *Allen's Synonyms and Antonyms* hopelessly out of date. Most students will require instruction and assistance to exploit the information contained in it, and adults, without having a special literary research project in mind, will probably end up exasperated.

V. Summary

Allen's Synonyms and Antonyms has historical interest and would be a useful adjunct to serious language and literary study, but it is no longer useful as a current source of synonyms. The maze-like arrangement of the book and its numerous cross-references will discourage most readers. High school students will need a dictionary of synonyms and antonyms or a more recent thesaurus—one such as *Webster's Collegiate Thesaurus* is current and also relevant for readers and writers today.

The Basic Book of Synonyms and Antonyms

Facts at a Glance

Full Title: **The Basic Book of Synonyms and Antonyms**.
Publisher: New American Library.
Editor: Laurence Urdang.
Edition Reviewed: © 1985; January 1986 printing.

Number of Volumes: 1.
Number of Entries: 4,000.
Number of Pages: 413.
Trim Size: 4¼″ × 7″.
Binding: paperback.

Price: $3.95.
Intended Readership: Middle school and up.
Sold in bookstores and other outlets; also sold to libraries and schools. ISBN 0-451-14064-8.

I. Introduction and Scope

Brief, concise, and easy to use, *The Basic Book of Synonyms and Antonyms* has about 4,000 entry words each with at least one example sentence. According to the preface, "it is intended as a guide to commonly used words in English, and those are almost always the most expressive," as opposed to rare, complicated, or archaic synonyms. This new revised edition expands the 1978 edition by 20 percent and updates the previous entries where relevant.

Laurence Urdang is well known in the field of language and lexicography. He is the editor of VER-BATIM, THE LANGUAGE QUARTERLY, and has written many highly acclaimed reference books including THE FACTS ON FILE DICTIONARY OF NUMERICAL ALLUSIONS (1986) and *-Ologies & -Isms* (1986), reviewed in *General Reference Books for Adults*, the companion to this Buying Guide. His works are known for concision and clarity, and this work is no exception. It continues with the same format and same concept as the earlier edition, but is here expanded to 4,000 words. Urdang's introductory remarks contain three important pieces of information about using the volume. He first states that there are no true synonyms—"there are words that can be substituted for other words, but they almost never have exactly the same meaning in the same context." Urdang then explains the differences between denotation and connotation; the fact that language functions at formal and informal levels; and the need to select the synonym with the right sense for the context. For example, **discharge** has several common meanings: "*vb.*

1. relieve, unload, unburden . . . **2.** fire, shoot . . . **3.** let go, dismiss. . . . " Example sentences, therefore, help the reader determine the sense of the context and use the word more effectively.

II. Format

This small, compact volume uses easy-to-read type in a conveniently readable format. The paper is adequate, with little show-through. However, the nature of the glued binding makes the rapid separation of pages from the binding, under repeated use, seem almost inevitable—a distinct drawback. Entry words are set in bold type, overhanging the text. The part of speech (*n.*, *adj.*, *vb.*) is abbreviated in italics, followed by the synonyms in lightface, an example sentence in italics, and, where appropriate, antonyms (indicated by **ant.**).

Clusters of common synonyms for·a main entry word are followed by an illustrative sentence; when different *senses* of a main entry word have synonym lists, these are numbered in boldface:

> **illustration** *n.* **1.** picture, photograph: *This book contains hundreds of illustrations.* **2.** example, explanation: *At least one illustration has been provided for each entry in this dictionary.*

Within a numbered group of synonyms, words belonging to the group that have slightly different characteristics, "as to the level of usage, appropriateness, or the grammatical or syntactic contexts in which they are found," are separated by a semi-colon. For example:

> **disciple** *n.* follower, supporter; student; pupil.
> **inn** *n.* hotel, lodge; motel.

There is a guide word in capital letters at the top of each page—the verso prints the first word on the page, the recto the last—which allows the reader to see the opening and closing entries on a double-page spread. Pages are numbered at the top inner margin.

III. Quality and Currency of Entries

Slang words are not included, nor are some words in current vogue such as *preppy* or *yuppie*, but these are not an important omission for a work that emphasizes *basic* vocabulary. More importantly, many words in common current use, for instance, *compute* and *program* in their computer technology context, are absent from this book. Newly added words in this revised edition include many that are variations of words used previously. For example: in the 1978 edition the words **accident, adore, advertisement, aim** and **ill** were included. This revised edition includes, in addition, **accidental, adoration, advertise, aimless, ill-advised, ill-at-ease, ill-natured,** and **ill-treated.** Totally new words included are: **abound, all-out, dote, forestall, foretell, mandatory, nebulous, prerequisite, revel in, snappy, surly, torrid, yellow** (cowardly), **zenith, zip,** and so forth. The additions make this the preferable edition to own and help to round out the vocabulary that is useful, according to the editor, "in simple, straightforward writing."

IV. Accessibility

The material in this thesaurus is easy to access because the boldface entry words and the substantially indented entries make skimming the pages easy. Thumb indexing is absent as is usual in paperbacks. The complete entry is also easy to read with elements so clearly indicated: bold type is used for numbering the different meanings and for identifying the antonyms and example sentences in italics. The antonyms correspond to the common meaning groups. If there is no antonym for the first set of words, but there is for the second set, the first set of antonyms is marked "**2.**" to correspond to the proper set of synonyms:

> **launch** *vb.* **1.** fire, drive, propel: *The rocket was launched to the moon at dawn.* **2.** initiate, originate, start, begin: *The senator launched his campaign for president early in February.* **ant. 2.** stop, finish, terminate.

Although the main entry word appears in an inflected form (**launched**) here, that is not usual in the illustrative sentences.

V. Summary

The Basic Book of Synonyms and Antonyms will be useful in homes and in schools. It is a handy desk reference that can be used by readers from fourth grade and up. While it lacks the complexity and number of words found in many large thesauruses, its very simplicity makes it a good source for quick reference. Although the book lacks many contemporary words and usages, its concentration on the words that are *common* in the English language as well as its example sentences placing the words in context are of particular value to middle school and older students.

A Concise Dictionary of Correct English

Facts at a Glance
Full Title: **A Concise Dictionary of Correct English.**
Publisher: Littlefield, Adams & Company (Quality Paperback Series, No. 349).
Editor: B. A. Phythian.
Edition Reviewed: © 1979.

Number of Volumes: 1.
Number of Entries: approximately 940.
Number of Pages: 166.
Trim Size: 5½″ × 8⁷⁄₁₆″.
Binding: paperback.

Price: $1.50.
Intended Readership: high school and up.
Sold in bookstores and to libraries and schools.
ISBN 0-822-60349-7.

I. Introduction and Scope

According to its preface, this 1979 reference work "is intended for those who would like to brush up their English grammar and be guided round some of the more common pitfalls in the use of English." Entries guide the user in grammatical correctness and stylistic conciseness and clarity. Many entries "require the reader to have a working knowledge of the principal parts of speech," and users lacking this knowledge are encouraged to study the work's entries under individual part-of-speech labels before looking at other entries.

The work's British editor, B. A. Phythian, has also edited A CONCISE DICTIONARY OF ENGLISH SLANG AND COLLOQUIALISMS and A CONCISE DICTIONARY OF ENGLISH IDIOMS. In the preface to *A Concise Dictionary of Correct English*, he acknowledges his indebtedness to other works on English usage, including Eric Partridge's USAGE AND ABUSAGE, Fowler's MODERN ENGLISH USAGE, and Gowers's COMPLETE PLAIN WORDS. Phythian's work is admirably up-to-date in its understanding of the constantly shifting nature of English usage. However, its focus is on British usage, and minimal attention is given to "Americanisms." The work is, therefore, of little real value to American students.

II. Format

Entries are arranged alphabetically. Boldfaced main entry words overhang the text. When any form of the entry word or phrase recurs within the entry, it is italicized. Also italicized are phrases containing the entry word, incorrect alternatives to the entry word, and words or phrases presented as correct alternatives for misused main entries. Words used within entries that have their own main entries appear in boldface, and cross-references, beginning with "See," are usefully provided in some cases. For some entries, illustrative sentences are provided. These are printed in roman type and indented from the left margin. A representative entry is the following:

> **degree**. The common phrase *to a less degree* should be used when two things are being referred to, because *less* is the comparative form (see **adjective 1, 3**):
>> Male cosmetics are widely used in America, and to a less degree in England.
>
> *Lesser* means *less than less*, and *to a lesser degree* should not be used unless this is the intended sense. See **less, lesser**.
>> The expression *to a more or less degree* is bad English because, though *a less degree* makes sense, *a more degree* does not.

Print is clear and adequate in size, with minimal show-through. White space is used advantageously to make pages easy to read. The volume does not open flat, but the pages do not separate easily from the binding of this sturdy paperback.

III. Quality and Currency of Entries

This usage guide provides solutions to many problems that writers encounter. For example, users are shown the distinction between **e.g.** and **i.e.**, **counsel** and **council**, **infer** and **imply**, **militate** and **mitigate**. Users are taught how to form the plurals of such words as **hero**, **crisis**, and **criterion**; how to apply rules of grammar and syntax; how to distinguish **active** from **passive** voice; and how to recognize a **cliché**, a **euphemism**, and figurative language such as the **simile**, the **metaphor**, and **onomatopoeia**.

The work is not intended for the novice in English grammar and usage. Although illustrative examples are often provided, some entries exclude or underemphasize concrete examples. For instance, after a brief definition of **mixed metaphor** ("a ludicrous mixture" of metaphors), the user is merely warned:

> Do not fall into the sort of error committed by the local politician who wrote to tell *The Times* that, at a recent event which had ended in a riot, the police had leaned over backwards to maintain a low profile!

It is left for the reader to identify and analyze the mixed metaphor. Another entry appears as follows:

> **officious** (meddlesome, over-zealous, interfering) should not be confused with **official** (properly authorised).

Without illustrative sentences, the entry may not provide sufficient distinguishing information to the user.

Most importantly, the American user should be aware that what the entries present is British usage. American users, particularly students, will be confused and misled by many of the entries. British spelling is retained. For example, under **gram**, **gramme** the user is told that "either spelling is acceptable"; under **humour**, **humourous**, only the British spellings are provided. The British slant also appears, for example, in the entry for **pound**, which stresses the term's application in British currency, and in the following entry:

> **Mr** and **Mrs** do not need full stops after them.

Not only does this provide the American user with incorrect usage information, it also uses the unfamiliar "full stop" for "period."

"Americanisms" receive minimal treatment in the work. For example, under **raise** the user is told

> An increase in wages is a *rise*. The use of *raise* in this sense is an Americanism.

Another entry begins:

> **stop off**, **stop over** are Americanisms which have established themselves firmly. *Stop off* means no more than *stop*, and the redundant *off* should be avoided. *Stop over* is slightly more useful, but if *over* means *overnight*, as it usually does, why not say so?

The most obvious strength of this 1979 work rests in its reflection of current trends in usage. The tendency toward dropping the hyphen when "words are taken into common usage (coeducation, hypermarket, cooperation)" is noted. Under **verb** the user is told that it is permissable to split an infinitive for the sake of fluency or clarity of expression.

IV. Accessibility

Information is easily located in this alphabetized and cross-referenced work. Boldfaced guide words at the top of each spread indicate the first and last entries on the spread.

V. Summary

A Concise Dictionary of Correct English is an informative, clearly written, and easily used guide to usage. However, the work's British slant seriously limits its usefulness for American users in general, and especially for students who may be struggling to ground themselves in American usage.

Dictionary of Problem Words and Expressions

Facts at a Glance

Full Title: **Dictionary of Problem Words and Expressions**.
Publisher: Washington Square Press.
Author: Harry Shaw.
Edition Reviewed: © 1975; September 1985 printing.

Number of Volumes: 1.
Number of Entries: over 1,500.
Number of Pages: 369.
Trim Size: 4⅛″ × 6¾″.
Binding: paperback.

Price: $4.95.
Intended Readership: students, writers, and general readers.
Sold in bookstores. ISBN 0-671-54558-2.

I. Introduction and Scope

Harry Shaw, editor, teacher, and writer, has published extensively on English composition and literature; his books include *Concise Dictionary of Literary Terms*, *Errors in English*, and *The Joy of Words*. His *Dictionary of Problem Words and Expressions* is designed to "alert you to faulty speech and writing habits you may have acquired and to confirm and strengthen you in good ones." The volume "singles out, defines, explains, and illustrates some 1,500 of the more common mistakes in word use made by speakers and writers of our language." Dissociating himself from "outmoded notions about 'grammar' and 'correctness,' " Shaw focuses on the effectiveness and appropriateness of diction that is "in *national*, *present* and *reputable* use." The intended audience includes students and business writers, as well as the general public.

In addition to the alphabetical listing of problem words and phrases, the volume contains a prefatory article offering sections titled "Wordiness," "Trite-

ness," "Troublesome Verbs," "Idiomatic Usage," "Euphemisms," and "Slang." Discussions are amplified by illustrative lists of wordy phrases (such as **at the present time** and **in this day and age**) and linguistically economical alternatives (**now, today**); trite expressions (**add insult to injury** and **in the long run**); principle parts of 150 troublesome verbs; idiomatic usages (especially helpful to non-native English speakers); euphemisms (**previously owned car**); and slang (**teenybopper** and **wacky**). Also included is a discussion, "You and the Way You Talk and Write," highlighting the so-called four commandments of effective communication: "Be concise. . . . Be original. . . . Be specific. . . . Vary the approach."

II. Format

Within the prefatory section, topics are indicated in large bold type. Illustrative lists appear in double- or triple-column format. Within the alphabetical listing, main entry words and phrases are boldfaced and overhang the text. When these words and phrases recur within the entry, they are italicized. Also italicized are synonyms and related words and solecisms (as in the indication that *more better* is unacceptable). Cross-references are introduced by *See* or *See also* with the word reference printed in small capitals.

Clear typefaces and ample white space make the work easy to read. Text shows through the pages but does not impede readability. The pages do not separate easily from the binding of this acceptably sturdy paperback.

III. Quality and Currency of Entries

Entries are particularly strong in their clear distinctions between commonly confused words and phrases. For example, the user seeking the correct use of "that" and "which" will find the triad **that, which, who** in proper alphabetical order with a clear discussion of usage. The discussion's definition of *restrictive clauses* ("those that define and limit what precedes by providing information necessary to full understanding") is noteworthily clear. Under **which**, a cross-reference directs the user to the entry for **that**.

Entries are also enhanced by the inclusion of illustrative sentences. For example, **complement** and **compliment** are distinguished in the following entry:

Complement implies something which completes: "This jewelry will *complement* your dress." A *compliment* is flattery or praise: Beulah enjoyed the *compliment* paid to her."

Similarly, **imply** and **infer** are clearly distinguished and illustrated:

> To *imply* is to suggest a meaning only hinted at, not explicitly stated. To *infer* is to draw a conclusion from statements, evidence, or circumstances. "Your remark *implies* that Bill was untruthful." "The officer *inferred* from the fingerprints that the killer was left-handed."

Entries are in some cases also enhanced with etymological information. In the case of **résumé, synopsis, summary**, for example, etymology usefully clarifies distinctions.

The work is up-to-date in its appropriate inclusion of colloquialisms in current English usage. For example, the list includes **being as, being as how, being that**:

> Each of these phrases borders on illiteracy; all are vague, wordy, and illogical. Say "*Because* (not *being as*, *being as how*, or *being that*) I am already here, I'll help."

In addition to providing alternatives for unacceptable usages, the work also discusses the use of acceptable colloquialisms, such as **un-huh, huh-uh**, and **O.K.**

However, the work's 1975 date inevitably results in some omissions. Excluded, for example, from the list of slang terms are *nerd*, *punk*, and *yuppie*, while outmoded terms such as **beatnik, hepcat**, and **she-bang** do appear. Current euphemisms—such as *funeral director*, *hearing impaired*, and *visually handicapped*—are also omitted. More substantively, the work does not reflect current emphasis on avoiding sexist language. For example, under **everybody, everyone**, the reader is told:

> Both pronouns, when used as subjects, require singular verbs; accompanying pronouns should also be singular: "everyone *has* (not *have*) an obligation to cast *his* (not *their*) vote."

In contrast, current works, advising against the use of *he*, *his*, and *him* as indefinite personal pronouns, help their users to avoid offense to portions of their audiences.

IV. Accessibility

The work begins with a contents listing detailing the subsections of the prefatory article and ensuring they will not be overlooked. Illustrative lists within this part of the work are alphabetized for easy access. Within the main body of the text, entries are also alphabetized; cross-references clearly direct the user to alternative forms.

In the prefatory article, boldfaced underlined running heads on each page repeat the topic titles. Guide words, also boldfaced and underlined, appear at the top of each page within the main text; these indicate the first and last terms entered on each double-page spread.

V. Summary

The *Dictionary of Problem Words and Expressions* is intelligent and engaging, as well as being an informative, clear, well-organized reference wordbook. It admirably fulfills its intention to address usage and problems in current spoken English; however, it excludes some more recent terms and trends in usage, such as avoiding sexist pronouns. Despite these omissions, the book's clarity and relative comprehensiveness—given its compact size and reasonable price—earn it commendation. Students from tenth grade and up will find this a useful and usable source. The work should prove a valuable addition to the classroom collection, as well as to the circulating paperback collection of the school or public library.

A Dictionary of Synonyms and Antonyms

Facts at a Glance

Full Title: **A Dictionary of Synonyms and Antonyms**.
Publisher: Warner Books.
Compiler: Joseph Devlin.
Editor: Jerome Fried.
Edition Reviewed: © 1961; 1982 printing.

Number of Volumes: 1.
Number of Words: over 3,000.
Number of Pages: 384.
Trim Size: 4¼" × 7".
Binding: paper.

Price: $2.95.
Intended Readership: grade 6 and up.
Sold in bookstores and other outlets; also sold to libraries and schools. ISBN 0-446-31310-6.

I. Introduction and Scope

A Dictionary of Synonyms and Antonyms with 5000 Words Most Often Mispronounced is intended to help readers in "finding the exact words they need to express their written and spoken thoughts, with a minimum expenditure of time and effort, and a maximum reward in efficiency and accuracy." The work lists over 3,000 frequently used English words along with many of their synonyms and antonyms. The volume also includes an article entitled "Word Formation," which briefly introduces etymology and lists and defines the main Latin, Greek, and Old English roots and derivatives, as well as Latin and Greek prefixes and suffixes. Appended at the back of the volume is a listing of 5,000 words that Americans frequently mispronounce. The volume's intended audience is students from the upper elementary level to college, as well as adults.

First published in 1938, the work was most recently revised in 1961. The potential buyer should be aware that the publisher's claim on the back cover that the word listings are "the most up-to-date . . . available" is no longer valid. Compiler Joseph Devlin is the author of HOW TO SPEAK AND WRITE CORRECTLY and DEVELOPMENT OF THE ENGLISH LANGUAGE. Editor Jerome Fried compiled THE BANTAM CROSSWORD DICTIONARY and coedited FUNK & WAGNALL'S STANDARD DICTIONARY OF FOLKLORE, MYTHOLOGY, AND LEGENDS.

II. Format

Entries are arranged alphabetically. Boldfaced main entry words overhang the text on double-column pages. The abbreviations *Syn.* and *Ant.* introduce listings of synonyms and antonyms. The following is a representative entry:

> **draw**—*Syn.* pull, haul, drag, attract, inhale, sketch, describe, move, bring, convey, lure, tow, tug, allure, induce, entice, trail. *Ant.* repel, repulse, alienate, estrange, rebuff, reject, leave, abandon.

The print size is adequate for adult readers, although younger users and non-native English speakers may find it too small. The book's good-quality, newsprint paper permits little show-through and the physical design allows generous margins for the text. Like most paperbacks, its spine must be cracked in order for the page to be fully and clearly visible. Pages may, therefore, begin to separate from the binding under heavy classroom or library use.

III. Quality and Currency of Entries

Nouns, verbs, and adjectives appear as main entries. Entries list from one to fifty synonyms and, for most entries, antonyms. Ordering within the listings appears to have no rationale. No definitions or illustrative examples are provided to differentiate among the listings, but the compiler's prefatory comments urge the user to consult a dictionary before using unfamiliar words gleaned from the listings. Parenthetical italicized usage labels helpfully identify slang, colloquialisms, and British and Australian terms.

Italicized part-of-speech labels follow main entry words in some cases, but not in others, with no apparent pattern. Coverage is uneven in other ways as well. For example, the entry term **beauty** is followed by eleven synonyms and no antonyms, while **ugly** commands 35 synonyms and 43 antonyms, among them **beauty**. These inconsistencies are likely to prove confusing and misleading to students.

The inclusion of slang and colloquialisms in the listings lends some currency to the work, although many of the words and phrases labeled *slang* are outdated clichés, such as "hit the hay" under **sleep** and "play the ponies" under **venture**. The volume lacks more than twenty-five years' worth of new idioms and terms, including the languages of astronautics and computer science.

IV. Accessibility

Two guide words in boldfaced capitals appear on each page, indicating the first and last entries on the page. No key to abbreviations is provided; however, since only a few easily deciphered abbreviations are used to identify parts of speech and restricted usage, this is not a serious drawback. No table of contents is provided to alert the user to the existence of the work's special features. The absence of cross-references makes the volume less useful for students and adult users alike.

V. Summary

A Dictionary of Synonyms and Antonyms is not recommended as a first choice for home, school, or library use. For adults with a reasonably large vocabulary, it often meets its aim of offering a useful—and quickly used—basis for appropriate word choice. A major drawback of the work, however, is its lack of new words and idioms that have entered the language in the past 25 years. For younger readers and non-native English speakers, the print may be too small, and these users will also lack the vocabulary to discriminate effectively among the synonyms and antonyms offered. An alternative for both student and adult users in need of a compact thesaurus is Laurence Urdang's THE BASIC BOOK OF SYNONYMS AND ANTONYMS, NEW REVISED EDITION. This more up-to-date reference work includes illustrative sentences that aid the user in selecting appropriate synonyms.

Funk & Wagnalls Standard Handbook of Synonyms, Antonyms, and Prepositions

Facts at a Glance

Full Title: **Funk & Wagnalls Standard Handbook of Synonyms, Antonyms, and Prepositions**.
Former Title: English Synonyms and Antonyms.
Publisher: Harper & Row (Thomas Y. Crowell).
Editor: James C. Fernald.
Edition Reviewed: © 1947; 3rd printing.

Number of Volumes: 1.
Number of Entries: approximately 1,700.
Number of Pages: 515.
Trim Size: 8½″ × 11″.
Binding: cloth.

Price: $13.95.
Intended Readership: secondary school students and up.
Sold in bookstores and other outlets; also sold to libraries and schools. ISBN 0-308-40024-9.

I. Introduction and Scope

The original version of this well-known work, prepared by Dr. James Champlain Fernald, was first published in 1896; a revised and enlarged second edition was published in 1914. The present edition was updated and enlarged by the Funk & Wagnalls editorial staff in 1947; the work has not been revised since.

No specific target audience is mentioned by the publishers, but the book appears geared to serious students, at the secondary level and above. There are approximately 1,700 main entries, and over 8,000 synonyms and 3,000 antonyms are accessible through the indexes.

Words listed as main entries include nouns, verbs, adjectives, adverbs, and prepositions. Each entry lists synonyms and provides a detailed discussion differentiating among them both denotatively and connotatively. Many entries also list antonyms; for some

the idiomatic use of prepositions with the main entry word is also described. For example, under **make**, preposition use is clarified as follows:

> Make *of*, *out of*, or *from* certain materials, *into* a certain form, *for* a certain purpose or person; made *with* hands, *by* hand; made *by* a prisoner, *with* a jackknife.

Not included among the entries are foreign words and phrases, slang, and colloquialisms.

II. Format

Within the body of the text, main entry words (termed "key-words") appear in large boldface capitals heading their entries. Part of speech is indicated only when the same word is entered as two different parts of speech; **reason**, for example is entered both as a noun and as a verb. Beneath the heading, also in boldface, appears the list of synonyms, set in three or four short columns. A discussion follows, of one or more paragraphs' length, distinguishing among the synonyms. The proper use of each synonym is explained and illustrated in phrases or sentences. After the discussion antonyms appear, for selected entries, in boldface, and clarifications of correct preposition use with the main entry word are also included.

The "Index of Synonyms" appears in triple-column format. Each index term and, for selected terms, each indented subentry, is followed by a page number indicating the location of the term under the appropriate main entry word. The columns are divided by vertical lines; dotted lines connect terms with page numbers.

Also triple-columned, the "Index of Antonyms" lists one or more pages for each entry on which the antonyms are discussed and provides occasional cross-references to the synonyms listed in the body of the text.

The hard-covered volume is sturdily bound and will withstand heavy use. Paper is of good quality with minimal show-through. Clear, adequate-sized typefaces and ample use of white space make the entries easy to read.

III. Quality and Currency of Entries

Information in the discussions is clearly presented, and careful distinctions are drawn among synonyms. The information on idiomatic preposition use, although only selectively provided, may have new currency: teachers have recently remarked a decline in the grasp of correct use of prepositions among native English speakers.

In other regards, however, the work's currency is impaired. The 1947 copyright date results in the exclusion of terms coined since World War II. Those terms that are included are themselves still current, but examples used in the discussions are in many cases out of date. For example, under **beneath** the following sentence appears, with a meaning that will strike people today as obsolete, at best:

Beneath or *below* may signify occupying a lower plane, as we speak of one marrying *below* or *beneath* his station.

Under **love**, we are told that

Love is used specifically for personal *affection* between the sexes in the highest sense, the *love* that normally leads to marriage, and subsists throughout all happy wedded life.

The discussion of **feminine** and its synonyms is similarly inappropriate for a contemporary audience:

We apply *female* to the sex, *feminine* to the qualities, especially the finer physical or mental qualities that distinguish the *female* sex in the human family, or to the objects appropriate for or especially employed by them. . . . *Womanish* denotes the undesirable; *womanly*, the admirable or lovely qualities of woman. *Womanly* tears would suggest respect and sympathy, *womanish* tears a touch of contempt. . . . *Womanlike* suggests *feminine* frailties or faults of character; *ladylike*, the characteristics of a lady.

IV. Accessibility

The volume combines the convenience of an alphabetical listing for its contents with copious indexing, like that of a conventional thesaurus. A "Special Note: Use the Index" clarifies the use of the index. Within the main text as well as within the indexes, two guide words are provided, in boldface, at the top margins of each double-page spread. These indicate the first and last entries on the spread. Page numbers, however, are located so close to the spine in the inner margins that the volume must be fully opened for them to be seen. The binding is sturdy enough to withstand the book's being opened thus, but the placement of page numbers interferes with the user's speed in locating a page referred to in the index.

V. Summary

The *Funk & Wagnalls Standard Handbook of Synonyms, Antonyms, and Prepositions* provides clear, careful distinctions among synonyms and valuable information on idiomatic preposition use; its information is easily located within the alphabetical listing with the aid of comprehensive indexes. However, the work is out-of-date in its exclusion of post-World War II coinages and in many of the examples used in its discussions. For the reference needs of today's students, a better choice would be the more comprehensive (250,000 synonyms and antonyms) and up-to-date DOUBLEDAY ROGET'S THESAURUS IN DICTIONARY FORM.

Joan Hanson Word Books

Facts at a Glance

Full Title: **Antonyms, Still More Antonyms, More Homonyms, Still More Homonyms, Homographs, British-American Synonyms, More Synonyms, Similes, More Similes, More Sound Words, Possessives.**
Publisher: Lerner Publications.
Author-illustrator: Joan Hanson.
Editions Reviewed: © 1972, 1973, 1976, 1979.

Number of Volumes: 11.
Number of Pages: 32 per volume.
Number of Illustrations: each title illustrated in two or three colors.
Trim Size: 7¼" × 7¼".
Binding: laminated paper over boards.

Price: $4.95 each.
Intended Readership: preschool through third grade.
Sold in bookstores, also sold to libraries and schools. ISBNs 0-8225-0276-3, 0-8225-1106-1, 0-8225-0287-9, 0-8225-1107-X, 0-8225-0278-X, 0-8225-0279-8, 0-8225-0289-5, 0-8225-1108-8, 0-8225-1112-6, 0-8225-1113-4, 0-8225-1115-0.

I. Scope and Format

The Joan Hanson Word Books series contains 11 titles intended for early readers that use illustrations to introduce children to a range of linguistic information. Volumes on antonyms, homonyms, homographs, synonyms, and other special kinds of words will amuse and intrigue children while preparing them to encounter these categories in conventional dic-

Joan Hanson Word Books

Sarah is as graceful as a swan.

❶ Amusing line drawings provide literal interpretation of a simile and illustrate the two-fold comparison

❷ A simple sentence introduces children to the use of similes

❸ Personal names are used in each sentence

tionaries. Introducing figurative language and such grammatical concerns as possessives, the series also encourages children to become more appreciative readers and more effective writers.

Each volume begins with one unillustrated page presenting a brief, clear definition of the volume's topic. For example, *Antonyms* begins with

an·to·nym [printed in red] (AN-tuh-nim) A word that means the opposite of another word. The antonym of *hard* is *soft*. *Tall* is the antonym of *short*.

Providing pronunciation, definition, and illustrative examples, these topic introductions are accessible to fairly young children although significantly more advanced than the books themselves. The passages do not shy away from necessary specialized language: for example, the text beginning *More Sound Words* incorporates the terms **echoic** and **onomatopoeia**. Although the youngest readers of the series will require an adult's assistance to make sense of these beginning texts, older children will understand them; the definitions, in a dictionary-like format, will also prepare older children for more advanced reference works.

The remainder of each volume consists of 26 illustrated pages, each containing a single word or phrase. In most cases, the two pages of each double spread are interrelated. In the case of antonyms, homonyms, homographs, and synonyms, this is the logical arrangement, but even in *Similes* the interrelationship is amusingly preserved in such a pairing as

Mary is always as hungry as a bear.
But Sam eats like a bird.

The books' paper is heavy and of good quality; they are sturdily bound and will withstand multiple use even by young children.

II. Authority

Joan Hanson, the series' creator, has written and illustrated over 50 books for children. The publisher, Lerner Publications Company, specializes in children's books, including educational works in the areas of geography, health science, and zoology.

III. Quality and Currency of Entries

Words selected for illustration are within the scope and interest of young readers, and will not date. *Antonyms*, for example, includes such simple pairs

as **up** and **down** and **hot** and **cold**; it also includes more challenging pairs, such as **create** and **destroy**. *Homographs* contains no pronunciation information for individual words, and some of its pairings may be beyond the grasp of many young readers. For example, **sow** is illustrated with a pig on one page and with a child sowing seeds on the other. **Refuse** shows a child refusing, with a shake of the head, a proffered spoonful of medicine; the companion page shows a child seated on a pile of garbage. This volume is more likely than the others to require adult explanation.

Similes and *More Similes* are fully accessible to young readers. They may particularly enjoy the use of personal names in *Similes* and seek out their own names and those of friends and relatives. A child encountering such phrases as "**waddle like a duck**" and "**flat as a pancake**" for the first time will also appreciate their connotative power in a way adults no longer can. (However, it would be helpful if the volume—or an adult working with the child reader—introduced the idea that overuse of these similes results in clichés.)

Some volumes in the series have more specialized applications than those on synonyms and antonyms. For example, *British-American Synonyms* is ideal for an American family traveling or working in Great Britain, for a classroom social studies or geography lesson, or a school hosting visiting British children. *More Sound Words*, as well as the simile books, could be used in introducing children to the reading and writing of poetry. *Possessives* provides the repetition children need to grasp the use of the apostrophe, while the illustrations make the repetition more palatable than it would otherwise be.

IV. Illustrations

Joan Hanson's drawings are fanciful and amusing, while they also function effectively in clarifying the range of usages the series covers. In *More Homonyms*, for example, a smiling child carries a wooden **board** on the left-hand page; on the right, the same child, now **bored**, twiddles her thumbs and wears an expression of excruciating ennui as a rabbit reads to her, ". . . and on and on and on." No minorities per se appear in the illustrations. The bored child and the other children depicted are more stylized than real, but they transcend the usual stereotypes.

Suggestions of motion enliven many of the drawings, while making them more communicative. For example, in *More Sound Words*, the onomatopoeia **Rat-a-tat-tat** is illustrated by a bird, with wings flapping, hovering over a drum that he is banging on with drumsticks held in his feet. On the facing page, illustrating **Clickety-clack**, another bird in stylish sunglasses rides a speeding skateboard. In many cases, the black line drawings are enhanced with touches of color. Only one additional color is used in each volume, with the exception of *British-American Synonyms*, where red and blue serve to distinguish the British (with Union Jacks) from the Americans (with Stars and Stripes).

V. Summary

The Joan Hanson Word Books are a pleasing and informative introduction to linguistic information for children. Although these small volumes are not and do not purport to be dictionaries, they will interest children in a range of the information they will encounter in children's—and more advanced—dictionaries. Useful in the home, particularly with parental involvement, the series is also a valuable adjunct to a library's word book collection. In the classroom, where the series can be put to specialized uses in reading, writing, and general language arts instruction, it will also be a very welcome resource.

The Merriam-Webster Pocket Dictionary of Synonyms

Facts at a Glance

Full Title: **The Merriam-Webster Pocket Dictionary of Synonyms.**
Publisher: Pocket Books.
Edition Reviewed: © 1972.

Number of Volumes: 1.
Number of Pages: 441.
Trim Size: 4¼" × 6¾".
Binding: paperback.

Price: $3.95.
Intended Readership: high school and up.
Sold in bookstores and other outlets; also sold to libraries and schools. ISBN 0-671-50445-2.

I. Introduction and Scope

According to its preface, the purpose of the compact paperback *The Merriam-Webster Pocket Dictionary of Synonyms* is "not to provide mere word-finding lists for consultants with a vague notion of the sort of work they seek." Rather, the work is intended to help readers make clear distinctions among words of similar denotation. In addition to the alphabetically arranged main entry paragraphs, this dictionary also includes numerous cross-reference entries. Antonyms are listed when these exist. The work is based on *Webster's New Dictionary of Synonyms*, originally published in 1968. This paperback edition shows no indication of updating since its 1972 publication date.

II. Format

Entries appear in two forms: the discriminating article and the cross-reference entry. Each article begins with a boldface main entry word and a boldface listing of words to be discriminated. A part-of-speech abbreviation follows the main entry word only when that word is entered more than once, in different part-of-speech applications. For example, the main entry word **abandon** is identified as a verb (*vb*) and followed by the list **abandon, desert, forsake.** (A cross-reference entry for **abandon** as a noun follows.) The main entry word is usually the most central in meaning or the one most typically used. Each list is followed by a statement of the meaning shared among the synonyms. For **abandon**, this appears as:

> *shared meaning*: to give up completely.

Each word is then discussed and illustrated in the order that the synonyms appear at the opening of the entry:

> **Abandon** can suggest complete disinterest in the future of what is given up ⟨the picnickers *abandoned* their lunch to the ants⟩ ⟨no decent man *abandons* his family⟩ **Desert** implies a relationship (as of occupancy or guardianship); it can suggest desolation ⟨*deserted* farms growing up to brush⟩. . . .

Frequently quotations from well-known writers are used to illustrate a synonym's meaning:

> **Forsake** implies a breaking of a close association by repudiation or renunciation ⟨all his knights and courtiers had *forsaken* him; not one came to his help—Matthew Arnold⟩. . . .

When the first word in the synonym list has one or more antonyms, these are listed at the end of the entry, where they are introduced by the abbreviation *ant.* Antonyms for other words from the synonym list appear in the cross-reference entries for those words.

Cross-references are provided within some of the discriminating articles, for senses other than the one discriminated. Cross-references also appear as separate entries that refer the reader to the appropriate discriminating article. In both cases, the word "see" introduces the cross-reference, and the word(s) to which the reader is referred appear in small capital letters.

Although the text is printed in a single column, readability is impaired by the small size of the print and the limited use of white space. The paper is of standard quality for mass market paperbacks. Although it is thin, it permits only minimal show-through of text. The pages do not separate easily from the binding of this adequately sturdy paperback.

III. Quality and Currency of Entries

The work's discriminating articles are carefully detailed, clearly and interestingly illustrated, and useful to the reader. They provide valuable guidance in the use of many standard American English words and their synonyms and antonyms. However, the dictionary's 1972 date results in limited currency. Under **gay**, for example, the reader is referred only to **lively**; nowhere is the homosexual connotation of the word described. Neither *compute* nor *computer* is entered, and terms relating to space technology are also excluded. The dictionary excludes slang and colloquialisms, which further limits its currency.

IV. Accessibility

The entries are alphabetized letter by letter. Pairs of guide words appear at the top of each page, indicating the first and last words entered on the page. These guide words are usefully printed in type larger than that used in the entries.

V. Summary

The Merriam-Webster Pocket Dictionary of Synonyms contains careful and well-illustrated articles discriminating synonyms for many standard American English words. Its use of quotations from well-known writers provides both interest and useful clarifications of synonyms. However, prospective buyers who are exasperated by frequent cross-referencing will dislike this work's extensive reliance on the technique. The work is not sufficiently current to meet the needs of some readers, and its print is small and cramped. A preferable alternative is Laurence Urdang's more recent BASIC BOOK OF SYNONYMS AND ANTONYMS, which is clear, concise, and easy to read.

The Random House Basic Dictionary of Synonyms & Antonyms

Facts at a Glance
Full Title: **The Random House Basic Dictionary of Synonyms & Antonyms**.
Former Titles: The Random House Vest Pocket Dictionary of Synonyms and Antonyms and *The Random House Dictionary of Synonyms and Antonyms*.
Publisher: Ballantine Books.
Editor: Laurence Urdang.
Edition Reviewed: © 1960; 4th printing, 1984.

Number of Volumes: 1.
Number of Entries: approximately 4,000.
Number of Words: 80,000.
Number of Pages: 137.
Trim Size: 4¼″ × 6⅞″.
Binding: paperback.

Price: $1.50.
Intended Readership: junior high, high school, and up.
Sold in bookstores and through direct mail. ISBN 0-345-29712-1.

I. Introduction and Scope

The Random House Basic Dictionary of Synonyms & Antonyms was copyrighted in 1960 and previously published as *The Random House Vest Pocket Dictionary of Synonyms and Antonyms* and *The Random House Dictionary of Synonyms and Antonyms*. Ballantine Books began publishing the paperback edition in 1981.

Of the 80,000 synonyms and antonyms included, about 4,000 are main entry words. The book is intended by the publishers for a "general" audience, but the vocabulary is suitable for junior and senior high school students. Laurence Urdang, the editor, states that "judicious use of this book will more than treble the average person's . . . vocabulary." Although the book is no longer current, the publisher claims on the cover that it is "comprehensive" and that it offers "everything for writers, speakers, students."

The word list is composed of standard English language words, and its main entries are ample for the vast majority of American students to refer to when searching for a synonym or antonym. The editor's brief introductory remarks will help readers access the vocabulary, although it does not cover new words or acquired meanings that have emerged in the last quarter of a century.

II. Format

The 127 pages that make up this book's synonym and antonym section are printed in double columns in type so small that it is difficult for both young people and adults to consult it without the use of a magnifying glass. In addition, margins are narrow, which also detracts from the book's readability. While there is little show-through in the pages, the paper is little better than newsprint and cannot be expected to stand up to hard use. The same may be said for the poorly glued binding that allows the pages to separate from the binding with minimal use. However, the extremely low sales price would certainly allow users to replace it frequently.

Main entries are listed in alphabetical order. Each entry appears in boldface type overhanging the text. Main entry words are followed by a list of synonyns, often subgrouped by numbers, and sometimes concluded by a short list of antonyms, all in lightface type.

In the four-paragraph introduction, the editor explains that synonyms are grouped according to the sense most commonly used and numbered from most common, or "strongest," to the least common, or "weakest," usage and meaning. The editor advises looking up the few antonyms in the main entry word list to find additional possibilities. The sections preceding the main entry dictionary contain "A Word of Caution" and a key to the seven "Abbreviations Used in This Book." In the cautionary section, the user is reminded that "there is no true synonym for any word in the English language," that context must be considered, and that a good dictionary must be consulted for any word unknown to the user.

III. Quality and Currency of Entries

The selection of words, both main entries parts of speech, and their synonyms and antonyms, correlates with basic English usage in junior and senior high school textbooks and most reading assignments in the areas of the humanities. If the student reads the directions for using the book or is taught or assisted, he or she can easily exploit its possibilities with very little effort.

However, the 1960 copyright date is only too evident in the book's entries. Because its word list ap-

pears not to have been expanded since that date, the book's contemporary vocabulary is virtually nonexistent. Obviously, this is a severe liability.

IV. Accessibility

The dictionary arrangement, with boldface, lower-case guide words near the top exterior margin of each page, above one of the double columns, simplifies locating a word in this small paperback book. The abbreviations used in the text are listed in the prefatory pages only. There is no thumb index, which is not a crucial drawback in such a small book, but the absence of cross-referencing does hinder the reader's full access to the book's contents.

There are no definitions, no pronunciations, and, only rarely, examples or explanations of any kind other than the part or parts of speech identified for the main entry word—again, these omissions present serious drawbacks to accessing words in this thesaurus. For example, for the main entry **ill**, twenty-one words in four numbered sense clusters are listed for the adjective form; seventeen words in three numbered clusters for the noun form; and nine words in four numbered clusters for the adverb form. The seven *antonyms* for **ill** are an unidentified mixture of all three parts of speech; and some of them appear as main entry words in a different form from their listings as antonyms.

The final pages of the book contain three special features: "Common Signs and Symbols" (with listings for **astronomy** and **astrology**, **biology**, **business**, **mathematics**, **medicine**, **money**, and **religion**; "Foreign Alphabets" with transliterations for the Greek, Hebrew, and Russian alphabets; and "Weights and Measures," complete with metric conversion factors.) All of these tables are of some use to the student reader, although their presence in a *thesaurus* comes as something of a surprise.

V. Summary

The Random House Basic Dictionary of Synonyms & Antonyms is an inexpensive, concise, quick, and very outdated reference source. Its print, paper, and binding are all of poor quality. While the book might still have some very limited value in younger-level basic writing classes, it cannot be recommended as a good resource for school or public library circulating paperback reference collections or for personal reference. This is a once-useful book that should be revised.

Scholastic Dictionary of Synonyms, Antonyms, Homonyms

Facts at a Glance

Full Title: **Scholastic Dictionary of Synonyms, Antonyms, Homonyms**.
Former Title: Webster's Synonyms, Antonyms, Homonyms.
Publisher: Scholastic Inc.
Editor: Molly Harrington.
Edition Reviewed: © 1965.

Number of Volumes: 1.
Number of Words: 24,000.
Number of Pages: 224.
Trim Size: $4\frac{3}{16}'' \times 6\frac{3}{4}''$.
Binding: paperback.

Price: $1.95.
Intended Readership: age 9 and up.
Sold in bookstores and through other outlets; also sold to libraries and schools. ISBN 0-590-01483-8.

I. Introduction and Scope

Originally published in 1953 (and revised in 1962) under the title *Webster's Synonyms, Antonyms, Homonyms*, the *Scholastic Dictionary of Synonyms, Antonyms, Homonyms* was last copyrighted in 1965 and has not been revised since. The publisher advises teachers that its 12,000 synonyms (2,500 of which appear as main entries), 10,000 antonyms, and 2,000 homonyms will be suitable for instructional purposes. The one-and-a-half page preface of the book explains to students the book's value in helping to improve writing and speaking skills by eliminating clichés and enlivening the vocabulary. It also briefly outlines the volume's structure and its use.

The word list is limited to common English language words excluding slang, idioms, and colloquialisms—and can only be categorized as narrow. Although the words included are not out-of-date, some synonyms are unlikely candidates for modern student use and the targeted audience; for example, **oleaginous** for **fat**. The book does not, of course, include new words or changes in meaning that have entered the language in the past two decades.

II. Format

The main entry word in the "Synonyms and Antonyms" section of the book appears in boldface and is followed, first, by synonyms and, second, by antonyms that are printed in italic and enclosed in parentheses. In the 23-page Part 2, "Homonyms," each homonym is briefly defined, as follows:

> **furs**, skins of beasts. **furze**, a shrub.

Homonyms are in boldface. No tips on usage appear, and it is only after careful examination that the user finds that some homonyms are listed in the main alphabet under all entries, as are **ewe**, **you**, and **yew**, while others, such as **chute** and **shoot**, are found only under the most commonly used homonym.

The main entries in the "Synonyms and Antonyms" section are followed by two to some twenty synonyms and one to ten antonyms. Parts of speech are given only after main entries that are spelled identically but have different meanings, for example, "**lie**—*n.*" and "**lie**—*v.*" The one- or two-word definitions for homonyms are the only definitions given in this book. Although accompanying use of a good dictionary is necessary if the information in this book is to be used accurately and intelligently, a recommendation for doing this is not provided in the book's preface, as it is in many other thesauruses.

III. Quality and Currency of Entries

The common words in the synonyms and antonyms section and the homonyms list along with the lack of complexity in usage and in format combine to make this book a basic, although not up-to-date, introduction to the world of synonyms, antonyms, and homonyms for grades five through eight. Its brevity and lack of distinctions of any kind, however, will not satisfy the needs of more diligent middle school students as well as A DICTIONARY OF SYNONYMS AND ANTONYMS by Joseph Devlin would, for example.

IV. Accessibility

With no thumb indexes, the user must approximate the location of the letter of the alphabet needed and, in addition, check the boldface main entries to find the word desired, as no running heads are provided to assist a reader's search for a word. Since the pages are printed in single columns, specific location of words is not seriously impeded.

The lack of cross-referencing and of an abbreviation key compound the problems of overall accessibility and hence the usefulness of this book. Very few of the synonyms and antonyms given for the main entries are themselves listed as main entries; with no cross-references, they will probably go unnoticed by students and teachers alike. Moreover, without a key to abbreviations, younger students may experience some difficulties in proper identification. The few abbreviations that do appear, however, are commonly used and should prove no great obstacle to older students. It will be advisable for students to check a good dictionary for both definitions and pronunciations when using this brief reference source.

V. Summary

Since it gives basic information on synonyms, antonyms, and homonyms in a very simplified form, the *Scholastic Dictionary* has some minimal value as a first introduction to language arts. However, its uses are extremely limited beyond the basic introductory level. Its word list is far from impressive, the number of synonyms provided varies inconsistently, and the list of words included dates back well over two decades.

Moreover, this small volume is very poorly packaged, its paper is little better than newsprint, and its badly glued pages come away from the spine with minimal handling. While its low price makes frequent replacement feasible, a more sturdy book would surely be preferable. For these reasons, the *Scholastic Dictionary of Synonyms, Antonyms, Homonyms* cannot be recommended for school and public libraries.

PART FIVE
Large-Print Reference Books

Chapter 12 Evaluations of Large-Print Reference Books

Large-Print Dictionaries

American Heritage School Dictionary: Large Print Edition

Facts at a Glance

Full Title: **American Heritage School Dictionary: Large Print Edition**.
Publisher: Houghton Mifflin.
Editor: P. Davis.
Edition Reviewed: © 1977.

Number of Volumes: 4.
Number of Entries: 30,000.
Number of Pages: 1,076.
Trim Size: 11½″ × 13¾″.
Binding: hardcover.

Price: $418.00.
Intended Readership: visually impaired; grades 5 through 9; also useful for older students with learning disabilities.

Available from the American Printing House for the Blind. Order No. L–0285 (text), L–0261 (activities book, $40.28); Also available from Library Reproduction Service (6 volumes) for $258.00. Order No. LRS 08170.

I. Introduction and Scope

The *American Heritage School Dictionary: Large Print Edition* is similar to the AMERICAN HERITAGE STUDENT'S DICTIONARY (1986) reviewed elsewhere in the Buying Guide.

The dictionary has been photoenlarged to 18-point type (guide words and entry words) and 15-point type (definitions). An activities book to accompany the dictionary can also be purchased from the American Printing House for the Blind. This ancillary material has been prepared in a single 102-page volume and set in 15- and 18-point type. The dictionary has also been enlarged to 18- to 20-point type and is available in six volumes from Library Reproduction Services.

The vocabulary for the *American Heritage School Dictionary* has been selected from materials that students would encounter in school. The typefaces used are varied and distinct: the entry word is in sans serif bold, the definition in serif lightface type, and the illustrative sentences in italic. All are well designed to enable the visually handicapped student to distinguish each element. Extrabold centered dots indicate syllable breaks in the entry words. Pronunciation is easy to read, with the accented syllable printed in boldface and also marked with an accent. A short pronunciation key is conveniently provided on each double-page spread. Bold guidewords appear at the top of each page.

The quality and comprehensiveness of the dictionary are well suited to prepare the student to move up to a higher level dictionary, such as THE LARGE TYPE AMERICAN HERITAGE BASIC DICTIONARY.

569

Beginning Dictionary: Large Print Edition

Facts at a Glance

Full Title: **Beginning Dictionary: Large Print Edition**.
Publisher: Houghton Mifflin.
Editor: Fernando de Mello Vianna, Editorial Director.
Edition Reviewed: © 1979.

Number of Volumes: 6.
Number of Entries: approximately 10,000.
Number of Pages: 877.
Number of Illustrations: over 1,500.
Trim Size: 11½″ × 8⅞″.
Binding: hardcover.

Price: $225.00.
Intended Readership: visually impaired; grades 3 through 6.
Available from Library Reproduction Service, LRS No. 07490.

I. Introduction and Scope

The *Beginning Dictionary* was originally developed by Houghton Mifflin to complement its reading and language arts series and intended for school use. In this edition the print is enlarged to 14-point for definitions and up to 20-point for guide letters. The *Beginning Dictionary* can provide the visually impaired youngster with necessary vocabulary balanced, according to the preface, "between familiar words and unfamiliar words the student is likely to encounter in reading."

An introduction, complete with special activities, encourages student interest as it conveys important information.

Word histories are interspersed in the wide margins of the dictionary. These are set apart from the text not only by their placement, but also by their boxed, shaded background. A short pronunciation key is also printed within a boxed shaded background at the lower left corner of each double-page spread.

Double lines, one bold and one extrabold, border the top and bottom of each page and direct the eye toward the body of the text. Boldface guide words head each page.

Each bold sans serif entry word is divided into syllables by centered dots. Pronunciation follows, enclosed within vertical bars. As another feature helpful for the visually impaired, the accented syllable is printed in boldface as well as marked with an accent

mark. Multiple meanings are introduced with easy-to-read boldface numerals. Homophones are printed in bold and preceded by a bold diamond and the words *These sound alike* in italic. Illustrative sentences are printed in sans serif italic. These type variations can help visually impaired students focus on their intended objectives. However, in the illustrative sentences, the entry word itself is not set in a distinctive type face, and this is a drawback.

Generous use of white space in the margins, broken up with various illustrations and photographs, adds to the dictionary's visual appeal. Accessibility is enhanced by the rectangular thumb tabs that bleed off the top edge of each page. Within each rectangle is the letter of the alphabet with which the words on that page begin.

The version of this dictionary designed for younger readers (six- and seven-year-olds), THE AMERICAN HERITAGE FIRST DICTIONARY, is reviewed in detail elsewhere in this BuyingGuide. The *Beginning Dictionary* can serve as an excellent resource for the visually handicapped or learning disabled student ready for expanded vocabulary development.

First Dictionary: Large Print Edition

Facts at a Glance

Full Title: **First Dictionary: Large Print Edition**.
Publisher: Macmillan.
Editors: W. D. Halsey and D. Morris.
Edition Reviewed: © 1978.

Number of Volumes: 3.
Number of Entries: approximately 1,500.
Number of Pages: 276.
Number of Illustrations: approximately 500.
Trim Size: 11½″ × 13¾″.
Binding: hardcover.

Price: $109.44.
Intended Readership: visually impaired; grades 1 and 2.
Available from the American Printing House for the Blind. Order No. M–2722.

I. Introduction and Scope

This large print version of the Macmillan *First Dictionary* has been photoenlarged to 19-point type by the American Printing House for the Blind. The enlargement has been made from the 1978 edition of the FIRST DICTIONARY, one in a series of school dictionaries developed by Macmillan.

The illustrations were designed to contribute substantively to the definitions, especially of "abstract and conceptual words." In the large print edition, the photoenlarged illustrations "have been reproduced without any attempt to clarify them." Thus some visually impaired readers will have to rely heavily on the verbal definitions for understanding. However, the illustrations are all captioned with complete sentences, which will aid the students in identifying the drawings. Both the varied placement of generous-sized illustrations and the use of symbols within the text directing the student to an illustration compensate somewhat for any lack of clarity in the enlarged version of the book.

The vocabulary words are listed alphabetically without syllable division. Each entry word is printed in extrabold type, with the definition and an illustrative sentence printed directly underneath. The entry word appears in boldface within the illustrative sentence and the definition (also a complete sentence).

Bold guide words appear at the top of each page. Wide outer margins guide the eye to the entry word. (For a review of the 1987 edition of the FIRST DICTIONARY and the identical MACMILLAN VERY FIRST DICTIONARY, see above in this Buying Guide.)

Holt School Dictionary of American English: Large Print Edition

Facts at a Glance

Full Title: **Holt School Dictionary of American English: Large Print Edition**.
Publisher: Holt, Rinehart and Winston.
Edition Reviewed: © 1981.

Number of Volumes: 5.
Number of Entries: 40,000.
Number of Pages: 1,156.
Number of Illustrations: approximately 1,450.
Trim Size: 11½″ × 13¾″.
Binding: hardcover.

Price: $450.70.
Intended Readership: visually impaired; ages 9 and up.
Available from the American Printing House for the Blind. Order No. L-3671.

I. Introduction and Scope

This large print edition of the *Holt School Dictionary of American English*, photoenlarged from the 1981 edition of that dictionary, is one of the more current dictionaries available in large type for upper elementary and middle school students. It has been reproduced in 12- to 19-point type and published in five volumes.

Many of the special features of the dictionary, including maps, charts, and tables, make it a useful reference source and teaching tool, as well as a dictionary, for visually impaired students. Interesting features such as charts of Indian cultures and tribes and of human body systems and a glossary of "Persons and Places in Mythology and Folklore" add to the dictionary's usefulness and appeal.

Definitions are clearly stated, and multiple meanings are indicated by boldface numerals. Idioms and word phrases are listed in boldface under the appropriate main entry word. A useful and convenient short pronunciation key is printed at the bottom of all right-hand pages. Further details are given in the review of the HOLT SCHOOL DICTIONARY OF AMERICAN ENGLISH elsewhere in this Buying Guide.

The Large Print Version of The Little Oxford Dictionary of Current English

Facts at a Glance

Full Title: **The Large Print Version of The Little Oxford Dictionary of Current English**.
Publisher: Oxford University Press (distributed by Ulverscroft).
Edition Reviewed: © 1969, fourth edition.

Number of Volumes: 1.
Number of Entries: approximately 25,000.
Trim Size: 5½″ × 8¾″.
Binding: hardcover.

Price: $18.95; $22.00.
Intended Readership: visually impaired; high school and up. Available from Ulverscroft Large Print Books.

I. Introduction and Scope

This version of *The Little Oxford Dictionary of Current English* is reprinted from the fourth edition (1969) of the dictionary. This edition, first compiled by

The Large Type American Heritage Basic Dictionary

❶ Easy-to-read extra bold print for each entry word

❷ Bold center rule divides the two-column text

❸ Homographs are indicated by superior number

❹ Inflected forms follow pronunciation and part-of-speech abbreviation

❺ Variant forms in boldface type are divided into syllables and followed by an abbreviated part-of-speech label

❻ Alternate pronunciations are supplied

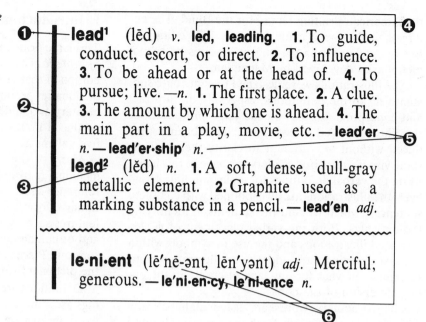

George Ostler and edited by Jessie Coulson, has been photographically enlarged to 16- and 18-point type.

This dictionary is a British publication, published by Oxford University Press, and available from a British large-print supplier, from whom further details can be obtained. Thus the spelling, pronunciation guides, use of words, and specialized meanings reflect their British origins. It can serve, however, as a concise reference source for those requiring basic definitions.

Multiple meanings are preceded by clear boldface numbers. Compound words, run-in entries, and guide words at the top of each page are also printed in boldface type. These are helpful features for the visually impaired.

Despite the dictionary's relatively small size and narrow margins, the strong, clear typeface gives the pages the visual clarity necessary for the large-print user. (See the review above, in the buying guide, of a more recent edition THE LITTLE OXFORD DICTIONARY OF CURRENT ENGLISH for more details.)

The Large Type American Heritage Basic Dictionary

Facts at a Glance

Full Title: **The Large Type American Heritage Basic Dictionary**.
Publisher: Houghton Mifflin.

Editors: Fernando de Mello Vianna, Editor-in-Chief; Anne D. Steinhardt and Pamela DeVinne.
Edition Reviewed: © 1981.

Number of Volumes: 1.
Number of Definitions: over 35,000.
Number of Pages: 312.
Trim Size: 8½″ × 10¹⁵⁄₁₆″.
Binding: paperback.

Price: $7.95.
Intended Readership: all ages. Approved by the National Association of Visually Handicapped for use by the partially seeing.
Sold in bookstores; also sold to libraries and schools. ISBN 0-395-31673-1.

I. Introduction

This dictionary, in the American Heritage family, is especially designed "for those who need or prefer large type." The cover states that "the Production Review Committee of National Aid to Visually Handicapped has found this publication to meet its criteria for use by the partially seeing."

There are over 35,000 highly condensed definitions of basic vocabulary words. These appear to be well selected for contemporary dictionary users. All main entries include pronunciations and parts of speech, and most have numbered, multiple meanings. Examples, guidance on usage (except for the guide to punctuation), and all etymologies are omitted, but a large-type, simplified style guide as well as several tables are included.

II. Authority

Houghton Mifflin's American Heritage dictionaries are respected and popular works, especially known for providing guidance on contemporary, educated use of language. This large-type dictionary was prepared by the publisher's American Heritage staff editors, under Fernando de Mello Vianna, who was also Editor-in-Chief of THE AMERICAN HERITAGE DESK DICTIONARY and a special consultant to the AMERICAN HERITAGE DICTIONARY: SECOND COLLEGE EDITION. Supervising Editor Anne D. Steinhardt and Associate Editor Pamela DeVinne are also staff editors for other American Heritage dictionaries.

III. Comprehensiveness

The dictionary includes, according to the publisher, over 35,000 definitions. This is between 5,000 and 25,000 fewer than typical pocket-size or paperback dictionaries. Considering the special purpose of this dictionary—for readers who are visually impaired—this quantity is acceptable for spelling or basic use but may be too limited for students in high school or college.

The omission of all etymologies, or word sources, and of usage examples is sensible here; ordinarily, these make entries more visually complex and difficult to read, because different typefaces, sizes, and symbols are required to distinguish this information from basic definitions.

A comparison of two segments of entries with those in the CONCISE AMERICAN HERITAGE DICTIONARY illustrates the reduced selection of entries for the large type edition, and may help buyers to judge whether that version is too limited for readers' use. The *Concise* includes the following eight-entry sequence:

lariat, lark[1]**, lark**[2]**, larkspur, larrup, larva, laryngitis, larynx**.

The large type edition reduces this to three entries:

lar·i·at, lark, lar·ynx (under this last entry, both editions include "—**la·ryn′ge·al** *adj*.").

In a second sample segment, the *Concise* offers

par, par., para-., parable, parabola, par·a·chute, pa·rade, par·a·dise, par·a·dox, par·af·fin, par·a·gon, and **par·a·graph**.

The *AHD Large Type* includes nine entries:

par, parable, par·a·chute, pa·rade, par·a·dise, par·a·dox, par·af·fin, par·a·gon, and **par·a·graph**.

The large-type edition excludes variations of words and combining forms as well as more difficult scientific or technical terms as main entries; however, occasional chemical and medical terms are entered, for example, **epinephrine** and **penicillin**. A considerable number of variant forms of words are included under main entries. For example, under the entry for discipline, the following also appear:

—*v*.—**plined,** —**plining** [and] —**dis′ci·pli·nar′i·an** *n*. —**dis′ci·pli·nar′y** *adj*.

IV. Quality and Currency of Entries

All definitions are condensed to short phrases or single words. They are generally clear and serviceable. The publisher states that definitions begin with "the current, central meaning" in cases where multiple meanings are listed.

The entries are organized in the following sequence: main entry divided into syllables; pronunciation with some alternatives; parts of speech; inflected forms or, in rare cases, idiomatic usage if the word usually appears in a phrase; definitions (numbered when necessary); and variant forms. An example is:

var·y (vâr′ē) *v*. —**ied,** —**ying. 1.** To cause or undergo change. **2.** To give variety to; diversify. **3.** To differ. —**var′i·ance** *n*. —**var′i·ant** *adj*. & *n*.

Definitions are usually unambiguous, although they do not attempt to encompass the range of nuances in words. For example, **evangelism** is defined as "The preaching of the Gospel," which omits such customary defining characteristics as *zealous* or *missionary*.

The absence of usage examples makes occasional definitions seem cryptic, as in the third definition provided for **sea**: "A vast amount or extent." Only rarely do homographs appear, but they are included as separate entries with superscript numbers: **pale**[1], **pale**[2].

V. Syllabication and Pronunciation

Main entries and their variant forms are divided into syllables by bold centered dots, and follow the breaks normally used in printing. Inflected forms of verbs are not syllabified. When variant forms of words are included, the part appearing in the main entry is not syllabified, but stress is indicated:

> **Eve·ry** *adj.* . . . . **eve′ry·bod′y, eve′ry·one′.**

Pronunciation is based on the symbols used in other American Heritage dictionaries. The publisher indicates that all pronunciations included "are acceptable in all circumstances." The criterion for acceptable pronunciation in American Heritage dictionaries is that of "educated speech" with regional variations. A list of spellings representing the full range of pronunciation symbols appears in the front of the dictionary for easy reference. The accompanying short explanation of the symbols indicates that variation in the pronunciation of the letter *y* is shown by: /y/. The dictionary includes typical variant pronunciations; **es·teem** (ĕ-stēm′, ĭ-stēm′) and **mem·oir** (mĕm′wär′, -wôr′). Bold primary stress marks ′ and lighter secondary stress marks ′ are shown as for **mem·oir** above.

VI. Special Features

There is a contents list at the front of the dictionary that is rather hard to find, since it is printed above the extensive copyright information. The two-and-one-half page "How to Use This Dictionary" guide is divided into five very short but lucid sections that explain main entries, variants, inflected forms, labels (only for parts of speech and word forms), and pronunciations with a spelling and symbol list that includes the schwa ə, unidentified by name, but with samples of its use for vowel sounds, for example: item and circus.

At the back of the dictionary is a five-page guide to the use of punctuation marks with short explanations (including preferred printing style for dashes) and with usage examples set off in italic print, numbered rules (three for the period and 21 for the comma). There is a two-page guide to the metric system and three pages of metric conversions, plus a handy list of U. S. states with their capital cities, date of joining the Union, and population (based on the 1980 census). All these features are printed in large type with a generous amount of white space that makes reading them easier. The clarity and size of these special features make them useful to upper elementary students as well as older, visually impaired readers.

VII. Accessibility

The design of this dictionary ensures that the entries and definitions are as visually accessible as possible. The main entry words are printed in large, readable, bold type which overhangs the text. They are arranged in simple, letter-by-letter alphabetical sequence. The text is printed in two wide columns separated by a bold vertical rule. Page numbers are centered at the top of each text page; variant spellings, inflected verb forms, and words associated with the main entry are printed in smaller boldface type.

The system of guide words is visually simplified to indicate first and last entries on each double-page spread. A single bold word appears near the outside margin at the top of each page: on the left, the guide word indicates the first entry to appear on the left-hand page; on the right, the guide word indicates the last word to appear on the right-hand page.

Within entries, numbered definitions are clearly visible, as are the inflected verb forms and variant forms of words.

VIII. Graphics and Format

The graphic design of this basic dictionary is simple and attractive. There are no pictures or other illustrations. The text is printed in 14-point type with entry words in bold 14-point. There is enough white space between lines to facilitate reading. The text columns are approximately 3¼ inches wide, which means that a reader can use a rectangular magnifying glass as small as 3½ to four inches wide without seeing any text distortion.

The guide to the dictionary is in larger type and so are the metric charts, with columns of unit names and measurements generously spaced. Although the punctuation rules are printed in a similar large type, they appear very dense on the page in a single wide-column format. The usage examples are in italic and can be distinguished with ease from the numbered rules.

IX. Summary

The *Large Type American Heritage Basic Dictionary* is visually accessible, attractive, and easy to read. Its definitions, although *very* basic, are reliable and will be useful to readers from upper elementary school age to adults who require larger type than is normally found in dictionaries. There are few frills beyond the basic meanings in this dictionary, but it is a solid work, clearly related to its respected larger companions in the American Heritage family and a good value for its modest price.

The Merriam-Webster Dictionary for Large Print Users

Facts at a Glance

Full Title: **The Merriam-Webster Dictionary for Large Print Users.**
Publisher: G. K. Hall.
Editor: Henry Bosley Woolf, Editor-in-Chief.
Edition Reviewed: © 1977.

Number of Volumes: 1.
Number of Entries: 57,000.
Number of Pages: 1,120.
Trim Size: 8¾" × 11".
Binding: hardcover.

Price: $29.50.
Intended Readership: visually impaired; upper junior high school and up.
Available directly from the publisher. ISBN 0-816-16459-2.

I. Introduction

The Merriam-Webster Dictionary for Large Print Users is a descendant of *Webster's Third New International Dictionary*. It contains over 57,000 entries covering the core of contemporary English usage. The definitions are based on the nearly 12 million examples of use entered in the Merriam-Webster citation files. Geographic and biographical information is excluded.

Originally published in 1975, the dictionary is intended primarily for large print users, particularly the visually impaired. As such it is most appropriate for public libraries serving a largely older population or libraries housing special collections for the visually handicapped. Its appreciably smaller vocabulary, however, could limit its usefulness among secondary and college level students.

II. Authority

The Merriam-Webster Dictionary for Large Print Users is a combined effort of G. K. Hall, a leading U.S. publisher of large print books, and the G. & C. Merriam Company, long recognized as a highly respected publisher of dictionaries. The Merriam-Webster staff of dictionary specialists was headed by Editor-in-Chief Henry Bosley Woolf.

The Webster's Third New International Dictionary, upon which the G.K. Hall large-print version is based, favors contemporary words and usage. Merriam-Webster's authority derives from a dedication to accuracy, clarity, and comprehensiveness.

III. Comprehensiveness

Webster's Third New International Dictionary contains close to 460,000 entries. *The Merriam-Webster Dictionary for Large Print Users* includes approximately 57,000 definitions. The bulk of the eliminated matter falls into scientific and technical categories. With its 1975 copyright date, the work excludes a number of terms such as *meltdown, modem,* and *robotics* that have gained current usage.

Etymologies in the dictionary appear in boldface brackets preceding the definition. The etymology gives the language from which words assimilated into English have come. Synonyms are indicated by a boldface **syn** near the end of the entry.

Four types of cross-references are used: directional, synonymous, cognate, and inflectional. In each case the cross-reference appears in small capitals. A directional cross-reference follows a light dash and directs the user to look elsewhere for additional information. A synonymous cross-reference follows a boldface colon and indicates that the definition referred to can be used as a substitute. A cognate cross-reference follows an italic **var of** and indicates a variant. An inflectional cross-reference follows an italic label and identifies an entry as an inflected form.

IV. Quality and Currency of Entries

The Merriam-Webster Dictionary for Large Print Users is designed for a general readership and is sufficient to meet the vocabulary needs of many readers. The serious high school or college student however, may find the relatively small number of entries inadequate for research purposes.

Definitions are introduced by a boldface colon, which also is used to separate two or more clarifications of a single sense. Definitions of a word that has more than a single sense are separated by boldface Arabic numerals. Multiple senses of a word are presented in historical order. The first known English language sense is entered first. For example:

> **Master** . . . n. **1 :** a male teacher . . . **2 :** one highly skilled.

Editors have attempted to make the definitions as readable as possible. Although the definitions are brief and verbal illustrations rare, there is little need to consult additional entries for clarification.

V. Syllabication and Pronunciation

Pronunciation is indicated between reversed virgules following the main entry word (for example, **dis·like** \dis -'lik\ vb). A pronunciation key is located in the front of the volume. However, it is not repeated on individual pages. A hyphen is used in the pronunciation to indicate the division of syllables. A high-set mark shows primary stress or accent while a low-set mark indicates secondary stress (for example, **jack·knife** \jak -'nif\ n). Syllables with neither a high-set mark nor a low-set mark are unstressed. An italic label following the pronunciation indicates a part of speech or another functional classification. Alternative pronunciations are included, although no preference is indicated.

VI. Special Features

The *A* to *Z* vocabulary in the *Merriam-Webster Dictionary for Large Print Users* is followed by several special feature sections. Included are population tables of the United States and Canada; a section on widely used signs and symbols; and tables covering the metric system, weights and measures, money, and the planets. While this type of information is occasionally useful, the population figures are out-of-date.

VII. Accessibility

Main entry words are in boldface type set flush with the left-hand margin of each column. They follow one another in letter-by-letter alphabetical order. A pair of guide words appears at the top of each page. When a main entry is followed by the word **or** and an alternative spelling, the two spellings are considered equal variants (**disk** or **disc**). When a variant spelling is joined to the main entry by the word **also** it indicates the second entry occurs less frequently (**surprise** also **sur·prize**. . . vb).

VIII. Graphics and Format

The outstanding characteristic of the Merriam-Webster enlarged print edition is the typography. The *A* to *Z* vocabulary features 18-point type guide words, 14-point type word entries, and 12-point type definitions. The special sections appear in 16-point type. The preface states that this conforms to the accepted standards for reference books for large print users as established by the National Association of Visually Handicapped. A brief perusal will verify the value of this work to the visually handicapped individual.

The dictionary is in a single volume and is durably bound. Its size prevents it from being easily transported, but the binding does permit it to lie flat on an open surface. The paper is of good quality, sufficiently opaque, and heavy enough to withstand frequent use.

IX. Summary

The Merriam-Webster Dictionary for Large Print Users is an authoritative and highly readable work well designed to meet the needs of a general audience, particularly the visually impaired. In graphics and format the Merriam/G.K. Hall version is superior to the WEBSTER'S NEW WORLD LARGE PRINT DICTIONARY OF THE AMERICAN LANGUAGE: SECOND CONCISE EDITION published by Prentice Hall. However, it is less comprehensive, containing about one half the entries incorporated into the latter. Students and others involved in extensive research may find this a significant shortcoming.

The dictionary is current only through the mid-1970s, but its general vocabulary is still suitable for public library holdings or any special collection serving the visually impaired.

My Second Pictionary

Facts at a Glance

Full Title: **My Second Pictionary**.
Publisher: Scott, Foresman.
Editors: M. Monroe and W. C. Greet.
Edition Reviewed: © 1964.

Number of Volumes: 2.
Number of Entries: 12,500.
Number of Pages: 392.
Trim Size: 11½″ × 13¾″.
Binding: hardcover.

Price: $153.14.
Intended Readership: visually impaired; lower elementary grades.
Available from the American Printing House for the Blind. Order No. 4-7551.

I. Introduction and Scope

The large print version of *My Second Pictionary*, edited by M. Monroe and W. C. Greet, is available in 17-point type from the American Printing House for the Blind. The dictionary is aimed toward the skills and interests of younger students and includes familiar words and concepts.

This is one of the dictionaries that the American Printing House for the Blind has reproduced mechanically, "without any attempt to clarify" the illustrations. They note this caveat to prospective purchasers of the dictionary prominently on the order form. Because the process of photographic enlargement can cause some distortion, many illustrations lack clarity, and this may render the picture dictionary of little use to the more seriously visually handicapped.

Teachers should note that ancillary material for this large print dictionary is also available: *My Second Pictionary Dictionary (Exercise Book)* edited by W. C. Greet et al., and published by Scott, Foresman (1971) is also available in 16-point type. At this writing, the 70-page exercise book can be purchased from the American Printing House for the Blind for $25.69. (See also the review of Scott, Foresman's MY PICTIONARY in this Buying Guide for a description of the publisher's dictionary for still younger children.)

Scott, Foresman Beginning Dictionary: Large Type Edition

Facts at a Glance

Full Title: **Scott, Foresman Beginning Dictionary: Large Type Edition**.

Former Title: Thorndike-Barnhart Beginning Dictionary.

Publisher: Scott, Foresman.

Editors: E. L. Thorndike and C. L. Barnhart.

Edition Reviewed: © 1979.

Number of Volumes: 6.
Number of Entries: 28,000.
Number of Pages: 1,396.
Number of Illustrations: approximately 1,200.
Trim Size: 11″ × 12½″.
Binding: hardcover.

Price: $290.16.
Intended Readership: visually handicapped; upper elementary school students (grades 3 through 6).
Available from the American Printing House for the Blind. Order No. 4-2269.

I. Introduction and Scope

This large type edition of the *Scott, Foresman Beginning Dictionary*, edited by E. L. Thorndike and C. L. Barnhart is a resetting of the 1979 *Scott, Foresman Beginning Dictionary*. (The 1988 edition of the SCOTT, FORESMAN BEGINNING DICTIONARY is reviewed elsewhere in the Buying Guide.) The type for this edition was entirely reset in 16-point type and all illustrations were redrawn. The dictionary is published in six volumes. It is listed in the reference circular of the National Library Service for the Blind and Physically Handicapped.

This basic dictionary is specifically designed to meet the educational needs of children in the upper elementary grades. However, the superior quality of the word list, definitions, and illustrations, and large-print format make it useful for developmental reading classes through the high school and adult levels, as well as for ESL programs.

Especially helpful features for the visually impaired are the generous use of white space around the varied illustrations and the frequent positioning of etymologies in distinctive boxes labeled "Word History."

The ragged right format guides the eye to the left and is an aid in finding entry words. Extra large boldface guide words at the top corners of each page can be especially helpful for the older elementary student. However, it would have been more helpful to the visually impaired if parts of speech, now printed in italics, had been printed in boldface to distinguish them from the italicized illustrative phrases. A convenient short pronunciation key is printed in the upper right corner of each double-page spread.

Since the large type edition is a resetting of the 1979 edition of the *Scott, Foresman Beginning Dictionary*, it does not have the currency of the newly revised 1988 edition.

For a complete description of the SCOTT, FORESMAN BEGINNING DICTIONARY © 1988 see the review elsewhere in the Buying Guide.

Webster's New Collegiate Dictionary: Large Print Edition

Facts at a Glance

Full Title: **Webster's New Collegiate Dictionary: Large Print Edition**.

Publisher: Merriam-Webster.

Edition Reviewed: © 1976.

Number of Volumes: 9.
Number of Entries: 150,000.

Number of Illustrations: 500.
Trim Size: 11″ × 13½″.
Binding: hardcover.

Price: $313.00.
Intended Readership: visually impaired; high school and up.
Available from Library Reproduction Service. LRS No. 04505.

I. Introduction and Scope

Webster's New Collegiate Dictionary is available from Library Reproduction Service in 14-point type, considered the minimum size for large-print material.

This dictionary is a comprehensive, abridged work based on an extensive citation file and list of authoritative historical sources from the venerable publisher.

It contains complete etymologies, extensive labels, synonyms, usage notes, cross-references, and numbered multiple meanings. Guide words in boldface type are printed at the top of each page. A bold rule draws the eye to the short pronunciation key conveniently placed at the lower right corner of each double-page spread. Various other elements, such as the use of the tilde to identify the entry word in illustrative sentences, also help attract the eye.

This *Webster's New Collegiate Dictionary*, while lacking somewhat in currency, would be a useful tool for the visually handicapped reader at the high school level and up. The edition is that preceding WEBSTER'S NINTH COLLEGIATE DICTIONARY, reviewed elsewhere in this Buying Guide.

Webster's Concise Family Dictionary: Large Print Edition

Facts at a Glance

Full Title: **Webster's Concise Family Dictionary: Large Print Edition**.
Publisher: Merriam-Webster.
Edition Reviewed: © 1975.

Number of Volumes: 5.
Number of Entries: 57,000.
Number of Pages: 856.
Trim Size: 11″ × 13½″.
Binding: hardcover.

Price: $214.00.
Intended Readership: visually impaired; high school and up.
Available from Library Reproduction Service. Order No. LRS 04452.

I. Introduction and Scope

Since the regular-print edition of WEBSTER'S CONCISE FAMILY DICTIONARY was originally set in larger-than-standard adult dictionary print, this large print version includes several features especially helpful for the visually impaired: syllable breaks of boldface entries are marked with extrabold centered dots; high-set and low-set marks indicate primary or secondary stress or accents; a boldface colon introduces a definition; and boldface numerals mark multiple senses of an entry word.

In this large print edition of *Webster's Concise Family Dictionary*, type sizes range from 14-point definitions to 20-point guide words. For those large print dictionary users who prefer a single volume and who are able to work with 12-point definitions, THE MERRIAM-WEBSTER DICTIONARY FOR LARGE PRINT USERS can be a satisfactory and less expensive alternative reference. The concise definitions and text format are essentially the same for both of these dictionaries.

While this large-print dictionary has been reprinted from the 1975 regular-print edition its "generally authoritative approach to the lexicon" makes it useful for the needs of those visually impaired readers who may not require a more extensive current vocabulary.

For a complete analysis, see the review of THE MERRIAM-WEBSTER DICTIONARY for an evaluation of the contents, and the review of WEBSTER'S CONCISE FAMILY DICTIONARY for comments on the regular-size type edition. See also the summary review of THE MERRIAM-WEBSTER DICTIONARY FOR LARGE PRINT USERS. All appear elsewhere in this Buying Guide.

Webster's New Elementary Dictionary: Large Type Edition

Facts at a Glance

Full Title: **Webster's New Elementary Dictionary: Large Type Edition**.
Publisher: G. & C. Merriam.
Edition Reviewed: © 1975.

Number of Volumes: 1.
Number of Entries: more than 32,000.
Number of Pages: 620.
Number of Illustrations: 1,200.
Trim Size: 10½" × 14".
Binding: hardcover.

Price: $88.00 single copy; $78.00 each for 2 or more copies.
Intended Readership: visually impaired; upper elementary students through high school; and ESL.
Available from Library Reproduction Service. Order No. LRS 08085.

I. Introduction and Scope

The large type version of the 1975 edition of *Webster's New Elementary Dictionary* is available from the Library Reproduction Service, a division of the Microfilm Company of California. Reproduced in 18-point type (main entries) and 16-point type (definitions), the more than 32,000 entries are bound in a single large-type volume.

The dictionary has been developed for students in grades four to six. The clear, precise definitions are easy to understand. Elements such as variant pronunciations, multiple senses, extensive use of special symbols and pronunciation marks may require some children to seek guidance or special instruction in order to use the dictionary. However, these elements would be useful for the bright upper elementary students and would help them prepare for more adult dictionaries. The large type work will be useful for those developmental programs working with junior high and senior high school students and ESL students.

Guide words are provided at the top of each double-column page; pronunciation keys are printed at the bottom. Page numbers are centered. Synonym paragraphs and "Word History" paragraphs follow the entry word and are set off from the body of the text by white space and paragraph indentation—both helpful features for the visually impaired.

A generous number of illustrations helps to break up the pages and attract the eye.

(See also WEBSTER'S ELEMENTARY DICTIONARY discussed above in the Buying Guide.)

Webster's New World Large Print Dictionary of the American Language: Second Concise Edition

Facts at a Glance

Full Title: **Webster's New World Large Print Dictionary of the American Language: Second Concise Edition**.
Publisher: Prentice Hall Press.
Editor: David B. Guralnik, General Editor.
Edition Reviewed: © 1979.

Number of Volumes: 1.
Number of Entries: over 105,000.
Number of Pages: 882.
Number of Illustrations: 612 black-and-white line drawings.
Trim Size: 9¾" × 13¾".
Binding: cloth.

Price: $29.95.
Intended Readership: visually impaired; high school and up.
Sold in bookstores; also sold to libraries. ISBN 0-671-41818-1.

I. Introduction

Webster's New World Large Print Dictionary is a larger typeface version of *Webster's New World Dictionary of the American Language: Second Concise Edition*. The latter, an abridgment of the 158,000 WEBSTER'S NEW WORLD DICTIONARY: SECOND COLLEGE EDITION (1970), was first published in 1975 and updated in 1979.

The version retains many of the features of the *Second College Edition*, including clear and reliable definitions. However, the etymologies are less extensive, and highly technical, and arcane terms as well as synonyms have been eliminated.

In the foreword, the publisher states that this dictionary in its original format was especially prepared for a wide range of general readers that includes secondary school students and learners of English as a Second Language (ESL).

II. Authority

Prentice Hall is the publisher of this large-print dictionary. Of all the Webster's dictionaries on the market, the *Webster's New World* volumes (originally published by World + Collins) and the Merriam-Webster, Inc. volumes are among the most reputable dictionaries. This work was prepared by David B. Guralnik along with the same permanent lexico-

Webster's New World Large Print Dictionary of the American Language: Second Concise Edition

❶ Etymology provided in brackets includes a meaning

❷ Inflected forms appear in boldface

❸ Colloquial usage is defined

❹ Variant word form is indicated

❺ Illustrative line drawing with label

❻ Idiomatic phrase is defined

dib·ble (dib′′l) *n.* [ME. *dibbel*, prob. < *dibben*, to dip] a pointed tool used to make holes in the soil for seeds, bulbs, or young plants: also called **dib′ber** —*vt.* **-bled, -bling** 1. to make a hole in (the soil) with a dibble 2. to plant with a dibble —*vi.* to use a dibble

dibs (dibz) *n.pl.* [< *dibstone*, a jack in a children's game] [Colloq.] a claim to a share of, or rights in, something wanted —*interj.* an exclamation announcing such a claim: chiefly a child's term

dice (dīs) *n.pl., sing.* **die** or **dice** [ME. *dis*, pl.: see DIE[2]] 1. small cubes of bone, plastic, etc. marked on each side with from one to six spots and used, usually in pairs, in games of chance 2. [*with sing. v.*] a gambling game played with dice 3. any small cubes —*vi.* **diced, dic′ing** to play or gamble with dice —*vt.* to cut (vegetables, etc.) into small cubes —**no dice** 1. no: used in refusing a request 2. no success, luck, etc. —**dic′er** *n.*

DIBBLE

graphical staff that produced the WEBSTER'S NEW WORLD DICTIONARY: SECOND COLLEGE EDITION, using the same database.

The entries were selected on the basis of their frequency of appearance in general interest publications. Only those terms that had gained stability in form and meaning by the late 1970s and that have demonstrated a potential for survival in the language were selected for inclusion.

III. Comprehensiveness

Over 105,000 vocabulary entries are included in the large-print volume. Since the copyright date is 1979, however, a number of terms that are now current are not included. For example, a perusal indicates no entries for *Alzheimer's disease, arbitrage, triathlon,* or *wind shear.*

Obsolete and archaic terms that are often found in standard works of literature or in biblical works have been included. Common technical terms encountered in general writings have been entered, prefaced by an abbreviated field label. A list of abbreviations immediately precedes the first page of the dictionary.

Numerous prefixes, suffixes, and combined forms have been entered, enabling the reader to determine the meanings of thousands of additional words too specialized for inclusion. To conserve space, words that are derived from main entries, such as nouns ending in **-tion**, adjectives ending in **-like**, or adverbs ending in **-ly** are run in to the end of the entry for the base word. Derivatives that have significant meanings not readily identifiable from the main term's separate parts are given in separate entries.

IV. Quality and Currency of Entries

The definitions in this large-print work are uniformly clear and accurate as well as being reasonably thorough, for example:

> **barter** . . . to trade by exchanging goods or services without using money.

This precise approach is accommodating to a broad readership, especially students. The definitions of longer entries have been arranged in an order that indicates how the word developed from its etymology and earliest meanings, for example:

> **Jupiter** . . . 1. the chief Roman god . . . 2. the largest planet of the solar system . . . .

Colloquial, slang, archaic, obsolete, or similar senses follow the general definitions. Occasionally, an obsolete sense may be given first to serve as a link between the etymology and the current senses. Where a primary sense of a word can easily be subdivided into several closely related meanings, this has been done. The words "especially" or "specifically" are frequently used to introduce such groupings or related senses. This procedure for listing definitions could be confusing for students who might expect to have the most common definition listed first.

V. Syllabication and Pronunciation

All syllables are divided by bold centered dots: e·lec·tron·ic, pudg·y. The editors note, however, that it is not customary in written or printed material to break a word after the first syllable or before the last, if that syllable consists of only a single letter or, in the case of lengthy words, two letters.

Pronunciations are given inside parentheses, immediately following the boldface entry. A single space is used between pronounced syllables. Primary and secondary stress are indicated by bold and lighter stress marks.

The editors state that pronunciations are "for the most part those found in the normal relaxed conversation of educated speakers." Common variants are also shown, as well as native pronunciations of foreign words and proper names. A "Guide to the Dictionary" includes a key to pronunciation; an abbreviated key appears at the bottom of every right-hand page of the vocabulary. The symbols in the key can be easily understood from the key words in which they are shown. This quick reference feature will be especially helpful to students.

VI. Special Features

Several pages preceding and following the lexicon include tables of weights and measures, time zones, and a guide to the mechanics of writing that briefly covers marks of punctuation, numbers, capitalization, abbreviations, and spelling. Also added is a table of alphabets providing the sounds of letters in Arabic, Hebrew, Greek, Russian, and German. This sort of information is readily available in various general almanacs and encyclopedias—often in more complete form. In general, these features add little value to the text.

VII. Accessibility

To increase accessibility in this dictionary, all entries—including proper names of persons and places, abbreviations, affixes, and unnaturalized foreign terms found within English contexts—have been arranged in one alphabetical listing. This eliminates the need to browse through various appendixes in order to pinpoint lexical information.

When variant spellings of a word fall some distance apart in the alphabetical listing, the definition appears with the spelling most frequently used in the U.S. Other spellings of the word are cross-referenced to the form most widely used. Cross-references often indicate that the variant is *British*, *dialectal*, *slang*, *obsolete*, or the like, for example:

centre . . . *Brit. sp.* of center.

When two variant spellings appear close to each other in alphabetical order and are used with nearly equal frequency, they are placed together at the head of the entry. In this case, neither spelling is considered to be more accurate, even though the first one listed may be the most often used (for example, thea·ter, theatre).

VIII. Graphics and Format

Over 600 black-and-white line drawings contribute to the reader's understanding of the vocabulary. They are used on a very selective basis when the editors felt that an illustration would help to expand or sharpen a definition. The actual sizes of animals have been given in feet or inches, and tools and instruments are shown in use in order to make clearer their function and relative size.

One cautionary note is in order concerning the graphics of this large print edition. Compared to the diminutive size of typeface found in most dictionaries, the print used in this work can rightly be termed "extra-large." The volume has 16-point type guide words, 11-point type word entries, and 11-point type definitions. However, when measured against the standard 16-point type for the main entry word found in most large print books, this version comes up short. In consequence, the visually impaired reader may find the text size unacceptable. THE MERRIAM-WEBSTER DICTIONARY FOR LARGE PRINT USERS, for instance, published by G. K. Hall, features 18-point type guide words, 14-point type word entries, and 12-point type definitions.

Generally, the main entry words in this *Webster's New World* are easily spotted and clearly divided into syllables. The opaque paper is of sufficient quality to eliminate reflections and firm enough to avoid crumpling of pages. Thumb indexing facilitates access to the text.

Physically, this is a sturdy book with a binding that should withstand heavy and sustained use and still allow the book to lie flat. Because of its large-size format, the dictionary is not easily transportable or stored, and handling it could be awkward for some readers. Its most appropriate location would be on a separate stand or table in a classroom, library, or home.

IX. Summary

The *Webster's New World Large Print Dictionary: Second Concise Edition* is a highly reputable dictionary that retains many of the outstanding features of WEBSTER'S NEW WORLD DICTIONARY: SECOND COLLEGE EDITION, upon which it is based.

In comparing this volume to G. K. Hall's MERRIAM-WEBSTER DICTIONARY FOR LARGE PRINT USERS, the prospective buyer should note two considerations. The graphics, in particular the size of the typeface in the G. K. Hall large-print dictionary, are of sufficient size to accommodate the visually impaired person, while the Prentice Hall *Webster's New World* edition has significantly smaller type; and although it causes less strain on the eye than most dictionaries, it is not likely to satisfy the majority of large print users who are visually impaired. On the other hand, the Prentice Hall *New World* vocabulary is more comprehensive; it includes nearly twice the number of entries to be found in the G. K. Hall volume.

The *Webster's New World Large Print Dictionary*, while current only through the 1970s, is a useful tool for general vocabulary. In content and format, it is appropriate for secondary school students as well as young adult collections where there is a need for a large-print dictionary.

The Weekly Reader Beginning Dictionary: Large Type Edition

Facts at a Glance

Full Title: **The Weekly Reader Beginning Dictionary: Large Type Edition**.
Publisher: Xerox Family Education Services.
Editor: William Morris, Editor-in-Chief.
Edition Reviewed: © 1973.

Number of Volumes: 2.
Number of Entries: approximately 5,000.
Number of Pages: 372.
Number of Illustrations: approximately 600.
Trim Size: $10\frac{5}{8}'' \times 13\frac{7}{8}''$.
Binding: hardcover.

Price: $145.56.
Intended Readership: visually impaired; grades 3 through 5.
Photocopies available from the American Printing House for the Blind. Order No. 4-8883.

I. Scope and Format

According to its foreword, *The Weekly Reader Beginning Dictionary: Large Type Edition* is designed for young readers and tells about "words likely to [be met in] day-to-day reading." Teachers and pupils were consulted to find which words they "wanted to know about," and their choice of categories covering animals, games, space travel, food, and so forth, is reflected in the lexicon. Objectives include showing young students "that words can be fun" and helping them "learn to use [words] accurately."

The format of the page is ideal for the visually handicapped. Boldface entry words appear separately in the left-hand margin, with the succeeding definition forming one wide column down the page. Many of the definitions contain more than one meaning of the entry word and are clearly numbered in boldface.

Entry words are set in 24-point boldface type, while definitions are set in 18-point type. Illustration labels are set in 14-point sans serif type.

There are no guide words, syllabication, pronunciations, part-of-speech labels, or etymologies, elements that are often not included in dictionaries for young readers at these age levels.

Each letter of the alphabet starts on a new page and is illustrated by a large-sized capital and lowercase example of the letter. Page numbers are centered at the top of each page.

While its large size might make it cumbersome for carrying and awkward for standard shelves, its large size and clarity are appealing features for the visually impaired student.

II. Authority

This large print edition of *The Weekly Reader Beginning Dictionary* has been photoenlarged from the 1973 edition of *The Weekly Reader Beginning Dictionary*. The original edition of the book was published by Grosset & Dunlap in a trade edition. A school and library edition entitled *The Ginn Beginning Dictionary* was also published originally in 1973 by Ginn and Company, a well-known publisher of educational texts. The work is now published by Xerox Family Education Services.

The dictionary is available in two volumes from the American Printing House for the Blind. It is also listed in the reference circular of the National Library Service for the Blind and Physically Handicapped.

III. Quality and Currency of Entries

Each entry is clearly defined with a simple word or short phrase appropriate for upper elementary grade readers. Illustrative sentences appear frequently, with the entry word printed in boldface italics. Homographs are treated as separate entries. For example:

grave . . . A place where a dead person or animal is buried.

grave . . . Serious. Bill's brother said it would be a *grave* mistake to drop out of school.

Inflected forms and variants are provided in boldface italic directly under the entry word.

care 1. Protection; charge. Will you take *care* of my bike next week?
2. Attention. Cross the busy street with *care*.
3. A worry or trouble. Ted doesn't have a *care* in the world.

care To want; to like. Would you *care* to go to the game?
cared
caring

In some instances an illustrative sentence will include another form of the entry word. In this case children will have to gain understanding of meaning by inference. For example, the entry word **satisfy** has the inflected forms **satisfied** and **satisfying** listed, but not the noun *satisfaction*. However, one of the illustrative examples includes the noun:

To make content; to fill a need. A cool drink of water will **satisfy** my thirst. Susan finds **satisfaction** in listening to records.

The dictionary includes many terms having to do with space, such as **retrorocket**, **launch pad**, **moonwalk**, **spaceman** (but not *spacewoman*!), **spaceship**, and **satellite;** however, *computer* is not included. Although the dictionary was copyrighted in 1973, its basic vocabulary contains the fundamentals needed for today's children in upper elementary grades and into the middle school years.

IV. Illustrations

Simple line drawings are used extensively in the generous margins. There are from one to seven illustrated words on each double-page spread. Illustra-tions are clearly labeled and are placed next to the appropriate word. A number of illustrations (see **washing machine** and **umbrella**) are printed with a background shading, which makes the labels difficult to read, especially for readers who are visually impaired.

V. Summary

The Weekly Reader Beginning Dictionary is a very basic, simple dictionary geared to the third to fifth grade student. The definitions and presentation, however, are sophisticated enough to satisfy the needs of students well into the middle school years. The book is appealing to the eye and accessible, despite some defects in the enlarged illustrations, and visually impaired students and those with certain kinds of learning disabilities, such as dyslexia, would be well served by the clear and appealing layout of this large-print dictionary. The student could logically progress from this dictionary to the LARGE TYPE AMERICAN HERITAGE DICTIONARY.

Large-Print Thesauruses

The Merriam-Webster Thesaurus for Large Print Users

Facts at a Glance

Full Title: **The Merriam-Webster Thesaurus for Large Print Users**.
Publisher: G. K. Hall.
Editors: E. Ward Gilman, Senior Editor; and Kathleen M. Doherty.
Edition Reviewed: © 1978.

Number of Volumes: 1.
Number of Entries: more than 50,000.
Number of Pages: 1,032.
Trim Size: $8\frac{3}{8}'' \times 10\frac{3}{4}''$.
Binding: cloth.

Price: $35.00.
Intended Readership: large print users, junior high school and up.
Available direct from the publisher. ISBN 0-816-16617-x.

I. Introduction and Scope

Based on the *Webster's Collegiate Thesaurus, The Merriam-Webster Thesaurus for Large Print Users* includes 50,000 entries and "is designed to meet the day-to-day requirements of those who need or prefer larger type and who want a compact and handy thesaurus," as the book's preface states. While retaining the basic features of the parent book, the large print edition simplifies and reorganizes the synonym list to include cross-references. It also eliminates unnecessary elements such as "specialized or abstruse entries" and "synonyms not likely to be of general interest." Ultimately, the book's authority lies in *Webster's Third New International Dictionary* and the Merriam-Webster research file of nearly 13 million words. The book (originally published in an attractive format by G. K. Hall and reviewed from a publisher's archival copy lent to the buying guide) conforms to the standards for reference books of the National Association for Visually Handicapped (NAVH).

II. Format

In addition to the preface, the book includes a 20-page "Explanatory Notes" section, which—with its examples—is necessary for the reader to understand the elements presented in the entries. It includes explanations of labels, punctuation, and symbols. A brief key to some of the abbreviations and symbols also appears on every left-hand page in the book.

The main portion of the book contains 1,000 pages of entries presented in large print in two-column format. The main entry words are in 14-point type, with 12-point type definitions. The columns are clearly separated from 18-point folios and guide words at the top of each page by a vertical black rule. The type (ranging from 12- to 18-point) is printed very black on good quality paper with minimal showthrough. This is a page made to order for the visually handicapped or for those who simply prefer larger print. Many other readers may also find it a pleasure to use this thesaurus.

The large-page format is well bound: the pages open easily and lie flat on a desk top.

III. Quality and Currency of Entries

Unlike *Roget's Thesaurus*, which is organized by large concepts, *The Merriam-Webster Thesaurus for Large Print Users* is organized alphabetically, like a dictionary. It is extremely well written and easy to use. Readers will find its lists of synonyms, related words, and cross-references helpful and rational, as well as instructive about the fine meanings of words. And far from limiting the browser, this more tightly constructed organization can send the reader on a most gratifying spree of page-turning in search of other words.

Here is an example of a representative main entry:

essentially *adv* **1** in regard to the essential points <essentially the problem is this: he is unreliable>
syn au fond, basically, fundamentally, in essence
rel actually, really
idiom at bottom
2 *syn* see ALMOST 2
rel substantially, virtually
idiom in the main

The entry consists of a main entry word, part-of-speech label, a sense number, a core meaning with brief, verbal illustration, and a list of synonyms (*syn*). Synonyms are followed by related words (*rel*), idiomatic equivalents (*idiom*), contrasted words (*con*), and antonyms (*ant*), where applicable.

A core meaning may be supplemented by a usage note and by two verbal illustrations if it is broad enough to cause confusion.

Secondary entries include main entry word, part-of-speech label, sense number when needed, and a "see" reference to the main entry where a list of synonyms that includes the secondary entry is given.

The editors state in the "Explanatory Notes" that "*No word may appear in more than one list at* [sic] *a main or secondary entry.*" Users will be grateful for the special thought and care that has gone into this simplifying rule.

Since this thesaurus was published in 1978, some words or idioms in current usage do not appear here. Verbs such as *access* and *program* are not used in their computer-related senses, for example. Because the book is concerned with the general vocabulary of the language, more technological, scientific, and other specialized words are also not found here.

However, because the established—as well as the new—meanings of words in the English language include so many senses and nuances, the editors state that "it is essential that the thesaurus be used in conjunction with an adequate dictionary."

IV. Accessibility

The "Explanatory Notes" make the thesaurus completely accessible to any reader. A simple key to some of the abbreviations and symbols used appears on the bottom of every left-hand page. Guide words in 18-point type appear at the top of every page. There is no thumb index, but because of the large print, generous use of white space, and bold main entry words overhanging the text, the alphabet is easy to follow.

V. Summary

The Merriam-Webster Thesaurus for Large Print Users contains a good compact vocabulary of the language in general use. The large-print format is excellent, with the dictionarylike organization providing a rich trove of synonyms and cross-references. Access to the book is well-planned and inviting, and the volume fulfills its purpose in making information easily readable for the visually handicapped. This thesaurus is highly recommended for library collections serving readers who require large print and is suitable for a larger group of students and adults who will find the format pleasing and exceptionally accessible.

Webster's New World Thesaurus: Large Print Edition

Facts at a Glance

Full Title: **Webster's New World Thesaurus: Large Print Edition**.
Publisher: World.
Editor: Charlton G. Laird.
Edition Reviewed: © 1974.

Number of Volumes: 4.
Number of Entries: 30,000.
Number of Pages: 544.
Trim Size: 8″ × 10″.
Binding: hardcover.

Price: $136.00.
Intended Readership: visually impaired; high school and up.
Available from Library Reproduction Service. Order No. LRS 08536.

I. Introduction and Scope

The large-print edition of *Webster's New World Thesaurus* is based on a work of the same title, originally published in 1971. Its type has been enlarged to 18-point size.

The volume includes a guide to the use of the thesaurus, and its entries are alphabetically arranged. Among its features are some that will be especially helpful to visually impaired readers. Main entry words are printed in boldface and overhang the text; pairs of bold guide words appear at the top of each page. The entries contain no illustrative phrases or sentences. Although this in some cases makes it more difficult for a reader to grasp nuances of meaning, the omission does visually simplify the entries. Librarians serving readers who prefer or require large

print will be interested in the fact that the Library Reproduction Service has decreased many of their prices (this volume was decreased from $168.00 to $136.00) to make their offerings more widely available.

For a review of the 1985 updating of the regular-print WEBSTER'S NEW WORLD THESAURUS, see above in this Buying Guide.

Large-Print Atlas

Hammond Large Type World Atlas

Facts at a Glance

Full Title: **Hammond Large Type World Atlas**.
Publisher: Hammond.
Edition Reviewed: © 1986.

Number of Pages: 144.
Number of Maps: 52.
Number of Indexes: 1.
Number of Index Entries: 3,100.
Trim Size: 9¾″ × 12¼″.
Binding: cloth.

Price: $24.95.
Intended Readership: visually impaired; elementary and up.
Sold in bookstores; also sold to libraries and schools. ISBN 0-843-71246-5.
No scheduled revision.

I. Introduction

Described on its dust jacket as "the only large type atlas on the market today," the *Hammond Large Type World Atlas* fills a significant gap for the visually impaired. It might also be an attractive starting atlas for the reluctant reader or slow learner. This work, first published in 1969 by Franklin Watts, features entirely different cartography from that used in other Hammond atlases in deference to its special format. It is 9¾″ by 12¼″ in size, with a sturdy, sewn hardcover binding and an attractive, easily readable two-color dust jacket. The editors claim that it "makes it easy for the reader to grasp the essential details of today's world." Thus, it was planned to be suitable for a wide-ranging audience. It contains 51 maps in its 144 pages, and carries a 1986 copyright.

II. Format

The *Hammond Large Type Atlas* contains 100 pages of political maps, each of which occupies two pages. The book is a manageable size and weight for both young and adult readers. It is bound in an attractive, sturdy hard cover; the heavy, nonglossy pages lie flat when open.

No legend is provided for map symbols, which include significant spot elevations (given in both feet and meters), various types of boundaries, large cities and capitals, scientific research stations, permanent and seasonal rivers and lakes, reefs, salt pans, canals, cataracts, and waterfalls. Natural features, such as mountain ranges, are indicated on the maps by name but not a symbol, nor is relief depicted. Most of these symbols are self-explanatory to the experienced atlas user but may present a stumbling block for the neophyte.

Although the publisher claims "the editors have succeeded brilliantly in assembling a vast amount of essential . . . information," in keeping with the needs of the visually impaired, this work presents only the most basic geographic information. As a result, the *Hammond Large Type World Atlas* necessarily lacks much of the detail one would expect in an atlas designed for normally sighted people or experienced atlas users.

III. Special Features

An eight-page gazetteer-index of the world lists countries, states, and other major geographic units; their area in square miles; population (based on "latest reliable figures obtainable"); capital or chief town; and map page and grid coordinate reference. Membership in the United Nations is also indicated. This easy-to-read table is useful for basic reference and will be particularly valuable to students of geography, political science, and current events.

IV. Geographic Balance

With eight maps, the United States receives by far the most extensive coverage, compared, for example, to one map each for Canada and one for the Soviet Union. Many countries are grouped on a single page. As an example of the *Hammond Large Type World Atlas*'s geographic bias, Europe has twelve maps in all, whereas Africa has only five.

V. Scale and Projections

Scales are presented only as bar scales, calibrated in miles and kilometers, making comparison of different areas difficult. In addition, a wide variety of scales is used. As a result, the inexperienced or inattentive user might suppose that the areas shown on various maps are similar in size. The average scale (excluding the world map) is about one inch to 150 miles, or 1 : 9,500,000. The smallest scale is that used for the world map, around one inch to 1,500 miles, or

1 : 95,000,000. The largest scale is approximately one inch to 14 miles, or 1 : 887,000.

Projections are not named (except for Antarctica), but the ones used represent the mapped areas without unacceptable distortion.

VI. Accuracy

Conventional anglicized spellings are used as much as possible, a convenience for the average American reader. The index, however, provides no cross-references from vernacular spellings to anglicized ones. Thus, the reader searching for Braunschweig, West Germany, for example, may not realize that it has a rarely used anglicized form, *Brunswick*, which is used in this atlas. Alternative names are rare, so that *Islas Malvinas*, for example, does not appear on the map in parentheses following *Falkland Islands*. Likewise, the now commonly used Pinyin spelling *Beijing* is ignored in favor of the traditional *Peking*.

The maps of France and Spain delineate and label the nation of Andorra but do not outline its borders in red as it does for Monaco. As a result, the reader might wonder whether Andorra is in fact a separate country. Curiously, both maps outline a small unlabeled area just to the east of Andorra, where no country exists. This is probably a cartographic error.

Official names of countries are not always used on the maps but are listed in the gazetteer-index, a convenient feature for reference. Placement of names of natural features is generally accurate. The Seychelles islands, in the Indian Ocean east of Africa, are only partially represented on the map by one of its island groups, Aldabra. Because *Seychelles* appears in parentheses after *Aldabra Islands* to indicate ownership, the reader might assume incorrectly that it is an alternative name for the Aldabra Islands. On the whole, however, the *Hammond Large Type* atlas is accurate and will serve readers well within the scope of its inherent limitations.

VII. Currency

The *Hammond Large Type* atlas accurately reflects the current world political situation, up to its 1986 copyright date, although, as is still the practice in many recent atlases, *Cambodia* is used rather than *Kampuchea*. Brunei became a member of the United Nations in 1984 but is not indicated as such in the gazetteer-index.

VIII. Legibility

Legibility is, of course, the principle goal of this atlas, and the editors have succeeded in achieving this objective. Print is dark, typefaces are sufficiently differentiated for the level of detail shown, and the pages are uncluttered. Colors are limited to blue, yellow, red, white, and black, a scheme that preserves clarity and consistency. Overall, the maps are visually pleasing. They are not contained by neat lines, and they fill the whole page; a half-inch margin on the inner edge of each page insures that nothing is lost in the gutter, but the margin is unnecessarily wide and the maps lose their continuity. Place names are often divided inconveniently (for example, *Norma* on the left page and *n, Oklahoma* on the right page), and borders and rivers sometimes appear disjointed. In most cases, however, a good match can be achieved by bunching the two pages of the map together. It should be noted, however, that frequent handling of this type can damage the pages.

National (and for the United States and Canada, state and provincial) borders are clearly marked, and natural features are indicated, although only by name; no shading or symbols are used except for spot elevations.

IX. Accessibility

The gazetteer-index includes some 315 entries arranged conveniently for ready reference. It includes countries and other areas of the world, such as U. S. states. The number of actual unique entries is somewhat smaller, since alternative names are entries rather than cross-references. For example, information entered for Vanuatu is duplicated in an entry for its previous name, New Hebrides, which is followed by the new name in parentheses.

The master index, located at the end of the atlas, contains approximately 2,700 entries listing all features that appear in the atlas except those included in the gazetteer-index. Most entries are indexed to the map having the largest scale; occasionally more than one reference is given. Entries usually include the name or abbreviation of the political unit or continent in which they are located. Many are modified by a word or abbreviation describing the type of feature, for example, "sea," "pen.," or "cap." There is no key to the abbreviations, but most of them will be obvious to experienced atlas users. Younger readers, however, are unlikely to know that "Vostok (sta.), Antarc.," for example, refers to a scientific research station.

Index entries cite page number and alphanumeric grid coordinates but not latitude and longitude coordinates. Three inset maps, at the same scale as their main maps, are included.

The editors' failure to provide cross-references from vernacular to anglicized versions of place names in the index (see *Accuracy*) is a major drawback and seriously limits accessibility if the reader is familiar only with the vernacular spelling.

X. Summary

The *Hammond Large Type World Atlas* is a large-format, large-type atlas designed for use by the visually impaired. Attractive, highly legible, and uncluttered in appearance, it serves its intended readers admirably within the limits imposed by its purpose. What would be a serious omission of detail in a more comprehensive atlas is a virtue in this volume.

Of necessity, maps in this atlas provide only the most general information. Prospective purchasers must decide whether simplicity and clarity outweigh detail and completeness, depending upon the needs of their patrons. Visually impaired readers might prefer to use a more detailed atlas with a magnifying lens. However, this title provides convenient ready reference for the visually impaired while doubling as an excellent source of outline or base maps for other uses.

The lack of map legends and the absence of index references from vernacular to anglicized place names are the two principal drawbacks of this volume. As a reference work for the visually impaired, it has been executed carefully, with close attention to the needs of its primary users, and represents good value at its price of $24.95.

Select Bibliography

Encyclopedias

American Reference Books Annual (ARBA). Edited by Bohdan S. Wynar. Littleton, Colo.: Libraries Unlimited, 1970—. Contains reviews of encyclopedias.

ARBA Guide to Subject Encyclopedias and Dictionaries. Edited by Bohdan S. Wynar. Littleton, Colo.: Libraries Unlimited, 1986.

Bennion, Bruce. "Performance Testing of a Book and Its Index as an Information Retrieval System," *Journal of the American Society for Information Science* (July 1980): 264–70.

Booklist: Including Reference Books Bulletin (Formerly, *Booklist and Reference and Subscription Books Reviews*). Chicago: American Library Association, 1905—. Semimonthly. Contains reviews of encyclopedias.

Bunge, Charles A. "Illustrated Reference Books: Technological, Intellectual and Economic Developments." *Reference Services Review* (Spring 1983): 89–98.

Cheyney, Frances Neel, and Wiley J. Williams. *Fundamental Reference Sources*. 2d ed. Chicago: American Library Association, 1980.

Collison, Robert L. "Encyclopedias." In *The New Encyclopaedia Britannica: Macropaedia* 6: 779–99. Chicago: Encyclopaedia Britannica, 1980.

Collison, Robert L. *Encyclopedias: Their History Throughout the Ages*. 2d ed. New York: Hafner, 1966.

Darnton, Robert. *The Business of Enlightenment: A Publishing History of the Encyclopédie, 1775–1800*. Cambridge: Harvard University Press, 1979.

Denenberg, Herbert S. "Consumers' Guide to Buying an Encyclopedia." *Caveat Emptor*, August–September 1979, 19–20.

Einbinder, Harvey. "Encyclopedias: Some Foreign and Domestic Developments." *Wilson Library Bulletin* (December 1980): 257–61.

"Encyclopedia Sales Frauds." *Consumer Reports*, March 1971, 172–74.

"Five Multivolume Children's Encyclopedias." *Booklist* (15 May 1983): 1233–43.

Flagg, Gordon. "Online Encyclopedias: Are They Ready for Libraries? Are Libraries Ready for Them?" *American Libraries* (March 1983): 134–36.

Free, John. "Computerized Encyclopedias." *Popular Science*, June 1983, 138–39.

Graham, Beryl Caroline. "Treatment of Black American Women in Children's Encyclopedias." *Negro History Bulletin* (April 1976): 596–98.

Grieves, Robert T. "Short Circuiting Reference Books." *Time*, 13 June 1983, 96.

Harmet, A. Richard. "Encyclopedia." In *The World Book Encyclopedia* 6: 216–22. Chicago: World Book–Childcraft International, 1980.

Harter, Stephen P., and Kenneth F. Kister. "Online Encyclopedias: The Potential." *Library Journal* (1 September 1981): 1600–602.

Horowitz, Lois. "Judging Books by More Than Covers." *Consumer's Digest*, October 1985, 46.

Instructor. Cleveland, Ohio: Instructor Publications, 1891—. Monthly. Contains reviews of encyclopedias especially appropriate for school use.

Isaacson, Richard H., ed. *Junior High School Library Catalog*. 5th ed. New York: H. W. Wilson Company, 1985.

Isaacson, Richard H., Ferne E. Hillegas, and Juliette Yaakov, eds. *Children's Catalog*. 15th ed. New York: H. W. Wilson Company, 1986.

Johnston, W. T., and Joy B. Trulock. "Buying an Encyclopedia." *Consumers' Research Magazine*, February 1975, 12–16.

Katz, William A. *Introduction to Reference Work*. Vol. 1, *Basic Information Sources*. 4th ed. New York: McGraw-Hill, 1982.

Kister, Ken[neth]. "Encyclopedias and the Public Library: A National Survey." *Library Journal* (15 April 1979): 890–93.

Kleinfield, N. R. "Encyclopedias with New Twist." *New York Times*, 30 May 1980, 1–D, 9–D.

Kraft, Linda. "Lost Herstory: The Treatment of Women in Children's Encyclopedias." *School Library Journal* (January 1973): 26–35.

Library Journal. New York: R. R. Bowker, 1876—. Semimonthly. Contains reviews of encyclopedias. "Reference Books of [year]" published annually in April issue.

Machalaba, Daniel. "Coming Soon: Encyclopedias That Can Talk." *Wall Street Journal*, 18 February 1981, 29.

Mathisen, Tyler. "All about Encyclopedias." *Money*, October 1983, 209–12.

Meacham, Mary. *Information Sources in Children's Literature: A Practical Reference Guide for Children's Librarians, Elementary School Teachers, and Students of Children's Literature*. Westport, Conn.: Greenwood Press, 1978.

Miller, Jerome K. "Popular Encyclopedias as a Source of Information about Copyright: A Critical Comparison." *RQ* (Summer 1983): 388–92.

Peterson, Carolyn Sue, and Ann D. Fenton. *Reference Books for Children*. Metuchen, N.J.: Scarecrow Press, 1981.

Purchasing an Encyclopedia: 12 Points to Consider. Chicago: American Library Association, 1979.

Reference Services Review. Ann Arbor, Mich.: Pierian Press, 1973—. Quarterly. Contains reviews of encyclopedias.

RQ. Chicago: Reference and Adult Services Division of the American Library Association, 1960—. Quarterly. Contains reviews of encyclopedias.

Santa Vicca, Edmund Frank. "The Treatment of Homosexuality in Current Encyclopedias." Ph.D. diss., University of Michigan, 1977. Ann Arbor, Mich.: University Microfilms, 1979.

Schlachter, Gail. "Reference Books." *RQ* (Fall 1985): 142.

School Library Journal. New York: R. R. Bowker, 1954—. Ten issues per year. Contains reviews of encyclopedias.

Sheehy, Eugene P., comp. *Guide to Reference Books*. 10th ed. Chicago: American Library Association, 1986.

Walford, Albert J. *Guide to Reference Material*. 3 vols. 4th ed. London: The Library Association, 1980.

Walsh, S. Padraig. *Anglo-American General Encyclopedias: A Historical Bibliography, 1703–1967*. New York: R. R. Bowker, 1968.

Whitelock, Otto V. St. "On the Making and Survival of Encyclopedias." *Choice* (June 1967): 381–89.

Wilson Library Bulletin. New York: H. W. Wilson, 1914—. Ten issues per year. Contains reviews of encyclopedias.

Wynar, Bohdan S., ed. *Recommended Reference Books for Small and Medium-sized Libraries and Media Centers 1987*. Littleton, Colo.: Libraries Unlimited, 1987.

Wynar, Christine Gehrt. *Guide to Reference Books for School Media Centers*. 2d ed. Littleton, Colo.: Libraries Unlimited, 1981.

Atlases

Alexander, G. L. *Guide to Atlases: World, Regional, National, Thematic: An International Listing of Atlases Published Since 1950*. Metuchen, N.J.: Scarecrow Press, 1971.

———. *Supplement: An International Listing of Atlases Published 1971 through 1975 with Comprehensive Indexes*. Metuchen, N.J.: Scarecrow Press, 1977.

American Cartographer. Falls Church, Va.: American Cartographic Association, 1974—. Semiannual. Contains reviews of atlases.

American Reference Books Annual (ARBA). Edited by Bohdan S. Wynar. Littleton, Colo.: Libraries Unlimited, 1970—. Contains reviews of atlases.

Base Line: A Newsletter of the Map and Geography Round Table. Chicago: American Library Association, 1980—. Six issues per year. Contains news and reviews of new atlases.

Booklist: Including Reference Books Bulletin (Formerly, *Booklist and Reference and Subscription Books Reviews*). Chicago: American Library Association, 1905—. Semimonthly. Contains reviews of atlases.

Carswell, R. J. B., G. J. A. de Leeuw, and N. M. Waters, eds. "Atlases for Schools: Design Principles and Curriculum Perspectives." *Cartographia* (Spring 1987).

Cartographic Journal. London: British Cartographic Society, 1964—. Semiannual. Contains reviews of atlases.

Cheyney, Frances Neel, and Wiley J. Williams. *Fundamental Reference Sources*, chap. 7, 284–87; see also Appendix, 315–18. 2d ed. Chicago: American Library Association, 1980.

Geography and Map Division Bulletin. Special Libraries Association. 1947—. Quarterly. Contains reviews of atlases; useful for the high school and young adult librarian.

Goméz-Ibáñez, Daniel A. "World Atlases for General Reference." *Choice* (July–August 1969): 625–30.

Isaacson, Richard H., ed. *Junior High School Library Catalog*. 5th ed. New York: H. W. Wilson Company, 1985.

Isaacson, Richard H., Ferne E. Hillegas, and Juliette Yaakov, eds. *Children's Catalog*. 15th ed. New York: H. W. Wilson Company, 1986.

Katz, William A. *Introduction to Reference Work*. Vol. 1, *Basic Information Sources*. 4th ed. New York: McGraw-Hill, 1982.

Kister, Ken[neth]. "Encyclopedias and the Public Library: A National Survey." *Library Journal* (15 April 1979): 890–93.

Meacham, Mary. *Information Sources in Children's Literature: A Practical Reference Guide for Children's Librarians, Elementary School Teachers, and Students of Children's Literature*. Westport, Conn.: Greenwood Press, 1978.

Peterson, Carolyn Sue, and Ann D. Fenton. *Reference Books for Children*. Metuchen, N.J.: Scarecrow Press, 1981.

Porter, Roy E. "How to Select an Atlas." *Library Journal* (1 November 1961): 3747–50.

RQ. Chicago: Reference and Adult Services Division of the American Library Association, 1960—. Quarterly. Contains reviews of atlases.

Schlachter, Gail. "Reference Books." *RQ* (Fall 1985): 142.

Schorr, Alan Edward. "General World Atlases." *Booklist* (15 December 1981): 564–67.

Sheehy, Eugene P., comp. *Guide to Reference Books*, 587. 10th ed. Chicago: American Library Association, 1986.

Walford, Albert J. *Guide to Reference Material*. 3 vols. 4th ed. London: The Library Association, 1980.

Walsh, S. Padraig. *General World Atlases in Print, 1972–1973*, 3–18. New York: R. R. Bowker, 1973.

Western Association of Map Libraries Information Bulletin. Santa Cruz, Calif.: Western Association of Map Libraries, 1968—. Three issues per year. Contains reviews of atlases.

Wynar, Bohdan S., ed. *Recommended Reference Books for Small and Medium-sized Libraries and Media Centers 1987*, 65, 69. Littleton, Colo.: Libraries Unlimited, 1987.

Wynar, Christine Gehrt. *Guide to Reference Books for School Media Centers*. 2d ed. Littleton, Colo.: Libraries Unlimited, 1981.

Dictionaries and Word Books

American Reference Books Annual. (*ARBA*). Edited by Bohdan S. Wynar. Littleton, Colo.: Libraries Unlimited, 1970—. Contains reviews of dictionaries.

ARBA Guide to Subject Encyclopedias and Dictionaries. Edited by Bohdan S. Wynar. Littleton, Colo.: Libraries Unlimited, 1986.

Bailey, Richard W. "Research Dictionaries." *American Speech* (Fall 1969): 166–72.

———, ed. *Dictionaries of English: Prospects for the Record of Our Language*. Ann Arbor: University of Michigan Press, 1987.

Barnhart, Clarence L. "General Dictionaries." *American Speech* (Fall 1969): 173–78.

Booklist: Including Reference Books Bulletin (Formerly, *Booklist and Reference and Subscription Books Reviews*). Chicago: American Library Association, 1905—. Semimonthly. Contains reviews of dictionaries.

Brewer, Annie M., ed. *Dictionaries, Encyclopedias, and Other Word-Related Books, 1966–1974*. Detroit, Mich.: Gale Research, 1975.

———, ed. *Dictionaries, Encyclopedias, and Other Word-Related Books*. 3 vols. 4th ed. Detroit, Mich.: Gale Research, 1987.

Chadbourne, Robert. "Keeping Up with Conversation: Merriam-Webster Is On the Job." *Wilson Library Bulletin* (September 1987): 41–44.

Chapman R. W. *Lexicography*. London: Oxford University Press, 1948.

Cheyney, Frances Neel, and Wiley J. Williams. *Fundamental Reference Sources*. 2d ed. Chicago: American Library Association, 1980.

Collison, Robert L. "Dictionaries before 1800." In *Encyclopedia of Library and Information Science*, edited by Allen Kent and Harold Lancour, 7: 170–91. New York: Marcel Dekker, 1972.

———. *Dictionaries of English and Foreign Language: A Bibliographical Guide to Both General and Technical Dictionaries with Historical and Explanatory Notes and References*. 2d ed. New York: Hafner, 1971.

Dillard, Joey Lee. *American Talk: Where Our Words Came From*. New York: Random House, 1976.

———. *Black English: Its History and Usage in the U.S*. New York: Random House, 1972.

Douglas, George H. "What's Happened to the Thesaurus?" *RQ* (Winter 1976): 149–55.

Evans, Bergen. "'dik-shə-,ner-ēs' ōld & 'n(y)ü." *Today's Education* (February 1970): 24–27.

Fillmore, C. J. "Types of Lexical Information." In *Semantics: An Interdisciplinary Reader in Philosophy, Linguistics, and Psychology*, edited by D. D. Steinberg and L. A. Jakobovits. London: Cambridge University Press, 1971.

Gimson, A. C. *An Introduction to the Pronunciation of English*. London: The English Language Book Society/Edward Arnold, 1980.

Guralnik, David B. "The Making of a Dictionary." *The Bulletin of the Cleveland Medical Library* (January 1977): 5–23.

Hartmann, R. R. K., and F. C. Stork. *Dictionary of Language and Linguistics*. New York: Halsted/ Wiley, 1972.

Hindmarsh, R. *Cambridge English Lexicon*. Cambridge: Cambridge University Press, 1980.

"Historical Introduction." In the *Oxford English Dictionary*, edited by James A. H. Murray et al., vii–xxvi. Oxford: Clarendon Press, 1933.

Horowitz, Lois. "Judging Books by More Than Covers." *Consumer's Digest*, October 1985, 46.

Hulbert, James R. *Dictionaries: British and American*. Rev. ed. London: Andre Deutsch, 1968.

Isaacson, Richard H., ed. *Junior High School Library Catalog*. 5th ed. New York: H. W. Wilson Company, 1985.

Isaacson, Richard H., Ferne E. Hillegas, and Juliette Yaakov, eds. *Children's Catalog*. 15th ed. New York: H. W. Wilson Company, 1986.

Katz, William A. *Introduction to Reference Work*. Vol. 1, *Basic Information Sources*. 2d ed. New York: McGraw-Hill, 1974.

Katzner, Kenneth. *The Languages of the World*. New York: Funk & Wagnalls, 1975.

Kister, Kenneth. *Dictionary Buying Guide*. New York: R. R. Bowker, 1977.

Kučera, Henry. "Computers in Language Analysis and in Lexicography." In *The American Heritage Dictionary: New College Edition*, xxxviii–xl. Edited by William Morris. Boston: Houghton Mifflin, 1976.

———. "The Mathematics of Language." In *The American Heritage Dictionary: Second College Edition*, 37–41. Boston: Houghton Mifflin, 1982.

Kučera, H[enry], and W. Francis. *Computational Analysis of Present-Day American English*. Providence, R.I.: Brown University Press, 1967.

Laird, Charlton Grant. *Language in America*. New York: World Publishing Company, 1970.

Landau, Sidney I. *Dictionaries: The Art and Craft of Lexicography*. New York: Scribners, 1984.

———. "Little Boy and Little Girl." *American Speech* (Fall/Winter 1970): 195–204.

———. "The Numbers' Game: Dictionary Entry Count." *RQ* (September 1964): 6, 13–15.

Library Journal. New York: R. R. Bowker, 1876—. Semimonthly. Contains reviews of dictionaries. "Reference Books of [year]" published annually in April issue.

Meacham, Mary. *Information Sources in Children's Literature: A Practical Reference Guide for Children's Librarians, Elementary School Teachers, and Students of Children's Literature*. Westport, Conn.: Greenwood Press, 1978.

Miller, Casey, and Kate Swift. *Words and Women: New Language in New Times*. New York: Anchor/ Doubleday, 1976.

Newman, Edwin. *A Civil Tongue*. New York: Bobbs-Merrill, 1976.

———. *Strictly Speaking: Will America Be the Death of English?* New York: Bobbs-Merrill, 1974.

Pei, Mario. *Words in Sheep's Clothing*. New York: Hawthorn, 1969.

Peterson, Carolyn Sue, and Ann D. Fenton. *Reference Books for Children*. Metuchen, N.J.: Scarecrow Press, 1981.

Pierson, Robert M. *Desk Dic·tio·nar·ies: A Consumer's Guide*. Chicago and London: American Library Association, 1986.

———. "Offensive Epithets in Six Dictionaries." *Reference Services Review* (Fall 1984): 41–48.

Read, Allen Walker. "Approaches to Lexicography and Semantics." In *Current Trends in Linguistics* 10: 145–205. The Hague: Mouton, 1972.

———. "Dictionary." In *Encyclopaedia Britannica: Macropaedia* 5: 713–22. Chicago: Encyclopaedia Britannica, 1977.

Rogers, Byron. "Eric Partridge and the Underworld of Language." *Horizon* (Winter 1976): 49–53.

RQ. Chicago: Reference and Adult Services Division of the American Library Association, 1960—. Quarterly. Contains reviews of dictionaries.

Schlachter, Gail. "Reference Books." *RQ* (Fall 1985): 142.

School Library Journal. New York: R. R. Bowker, 1954—. Ten issues per year. Contains reviews of dictionaries.

Sheehy, Eugene P., comp. *Guide to Reference Books*. 10th ed. Chicago: American Library Association, 1986.

Shipley, Joseph T. *In Praise of English: The Growth and Use of Language*. New York: Times Books, 1977.

Sledd, James, and Wilma R. Ebbitt. *Dictionaries and That Dictionary*. Chicago: Scott, Foresman, 1962.

Smitherman, Geneva. *Talkin and Testifyin: The Language of Black America*. Boston: Houghton Mifflin, 1977.

Starnes, DeWitt T., and Gertrude E. Noyes. *The English Dictionary from Cawdrey to Johnson, 1604–1755*. Chapel Hill: University of North Carolina Press, 1946.

Stoller, Paul, ed. *Black American English: Its History and Its Usage in the Schools and in Literature*. New York: Dell, 1975.

Stubbs, K. L. "Dictionaries after 1800." In *Encyclopedia of Library and Information Science*, edited by Allen Kent and Harold Lancour, 7: 191–207. New York: Marcel Dekker, 1972.

U.S. General Services Administration. Federal Supply Service. *Federal Specification: Dictionaries, English*. Washington, D.C.: Government Printing Office, 28 June 1974. (Superintendent of Documents Number: GS 2.8 G-D-331D.)

Walford, Albert J. *Guide to Reference Material*. 3 vols. 4th ed. London: The Library Association, 1980.

Wells, Ronald A. *Dictionaries and the Authoritarian Tradition: A Study in English Usage and Lexicography*. The Hague: Mouton, 1973.

West, M. *A General Service List of English Words*. London: Longman, 1953.

Whittaker, Kenneth. *Dictionaries*. New York: Philosophical Library, 1966.

Wilson Library Bulletin. New York: H. W. Wilson Company, 1914— . Ten issues per year. Contains reviews of dictionaries.

Wynar, Bohdan, S., ed. *Recommended Reference Books for Small and Medium-sized Libraries and Media Centers 1987*. Littleton, Colo.: Libraries Unlimited, 1987.

Wynar, Christine Gehrt. *Guide to Reference Books for School Media Centers*. 2d ed. Littleton, Colo.: Libraries Unlimited, 1981.

List of Publishers

Airmont Publishing Co., Inc.
401 Lafayette Street
New York, NY 10003
(212) 598-0222
Webster's Scholastic Dictionary

American Map Corporation
46-35 54th Road
Maspeth, NY 11378
(718) 784-0055
Colorprint Scholastic World Atlas
Colorprint Student's Atlas of the World
Colorprint World Atlas

American Printing House for the Blind, Inc.
1839 Frankfort Avenue
P.O. Box 6085
Louisville, KY 40206-0085
(502) 895-2405
The American Heritage School Dictionary
First Dictionary
Holt School Dictionary of American English
My Second Pictionary
Roget's Thesaurus of English Words and
*   Phrases*
Scott, Foresman Beginning Dictionary
The Weekly Reader Beginning Dictionary

Avon Books
(A Division of the Hearst Corp.)
1790 Broadway
New York, NY 10019
(212) 399-4500
The Concise Columbia Encyclopedia

Ballantine/Del Rey/Fawcett Books
(A Division of Random House, Inc.)
201 East 50th Street
New York, NY 10022
(212) 751-2600
The Random House Dictionary
Webster's Super New School and Office
Dictionary

Bantam Books
666 Fifth Avenue
New York, NY 10103
(212) 765-6500
The Scribner-Bantam English Dictionary

Barnes & Noble Books
(An imprint of Harper & Row, Publishers, Inc.)
10 East 53rd Street
New York, NY 10022
(212) 207-7000
Allen's Synonyms and Antonyms
Webster's Dictionary for Everyday Use

Berkley Publishing Group
(A subsidiary of the Putnam Publishing Group)
200 Madison Avenue
New York, NY 10016
(212) 686-9820
Webster's II New Riverside Dictionary

Bob Jones University Press
1700 Wade Hampton Boulevard
Greenville, SC 29614
(803) 242-5100
The Christian Student Dictionary

Columbia University Press
562 West 113th Street
New York, NY 10025
(212) 316-7100
The Concise Columbia Encyclopedia (see
    Avon)

CompuServe, Inc.
5000 Arlington Centre Boulevard
P.O. Box 20212
Columbus, OH 43220
(800) 848-8199 (outside Ohio)
(614) 457-0802 (in Ohio)
Academic American Encyclopedia (online)

Delair Publishing Co.
2085 Cornell Avenue
Melrose Park, IL 60160
(312) 921-2505
(312) 666-4200
> *The New Color-Picture Dictionary for Children*

Dell Publishing Co., Inc.
1 Dag Hammarskjold Plaza
New York, NY 10017
(212) 605-3000
> *The American Heritage Dictionary*

Dialog Information Services, Inc.
3460 Hillview Avenue
Palo Alto, CA 94304
(800) 982-5838 (outside California)
(800) 227-1927 (in California)
> *Academic American Encyclopedia* (online)
> *Everyman's Encyclopedia* (online)

Doubleday & Company, Inc.
666 Fifth Ave.
New York, NY 10103
(212) 984-7561
> *The Doubleday Children's Picture Dictionary*
> *The Doubleday Children's Thesaurus*
> *The Doubleday Dictionary for Home, School, and Office*
> *The Doubleday Roget's Thesaurus in Dictionary Form*
> *The Thorndike Barnhart Handy Pocket Dictionary*

Dow Jones News/Retrieval
P.O. Box 300
Princeton, NJ 08540
(609) 520-4000
> *Academic American Encyclopedia* (online)

EDC Publishing (A division of Educational Development Corp.)
10302 E. 55 Place
Tulsa, OK 74146
(918) 622-4522
> *The First Thousand Words: A Picture Word Book*

Encyclopaedia Britannica Educational Corp.
North Michigan Avenue
Chicago, IL 60611
(312) 347-7400
> *Britannica Atlas*
> *Compton's Encyclopedia*
> *Compton's Precyclopedia*
> *New Encyclopaedia Britannica*
> *The Young Children's Encyclopedia*

Facts on File, Inc.
460 Park Avenue South
New York, NY 10016
(212) 683-2244
> *Maps on File*

Fawcett Books (see Ballantine)

J. G. Ferguson Publishing Co.
111 East Wacker Drive
Chicago, IL 60601
(312) 861-0666
> *Webster Comprehensive Dictionary: Encyclopedic Edition*
> *Webster Comprehensive Dictionary: International Edition*
> *Webster Illustrated Contemporary Dictionary*

The Frontier Press Company
P.O. Box 1098
Columbus, OH 43216
(614) 864-3737
> *The Lincoln Library of Essential Information*

Funk & Wagnalls, Inc.
70 Hilltop Road
Ramsey, NJ 07446
(201) 934-7500
> *Funk & Wagnalls New Encyclopedia* (see also Harper & Row, Publishers, Inc.)

Gage Educational Publishing Company
164 Commander Boulevard
Agincourt, Ontario
Canada M1S 3C7
(416) 293-8141
> *The Gage Atlas of the World*
> *The Macmillan School Atlas*

General Videotex Corporation
3 Blackstone Street
Cambridge, MA 02139
(617) 491-3393
> *The Kussmaul Encyclopedia* (online)

Ginn (see Silver Burdett & Ginn, Inc.)

Graphic Learning International
One Galleria Tower
Suite 1425
Dallas, TX 75240
> *Concise Earthbook*
> *Earthbook*

Grolier Inc.
Sherman Turnpike
Danbury, CT 06816
(203) 797-3500
Academic American Encyclopedia
Encyclopedia Americana
The New Book of Knowledge

Grolier Electronic Publishing, Inc.
95 Madison Avenue
Suite 1100
New York, NY 10016
(212) 696-9750
Academic American Encyclopedia (CD-ROM)
Academic American Encyclopedia (online)

Grosset & Dunlap, Inc.
51 Madison Avenue
New York, NY 10010
(212) 689-9200
The Clear and Simple Thesaurus Dictionary
The Grosset Webster Dictionary
Tell Me Why: Answers to Hundreds of Questions Children Ask

G. K. Hall & Company
(A Division of Macmillan Publishing Company)
70 Lincoln Street
Boston, MA 02111
(617) 423-3990
The Merriam-Webster Dictionary for Large Print Users
The Merriam-Webster Thesaurus for Large Print Users

Hammond Inc.
515 Valley Street
Maplewood, NJ 07040
(201) 763-6000
Ambassador World Atlas
Citation World Atlas
Comparative World Atlas
Diplomat World Atlas
Hammond Headline World Atlas
Hammond Large Type World Atlas
Hammond New Horizon World Atlas
Hammond World Atlas: Gemini Edition
Intermediate World Atlas
International World Atlas
The Whole Earth Atlas
Wonderful World of Maps
World Atlas for Students

Harcourt Brace Jovanovich
Orlando, FL 32887
(305) 345-2000
The HBJ School Dictionary

Harper & Row Publishers, Inc.
10 East 53rd Street
New York, NY 10022
(212) 207-7000
Funk & Wagnalls Standard Handbook of Synonyms, Antonyms, and Prepositions
Roget's International Thesaurus: Fourth Edition

Holt, Rinehart and Winston
383 Madison Avenue
New York, NY 10017
(212) 872-2000
Holt School Dictionary of American English

Houghton Mifflin Company
One Beacon Street
Boston, MA 02108
(617) 725-5000
The American Heritage Children's Dictionary
The American Heritage Desk Dictionary
The American Heritage Dictionary: Second College Edition
The American Heritage First Dictionary
The American Heritage Picture Dictionary
The American Heritage Student's Dictionary
The Concise American Heritage Dictionary
The Large Type American Heritage Basic Dictionary
The Right Word II: A Concise Thesaurus
Roget's II: The New Thesaurus
Webster's II New Riverside Pocket Dictionary
Webster's II Riverside Children's Dictionary

David S. Lake Publishers
19 Davis Drive
Belmont, CA 94002
(415) 592-7810
Fearon New School Dictionary

Langenscheidt Publishers, Inc.
46-35 54th Road
Maspeth, NY 11378
(718) 784-0055
Langenscheidt's Lilliput Webster English Dictionary (see *The Little Webster*)
The Little Webster

Lerner Publications Co.
241 First Avenue, N
Minneapolis, MN 55401
(612) 332-3344
    Joan Hanson Word Books
        Antonyms
        British-American Synonyms
        Homographs
        More Homonyms
        More Similes
        More Sound Words
        More Synonyms
        Possessives
        Similes
        Still More Antonyms
        Still More Homonyms

The Library Reproduction Service of the
  Microfilm Company of California
1977 South Los Angeles Street
Los Angeles, CA 90011
(213) 749-2463
    The American Heritage School Dictionary
    Beginning Dictionary
    Scott, Foresman Beginning Dictionary
    Webster's Concise Family Dictionary
    Webster's New Collegiate Dictionary
    Webster's New Elementary Dictionary
    Webster's New World Thesaurus

Littlefield, Adams & Company
81 Adams Drive
Totowa, NJ 07512
(201) 256-8600
    A Concise Dictionary of Correct English

Longman, Inc.
Longman Building
95 Church Street
White Plains, NY 10601
(914) 993-5000
    Longman Dictionary of American English

Macmillan Publishing Co., Inc.
866 Third Avenue
New York, NY 10022
(212) 702-2000
    Beginning Dictionary
    Collier's Encyclopedia
    Macmillan Dictionary
    Macmillan Dictionary for Children (see
        Beginning Dictionary; see also *Childcraft*)
    Macmillan Dictionary for Students
    Macmillan First Dictionary
    The Macmillan Picture Wordbook

    The Macmillan School Atlas
    Macmillan School Dictionary
    *Macmillan Very First Dictionary: A Magic
        World of Words*
    Merit Students Encyclopedia
    Picture Dictionary (see *The Macmillan
        Picture Wordbook*)

G. & C. Merriam & Co.
47 Federal Street
Springfield, MA 01102
(413) 734-3134
    *The Merriam-Webster Pocket Dictionary of
        Synonyms*
    Webster's Beginning Book of Facts
    Webster's Concise Family Dictionary
    Webster's Elementary Dictionary
    Webster's Intermediate Dictionary
    Webster's Ninth New Collegiate Dictionary
    Webster's School Dictionary
    Webster's School Thesaurus
    Webster's Vest Pocket Dictionary

National Geographic Society
17 & M Sts., NW
Washington, DC 20036
(202) 857-7000
    National Geographic Atlas of the World

National Library Service for the Blind and
  Physically Handicapped
The Library of Congress
Washington, DC 20542
    (Write for list of titles currently available.)

National Textbook Co.
4255 W. Touhy Avenue
Lincolnwood, IL 60646
(312) 679-5500
    English Picture Dictionary
    Everyday American English Dictionary

Thomas Nelson, Inc.
Nelson Place at Elm Hill Pike
Nashville, TN 37214
(615) 889-9000
    Nelson's New Compact Roget's Thesaurus
    *Webster's New Compact Dictionary for
        School and Office*
    Webster's Vest Pocket Dictionary

New American Library
1633 Broadway
New York, NY 10019
(212) 397-8000
> *The Basic Book of Synonyms and Antonyms*
> *The New American Desk Encyclopedia*
> *The New American Roget's College Thesaurus*
> *in Dictionary Form*
> *New American Webster Handy College*
> *Dictionary*

New Century Publishers, Inc.
(A Division of New Century Education Corp.)
220 Old New Brunswick Road
Piscataway, NJ 08854
(201) 981-0820
> *The New Century Vest-Pocket Webster*
> *Dictionary*

Oxford University Press, Inc.
200 Madison Avenue
New York, NY 10016
(212) 679-7300
> *The Large Print Version of The Little Oxford*
> *Dictionary of Current English*
> *The Little Oxford Dictionary of Current*
> *English*
> *Open Sesame Picture Dictionary*
> *The Oxford Children's Dictionary: Second*
> *Edition*
> *Oxford Student's Dictionary of American*
> *English*

Pocket Books
(A Division of Simon & Schuster, Inc.)
1230 Avenue of the Americas
New York, NY 10020
(212) 698-7000
> *The Merriam-Webster Dictionary*
> *Roget's Pocket Thesaurus*

Prentice Hall Press (A Division of Simon &
Schuster, Inc.)
Englewood Cliffs, NJ 07632
(201) 592-2000
> *Prentice-Hall New World Atlas*
> *Prentice-Hall Pocket Atlas of the World*
> *Webster's New World Compact School &*
> *Office Dictionary*
> *Webster's New World Dictionary: Second*
> *College Edition*
> *Webster's New World Handy Pocket*
> *Dictionary (see Webster's New World*
> *Pocket Dictionary)*
> *Webster's New World Large Print Dictionary:*
> *Second Concise Edition*
> *Webster's New World Pocket Dictionary*
> *Webster's New World Thesaurus*

Rand McNally & Company
8255 Central Park Avenue
Skokie, IL 60076
(312) 673-9100
> *Rand McNally Children's Atlas of the World*
> *Rand McNally Classroom Atlas*
> *Rand McNally Family World Atlas*
> *Rand McNally Goode's World Atlas*
> *Rand McNally Images of the World*
> *Rand McNally Quick Reference World Atlas*
> *Rand McNally Students World Atlas*

Random House, Inc.
201 East 50th Street
New York, NY 10022
(212) 751-2600
> *The Cat in the Hat Beginner Book Dictionary*
> *My First Picture Dictionary*
> *The Random House American Dictionary:*
> *New Revised Edition*
> *The Random House Basic Dictionary of*
> *Synonyms and Antonyms*
> *The Random House College Dictionary:*
> *Revised Edition*
> *The Random House Concise World Atlas*
> *The Random House Dictionary: Concise*
> *Edition*
> *The Random House Mini World Atlas*
> *The Random House School Dictionary*
> *The Random House Thesaurus: College*
> *Edition*
> *The Random House Thesaurus: A Dictionary*
> *of Synonyms and Antonyms*
> *The Sesame Street Dictionary*

Scholastic Inc.
730 Broadway
New York, NY 10003
(212) 505-3000
> *New Scholastic Dictionary of American*
> *English (see also Holt School Dictionary of*
> *American English)*
> *Scholastic Dictionary of Synonyms,*
> *Antonyms, Homonyms*

Scott, Foresman and Company
1900 East Lake Avenue
Glenview, IL 60025
(312) 729-3000
> *In Other Words: A Beginning Thesaurus*
> *In Other Words: A Junior Thesaurus*
> *My First Picture Dictionary*
> *My Pictionary*
> *My Second Picture Dictionary*
> *Scott, Foresman Advanced Dictionary*
> *Scott, Foresman Beginning Dictionary*

Scott, Foresman Intermediate Dictionary
Scott, Foresman World Atlas

The Scribner Book Companies, Inc.
(A Subsidiary of Macmillan Inc.)
115 Fifth Avenue
New York, NY 10003
(212) 614-1300
Scribner Beginning Dictionary (see *Beginning Dictionary*)

Sharon Publications, Inc.
1086 Teaneck Road
Teaneck, NJ 07666
(201) 833-1800
Students' Webster Dictionary of the English Language
Students' World Atlas

Silver Burdett & Ginn
(A Subsidiary of Simon & Schuster, Inc.)
250 James Street
Morristown, NJ 07960-CN1918
(201) 285-7700
My Picture Dictionary
My Second Picture Dictionary

Simon & Schuster, Inc.
1230 Avenue of the Americas
New York, NY 10020
(212) 698-7000
Webster's New World Dictionary for Young Readers
Webster's New World Dictionary: Student Edition
Webster's New World Vest Pocket Dictionary

The Southwestern Company
P.O. Box 820
Nashville, TN 37202
(615) 790-4000
The Volume Library

Standard Education Corporation
200 West Monroe Street
Chicago, IL 60606
(312) 346-7440
New Standard Encyclopedia

Troll Associates
100 Corporate Drive
Mahwah, NJ 07430
(201) 592-4000
New Talking Cassette Encyclopedia

U.S. Department of State
Distributed by the Superintendent of Documents
U.S. Government Printing Office
Washington, DC 20402
Background Notes on the Countries of the World

Ulverscroft Large Print Books
(A Subsidiary of F. A. Thorp)
The Green, Bradgate Road
Anstey, Leicester, England LE7 7FU
The Large Print Version of The Little Oxford Dictionary of Current English

Van Nostrand Reinhold Co., Inc.
(A Division of International Thompson Organization, Inc.)
115 Fifth Avenue
New York, NY 10003
(212) 254-3232
VNR Pocket Atlas

Viking-Penguin Inc.
40 W. 23 Street
New York, NY 10010
(212) 337-5200
New Penguin World Atlas
The Penguin Pocket Thesaurus
The Penguin Roget's Thesaurus of English Words and Phrases
Viking Children's World Atlas
Viking Student World Atlas

Voluntad Publishers, Inc.
(see National Textbook Company)

VU/TEXT Information Services, Inc.
1211 Chestnut Street
Philadelphia, PA 19107
(800) 258-8080 (outside Pennsylvania)
(215) 665-3300 (in Pennsylvania)
Academic American Encyclopedia (online)

Wanderer Books
(An imprint of Simon & Schuster, Inc.)
1230 Avenue of the Americas
New York, NY 10020
Simon & Schuster Young Readers' Atlas
Simon & Schuster's Young Readers' Illustrated Dictionary
The Simon & Schuster Young Readers' Thesaurus

Warner Books, Inc.
666 Fifth Avenue
New York, NY 10103
(212) 484-2900
 A Dictionary of Synonyms and Antonyms
 Webster's New World Dictionary of the
  American Language
 Webster's New World Thesaurus

Washington Square Press
(An imprint of Pocket Books)
1230 Avenue of the Americas
New York, NY 10020
 Dictionary of Problem Words and
  Expressions

World Book, Inc.
510 Merchandise Mart Plaza
Chicago, IL 60654
(312) 245-3456
 Childcraft Dictionary (see *Macmillan*
  Dictionary for Children)
 Childcraft: The How and Why Library
 The World Book Dictionary
 The World Book Encyclopedia

Acknowledgments

Page numbers are followed by titles listed in alphabetical order.

Page 81 from volume 7, page 137 in *Academic American Encyclopedia*. Copyright © 1987 by Grolier Incorporated. Reprinted by permission of Grolier Incorporated.

Page 315 from *The American Heritage Children's Dictionary*. Copyright © 1986 by Houghton Mifflin Company. Reprinted by permission of Houghton Mifflin Company.

Page 318 from *The American Heritage Desk Dictionary*. Copyright © 1981 by Houghton Mifflin Company. Reprinted by permission of Houghton Mifflin Company.

Page 322 from *The American Heritage Dictionary*. Copyright © 1981 by Houghton Mifflin Company. Reprinted by permission of Houghton Mifflin Company.

Page 326 from *The American Heritage Dictionary, Second College Edition*. Copyright © 1985 by Houghton Mifflin Company. Reprinted by permission of Houghton Mifflin Company.

Page 332 from *The American Heritage First Dictionary*. Copyright © 1986 by Houghton Mifflin Company. Reprinted by permission of Houghton Mifflin Company.

Page 334 from *The American Heritage Picture Dictionary*. Copyright © 1986 by Houghton Mifflin Company. Reprinted by permission of Houghton Mifflin Company.

Page 336 from *The American Heritage Student's Dictionary*. Copyright © 1986 by Houghton Mifflin Company. Reprinted by permission of Houghton Mifflin Company.

Page 338 from *Beginning Dictionary*. Copyright © 1987 by Macmillan Publishing Company. Reprinted by permission of Macmillan, Inc.

Page 340 from *The Cat in the Hat Beginner Book Dictionary*. Copyright © 1964 by Random House, Inc. Reprinted by permission of Random House, Inc.

Page 341 from *Childcraft Dictionary*. Copyright © 1982, 1980, 1979, 1978, 1977, 1976, 1975 by Macmillan Publishing Company. Reprinted by permission of Macmillan, Inc.

Page 343 from *The Christian Student Dictionary*. Copyright © 1982 by Bob Jones University Press. Reprinted by permission of Houghton Mifflin Company and Bob Jones University Press.

Page 98 from volume 20, page 591 in *Collier's Encyclopedia*. Copyright © 1986 by Macmillan Educational Company. Reprinted by permission of Macmillan Educational Company.

Page 106 from volume 9, page 254 in *Compton's Encyclopedia*. Copyright © 1987 by Encyclopaedia Britannica, Inc. Reprinted by permission of Encyclopaedia Britannica, Inc.

Page 347 from *The Concise American Heritage Dictionary*. Copyright © 1987 by Houghton Mifflin Company. Reprinted by permission of Houghton Mifflin Company.

Page 116 from page 369 in *The Concise Columbia Encyclopedia*. Copyright © 1983 by Columbia University Press. Reprinted by permission of Columbia University Press.

Page 351 from *Doubleday Children's Picture Dictionary*. Copyright © 1986 by Grisewood & Dempsey, Ltd. Reprinted by permission of Doubleday, a division of Bantam, Doubleday, Dell Publishing Group, Inc.

Page 353 from *Doubleday Dictionary for Home, School, and Office*. Copyright © 1975 by Doubleday, a division of Bantam, Doubleday, Dell Publishing Group, Inc. Reprinted by permission of the publisher.

Page 123 from volume 16, page 420 in *Encyclopedia Americana*. Copyright © 1987 by Grolier Incorporated. Reprinted by permission of Grolier Incorporated.

Page 362 from *Fearon New School Dictionary*. Copyright © 1987 by David S. Lake Publishers. Reprinted by permission of David S. Lake Publishers.

Page 365 from *The First Thousand Words: A Picture Word Book*. Copyright © 1983 by Usbourne Publishing Limited. Reprinted by permission of Education Development Corporation and Hayes Publishing.

Page 133 from volume 15, page 445 in *Funk & Wagnalls New Encyclopedia*. Copyright © 1986 by Funk & Wagnalls Inc. Reprinted by permission of Funk & Wagnalls Inc.

Page 369 from *The HBJ School Dictionary*. Copyright © 1985 by Harcourt Brace Jovanovich. Reprinted by permission of Harcourt Brace Jovanovich.

Page 431 from *The Random House School Dictionary*. Copyright © 1984, 1978, 1973, 1971, 1970 by Random House, Inc. Reprinted by permission of Random House, Inc.

Page 442 from *Scribner-Bantam English Dictionary*. Copyright © 1979, 1977 by Bantam Books, Inc. Reprinted by permission of Bantam Books, Inc.

Page 445 from *The Sesame Street Dictionary*. Copyright © 1980 by Children's Television Workshop. Reprinted by permission of Random House, Inc.

Page 447 from *Simon & Schuster Illustrated Young Readers Dictionary*. Copyright © 1984 by Kingfisher Books Ltd. Reprinted by permission of Simon & Schuster, Inc.

Page 456 from *Webster Comprehensive Dictionary: Encyclopedic Edition*. Copyright © 1984 by J. G. Ferguson Publishing Company. Reprinted by permission of J. G. Ferguson Publishing Company.

Page 465 from *Webster's Concise Family Dictionary*. Copyright © 1975 by Merriam-Webster, Inc. Reprinted by permission of Merriam-Webster, Inc., publisher of the Merriam-Webster® dictionaries.

Page 466 from *Webster's Dictionary for Everyday Use*. Copyright © 1963, 1964, 1965, 1966, 1971, 1974, 1975, 1977, 1980, 1981 by Ottenheimer Publishers, Inc. Reprinted by permission of Ottenheimer Publishers, Inc.

Page 467 from *Webster's Elementary Dictionary*. Copyright © 1986 by Merriam-Webster, Inc. Reprinted by permission of Merriam-Webster® dictionaries.

Page 471 from *Webster's Intermediate Dictionary*. Copyright © 1986 by Merriam-Webster, Inc. Reprinted by permission of Merriam-Webster, Inc., publisher of Merriam-Webster® dictionaries.

Page 476 from *Webster's New World Compact School & Office Dictionary*. Copyright © 1982, 1977, 1974, 1971, 1970, 1967 by Simon & Schuster, Inc. Reprinted by permission of Simon & Schuster, Inc.

Page 479 from *Webster's New World Dictionary of the American Language: Second College Edition*. Copyright © 1986 and 1970, 1972, 1974, 1976, 1978, 1979, 1980, 1982, 1984 by Simon & Schuster, Inc. Reprinted by permission of Simon & Schuster, Inc.

Page 485 from *Webster's New World Dictionary: Student Edition*. Copyright © 1976, 1981 by Simon & Schuster. Reprinted by permission of Simon & Schuster, Inc.

Page 488 from *Webster's New World Dictionary of the American Language*. Copyright © 1984, 1979, 1977, 1975, 1973, 1971 by Simon & Schuster, Inc. Reprinted by permission of Simon & Schuster, Inc.

Page 490 from *Webster's New World Dictionary for Young Readers*. Copyright © 1983, 1979 by Simon & Schuster, Inc. Reprinted by permission of Simon & Schuster, Inc.

Page 496 from *Webster's Ninth New Collegiate Dictionary*. Copyright © 1987 by Merriam-Webster, Inc. Reprinted by permission of Merriam-Webster, Inc., publisher of the Merriam-Webster® dictionaries.

Page 503 from *Webster's School Dictionary*. Copyright © 1986 by Merriam-Webster, Inc. Reprinted by permission of Merriam-Webster, Inc., publisher of the Merriam-Webster® dictionaries.

Page 506 from *Webster's II New Riverside Dictionary*. Copyright © 1984 by Houghton Mifflin Company. Reprinted by permission of Houghton Mifflin Company.

Page 508 from *Webster's II Riverside Children's Dictionary*. Copyright © 1984 by Houghton Mifflin Company. Reprinted by permission of Houghton Mifflin Company.

Page 517 from *The World Book Dictionary*. Copyright © 1987 by the publisher. Courtesy of World Book, Inc.

Page 198 from volume 16, page 71 in *The World Book Encyclopedia*. Copyright © 1987 by World Book, Inc. Reprinted by permission of World Book, Inc.

Page 580 from *Webster's New World Large Print Dictionary of the American Language: Second Concise Edition*. Copyright © 1975, 1977, 1979 by Simon & Schuster, Inc. Reprinted by permission of Simon & Schuster, Inc.

Index

Titles with full reviews in this Buying Guide appear below in small capital letters. All other titles are in italics. Abbreviations of titles are fully cross-referenced (for example, "AHD. See *American Heritage Dictionary.*"). Boldface page numbers indicate facsimiles and other illustrations.